Global Knowledge™ Certificati

C000019231

1999 CNE NETWARE 5 CERTIFICATION

CORE EXAMS (ALL REQUIRED)	Number of Questions	Passing Score	Time Allowed
Exam 50-632: Networking Technologies	82	620	120
Exam 50-634: NDS Design and Implementation	69	620	105
Exam 50-635: Service & Support	78	608	120
Exam 50-639: NetWare 5 Administration	80	614	120
Exam 50-640: NetWare 5 Advanced Administration	78	596	120
ELECTIVE EXAMS (1 REQUIRED):			
Exam 50-636: intraNetWare: Integrating Windows NT	70	620	90
Exam 50-618: GroupWise 5 Administration			
Exam 50-628: Network Management Using ManageWise			
Exam 50-629: Securing Intranets with BorderManager			

COMPLETE COVERAGE IN THIS STUDY GUIDE

For complete information on CNE NetWare 5 Certification, visit **www.novell.com** and click on Training and Services.

CNE NetWare 5™
Study Guide

Osborne/McGraw-Hill is an independent entity from Microsoft Corporation, and not affiliated with Microsoft Corporation in any manner. This publication and CD may be used in assisting students to prepare for a Microsoft Certified Professional Exam. Neither Microsoft Corporation, its designated review ICV, nor Osborne/McGraw-Hill warrants that use of this publication and CD will ensure passing the relevant Exam. Microsoft is either a registered trademark or trademark of Microsoft Corporation in the United States and/or other countries.

Syngress Media, Inc.

Osborne/McGraw-Hill

Berkeley   New York   St. Louis   San Francisco   Auckland   Bogotá   Hamburg   London   Madrid   Mexico City
Milan   Montreal   New Delhi   Panama City   Paris   São Paulo   Singapore   Sydney   Tokyo   Toronto

Osborne/**McGraw-Hill**
2600 Tenth Street
Berkeley, California 94710
U.S.A.

For information on translations or book distributors outside the U.S.A.,
or to arrange bulk purchase discounts for sales promotions, premiums,
or fund-raisers, please contact Osborne/**McGraw-Hill** at the above address.

CNE NetWare 5 Study Guide

Copyright © 1999 by The McGraw-Hill Companies. All rights reserved.
Printed in the United States of America. Except as permitted under the
Copyright Act of 1976, no part of this publication may be reproduced or
distributed in any form or by any means, or stored in a database or retrieval
system, without the prior written permission of the publisher, with the
exception that the program listings may be entered, stored, and executed in a
computer system, but they may not be reproduced for publication.

1234567890 DOC DOW 90198765432109

ISBN 0-07-211923-3

Publisher	**Technical Editor**	**Computer Designers**
Brandon A. Nordin	Daniel Cheung	Jani Beckwith
		Gary Corrigan
Editor-in-Chief	**Copy Editor**	
Scott Rogers	Eileen Kramer	**Illustrators**
		Beth Young
Acquisitions Editor	**Proofreader**	Brian Wells
Gareth Hancock	Linda Medoff	
	Paul Medoff	**Series Design**
Editorial Assistants		Roberta Steele
Stephane Thomas	**Indexer**	Arlette Crosland
Debbie Escobedo	Jack Lewis	
		Cover Design
		Regan Honda

Novell NetWare, GroupWise, and ManageWise are registered trademarks; NDS, Novell
Directory Services, and Novell BorderManager are trademarks; CNE is a registered service
mark; and Certified Novell Engineer, CNI, and CAN are service marks of Novell, Inc., in the
United States and in other countries.

Screen shots from NetWare 5 software, © 1998, Novell, Inc. All Rights Reserved. Reprinted
and used with permission

Information has been obtained by Osborne/**McGraw-Hill** from sources believed to be reliable.
However, because of the possibility of human or mechanical error by our sources,
Osborne/**McGraw-Hill**, or others, Osborne/**McGraw-Hill** does not guarantee the accuracy,
adequacy, or completeness of any information and is not responsible for any errors or
omissions or the results obtained from use of such information.

FOREWORD

From Global Knowledge

At Global Knowledge we strive to support the multiplicity of learning styles required by our students to achieve success as technical professionals. In this series of books, it is our intention to offer the reader a valuable tool for successful completion of the CNE exams.

As the world's largest IT training company, Global Knowledge is uniquely positioned to offer these books. The expertise gained each year from providing instructor-led training to hundreds of thousands of students worldwide has been captured in book form to enhance your learning experience. We hope that the quality of these books demonstrates our commitment to your lifelong learning success. Whether you choose to learn through the written word, computer-based training, Web delivery, or instructor-led training, Global Knowledge is committed to providing you the very best in each of those categories. For those of you who know Global Knowledge, or those of you who have just found us for the first time, our goal is to be your lifelong competency partner.

Thank you for the opportunity to serve you. We look forward to serving your needs again in the future.

Warmest regards,

President and Chief Operating Officer, Global Knowledge

The Global Knowledge Advantage

Global Knowledge has a global delivery system for its products and services. The company has 28 subsidiaries, and offers its programs through a total of 60+ locations. No other vendor can provide consistent services across a geographic area this large. Global Knowledge is the largest independent information technology education provider, offering programs on a variety of platforms. This enables our multi-platform and multi-national customers to obtain all of their programs from a single vendor. The company has developed the unique Competus™ Framework software tool and methodology which can quickly reconfigure courseware to the proficiency level of a student on an interactive basis. Combined with self-paced and on-line programs, this technology can reduce the time required for training by prescribing content in only the deficient skills areas. The company has fully automated every aspect of the education process, from registration and follow-up, to "just-in-time" production of courseware. Global Knowledge, through its Enterprise Services Consultancy, can customize programs and products to suit the needs of an individual customer.

Global Knowledge Classroom Education Programs

The backbone of our delivery options is classroom-based education. Our modern, well-equipped facilities staffed with the finest instructors offer programs in a wide variety of information technology topics, many of which lead to professional certifications.

Custom Learning Solutions

This delivery option has been created for companies and governments that value customized learning solutions. For them, our consultancy-based approach of developing targeted education solutions is most effective at helping them meet specific objectives.

Self-Paced and Multimedia Products

This delivery option offers self-paced program titles in interactive CD-ROM, videotape and audio tape programs. In addition, we offer custom development of interactive multimedia courseware to customers and partners. Call us at 1 (888) 427-4228.

Electronic Delivery of Training

Our network-based training service delivers efficient competency-based, interactive training via the World Wide Web and organizational intranets. This leading-edge delivery option provides a custom learning path and "just-in-time" training for maximum convenience to students.

ARG

American Research Group (ARG), a wholly-owned subsidiary of Global Knowledge, one of the largest worldwide training partners of Cisco Systems, offers a wide range of internetworking, LAN/WAN, Bay Networks, FORE Systems, IBM, and UNIX courses. ARG offers hands on network training in both instructor-led classes and self-paced PC-based training.

Global Knowledge Courses Available

Network Fundamentals

- Understanding Computer Networks
- Telecommunications Fundamentals I
- Telecommunications Fundamentals II
- Understanding Networking Fundamentals
- Implementing Computer Telephony Integration
- Introduction to Voice Over IP
- Introduction to Wide Area Networking
- Cabling Voice and Data Networks
- Introduction to LAN/WAN protocols
- Virtual Private Networks
- ATM Essentials

Network Security & Management

- Troubleshooting TCP/IP Networks
- Network Management
- Network Troubleshooting
- IP Address Management
- Network Security Administration
- Web Security
- Implementing UNIX Security
- Managing Cisco Network Security
- Windows NT 4.0 Security

IT Professional Skills

- Project Management for IT Professionals
- Advanced Project Management for IT Professionals
- Survival Skills for the New IT Manager
- Making IT Teams Work

LAN/WAN Internetworking

- Frame Relay Internetworking
- Implementing T1/T3 Services
- Understanding Digital Subscriber Line (xDSL)
- Internetworking with Routers and Switches
- Advanced Routing and Switching
- Multi-Layer Switching and Wire-Speed Routing
- Internetworking with TCP/IP
- ATM Internetworking
- OSPF Design and Configuration
- Border Gateway Protocol (BGP) Configuration

Authorized Vendor Training

Cisco Systems

- Introduction to Cisco Router Configuration
- Advanced Cisco Router Configuration
- Installation and Maintenance of Cisco Routers
- Cisco Internetwork Troubleshooting
- Cisco Internetwork Design
- Cisco Routers and LAN Switches
- Catalyst 5000 Series Configuration
- Cisco LAN Switch Configuration
- Managing Cisco Switched Internetworks
- Configuring, Monitoring, and Troubleshooting Dial-Up Services
- Cisco AS5200 Installation and Configuration
- Cisco Campus ATM Solutions

Bay Networks

- Bay Networks Accelerated Router Configuration
- Bay Networks Advanced IP Routing
- Bay Networks Hub Connectivity
- Bay Networks Accelar 1xxx Installation and Basic Configuration
- Bay Networks Centillion Switching

FORE Systems

- FORE ATM Enterprise Core Products
- FORE ATM Enterprise Edge Products
- FORE ATM Theory
- FORE LAN Certification

Operating Systems & Programming

Microsoft

- Introduction to Windows NT
- Microsoft Networking Essentials
- Windows NT 4.0 Workstation
- Windows NT 4.0 Server
- Advanced Windows NT 4.0 Server
- Windows NT Networking with TCP/IP
- Introduction to Microsoft Web Tools
- Windows NT Troubleshooting
- Windows Registry Configuration

UNIX

- UNIX Level I
- UNIX Level II
- Essentials of UNIX and NT Integration

Programming

- Introduction to JavaScript
- Java Programming
- PERL Programming
- Advanced PERL with CGI for the Web

Web Site Management & Development

- Building a Web Site
- Web Site Management and Performance
- Web Development Fundamentals

High Speed Networking

- Essentials of Wide Area Networking
- Integrating ISDN
- Fiber Optic Network Design
- Fiber Optic Network Installation
- Migrating to High Performance Ethernet

DIGITAL UNIX

- UNIX Utilities and Commands
- DIGITAL UNIX v4.0 System Administration
- DIGITAL UNIX v4.0 (TCP/IP) Network Management
- AdvFS, LSM, and RAID Configuration and Management
- DIGITAL UNIX TruCluster Software Configuration and Management
- UNIX Shell Programming Featuring Kornshell
- DIGITAL UNIX v4.0 Security Management
- DIGITAL UNIX v4.0 Performance Management
- DIGITAL UNIX v4.0 Intervals Overview

DIGITAL OpenVMS

- OpenVMS Skills for Users
- OpenVMS System and Network Node Management I
- OpenVMS System and Network Node Management II
- OpenVMS System and Network Node Management III
- OpenVMS System and Network Node Operations
- OpenVMS for Programmers
- OpenVMS System Troubleshooting for Systems Managers
- Configuring and Managing Complex VMScluster Systems
- Utilizing OpenVMS Features from C
- OpenVMS Performance Management
- Managing DEC TCP/IP Services for OpenVMS
- Programming in C

Hardware Courses

- AlphaServer 1000/1000A Installation, Configuration and Maintenance
- AlphaServer 2100 Server Maintenance
- AlphaServer 4100, Troubleshooting Techniques and Problem Solving

v

ABOUT THE CONTRIBUTORS

Syngress Media creates books and software for Information Technology professionals seeking skill enhancement and career advancement. Its products are designed to comply with vendor and industry standard course curricula, and are optimized for certification exam preparation. You can contact Syngress via the Web at http://www.syngress.com.

Melissa Craft is a consulting engineer for MicroAge in Phoenix, Arizona. She has a bachelor's degree from the University of Michigan. After relocating to the Southwest, Melissa became increasingly involved with technology, and obtained several certifications: CNE-3, CNE-4, CNE-GW, MCNE, Citrix, and MCSE. Melissa Craft is a member of the IEEE, the Society of Women Engineers, and American MENSA, Ltd.

Justin Grant is an Internetworking Practice Manager with Xerox Connect where he leads the Internetworking Services Group at their Louisville, Kentucky branch. Xerox Connect, Inc., a wholly owned subsidiary of Xerox Corporation, is a national systems integrator providing enterprise-wide technology solutions for businesses with complex computing needs. With over 1,500 engineers, developers, and consultants in 30 branches nationwide, Xerox Connect helps its clients meet the challenges of planning, building, and managing state-of-the-art technologies. As a Novell Enterprise Consulting Partner, Xerox Connect ensures its clients the highest caliber of Novell solutions and professional services expertise in the industry. Justin has many years of networking experience, and his certifications include several CNA's, CNE's, Master CNE's and a CNI. His focus is on delivering enterprise solutions using Novell technology. Justin can be reached at the following address: justin.grant@connect.xerox.com.

Todd Meadors teaches full-time computer classes for DeKalb Technical Institute, outside Atlanta, Georgia. He holds CNE and MCSE certifications, and he has an MBA and MS in Computer Information Systems (CIS). He credits LANOP The Computer Lab for assisting him in obtaining the MCSE. He would like to dedicate his sections of the book to his family: Micki, Zac, and Jessie.

James Vogan Tysinger is a CNE who resides in Sacramento, California, with his wife Kathleen, son Conor, and daughter Grace. He currently works as a network engineer and administrator on Novell, Windows NT, and Macintosh networks. He would like to dedicate his sections of the book to his Uncle, Jim Vogan, who introduced him to the world of computers beginning with that first Apple][.

Brian Frederick is a Systems Engineer for Entre Information Systems, a midwest network solution provider and Novell Platinum Partner. He is an MCNE as well as an MCSE. Brian has been in the networking field for over 7 years. He has written a book on MCSE certification and has also coauthored other books on the various Microsoft certification exams.

Darin McGee is a Senior Network Engineer under contract with the FCC. He holds the CNP, MCNE, MCSE+Internet, NCIP, and A+ certifications. Darin has been working with computers since 1979, when he taught himself the BASIC programming language on a Tandy TRS-80. Darin can be reached at darin@tolder.com.

Jim Queen is a NetWare Master CNE with over 14 years of networking experience, specializing in the support of NetWare 4, NetWare 5, and directory services in WAN environments. He is the President of Network Data Services, Inc., based in Dallas, Texas and can be reached at jqueen@ndsvcs.com.

Vernon Hall graduated with a B.S. in Computer Science from James Madison University in 1992 and has been working as a consultant and network engineer for the past six years. He has been designing, installing, and supporting large Novell NetWare internetworks the entire time, and has worked with NetWare versions 3.11 through NetWare 5. He currently holds both CNE and MCSE certifications. Vernon has also worked extensively with Windows NT since its early versions, and specializes in implementing networks where NetWare and NT coexist. He is currently working as the Director of MIS for M.C. Dean, Inc. in Chantilly, Virginia.

Dorothy McGee has worked in the computer industry for more than 12 years and currently holds CNA, CNE, MCNE, MCP, MCP+Internet, MCSE and A+ certifications.

Technical Reviewer and From the Classroom Contributor

Daniel Y. Cheung (CNI, CNE, MCNE, MCP, MCT) has been a networking consultant since 1996 and a technical trainer since 1995. Daniel is currently an instructor in computer networking at University of New England-Westbrook College, Portland, Maine, as well as a freelance writer and editor. Dan spent ten years working in bank financial accounting systems and served six years on active duty as a Captain in the United States Army. He has a BA from Cornell University, Ithaca, NY, and has also attended Northwestern University-University College, Evanston, IL, and the University of Alaska-Anchorage, Anchorage, AK. Dan is also a competitive rower (sculling).

ACKNOWLEDGMENTS

We would like to thank the following people:

- Richard Kristof of Global Knowledge for championing the series and providing us access to some great people and information, and to Shelly Everett for her assistance.

- All the incredibly hard-working folks at Osborne/McGraw-Hill: Brandon Nordin, Scott Rogers, and Gareth Hancock for their help in launching a great series and being solid team players, as well as Emily Rader, Betsy Manini, and Mark Karmendy for their help in fine-tuning the book.

- Marcy Shanti at Novell for being patient and diligent in answering all our questions.

CONTENTS

Foreword. . . . .   *iii*

About the Contributors. . . . .   *vii*

Acknowledgments. . . . .   *xi*

Preface . . . .   *xxxxi*

Part I
NetWare 5 Administration   I

I   Introduction to intraNetWare   3

Administrator Responsibilities   4

    Reactive Administration   5

    Proactive Administration   6

Network Resources and Services   8

Introduction to Novell Directory Services   9

    NDS Structure   10

    Leaf Objects   11

    Object Properties and Values   15

    The NDS Database   17

Introduction to a Tree Structure   18

How the Directory Tree Affects Resource Access   20

    Rights Within NDS   20

Certification Summary   22

Two-Minute Drill   24

Self Test   27

2   Enabling Network Access   31

Enabling Network Communication (IPX/IP)   32

Client 32 Overview   33

    Multiple Link Interface Driver (MLID)   34

    Link Support Layer   35

    IPX Protocol or IP Compatibility Protocol   35

    NetWare Client Software   35

Client 32 Installation Procedure for Windows 95 37
Client 32 Installation Procedure for Windows NT 41
Login Concepts 42
    Restrictions in NDS 43
    Intruder Detection 45
Login Process 47
Browser Client Installation 49
Certification Summary 50
Two-Minute Drill 52
Self Test 54

3   Managing User Accounts **57**
Introduction to User Object Management 58
    Understanding User Object Context 59
    Network Administrator Utilities 62
Creating User Objects 63
    NetWare Administrator 69
    NetAdmin 71
    Console One 72
    UIMPORT 73
Adding Licenses 74
Introduction to Network Security 77
    Security for User Objects 78
Login Security 79
Certification Summary 80
Two-Minute Drill 82
Self Test 85

4   Managing Network Printing **89**
Network Printing Overview 90
    Print Queues and Print Servers 90
    New Technology Directions 105
Introduction to Novell Distributed Print Services 105
    Benefits of NDPS 105
    NDPS Structure 107
Setting Up NetWare Distributed Print Services (NDPS) 109
    Setting Up NDPS During Server Installation 109
    Completing NDPS Setup from the Workstation 110

Managing NDPS 114
Certification Summary 121
Two-Minute Drill 122
Self Test 125

5   Managing the File System **129**
Introduction to Managing the Network File System 130
    File System Components 130
File System Management Utilities 132
    NLIST 132
    NDIR 134
    FILER 135
    NetWare Administrator 137
Displaying File System Information 138
Accessing the File System 141
Managing the Directory Structure 144
Managing Files 144
Managing Volume Space Usage 146
Certification Summary 150
Two-Minute Drill 151
Self Test 154

6   Managing File System Security **157**
Introduction to File System Security 158
Planning File System Rights 158
    Inheritance and Filters 163
    Security Equivalence 163
    Effective Rights 165
    Rules for Planning 167
Planning File System Attribute Security 168
    File and Directory Attributes 168
    Planning File System Attributes 172
Implementing File System Security 174
    Trustee Rights 175
    File System Attributes 175
Certification Summary 177
Two-Minute Drill 178
Self Test 181

7 Creating Login Scripts **185**

Login Script Overview 186
    Container Script 187
    Profile Script 188
    User Scripts 190
    Default Login Script 192
Designing Login Script Systems 193
    Login Script Commands 197
    Cascading Container Scripts 200
Creating, Executing, and Debugging Login Scripts 202
Login Scripts and the GUI Login Utility 207
Certification Summary 208
Two-Minute Drill 209
Self Test 212

8 Remote Management of Workstations (NEBO) 215

Introduction to the Z.E.N.works Desktop
    Management Utilities 216
    Z.E.N.works Features 216
    Installing Z.E.N.works 217
Remote Control Access Utilities (NEBO) 221
Creating Workstation Objects 221
Using Login Scripts to Register Workstations in
    Novell Directory Services 226
Configuring Workstations for Remote Control Access 227
Using the Help Request Application to Log
    Workstation Problems 232
Synchronizing a Workstation with Its NDS Object 237
Certification Summary 239
Two-Minute Drill 241
Self Test 243

9 Configuring Network Applications for Users ... 247

Introduction to the NetWare Application Launcher (NAL) ... 248
    NAL Features 250
    Enabling NAL 254
Configuring NDS and the File System for NAL 256
    snAppShot Basics 256

Simple vs. Complex Applications 263

NDS Object and Property Rights 264

Application Objects 269

File System Rights 275

Launching Network Applications with NAL 277

Certification Summary 277

Two-Minute Drill 280

Self Test 283

**10 Using Workstation Manager to Manage
Workstations** **287**

Introduction to Workstation Manager 288

Installing and Configuring Multiple Clients with

Workstation Manager 291

Enabling Workstation Manager Policies 293

Configuring the Novell Client 296

Managing Workstation Inventory 299

Managing Profiles and Policies with NDS 302

Desktop Management 302

System Policies 304

Scheduling Workstation Application Upgrades 307

Dynamically Configuring Printers and Print Queues 308

Windows NT User Management 309

Certification Summary 311

Two-Minute Drill 312

Self Test 314

11 Managing NDS Security **317**

Introduction to NDS Security 318

Controlling Directory Access with Object Trustee and NDS Rights

Assignments 320

Object Rights 323

Property Rights 324

NDS Default Rights 325

[Public] Trustee 326

Default Object Rights 326

Default Property Rights 327

NDS Rights Inheritance 328
    Security Equivalence 330
Blocking Inherited Rights 332
Determining an Object's Effective Rights 334
Guidelines for Implementing NDS Security 336
Troubleshooting NDS Security 337
Certification Summary 338
Two-Minute Drill 340
Self Test 343

12 Managing Resources in a Multicontext
Environment **345**
How the Directory Tree Affects the Network 347
    Just How Is That Directory Tree Made Up Again? 348
    Object Interaction in the Directory Tree 352
How the Directory Tree Affects
    NDS Planning and Design 354
Setting Context for Resource Access 354
    Current Context and Object Context 356
    Contextless Login with NetWare 5 356
Shortcuts to Accessing and Managing Resources 357
    Naming Concepts 357
    Those Dots Are Confusing 359
Guidelines for Setting Up Resources 360
    Configuring NDS for Login 361
    Configuring NDS for Resource Access 361
Summary of Actions and Rights Needed 363
Using Correct Naming in Login Scripts 363
Certification Summary 364
Two-Minute Drill 364
Self Test 367

13 Performing a Simple Installation **373**
Common Install Interface Overview 374
Comparing Simple and Custom Installations 375
    Simple Installations 375
    Custom Installations 379

Using the GUI Installation Utility to Perform a

Simple Install 382

    Setting Up the Hardware 383

    Creating the NetWare Partition and Volume SYS: 384

    Server Name 385

    Installing the File System 385

Certification Summary 392

Two-Minute Drill 393

Self Test 396

Part II
NetWare 5 Advanced Administration 399

14 Upgrading NetWare 3.1x to NetWare 5

Server **401**

Upgrade Overview 402

    In-Place Upgrade Method 403

    Across-the-Wire Migration Method 404

Hardware and Software Requirements for a

NetWare 5 Server 405

    Hardware Requirements 406

    Software Requirements 408

Upgrade Prerequisites 408

    Client Software Considerations 408

    In-Place Upgrade Preparation 409

    Preparing to Migrate Across the Wire 411

Install Files 415

Upgrade Steps 415

    In-Place Upgrade Steps 415

    Across-the-Wire Migration Steps 418

After the Upgrade 421

Confirm the Upgrade 422

Certification Summary 422

Two-Minute Drill 423

Self Test 426

15 Upgrading from Queue-Based Printing to NDPS **429**

Overview of the Upgrade 430
    Designing the NDPS System 431
    Creating NDPS Objects 432
    Upgrading the Clients 434
Gathering Current Printing Information 435
Configuring Your Current Printing Information 437
Migrating Printing Components 439
    Interoperability with Print Queue Components 441
    NDPS Migration Scenarios 442
    Migration 443
Testing Migrated Components 446
Removing the Old Printing Environment 447
Certification Summary 449
Two-Minute Drill 450
Self Test 452

16 Performing a Custom Installation **455**

Installing NetWare 5 Using the Custom Option 456
    Custom Installation Steps 457
Modifying Volume Parameters 457
    Volume Types 458
    Creating a Volume 458
    Mounting a Volume 459
Integrating Multiple Protocols 460
    Configuring the Internet Protocol (IP) 460
    Configuring the Internetwork Packet eXchange
        (IPX) Protocol 461
    IPX Compatibility, DNS, and SNMP 462
Certification Summary 463
Two-Minute Drill 463
Self Test 466

17 Setting Up the Network File System **469**

Introduction to Planning 470
System-Created Directories 477
Possible Directory Structures 479

Creating Additional Volumes 482
Designing Directory Structures 485
Certification Summary 487
Two-Minute Drill 487
Self Test 490

18 Using the Server Console **493**
NetWare Server Overview 494
Executing Console Commands 496
    Navigating the Server Console 497
    Navigating Console One 497
Loading and Unloading NLMs 497
Server Configuration Files 498
Customizing the Server Configuration Files 499
Creating Server Batch Files 501
Accessing the Server Console from a Workstation 501
    Navigating the Console with RCONSOLE 503
Protecting Your Server 504
    Using SECURE CONSOLE 505
    Using SCRSAVER to Secure the Server 505
Loading Support for Java Applications on the
    NetWare 5 Server 506
Using the NetWare ServerTop 506
Certification Summary 507
Two-Minute Drill 507
Self Test 510

19 Optimizing the Network and Server **513**
Memory Overview 514
    More and More Memory 515
    Server Performance 515
    Types of Memory 515
Memory Allocation and Deallocation 516
Virtual Memory 517
    Configuring Virtual Memory 518
    Disk Thrashing 518
Monitor Statistics 519

Server Buffer and Packet Parameters 521
    Increasing Maximum Packet Buffers 522
    Minimum Packet Receive Buffers 523
Block Suballocation 523
Enabling File Compression 524
    Disabling File Compression 525
    Using NetWare Administrator to Configure
      File Compression 525
Packet Burst 527
Large Internet Packets 528
Certification Summary 529
Two-Minute Drill 530
Self Test 533

20 Backing Up Servers and Workstations **535**
Introduction to Storage Management Services 536
Choosing a Backup Strategy 538
    Time Requirements 538
    Time Requirements for Restoration 540
    Backup Security Rights 540
Backing Up a NetWare Server 541
    Backing Up Your Servers and Workstations 541
    Backup Terminology 542
    NetWare Backup/Restore Program Guidelines 543
    Backing Up a Novell NetWare 5 Server 543
Restoring Data 545
Certification Summary 547
Two-Minute Drill 547
Self Test 549

21 Using DNS/DHCP Services **551**
DNS/DHCP Overview 552
    Domain Name Service 552
    Dynamic Host Configuration Protocol 553
Installing DNS/DHCP Services 553
Configuring and Starting DHCP Services 556
    Creating the DHCP Server Object 558
    Creating the Subnet Object 559
    Creating the Subnet Address Range (SAR) Object 560

Exporting and Importing DHCP Databases 561

Configuring and Starting DNS Services 562

Exporting and Importing DNS Databases 564

Certification Summary 564

Two-Minute Drill 565

Self Test 567

22 Installing a Web Server **569**

Introduction to the FastTrack Web Server 570

Installing the FastTrack Web Server 570

    Minimum Requirements 571

    Installation 572

Configuring the FastTrack Web Server 574

    Admin Preferences 576

    Global Settings 577

    Users and Groups 578

    Keys and Certificates 579

    Cluster Management 581

Troubleshooting the Web Server 581

Certification Summary 585

Two-Minute Drill 586

Self Test 588

23 Securing the Directory Tree **591**

NDS Default Rights 592

    Trustee Assignments 594

    Security Equivalence 596

    Inherited Rights 596

    Inherited Rights Filter 597

    Effective Rights 597

    Inheritable Rights 597

Guidelines for Implementing NDS Security 599

Centralized Versus Distributed Administration 600

Suggested Administrative Roles and Rights Assignments 603

    Container Administrators 603

    File System Administrator 604

    Installers 605

    The Help Desk 607

Password Administrators 608
Partition Administrators 609
Certification Summary 609
Two-Minute Drill 611
Self Test 612

24   Maintaining NDS **615**
Understanding Replication and Synchronization 616
Replication 617
Synchronization 627
Preventative Maintenance 628
Before NDS Is Installed 628
After NDS Is Installed 629
Troubleshooting NDS Inconsistencies 631
Readily Apparent Problems and Symptoms
of Problems with NDS 631
NDS Problems That Take Some Detective Work 632
Repairing NDS 634
DS Repair 635
NDS Manager 636
Recovering from a Crashed SYS: Volume 637
Certification Summary 639
Two-Minute Drill 640
Self Test 643

25   Mobile Clients **647**
Introduction to Mobile Clients 648
Remote Node versus Remote Control 648
Connecting Remotely 651
Using Remote Connections 652
Remote Clients 654
Installing NetWare Connect on the Server 656
Server Product Installation 656
Configuring NetWare Connect 660
Configuration at the Server Console 660
Configuration Within NetWare Administrator 663
Certification Summary 666
Two-Minute Drill 667
Self Test 669

Part III
Networking Technologies 671

26 Network Services 673

Networking Technologies 674
    Computer Networking Models 674
    Network Sizes 675
    Network Components 676
Network Services 676
    File Services 677
    Print Services 678
    Message Services 679
    Application Services 679
    Database Services 680
Network Management 680
    Configuration Management 680
    Fault Management 681
    Security Management 681
    Accounting Management 681
    Performance Management 681
Certification Summary 682
Two-Minute Drill 683
Self Test 684

27 Transmission Media and Connections 687

Media Types 688
    Cost 688
    Installation 689
    Capacity 689
    Attenuation 689
    Electromagnetic Interference 689
Cable Media 690
    Twisted-Pair Cable 690
    Coaxial Cable 693
    Fiber-Optic Cable 694
Wireless Media 696
    Radio Wave Transmissions Systems 696
    Microwave Transmission Systems 696
    Infrared Transmission Systems 697

Public and Private Network Services 697
Transmission Media Connections 697
    Network Connectivity Devices 698
    Internetwork Connectivity Devices 700
Certification Summary 701
Two-Minute Drill 702
Self Test 703

28 The OSI Model's Lower Layers **705**
The OSI Model 706
    Protocol Stacks 707
    Peer Layer Communication Between Stacks 708
The Physical Layer 709
    Connection Types 710
    Physical Topology 710
    Bit Synchronization 717
    Baseband and Broadband Transmissions 718
    Multiplexing Methods 718
The Data Link Layer 718
    Logical Topology 719
    Media Access Control 719
    Data Link Layer Addressing 720
    Transmission Synchronization 721
    Connection Services 722
Certification Summary 722
Two-Minute Drill 724
Self Test 726

29 The OSI Model's Middle Layers **729**
The Middle Layers of the OSI Model 730
The Network Layer 730
    Network Layer Addressing 731
    Service Addressing 732
    Switching 732
    Routing 734
    Route Discovery 735

Connection Services 736
Gateway Services 736
The Transport Layer 738
Transport Layer Addressing 738
Address/Name Resolution 738
Message Segment Development 739
Connection Services 739
Certification Summary 740
Two-Minute Drill 743
Self Test 745

30 The OSI Model's Upper Layers **747**
Upper Layers of the OSI Model 748
The Session Layer 748
Dialog Control 749
Session Administration 749
The Presentation Layer 751
Data Translation 751
Encryption 752
The Application Layer 753
Service Advertising 753
Service Use Methods 754
Certification Summary 755
Two-Minute Drill 756
Self Test 757

Part IV
Networking Directory Services Design and
Implementation **759**

31 Assessing the Network **761**
Defining the NetWare Design and Implementation Process ... 762
System Design Life Cycles 763
The NetWare Design and Implementation Process 766
Identifying the Design and Implementation Team 771
Assessing Business Needs 776

Previewing Case Company Information 777
Certification Summary 779
Two-Minute Drill 780
Self Test 781

32   Defining and Justifying the Network Solution .. 783

Defining a Network Solution 784
Creating a Design and Implementation Schedule 788
   Design Phase 788
   Implementation Phase 790
Calculating the Costs, Benefits, and Risks 792
Selling the Solution 794
Launching the Design and Implementation Process 795
Certification Summary 795
Two-Minute Drill 796
Self Test 798

33   Designing the Directory Tree 801

Creating a Naming Standards Document 802
NDS Naming Standard 804
   Tree and Container Units 805
   Server and Volume Names 808
   Leaf Object Names 809
Guidelines for the Upper Layers 815
Assessing Other Design Considerations 818
Certification Summary 820
Two-Minute Drill 821
Self Test 822

**34   Implementing Time Synchronization
     Strategies 825**

Determining a Partition Boundary Strategy 826
   A Brief Review of the NDS Database 826
   Partitioning Issues 830
Reviewing Time Synchronization Issues 837
   Time Setup in an IPX Environment 838
   Time Setup in an IP or Mixed IP/IPX Environment ... 839

Planning a Time Synchronization Strategy 840

Certification Summary 845

Two-Minute Drill 846

Self Test 849

35   Creating an Accessibility Plan 853

Creating a User Accessibility Needs Analysis Document 854

    Application Needs 854

    Physical Network Needs 855

    Needs to Access Legacy Network Services 855

Creating an Accessibility Guideline Document 856

Creating an Administrative Strategies Document 859

    Common Login Scripts 859

    Security Guidelines 860

    Design Strategy for Legacy Services 862

Certification Summary 866

Two-Minute Drill 866

Self Test 869

36   Conducting a NetWare Implementation 871

Creating the Directory Tree 872

    Assessing the Situation 872

    Defining the Network Solution 874

    Designing the Directory Tree 879

Managing Partitions and Replicas 883

    Partitions 883

Implementing and Managing Time Synchronization 886

    The Novell Time Synchronization Model 887

    NetWare 5 Time Synchronization 889

Merging NDS Trees 890

    Running DSMERGE 892

Providing Network Access 894

    File System Rights 895

    NDS Rights 895

Certification Summary 896

Two-Minute Drill 897

Self Test 899

Part V
NetWare Service and Support **901**

37 Network Troubleshooting **903**

Preventing Problems 904
  Problems in the Physical Environment 904
  Electrical Problems 905
  Viruses 908
  Security 909
Troubleshooting the Network 910
  The Novell Troubleshooting Model 910
  Diagnostic Tools 912
Reference Sources 913
  The Support Connection CD 913
  NetWire on CompuServe 914
  Novell's Web Site 917
  The Support Source 920
Certification Summary 925
Two-Minute Drill 925
Self Test 927

**38 Installing and Troubleshooting Network Interface
  Cards and Cables** **931**

Ethernet Networks 932
  How Ethernet Works 932
  Ethernet Cabling Types 934
  10Base5 (Thicknet) Ethernet 934
  10Base2 (Thinnet) Ethernet 935
  10BaseT / 100BaseTX (Twisted-Pair) Ethernet 936
  100Base-T4 (Twisted-Pair) Ethernet 939
Token Ring Networks 940
  How Token Ring Works 941
  Token Ring Cabling Types 942
  Network Card Types 944
  Troubleshooting Ethernet 949
  Troubleshooting Token Ring 950
FDDI Networks 950
ATM Networks 952

Certification Summary 954
Two-Minute Drill 954
Self Test 957

39 Installing and Troubleshooting Network Storage Devices 961

Hard Drives 962
    Hard Drive Interface Types 964
    Setting Jumpers on the Hard Drive and Controller Card 969
    Hard Drive Cabling 976
    Formatting the Hard Drive 976
Using RAID Devices 978
    Disk Mirroring and Disk Duplexing 979
CD-ROM Drives on NetWare 982
Magneto-Optical Drives 984
Certification Summary 984
Two-Minute Drill 984
Self Test 986

40 Troubleshooting the DOS Workstation 989

The Workstation's Communication with the Server 990
    What Occurs During the INSTALL Process? 990
    Files and Programs Used on DOS Workstations 993
    Setting Up a Workstation's NIC 998
    NetWare's Watchdog Feature for Workstations 1000
    Using the Remote Boot Feature 1002
    Using TRACK for Troubleshooting 1002
Troubleshooting Hardware Conflicts 1004
    Types of PC Memory 1005
DOS Versions 1005
Certification Summary 1006
Two-Minute Drill 1006
Self Test 1008

41 Troubleshooting Network Printing 1011

An Overview of Network Printing 1012
General Printer Troubleshooting 1017

Troubleshooting Print Queues 1019

Troubleshooting Print Server and Printer Objects 1023

Certification Summary 1026

Two-Minute Drill 1027

Self Test 1028

**42 Troubleshooting the Server and
the Network** **1031**

Installing Server Software Updates 1032

    Operating System Updates 1033

    Device Driver Updates 1035

Understanding Server Abends and Lockups 1036

    Server Lockups 1040

    Troubleshooting Server Abends and Lockups 1041

Troubleshooting Performance Bottlenecks 1044

    Disk I/O Problems 1045

    Network I/O Problems 1045

    CPU Problems 1046

    Bus I/O Problems 1046

Using LANalyzer to Diagnose Performance Problems 1047

    Network Errors 1048

    Determining Baseline Network Performance 1048

    Diagnosing Overloaded Servers and Networks 1049

Developing Disaster Recovery Options 1049

    Planning for a Disaster 1049

    Recovering from a Disaster 1050

Certification Summary 1053

Two-Minute Drill 1053

Self Test 1056

**Part VI
IntranetWare: Integrating
Windows NT** **1059**

**43 Introduction to
Windows NT** **1061**

Windows Product Overview 1062

    Windows 95 1063

Windows NT Workstation 4.0 1064

Windows NT Server 4.0 1066

Logging In to Windows NT 1067

Windows NT Default Accounts 1069

Administrator Account 1069

Guest User Account 1070

Initial User Account (NT Workstation) 1071

The Windows Registry 1071

Subtree 1072

Hive 1073

Editing the Registry 1074

Windows NT Utilities and Programs 1074

My Computer 1075

Windows NT Explorer 1076

Network Neighborhood 1077

Control Panel 1077

Disk Administrator 1079

Adminstrative Wizards 1080

Server Manager 1080

Event Viewer 1081

System Policy Editor 1082

Adding Users to the Local Workstation 1083

Certification Summary 1086

Two-Minute Drill 1086

Self Test 1090

44   Introduction to Windows NT

Networking **1093**

Windows NT Networking Models 1094

The Workgroup Model 1094

The Domain Model 1096

Supported Protocols in Windows NT 1098

NetBEUI 1100

NWLink IPX/SPX Compatible 1100

TCP/IP 1101

Other Protocols Used on a Windows NT Network 1102

Supported File Systems in Windows NT 1102

FAT 1103

NTFS Overview 1104

FAT Versus NTFS 1105

Using Disk Administrator to Manage the File System 1105

Partitioning the Hard Disk 1106

Volume Sets 1107

Creating Shares and Granting Permissions 1107

Creating Shares for Resource Access 1108

Granting Permissions 1112

Certification Summary 1116

Two-Minute Drill 1116

Self Test 1119

45 Windows NT Domain

Networking **1123**

NT Directory Services (NTDS) 1124

Single Network Logins 1126

Integration with Windows NT-Based Applications 1126

Single Point of Administration 1126

Directory Replication 1127

Domain Server Roles 1127

Primary Domain Controller (PDC) 1127

Backup Domain Controllers (BDC) 1128

Member Servers 1129

Setting Up Domain Controllers 1130

The Domain Logon Process 1131

Creating and Administering Domain User Accounts ... 1133

Local Groups 1135

Global Groups 1138

Adding a Workstation or Server to a Domain 1142

Certification Summary 1144

Two-Minute Drill 1145

Self Test 1147

46 Managing Windows NT

Security **1149**

Windows NT Security 1150

Windows NT Security Components 1152

Resource Access Controls 1154

Policies 1155
    Account Policies 1156
    User Rights Policies 1158
    Audit Policies 1159
User Profiles 1161
System Policies 1165
Certification Summary 1167
Two-Minute Drill 1167
Self Test 1170

**47 Multiple Domain Windows
NT Networking** **1173**
Trusts 1174
    Trusted Versus Trusting 1174
    Using Groups with Trust Relationships 1177
    Setting Up Trust Relationships 1178
Domain Models 1180
    Single Domain Model 1182
    Single Master Domain Model 1184
    Multiple Master Domain Model 1186
    Complete Trust Model 1188
Certification Summary 1190
Two-Minute Drill 1190
Self Test 1193

48 Integrating Windows NT Workstations **1197**
Benefits of Integrating Windows NT Workstations
    with NDS 1198
NDS Integrated Messaging Multiprotocol Support
    Management 1199
32-Bit NetWare Administrator on an NT Workstation 1199
    Management of Local NT Workstation User
        Accounts in NDS 1200
    Distribution and Management of Network
        Applications 1201
Windows NT Workstation Benefits 1202
    Providing Access to NetWare Services 1202

Introduction to the NetWare Client for Windows NT 1202
Installing the NetWare Client for Windows NT 1203
Updating the Client with Automatic Client
Update (ACU) 1204
Managing Windows NT Workstation Users and Desktops . . . 1204
Introduction to the Novell Workstation Manager 1205
NWGINA 1206
Snap-In for the NT Client Configuration Object 1206
Creating and Configuring the NT Client
Configuration Object 1207
Associating Users with the NT Client
Configuration Object 1207
Managing User Profiles and System Policies 1208
Introduction to the Novell Application Launcher (NAL) 1208
Installing and Configuring NAL 1208
Certification Summary 1210
Two-Minute Drill 1210
Self Test 1212

**49 Integrating NetWare and Windows
NT Domains** **1215**
Benefits of Integrating Windows NT
Domains with NDS 1216
Reducing Redundant Administration by Managing
Windows NT Domains from NetWare
Administrator 1216
Allowing Access to Both Windows NT and NetWare
Resources and Services 1217
Introduction to the Novell Administrator for Windows NT . . 1217
NDS Schema Extensions 1218
NetWare Administrator Snap-In Service 1218
NDS Event Monitor 1219
NDS Object Replication Service 1219
Integration Utility 1220
Integration Security 1220
Installing and Configuring Novell Administrator for
Windows NT 1221

Synchronizing NetWare and Windows NT Users
and Groups 1224
Integrating NDS Users to Windows NT 1225
Integrating Windows NT Users to NDS 1225
Synchronizing Existing NDS Users with Existing
Windows NT Users 1226
Configuring User Properties 1227
Replicating New NDS Users to Windows NT 1228
Using NetWare Administrator 1228
Certification Summary 1229
Two-Minute Drill 1230
Self Test 1233

A   Self-Test Answers **1237**
Answers to Chapter 1 Self Test 1238
Answers to Chapter 2 Self Test 1238
Answers to Chapter 3 Self Test 1239
Answers to Chapter 4 Self Test 1239
Answers to Chapter 5 Self Test 1240
Answers to Chapter 6 Self Test 1241
Answers to Chapter 7 Self Test 1241
Answers to Chapter 8 Self Test 1242
Answers to Chapter 9 Self Test 1243
Answers to Chapter 10 Self Test 1243
Answers to Chapter 11 Self Test 1244
Answers to Chapter 12 Self Test 1245
Answers to Chapter 13 Self Test 1245
Answers to Chapter 14 Self Test 1246
Answers to Chapter 15 Self Test 1247
Answers to Chapter 16 Self Test 1247
Answers to Chapter 17 Self Test 1248
Answers to Chapter 18 Self Test 1248
Answers to Chapter 19 Self Test 1249
Answers to Chapter 20 Self Test 1249
Answers to Chapter 21 Self Test 1250

Answers to Chapter 22 Self Test 1250
Answers to Chapter 23 Self Test 1251
Answers to Chapter 24 Self Test 1252
Answers to Chapter 25 Self Test 1253
Answers to Chapter 26 Self Test 1253
Answers to Chapter 27 Self Test 1254
Answers to Chapter 28 Self Test 1254
Answers to Chapter 29 Self Test 1255
Answers to Chapter 30 Self Test 1255
Answers to Chapter 31 Self Test 1256
Answers to Chapter 32 Self Test 1256
Answers to Chapter 33 Self Test 1257
Answers to Chapter 34 Self Test 1257
Answers to Chapter 35 Self Test 1258
Answers to Chapter 36 Self Test 1259
Answers to Chapter 37 Self Test 1260
Answers to Chapter 38 Self Test 1260
Answers to Chapter 39 Self Test 1261
Answers to Chapter 40 Self Test 1262
Answers to Chapter 41 Self Test 1262
Answers to Chapter 42 Self Test 1263
Answers to Chapter 43 Self Test 1264
Answers to Chapter 44 Self Test 1265
Answers to Chapter 45 Self Test 1266
Answers to Chapter 46 Self Test 1266
Answers to Chapter 47 Self Test 1267
Answers to Chapter 48 Self Test 1268
Answers to Chapter 49 Self Test 1269

B   About the CD **1271**
Test Type Choices 1272
    Live 1272
    Managing Windows 1272
    Saving Scores as Cookies 1273
    Using the Browser Buttons 1273

	JavaScript Errors	1273
	Practice	1273
	Review	1274
	Scoring	1274
C	**About the Web Site**	**1275**
	Access Global Knowledge Network	1276
	What You'll Find There...	1276
D	**The Career Center**	**1277**
	The "Help Wanteds": Planning Your Attack	1278
	The Job Search	1278
	Networking 101	1279
	Using Placement Services	1280
	Going Online	1281
	Getting the Advice of Peers	1282
	The Interview	1282
	Working with a Headhunter	1283
	Preparing for the Interview	1285
	Acing the Interview	1285
	Following Up on the Interview	1287
	Glossary	**1289**
	Index	**1313**

PREFACE

This book's primary objective is to help you prepare for and pass the required CNE exams, so you can begin to reap the career benefits of certification. We believe that the only way to do this is to help you increase your knowledge and build your skills. After completing this book, you should feel confident that you have thoroughly reviewed all of the objectives that Novell has established for the exam.

In Every Chapter

We've created a set of chapter components that call your attention to important items, reinforce important points, and provide helpful exam-taking hints. Take a look at what you'll find in every chapter:

- Every chapter begins with the **Certification Objectives**—what you need to know in order to pass the section on the exam dealing with the chapter topic. The Certification Objective headings identify the objectives within the chapter, so you'll always know an objective when you see it!

- **Exam Watch** notes call attention to information about, and potential pitfalls in, the exam. These helpful hints are written by CNEs and MCNEs who have taken the exams and received their certification— who better to tell you what to worry about? They know what you're about to go through!

- **On the Job** notes point out procedures and techniques important for coding actual applications for employers or contract jobs.

EXERCISE

- **Certification Exercises** are interspersed throughout the chapters. These are step-by-step exercises that mirror vendor-recommended labs. They help you master skills that are likely to be an area of focus on the exam. Don't just read through the exercises; they are hands-on practice that you should be comfortable completing.

Learning by doing is an effective way to increase your competency with a product.

■ **From the Classroom** sidebars describe the issues that come up most often in the training classroom setting. These sidebars give you a valuable perspective into certification- and product-related topics. They point out common mistakes and address questions that have arisen from classroom discussions.

■ The **Certification Summary** is a succinct review of the chapter and a re-statement of salient points regarding the exam.

■ The **Two-Minute Drill** at the end of every chapter is a checklist of the main points of the chapter. It can be used for last-minute review.

■ The **Self Test** offers questions similar to those found on the certification exams, including multiple choice, true/false questions, and fill-in-the-blank. The answers to these questions, as well as explanations of the answers, can be found in Appendix A. By taking the Self Test after completing each chapter, you'll reinforce what you've learned from that chapter, while becoming familiar with the structure of the exam questions.

Some Pointers

Once you've finished reading this book, set aside some time to do a thorough review. You might want to return to the book several times and make use of all the methods it offers for reviewing the material:

1. *Re-read all the Two-Minute Drills,* or have someone quiz you. You also can use the drills as a way to do a quick cram before the exam.

2. *Re-read all the Exam Watch notes.* Remember that these are written by CNEs who have taken the exam and passed. They know what you should expect—and what you should be careful about.

3. *Re-take the Self Tests.* Taking the tests right after you've read the chapter is a good idea, because it helps reinforce what you've just learned. However, it's an even better idea to go back later and do all

the questions in the book in one sitting. Pretend you're taking the exam. (For this reason, you should mark your answers on a separate piece of paper when you go through the questions the first time.)

4. *Complete the exercises.* Did you do the exercises when you read through each chapter? If not, do them! These exercises are designed to cover exam topics, and there's no better way to get to know this material than by practicing.

5. *Check out the Web site.* Global Knowledge Network invites you to become an active member of the Access Global Web site. This site is an online mall and an information repository that you'll find invaluable. You can access many types of products to assist you in your preparation for the exams, and you'll be able to participate in forums, online discussions, and threaded discussions. No other book brings you unlimited access to such a resource. You'll find more information about this site in Appendix C.

How to Take a Novell CNE Certification Examination

Good News and Bad News

If you are new to Novell certification, we have some good news and some bad news. The good news is that Novell's CNE certification is one of the most highly recognized and respected IT credentials you can earn. It sets you apart from the crowd and marks you as a valuable asset to your employer and customers. Not only will you gain the respect of your peers, the CNE certification can have a positive effect on your income potential.

The bad news is that CNE certification tests are not easy. You may think you can read through some study materials, memorize a few facts, and pass the examinations. After all, these certification exams are just computer-based, multiple-choice tests, so they must be easy. If you believe this, you are wrong. Unlike many standardized tests you may have been exposed to in school, the questions on CNE certification exams go beyond merely processing factual knowledge.

The purpose of this introduction is to teach you how to take a CNE certification exam. To be successful, you need to know something about the purpose and structure of these tests. We will also look at the latest testing methodologies used in Novell testing. Using simulations and adaptive testing, Novell is enhancing both the validity and security of the certification process. These factors have some important effects on how you should prepare for an exam, as well as your approach to each question during the test.

We'll start by looking at the purpose, focus, and structure of Novell certification tests, and examine the effect these factors have on the kinds of questions you will see. We will define the structure of examination questions, and investigate some common formats. Next, we will present a strategy for answering these questions. Finally, we will give some specific guidelines on what you should do on the day of your test.

Why Vendor Certification?

The Novell CNE program, like the certification programs from Lotus, Microsoft, Oracle, and other software vendors, is maintained for the ultimate purpose of increasing an organization's profits and/or maximizing their productivity and efficiency. A successful vendor certification program accomplishes this goal by helping to create a pool of experts in a company's software, and by "branding" these experts so that companies using the software can identify them and be assured of a baseline level of knowledge, albeit a rather high one.

We know that vendor certifications have become increasingly popular in the last few years because it helps employers find qualified workers, and because it helps software vendors, like Novell, to sell their products. But why should you be interested in vendor certification rather than a more traditional approach like a college or professional degree in computer science? A college education is a broadening and enriching experience, but a degree in computer science does not prepare students for most jobs in the IT industry.

Computer and telecommunications technology have been developing at a rapid pace. The problem is that, if a first-year student learns about a specific computer program, it probably will no longer be in wide use when he or she graduates. Although some colleges are trying to integrate vendor certification into their curriculum, the problem is not really a flaw in higher education, but a characteristic of the IT industry. Computer software is changing so rapidly that a four-year college just can't always keep up. Most of the jobs today in the IT industry did not even exist five years ago.

A characteristic of the Novell certification program is an emphasis on understanding fundamental concepts and then applying them to specific job tasks rather than merely gathering knowledge. It should not come as a surprise, but most potential employers do not care how much you know about the theory of operating systems, testing, or software design. As one IT manager put it, "I don't really care what my employees know about the theory of our network. We don't need someone to sit at a desk and think about it. We need people who can actually do something to make it work better."

You should not think that this attitude is some kind of anti-intellectual revolt against book learning. Knowledge is a necessary prerequisite, but it is not enough. More than one company has hired a computer science graduate as a network administrator only to learn that the new employee has no idea how to add users, assign permissions, or perform the other everyday tasks necessary to maintain a network. One must be able to apply that knowledge to making the network work for the benefit of the organization that it supports. In addition to being up-to-date on technical developments, Novell certification is also job-task oriented.

The timeliness of Novell's certification program is obvious, and is inherent in the fact that you will be tested on current versions of software in wide use today. The job-task orientation of Novell certification is almost as obvious, but testing real-world job skills using a computer-based test is not easy.

Computerized Testing

Considering the popularity of Novell certification, and the fact that certification candidates are spread around the world, the only practical way to administer tests for the certification program is through Sylvan Prometric and Virtual University Enterprises (VUE) testing centers. Sylvan Prometric and VUW provide proctored testing services for Novell, Oracle, Novell, Lotus, and the A+ computer technician certification. Although the IT industry accounts for much of Sylvan's revenue, the company provides services for a number of other businesses and organizations, such as FAA preflight pilot tests. In fact, most companies that need secure test delivery over a wide geographic area use the services of Sylvan Prometric. In addition to delivery, Sylvan Prometric also scores the tests and provides statistical feedback on the performance of each test question to the companies and organizations that use their services.

Typically, several hundred questions are developed for a new Novell certification exam. The questions are first reviewed by a number of subject-matter experts for technical accuracy, and then are presented in a beta test. The beta test may last for several hours, due to the large number of questions. After a few weeks, Novell Education uses the statistical feedback from the testing services to check the validity of the beta questions.

Questions are discarded if most test takers get them right (too easy) or wrong (too difficult), and a number of other statistical measures are taken of each question. Although the scope of our discussion precludes a rigorous treatment of question analysis, you should be aware that Novell and other vendors spend a great deal of time and effort making sure their examination questions are valid and relevant to today's IT needs. In addition to the obvious desire for quality, the fairness of a vendor's certification program must be legally defensible.

The questions that survive statistical analysis form the pool of questions for the final certification exam.

Test Structure

The kind of test we are most familiar with is known as a *form* test. For Novell certification, a form test usually consists of 50–80 questions and takes 60–90 minutes to complete, depending on the test. If there are 240 questions in the final pool for an examination, then four forms can be created. Thus, candidates who retake the test probably will not see the same questions. Until recently, form tests did not allow you to mark questions and go back to review it. Some of the newer form tests allow you to revisit a question and even change your response. Be careful not to waste time "retaking" the test, but do take the opportunity to make sure you marked "A" and not "B." The temptation to reread and change is great, but avoid it.

Eventually, when enough people sit for the exam, adaptive tests are developed and administered. *Adaptive tests* are also drawn from a pool of different versions. An adaptive test will have a minimum of 15 questions and a maximum of 25. The time limit varies from test to test; however, most of the tests are 30 minutes in duration, with the Service and Support test being close to two hours. You must mark a response for each question; otherwise, you will be prompted to do so and the test will not give you the next question until you do. Just as important, don't exceed the time limit; if you do, the test will be marked as "failed" due to exceeding the time limit even if you have accumulated enough points to pass. Novell Education endeavors to have every CNE test become adaptive, although, some tests, due to the low number of candidates taking them, may remain as form tests.

The questions in a Novell adaptive test are assigned weighted values. The more difficult questions or ones that require more complex actions and analysis are given a greater weight in computing your final score. When you finish all the questions, your test is scored and you will see a message that tells you how you scored and whether you passed.

When an adaptive test begins, you are first given a simple or moderately simple question. If it is answered correctly, a more difficult question or action requiring more complex actions is presented. An incorrect response results in a question from the next lower level. When 15–20 questions have been answered in this manner, the scoring algorithm is able to predict, with a high degree of statistical certainty, whether you would pass or fail if all the questions in the form were answered. When the required degree of certainty is attained, the test ends, gets scored, and you receive either a pass or fail based on the total points achieved.

CNE adaptive tests also generally have five categories of questions. Typically, in order to pass, correct responses must be given in three out of the five categories. If you are pursuing a CNI certification, you must give correct responses in all of the categories. Be careful which version of the test you register for. The CNI version of the test asks identical questions as the CNE version; however, a higher passing threshold score is required, and even if you score high enough to pass the CNE version of the test, your test will be scored as "failed" with no credit applied toward CNE certification.

Adaptive testing has some definite advantages for everyone involved in the certification process. Adaptive tests allow Sylvan Prometric to deliver more tests with the same resources, as certification candidates often are in and out in 30 minutes or less. For Novell, adaptive testing means that fewer test questions are exposed to each candidate, and this can enhance the security, thus safeguarding the validity of certification tests.

One possible problem you may have with adaptive testing is that you are not allowed to mark and revisit questions. Since the adaptive algorithm is interactive, and all questions but the first are selected on the basis of your response to the previous question, it is not possible to skip a particular question or change an answer.

Question Types

Computerized test questions can be presented in a number of ways. Some of the possible formats are used on Novell certification examinations, and some are not.

True/False

We are all familiar with true/false questions, and the inherent 50 percent chance of guessing the correct answer.

Multiple Choice

The majority of Novell certification questions are in the multiple-choice format, with either a single correct answer or multiple correct answers. There is an interesting variation on multiple-choice questions with multiple correct answers and you are asked to select *all that apply*, and you are not told how many to choose. These tend to be the most challenging.

EXAMPLE:

Which two of the following are Leaf objects? (Choose two.)

or

Which of the following commands can be used at the server console? (Choose all that apply.)

You may see both variations on Novell certification examinations, but the trend seems to be toward the first type, where candidates are told explicitly how many answers are correct. Questions of the "choose all that apply" variety are more difficult, and can be confusing.

Graphical Questions

One or more graphical elements are sometimes used as exhibits to help present or clarify an exam question. These elements may take the form of a database diagram, flow charts, or screenshots from the software on which you are being tested. It is often easier to present the concepts required for a complex performance-based scenario with a graphic than with words.

Test questions called *performance-based,* actually incorporate simulated graphical utilities as part of the answer. These questions ask the certification candidate to perform administrative tasks on the simulated utility to answer the question. For example, you might be asked to grant NDS object rights to a User object. The answer is correct if any combination of steps will lead to the desired result. These questions do not necessarily test which technique you used, but rather, whether the task was accomplished.

Short-Answer Questions

Another kind of question you sometimes see on Novell certification examinations requires a typed-in answer. An example of this type of question might be to type in a server console command, a text box in a dialogue box, or even to complete a statement's blank spaces.

Knowledge-Based and Performance-Based Questions

Novell Education develops a blueprint for each Novell certification examination with input from Novell's internal personnel, current CNEs and MCNEs (Master Certified Novell Engineers), managers at some of Novell's biggest customers, and CNIs (Certified Novell Instructors). This blueprint defines the content areas and objectives for each test, and each test question is created to test a specific objective. The objectives for each test can be found at Novell Education's web site.

Some objectives demand a knowledge-based question. For example, objectives that use verbs like *list* and *identify* tend to test only what you know, not what you can do.

EXAMPLE:

Objective: Explain how file system security works.
Which two of the following are file system rights that allows a user to run an executable file with an EXE extension? (Choose two.)

    A. Access Control

    B. Read

    C. Modify

    D. File Scan

    E. Browse

Correct answers: **B** and **D**

Other objectives use action verbs like *connect, configure,* and *troubleshoot* to define job tasks. These objectives can often be tested with either a knowledge-based question or a performance-based question.

EXAMPLE:

Objective: Troubleshoot NDS database inconsistencies.
Knowledge-based question: Which of the following symptoms might indicate that replicas are out of synchronization?

    A. Dirty Cache Buffers are consistently at 90.

    B. Client login takes dramatically longer than usual.

    C. The SYSCON utility is no longer available.

    D. An SNMP Trap message is received.

Correct answer: **B**

Performance-based questions typically require an action done on a simulated GUI-based utility, such as NetWare Administrator, to perform a task, such as granting object rights to a user. However, the functions are limited to the task at hand, and the <Help> button is disabled.

Even in this simple example, the superiority of the performance-based question is obvious. Whereas the knowledge-based question asks for a single fact, the performance-based question presents a real-life situation and requires that you make a decision based on this scenario. Thus, performance-based questions give more bang (validity) for the test author's buck (individual question).

Testing Job Performance

We have said that Novell certification focuses on timeliness and the ability to perform job tasks. We have also introduced the concept of performance-based questions, but even performance-based, multiple-choice questions do not really measure performance. Another strategy is needed to test job skills.

Given unlimited resources, it is not difficult to test job skills. In an ideal world, Novell would fly CNE candidates to one of their sites, place them in a controlled environment with a team of experts, and ask them to plan, set up, administer, and document a network. In a few days at most, the experts could reach a valid decision as to whether each candidate should be granted CNE status. Obviously, this is not likely to happen.

Closer to reality, another way to test performance is by using the actual software, and creating a testing program to present tasks and automatically grade a candidate's performance when the tasks are completed. This *cooperative* approach would be practical in some testing situations, but the same test that is presented to CNE candidates in Chicago must also be available in Tokyo and Sydney. Many Sylvan Prometric testing locations around the world do not have all of the equipment needed to set up a complete NetWare network, much less provide the complex networked solutions required by cooperative testing applications.

The most workable solution for measuring performance in today's testing environment is a *simulation* program. When the program is launched during a test, the candidate sees a simulation of the actual software that looks and behaves just like the real thing. When the testing software presents a task, the simulation program is launched and the candidate performs the required task. The testing software then grades the candidate's performance on the required task and moves to the next question. In this way, a Windows 3.1 simulation program can mimic the look and feel of a network operating system, a Windows NT Workstation, a complicated network, or even the entire Internet.

Novell has included simulation questions on the certification since the first tests for the earlier CNE4 certification tests. Simulation questions provide many advantages over other testing methodologies, and simulations are expected to become increasingly important in the Novell CNE Program. For example, studies have shown that there is a very high correlation between the ability to perform simulated tasks on a computer-based test and the ability to perform the actual job tasks. Thus, simulations enhance the validity of the certification process.

Another benefit of simulations is in the area of test security. It is just not possible to cheat on a simulation question. In fact, you will be told exactly what tasks you are expected to perform on the test.

Study Strategies

There are appropriate ways to study for the different types of questions you will see on a Novell certification examination.

Knowledge-Based Questions

Knowledge-based questions require that you memorize facts. There are hundreds of facts inherent in every content area of every Novell certification examination. There are several keys to memorizing facts:

- *Repetition* The more times your brain is exposed to a fact, the more likely you are to remember it.

- *Association* Connecting facts within a logical framework makes them easier to remember.

- *Motor Association* It is often easier to remember something if you write it down or perform some other physical act, like clicking a practice test answer.

We have said that the emphasis of Novell certification is job performance; however, there are many knowledge-based questions on Novell certification exams. A few of the CNE tests contain nearly all knowledge-based questions. The Networking Technologies and Fundamentals of Internetworking (not required for CNE) tests are prime examples of tests that test your ability to recall technical minutiae.

Simulations

Simulation questions really do measure your ability to perform job tasks. You *must* be able to perform the specified tasks. There are two ways to prepare for simulation questions:

1. Get experience with the actual software. If you have the resources, this is a great way to prepare for simulation questions.

2. Use practice tests. Practice tests are available that provide practice with the same simulation engine used on Novell certification exams. This approach has the added advantage of grading your efforts.

Using Practice Tests

Practice tests are invaluable aids to help you prepare for the real thing. They are very helpful in giving you an idea of the type of questions that you might encounter on the test and the depth of knowledge required. Use practice tests to get an idea of what topics you should concentrate on in your preparation. Most practice tests will give you an analysis of the question and cite specific references, which you can look up. One common pitfall is to memorize the answers to practice tests. This can lead to disastrous test scores, since you can be lulled into a false sense of security. If you use practice tests, analyze the questions and topics that you scored poorly on, and actually go to the cited reference. Also, don't forget to analyze those questions you answered correctly, and check to see if you answered the question correctly because you truly understood the concepts presented, or if you just got lucky.

Signing Up

Signing up to take a Novell certification examination is easy. Sylvan operators in each country can schedule tests at any testing center. There are, however, a few things you should know:

- If you call Sylvan during a busy time period, you may be in for a long wait. Sylvan does an excellent job, but everyone in the world seems to want to sign up for a test on Monday morning.

- You will need your Social Security number or some other unique identifier to sign up for a Sylvan test, so have it at hand.

- Pay for your test by credit card if at all possible. This makes things easier, and you can even schedule tests for the same day you call, if space is available at your local testing center.

- Know the number and title of the test you want to take before you call. This is not essential, and the Sylvan operators will help you if they can. Having this information in advance, however, speeds up the registration process and reduces the risk that you will accidentally register for the wrong test.

Taking the Test

Teachers have always told you not to try to cram for examinations, because it usually does no good. If you are faced with a knowledge-based test requiring only that you regurgitate facts, cramming can mean the difference between passing and failing. This is not the case, however, with Novell certification exams. If you don't know it the night before, don't bother to stay up and cram.

Instead, create a schedule and stick to it. Follow these guidelines on the day of your exam:

1. Get a good night's sleep. The scenario questions you will face on a Novell certification examination require a clear head.

2. Remember to take two forms of identification—at least one with a picture. A driver's license with your picture, and Social Security or credit cards are acceptable.

3. Leave home in time to arrive at your testing center a few minutes early. It is not a good idea to feel rushed as you begin your exam.

4. If you are given a practice exam when you register on the testing workstation, take the 15-minute exam. It is a good way to check the "feel" of the mouse and keyboard, or to find out if they work properly at all. If nothing else, you have the opportunity to score 100% at least once that day.

5. Do not spend too much time on any one question. If you are taking a form test, take your best guess and mark the question so you can come back to it if you have time. You cannot mark and revisit questions on an adaptive test, so you must do your best on each question as you go.

6. If you do not know the answer to a question, try to eliminate the obviously wrong answers and guess from the rest. If you can eliminate two out of four options, you have a 50 percent chance of guessing the correct answer.

7. For all questions, read the question carefully to ensure you understand what is being asked, look over all the answers, before selecting an answer, re-read the question, then mark your answer.

8. Keep track of the time on the computer. Anyone not completing all questions will get a failing score.

9. If the test is adaptive and you are at question #25, check how much time you have left and use as much of it as possible to think about the question before selecting your answer. If you have gotten this far, it is your last chance to pass. The adaptive testing algorithm has calculated that you have a chance to pass, if you answer the question correctly.

Finally, I would advise anyone attempting to earn Novell certification to adopt a philosophical attitude. Even if you are the kind of person who never fails a test, you are likely to fail at least one Novell certification test somewhere along the way. Do not get discouraged. If Novell certification were easy to obtain, more people would have it, and it would not be so respected and valuable to your future in the IT industry.

CNE
CERTIFIED NOVELL ENGINEER

Part I

NetWare 5 Administration

CERTIFIED NOVELL ENGINEER

1

Introduction to intraNetWare

CERTIFICATION OBJECTIVES

1.01   Administrator Responsibilities

1.02   Network Resources and Services

1.03   Introduction to Novell Directory
        Services

1.04   Introduction to a Tree Structure

1.05   How the Directory Tree Affects
        Resource Access

W elcome to an adventure in learning! The Certified Novell Engineer (CNE) is one of the most widely known and respected professional credentials in the information systems industry today. This is a learning adventure because CNEs must have historical knowledge of computing and be familiar with the most recent innovations. Therefore, this book covers a wide variety of subjects, but the central theme of each topic is networking.

Networking is Novell's core business and it leads the market in server network operating system (NOS) software. Novell's NetWare servers are the core of networks around the world. NetWare 5 is Novell's latest network server product. With all the changes and added functionality to this product, even an experienced administrator or engineer will need to brush up. Some of these product additions will change administration methods. What will not change is the need for competent network management and end-user support.

CERTIFICATION OBJECTIVE 1.01

Administrator Responsibilities

Back in the early days of networking, the administrator's primary responsibility was simply to keep the server up and running. The job has evolved over the years to include many more tasks and responsibilities.

A network used to be a single server and a bunch of workstations. While some workstations were attached to the network and could use server resources, many were stand-alone. As needs arose for server resources and different functions that the network could provide, enterprise networks included many servers and many workstations, not necessarily all running the same operating system. Now, the administrator adds workstation maintenance to the list of duties, and responsibility for increased numbers and types of servers.

Another change to networking was added distance. Many local area networks (LANs) became wide area networks (WANs). Distribution of network resources required distribution of the administration. Enterprise networks grew and administration needs grew with them. Hierarchical network management is fairly common in large, complex networks. Each administrator handles only a portion of the administration tasks, while other administrators handle the rest. Administrative tasks can be divided into two categories:

- Reactive
- Proactive

Reactive Administration

Reactive administration is the collection of tasks that fix problems as they arise. It is "reactive" to the situation at hand. The types of tasks that fall under this heading include

- Responding to help desk calls
- Answering end-user questions
- Bringing up a downed server
- Salvaging an accidentally deleted file
- Resetting an end user's password
- Reestablishing network connectivity, after it has failed
- Resolving issues when servers run out of disk space
- Setting up printing resources and redirecting print jobs
- Recovering from disasters such as from fire, flood, hack attacks, and viruses

Reactive administration includes many more tasks than this, and makes up the bulk of the administrative tasks for a network. In general, when something is not right on the network, and it needs to be corrected, then it is a reactive administrative task.

Proactive Administration

Proactive administration is the collection of tasks that attempts to prevent errors and avoid problems on the network. Proactive administration results in less-reactive administration. Some examples of proactive administration include

- **Installation** Setting up servers, workstations, applications, and wiring.

- **Capacity planning** Examining the network growth trends and disk space usage; analyzing and estimating the future needs for storage space.

- **Disaster recovery planning** Preparing for a disaster that could incapacitate the network or a majority of the business-critical functions.

- **End-user training** Keeping end users updated and informed of network usage procedures to reduce support calls.

- **Performance monitoring and optimization** Consistent review and analysis of server statistics to detect potential faults and server bottlenecks, and then modifying settings to improve performance.

- **Novell Directory Services design** Consistent review and analysis of Novell Directory Services design and partitioning structure in order to provide optimal performance with sufficient backup in case of an individual server error.

- **Bandwidth capacity planning** Examining the network growth trends and network bandwidth usage; moving resources closer to users so that bandwidth usage is optimized.

- **Scheduled maintenance** Sometimes taking down a server and rebooting it to flush out information that has been stuck in memory due to poor programming of some server application. This process of rebooting ends up enhancing the network server's response time. Other maintenance tasks may include updating drivers, applying patches, or adding small hardware upgrades such as additional RAM.

- **Security auditing**   Reviewing the network for security breaches to ensure that information is protected.

- **Backup and data recovery**   Maintaining a backup method for critical data and a restoration procedure, in case of server failure or data loss.

- **Documentation**   Establishing and updating documentation of the network infrastructure, server settings, security access, and other network issues.

on the **job**

Many times, a company will not do proactive administration on a consistent basis, and sometimes not at all. Administrators get caught up in the day-to-day business needs of end users (that is, doing reactive administration) and put off proactive tasks. The result is that reactive administration tasks increase, and end users become dissatisfied. Finally, management throws up its hands and calls in a consultant. A good consultant performs a network analysis and makes recommendations for the network that might have surfaced from proactive network administration. I like to call this preventative computing. The comparison is that in preventative dentistry, the dentist asks you to floss only the teeth that you want to keep. In preventative computing, you need perform proactive tasks on only the network components you want to keep online.

Some enterprises have recognized the need for proactive administration and provide separate administrators to handle these tasks. The proactive administrators are not besieged by end-user requests and can concentrate on preventing serious errors from occurring on the network.

Note that proactive and reactive administrative tasks may affect the same issue. For instance, proactive security planning may set a policy that passwords will be changed every 30 days, and that the account will be locked out if the wrong password is entered more than three times. A reactive task for security is resetting a password when the user is locked out from his account because he entered it incorrectly several times at the login screen.

CERTIFICATION OBJECTIVE 1.02

Network Resources and Services

Sharing resources and services is a powerful method to enhance productivity. The terms *resources* and *services* tend to be used interchangeably. However, there is a distinction. A *resource* is an entity that exists on the network. A *service* provides access to the resource. For example, a printer is a resource on the network. The program or function that makes it possible for people to print documents on that printer is the printing service. In NetWare 5, the printing service is provided by Novell Distributed Printing Services (NDPS). In order to print on a network, both components are required. Usually, both a resource and a service must be up and running in order for the resource to be used.

Table 1-1 lists some common resources and their associated services. There are many other services and resources than the ones listed in Table 1-1. NetWare typically provides services through NetWare Loadable Modules (NLMs) on the NetWare server. NLMs are applications that run on a NetWare server.

TABLE I-I	Resource	Service
Network Resources and Their Associated Services	Printer	Printing service
	Server	Shared disk space; file service
	Modem	NetWare Connect shared modem service, or third-party FAX service
	HTML (Hypertext Markup Language) document	Web server service
	IP address	DHCP Service (Dynamic Host Control Protocol used to distribute IP addresses dynamically)
	CD-ROM drive	CD-ROM volume-sharing service
	Database	Database service

FROM THE CLASSROOM

What Is NDS?

Novell Directory Services (NDS) is a hierarchical database that contains information about all of the "entities" that make up a NetWare 4.*x* or 5 network. The key word is *database*; every object below the [Root] is represented in the Directory database by a record that contains the object's name and properties. If you think of the record identifier as the object name and the field names as the object's properties (or details), you will have made a major step in understanding the nature of NDS.

For those of you who are not familiar with database structures, take a look at your driver's license. It has your name (object name) and information about you (details/properties), such as what you look like, what type of vehicles you are authorized to operate (object rights), where you reside, and which state issued the license (context). In the case of a driver's license, it looks just like a User object in the NDS tree.

—*By Dan Cheung, CNI, MCNE, MCT*

CERTIFICATION OBJECTIVE 1.03

Introduction to Novell Directory Services

Novell Directory Services (NDS) is the service used by NetWare to organize resources throughout an entire network. It is a database that contains user IDs and network resources such as printers, print queues, servers, and volumes where objects may be granted access to other objects for security purposes. Because all network resources are organized in NDS, this is the most efficient place to manage security among network resources, users, groups, and other objects.

NDS allows users a single login authentication. In older versions of NetWare, resources were organized on an individual server basis. This created the need for multiple loginIDs—one for each server to which a user was granted access. NetWare 4 includes NDS, which combines all resources in one directory and enables each user's login to check one directory for access information—for example, a single login ID needed for authentication to any resource on the enterprise network.

NDS enables the following:

■ Single login authentication to enterprise network resources

■ Single point of administration for enterprise network resources

NDS Structure

NDS stores network resources in a tree structure that is similar to a directory tree. There are two types of objects within the tree:

■ Leaf objects

■ Container objects

A *container object* in NDS is like a directory (or folder) in a directory tree. It can contain leaf objects or other container objects. Container objects are used to organize the tree structure. Table 1-2 defines the [Root] and container objects.

TABLE 1-2		
The [Root] and Container Objects		

Object	Abbreviation	Description
[Root]		The top of the NDS tree. There is only one root object. It is created during the first server installation into the NDS tree. The [Root] can contain only Country objects or the Organization object. It does not contain any leaf objects other than Alias objects, if the Alias represents a Country or an Organization.
Country	C	Special container object for country locations. Country objects can be placed only in the root. Country objects are optional.

Object	Abbreviation	Description
Organization	O	A high-level container object placed directly in the root or under country units. This object usually represents the company.
Organizational Unit	OU	Container objects placed below the Organization-level unit. This creates a subgroup within the tree in order to organize the network resources.

TABLE 1-2

The [Root] and Container Objects *(continued)*

Leaf objects represent resources in the NDS tree. A leaf object does not contain any other objects. A leaf object is analogous to a file in a directory tree, since it cannot contain any other files or folders. Some developers have created NDS-aware programs that add leaf objects (for example, resources) to the NDS tree.

exam
Watch

Container objects can contain other container objects, as well as leaf objects. Leaf objects are end points in the NDS tree and cannot contain any objects whatsoever.

Leaf Objects

Directory leaf objects are objects that do not contain any other objects. These represent actual network entities such as users, servers, printers, and computers. Table 1-3 describes the different types of leaf objects available in NDS.

Leaf Object	Description
Alias	The Alias object is essentially a pointer to another leaf object in the tree. An alias is used to ease access to network resources since it makes the leaf object that the alias represents appear as though it exists in the context of the Alias object.
Application	This object is not part of the base schema, but is added when using the NetWare Application Launcher (NAL). It represents an executable application that the end user must be granted rights to before it appears in the NAL window on the end-user's workstation.

TABLE 1-3

Leaf Objects Available in NDS

TABLE 1-3	**Leaf Object**	**Description**
Leaf Objects Available in NDS *(continued)*	Bindery	The Bindery object is provided for backward compatibility to older versions of NetWare. It is commonly created during migrations and upgrades of existing NetWare 2.*x* and 3.*x* servers, or placed there by bindery-based programs.
	Bindery Queue	The Bindery Queue is a print queue that was migrated from a NetWare 2.*x* or 3.*x* server. This object is for backward compatibility.
	Computer	This object is a computer on the network that is not a server, such as a workstation or router.
	Directory Map	An object that represents a directory path in the file system on a volume. Directory Maps can ease administration of files, since files can be moved to other volumes and the move would be transparent to end users because the Directory Map name would not need to be changed. When mapping drives within a login script, using a Directory Map name allows the physical location of the files to change without editing the login script later.
	Group	The Group object represents a list of multiple User objects that can be located in any context within the NDS tree. Group objects are convenient for assigning the same rights to an entire list of individuals, and are useful in login scripts.
	NetWare Server	The NetWare Server object denotes a server running the NetWare operating system on the network. This object is automatically created when a server is installed into the NDS tree. It is useful for storing information about the server, such as physical location and provided services. Other objects, such as Volume and Directory Map, point to their associated NetWare Server object.

TABLE 1-3	Leaf Object	Description
Leaf Objects Available in NDS *(continued)*	Organizational Role	The Organizational Role object enables the definition of a position that is person-independent. When a person is placed in that position, the User object is associated with the Organizational Role object and automatically receives the Organizational Role object rights. If there is a position that is filled by consistently changing personnel, the creation of this object can facilitate the management of the rights needed for it.
	Print Server	The Print Server object represents a network print server.
	Printer	The Printer object represents a network printer.
	Print Queue	The Print Queue object signifies a network print queue.
	Profile	The Profile object is a login script object that can be assigned to a user property. The script contained in the Profile object is executed when any assigned user logs in to the network after the system login script and before the user login script. The Profile object is useful for a group of users that need a common login script function.
	Unknown	The Unknown object is exactly that: an object that NDS cannot validate or identify as belonging to the object classes defined within the schema.
	User	The User object must be created for each individual login ID required on the network. This object represents a person who logs in to the network and allows network security to be granted for resources.
	Volume	The Volume object is a volume on a network server. When a NetWare Server is installed, the installation process automatically creates a Volume object for each volume built at installation. Information about the volume's files and directories is available from within the NetWare administrator program by examining the properties of this object.

e x a m
Ⓦatch

An object's context is a description of the location of that object in the NDS tree.

The NDS *schema* is the structure of objects that can be stored within the directory tree, as illustrated in Figure 1-1. The schema defines the following information about objects:

- **Attribute information**   The information that an object can or must have associated with it
- **Inheritance**   How rights and properties may be inherited from designated objects
- **Naming**   The object's reference name
- **Subordination**   The location of objects within the NDS tree

Object classes contain the above information within the schema. An object class is the type of object that can be within the tree, such as a User object or an Organizational Unit object. For example, a User object has the following elements:

- Attribute information such as first name, last name, and user login script
- Inheritance information stating that User objects can inherit rights from an Organizational Role object (as well as from others)
- Naming that is selected at creation
- Subordination of the User object stating that this is a leaf object

o n t h e
Ⓙo b

The NDS schema is expandable. Some NDS-aware applications will change the schema to suit their own purposes—adding object classes to the schema and then the objects to the tree for use. This does not harm existing servers in the directory nor does it affect servers installed into the tree after the schema has changed. However, when merging two NDS trees, the schemas must be identical. This can be a problem if a program was installed and changed the schema of one tree, but was never installed into the other tree. When NDS was new, there were no tools to manage the schema, maintain the directory, or even merge trees. Now there are DSREPAIR and DSMERGE utilities to handle tree and schema issues.

FIGURE 1-1

NDS tree structure

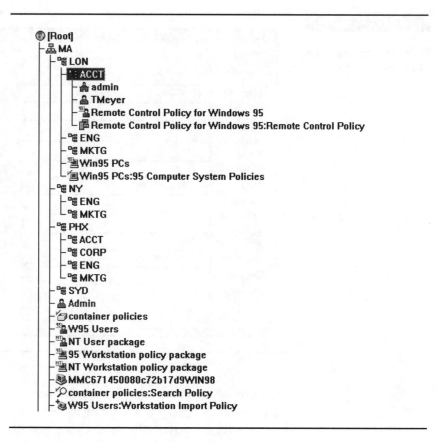

Object Properties and Values

The attribute information of NDS objects is a collection of *properties*. The data contained within each property is its *value*. This information is stored within the NDS tree and can be viewed for each object through the NetWare administrator in the form of dialog boxes, as shown in Figure 1-2.

Each NDS object consists of various properties that have corresponding values. Some values must be input into NDS upon object creation. Other values are optional. The properties for an object always exist and can be modified in the future. One benefit of NDS is the maintenance of an inventory of all network resources and users. Since NDS allows searching of its database, an administrator can easily locate all User objects that have a

FIGURE 1-2

Dialog box showing values
of an object's properties

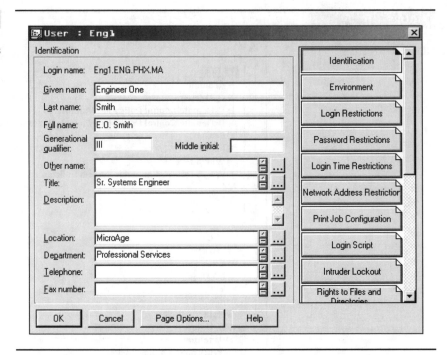

specific value for a property. This is convenient if, for example, the
administrator is managing a building move for a group of users, and the
inventory is readily available. Some User properties and values are given in
Table 1-4.

TABLE 1-4   Example of Some User Properties and Values from Figure 1-2

Property	Value	Editable?	Required at Object Creation?
Login name	Eng1.ENG.PHX.MA	No	Yes
Given name	Engineer One	Yes	No
Last name	Engineer	Yes	Yes
Full name	E.O. Smith	Yes	No
Generational qualifier	III	Yes	No
Middle initial		Yes	No

| TABLE 1-4 | Example of Some User Properties and Values from Figure 1-2 *(continued)* |

Property	Value	Editable?	Required at Object Creation?
Other name		Yes	No
Title	Sr. Systems Engineer	Yes	No
Description		Yes	No
Location	MicroAge	Yes	No
Department	Professional Services	Yes	No
Telephone		Yes	No
Fax number		Yes	No

The NDS Database

NDS is actually a database that contains objects, their properties and values, and their organization in the tree structure. The NDS database is in a file format, just like any other database. These files can be found in the SYS volume under the _NETWARE directory. You can access this directory and view file sizes:

1. Launch NetWare Administrator.

2. Click the Tools menu.

3. Select Remote Console.

4. Select the Server from the Available Servers window. If the server does not appear, make sure that the REMOTE.NLM and RSPX.NLM have been loaded on the server.

5. Press ALT-F1.

6. Select Directory Scan.

7. Type **SYS:_NETWARE** in the space provided. The files in that directory will appear in a blue dialog box, as shown in Figure 1-3.

FIGURE 1-3

NDS Database file scan

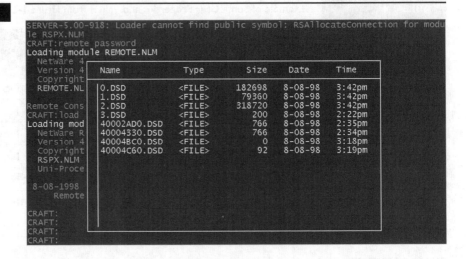

```
SERVER-5.00-918: Loader cannot find public symbol: RSAllocateConnection for modu
le RSPX.NLM
CRAFT:remote password
Loading module REMOTE.NLM
  NetWare 4
  Version 4
  Copyright
  REMOTE.NL
Remote Cons
CRAFT:load
Loading mod
  NetWare R
  Version 4
  Copyright
  RSPX.NLM
  Uni-Proce

8-08-1998
     Remote

CRAFT:
CRAFT:
CRAFT:
CRAFT:
```

Name	Type	Size	Date	Time
0.DSD	<FILE>	182698	8-08-98	3:42pm
1.DSD	<FILE>	79360	8-08-98	3:42pm
2.DSD	<FILE>	318720	8-08-98	3:42pm
3.DSD	<FILE>	200	8-08-98	2:22pm
40002AD0.DSD	<FILE>	766	8-08-98	2:35pm
40004330.DSD	<FILE>	766	8-08-98	2:34pm
40004BC0.DSD	<FILE>	0	8-08-98	3:18pm
40004C60.DSD	<FILE>	92	8-08-98	3:19pm

An important concept to understand is that the NDS database can be distributed across multiple servers. Not only can it be split into parts, but also each part can be copied. This is beneficial because when one server with a part of the NDS database (called a *replica*) on it goes down, the resources in that replica can still be accessed. For example, users may still log in, and printers can print. The process of dividing the database into multiple parts is called *partitioning*.

CERTIFICATION OBJECTIVE 1.04

Introduction to a Tree Structure

Figure 1-4 illustrates an NDS tree structure viewed from within the NetWare Administrator. Throughout this book, various tree structures will be depicted in order to demonstrate different NDS-related concepts. They all share a common hierarchical structure, but can be set up in different ways to suit the enterprise environment that they represent.

FIGURE 1-4

Example of an NDS tree
structure

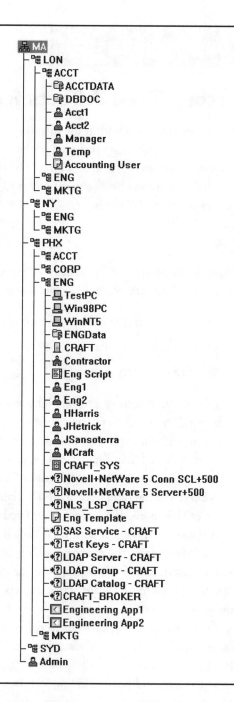

- MA
  - LON
    - ACCT
      - ACCTDATA
      - DBDOC
      - Acct1
      - Acct2
      - Manager
      - Temp
      - Accounting User
    - ENG
    - MKTG
  - NY
    - ENG
    - MKTG
  - PHX
    - ACCT
    - CORP
    - ENG
      - TestPC
      - Win98PC
      - WinNT5
      - ENGData
      - CRAFT
      - Contractor
      - Eng Script
      - Eng1
      - Eng2
      - HHarris
      - JHetrick
      - JSansoterra
      - MCraft
      - CRAFT_SYS
      - Novell+NetWare 5 Conn SCL+500
      - Novell+NetWare 5 Server+500
      - NLS_LSP_CRAFT
      - Eng Template
      - SAS Service - CRAFT
      - Test Keys - CRAFT
      - LDAP Server - CRAFT
      - LDAP Group - CRAFT
      - LDAP Catalog - CRAFT
      - CRAFT_BROKER
      - Engineering App1
      - Engineering App2
    - MKTG
  - SYD
  - Admin

How the Directory Tree Affects Resource Access

Resources are stored within the directory tree in the form of objects. Because all resources are included in that tree, the most efficient method of associating access rights to an object is by handling it within the tree. NDS enables an administrator to grant access to network resources by adjusting properties of the NDS objects.

Rights Within NDS

Rights is the term used for security access to various network resources. The following rights are available in NetWare:

- File-system directory rights and file rights
- NDS object rights
- NDS property rights

File-system directory and file rights are much the same as they were in older bindery-based NetWare systems. Users and groups can be granted the rights to perform various actions on files and directories, such as to browse the directory or file in their Explorer, or modify or delete the file. These rights are examined in greater detail in Chapter 6.

NDS is a hierarchical tree. Any NDS rights assigned will flow down through the tree. This should be carefully considered when designing an NDS tree.

A *trustee* is any object within NDS that is granted rights to another object. Most often, the trustee is a User or Group object, which makes it easier to understand. However, a trustee can also be any NDS object. Rights can be granted to NetWare Server objects and container objects just as easily as to users and groups.

Object rights enable a trustee to perform actions on an NDS object. The object rights are Browse, Create, Delete, Rename, and Supervisor. Except for the Supervisor rights, these object rights allow a trustee to browse, create, delete, and rename any object, but not edit the properties of the object. The Supervisor rights allow a trustee to edit properties as well as perform all other object actions.

exam

atch

The [Public] trustee is not an object, but is a way to assign rights to users who have not yet logged in to the NetWare network.

Property rights allow a trustee to access the values of the property information stored within NDS. The property rights are Compare, Read, Write, Add or Delete Self, and Supervisor. If some information about an object is confidential, such as a user's home telephone number, then users can be prevented from seeing that property by denying all Read rights to it. At the same time, other information, such as the user's business telephone number, can be allowed.

Inherited Rights Filter (IRF) is the system used to prevent rights from flowing down the tree from a parent container object. The IRF lists those rights that should not be inherited.

Security Equivalence is the ability to grant an object all the rights that another object has, simply by making them equivalent. The practice of making an object equivalent to the root of the tree grants that object all administrative and supervisory rights to every object in the tree, although this is not considered good practice.

Effective rights are the actual rights that an object has, which include rights that have been inherited, rights that have been filtered, and rights that have been directly granted to the object or granted through Security Equivalence.

An *Access Control List (ACL)* is the information about who has rights to access the NDS object information. It is stored as a property within the object and contains both trustee assignments and the Inherited Rights Filter. To change the trustees of an object, simply edit the ACL property of the object as indicated in Exercise 1-1.

EXERCISE 1-1

Viewing the Access Control List

1. Right-click an object in the NDS tree within the NetWare Administrator program.

2. Select Trustees of this Object.

3. The dialog box in Figure 1-5 will appear. Note that you may view both the Effective rights and the Inherited Rights Filter by clicking the designated buttons.

FIGURE 1-5

Access Control List (ACL)
dialog box showing
properties list

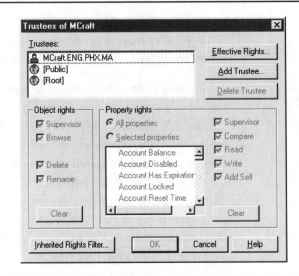

4. To add or remove an object from the ACL, click the Add Trustee
   or Delete Trustee buttons.

5. In order to change the property rights, such as removing the Read
   property rights for the Telephone number property, click the
   Selected Properties radio button, and then select the Telephone
   property. After the property is selected, click the Read check box so
   that it is unchecked.

6. Click OK when changes to the ACL are complete.

CERTIFICATION SUMMARY

A network administrator's many responsibilities fall into two categories:
reactive administration and proactive administration. Reactive duties
address problems as they occur. Proactive duties plan changes to the
network in order to avoid problems. Examples of reactive administration are

- Salvaging a deleted file
- Bringing up a server that has gone down
- Fixing a jammed printer and redirecting the prints sent to it

Examples of proactive administration are

■ Documenting the network security policies

■ Backing up server data

■ Monitoring server performance, etc.

A network resource is an entity on the network, such as an HTML Web page or a printer. A network service is the way that this resource can be accessed, often in the form of a server application, such as a Web server program, or the Novell Distributed Printing Services (NDPS).

Novell Directory Services (NDS) is the database of all network resources, users, and other network objects. It is organized in a hierarchical tree structure. There are three types of objects: [Root], container, and leaf objects. The [Root] is a placeholder that delineates the top of the NDS tree. Container objects are used to organize the network resources into the tree structure. They can contain leaf objects and other container objects. Leaf objects are end points in the tree and cannot contain any other object. Some container objects are Organization, Organizational Unit, and Country. Some of the most common leaf objects are User, Group, NetWare Server, Volume, Directory Map, and Profile.

There are other types of leaf objects that can exist in a directory tree, as well. The list of the container and leaf object types, plus their associated properties, in an NDS database is called the schema. The schema can change, since developers may create other NDS objects for application use.

The attribute types for each object are called properties. The information for a property is called the property's value. For example, a *property* of a User object is a First Name. For a User object HHarris (representing a network user named Heather Harris), the *value* of the First Name *property* would be Heather.

NDS allows objects to be granted access to other objects within the tree. The object rights grant an object the ability to perform actions such as creating, browsing, or deleting the object. The property rights grant an object the ability to edit or browse property values. To view the Access Control List of an object, right-click the object inside the NetWare Administrator program and select Trustees of this Object.

✓ TWO-MINUTE DRILL

❏ Hierarchical network management is fairly common in large, complex networks. In hierarchical network management, each administrator handles only a portion of the administration tasks, while other administrators handle the rest.

❏ Administrative tasks can be divided into two categories: *reactive administration,* the collection of tasks that fix problems as they arise (and which makes up the bulk of the administrative tasks for a network) and *proactive administration,* the collection of tasks that attempts to prevent errors and avoid problems on the network. Proactive administration results in less-reactive administration.

❏ A resource is an entity that exists on a network. A service provides access to the resource. Usually both a resource and a service must be up and running in order for the resource to be used.

❏ NetWare typically provides services through NetWare Loadable Modules (NLMs) on a NetWare server. NLMs are applications that run on a NetWare server.

❏ Novell Directory Services (NDS) is the service used by NetWare to organize resources throughout an entire network. It is a database that contains user IDs and network resources, where objects may be granted access to other objects for security purposes.

❏ NDS is the most efficient place to manage security among network resources, users, groups, and other objects.

❏ NDS allows users a single login authentication, and provides administrators with a single point of administration for an enterprise network, by combining all network resources in one directory and enabling each user's login to check one directory for access information.

❏ NDS stores network resources in a tree structure similar to a directory tree. There are two types of objects within the tree: leaf objects and container objects. Container objects are used to organize the tree structure. Leaf objects represent resources in the NDS tree.

❑ A leaf object does not contain any other objects and is analogous to a file in a directory tree. Leaf objects represent actual network entities such as users, servers, printers, and computers. Some developers have created NDS-aware programs that add leaf objects (for example, resources) to the NDS tree.

❑ The NDS *schema* is the structure of objects that can be stored within the directory tree. The schema defines attribute information, inheritance, naming, and subordination.

❑ The NDS schema is expandable. When merging two NDS trees, the trees' schemas must be identical. The DSREPAIR and DSMERGE utilities handle tree and schema issues.

❑ Object classes contain the information within the schema. An object class is the type of object that can be within the tree.

❑ The attribute information of NDS objects is a collection of properties. The properties for an object always exist and can be modified in the future. The data contained within each property is its value. Some values must be input into NDS upon object creation. Other values are optional. Attribute information is stored within the NDS tree and can be viewed for each object through the NetWare administrator.

❑ One benefit of NDS is maintenance of an inventory of all network resources and users. NDS allows searching of its database, enabling an administrator to easily locate all User objects that have a specific value for a property.

❑ NDS is a database that contains objects, their properties and values, and their organization in the tree structure. The NDS database, like any other database, is in a file format. The NDS database files can be found in the SYS volume under the _NETWARE directory.

❑ The NDS database can be distributed across multiple servers. It can be split into parts, and each part can be copied. The process of dividing a database into multiple parts is called *partitioning*. Partitioning is beneficial because it enables the resources in a replica to be accessed even if the replica itself goes down.

❑ NDS enables an administrator to grant access to network resources by adjusting properties of the NDS objects.

❑ The following rights are available in NetWare: file system directory rights and file rights, NDS object rights, and NDS property rights.

❑ NDS is a hierarchical tree, and any NDS rights assigned will flow down through the tree.

❑ A trustee is any object within NDS that is granted rights to another object. Most often, the trustee is a User or Group object, which makes it easier to understand. However, rights can be granted to NetWare Server objects and container objects just as easily as to users and groups.

SELF TEST

The following Self-Test questions will help you measure your understanding of the material presented in this chapter. Read all the choices carefully, as there may be more than one correct answer. Choose all correct answers for each question.

1. What is not a proactive responsibility of a network administrator?

   A. Planning for a new storage system

   B. Resetting a user's password because he forgot it

   C. Installing a new server into the tree

   D. Monitoring server performance

2. Joel has a new job as Desk-side Support Administrator in an enterprise network of over 5,000 users. He has the responsibility of being dispatched to help end users with computer problems that the help desk cannot resolve over the phone. There are two other administrative groups: Server Support and Network Planning. Mary, a Phoenix end user, has approached Joel about redesigning the Novell Directory Services tree so that she can be in the same Organizational Unit as her New York counterpart and have instant access to the same resources. Joel has the administrative ability to make the change. What should he do? (Select the best answer.)

   A. Make the change; he has the ability.

   B. Do not make the change; he doesn't believe it is good for the tree design.

   C. Hand it to the Server Support group, since Mary needs server resource access.

   D. Hand it to the Network Planning group, since it will make a change to the NDS design at the Organizational Unit level.

3. Which of the following is a network resource?

   A. Novell Storage Services

   B. Printer attached to the server

   C. Novell Distributed Printing Services

   D. Netscape Web Server program

4. What is needed in order to gain access to an IDE CD-ROM on a NetWare server from another network station?

   A. One thing: the CD-ROM hardware must be installed and working on the server.

   B. One thing: the CD-ROM sharing program must be loaded on the server.

   C. Two things: both the CD-ROM hardware and the sharing program must be installed on the server.

   D. Nothing. It cannot be done.

5. What is NDS?

   A. Novell Distributed Storage—a new service to distribute files transparently between servers and mainframes

   B. NetWare Database Security—a C2-level secured database

   C. Novell Directory Services—the distributed database used to store userIDs, printers, servers, and other objects, and organize them for security on an enterprise network

D. New Directory Storage—a technology to store directories of network resources on workstations

6. Which of the following network resources cannot be organized in NDS?

A. Files and directories

B. Printers

C. Applications

D. Workstation computers

E. None of the above

F. All of the above

7. Gene is a user on a NetWare network. Because of the network setup, the administrator gave Gene four userIDs in order to access four separate servers, all on the same Ethernet network segment. Is Gene using NDS on a NetWare 5 network to gain network access?

A. Yes. However, the four separate servers are in four separate NDS trees.

B. No. He is using a NetWare 2.x or 3.x network for at least three of the servers.

C. No. He may be using NetWare 5 servers, but he must be using a bindery-based login to require a separate ID per server.

D. Any of the above.

E. None of the above.

8. The root object is a special _____ object in NDS. It cannot contain any _____

objects other than an Alias object, but can contain either a _____ or _____ object.

A. Container-like, leaf, country, organization

B. Leaf, container, user, NetWare Server

C. Container, leaf, organization, organizational unit

D. Container, container, user, group

9. Jan is adding a new business unit to her NDS tree. It will receive its own Organizational Unit and a new NetWare Server. In this business unit, there are several students who share an auditing position for the server training files on a rotating basis. How should Jan plan for the constantly changing access needs?

A. Jan should create a Directory Map object to give the students a shortcut to the training files.

B. Jan should create an Organizational Role object to have the auditing access, and assign the students to the role whenever their turn comes up.

C. Jan should create a Group and grant them all the same access.

D. Jan should create two Groups and change the members of both groups as the auditing role changes.

10. Patti is an end user who created her own login script within her User object in the NDS tree. She showed her boss, Ed, the way the script automated various functions for her and he has asked you, the network administrator, to make sure that 12 other people in his department are

given the same script. It is possible that he may add more users in the future with this requirement. How should you manage this request?

A. Speak with Patti about her script so that you can rewrite it in each of the user's objects.

B. Create an Organizational Role and add to it the users who need the script.

C. Create a Profile object. Open up Patti's User object, open the Login Script property, highlight the script and press CTRL-C to copy it, and then open the Profile object and press CTRL-V to paste the script. Open each of the designated end users' User objects and assign the Profile to the user.

D. Compile the script. Create an Application object that points at the compiled script. Grant each of the designated users access rights to the Application object by right-clicking it, selecting Trustees of this Object, and then clicking the Add Trustee button.

11. What is a schema?

A. A new kind of printer

B. A special Directory Map object

C. A template for a profile script

D. The structure of NDS objects

12. A _____ represents a network resource. A _____ is a field available in the object to store information. The _____ is the information stored in the _____.

A. Object, property, value, property

B. Property, object, value, object

C. Value, property, object, value

D. Object, value, property, container

13. What are rights?

A. Correct network procedures

B. Security access that can be granted in NDS

C. Schema control factors

D. User object trustees

14. What rights are available to be granted to objects in NDS?

A. Property rights and file system rights

B. File and directory rights

C. NDS object rights and NDS property rights

D. NDS object rights, NDS property rights, file, and directory rights

15. Jack is a network administrator. He has been notified by Human Resources (HR) of a new policy that all home telephone numbers stored in the Novell Directory are no longer allowed to be seen by any users other than HR and the network administrator. How will Jack enable the correct security?

A. He will edit the object rights of the User objects.

B. He will create an Inherited Rights Filter.

C. He will edit the property rights of the Telephone property of the User objects.

D. It cannot be done.

CERTIFIED NOVELL ENGINEER

2

Enabling Network Access

CERTIFICATION OBJECTIVES

2.01   Enabling Network Communication (IPX/IP)

2.02   Client 32 Overview

2.03   Client 32 Installation Procedure for Windows 95

2.04   Client 32 Installation Procedure for Windows NT

2.05   Login Concepts

2.06   Login Process

2.07   Browser Client Installation

One of the first things end users do when they arrive at the enterprise network is log in. Logging in gives them access to files, printers, e-mail, databases, and other network resources. Some enterprises require that no data be kept anywhere but on the servers, and in those enterprises, the *only way* that an end user can get to work is by logging in. There are several things that an administrator has to provide in order to enable login authentication:

- A network protocol must be enabled on the network, server, and workstation
- A network client program must be installed on the workstation
- The server must be enabled for logins
- If using an intranet or Internet access, both IP and a browser must be installed on the workstation

CERTIFICATION OBJECTIVE 2.01

Enabling Network Communication (IPX/IP)

In order for workstations to access network resources, they need a method of communication with the server. This method of communication is a *protocol*. Older versions of NetWare used only the Internet Packet Exchange/Sequenced Packet Exchange (IPX/SPX) protocol. Administrators have added Transmission Control Protocol/Internet Protocol (TCP/IP), the protocol used on the Internet, to satisfy the growing need for businesses to communicate with the Internet. The result is that NetWare networks must run multiple protocols. There is a perception that TCP/IP is easier to maintain since routers are optimized for Internet traffic. So, with NetWare version 5, Novell has stepped up to the challenge and begun to provide TCP/IP as a base communications protocol for NetWare networks. IP compatibility mode can run on a NetWare 5 server, and all IPX dependencies are no longer present. The IP compatibility mode can run on a NetWare client using an IP compatibility mode driver, allowing the client to access any NetWare server running IP compatibility mode.

Workstations access the network through client software. NetWare 5 comes with client access software for many different workstation operating systems, including DOS, OS/2, Microsoft Windows 95/98, and Microsoft Windows NT 4.

CERTIFICATION OBJECTIVE 2.02

Client 32 Overview

When Microsoft introduced Windows 95, Novell immediately followed with the NetWare Client 32. The 32 stands for *32-bit*, which means that the client software is not a standard DOS or Windows 3.*x* 16-bit application. Microsoft Windows 95 already included a 32-bit client for NetWare, but Novell's version came with additional access components. For example, Microsoft's initial version did not allow the end user to browse the NDS tree; it was only a bindery-compatible client. Novell's version was immediately compatible with NDS.

Client 32 was popular due to the graphical utilities and speed. Novell then created a Client 32 for DOS and Windows 3.1*x*. And after Microsoft released Windows NT 4, Novell released a 32-bit client for that operating system.

Client 32 requires the following workstation components:

- DOS 5 or later, Windows 3.1*x*, Windows 95/8, or Windows NT 4
- 386 or later processor
- Network Interface Card (NIC)
- Available RAM of 5MB for DOS or Windows 3.1*x*, or 6MB for Windows 95/8

Client 32 includes several software components called NetWare Loadable Modules (NLMs). Client 32 supports the NetWare Open Data-link

Interface (ODI) specification. ODI is a modular client specification, allowing multiple protocols to be used with a single NIC. It requires four components for network connectivity:

- **Network Interface Card driver, known as a Multiple Link Interface driver (MLID)**   A file with a .LAN extension specific to the type of card used

- **Link Support Layer driver**   LSLC32.NLM

- **IPX protocol driver**   IPX.NLM or IP compatibility mode protocol driver, IPHLPR.NLM

- **Main client software**   CLIENT32.NLM

on the job

An older ODI client software from NetWare was the Virtual Loadable Module (VLM) software. VLMs were DOS 16-bit client software pieces.

Multiple Link Interface Driver (MLID)

The MLID is the software that transmits data onto the network through the Network Interface Card (NIC). It communicates directly with the NIC hardware. This software component is different for each NIC used. For example, an Ethernet card will not use the same NIC driver software as a Token-Ring card, and the driver for various Ethernet cards may be different between vendors or even types of cards from the same manufacturer. Even though the MLID is an NLM, the file does not use the .NLM extension. Instead it uses a .LAN extension. This represents the Physical layer of the OSI (Open Systems Interconnection) protocol stack model.

on the job

Sometimes using the ODI drivers for the NetWare Client 32 causes access problems with existing client software for Microsoft NT networks. This is normally due to the MLID driver not being compatible with the other network client software. In order to force Client 32 to install using an existing (and already functioning MLID) NIC driver, use the /N switch after invoking setup. This forces Client 32 to use the existing Microsoft client NIC driver and keeps the Microsoft client software working correctly. On the other hand, if you want to force an ODI driver, use the /O switch.

Link Support Layer

The Link Support Layer (LSL) communicates at the Data Link layer of the OSI model. This connection between the IPX or IP protocol and the MLID is handled by LSLC32.NLM.

IPX Protocol or IP Compatibility Protocol

IPX.NLM and IPHLPR.NLM provide the IPX and IP protocols. These protocols work at the Network layer of the OSI model. They transmit data between the NetWare client software and the Link Support Layer.

NetWare Client Software

Network applications interface directly with the NetWare client software (see Figure 2-1), which can work at the upper layers of the OSI protocol stack reference model. These layers are all above the Network layer—Transport, Session, Presentation, and Application. This software enables the mapping of drives, capturing network printers, and access to other network resources. The Client 32 is NDS-compliant, and allows NDS applications such as the NetWare administrator or NDS Manager to run on the workstation. Bindery-based client software will not allow the workstation to browse the NDS tree, or run any other NDS utilities.

exam
ⓦatch

The four components needed to supply client access to NetWare's ODI specification are, in this order, MLID, LSLC32.NLM, IPX.NLM/IPHLPR.NLM, and CLIENT32.NLM.

All Client 32 software can install automatically using existing configuration or newly edited configuration files. The command is SETUP /ACU. The /ACU switch stands for Automatic Client Update and is also used for upgrading an existing Client 32 installation.

FIGURE 2-1

Modular software
communication for Client 32

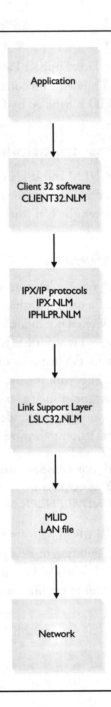

Client 32 Installation Procedure for Windows 95

There are a few different ways to install Client 32 on a workstation:

- **Over the network and attended** If using the Microsoft Client for NetWare networks on Windows 95/98, the workstation may be able to access the NetWare 5 server and load the NetWare Client 32 over the network. This is dependent on whether the server is running in Bindery mode, or if the workstation has an added NDS Access Services component—lately added by Microsoft as a downloadable component—or part of Windows 98.

- **Over the network and unattended** The same rules apply for an unattended setup as the attended version. Unattended installations use an /ACU switch after the SETUP program is invoked. Optionally, the administrator may edit some configuration files to set properties, such as the Preferred Server.

- **Using diskettes or CD** Client 32 can be installed from diskettes or the NetWare 5 installation CD.

- **As part of the workstation install** Client 32 can be integrated into the Microsoft Windows 95/98 installation process.

The most common installation is run over the network and attending the setup. This usually involves the administrator copying the installation files to a network server volume. Table 2-1 depicts the optional components available with the Windows 95 version client.

TABLE 2-1	Component	Description
Optional Windows 95 Client 32 Components	Novell Workstation Manager	A single administrative utility for managing user and desktop information
	Novell Distributed Print Services (NDPS)	A new printing service enabling bi-directional, real-time communication with network printers

TABLE 2-1

Optional Windows 95
Client 32 Components
(continued)

Component	Description
Novell NetWare/IP Protocol	Support for NetWare/IP requester networks
Novell SNMP Agent	SNMP agent that works on both IPX and IP networks
Host Resources MIB	Enables a management console to poll SNMP clients for inventory information
Network Management Responder (NMR)	Supplies operating system, BIOS, and other information to the management console
Novell Target Service Agent (TSA)	Used for backing up workstations
Novell NDS Provider for Active Directory Service Interfaces (ADSI)	Enables ADSI client applications to access NDS information
Novell Remote Control Agent	Allows other workstations to take control remotely of this workstation

Exercise 2-1 outlines the process for installing the Client 32 on a Windows 95 workstation.

EXERCISE 2-1

Windows 95 Client 32 Installation

1. To access the Client 32 setup files, place the CD in a server's shared CD-ROM drive.

2. Access the server's CD-ROM drive by browsing in the Network Neighborhood; or right-click the Network Neighborhood, selecting Map Network drive, and type in the name of the resource in the format: \\SERVER\CDROM_VOLUME_NAME.

3. The English language setup files for Windows 95 are in the path PRODUCTS\WIN95\IBM_ENU on the NetWare 5 installation CD-ROM. Run the SETUP.EXE file from this location.

FIGURE 2-2

Client 32 license screen

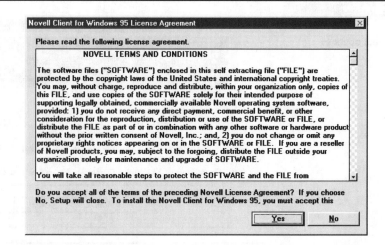

4. The first screen to appear is the license acceptance, as shown in Figure 2-2. Click Yes.

5. There are two options for installation: Typical and Custom. If using a standard IPX network, the Typical installation is usually sufficient. However, to view all the possible installation options, select Custom now and click Next.

6. The next screen depicts the IP addition to NetWare networking. The possible selections are IP, IP & IPX, and IPX (see Figure 2-3). Select the appropriate protocols, and click Next.

7. The next option is to install an NDS-compatible or bindery-compatible client. For NetWare 5, select the NDS option and click Next.

8. NetWare has several components available to install, as illustrated in Figure 2-4. Click the appropriate options and click Install.

9. The client installs and then prompts to reboot. After rebooting, the setup is complete.

FIGURE 2-3

Protocol options

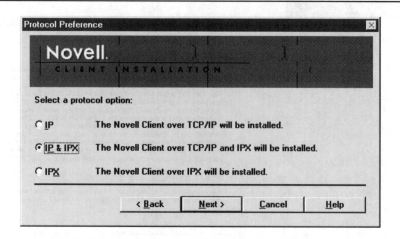

FIGURE 2-4

Optional components

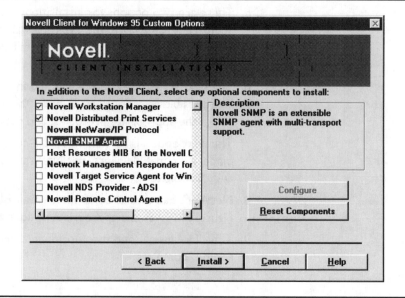

Client 32 Installation Procedure for Windows NT

Exercise 2-2 outlines the installation procedure for the Client 32 software on Microsoft Windows NT 4. The client can be loaded over the network, if the Microsoft Client Service for NetWare is loaded, in both an attended or unattended mode. The client can be integrated with a network installation of Windows NT, or manually installed from diskettes or CD.

Client 32 for NT uses the IPX/SPX compatible protocol that comes as part of the Windows NT operating system. It is recommended, but not necessary for diskette or CD installs, that the Microsoft Client Service for NetWare be set up prior to installing Client 32. To verify that it is installed, right-click on the Network Neighborhood and select Properties. Click the Services tab to view which clients are installed (see Figure 2-5).

FIGURE 2-5

Client Service for NetWare

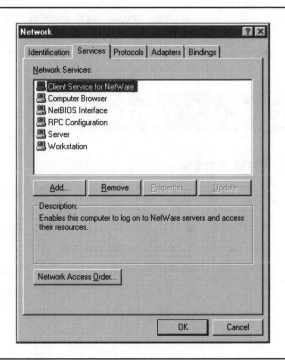

EXERCISE 2-2

Microsoft Windows NT 4 Client 32 Installation

1. From the Network Neighborhood, browse to the shared CD-ROM where the NetWare 5 installation CD resides. Open the PRODUCTS\WINNT\I386 folder and double-click the SETUPNW.EXE program. You may also click Start | Run, type in the full path to the SETUPNW program, and press ENTER.

2. The first screen is the software license agreement. Accept the agreement and click Next.

3. As shown here, the Client 32 software will notify you that it is removing the existing Microsoft Client Service for NetWare. Click Yes.

4. Not only is the existing client removed, but new keys are added to the registry, and files are copied to the workstation hard drive.

5. After the Client is installed, it prompts to reboot or close the installation program. In order for the Client to work, the workstation must be rebooted, so select reboot.

CERTIFICATION OBJECTIVE 2.05

Login Concepts

There are several different security controls in NetWare:

- **File system security** Manages the access to files and directories on NetWare servers

- **NDS security** Manages the rights granted to objects so that they can manipulate other objects, and manages the rights granted to objects so that they can view or edit the property values of other objects

■ **Server security** Manages how users can access the server console, either remotely or with direct password protection at the server

■ **Login security** Manages how users can authenticate into the network

The authentication process manages login security. Authentication is configured through the restrictions and rules set within NDS, with properties of objects such as users who log in and container objects that contain user objects somewhere beneath them.

Restrictions in NDS

Several NDS restrictions establish network security. The Login Restrictions properties in the User object (see Figure 2-6) enable the administrator to restrict whether a user may log in at all. The administrator may disable the ID, force it to expire on a given date, or limit how many concurrent logins the user may have.

FIGURE 2-6

Login Restrictions properties for User objects

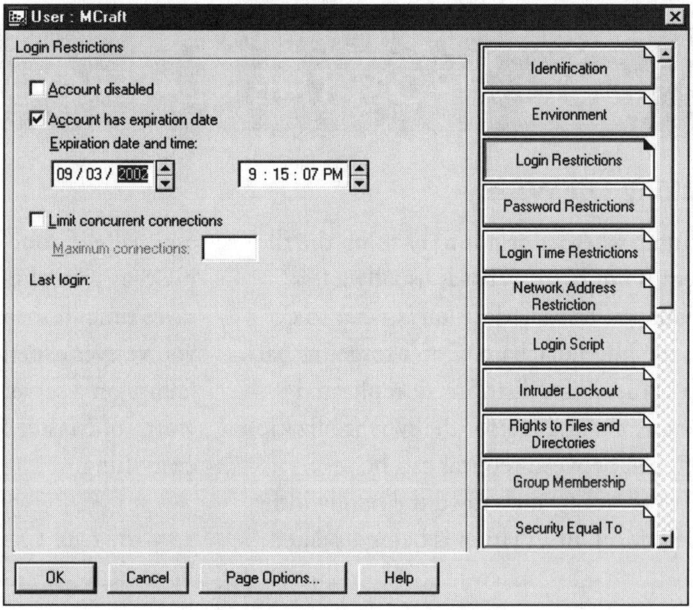

The Password Restrictions properties allow the administrator to establish password policies on a per-user basis. The administrator may set whether a user can change their password, how often the password will be required to change, or how many grace logins the user is allowed with the old password before they must change it.

Login Time Restrictions properties offer the administrator a method of restricting logins on a time basis. Login time restrictions are used for handling daily backups or weekly scheduled maintenance of the servers. They effectively avoid some loss of data by making sure that no files are open when other processes need to access them or when the server is suddenly taken offline. In Figure 2-7, the shaded area shows that logins are restricted between 12:00 A.M. and 3:30 A.M. each weekday.

A network address restriction uses the network node address of a workstation, and limits the network access for a user to only the workstations having those addresses listed. For high-security networks, using a network address restriction can make sure that a user does not log in without authorization.

FROM THE CLASSROOM

Backing Up Wisely

Deciding whether or not to back up the file system is not hard. What is usually a less obvious, yet critical, decision is what to do with the NDS database. Don't forget to back it up. True, it is a distributed, replicated database, but waiting for the synchronization to happen between replicas can be time-consuming and crowd the bandwidth while critical information is being updated, especially if done over WAN links. Including NDS as part of the backup is prudent and saves time in the long run, particularly if you've ever experienced a catastrophic disk failure on a server containing several partitions worth of Master Replicas and have to restore everything.

—*By Dan Cheung, CNI, MCNE, MCT*

FIGURE 2-7

Example of a login time
restriction

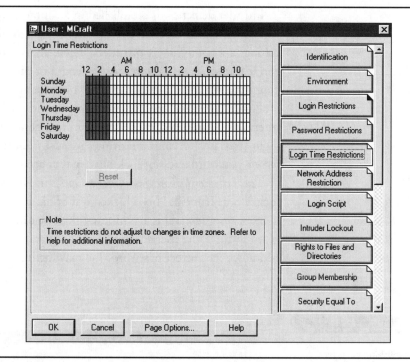

Intruder Detection

An *intruder* is anyone who attempts to log in to the network using an
invalid password. NetWare can lock an account when an invalid password is
used too many times for a user ID. This is to protect the network from
hackers trying to figure out a password.

on the
job

*Intruder detection is both a blessing and a curse. One thing for sure, it
definitely works. The problem is that many users forget their
password, or mistype it too many times and unintentionally lock
themselves out. Most do not realize that they have locked their user
ID and call the administrator or the help desk to ask why the network
is down. If you intend to use intruder lockout, this is simply one of the
added administrative tasks to be aware of, and one of the first things
to look at when a user calls about not being able to log in.*

Intruder detection is established in a container object, through the Intruder Detection property, as demonstrated in Figure 2-8. The default settings are *not* to detect intruders. There are two reset intervals. The *intruder attempt reset interval* is the length of time to wait before starting to count the number of incorrect password attempts again. For example, if Joe is allowed seven incorrect login attempts, and the intruder attempt reset interval is 30 minutes, then the 30-minute period starts from the first bad login attempt. Joe can try six times in a 30-minute period to log in with the wrong password and not lock out the user account.

The *intruder lockout reset interval* kicks in after the user account has been locked out. If Joe has been locked out of his account, and the intruder lockout reset interval is 15 minutes, then he can wait 15 minutes. At that point in time, the user account will no longer be locked out, and provided he knows the correct password, Joe may log in.

FIGURE 2-8

Establishing intruder detection in an organizational unit

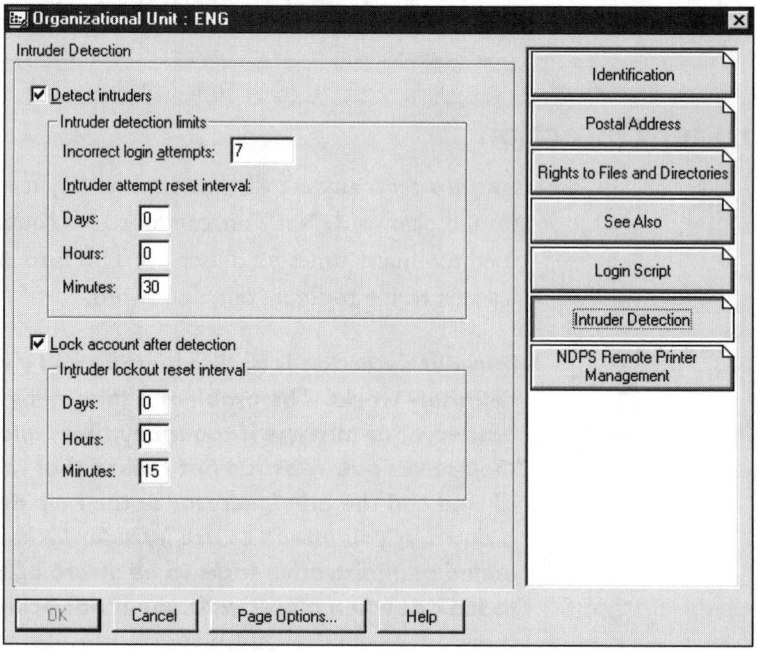

Login Process

Novell Directory Services enables users to have a single login to gain access to any enterprise-wide network resource. *Authentication* is the process that enables the single login capability.

When a user logs in to the network, it may appear that the password is sent to the server and that the server clears the user for access. However, for security reasons, the password is not sent across the network. Instead, an encrypted user code of the user's information—including user name, password, workstation, and other details—is created from the login process. The authenticating server performs the same process to create a user code. The server compares its user code to the workstation version and, if it matches, the user is granted access.

on the **job**

Note that the authenticating server will perform the comparison of the user code. The authentication process is a key concept in network design. In one global network I worked on, I found that every third login attempt I made ended up being authenticated in Sydney, Australia, even though I was in Phoenix, or in Miami. It turned out that the partitioning scheme had not been completed in Phoenix, but had been completed in Sydney. As a result, there were more servers with replicas of my user ID's context sitting in Sydney. They authenticated more often because there were more of them available for authentication even though the slow bandwidth might normally prevent this from happening. Once the partitioning scheme was completed in Phoenix and Miami, the Sydney-authentication-syndrome stopped occurring.

As illustrated in Figure 2-9, when a user logs in there are several scripts that will be run in a specific order.

1. **Container login script**   The script defined in the container object that the user resides in

2. **Profile login script**   A script that is in a Profile object and assigned to a user

3. **User login script**   A script that is written in the Login Script property of the User object itself

4. **Default login script**   A script that will run if NetWare does not find a user login script for the User object

The following is a list of commands found in the default login script:

```
MAP DISPLAY OFF
MAP ERRORS OFF
REM (Set first drive to most appropriate directory.)
MAP *1:=SYS
MAP *1:=SYS:%LOGIN_NAME
IF "%1"="SUPERVISOR" THEN MAP *1:=SYS:SYSTEM
MAP S1:=SYS:PUBLIC
MAP S2:=S1:%MACHINE\%OS\%OS_VERSION
MAP DISPLAY ON
MAP
```

FIGURE 2-9

Logical cascade of login scripts

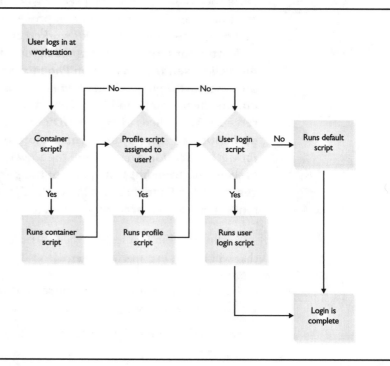

QUESTIONS AND ANSWERS

Justine is the administrator of a NetWare 5 network. She has created a profile script that runs a CAPTURE command for the Graphics Department's color laser printer. Justine then assigns the profile script to the users within the Graphics Department. There is no container script or user script being run. When Justine tests the script, she gets an error that the external command CAPTURE cannot be executed. CAPTURE is in the Public directory, and when Justine checks, there is a mapping to SYS:PUBLIC. Why does she get this error and how can she fix it?

Justine was depending on the default login script to provide the mapping to the Public directory. However, because the profile script executes before the default login script, it did not have a mapping to SYS:PUBLIC when it was trying to find the CAPTURE command. In order to fix this, Justine can add the Search drive mapping to the profile script. Or, to prevent errors like this from happening in the future, she can place the commands she wants to have in the container script for all users and add the NO DEFAULT line so that the default script will not run for users in that container.

CERTIFICATION OBJECTIVE 2.07

Browser Client Installation

A Web browser, Netscape Navigator 4.04, is part of the client installation options on the NetWare 5 CD. The steps for installing the browser client are outlined in Exercise 2-3.

EXERCISE 2-3

Netscape Navigator 4.04 Installation

1. Open the Network Neighborhood and locate the server with the shared CD-ROM where the NetWare 5 CD resides.

2. Open the Products folder, then the Netscape folder, the Win32 folder, and finally the English folder.

3. Double click on the N32E404.EXE file. Netscape will install automatically.

Previous versions of NetWare did not include a Web browser. The need simply was not prevalent in an IPX-based network. With Internet and intranet access needs becoming more accepted in networks, including a

Web browser on a client workstation has become necessary. This completes the client software needed to access a NetWare 5 server configured as a Web server. New to NetWare 5 is the publishing of Help files and server documentation in HTML (Hypertext Markup Language) format. To view the documentation, a Web browser is required.

CERTIFICATION SUMMARY

The communication between the workstation and the server is through a protocol. NetWare 5 can use both the IPX protocol and the IP protocol from the client to access a server running the same protocol. The IP protocol is new to NetWare 5 in the sense that the server and the workstation do not need to have IPX running for network access.

Client 32 is a 32-bit software application that is available for DOS, Windows 3.1x, Windows 95/98, and Windows NT 4 workstations.

Client 32 has four components for network communication that translate to a layer of the OSI reference model for protocol stacks. The specification for the four components is called ODI, or Open Data-link Interchange. These four components are

1. **MLID (Multiple Link Interface Driver)**   Physical layer

2. **LSL (Link Support Layer)**   Data Link layer

3. **IPX or IP (Protocol)**   Network layer

4. **Client 32 (Client access software)**   Upper layers of the protocol stack: Transport, Session, Presentation, and Application

The applications that provide the components are called NetWare Loadable Modules (NLMs). The files that provide each layer are .LAN files for the MLIDs specific to the cards being loaded. This file is still an NLM even though the file has a .LAN extension. LSLC32.NLM provides Link Support Layer communication. IPX.NLM and IPHLPR.NLM provide

Network layer services. CLIENT32.NLM supplies the client access software interface and upper layers.

The Windows 95 Client 32 can be installed from CD or diskette, over the network, and can be integrated with an installation of Windows 95/98. The installation can run in an unattended mode using a switch after the setup program. The command is SETUP /ACU. The /ACU switch stands for Automatic Client Update and is used for upgrading an existing Client 32 installation.

Windows 95 setup files for Client 32 are located on the NetWare 5 CD-ROM. It is typical for an administrator to copy them to a network server for installation.

Windows NT setup files for Client 32 are located in a different directory on the CD. The setup executable for the NT version of Client 32 is SETUPNW.EXE.

Login security within NetWare is above and beyond file security and NDS security. Properties of user objects and container objects will configure how login security works. These things include password restrictions, login time restrictions, intruder detection, and network address restrictions.

The login process begins with authentication. The user's password is never sent over the network wire. Instead, a complex process at the workstation creates an encrypted package of the user's information and typed-in password. The server is notified of the login attempt, creates the same encrypted package, and compares it to the one from the workstation. A match allows the login to occur. Once the user logs in, the authenticating server will check for a container login script and run it, if there is one. Then it will look for a profile script and run it, if there is one, and for a user login script and run it, if there is one. If there is no user script, the login process will run a default login script.

To provide the network an access method to HTML documents, NetWare 5 comes with Netscape Navigator, version 4.04.

TWO-MINUTE DRILL

❑ In order for workstations to access network resources, they need a protocol, or method of communication with the server. Older versions of NetWare used only the IPX/SPX protocol. Administrators have added TCP/IP, the protocol used on the Internet. Consequently, NetWare networks must run multiple protocols.

❑ NetWare 5 comes with client access software for many different workstation operating systems, including DOS, OS/2, Microsoft Windows 95/98, and Microsoft Windows NT 4.

❑ MLID is the software that transmits data onto the network through the Network Interface Card and communicates directly with the NIC hardware. This software component is different for each NIC used. Even though the MLID is an NLM, it does not use the .NLM extension. Instead it uses the .LAN extension. This represents the Physical layer of the OSI protocol stack model.

❑ Network applications interface directly with the NetWare client, which can work at the upper layers of the OSI protocol stack reference model. These layers are all above the Network layer—Transport, Session, Presentation, and Application. The NetWare client enables the mapping of drives, capturing network printers, and access to other network resources

❑ The Client 32 is NDS compliant, and allows NDS applications such as the NetWare administrator or NDS Manager to run on the workstation. Bindery-based client software will not allow the workstation to browse the NDS tree or run any other NDS utilities.

❑ There are a few different ways to install Client 32 on a workstation: Over the network and attended, over the network and unattended, using diskettes or CD, or as part of the workstation install. The most common installation is run over the network and attending the setup, which usually involves the administrator copying the installation files to a network server volume.

❑ Client 32 for NT uses the IPX/SPX compatible protocol that comes as part of the Windows NT operating system. It is recommended, but not necessary for diskette or CD installs, that the Microsoft Client Service for NetWare be set up prior to installing Client 32.

❑ There are several different security controls in NetWare: file system security, NDS security, server security, and login security. The authentication process manages login security. Authentication is configured through the restrictions and rules set within NDS, with properties of objects, such as users who log in and container objects that contain user objects somewhere beneath them.

❑ Several NDS restrictions establish network security. The Login Restrictions properties in the User object enable the administrator to restrict whether a user may log in at all. The Password Restrictions properties allow the administrator to establish password policies on a per-user basis. Login Time Restrictions properties offer the administrator a method of restricting logins on a time basis. The benefit of a login time restriction is for handling daily backups or weekly scheduled maintenance of the servers. It effectively avoids some data loss by making sure that no files are open when other processes need to access them, or when the server is suddenly taken offline.

❑ An intruder is anyone who attempts to log in to the network using an invalid password. NetWare can lock an account when an invalid password is used too many times for a user ID. This protects the network from hackers trying to figure out a password. Intruder detection is established in a container object, through the Intruder Detection property. The default settings are *not* to detect intruders.

❑ Novell Directory Services enable users to have a single login to gain access to any enterprise-wide network resource. Authentication is the process that enables the single login capability.

❑ When a user logs in, there are several scripts that will be run in a specific order: container login script, profile login script, user login script, and default login script.

❑ A Web browser, Netscape Navigator 4.04, is one of the client installation options on the NetWare 5 CD and completes the client software needed to access a NetWare 5 server configured as a Web server. Previous versions of NetWare for IPX-based networks did not include a Web browser. With Internet and intranet access becoming more important, including a Web browser on a client workstation has become necessary. New to NetWare 5 is the publishing of Help files and server documentation in HTML format. To view this documentation, a Web browser is required.

SELF TEST

The following Self-Test questions will help you measure your understanding of the material presented in this chapter. Read all the choices carefully, as there may be more than one correct answer. Choose all correct answers for each question.

1. What are NLMs?

    A. NetWare Link Multistations

    B. Novell Link Multistations

    C. Nameable Loaded Machinations

    D. NetWare Loadable Modules

2. What is the ODI specification?

    A. Open Data-link Interchange—a modular approach to client software

    B. Open Systems Interconnection—a standard for the protocol reference model

    C. Open Shortest Path First—a TCP/IP routing protocol

    D. Overrun Data Interrupt—a way to prevent excessive data on the network during login

3. When using ODI with four protocols: DLC, TCP/IP, IPX/SPX, and NetBEUI, how many NICs are required?

    A. 4

    B. 2

    C. 1

    D. 0, can't be done

4. Which of the following is the NLM known as an MLID?

    A. LSLC32.NLM

    B. CLIENT32.NLM

    C. IPX.NLM

    D. TOKEN.LAN

5. What OSI reference model layers does the CLIENT32.NLM handle?

    A. Physical and Data Link

    B. Network only

    C. Transport, Session, Presentation, and Application

    D. Application only

6. What is the order for the ODI components?

    A. MLID, LSL, IPX or IP, CLIENT32

    B. LSL, MLID, IPX or IP, CLIENT32

    C. CLIENT32, MLID, IPX or IP, LSL

    D. IPX or IP, CLIENT32, LSL, MLID

7. True or False. When installing Client 32 on a Windows 95 workstation, NDPS is automatically part of the installation.

    A. True

    B. False

8. Taylor is the network administrator for a large network. Frequently, she is requested by HR to remove accounts for users because they are going on leave. Just as frequently, she is then notified to re-create

the accounts, add the old permissions, and re-establish the same properties as the user had before. This is a login security requirement, because HR policy states that users on leave are not allowed to log in to the network while on leave. Can Taylor make this process easier, yet still maintain the HR policy?

A. Yes, she can do so by managing the Intruder Detection property of the end user's container.

B. Yes, she can do so by managing the Login Restrictions property for Account Disabled of the end user's object.

C. No; it cannot be done.

D. Yes, she can do so by managing the root object of the tree.

9. Every night at 2:00 A.M., the backup of three NetWare servers takes place on Dan's network. Dan has enabled remote access services, and occasionally a user will be logged in at that late hour. The backup process fails if it finds too many open files, which Dan finds out will happen when a user is logged in. How can Dan manage the backup so that it does not fail, plus provide maximum hours of remote access?

A. He can turn off the remote access modems each night and turn them on in the morning.

B. He can mark each remote user's account as Disabled before he leaves for the night.

C. He can edit the remote user's login time restrictions and mark off the time period that the backup takes place.

D. He cannot do this.

10. Gordon is the teacher in a class that uses a NetWare network for training users on applications. The classroom container login script looks at the node address of the NIC in order to map the workstation to specific files that the student worked on last. Gordon wants to make sure that students do not log in to other people's workstations. Can he do this?

A. Yes, he can do this by editing the network address restrictions of the users.

B. Yes, he can do this by editing the container login script further.

C. Yes, he can do this by editing the login time restrictions of the users.

D. No; it cannot be done.

11. Where do intruder detection policies get established?

A. In each User object

B. In a Group object

C. In the public trustee

D. In the container object

12. The PHX organizational unit has set the intruder detection lockout to start after four incorrect login attempts during a 20-minute period and to last for four hours. Joe.PHX.MA has forgotten his password. He tries a couple of times to log

in, gives up, and goes to an hour-long meeting. When he comes back, he tries three more times, and then gets it right on the fourth attempt and logs in. Why didn't his account get locked out?

A. Because it was locked out for 20 minutes and then was available again automatically

B. Because he never had four incorrect passwords during a 20-minute period, and the intruder attempt reset interval was changed from 2 to 0 when 20 minutes passed since the first login attempt

C. Because intruder detection was disabled

D. Because the intruder detection was set for the PHX organizational unit container, not the MA organization container

13. Terry works for a bank that has strict security policies. He is considering putting NetWare 5 servers into the network, but is concerned that sniffers can grab people's passwords, which would violate security. How can you respond to Terry's concern?

A. Tell Terry about the login process of authentication that uses an encrypted user code and never sends a user's password over the wire.

B. Tell Terry about a new product, NetSecure, that can be added to encrypt all end-user traffic, including password authentication.

C. Tell Terry how all other network operating systems have the same type of login scenario.

D. Tell Terry that there is really nothing that can be done about capturing passwords on the wire.

14. When a user logs in to the NetWare network, the following scripts are run in the following order:

A. Default login script; system login script; user login script

B. System login script; user login script; or if there is no user script, the default login script

C. Container login script, if it exists; profile login script, if it exists; user login script, if it exists; or if there is no user script, the default login script

D. Profile script, if it exists; container login script or the default script, if there is no container script; user login script

3

Managing User Accounts

CERTIFICATION OBJECTIVES

3.01   Introduction to User Object
       Management

3.02   Creating User Objects

3.03   Adding Licenses

3.04   Introduction to Network Security

3.05   Login Security

I t does not matter if a network is brand new, or if it is decades old; administrators must still manage users and their accounts on a network. Changes to names, titles, departments, and security access to files, and new installations happen all the time. Under NetWare, the management of user accounts occurs in the Novell Directory Services (NDS) tree.

Introduction to User Object Management

A User object represents a person who accesses the network. The name of the User object is the loginID. The way that users are granted security is through the User object properties. The NDS database enables the collection of user-related data, such as telephone numbers and locations.

FROM THE CLASSROOM

User Context and Network Resources

User context is nothing more than where that user's User object resides in the Directory. Another way to look at this concept is "Context=Immediate parent container and all containers in a direct hierarchical line to [Root]". That is, context is container names. Two different words describing the same concept.

User context is important because it gives information on all relevant containers that are in the User object's NDS hierarchy to [Root]. Knowing this will help greatly when you are troubleshooting NDS Object rights because containers can be made trustees of NDS objects

and the NetWare file system, which means that all subordinate objects get the same rights.

User context also gives a precise idea of where the user is located in relationship to the network's physical resources, provided that the NDS tree structure follows Novell's recommendations for designing and implementing NDS. Remember, always strive to place users in the same context as the resources they use.

—By Dan Cheung, CNI, MCNE, MCT

Understanding User Object Context

When a Novell Directory Services tree is organized into more than one container object, locating and accessing network resources becomes difficult. The NDS tree must be told how to find the other resource from the current location in the tree, or *context*. Users must know their account's context in order to log in to a workstation that is set to a different context.

QUESTIONS AND ANSWERS

Jeff is from Phoenix and is visiting the New York branch office. He borrows a workstation that is set to access the New York context. Jeff tries to log in the same way he does in the Phoenix office by inputting his username and password. The login fails. Why?	The NDS tree looked for Jeff's ID in the borrowed workstation's context, but Jeff's ID is located in the Phoenix context. The Phoenix user must know his user account's context for the login program to find it in NDS.

In Figure 3-1, the lower portion of the login screen shows the workstation's current context. The upper portion of the screen displays the user HHARRIS's Typeful Distinguished Name. User accounts can use either a Distinguished Name or a Relative Distinguished Name to navigate through the NDS tree from the current context to reach the user account's context. A *Distinguished Name* begins with a leading period, starts with the common name of the resource, and then lists each container unit up the tree to the [Root]. Each object has a unique Distinguished Name in the tree. A Distinguished Name can locate an object no matter what the current context is set at. A Distinguished Name for the User object named HHARRIS in Figure 3-1 is

```
.CN=HHARRIS.OU=ENG.OU=PHX.O=MA
```

In this example, the context of the HHARRIS user is OU=ENG.OU=PHX.O=MA. The context of a workstation can be set to .OU=ACCT.OU=TOK.O=MA, and the user account's context will still be .OU=ENG.OU=PHX.O=MA.

FIGURE 3-1

NDS login example

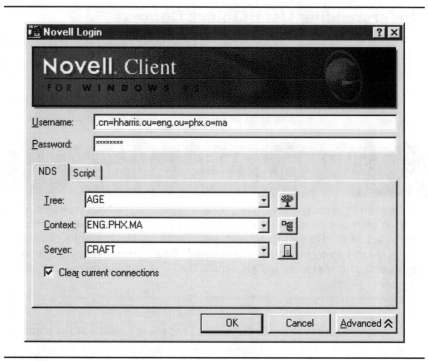

exam
ⓦatch

A Distinguished Name will always be able to find a resource regardless of the current context.

Use a Relative Distinguished Name to navigate from a workstation's context to an account's or another network resource's context. A *Relative Distinguished Name* lists the path from the current context to the object, does not contain a leading period, and can have an ending period. The Relative Distinguished Name can be confusing because it starts with the object that it is trying to reach, although it is intended to lead to that object from the current context. Remember that this type of name is locating a resource in a context *relative* to the current context. As illustrated in Figure 3-2, if user HHARRIS was logging in to a workstation with the context .OU=ACCT. OU=TOK.O=MA, the Relative Distinguished Name would be

```
CN=HHARRIS.OU=ENG.OU=PHX.
```

When HHARRIS is logging in to a workstation in the .OU=ENG. OU=PHX.O=MA context, it is not necessary for her to use anything other than her user account ID HHARRIS. Users traditionally do not use

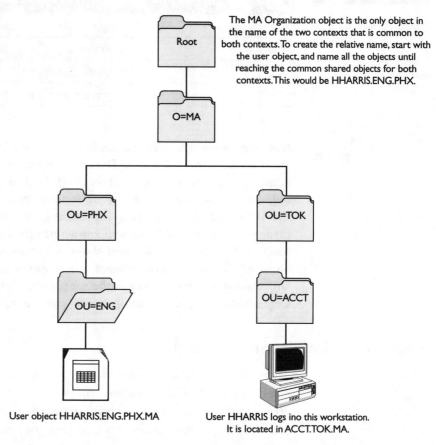

FIGURE 3-2

NDS location with Relative
Distinguished Name

The MA Organization object is the only object in the name of the two contexts that is common to both contexts. To create the relative name, start with the user object, and name all the objects until reaching the common shared objects for both contexts. This would be HHARRIS.ENG.PHX.

User object HHARRIS.ENG.PHX.MA

User HHARRIS logs ino this workstation. It is located in ACCT.TOK.MA.

anything other than their account ID, or User object name, when logging in to a network. For this reason, you should ensure that users are located in the same context as the network resources they access most often.

So far, all names used have been Typeful Names. *Typeful* refers to the use of the abbreviation for the container object and leaf object names. The abbreviations are followed by an equal sign (=), and each object in the name is separated by a dot (.). The abbreviations used most often are listed in Table 3-1.

Typeless Names do not use the abbreviation. An example of a Typeless Name for user HHARRIS is .HHARRIS.ENG.PHX.MA.

TABLE 3-1	Typeful Abbreviation	Resource Type
	O	Organization
Typeful Abbreviations	C	Country
	OU	Organizational Unit
	CN	Common Name (used for leaf objects)

Notice how quickly Distinguished Names grow in size when adding more layers to an NDS tree. The only way to keep the size of names manageable is to use the shortest possible names for container objects. It is not uncommon for national or global companies to use the IATA Code for airports to represent cities, since these codes are three characters and fairly well known or understood by end users. Los Angeles becomes LAX, and Newark becomes EWR. Usually the name of the Organization object is designated as being a long name. Unfortunately, this can cause the most problems because the Organization object shows up in every single object in the tree.

Network Administrator Utilities

There are several utilities included in NetWare 5 for administration of User objects. New to the NetWare operating system is the ability to manage User objects at the server console. The utility used for this is called Console One. It is a Java application loaded from the Java graphical screen on the console. This application can browse and display the entire NDS tree, as well as access other trees that exist on the network.

With NetWare 3.1x, the main administrative utility was SYSCON, which was a DOS-based text menu utility. In NetWare 5 and NetWare 4.x, the main administrative utility is a graphical application called NetWare Administrator. These more recent versions also include a DOS-based menu utility called NetAdmin.

CERTIFICATION OBJECTIVE 3.02

Creating User Objects

User objects can be created under any container object, except for the [Root] object of the NDS tree. The user's context should be the same as the one at the workstation they normally log in to. For bindery logins, the workstation and server that the user is logging in to should be set to the same context as the User object. The User object creation process includes the option for creating a user's home directory. As part of the process, the User object is granted all file system rights (except Supervisor) to fully manage all files and subdirectories in the new home directory.

exam
Ⓦatch

User objects cannot be created in the [Root] object.

When users are created, there are subsequent information fields that can be completed in NDS. This information manages the user's security access to network resources, as well as other objects' access to the User object. If using a user template during the User object creation, default properties for the User object are automatically applied. Table 3-2 describes the User object fields.

QUESTIONS AND ANSWERS

Jane created a User object in the NDS tree. She named the object JL4788, which was the end user's employee ID. The user's name is Taylor Meyer. Jane instructed Taylor to log in as Tmeyer, but Taylor was unable to log in. What went wrong?	Jane had named the User object JL4788. In NDS, the name of the User object is the login name. Jane can either instruct Taylor to log in as JL4788 or rename the User object to Tmeyer.

TABLE 3-2	User Property	Property Set Page	Description
User Object Properties	Account Balance	Account Balance	The Account Balance is a property used for the network usage accounting system. It displays the remaining network usage credit.
	Account Disabled	Login Restrictions	Checking this box will disable a user account from being able to log in, but will retain all other properties of the User object, in case it should be enabled in the future.
	Account has expiration date	Login Restrictions	When this field is completed, a user's ID will expire on a predetermined date without requiring an administrator to mark the account disabled.
	Account Locked	Intruder Lockout	This marks the status of a User object that has been locked out by a number of incorrect login attempts that exceeds the number set in the container object Intruder Detection Rules property.
	Account Reset Time	Intruder Lockout	This property lists the time interval that must elapse before the account will no longer be locked out.
	Allow Unlimited Credit	Account Balance	This property enables a user to have unlimited access to network resources when Accounting is enabled, regardless of the credit set in the Account Balance property.
	Allow user to Change Password	Password Restrictions	When checked, this property enables a user to change his or her own password.

TABLE 3-2

User Object
Properties *(continued)*

User Property	Property Set Page	Description
City	Postal Address	Name of the user's city.
Date Password Expires	Password Restrictions	This property lists the date that the User object's password expires, at which point the user will be prompted to change passwords.
Days Between Forced Changes	Password Restrictions	Number of days that a password can be used.
Default Queue	Environment	Unless the user specifies a different queue, print jobs go here.
Default Server	Environment	This property lists the server that the workstation will authenticate to when the user logs in to NDS.
Department	Identification	The business unit the user belongs to.
Description	Identification	Notes about the user.
E-mail Address	E-mail Addresses	Multiple e-mail addresses of the user can be listed here.
FAX Number	Identification	User's fax number.
Full Name	Identification	User's entire name.
Generational Qualifier	Identification	The part of a user's name that represents his generation, e.g., Jr., Sr., or III.
Given Name	Identification	User's first name.
Grace Logins Allowed	Password Restrictions	Number of logins allowed with an old password before the user is forced to change the password or lock out the account.
Group Membership	Group Membership	Groups that this User object is a member of.

TABLE 3-2

User Object
Properties *(continued)*

User Property	Property Set Page	Description
Home Directory	Environment	Location of the User object's personal directory—both volume and path to the directory. The directory can be created at the same time as the User object, or created separately and manually entered in this field.
Incorrect Login Attempts	Intruder Lockout	Accrued number of incorrect login attempts made consecutively before the interval is reset.
Initial	Identification	User's middle initial.
Language	Environment	Language the network messages are displayed in from NDS.
Last Intruder Address	Intruder Lockout	Lists the network address of the workstation where the last wrong password was entered.
Last Login	Login Restrictions	Date and time that the user last logged in to NDS.
Last Name	Identification	This property is required during object creation. It is the last name, or *surname,* of the user.
Limit Concurrent Connections	Login Restrictions	Check this box if the user should be restricted to logging in at a single or static number of workstations.
Location	Identification	Any location identification for the user can be entered here, such as a building name or a mail stop.
Login Script	Login Script	User's personal login script.

User Object
Properties *(continued)*

User Property	Property Set Page	Description
Login Time Restriction	Login Time Restriction	This property enables the administrator to limit what times the user can have access to the network.
Low Balance Limit	Account Balance	When using accounting, if a user's balance reaches this number, the user is denied network access until the balance is increased.
Mailing Label Information	Postal Address	Information to be used on a mailing label for this user.
Maximum Connections	Login Restrictions	The maximum number of workstations that this User object can be logged in to simultaneously.
Minimum Password Length	Password Restrictions	The minimum number of characters that a user's password is allowed to have.
NDPS Printers	NDPS Printer Access Control	The user's access to printers can be changed here by toggling on and off whether the user is a manager, operator, or user of the printer.
NetWare Registry Editor	NetWare Registry Editor	Values listed here are inserted into the user's Registry.
Network Address	Environment	The network address of the workstation where the user last logged in.
Network Address Restrictions	Network Address Restrictions	The network addresses listed are the only network addresses that the User object will be allowed to log in to. If no addresses are listed, the user can log in anywhere.

TABLE 3-2

User Object
Properties *(continued)*

User Property	Property Set Page	Description
Other Name	Identification	This space can be used for nicknames or other identification information.
Postal (zip) Code	Postal Address	User's ZIP code.
Postal Office Box	Postal Address	User's P.O. box.
Print Job Configuration	Print Job Configuration (Non NDPS)	Names of the various print jobs that the user can utilize.
Profile	Login Script	The name of a profile object is listed here. When the login script process executes, this profile script executes after the Organizational Unit script and before the user profile script.
Remaining Grace Logins	Password Restrictions	The number of grace logins remaining before the account is locked out or the user is forced to change passwords.
Require a Password	Password Restrictions	When checked, this property requires the user to have a password.
Require Unique Password	Password Restrictions	When checked, this requires that passwords are not reused.
Security Equal To	Security Equal	All the objects in NDS that the User object has been specified as being equivalent to.
See Also	See Also	List of objects related to this User object.
State or Province	Postal Address	User's state.
Street	Postal Address	User's street address.
Telephone	Identification	User's telephone number.
Title	Identification	User's business title or designation.

NetWare Administrator

The NetWare Administrator is a graphical tool for viewing the Novell Directory Services tree and making changes to the objects within it. Any changes made to NDS objects can be made from within the NetWare Administrator. This program is called NWADMIN, short for NetWare Administrator. The utility for Windows 95 is NWADMN95.EXE and the NT utility is NWADMNNT.EXE. There is also a utility that can be used under any 32-bit NetWare client for Windows called NWADMN32.EXE.

The NetWare Administrator program is in the SYS: volume of a NetWare 5 server. Depending on which operating system version is required, the executables are located in subdirectories of SYS:PUBLIC: Win95, WinNT, and Win32.

EXERCISE 3-1

Creating a User in NWADMN32.EXE

1. To start NetWare Administrator, choose Start | Run, type **F:\Public\Win32\NwAdmn32**, and then click OK.

2. Navigate through the tree to the container where you would like to place the User object. Containers can be expanded by double-clicking them.

3. Press the INSERT key, select User, and click OK. You'll see the New Object dialog box shown in Figure 3-3. Alternatively, choose Object | Newselect User, and click OK. Or you may click the Create User button on the toolbar.

4. Type the Login name and the Last name in the Create User dialog box shown in Figure 3-4. Note that the Login name is not necessarily the user's first name. This should be in accordance with your naming standards for NDS. Typically, large enterprises use the first one or two initials of a person's name and the first five characters of the last name and concatenate them to create a login name.

5. If using a template, check the User template box and select the template object from the tree. If creating a home directory, check the Create Home Directory box and locate the home directory parent volume and directory from the Path button. To add more details for the user, check Define additional properties. Note that you cannot add more details for a new user *and* select Create another User. These options are mutually exclusive.

6. Click the Create button.

FIGURE 3-3

Object insert window

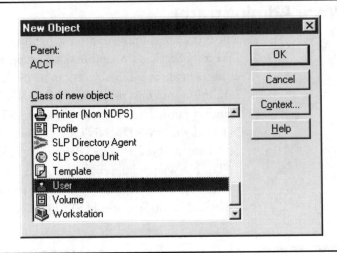

FIGURE 3-4

User object
creation window

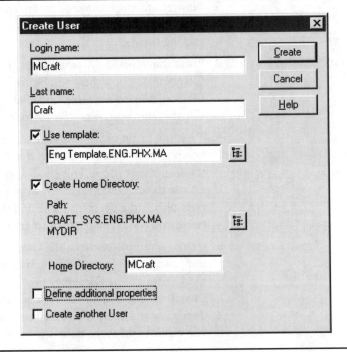

NetAdmin

The DOS version of the NetWare administrator is NETADMIN.EXE. This utility is located in SYS:PUBLIC, along with many of NetWare 5's DOS utilities. It is a text-menu application (see Figure 3-5) that allows administration of NDS objects. The NetAdmin utility is useful if, for whatever reason, the GUI applications are unusable.

<table>
<tr><td>EXERCISE 3-2</td></tr>
</table>

Creating a User in **NETADMIN.EXE**

1. Choose Start | Run, type **F:\public\netadmin**, and click OK.

2. Using the arrow keys, move the cursor down to Change Context and press ENTER.

3. Either type in the preferred context, or press INSERT to navigate with the arrow keys to the preferred context, and press F10. You will be returned to the original menu.

4. Use the arrow keys to navigate to the Manage Objects option and press ENTER.

5. Press the INSERT key.

6. Select User using the arrow keys and press ENTER.

7. Enter both the Login name and Last name (required), and any other information. Press ENTER after each option is entered.

8. When complete, press F10.

<table>
<tr><td>FIGURE 3-5</td></tr>
</table>

DOS version of NetAdmin
User object utility

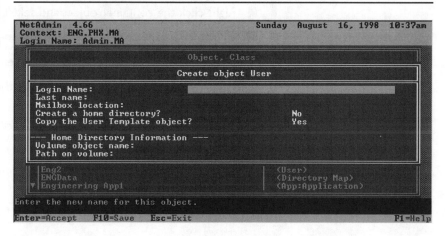

Console One

Console One is a Java utility that runs on a NetWare 5 console screen. NetWare 5 is the first version of the NetWare operating system that enables an administrator to manage User objects from the server console. User objects, group objects, and containers can all be created and managed from Console One. Console One can display other NDS trees, and allow user, group, and container object creation and editing.

EXERCISE 3-3

Creating a User Object from Console One

1. Start Console One by choosing the Start menu on the X-Window Java-based console and select Console One.

2. From the Console One window, expand the Trees folder in the left-hand pane by clicking the dot to the left of the Trees folder.

3. Expand the tree that you wish to create a User object in.

4. The Console One application will prompt for a user name, context, and password.

5. After logging in to the selected tree, the tree expands to show the Organization object. Continue expanding container objects until the one in which the User object will reside is displayed in the left pane. Then select that container object by clicking it. The objects within the container will appear in the right-hand pane of Console One.

6. There are three separate ways to initiate the new user dialog box.

   ■ Right-click the container object and select New | User.

   ■ Click the Create User button on the Console One toolbar.

   ■ Select New User object from the File menu.

7. The User dialog box will appear. Complete the two mandatory fields for login name and last name.

8. Check the Define Additional Properties check box.

9. Click Create.

10. The User dialog box will appear in which additional properties, such as Given Name, can be entered. When you have finished, click OK.

UIMPORT

UIMPORT is a utility for migrating a large number of users from an existing database into NDS. This is particularly helpful when migrating from one operating system to NetWare 5, or when adding a large number of users to the NetWare network. An existing database can be utilized for the UIMPORT process, which consists of three stages, as illustrated in Figure 3-6:

1. Export the data from the database into a delimited ASCII text file. The data may need to have fields excluded before the export process, or deleted after, depending on the database export capabilities. The data may need to be checked for special characters, such as quotation marks and commas, since they may shift the imported data into the wrong user properties. If special characters are found, they should be deleted.

2. Create a control file that describes each of the fields for the delimited ASCII text file applicable to NDS. The import control file specifies which character is used as the field separator. Note that this character is normally a comma, but can be another special character. The two required fields are First Name and Last Name.

3. Run UIMPORT against the control and data files, which will create the User objects in the Novell Directory Services tree.

To run UIMPORT, the user must have Create object rights or the Supervisor object rights to the container that users will be created in. Make sure the workstation used is set to the correct context using the CX command. UIMPORT is run at a DOS prompt window. The command to use when running UIMPORT is

```
UIMPORT [ControlFilename] [DataFileName] [/C]
[LogFileName.LOG]
```

We have already described the control and data files. The /C switch is used to allow UIMPORT to have continuous output and not stop for responses. A log file describing the success or failure of the imported User objects must be described at the end of the command with an attached .LOG file extension.

FIGURE 3-6   Three-step UIMPORT process

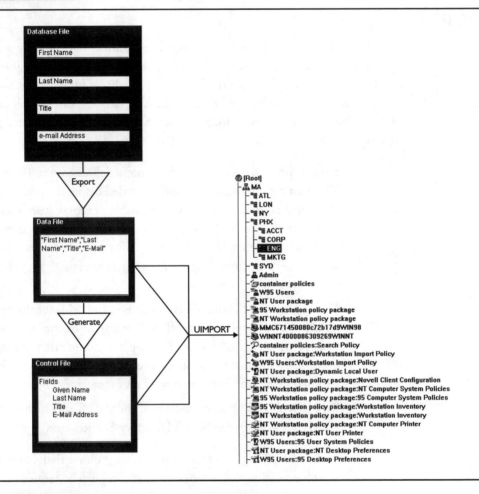

CERTIFICATION OBJECTIVE 3.03

Adding Licenses

New to NetWare 5 is a licensing management capability. NetWare Licensing Services (NLS) provides the following:

- A single utility for NetWare product license management

- Consistent licensing for NetWare products

- Licensing provisions for any other products meeting NLS requirements

This utility can be used on 32-bit operating systems (Windows 95, Windows 98, and Windows NT). The NLS 32-bit executable name is NLSMAN32.EXE. This utility is located in the SYS: volume under the PUBLIC\WIN32 directory.

Figure 3-7 displays the NLS Manager initial screen. Licenses for NetWare and NetWare server products are stored within a license container within NDS. The first screen enables *walking* the NDS tree for licenses, which simply means that the NDS database is searched for license containers in all containers below the NDS container object selected.

Follow these steps to add a license to NetWare:

1. From the workstation, choose Start I Run.

2. Type **F:\PUBLIC\WIN32\NLSMAN32.EXE** and press ENTER.

3. Allow the NLS Manager to walk the tree from the [Root] by accepting the default selections and clicking OK.

4. Choose the View menu and select Tree View of Licenses.

FIGURE 3-6

NLS Manager

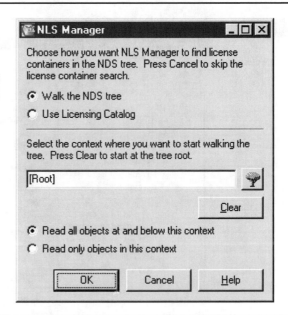

5. Choose the Actions menu and select Install License Certificate.

6. In the resulting dialog box, shown in Figure 3-8, type the path to the disk that holds the new license in the upper box (normally, this is A:\); then type the context in the tree where this license should be installed.

7. Click OK.

Because the licensing information is stored in NDS, the NetWare Administrator has integrated the NLS Manager functionality into its program. To add a license from within NetWare Administrator, highlight the container for the license that you are going to add. Then choose the Tools menu and select Install License, as shown in Figure 3-9. The remaining dialog boxes are identical to the NLS Manager dialog boxes.

FIGURE 3-7

Installing a license using NLS Manager

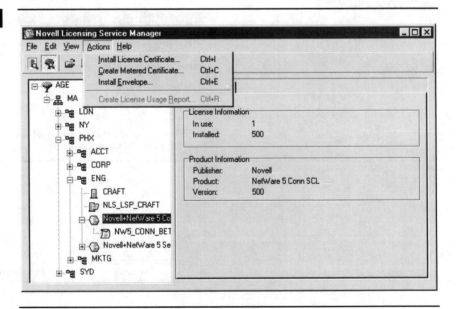

FIGURE 3-8

Installing a license using
NetWare Administrator

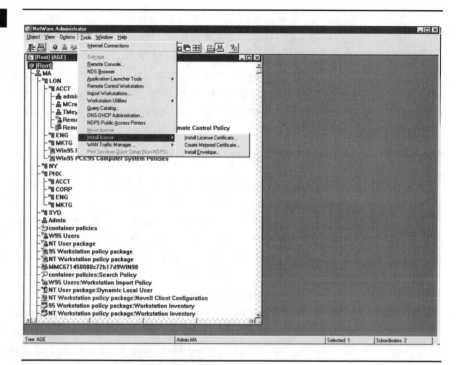

Introduction to Network Security

There are several types of network security. All levels of security share the
same goal: to control access to network resources. There are four types of
security:

- **Login security**   General or public network resource access
- **Server security**   Console accessibility
- **File system security**   Explicit access to files and directories on
  NetWare servers
- **NDS security**   Rights to objects and properties of objects in NDS

When a User object is created, the properties of the object determine the login security that will be applied to it. Server security is not affected by User object creation. File system security involves rights to files and directories granted to users. NDS security is the granting of object and property rights to users. Both file system security and NDS security are applied immediately to the User object when it is created.

Security for User Objects

For a User object, the Access Control List determines what other objects in Novell Directory Services have rights to it. A User object's container may affect the rights that are assigned to a user in that container. When a container object has been assigned file system or NDS rights, all objects—either leaf or container objects —automatically inherit the container's rights. This is called *implied security equivalence.* When assigning file system rights, the administrator may apply them to the container object so that all new users in that container will receive the same file system rights. The container object has the Read property rights to its own login script. Newly created User objects inherit this so that they may run the container login script. The New User object receives other default rights at creation, as described in Table 3-3. Other objects in the tree receive further rights at the creation of a new user.

If an administrator does not want a user to be able to change the user login script or manage print jobs, or have full file system rights to the user's home directory, then these rights must be revoked after the User object is created.

TABLE 3-3	Trustee	Rights
Default Rights at User Object Creation	[Public]	Browse object rights to the tree [Root] object. This enables a user to browse for the correct context before logging in.
		Read property rights to the User's Default Server property to enable the correct authenticating server at login.
		Read property rights to the NetWare server's network address property, to locate the authenticating server at login. Note: [Public] trustee rights are available to the user before login.

TABLE 3-4	Trustee	Rights
Default Rights at User Object Creation *(continued)*	Container	Read property rights to its own login script, so the script can be run. Read and File Scan file system rights to SYS:PUBLIC. Note: Container trustee rights are inherited by the User object after login.
	[Root]	Browse object rights to the User object.
	New User object	Browse object rights to itself. Read property rights to all its own property rights. Read and Write property rights to login script—users are allowed to write their own login scripts. Read and Write property rights to the Print Job Configuration property for users to manage their own non-NDPS print jobs. All file system rights to the user's own home directory, if created.

CERTIFICATION OBJECTIVE 3.05

Login Security

Before logging in, every user is granted some default rights to the NDS tree to enable logging in through the [Public] trustee. The [Public] trustee is unique because it is not an object, but a trustee assignment that is applied to all users, whether logged in or not. If creating a completely nonsecured network, further rights can be assigned to the [Public] trustee, and users will not be required to log in at all.

The default properties for a User object do not require any login security. The User object is not required to have a password. An efficient method to apply default login security is to create a template object for the user and establish the login security requirements.

The types of security measures that affect login security are

- Login passwords
- Login time restrictions
- Network address restrictions
- Intruder detection and lockout
- Account expiration and lockout

To set up these options, double-click any User object in the NDS tree that you want to change. The options that apply to intruder detection are in the container object properties. The options that apply to the remainder are in the User object properties, under the following:

- Password Restrictions to set up passwords for logging in
- Network Address Restrictions to restrict the login locations
- Login Restrictions, which can disable the account, limit the number of concurrent logins, or set an expiration date for the User object account
- Login Time Restrictions to disable logins during restricted hours

Each of these options is available in a Template object. The Template object can be created for each different type of user, such as students and teachers, or for each container object in the tree. If each user is to have identical basic restrictions, the administrator may opt to create a single template for the entire NDS tree. If you're not using a template and want to have login security, you must edit each individual User object account because login security is not enabled by default.

CERTIFICATION SUMMARY

NetWare User object management occurs in the NDS tree. The single point of administration for User objects is the NetWare Administrator program, also referred to as NWAdmin. NWAdmin is available in Windows 95–, Windows NT–, and Client 32– compatible executables.

The User object context is necessary for users to understand their login process. The user's context is the place where the User object is located in the NDS tree. The User object has a Distinguished Name that describes the name and context together. The Distinguished Name can be used by a user to log in from any point in the tree. A Relative Distinguished Name is created when a user traces a User object context to the point in the tree where it shares a container with the current login context. The Relative Distinguished name is dependent on the other context. Names for User objects can be *Typeful,* including the abbreviations for the object and containers, or *Typeless,* which does not include the abbreviations.

User objects can be created in the NWAdmin programs under the SYS:PUBLIC directory in the Win32, Win95, and WinNT directories. They can also be created using NETADMIN, a DOS menu program; and on the NetWare Server console, they can be created using Console One, a Java application that runs on the server. Large numbers of users can be imported directly into the NDS tree using UIMPORT. This is especially helpful if there is an existing database of users.

NetWare has a new licensing structure that is integrated into Novell Directory Services. Licenses are stored in a license container in the NDS tree and can be installed into the tree using the NLS Manager or NWAdmin.

There are several aspects to network security: login security, NDS security, file system security, and server security. NDS security is applied through object rights and property rights in the tree. File system security involves rights to files and directories granted to users.

Login security is managed through the properties of the individual User objects that are created, except for intruder detection, which is handled as a property of the container object for end users. Login security involves the following property pages in a User object: Password Restrictions, Network Address Restrictions, Login Restrictions, and Login Time Restrictions.

TWO-MINUTE DRILL

❑ When a Novell Directory Services tree is organized into more than one container object, it must be told how to find the other resources from the current context. Users must know their account's context in order to log in to a workstation that is set to a different context.

❑ User accounts can use either a distinguished name or a relative distinguished name to navigate through the NDS tree from the current context to reach the user account's context.

❑ A Distinguished Name begins with a leading period, starts with the common name of the resource, and then lists each container unit up the tree to the [Root]. Each object has a unique Distinguished Name in the tree. A Distinguished Name can locate an object no matter what the current context is set at.

❑ A Relative Distinguished Name lists the path from the current context to the object, does not contain a leading period, and can have an ending period. A Relative Distinguished Name can be confusing because it starts with the object that it is trying to reach, although it is intended to lead to that object from the current context. Remember that this type of name is locating a resource in a context relative to the current context.

❑ *Typeful* refers to the use of the abbreviation for the container object and leaf object names. The abbreviations are followed by an equal sign (=), and each object in the name is separated by a dot (.). Typeless Names do not use the abbreviation.

❑ NetWare 5 is the first version of the NetWare operating system that enables an administrator to manage User objects from the server console through the Console One utility. Console One is a Java application that runs on a NetWare 5 console screen.

❑ User objects can be created under any container object, except for the [Root] object of the NDS tree. The user's context should be the same as the one at the workstation they normally log in to. For bindery logins, the workstation and server that the user is logging into should be set to the same context as the User object. The User object creation process includes the option for creating a user's home directory. As part of the process, the User object is granted all file system rights (except Supervisor) to fully manage all files and subdirectories in the new home directory.

❑ The NetWare Administrator (called NWADMIN) is a graphical tool for viewing the Novell Directory Services tree, and making changes to the objects within it. Any changes made to NDS objects can be made from within the NetWare Administrator. The utility for Windows 95 is NWADMN95.EXE. The utility for Windows NT is NWADMNNT.EXE. The NWADMN32.EXE utility can be used under any 32-bit NetWare client for Windows.

❑ The NetWare Administrator program is found in the SYS: volume of a NetWare 5 server. Depending on which operating system version is required, the executables are located in subdirectories of SYS:PUBLIC: Win95, WinNT, and Win32.

❑ The DOS version of the NetWare Administrator program is NETADMIN.EXE. This utility is located in SYS:PUBLIC, along with many of NetWare 5's DOS utilities. It is a text-menu application that allows administration of NDS objects. The NetAdmin utility is useful if the GUI applications are unusable.

❑ UIMPORT is a utility used for migrating a large number of users from an existing database into NDS. This is particularly helpful when migrating from one operating system to NetWare 5 or when adding a large number of users to the NetWare network.

❑ NetWare Licensing Services (NLS) is a new licensing capability in NetWare 5 that provides a single utility for NetWare product license management, consistent licensing for NetWare products, and licensing provisions for any other products meeting NLS requirements. NLS can be used on 32-bit operating systems. The NLS 32-bit executable name is NLSMAN32.EXE. NLS is located in the SYS: volume under the PUBLIC\WIN32 directory.

❑ There are four types of security: login security, server security, file system security, and NDS security. The properties of a user object determine the login security that will be applied to it. Server security is not affected by User object creation. File system security involves rights to files and directories granted to users. NDS security is the granting of object and property rights to users. Both file system security and NDS security are applied immediately to the User object when it is created.

❑ The Access Control List determines what other objects in Novell Directory Services have rights to a User object. A User object's container may affect the rights that are assigned to a user in that container. When a container object has been assigned file system or NDS rights, all objects—either leaf or container objects—automatically inherit the container's rights (implied security equivalence).

❑ Every user is granted some default rights to an NDS tree to enable logging in through the [Public] trustee. The [Public] trustee is unique because it is a trustee assignment applied to all users. If creating a completely nonsecured network, further rights can be assigned to the [Public] trustee, and users will not be required to log in at all. An efficient method to apply default login security is to create a template object for the user and establish the login security requirements.

❑ The security measures affecting login security are login passwords, login time restrictions, network address restrictions, intruder detection and lockout, and account expiration and lockout.

SELF TEST

The following Self-Test questions will help you measure your understanding of the material presented in this chapter. Read all the choices carefully, as there may be more than one correct answer. Choose all correct answers for each question.

1. If the User object naming convention is the first four letters of a user's first name concatenated with the first four letters of the user's last name, and the user is named Justine Herfurth, what is the login name?

    A. JHerfurth

    B. JustineH

    C. JustHerf

    D. Justine

2. What is a *context*?

    A. The location in the NDS tree

    B. A workstation

    C. The network segment

    D. The Organizational Unit

3. When logging in to the tree, what information is required for NDS to find the User object?

    A. The login time restriction

    B. Intruder detection policies

    C. Default printer object

    D. The User object's context

4. What makes up a Distinguished Name?

    A. The abbreviations for each object described, including an equal sign (=)

    B. No abbreviations included

    C. A leading period and the username, then each container object until the [Root] is reached, each separated by periods

    D. No leading period, the username, and each container object until the [Root] of the current context and the User object context are reached, each separated by periods, and ending in a period

5. What is a Relative Distinguished Name?

    A. The abbreviations for each object described, including an equal sign (=)

    B. No abbreviations included

    C. A leading period and the username, then each container object until the [Root] is reached, each separated by periods

    D. No leading period, the username, and each container object until the [Root] of the current context and the User object context are reached, each separated by periods, and ending in a period

6. What is a Typeful Name?

    A. The abbreviations for each object described, including an equal sign (=)

    B. No abbreviations included

    C. A leading period and the username, then each container object until the [Root] is reached, each separated by periods

    D. No leading period, the username, and each container object until the [Root] of the current context and the User object context are reached, each separated by periods, and ending in a period

7. What is a Typeless Name?

   A. The abbreviations for each object described, including an equal sign (=)

   B. No abbreviations included

   C. A leading period and the username, then each container object until the [Root] is reached, each separated by periods

   D. No leading period, the username, and each container object until the [Root] of the current context and the User object context are reached, each separated by periods, and ending in a period

8. True or False. User objects can be created and managed at the server console.

   A. True

   B. False

9. Which of the following is a NetWare Administrator program that lists the NDS objects in a tree structure?

   A. SYS:PUBLIC\WIN32\NLSMAN32.EXE

   B. SYS:PUBLIC\NLIST.EXE

   C. SYS:SYSTEM\SERVER.EXE

   D. SYS:PUBLIC\WIN32\NWADMN32.EXE

10. Which option in the NDS administration utility for DOS, NETADMIN, is used to initiate User object creation?

    A. Change Context

    B. Insert User Object

    C. Manage Objects

    D. Install User

11. Which of the following statements is false?

    A. Console One is a Java utility.

    B. Console One can view the NDS tree of only the server it is running on.

    C. Console One runs on a NetWare 5 Server console.

    D. Console One can manage User objects, groups, and containers.

12. What is UIMPORT used for?

    A. Importing a large number of users from an existing database to NDS

    B. Migrating a NetWare 3.x Server to NetWare 5

    C. Importing utilities into NetWare that normally run under Windows NT

    D. Importing unused licenses from one context to another

13. Which of the following are steps for importing users with UIMPORT?

    A. Run the data file and control file against UIMPORT.

    B. Edit the NDS tree properties to accept UIMPORT data.

    C. Extract data into a delimited ASCII text file from the existing user database.

    D. Generate a control file describing the fields in the data file.

14. What does NLS provide?

    A. NetWare Login Security—a single administration point for login and intruder detection

    B. NetWare License Services—a single administration point for handling licenses for NetWare and NetWare products

    C. Novell Logic Services—a database engine for User object creation

    D. Novell Login Services—the ability to log in from any context

15. What can an administrator do to make all users in a container have identical NDS object, NDS property, and file system rights?

    A. Edit each User object to add the rights

    B. Apply the rights to the [Public] trustee

    C. Apply the rights to the container object in which the users are located

    D. Apply the rights to the [Root]

4

Managing Network Printing

CERTIFICATION OBJECTIVES

4.01	Network Printing Overview
4.02	Introduction to Novell Distributed Print Services
4.03	Setting Up NetWare Distributed Print Services (NDPS)
4.04	Managing NDPS

M anaging print services is one of the most critical network functions. Printing is one of the few outputs on a network, and even with the movement towards paperless offices, printing is an essential service for network users.

Network Printing Overview

Sharing printers on a network is much more efficient than individual users having their own printers, reducing the costs for business overall, since one printer can serve many users, as illustrated in Figure 4-1. This is one reason that businesses invest in network hardware and software. The NetWare operating system has an extensive history in efficiently serving printers to network users.

Print Queues and Print Servers

Older versions of the NetWare printing system were based on print queues and print servers. Along with Queue and Server objects, a Printer object was included in NDS as a resource object. The printing services NetWare provided were complex. They required the creation of each individual print queue, Printer object, and print server. These printing service objects had to be linked together to provide a path for a print job to follow from the workstation to the printed output. Printing involved three objects in NDS:

- Print Queue object
- Print Server object
- Printer object

The *print queue* is a storage area that receives print jobs from multiple users and lines them up or queues them for printing. This is how the print queue enables multiple users on a single printer. Because the print jobs are stored, the workstation is not held up waiting for printing before its print

FIGURE 4-1   A NetWare printer can be accessed by multiple users

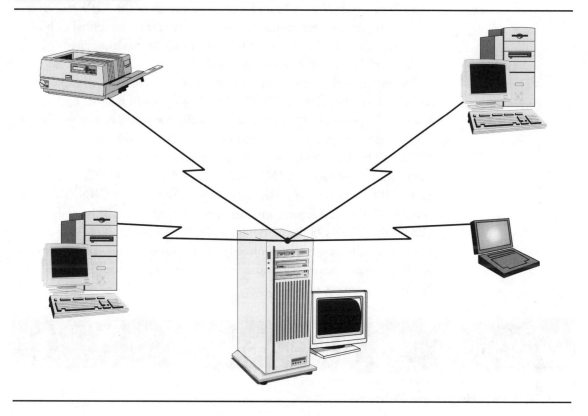

jobs can be processed. The actual data for the print jobs is stored on a NetWare server volume.

A NetWare Print Queue object represents a subdirectory under the volume_name:QUEUES\ directory, which gets created when the first Print Queue object is created. The individual queue directories are assigned hexadecimal numbers as directory names so they may appear as seemingly random numerals and letters.

The print queue sends the print jobs to a *print server*. The print server accepts the job and sends it to the correct printer. Whereas the print queue is a storage area, the print server is a service that manages the print action. The PSERVER.NLM NetWare loadable module runs the NetWare server.

The *Printer object* represents a network printer. It is configured in NDS, along with the Print Server and Print Queue objects, to define the connections between the various components.

Printers can either be connected to a NetWare server directly or connected to a workstation. PSERVER.NLM works with either option, however the printer is denoted as either locally connected or remote. When a printer is connected to the server directly, the server must also run the NPRINTER.NLM. When a printer is connected to a workstation, the workstation must run NPRINTER.EXE. For Windows 95 PCs, there is a 32-bit NPRINTER executable, NPTWIN95.EXE. The NPRINTER.EXE and NPTWIN95.EXE programs are stored in the SYS:PUBLIC and SYS:PUBLIC\WIN95 directories on a NetWare 5 Server. Note that printers can also be connected directly to the network using special network printing cards or boxes that utilize their own software, which integrates with NetWare's printing architecture.

FROM THE CLASSROOM

NDPS Printing New Feature

The NetWare print queue has been a workhorse of many NetWare networks since it was introduced. Some popular third-party print servers even encourage using NetWare print queues instead of creating them with the utility that comes with the hardware. So why the switch to NDPS? The short answer is that NDPS is an improvement in administering networked printing. One notable new feature is the Public Access Printer, which is managed through NetWare Administrator, but a user need not be authenticated to NDS to be able to print. This is a convenience for roaming users who carry a laptop computer from location to location, who may not be able to log in easily because their User object resides in a container other than their current locale. It is also useful for users who cannot otherwise log in to NDS without additional effort by the local administrator.

—By Dan Cheung, CNI, MCNE, MCT

EXERCISE 4-1

Setting up Remote Workstation Printing on the Server

1. First, you must create the printing objects. To create objects, open the NetWare administrator by choosing Start | Run, type **SYS:PUBLIC\WIN32\NWADMN32.EXE**, and press ENTER.

2. Navigate to the appropriate context and press the INSERT key.

3. Select Printer (non-NDPS) and click OK.

4. Type an appropriate name that does not already exist in that context and click Create.

5. You will be returned to NetWare Administrator still in the same context. Press INSERT.

6. Select Print Queue and click OK.

7. Type an appropriate name (not already in that context).

8. Click the Print Queue volume button and select a server volume; then click OK. If a server is not in that context, you will need to navigate the tree to find a volume. The volume will be the physical place where print jobs are stored.

9. Click Create.

10. You will be returned to the NetWare Administrator in the same context. Press the INSERT key.

11. Select Print Server (non-NDPS) and click OK.

12. Type an appropriate name (not already in that context) and check off the Define Additional Properties check box; then click Create.

13. The Print Server properties box will appear. Click the Assignments property page.

14. Click the Add button.

15. Select the printer you created and click OK.

16. Click OK to close the Print Server properties.

17. In the NetWare Administrator, select the Printer object and double-click it to display its properties. Alternatively, select the Object menu and the Properties option.

18. Click the Assignments property page button.

19. Click the Add button, select the print queue you created, and click OK.

20. Click the Configuration property page button.

21. Under Printer Type, select Other/Unknown. This option states that the printer will be a remote printer. If the printer is connected to a network printing box or card, this would also be selected. If the printer is connected directly to the NetWare Server, select either Serial or Parallel.

22. Click OK.

23. At the server console prompt, type **LOAD PSERVER** and the Distinguished Name of the print server object. This object might be .PSRVR.ENG.PHX.MA, which makes the entire command **LOAD PSERVER .PSRVR.ENG.PHX.MA**.

If you look at the Print Server object properties and click the Print Layout property page, the result of Exercise 4-1 will be the same as that shown in Figure 4-2.

FIGURE 4-2

Print layout for a
non-NDPS print server

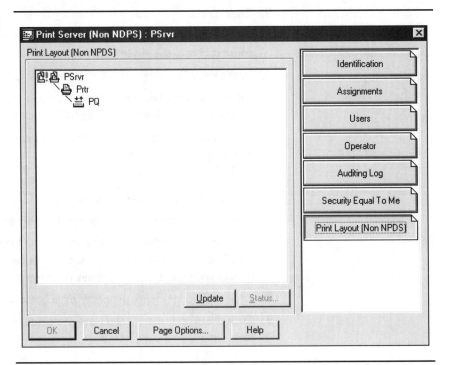

Setting Up Remote Workstation Printing at the Workstation

1. At the Windows 95/98 workstation that will be running the printer, log in to the network.

2. If not already mapping a drive to SYS, right-click the Network Neighborhood icon, and select Map Network Drive. Select drive F: Type the server name and SYS volume in the UNC format (Universal Naming Convention), which is *SERVERNAME*\SYS, and click OK.

3. Choose Start | Run, type **F:\PUBLIC\WIN95\NPTWIN95.EXE**, and press ENTER or click OK.

4. The NPRINTER Manager will start. The first screen will prompt you to select the NDS PRINTER object. Navigate through the tree to locate the Printer object and click OK.

5. Make sure that the Activate When Nprinter Manager Loads check box is on so that the same printer will become active each time NPTWIN95 is executed.

6. Click OK and workstation printing will become active.

Several NDS options can manage and configure printing to work correctly for the environment that it is serving. These options are available through the properties of the Printer, Print Queue, and Print Server objects. The Print Server property options are described in Table 4-1. Print Queue object properties are summarized in Table 4-2. Printer object properties are described in Table 4-3.

Users can attach to print queues in order to print documents to the network printer. The DOS utility for this process is CAPTURE.EXE. It redirects print jobs sent to the LPT port of the workstation to a network print queue and has multiple switches to control how print jobs are handled. Table 4-4 describes some of the switches for the CAPTURE command.

Capturing a printer in Windows 95 is somewhat different. It is integrated into Client 32. In the Network Neighborhood properties, which is the same as the network icon in control panel, the properties of the

TABLE 4-1

Print Server Properties

Print Server Property	Page	Function
Advertising Name	Identification	Name that is viewed from workstation browsing
Other Name	Identification	Another name used for the print server
Network Address	Identification	IPX network and node address of the print server
Description	Identification	Description of the print server
Location	Identification	Location information
Department	Identification	Department using this print server
Organization	Identification	Business unit using this print server
Version	Identification	Version of the PSERVER.NLM being used
Status	Identification	Whether the print server is currently running or not
Change Password button	Identification	Used to set a password that is required when PSERVER.NLM is loaded at the server console
Assignments	Assignments	The printers that are managed by this print server
Users	Users	The users, or their containers, that are granted permissions to use the print server
Operator	Operators	The operators of the print server
Auditing Log	Auditing Log	Offers powerful auditing features for printing, such as usage of the printer, printing successes, and which printer the job was directed to
Security Equal To	Security Equal To	Objects having the same security as the print server
Print Layout	Print Layout	Displays a graphical map of the connected printing objects

TABLE 4-2

Print Queue
Object Properties

Print Queue Property	Property Page	Function
Name	Identification	NDS Fully Distinguished Name of the Print Queue object
Volume	Identification	Volume where print jobs are stored until they can be printed
Other Name	Identification	Another name for the Print Queue object
Description	Identification	A description for the print queue
Location	Identification	Location information for the print queue
Department	Identification	Department that uses this print queue
Organization	Identification	Business unit that uses this print queue
Operator Flags	Identification	Check boxes to enable/disable printing to the queue: allows users to submit print jobs; allows service by current print servers; allows new print servers to attach
Assignments	Assignments	Displays the connected Print Server and Printer objects
Operator	Operator	Operators for the print queue
Users	Users	Authorized users of the print queue
Security Equal	Security Equal	Lists NDS objects with equivalent security
Job List	Job List	Displays current print jobs and their details; allows print jobs to be held, resumed, or deleted through appropriate buttons

TABLE 4-3

Printer Properties

Printer Property	Property Page	Function
Name	Identification	NDS Fully Distinguished Name of the Printer object.
Other Name	Identification	Another name for the Printer object.
Description	Identification	Printer description.
Network address	Identification	IPX network and node address for the printer.
Location	Identification	Location information for the printer.
Department	Identification	Department that uses this printer.
Organization	Identification	Business unit that uses this printer.
Print Queues	Assignments	The print queues that feed jobs to this printer; Priority shows which print queues will have the highest priority when submitting jobs to the printer.
Default Print Queue	Assignments	The default print queue captured when a user captures the Printer object rather than a print queue
Printer Type	Configuration	The type of printer port that the printer is attached to: If attached to the server, use serial or parallel; if attached to a workstation or network printing device, select other/unknown
Communication	Configuration	The specifics of the printer port/type; for example, the parallel port communication allows you to select which LPT port.
Banner Type	Configuration	Specifies whether the banner is in ASCII text format or PostScript. PostScript can be used only on compatible printers.
Service Interval	Configuration	How often, in seconds, the printer checks for new jobs in the print queue.

TABLE 4-3	Printer Property	Property Page	Function
Printer Properties *(continued)*	Buffer Size in KB	Configuration	The size of the data store buffer; a RAM buffer of the print server (either server or workstation) between 3 and 20K.
	Starting Form	Configuration	Default form for the printer.
	Network address restriction	Configuration	The network addresses this printer is restricted to using.
	Service Mode for Forms	Configuration	How to manage the way forms are changed.
	Notification	Notification	List users who are notified of printer errors.
	Page Description Language	Features	Printer languages supported by the printer.
	Memory in KB	Features	The amount of RAM that is installed in the printer.
	Supported Type Faces	Features	The printer fonts the printer can use.
	Supported Cartridges	Features	The font cartridges the printer can use.
	Security Equal	Security Equal	List of NDS objects with equivalent security.
	See Also	See Also	Other objects to reference with this Printer object.

NetWare Client include a Default Capture page and a couple of Advanced Settings to manage printing (see Figure 4-3).

The Windows 95 client enables the user to specify the standard configuration to use for printing whenever a capture is made. These settings are specified in the Default Capture page of the NetWare Client properties. As shown in Figure 4-3, the Default Capture page displays many of the

TABLE 4-4	CAPTURE Switch	Function
Capture Switches	/AU or /NA	Autoendcap or No Autoendcap; /AU enabled by default. This enables an application to send a job as soon as it is finished printing. If an application does not support this, use /NA to turn it off.
	/B=*text* or /NB	The banner is a leading page describing the print job. The /NB switch turns off the banner. The /B=*text* adds text to the bottom of the banner.
	/C=*number*	Specifies the number of copies to print the print job.
	/CR=*filename*	Redirects the print job to a file.
	/D	Displays the details about the captured printer port.
	/EC	/EC L=*port* Ends capture of the printer port. /EC ALL Ends capture of all printer ports. /ECCA Ends the capture and cancels the print job.
	/F=*number* or *name*	Specifies the form to use.
	/FF or /NFF	/FF forces a form feed, or blank sheet of paper, after the print. /NFF turns this off. Most applications already have a built-in form feed.
	/? or /H	Displays the help screen.
	/HOLD	Holds the print jobs. They can be released later through NetWare Administrator.
	/J=*name*	Selects a print job configuration to use.
	/K	Keeps a print job and sends it to the queue, even if the capture does not end correctly.
	/L=*number* or /LPT*n*	Selects a printer port, using the logical ports 1 through 9.
	/NAM=*name*	Specifies the name to be printed on the banner page at the top.
	/NOTI or /NNOTI	/NOTI notifies the user that the print job has completed. /NNOTI turns this feature off.
	/P=*name*	Use this option when capturing a port to an NDS Printer object (excludes using the /Q option).
	/Q=*name*	Use this option when capturing a port to a print queue (excludes using the /P option).

TABLE 4-4

Capture Switches
(continued)

CAPTURE Switch	Function
/S=*name*	If using a bindery-based queue, this specifies which server the queue is attached to.
/SH	Displays each captured printer port configuration.
/T=*number* or /NT	Specifies the number of spaces to use for tab characters in the print job. Most applications do not require this, and the /NT parameter applies.
/TI=*number*	Specifies the timeout in number of seconds after which time the print job is considered ended because no data was sent during that period.

FIGURE 4-3

Default Capture in
NetWare Client 32
properties

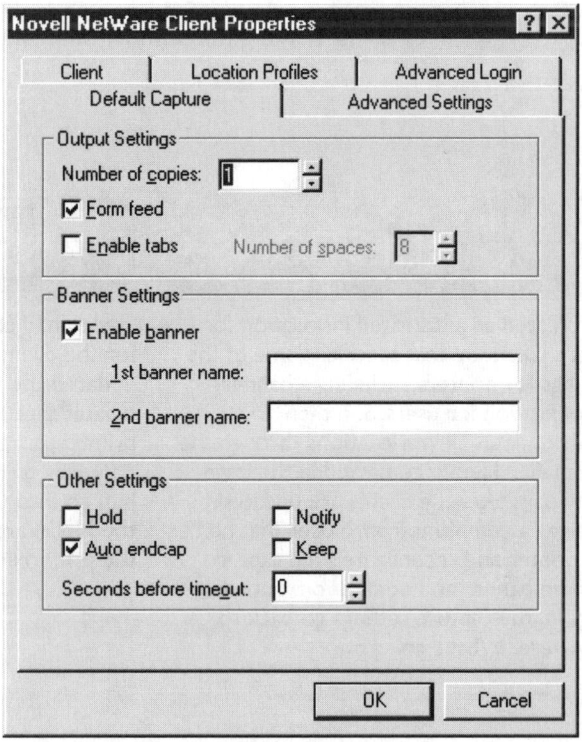

same parameters that are available in the CAPTURE command. These include the following:

- The number of copies
- Enabling a form feed
- Specifying the number of spaces for tabs
- Banner settings
- Placing print jobs on hold as they are submitted
- Autoendcap to allow print jobs to be submitted as soon as the application is ready
- Whether to notify the user
- Whether to keep the job in the queue, even if the station disconnects improperly
- Specifying the number of seconds for a timeout on the print job

QUESTIONS AND ANSWERS

Taylor has created an automated installation for the NetWare Client 32 that specifies some of the default settings for printers, including a banner page and notification for users. She then automatically updates all workstations through the addition of an ACU Setup command in the login script. A few days after the clients are updated, Taylor receives a complaint from a user that he has captured a printer and reconfigured the capture settings for the banner and notification, but each time he logs in, the capture settings go back to where they were. What's going on?

Taylor had configured the default capture settings for the client. When the files installed, they updated the user's workstation settings. The default capture settings are inherited by each new print capture performed at the workstation. The only way to change this for the user is to have him go into the Default Capture settings page for the NetWare Client 32 properties and change to the preferred settings there.

The Windows 95 Client 32 Advanced Settings page includes several printing management settings. Many of these settings could possibly affect the performance of printing, merely by optimizing the workstation, such as enabling Large Internet Packets and Packet Burst. Others affect printing directly and are listed here:

- **Network Printers** This parameter allows you to select the number of LPT ports that the Windows 95 client will allow capturing to. The default is three. The values are 1 through 9.

- **Print Header** This sets the size of the buffer used to initialize the print job. Increase this buffer when printing large or complex print jobs.

- **Print Tail** This sets the size of the buffer used to hold the information needed to reset the print job.

on the **Job**

Since legacy NetWare printing uses Sequenced Packet Exchange (SPX), large or complex prints that do not print correctly can sometimes be fixed by adjusting the SPX parameters of the IPX/SPX 32-bit protocol properties. Specifically, increasing the SPX connections parameter to 60 or above can correct some printing problems.

EXERCISE 4-3

Capturing a Printer Port in Windows 95

1. Right-click the Network Neighborhood icon.

2. Select Novell Capture Printer Port from the pop-up menu (see Figure 4-4).

3. The first available port will appear in the upper part of the dialog box. If you wish to select a different port, select it from the drop-down list.

4. The second portion of this dialog box should be completed with the name of the server and print queue as displayed in Figure 4-5.

5. Click the Capture button.

6. You can click the Settings buttons and customize the capture settings, if desired. If the defaults are OK, click Close.

FIGURE 4-4

Network Neighborhood
pop-up menu

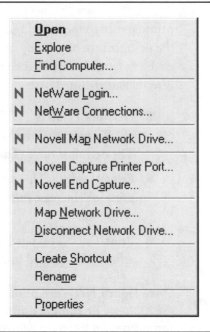

FIGURE 4-5

The Capture Printer
Port dialog box

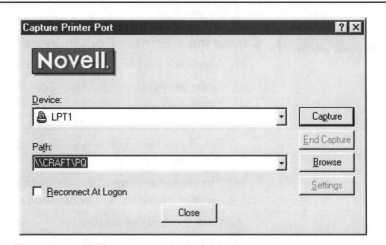

New Technology Directions

NetWare's print queue-based printing architecture was efficient, and Novell's NetWare operating system was well known for its printing services. However, newer technology demanded that a printing system be created that could incorporate bidirectional communication with more intelligent printers, and desktop printers have begun moving in this direction. Integration with Microsoft Windows operating systems, the most widely installed desktop operating systems, was a requirement. In extending the single-seat administrative concept of Novell Directory Services, a management solution was also in order for printing.

CERTIFICATION OBJECTIVE 4.02

Introduction to Novell Distributed Print Services

Novell Distributed Print Services (NDPS) is the next generation for printing within a NetWare 5 environment. This printing architecture was designed by the partnership of Novell, Hewlett-Packard, and Xerox. The goals for NDPS were as follows:

- Take advantage of built-in printer intelligence
- Centrally manage network printers
- Improve network print performance
- Facilitate network printer usage for end users

Benefits of NDPS

NDPS leverages the power of Novell Directory Services, and the single point of administration advantage that it offers. The NDPS Printer object is the main focus of NDPS administration. The bidirectional and intelligent communication built into printers feeds information into the NDPS object.

From there, the administrator can view proactive information and review printer messages without having to get up to visit the printer and view its information panel. The administrator can move, pause, copy, and delete print jobs. Event notification features of NDPS can even submit an e-mail, write an event to a log file, and prompt a pop-up window on the administrator's workstation. The event notification features can include FAX and beeper notification, if a third-party application has been integrated with NetWare 5.

With NDPS, administrators can install common Windows drivers for the printer and configure the printer setup so that the correct printer driver automatically installs when the user first attempts to print. The NDPS client software is integrated with the Novell NetWare Client 32 software. This software also enables the user to view printer status, job status, and other printer details, as well as reroute their own print jobs. DOS printing still requires the legacy Novell NetWare print queue environment.

End users can benefit from print-job scheduling features of NDPS. There is the ability to schedule print jobs in a first-in, first-out basis, or prioritize them based on the smallest sizes first.

On the network, there is an improved performance for the network in general. NDPS reduces network traffic that is associated with SAP (Service Advertising Protocol) broadcasts. Even NDPS printers connected to HP JetDirect cards, network printing devices connected directly to the network, are not required to use SAP under NDPS, thus reducing bandwidth. Instead, under NDPS, a new printer is registered with the NDPS Service Registry that notifies clients of printer availability.

NDPS provides support for all Internet Engineering Task Force (IETF) standard management information base (MIB) Printer objects. This means that any NDPS printer can also be managed through Simple Network Management Protocol (SNMP). With a draft of the Internet Printing Protocol (IPP) still in the IETF standards committee, Novell is actively participating in IPP development. NDPS already includes many IPP-like principles. Novell's current plans include adding support for IPP.

QUESTIONS AND ANSWERS

Justine is an engineer who is migrating an Enterprise network from a mixed legacy NetWare 3.x and NetWare 4.x network to NetWare 5. The internetwork includes an Ethernet segment that historically performs poorly during main business hours. Justine notes that this segment includes a large number of printers and decides to migrate the servers that manage those printers first. Why would she decide to do this?

Justine knew that in migrating the servers, she could also migrate the printers to NDPS and immediately receive a performance bonus on that segment of the network. This is because NDPS does not need to use SAP, whereas legacy printing is known to consume excess traffic due to SAP usage.

NDPS Structure

Novell Distributed Printing Services was designed to have an architecture that was independent of the operating system. This makes NDPS portable to other environments. The following components make up the NDPS structure:

- Printer Agent
- Printer Gateways
- NDPS Manager
- NDPS Broker
- Print Client

The *Printer Agent* is the center of NDPS, and it combines the same functions performed by the legacy NetWare printer, print queue, print server, and spooler. The Printer Agent can be software running on the server, or firmware embedded in a network printing device. A Printer Agent can make printers publicly available by not being registered as an NDS object. In contrast, a controlled access printer uses a Printer Agent that is an object within NDS.

Printer gateways enable communication between non-NDPS printers and NDPS clients so that NDPS clients can place jobs in print queues. The two types of gateways are third-party gateways and the Novell gateway:

- Third-party gateways were developed by printer manufacturers to support network attached printers (plug-and-print) to provide access to printers that are not NDPS aware (currently, NetWare 5 ships with the Hewlett-Packard and the Xerox gateways).

- The Novell gateway supports a printer without an embedded printer agent that is connected to a NetWare server or workstation, including NPRINTER and queue-based printers connected directly to the network.

The Novell gateway utilizes a *Print Device Subsystem (PDS)* and *Port Handler*. The PDS stores printer information in a database. The PDS information is then used for the Printer Agents created for each of the NDPS printers. The Port Handler portion of the gateway makes sure that there is communication between PDS and the printer.

The *NDPS Manager* is where Novell Distributed Print Services Printer Agents are created and managed. The NDPS Broker provides three services:

- **Service Registry Service (SRS)**   SRS permits public access printers (those without NDS object-based Printer Agents) to advertise themselves. When a printer is required, the workstation NDPS client contacts SRS and retrieves a list of all registered printers.

- **Event Notification Service (ENS)**   ENS provides the means for event notification configuration for users that may or may not be the print job owner.

- **Resource Management Service (RMS)**   RMS enables resources to be stored in a central location and distributed to network nodes, such as client workstations and printers. The resources that can be stored and shared are such things as printer drivers, banners, and fonts.

The NDPS client software is integrated with the NetWare 5 client software. The NDPS Print Client includes an agent for the Printer Service Requester. The client transmits print jobs to the Printer Agent.

CERTIFICATION OBJECTIVE 4.03

Setting Up NetWare Distributed Print Services (NDPS)

There are two areas where Novell Distributed Print Services must be set up in order for it to function. First, NDPS files must be installed on a NetWare server, either during server installation or later through the NetWare Configuration NLM. Then, NDPS must be set up so printers can be shared.

Setting Up NDPS During Server Installation

When installing a network server, the installation program reaches a point where it prompts for additional products to be installed. This is a critical point for NDPS, since it is listed in the products available for installation. If a server did not have NDPS installed when it was set up, it is still possible to load the product.

EXERCISE 4-4

Installing NDPS Files on a NetWare 5 Server

1. Load NWCONFIG.NLM at the server console.
2. Select Product Options from the menu.
3. The resulting menu should include an option for Install Novell Distributed Print Services (NDPS) in the upper box (see Figure 4-6).
4. In the lower box, select Choose an item or product listed above.

FIGURE 4-6

NetWare configuration
menu product installation

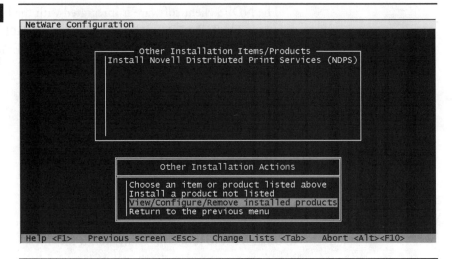

```
NetWare Configuration

                  ┌──── Other Installation Items/Products ────┐
                  │Install Novell Distributed Print Services (NDPS)│
                  │                                           │
                  │                                           │
                  │                                           │
                  │                                           │
                  │                                           │
                  │                                           │
                  └───────────────────────────────────────────┘

            ┌──────── Other Installation Actions ────────┐
            │Choose an item or product listed above      │
            │Install a product not listed                │
            │View/Configure/Remove installed products    │
            │Return to the previous menu                 │
            └────────────────────────────────────────────┘

    Help <F1>    Previous screen <Esc>    Change Lists <Tab>    Abort <Alt><F10>
```

5. The cursor will move to the upper box, in which you should select Install Novell Distributed Print Services (NDPS).

6. The NWCONFIG program will prompt for the path to the installation files. Verify that the correct path is being prompted, or press F3 and type the correct path.

7. Files will copy, and NDPS will be ready for further configuration through NetWare Administrator.

on the
○○b

INSTALL.NLM is no longer used in NetWare 5. It has been replaced by NWCONFIG.NLM.

Completing NDPS Setup from the Workstation

NDPS objects are set up in the NetWare Administrator, which is run from the workstation. The workstation setup for NDPS is easiest to initiate from the creation of the NDPS Manager and an NDPS printer.

Creating NDPS Objects

1. Choose Start | Run, type
   F:\PUBLIC\WIN32\NWADMN32.EXE, and press ENTER.

2. Navigate to the context where you wish to place the NDPS objects.

3. Press the INSERT key.

4. Select NDPS Broker from the list of objects.

5. Type in an appropriate name and press ENTER.

6. You will be returned to NetWare Administrator; press the INSERT key.

7. Select NDPS Manager from the list of objects.

8. Type an appropriate name and press ENTER.

9. At the NetWare Administrator window, press the INSERT key.

10. Select NDPS Printer from the list of objects (see Figure 4-7).

11. Make sure that the Create New Printer Agent is selected in order to set up the NDPS Printer Agent; then click Create.

FIGURE 4-7

NDPS printer creation

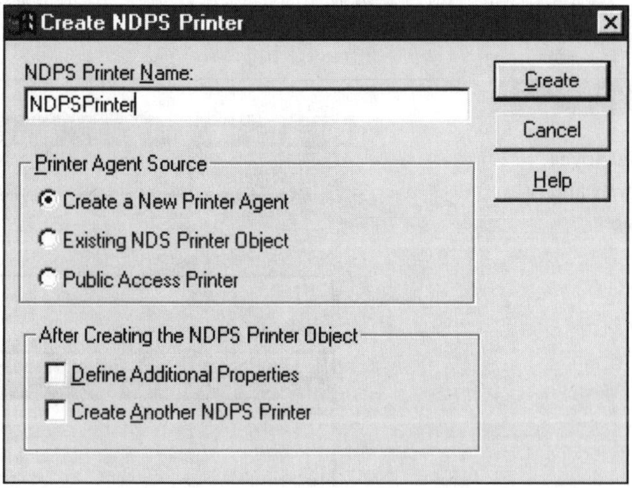

12. The NDPS Printer Agent prompts for the correct gateway and NDPS Manager (see Figure 4-8). For NDPS Manager Name, click the button to the right of the box and navigate until the NDPS Manager object is selected. This printer will be a printer connected locally to the server, in which case the Novell gateway should be selected. The other two gateways are for use with Hewlett-Packard and Xerox printers attached directly to the network. Click OK.

13. The next screen, shown in Figure 4-9, prompts for the configuration of the PDS (Print Device Subsystem) and Port Handler. Select the printer type in the upper box, and click OK.

14. The next screen configures the printer connection. Select Local (physical connection to the server) and the appropriate physical port (most likely LPT1); then click Next.

15. At the next dialog box, accept the default parameters for PSERVER emulation and click Finish.

16. The NetWare Administrator next prompts for the resource drivers to be distributed by the Resource Management Service. Click the Windows 95 Driver tab and select the appropriate driver. Click OK.

FIGURE 4-8

Selecting the Novell printer gateway and NDPS Manager

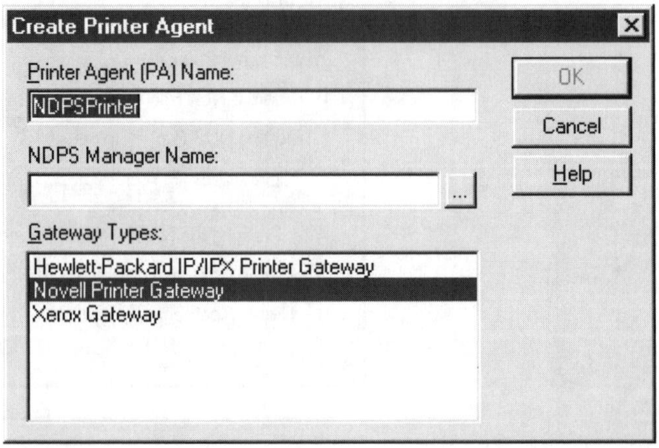

FIGURE 4-9

FIGURE 4-9

PDS and Port Handler
configuration screen

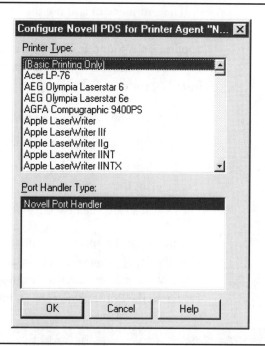

In order to use an NDPS printer from a workstation, the user simply has to browse through the Network Neighborhood tree and double-click the NDPS printer. The following dialog box appears to the user:

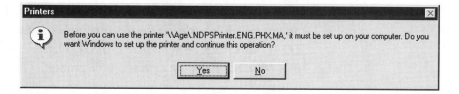

After clicking Yes in this dialog box, the printer automatically installs its driver and prompts you to verify the name to use for the printer in the client workstation's Printers folder. This process alone is a vast improvement over the legacy printing method from the end user's standpoint.

The end user can also use the Novell Printer Manager from the workstation to install printers and manage their print jobs. This application is found in SYS:PUBLIC\WIN32. The executable name is NWPMW32.EXE. When it is running on the workstation, the user can install a printer as follows:

1. Click the Printer menu and select New.

2. Click the Add button, which extends the dialog box.

3. Click the Browse button and navigate to the NDPS printer object to print on.

4. Click OK; then click Install.

The installed printers show up in the Novell Printer Manager window. To view the list of print jobs, double-click the printer icon. To see the current status of the printer, select the Printer menu and click Information. To configure the Printer object, select the Printer menu, and click Configuration.

CERTIFICATION OBJECTIVE 4.04

Managing NDPS

There are two NLMs that are loaded on the server for NDPS functionality. One is NDPSM.NLM, which is the NDPS Manager NLM and loaded at the server console prompt by typing **LOAD NDPSM**. The other is the broker, which is loaded at the server console prompt using the command **LOAD BROKER** *.BROKERNAME*.OU.O. To verify that they are loaded, type **MODULES** at the server console prompt.

The NDPS NLMs, as well as most of the NLM files for NetWare, are stored in the SYS:SYSTEM directory or in the C:\NWSERVER directory. The server will search the NWSERVER and SYSTEM directories first for NLMs. If an NLM is moved to another directory, the LOAD command must include the path to the NLM file. The administrator can also execute a SEARCH ADD volume:path command on the console so that all subsequent LOAD commands will also search that path for the NLM file before reporting that the file is not found.

The NDPS Manager displays the printer status at the server. The printer shown in Figure 4-10 has gone offline.

The NDPSM.NLM offers several options to manage the NDPS printing. The first menu offers the options for Printer Agent List, NDPS Manager Status and Control, and Exit. To view an individual printer's status, such as that depicted in Figure 4-10, select a printer from the Printer Agent List.

To view further details of the NDPSM.NLM, select NDPS Manager Status and Control. This screen displays how long the NDPS Manager has been up and running. It also shows the number of attached printer agents and the current status of the NDPS Manager. The final option in this screen is Database options. Select this for further features as shown in Figure 4-11.

These options, which consist of a database file and an index file, are available for advanced troubleshooting of NDPS Manager. The Examine Database option will display database statistics. The Backup Database Files option copies the NDPS Manager database files. The Auto Backup option displays another menu of automatic backup for NDPS Manager database files. When requiring an NDPS Manager Database Restore, select the Restore Database from Backup option. The Resynchronize Database Files

---

FIGURE 4-10

NDPS printer status at the NDPSM.NLM server

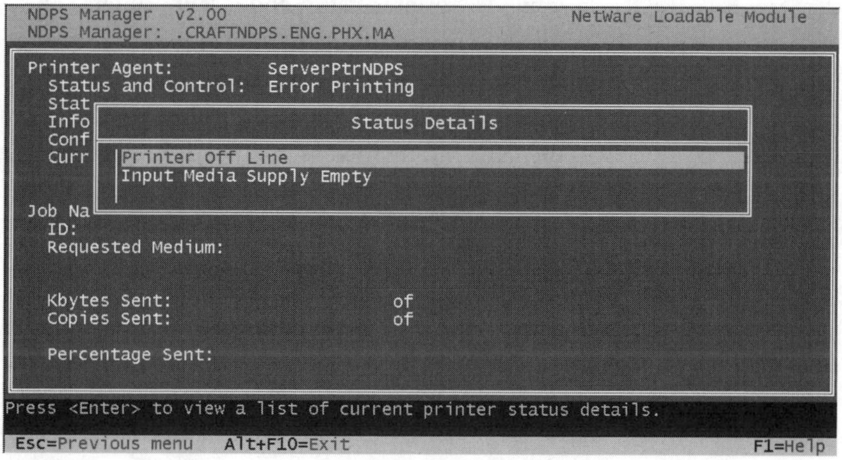

```
NDPS Manager  v2.00                              NetWare Loadable Module
NDPS Manager: .CRAFTNDPS.ENG.PHX.MA

  Printer Agent:          ServerPtrNDPS
   Status and Control:  Error Printing
   Stat
   Info                      Status Details
   Conf
   Curr   Printer Off Line
          Input Media Supply Empty

  Job Na
   ID:
   Requested Medium:


   Kbytes Sent:                      of
   Copies Sent:                      of

   Percentage Sent:

Press <Enter> to view a list of current printer status details.

Esc=Previous menu    Alt+F10=Exit                           F1=Help
```

FIGURE 4-11

Database options for the
NDPS Manager

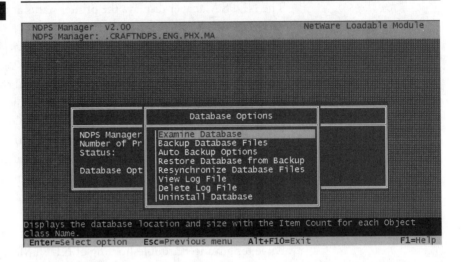

```
NDPS Manager  V2.00                              NetWare Loadable Module
NDPS Manager: .CRAFTNDPS.ENG.PHX.MA

                            ┌─────────── Database Options ───────────┐
              NDPS Manager  │Examine Database                        │
              Number of Pr  │Backup Database Files                   │
              Status:       │Auto Backup Options                     │
                            │Restore Database from Backup            │
              Database Opt  │Resynchronize Database Files            │
                            │View Log File                           │
                            │Delete Log File                         │
                            │Uninstall Database                      │
                            └────────────────────────────────────────┘

Displays the database location and size with the Item Count for each Object
Class Name.
 Enter=Select option    Esc=Previous menu    Alt+F10=Exit            F1=Help
```

builds a new Index file from the database file. To review the NDPS events,
select View Log File. Delete the log file if it has become too large. Uninstall
Database removes the NDPS Manager and its supporting files from the
NetWare 5 server.

The Novell Printer Manager enables users to manage their own print
jobs, view printer status, and install printers. The NetWare Administrator
provides further configuration and management of NDPS printing objects.
In particular, when viewing the NDPS Printer object properties, the Job
List and Set Defaults buttons in the Printer Control property page display
the same information as the Novell Printer Manager Information and
Configuration options. Table 4-5 describes NDPS Broker properties. The
NDPS Manager properties are summarized in Table 4-6. Table 4-7
summarizes NDPS printer properties.

TABLE 4-5

NDPS Broker Properties

NDPS Broker Property	Property Page	Function
Name	Identification	NDS name for the NDPS Broker object.
SAP Name	Identification	Name to use for SAP (Service Advertising Protocol).
Description	Identification	Description information for NDPS Broker.
Location	Identification	Location information for NDPS Broker.
Status/Unload	Identification	Allows the administrator to unload the NDPS Broker NLM from the server.
Managers	Access Control	Lists users given manager access to the NDPS Broker.
Service Registry Service	Service Registry Service	Displays the services registered and availability. When a service option is selected, the address for the service information will display a MAC or IP address. A Disable button allows the administrator to select a service and turn it off.
Event Notification Service	Event Notification Service (ENS)	Displays which events are loaded. The administrator can load more services, unload the ones currently loaded, or disable the ENS altogether.
Resource Path	Resource Management (RMS)	Shows the path where resources are located on the network.

TABLE 4-6

NDPS Manager Properties

NDPS Manager Property	Property Page	Function
Name	Identification	The NDS Fully Distinguished Name for the NDPS Manager.
Version	Identification	The version of the software loaded for the NDPS Manager.
Net Address	Identification	The network and node address of the NDPS Manager.
Description	Identification	Description information for the NDPS Manager.
Location	Identification	Location information for the NDPS Manager.
Volume	Identification	Volume where the NDPS Manager files exist.
Status/Unload	Identification	The status shows whether the NDPS Manager is active. The Unload button enables the administrator to unload the NDPSM.NLM from NetWare Administrator.
Role	Access Control	Lists the users who have manager control over the NDPS Manager.
Printer Agent List	Printer Agent List	Lists the printers that are being served to the network.

TABLE 4-7

NDPS Printer Properties

NDPS Printer Property	Property Page	Function
DS Name	Printer Control	Identification button—NDS name for the NDPS printer
Printer Agent	Printer Control	Identification button—name of the NDPS Printer object
NDPS Manager	Printer Control	Identification button—name of the NDPS Manager object
Description	Printer Control	Identification button—description information for the NDPS printer

TABLE 4-7

NDPS Printer Properties
(continued)

NDPS Printer Property	Property Page	Function
Location	Printer Control	Identification button—location information for the NDPS printer
Manufacturer	Printer Control	Identification button—manufacturer name communicated from the printer
Model	Printer Control	Identification button—model name communicated from the printer
Net Address	Printer Control	Identification button—IPX network and node address
Printer Control DLL name	Printer Control	Identification button—DLL snap-in for the printer
Spooling location	Printer Control	Spooling button—volume for spool files
Disk space available	Printer Control	Spooling button—space available on volume where spool files are located
Limit disk space	Printer Control	Spooling button—limits the disk space for the spool files
Scheduling	Printer Control	Spooling button—selects the scheduling type for the printer
Queue compatibility	Printer Control	Spooling button—selects NetWare print queues to service as a backward compatibility feature
Job List	Printer Control	Job List button—lists the current print jobs and their status
Update Console	Printer Control	Updates the console with current information
Features	Printer Control	Features button—displays the printer's features as communicated to NDPS by the printer, including the amount of RAM

TABLE 4-7

NDPS Printer Properties
(*continued*)

NDPS Printer Property	Property Page	Function
Advanced	Printer Control	Features button—displays advanced printer features
Set Defaults	Printer Control	Set Defaults button—enables the administrator to select the printer configuration to be passed to users, including the number of copies and banner pages
Media	Printer Control	Media button—enables the administrator to limit the type of media loaded on the printer
Status	Printer Control	Status of the printer
Access Control	Access Control	Ability to establish managers, operators, and users for the printer
Configuration	Configuration	Creation and management of print job configurations
Container for remote config	NDPS Remote Printer Mgmt	NDS container object in which to store the remote configuration
Remote Printer Options	NDPS Remote Printer Mgmt	Automatically installs or removes this printer to workstations in the container listed

CERTIFICATION SUMMARY

Network printing is the ability to print from a workstation to a printer that is connected somewhere else on a network. The printer can be attached to another workstation, a server, or be attached directly to the network.

Legacy printing structure in Novell NetWare included Printer, Print Queue, and Print Server objects in NDS. These objects are linked together so that prints are spooled under the Print Queue object, served out to the network by the Print Server object, and then printed to the Printer object.

New technology, such as bi-directional communication, central management solutions, and intelligence in printers and network-attached print devices, has forced a new look at the way Novell NetWare handles printing. Novell, in partnership with Hewlett-Packard and Xerox, created Novell Distributed Print Services (NDPS), which incorporates new technology functions.

NDPS offers a single point of administration through its integration with NDS. It can communicate with printers directly, give notification of printer events, distribute printing resources such as print drivers automatically to clients, and reduce bandwidth consumption through the replacement of SAP with SRS. There are several components to NDPS:

- **Printer agent**   A combination printer, print server, and print queue
- **Printer gateways**   Print device subsystem and port handlers that enable communication between client workstations and printer
- **NDPS Manager**   The software or firmware that manages the printer agent(s)
- **NDPS Broker**   The Service Registry Service, Event Notification Service, and Resource Management Service
- **Print Client**   Integrated with the NetWare Client 32, and using a printer service requestor agent to access print services

To set up NDPS, the files for NDPS must be copied on a server first. If this is not done during the server installation, the files can be installed through the Product Install option in the NWCONFIG.NLM on the server console. The three NDS objects that must be created for NDPS are NDPS Broker, NDPS Manager, and NDPS Printer. This is done in the NetWare Administrator.

NDPS is also managed from the NetWare Administrator. It provides the single seat of administration. Print jobs can be configured, managed, moved, and deleted. The NDPS Printer object will display the status of the printer and other relevant printer information that can be useful in managing printing. The NDPS Broker and NDPS Manager objects enable configuration management of printing. The NDPS Manager NLM (NDPSM.NLM) loaded on the server offers some administration capabilities over the printer agents it manages. End users can use the Novell Printer Manager to list and manage their own print jobs.

TWO-MINUTE DRILL

❑ Older versions of the NetWare printing system were based on print queues and print servers. Along with Queue and Server objects, a Printer object was included in NDS as a resource object.

❑ The printing services NetWare provided required the creation of each individual Print Queue, Printer, and Print Server object. These printing service objects had to be linked together to provide a path for a print job to follow from the workstation to the printed output.

❑ The print queue is a storage area that receives print jobs from multiple users, and lines them up or queues them for printing.

❑ The print server is a service that manages the print action. The print server accepts the job and sends it to the correct printer.

❑ The Printer object represents a network printer. It is configured in NDS, along with the Print Server and Print Queue objects, to define the connections between the various components.

❑ Several NDS options can manage and configure printing to work correctly for the environment that it is serving. These options are available through the properties of the Printer, Print Queue, and Print Server objects.

❑ Users can attach to print queues in order to print documents to the network printer using the DOS utility CAPTURE.EXE. CAPTURE.EXE redirects print jobs sent to the LPT port of the workstation to a network print queue, and has multiple switches to control how print jobs are handled.

❑ Capturing a printer in Windows 95 is integrated into Client 32. In the Network Neighborhood properties, the properties of the NetWare Client include a Default Capture page and two Advanced Settings to manage printing.

❑ The Windows 95 client enables the user to specify the standard configuration to use for printing whenever a capture is made. These settings are specified in the Default Capture page of the NetWare Client properties.

❑ The Windows 95 Client 32 Advanced Settings page includes several printing management settings. They are Network Printers, Print Header, and Print Tail.

❑ NDPS leverages the power of Novell Directory Services (NDS), and the single point of administration advantage that it offers. The NDPS Printer object is the main focus of NDPS administration. The bidirectional and intelligent communication built into printers feeds information into the NDPS object. From there, the administrator can view proactive information and review printer messages.

❑ With NDPS, administrators can install common Windows drivers for the printer and configure the printer setup so that the correct printer driver automatically installs when the user first attempts to print.

❑ End users can schedule print jobs in a first-in, first-out basis or prioritize them based on the smallest sizes first.

❑ NDPS reduces network traffic that is associated with SAP (Service Advertising Protocol) broadcasts.

❑ NDPS provides support for all IETF (Internet Engineering Task Force) standard MIB (management information base) Printer objects. This means that any NDPS printer can also be managed through SNMP (Simple Network Management Protocol).

❑ Novell Distributed Printing Services has an architecture that is independent of the operating system. This makes NDPS portable to other environments. The components of the NDPS structure are Printer Agent, Printer Gateways, NDPS Manager, NDPS Broker, and Print Client.

❑ The Printer Agent combines the same functions performed by the legacy NetWare printer, print queue, print server, and spooler. The Printer Agent can be software running on the server, or firmware embedded in a network printing device. A Printer Agent can make printers publicly available by not being registered as an NDS object. In contrast, a controlled access printer uses a Printer Agent that is an object within NDS.

❑ Printer Gateways enable communication between non-NDPS printers and NDPS clients so that NDPS clients can place jobs in print queues. The two types of gateways are third-party gateways and the Novell gateway.

❑ There are two areas where Novell Distributed Print Services must be set up in order for it to function. First, NDPS files must be installed on a NetWare server, either during server installation or later through the NetWare Configuration NLM. Then, NDPS must be set up so printers can be shared.

❑ There are two NLMs that are loaded on the server for NDPS functionality. One is NDPSM.NLM, which is the NDPS Manager NLM. The other is the broker.

❑ The NDPSM.NLM offers several options to manage the NDPS printing. The first menu offers the options for Printer Agent List, NDPS Manager Status and Control, and Exit. NDPS Manager Status and Control displays how long the NDPS Manager has been up and running. It also shows the number of attached printer agents and the current status of the NDPS Manager.

❑ Database options are available for advanced troubleshooting of NDPS Manager. The Examine Database option will display database statistics. The Backup Database Files option copies the NDPS Manager database files. The Auto Backup options displays another menu of automatic backup for NDPS Manager database files.

❑ The Novell Printer Manager enables users to manage their own print jobs, view printer status, and install printers. The NetWare Administrator provides further configuration and management of NDPS printing objects.

SELF TEST

The following Self-Test questions will help you measure your understanding of the material presented in this chapter. Read all the choices carefully, as there may be more than one correct answer. Choose all correct answers for each question.

1. How does network printing reduce costs?

   A. It reduces the costs of consumables, such as toner and paper.

   B. It increases the uptime of network printers.

   C. The ability to share printers enables multiple users to share a single resource.

   D. It does not reduce costs.

2. Select the best description for a print server.

   A. A storage area for print jobs

   B. The service that manages the print action

   C. The printing device

   D. An object in NDS that uses Service Registry Service

3. What is the purpose of the Print Queue Volume of a Print Queue object?

   A. It is the allowable size of a single print job.

   B. It is the allowable size for the entire set of print jobs.

   C. It is the place where print drivers are stored.

   D. It is the NetWare volume that stores the print jobs before they are serviced.

4. When creating a non-NDPS Printer object, when should the Printer Type be Other/Unknown?

   A. When the printer is connected to a workstation

   B. When it is an AppleTalk printer.

   C. When it is a UNIX printer.

   D. When the printer is connected to a server's serial port.

5. How does a user install the NDPS client software?

   A. The NDPS Manager NLM adds the installation to the login script of a container unit, automatically installing it on clients.

   B. At the setup of NDPS, the Resource Management Service distributes the NDPS client automatically.

   C. The user navigates to SYS:PUBLIC\WIN32 and executes the NWPMW32.EXE application.

   D. The user installs/updates NetWare Client 32. NDPS client is integrated with the NetWare Client 32 that comes with NetWare 5.

6. Select the NDPS component that acts as a legacy NetWare print queue, print server, and printer.

   A. Printer Agent

   B. Printer Gateway

   C. NDPS Broker

   D. NDPS Manager

7. Select the NDPS component that enables communication from the client to the non-NDPS printer through PDS and a port handler.

   A. NDPS Client
   B. Printer Gateways
   C. NDPS Broker
   D. NDPS Manager

8. Which of the following are services offered by the NDPS Broker? Select all that apply.

   A. PDS
   B. RMS
   C. ENS
   D. SRS

9. Which NDPS Broker service enables the automatic download and installation of printer drivers to a workstation?

   A. RMS
   B. ENS
   C. SRS
   D. None. NDPS Broker does not handle this.

10. If NDPS files were not copied during the initial NetWare 5 installation, which of the following commands will begin the product installation at the server console?

    A. LOAD INSTALL
    B. LOAD PINSTALL
    C. LOAD NWADMIN
    D. LOAD NWCONFIG

11. Which of the following are gateway options included in the Printer Agent installation dialog box? Select all that apply.

    A. Novell Printer Gateway
    B. Hewlett-Packard IP/IPX Gateway
    C. Xerox Gateway
    D. IBM Printer Gateway

12. Which of the following menu options from the NDPS Manager NLM database options will create a new index file?

    A. Examine Database
    B. Auto Backup Database
    C. Restore Database from Backup
    D. Resynchronize Database Files

13. Chris is a network administrator with a new NetWare 5 network in two offices of 80 users using NDPS. All the printing services are managed by two servers sharing an NDPS broker that are set aside to handle printing on the network. One Monday morning, Chris is alerted that in one of the offices no printers can print. Which of the following NDS properties could help Chris determine the cause of the printer problems?

    A. The Status/Unload property of the NDPS Broker
    B. The Status/Unload property of the NDPS Manager
    C. The Status properties of the NDPS Printer objects
    D. The Information option of the Novell Printer Manager

14. Which of the following properties represents the storage area for a printer object?

    A. The Print Queue Volume

    B. The Container for Remote Configuration

    C. The Spooling Location

    D. The Access Control

15. Where can the administrator set default properties for the way that a print job is handled in NDPS printing?

    A. By setting up the Default Capture settings for each of the clients

    B. By specifying the Job List in the Novell Printer Manager

    C. By Setting Defaults in the Printer Control page of the Printer object

    D. There is no way that this can be done.

MICROSOFT CERTIFIED SYSTEMS ENGINEER

5

Managing the File System

CERTIFICATION OBJECTIVES

5.01   Introduction to Managing the
        Network File System

5.02   File System Management Utilities

5.03   Displaying File System Information

5.04   Accessing the File System

5.05   Managing the Directory Structure

5.06   Managing Files

5.07   Managing Volume Space Usage

The most critical resources offered by a network operating system are the shared files being accessed by end users. NetWare administrators are typically responsible for setting up the file system on the server, granting access rights to end users, and managing the files and directories. The NetWare file system is the operating system component that makes these tasks possible.

CERTIFICATION OBJECTIVE 5.01

Introduction to Managing the Network File System

NetWare's file system is the organization of disk storage on the network. Servers provide files to workstations through the file system. Workstations are typically DOS-based or DOS-compatible PCs, but there are many other types of workstations running a variety of operating systems, such as OS/2, Mac OS, and UNIX, that need to access those same files. As a result, the NetWare file system is DOS compatible and extensible for access by other workstation operating systems.

File System Components

During the NetWare server installation, the server hard drive is partitioned to create (1) a DOS partition, from which the NetWare operating system is booted, and (2) a NetWare partition, where the NetWare file system resides. Once the NetWare operating system starts, the NetWare disk drivers are loaded, and the NetWare partitions are ready to be accessed. The NetWare partition is a hard disk drive space allocation, so that a logical structure can be applied to it. When adding a new physical disk drive, the administrator can use NWCONFIG.NLM (see Figure 5-1) to create a NetWare partition on that new drive. There is only one NetWare partition per disk drive.

Volumes are the fundamental units of storage on the NetWare server. The volume name is comparable to a disk drive letter in DOS. Just as a disk can have several disk drive letters representing the logical divisions on the disk, there can be several volumes per disk in NetWare. However, unlike DOS drives, a volume can span across more than one disk drive.

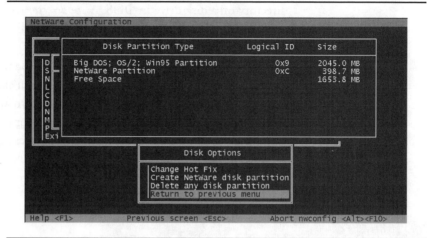

FIGURE 5-1

NetWare partition in
NWCONFIG.NLM

At installation, the volume is configured after a NetWare partition is created, since the volume will occupy space within the NetWare partition of a physical disk drive. The first volume is always named SYS:. Additional volumes can be named anything that the installer decides that and meets NetWare's volume-naming criteria.

on the

job

Many enterprise networks use naming conventions for each of the volumes on servers. Some common naming conventions include naming volumes in sequence: SYS:, VOL1, VOL2, VOL3; naming volumes for their data contents: SYS:, APPS, DATA, UTILS; or naming volumes for the business unit: SYS:, ENG, ACCT, OPS. The main focus in creating multiple volumes is to separate end-users' data from the system applications and utilities that exist on SYS:.

Within Novell Directory Services, a volume object corresponds to a physical volume on a NetWare server's hard drive. The default volume object name is a concatenation of the server name, an underscore, and the volume name. For example, for the BASE volume on a server named DATA, the volume object would be named DATA_BASE. The names of servers must be unique, and since every server must have a SYS: volume, by concatenating the server name and volume name, several servers can exist in the same NDS context without repetition of a volume object name.

Data can exist in the root of a volume or in various data repositories called directories. A *directory* on a NetWare volume is the same as a directory on a disk drive in DOS. A *subdirectory* is a directory contained by another directory. The terms directory and subdirectory are considered interchangeable.

Directories and subdirectories are logical mechanisms that store and organize files. A *file* is a unit of data that can be an executable application or a document, graphic, or database. The filename format under DOS is eight characters for the filename and three characters for the extension. The extension typically identifies the type of file. For example, a batch file ends in the letters .BAT. Under Windows 95, Windows NT, UNIX, Macintosh, and OS/2 operating systems, longer filenames, with extensions, are supported.

CERTIFICATION OBJECTIVE 5.02

File System Management Utilities

There are a wide variety of utilities included in NetWare that manage network resources, including the files stored on NetWare servers. There are two command-line utilities, a DOS utility, and the NetWare Administrator, which can be used for file system management.

NLIST

NLIST is a command-line search tool for NDS objects that can be found in the SYS:PUBLIC directory. Although generally used for NDS searching, NLIST can display some file system data. It is useful for showing volume object information. To view volume information in a specific context, type **NLIST VOLUME /CO .OU.OU.O /D**. This command will show detailed volume information for all the volumes in the .OU.OU.O context. The following is the output of this command:

```
Object Class: Volume
Current context: ENG.PHX.MA
Volume: CRAFT_SYS:
    Name: CRAFT_SYS:
    Name: SYS:
    Object Trustees (ACL):
        Subject: [Root]
```

```
        Property: Host Resource Name
        Property Rights: [ R    ]
  Object Trustees (ACL):
        Subject: [Root]
        Property: Host Server
        Property Rights: [ R    ]
  GUID:
        Value:
0000: 01 A3 AE 38 F5 2E D2 11  B9 87 00 80 C6 05 A9 4F   .£®8õ.Ò.¹‡.?Æ.©O
        Host Resource Name: SYS:
        Host Server: CRAFT
        Object Class: Volume
        Object Class: Resource
        Object Class: Top
        Revision: 5
        Used By:
        Volume Name: [Root]
        Path:
        Name Space Type: DOS
-------------------------------
One Volume object was found in this context.
```

The administrator can use NLIST to display specific volume properties. In order to view all of NLIST's features, type **NLIST /? ALL** at the F:\PUBLIC prompt (assuming the SYS: volume is mapped to F:). The output is shown in Figure 5-2.

FIGURE 5-2

NLIST Help screen

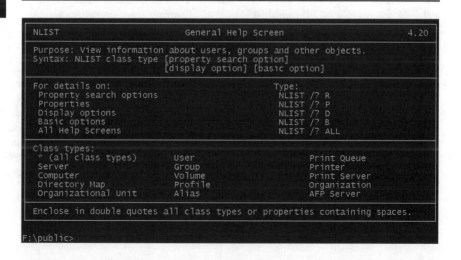

NDIR

Anyone familiar with DOS knows that the DIR command lists all the files in a directory. In NetWare 5, the NDIR command is similar in function. NDIR enables viewing information about files, directories, and volumes. However, the NDIR command can also be used to display additional NetWare file system information that the DOS DIR command cannot. Table 5-1 describes all the NDIR switches available. NDIR also allows manipulating a directory search through the following:

- The display format of the resulting search
- The sort order
- Search filters (restrictions) and attribute filters
- Logical operators

TABLE 5-1   NDIR Switches and Their Functions

NDIR Switch	Syntax	Function
/DA	NDIR [path] [/DA]	Displays date information.
/R	NDIR [path] [/R]	Displays filters, rights, and file attributes.
/MAC	NDIR [path] [/MAC]	Displays Apple Macintosh-formatted files.
/L	NDIR [path] [/L]	Displays long filenames.
/D	NDIR [path] [/D]	Displays file details.
/COMP	NDIR [path] [/COMP]	Displays compressed file information.
attributes	NDIR [path] [/attributes]	Displays files with desired attributes. Options include RO–read only, RW–read write, SY–system, H–hidden, X–execute only, A–archive needed, Ds–don't suballocate, T–transactional, P–purge, Sh–shareable, I–indexed, Ci–copy inhibit, Di–delete inhibit, Ri–rename inhibit, Co–compressed file, Ic–immediate compressed, Dc–don't compress, Cc–can't compress, Dm–don't migrate, and M–file migrated.

TABLE 5-1		NDIR Switches and Their Functions *(continued)*
NDIR Switch	**Syntax**	**Function**
Sort options	NDIR [*path*] [/REV] [SORT *option*]	Displays files in the desired sort order. /REV will put the sort in reverse order. The word SORT is required. Sort options include AC–date last accessed, AR–date archived, CR–created/copied date, OW–owner, SI–size, UP–last updated date, and UN–not sorted.
Logical operators	NDIR [*path*] [/*options* [NOT] *operator value*]	This use of NDIR allows the user to filter the results based on the logical operator and value selected. The options that can be filtered are the same as the sort options except that UN is not an option, and NAM for name space is an option. The operators are: LE–less than, GR–greater than, EQ–equal to, BEF–before, and AFT–after. The [NOT] is optional.
/FO	NDIR [*path*] [/FO]	View files only.
/DO	NDIR [*path*] [/DO]	View directories only.
/S	NDIR [*path*] [/S]	View information in subdirectories too.
/C	NDIR [*path*] [/C]	Continuous. Don't pause during the directory screen output.
/VOL	NDIR [*path*] [/VOL]	View volume information.

To view the help information at any time, type **NDIR /?** at a DOS prompt. The NDIR /? ALL command will display several screens worth of information discussing the usage and syntax for NDIR. The first screen is shown in Figure 5-3.

FILER

The FILER utility in the SYSSYS::PUBLIC directory is a DOS menu-based utility. It can search for files, create new directories, delete files and directories, and salvage files.

FIGURE 5-3

NDIR Help screen

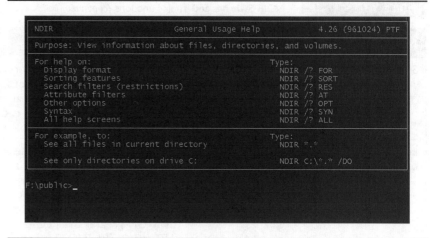

```
NDIR                        General Usage Help          4.26 (961024) PTF

Purpose: View information about files, directories, and volumes.

For help on:                                     Type:
   Display format                                NDIR /? FOR
   Sorting features                              NDIR /? SORT
   Search filters (restrictions)                 NDIR /? RES
   Attribute filters                             NDIR /? AT
   Other options                                 NDIR /? OPT
   Syntax                                        NDIR /? SYN
   All help screens                              NDIR /? ALL

For example, to:                                 Type:
   See all files in current directory            NDIR *.*

   See only directories on drive C:              NDIR C:\*.* /DO


F:\public>_
```

EXERCISE 5-1

Viewing File Information from FILER

1. Start FILER by choosing Start | Run, type [path to **SYS:PUBLIC** or mapped drive letter:]**FILER** and press ENTER, or type **FILER** at the command (DOS) prompt.

2. In the first menu, select Manage Files and Directories; then press ENTER.

3. The current path will display in the upper-left corner of the screen. Navigate through the path by selecting the two dots (..) to move back a directory or pressing ENTER when a directory is highlighted to browse that directory.

4. Select a file and press the F10 key. To select multiple files, mark them by pressing the F5 key when each file is selected; then press F10 after all files are marked.

5. The F10 key brings up a small menu that enables the user to copy, move, view, display the rights, or display the file information. Select View | Set File Information and press ENTER. The screen shown in Figure 5-4 will be displayed.

The most valuable feature of FILER is the ability to undelete files from NetWare volumes. In older versions of NetWare, this feature was a separate utility called SALVAGE, but it is now integrated into FILER. The option in the first menu is still Salvage Deleted Files.

FIGURE 5-4

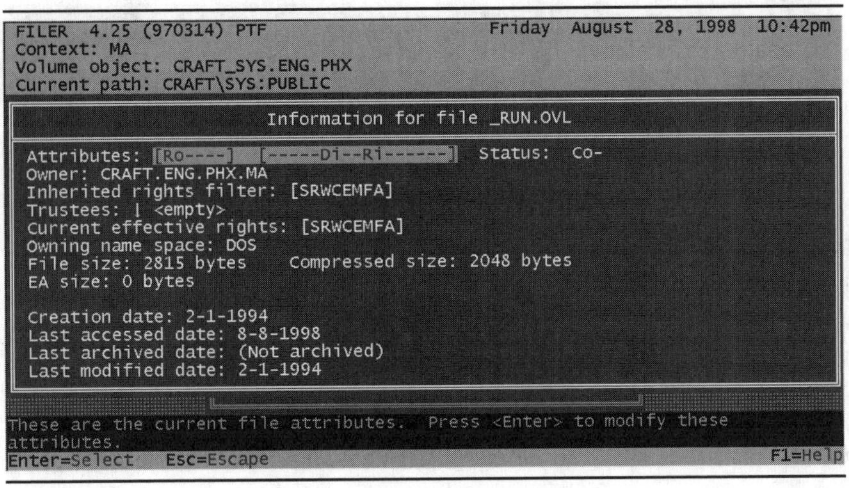

File information in FILER

```
FILER 4.25 (970314) PTF                    Friday  August  28, 1998  10:42pm
Context: MA
Volume object: CRAFT_SYS.ENG.PHX
Current path: CRAFT\SYS:PUBLIC
┌──────────────────────────────────────────────────────────────────────────┐
│                       Information for file _RUN.OVL                         │
├──────────────────────────────────────────────────────────────────────────┤
│  Attributes: [Ro----]  [-----Di--Ri------]   Status:  Co-                  │
│  Owner: CRAFT.ENG.PHX.MA                                                    │
│  Inherited rights filter: [SRWCEMFA]                                        │
│  Trustees: | <empty>                                                        │
│  Current effective rights: [SRWCEMFA]                                       │
│  Owning name space: DOS                                                     │
│  File size: 2815 bytes     Compressed size: 2048 bytes                     │
│  EA size: 0 bytes                                                           │
│                                                                            │
│  Creation date: 2-1-1994                                                    │
│  Last accessed date: 8-8-1998                                               │
│  Last archived date: (Not archived)                                         │
│  Last modified date: 2-1-1994                                               │
│                                                                            │
│                                                                            │
├──────────────────────────────────────────────────────────────────────────┤
│These are the current file attributes.  Press <Enter> to modify these       │
│attributes.                                                                  │
Enter=Select    Esc=Escape                                           F1=Help
```

EXERCISE 5-2

Salvaging Files

1. If drive F: is not mapped to volume SYS:, then right-click Network Neighborhood, select Novell Map Network Drive, select drive F: under Device, and type **\\SERVERNAME\SYS:** in the Path area; then click Map.

2. Start FILER by selecting Start | Run and type **F:\PUBLIC\FILER**; then press ENTER.

3. Select Salvage Deleted Files and press ENTER.

4. Select View | Recover Deleted Files and press ENTER.

5. FILER will prompt for a filename or file pattern to filter. If only looking for an executable file, type ***.EXE** and press ENTER.

6. The next screen enables you to browse through the directories for deleted files that match the pattern you have entered. Select a file and press INS to salvage that file. To select multiple files, highlight each and press F5.

NetWare Administrator

The NetWare Administrator application enables the viewing of files and directories that exist within NetWare volumes. Files and directories can be managed, copied, moved, salvaged, and deleted. To view files and directories,

QUESTIONS AND ANSWERS

Dan, the CEO, calls up Cheryl, his network administrator, and explains that he was in the Windows 95 Explorer and pressed the DEL key when he meant to press the HOME key. Now, all his files in his home directory have disappeared. Dan is worried that all his data is gone and that he won't be able to get it back before his meeting in half an hour because he knows it takes much longer than that to restore data from tape. What can Cheryl do to reassure Dan?	Cheryl can tell Dan that she will run FILER and salvage his deleted files. It should take her no more than a few minutes.

double-click the volume object. The files in the volume are displayed, as shown in Figure 5-5. Double-click a directory to display the files within that directory. To view the file or directory information, right-click the file or directory icon and select Details from the pop-up menu.

Files can be undeleted from within the NetWare Administrator. To undelete a deleted file, the administrator can select the directory the file was deleted from, click the Tools menu, and select the Salvage option. The dialog box that appears enables the administrator to sort and select the files to be salvaged, as well as identify the user who deleted the file.

CERTIFICATION OBJECTIVE 5.03

Displaying File System Information

File system information is available for each file and directory in the volume objects. The information about a directory or a file is available in the NetWare Administrator, as the Details of that object, as illustrated in Figures 5-6 and 5-7. An object's details can be viewed by highlighting that object, selecting the Object menu, and choosing the Details option. Directory and file properties are defined in Tables 5-2 and 5-3.

FIGURE 5-5

Files and directories viewed
in NetWare Administrator

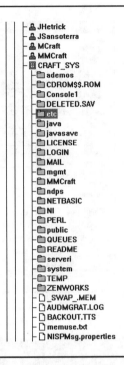

FIGURE 5-6

Directory information

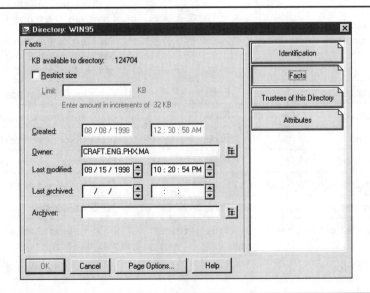

FIGURE 5-7

File information

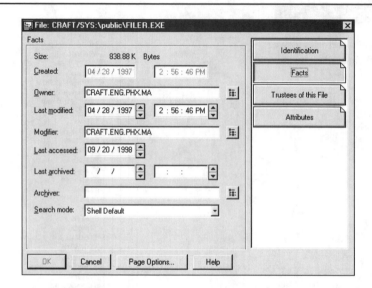

TABLE 5-2 Directory Object Properties

Directory Property	Property Page	Function
Identification	Identification	Name space and the name format of the directory in that name space. For the DOS name space, long filenames are truncated.
KB available to directory	Facts	Amount of space available for that directory, before it reaches the space limit value or the limit of the disk drive.
Restrict Size	Facts	Amount of disk space that the directory is limited to.
Created	Facts	Date and time the directory was created.
Owner	Facts	NDS object owning the directory.
Last modified	Facts	Date the directory was last modified.
Last archived	Facts	Date the directory was last archived.
Archiver	Facts	NDS object that last archived the directory.
Trustees of this directory	Trustees	NDS objects that have access, or trustee, rights to this directory.
Attributes	Attributes	Directory attributes that are applied to this directory.

| TABLE 5-3 | File Object Properties |

File Property	Property Page	Function
Identification	Identification	Name space and the name format of the file in that name space. For the DOS name space, long filenames are truncated.
Size	Facts	File size.
Created	Facts	Date and time that the file was created.
Owner	Facts	NDS object designated as file owner.
Last Modified	Facts	Date and time the file was modified.
Modifier	Facts	NDS object that last modified the file.
Last accessed	Facts	Date the file was last accessed.
Last archived	Facts	Date the file was last archived.
Archiver	Facts	NDS object that last archived the file.
Search Mode	Facts	Search settings for this file.
Trustees of this file	Trustees of this file	NDS objects granted access, or trustee, rights to this file.
Attributes	Attributes	File attributes.

exam
Watch

Directories can be restricted from growing in size by checking the Restrict Size check box in the directory's Facts property page and then typing in the maximum size the directory should reach.

CERTIFICATION OBJECTIVE 5.04

Accessing the File System

A workstation can access the NetWare 5 server through browsing the Network Neighborhood or mapping a drive, as long as the logged-in user or [public] trustee has been granted rights to those files. After Client 32 is installed in Microsoft Windows 95, as well as Windows 98 and Windows NT 4, the Network Neighborhood is able to browse through the NetWare 5 servers, their volumes, directories, and files.

Some applications require a drive letter in order to function properly. For those applications, the user can map a drive letter to the volume and directory. In Windows 95, a drive can be mapped by right-clicking the Network Neighborhood icon on the desktop and selecting Novell Map Network Drive. In the drive letter space, select a letter. In the Path space, type the UNC (Universal Naming Convention) name for the server and volume in the *SERVERNAME\VOLUME* format.

Drives can be mapped from a DOS prompt using the MAP command. This can even be done using a Windows 95 DOS prompt window and from within a login script. The MAP command, which is located in the SYS:PUBLIC directory, enables a user to map root drives and search drives:

- **Root drive**   A root drive is the way to make a subdirectory on a NetWare volume appear to be the root of the drive. The way to do this is by typing **MAP R K:=SYS:PUBLIC\WIN32** and pressing ENTER. When viewing the R: drive, all the files that are in the SYS:PUBLIC\WIN32 directory appear at the root of K:\.

- **Search drive**   Search drives enable applications to look in that drive for an executable file or command. If a file such as FILER.EXE is in SYS:PUBLIC, and a search drive Z: is mapped to SYS:PUBLIC, then typing **FILER** at the DOS prompt, regardless of the current directory, will automatically search in the SYS:PUBLIC directory and start FILER, even if the user is currently in the C: drive. To map the next available search drive to the PUBLIC directory, type **MAP INS S16:=SYS:PUBLIC**.

The syntax for the map command is: MAP [*option* | /VER] [search:=[*drive:*=]] | [*drive:*=] [*path*] [/W]. To see which drives are mapped to which servers, type **MAP** and press ENTER. MAP can be used with Directory Map objects by mapping the drive letter to the NDS name of the Directory Map object, such as MAP M:=.name.ou.o. Table 5-4 lists the MAP command options.

| TABLE 5-4 | MAP Command Options |

Option Switch	Function
INS	Inserts a search drive at the level indicated. There can be up to 16 NetWare search drives, S1 through S15. If S16 is indicated, and there are fewer than 15 search drives mapped, then the search drive is added to the end of the list and the next ordinal "S[*Next number in order*]:" is assigned to that directory path.
DEL	Deletes the drive mapping for the drive letter selected.
N	Maps the next available drive letter.
R	Makes the path a root directory.
P	Maps to a physical volume.
C	Changes a regular drive mapping to a search drive mapping and vice versa.
/VER	Displays version information.
/W	Do not change the master environment.

QUESTIONS AND ANSWERS

Jesse was browsing through her Network Neighborhood and attempted to execute the GLOW.EXE file. The file returned an error that the BRITE.DLL could not be found, but Jesse can see the BRITE.DLL file in the GLO directory. What can Jesse do to fix this problem?

The GLOW program requires the ability to search its local drive for the BRITE.DLL by referencing the current drive letter. To make the GLOW.EXE file execute, Jesse can map a drive.

Managing the Directory Structure

DOS commands can be used on a drive mapping the same way that they are used on local drives. A subdirectory can be created using the MD command, and the user can move about the directory structure using the CD command. Directories can be deleted using the RD command. In Windows 95, the same method of managing a local directory in the Explorer works for mapped network drives.

The directory structure can also be managed using the NetWare Administrator. To create a directory from the NetWare Administrator, navigate to the Volume object or one of its subdirectories, and press the INSERT key. A dialog box appears for the name of the directory and check boxes to define additional properties or create another directory. To delete a directory in the NetWare Administrator, select the directory and press the DELETE key. To rename the directory, highlight it, click the Object menu, and select Rename. Moving and copying are also available in the Object menu for the directory.

Renaming directories can be tricky from a DOS prompt. There is no easy way to do it in DOS. However, NetWare includes a DOS command-line utility in the SYS:PUBLIC directory called RENDIR.EXE, which is specifically used for renaming directories. The syntax for this command is RENDIR directory [TO] newdirectory. Note that renaming home directories using RENDIR or the NetWare Administrator will not change the value of the home directory for a user object. To change the value, you must edit the user object property for home directory.

Managing Files

Files can be browsed, copied, moved, and deleted from the NetWare Administrator. To browse the files in NetWare Administrator, double-click

FROM THE CLASSROOM

DOS XCOPY vs. NetWare NCOPY and Other File System Management Utilities

When to use local workstation operating system utilities versus NetWare utilities for managing the file system can be a puzzling choice if you are not aware of how each works. One of the reasons that might lead to confusion is that NetWare is aware of most DOS and Windows 95 file system management compiled into COMMAND.COM and for Windows NT, comparable commands compiled into CMD.COM. This makes it very easy to use the utilities built into your local workstation operating system, sometimes at the expense of taking advantage of some of the benefits that the NetWare utilities provide. A simple way to approach the dilemma is to determine: Where are the files and directories physically

stored, and where should the processing be taking place? If the answer, is "on a NetWare server" to either, choose to use the NetWare utility. Additionally, if a NetWare utility is used, the bulk of the processing of the command is done on the server, not the workstation. This can have enormous implications when managing files and directories between multiple servers and sites. There will always be exceptions to the general rule, but for most situations, improve your efficiency and make the network work for you by using NetWare commands and utilities for the server file system and use local O/S commands and utilities for local workstation file management.

—By Dan Cheung, CNI, MCNE, MCT

the volume object and each subdirectory until the desired files are displayed. When a file is double-clicked, it opens the file information page, not the file itself.

EXERCISE 5-3

Copying a File in NetWare Administrator

1. It is assumed that F: is mapped to SYS:. Choose Start | Run, type **F:\PUBLIC\WIN32\NWADMN32.EXE**, and press ENTER.
2. Navigate through the tree until you reach the desired volume object.
3. Double-click the volume object to expand the file structure beneath it.

4. Continue to browse by double-clicking directories until you find the file you want to copy. Select this file by highlighting it.

5. Press the F8 key. Alternatively, choose the Object | Copy.

6. The radio buttons at the top of the resulting dialog box (Figure 5-8) allow you to change the command from copy to move, if desired. The central box displays the selected files. The check box at the bottom enables the user to retain the original trustee assignments.

7. Press the button to the right of the Destination box and browse to the desired destination of the file copy.

NetWare has a comprehensive command-line utility for copying files on NetWare volumes. This command, NCOPY, is similar to the DOS COPY command, but maintains NetWare file attributes.

CERTIFICATION OBJECTIVE 5.07

Managing Volume Space Usage

In Novell Directory Services, there are objects that represent the volumes on each server. Each volume object has properties as described in Table 5-5.

FIGURE 5-8

Move/Copy dialog box

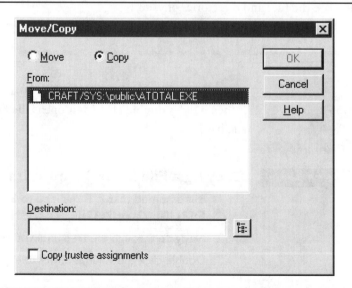

TABLE 5-5 Volume Object Properties

Volume Property	Property page	Function
Name	Identification	NDS name of the volume object.
Host server	Identification	NDS name of the server object housing the volume.
Version	Identification	NetWare version.
Host volume	Identification	Name of the actual volume.
Other name	Identification	Other name for the volume.
Location	Identification	Location information for the volume.
Department	Identification	Department that uses or manages the volume.
Organization	Identification	Business unit that uses or manages the volume.
Statistics	Statistics	Display percentage of disk space, block size, name spaces, and compressed files for the volume.
Created on	Dates and Times	Date and time that the volume was created.
Owner	Dates and Times	Owner of the volume. This value can be modified.
Modified on	Dates and Times	Date and time that the volume was last modified.
Archived Last On	Dates and Times	Date and time that the volume was last backed up.
Archived Last By	Dates and Times	The person who last backed up the volume.
User Space Limits	User Space Limits	Add and modify the space limits for users in this property page.
Trustees of the root directory	Trustees of the root directory	Lists the users and their rights to the root of the volume.
Attributes	Attributes	Lists the attributes of the root directory of the volume.
See Also	See Also	Other NDS objects that are related to the volume object.
Security Equal	Security Equal	Objects that have security equivalence to the volume.

FIGURE 5-9   Volume statistics

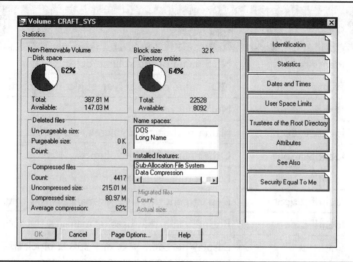

Volumes can be directly managed within NDS. The Statistics property page, shown in Figure 5-9, displays information that can assist in troubleshooting problems with the server. For example, if a user cannot save a file with a long name to a directory within the volume, the administrator simply needs to view the Name Spaces information. That would determine whether the Long Name name space was installed on that volume. If the name space was not there, then the file-save issue could be resolved by adding that name space.

Volume space can be managed by adding users and their respective space limitations to the User Space Limits property page of the Volume object.

EXERCISE 5-4

Restricting a User's Volume Space Usage

1. If the SYS: volume is not already mapped to drive F:, then right-click the Network Neighborhood icon, select map drive, ensure F: is the drive selected, and type **\\SERVERNAME\SYS:** in the Path space.

2. Choose Start | Run, type **F:\PUBLIC\WIN32\NWADMN32.EXE**, and press ENTER.

3. In the NetWare Administrator, navigate through the tree until you reach the context where the target volume resides.

4. Highlight the volume object and right-click it; then select Details from the pop-up menu. Alternatively, highlight the volume object, click the Object menu, and select Details.

5. Click the User Space Limits property page button.

6. In the Search Context space, type the context where the user objects reside. Alternatively, click the button to the right of the Search Context space, navigate until the container holding the user objects appears in the left-hand window pane, select it, and click OK.

7. A list of user objects will appear in the User Space Limits window, as shown in Figure 5-10. Select the user object in order to apply the limits.

FIGURE 5-10   User's space limits on a volume

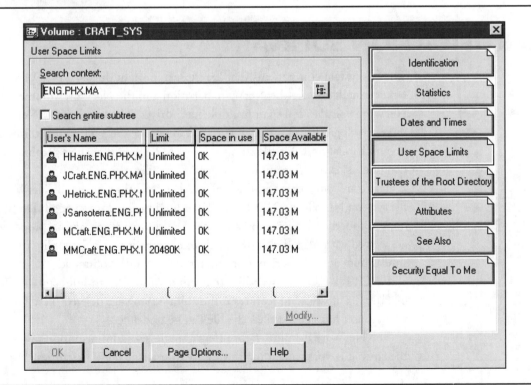

8. Click Modify.

9. Check the Limited Volume Space check box, as shown here:

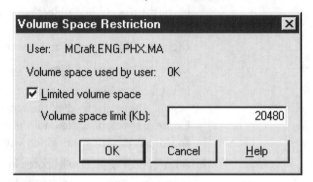

10. Type **20480** in the Volume Space Limit.

11. Click OK.

12. The Limit column for the user will state 20480K, rather than Unlimited.

CERTIFICATION SUMMARY

The file system components that are most important during a NetWare server installation are the NetWare partition and the NetWare volume. NetWare volumes can span multiple hard drives. The volume in a NetWare server is a logical structure that contains directories and files. Directories are organizational units for file storage. Files are data units such as graphics, documents, executable applications, and text files.

There are two command-line utilities that can help manage the NetWare file system: NLIST and NDIR. NLIST is used mainly for viewing NDS object properties from a command line. The volume object and its properties are viewed with NLIST. NDIR is a directory search and listing utility that is similar but contains more options than the DOS DIR command.

FILER is a DOS menu utility that can manage files and directories. One of FILER's most useful features is the ability to salvage deleted files. That is, when a user has deleted files, the file can be undeleted.

The NetWare Administrator offers a single-seat administration point of the entire network, including the ability to manage files, directories, and volumes. Files and directories can be browsed, moved, copied, renamed, and deleted.

Other utilities that can be used for file management are NCOPY, RENDIR, and MAP. NCOPY allows a user to copy files and directories on NetWare drives. RENDIR can rename directories. MAP is the command-line utility to connect drive letters to NetWare volumes. It can be used to map root drives and search drives to assist in the way applications work from the network.

The User Space Limits properties of the volume object in the NetWare Administrator restricts the amount of space that each user is allowed on a volume. The Statistics property page displays other troubleshooting information.

TWO-MINUTE DRILL

- ❑ NetWare's file system is the organization of disk storage on the network. Servers provide files to workstations through the file system. Workstations are typically DOS-based or DOS-compatible PCs, but there are many other types of workstations running a variety of operating systems that need to access those same files. NetWare file system is DOS compatible and extensible for access by other workstation operating systems.

- ❑ During the NetWare server installation, the server hard drive is partitioned to create (1) a DOS partition, from which the NetWare operating system is booted, and (2) a NetWare partition, in which the NetWare file system resides. Once the NetWare operating system starts, the NetWare disk drivers are loaded, and the NetWare partitions are ready to be accessed. The NetWare partition is a hard disk drive space allocation, so that a logical structure can be applied to it.

- ❑ Volumes are the fundamental units of storage on the NetWare server. The volume name is comparable to a disk drive letter in DOS. Just as a disk can have several disk drive letters representing the logical divisions on the disk, there can be several volumes per disk in NetWare. Unlike DOS drives, a volume can span across more than one disk drive.

❑ Within Novell Directory Services, a volume object corresponds to a physical volume on a NetWare server's hard drive. The default volume object name is a concatenation of the server name, an underscore, and the volume name. The names of servers must be unique, and since every server must have a SYS: volume, by concatenating the server name and volume name, several servers can exist in the same NDS context without repetition of a volume object name.

❑ A directory on a NetWare volume is the same as a directory on a disk drive in DOS. A subdirectory is a directory contained by another directory.

❑ There are a wide variety of utilities included in NetWare that manage network resources, including the files stored on NetWare servers. There are two command-line utilities, a DOS utility, and the NetWare Administrator that can be used for file system management. NLIST is a command-line search tool for NDS objects that can be found in the SYS:PUBLIC directory.

❑ NDIR enables viewing information about files, directories, and volumes. However, the NDIR command can also be used to display additional NetWare file system information that the DOS DIR command cannot.

❑ The FILER utility in the SYS:PUBLIC directory is a DOS menu-based utility. It can search for files, create new directories, delete files and directories, and salvage files. The most valuable feature of FILER is the ability to undelete files from NetWare volumes. In older versions of NetWare this feature was a separate utility called SALVAGE, but it is now integrated into FILER. The option in the first menu is still Salvage Deleted Files.

❑ The NetWare Administrator application enables the viewing of files and directories that exist within NetWare volumes. Files and directories can be managed, copied, moved, salvaged and deleted.

❑ File system information is available for each file and directory in the volume objects. The information about a directory or a file is available in the NetWare Administrator, as the Details of that object. An object's details can be viewed by highlighting that object, selecting the Object menu, and choosing the Details option.

❑ A workstation can access the NetWare 5 server through browsing the Network Neighborhood, or mapping a drive, as long as the logged-in user or [public] trustee has been granted rights to those files. After Client 32 is installed in Microsoft Windows 95, as well as Windows 98 and Windows NT 4, the Network Neighborhood is able to browse through the NetWare 5 servers, their volumes, directories, and files.

❑ Drives can be mapped from a DOS prompt using the MAP command. This can even be done using a Windows 95 DOS prompt window and from within a login script. The MAP command, which is located in the SYS:PUBLIC directory, enables a user to map root drives and search drives.

❑ DOS commands can be used on a drive mapping the same way that they are used on local drives. A subdirectory can be created using the MD command, and the user can move about the directory structure using the CD command. Directories can be deleted using the RD command. In Windows 95, the same method of managing a local directory in the Explorer works for mapped network drives.

❑ The directory structure can also be managed using the NetWare Administrator. To create a directory from the NetWare Administrator, navigate to the Volume object or one of its subdirectories, and press the INSERT key.

❑ There is no easy way to rename directories in DOS. NetWare includes a DOS command-line utility in the SYS:PUBLIC directory called RENDIR.EXE, which is specifically used for renaming directories.

❑ Files can be browsed, copied, moved, and deleted from the NetWare Administrator. To browse the files in NetWare Administrator double-click the volume object and each subdirectory until the desired files are displayed. When a file is double-clicked, it opens the file information page, not the file itself.

❑ Volumes can be directly managed within NDS. The Statistics property page displays information that can assist in troubleshooting problems with the server. Volume space can be managed by adding users and their respective space limitations to the User Space Limits property page of the Volume object.

SELF TEST

The following Self-Test questions will help you measure your understanding of the material presented in this chapter. Read all the choices carefully, as there may be more than one correct answer. Choose all correct answers for each question.

1. Which of the following is the largest storage unit on a NetWare server?

   A. NetWare partition

   B. Volume

   C. Directory

   D. File

2. Which of the following is the name of the first volume on every NetWare 5 server?

   A. SYSTEM

   B. PUBLIC

   C. SYS:

   D. ETC

3. Which of the following can be used to manage the NetWare file system? Select all that apply.

   A. NLIST

   B. NDIR

   C. FILER

   D. NetWare Administrator

4. Which command will display volume details at the DOS prompt?

   A. NLIST VOLUME /CO .OU.OU.O /D

   B. NDIR VOLUME: /D

   C. MAP V:=VOLUME:

   D. NCOPY VOLUME:DIR VOLUME:DIR2 /S

5. Joe can't find a file that he last looked at on September 22, 1998. He doesn't remember the name. What command should Joe try at the command line to find the file?

   A. NDIR *.* /AC EQ 092298

   B. NDIR *.* /AR BEF 092398

   C. NLIST *.* /AC EQ 092298

   D. NLIST *.* /AR AFT 092198

6. What command can Shelly use to determine the space available in her home directory, which is mapped to H:?

   A. VOLUMES

   B. NDIR H:\ /SPA

   C. NLIST VOLUME /CO .ou.ou.o /D

   D. NDIR H:\ /VOL

7. Frank wants to undelete a file on a NetWare volume, but his DOS UNDELETE command doesn't work. What utility will undelete the file?

   A. NetWare's UNDELETE command

   B. NetWare's SALVAGE command

   C. NetWare's NDIR command

   D. NetWare's FILER utility

8. Which file management feature cannot be achieved in the NetWare Administrator program?

   A. File moves

   B. File and directory copies

   C. Renaming a directory

   D. Salvaging deleted files

   E. All of the above

   F. None of the above

9. Chris was trying to copy a file to a directory, but the copy did not work. How can Chris check to see if the directory has a space limitation?

   A. Use the NDIR command.

   B. Use the NLIST command.

   C. Use the NetWare Administrator Directory properties.

   D. It cannot be done.

10. George is the administrator of a NetWare network. One of the users has called because a file has been modified since he last used it, and it is in his home directory. The user wants to know who has modified this file and how the person gained access to his home directory. How can George help the user?

    A. George can view this information using NDIR.

    B. George can see this using NLIST.

    C. George can look at the home directory's properties in NetWare Administrator.

    D. George can look at the changed file's properties in NetWare Administrator.

11. Joe has created a group of home directories with the same name as the user's ID under the HOME directory in the FILES volume of his NetWare 5 server named THE_X. How can Joe map each user's home directory so that they do not see the HOME directory or other user's directories underneath it?

    A. MAP INS S16:=H:=THE_X/FILES: HOME*username*

    B. MAP DEL H:=THE_X/FILES:HOME*username*

    C. MAP C H:

    D. MAP R H:=THE_X/FILES:HOME*username*

12. Julie uses the command line often and wants to have command-line access to her home directory files. Which of the following commands will give her instant access to the files without having to change to the H: directory or map another drive?

    A. NDIR H: /D

    B. NLIST VOLUME /CO .Ou.O

    C. MAP INS S16:=SERVER/ VOLUME:PATH\HOMEDIR

    D. MAP C H:

13. Kathy just got married and her name has changed. According to the naming conventions, Kathy's user ID and home directory should change as well. When George renames Kathy's home directory

using RENDIR, the directory no longer maps in the login script to H:. What can George do to make this work?

A. George can change the user ID and the home directory back to Kathy's old name. They can't be changed.

B. George can edit the home directory property in the user object so that it uses the new home directory name. George should also look at the login script to verify that it is mapping to the home directory property, and not to the old login name.

C. George must run an NDIR command to reset the properties of the home directory.

D. George should have used the NetWare Administrator, not RENDIR, since it automatically synchronizes the names within NDS.

14. Jan has meticulously selected 438 files to be moved from one directory to another. She accidentally selected the Copy command in NetWare Administrator. Is Jan going to have to start over?

A. No, Jan can select the Move radio button and dynamically change to a Move command from a Copy command.

B. Yes, there is no way Jan can change from a Copy to a Move.

15. David is a NetWare administrator for a large enterprise NetWare 5 network. He has been tasked with restricting the space for every user at Headquarters (who are all in the HQ container) to 100MB on the HOME volume, which is used for home directories. How can David do this?

A. He can run the DSPACE utility against each user's ID and restrict the space for each user.

B. He can run the VOLUMES command and restrict a group of users he created to 100MB.

C. He can use the NetWare Administrator and restrict the user space limits for the HOME volume for each user existing in the HQ container.

D. He can use NetWare Administrator and restrict the space limits for the HQ container itself, which is then inherited by all the users in that container.

6

Managing File System Security

CERTIFICATION OBJECTIVES

6.01	Introduction to File System Security
6.02	Planning File System Rights
6.03	Planning File System Attribute Security
6.04	Implementing File System Security

Every network administrator must determine which users should be granted access to specific directories and files. An equally critical task is determining who should be denied access to certain directories and files. The network administrator must strike a balance between the needs of users to access files and the need to maintain security to protect the shared files and directories from deliberate or inadvertent abuse. This is the basis for fileservers; that is, serving files. Exactly how files are secured varies somewhat from system to system.

Introduction to File System Security

Once a NetWare administrator understands file system security, it becomes apparent that files shared on a NetWare server can be more secure than ones on a workstation. For example, when a file exists on a NetWare server, a casual user cannot access it from the server console, which is usually the case on a workstation. When a file is on a server, the user must pass through login security and be granted access rights to use the file. NetWare file system attributes offer the ability to prevent file changes, even when a user has the access rights to make those changes. Beyond that, a network file has the flexibility to be shared among several users, then secured from the remainder of the network users. This flexibility, combined with security, makes for a powerful file management tool. Within NetWare, there are two layers of file system security:

- Trustee rights to the file system
- File system attribute security

Planning File System Rights

File system rights are the basic tools for securing files and directories. Planning the file and directory rights correctly will determine whether files are accessible by the appropriate end users, and protected from all other users. You must understand basic file system security to effectively implement security.

Before a user can access a file or directory on a NetWare volume, some rights to that file must be granted to the user's NDS object, as illustrated in Figure 6-1. Rights can be granted to users, groups, and containers, or any other object in NDS. The NDS object is considered a *trustee* of the file or directory when granted rights to it.

When a right is granted to a group or a container, any user who is a member of the group or who exists in that container will also receive those rights. When a right is granted to the [public] trustee, all users, whether logged in or not, will receive it. It is preferred that groups and containers, rather than individual users, be granted explicit rights, since it facilitates planning and maintenance. The rights that can be granted to access a file or directory are listed in Table 6-1.

FIGURE 6-1

File system trustee rights

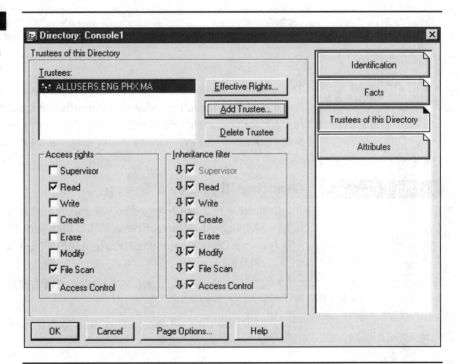

	Right	Abbreviation	What Is Granted
TABLE 6-1	Read	R	Trustee is able to read data from the file
Trustee Rights to Files and Directories	Write	W	Trustee is able to write data to an existing file
	Create	C	Trustee can create a new file or subdirectory
	Erase	E	Trustee can delete an existing file or subdirectory
	Modify	M	Trustee can rename a file or change the file attributes
	File Scan	F	Trustee can list the contents of a directory, such as when using the DIR or NDIR commands, or view the files in a directory from Explorer
	Access control	A	Trustee can grant or revoke rights to other trustees
	Supervisor	S	Supervisor right implies all rights, and cannot be filtered

exam
⚠atch

The minimal rights required both to list files and execute them are Read and File Scan. In order to remember the trustee rights, remember the words FEW SCRAM. F-file scan E-erase W-write S-supervisor C-create R-read A-access control M-modify.

EXERCISE 6-1

Granting Rights to a Group

1. If drive F: is not mapped to volume SYS, then right-click Network Neighborhood, select Novell Map Network Drive, select drive F: under Device, type **\\SERVERNAME\SYS** in the Path area, and click Map.

2. Choose Start | Run, type **F:\PUBLIC\WIN32\NWADMN32**, and press ENTER.

3. Navigate through the tree to the desired context where the SYS Volume object exists.

4. Double-click the Volume object to expand the files below it.

5. Select the Public folder and right-click it.

6. Select Details.

7. Click the Trustees of this Directory property page button.

8. Click Add Trustee.

9. From the resulting dialog box, navigate the tree until the desired Group object is found.

10. Select the Group object and click OK. Note that when you are returned to the property page, the group has been added to the Trustees window, selected, and the Access rights check boxes are active. The Read and File Scan rights are selected by default.

11. With the Group object highlighted in the Trustees window, click the following rights under Access rights: Write, Create, and Modify.

12. Click OK.

EXERCISE 6-2

Granting Trustee Rights from a User Object

1. If drive F: is not mapped to volume SYS, then right-click Network Neighborhood, select Novell Map Network Drive, select drive F: under Device, type **\\SERVERNAME\SYS** in the Path area, and click Map.

2. Choose Start | Run, type **F:\PUBLIC\WIN32\NWADMN32**, and press ENTER.

3. Navigate through the tree to the desired context where the User object exists.

4. Double-click the User object to bring up the Details window.

5. Click the Rights to Files and Directories property page button (see Figure 6-2).

6. Click the Find button to find the Volume objects.

7. The context where the User object exists will be shown as the default context to find Volume objects in. Click the button to the right of the Context path to navigate to a different NDS context. When the correct context is displayed, click OK.

8. Next to the Files and Directories display area, click Add.

9. Double-click the Volume object in the right pane window to expand the files and directories below it. Navigate through the directories until the correct file or directory is displayed in the left pane window.

10. Select the file or directory from the left pane window; then click OK.

11. The directory or file will be displayed in the Files and Directories display area. It will be highlighted, and the user's rights to it will be checked in the Rights area. The default rights are Read and File Scan.

12. Check the Supervisor right.

13. Click OK to apply the rights to the User object.

FIGURE 6-2

Rights to Files and Directories property page

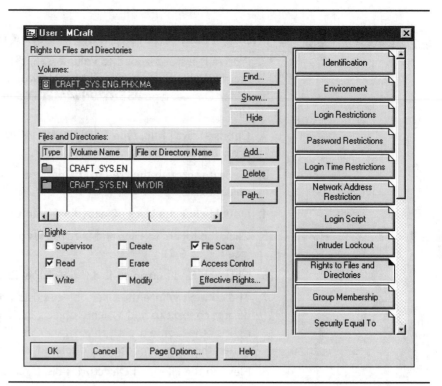

Inheritance and Filters

Rights flow down the directory structure. When a user is granted a right to a directory, that right automatically flows down to the subdirectories. For example, if a user has Read and File Scan rights in SYS:PUBLIC, then the user will also have Read and File Scan rights to the WIN32 subdirectory of SYS:PUBLIC. This is called *inheritance.*

An *Inherited Rights Filter (IRF)* controls inheritance. The IRF blocks rights from flowing down the file directory structure. When a right is listed in the IRF, users can inherit it. When a right is not included in the IRF, then it is effectively blocked from being inherited. If that right is required by a user, then the user must be explicitly granted that right at that subdirectory.

exam
ⓌatCh

When planning rights to the file system, keep in mind how inheritance works. It is best not to grant users rights at the root of a volume or high-level directory. Granting users rights at a lower level is easier to control when adding directories later on. Give each trustee only the rights needed at each level.

Security Equivalence

NetWare has the capability of enabling one trustee to have the rights given to another trustee by setting the first trustee as *security equivalent* to the second. This is *explicit* security equivalence. Each User object has a Security Equal To property in NDS. When adding other NDS objects to this property, the user receives the same rights as those objects.

Two other types of security equivalence occur in NDS. When a User object is a member of a group, the User object becomes security equivalent to the Group object. When a User object is an occupant of an Organizational Role object, the User object becomes security equivalent to the Organizational Role object.

Each security equivalence is listed in the Security Equal To property of the User object, as illustrated in Figure 6-3.

Implied security equivalence occurs when rights that have been granted to a container object automatically flow to its child objects. In Novell

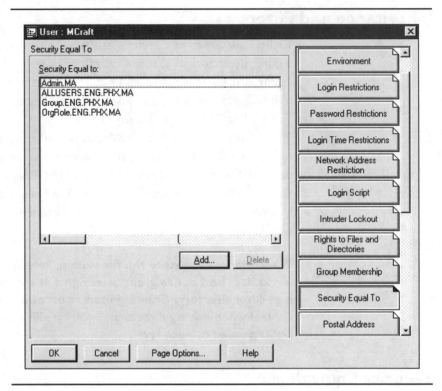

FIGURE 6-3

Security Equal
To property

Directory Services a container object is considered a parent to the objects within it, and they are considered children of the container. Implied security equivalence is not listed in the Security Equal To property of the User object.

exam
Watch

Security equivalence is not transferable; for example, if User Bob has been made a trustee of the SYS:ANSEU directory with Read, Write, Create, Erase, Modify and File scan [-RWCEMF-] rights granted, and User Tom has been granted only Read and File scan [-R———F-] rights, and is later made security equivalent to User Bob, then Tom gets [-RWCEMF-] rights. If User Bruce is made security equivalent to Tom, Bruce does not get the same rights to SYS:ANSEU, as Bob [-RWCEMF-], he gets the same rights as Tom, [-R———F-], because those were the rights granted to the trustee Tom.

Making a User Object Security Equivalent to Administrator

1. If drive F: is not mapped to volume SYS, then right-click Network Neighborhood, select Novell Map Network Drive, select drive F: under Device, type **\\\\SERVERNAME\\SYS** in the Path area, and click Map.

2. Choose Start | Run, type **F:\PUBLIC\WIN32\NWADMN32**, and press ENTER.

3. Navigate through the tree to the desired context.

4. Select a User object to be made equivalent to the Admin object.

5. Click the Object menu and select Details.

6. Click the Security Equal To property page button.

7. Click the Add button.

8. Navigate through the tree until the Admin object appears in the left pane under available objects.

9. Click the Admin object and then click OK.

10. Click OK to exit the User object properties and save the security equivalent changes.

Effective Rights

Effective rights are the actual trustee rights that are in effect when a user accesses a file or directory. A user's effective rights are calculated from

Rights granted through security equivalence
Plus rights granted to the [public] trustee
Plus rights granted to groups the user is a member of
Plus rights granted to the user's container
Plus rights explicitly granted to the user
Plus rights inherited from upper directory minus rights filtered by the IRF

In order to calculate effective rights, the flow of rights must be traced down the directory structure shown in Figure 6-4.

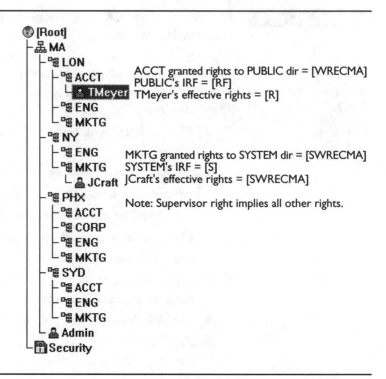

FIGURE 6-4

Effective rights example

---

exam
ⓦatch

Effective rights are calculated from the explicitly granted rights, plus those granted through security equivalence, group membership, and container membership, plus those inherited from upper directories, minus those filtered by the IRF. The NetWare exams always include a couple of questions about determining the effective rights of users and planning the rights for the NetWare file system.

Calculating effective rights is a skill that is absolutely required for planning and administering a NetWare network. The following example will use the Jcraft user in the .OU=MKTG.OU=NY.O=MA context shown in Figure 6-4.

Jcraft is granted the explicit rights to the SYS:PUBLIC\WIN32 directory for Write [W]. Jcraft is granted the rights for Read, Create, File Scan, and Modify [RCFM] for the SYS:PUBLIC directory. The IRF for the

SYS:PUBLIC\WIN32 directory is [RF]. Jcraft belongs to the ALLUSERS group that is granted the Read and File Scan rights [RF] for SYS:PUBLIC, and Read, File Scan, and Access Control [RFA] for SYS:PUBLIC\WIN32. What are Jcraft's effective rights fir SYS:PUBLIC\WIN32? Table 6-2 provides the process of determining Jcraft's effective rights for SYS:PUBLIC\WIN32.

Jcraft's effective rights are Read, Write, File Scan, and Access Control.

Rules for Planning

The rules for planning rights can be simplified into the following steps:

1. Design the file system so that there is limited access at the root of NetWare volumes.

2. Grant greater file system access at lower levels of the directory structure.

3. To protect files, do not grant unnecessary rights at any level.

4. Use inheritance to your advantage, granting explicitly as few times as possible within the directory structure.

TABLE 6-2			
	Calculations	**Directory**	**Rights**
Calculating Effective Rights	To calculate the effective rights, start with the explicit rights.	SYS:PUBLIC\WIN32	[W]
	Add the inherited rights that are granted to the user for the parent directory, subtracting the rights blocked by the IRF.	SYS:PUBLIC –SYS:PUBLIC\WIN3 2 IRF blocked rights	[RCFM] only [RF] allowed
	Add the rights granted through security equivalence, either implied or explicit.	SYS:PUBLIC\WIN32	[RFA]
	Effective rights	SYS:PUBLIC\WIN32	[RWFA]

5. Plan rights for the [Public] trustee, [root], container objects, organizational role objects, and groups first; then for individual users.

6. Consider the effect that security equivalence will have on the rights granted.

7. Filter rights only when absolutely necessary; that is, try to keep the directory structure with the fewest rights at the top.

CERTIFICATION OBJECTIVE 6.03

Planning File System Attribute Security

File system attributes add another layer of security to the network. *File attributes* can be applied to a file and are applicable no matter what rights a trustee has been granted to a file. For example, if a user has been granted the Supervisor right to a directory, but a file has been flagged Read Only, the user cannot delete or rename that file, until or unless that attribute has been changed.

There is a similar system under DOS. A file on a DOS, Windows 95/98, or NT workstation can have attributes set to prevent it from being seen (Hidden), to be a system file (System), to not be deleted or renamed (Read Only), or to be used as normal (Read/Write). NetWare enables these same types of rights plus many more to be set on both files and directories. Some of these attributes are applicable only to files, and others are applicable only to directories.

File and Directory Attributes

Some file attributes are the same as directory attributes. Other attributes are applicable only to files or only to directories. Table 6-3 shows the file system attributes and whether they are applicable to files, directories, or both; the symbol for that attribute; and what function it provides for the file.

TABLE 6-3
File and Directory Attributes

Atribute	File / Dir	Symbol	Function
Archive Needed	File	A	Whenever a file is changed, this attribute is set automatically by NetWare. This flags the file for backup during incremental or differential backups.
Copy Inhibit	File	Ci	Prohibits the trustee from copying the file.
Can't Compress	File	Cc	If no significant amount of space can be saved through compression, NetWare sets this attribute automatically.
Don't Compress	File / Dir	Dc	Prevents the file from being compressed.
Delete Inhibit	File / Dir	Di	Prohibits the trustee from deleting the file.
Don't Migrate	Dir	Dm	If optical storage is being used, this attribute prevents a file from being migrated to it.
Don't Suballocate	File	Ds	Causes the file to be written to entire blocks, and ignores the use of block suballocation.
Hidden	File / Dir	H	Hides a file from being seen in the Explorer or during a DIR or NDIR search.
Immediate Compress	File / Dir	Ic	Compresses the file as soon as it is written.
Indexed	File	I	Starts a turbo FAT- indexing feature on the file.
Migrated	File	M	Shows that the file has been migrated to another storage device (optical storage).

TABLE 6-3			

File and Directory
Attributes *(continued)*

Atribute	File / Dir	Symbol	Function
Purge	File / Dir	P	Causes a file to be erased from the file system as soon as it is deleted, and cannot be recovered through the SALVAGE feature of NetWare Administrator or FILER.
Rename Inhibit	File / Dir	Ri	Prevents users from renaming a file.
Read Only	File	Ro	Protects a file from being moved, written to, renamed, or deleted. It automatically includes the Ri and Di attributes.
Read/Write	File	Rw	Allows the file to be moved, written to, renamed, or deleted.
Shareable	File	S	Enables multiple users to access a file simultaneously.
System	File / Dir	Sy	Indicates that the file is used by the System, and includes the Read Only and Hidden attributes.
Transactional	File	T	Shows that the file is a TTS (Transaction Tracking System) protected file. It is used only with applications that support TTS.
Execute Only	File	X	Prevents a file from being modified, renamed, erased, or copied. After it is set, this attribute cannot be removed.

QUESTIONS AND ANSWERS

Stephanie is an administrator of a NetWare network. She has a group of graphics design users that print very large files. Whenever Stephanie wants to salvage a file, she finds that only the most recently deleted files are available to be salvaged. When she browses through the files, she finds many extremely large files available in the Queues directory. What can Stephanie do to manage her file system?	Stephanie can flag the Queues directory to be purged immediately. This will keep the large print jobs from taking up space in the deleted files area in the NetWare file system.

EXERCISE 6-4

Setting Attributes for a File and a Directory

1. If drive F: is not mapped to volume SYS, then right-click Network Neighborhood, select Novell Map Network Drive, select drive F: under Device, type **\\SERVERNAME\SYS** in the Path area, and click Map.

2. Choose Start | Run, type **F:\PUBLIC\WIN32\NWADMN32**, and press ENTER.

3. Navigate through the tree to the desired context where the SYS Volume object resides.

4. Double-click the SYS Volume object to expand the files and directory structure below it.

5. Select the ETC directory and right-click it.

6. Select Details.

7. Click the Attributes property page button (see Figure 6-5).

8. Check the Immediate Compress attribute.

9. Click OK.

10. You are returned to the NetWare Administrator window. Navigate down to the Public directory and select the ATOTAL.EXE file.

11. Double-click the file to bring up the File properties dialog box.

12. Click the Attributes property page button.

13. Note that there are more attributes available for files than directories (see Figure 6-6). Check the Don't Compress and Shareable attributes.

14. Click OK.

Planning File System Attributes

The file system attributes should be planned according to the way the files are used by the end users. For instance, mission-critical files should never be placed in a directory marked for purging, and they should possibly be flagged as Delete Inhibit and Rename Inhibit, if they should not be deleted

FIGURE 6-5

Directory attributes

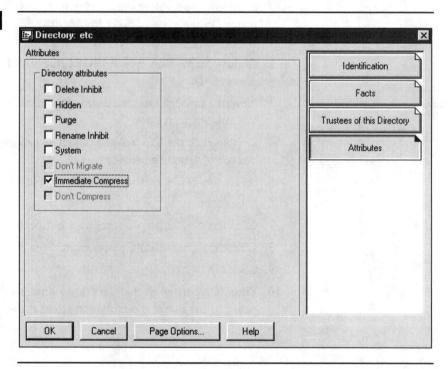

FIGURE 6-6

File attributes

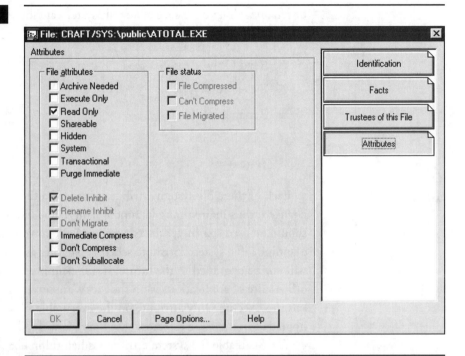

File: CRAFT/SYS:\public\ATOTAL.EXE

Attributes

File attributes
- ☐ Archive Needed
- ☐ Execute Only
- ☑ Read Only
- ☐ Shareable
- ☐ Hidden
- ☐ System
- ☐ Transactional
- ☐ Purge Immediate

- ☑ Delete Inhibit
- ☑ Rename Inhibit
- ☐ Don't Migrate
- ☐ Immediate Compress
- ☐ Don't Compress
- ☐ Don't Suballocate

File status
- ☐ File Compressed
- ☐ Can't Compress
- ☐ File Migrated

Identification

Facts

Trustees of this File

Attributes

OK   Cancel   Page Options...   Help

FROM THE CLASSROOM

Inherited Rights Filter (IRF) and Calculating Effective Rights

Effective Rights determine what a user can actually do in a particular directory or to a particular file. File System Rights may have been acquired through inheritance, a trustee assignment, or security equivalence. Inherited Rights Filters (IRFs) are applied to directories or files to *prevent* effective rights from flowing downward from a *parent* directory. (Inherited rights can flow all the way from the volume root.) The only ways to get around IRFs is to either make a new trustee assignment and grant rights, or make the object security equivalent to another object that is already a trustee of the directory or file.

—By Dan Cheung, CNI, MCNE, MCT

or renamed. There are several key file system attributes that can secure the file system:

- Read Only
- Delete Inhibit
- Rename Inhibit
- Execute Only
- System

Each of these file system attributes prevents a file or its name from being changed, thus maintaining its functionality. The Execute Only attribute should be used sparingly, since it cannot be removed once set. When planning a file system attribute scheme, flag files as Execute Only if they will not be upgraded in the future. If, for example, a network source for an office suite of applications is on the NetWare server, and the administrator sets the Execute Only attribute on the executable files, when the suite is upgraded in the same directory, the upgrade will fail.

The Shareable file system attribute is helpful in enabling applications to work appropriately. Some applications are not created for use in a networked system and do not natively support multiple users. To make the application work correctly, flag all the files in the applications directory as Shareable.

CERTIFICATION OBJECTIVE 6.04

Implementing File System Security

File system security can be assigned in the NetWare Administrator program for both trustee rights and file system attributes. The NetWare Administrator offers a single point of administration for the entire NetWare network. The NetWare Administrator offers the ability to set both trustee rights to files and directories, and the ability to set file system attributes on both files and directories. The NetWare Administrator methods were reviewed in the exercises given previously. There are other ways to implement file system security, using command-line utilities offered in NetWare.

Trustee Rights

Trustee rights are usually implemented in the NetWare Administrator by adding the file or directory to the Rights to Files and Directories property page for users, groups, organizational roles, and organizational units. After adding the file to that property, the administrator selects the rights to be applied for that user to the file. If the administrator prefers, the rights can be assigned to the file or directory by using the Trustees of this File or Trustees of this Directory property page and adding the user, group, organizational role, or organizational unit to the list, and then selecting the applicable trustee rights.

Sometimes it is easier for an administrator to use a command-line utility, and NetWare offers a DOS command-line utility for assigning trustee rights. It is available in the SYS:PUBLIC directory and is called RIGHTS.EXE. Using the RIGHTS command enables an administrator to grant, revoke, and view rights information at a DOS prompt. The administrator can also set the IRF and see which rights are inherited. A useful troubleshooting tool, RIGHTS, enables the user to view the current effective rights for a file or directory.

To assign a right with the RIGHTS command, use the following syntax:

```
RIGHTS path to file + rights symbols /NAME=NDS distinguished name of User object
```

To view the currently assigned trustee rights, simply type **RIGHTS** at the prompt.

File System Attributes

In the NetWare Administrator, file system attributes are set from the Attributes property page of the file or directory. This can be somewhat cumbersome to manage, if, for example, you want to apply the Execute Only attribute to .EXE files, or if you want to apply a Shareable attribute to an entire directory system of hundreds of files in multiple subdirectories. NetWare offers a DOS command-line utility for changing file system attributes. It is the FLAG.EXE utility in the SYS:PUBLIC directory.

FLAG is similar to the DOS ATTRIB command. It can modify the file system attributes on either files or directories. To see the entire slew of FLAG options, type **FLAG /? ALL** at the DOS prompt. FLAG is most helpful for applying a single attribute to multiple files in multiple subdirectories, since a single command can affect hundreds of files at once. When using the FLAG command, please note that the N flag is not an attribute. Instead it is a flag that automatically assigns the default file attributes to a file. These are Shareable and Read/Write.

| EXERCISE 6-5 | **Using the FLAG Command on Multiple Files** |

1. If drive F: is not mapped to volume SYS, then right-click Network Neighborhood, select Novell Map Network Drive, select drive F: under Device, type **\\\SERVERNAME\SYS** in the Path area, and click Map.

2. On a Windows 95 workstation, open a DOS prompt window by choosing Start | Programs | MS-DOS Prompt.

3. At the prompt, type **F:** and press ENTER.

4. If the prompt does not read **F:\PUBLIC**, then type **CD\PUBLIC** and press ENTER.

5. In this exercise, the F:\QUEUES directory will be flagged so that it will purge print files immediately. There is normally no need to keep them salvageable. Also, the files in PUBLIC and its subdirectories will be flagged as Read Only and Shareable. To flag the QUEUES directory, type **FLAG F:\QUEUES*.* P /DO** and press ENTER.

6. To flag the files in F:\PUBLIC and its subdirectories as Read Only and Shareable, type **FLAG F:\PUBLIC*.* Sh RO /FO** and press ENTER.

CERTIFICATION SUMMARY

The file system security has two layers. One layer is the granting of access to end users, who are then called *trustees*. A trustee can also be a Group object, Organizational Role object, Organizational Unit object, and many other objects within Novell Directory Services (NDS).

Trustee rights for files and directories are Supervisor, Read, Write, Create, Erase, Modify, File Scan, and Access Control [SRWCEMFA]. The Supervisor right includes all other access rights. Read and File Scan are the minimum rights required to see a file and execute it. Write allows changes to be made to the file. Create allows a user to create a new file or directory. Erase enables the user to delete a file or directory. Modify allows the user to change the file attributes. Read allows the user to open the file. File Scan allows the user to see the files listed in a directory listing or the Explorer. Access Control enables a user to grant other NDS objects trustee rights to that file or directory.

Trustee rights can be granted explicitly to a user. A trustee right granted to a user at an upper-level directory is inherited at lower-level directories, thus simplifying the need for explicit granting of rights. However, when planning the trustee rights for a directory, inheritance must be considered in order to avoid security problems. The Inherited Rights Filter, or IRF, is used to block rights from being inherited. For those rights to be granted to a trustee, the rights must be granted explicitly at that directory.

Security equivalence is a NetWare function that allows the administrator to make one trustee equal to another. Security equivalence can be granted through group membership, organizational role occupancy, or it can be an explicit addition to the Security Equal To property page of the User object. Implied security equivalence is where a User object automatically receives the trustee rights granted to the parent container object in NDS. Explicit security equivalence will appear in the Security Equal To property; implied security equivalence will not.

Effective rights are the actual rights in effect for any given file or directory that a trustee is accessing. The rights are calculated from the explicit rights granted the trustee, plus the Security Equivalence rights granted to the security-equivalent objects and the inherited rights from upper directories; that is, the inherited rights filter blocked rights.

Trustee rights should be carefully planned, with the file system organized to keep secured files separate from less secure files. Trustee rights should be granted stringently at the top of the directory structure, and more generously below it, so that inheritance will not accidentally grant access to files that should be secure.

File system attributes in NetWare are similar to the file system attributes available in DOS, except that there are many more of them. The file system attributes can be applied to files and directories and control how they are used, regardless of the trustee rights granted to a user. For example, if a user is granted the Erase Trustee right, and a file system attribute for a file is Delete Inhibit, the user cannot delete the file. File system attributes should be planned according to the way that the files will be used.

Both trustee rights and file system attributes can be set in the NetWare Administrator. The RIGHTS command-line utility can be used to grant, revoke, or display trustee rights from a DOS prompt. The FLAG command-line utility can be used to set the file system attributes of files and directories. It is useful in that the administrator can set attributes on multiple files or directories.

TWO-MINUTE DRILL

- ❑ NetWare file system attributes offer the ability to prevent file changes, even when a user has the access rights to make those changes. A network file has the flexibility to be shared among several users, and then secured from the remainder of the network users.

- ❑ File system rights are the basic tools for securing files and directories. Planning the file and directory rights correctly will determine whether files are accessible by the appropriate end users and protected from all other users.

❑ Rights can be granted to users, groups, and containers, or any other object in NDS. The NDS object is considered a trustee of the file or directory when granted rights to it.

❑ When a right is granted to a group or a container, any user who is a member of the group or who exists in that container will also receive those rights. When a right is granted to the [public] trustee, all users, whether logged in or not, will receive it.

❑ Groups and containers, rather than individual users, should be granted explicit rights, since it facilitates planning and maintenance.

❑ Rights flow down the directory structure. When a user is granted a right to a directory, that right automatically flows down to the subdirectories. This is called *inheritance*.

❑ An Inherited Rights Filter (IRF) controls inheritance. The IRF blocks rights from flowing down the file directory structure. When a right is listed in the IRF, users can inherit it. When a right is not included in the IRF, then it is effectively blocked from being inherited.

❑ NetWare has the capability of enabling one trustee to have the rights given to another trustee by setting the first trustee as security equivalent to the second. This is explicit security equivalence. Each User object has a Security Equal To property in NDS. When adding other NDS objects to this property, the user receives the same rights as those objects.

❑ Two other types of security equivalence occur in NDS. When a User object is a member of a group, the User object becomes security equivalent to the Group object. When a User object is an occupant of an Organizational Role object, the User object becomes security equivalent to the Organizational Role object.

❑ Implied security equivalence occurs when rights that have been granted to a container object automatically flow to its child objects. In Novell Directory Services a container object is considered a parent to the objects within it, and they are considered children of the container. Implied security equivalence is not listed in the Security Equivalent To property of the User object.

❏ Effective rights are the actual trustee rights that are in effect when a user accesses a file or directory.

❏ File system attributes add another layer of security to the network. File attributes can be applied to a file and are applicable no matter what rights a trustee has been granted to a file.

❏ There is a similar system under DOS. A file on a DOS, Windows 95/98, or NT workstation can have attributes set to prevent it from being seen (Hidden), to be a system file (System), to not be deleted or renamed (Read Only), or to be used as normal (Read/Write).

❏ The file system attributes should be planned according to the way the files are used by the end users. There are several key file system attributes that can secure the file system. They are Read Only, Delete Inhibit, Rename Inhibit, Execute Only and System.

❏ File system security can be assigned in the NetWare Administrator program for both trustee rights and file system attributes. The NetWare Administrator offers a single point of administration for the entire NetWare network. The NetWare Administrator offers the ability to set both trustee rights to files and directories, and the ability to set file system attributes on both files and directories.

❏ Trustee rights are usually implemented in the NetWare Administrator by adding the file or directory to the Rights to Files and Directories property page for users, groups, organizational roles, and organizational units.

❏ In the NetWare Administrator, file system attributes are set from the Attributes property page of the file or directory.

❏ NetWare offers a DOS command-line utility for changing file system attributes. It is the FLAG.EXE utility in the SYS:PUBLIC directory. FLAG is similar to the DOS ATTRIB command. It can modify the file system attributes on either files or directories.

SELF TEST

The following Self-Test questions will help you measure your understanding of the material presented in this chapter. Read all the choices carefully, as there may be more than one correct answer. Choose all correct answers for each question.

1. Which of the following NDS objects can be trustees?

   A. User object

   B. Group object

   C. Organizational Unit

   D. Organization

   E. All of the above

   F. None of the above

2. Laura is a network administrator for a NetWare 5 network. She has received a request from her management to make a file accessible to users that are not going to be granted login access to the network. How can Laura achieve this?

   A. She cannot. There is no way to grant access to a file without logging in first.

   B. She can grant the Read and File Scan rights to the Organization container.

   C. She can grant the Read and File Scan rights to [public].

   D. She can grant the Read and File Scan rights to [root].

3. Which of the following is not a trustee right?

   A. Read Only

   B. Write

   C. Create

   D. Supervisor

4. What is inheritance?

   A. It is when the Read trustee right automatically includes the File Scan right.

   B. It is when a group right is automatically given to a group member.

   C. It is when the parent organizational unit rights are automatically given to the child objects.

   D. It is when the trustee rights granted at an upper-level directory automatically flow down the directory tree.

5. How is inheritance controlled?

   A. Through trustee rights

   B. Through the IRF

   C. Through file system attributes

   D. Through security equivalence

6. Which of the following security equivalence objects do not show up in the Security Equal To property page?

   A. Group objects

   B. Organizational role objects

   C. Parent Organizational Units

   D. Any explicitly added security-equivalent objects

7. What are effective rights?

   A. File system attributes

   B. File system attributes and trustee rights combined

   C. Rights granted to the [public] trustee

   D. Rights that are in effect for a file or directory

8. User Aconat is explicitly granted [EC] to the VOL1:DATA\DB directory. Aconat is granted [RFM] for VOL1:DATA, and the IRF for the VOL1:DATA\DB is [RF]. He is a member of the group DBUSERS, which is granted [RFCW] to the VOL1:DATA\DB directory. What are Aconat's effective rights to VOL1:DATA\DB?

   A. [EC]

   B. [RFECWM]

   C. [RFM]

   D. [RFECW]

9. George is planning trustee rights on a server that he is adding to the network. George has two business units that need to keep their files on the server, but secured from all other users outside their business units. George has decided to place these directories in the VOL1:DATA\GROUPS\BU1 and VOL1:\DATA\GROUPS\BU2 directories. Since all other data is public, George has placed this data in the VOL1:DATA\PUBLIC. George has decided to grant [RWECF] to the [public]

trustee at the VOL1:DATA directory level. Does this meet with the security scheme George has been asked to provide?

   A. Yes, for both business units

   B. Yes for one business unit, no for the other

   C. No for both business units

10. A user DavidH has been granted [RWECF] to the DATA:DIR\DB directory. All files in that directory have been flagged with the Di, Ri, and S attributes. Will DavidH be able to erase any files?

   A. Yes, he has been granted the Erase trustee right.

   B. Yes, the S attribute allows him to have Supervisor trustee rights.

   C. No, the S attribute and the Ri attribute override all other trustee rights.

   D. No, the Di attribute overrides the E trustee right.

11. What is the A attribute used for?

   A. It is required for Access control, so that users can grant further trustee rights.

   B. It is used as a flag for backups.

   C. It is used to indicate a system file.

   D. It is required for allowing changes to the file.

12. Which two attributes are automatically included when Read Only is set?

    A. Archive Needed and System

    B. Archive Needed and Delete Inhibit

    C. Delete Inhibit and Rename Inhibit

    D. Rename Inhibit and System

13. Why should an administrator be careful when applying the X attribute to files?

    A. Because it can delete files

    B. Because it gives users more access to files and they can delete them

    C. Because it can migrate a file to another storage system

    D. Because it cannot be removed

14. Which of the following commands can be used to make a user a trustee of a file?

    A. RIGHTS

    B. FLAG

    C. NDIR

    D. NLIST

15. When using FLAG, what does the N flag mean?

    A. It is a new NetWare 5 attribute for Normal.

    B. It is a switch to undo the last flag executed.

    C. It is an easy way to apply Read/Write and Shareable attributes.

    D. It is not a flag.

7

Creating Login Scripts

CERTIFICATION OBJECTIVES

7.01   Login Script Overview

7.02   Designing Login Script Systems

7.03   Creating, Executing, and Debugging
        Login Scripts

7.04   Login Scripts and the GUI
        Login Utility

Through Novell Directory Services, NetWare 5 offers a single login to the network. That single login enables authentication for access to any NetWare 5 server, printers, and other network resources. In environments with multiple resources, or with end users that require transparent access to resources, the administrator needs to be able to automate how users attach to resources.

Login scripts can be used to

- Attach to resources such as network drives and printers
- Set workstation environment variables
- Display messages
- Execute applications

CERTIFICATION OBJECTIVE 7.01

Login Script Overview

Several types of login scripts can execute when logging in to Novell Directory Services. There is an order to the execution, which makes the login scripts a scalable tool that can be used in global enterprise networks. The login script order is

1. Container script that contains the User object (if it exists)
2. Profile script (if it exists)
3. User script (if it exists) or default script (if user script does not exist)

Login scripts are generally located within Novell Directory Services as properties of objects. The only exception to this rule is the default login script, which has historically been compiled within the login executable of the workstation client.

Container Script

The Container Script is a property of the container object. Both the Organization and the Organizational Unit objects have a Login Script property. These are all container scripts.

A container script executes for a user who is a child object of that container object. For example, in the NDS tree in Figure 7-1, the user TMeyer is a child of the ACCT container. As such, TMeyer executes the Login Script property of the ACCT container. In contrast, user JSansoterra is a child of the ENG container and executes the Login Script property of the ENG container.

In order to access the Container Script property, in NetWare Administrator, browse through the NDS tree until the target container is located. Right-click the container and select Details from the pop-up menu. In the resulting dialog box (see Figure 7-2), click the Login Script button. If the container does not have a login script, this window will be blank.

FIGURE 7-1

Container script execution

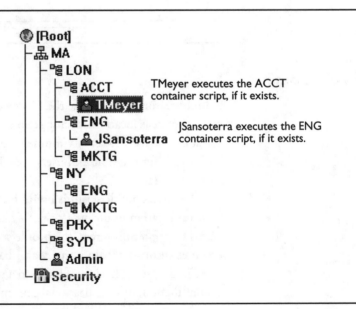

[Root]
MA
LON
ACCT
TMeyer — TMeyer executes the ACCT container script, if it exists.
ENG
JSansoterra — JSansoterra executes the ENG container script, if it exists.
MKTG
NY
ENG
MKTG
PHX
SYD
Admin
Security

FIGURE 7-2

Container Script property

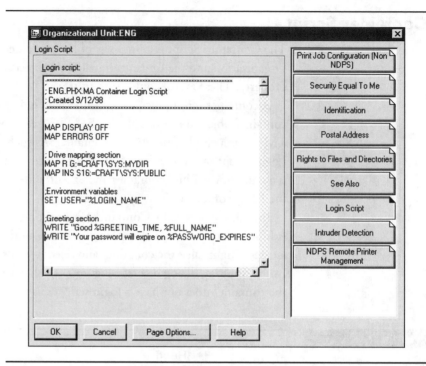

Organizational Unit:ENG

Login Script

Login script:

```
;**********************************************************
; ENG.PHX.MA Container Login Script
; Created 9/12/98
;**********************************************************

MAP DISPLAY OFF
MAP ERRORS OFF

; Drive mapping section
MAP R G:=CRAFT\SYS:MYDIR
MAP INS S16:=CRAFT\SYS:PUBLIC

;Environment variables
SET USER="%LOGIN_NAME"

;Greeting section
WRITE "Good %GREETING_TIME, %FULL_NAME"
WRITE "Your password will expire on %PASSWORD_EXPIRES"
```

Print Job Configuration (Non NDPS)

Security Equal To Me

Identification

Postal Address

Rights to Files and Directories

See Also

Login Script

Intruder Detection

NDPS Remote Printer Management

OK   Cancel   Page Options...   Help

Profile Script

Administrators typically use the Profile object for special-purpose login scripts, such as location-specific scripts or even a global script. The profile script can be used to set environment variables, map drives, and execute commands for multiple end users. The Profile Script is a property of the Profile object.

A location-specific script is useful for grouping users based on their physical location in the enterprise. When designing printing services and access to printer resources, the profile script enables users to run the printer captures through a login script that is based on the printers closest to them (see Figure 7-3). This is preferable to a script that is run based on a business unit affiliation, or organizational unit membership.

The profile script also allows an administrator to create a script that can be used by several users in any context of the tree. Whenever a change is

FIGURE 7-3

Profile script

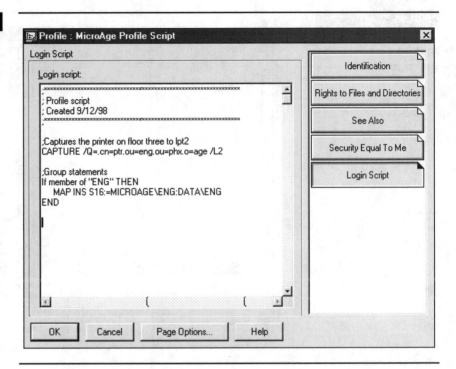

needed, the profile script needs to be changed only once. In contrast, if an administrator has created identical user scripts instead of a profile script, each user script must be edited if change is required.

A profile script is assigned to a user through the User object's Login Script property page.

EXERCISE 7-1

Assigning a Profile Script to a User Object

1. If drive F: is not mapped to volume SYS, then right-click the Network Neighborhood icon, select Novell Map Network Drive, select drive F: under Device, and type **\\\\SERVERNAME\\SYS** in the Path area; then click Map.

2. Choose Start | Run, type **F:\\PUBLIC\\WIN32\\NWADMN32**, and press ENTER.

3. Navigate through the tree until the User object is located.

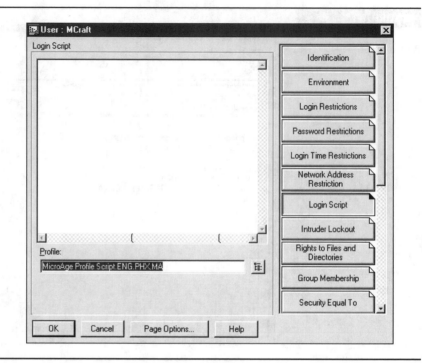

FIGURE 7-4

Assigning a profile script to
User object

4. Double-click the User object.

5. Click the Login Script property page button.

6. Click the button to the right of the Profile script box.

7. Navigate through the NDS tree until the Profile object is selected.

8. Click OK.

9. Click OK to close the User object details and save the changes
   made (see Figure 7-4).

User Scripts

A user Login Script is a property of the User object in Novell Directory
Services (see Figure 7-5). It executes for the individual User object and
never for any other user.

FIGURE 7-5

User login script

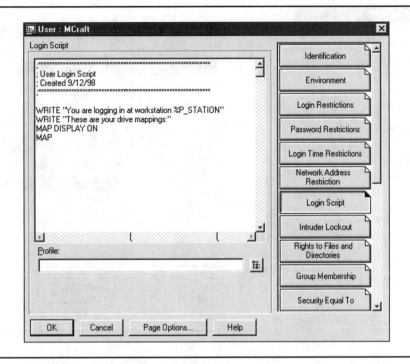

When designing an enterprise network login system, most network designers choose not to include user login scripts because they are difficult to maintain for a growing network. Network resources can be added, moved, or changed. Changes in network resources directly affect how a script is designed. For example, if a database application is added to the network that requires an environment variable to be set for each user accessing the application, a line would have to be added to each individual's login script. The larger the number of users that access the application, the more scripts to be changed. In contrast, if using a container or profile script, the line would have to be added only once to a single script.

exam
atch

When a user logs in, up to three scripts can execute. The user script is the last of these and the most difficult to maintain.

Each user is given access to his or her own user Login Script property, as shown in Figure 7-6. The default property rights for the user's own Login

FIGURE 7-6

A user's property rights to
his or her own login script

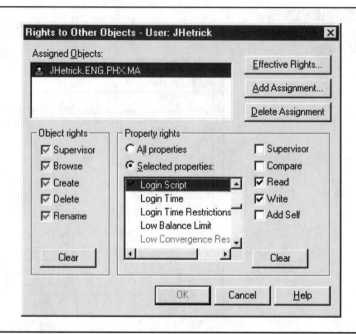

Script property in Novell Directory Services are Read and Write. This
enables the user to write his or her own login script.

Default Login Script

The default login script is compiled as part of the login executable. It
provides the minimal resource access a user might need when connecting
and logging in to the network. Because the default login script is compiled,
there is no way to change the script commands. The following is the list of
commands that are in the default login script:

```
MAP DISPLAY OFF
MAP ERRORS OFF
REM Set 1st drive to most appropriate directory
MAP *1:=SYS
MAP *1:=SYS:%LOGIN_NAME
IF "%1"="SUPERVISOR" THEN MAP *1:=SYS:SYSTEM
MAP S1:=SYS:PUBLIC
```

```
MAP S2:=S1:%MACHINE\%OS\%OS_VERSION
MAP DISPLAY ON
MAP
```

Knowing which directories are mapped in the default login script is critical to designing effective container and profile login scripts. If there is a drive letter conflict between the different login scripts, then the last executed script will determine which directory path gets mapped.

If there is no user login script, the default login script runs. Because a network designer might not want the default login script to run, there is a way to stop it. This is accomplished by placing the statement NO_DEFAULT in either the container login script or the profile login script that the users run prior to the default script.

QUESTIONS AND ANSWERS

Stacy is designing a login script system for an enterprise network, and has decided to utilize only the container script. She has a requirement to make sure that no one has drive mappings to the SYS: volume through the login script. Stacy creates a short container script that consists of one line: MAP R:=VOL1:GROUP, and then she tests it. When she types the MAP command at the prompt, she sees that the F: and Z: drives have been mapped to SYS:. What can Stacy do to meet the requirement to not map drives to SYS?

The extra SYS: drive mappings are from the default login script. Stacy needs to add the NO_DEFAULT command to the container script to avoid executing the default script.

CERTIFICATION OBJECTIVE 7.02

Designing Login Script Systems

NetWare includes many login identifier variables for customizing a login script. Administrators use the login identifier variables in order to use a standard login script for multiple users. This system is both flexible and efficient. Table 7-1 defines the login identifier variables and their uses.

TABLE 7-1

Login Variables

Login Variables	Function
%ACCESS_SERVER	Represents the functionality of the access server. If it returns a TRUE, the server is functional. If FALSE, the server is not functional.
%ACCOUNT_BALANCE	Represents the account balance, if the accounting feature has been implemented.
%ALLOW_UNLIMITED_CREDIT	Represents the Unlimited Credit property value of the User object, if the accounting feature has been implemented.
%AM_PM	Represents the current time of A.M. (morning) or P.M. (evening).
%CN	Represents the NDS Common Name of the user logging in.
%DAY_OF_WEEK	Represents which day of the week it is Sunday, Monday, Tuesday, Wednesday, Thursday, Friday, or Saturday.
%DESCRIPTION	Represents the value of the Description property of the User object that is logging in.
%ERROR_LEVEL	Displays an error level, where 0 = no error.
%FILE_SERVER	Represents the preferred server set at the workstation.
%FULL_NAME	Represents the contents of the Full Name property of the User object that is logging in.
%GREETING_TIME	Represents "morning," "afternoon," "evening," or "night" depending on the current time of day.
%HOME_DIRECTORY	Represents the Home Directory property of the User object.

TABLE 7-1	Login Variables	Function
Login Variables *(continued)*	%HOUR	Represents the current hour in a 12-hour format; for example, 1:00 P.M. is depicted as 1.
	%HOUR24	Represents the current hour in a 24-hour format; for example, 1:00 P.M. is depicted as 13.
	%L	Represents the locality.
	%LANGUAGE	Represents the language used by the workstation.
	%LAST_NAME	Represents the Last Name property of the User object that is logging in.
	%LOGIN_CONTEXT	Represents the context that the User object exists in.
	%LOGIN_NAME	Represents the Login Name property of the User object that is logging in; this value is truncated to 8 characters.
	%MACHINE	Represents the machine type of the workstation; for example, IBM_PC.
	MEMBER of "GROUP"	Typically used with an IF statement to execute a number of commands for User objects that are members of the stated group.
	%MINUTE	Represents the minutes portion of the current time; for example, 1:15 P.M., this would be 15.
	%MONTH	Represents the number of the current month, from 1 through 12; for example, the month of April would be 4.
	%MONTH_NAME	Represents the current month: January, February, March, April, May, June, July, August, September, October, November, or December.
	%NDAY_OF_WEEK	Represents the numeric value of the day of the week.

TABLE 7-1

Login Variables *(continued)*

Login Variables	Function
%NETWORK	Represents the physical network address.
%OS	Represents the workstation operating system; for example, MS-DOS version 6.22 would be MSDOS.
%OS_VERSION	Represents the version of the operating system; for example, MS-DOS version 6.22 would be 6.22.
%P_STATION	Represents the network address of the network interface card in a workstation.
%PASSWORD_EXPIRES	Represents the number of days left before the password will expire.
%PASSWORD_MINIMUM_LENGTH	Represents the number of characters that a password must have in order to be accepted by NetWare.
%PASSWORD_REQUIRED	Represents whether NetWare requires a password for that User object.
%PASSWORD_UNIQUE_REQUIRED	Represents whether NetWare requires a unique password for that User object.
%PROFILE	Represents the value of the Profile property for the User object that is logging in.
%REQUESTER_CONTEXT	Represents the workstation's context setting.
%SECOND	Represents the seconds value of the current time. If the current time is 1:15:23 P.M., this value is 23.
%SECURITY_EQUALS	Represents the security equivalence assignments of the User object that is logging in.
%SHORT_YEAR	Represents the last two digits of the year. If the current year is 1999, this value is 99.

	Login Variables	Function
TABLE 7-1 Login Variables *(continued)*	%STATION	Represents the connection number that the workstation has made on the authenticating server.
	%TELEPHONE_NUMBER	Represents the value of the Telephone Number property of the User object that is logging in.
	%TITLE	Represents the Title property of the User object that is logging in.
	%USER_ID	Represents the number assigned to the user.
	%YEAR	Represents the four-digit year.

Note that many of the login variables are actually NDS properties of the User object. Property values of NDS objects can be used as variables in login scripts. However, not all properties are supported. They can be used the same as any login identifier variable. When the schema is extended to include additional properties, this capability makes NetWare scripting flexible. If a network administrator wants to use an NDS property as a login variable but it contains a space in the property name, the administrator simply encloses the property name in quotation marks or replaces the spaces with underscores.

exam
Watch

Login script variables, such as %HOME_DIRECTORY or %DAY_OF_WEEK, are used to extend the way a container script can be used. Usually, each user is granted a home directory that is completely separate from all other users' home directories. In order to map each home directory correctly, the administrator can use the %HOME_DIRECTORY variable with the MAP command in the container login script.

Login Script Commands

NetWare login scripting supports commands that can be used on a command line. One of the most common is MAP, which is used to connect network drives. The login script actually uses an internal version of MAP.

When used in a login script, the MAP command is used the same way as it is on the command line.

In a login script, the command for mapping a root drive is

```
MAP R G:=SERVER\VOLUME:DIR\SUBDIR
```

In a login script, the command for mapping a search drive is

```
MAP INS S16:=SERVER\VOLUME:DIR
```

In a login script, the command for mapping a standard drive is

```
MAP J:=SERVER\VOLUME:DIR
```

There are two MAP commands that work in a login script that do not work on the command line. These are

```
MAP DISPLAY OFF or MAP DISPLAY ON
MAP ERRORS OFF or MAP ERRORS ON
```

The MAP DISPLAY ON/OFF toggles whether the user will see drive mapping during the login script execution. The MAP ERRORS ON/OFF toggles whether the user will see the drive map errors during the login script execution. Neither of these script commands works on the command line.

The FIRE PHASERS command works only in a login script. When using this command, the computer will issue a beeping sound. Up to nine sounds can be executed by adding a number between 1 and 9 after the FIRE PHASERS command. So, for a login script to promote seven beeps, the command would be FIRE PHASERS 7.

In order to run an external, or DOS, command from a login script, the command must be preceded by a pound sign (#). To change the current context from within the login script, use the CONTEXT command. To set the user to the NY Organizational Unit in the MA Organization, the command is CONTEXT.NY.MA. The WRITE command is used to display a single text line during the login script execution. To display the

word Hello, the command is WRITE "Hello". The DISPLAY and
FDISPLAY commands will show a text file during login script execution.
The difference between DISPLAY and FDISPLAY is

- DISPLAY shows a text file in raw format.

- FDISPLAY filters out codes such as unprintable characters and
printer codes and displays the remaining text of the file.

on the **Job**

*If the # symbol is used to execute a command external to the
commands compiled with the login executable, make sure that a
search drive is mapped to the directory where the external command
resides; otherwise, a login script command-execution error will result.*

To show a tip-of-the-day text file, the administrator can add the
command DISPLAY SERVER\SYS:PUBLIC\TIP.TXT to the login script.
A REM, a REMARK, a semicolon (;), or an asterisk (*) can all be used as
comment indicators. The text following these will be ignored. This is
helpful if an administrator wants to temporarily stop using a login script
command, but enable it later.

The logic that a login script uses is embodied in the IF, THEN, ELSE
command set. This set will execute a command based on a condition.
The syntax is

IF *condition* THEN *command* [ELSE] *command* END

The ELSE is optional. For example, if the admin user wants a MAP
command to run for the SVC group or a different MAP command for
everyone else, the condition is MEMBER OF SVC; the command is
MAP drive letter = SERVER\VOLUME:GROUP\SVC; and the ELSE
command is MAP drive letter = SERVER\VOLUME:GROUP\ALL,
which creates the following:

```
IF MEMBER OF SVC THEN
     MAP G:=SERVER\VOLUME:GROUP\SVC
ELSE
     MAP G:=SERVER\VOLUME:GROUP\ALL
END
```

QUESTIONS AND ANSWERS

Jenny has just completed a course in network administration and has decided to create a new login script that contains the following line:

`#MAP R G:=SYS:PUBLIC.`

The login script executes, but instead of a smooth drive mapping within the login window, a DOS window pops up. Why?

Jenny has erroneously invoked the external MAP command instead of the login script version. She should remove the # sign from the MAP statement.

Cascading Container Scripts

One way to scale a login script process across an enterprise is to design login scripts to include the scripts within other containers (see Figure 7-7). This is done with an INCLUDE command. The idea is to create a series of login scripts that start at the user's container and lead up the tree to the organization container script. This way, any commands that must be run for every user in the network can be placed in the organization container script. The INCLUDE command can extend to text files that are written with the standard login script structure. For example, adding the line INCLUDE SYS:PUBLIC\SCRIPTS\SAMPLE.TXT to a container script will run those script commands before moving to the next script, which would be a profile script, if it exists.

FIGURE 7-7 Cascading login scripts

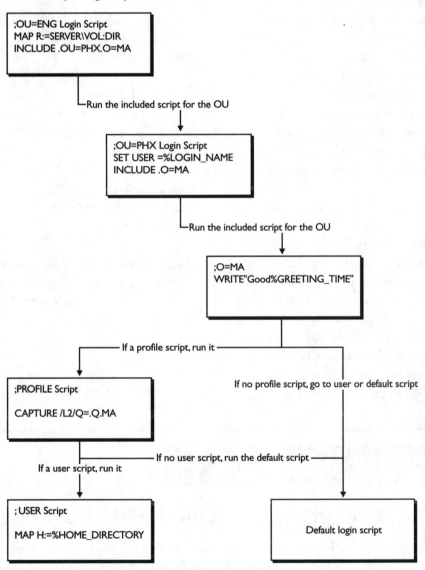

When logging in, a User object always executes in the parent container object's login script first.

;OU=ENG Login Script
MAP R:=SERVER\VOL:DIR
INCLUDE .OU=PHX.O=MA

Run the included script for the OU

;OU=PHX Login Script
SET USER =%LOGIN_NAME
INCLUDE .O=MA

Run the included script for the OU

;O=MA
WRITE"Good%GREETING_TIME"

If a profile script, run it

If no profile script, go to user or default script

;PROFILE Script

CAPTURE /L2/Q=.Q.MA

If no user script, run the default script

If a user script, run it

; USER Script

MAP H:=%HOME_DIRECTORY

Default login script

FROM THE CLASSROOM

Container Login Script Pitfalls to Avoid

Container objects provide the most common and manageable venue for login scripts. If the NDS tree is designed according to Novell's recommended method, User objects will be naturally grouped according to resource proximity and usage. Also, there are typically fewer containers than User objects; therefore, login script management and administration are simpler than managing a multitude of user login scripts.

However, don't forget that container login scripts aren't inherited by users in subordinate organizational objects. In order to use a container login script, the User object must have that container as its immediate parent object, and cannot use the container login script of the container that the user's parent container is in. The Read Selected Property right to the container object's Login Script property is not inherited by a subordinate container object's users. For example,

If O=Chicago has a container login script and one of the commands is NO_DEFAULT,

And if OU=Downtown.O=Chicago has a container login script with NO_DEFAULT as one of its commands,

But OU=Naperville.O=Chicago does not have a container login script and there are no user login scripts and no profile login scripts assigned to any user,

Then, when CN=Mark.OU=Naperville. O=Chicago logs in, Mark does not run any container login scripts. Instead, Mark uses the default login script.

—By Dan Cheung, CNI, MCNE, MCT

CERTIFICATION OBJECTIVE 7.03

Creating, Executing, and Debugging Login Scripts

All login scripts use the same scripting language, which makes it easy to transfer the contents of a profile script to a container script, for example.

This is important to remember. When testing a login script, it is in the administrator's best interest not to create a new login script, nor to add new login script commands, to the Login Script property of an organizational unit. This avoids two things:

- Users accidentally running the unproven login script
- Bad logic causing the login script to lock users out of the network

The best practice when creating and debugging a login script is to create the script in a Profile object, and assign that object to a test User object. If the administrator wants to skip the container object script, the administrator can do either of the following:

- Place the test User object in a test container object that does not have a login script, or
- Add the following statements:

```
IF %LOGIN_NAME = "TESTUSER" THEN
EXIT
                    END
```

Even though you are skipping the container script in order to test the profile script, the new script should always be tested with any other scripts that will be executed. If the new script will be a user script, a good practice is to copy it to the user Login Script property of a test user in the same context as the user that will eventually use it. If the new script will be a profile script, it should be tested with the container script and user or default login scripts, if any are used. If the new script will be a container script, it should be tested with the profile, user, or default login scripts, if any of them are used.

EXERCISE 7-2

Creating, Executing, and Debugging a Login Script

1. If drive F: is not mapped to volume SYS:, then right-click the Network Neighborhood icon, select Novell Map Network Drive, select drive F: under Device, and type **\\\SERVERNAME\SYS** in the Path area; then click Map.

2. Choose Start | Run, type **F:\PUBLIC\WIN32\NWADMN32,** and press ENTER.

3. Create the Profile object by navigating through the tree to a context, press INSERT, and select Profile. From the dialog box, give the profile the name TEST and click Create.

4. Create a group (to use in testing an If MEMBER OF "group" statement) in the same context by pressing INSERT and selecting Group. Give the group the name **GRP**.

5. Create the User object in the same context by pressing INSERT and selecting User. From the dialog box, give the user the name **TESTUSER**, the last name **TEST**, and check off the box for Define Additional Properties.

6. The User object will be created and the User Details dialog box will appear. Click the Login Script property page button.

7. Click the button to the right of the Profile field and select the TEST Profile object to assign it to the user. An error will appear about the user not having the Read property rights. Click OK to continue.

8. Click the Group Membership property page button. Click the Add button and select the GRP Group object. Click OK.

9. Click OK to save changes and exit the user details.

10. Assign the user Read rights to the Profile object by right-clicking the TESTUSER and selecting Rights to Other Objects. Click OK to search in the current context. Click Add Assignment. Select the TEST script and click OK. Click the Selected Properties radio button; then scroll down to the Login Script property. Select it and check off the Read box to the right of the scrolling window. Click OK.

11. Write the test script by double-clicking the Profile object, and clicking the Login Script property page button; then type the following into the window area:

```
**************************************************
; Test script
; Created 9/12/1998
; **********************************************
WRITE "It is %HOUR:%MINUTE %AM_PM."
WRITE "Good %GREETING_TIME, %FULL_NAME."
```

```
WRITE "Your network address is %NETWORK_ADDRESS."
WRITE "Your workstation is %P_STATION."
WRITE "You have %PASSWORD_EXPIRES days until your password expires."
MAP INS S16:=SERVER\SYS:PUBLIC
MAP H:=HOME_DIRECTORY
IF MEMBER OF ".GRP.ENG.PHX.MA" THEN
      MAP INS S16:=SERVER\SYS:SYSTEM
      SET USER=%LOGIN_NAME
END
FIRE PHASERS 8
PAUSE
DAY_OF_WEEK = "Monday" THEN
      RIGHTS SERVER\SYS:PUBLIC
END
```

12. Note that the semicolon (;) is understood to be a REMARK. Statements beginning with a semicolon do not execute. Make sure to replace the SERVER with an actual server name, and to replace the MONDAY with the current day of the week.

13. This script will execute when the TESTUSER user logs in. To log in as TESTUSER, right-click the Network Neighborhood icon and select NetWare Login. Type in the name **TESTUSER** and click OK. If the TESTUSER is in a different context, then put in the Fully Distinguished Name: **TESTUSER.OU.O**.

14. The results should resemble Figure 7-8.

15. The error was a result of the SET USER=%LOGIN_NAME command not having the appropriate quotation marks. Log in as an administration-level user, run NetWare administrator, double-click the TEST profile, and change the command to **SET USER="%LOGIN_NAME"** Also move the PAUSE statement to below the END statement. Click OK to save the changes.

16. Follow Step 13 again to log in to the network as TESTUSER. The results will be similar to Figure 7-9.

17. The first error is due to the fact that there is no IF command logic applied. Change that line to **IF DAY_OF_WEEK="Monday" THEN**.

18. The second error is due to the fact that the LOGOUT command is an external DOS command and requires the pound sign (#) in front of it. Change that line to **#LOGOUT**. To prevent the script from pausing further, delete the PAUSE line.

FIGURE 7-8

Login script results with first error

FIGURE 7-9

Login script results with final errors

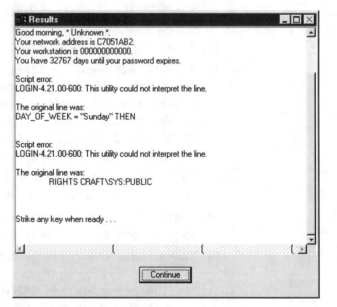

19. Test the script again, following the login procedures in Step 13. There should be no further errors, and a DOS window should pop up displaying the user's rights to the SYS:PUBLIC directory.

CERTIFICATION OBJECTIVE 7.04

Login Scripts and the GUI Login Utility

GUI login utility script variables are available to use with a login script. Older versions of NetWare assumed that a DOS client would be used, with a text-based login script. This enabled the user to execute the login command from a prompt and follow it with variables, such as LOGIN BLDG1 FLOOR3. The login script would interpret the BLDG1 and FLOOR3 expressions as the %2 and %3 variables, respectively, in the script. Then, assuming that the script was set up to capture printers and map drives based on the building and floor, these variables would set that user's location environment accordingly.

DOS clients are becoming more rare. Most network clients, such as Microsoft Windows 95/98 or Microsoft Windows NT 4, utilize a GUI login. The difficulty with the GUI login utility is that the login command is not invoked at the command line. In order to use variables, the login script utility requires a place to put them. It is prompted from the Variables button on the Script tab of the login utility, shown in Figure 7-10.

As seen in Exercise 7-2, the execution of an external DOS command from a GUI login utility will bring up a DOS window. If multiple external DOS commands must be executed, they will each bring up their own DOS window. In order to execute multiple external DOS commands in a single window, the administrator must create a batch file and execute the batch file from the login script.

When the FIRE PHASERS command executes for the GUI login utility, it does not execute the machine beep. Instead, it executes a PHASERS.WAV file. If another sound file is desired, the PHASERS.WAV file should be replaced on the network client workstation.

FIGURE 7-10

Location of variables for
GUI login utility

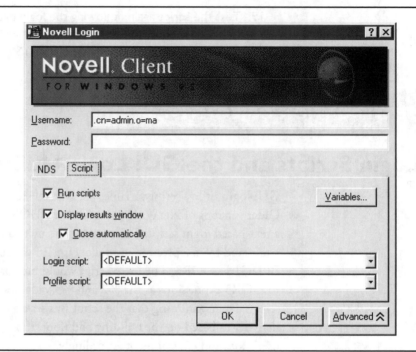

CERTIFICATION SUMMARY

There are four types of login scripts: container scripts, profile scripts, user scripts, and the default login script. The container script of the user's parent container executes first, if it exists; the profile script executes next, if it exists; the user login script executes next, if it exists; and, finally, if there is no user script, the default login script executes. The administrator can disable the default login script by using the NO_DEFAULT statement in a container or profile script that executes before the default login script normally would execute.

The container script is written within the Login Script property of a container, either an organization or an organizational unit. The profile script is written within the Login Script property of a Profile object. A profile script is assigned to a user in the Profile Script property of the Login Script property page of a User object. The user login script is on that same property page. The default login script is compiled within the login executable.

Login scripts use several variables, and can even use some NDS properties in order to make the scripts flexible and efficient. The login scripting language uses a few commands, and can execute external DOS commands by using the pound sign (#) in front of the command within the script.

Using the INCLUDE statement, a login script system can be designed for an enterprise network. The INCLUDE statement will run another container object's login script, effectively cascading from one to another.

It is best to take care in creating new login scripts. If possible, use a test user and a profile script so that other users are not affected by the new commands. The PAUSE command is useful for stopping the login script between new commands in order to view the errors that may be occurring.

The GUI login utility executes login scripts within a window, which is very different from the way a text-based DOS client might execute a login script. Aside from DOS commands executing external DOS windows, the GUI login utility uses a different way of executing login script variables.

 # TWO-MINUTE DRILL

- ❑ NetWare 5 offers a single login to the network through Novell Directory Services. This single login enables authentication for access to any NetWare 5 server, printers, and other network resources.

- ❑ Login scripts can be used to attach to network resources, set workstation environment variables, display messages, and execute applications.

- ❑ Several types of login scripts can execute when logging in to Novell Directory Services. The login script order of execution is
  1. Container script that contains the User object (if it exists)
  2. Profile script (if it exists).
  3. User script (if it exists) or default script (if user script does not exist).

❑ The Container Script is a property of the container object. Both the Organization and the Organizational Unit objects have a Login Script property. These are all container scripts. A container script executes for a user who is a child object of that container object.

❑ The profile script can be used to set environment variables, map drives, and execute commands for multiple end users. The Profile Script is a property of the Profile object. A location-specific script is useful for grouping users based on their physical location in the enterprise.

❑ The profile script also allows an administrator to create a script that can be used by several users in any context of the tree. Whenever a change is needed, the profile script needs to be changed only once.

❑ A user Login Script is a property of the User object in Novell Directory Services. It executes for the individual User object, and never for any other user.

❑ When designing an enterprise network login system, most network designers choose not to include user login scripts because they are difficult to maintain for a growing network. Each user is given access to his or her own user Login Script property. The default property rights for the user's own Login Script property in Novell Directory Services are Read and Write.

❑ NetWare includes many login identifier variables for customizing a login script. Administrators use the login identifier variables in order to use a standard login script for multiple users. Property values of NDS objects can be used as variables in login scripts. However, not all properties are supported.

❑ NetWare login scripting supports commands that can be used on a command line. One of the most common is MAP, which is used to connect network drives. The login script actually uses an internal version of MAP.

❑ One way to scale a login script process across an enterprise is to design login scripts to include the scripts within other containers. This is done with an INCLUDE command.

❑ All login scripts use the same scripting language, which makes it easy to transfer the contents of a profile script to a container script, for example.

❑ GUI login utility script variables are available to use with a login script. Older versions of NetWare assumed that a DOS client would be used, with a text-based login script. This enabled the user to execute the login command from a prompt and follow it with variables.

❑ Most network clients, such as Microsoft Windows 95/98 or Microsoft Windows NT 4, utilize a GUI login. The difficulty with the GUI login utility is that the login command is not invoked at the command line. In order to use variables, the login script utility requires a place to put them. It is prompted from the Variables button on the Script tab of the login utility.

SELF TEST

The Self-Test questions will help you measure your understanding of the material presented in this chapter. Read all the choices carefully, as there may be more than one correct answer. Select all correct answers for each question.

1. What is the execution order of login scripts?

    A. Profile, Container, User, then Default

    B. Default, Container, Profile, then User

    C. Container, Profile, User or Default

    D. Container or Default, Profile, then User

2. The administrator wrote a login script for the container .ACCT.NY.MA. Will user .JohnR.NY.MA be able to execute this script first?

    A. Yes, container scripts execute first.

    B. No, the User object is in the wrong container.

3. Harold is an administrator who wants to create a script that will execute for users based on their location variable. Which of the following is most appropriate for a location specific script?

    A. Container script

    B. Profile script

    C. User script

    D. Default script

4. Gordon has created a profile script and wants to assign it to all the members of the BOOKING group. How can Gordon assign this profile script?

    A. Gordon can assign the profile to the Group object's parent organizational unit's Login Script property page Profile property.

    B. Gordon can assign the profile to the Group object's Login Script property page Profile property.

    C. Gordon can assign the profile to each user's parent organizational unit's Login Script property page Profile property.

    D. Gordon can assign the profile to each user's Login Script property page Profile property.

5. Why are user login scripts difficult to maintain?

    A. Because there can be multiple scripts requiring changes when network resources change.

    B. Because they may not execute if the default script is present.

    C. Because the user will not execute the same commands as the rest of the users in the same container object.

    D. They are not difficult to maintain.

6. Jack has decided to use both a container login script and the default login script for his login script system. In some containers, he decides to change the default script because those commands execute after the container script. How can Jack change the default script?

    A. By editing the login script properties of the default profile script.

    B. By editing the login script properties of the [root].

    C. By editing the login script properties of the Organization object.

    D. He cannot change the default script.

7. If the administrator wanted to display the context that the User object belongs to, which login script variable can be used?

    A. %LOGIN_CONTEXT

    B. CONTEXT

    C. %REQUESTER_CONTEXT

    D. %CN

8. Linda is the new network administrator for a NetWare 5 network. In reviewing the login scripts, she finds that each user has a login script mapped within his or her own user login script, and that is the user script's only command. How can Linda streamline this login script system?

    A. She can use a profile script instead.

    B. She can use the %HOME_ DIRECTORY variable in the container script instead.

    C. She can use the %OS variable in the container script instead.

    D. She cannot streamline it any further.

9. Which of the following commands will hide drive mappings as they execute?

    A. MAP DISPLAY ON

    B. MAP ERRORS ON

    C. MAP DISPLAY OFF

    D. MAP ERRORS OFF

10. Which of the following characters is required for an external DOS command to be executed from a login script?

    A. *

    B. ;

    C. #

    D. _

11. Which of the following login script commands will display a text file in raw format?

    A. ECHO

    B. FDISPLAY

    C. DISPLAY

    D. WRITE

12. Which command will execute the MA organization login script after another login script?

    A. INCLUDE .MA

    B. INCLUDE .LOGIN.MA

    C. INCLUDE LOGINSCRIPT.MA

    D. INCLUDE %LOGIN_SCRIPT.MA

13. Why should an administrator use a profile script to test a login script?

A. Because a profile script is automatically global.

B. Because it prevents users from accidentally running an unproven script.

C. Because the default script will nullify a container test script.

D. The administrator should not use the profile script to test.

14. After upgrading all the DOS clients using NETX and VLMs to Windows 98 and the NetWare Client 32, George realized that his mobile clients could no longer execute the LOGIN REMOTE command to avoid the network printer capture and unnecessary drive map commands. How can George use this method with the GUI login utility?

A. He cannot. Such variables are not supported.

B. He can teach users to change the context in the login screen.

C. He can teach users to change the variables from the Variables button on the Script tab.

15. Can you change the beeping sound that the FIRE PHASERS command makes for Windows 95 users using the NetWare Client 32?

A. No, it is from the internal machine components.

B. Yes. It can be changed by using a different PHASERS.WAV file.

8

Remote Management of Workstations (NEBO)

CERTIFICATION OBJECTIVES

8.01   Introduction to the Z.E.N.works
        Desktop Management Utilities

8.02   Remote Control Access
        Utilities (NEBO)

8.03   Creating Workstation Objects

8.04   Using Login Scripts to Register
        Workstations in Novell
        Directory Services

8.05   Configuring Workstations for
        Remote Control Access

8.06   Using the Help Request Application
        to Log Workstation Problems

8.07   Synchronizing a Workstation with Its
        NDS Object

Network administrators have long been asking for management utilities that make network management easier. Networks have gotten larger, and computing needs have become more complex with changes in technology. Novell has created Z.E.N.works, or Zero Effort Networks, in response to this business requirement.

Introduction to the Z.E.N.works Desktop Management Utilities

Z.E.N.works is a utility set that automates installing and managing network clients. Z.E.N.works is a time saver for administrators, reducing the cost of ownership for enterprise networked workstations. For example, when a change needs to be replicated to 10,000 client workstations that would take the administrator ten minutes at each workstation, it would take several months to perform. An automating utility such as Z.E.N.works can push many types of workstation changes to the desktop without the administrator personally visiting each desk.

Z.E.N.works Features

The main purpose of Z.E.N.works is to reduce the cost involved with managing workstations on a network. There are several interrelated processes that it uses to achieve this purpose:

- Software management and distribution
- Desktop management and maintenance, using remote control
- Help desk application

Z.E.N.works is enabled for Novell Directory Services; in fact, much of it is integrated within NDS and managed using the NetWare Administrator. This adds a level of security to remote control features and software management and distribution.

NDS provides a framework of hierarchical relationships for network resources. Users are granted access to resources through their explicit rights and those granted from group memberships, security equivalence, and inheritance. Z.E.N.works builds on this relationship framework, adding

- Application access information
- Printer access information
- Help Desk information
- Windows PC configuration
- Remote access security applied to a workstation

Z.E.N.works adds workstation objects to NDS, and depends on them for features such as remote control. The workstation object is independent of the user who logs in at it. The workstation object can assist with

- Inventorying network hardware
- Applying policies to the workstation operating system
- Setting the preferred tree and context on the workstation

Installing Z.E.N.works

Z.E.N.works is included with NetWare 5 on the NetWare 5 installation CD. The version of Z.E.N.works that comes with the NetWare 5 CD is the Z.E.N.works Starter Kit, a cut-down version of the fully featured Z.E.N.works, which is a separate purchase item in the current market release version. The Z.E.N.works client is located in the directory D:\PRODUCTS\ZENWORKS, if D: is the letter indicating the CD-ROM drive.

EXERCISE 8-1

Installing Z.E.N.works

1. Place the NetWare 5 installation CD in the CD-ROM drive.

2. Choose Start | Run, type **D:\PRODUCTS\ZENWORKS\SETUP.EXE**, and press ENTER (or replace D: with the drive letter that the CD-ROM drive uses).

3. The initial screen warns you to close all programs that may be running from the SYS:PUBLIC directory, and any Windows programs as well. Verify that these programs are closed, and click Next.

4. Click Yes to accept the license agreement.

5. There are three setup types presented next, as shown in Figure 8-1: Typical, Compact, and Custom. Select Custom and click Next.

6. The next screen shows the options that can be installed. Accept the default options, as displayed in Figure 8-2.

on the
Job

To get the latest network client that is installed with NetWare 5, use the option during Z.E.N.works installation to copy clients to the network.

7. The next screen shows the NetWare operating system options that Z.E.N.works can install (see Figure 8-3). Again, accept the defaults.

FIGURE 8-1

Z.E.N.works setup options

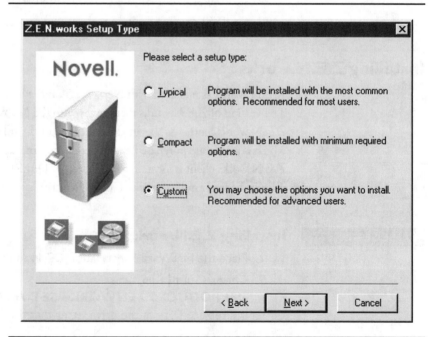

FIGURE 8-2

Z.E.N.works
 installation options

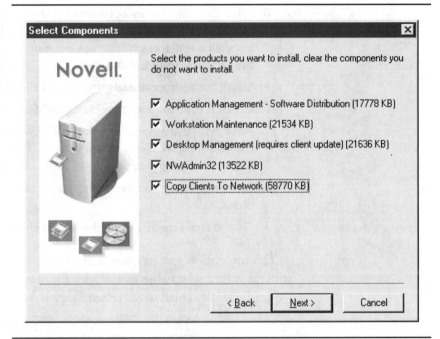

FIGURE 8-3

NetWare operating system
options

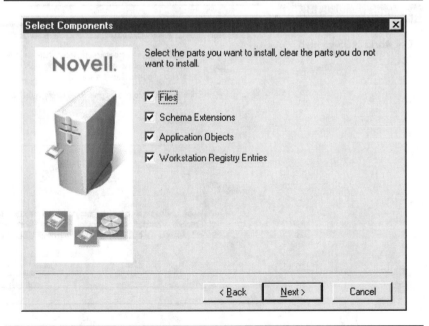

8. After this, Z.E.N.works prompts for the servers to install. These are listed in the format TREE/SERVER, so that Z.E.N.works can be installed to different NDS trees in a multitree environment. Select the server(s) to install and click Next.

9. Select the appropriate language(s) and click Next.

10. Click Next at the summary dialog and files will start copying.

11. After files have stopped copying, Z.E.N.works presents a screen like the one in Figure 8-4 requesting the context(s) in which to grant users the appropriate rights. Accept the default and click OK.

12. Next, the dialog acknowledging that rights were assigned pops up; click OK.

13. On the final screen, accept the default check boxes and click Finish.

This installation process extends the schema of the selected NDS tree(s) with the Z.E.N.works objects, and adds the functionality to it. All the required files are copied to the selected server(s).

FIGURE 8-4

Z.E.N.works NDS-granted rights

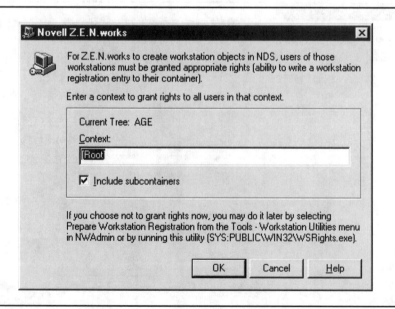

Remote Control Access Utilities (NEBO)

When choosing a remote control management package, consider three issues:

- **Security**   Whether users must be authorized before accessing a remote workstation

- **Bandwidth**   Whether the remote control application causes traffic problems

- **Ease of use**   Whether it is easy to navigate the remote control application

Because Z.E.N.works uses NDS, it is secured through login authentication. Remote control works only if the user has been granted appropriate object rights to the workstation object. This answers the security issue.

Regarding the issue of bandwidth, there is no excess traffic causing bandwidth problems because a remote control agent is not required to advertise constantly. Instead, the IP and IPX addresses of the workstation are stored in NDS. When remote control is initiated, it uses this information instead. Z.E.N.works is fairly easy to use. It uses the NetWare Administrator as the single point for network management. In order to execute remote control, the authorized user simply navigates the NDS tree to the appropriate workstation object, accesses the workstation object details, and clicks Remote Control.

Creating Workstation Objects

Workstation objects are required for Z.E.N.works to perform workstation management and remote control. The workstation objects are created automatically after the following steps are executed:

1. Users are granted the Write right to the WM:Registered Workstation attribute of the parent container object for the workstation. This can be executed during Z.E.N.works installation (see Exercise 8-1, Step 11). It can also be executed from within the NetWare Administrator by choosing Tools | Workstation Utilities to view the pop-up submenu, and choosing the Prepare Workstation Registration utility shown in Figure 8-5.

2. Alternatively, an administrator can execute the WSRIGHTS.EXE application from SYS:PUBLIC.

3. Workstations register with NDS. This is done with the Workstation Registration program executed at the workstation. The executable is WSREG32.EXE for Windows 95/98 or NT workstations, WSREG16.EXE for Windows 3.1x, and it can be pushed to workstations through a login script. The Workstation Registration application will also appear in the NetWare Application Launcher (NAL) window (see Figure 8-6). NAL is executed from the SYS:PUBLIC directory. The NAL executable is NAL.EXE. The registration creates a workstation entry in the container object's Workstation Registration page where the user's User object exists.

FIGURE 8-5

Prepare Workstation
Registration dialog box

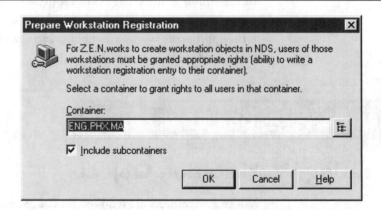

FIGURE 8-6 Workstation registration application in NAL

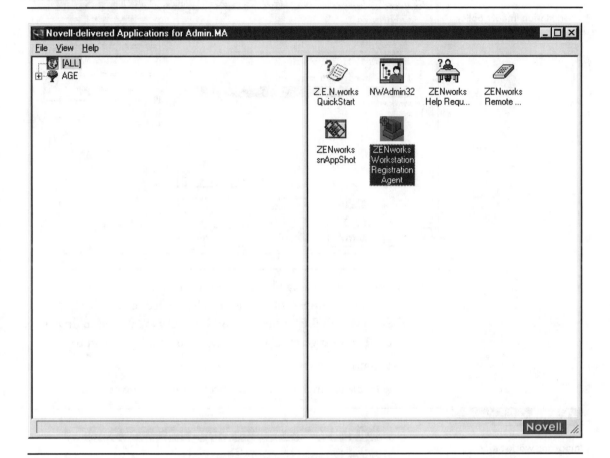

4. Workstations are imported into NDS as objects. The workstation import policy must be created and associated with the affected users. This is done by creating a policy package for users and then editing the details of the workstation import policy (see Figure 8-7). The details include the name format that the workstations will have when they are finally imported into NDS.

5. The administrator must import the workstations (see Figure 8-8) using NetWare Administrator. Choose Tools | Import Workstations.

FIGURE 8-7

Workstation import policy
in user policy package

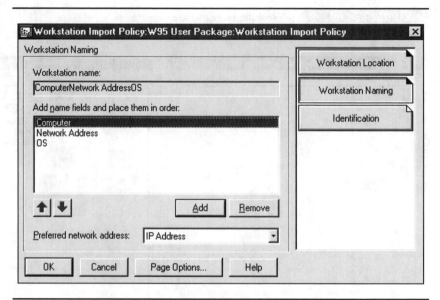

6. Automatic imports can be scheduled using the Application Launcher. An Application object can be created to launch theWSIMPORT.EXE file. If SYS:PUBLIC was mapped to drive F:, and the context was OU.OU.O, the command line would be

```
F:\PUBLIC\WSIMPORT.EXE " OU.OU.O" /s-
```

The /s- switch includes all the subcontainers for the context.

FIGURE 8-8

Importing workstations

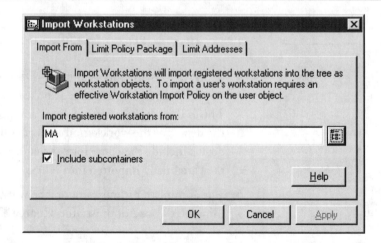

7. The import process adds a Distinguished Name to the workstation entry in the container object; then adds that workstation object to the NDS tree. Each workstation name is in the same format that the workstation import policy dictates. This workstation import policy is the one created for the user policy package associated with the user who first ran the workstation registration package.

8. After the workstation entry has been imported to a workstation object in NDS, the workstation registration program must be run a second time. This time, the workstation registration program finds the object's Distinguished Name and stores it locally on the workstation. Finally, it updates the workstation object so that the registration time, network address, last server, and last user are captured, and this information is captured *each time* the workstation runs the registration program.

9. Verification that the workstation registration was successful is done by viewing the C:\WSREG32.LOG on Windows 95/98 or Windows NT, and the C:\WSREG16.LOG on DOS or Windows 3.1*x*. It is created on each workstation that has been registered. Here is an example of this verification message:

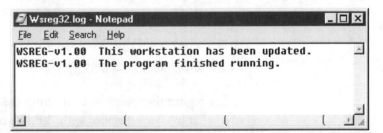

QUESTIONS AND ANSWERS

Heather has installed Z.E.N.works to a server located in .OU=ACCT.OU=LON.O=MA. When she was prompted for the container, she selected that server's container; then completed the installation. When Heather added the WSREG32.EXE file to the login script, her end users in the .OU=ENG.OU=LON.O=MA container complained that they were receiving errors during login. Why?

Heather did not run the WSRIGHTS.EXE file or the Prepare Workstation Registration utility from NetWare Administrator on the .ENG.LON.MA context.

CERTIFICATION OBJECTIVE 8.04

Using Login Scripts to Register Workstations in Novell Directory Services

The workstation must register to capture the following information:

- Registration time
- Network address
- Last server
- Last user

This demonstrates the need to run the registration program every time a user logs in to the network. NetWare 5 offers the ability to run the registration program from a login script to automate this process.

The logic of the login script must recognize the type of workstation operating system and run the correct registration program. The registration programs are

- Windows NT or Windows 95/98—WSREG32.EXE
- Windows 3.1x—WSREG16.EXE

The registration program is run from the SYS:PUBLIC directory of a server that has been installed with Z.E.N.works. It works in conjunction with the WSREG32.DLL file in the WINDOWS\SYSTEM32 directory (or WINDOWS\SYSTEM directory).

The following login script commands will apply this logic:

```
********************************
*Workstation Registration Login Script *
********************************
MAP DISPLAY OFF
MAP ERRORS OFF
MAP F:=SERVER\SYS:PUBLIC
```

```
IF " %PLATFORM" =" W95" THEN BEGIN
    #F:\PUBLIC\WSREG32.EXE
END
IF " %PLATFORM" =" WNT" THEN BEGIN
    #F:\PUBLIC\WSREG32.EXE
END
IF " %PLATFORM"=" WIN" THEN BEGIN
    #F:\PUBLIC\WSREG16.EXE
END
IF " %PLATFORM" =" DOS" THEN BEGIN
    #F:\PUBLIC\WSREG16.EXE
END
```

CERTIFICATION OBJECTIVE 8.05

Configuring Workstations for Remote Control Access

In order to control a workstation remotely, the administrator must enable the Remote Control Agent on the workstation. Table 8-1 lists the Remote Control Agents for each platform.

In addition to these launch methods, installing the new client for NetWare 5 that is included with Z.E.N.works will copy the Remote Control Agent (shown here) to the workstation, add it to the startup folder, and run it automatically for Windows 95.

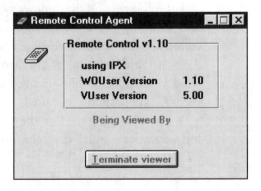

TABLE 8-1 Remote Control Agents	Operating System	Agent Type	Launch Method
	Windows 3.1	Application SYS:PUBLIC\WUSER.EXE	NetWare Application Launcher Scheduled action Login script Manually run
	Windows 95	Application SYS:PUBLIC\WUSER.EXE	NetWare Application Launcher Scheduled action Login script Run manually
	Windows 98	Application SYS:PUBLIC\WUSER.EXE	NetWare Application Launcher Scheduled action Login script Run manually
	Windows NT 4	Service SYS:PUBLIC\NTSTACFG.EXE	Installed on the workstation and run automatically as an NT service

exam
Match

The NTASCFG.EXE file is the installation file for the Novell WUser Service in NT. It can be found in the NT Control Panel Services icon, and runs at the operating system initialization.

For full-screen DOS windows to be remote-controlled on Windows 3.1 and Windows 95 workstations, the administrator must install a driver in addition to the standard Remote Control Agent. If the Remote Control Agent is initialized using NAL, then the driver enabling full-screen DOS window remote control is installed automatically. The difficulty occurs if the NAL application is not used.

When initializing the Remote Control Agent from another method, login script or manual, the following steps will enable full-screen DOS window remote control:

1. Copy SYS:PUBLIC\VUSER.386 and SYS:PUBLIC\VUSER98.386 to the Windows system directory on the workstation.

2. Choose Start | Run and type **NOTEPAD C:\WINDOWS\SYSTEM.INI**. Locate the [386Enh] section and add the following line (substitute the appropriate windows system directory path, if different): **device=c:\windows\system\vuser.386**

For Windows NT, the Remote Control Agent is not explicitly run. It is a service that is installed and runs whenever Windows NT runs. As a service, the NT Workstation can be remotely controlled as soon as the service initializes. The Remote Control Agent installation program is SYS:PUBLIC\NTSACFG.EXE. This program registers the Novell WUser Agent service in Windows NT, and can subsequently be found in the Start | Settings | Control Panel | Services icon.

The other portion of enabling remote control is the creation and application of a remote control policy. This is done within the NDS User Policy Package associated with the users and types of workstations that they use.

<table>
<tr><td>EXERCISE 8-2</td></tr>
</table>

Remote Control Policy

1. If drive F: is not mapped to volume SYS:, then right-click the Network Neighborhood icon, select Novell Map Network Drive, select drive F: under Device, type **\\SERVERNAME\SYS** in the Path area, and then click Map.

2. Choose Start | Run and type **F:\PUBLIC\NAL**.

3. In the Application Launcher window, select NWAdmin32 and double-click it to launch the NetWare Administrator.

4. Navigate the tree to the desired context and highlight the Organizational Unit.

5. Choose Object | Create. Alternatively, press the INSERT key.

6. From the Object Creation dialog box, select Policy Package (this is a new object added to the schema with the installation of Z.E.N.works).

7. The next dialog box, shown here, prompts you to select the type of policy package to create. Select a user policy package—either Win31, Win95, or WinNT. Make sure to check the Define Additional Properties box.

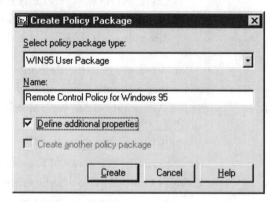

8. Click the Create button.

9. The details for a user policy package will appear, as shown in Figure 8-9.

10. Check the Remote Control Policy box; then click the Details button. The dialog box shown in Figure 8-10 will appear.

11. If the default details are acceptable, simply click Cancel. Otherwise, check or uncheck the boxes until the correct remote control features are selected; then click OK.

12. You will be returned to the user policy package details window. Select the Associations button.

13. Click the Add button and add the appropriate users to be associated with this user policy package.

14. Click OK.

15. The workstation remote control policy must also be created and associated with a workstation in order to enable remote control. To create the workstation policy, choose Object | Create.

16. From the Object Creation dialog box, select policy package, and then select the appropriate type of workstation package: Win31, Win95, or WinNT. Make sure to check the Define Additional Properties box and click Create.

FIGURE 8-9

User policy package details

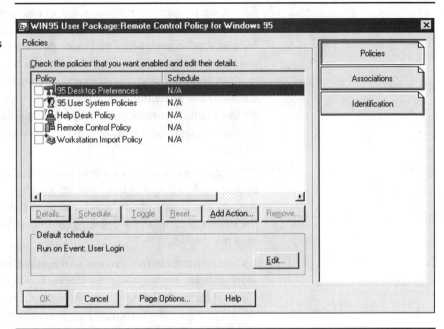

FIGURE 8-10

Remote Control
Policy details

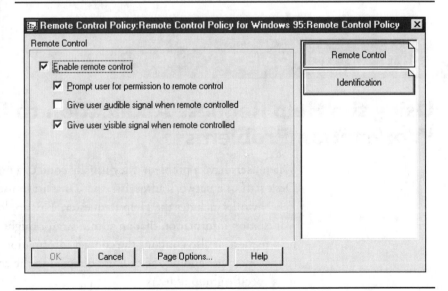

17. Check the box for the Remote Control Policy, as shown in Figure 8-11. Click the Details button and enable the correct remote control policy for that workstation. Note that these details are identical to those in the User package remote control policy. Also, these policies do not need to be identical to the user remote control policies. NDS will automatically select the most restrictive policies and enable them. So, if a user remote control policy requires notification but a workstation remote control policy does not, the user will be notified to adhere to security.

18. After applying the remote control policy details, click OK. You will be returned to the workstation policy package details. Click the Associations button. Add the workstations that are associated to the users selected for the previous user policy package. Click OK to save the changes.

19. To use remote control on one of the associated user's workstations, double-click the workstation and click the Remote Control button to bring up the Remote Control property page, shown in Figure 8-12. (Note: This is another extension to the schema that Z.E.N.works brings to NDS.)

20. Click the Remote Control button to initiate remote control of the workstation.

CERTIFICATION OBJECTIVE 8.06

Using the Help Request Application to Log Workstation Problems

When users have a problem, they usually contact a member of the Help Desk staff or a network administrator. To assist in users' requests for help, Z.E.N.works includes the Help Requester. This application contains the workstation information that an administrator might need for logging the help request. It also contains the contact information for the administrator, so that messages and phone calls are directed to the correct administrator for a specific group of users.

The Help Request application is automatically added to the NetWare Application Launcher (NAL) as an object. All NAL applications are objects

FIGURE 8-11

Workstation policy package
for remote control

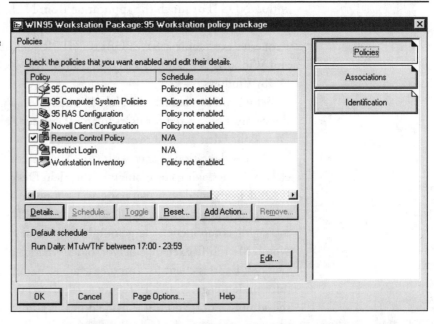

FIGURE 8-12

Using remote control on
a workstation

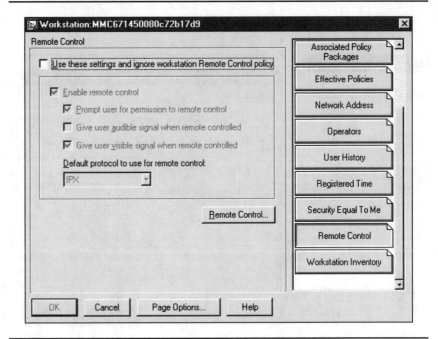

within NDS. To launch the application from NAL, the users must be granted the appropriate object rights to the application. The actual Help Requester executable is SYS:PUBLIC\HLPREQ32.EXE for Windows 95 and Windows NT, and SYS:PUBLIC\HLPREQ16.EXE for DOS\Windows 3.1*x*.

Before you can launch the Help Requester, an appropriate Help Desk Policy must be created for users in an NDS User Policy Package. The Help Desk Policy details are shown in Figure 8-13.

The configuration properties for the Help Desk Policy enable the electronic messaging component of the Help Desk Request. The Trouble ticket delivery mode has two options: Groupwise 5, which is a Novell messaging and groupware application, and MAPI, which is a standard messaging component. A large number of e-mail systems use MAPI: Lotus Notes, Microsoft Exchange Server, older versions of GroupWise, and Outlook Express client for Internet Mail, to name just a few. The information page, shown in Figure 8-14, shows the contact information for the administrator, and this e-mail address is automatically used for the messages sent from the Help Requester application.

FIGURE 8-13

Help Desk Policy details

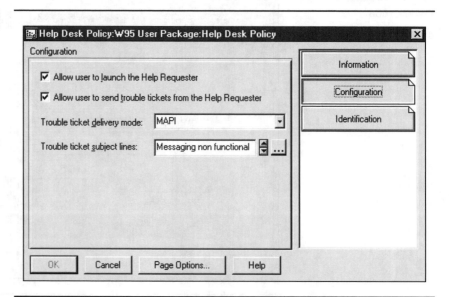

FIGURE 8-14

Help desk information page

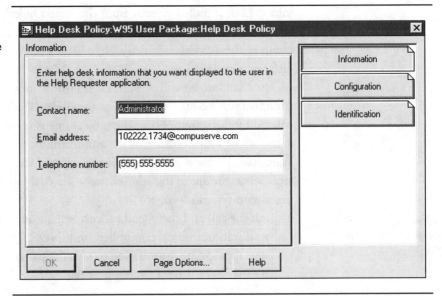

From the Help Requester application, the user can click the Call or Mail button to request help. The Call button will display a dialog box with the contact information for the Administrator (see Figure 8-15). This

FIGURE 8-15

Call for Help dialog box

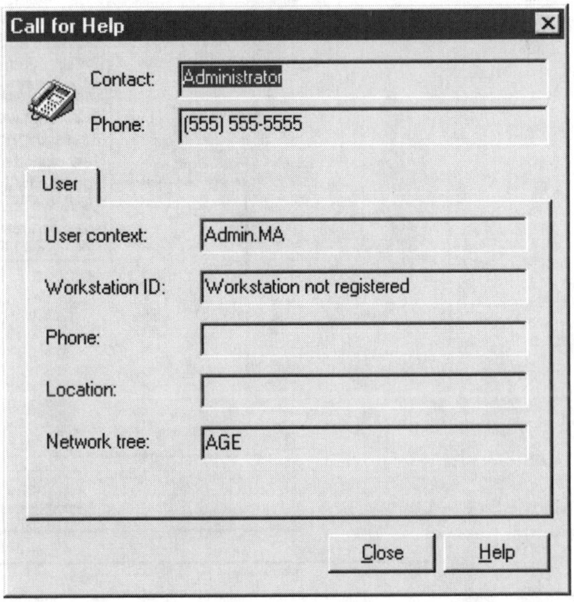

information is pulled directly from the Help Desk Policy. Since there can be multiple help desk policies assigned to different administrators, each group of users associated with a Help Desk Policy can be administered by a different person.

The Mail button will prompt an electronic message to be sent to the administrator's e-mail address. The user's e-mail address is automatically entered by the system. Next, the subject line is selected from a drop-down menu of the subject lines that the administrator added to the Help Desk Policy (see Figure 8-16). This practice automatically organizes the help requests according to the administrator's needs. Finally, there is space for the user to type a message.

Both the call and the e-mail address will automatically include the user and workstation information pulled from NDS. This allows the user to have the appropriate information to give the person at the Help Desk, which expedites the help request process.

FIGURE 8-16

Mail for Help dialog box, with predetermined subject lines

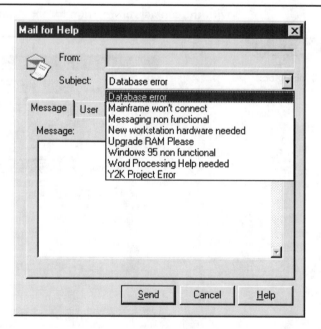

FIGURE 8-17

Previous help requests are maintained by the Help Requester

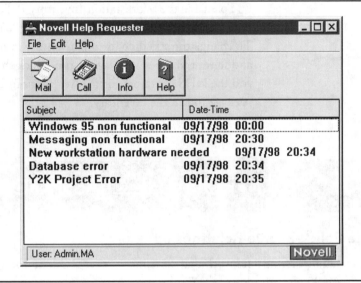

The Help Requester maintains a list of previously logged help requests, as shown in Figure 8-17. The end user can double-click the line of a previous request and view the information that was logged for that request.

CERTIFICATION OBJECTIVE 8.07

Synchronizing a Workstation with Its NDS Object

Z.E.N.works brings a Workstation Inventory Policy to NDS. This policy polls the workstation for information and stores it within the workstation object, which integrates it with the workstation import policy. Once a workstation has been imported into NDS, each time the Workstation Registration program runs, the workstation will provide NDS with updated Workstation Inventory information. This synchronization between the workstation and NDS objects is accomplished by the Workstation Registration application.

To enable the Workstation Inventory Policy, open the Workstation Policy package. Check the box next to the Workstation Inventory Policy. To change the schedule for the inventory event, click the schedule button and select the times and days to run. Click the Associations page button and add the NDS container for the workstations in order to finalize the policy package to run the inventory.

FROM THE CLASSROOM

The Policy-Profile Relationship

When administering a network that contains Windows 95 and Windows NT Workstation clients, the terms "policies" and "profiles" come up often, along with a question or dilemma over which to use. Understanding what each does will make the choice easier. In the simplest terms, profiles determine what a user sees on a computer's desktop: shortcuts to executables, "Start Menu" shortcuts, wall-paper, and other items. A *profile*—the desktop's "appearance"—can be modified while the user's session is in effect, although whether that same desktop appears when the same user's next session starts depends on whether the administrator enabled the profile as mandatory or roaming. Nevertheless, the user is able to change the desktop's appearance, pretty much at will, during a given session. A policy can be thought of as the parameters, or limits put on a user, or a specific machine, how the registry settings can be changed, including a currently loaded profile. Think of profiles as changes made to the registry and policies as restrictions placed on a user's or machine's ability to access and use the tools (Control Panel) used to modify the system registry. Z.E.N.works offers the administrator another tool to manage and administer policies via NDS.

—By Dan Cheung, CNI, MCNE, MCT

CERTIFICATION SUMMARY

Z.E.N.works enables centralized administration of workstations and their users. This includes the ability to manage and distribute software, manage desktops, remote control workstations, and enable help desk support for end users.

Z.E.N.works Starter Kit is included with NetWare 5 and can be installed from the NetWare 5 CD-ROM. When Z.E.N.works is installed, it is installed from a workstation onto a server. It extends the schema of NDS and adds new objects, which are the policy packages and the workstation objects through which Z.E.N.works manages the network.

One of the biggest benefits of Z.E.N.works is the ability to remote control workstations. Using remote control with Z.E.N.works is very secure, due to the use of NDS secured objects. A user must be granted access to a workstation object in the NDS tree in order to take remote control of the workstation. Z.E.N.works also avoids excess bandwidth consumption through remote control. Instead of using an advertising protocol on the network for the remote control agent, Z.E.N.works relies on the workstation object's network address for locating the workstation.

In order to take remote control of a workstation, it first must be created as a workstation object in NDS, which is a five-step process:

1. The users must be granted access to the registered objects. This is done through the NetWare Administrator using the Prepare Workstation Registration option, or the WSRIGHTS.EXE executable can be run from SYS:PUBLIC.

2. The workstations must then register with NDS. This is done through the Workstation Registration application available in NAL, or it can be run from the WSREG32.EXE or WSREG16.EXE files run from SYS:PUBLIC.

3. The workstations must then be imported into NDS using the NetWare Administrator to create a Workstation Import Policy and associate it to users, and then running the Tools | Import Workstations utility. The import can be done using the WSIMPORT.EXE file in SYS:PUBLIC.

4. The workstations must then register with NDS a second time, and continue to run each time the workstation logs in. This can be done through a login script, utilizing a line such as IF %PLATFORM = "WIN95" THEN WSREG32.EXE END to run the command, or it can be launched from NAL or manually executed.

5. To be successful, the workstation import must be verified. Each workstation has a log written to the root of C: called WSREG32.LOG or WSREG16.LOG, which are text files viewable in Notepad.

To configure a workstation for remote control, both NDS and the workstation must be involved. In NDS, the remote control policy must be created for both a workstation and for a user policy package. Then each of the workstation policies and the user policy must be associated to the respective workstations and users. The security restrictions are such that if a security restriction is higher on either the workstation or the User object in NDS, then the higher level of security is applied to the remote control.

The second part of enabling remote control is to run the Remote Control Agent on the workstation. For NT workstations, this is a service called NTASCFG.EXE. For Windows 3.x and Windows 95/98, the application is WUSER.EXE.

To remotely control a workstation, locate the workstation object in NDS and view its details. Click the Remote Control page button and then click the Remote Control button.

Z.E.N.works includes a Help Requester application that allows users to contact the appropriate administrators for help. This is enabled using a Help Desk policy. The Help Requester application is installed as an object in NDS and appears in the NetWare Application Launcher window. The Help Requester can initiate an e-mail to the administrator with preconfigured subjects, or it can give the end user the information needed to access the administrator via phone.

The workstation must be synchronized with its NDS object in order for the Z.E.N.works remote control policy to work. The workstation inventory policy also requires synchronization. This synchronization is established by the WSREG32.EXE or WSREG16.EXE executables, and it can be launched from the NAL window.

TWO-MINUTE DRILL

❑ Z.E.N.works is a utility set that automates installing and managing network clients. Z.E.N.works is a time saver for administrators, reducing the cost of ownership for enterprise networked workstations.

❑ Z.E.N.works uses several interrelated processes to reduce the cost involved with managing workstations. They are software management and distribution, remote-control desktop management and maintenance, and a Help Desk application.

❑ Z.E.N.works is enabled for Novell Directory Services. Much of it is integrated within NDS and managed using the NetWare Administrator.

❑ Z.E.N.works builds on the NDS hierarchical relationship framework by adding application access information, printer access information, Help Desk information, Windows PC configuration, and Remote access security applied to workstations.

❑ The Z.E.N.works Starter Kit is included on the NetWare 5 installation CD. Z.E.N.works Starter Kit is a cut-down version of the fully featured Z.E.N.works. The Z.E.N.works client is located in the directory D:\PRODUCTS\ZENWORKS, if D: is the letter indicating the CD-ROM drive.

❑ Workstation objects are required for Z.E.N.works to perform workstation management and remote control.

❑ The workstation must register to capture registration time, network address, last server, and last user information, requiring the registration program to run every time a user logs into the network. NetWare 5 offers the ability to run the registration program from a login script to automate this process.

❑ The logic of the login script must recognize the type of workstation operating system and run the correct registration program, either WSREG32.EXE for Windows NT or Windows 95/98, or WSREG16.EXE for Windows 3.1x.

❑ In order to control a workstation remotely, the administrator must enable the Remote Control Agent on the workstation. Installing the new client for NetWare 5 that is included with Z.E.N.works will copy the Remote Control Agent to the workstation, add it to the startup folder, and run it automatically for Windows 95.

❑ For full-screen DOS windows to be remote-controlled on Windows 3.1 and Windows 95 workstations, the administrator must install a driver in addition to the standard Remote Control Agent. If the Remote Control Agent is initialized using NAL, then the driver enabling full-screen DOS window remote control is installed automatically. The difficulty occurs if the NAL application is not used.

❑ Z.E.N.works includes the Help Requester, an application that contains the workstation information that an administrator might need for logging the help request. It also contains the contact information for the administrator, so that messages and phone calls are directed to the correct administrator for a specific group of users.

❑ Z.E.N.works brings a Workstation Inventory Policy to NDS. This policy polls the workstation for information and stores it within the workstation object, which integrates it with the workstation import policy. Once a workstation has been imported into NDS, each time the Workstation Registration program runs, the workstation will provide NDS with updated Workstation Inventory information.

SELF TEST

The following Self-Test questions will help you measure your understanding of the material presented in this chapter. Read all the choices carefully, as there may be more than one correct answer. Choose all correct answers for each question.

1. How does Z.E.N.works manage desktops?

   A. It runs as a special utility installed on each workstation.

   B. It maintains a database of workstation assets that it uses for management.

   C. It integrates with NDS.

   D. It is a server-based messaging application for help desk requests.

2. Which of the following is not a feature of Z.E.N.works?

   A. Application access information

   B. Help Desk information

   C. Remote access security applied to a workstation

   D. Teleconference Help Requests

3. Can the schema extensions be avoided in Z.E.N.works?

   A. Yes, the installer can clear this option during installation.

   B. Yes, the administrator can remove the schema extensions through the NetWare Administrator Tools menu.

   C. No, the schema extensions must be installed for Z.E.N.works to function.

4. If there are multiple trees on a network, can Z.E.N.works be installed to more than one of those trees simultaneously with the others?

   A. No, each tree must be installed separately.

   B. No, each server must be installed separately, and each server must exist in only one tree.

   C. Yes, Z.E.N.works can be installed to more than one tree simultaneously.

5. Which of the following are the three main features to consider for remote control software?

   A. Security

   B. Ease of use

   C. Protocols used

   D. Bandwidth

6. Why does Z.E.N.works not use as much bandwidth as traditional remote control applications?

   A. It compresses data.

   B. It uses NDS so that the agent doesn't advertise.

   C. It encrypts data.

   D. It uses SAP.

7. Which of the following applications grants users the Write right to the WM:Registered Workstation attribute of the container object for the workstations?

A. WSIMPORT.EXE

B. WSREG32.EXE

C. WSRIGHTS.EXE

D. WSREG16.EXE

8. Which of the following applications will register a Windows NT workstation?

A. WSIMPORT.EXE

B. WSREG32.EXE

C. WSRIGHTS.EXE

D. WSREG16.EXE

9. Which of the following steps must be run before importing a workstation?

A. Create a workstation import policy in a workstation policy package.

B. Create a workstation import policy in a container policy package.

C. Create a workstation import policy in a user policy package.

D. No steps are required.

10. Veronica is a network administrator who has just implemented Z.E.N.works on her NetWare 5 network. She has decided to import workstations and has run a test on her own workstation. How can she verify that the workstation was registered successfully?

A. She can check her User object in NDS for past activity.

B. She can check the details of the container object in NDS for past activity.

C. She can run the WSREG32.EXE command.

D. She can check the WSREG32.LOG file on her workstation's C: drive.

11. The following is the installation file for the service for the Remote Control Agent for NT workstations:

A. NTASCFG.EXE

B. WUSER.EXE

C. WSREG32.EXE

D. WSREG16.EXE

12. Where does the Remote Control Policy reside in NDS?

A. The Container Policy Package

B. The User Policy Package

C. The Workstation Policy Package

D. An Application object

13. Do the remote control policies for user policy packages and workstation policy packages have to be identical when a user is using a workstation?

A. Yes, they must be identical.

B. No, they can differ, and the workstation policy overrides that of the user.

C. No, they can differ and the user policy overrides that of the workstation.

D. No, they can differ, and the most restrictive policy options are always in effect.

14. Which of the following is the Help Requester application for Windows 3.1?

A. HLPREQ16.EXE

B. HLPREQ32.EXE

C. WUSER.EXE

D. WSREG16.EXE

15. How does a workstation synchronize with its NDS object?

    A. It uses the workstation registration program each time it logs in.

    B. It uses IPX to synchronize.

    C. It uses NDS to locate the workstation and synchronize.

    D. It uses SAP to synchronize.

9

Configuring
Network
Applications
for Users

CERTIFICATION OBJECTIVES

9.01   Introduction to the NetWare
        Application Launcher (NAL)

9.02   Configuring NDS and the File System
        for NAL

9.03   Launching Network Applications
        with NAL

M anaging applications on an enterprise network can be a difficult business. When it comes to an application upgrade, manually upgrading each workstation requires time for each one; and, as the number of workstations increases, the distribution time for the application increases. Keeping the application installation method and components consistent across large numbers of client workstations is nearly impossible when the installation is manual. When the software manufacturer creates a patch to the software, the administrator must distribute that as well. This leaves the network in various stages of application versions, causing support problems for help desk staff.

Z.E.N.works includes the NetWare Application Launcher (NAL) to address these issues. NAL includes the ability to

- Configure consistent, automatic application installation executables
- Manage upgrades
- Apply NDS security to applications in order to control their distribution

CERTIFICATION OBJECTIVE 9.01

Introduction to the NetWare Application Launcher (NAL)

NAL offers a software delivery process secured by and centrally managed through NDS. The administrator uses NetWare Administrator to create and distribute applications. The end user uses the NetWare Application Launcher to access and execute those applications.

Users find NAL very easy to use. The application does not appear in the NAL window unless the user has been associated to the Application object in NDS, or inherited that association. In addition, only the application icon that is specific to the workstation operating system appears.

For example, if a user moves between a Windows NT workstation and a Windows 3.1 workstation, when he or she uses Windows NT, the applications in NAL will be only those that the administrator has specified

FROM THE CLASSROOM

Networked Applications and Search Drive Mappings

Before NAL was introduced by Novell in NetWare 4.11, network administrators had to worry about running out of search drive mappings and configuring each workstation to properly run applications. Because the number of network search drive mappings is limited to 16, writing login scripts can become complex, if not convoluted, to accommodate the application needs of users. Fortunately, any applications launched through NAL do not require a search drive mapping to the directory containing the executable; and, as a matter of fact, they can be accessed from another server altogether if load balancing or fault tolerance are enabled. NAL has relieved the administrator from being concerned about the limit on network search drive mappings.

—By Dan Cheung, CNI, MCNE, MCT

for distribution to NT workstations. When he or she is using Windows 3.1, the applications in NAL will not include any of the Windows NT–specific applications, but may include other applications that were specified for Windows 3.1. This intelligence prevents users from complaining about an application failure when the application *should have* failed.

Users only have to double-click an icon in the NAL window to launch the application. If the application does not launch, the user can click the File menu and select the Verify option. The Verify option will display any configuration errors with the Application object, as shown here:

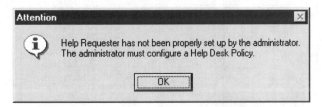

The application icons in the NAL window represent the Application objects in NDS. Each Application object includes information about drive mappings, printer captures, application switches, and so on. The administrator can deliver new applications simply by creating Application objects and configuring them in NetWare Administrator, which continues as the single seat of administration.

The NAL application is SYS:PUBLIC\NAL.EXE. It can be executed as part of the login script. Figure 9-1 displays the NAL window.

NAL Features

NAL features the following capabilities:

- Software distribution
- Application management
- Single seat of administration
- Secured applications

FIGURE 9-1

NAL window

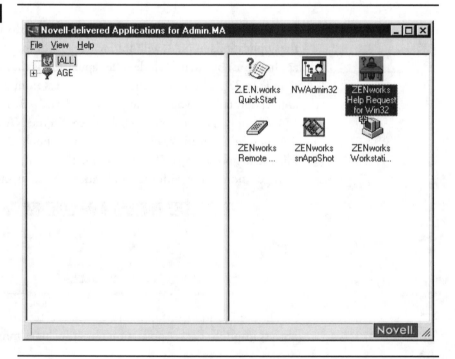

Software distribution is the ability for network administrators to *push* or *pull* applications to desktop workstations. Pushing an application is installing an application in an unattended manner (for example, requiring no one to select options during installation) over a network to a workstation. Pulling an application is installing an application over a network to a workstation in an attended manner, by having the person at the workstation prompt for installation and/or select options during installation. Automated installation templates can be generated for custom applications through the use of snAppShot templates. Software distribution can be scheduled for after-business or off-peak hours, which enables management of the network bandwidth.

Administrators use NAL to manage applications. It offers the ability to modify registry entries and .INI files, create custom drive mapping and printer captures for the application, and return the workstation to its previous state (of drive mappings, etc.) after the application is exited. Applications are managed according to the operating systems that they are enabled for: Windows 3.1*x*, Windows 95, or Windows NT Workstation 4.

In NAL, NetWare Administrator is the single seat of administration. Applications are created as Application objects in the NDS tree in the same manner as other network resources.

NDS delivers security to applications, using NDS as the foundation. Users must be granted rights to the Application object in order to use it.

Users mainly access NAL through its workstation component, the NAL window that displays the icons available to that user. If the administrator grants permission, users can extend the functionality of the NAL Window by creating personal folders, as in Figure 9-2. Users must have the ability to create personal folders granted to them in NDS. Then, it is a matter of the user selecting the NAL File menu and the New Personal Folder option and typing in the name for that folder. Folders appear under the Personal icon and can be created in a tree configuration. Users can drag application icons from the right pane and drop on the desired personal folder in the left pane of NAL to organize.

FIGURE 9-2

NAL personal folders

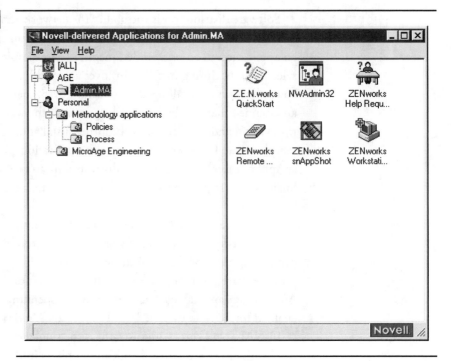

NAL.EXE uses a wrapper technology. It handles initialization and executes the correct program for the operating system. For example, a user at a Windows 3.1 workstation will execute NAL.EXE, which will execute NALW31.EXE, and then exit, leaving only NALW31.EXE to run. Table 9-1 lists the executables for each operating system.

As a wrapper, NAL selects which application icons to display for the user depending on the operating system currently being used. The wrapper also updates the files on the workstation from those in the SYS:PUBLIC\NALLIB directory. Local workstation files are only updated if the network version is newer than the local version.

The wrapper technology will not launch the NAL Explorer, which is an add-on to the Windows 95/98/NT4 Explorer. Instead, the NALEXPLD.EXE application must be explicitly launched, but only for Windows 95, 98, or

TABLE 9-1	Operating System	NAL-Launched Executable	NAL Explorer
Operating Systems and Associated NAL Executables	Windows 3.1	NALW31.EXE	N/A
	Windows for Workgroups 3.11	NALW31.EXE	N/A
	Windows 95	NALW95.EXE	NALEXPLD.EXE
	Windows NT Workstation 4	NALWIN32.EXE	NALEXPLD.EXE
	Windows 98	NALWIN32.EXE	NALEXPLD.EXE

NT 4. Windows 3.1*x* does not contain an Explorer interface. NAL Explorer shows the NAL applications directly in the Windows Explorer under the Application Explorer icon, which is added as a top-level folder, such as Figure 9-3 exhibits.

FIGURE 9-3

NAL Explorer

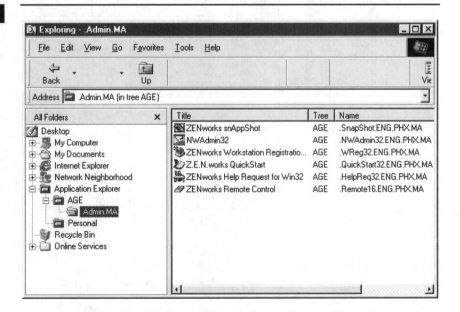

Enabling NAL

As a component of Z.E.N.works, NetWare Application Launcher is installed when Z.E.N.works is installed. After installation, the administrator must enable NAL for use by end users.

When Z.E.N.works is installed, the NDS schema is extended to include properties for the NAL on User, Group, Organizational Unit, Organization, and Country objects. There are two property pages that affect NAL:

■ Launcher Configuration (illustrated in Figure 9-4)

■ Applications

The default state for the Launcher Configuration is not to have any settings. In order to add a setting, the administrator would click Edit and

FIGURE 9-4

Launcher Configuration

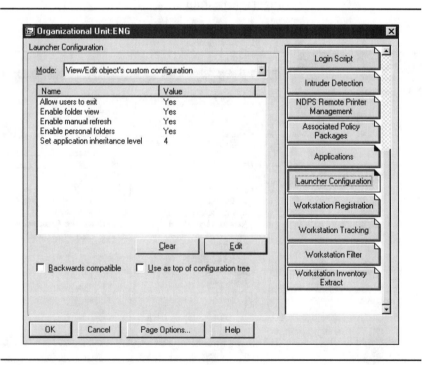

select the options from the configuration dialog box, and then select the corresponding value. When exiting the dialog box, these selections will appear in the Launcher Configuration property page.

In order to place application icons into the NAL window for users, the applications must be added to the Applications property page, shown in Figure 9-5. There are check boxes on this page that configure where the applications will appear on the end users' desktops. Applications are, by default, placed in the Application Launcher window. They can also be placed on the Start menu, the desktop, or the system tray. In addition, the Applications page includes an option to force the application to run. The administrator must click the Add button and locate Application objects for these applications to appear on this page.

FIGURE 9-5

Applications property page

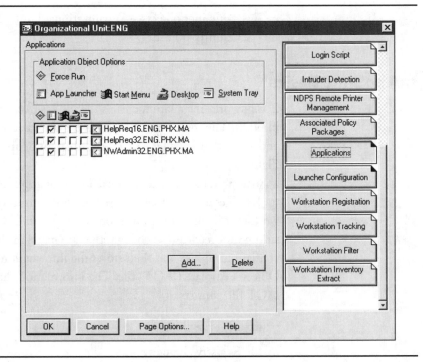

Configuring NDS and the File System for NAL

Delivering applications to end users is the main function for NAL. An application appearing in the NAL window depends on Application objects being created and the correct NDS and file system rights being applied so that they can be used. Creating an application can be done through the NetWare Application Launcher snAppShot, or by creating a simple Application object in NDS. Further configuration is all handled in the NetWare Administrator by editing properties of

- Application objects
- User objects
- Group objects
- Container objects—Organizational Unit, Organization, and Country objects

snAppShot Basics

Z.E.N.works installation creates the NAL snAppShot Application object in NDS. The installing User object is granted access to the application, and when that installer runs NAL, snAppShot appears as an icon, as in Figure 9-6.

snAppShot simplifies the installation of applications that make changes to .INI files and the Registry. snAppShot runs in the background on a client workstation while an application is being installed. During installation, snAppShot records the changes that are made to the workstation's configuration files and then stores the information in a binary Application Object Template (.AOT) file. The information that is recorded in the .AOT file consists of

- .INI file changes
- Registry changes

FIGURE 9-6

Z.E.N.works
snAppShot icon

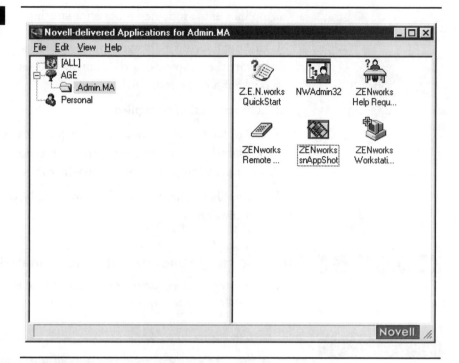

- Text file changes
- List of the files copied during installation
- Application object name and description
- Macros defined during application installation

snAppShot also records the new files added to the workstation and stores them as .FIL files. The configuration information can be stored in an .AXT file. This is a text-based template that the installer can edit before the file is imported as an object into NDS.

exam
watch

An .AOT file is an Application Object Template written in binary format and created by snAppShot. An .AOT file represents the changes made to the configuration files of a workstation during an applications installation.

snAppShot uses a four-step process for creating applications.

1. snAppShot runs a discovery process to see what is on the workstation before the setup process is executed. This sets a baseline with which snAppShot can compare later.

2. The application is installed.

3. snAppShot runs a second discovery process to see what is on the workstation after the setup process is executed. This automatically prompts a comparison of the two discoveries.

4. snAppShot writes the .AOT file to store the configuration information.

EXERCISE 9-1

Running snAppShot on a 32-Bit Application

1. From the NAL window, double-click the Z.E.N.works snAppShot icon. You will see the dialog box in Figure 9-7.

FIGURE 9-7

Z.E.N.works snAppShot

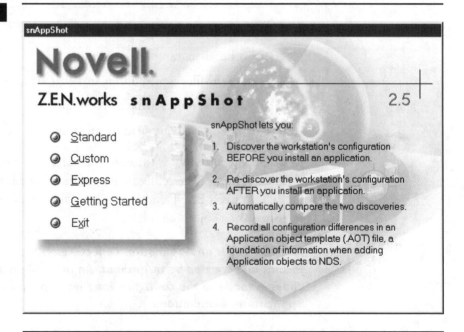

snAppShot

Novell.

Z.E.N.works **snAppShot**   2.5

- ● Standard
- ● Custom
- ● Express
- ● Getting Started
- ● Exit

snAppShot lets you:

1. Discover the workstation's configuration BEFORE you install an application.

2. Re-discover the workstation's configuration AFTER you install an application.

3. Automatically compare the two discoveries.

4. Record all configuration differences in an Application object template (.AOT) file, a foundation of information when adding Application objects to NDS.

2. The Standard option will use Novell's default options. The Custom option allows the administrator to specify drive mappings, registry information, and other configurations as part of the installation. The Express option uses a previously created Preferences file for the configuration information. Select the Custom option.

3. The next screen will prompt for the preferences file. Accept the snAppShot Default Settings by clicking Next.

4. This screen prompts for an Application object name and an icon title. When the first dialog box is completed, the second one will default to the first name; however, these can be different, as in Figure 9-8. Click Next.

5. A dialog box requesting a storage folder for the application files is prompted for next. This storage folder can be on the workstation temporarily, or on a server. Depending on how large the application is and the size of the local server's SYS: volume, it is best not to place this folder on a SYS: volume since it could cause SYS: to run out of space, which can cause the server to stop functioning. After selecting a storage folder, click Next. If prompted to create the folder, click OK.

FIGURE 9-8

Application object name

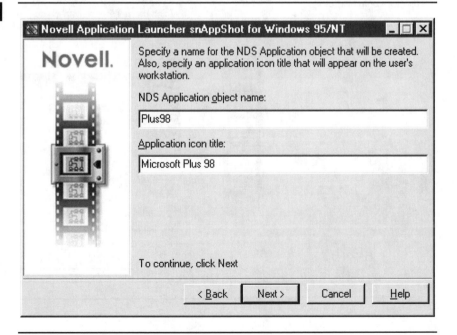

6. A dialog box will suggest placing the .AOT file in the storage folder and give it a default name, which is the same as the Application object name. Click Next.

7. The next screen prompts for the configuration information to capture during setup (Figure 9-9). By default, all boxes are checked. It is recommended that you retain these settings. Click Next.

8. The next shot will state which drives to scan for file and configuration changes. The default drive letter is C:. Except in cases in which the standard desktop configuration has multiple drives or program files stored on the server, this is the correct setting. Click Next.

9. In order to save Preferences as its own file, the administrator can click the Save Preferences button on the next dialog box. Review the settings and click Next.

FIGURE 9-9

snAppShot configuration selections

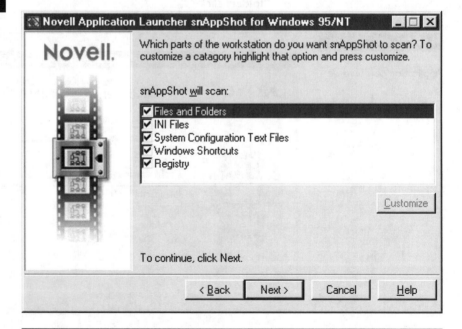

10. snAppShot will start scanning the configuration, as in Figure 9-10.

11. After scanning is complete, the snAppShot process will prompt to start the application installation, as in Figure 9-11. Click the Run Application Install button.

12. From the dialog box, browse through the file folders and select the application setup executable. Install the application through the normal method. snAppShot remains running in the background. When the application installation is complete, switch to the snAppShot screen and click Next.

13. The first dialog box displayed after that asks you to specify how the .INI files, registry entries, and folder and file entries should be handled—the default is to copy the entries always. Each setting should be reviewed for which action is appropriate; then click Next.

14. The next screen asks you to select the directory for file installation on the workstation. There is no problem with leaving this blank. Complete this screen and click Next.

FIGURE 9-10

snAppShot discovery process

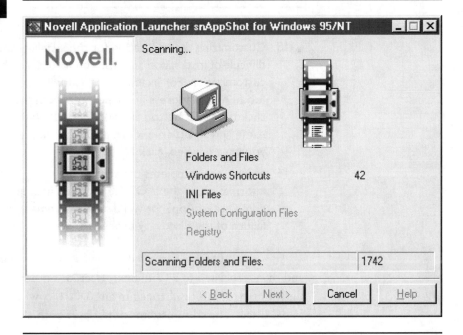

FIGURE 9-11

Starting the application
installation

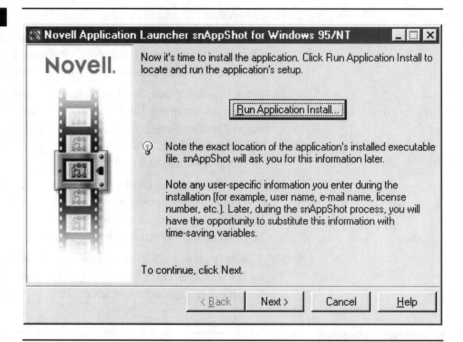

15. Customizing the application for the installing user is the most difficult of installation actions. The next dialog box allows this customization. For example, if the installer is asked during installation for an e-mail address and types **xyz@corp.com**, the installer can click the ADD button and add **E-MAIL ADDRESS** to the variable name and **xyz@corp.com** as the variable to be replaced. When you have finished, click Next.

16. snAppShot completes the second discovery process and records the information to the .AOT file specified in step 6. When it is complete, snAppShot will display a summary with the success or failure of the discovery processes.

After the .AOT file is created, it can be imported into NDS as an object and then associated to a Container, User, or Group object. Since the .AOT file is binary, it can be changed to an .AXT file, which is text based, in order to be edited. The administrator can import both .AOT and .AXT files into the NetWare Administrator as Application objects. In order to change an .AOT file to an .AXT file, a tool is available in the NetWare Administrator under Tools | Application Launcher Tools | AOT/AXT File Tools | AOT > AXT. The file can be changed back to an .AOT file using the same menu AXT > AOT option.

exam
ⓦatch

snAppShot performs a baseline discovery, the application installation, a postinstallation discovery, comparison of the discoveries, and writes an .AOT file with the configuration changes.

Simple vs. Complex Applications

Simple applications are those that do not require any configuration file changes or supporting files such as .DLL files. An example of these applications is RCONSOLE.EXE included in NetWare 5. Setting up a simple application does not require snAppShot. Instead, the administrator creates an Application object in NDS and then associates it to the User, Group, or container object.

exam
ⓦatch

When an application is associated with a container object or with a Group object, any User objects added later as members of the container object or the group automatically are granted access to the network Application object through inheritance.

Complex applications are those applications that require any configuration file changes and files to be copied to the workstation. Complex applications require snAppShot.

EXERCISE 9-2

Create a Simple Application Object

1. In NetWare Administrator, navigate to the context in which the application will reside.

2. Right-click the container object and select Create from the pop-up menu.

3. Select Application from the Object Creation dialog box, and then click OK.

FIGURE 9-12

Creating simple applications
with the Application object
creation wizard

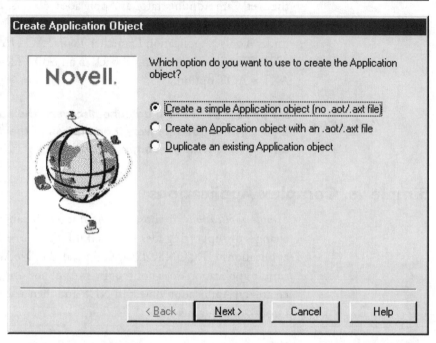

4. The Application object creation wizard starts. Select the first option for simple application creation (Figure 9-12). Click Next.

5. In the next screen, type the name for the Application object and then state the path to the application executable. Note that the path should be in a universally accessible format, such as \\SERVER\VOL\PATH\APPLICATION.EXE.

6. Click Next. The Application object is created and ready for use.

NDS Object and Property Rights

When the network administrator installs Z.E.N.works, the administrator's User object requires the Supervisor Object right to the NDS tree [Root]. This is due to the fact that Z.E.N.works extends the NDS schema.

NDS rights are not required for accessing the Application objects; however, associations are required for the application icons to appear in the NAL window. Associations are set on the User, Group, or container object Applications page. To enable an application for all users within a container object:

1. Right-click the container.

2. Select details.

3. Click the Applications property page.

4. Click the Add button.

5. Navigate the tree until the desired Application object is available in the left pane window.

6. Click the Application object and then click OK.

7. The Application object will appear in the Applications window.

8. Select the options for the Application to launch from, or leave the default for the application to appear in the Launcher (NAL) window.

The Launcher can be further configured in NDS through the Launcher Configuration property page. Table 9-2 lists the defaults for Launcher configuration.

The Set Application Inheritance Level affects NDS inheritance by limiting the number of levels that the tree is "walked" for custom settings. NDS Inheritance for NAL works in this manner:

■ NAL seeks configuration settings at the lowest object, the leaf object, or the lowest container object.

■ Then NAL walks the tree toward the [Root], collecting the custom settings at each level.

■ NAL continues until it reaches an object that has been designated as the "top" of the inheritance tree.

■ When NAL finds a custom setting, it applies it. If it does not find a custom setting for an option, it uses the defaults shown in Table 9-2.

TABLE 9-2

Launcher Configuration
Options

Configuration Option	Function	NDS Default
Allow Users to Exit	Allows users to exit NAL	Yes
Display Icon on Desktop	Displays the Application Explorer icon on the desktop	Yes
Display Start Menu	Shows the Start menu icons in the NAL window	No
Enable Folder View	Shows folders in left pane	Yes
Enable Manual Refresh	Allows users to select F5 to refresh NAL and look for new applications	Yes
Enable Personal Folders	Allows users to create personal folders	No
Enable Timed Refresh	Automatically refreshes NAL to look for new applications	No
Enable Log In	Allows users to log in from NAL File menu	Yes
Expand Folder View on Startup	Expands the tree view when NAL starts up	No
Name Icon on Desktop	Changes the Application Explorer icon name	Application Explorer
Read Group Objects for Applications	Enables the user to read Group objects for the associated Application objects	Yes
Save Window Size and Position	Retains the window size upon reboot	Yes
Set Application Inheritance Level	Sets the number of the levels of tree to walk to look for applications	1

	Configuration Option	Function	NDS Default
TABLE 9-2 Launcher Configuration Options *(continued)*	Set Refresh Frequency	Sets the number of seconds to wait between timed refreshes	3600 seconds
	Specify E-Mail Attribute	Sets the e-mail contact	Mailbox ID

The administrator can designate an object as the top of the inheritance tree by selecting the option Use Object as Top of Inheritance Tree on the object's Launcher Configuration property page. When the Set Application Inheritance Level for a User object is set to 0, NAL does not look for Application objects. When it is set to 1, NAL looks only in the immediate container for Application objects. When set to 2 or higher, NAL will navigate the tree toward the [Root] for that same number of levels. If the Set Application Inheritance Level is set to −1, NAL always looks all the way to the [Root].

Because applications can be applied to a User object through explicit association, or through the inherited applications from Group objects or parent container object, the administrator cannot see all the applications at once within the User object or the container objects. Instead, NetWare Administrator contains a tool to view the inherited applications.

EXERCISE 9-3

View the Inherited Applications for a User

1. In NetWare Administrator, navigate the tree until the User object is displayed.
2. Click the User object so that it is highlighted.
3. Click the Tools menu.
4. Click Application Launcher Tools.
5. Select Show Inherited Applications.
6. Click the plus signs next to the container objects displayed in order to view the Application objects (Figure 9-13).

FIGURE 9-13

Displaying inherited applications

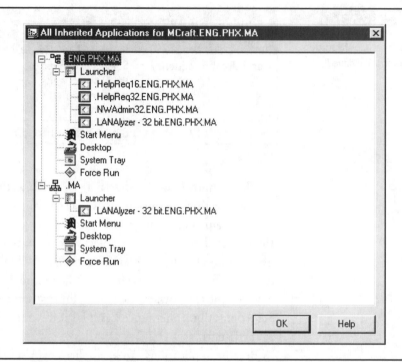

QUESTIONS AND ANSWERS

An end user has called the network administrator and complained that her workstation is running an application on startup and it is hanging her PC. How can the administrator find the application that is running, and how can he or she fix it?	After checking the login scripts, the administrator would open NetWare Administrator, highlight the User object, and then select Tools | Application Launcher Tools | Show Inherited Applications. The Administrator would look for applications that are shown in the Force Run area for each container. Then, the administrator would open the User object and select the Launcher Configuration property page. The administrator would edit the Set Application Inheritance Level option to a number that does not reach the container level that has the offending Application object in it, or to a 0 to avoid all Application objects.

Application Objects

There are two NAL objects in the NDS schema:

- Application folders
- Application objects

The administrator may wish to organize applications for the end users in a hierarchical folder structure, which is much the same as a file directory structure. In order to do this, the administrator creates an Application Folder object in a container and then creates folders within the Folders property page in a tree structure. After the tree structure of folders is created, the administrator can add Application objects to the folders. Once a folder is populated by an Application object, it will appear in the NAL window (Figure 9-14).

FIGURE 9-14

Application Folder object

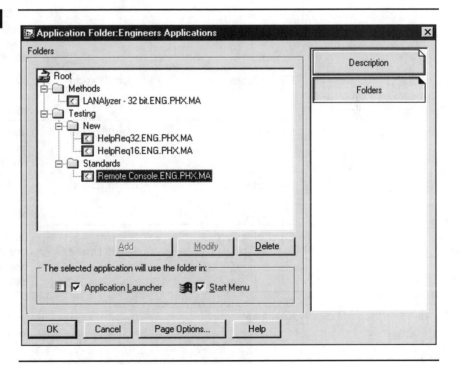

Application objects have an extensive list of properties. Many of these are directly related to the application's configuration settings. Table 9-3 lists the Application object properties.

TABLE 9-3

Application Object
Properties *(continued)*

Property	Property Page	Function
Application Icon Title	Identification	Displays the title of the icon in NAL.
Path to executable file	Identification	Represents the path and file for the application.
Install Only	Identification	Excludes the path to the executable; is used with snAppShot to copy files to a local workstation.
Run Once	Identification	Utilizes a version stamp to add information to the HKCU\SOFTWARE\NET WARE\NAL in order to prevent the application from running more than once for that user.
Order Icons	Identification	Places this icon in a certain order in the NAL window.
Icon Order	Identification	Identifies which place the icon is placed in the NAL window.
Application Icon	Identification	Enables the administrator to change the icon used in NAL.
Operating System	System Requirements	Enables the administrator to select which operating systems will be allowed to execute this application.
Display icons on machines with RAM	System Requirements	Specifies the minimum amount of RAM required for the application.

TABLE 9-3

Application Object
Properties *(continued)*

Property	Property Page	Function
Display icons on machines with free disk space	System Requirements	Specifies the minimum amount of free disk space required for up to three disk drives in order for the application to run on a workstation—useful for installation files.
Command Line Parameters	Environment	Specifies startup switches for the executable.
Working directory	Environment	Displays the working directory used as the default for a File | Save.
Run	Environment	Selects the window size as normal, minimized, or maximized.
Windows NT WOW	Environment	Selects a Shared (unprotected) 16-bit DOS virtual DOS machine (VDM) or Separate (protected) VDM session for Windows NT. If an application crashes in a Shared VDM, all of the applications sharing it will fail at the same time.
Enable error logging to file	Environment	Specifies a file to be used as an error log.
Clean up Network Resources	Environment	NAL will clean up resources such as mapped drives and captured printers.
Monitor Module	Environment	When an executable uses a wrapper technology, wherein one application spawns the next, the Monitor Module Name selects which executable to monitor for the network resource cleanup.

TABLE 9-3

Application Object
Properties *(continued)*

Property	Property Page	Function
Show Distribution Progress	Distribution	Turns on a progress bar for the users when a new application is being distributed to a workstation.
Prompt user before distribution	Distribution	Allows a user to confirm the distribution of an application.
Distribute Always	Distribution	Forces the application to be distributed every time.
Prompt user for reboot	Distribution	Allows or disallows the user to confirm for a reboot.
Use version stamp to trigger distribution	Distribution	If an administrator makes changes to an application, can redistribute those changes by assigning a later version number.
Folders	Folders	Allows the administrator to create a custom folder for the application or link it to an Application Folder object.
Description	Description	Displays detailed, custom information about the application.
Drives	Drives/Ports	Enables custom drive mappings.
Ports	Drives/Ports	Enables custom printer captures.
Run Before Launching	Scripts	Allows the administrator to create a script using NetWare's scripting language to execute prior to the application.

TABLE 9-3

Application Object
Properties *(continued)*

Property	Property Page	Function
Run After termination	Scripts	Allows the administrator to create a script using NetWare's scripting language to execute after the application exits.
Enable Load Balancing	Fault Tolerance	With multiple application servers, this option allows distribution of the application "load" across multiple servers.
Enable Fault Tolerance	Fault Tolerance	With multiple application servers, this option allows a different server to be selected if the initial one crashes.
Contacts	Contacts	User objects that are contacts for the application.
Associations	Associations	User, Group, and container objects allowed to use the application.
Administrator Notes	Administrator Notes	Text field that is not viewable by users that can be used to track changes to the Application object.
Macros	Macros	Customizable fields used in the distribution of the application.
Registry Settings	Registry Settings	Modifications to the registry are displayed, and can be edited, in this property page.
INI Settings	INI Settings	Modifications to .INI files are displayed and can be edited in this property page.

TABLE 9-3

Application Object
Properties *(continued)*

Property	Property Page	Function
Application Files	Application Files	Displays files that are targeted to be copied to the workstation upon application distribution.
Text Files	Text Files	Modifications to text files are displayed and can be edited in this property page.
Schedule	Schedule	Enables restriction of times for the application to run. This can be used to keep distributions from occurring during peak network usage hours.
Icons/Shortcuts	Icons/Shortcuts	Used to specify which icons and shortcuts are placed on a workstation at distribution.
File Rights	File Rights	Enables custom file rights needed to run the application. The user will gain these rights during the application execution.
Termination	Termination	Enables a custom exit from an application, such as sending a message to the user to save his or her data before closing.
Application Site List	Application Site List	When an enterprise network consists of multiple sites that users travel between, the use of an application site list will enable the nearest server to a user to execute an application, rather than a static server.

FIGURE 9-15

Application object
properties

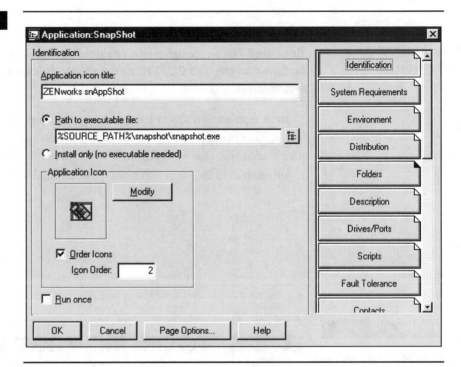

Application objects are the core of an application and its distribution. The Application object properties can customize the behavior of the Application object (Figure 9-15). Multiple Application objects can be created for the same application, but simply be customized according to the Application object settings in order for the application to work on different systems.

File System Rights

When Z.E.N.works installs, it automatically places the NAL files in the SYS:PUBLIC directory of the servers on which it is installed. By default, all users are granted the read and file scan rights to this directory. However, in an enterprise network, the file system rights may not be set up for all file servers the same way. The administrator must ensure that NAL files are in a file server directory in which users have the Read and File Scan rights.

exam

@atch

Read and File Scan rights are required to execute NAL.EXE. NAL is installed to the SYS:PUBLIC directory by default during Z.E.N.works installation.

Each Application object has a property page for File system rights (Figure 9-16). These file system rights are automatically granted to a user while that user is accessing that application. The administrator simply adds the rights required to the File Rights property page of the Application object.

FIGURE 9-16

Application object file rights

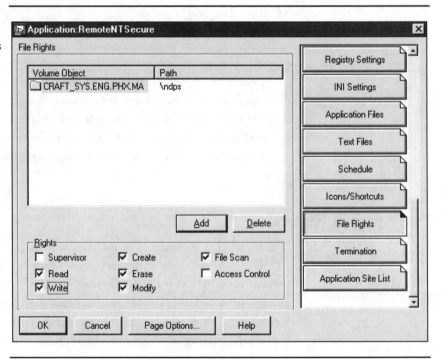

Launching Network Applications with NAL

In addition to configuring NDS, the administrator must make sure that the correct file system rights are applied to the NAL files for users, and that NAL is executed from the correct login scripts. The login script syntax in a pure Windows environment (that is, Windows 3.1*x*, Windows 95/98, or Windows NT 4), is @\\SERVER\SYS\PUBLIC\NAL.EXE. In a mixed environment, the administrator will want to specify an IF %PLATFORM="WIN95" THEN statement before the NAL executable line, and an END statement after, replacing WIN95 with WIN31 or WINNT or WIN98 for the other operating systems. The @ command is used instead of a # command, since it will allow the login script to continue process during the execution of the external command. The # command waits until the external command completes before going forward. The NAL.EXE switches and their functions are listed Table 9-4.

From the end user's perspective, the NAL window is automatically launched upon login when NAL is executed from a login script. The user simply navigates through folders in the left pane of the NAL window, if folders have been enabled. Upon finding the application, the user can double-click selected applications in the right pane in order to execute the application.

CERTIFICATION SUMMARY

NetWare Application Launcher (NAL) is the component of Z.E.N.works that handles application management and software distribution. NAL centralizes application administration by creating Application objects in Novell Directory Services (NDS). The Application objects can then be secured using NDS Security.

NAL is installed as a component of Z.E.N.works. Users will require the Read and File Scan file system rights to the NAL files. Applications will need to be created and associated to container, Group, or User objects.

TABLE 9-4	Switch	Syntax	Function
NAL Switches	/a	NAL /A=*Application object Distinguished Name* NAL /A=*tree; Application object Distinguished Name*	Runs the specified application. If NAL is not running, it is started minimized while the application runs.
	/c	NAL /C="Customized Title"	NAL loads with a title bar using this display.
	/h	NAL /H	Hides NAL while running.
	/min	NAL /MIN	Runs NAL minimized.
	/max	NAL /MAX	Runs NAL in full screen.
	/norm	NAL /NORM	Runs NAL in normal screen window.
	/s	NAL /S	Makes NAL the OS shell, displaying shutdown instead of exit.
	/u	NAL /U	Unloads NAL after all NAL-launched applications have exited.
	/u!	NAL /U!	Unloads NAL and leaves any NAL-launched applications open.

QUESTIONS AND ANSWERS

Tyler has implemented NAL on his network, and has created a container login script with the line NAL /C="NetWare Secured Programs for Tyler". An error occurs with the line, and when Tyler fixes that error he finds that everyone has his name on his or her title bar. What did Tyler do to fix the original error, and how can he fix the name problem?

Tyler realized that NAL was not being executed as an external command. He changed the line to @\\SERVER\SYS\PUBLIC\NAL /C="NetWare Secured Programs for Tyler". In order to change the name problem, Tyler should write the following command:
@\\SERVER\SYS\PUBLIC\NAL /C="NetWare Secured Programs for %FULL_NAME"

snAppShot is the application included with NAL that is used to configure applications for software distribution. snAppShot uses the following steps:

1. It discovers the baseline preinstallation configuration.

2. It installs the application.

3. It discovers the postapplication configuration and comparison.

4. It writes the configuration information to an .AOT file.

The information stored in an .AOT file is registry settings, .INI file changes, text file changes, macro information, and files and folders to be copied. The .AOT file is a binary file. It can be transferred to an .AXT file, which is text based, and vice versa. The tools for file conversion are in the NetWare Administrator.

There are two types of applications: simple and complex. A simple application is one that does not require any configuration on the workstation in order to run. A complex application may require registry entries, .INI file changes, text file changes, and multiple files to be copied. Creating an Application object in NDS is done with the Application object creation wizard. This is initialized in the NetWare Administrator.

The container, User, and Group objects all have NDS properties that are related to NAL. These are located in the Launcher configuration page and the Applications property page. These properties are inherited from the lowest leaf object and walked up the tree toward the [Root]. Inheritance can be controlled through the Set as Top of Inheritance Tree or Set Application Inheritance Level in these property pages.

The Application object and the Application Folder object are both NDS schema extensions for NAL use. The Application Folder object is used to organize applications in the NAL window for end users. The Application object includes configuration information for applications. Multiple Application objects can be created for a single executable file.

NAL.EXE has multiple switches used to configure how the NetWare Application Launcher is executed. These switches can be used in a login script. Launching an application can either be done from the command line or by double-clicking application icons in the NAL window.

TWO-MINUTE DRILL

❑ NAL offers a software delivery process secured by and centrally managed through NDS. The administrator uses NetWare Administrator to create and distribute applications. The end user uses the NetWare Application Launcher to access and execute those applications.

❑ An application does not appear in the NAL window unless the user has been associated to the Application object in NDS or has inherited that association. Only the application icon that is specific to the workstation operating system appears.

❑ Users double-click an icon in the NAL window to launch an application. If the application does not launch, the user can click the File menu and select the Verify option. The Verify option will display any configuration errors with the Application object. If the administrator grants permission, users can extend the functionality of the NAL Window by creating personal folders.

❑ The application icons in the NAL window represent the Application objects in NDS. Each Application object includes information about drive mappings, printer captures, application switches, and so on. The administrator can deliver new applications by creating Application objects and configuring them in NetWare Administrator.

❑ Software distribution is the ability for network administrators to push or pull applications to desktop workstations. Automated installation templates can be generated for custom applications by using snAppShot templates. Software distribution can be scheduled for after-business or off-peak hours, which enables management of the network bandwidth.

❑ NAL offers the ability to modify registry entries and .INI files, create custom drive mapping and printer captures for the application, and return the workstation to its previous state after the application is exited. Applications are managed according to the operating systems that they are enabled for.

❑ NDS delivers security to applications, using NDS as the foundation. Users must be granted rights to the Application object in order to use it.

❑ NAL.EXE uses a wrapper technology. NAL selects which application icons to display for the user depending on the operating system currently being used. The wrapper also updates the files on the workstation from those in the SYS:PUBLIC\NALLIB directory. Local workstation files are only updated if the network version is newer than the local version.

❑ NetWare Application Launcher is installed when Z.E.N.works is installed. After installation, the administrator must enable NAL for use by end users.

❑ When Z.E.N.works is installed, the NDS schema is extended to include properties for the NAL on User, Group, Organizational Unit, Organization, and Country objects. There are two property pages that affect NAL: Launcher Configuration, and Applications.

❑ The main function for NAL is delivering applications to end users. An application appearing in the NAL window depends on Application objects being created and the correct NDS and file system rights being applied so that they can be used.

❑ Z.E.N.works installation creates the NAL snAppShot Application object in NDS. The installing User object is granted access to the application; and when that installer runs NAL, snAppShot appears as an icon.

❑ snAppShot simplifies the installation of applications that make changes to .INI files and the Registry. snAppShot runs in the background on a client workstation while an application is being installed. During the installation, snAppShot records the changes that are made to the workstation's configuration files and then stores the information in a binary Application Object Template (.AOT) file.

❑ snAppShot also records the new files added to the workstation, and stores them as .FIL files. The configuration information can be stored in an .AXT file, a text-based template that the installer can edit before the file is imported as an object into NDS.

❑ After the .AOT file is created, it can be imported into NDS as an object and then associated to a Container, User, or Group object. Since the .AOT file is binary, it can be changed to an .AXT file, which is text based, in order to be edited. The administrator can import both .AOT and .AXT files into the NetWare Administrator as Application objects.

❑ Simple applications are those that do not require any configuration file changes or supporting files such as .DLL files. An example of these applications is RCONSOLE.EXE, included in NetWare 5. Setting up a simple application does not require snAppShot.

❑ When the network administrator installs Z.E.N.works, the administrator's User object requires the Supervisor Object right to the NDS tree [Root] because Z.E.N.works extends the NDS schema.

❑ Associations are required for the application icons to appear in the NAL window. Associations are set on the User, Group, or container object Applications page. The Launcher can be further configured in NDS through the Launcher Configuration property page.

❑ The Set Application Inheritance Level affects NDS inheritance by limiting the number of levels that the tree is "walked" for custom settings. The administrator can designate an object as the top of the inheritance tree by selecting the option Use Object as Top of Inheritance Tree on the object's Launcher Configuration property page.

❑ To organize applications in a hierarchical folder structure, the administrator creates an Application Folder object in a container and then creates folders within the Folders property page in a tree structure. After the tree structure of folders is created, the administrator can add Application objects to the folders.

❑ Application objects have an extensive list of properties. Many of these are directly related to the application's configuration settings. The Application object properties can customize its behavior. Multiple Application objects can be created for the same application, but simply be customized according to the Application object settings in order for the application to work on different systems.

❑ Z.E.N.works automatically places the NAL files in the SYS:PUBLIC directory of the servers on which it is installed. By default, all users are granted the read and file scan rights to this directory. The administrator must ensure that NAL files are in a file server directory in which users have the Read and File Scan rights.

SELF TEST

The Self-Test questions will help you measure your understanding of the material presented in this chapter. Read all the choices carefully, as there may be more than one correct answer. Select all correct answers for each question.

1. What is required for a user to see an icon for an application in the NAL window?

    A. Read and File Scan rights to the application

    B. Browse NDS Property rights to the Application object

    C. Association to the Application object in a container unit below the leaf object in the NDS tree

    D. Association to the Application object in a container unit above the leaf object in the NDS tree

2. Jay has used a Windows 3.1 workstation for the past year with NAL. Yesterday, the administrator upgraded his workstation to Windows NT 4 Workstation, also using NAL. Will Jay see the exact same applications as he saw in the NAL window under Win31? (Choose all that apply.)

    A. Yes, all applications associated to Jay will appear in the NAL window.

    B. Yes, but on the condition that the applications have been configured for both Windows 3.1 and Windows NT Workstation 4.

    C. No, applications that are configured for Windows 3.1 only will not appear in Windows NT 4.

    D. No, applications cannot be configured for more than one operating system at once.

3. If the administrator is running Windows NT, which application will she use to configure applications for the NetWare Application Launcher?

    A. NAL.EXE

    B. NALWIN32.EXE

    C. NWADMNNT.EXE

    D. SNAPPSHOT

4. What does NAL's technology do?

    A. The wrapper technology for NAL.EXE detects the operating system (OS) and launches the correct OS-specific NAL executable.

    B. The wrapper technology for NAL.EXE detects the application associations and lists them in the NAL window.

    C. The wrapper technology for NAL.EXE detects the inheritance level and displays the applications that are inherited in the NAL window.

    D. The wrapper technology for NAL.EXE detects the differences between the pre- and post-installation state of the OS and writes a configuration file.

5. What file is used to detect configuration changes after an application installs?

   A. NAL.EXE

   B. NALWIN32.EXE

   C. NWADMNNT.EXE

   D. SNAPPSHOT

6. What type of file does snAppShot use to store configuration changes?

   A. .FIL file

   B. .AOT file

   C. .EXE file

   D. .INI file

7. How many discovery processes will snAppShot run for a single application installation?

   A. 1

   B. 2

   C. 3

   D. 4

8. True or False. Simple applications require snAppShot to run in order to create applications.

   A. True

   B. False

9. In an enterprise in which inheritance is set to travel all the way to the tree [Root], which property page will enable an application to be seen by all users of the container object .OU=ACCT.OU=LON.O=MA?

   A. The Applications property page of .CN=ACCT.OU=PHX.O=MA

   B. The Applications property page of .CN=ALLUSERS.OU=NY.O=MA

   C. The Associations property page of .OU=ENG.OU=LON.O=MA

   D. The Applications property page of .O=MA

10. What can the administrator do to organize applications in a specific way without users being able to change the system?

   A. Enable and set up personal folders

   B. Create special Application objects

   C. Create an Application Folder object and organize folders and Application objects within it.

   D. Configure the Launcher Configuration properties

11. How can the application icon be changed in the NAL window?

   A. The user selects File | Properties | Application icon and selects a new icon.

   B. The user selects Edit | Application icon and selects a new icon.

   C. The administrator edits the Application Icon property of the Application Folder object.

   D. The administrator clicks the Application icon button on the Identification page of the Application object.

12. George is consulting with a client who is adamant about not using NAL for his

custom application. The client tells him that the application requires different custom switches and the users must be able to have flexibility in its execution. On the other hand, the client wants his applications secured and knows NAL will use this. What can George do with NAL to make this work for his client?

A. George cannot make this work for his client.

B. George can create Application objects that prompt for the switches.

C. George can show the client the Command Line Parameters property on the Environment page of the Application object and then create Application objects for each custom switch required by the client.

13. Which Application object property will display a moving bar during application execution?

A. Monitor Module

B. Show Distribution Progress

C. Clean Up Network Resources

D. Distribute Always

14. Which of the following commands will execute an application during the login script execution?

A. @\\SERVER\SYS\PUBLIC\NAL /A=.APP.OU.O

B. #SERVER\SYS:PUBLIC\NAL /C="Application"

C. NAL /U!

D. @\\SERVER\SYS:PUBLIC\NAL /H

15. Which of the following commands will unload NAL immediately and leave any NAL-launched applications open?

A. @\\SERVER\SYS\PUBLIC\NAL /A =.APP.OU.O

B. #SERVER\SYS:PUBLIC\NAL /C= "Application"

C. NAL /U!

D. @\\SERVER\SYS:PUBLIC\NAL /H

10

Using Workstation Manager to Manage Workstations

CERTIFICATION OBJECTIVES

10.01	Introduction to Workstation Manager
10.02	Installing and Configuring Multiple Clients with Workstation Manager
10.03	Managing Workstation Inventory
10.04	Managing Profiles and Policies with NDS
10.05	Scheduling Workstation Application Upgrades
10.06	Dynamically Configuring Printers and Print Queues
10.07	Windows NT User Management

W hen Microsoft Windows NT Workstation became more popular for business workstations, it presented a challenge for NetWare. Each NT workstation had its own local security for end users, requiring a mandatory local logon to the local security database. Additionally, the NT workstation could belong to an NT domain and use domain security for end users, which requires logging in to an NT domain but provides a level of workstation management. NT Workstation was created to be a high-performance desktop operating system that can act as a peer server in a workgroup or member of an NT Domain. However, NT workstations are not built to accept another enterprise network security. Novell came out with Workstation Manager to add these and other benefits to NetWare through Novell Directory Services.

Workstation Manager does more than manage NT workstations. It has been extended, as a portion of the Z.E.N.works package, to manage Windows 95 workstations. Although not all aspects of NT workstation management are applicable to Windows 95, most are, and these capabilities are part of the current Z.E.N.works Workstation Manager component.

Introduction to Workstation Manager

Workstation Manager adds the ability to NetWare to manage workstations through the use of Novell Directory Services (NDS). Although originally created in response to the need to manage NT workstations, Workstation Manager manages Windows 95 workstations, as well. Workstation Manager services are listed in Table 10-1.

Workstation Manager is integrated into Novell Directory Services. All aspects of managing workstations are available as objects in the NDS tree when using the NetWare Administrator. The objects that are used by Workstation Manager are policy package objects. The applicable objects are listed in Table 10-2.

TABLE 10-1

Workstation
Manager Services

Service	Operating System	Function
Workstation Inventory	Windows NT and Windows 95	Maintains an inventory of workstation hardware and applications within NDS
Password Synchronization	Windows NT	Synchronizes passwords between NetWare and NT user accounts
User Account Management	Windows NT	Eliminates need for users to be located in the local or SAM domain
Activity Scheduling	Windows NT and Windows 95	Enables the scheduling of actions to be executed on a workstation
Desktop Management	Windows NT and Windows 95	Manages the desktop settings
System Policy Management	Windows NT and Windows 95	Enables centralized control of native system policies

TABLE 10-2

User and
Workstation Policies

Policy Package	Policy	Function
NT User Package	Dynamic Local User	Enables local user management
NT User Package	NT Desktop Preferences	Manages the desktop
NT User Package	NT User Printer	Creates and configures printers for NT users
NT User Package	NT User System Policies	Manages native NT system policies
NT User Package	Workstation Import Policy	Enables a user to import Workstation objects into NDS, applying a name standard

TABLE 10-2

User and
Workstation Policies
(continued)

Policy Package	Policy	Function
NT Workstation Package	Novell Client Configuration	Configures the protocol and components of the Novell client
NT Workstation Package	NT Computer Printer	Creates and configures a network printer for a workstation
NT Workstation Package	NT Computer System Policies	Manages the computer-based system policies native to NT
NT Workstation Package	Restrict Login	Allows administrator to restrict user logins
NT Workstation Package	Workstation Inventory	Manages and maintains the inventory of workstation hardware and software
95 User Package	95 Desktop Preferences	Manages the Windows 95 desktop
95 User Package	95 User System Policies	Manages the Windows 95 User System Policies
95 User Package	Workstation Import Policy	Enables a user to import Workstation objects into NDS, applying a name standard
95 Workstation Package	95 Computer Printer	Creates and configures a network printer for a workstation
95 Workstation Package	95 Computer System Policies	Manages the computer-based system policies native to 95
95 Workstation Package	Novell Client Configuration	Configures the protocol and components of the Novell client
95 Workstation Package	Restrict Login	Allows administrator to restrict user logins
95 Workstation Package	Workstation Inventory	Manages and maintains the inventory of workstation hardware and software

CERTIFICATION OBJECTIVE 10.02

Installing and Configuring Multiple Clients with Workstation Manager

The Workstation Manager installs as a service under NT. It is a network client service under Windows 95. After the Windows NT Workstation Manager service authenticates to NDS, it periodically polls NDS to update scheduled actions and any other changes that should be made to the workstation. The polling schedule can be between 1 and 60,000 minutes. The default is 10 minutes.

Workstation Manager is an option in the installation of the NetWare 5 client. In order to install Workstation Manager, the administrator simply runs the NetWare 5 client setup with the /W switch, or selects the Custom installation option and then selects Workstation Manager from the list of optional components (see Figure 10-1). The installation switches and functions are given in Table 10-3.

In order to install Workstation Manager on multiple clients, the administrator may opt to use a login script installation method. The /ACU switch is the key to making this installation method work. The /ACU switch installs the updated client software if the existing client is older than the current version. This means that the login script does not need any logic for determining whether the workstation has already installed the client. A

TABLE 10-3	Installation Switches	Function
Installation Command Parameters	/U:[path to unattend file for Windows NT only]	Uses a text file, usually UNATTEND.TXT, to specify the setup specifications.
	/ACU	ACU stands for Automatic Client Update—this will automatically install the NetWare client without requiring input from the installer. ACU will upgrade an existing client setup and retain existing settings.
	/W	Installs the Workstation Manager component.
	/?	Displays the command-line help text.

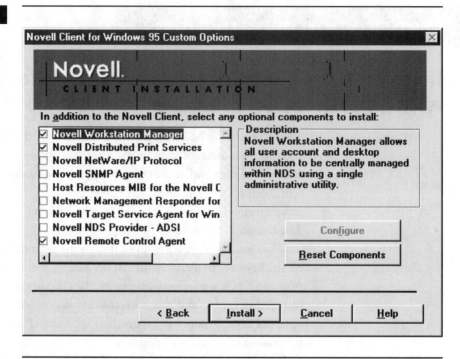

FIGURE 10-1

Installation of client with
Workstation Manager

login script for installing the client might look like the following if the
client files were on a server below PUBLIC in the respective operating
system–specific directories:

```
**********************************************************
** LOGIN SCRIPT FOR INSTALLING NETWARE CLIENT32  **
** including Workstation Manager - created October 3, 1998 **
**********************************************************
; Mapping drives section
MAP ERRORS OFF
MAP DISPLAY OFF
MAP INS S16:=X:=SERVER/SYS:PUBLIC
IF %PLATFORM = "WINNT" THEN BEGIN
     X:\PUBLIC\WINNT\I386\SETUPNW /W /ACU
END
IF %PLATFORM = "WIN95" THEN BEGIN
     X:\PUBLIC\WIN95\SETUP /W /ACU
END
MAP DISPLAY ON
MAP
```

Enabling Workstation Manager Policies

In order to begin using Workstation Manager, the NetWare Administrator needs to have policy packages created and associated to the appropriate users and workstations. The difference between a workstation policy package and a user policy package is that a *user policy package* will follow a roving user around the network. A *workstation policy package*, on the other hand, will be applied to the same workstation no matter which user logs in. Workstations must be imported into NDS as objects before the workstation policies become effective.

Policy packages can be created for different containers, and multiple policy packages can exist in the same container. This allows a network environment to use the existing network management structure already in place, whether that is a centralized or distributed administrative network.

In order to import workstations, the administrator must create a Workstation Import Policy for workstations, both NT and Windows 95. This policy exists in the NT User Package and the 95 User Package. Figures 10-2 and 10-3 show the user policy package pages for Windows 95 and Windows NT.

QUESTIONS AND ANSWERS

Jerry is a network administrator for two business units within a large network environment. Both of the business units exist in a single container, of which Jerry is the sole administrator. The network planning group is implementing Workstation Manager and has distributed a policy to Jerry that all workstations must use the business unit as part of the workstation's name to comply with the naming standards. They have asked Jerry to implement Workstation Manager. Jerry wants to create a separate container for one of the business units, move all the User objects, and change the context on the workstations. Is this necessary, and why or why not?

No, it is not necessary to create another container. Jerry can implement Workstation Manager through two user policy packages, one created for each business unit. He can associate the packages to the appropriate users. In each user policy package, he would create a Workstation Import Policy with a custom naming convention using the business unit name. Then, Jerry would create a login script to register workstations upon a user's login. The import process would pull the correct naming convention from the Workstation Import Policy.

FIGURE 10-2

Windows 95 User Package

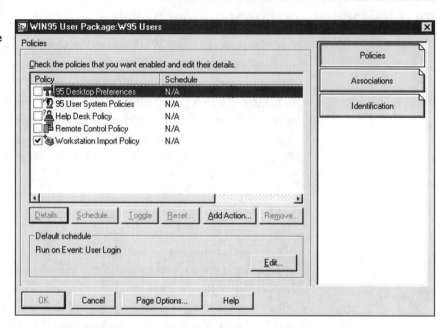

FIGURE 10-3

Windows NT User Package

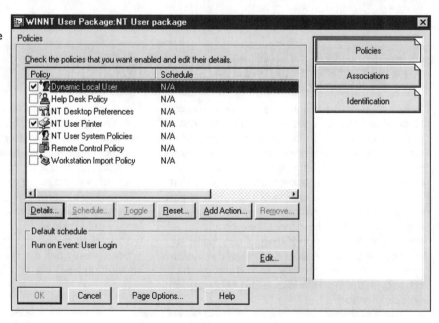

To register workstations, the administrator follows these steps:

1. The administrator must enable NDS to allow workstation registration. That option is in the NetWare Administrator Tools menu.

2. Some method, usually through the login script, must execute Workstation Registration application—SYS:PUBLIC\ WSREG32.EXE—on the workstations.

3. The administrator must import the Workstation objects into NDS, again through an option within the NetWare Administrator Tools menu.

4. The workstations must continue to register with NDS in order to update their respective objects. If a login script method was used for the initial workstation registration, then it may be used thereafter.

When the Workstation objects have been imported, the workstation policies must be associated to them. Instead of having to associate each individual Workstation object with a workstation policy package, the administrator can associate the container object with the workstation policy package, as outlined in Exercise 10-1.

EXERCISE 10-1

Associating Workstation Objects to a Workstation Policy

1. In the NetWare Administrator, navigate through the NDS tree to the container object that will contain the workstation policy package.

2. Choose the Object menu and select Create.

3. From the Object Creation dialog box, select Policy Package.

4. From the dialog box that appears, select Win95 Workstation Package from the top drop-down box, type a name in the next box, and check off the box for Define Additional Properties.

5. Click Create.

6. The policy package details will appear. Click the Associations button on the right pane.

7. Click the Add button.

8. In the right pane of the dialog box that appears, browse for the context that contains the Workstation objects.

9. Both container objects and Workstation objects will appear in the left pane of the dialog box. Either select the container for the Workstation objects, if all of the workstations in that container will use this policy package, or select the individual Workstation object. Click OK.

10. If a Workstation object is already associated with a policy package, a message requesting policy replacement appears, as shown here. Click Yes.

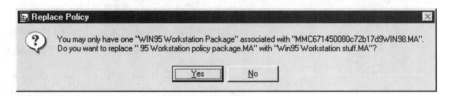

Configuring the Novell Client

Workstation Manager includes a computer-based policy in the workstation policy package for either NT or 95 that manages the configuration of the Novell client. Any client parameters on the workstation that the administrator might adjust are available in the Novell Client Configuration policy (see Figure 10-4). Further, the policy uses the exact same dialog box as is used at the client, so the interface is identical to what the administrator is familiar with.

The various client options will facilitate the selection of the tabs for the GUI login. In addition to configuring the NetWare client, the Novell Client Configuration policy facilitates configuration of

- NetWare/IP
- IP Gateway
- IPX Compatibility Adapter
- Target Service Agent

Each of these components can be used in conjunction with the Novell client to provide full network connectivity and resource access. NetWare/IP, IP Gateway, and the IPX Compatibility Adapter are all protocol related, thus enabling full network connectivity. The Target Service Agent is the client

FIGURE 10-4

Novell Client
Configuration policy

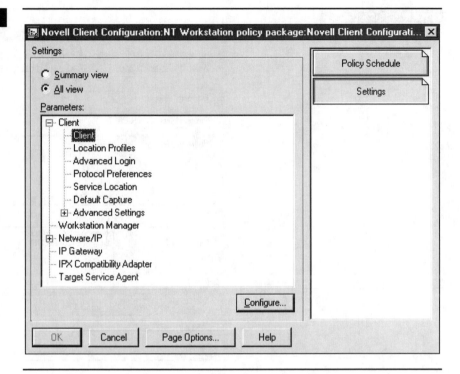

portion of back up. It enables NetWare Servers to backup workstations onto the server's archive system, which is usually a tape drive.

In order to change a component of the Novell client, the protocol components, or the Target Service Agent, the administrator must select a component from the list and click the Configure button. This will bring up a dialog box similar to the client selection depicted in Figure 10-5.

Each of the tabbed dialog box pages is a network client configuration tab available locally at the workstation through the Network icon in the Control Panel. The administrator may make the selections in this dialog box, and then allow NDS to apply the client configuration.

FIGURE 10-5

Client Options

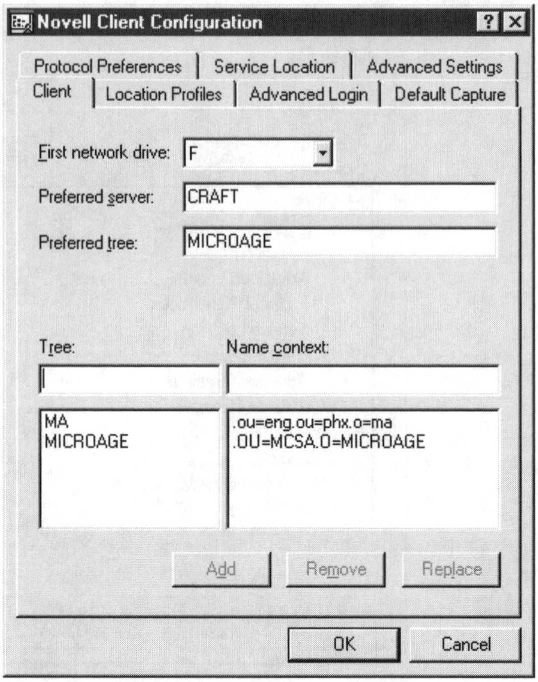

Novell Client Configuration

| Protocol Preferences | Service Location | Advanced Settings |
| Client | Location Profiles | Advanced Login | Default Capture |

First network drive: F

Preferred server: CRAFT

Preferred tree: MICROAGE

Tree:

Name context:

MA
MICROAGE

.ou=eng.ou=phx.o=ma
.OU=MCSA.O=MICROAGE

Add   Remove   Replace

OK   Cancel

QUESTIONS AND ANSWERS

Gail is planning an upgrade of all 7 NetWare 4.11 servers to NetWare 5, the addition of 12 new NetWare 5 servers, and a full Z.E.N.works installation. This upgrade and these additions will include a full redesign of the NDS tree; no user will be in the same context. Gail is not sure whether she should implement Z.E.N.works with Workstation Manager first, or as part of the server upgrade. What will Gail gain by implementing Z.E.N.works first?

If Gail implements Z.E.N.works first, installing clients and importing workstations' objects can all be done through the login script. When the servers are upgraded and the tree redesigned, the Novell Client Configuration policy for the workstations can automatically push out the new context to the workstations. An alias in the old context can help the first login for users in order to implement the new context through the workstation Novell Client Configuration policy. If Gail does not implement Z.E.N.works first, she may have to visit each of the workstations to make the changes.

CERTIFICATION OBJECTIVE 10.03

Managing Workstation Inventory

One of the most complicated network management functions is maintaining a functional and up-to-date inventory of hardware and software that exists on the network. Server hardware and software is not nearly as complex to maintain as workstations:

- Server upgrades affect many people when they are taken offline, so they occur less often.

- Only the administrator(s) have the access to upgrade servers.

- There are typically fewer servers than workstations on a network.

- Workstations can be upgraded by anyone except when extreme restrictions and security measures have been taken.

The more workstations on a network, the more likely an inventory will be outdated quickly. If there is high growth in the organization, the inventory will easily become difficult to manage manually from the moves, adds, and changes, as well as the new installations.

Novell's Workstation Manager offers an automated workstation inventory to address these challenges. Creating a Workstation Inventory policy within the workstation policy package enables the Workstation Inventory and governs the schedule for inventory updates (see Figure 10-6).

The Workstation Inventory itself is maintained within the Workstation objects. To view a workstation's current hardware and software, the administrator can open the Workstation Object Details and then select the Workstation Inventory button on the right-hand pane (see Figure 10-7).

The Workstation Inventory policy schedules when the inventory updates will be sent to Novell Directory Services. All inventory information is stored within the Workstation objects.

FIGURE 10-6

Workstation
Inventory policy

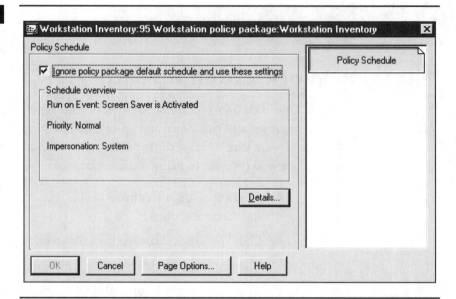

FIGURE 10-7

Workstation Inventory
property page

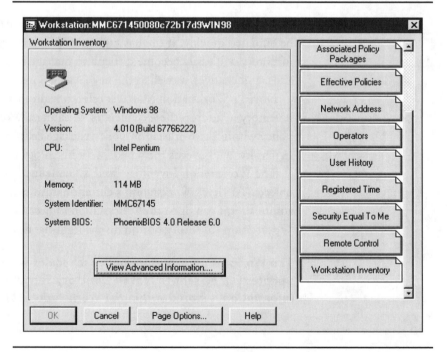

There is detailed information about the workstation available to an administrator when the View Advanced Information button is clicked (see Figure 10-8):

■ Drives available on the workstation

■ Buses, such as PCI or ISA

■ Services or devices on the workstation

■ Resources utilized, such as IRQ, I/O Port, DMA, or memory

■ Display adapter information, including the display adapter BIOS and driver settings

FIGURE 10-8

Advanced Inventory
information

Managing Profiles and Policies with NDS

User profiles are a feature of both Windows NT and Windows 95 that allows a network administrator to control the desktop settings for users of each workstation they log in to on the network. System policies is another feature of both operating systems that enables centralized control of both user and computer configuration of the operating system. Both user profiles (desktop settings) and system policies are part of the Workstation Manager NDS policies.

Desktop Management

Desktop settings are managed through the user policy package in the Desktop Preferences policy. For Windows NT, desktop settings are stored in a user profile that can be set up to be "roaming." That is, instead of storing the settings on each workstation that the user logs into, the profile is stored a single time on a NetWare server or the user's home directory. If storage space is an issue on individual workstations, the use of roaming profiles will minimize the impact of roaming users on a network. An administrator simply clicks the Roaming Profile button of the NT Desktop Preferences to configure how the desktop settings are stored.

In the Roaming Profiles options, the administrator can enable roaming profiles and then configure where they are stored on the network (see Figure 10-9). The storage options for profiles are in the user's home directory or on a NetWare server in another directory.

To set up a user profile or desktop settings, the administrator would configure a Desktop Preferences policy (see Figures 10-10 and 10-11) in the user policy package. All settings are downloaded to the user's current workstation the next time that user logs in to the network.

The Desktop Preferences policy has a Control Panel properties page that is similar to Windows Control Panel features. There are some differences, however.

For example, in the Accessibility Properties page for Accessibility Options, the three available option areas—StickyKeys, FilterKeys, and

FIGURE 10-9

NT roaming profiles

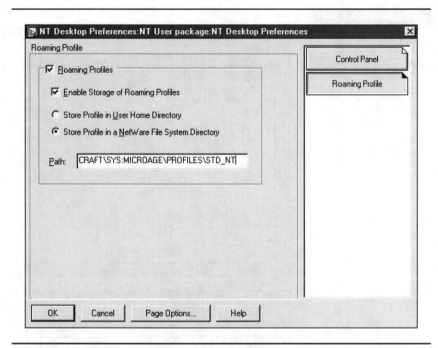

FIGURE 10-10

NT Desktop Preferences

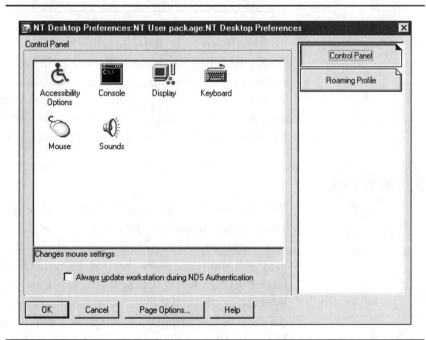

FIGURE 10-11

Windows 95
Desktop Preferences

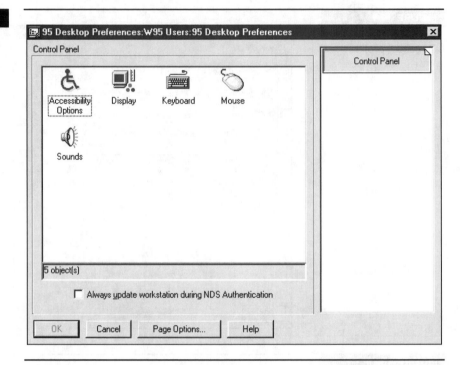

ToggleKeys—must be activated before the associated options can be configured. The administrator must check the box with the "use" for that option; then click Settings to configure them. In nearly all other aspects, the settings modified in this page are identical to the settings that can be modified when sitting at a workstation console and editing the same or similar Control Panel options. The desktop options are listed and defined in Table 10-4.

System Policies

Both Windows NT and Windows 95 can be configured to look for a system policy file to control how the workstation works. With the NetWare client and Workstation Manager, they can be configured to look for a policy file, even with a different name than the default, NTCONFIG.POL for NT or CONFIG.POL for 95, on the network in a specified directory. This is done by enabling and configuring a workstation computer system policy where the Remote Update option is edited for a manual update, as shown in Figure 10-12.

TABLE 10-4	Feature	Operating System	Function
Desktop Options Available for Windows NT and Windows 95	Accessibility Options	Windows NT Windows 95	Configures options that facilitate the use of the workstation by users with disabilities
	Console	Windows NT	Configures the way the DOS prompt window appears to users, such as colors, buffers, and whether the DOS prompt is in a window or a full screen
	Display	Windows NT Windows 95	Configures screen colors, wallpaper, screensaver, and other display options
	Keyboard	Windows NT Windows 95	Configures character repeat action and the cursor blink rate
	Mouse	Windows NT Windows 95	Configures the mouse click options and pointer styles
	Sounds	Windows NT Windows 95	Allows the selection of a sound scheme

FIGURE 10-12

Configuring a remote update of system policies

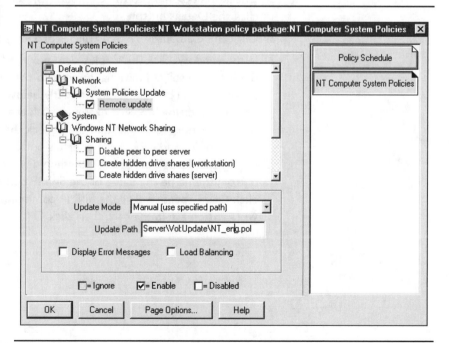

To set up system policies, the administrator can enable either, or both, a user policy and a workstation policy. Computer system policies configure the items that are found in the HKEY_LOCAL_MACHINE hive of the Registry. User System Policies configure items that are found in the HKEY_CURRENT_USER hive of the Registry. These policies are applied each time a user logs in to the network.

Creating a Computer System Policy

1. In the NetWare Administrator, navigate to the container in which the workstation policy package will reside.

2. Press the INSERT key.

3. Select Policy Package from the Object Creation dialog box; then click OK.

4. From the drop-down box at the top of the dialog box, select either a Win95 Workstation Package or a WinNT Workstation Package. In the next box, type a name for the policy package; check off the box to define additional properties; then click Create.

5. Check the box next to the Computer System Policies option; then click the Details button.

6. Click the Computer System Policies property page button.

7. In the window, click the + (plus sign) next to the options to expand the list; then select individual options to configure them. Some properties will be configurable directly below the window; others will need a dialog box. For example, click the + next to Network, then the + next to SNMP; and then check the box next to Communities and click the Properties button below the window to display the dialog box. In the Communities dialog box, click the Add button; then type the name of the SNMP community in the box and click OK. Repeat until all the SNMP communities for the workstation are in the box; then click OK.

Scheduling Workstation Application Upgrades

Any application execution can be scheduled for workstations or for users. This is done in the user policy package or workstation policy package. The administrator just adds an action to the policy package.

exam
Ⓦatch

When an action is scheduled for a user, it will apply to that user wherever the user logs in on the network. When an action is scheduled for a workstation, it will apply to the workstation, regardless of which user logs in.

EXERCISE 10-3

Adding an Action

1. In NetWare Administrator, navigate the NDS tree to the context with a workstation or user policy package.
2. Double-click the policy package to display its details.
3. Click the Add Action button.
4. Type a name for the action in the dialog box and click Create. Note that the action item appears in the window with a check box next to it.
5. Highlight the new action and click the Details button.
6. Check the box for Ignore package default schedule; then click the Details button.
7. On the General tab, click the Impersonation drop-down box and select System; then click Apply.
8. Click the Schedule tab and select the Event button, make sure the drop-down box displays User Login, and click Apply.
9. Click the Advanced tab and check off the box for Disable the Action after Completion. (This makes the action run only once.)
10. Click the Items tab, and click the Add button.
11. In the Item Properties dialog box, place the name of the application in the Name box, the UNC (Universal Naming Convention) in the form of \\server\volume\path for the Working Directory box, and any switches in the Command Parameters box. Select Above Normal from the Priority drop-down box.

12. Click OK to close the dialog box; then click Apply and Close to close the Action dialog box.

13. Click OK to close the Action and then click OK to close the policy package and save all the changes.

Dynamically Configuring Printers and Print Queues

Print management is a part of the Z.E.N.works Workstation Manager component. This is set up so that printers can be created for Windows 95 workstations, Windows NT workstations, and Windows NT users. There is currently no Windows 95 user printer.

The user printer for NT will follow the user around the network wherever they log in. The workstation printers will be available at those workstations regardless of the user logged in. In an environment where multiple users log in at a stationary workstation, the use of a computer-based printer makes printing transparent to the users. A printer can be moved, added, or changed on the network without the users being unable to print.

To create a printer, the administrator views the details of a workstation policy package and then checks off the Computer Printer option (see Figure 10-13). By clicking the Details button, the administrator can add and configure the printer for the user. The Add button allows the administrator to browse through the NDS tree for a Print Queue object. The New Driver button lets the administrator upgrade the printer driver with a few mouse clicks. When the administrator clicks the NetWare Settings button, he or she can change the NetWare print settings, such as whether to notify the user when printing has completed or whether to include a banner with the printout.

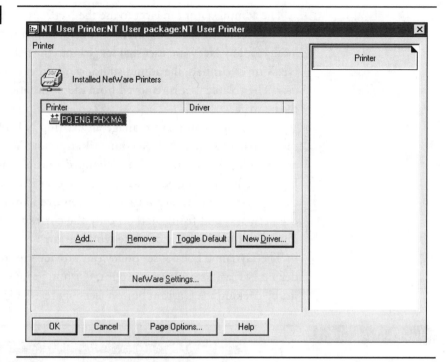

FIGURE 10-13

Printer configuration
options

CERTIFICATION OBJECTIVE 10.07

Windows NT User Management

Those Windows NT users who require access to NetWare 5 servers would
have traditionally required two user loginIDs: one for NetWare and one for
the NT workstation or domain. Workstation Manager and the NT client
can simplify the login process by transparently extending the Windows NT
login to include the execution of the NetWare login.

The WinNT User Package includes a Dynamic Local User policy. This
policy governs whether a local NT workstation user is created after the user
is authenticated to NDS. When the Enable Dynamic Local User is checked
in this policy, then the workstation is checked to see if the user exists with
the credentials (name, full name, and description) specified. If not, the user
is created. If so, the user is authenticated.

The administrator can elect to use the NetWare credentials of any user existing in Novell Directory Services. This would create a matching user locally for any NetWare user that logged into the network. When using the NetWare credentials, the administrator can further elect to create a *volatile* user. The volatile user is removed from the workstation after logging out of the network.

The administrator can manage an existing NT account by checking the Manage Existing NT Account (if any) box. Workstation group assignments for the account are changed to those specified in the Dynamic Local User policy. If a volatile user is checked in addition to this option, the local account will be removed after the user logs out of the network, and from then on only the corresponding NDS User object will be able to access the workstation.

The Dynamic Local User policy can provide group membership to any default NT workstation user groups. Custom groups can be added to the list by clicking the Custom button (see Figure 10-14).

FIGURE 10-14

Dynamic local users in Windows NT

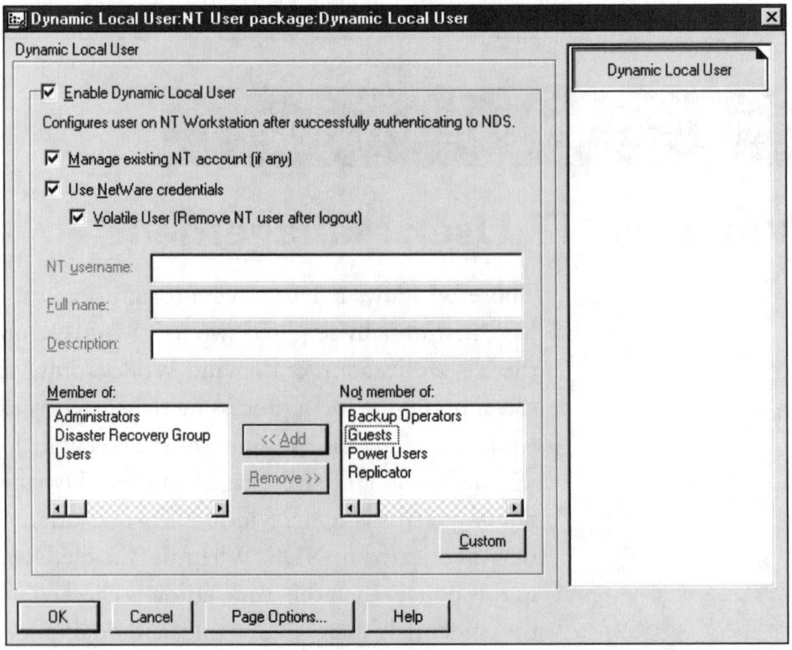

CERTIFICATION SUMMARY

Workstation Manager was originally created to manage Windows NT workstations. It has been extended to Windows 95 workstations and incorporated within the Z.E.N.works package.

Workstation Manager enables workstation management through policies created for users and workstations. These policies can manage the users' desktop settings, system policies, client configuration, Workstation Inventory, and printers. The policies can also schedule updates to workstation software and manage user synchronization between the Novell Directory Services (NDS) users and NT workstation local or domain users.

The installation of Workstation Manager is a function of installing Z.E.N.works on the server and installing the client on the workstations. In order to include Workstation Manager with the client installation, the administrator can create an unattended installation for the client using an /ACU command parameter, and use the /W command parameter to include Workstation Manager. The Workstation Manager component runs as a service on Windows NT (available within the Services icon in the Control Panel) and as a network service under Windows 95 (available within the Network icon in the Control Panel).

Workstation Manager includes the ability to configure the client from within the NetWare Administrator through a Novell Client Configuration policy in the workstation package. This can effectively configure any client option remotely that the administrator could configure locally. The changes are applied with the user login, but do not become active until the next time the client reboots.

Workstation Manager includes a Workstation Inventory capability that can poll the workstation for software and hardware configuration information. It is updated whenever the schedule is set to update.

Native Windows 95 and Windows NT system policies and desktop settings can be configured from within the NetWare Administrator using

- Desktop Preferences policies in the user package
- User System Policies in the user package
- Computer System Policies in the workstation package

The administrator can schedule application upgrades, or any application execution, to occur on an NT or 95 workstation through the use of user- or workstation-added actions. Actions that are added to a user package will take place regardless of where the user logs in. Actions that are added to a workstation package will take place on that specific workstation regardless of which user is logged in to the workstation.

The administrator can use printer policies to configure print queues for NT users, or for Windows 95 and Windows NT workstations. The policy includes the ability to update printer drivers for printers on the network.

Windows NT users exist locally on NT workstations and on NT domains. The Workstation Manager's Dynamic Local User policy in the WinNT User Package enables synchronization of these accounts, or even the ability to use only the NDS user. Volatile users can be created that are removed immediately upon logout from the NT Workstation.

 # TWO-MINUTE DRILL

- ❏ Workstation Manager adds the ability to manage workstations to NetWare through the use of Novell Directory Services (NDS).

- ❏ The Workstation Manager installs as a service under NT. It is a network client service under Windows 95. After the Windows NT Workstation Manager service authenticates to NDS, it periodically polls NDS to update scheduled actions and any other changes that should be made to the workstation.

- ❏ In order to begin using Workstation Manager, the NetWare Administrator needs to have policy packages created and associated to the appropriate users and workstations.

- ❏ Workstation Manager includes a computer-based policy in the workstation policy package for either NT or 95 that manages the configuration of the Novell Client. Any client parameters on the workstation that the administrator might adjust are available in the Novell Client Configuration policy.

❑ One of the most complicated network management functions is maintaining a functional and up-to-date inventory of hardware and software that exists on the network. Server hardware and software is not nearly as complex to maintain as that of workstations.

❑ User profiles are a feature of both Windows NT and Windows 95 that allows a network administrator to control the desktop settings for users of each workstation they log into on the network.

❑ Desktop settings are managed through the user policy package in the Desktop Preferences policy. For Windows NT, desktop settings are stored in a user profile that can be set up to be "roaming."

❑ Both Windows NT and Windows 95 can be configured to look for a system policy file to control how the workstation works. With the NetWare client and Workstation Manager, they can be configured to look for a policy file, even with a different name than the default—NTCONFIG.POL for NT or CONFIG.POL for 95—on the network in a specified directory.

❑ Any application execution can be scheduled for workstations or for users. This is done in the user policy package or workstation policy package.

❑ Print management is a part of the Z.E.N.works Workstation Manager component. This is set up so that printers can be created for Windows 95 Workstations, Windows NT Workstations, or Windows NT Users.

❑ Those Windows NT users who require access to NetWare 5 servers would have traditionally required two user loginIDs—one for NetWare and one for the NT workstation or domain. Workstation Manager and the NT client can simplify the login process by transparently extending the Windows NT login to include the execution of the NetWare login.

SELF TEST

The following Self Test questions will help you measure your understanding of the material presented in this chapter. Read all the choices carefully, as there may be more than one correct answer. Choose all correct answers for each question.

1. Which application is used for Workstation Manager management?

   A. NLIST

   B. NWORKMAN

   C. NetWare Administrator

   D. Workstation Manager

2. Which of the following policies exists within an NT User Package?

   A. NT Desktop Preferences

   B. NT Computer Printer

   C. NT Computer System Policies

   D. Restrict Login

3. What is the default polling schedule for the Workstation Manager client component?

   A. 1 second

   B. 10 minutes

   C. 60,000 seconds

   D. 20 minutes

4. George wants to update NetWare/IP options for all the workstations on his network. If he has Workstation Manager implemented, which of the following policies will let him do this?

   A. 95 User System Policies

   B. NT User System Policies

   C. Workstation Inventory

   D. Novell Client Configuration

5. If Susan creates a Workstation Inventory policy, how will she see the inventory?

   A. A Workstation Inventory object will contain the network inventory for that container.

   B. Each Workstation Inventory object will contain the inventory of the workstations they affect.

   C. Each Workstation object will have an Inventory property page with the individual information.

   D. A separate inventory database is created in SYS:PUBLIC\INV.DB.

6. Which of the following does not represent information seen in the Workstation Inventory?

   A. Drive Configuration

   B. Buses

   C. NetWare Client Configuration

   D. IRQ Resources

7. How does Workstation Manager handle roaming users and profiles on NT?

   A. The NT Desktop Preferences policy manages roaming profiles.

   B. The NT Workstation Inventory policy manages roaming profiles.

   C. The Dynamic Local User policy creates a roaming profile.

D. Roaming users and profiles cannot be supported.

8. If Tom wants to create a new policy file named TOM.POL for a group of 95 workstations, what must he update?

A. Tom must create a Dynamic Local User policy with a remote update option pointing to the file.

B. Tom must create an NT Computer System Policies policy with a remote update option pointing to the file.

C. Tom must create a 95 Computer System Policies policy with a remote update option pointing to the file.

D. Tom must create a 95 User System Policies policy with a remote update option pointing to the file.

9. Taylor created a new action to run once in NT Actions, which is an NT User Package, so that it will update all workstations. Then Taylor logged in to three NT workstations in succession, but the action did not execute each time. Why?

A. The NT Actions policy had already executed the run-once option for the user, so it did not need to execute again.

B. Taylor did not use the correct command parameters.

C. The NT Actions policy executed only for those workstations that had a search drive mapped to the executable's directory.

D. The NT Actions policy did not include its own login script, which would have ensured execution.

10. Justine is consulting for a firm that has just implemented Workstation Manager. The network administrator has called her in a panic. At a Workstation Manager seminar during the morning, the administrator had seen more than 12 options in the seminar teacher's workstation policy package, but in the administrator's own workstation policy packages, there were always less than 9, and some had more than others. What caused the differences?

A. The workstation policy packages on the administrator's network are corrupt.

B. NDS must be synchronized before all policies will appear in the policy package.

C. Each time a new action is added to a workstation policy package, it adds an item to the list. So these numbers vary based on usage.

D. The administrator has somehow changed the workstation policy package schema within NDS, and it must be edited.

11. The workstation policy packages on the administrator's network are corrupt.

A. NDS must be synchronized before all policies will appear in the policy package.

B. Each time a new action is added to a workstation policy package it adds an item to the list, so these numbers are variable based on usage.

C. The administrator has somehow changed the workstation policy package schema within NDS, and it must be edited.

12. Penny wants to update an application, but the update application requires some switches in order for it to run unattended. How can she do this with one action?

    A. She can put the switches in the Name dialog box.

    B. She can put the switches in the Command Parameters dialog box.

    C. She can add the switches in with Priority.

    D. She can change the Event requirements to include the switches.

13. Which policy will configure a printer and print queue on Windows 95?

    A. The 95 User Printer

    B. The NT User Printer

    C. The 95 Computer Printer

    D. The NT Computer Printer

14. Which of the following buttons can enable a banner page for the print queue?

    A. Add

    B. Toggle Default

    C. New Driver

    D. NetWare Settings

15. Which of the following policies is used to manage NT user accounts?

    A. Dynamic Local User

    B. NT User System Policies

    C. NT Computer System Policies

    D. Restrict Login

16. Which of the following options removes a user when the user logs out?

    A. Enable Dynamic Local User

    B. Manage Existing NT Account (if any)

    C. Volatile User

    D. Use NetWare Credentials

11

Managing NDS Security

CERTIFICATION OBJECTIVES

11.01　Introduction to NDS Security

11.02　Controlling Directory Access with Object Trustee and NDS Rights Assignments

11.03　NDS Default Rights

11.04　NDS Rights Inheritance

11.05　Blocking Inherited Rights

11.06　Determining an Object's Effective Rights

11.07　Guidelines for Implementing NDS Security

11.08　Troubleshooting NDS Security

T o manage a NetWare 5 network effectively, you must have a thorough understanding of Novell Directory Services (NDS). By virtue of their integration, NDS and NetWare 5 are nearly synonymous.

On the surface, NDS appears to be simply a directory of the NetWare network resources and users. Much like an inventory, the NDS directory seems to be a mere listing of what is on the network. However, as we'll see, that is just a surface evaluation. In fact, NDS provides a comprehensive set of administrative tools that can manage a global enterprise network as easily as a single server network with a few client workstations. NDS provides a single seat of administration, regardless of the number of users, workstations, or servers. Additionally, NDS will secure the resources on the network.

Introduction to NDS Security

NDS provides security to an enterprise network by creating a hierarchical tree structure for all network resources to reside in (see Figure 11-1). Since all network resources reside in a single structure, they can also be managed from a single seat of administration. The NetWare Administrator program is the primary means for the single seat of administration for NetWare 5. An administrator who has access to the entire NDS tree can execute the NetWare Administrator program from any network client and manage any network resource, even if that resource is located halfway around the world.

Three types of objects exist in the NDS tree structure:

■ **[Root]**   The root of the NDS tree, contains either Country or Organization container objects and very limited types of leaf objects

FIGURE 11-1

NDS hierarchical tree
structure

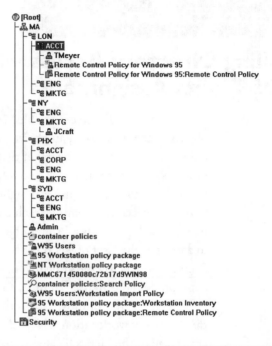

- **Container objects** Objects that can contain either container objects or leaf objects
- **Leaf objects** Objects that represent a network resource

The NDS container objects organize the leaf objects into manageable units. Designs for NDS trees can be based on location, business unit, or other functional criteria, which demonstrates the flexibility of the NDS architecture.

NDS security is established for each leaf object within the NDS tree. Security can be applied at a container object level, which then influences the security of the child objects contained within the parent container, thus simplifying the management of security.

Controlling Directory Access with Object Trustee and NDS Rights Assignments

Security in the NDS tree is established for an object by granting *rights* to objects in the tree. When an object has been granted rights to another object, it is considered a *trustee* of that object. An object must be a trustee in order to access other network resources. Objects can also be trustees of themselves. Object and property rights do not necessarily have to be granted to other objects. For example, each user is a User object within the NDS tree and each printer is a Printer object in the NDS tree. For a user to print to a printer, the User object must be granted appropriate rights to the Printing objects. By the same token, an object must be granted the appropriate rights to itself in order to make changes to its own status.

The NetWare Administrator is the tool used to administer the NDS tree from any workstation within the enterprise network. One major advantage of the hierarchical structure is the capability to create container administrators. Distributing administrators in this way creates a hierarchical administration structure, which is comparable to the way enterprises organize their network managers.

Container administrators are User objects that have been granted Supervisor rights to a container object and all the objects within that container, but not to any other container objects within the tree. Figure 11-2 illustrates this process. Using an Organizational Role object for the container administrators allows multiple container administrators to have the same rights and facilitates alternating administrators. For example, when creating a container administrator with Supervisor rights granted to the Organizational Role, the Organizational Role will have Supervisor rights to the file system of any servers within that container. In order to create a container administrator using an Organizational Role object, follow Exercise 11-1.

FIGURE 11-2   Container administration

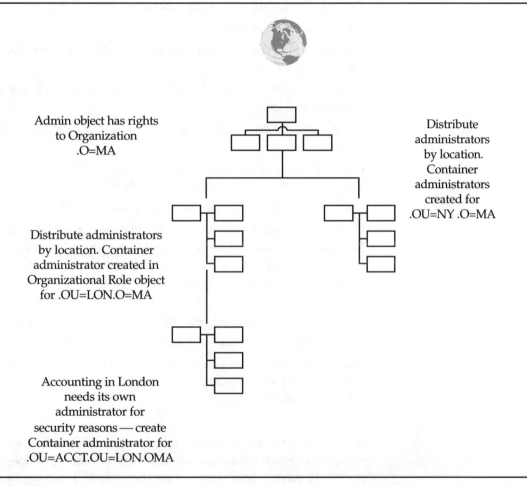

Admin object has rights
to Organization
.O=MA

Distribute
administrators
by location.
Container
administrators
created for
.OU=NY .O=MA

Distribute administrators
by location. Container
administrator created in
Organizational Role object
for .OU=LON.O=MA

Accounting in London
needs its own
administrator for
security reasons — create
Container administrator for
.OU=ACCT.OU=LON.OMA

EXERCISE 11-1   ## Creating a Container Administrator

1. In the NetWare Administrator, browse to the container that will be administered. The Organizational Role object should be created in the container where it will have administrative rights.

2. Choose the Object menu and select Create.

3. Select Organizational Role from the Object Creation dialog box.

4. Give the Organizational Role an appropriate name.

5. Click the Create button.

6. The object should appear in the container. Right-click it and select Rights to Other Objects.

7. The Search Context dialog box will default to the current container context. Click OK.

8. In the Rights to Other Objects dialog box, click the Add Assignment button.

9. In the right pane of the Select Object dialog box, double-click the up arrow until the container object is available in the left pane.

10. Click the container object in the left pane and click OK.

11. Under the Object Rights section, check Browse, Create, Delete, and Rename. If you want the Organizational Role to have the ability to manage the file system rights of any servers in that container, or if the Supervisor rights are required in this container, also check Supervisor.

12. Click OK to save the new object rights.

13. Double click the Organizational Role object to view its details.

14. Click the button with three dots next to the Occupant box. Using this button will allow the addition of multiple occupants to the Organizational Role object.

15. Click Add.

16. Select the User objects in the left pane of the next dialog, which will occupy the Organizational Role object. It may be necessary to navigate the tree in the right-pane window if the User objects do not exist in the same container context. Click OK. Repeat until all occupants are added.

17. The User objects will appear in the Occupant dialog box. Click OK.

18. Click OK to save the occupant changes to the Organizational Role object.

e x a m

ⓦ a t c h

The administrator can change object rights by selecting either Rights to Other Objects or Trustees of this Object. The Rights to Other Objects will show the NDS rights that the current object has granted to other objects in the tree. The Trustees of this Object will display the objects that have been granted rights to the currently selected object in the tree.

Object Rights

In Exercise 11-1, the container administrator was granted object rights to all objects within a container. Object rights are shown in Table 11-1.

The object rights are the basic rights needed to change objects within the tree. When a User object is granted rights within the NDS tree, the user who logs in with that User object ID will have those same rights to the other

TABLE 11-1	Right	Abbreviation	Function
Object Rights	Supervisor	S	All object rights are included in the Supervisor rights. In addition, the rights to the file system of any servers in the context where this right is applied are included. The Supervisor rights imply all property rights to that object.
	Browse	B	Browse objects in the NDS tree.
	Create	C	Create new child objects. Applicable only to container objects (leaf objects cannot have objects created in them).
	Delete	D	Delete objects such as User objects in the NDS tree. Requires Write property rights for all properties.
	Rename	R	Rename objects in the NDS tree.
	Inheritable	I	Describes whether a right can be inherited by lower-level objects in the NDS tree. This right is enabled only for [Root] and container objects.

objects in the tree. The Browse rights are the most important, since they allow the basic access of seeing the objects in the tree. If a user does not have the Browse rights to objects, they will not be able to view the resource or any of its details. In fact, the Browse rights are required for a user to even know whether a resource is on the network.

Property Rights

Each NDS object has specific attributes or *properties*, which are listed in Table 11-2. An example of a User object property is the Login Script property, which represents the user login script. Before an object can view or modify a property, it must have rights to that property. For example, a User object must be granted Write property rights to the User object's own Login Script property in order for that user to be able to create, modify, and use their own user login script.

exam
ⓦatch

By default, NDS objects are not automatically granted full rights to their own properties.

TABLE 11-2	Right	Abbreviation	Function
	Supervisor	S	Entails all other property rights to that property.
Property Rights	Compare	C	Allows comparison of the property value to a given value in order to return a true or false.
	Read	R	Allows viewing of the property value. The Read rights incorporate the Compare rights.
	Write	W	Allows modification, addition, or deletion of any property value.
	Add Self	A	When granted this right, the trustee object can add or remove itself as a value of the applicable property. The Write rights are implied by this right.

FIGURE 11-3

Object and property rights

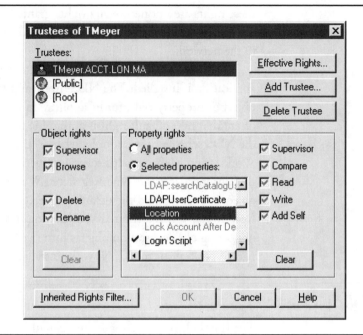

As illustrated in Figure 11-3, a trustee can be granted property rights to all properties or to selected properties. Using a selected property method for granting rights can fine-tune security. Note that in some cases, a trustee can inherit all property rights from a parent object and be granted explicit rights to selected properties.

CERTIFICATION OBJECTIVE 11.03

NDS Default Rights

When NDS installs the first time, it provides object and property rights that are generally sufficient for the network resource access required by users. Although the default NDS rights are available to users when they log in, these rights are not necessarily rights granted explicitly to User objects. Instead, some of the rights are granted to other objects to allow user access to the network.

The default rights for NDS may be extended when an NDS-aware application is installed. The NDS-aware application may add a default object or property right for its application to work appropriately. More often, that new default right is applicable to a new property or object within the NDS schema. For example, when Z.E.N.works is installed, the Workstation Manager adds several properties to container objects. One of these properties is the WM:Registered Workstation property. The container object is then granted the default property rights of Write, Compare, and Read to the WM:Registered Workstation property. This enables the importing of Workstation objects into the NDS tree. These rights are not part of NDS prior to Z.E.N.works installation.

[Public] Trustee

The [Public] trustee is not an object within the NDS tree. It is a special trustee rights holder that is applicable to all users, whether or not they have logged in to the network. By default, then, each User object is security equivalent to [Public]. Any rights granted to [Public] are valid rights for everyone. Since [Public] is not an object within the NDS tree, but a trustee rights holder, the only way to grant or revoke rights to [Public] is to right-click the object and select Trustees of this Object. Then, after selecting Add Trustee, the [Public] trustee will appear as one of the available trustee options. Both object rights and property rights can be granted to [Public] in this way.

Default Object Rights

The [Public] trustee is granted Browse Object rights to the [Root] of the NDS tree. This right enables users to see objects in the tree before and after logging in. Users are thus able to browse for their context before they log in.

The NDS tree [Root] is granted the Browse and Inheritable object rights to all NDPS printer, and non-NDPS Printer, Print Queue, and Print Server objects. This enables enterprise-wide printing.

When a User object is created, it is granted the Browse Object rights to itself. This allows the User object to "see" itself in the NDS tree.

Default Property Rights

By default, the [Public] trustee is granted Read rights to each User object's Default Server property and Read rights to each NetWare Server object's Network Address property. The combination of these two rights allows the login process to locate the default server name, and, secondarily, to find that server on the network through its Network Address property.

[Root] is granted Read property rights to each User object's Group Membership property and Read property rights to each User object's Network Address property. [Root] is also granted Read property rights to each Group object's Members property. These property rights enable members of groups to be located on the network.

Container objects are granted Read property rights to their own Login Script property. This is required for User objects to inherit that right at login and be able to read and execute the container login script. Container objects are also granted Read property rights to the Print Job Configuration property. Since some print job configurations are created for a container, inheritance allows User objects to use the print job configuration.

New User objects are granted the following property rights that enable the object to read its own properties and modify the user login script and user print job configuration:

- Read property rights to all of the User object's own properties
- Read and Write property rights to the User object's own login script
- Read and Write property rights to the User object's own Print Job Configuration property

NDS Rights Inheritance

Inheritance is the facility by which NDS passes rights (object rights, property rights, and/or file system rights) from one object to another. Rights flow down the NDS tree from as high as the NDS tree [Root] through container objects to leaf objects. Figure 11-4 displays object rights inheritance, which could apply to any NDS object.

FIGURE 11-4	Inherited object rights

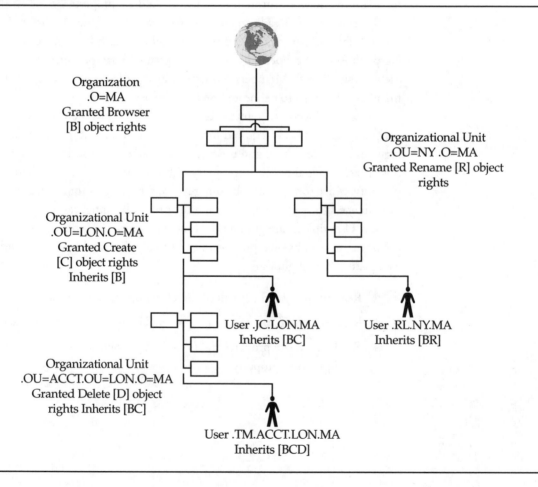

Organization
.O=MA
Granted Browser
[B] object rights

Organizational Unit
.OU=NY .O=MA
Granted Rename [R] object
rights

Organizational Unit
.OU=LON.O=MA
Granted Create
[C] object rights
Inherits [B]

User .JC.LON.MA
Inherits [BC]

User .RL.NY.MA
Inherits [BR]

Organizational Unit
.OU=ACCT.OU=LON.O=MA
Granted Delete [D] object
rights Inherits [BC]

User .TM.ACCT.LON.MA
Inherits [BCD]

An *explicit right* is a trustee assignment that has been granted to an object directly. An *inherited right* is a trustee assignment that was granted to an upper-level object and is received by the lower-level object through the NDS flow-down relationship. Property rights can be inherited the same as object rights. Figure 11-5 demonstrates a property right inheritance using a Login Script property as an example.

FIGURE 11-5   Property rights inheritance

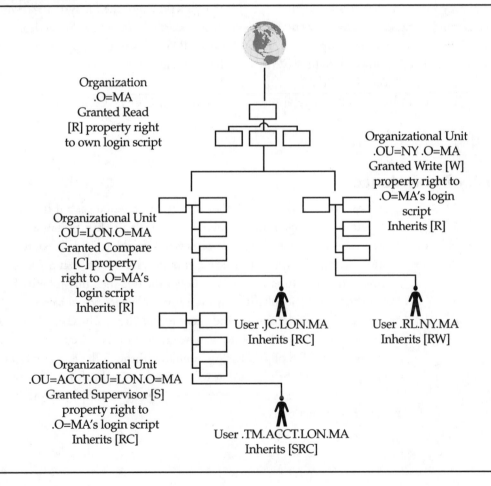

Organization
.O=MA
Granted Read
[R] property right
to own login script

Organizational Unit
.OU=NY .O=MA
Granted Write [W]
property right to
.O=MA's login
script
Inherits [R]

Organizational Unit
.OU=LON.O=MA
Granted Compare
[C] property
right to .O=MA's
login script
Inherits [R]

User .JC.LON.MA
Inherits [RC]

User .RL.NY.MA
Inherits [RW]

Organizational Unit
.OU=ACCT.OU=LON.O=MA
Granted Supervisor [S]
property right to
.O=MA's login script
Inherits [RC]

User .TM.ACCT.LON.MA
Inherits [SRC]

FROM THE CLASSROOM

When NDS Rights Flow into the File System

NDS security and NetWare File System security are administered separately. They even have different sets of rights that can be granted to trustees. There is one major point at which NDS rights flow into the file system. The simplest way to accomplish this is to grant Supervisor object rights for a parent container of a Server object to a trustee. However, if an object has the effective property right of Write to a Server object's Trustee List (ACL) property, then that object has the Supervisor

File System Rights to all volumes on that server. In the file system, unlike NDS, the Supervisor rights cannot be blocked by an IRF or a new trustee assignment lower in the directory structure. This is the point at which NDS rights flow into the file system, so you don't necessarily have to have Supervisor effective NDS rights to have Supervisor rights in the file system.

—By Dan Cheung, CNI, MCNE, MCT

Security Equivalence

It is easy to confuse *security equivalence* with inheritance, but they are not the same. Although both are methods of passing rights from one object to another, security equivalence applies when an object is made equivalent to another object's explicit trustee assignments, but not to that object's inherited rights. Inheritance flows down the tree such that inherited rights can continue to be inherited by even further lower-level objects.

User objects are security equivalent to the Group objects of which they are members. Any NDS object can be granted explicit security equivalence to any other NDS object, leaf, or container through the Security Equal To property page of the object that will receive new rights from other objects. There is an implied security equivalence between a leaf object and its direct parent container object.

Making a User Security Equivalent to the Admin Object

1. In the NetWare Administrator, navigate the tree until you locate the User object.

2. Double-click the User object to display its details. Alternatively, highlight the User object, choose the Object menu, and select Details or right-click the User object and select Details from the pop-up menu.

3. Click the Security Equal To property page, shown in Figure 11-6.

4. Click the Add button.

5. Navigate through the tree until the Admin object is displayed in the left-pane window.

6. Click the Admin object and click OK.

7. Click OK to save the changes to the User object and close the Details window.

FIGURE 11-6

Security Equivalence
property page

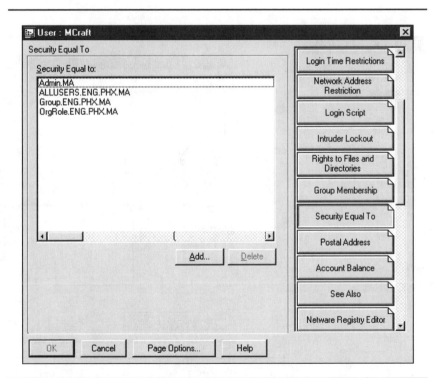

CERTIFICATION OBJECTIVE 11.05

Blocking Inherited Rights

The Inherited Rights Filter (IRF) is used to prevent inherited rights from traveling down the tree structure. The IRF is started from the Trustees dialog box, shown in Figure 11-7. The IRF can block any inherited rights, but cannot block those that are granted explicitly or through security equivalence. The fact that child leaf objects are implied to be security equivalent to their parent container objects means that those rights are not blocked by the IRF.

The IRF is applied for each object through the Trustees of this Object option using the IRF dialog box shown in Figure 11-8. When a right is checked off, that means it can be inherited. When the check box is clear next to a right, the right is filtered out and cannot be inherited.

FIGURE 11-7

IRF is started from the Trustees dialog box

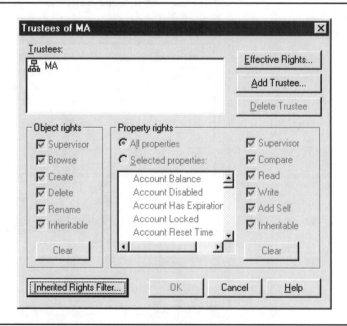

FIGURE 11-8

The IRF dialog box

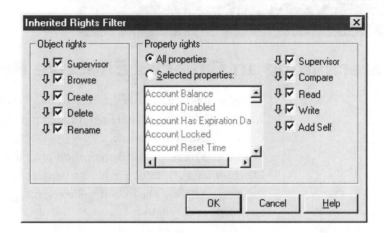

Both object rights and property rights can be filtered. The rights that this affects are those that are inherited from upper level containers. When a right is explicitly granted, even though the IRF blocks that right, the object still has that right. For example, when setting up a container administrator, you may want to filter out upper-level administrators. The container administrator would make sure to have explicit supervisor rights to the container and then set up an IRF for that container with the Supervisor rights check box cleared. Although the IRF does not allow the Supervisor right, the container administrator has an explicit trustee assignment and maintains Supervisor capabilities.

QUESTIONS AND ANSWERS

Janet is the network administrator for an aeronautical design firm. The research and development business unit of the firm works on some projects that are considered top secret within the company. Janet has been informed that all resources within the R&D organizational unit are to be hidden from all other users. How can Janet achieve this but still be able to manage it herself?

The R&D organizational unit will require Browse object rights and Supervisor object rights (since it implies the Browse right) to be filtered for all objects in the tree. Before filtering the Browse right, Janet will need to explicitly grant her own User object the Browse and Supervisor rights to that container unit.

Determining an Object's Effective Rights

Effective rights are those rights that are in effect for any NDS object. Effective rights can be inherited, filtered out, explicitly granted, or applied through security equivalence.

Effective rights are the combination of all the rights available to an object. Determining the effective rights is a matter of adding and subtracting the appropriate rights. The following steps should give you the effective rights for an object:

1. Determine the inherited rights.

2. Subtract the rights that are filtered out by the IRF.

3. Add the rights explicitly granted to the object.

4. Add the rights granted through security equivalence; that is, parent container object rights, group rights of which the object is a member, and explicit rights of objects to which this object is Security Equal To.

exam
ⓦatch

Effective rights = (inherited rights – IRF) + explicit trustee assignments + security equivalence rights.

In Figure 11-9, each user has been granted identical rights at the organization level. In figuring what object rights the users have within their own contexts, the IRF will apply. The NY context IRF allows [SB] to flow down. That means that user RL's inherited rights are [SB]. Add RL's explicit [SB] and security equivalence [CDR] rights to obtain the effective rights of [SBCDR] within RL's own context. User object JC will have the inherited [SBCDR] rights filtered by the IRF [B]. Add the security equivalence rights of [CDR] and no explicit rights for the effective rights of [BCDR]. For User object TM, all rights except Browse are filtered out through the .LON.MA

FIGURE 11-9   IRF and effective rights

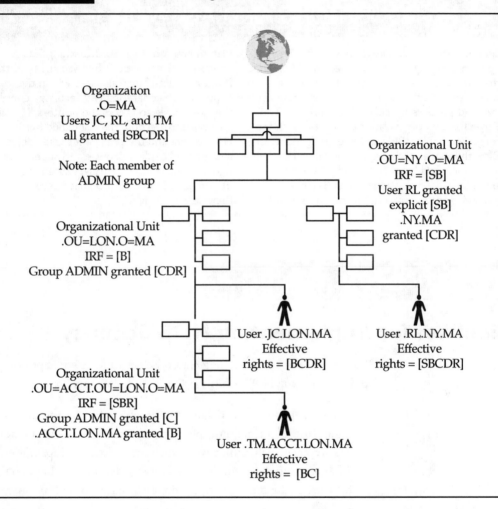

Organization
.O=MA
Users JC, RL, and TM
all granted [SBCDR]

Note: Each member of
ADMIN group

Organizational Unit
.OU=NY .O=MA
IRF = [SB]
User RL granted
explicit [SB]
.NY.MA
granted [CDR]

Organizational Unit
.OU=LON.O=MA
IRF = [B]
Group ADMIN granted [CDR]

User .JC.LON.MA
Effective
rights = [BCDR]

User .RL.NY.MA
Effective
rights = [SBCDR]

Organizational Unit
.OU=ACCT.OU=LON.O=MA
IRF = [SBR]
Group ADMIN granted [C]
.ACCT.LON.MA granted [B]

User .TM.ACCT.LON.MA
Effective
rights = [BC]

IRF. Then the [B] rights are also allowed to be inherited through the
.ACCT.LON.MA IRF. Through security equivalence, the TM user receives
both [B] and [C]. The final effective rights for TM in that context are [BC].

QUESTIONS AND ANSWERS

Marian is a network administrator who has been tasked with ensuring that the printers on F3 are not able to be seen by any users except the on that floor. However, both Marian and the president on Floor2 need supervisor access to the printer. The NDS tree has two organizational units beneath the SEC organization: EastBldg and WestBldg. Beneath EastBldg, there are three organizational units: Floor1, Floor2, and Floor3. Beneath WestBldg, there are three organizational units: Basement, Floor1, and Floor2. How can Marian set this up?	Marian granted the Floor3.EastBldg.SEC container object explicit Browse rights to the Printer objects. Since all users within the container object are implied security equivalent, they were able to access the printers. Marian also created a group that contained her own User object and the president's User object, and granted explicit Browse and Supervisor rights to the printers. Finally, Marian created an IRF on each Printer object that filtered out the Browse object rights.

CERTIFICATION OBJECTIVE 11.07

Guidelines for Implementing NDS Security

NDS security is the key to keeping enterprise network resources protected. When implementing NDS security, it is best to follow some basic guidelines:

- Do not depend on the default Admin object for the administrative login. Instead, create multiple administrator objects with names that are not necessarily indicative of their administrative capabilities. After creating the administrators, disable the Admin object so that hackers, or the merely curious, do not attempt to find its password.

- Use Group or Organizational Role objects to assign explicit rights. This facilitates granting multiple User objects the same rights as the original user. Adding a member or occupant is a much simpler task than determining which rights need to be granted and then granting them to multiple users.

- Avoid using security equivalence through the Security Equal To property page. The rights granted through security equivalence are difficult to track. For example, when a user has been granted security equivalence to an object, if that other object's rights are changed later on, the user's rights will change, seemingly without cause.

- Do not grant more rights than are required.

- Avoid granting rights at the [Root] or Organization level. Keep these rights to a minimum, and increase rights as needed while "walking" down the NDS tree. By keeping rights to a minimum at the upper levels of the tree, it is easier to control inheritance without IRFs.

- Avoid using IRFs, except where absolutely necessary. When there are security problems, many times in troubleshooting the problem the IRF is forgotten, and the problem goes unsolved or managed by granting too many rights when it was not required.

- Beware of assigning rights to the [Public] Trustee. Any rights assigned to the [Public] Trustee are available to users who have not yet logged into the network.

CERTIFICATION OBJECTIVE 11.08

Troubleshooting NDS Security

If NDS security has been planned prior to implementation, it is much less likely to require troubleshooting.

There is a basic four-step model to troubleshooting NDS security:

1. Gather information

2. Develop a plan of attack

3. Execute the plan

4. Document the solution or return to Step 1 and start over

The first step is to gather information about the security problem. What is the user attempting to do? Does the user have too much access? Does the user have too little access? Is the security of another object the problem?

The history of the problem is valuable in troubleshooting. Did this problem always exist, or did the security work before and now has changed? When did the problem start occurring? Have any changes to network security been made around this time?

If the security worked before and has suddenly changed, the plan of attack should concentrate on the changes that were made during the same time period. If the problem has always existed, the plan of attack would most likely be to start with a layout of the effective rights for both objects and properties as they apply to the target NDS objects.

If there were prior security changes, the plan execution would most likely reverse the security changes and test the results. If the problem has always existed, the plan would be to determine

- Which effective rights are required
- Which effective rights are actually there
- Which rights must be added or removed

Then the plan would be to change the rights so that the correct effective rights are in effect, and then to verify that they are the correct rights.

Finally, the verified solution should be documented to avoid the same issue from recurring.

CERTIFICATION SUMMARY

Novell Directory Services (NDS) is the key to network security. NDS is set up as a hierarchical tree consisting of container and leaf objects. The container objects organize the leaf objects into the hierarchy, and each object has properties.

NDS security is implemented by assigning trustee rights to the NDS objects or the properties of those objects. The object rights are Supervisor

[S], Browse [B], Create [C], Delete [D], Rename [R], and Inherited [I]. Object rights apply to actions that can be done to the objects themselves, not to the values within those objects. The only exception to this rule is that the Supervisor right will allow actions to be taken on the object's properties.

Property rights are Supervisor [S], Compare [C], Read [R], Write [W], and Add Self [A]. The Supervisor right includes all other rights. Property rights are required for an NDS object to view or modify the values of an object's property.

When NDS installs the first time, it includes some default security assignments that are designed to allow users the flexibility and access required to use the network. These rights are applicable to a special trustee, the [Public] Trustee. The [Public] Trustee is not an object, but a trustee assignment that is automatically granted to all users, whether or not they have logged in to the network.

NDS object and property rights can flow down the NDS tree and be *inherited* by objects. Although similar, security equivalence is the application of rights through making one object equal to the explicit trustee assignments that have been granted to another object.

Inherited rights can be blocked through the use of an Inherited Rights Filter (IRF). However, the IRF does not block rights that have been granted through security equivalence.

Effective rights are the trustee assignments in effect when an object is being accessed by another object. The effective rights are calculated by adding the inherited rights, subtracting the IRF blocked rights, and adding the explicit trustee assignments and the rights granted through security equivalence.

There is a four-step process for troubleshooting NDS security problems:

1. Gather the information.

2. Develop a plan of attack.

3. Execute the plan.

4. Document the results or return to Step 1.

TWO-MINUTE DRILL

❏ NDS provides security to an enterprise network by creating a hierarchical tree structure for all network resources to reside in. All network resources reside in a single structure and can be managed from a single seat of administration. The NetWare Administrator program is the primary means for the single seat of administration for NetWare 5. An administrator who has access to the entire NDS tree can execute the NetWare Administrator program from any network client and manage any network resource

❏ Three types of objects exist in the NDS tree structure: [Root], container objects, and leaf objects. The NDS container objects organize the leaf objects into manageable units. Designs for NDS trees can be based on location, business unit, or other functional criteria.

❏ NDS security is established for each leaf object within the NDS tree. Security can be applied at a container object level, which then influences the security of the child objects contained within the parent container.

❏ Security in the NDS tree is established for an object by granting rights to objects in the tree. When an object has been granted rights to another object, it is considered a trustee of that object. An object must be a trustee in order to access other network resources. Objects can also be trustees of themselves. Object and property rights do not necessarily have to be granted to other objects.

❏ Container administrators are User objects that have been granted Supervisor rights to a container object and all the objects within that container, but not to any other container objects within the tree.

❏ The object rights are the basic rights needed to change objects within the tree. When a User object is granted rights within the NDS tree, the user who logs in with that User object ID will have those same rights to the other objects in the tree. The Browse rights are the most important, since it allows the basic access of seeing the objects in the tree.

❑ Each NDS object has specific attributes or properties. An example of a User object property is the Login Script property, which represents the user login script.

❑ A trustee can be granted property rights to all properties or to selected properties. Using a selected property method for granting rights can fine-tune security. In some cases, a trustee can inherit all property rights from a parent object and be granted explicit rights to selected properties.

❑ When NDS installs the first time, it provides object and property rights that are generally sufficient for the network resource access required by users. Although the default NDS rights are available to users when they log in, these rights are not necessarily rights granted explicitly to User objects. Instead, some of the rights are granted to other objects to allow user access to the network. The default rights for NDS may be extended when an NDS-aware application is installed.

❑ The [Public] trustee is not an object within the NDS tree. It is a special trustee rights holder that is applicable to all users, whether or not they have logged in to the network yet. By default, then, each User object is security equivalent to [Public]. Any rights granted to [Public] are valid rights for everyone.

❑ The [Public] trustee is granted Browse Object rights to the [Root] of the NDS tree. This right enables users to see objects in the tree before and after logging in. Users are thus able to browse for their context before they log in.

❑ By default, the [Public] trustee is granted Read rights to each User object's Default Server property and Read rights to each NetWare Server object's network address property. The combination of these two rights allows the login process to locate the default server name and find that server on the network through its Network Address property.

❑ Inheritance is the facility by which NDS passes rights (object rights, property rights, and/or file system rights) from one object to another. Rights flow down the NDS tree from as high as the NDS tree [Root] through container objects to leaf objects.

❑ An explicit right is a trustee assignment that has been granted to an object directly. An *inherited right* is a trustee assignment that was granted to an upper-level object and is received by the lower-level object through the NDS flow-down relationship. Property rights can be inherited the same as object rights.

❏ It is easy to confuse security equivalence with inheritance. Security equivalence applies when an object is made equivalent to another object's explicit trustee assignments, but not to that object's inherited rights.

❏ User objects are security equivalent to the Group objects of which they are members. Any NDS object can be granted explicit security equivalence to any other NDS object, leaf, or container through the Security Equal To property page of the object that will receive new rights from other objects. There is an implied security equivalence between a leaf object and its direct parent container object.

❏ The Inherited Rights Filter (IRF) is used to prevent inherited rights from traveling down the tree structure. The IRF is started from the Trustees dialog box. The IRF can block any inherited rights, but cannot block those that are granted explicitly or through security equivalence.

❏ Effective rights are those rights that are in effect for any NDS object. Effective rights can be inherited, filtered out, explicitly granted, or applied through security equivalence. Effective rights are the combination of all the rights available to an object. Determining the effective rights is a matter of adding and subtracting the appropriate rights.

❏ NDS security is the key to keeping enterprise network resources protected. When implementing NDS security, it is best to follow some basic guidelines: Do not depend on the default Admin object for the administrative login. Use Group or Organizational Role objects to assign explicit rights. Avoid using security equivalence through the Security Equal To property page. Do not grant more rights than are required. Avoid using IRFs, except where absolutely necessary. Beware of assigning rights to the [Public] Trustee.

❏ There is a basic four-step model to troubleshooting NDS security:

   1. Gather information.

   2. Develop a plan of attack.

   3. Execute the plan.

   4. Document the solution or return to Step 1 and start over.

SELF TEST

The Self-Test questions will help you measure your understanding of the material presented in this chapter. Read all the choices carefully, as there may be more than one correct answer. Select all correct answers for each question.

1. How does NDS establish security?

   A. Through rights for container objects

   B. Through trustee assignments for User objects

   C. Through rights granted for each NDS object

   D. Through file system rights

2. What is the term for an object that has been granted rights to another object?

   A. Security equivalence

   B. Trustee

   C. Inherited Rights Filter

   D. Effective rights

3. Which of the following objects facilitates applying rights to multiple users?

   A. Organizational Role

   B. User object

   C. Workstation policy

   D. User policy

4. Which of the following is not an object right?

   A. Supervisor [S]

   B. Create [C]

   C. Browse [B]

   D. Read [R]

5. Which of the following is not a property right?

   A. Create [C]

   B. Read [R]

   C. Write [W]

   D. Supervisor [S]

6. George wants to allow every user, whether logged in or not, to be able to print to the graphics printer. Aside from enabling anyone to be able to place print jobs in the queue, how can he accomplish this?

   A. NDS will not support this.

   B. George can grant the [S] object right of the printer to the [Root].

   C. George can grant the [B] object right of the Printer objects to [Public].

   D. George can grant the [SBCDR] object rights of the Printer objects to the group "Everyone."

7. What is the default object right granted to [Public] for the tree [Root]?

   A. Supervisor [S]

   B. Browse [B]

   C. Create [C]

   D. Delete [D]

8. What are the default rights for a User object to its own Login Script property?

   A. Read [R] and Compare [C]

   B. Supervisor [S] and Read [R]

   C. Write [W] and Add Self [A]

   D. Read [R] and Write [W]

9. What is the method through which rights flow down the NDS tree?

   A. Security equivalence

   B. Inheritance

   C. Trustee assignments

   D. Inherited Rights Filter

10. What is the method through which an object is granted the same rights as another object's explicit trustee assignments?

    A. Security equivalence

    B. Inheritance

    C. Trustee assignments

    D. Inherited Rights Filter

11. What is used to block inherited rights?

    A. Explicit security equivalence

    B. Implied security equivalence

    C. Trustee assignments

    D. Inherited Rights Filter

12. What are the actual rights that an NDS object has when it is accessing another object?

    A. Trustee assignments

    B. Inherited rights

    C. Effective rights

    D. Security equivalent rights

13. When determining the effective rights, which are subtracted?

    A. Inherited rights

    B. Trustee assignments

    C. Implied security equivalence

    D. IRF

14. Aaron is a network administrator who has changed the rights for a User object. The next morning, three other users call Aaron to complain that there were problems with network access. Aaron called the user whose rights he changed and finds that there are no problems. What may have happened? Select the best option.

    A. Someone else changed those three users' rights.

    B. A group that all three users belonged to was deleted.

    C. The users depended on the security equivalence to the changed user.

    D. A change was made to the Organization container object.

15. Which of the following is not a troubleshooting step?

    A. Create a test security scenario.

    B. Gather information.

    C. Document the solution.

    D. Execute a plan of attack.

CERTIFIED NOVELL ENGINEER

12

Managing Resources in a Multicontext Environment

CERTIFICATION OBJECTIVES

12.01   How the Directory Tree Affects the Network

12.02   How the Directory Tree Affects NDS Planning and Design

12.03   Setting Context for Resource Access

12.04   Shortcuts to Accessing and Managing Resources

12.05   Guidelines for Setting Up Resources

12.06   Summary of Actions and Rights Needed

12.07   Using Correct Naming in Login Scripts

I n today's networking environment, multiple local area networks (LANs), are linked together to form wide area networks (WANs). These networks can become cumbersome and overly complex to administer if they are not planned carefully. Remember that the building block of this network system, the *directory tree*, is basically a database of objects. Every object in a directory has a relationship to every other object in the directory. We will look at how objects interact within the same tree and how they interact with different trees. We will also talk about the location of an object in the directory, or the *context*, as it is more commonly known.

Understanding how context affects an object's behavior on the network is essential for effective network administration. For example, knowing a user object's context is vital in implementing a container login script that the user will execute at login.

First, let's review Chapter 1 briefly. When we talk about a directory tree, think in terms of a real tree. Like a real tree, all directory trees start out with the [Root]s. From here, the tree branches out in various units, as shown in Figure 12-1. The first is the tree trunk, or Organization (EMA is the name of our organization in Figure 12-1). A directory tree can have multiple Organization objects, but it's not recommended except under special circumstances. The thicker, heavier branches from the trunk are called Organizational Units (PROD and DEVELOPMENT in Figure 12-1). The smaller branches can be other Organizational Units. Eventually, each of these branches will have leaves on them. Leaf objects are various object types such as users, printers, and volumes.

First, we will see how the directory tree affects the network. When designing and administering your network, you will always fall back on the directory tree when you make updates and changes. Although a directory tree can be organized however you want to organize it, we will see that proper planning and a commonsense approach make future administration of the network easier and more efficient.

FIGURE 12-1

A simple diagram of a
directory tree

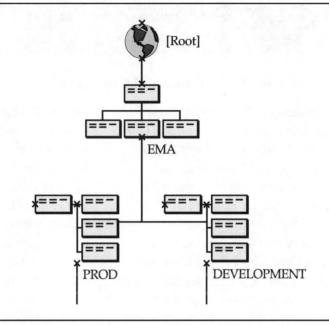

CERTIFICATION OBJECTIVE 12.01

How the Directory Tree Affects the Network

I cannot emphasize enough that the directory tree is the nervous system of
the NetWare world. Every object on the network from client Windows NT
workstations to the SYS: volume has an object in the directory. This means
that the more complex the directory tree, the harder network
administration. When organizing objects in the directory tree, remember to
use logic and commonsense when planning the various branches, or

FROM THE CLASSROOM

NDS Tree Design Fundamental Concepts

When evaluating an NDS tree's proposed design, or an existing tree's design, don't forget that the "D" in NDS stands for "Directory." Frequently, initial NDS tree designs are based on an organization chart that reflects management reporting relationships. An NDS tree based solely on that document would be fine if the network were supporting an organization with only a single location and no chance of expanding its physical plant structure, and with no plans for expanding its network.

For a more complex organization, a better prototype would be the interoffice mail distribution system's route diagram. Usually, delivery of office mail is based on location

codes, which may be further subdivided into floors, buildings, suites, rooms, or cubicles, much the same way that the NDS tree is organized into containers and subcontainers. Although knowing the title of the sender or recipient may help expedite the speed of delivery, not knowing the physical location of the recipient's *IN* box will effectively stop the delivery. Managers and their immediate subordinates are not necessarily collocated.

NDS trees are designed to aid the delivery of networked services, just as interoffice mail is designed to provide physical mail delivery services, and thus should be designed similarly.

—By Dan Cheung, CNI, MCNE, MCT

Organizational Units. If you think you need only one Organizational Unit, then NDS gives you the option to create only one Organizational Unit, with the flexibility to create more in the future.

Just How Is That Directory Tree Made Up Again?

For exam purposes, as well as real world, everyday administration, you must know and live the NDS tree. For that reason, we'll go over this one more time to make sure you understand it upside down and inside out.

The first, or top-level, object in the directory tree is the [Root] object. The [Root] is created when the first server is installed in the Directory tree. Once it is created, it cannot be deleted, renamed, or moved elsewhere in the directory tree. Since the directory is hierarchical in nature, the [Root] object has other objects under it, or within it. Figure 12-2 shows the start of a Directory tree. A globe represents the [Root]. Below the [Root] we have our Organization object. Remember that the [Root] object can hold only specific container objects. The two types of container objects that can exist directly under [Root] are Country and Organization objects. Only one leaf object can exist directly under [Root], an Alias object, which must point to another Country or Organization object in the tree. An Alias object pointing to any other type of object is not allowed at this level.

Container objects are just that—they contain other objects. (See Table 12-1 for a complete list of NetWare object types.) A container object in the directory tree holds other NDS objects. As illustrated in Figure 12-3, the hierarchical fashion of the directory tree takes shape when you start to branch out with the various container objects. NetWare has three types of container objects: Country, Organization, and Organizational Unit.

The Country object is optional and not widely used. It can be used to designate a locale for the tree, if the NDS tree is being designed with eventual merging into a global WAN in mind (this is not a typical scenario and beyond the scope of this chapter). The Organization object is required, and can be the company name, a location, a division of a company, or even a college or university. Although multiple organizations can exist in a single directory tree, most have only one. (There are some instances when two or more are needed, but those are special cases not discussed here.) The Organizational Unit is similar in the sense that it is a branch in the tree. There can also be multiple Organizational Units per directory tree. Organizational Units can contain other Organizational Units. This is where network administration can become complicated when you have multicontext environments. The final piece to the tree is the leaf object. A

FIGURE 12-2

The [Root] and
Organization objects

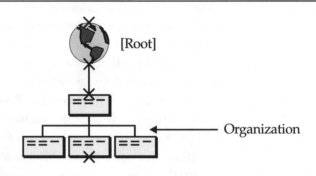

[Root]

Organization

leaf object represents an individual entity or resource in the tree like a
printer, user, or server. Once you reach a leaf, there is no further branching

TABLE 12-1

Definition of NetWare
Object Types

Object Type	Definition
[Root]	Top of the Novell Directory Services structure; sometimes referred to as the entry point to the directory tree
Country	A container object that designates the locale or country where the directory tree resides
Organization	Must be present and there can be only one in a directory tree; designates the tree name if no Country object is used
Organizational Unit	Represents a certain group of objects within a directory tree; can be multiple and can contain other Organizational Units
Leaf object	Actual network resources, such as users, servers, printers, and volumes

FIGURE 12-3   Branches of the NDS directory tree

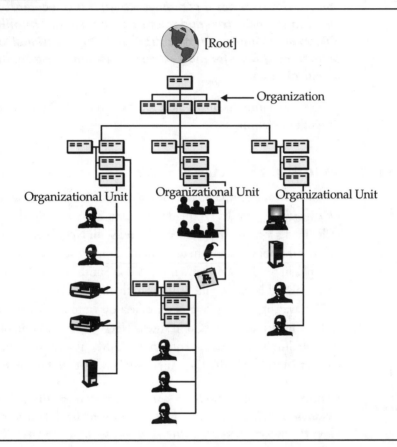

of the tree. In some cases, you may have duplicate leaf objects in different Organizational Units. However, this is not recommended because it may cause problems in searching for resources. The thing to remember here is that location makes the difference. You will notice that managing an object in your NDS tree is a matter of location, location, location.

exam **Match**

Volume objects and Group objects are not containers; they are leaf objects. [Root] is not a container either; it is the demarcation between the NDS tree and the rest of the world. The only container objects are Country, Organization, and Organizational Unit; this is a point of confusion for most students and can cause incorrect answers on Novell tests.

Next, we'll discuss how object location in the NDS directory tree affects network operation.

Object Interaction in the Directory Tree

As with any other NDS object, each leaf object has a name, called a *Distinguished Name*. Its Distinguished Name also uniquely identifies it, including its location in the directory tree. With NetWare, you always have to think of the object's name in terms of location in the directory tree. For example, in real life, a person's name is Bob Smith and, in NetWare terms, his Distinguished Name would be Bob Smith on 123 Main St., Anytown, U.S.A.

This way of naming isolates the object down to its location or context within the directory tree. Context tells NetWare the location of an object. In the Bob Smith example, his context is 123 Main St., Anytown, U.S.A. If he moves to 456 University Dr., Anytown, U.S.A., then his context has changed.

exam **Match**

Context and the immediate parent container of the object are synonymous. It should also be stressed that both leaf and container objects have a context. Some students walk away with the notion that only leaf objects can have a context.

When you consider two different objects in a directory tree, you have to understand the concept of context. Figure 12-4 shows a directory tree containing two objects with the same Common Name, which implies that their Distinguished Names are different. Otherwise, they could not exist in the same directory tree.

In Figure 12-4, notice that the two objects are both named HP_LJ_5. That is, their Common Names are HP_LJ_5 and HP_LJ_5. One resides in the Accounting container and the other resides in the Administration container. The difference is in their locations. The Distinguished Name of

FIGURE 12-4

Two objects with the same Common Name but with different Distinguished Names

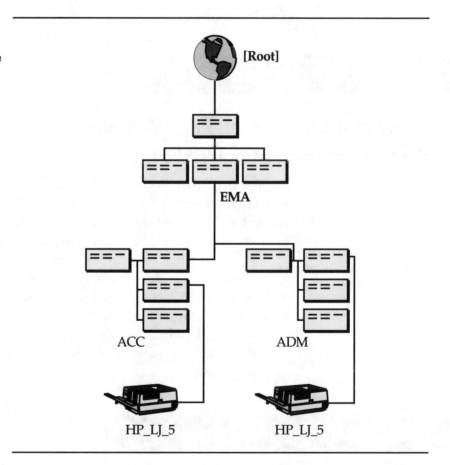

one is HP_LJ_5.ACC.EMA, and the other is HP_LJ_5.ADM.EMA. They reside in different containers so they can have the same common name, just as Michele, who lives in Illinois, and Michele, who lives in Maine, have the same first name, but their respective contexts identify them as two different people.

The key point here for exam and real-life purposes is to make sure you take context into account when designing your login scripts and overall resource access. Next, we will look at how the directory tree can affect NDS planning and design.

CERTIFICATION OBJECTIVE 12.02

How the Directory Tree Affects NDS Planning and Design

Planning an effective directory tree is essential to planning NDS. When planning how a directory tree will be laid out, consider where you want your leaf objects to reside and how many Organizational Units you will have, and where they will be located in relation to each other.

When you first draw out a directory tree for your network, you will have to know how many branches you need. To do this, you have to consider a couple of things. First, how many objects will you have and how do you want to group them? Once you determine this, you can draw out your basic directory tree. The other thing you need to do is think ahead to future network growth. Does your design have the flexibility to grow and change with your network?

CERTIFICATION OBJECTIVE 12.03

Setting Context for Resource Access

Remember that context is your location in the directory tree. Where you reside, and where other objects reside, determines how an NDS object has to be configured. When configuring how users will access resources, you have to keep in mind where the resources reside. An example of this is a printer that may exist in a different Organizational Unit in the directory tree. Figure 12-5 shows our directory tree with a user in the Accounting container and a printer in the Administration container. If user BSmith wants to print a document on the printer in the Administration container, then BSmith would be printing to a container outside of his context. In this

FIGURE 12-5

User in different context than the resource being accessed (printer)

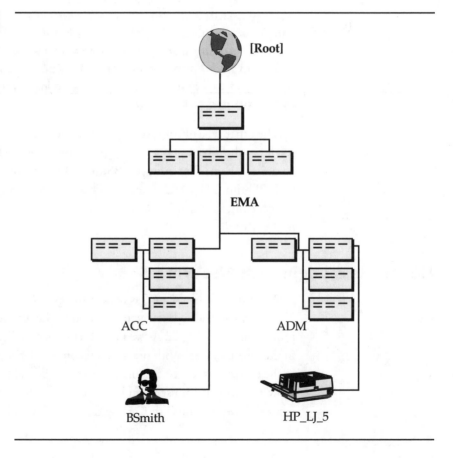

case, would you have to change BSmith's context? No, you can use the name of the printer: HP_LJ_5.ADM.EMA.

Current Context and Object Context

There are two types of contexts within Novell Directory Services. The first is Current context. *Current context* is where you currently are in the directory tree. Even though BSmith's context is the Account container (ACC.EMA), he could change his Current context to ADM.EMA.

exam
Ⓜatch

This concept is critical to understand correctly. A common classroom analogy is stated like this: "Current context is like perspective, it is your view of where other objects are in relation to your current position. In other words, think of how you would give directions to 123 Main if you were standing at 345 Main, versus if you were standing at 678 Elm and you had to give instruction in terms of left or right turns and distance only."

The other type of context is *Object context*, which is where the object resides in the directory tree. The Object context is the long form of an object's name. For example, BSmith's Object context is CN=BSmith.OU=ACC.O=EMA. Therefore, you can identify the Object context by starting with the object and listing every container back to the [Root].

Contextless Login with NetWare 5

A new feature of NetWare 5 is *contextless login*. With previous versions of NetWare, you had to know your location in the directory tree or have the proper context to log in. As we have discussed, an object can reside anywhere in the directory tree. With previous versions of NetWare, you had to be set up in the correct context or the login process would fail to find the User object.

With NetWare 5, users can log in anywhere on the network, regardless of context. This is done with Catalog Services. We will not go into detail here but, for the exam, know that NetWare 5 has contextless login. With contextless login you can authenticate from any point on the network simply by typing your login name and password, without knowing the location of your User object in the NDS tree.

CERTIFICATION OBJECTIVE 12.04

Shortcuts to Accessing and Managing Resources

NetWare 5 has some shorter methods than those we've mentioned for accessing the various resource types. There are a couple of naming concepts to become familiar with, and different ways to get to the same part of the directory tree. Here, we will look at these different naming concepts and some useful things to know for navigating the NDS directory tree.

Naming Concepts

For some of you, this may seem like a redundant review; but for concise exam preparation, we must cover this again. The directory tree has some naming concepts that engineers and administrators need to be familiar with.

Distinguished Names

The Distinguished Name is the complete directory path from the object back to the [Root]. For example, Figure 12-6 shows a small directory tree. The User object TRobins is located down the tree under a couple of different Organizational Units. Tracing from his object back to the [Root], we see that his Distinguished Name would be

```
.CN=TRobins.OU=MKTNG.OU=HDQTRS.O=EMA.
```

or

```
TRobins.MKTNG.HDQTRS.EMA
```

FIGURE 12-6	Distinguished Name example user TRobins in the MKTNG HDQTRS EMA container

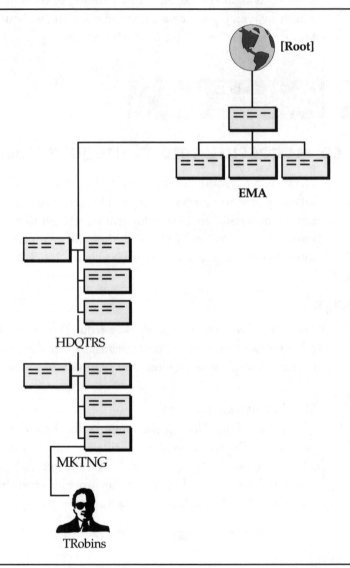

With Distinguished Names, there is also a short form known as the Relative Distinguished Name. The *Relative Distinguished Name* is a shorter, incomplete form of a Distinguished Name. Now that I have you thoroughly confused, let me explain.

A Relative Distinguished Name is from the object up to the current context. So if our user TRobins has a Current context of HDQTRS.EMA, then his Relative Distinguished Name would be

```
CN=TRobins.OU=MKTNG
```

exam
Ⓦatch

To keep the various naming concepts straight, remember this formula: Relative Distinguished Name + Current context = Distinguished Name.

Typeful Names and Typeless Names

The other type of naming concept to know for the exam is *Typeful Naming*. As we have seen, there are different ways to spell out a complete Distinguished Name. One way uses the attribute abbreviations. For example, TRobins is the Common Name, or CN. The Organizational Units are OU. Typeful Names are basically names that include the attribute abbreviation along with the name of the object. For example,

```
.CN=BSmith.OU=HOME.O=PLATE
```

A *Typeless Name* is a name without the attribute abbreviations. For example,

```
.BSmith.HOME.PLATE
```

These two types of naming are essentially telling us the same thing. The Typeful Name simply denotes the object type, which can help us avoid confusion when there are container and leaf objects in the same tree with similar or identical names.

Those Dots Are Confusing

You may have noticed that there are sometimes dots preceding or following the name. Let's review how the dots make up the various name types.

TABLE 12-2	Distinguished Name	Relative Distinguished Name
Dots and Distinguished Names	Leading dots required	Leading dots not allowed
	Trailing dots not allowed	Trailing dots optional

Table 12-2 shows the basic relationship between the trailing and leading dot.

Here is a summary of how dots are used in NetWare object names:

- Distinguished Names must have a leading dot. The leading dot means that the name is complete and includes all containers leading to [Root].

- Trailing dots can be used only with Relative Distinguished Names because they modify the current context. A trailing dot moves the context up one level in the tree.

- Other dots within a name are simply separators. They separate each object in the tree's hierarchy.

exam
Watch

Naming concepts and dots can be somewhat confusing, so be sure you are clear on this for the exam. For the exam, you may see at least one, maybe even two questions in regard to naming concepts. Review this material and make sure you understand the naming concepts. You will be asked, for example, which of the following is the Typeful Distinguished Name for user JSmith. Then you will be given a directory tree to look at and some choices to choose from. Use the scratch paper you are given during the exam to draw out the complete name on paper if that is easier for you.

CERTIFICATION OBJECTIVE 12.05

Guidelines for Setting Up Resources

When setting up and designing your tree, there are many things you must take into account. The goal of proper NDS tree design is to make it simple for your users to access resources while at the same time making it easy for you to administer.

To design and implement a successful NDS tree, you must organize the network resources carefully. This means placing resources as near as possible to the users who need access to them. The hierarchical nature of the NDS tree allows this to be done. One problem some administrators run into is organizing too much. Don't break your tree up into too many branches. Using common sense and good organization will make the tree come together.

Configuring NDS for Login

When considering where to place objects in your directory tree, keep the login process in mind. When designing login scripts you have to be careful when providing access to resources for certain users. The more contexts you have to deal with, the more complicated your login script.

When designing login scripts, you want to be able to give access to resources in a fashion that is simple to administer and change.

Configuring NDS for Resource Access

Figure 12-7 shows a directory tree with our user TRobins in the HDQTRS container. We also see a DOWNTOWN container that has some resources such as printer, volume, and server.

Now, if TRobins works in the downtown office where the printer, server, and volume that he accesses daily are located, it would make more sense for his User object to be in the DOWNTOWN container. On the flip side, if TRobins is a user who works at headquarters but accesses resources in the downtown office only occasionally, then the placement of his User object, shown in Figure 12-7, may be appropriate. The main thing to remember is to *keep users near the resources they access most often in the directory tree.*

FIGURE 12-7   User and resources residing in different contexts

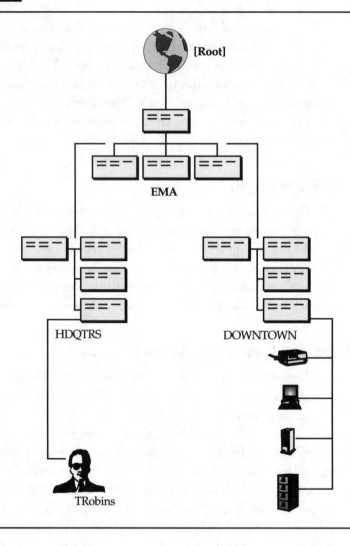

CERTIFICATION OBJECTIVE 12.06

Summary of Actions and Rights Needed

When it comes to configuring your directory tree for a multicontext environment, be sure to use proper naming when giving rights to users. The first step is to make sure you have the proper context set for a user. As long as you know where the user resides, and the current context is set appropriately, assigning the appropriate rights is easy. This is especially because the NWADMIN application is GUI driven.

CERTIFICATION OBJECTIVE 12.07

Using Correct Naming in Login Scripts

When it comes to login scripts, especially in a multicontext environment, you have to be sure you use the proper naming to get to the various resources that are needed by a user for a group of users.

The easiest way to do this is to use the Typeful Distinguished Name when identifying objects in the NDS tree. For example, to capture a printer in a login script, use the Typeful Distinguished Name. That way, if anyone else has to look at the login script, they can identify exactly what the NDS path is for that object.

There are different types of login scripts. Make sure you understand what each login script is and how it differs from the others. These are the login scripts, in order of execution:

- Container login scripts
- Profile login scripts
- User login scripts
- Default login script (executes only if a user login script does not exist)

Container login scripts are login scripts that customize settings for all users in a container. *Profile login scripts* are a way to customize certain items for groups of users. The profile login script allows administrators to have users share a common login script even though they aren't in a common context or members of the same group objects in the directory. *User login scripts* are scripts with individual login properties. The *default login script* is executed for any user who does not have an individual user login script.

Profile login scripts tend to confuse many people, especially those who have NetWare 3.x experience. Profile login scripts are a way to add login script commands for selected users. A profile login script can be used by multiple users who are not members of the same group.

CERTIFICATION SUMMARY

This part of the Administration exam is by far one of the easier parts as long as you nail a couple of things. The first is the different types of naming: Distinguished, Relative Distinguished, Typeless, and Typeful.

The second thing is to understand how context affects object interaction in the directory tree. Remember that there is Object context, or where an object resides in the directory tree. There is also Current context, which is the current location in the directory tree.

Also be sure to understand how the login scripts work and the different types of login scripts. This will not be seen as much on the exam, but it is good to know when looking at the scenario questions.

TWO-MINUTE DRILL

❑ The directory tree is the nervous system of the NetWare world. Every object on the network has an object in the directory. The more complex the directory tree, the harder network administration is.

❑ Container objects hold other NDS objects. The hierarchical fashion of the directory tree takes shape when various container objects branch out. NetWare has three types of container objects: Country, Organization, and Organizational Unit.

❑ The Country object is optional and not widely used. It can be used to designate a locale for the tree if the NDS tree is being designed with eventual merging into a global WAN in mind.

❑ The Organization object is required and can be, for example, the company name, a location, or a division of a company. Although multiple Organizations can exist in a single directory tree, most have only one.

❑ The Organizational Unit is a branch in the tree. There can also be multiple Organizational Units in the directory tree. Organizational Units can contain other Organizational Units. This is where network administration can become complicated when you have multicontext environments.

❑ The leaf object represents an individual entity or resource in the tree like a printer, user, or server.

❑ Each NDS object has a Distinguished Name, which uniquely identifies the object, including its location in the directory tree. With NetWare, always think of the object's name in terms of its location in the directory tree.

❑ Context is your location in the directory tree. Where you reside and where other objects reside determine how an NDS object has to be configured.

❑ There are two types of contexts within Novell Directory Services: Current context, where you currently are in the directory tree, and Object context, where the object resides in the directory tree.

❑ A new feature of NetWare 5 is contextless login. With previous versions of NetWare, you had to know your location in the directory tree or you had to have the proper context to log in. With NetWare 5, users can log in anywhere on the network, regardless of context. With contextless login, you can authenticate from any point on the network simply by typing your login name and password, without knowing the location of your User object in the NDS tree.

❑ The Distinguished Name is the complete directory path from the object back to the [Root].

❑ The Relative Distinguished Name is a shorter, incomplete form of a Distinguished Name. A Relative Distinguished Name is from the object up to the Current context.

❑ Typeful Names are names that include the attribute abbreviation along with the name of the object. A Typeless Name is a name without the attribute abbreviations.

❑ Distinguished Names must have a leading dot. The leading dot means that the name is complete and includes all containers leading to [Root].

❑ Trailing dots can be used only with Relative Distinguished Names because they modify the current context.

❑ Other dots within a name separate each object in the tree's hierarchy

❑ Place resources as near as possible to the users who need access to them. When considering where to place objects in your directory tree, keep the login process in mind. The more contexts you have to deal with, the more complicated the login script.

❑ When configuring a directory tree for a multicontext environment, be sure to use proper naming when giving rights to users. The easiest way to do this is to use the Typeful Distinguished Name when identifying objects in the NDS tree.

❑ There are four different types of login scripts. They are, in order of execution, Container login scripts, Profile login scripts, User login scripts, and Default login scripts.

SELF TEST

The Self-Test questions will help you measure your understanding of the material presented in this chapter. Read all the choices carefully, as there may be more than one correct answer. Select all correct answers for each question.

1. A user JGreen resides in the Finance Organizational Unit, which is under the SmithnSon Organization. What is the full NDS name of JGreen in the directory?

   A. FINANCE.JGREEN.SMITHNSON
   B. SMITHNSON.JGREEN.FINANCE
   C. JGREEN.FINANCE.SMITHNSON
   D. JGREEN

2. A user JGreen resides in the Finance Organizational Unit, which is under the SmithnSon Organization. What is the Common Name of JGreen in the directory?

   A. FINANCE.JGREEN.SMITHNSON
   B. SMITHNSON.JGREEN.FINANCE
   C. JGREEN.FINANCE.SMITHNSON
   D. JGREEN

3. What naming concept does this name follow (select two):
   CN=JDOE.OU=SHOES.OU=SALES.O=STORE

   A. Typeful Name
   B. Relative Distinguished Name
   C. Distinguished Name
   D. Typeless Name

4. Given the following information, what is the Typeless Distinguished Name for JMiller?

   ■ JMILLER object resides in the Organizational Unit of MANAGEMENT.

   ■ The Organization Name is EMA.

   ■ There is an Organizational Unit under EMA named CHICAGO that contains the Organizational Unit Management.

   A. .JMILLER.MANAGEMENT.CHICAGO.EMA
   B. JMILLER.MANAGEMENT.CHICAGO.EMA
   C. .JMILLER.CHICAGO.EMA
   D. JMILLER.MANAGEMENT.EMA

5. How would user JFreder, who is in the ABCD container under the 1234 Organization, use a printer LXM_1024 that is in the EFGH container under the 1234 Organization?

   A. Simply use the Relative Distinguished Name of .LXM_1024.ABCD.1234.
   B. Use the .LXM_1024.EFGH.1234 name to access the resource.
   C. Simply select the printer and print.
   D. Change her context to [Root] and then use the Common Name of the printer.

FIGURE 12-8   What happens to the TRobbins User object?

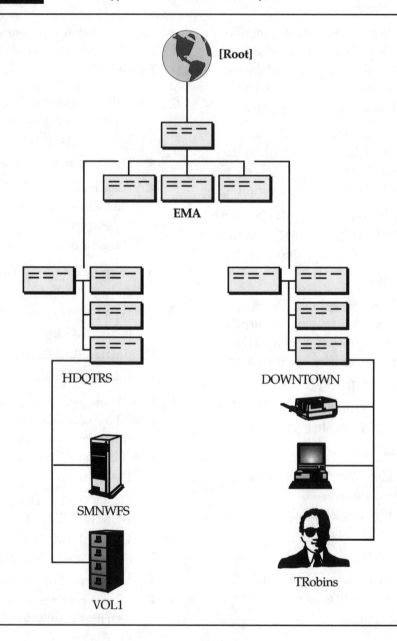

6. Refer to Figure 12-8 (on the facing page) for the following question: The user TRobins resides in the DOWNTOWN container. He accesses resources primarily on the SMNWFS server in VOL1. He is physically located at Headquarters. Once in a while he will print to a printer in the downtown office. Hundreds of users in the HDQTRS container access the SMNWFS server and volumes. With this information, what should be done with the TRobins User object?

   A. Nothing. Leave the object where it is.

   B. Move him to the HDQTRS container since he accesses resources primarily in that container and this will place the user near the resources.

   C. Leave the User object in the DOWNTOWN container and move the VOL1 and SMNWFS objects to the DOWNTOWN container so the user is near the resources.

   D. Move the TRobins User object under the EMA Organization object since he accesses resources in both containers.

7. Which of the following is not a type of login script?

   A. Profile

   B. Default

   C. Container

   D. Root

8. Which of the following is the correct Relative Distinguished Name given the following information?

   ■ Common Name=JDOE

   ■ Current Context = EMA

   ■ Organizational Unit that JDOE resides in = MKTNG

   ■ Organization (that MKTNG is in) = EMA

   A. .JDOE.EMA

   B. JDOE.MKTNG

   C. JDOE.MKTNG.EMA

   D. .JDOE.MKTNG

9. NetWare 5 offers the ability to log in from anywhere in the directory tree regardless of context. This is known as

   A. NW5LOGIN

   B. NetWare contextless login

   C. Contextless login

   D. NetWare5 Cfree login

10. To determine where an object is located in the directory tree, you need to know the object's _____?

   A. Common Name

   B. Current context

   C. Object context

   D. Login name

11. This type of object can exist directly under the [Root] object:

   A. Organization

   B. Organizational Unit

   C. Leaf object

   D. NetWare volume

FIGURE 12-9   What is BSmith's Current context?

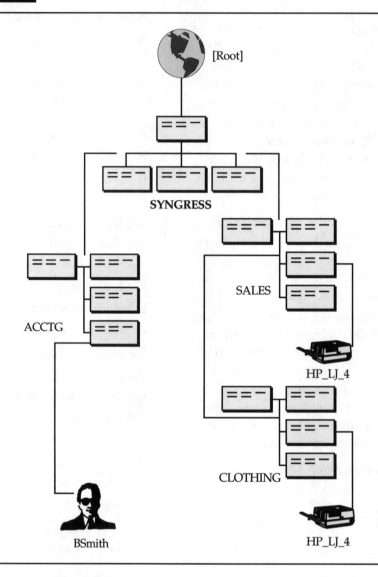

12. Given the following information, what is BSmith's current context (refer to Figure 12-9 on the facing page): Bob's current context is the same as the HP_LJ_4.

    A. .BSMITH.CLOTHING.SALES. SYNGRESS

    B. .BSMITH.ACCTG.SYNGRESS

    C. .BSMITH.CLOTHING

    D. .BSMITH.HP_LJ_4.CLOTHING. SALES.SYNGRESS

13. If SJones resides in the FRESHMAN container and the Current context is BUSINESS.UNI, then what is his Relative Distinguished Name?

    A. .SJONES.FRESHMAN. BUSINESS.UNI

    B. SJONES.FRESHMAN. BUSINESS.UNI

    C. .SJONES.FRESHMAN

    D. SJONES.FRESHMAN

14. The highest point in the directory tree is called the

    A. Country

    B. Root

    C. Container

    D. Organizational Unit

15. An object that is sometimes used above the Organization but still below the [Root] that signifies a location is the

    A. Organizational Unit

    B. [Root]

    C. Country

    D. Leaf object

13

Performing a Simple Installation

CERTIFICATION OBJECTIVES

13.01   Common Install Interface Overview

13.02   Comparing Simple and Custom
        Installations

13.03   Using the GUI Installation Utility to
        Perform a Simple Install

I n this chapter, we will describe the steps and options for installing NetWare 5. In the first section, we will discuss the common install interface overview. In the second section, we will compare simple and custom installation methods, and in the third section, we will use the GUI (Graphical User Interface) to perform a simple installation.

CERTIFICATION OBJECTIVE 13.01

Common Install Interface Overview

NetWare 5 offers two installation methods: a GUI installation and a text-based installation. The latter option is for servers that do not have sufficient RAM or processor speed.

The GUI installation looks at processor speed and RAM. If your processor does not rate at least a 1500, and you do not have a minimum of 47MB of RAM, the server installation program runs only in text mode.

The GUI server installation program starts out in text screens. These screens are used to gather information about the server, type of installation (new server or upgrade), and regional settings (country, code page, and keyboard); then it automatically checks for hardware devices, such as storage devices, platform support modules, and network boards. After the appropriate drivers are detected and loaded, you create a NetWare partition and volume (SYS:). After the program creates your partition and volume, it mounts the volume and copies the Java Virtual Machine (JVM) files to the server. These files are required to continue the GUI part of the installation.

After the files for the JVM are installed, the GUI screens are loaded. The first screen is where we name our server. The subsequent screens are where we choose our protocols (IP, IPX, or both), time zone information, and NDS information; license our server; and then choose whether to install any additional products (such as remote access or online documentation). After we complete these steps, we can choose to finish our installation or continue and customize our settings.

CERTIFICATION OBJECTIVE 13.02

Comparing Simple and Custom Installations

When installing NetWare 5, you have two installation methods to choose from: *Simple Installation* and *Custom Installation.* We will compare these two methods so you can decide which method meets your requirements.

Whether you are choosing a Simple or a Custom Installation, the basic process is the same. All NetWare 5 installations start out as Simple Installations. After you complete the Simple Installation, you can then choose to invoke the *Custom* Hallway (the new term for custom install). This part of the installation is where you can modify or customize your NetWare 5 server.

Simple Installations

A Simple Installation is quick and requires minimal user input. The installation program assumes a series of default parameters, which we will discuss next.

Server ID Number

The *Server ID Number* is randomly generated by the NetWare installation program. This number is a unique number that identifies the server on a network. (The Server ID Number was called the *Internal IPX Number* in older versions of NetWare.)

Volume (SYS:)

The installation program creates a SYS: volume by default. The volume is used to house the NetWare operating system and support files.

One Partition

The installation program creates a single partition by default. The partition holds the SYS: volume.

Block Size

The block size depends on the size of your volume. Novell recommends using the defaults shown in Table 13-1.

Using the defaults minimizes RAM and disk space. If you feel it is necessary to adjust the block size, keep in mind:

- Smaller block sizes require more server memory to track the File Allocation Table (FAT) and Directory Entry Table (DET).

- Larger block sizes use less RAM, but they waste more disk space unless you use block suballocation.

This is why volumes take time to mount—the server is building the FAT and DET. This does not apply to an NSS volume.

QUESTIONS AND ANSWERS

I have the minimum amount of RAM and I want to increase performance.	Set your volume block size to a larger limit.
I only have 32MB of RAM.	You need a minimum of 64MB to install the server.
The server installation did not detect all of my hardware.	Supply the driver from the device manufacturer.

TABLE 13-1

Default Volume and Block Sizes

Volume Size	Block Size
0–31MB	4K or 8K
32–149MB	16K
150–499MB	32K
Over 500MB	64K

Suballocation (Default: Enabled)

Block suballocation helps the NetWare 5 operating system conserve space by allowing fragments of data to share the same disk block. Disk blocks are divided into 512-byte suballocated blocks.

For example, if you were not using suballocation, a 5K file would require two 4K blocks (if the volume had its block size set to 4K), wasting 3K.

With block suballocation enabled, your 5K file uses only 5K. It uses one 4K block and two 512-byte suballocated blocks to form another 4K block. The suballocated block has 3K available for other files to use for their suballocated files.

on the **Job**

Regardless of file size, when it is saved to disk, it must occupy an empty disk block. If the file is larger than the block size, then the remaining data gets saved to a suballocated block.

File Compression (Default: Enabled)

With *file compression* enabled, files that are not used within a specified time are compressed to save disk space. When you access a compressed file, the NetWare 5 server automatically decompresses the file for use. The file will be compressed again only after it has remained unused for the specified time for file compression.

File compression is a valuable tool to save disk space. However, once you enable file compression, the only way to remove it is to delete and recreate the volume.

This option can be disabled using the Custom Hallway feature of NetWare 5.

Data Migration (Default: Disabled)

By default data migration is disabled. *Data migration* is the process of moving unused data to an external storage device (such as a disk, optical jukebox, or tape). The data movement is transparent to NetWare. NetWare perceives the data as local. When a user requests a file that has been moved to an external device, it is retrieved and delivered to the user making the request.

This option can be enabled using the Custom Hallway feature of NetWare 5.

Protocols

A *protocol* is a language your server uses to communicate with other servers and workstations on your network. A *frame type* is an identifier for a protocol.

In NetWare 5, you can use TCP/IP as your protocol, and its frame type is Ethernet_II. You can also use IPX/SPX as your protocol, and its frame type is Ethernet 802.2. NetWare 5 will allow you to run both TCP/IP and IPX/SPX at the same time for compatibility with older networks that use only IPX/SPX or newer networks that only run TCP/IP. However, it is recommended that you choose one protocol for your server. This will increase the performance of your NetWare 5 server.

exam
ⓦatch

By default NetWare 5 sets a compatibility mode. This allows IPX clients to work with an IP server. You can change this option to allow only one protocol.

Directory Services

Be default, your server is configured as a *Single Reference Time Server* if it's the first server in your tree. Any subsequent server installed into the tree will be configured, by default, as a *Secondary Time Server*. These options can be changed using the Custom Hallway feature of NetWare 5. The NetWare 5 Simple Installation also autodetects hardware, as we'll discuss next.

Storage Devices

The NetWare 5 installation program automatically detects and loads the appropriate drivers for many of your storage devices (such as hard disks, tape drives, and optical disks). If your device is not recognized by the NetWare 5 installation program, you will be prompted for a CDM (Custom Device Module) or a HAM (Host Adapter Module) driver. These are the drivers supplied by the device manufacturer.

All of this is part of NetWare Peripheral Architecture (NWPA), which provides more flexibility and functionality in storage device support.

Network Boards

The NetWare 5 installation program automatically detects and loads the appropriate drivers for many of your network boards. If the NetWare 5 installation program does not recognize your network board, you will be prompted for a driver that was supplied by the device manufacturer.

Platform Support Modules

Some hardware configurations and some multiprocessor configurations require a Platform Support Module or PSM. The NetWare 5 installation program automatically detects for the need of a PSM and loads the driver. If your installation does not load a PSM, your server does not require one.

Custom Installations

As we saw earlier, all Custom Installations start out as Simple Installations. After we complete the Simple Installation, we have the option to enter the Custom Hallway, illustrated in Figure 13-1. This is where we can customize our NetWare 5 server to fit our needs. We can install optional programs, configure our protocols, modify our Directory Services, and make changes to our server's file system. In this subsection, we will talk about what changes you can make and why you might want to. Please keep in mind that the Simple Installation is designed for most business needs.

on the **job**

If the network is going to be a Wide Area Network, or is projected to become a medium or large Network, the Custom Installation becomes the installation method of choice. Generally, Simple Installations are performed for small networks where the company or organization is fairly static and future growth is not anticipated.

Server ID Number

The Server ID Number is randomly generated by the NetWare installation program. Highlighting the Operating System option of the Custom

FIGURE 13-1

Entering the Custom
Hallway after Simple
Installation

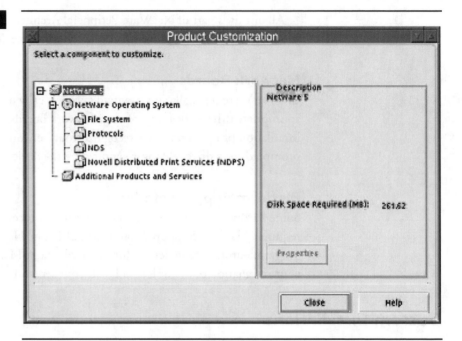

Hallway screen will allow you to change this number. The number
generated by the installation program is usually sufficient. However, if your
company uses a filtering method or registered numbers, this is where you
would change the number.

Language
To add additional language support for your new NetWare 5 server, you
choose the Language Tab and select from the following supported languages:

- English
- German
- Italian
- Spanish
- French
- Portuguese

File System

Select one of the following options to view the file system:

- Disk View
- Volume View
- Partition View

From any of the views, you can do the following:

- Create a new partition
- Create a new volume
- Edit a volume or partition
- Delete a volume or partition

Modifying Block Size

For optimal performance it is safer to let NetWare configure your block size.

Disabling Suballocation

As we discussed previously in the section "Suballocation (Default: Enabled)," suballocation is a tool that allows you to save valuable disk space by allowing multiple file fragments to share the same disk block. By default this option is enabled, and this is where you would disable this option.

Disabling File Compression

File compression is enabled by default. As we discussed previously in the section " File Compression (Default: Enabled)," file compression is another way of saving disk space by compressing unused files and decompressing them when accessed by a user. Once file compression is enabled, the only way to remove it is to delete and recreate the volume.

Enabling Data Migration

Data migration is disabled by default. As we discussed previously in the section "Data Migration (Default: Disabled)," data migration is another way of saving disk space by migrating unused files to an offline or near-line storage device. If you have such a device on your NetWare 5 server, you would enable this option here.

Customizing Protocols

You can add, remove, or customize your protocol selections here.

Modifying Directory Services

As we discussed previously in the section "Directory Services," your first server will be configured by default as a Single Reference and the other server installed into the tree will be configured as a Secondary Time Server thereafter.

CERTIFICATION OBJECTIVE 13.03

Using the GUI Installation Utility to Perform a Simple Install

In this section, we will follow the steps to perform a Simple Installation using the GUI utility. Before we install NetWare 5, we must check that our equipment meets the minimum requirements:

- 486/66 or higher processor
- VGA or SVGA monitor (SVGA recommended)
- 250MB of hard disk space
- 32MB of RAM (48MB recommended)
- Novell tested and approved network board
- PS/2 or serial mouse (optional but recommended)
- CD-ROM drive capable of reading ISO 9660–formatted CD-ROM disks

If we have the right equipment, we are ready to start the installation.

Setting Up the Hardware

In the following sections, we will walk through the process of preparing the hardware for NetWare 5 installation.

Creating the DOS Partition

Our first step in creating a NetWare 5 server is creating the DOS partition. To create a DOS partition, we must boot our computer with DOS version 3.3 or higher. After we boot our computer with the DOS disk, we must use the FDISK command to create a 50MB active DOS partition. This 50MB will hold all of the necessary files NetWare 5 will need to boot. After we have created our 50MB partition, we must reboot our computer and format the partition. To accomplish this, we must use our DOS disk and type the following command: **FORMAT C: /s**. This will copy the necessary files to our computer so it can boot.

Although 50MB may be sufficient to install and run the server, realistically, most production servers should have at least 100MB, or larger, DOS partitions. This is to accommodate large files and directories that may be needed for future needs, such as storing the core dump information in case of an abend (Abnormal End).

After we have completed the DOS partition and successfully rebooted it, we must install our CD-ROM drivers on our DOS partition. The drivers we need were supplied with the CD-ROM.

Make sure the installation program for your CD-ROM did not give the CD-ROM a logical name of CDROM. This will conflict with the NetWare 5 operating system because it has a file named CDROM.

Starting the Installation

Insert the NetWare 5 CD-ROM in the drive. Change to the drive letter for the CD-ROM and type **INSTALL**.

Choosing Regional Settings

This is where you will choose your country, keyboard mapping, and code page for your language and computer. Most installations will accept the default settings. If you require advanced customization, press the F3 key and choose your settings.

Autodetecting Storage Devices

The NetWare 5 installation program will autodetect most storage devices, hard disks, tape drives, and CD-ROM drives. If the NetWare 5 installation program does not detect your device, you must provide the driver that was supplied by the device's manufacturer. NetWare 5 no longer supports DSK drivers. NetWare 5 supports only Host Adapter Modules (HAMs) or Custom Device Modules (CDMs). This is part of NetWare 5 NWPA (NetWare Peripheral Architecture), and allows for more flexibility in driver support.

After you have loaded and configured your storage devices, it is time to load and configure your network adapter (NIC). Just like the storage devices, NetWare 5 will autodetect most network boards. If the NetWare 5 installation program does not detect the device, you must provide the driver that was supplied by the device's manufacturer. Your server will require a separate driver for each NIC you have installed in the server.

After NetWare has the appropriate driver selected for our network card we must select a *port value* (a memory location that is associated with a hardware port) and a *slot number* (a number that identifies each piece of hardware). Network card devices that cannot be detected are not assigned a slot number. A slot number can be detected for PCMCIA, PnP ISA, EISA, PCI, and MCA. We must also select an *INT* (Interrupt or IRQ), which is how the device makes its requests known to the computer. No other device in the system can share an IRQ. IRQs are set through the device software.

Now we are ready to start configuring our server.

Creating the NetWare Partition and Volume SYS:

A *partition* is a logical division of a hard disk into smaller sections. You can have up to four partitions on a single drive.

A *volume* divides partitions into smaller sections. NetWare requires one volume named SYS: and it is automatically created. You can have up to eight volumes on one partition.

NetWare Partition

During the first part of the installation, a single partition is created. You will have an opportunity to create additional partitions later during the installation. You can also create additional partitions after the installation using NWCONFIG.NLM.

Volume SYS:

The NetWare 5 server requires a volume named SYS:, which is automatically created and requires 150MB of disk space. This volume will take up all available disk space of the partition unless you specify a different amount. I recommend you do not use all available space. This will allow you to create another volume for data and users. Novell recommends keeping your volume SYS: separate from your data volumes. You will have an opportunity to create additional volumes later during the installation.

Server Name

Figure 13-2 illustrates the Server Properties screen. The first of the GUI screens, this is where we name our server. This name must be unique; no other server on your network can have the same name. The name can be between 2 and 47 characters long and can use dashes and underscores.

Installing the File System

At this point, we should have our partition and volume created. If we want to continue and create more partitions and volumes, we may do so at this point. For now we will continue and install the file system.

Installing and Configuring Protocols

NetWare 5 is the first NetWare server operating system to process pure IP. NetWare 5 still supports IPX, but now you can settle on just one protocol

FIGURE 13-2

Using the Server Properties
screen to name the server

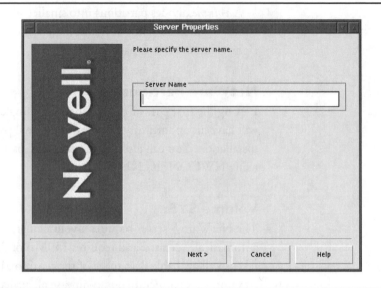

for your network or both. Your NetWare 5 server will allow both protocols
to be bound to the same NIC.

Compatibility

NetWare 5 offers a compatibility mode (CMD) that can be installed on
your NetWare 5 server. This will allow your IP clients to transmit and
receive data on your IPX segments, as well as allow your IPX clients to
transmit and receive data on your IP segments. CMD also allows your
legacy NWIP clients to send and receive data across your network.

IP (Internet Protocol)

Using IP allows your network to send and receive data with other networks
using IP. These networks include UNIX, Windows NT, and mainframes.
To use IP, you will need an IP address, a subnet mask, and a gateway or
router address.

IPX (Internet Packet Exchange)

NetWare 5 still supports IPX, which allows you to communicate with applications that were written for IPX. If you have applications that were written for IPX only and some written for IP only, you should run both protocols. If you run only IP, all IPX traffic will need to be encapsulated using the IP protocol.

Selecting and Configuring Protocols

Use the Protocols screen (illustrated in Figure 13-3), to select your protocol or protocols of choice. Highlight your NIC listed under the protocol of choice. To the right on the screen, click Bind Protocol. If you were using IP as your protocol, you would be prompted to enter your IP address, Subnet Mask, and Router Address.

FIGURE 13-3

The Protocols screen showing the NIC highlighted under the protocol of choice

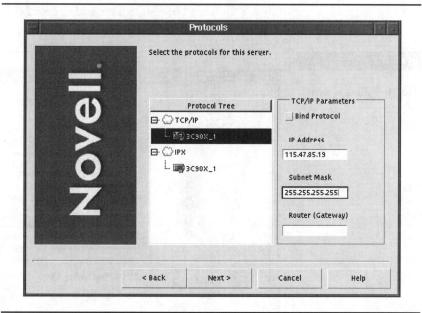

If you were using IPX, NetWare will automatically load and bind all detected IPX frame types for your NIC.

Time Zone

Figure 13-4 shows the Time Zone screen, in which you will select your server's time and time zone. This is important for many reasons. If you live in an area with daylight savings time, your server will know when to change its time in the spring and fall.

NDS Installation

The Novell Directory Services (NDS) provides global access to all networking resources. It governs file system rights, login restrictions, and access to network resources.

To install NDS, you must first choose whether to install this server into an existing NDS tree or create a new NDS tree, as shown in Figure 13-5. Choose Create a New NDS Tree and choose NEXT. Now supply NetWare with your Tree Name, Container Name, and Admin Password (see Figure 13-6).

FIGURE 13-4

The Time Zone screen

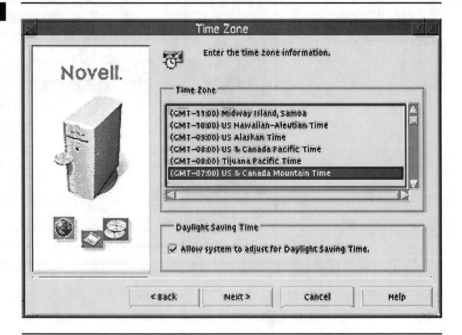

FIGURE 13-5

NDS Install screen showing options for installing NDS

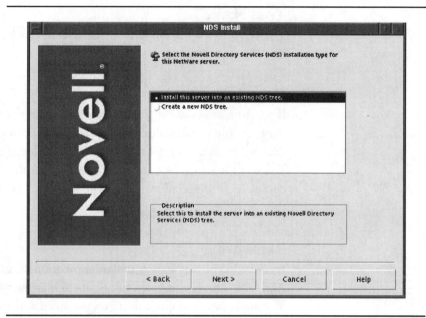

FIGURE 13-6

Creating a new NDS tree

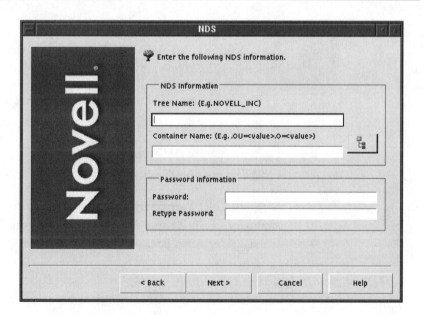

Tree Name

The NDS tree is the top level of available network resources, and the tree name must be unique.

Containers

If you think of your NDS tree as a file cabinet, the containers are like drawers. You use containers in the same fashion you would use your file drawers, to separate resources by function or location or a mixture thereof. You want to name the containers based on your company profile. After we complete the installation, you can go back and add or subtract containers to fit your needs.

Password

By default, the NetWare installation program creates a user named ADMIN. This user is given full rights to manage your server and NDS tree. You are required to give this user a password and you will have to reenter the password to ensure that you typed it correctly. You can change the password later, after the installation.

Finalizing the Server Installation

After we have given our ADMIN a password, we choose NEXT, and the server does the following:

- Checks the NDS tree name to make sure it is unique
- Sets the time
- Initializes NDS
- Extends NDS schemas

After your NetWare 5 server completes its checks, it will display an NDS summary screen. Be sure to write down all of this information so you can manage your server later.

Licensing the Server

The License screen is very important to your installation. If you do not have a server license, your server will default to a run-time version and allow only two connections.

Never use a server license more than once because the server will broadcast a License Violation message.

Adding Other Products and Services

This screen (shown in Figure 13-7) will allow you to install additional products, such as remote access, NetWare online documentation, and Novell distributed Print Services (NDPS). Place a check mark next to the options you wish to install and click the NEXT button.

FIGURE 13-7

Installing additional products and services

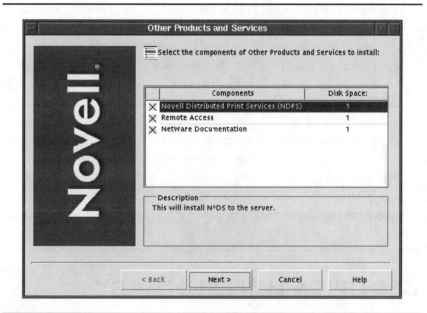

Summary Screen

Review the Summary screen. After you accept the summary, your server will perform a main file copy and then return you to the server console.

Congratulations, you have just installed a NetWare 5 server! To modify your server further, invoke the Custom Hallway and further enhance your server configuration. For more information, see Chapter 16.

FROM THE CLASSROOM

Preparing the Server Hard Drive for NetWare 5 Installation

Before installing NetWare 5 on your server, the hardware needs to be cataloged and prepared for the installation. The server's hard drive is no exception. Follow the manufacturer's instruction carefully to make sure that all manually configured settings have been performed and the information recorded is in an easily accessible place. Use the DOS FDISK.EXE utility to verify that the server hard drive(s) has a DOS partition and the remaining disk space is unformatted free space (that's where the NetWare Partition will be created during the installation process).

A 50MB DOS partition (minimum size for a successful installation) may not be large enough for a production server. You might want to have additional DOS partition space to accommodate future server service pack files, patches, fixes, and drivers for devices that are called by the server boot files prior to the SYS: volume mounting. Also, make the DOS partition large enough to store a server core dump image file. It will take up as much space as the amount of installed RAM on the server. In other words, a core dump from a server with 128MB RAM will need 128MB of storage space (assuming that you don't have another storage device to write this file to).

—Dan Cheung, CNI, MCNE, MCT

CERTIFICATION SUMMARY

In this chapter, we have described the steps and options for installing NetWare 5, including the common install interface, simple and custom installation methods, and using the Graphical User Interface to perform a simple installation.

NetWare 5 offers a GUI installation and a text-based installation. The text-based installation is for servers that do not have sufficient RAM or processor speed.

The GUI server installation program starts out in text screens that are used to gather information about the server, type of installation, and regional settings. The server installation program then automatically checks for hardware devices, and detects and loads the appropriate drivers.

After the appropriate drivers are detected and loaded, a NetWare partition and volume (SYS:) are created. After the installation program creates the partition and volume, it mounts the volume and copies the Java Virtual Machine (JVM) files to the server.

The GUI screens are then loaded. The first screen is where the server is named. The subsequent screens are where protocols, time zone information, NDS information, license information, and additional product installations are specified. The installation can then finish or continue with customization.

There are two installation methods for NetWare 5: Simple Installation and Custom Installation. All NetWare 5 installations start out as Simple Installations. After the Simple Installation is completed, the Custom Hallway can be invoked, in which the NetWare 5 server can be modified or customized.

A Simple Installation is quick and requires minimal user input. The installation program assumes a series of default parameters. Simple Installation is designed for most business needs.

The Custom Hallway can be used to install optional programs, configure protocols, modify Directory Services, and make changes to the server's file system.

TWO-MINUTE DRILL

❑ NetWare 5 offers two installation options: text-based and GUI.

❑ All installation options start out in text screens.

❑ The Server ID Number is a randomly generated number.

❑ The Server ID Number was called the Internal IPX Number in older versions of NetWare.

❑ A volume divides partitions into smaller sections.

❑ The Installation Program creates a SYS: volume by default.

❑ A partition is a logical division of a hard disk.

❑ The Installation Program creates a single partition by default.

❑ Novell recommends using the default block sizes.

❑ Smaller block sizes require more server memory.

❑ Larger block sizes use less memory.

❑ Block suballocation allows a NetWare 5 operating system to conserve space.

❑ Suballocation is enabled by default.

❑ File compression is another valuable tool for saving disk space.

❑ File compression is enabled by default.

❑ NetWare 5 supports IP and IPX/SPX.

❑ By default, NetWare 5 sets a compatibility mode for IP/IPX clients.

❑ By default, NetWare 5 sets your server as a Single Reference Time Server for the first server.

❑ All subsequent servers are Secondary Time Servers.

❑ NetWare 5 autodetects many storage devices and loads the appropriate drivers.

❑ NetWare 5 autodetects many network boards and loads the appropriate drivers.

❑ Novell NetWare 5 supports the following languages: English, German, Italian, Spanish, French, and Portuguese.

❑ To install NetWare 5, your computer will need the following minimum hardware: 486/66 or higher processor, VGA or SVGA monitor, 250MB of HDD space, 32MB of RAM (48MB recommended), NIC, PS/2 or serial mouse, and a CD-ROM drive.

❑ To start the GUI installation, type **INSTALL**. To perform a text-based install, type **INSTALL/T** .

❑ Port value is a memory location assigned with a hardware port.

❑ Slot number is a number that identifies each piece of hardware.

❑ INT is an interrupt request line to the processor.

❑ The SYS: volume requires 150MB of disk space.

❑ The server name can be between 2 and 47 characters long and can use dashes and underscores.

❑ The NDS tree name must be unique.

❑ By default, NetWare creates an ADMIN user.

❑ Never use the same server license more than once.

SELF TEST

The Self-Test questions will help you measure your understanding of the material presented in this chapter. Read all the choices carefully, as there may be more than one correct answer. Select all correct answers for each question.

1. How many install interfaces are available for installing NetWare 5?

   A. 1

   B. 2

   C. 3

   D. 4

2. What is the Server ID Number?

   A. A common number used by all servers on the network

   B. A user definable number for each server

   C. A randomly generated number for each server

   D. A number that identifies each server on the network

3. What is the name of the default volume?

   A. System

   B. Volume 1

   C. SYS

   D. SYS:

4. How many partitions are created by default?

   A. 1

   B. 2

   C. 3

   D. 4

5. What is the default block size of a 120MB hard disk?

   A. 4K

   B. 16K

   C. 32K

   D. 64K

6. When using suballocation, what is the size of the suballocated blocks?

   A. 1,024K

   B. 500K

   C. 512 bytes

   D. 10 bytes

7. What is the default setting for file compression?

   A. Enabled

   B. Disabled

8. What type of devices does data migration use?

   A. Jukeboxes

   B. Optical Drives

   C. Tape Drives

9. What is NetWare's default frame type for TCP/IP?

   A. Ethernet_II

   B. Ethernet_SNAP

   C. Ethernet 802.3

   D. Ethernet 802.2

10. What is NetWare's default frame type for IPX?

    A. Ethernet_II

    B. Ethernet_SNAP

    C. Ethernet 802.3

    D. Ethernet 802.2

11. What does CDM stand for?

    A. Custom Data Module

    B. Custom Device Module

    C. Computer Display Module

    D. Custom Display Module

12. What does HAM stand for?

    A. Host Adapter Module

    B. Host Amplitude Module

    C. Hardware Adapter Module

13. What languages are supported by NetWare 5?

    A. Spanish

    B. German

    C. Italian

    D. French

    E. Portuguese

14. What is the minimum processor needed for NetWare?

    A. 486/66

    B. 386/33

    C. Pentium 133

    D. Pentium II

15. What is a port value?

    A. A value between 1 and 10

    B. A value for identifying a hardware device

    C. A memory request line

    D. A memory location associated with a hardware port

16. What is a slot number?

    A. A number between 1 and 5

    B. A value identifying a hardware device

    C. The actual slot in the main board

    D. A number that identifies each piece of hardware

17. How many characters can the server name be?

    A. 17

    B. 27

    C. 37

    D. 47

Part II

NetWare 5
Advanced
Administration

CERTIFIED NOVELL ENGINEER

14

Upgrading NetWare 3.1x to NetWare 5 Server

CERTIFICATION OBJECTIVES

14.01	Upgrade Overview
14.02	Hardware and Software Requirements for a NetWare 5 Server
14.03	Upgrade Prerequisites
14.04	Install Files
14.05	Upgrade Steps
14.06	After the Upgrade
14.07	Confirm the Upgrade

Many companies have been content with the performance of NetWare 3. Although the benefits and features of intraNetWare vastly improved NetWare 3's performance, as well as simplified global administration through NDS, upgrading from the NetWare 3 bindery services to an NDS-based platform may be worthwhile for your company.

Novell has introduced NetWare 5 with some enhanced features, such as pure IP and a GUI server interface, and has also made it quite simple to upgrade or migrate from the bindery-based NetWare 3 environment to NetWare 5.

For those who are presently operating in a mixed bindery and NDS environment, a lot of planning work has been eliminated. Organizations that have been running NetWare networks in a pure Bindery mode will require a little more planning for their NDS tree(s) design. Once this has been completed, the transition is a lot smoother than you might expect. The process has also been simplified with the upgrade and migration utilities bundled with NetWare 5.

This chapter is designed to assist administrators and NetWare CNE candidates to develop the skills necessary to perform a server upgrade or migration to the NetWare 5 NDS structure from a NetWare 3.1x bindery-based system. We will discuss in detail the two methods used and the necessary steps it takes to successfully complete the upgrade. We will also cover the basic requirements for hardware and software, as well as preliminary preparation needed before the upgrade is performed. At the end of this chapter, you will be able to perform the tasks necessary to successfully complete the upgrade or migration.

CERTIFICATION OBJECTIVE 14.01

Upgrade Overview

You must first become familiar with the two methods of upgrading. Although you may sometimes hear each term used in the same context as the other, there are several important differences between an upgrade and a migration. The method you choose will be the starting point for the NetWare 5 installation.

In-Place Upgrade Method

A typical upgrade involves the installation of NetWare 5 on an existing server. The old system files are simply overwritten with the Bindery objects and file system upgraded to an NDS structure. This method of upgrading is known as an *in-place upgrade.*

The NetWare 5 CD includes the installation program, INSTALL.BAT, which will perform an in-place upgrade on the following NetWare operating systems:

- NetWare 3.1*x*
- NetWare 4.*x*
- intraNetWare (NetWare 4.11)
- intraNetWare for Small Business

The installation program runs as a Java-based GUI window. At a certain point in the installation program, you will be required to select the type of installation. It is at this step that you choose whether to upgrade an existing NetWare 3.1*x* server.

In-Place Upgrade Process

The in-place upgrade process is summarized by the following procedures:

1. The minimum software and hardware requirements must be met.

2. Network preparation for the NetWare 5 server (required if upgrading into an existing NetWare 4.1*x* NDS server environment).

3. Server preparation.

4. Start the installation program by running the INSTALL.BAT program file.

5. Follow the instructions indicated on each screen.

Advantages to In-Place Upgrade

- No additional hardware is needed if the existing server meets the requirements for a NetWare 5 server.

- Disk compression and suballocation can be used on the existing volumes.

Disadvantages to an In-Place Upgrade

- Data loss can result if a power outage occurs and the backups are defective.

- You cannot upgrade NetWare 2 server or non-NetWare servers using the installation program of NetWare 5. You must first upgrade to NetWare 3.x or NetWare 4.x, before upgrading to NetWare 5.

Across-the-Wire Migration Method

Migrating to NetWare 5 is another method of upgrading. You will be upgrading the bindery and file system from an existing NetWare 3.x server to another server that has NetWare 5 installed on it. This process is done over the network and is commonly referred to as an *across-the-wire migration.*

Novell has simplified the process of migrating across the wire by including an easy-to-use program called the *Novell Upgrade Wizard.* This graphical modeling and upgrade utility allows you to move the NetWare 3.x bindery, passwords, security rights, and volumes to a previously installed NetWare 5 server and NDS tree. The simple drag-and-drop functionality of the Novell Upgrade Wizard is used to perform these moves.

Migration Process

The migration process is summarized by the following procedures:

1. Install the Novell Upgrade Wizard utility.

2. Make preparations for the NetWare 5 migration.

3. Start the Novell Upgrade Wizard utility.

4. Create a project with the utility.

5. Drag and drop objects in the Project window.

6. Verify that there will be no NDS errors or conflicts.

7. Start the migration process.

Advantages of Across-the-Wire Migration

■ The source server remains intact during the migration process. If the connection is lost during the migration or a power outage occurs, all bindery and file system information is still available.

■ With the graphical modeling features of the Novell Upgrade Wizard, the new server structure can be designed before the migration is actually started.

■ Server volumes can be migrated all at once or selected individually.

■ Multiple servers can be migrated to a single server that has more powerful hardware.

■ NDS conflicts and errors are checked by the Novell Upgrade Wizard and will give you options for resolving them.

Disadvantage of Across-the-Wire Migration

■ Extra hardware is required. Another server is necessary with across-the-wire migration.

CERTIFICATION OBJECTIVE 14.02

Hardware and Software Requirements for a NetWare 5 Server

To ensure that the server upgrade process will operate properly, you must check the existing server's hardware to see if it meets the NetWare 5 minimum requirements. When migrating to a new hardware platform on which NetWare 5 is installed, you would have already determined what hardware is needed based upon the minimum recommended requirements of the NetWare 5 operating system and features that were implemented.

On an existing server, it is just as important to make sure that there is enough hardware presently installed or there is enough available space to add new hardware before proceeding with the upgrade.

Hardware Requirements

Table 14-1 lists the minimum and recommended hardware requirements for a NetWare 5 server.

 on the **Job**

Although it is not required, a PS/2 or serial mouse is recommended.

TABLE 14-1	Minimum Hardware Requirements	Recommended Hardware Requirements
Minimum and Recommended Hardware Requirements for NetWare 5 Server	PC-compatible machine with a Pentium processor	Server-class computer with a Pentium processor
	64MB of RAM	128MB if you plan to run Java-based applications
	30MB DOS boot partition	50MB (see the next section, "DOS Boot Partition," to determine optimal size)
	200MB of free disk space for the SYS volume	400MB of free disk space; also consider space needed for optional products yet to be installed
	VGA display adapter	SVGA high-resolution adapter
	One or more network interface cards	
	CD-ROM drive capable of reading ISO 9660-formatted disks	

DOS Boot Partition

A DOS boot partition is still needed to load the NetWare 5 operating system. When upgrading an existing server from NetWare 3, you must make sure that the DOS partition is large enough to accept all files needed in the C:\NWSERVER directory to boot the server.

As listed in Table 14-1, the DOS partition must have a minimum of 30MB free. 50MB of free space would be more comfortable to work with without having to remove other files stored on the local drive.

You may also want to consider a larger boot partition for troubleshooting purposes. This will allow you to perform a memory dump to the local drive when troubleshooting server problems. Figure 14-1 illustrates a formula to help determine the optimal size of the DOS boot partition.

FIGURE 14-1

Boot partition size formula for NetWare 5 server

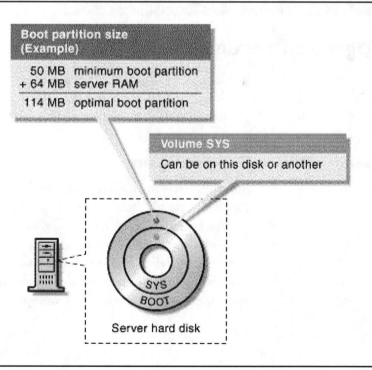

Software Requirements

It is necessary to have certain software immediately available to you before the upgrade or migration process can begin. The list below contains the software you will need before starting the NetWare 5 installation:

■ Drivers to access CD-ROM from DOS

■ NetWare 5 CD-ROM

■ License disk for NetWare 5

■ Novell Client for DOS and Windows 3.1x (required if upgrading from the network)

■ Novell Upgrade Wizard (if migrating across the wire)

CERTIFICATION OBJECTIVE 14.03

Upgrade Prerequisites

Before you begin the upgrade to NetWare 5, there are certain tasks that should be completed. These tasks differ depending on the upgrade method you have chosen.

Client Software Considerations

Although NetWare 5 still supports bindery client connections, upgrade your workstation's client software if you have not already done so. This can be done either before or after the upgrade is completed.

When using the Novell Upgrade Wizard to migrate a NetWare 3.1x server to NetWare 5, the workstation that will be running this utility must have the minimum client software requirements installed on it. Table 14-2 shows the client versions based on the operating system on the workstation.

TABLE 14-2	Operating System	Client Version
	Windows 95	Novell Client v2.2 or higher
Minimum Client Versions for NetWare 5 Server	Windows NT	Novell Client v4.11 or higher

In-Place Upgrade Preparation

Depending on your present environment, you may have additional steps to take before proceeding with the upgrade. If your network environment contains all NetWare 3.1x servers, only the server needs preparation. If you plan to install into an existing NDS tree that contains NetWare 4.x servers, you need to make preparations on the other servers as well.

Upgrading into an Existing NDS Structure

If your NetWare 5 server is going to be part of an existing NDS tree that contains NetWare 4.1x servers, it is recommended that certain tasks be completed on the NetWare 4.1x servers before you introduce the NetWare 5 server to the existing NDS tree:

1. Create a backup of the existing NDS structure from the server that contains the master replica of the partition to which you will be installing the NetWare 5 server.

2. Update the DS.NLM on the existing NetWare 4.1x servers to v5.99 or higher.

3. Obtain the following information:

   ■ Tree name that the server will be installed in

   ■ The NDS context for the upgraded server

   ■ The Administrator's username and password

4. Install Novell Licensing Services on the existing NetWare 4.1x servers.

QUESTIONS AND ANSWERS

Matt tested the upgrade of a NetWare 4.1 network to NetWare 5 in his lab. First, he installed NetWare 4.1 on three servers into the TEST tree. He attempted to upgrade the server containing the Master replica to NetWare 5. The attempt failed. What was the problem?	Matt installed NetWare 4.1 but did not install any patches, including the patch for the DS.NLM. With the "vanilla" installation of NetWare 4.1, the DS.NLM was not a recent enough version to communicate with the NetWare 5 version of DS.NLM.

Server Preparation

Follow the procedure that is outlined below to prepare for upgrading the NetWare 3.1*x* server to NetWare 5:

1. Document the new or existing NDS structure that your NetWare 3.1*x* server will be upgraded to.

2. Make sure the existing server meets all hardware and software requirements.

3. Make at least two full backups of your existing NetWare server and include files on the DOS partition.

4. Document hardware settings for the server's network board(s).

5. Log in to the server as a user with supervisor security equivalence.

6. Disable login and broadcast a console message requesting users to log out of the server that is being upgraded.

7. Check for any NetWare 5 compatibility issues with existing third-party NLMs, disk drivers, or LAN drivers.

8. Check the CONFIG.SYS file on the local drive and make sure it contains the following commands: FILES=40 and BUFFERS=30.

By using the CONFIG.NLM utility, you can get your existing NetWare server's configuration information, including NCF files, INETCFG configuration information, speed rating, total RAM, set parameters, modules list, disk information, volume information, name space information, LAN information, and system files. When CONFIG.NLM is loaded, it will create a file in the SYS:SYSTEM directory called CONFIG.TXT.

Preparing to Migrate Across the Wire

Since a migration involves upgrading the bindery and volume information from a NetWare 3.1x server to another server that has NetWare 5 already installed, you will be using the Novell Upgrade Wizard to complete this task as outlined in Exercise 14-1.

EXERCISE 14-1

Across-the-Wire Migration

1. Install the Novell Upgrade Wizard (see Figure 14-2) on the workstation you will use for the migration. Follow the steps below to load the utility:

   a. Insert the NetWare 5 Operating System CD-ROM in the workstation's CD-ROM drive.

   b. Browse to the \PRODUCTS\UPGRDWZD directory on the CD-ROM.

   c. Run the self-extracting UPGRDWZD.EXE file.

   d. Click Next.

   e. Click Accept to accept the license.

FIGURE 14-2

Novell's Upgrade Wizard

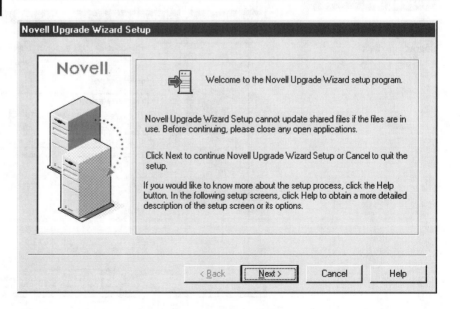

   f. Click Finish to install the Upgrade Wizard onto the hard drive of the workstation.

   g. Click OK to complete.

2. Choose Start | Programs | Novell | Novell Upgrade Wizard to start the upgrade process.

3. At the first screen, select Create a New Upgrade Project.

4. Give the project a name by typing it into the dialog box and click Next (see Figure 14-3).

5. Select a source server to migrate FROM and a destination tree to migrate TO and click Next.

6. Select the appropriate items to migrate: print configuration, User and Group objects, and security password information during next few dialog pages. Only objects in the Source area that are moved to the Destination area of the window are migrated.

7. Run the verification process to discover errors.

8. The Upgrade Wizard will migrate the selected Bindery items over the wire to the NDS tree.

FIGURE 14-3

Creating the
upgrade project

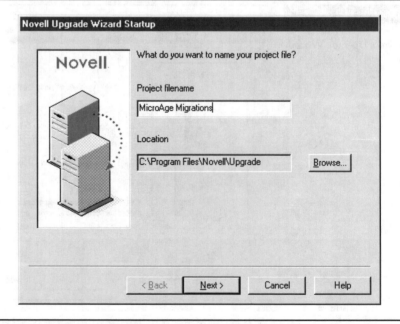

Prerequisites for the migration include the following:

1. Create a backup of NDS and the volumes on the NetWare 5 server to which the NetWare 3.1*x* server will be migrated.

2. Obtain the following information:

   - Tree name that the server will be installed in

   - The NDS context for the upgraded server

   - The administrator's username and password

3. If several servers will be migrated to the same NDS context, complete the following before migrating:

   a. Consolidate individual usernames that exist on different NetWare 3.1*x* servers.

   b. Rename different users that have the same names on different servers to prevent duplicate NDS usernames in the same context.

4. Upgrade client workstations.

5. Verify that you have Supervisor Equivalent rights to both the NetWare 3.1*x* and NDS tree.

6. Turn SAP filtering off if the servers involved are on different LAN segments. If SAP cannot be disabled, make sure that your client's default or preferred server is on the same LAN segment as the servers being migrated to and from.

7. Update NLMs on all NetWare 3.1*x* servers to be migrated. These NLMs are located in the PRODUCTS\NW3X directory where the Novell Upgrade Wizard was installed.

8. Unload the following NLMs on each NetWare 3.*x* server to be migrated. Unload each NLM in the order listed below:

   a. TSA311.NLM or TSA312.NLM

   b. SMDR.NLM

   c. SMDR31X.NLM

   d. SPXS.NLM

   e. TLI.NLM

      f. AFTER311.NLM

      g. CLIB.NLM

      h. A3112.NLM

      i. STREAMS.NLM

9. Load the new TSA312.NLM to update the NLMs that were copied in Step 8.

10. Load and add any additional name spaces on the destination NetWare 5 server volume(s) that the NetWare 3.1x server volume(s) will be migrated to. This must be done in order to properly migrate files that use non-DOS naming conventions.

11. Decide which objects will be upgraded. The Novell Upgrade Utility allows you to select which Bindery object or volume to migrate.

FROM THE CLASSROOM

IPX/SPX During a Migration or Upgrade to NetWare 5

One of the major changes that occurred when Novell developed NetWare 5 is the use of pure IP in network communications. In previous versions of NetWare, IPX/SPX was a required protocol suite for network communication. Even when TCP/IP was enabled on a server, IPX/SPX was still required to encapsulate IP and UDP (another Transport Layer protocol in the Internet Protocol Stack) packets to be properly processed by NetWare servers. NetWare 5 can run pure IP natively, without IPX/SPX being bound to LAN drivers, thus reducing the network's and server's overhead. However, this has important ramifications during the upgrade/migration to NetWare 5.

Until all the non-NetWare 5 servers are upgraded, IPX/SPX must remain bound to the LAN drivers loaded on the NetWare 5 servers. Once all servers are upgraded, then all extra protocols can be removed, until only TCP/IP remains. Also, don't forget, for Ethernet LANs and WANs, NetWare 3.11 and earlier, use frame type Ethernet_802.3; and for NetWare 3.12 and later, use frame type Ethernet_802.2 as defaults. Make sure that the appropriate frame types get bound to the NetWare 5 servers while the network is in transition.

—By Dan Cheung, CNI, MCNE, MCT

CERTIFICATION OBJECTIVE 14.04

Install Files

The installation process copies files from the CD, or from a network drive, to the hard drive in two separate areas. The first area is where files are copied to the boot partition. The second area is where files are copied to the SYS volume of the server.

Many NetWare files that were used in older versions of NetWare use the same names as NetWare 5 files, but have been enhanced. Old files are moved to an archive subdirectory on the boot partition, and under the SYS:SYSTEM directory. Some drivers, such as .DSK drivers, have been completely replaced by a new architecture—in this case, .CDM and .HAM drivers. Such files are not initialized until after the server has been rebooted.

CERTIFICATION OBJECTIVE 14.05

Upgrade Steps

Once you are confident you have made all the necessary preparations, you are ready for the upgrade itself. This section will describe the steps for both an upgrade and a migration to NetWare 5.

In-Place Upgrade Steps

The steps in Exercise 14-2 are used to upgrade an existing NetWare 3.1x server to NetWare 5.

EXERCISE 14-2

Upgrade to NetWare 5

1. Take down the server and exit to DOS.

2. Insert the CD-ROM containing the NetWare 5 Operating System. If you are accessing the installation files from another server on the network, you will need to log in to that server via a DOS client on the server to be upgraded and map a drive to the network directory containing the installation files.

3. Execute the installation program, INSTALL.BAT, by typing **INSTALL** at the CD-ROM drive or network drive prompt.

4. Select the language and accept the license agreement.

5. Choose Upgrade from 3.1x or 4.1x by selecting Modify from the Options menu. Figure 14-4 is an example of the screens that you will see during the in-place upgrade.

6. Select the mouse type and video mode that your server will be using.

7. Allow the installation program to run a file copy process.

8. Select and configure a storage adapter. You may also select a platform support module and a PCI hot plug module at this point, if they are required.

Support for .DSK drivers has been discontinued. NetWare 5 uses NWPA (NetWare Peripheral Architecture) that requires a software driver called a HAM (Host Adapter Module) to allow communications between the computer (host) and the storage device linked to it. The storage devices will use a CDM (Custom Device Module) drive to communicate with the storage adapter.

FIGURE 14-4

Initial installation screen

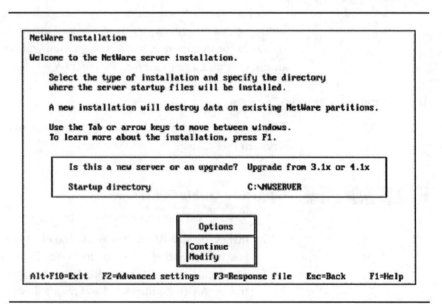

9. Select and configure the storage device(s) that will be used. The SYS: volume will be mounted at this point.

10. Select the correct network board and configure. If necessary, load any special NLMs for the network adapter.

11. Allow the installation program to run a file copy process and load the Java virtual machine console. When the installation program runs, all of the old driver files in the SYS:SYSTEM directory are copied to the SYS:SYSTEM|DRIVERS.OLD directory.

12. In the Mount Volumes window, select No if you plan to install products and services on another volume besides SYS.

13. In the Protocols window, choose your network board icon and configure the IP parameters for that board, if you have decided to run IP on this server. IPX frame types will automatically be detected and bound to the network board(s).

exam
ⓦatch   *IPX cannot be removed with the installation program but can be removed at a later time, after NetWare 5 has been installed and rebooted.*

14. Set the time zone information.

15. Upgrade and configure NDS on the server according to your documentation. If this is the first NetWare 5 server installed into an existing NDS structure containing NetWare 4.*x* server, the schema must be modified. You will be prompted to do this.

16. At the License window, browse to the drive containing the .NLF License file for your server and add the license. You can choose not to install a license at this time and use the NetWare Administration utility to do this later. However, until you add a license, this will allow only two user connections at any given time.

17. Select any additional products and services you want installed.

18. At the Summary screen, you can view and customize the products and services that you have chosen to install. You may be required to supply additional CD-ROMs, depending on the products and services selected.

19. Allow the file copy process to complete without interruption. If prompted to replace any existing files, select to replace all existing files.

20. Reboot the server when prompted.

Across-the-Wire Migration Steps

The Novell Upgrade Wizard will be used in across-the-wire migration when upgrading to NetWare 5. Once you have completed the preliminary preparations, you will be ready to do the migration.

Launch the Novell Upgrade Wizard Utility

Launch the NetWare Upgrade Wizard from your workstation by choosing Start | Programs | Novell | Novell Upgrade Wizard. You can begin to create a new upgrade project from the Startup dialog box that appears from launching the utility.

Create a New Upgrade Project

Create a new project by doing the following:

1. Choose Create | New | Upgrade | Project in the Startup dialog box; then click OK.

2. Type in a project name and then Browse to the location where you want to save the project; click Next.

3. On the next screen, choose the source server(s) and the destination tree from the drop-down lists; then click Next. If the bindery server or the NDS tree is displayed, click the Server or Tree button to browse and log in to them.

4. Click Create to create the project.

Moving Objects in the Project Window

If you have already logged in to the source server(s) and the destination NDS tree, you can begin moving the objects around. You do this by dragging and dropping the Bindery object(s) and volume data from the source server(s) to the desired location(s) in the destination NDS tree. Figure 14-5 demonstrates how objects are moved around in the Project window.

If you have prepared in advance, the container object(s) will be there. If the container has not yet been created, right-click the parent object and create a new container or folder.

The Verification Process

Verify that the migration can proceed as indicated in the Project window by completing the tasks in Exercise 14-3.

EXERCISE 14-3

Verifying the Migration

1. Click Verification from the toolbar or select Project | Verify.

2. Click Next at the Overview page.

3. If you will be upgrading the NetWare 3.1x print information, select a volume in the tree browser; then click Next. If not, deselect the box on the page.

4. If you have configured a template object for the users being upgraded, locate and click the template object; then click Next. If not, deselect the box on the page.

FIGURE 14-5

Migration Project window

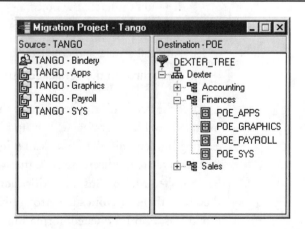

5. To create a user template, mark the box on the page, enter a name for the template, and click Next.

6. Mark the box to indicate how you want to handle conflicts between duplicate files; then click Next.

7. Enter passwords to the source server(s) and destination tree; then click Next.

8. Mark the boxes to select the categories you want verified; then click Next.

9. When a naming conflict is found between same object types, correct it by selecting one of the following options:

   ■ Let the wizard rename the object automatically.

   ■ Don't migrate the object.

   ■ Merge the objects and maintain the bindery properties.

   ■ Merge the objects and maintain the NDS properties. Each object is renamed by default if a resolution is not selected. If no conflict occurs, the list box will be empty.

10. Click Next.

11. When a naming conflict is found between *different object types*, correct it by selecting one of the following options:

    ■ Let the wizard rename the object automatically.

    ■ Don't migrate the object.

12. Click Next.

13. After all errors and conflicts have been resolved, click Next.

14. Read through the verification summary page; then click Finish.

After the verification is completed, the objects that can or cannot be migrated are listed for review. It is up to the installer to "clean up" the existing bindery in order for a clean migration to take place. That means that if there are duplicate userIDs that will be migrated, the migration will fail. So, the installer runs the verification to find out what errors will occur, then fixes them to avoid such errors. Fixes can include renaming userIDs, group IDs, or print queue information, as well as deleting those objects. It is highly recommended to rename objects rather than delete them, except in cases where two servers are migrated to the same context and contain essentially the same user and group data.

QUESTIONS AND ANSWERS

Cheri upgraded two NetWare 3.12 servers to NetWare 5 using the Upgrade Wizard. She knew that the user data was correctly imported with the first upgrade, but neglected to run the verification process before migrating the second server. Cheri was surprised to see that there were multiple errors on nearly every user for the second migration. What happened?	Cheri migrated the users and groups of both servers to the same context in the new NetWare 5 Novell Directory Services tree. Previously, the servers had duplicates of each user and group in order to facilitate access for all the users to either server. However, when migrating the second time, the userIDs already existed, so they produced an error.

Migrating Across the Wire

Migrate the bindery and file system across the wire by completing the following steps:

1. Click Upgrade from the toolbar or select Project | Upgrade.

2. After reading the Overview page, click Next.

3. As the program goes through the verification process again, resolve any remaining errors and conflicts.

4. Start the upgrade process by clicking on Upgrade. The upgrade process can be stopped at any time by clicking Stop and Yes to confirm. All bindery and file information that has been copied to NDS up to that point will remain there until manually deleted.

CERTIFICATION OBJECTIVE 14.06

After the Upgrade

After the upgrade process has been completed, you should perform any post-upgrade procedures. Below are a few post-upgrade tasks:

■ Make any necessary changes to the login script.

■ Modify printing configuration.

- Check the information on the users that were upgraded.

- Check the file information that was upgraded.

- Check any third-party applications that were running on the NetWare 3.1*x* server.

- Move any other objects to other locations in the NDS tree that you may need.

- Upgrade the client software if you have not done so already.

CERTIFICATION OBJECTIVE 14.07

Confirm the Upgrade

After completing the upgrade, confirm that it was successful by sample testing to ensure that

- You can log in to the NetWare 5 server.

- Drives are being mapped correctly as specified in the login script.

- User accounts and restrictions are configured properly.

- Directory and file attributes are set correctly.

- All applications run properly.

- The printing environment has migrated correctly.

CERTIFICATION SUMMARY

In this chapter, we have discussed the two methods used to perform an upgrade from NetWare 3.*x* to NetWare 5.

- Using the installation program, INSTALL.BAT, from the NetWare 5 CD-ROM, you can perform an *in-place upgrade*. This method will overwrite the system files on an existing server and upgrade the bindery and file system to an NDS structure.

■ The Novell Upgrade Wizard is used during an *across-the-wire migration*. This upgrade method can take the bindery and volume information from multiple NetWare 3.1*x* servers and upgrade them to another more powerful server that has had NetWare 5 already installed.

Although Novell has simplified the process for both methods, you should still have a plan in place that conforms to the requirements and prerequisites before beginning the upgrade.

TWO-MINUTE DRILL

❑ Novell has introduced NetWare 5 with some enhanced features, such as pure IP and a GUI server interface, and has also made it quite simple to upgrade or migrate from the bindery-based NetWare 3 environment to NetWare 5.

❑ A typical upgrade involves the installation of NetWare 5 on an existing server. The old system files are simply overwritten with the bindery objects and file system upgraded to an NDS structure. This method of upgrading is known as an in-place upgrade.

❑ Migrating to NetWare 5 is another method of upgrading. You upgrade the bindery and file system from an existing NetWare 3.*x* server to another server that has NetWare 5 installed on it. This process is done over the network and is commonly referred to as an across-the-wire migration.

❑ To ensure that the server upgrade process will operate properly, you must check the existing server's hardware to see if it meets the NetWare 5 minimum requirements. When migrating to a new hardware platform on which NetWare 5 is installed, you would have already determined what hardware is needed in order to install NetWare 5.

❑ The software programs needed for a NetWare 5 installation are drivers for accessing a CD-ROM drive from DOS, NetWare 5 CD-ROM, license disk for NetWare 5, Novell Client for DOS and Windows 3.1*x* (required if upgrading from the network), and Novell Upgrade Wizard (if migrating across the wire).

❏ Although NetWare 5 still supports bindery client connections, it is recommended that you upgrade your workstation's client software before upgrading to NetWare 5. This can be done either before or after the upgrade is completed.

❏ When using the Novell Upgrade Wizard to migrate a NetWare 3.1x server to NetWare 5, the workstation that will be running Novell Upgrade Wizard must have the minimum client software requirements installed on it.

❏ If your network environment contains all NetWare 3.1x servers, only the server needs preparation. If you plan to install into an existing NDS tree that contains NetWare 4.x servers, you need to make preparations on the other servers as well.

❏ Since a migration involves upgrading the bindery and volume information from a NetWare 3.1x server to another server that has NetWare 5 already installed, you use the Novell Upgrade Wizard.

❏ The installation process copies files from the CD, or from a network drive, to the hard drive in two separate areas. The first area is where files are copied to the boot partition. The second area is where files are copied to the SYS: volume of the server.

❏ After completing the upgrade process, perform any required post-upgrade procedures, including the following:

  ❏ Making any necessary changes to the login script

  ❏ Modifying printing configuration

  ❏ Checking user information for users that were upgraded

  ❏ Checking file information for files that were upgraded

  ❏ Checking third-party applications that were running on the NetWare 3.1x server

  ❏ Moving any other objects to other locations in the NDS tree that you may need

  ❏ Upgrading the client software if you have not done so already

❑ After completing the upgrade, verify that it was successful by logging in to the NetWare 5 server, confirming that drives are mapped correctly as specified in the login script, confirming that user accounts and restrictions are configured properly, confirming that directory and file attributes are set correctly, confirming that all applications run properly, and confirming that the printing environment has migrated correctly.

SELF TEST

The Self-Test questions will help you measure your understanding of the material presented in this chapter. Read all the choices carefully, as there may be more than one correct answer. Select all correct answers for each question.

1. Which method is used to upgrade an existing server to NetWare 5?

   A. Across-the-wire-migration

   B. In-place upgrade

   C. Custom upgrade

   D. Same-server migration

2. The installation program, INSTALL.BAT, can upgrade which of the following NetWare operating systems? (Choose all that apply.)

   A. NetWare 2.x

   B. NetWare 3.1x

   C. NetWare 4.x

   D. intraNetWare

   E. intraNetWare for Small Business

   F. All of the above

3. What are the advantages to the in-place upgrade? (Choose all that apply.)

   A. The source server remains intact during the entire upgrade process.

   B. No additional hardware is needed if the existing server meets the minimum requirements.

   C. Disk compression and suballocation can be used on existing volumes.

   D. Server volumes can be migrated all at once or individually selected.

4. Which of the following is not a disadvantage of an in-place upgrade?

   A. Loss of data can occur if power is lost.

   B. NetWare 2 and non-NetWare servers cannot be upgraded to NetWare 5.

   C. Additional hardware may not be needed if the existing server meets minimum requirements.

5. Which term best describes the upgrade method in which the bindery and file system from an existing NetWare 3.1x server is upgraded to another server that has NetWare 5 already installed?

   A. Same-server migration

   B. In-place upgrade

   C. Across-the-wire migration

   D. Custom migration

6. What utility is used to upgrade a server from NetWare 3.1 to NetWare 5 across the wire?

   A. NetWare Administrator

   B. Windows 95 Upgrade Tool for NetWare

   C. INSTALL.BAT

   D. Novell Upgrade Wizard

7. Which of the following are advantages of an across-the-wire migration? (Choose all that apply.)

A. Multiple servers can be migrated into a single, more powerful server.

B. All volumes must be migrated at the same time.

C. The source server remains intact during the migration process.

D. The new server structure can be designed before the migration by using the Novell Upgrade Wizard.

E. The Novell Upgrade Wizard can be used to check and resolve NDS conflicts and errors before performing the migration.

8. Which of the following is the only disadvantage of across-the-wire migration?

A. Extra hardware is required.

B. Data loss is possible if a power outage occurs or the backups are defective.

C. NDS conflicts will almost always occur, forcing you to manually resolve them.

D. Bindery objects cannot be upgraded using the Novell Upgrade Wizard.

9. Which is not a minimum hardware requirement for a NetWare 5 server?

A. PC-compatible machine with a Pentium processor

B. 64MB of RAM

C. A PS/2 or serial mouse

D. One or more network interface cards

10. Which of the items below are software requirements before the upgrade can begin?

A. NetWare 5 CD-ROM

B. License diskette

C. Drivers to access CD-ROM from DOS

D. Novell Upgrade Wizard (if migrating across the wire)

E. All of the above

11. What is the name of the self-extracting file used to install the Novell Upgrade Wizard on a workstation?

A. WIZARD.EXE

B. INSTALL.BAT

C. SETUP.EXE

D. UPGRDWZD.EXE

12. What is the first step you take when starting the in-place upgrade?

A. Run the INSTALL.BAT installation program.

B. Select the mouse and video mode that your server will be using.

C. Take down the server and exit to DOS.

D. Select and configure a storage adapter.

13. How do you launch the Novell Upgrade Utility on your workstation?

A. Type **UPGRADE** at a DOS prompt.

B. Choose Start | Programs | Novell | Novell Upgrade Wizard.

C. Type **INSTALL** at the server's console.

D. Run the UPGRDWZD.EXE self-extracting file.

14. What must you do to ensure that the migration can proceed as indicated in the Project window of the Novell Upgrade Wizard?

   A. Run a verification process from within the Project window.

   B. Do nothing; this step is not necessary.

   C. Choose Start | Run | and type **Verify**.

   D. Choose Start | Programs | Novell | Verify.

15. Which item below is not a post-upgrade task?

   A. Checking that file information was upgraded

   B. Upgrading client software

   C. Making any necessary changes to the login script

   D. Rebooting the server

CERTIFIED NOVELL ENGINEER

15

Upgrading from Queue-Based Printing to NDPS

CERTIFICATION OBJECTIVES

15.01 Overview of the Upgrade

15.02 Gathering Current Printing Information

15.03 Configuring Your Current Printing Information

15.04 Migrating Printing Components

15.05 Testing Migrated Components

15.06 Removing the Old Printing Environment

N ovell's Distributed Printing Services (NDPS) was created in response to the need to simplify printer management and reduce printing costs. NDPS utilizes Novell Directory Services (NDS) for providing printing services and managing them from a single NDS object. In addition, NDPS brings new features:

- It can be used in a pure IP environment
- It makes available automatic printer driver downloads
- It supports bidirectional printing

Upgrading to NDPS is a worthwhile investment in effort for an existing print-queue–based NetWare network. The fact that it is included as part of NetWare 5 makes it easier to implement as part of an enterprise-wide network upgrade.

CERTIFICATION OBJECTIVE 15.01

Overview of the Upgrade

In any network system upgrade, one of the first tasks to perform is planning the new system. Protocol choice is a primary area to review. NDPS and NetWare 5 both support a pure IP environment, a pure IPX environment, or a combination of both protocols.

The final system design will depend on the printers already in use within the enterprise network and the protocols used by them. Under NetWare 5, NCP (NetWare Core Protocol) is capable of travelling on top of either IPX or IP. Any application, including the NDPS printing environment, that does not require direct interface with IPX or SPX, can run in a pure IP environment. Those applications that do require IPX interface, such as queue-based printing, can run in NetWare 5's Compatibility mode. Compatibility mode allows IPX-based applications to communicate with the IPX protocol stack counterparts on the client or server without IPX packets being sent directly on the wire.

Designing the NDPS System

Security and management of NDPS components is handled in the NetWare Administrator because the NDPS components are integrated in NDS. Designing the NDPS components' location in the tree, and on which servers they will be run, is a key step for a fully functional NDPS implementation.

Security

Like any object in the NDS tree, the NDPS printers can be made available to all users, or they can be locked down so they are available to a select group. There are three roles associated to the security of NDPS printers:

- **Manager**   Maintains complete control of the NDPS component
- **Operator**   Has administrative control of the NDPS printer
- **User**   Is granted printing privileges to the NDPS printer

Broker Distribution

The *broker* is the component of NDPS that makes the Service Registry Service, Event Notification Service, and Resource Management Service available to end users:

- The Service Registry Service (SRS) holds and advertises printer registration information (device type, address, and device-specific information) for public access servers so that users and administrators can find them. SRS prevents the need for SAP (Service Advertising Protocol), minimizing bandwidth utilization. When a client needs to send a print job to a printer, it contacts an SRS to retrieve the list of registered NDPS printers.

- The Event Notification Service (ENS) provides event notification for print jobs and status. ENS can be configured to notify the users that sent the print job or to notify administrators about any printer events.

- The Resource Management Service (RMS) allows centralized printing resources such as print drivers, PDFs (printer definition files), and banners to be downloaded to clients or printers.

Brokers are not required on all servers. However, the brokers will need to be distributed so that NDPS services are available when and where needed.

When installing a broker, the installer must have the Browse and Create object rights for the container in which the broker will reside. The installer will require file system rights of Read, Write, Modify, Create, and File Scan at the root of the server SYS: volume. The broker will store its databases in the SYS:NDPS/RESDIR directory, which is created at the time the Broker object is created.

When NDPS is installed for the first time into an NDS tree, the installation creates a broker on the server. After that, NDPS installations on new servers will follow a process to determine whether an additional broker is needed. First, it checks all NDPS brokers until one is found that is within three hops of the server that the installer has Supervisor rights to. At this point, the NDPS installation skips creating a broker. If a broker is not found, NDPS installation creates a new one.

Brokers can be moved to different NDS containers, as needed. The NetWare Administrator is the program used to move the Broker object (see Figure 15-1). When a Broker object is moved from one location to another in NDS, a corresponding change must be made on the server in the AUTOEXEC.NCF file. The LOAD BROKER or BROKER command will not have the new location or name of the broker, and that line should be changed.

If a system has multiple locations separated by WAN links, it is best to maintain a broker at each separate location. For example, if there are three buildings in Phoenix, one in London, and two in New York, and there are printers in each location, then the minimum number of NDPS brokers will be six. This corresponds to one NDPS broker in each building.

Creating NDPS Objects

The NDPS Manager makes printer agents available from a NetWare 5 Server. The NDPS Manager must be created as an object in an NDS tree

FIGURE 15-1

Broker object

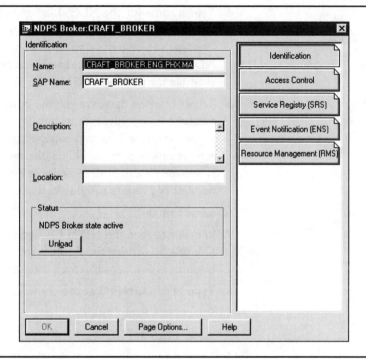

before server-based printer agents can be created. The NDPS Manager object stores the information that is used by NDPSM.NLM on the server and can control an unlimited number of printer agents.

Each NDPS Manager object can be loaded on a single server with the NDPSM.NLM module. If the NDPS Manager controls a printer that is local to the server, then the NDPS Manager object can be loaded only on the server to which that printer is attached.

EXERCISE 15-1

Creating the NDPS Manager Object

1. In the NetWare administrator, navigate to the container in which the NDPS Manager will reside and select it.

2. From the Object menu, select the Create option.

3. From the New Object dialog box, select NDPS Manager.

4. Type a name for the NDPS Manager object and browse; then select the server that will be assigned to this object. Note that the NDPS Manager can be moved to another server but, when it moves, the NDPS database moves and any local printers will no longer be available for printing.

5. Browse for the database volume in which the NDPS Manager database will reside. It must be a volume on the previously selected server, and it will contain configuration information for the Printer Agents assigned to the NDPS Manager object. Make sure that there is between 3 and 5MB of available disk space so that even a large number of printers can be managed.

6. Click Create.

7. In order to load the NDPS Manager automatically, start Remote Console by clicking the Tools menu in NetWare Administrator and begin a session or walk to a server console for the next steps.

8. Type **NWCONFIG** at the console.

9. Select NCF Files Options.

10. Select Edit AUTOEXEC.NCF.

11. Scroll down to the end of the file and add the line: **NDPSM {NDPS manager name and context}**.

Before an NDPS printer can be created, there must be an NDPS Manager.

The following methods can be used to create NDPS printers:

- Use NetWare Administrator and create the NDPS printer as a new object.

- Use NDPSM.NLM on the server console.

- Use the Novell Upgrade Wizard, which can be downloaded from Novell's Web site.

Upgrading the Clients

Client workstations must have their NetWare client software upgraded to the NetWare 5 client in order to print to NDPS printers. If there are a large number of workstation clients, the NetWare client software upgrade may be implemented in phases. NDPS can have the server components implemented in tandem with the maintenance of existing queue-based printing components.

QUESTIONS AND ANSWERS

Kelsey created an NDPS printing system using a new NetWare 5 Server on an existing NetWare 4.11 network. When she migrated the first group of users to the new server, the workstations were able to use the file services but none could print. What was Kelsey's error?	Kelsey did not upgrade the workstations to a NetWare client that included NDPS components. The older NetWare clients are able to attach to the new file server and use files and directories, but they cannot print to NDPS printers. They would still be able to print to a legacy print queue, however.

CERTIFICATION OBJECTIVE 15.02

Gathering Current Printing Information

In determining the location of brokers, printers, servers, workstation clients, and routers, the designer should have a written record of the existing network resources and components. Taking that written record and drawing a diagram of those components with the changes expected by NDPS will assist in the final configuration determination (see Figure 15-2).

A list of the printers currently in use, their configurations, and how they are used by end users will show which printers can be migrated to NDPS and which cannot. For example, if New York has seven identical printers on the second floor, and 14 users print to four of the printers with DOS-based applications, then at least one printer must remain as a queue-based printer to serve those end users. If some of the users are on one side of the building in the HR group and the others are on the other side of the building in Accounting, then two printers will be more effective for servicing the DOS-based application print jobs.

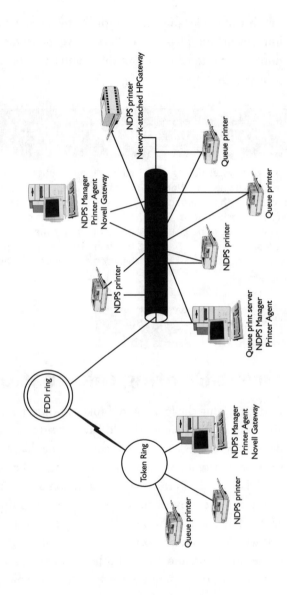

FIGURE 15-2

Sample network diagram

Configuring Your Current Printing Information

To make a tree location diagram, draw the tree's containers and place the potential NDPS Printing objects within them. The tree location diagram will depict how the printers will be placed in containers and whether they will be placed with the users that send print jobs to them.

The diagram can contain the NDPS Manager, the NDPS Broker, printer users (grouped together), printer Managers and Operators, and printer configurations (see Figure 15-3). There may be some simplification or reorganization of the tree, until you reach an optimal configuration.

Table 15-1 compares the characteristics of NDPS printers and queue printers.

TABLE 15-1	Queue-Based Printers	NDPS Printers
Queue-Based Printers vs. NDPS Printers	Tend to be public and available to all users	Uses NDS security to restrict access to certain users; hierarchy of management by assigning managers and operators
	Minimal administration required	Offers event and status notification to further minimize administration requirements
	Available through gateways when used with NDPS	Supports multiple configurations
	No capabilities for configuring clients	Automatic download of printer drivers to client

FIGURE 15-3

Sample tree diagram

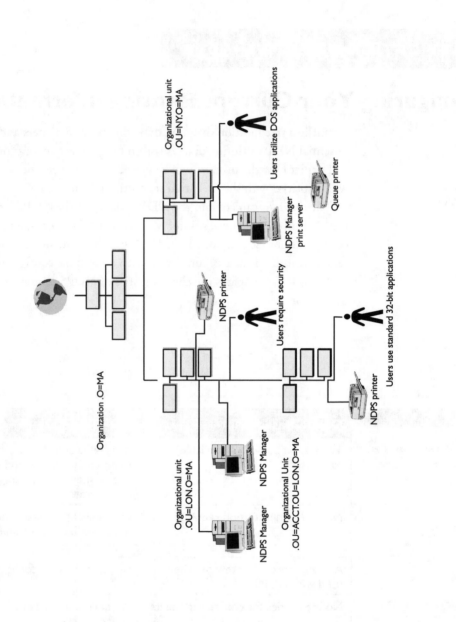

Migrating Printing Components

When NetWare 5 is installed, NDPS version #2 is included as part of the typical installation. If, however, NDPS was not installed at the server's installation, it can be added later since the NDS schema is extended to accept NDPS objects whether the server has NDPS installed on it or not. In order to add NDPS later, follow these steps:

1. Map a drive to the root of the SYS: volume on the target NetWare 5 Server.

2. Access the NetWare 5 CD-ROM.

3. Copy the CD-ROM's directory of PRODUCTS\NDPS to the root of the SYS: volume.

4. Unzip each of the ZIP files in the RESDIR directory that was copied to the SYS: volume.

Deciding which gateways to use in the NDPS design is one step in the strategy for implementation. Third-party gateways are a good option for the printers that they support. When NDPS-embedded printers are available, the gateways that are used with them will provide the best access. The protocols that the gateways support will make the final determination as to whether they can be implemented in your environment. For example, if the gateway supports only IP, and the environment is IPX, then that gateway would not work in the environment and another should be selected.

When a pure IP gateway is required, and the third-party gateway does not work in an IP environment, then the Novell gateway can be used and configured to communicate with the printer using LPR (Line Printer Remote protocol). This, in turn, requires that the printer be configured to communicate using the same protocol.

The following is the strategy to use when deploying NDPS:

1. Design the NDPS printing system.

2. Migrate servers first, since NDPS components and print servers can exist on the same server simultaneously.

3. Create NDPS components using the NetWare Administrator.

4. Set up the NDPS printer agents in the NDPS Manager to retrieve prints from print queues as well as service NDPS printers (see Figure 15-4).

5. Gradually migrate end users in printer-sharing workgroups to have the NDPS client software.

6. Change the users' setup to print directly to NDPS printers. Set up users who require DOS applications to utilize both queues and NDPS.

7. Remove the legacy printer and Print Server objects that are no longer used. Retain any queues needed for DOS applications.

8. Remove login script CAPTURE statements, as needed.

9. Add or move brokers and other NDPS components throughout the NDS tree to optimize the design.

| FIGURE 15-4 | Using the NDPS printer agent and queues during transition |

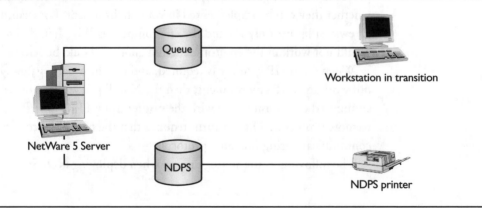

exam
ⓜatch *The NetWare Loadable Modules for the NDPS Manager and Print Servers—NDPSM.NLM and PSERVER.NLM—can be loaded on the same server at the same time.*

EXERCISE 15-2

Creating an NDPS Printer

A public access printer is one to which any user may send print jobs. Public access printers are not associated with an NDS Printer object. Controlled access printers do have an associated Printer object and can take advantage of NDS security. In order to create a controlled access printer, an NDPS broker and NDPS Manager must be installed and active.

1. In NetWare administrator, navigate to a container that holds the NDPS Manager object.

2. Double-click the NDPS Manager.

3. Click the Printer Agent List button.

4. Click New.

5. Type a name in the NDPS Printer Name field, select the gateway type, and click OK.

6. Select the printer type that matches the printer, or the nearest equivalent, and the port handler.

7. Select the printer driver for each desktop operating system on the network.

8. Click Continue and the printer agent will appear in the Printer Agent window. Click OK to save the changes and close the Details of the NDPS Manager.

Interoperability with Print Queue Components

Legacy printing components offered printing services by linking printers to print queues, and print queues to print servers. *Print servers* run on NetWare servers and manage the print jobs. *Queues* are file storage areas on the server where print jobs are temporarily stored before being processed by the printer. NDPS combines the components into a *printer agent*. Users are able to send print jobs directly to NDPS printers.

NDPS does not require queues, but is backward compatible with queue-based printing. Implementing NDPS requires no disruption to the current printing configuration on the network because the two types of systems can exist and be used simultaneously.

It is possible to print through NDPS to an existing queue, which enables access to systems that require a print queue. NDPS can service existing print queues, so client software does not have to be updated before the server components are installed.

NDPS Migration Scenarios

The flexibility and coexistence of queue-based and NDPS printing components enables several migration scenarios.

If implementing NetWare 5 and NDPS in an existing NetWare 3.x environment, and if there is no need for queue-based printing, then the migration can be accomplished fairly easily. In a small network with few printers to migrate, it is just as easy to implement NDPS as it is to implement an entirely new system. In a large network, or in one that uses a complex printing design, the Novell Upgrade Wizard (bundled with NetWare 5 or downloadable from http://www.novell.com) can migrate the printers from the old bindery system to the new NDS tree.

When implementing NetWare 5 and NDPS in an existing NetWare 4.x queue-based printing system, the simplest way to migrate printers to NDPS is to use a gateway. NetWare 5 ships with HP and Xerox gateways, as well as the Novell gateway. If there is no applicable third-party gateway, then the Novell NDPS gateway is a good option.

exam
watch

An NDPS gateway is a software component that allows NetWare NDPS clients to print to non-NDPS-aware printers. The Novell gateway supports legacy printers using the LPR/LPD protocol over IP and the RP protocol over IPX. The Novell gateway will allow jobs to be sent to legacy print queues.

When implementing NetWare 5 and NDPS on a new network, or one that does not include any Novell NetWare servers, NDPS can be implemented as the primary printing solution.

Migration

Migration is the process of changing from legacy queue-based printing to NDPS printing. Standard queue-based printing is shown in Figure 15-5. There are three types of printing setups common to the legacy system:

■ **Server-attached printers**   Workstations send print jobs to the print queue, which forwards them through the print server (a server running PSERVER.NLM) to the server running NPRINTER.NLM and attached printer.

■ **Workstation-attached printers**   Workstations send print jobs to the print queue, which forwards them through the print server to the workstation that is running NPRINTER.EXE and attached printer.

■ **Network-attached printers**   Workstations send print jobs to the print queue, which is polled by the network-attached printer running in queue-server mode.

In any of these three configurations, a gateway can be used to begin the migration to NDPS (see Figure 15-6). The strategy for each type of printer is somewhat different.

After the gateway is installed, server-attached printers must have an NDPS Manager installed directly on the server to manage the local printers. The printer agent and gateway are installed and the clients updated so that the clients can pass print jobs through to the server-attached printer.

Workstation-attached printers will be running NPRINTER.EXE at first and may continue in that mode. Alternatively, they may be configured as LPR printers running over IP.

For network-attached printers, the third-party gateway is the best option. If the Novell gateway is the only option, then the protocol running on the network should determine how the printer should be configured. The options are either as an LPR printer over IP, or an RP printer over IPX.

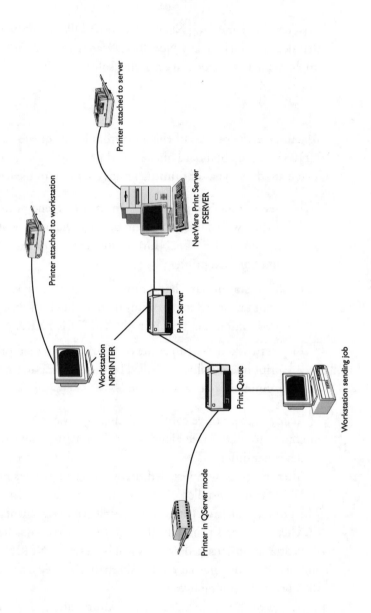

FIGURE 15-5

Legacy queue-based printing setup

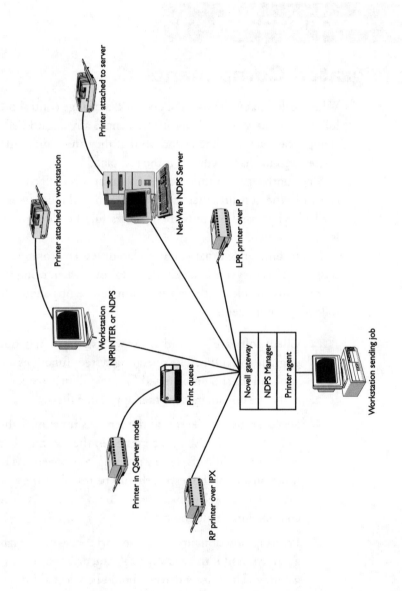

FIGURE 15-6   NDPS gateway used in migration

CERTIFICATION OBJECTIVE 15.05

Testing Migrated Components

When making any change on a network, a change control process should be followed. *Change control* is meant to manage any negative effects that changes can have on the network so that they are minimized. One of the major steps in change control is the test plan.

Since both legacy printing components and NDPS components can coexist in the network, there can be a level of redundancy or "backout" available. That is, if the tests are unsuccessful, the old printing environment is easily restored.

It is recommended that you use a lab or test environment whenever possible. This prevents confusion by end users when printers suddenly become unavailable. In the lab environment, testing should be done on the following components:

- **Client software** Test that the workstation is functional after the upgrade to NDPS. The operating system functions and standard applications should be tested for their ability to open, save, print, and close documents or other applicable files.

- **Server software** Test that the server is functional after the upgrade to NDPS. Servers should be tested in their standard configurations, with and without the legacy printing components. The standard functionality of the servers should be tested. If the server is used as a mail server as well as print server, both mail and printing components should be verified.

- **Printing functionality** Test the printers with the native third-party gateways, and if there is any problem, also test them with the Novell gateway. The printer drivers should be selected for each workstation operating system used on the network. Test the automatic download and use of the drivers that are set up, and test for the optimal drivers for the network environment.

QUESTIONS AND ANSWERS

Logan created a new NDPS printing environment in his lab. He used a NetWare 5 Server, a locally attached HP LaserJet 6 printer, and a Windows NT 4 workstation. He tested all functionality of each component and then proceeded to implement NDPS in the network. When the first group was migrated, four users called Logan with problems for an application running on their Windows 98 workstations that was not able to print to a network-attached printer. What steps should Logan have taken to prevent these errors?	Logan did not duplicate the enterprise network environment in his lab. He used server-attached printers when the network had network-attached printers, and he used Windows NT 4 when the workstations were using Windows 98. Logan should have duplicated each type of printer/workstation/server configuration, and then tested it before implementing it on the network.

CERTIFICATION OBJECTIVE 15.06

Removing the Old Printing Environment

When you no longer need to maintain a redundant or "backout" printing system, the old printer components can be removed. The first components to remove are the print servers. Rather than remove their NDS objects, the servers that were acting as print servers should no longer have PSERVER.NLM loaded. Since it is likely that the PSERVER.NLM load line was automated, the administrator will likely have to remove the LOAD PSERVER.NLM *<print server name>* from the AUTOEXEC.NCF.

It is recommended that you do not remove the print servers from NDS for a few weeks to verify that no one needs them. However, once it is fairly certain that no one needs the print server components, they can be deleted from NDS. At the same time, the printers can be deleted from NDS.

Print queues can still be used in the NDPS environment. For that reason, care should be taken before removing them completely. So, rather than remove the print queue, it can be disabled through its NDS properties first. To disable a print queue, double-click the Print Queue NDS object in NDS and deselect the Operator flag that states "Allow Users to Submit

Print Jobs." After a period of time, such as one or two weeks, if the print queue is not needed, delete it from the NDS tree (see Figure 15-7).

Print queues use a directory on the file server as temporary storage for the print jobs. These directories, which are subdirectories of the QUEUES directory in the volume to which the print queue has been assigned, will be removed automatically when the print queue object is deleted.

exam
ⓦatch

Do not remove print queues to which users send print jobs from DOS programs. NDPS will not allow a user to redirect printing to an LPT port, but NetWare's legacy print-queue–based printing will. DOS programs nearly always print to LPT ports.

FIGURE 15-7

Disabling a print queue

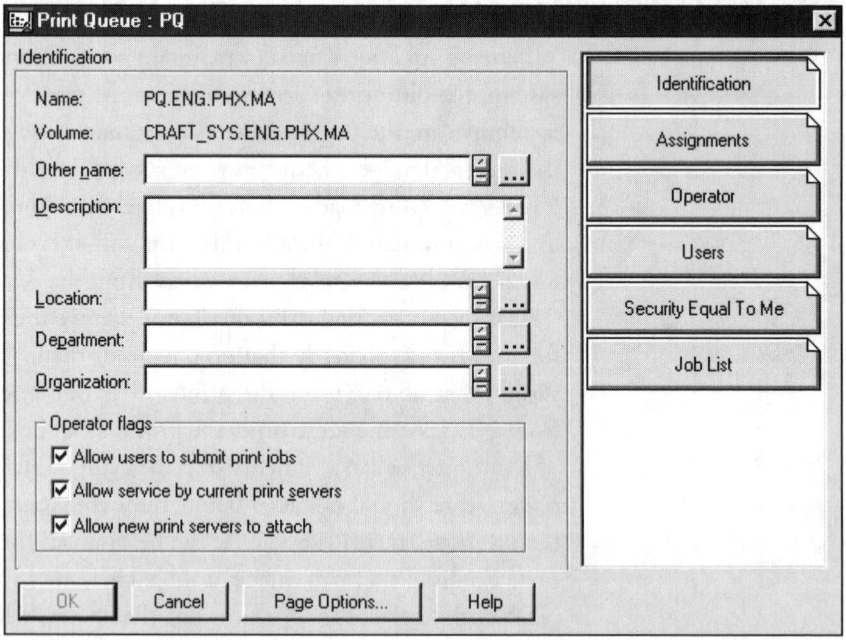

CERTIFICATION SUMMARY

Novell Distributed Printing Services (NDPS) are a new printing function under NetWare 5 that increase the manageability and capabilities of NetWare print services.

NDPS implementation requires that both client software and server printing components be upgraded or migrated. The client software must be upgraded to the NetWare client that comes with NetWare 5 or a later version that supports NDPS.

The upgrade includes a design component in which the new system is considered from a physical topology perspective, as well as from an NDS tree perspective. The physical location of printers, the security requirements, and the logical placement of the printer components contribute to the design of the NDPS printing system.

Novell Directory Services (NDS) offers three levels of security: users, operators, and managers. The *users* of an NDS printer can send print jobs to it. The *operators* are able to access the administrative options for the NDPS printer. *Managers* have full access to the NDPS printer.

The NDPS *broker* uses a default system to determine when a new broker is needed. When an NDPS manager is created, the system checks all NDPS brokers until one is found that is within three hops of the server that the installer has Supervisor rights to. If it is not found, NDPS installation creates a new broker. If the default system does not create a broker when one is needed, then one should be manually created and used.

The upgrade process should start with the creation of server printing components. That would include creating the NDPS brokers, NDPS managers, and NDPS printers.

The current printing configuration is used to determine the final configuration of NDPS printing components. The current printing configuration will reveal the need for which types of gateways and printing configuration will be needed.

NDPS printing components are compatible with legacy print-queue-based components. This means that during migration, the legacy components can remain in place until they are removed.

There are three types of printers that can be migrated:

- Server-attached printers
- Workstation-attached printers
- Network-attached printers

The migration for each printer will depend on the protocols in use on the network, the gateways available for the printer type, and the security requirements.

Printing components that are eligible for migration must be tested in a non-production environment prior to implementation. All components—server, workstation, and printer—should be tested in a lab environment for functionality and impact to the existing environment. Eventually, legacy Print Server, Printer, and Print Queue objects should be removed from NDS. Before removing the components, the print servers and print queues can be disabled in case they need to be reinstated in the legacy environment.

✓ TWO-MINUTE DRILL

- ❏ Novell's Distributed Printing Services (NDPS) was created in response to the need to simplify printer management and reduce printing costs.
- ❏ In any network system upgrade, one of the first tasks to perform is planning the new system.
- ❏ Security and management of NDPS components is handled in the NetWare Administrator because the NDPS components are integrated in NDS.
- ❏ Like any object in the NDS tree, the NDPS printers can be made available to all users, or they can be locked down so they are available to a select group.
- ❏ The NDPS Manager makes printer agents available from a NetWare 5 Server.
- ❏ Client workstations must have their NetWare client software upgraded to the NetWare 5 client in order to print to NDPS printers.

❑ In determining the location of brokers, printers, servers, workstation clients, and routers, the designer should have a written record of the existing network resources and components.

❑ When NetWare 5 is installed, NDPS version #2 is included as part of the typical installation.

❑ A public access printer is one to which any user may send print jobs. Public access printers are not associated with an NDS Printer object.

❑ *Print servers* run on NetWare servers and manage the print jobs.

❑ *Queues* are file storage areas on the server where print jobs are temporarily stored before being processed by the printer.

❑ NDPS combines the components into a *printer agent*.

❑ An NDPS gateway is a software component that allows NetWare NDPS clients to print to non-NDPS-aware printers.

❑ *Change control* is meant to manage any negative effects that changes can have on the network so they are minimized.

SELF TEST

The following Self-Test questions will help you measure your understanding of the material presented in this chapter. Read all the choices carefully, as there may be more than one correct answer. Choose all correct answers for each question.

1. What application is used to manage and secure NDPS components?

   A. NDS Manager

   B. Z.E.N.works

   C. NetWare Administrator

   D. Workstation Manager

2. What role of security does the operator have?

   A. Can send print jobs to the printer only

   B. Has administrative control over the NDPS printer

   C. Has complete control over the NDPS Printer object

   D. None

3. Which services does the broker make available for NDPS?

   A. ENS, RMS, SRS

   B. NASI, NIAS, NCS

   C. ENS, NASI, NCS

   D. RMS, ARAS, PPPRMS

4. Where does the Broker object store its databases?

   A. SYS:QUEUES

   B. VOL1:QUEUES

   C. SYS:NDPS

   D. SYS:NDPS\RESDIR

5. What must be created before an NDPS printer agent is available on a NetWare 5 server?

   A. Print Server

   B. NDPS Manager

   C. Print Queue

   D. NDPS Printer

6. Which of the following configurations will be NDPS enabled?

   A. Windows 95 workstation using the Microsoft Client for NetWare

   B. Windows NT 4 workstation using the NetWare 5 Client for NetWare

   C. Windows 98 workstation using the NetWare 4 version Client for NetWare

   D. DOS/Windows 3.1 workstation using a VLM client

7. What will show which printers can or cannot be migrated to NDPS?

   A. A list of all the printer drivers used

   B. Floor plans of the building with printer locations marked off

   C. A list of the printers and their uses by end users

D. The server capacity utilization chart

8. Which of the following is available from NDPS printers?

   A. Security through NDS

   B. Automatic download of printer drivers to the client

   C. Management capabilities

   D. All of the above

9. On a NetWare 5 network, does the schema need to be extended to include NDPS objects?

   A. Yes; NDPS is not a default component of NetWare 5.

   B. No; NDPS is a default component of NetWare 5.

10. Which of the following statements accurately depicts how NDPS and legacy printing components can be placed in a network?

   A. NDPS components must be on separate servers from legacy components.

   B. NDPS components cannot be in the same NDS tree as Print Queue objects.

   C. NDPS components and legacy print queue components can coexist on the same server.

   D. All legacy components must be removed before NDPS components can be installed.

11. Which program can be used to migrate queue-based components to NDPS when NetWare 3.x is being migrated to NetWare 5?

   A. NetWare Administrator

   B. NDS Manager

   C. Novell Upgrade Wizard

   D. NDPS Manager

12. Which of the following gateways can be used with any printer?

   A. HP gateway

   B. Novell gateway

   C. Xerox gateway

   D. Third-party gateways

13. Which program must a server run in order to share its own server-attached printer on the network in the legacy queue-based system?

   A. NPRINTER.EXE

   B. PSERVER.NLM

   C. QUEUE.NLM

   D. NPRINTER.NLM

14. After the server-attached printer has been migrated to the NDPS system, what program must be loaded on the server in order to share out the server-attached printer?

   A. PSERVER.NLM

   B. NPRINTER.NLM

   C. NDPS Manager

   D. NDPS Broker

15. What is the best method of removing a print queue from a network?

   A. Disable the queue first; then remove it from NDS, which removes the queue directory.

   B. Remove it from NDS, but maintain the queue directory.

   C. It cannot be removed.

   D. If you remove the print servers, the queues will not be usable.

CERTIFIED NOVELL ENGINEER

16

Performing a Custom Installation

CERTIFICATION OBJECTIVES

16.01   Installing NetWare 5 Using the Custom Option

16.02   Modifying Volume Parameters

16.03   Integrating Multiple Protocols

hen you're ready to install your server, you will see the need to customize certain components of the network operating system. In today's networking environments there are many different components that may be used. Some companies need Internet components such as DNS or DHCP for name resolution and IP address assignment. Other companies simply need a server with the capability to share information and printing.

In this chapter, we will look at the options available to customize and configure the server for your clients' needs. For the exam, we will look at making changes to the file system by modifying and configuring the volumes on a NetWare server. We will also focus on implementing different protocols and the options available to configure them. Other customization options such as configuring the NDS and Novell Distributed Print Services are covered elsewhere in this book.

Installing NetWare 5 Using the Custom Option

With NetWare 5, the custom install option is a little different than in previous versions of NetWare. Earlier in this book we looked at a simple installation. When you first start the installation, you'll do some basic entry information such as regional settings and server ID. Once all the basic information is entered, you will be able to customize the following options:

- NetWare Operating System
- File System
- Protocols
- NDS
- NDPS
- Additional products and services

These options can be customized once you reach the summary screen of the installation. With each option you have a Customize button that opens a window.

From the dialog box you can select the Properties button on each of the items listed and see a new list of options.

Custom Installation Steps

To customize your NetWare installation you simply select the Customize button on the summary screen during the installation. There are other configuration tasks, such as selecting certain options or entering information.

For example, when you select Properties on the NetWare Operating System option, you will see five tabs with various information. The first of these is the Server Properties Tab, which allows you to enter a server ID number.

The second is a Language Tab, which simply asks you to select which language you want installed for the server and for administration.

NetWare 5's GUI makes configuration and customization a lot easier for inexperienced network administrators. This new interface approach to network management and configuration at the server is becoming widely accepted.

One of the last three tabs on the NetWare Operating System Properties is Console One, which allows an administrator to choose whether to load Console One when the server reboots. The other two tabs are License and Components, which give you options to install connection licenses or additional components that we will talk about shortly (file system, protocols, and NDS).

CERTIFICATION OBJECTIVE 16.02

Modifying Volume Parameters

As a network administrator, occasionally you may see different server configurations, and you must be able to modify the file system and customize the volumes accordingly.

You may have one server that does not need block suballocation and another that requires block suballocation but not compression on the volume. The File System Properties give you the flexibility to make changes to your volumes and configure them the way you want them.

You can customize the following components with the NetWare File System:

■ View free space

■ Create, modify, or delete a partition

■ Create, modify, or delete a volume

■ Mount a volume

In this section, we will focus on two of these. For exam purposes, our focus will be on the volume parameters and how they may impact your server.

Volume Types

A volume divides a partition. With the volume parameters you can work with two type of volumes:

■ **Traditional volume**   A traditional volume can be created within a NetWare partition.

■ **NSS volume**   NSS volumes can be created in NetWare NSS partitions.

exam
ⓜatch

The thing to remember is that a traditional volume can be created only on a traditional partition, and an NSS volume can be created only on an NSS partition.

Creating a Volume

If you have a partition that has free space available, you can select it and then click on the New Volume button to create a volume. When creating a volume, you will have some decisions to make.

Exercise 16-1 will walk you through creating a new volume. Make sure you have a server with free space available on a traditional NetWare partition. We will create a traditional NetWare volume with a size of 500MB, with migration and compression turned off, and suballocation turned on.

EXERCISE 16-1

Creating a Traditional Volume

1. Open the Customization Options and select the File System.

2. Select the Properties button, and you will see a breakdown of the volumes and free space.

3. Select the free space on a traditional NetWare partition that has at least 500MB free.

4. Click on New Volume.

5. In the New Volume window enter the following information:

    a. Volume Name: **OMHI**

    b. Space to Use: **250**

    c. Make sure that Migration and Compression are turned off and that Suballocation is turned on.

    d. Make sure that the Mount Volume on Creation is selected.

6. Click the OK button, and your volume should be created and mounted.

Mounting a Volume

It's easy to forget that you must *mount* a volume in order to use it. One of the options under the File System properties is to Mount Volumes.

You can mount volumes before or after the installation is complete (or when the server reboots). Base your timing on what is going to be done next during the installation. If you plan on installing other options on the server and need to use the new volume you created, then mount the volume before you try to add the components. If, on the other hand, you are installing components only to the SYS: volume, you can probably wait until after the installation to mount the volume.

CERTIFICATION OBJECTIVE 16.03

Integrating Multiple Protocols

For complete functionality, networking today may require more than one protocol to be installed. When installing NetWare you have the option to select and configure which protocols your server will use. Highlighting the Protocols option under the Customization window to open the Protocol Properties dialog box.

The four tabs of this dialog box let you configure if and how a server will communicate on the network. NetWare 5 introduced support for native IP and IPX protocols. The general installation configures the basic functionality, but you may also need to configure some enhancements.

The first tab is the Protocols tab, where you can configure the IPX and IP components of a NetWare server. On the left, you see the server and network adapter cards that are installed in it. If multiple network cards are installed, highlight each individual network card to see its properties.

Configuring the Internet Protocol (IP)

In the middle of the Protocols tab is the IP information. At least two of the three components are required to use IP. The first is the IP address of the network card. The IP address is made up of four octets, which means that an IP address is a 32-bit number. Remember that an octet is a number consisting of four bits. The bits are made up of zeros and ones, but the values are represented in decimal value from 0 to 255. An IP address looks like 208.163.10.41 and each number is an octet.

The second component of successful IP configuration is the subnet mask. A *subnet mask* tells us that the IP address is made up of two parts. One part is the network address, which can be compared to a street. For example, Bob and Tim live on Main Street and their network address is Main Street. The other part of the IP address is the *host address*. The host address is similar to a house number. Bob's house number is 111 and Tim's is 214. This differentiates them on the street. So looking at 208.163.10.41, we have to know which part is the network address and which part is the host address. For two or more computers to be on the same network (or subnet) they must have a portion of the address in common, just as Bob and Tim both live on Main Street. A subnet mask masks each portion of the address. For example, with a subnet mask of 255.255.0.0 we know that every IP address on our network starting with 208.163 are on the same network. Any other computers starting with two different octets are on another network. The most common subnet masks are

- 255.0.0.0
- 255.255.0.0
- 255.255.255.0

Subnet masks tell us where to break the address up. The corresponding locations in the IP address that are the same as the subnet mask value of 255 are the network portion of the address. The corresponding locations in the IP address that are the same as the subnet mask value of 0 are the host address. For more details on IP addressing and subnetting check your local bookstore. There are many books on the subject.

The last component of IP is the *gateway*, which is the IP address of a router that connects the network to another network such as the Internet. The IP address of the router tells the server where to direct traffic to reach another network. This is a component that may or may not need to be configured, depending on your network configuration.

Configuring the Internetwork Packet eXchange (IPX) Protocol

The IPX protocol is the most commonly associated with Novell networks. IPX has been the default NetWare protocol for a long time. The right-hand section of the Protocols tab has the IPX configuration information. There are different frame types that can be used with IPX, with Ethernet_802.2 being the most common, since the introduction of NetWare 3.12.

Along with the frame type is the network address or cable segment of that frame type. The IPX network number tells your server what cable segment it is on so you can differentiate between two Ethernet network cards in a server. Maybe one is a 10 Mbps card whose segment (or IPX network number) is 00000010, and the other card is a 100 Mbps card whose IPX network number is 00000100. This can help distinguish between cable segments when you're troubleshooting and configuring the network.

IPX Compatibility, DNS, and SNMP

The last three tabs in the Protocol Properties screen are the IPX Compatibility tab, the Domain Name Service tab, and the SNMP tab. These tabs allow further configuration options, but for the exam we will only hit on a couple of key areas.

The IPX Compatibility tab enables a new feature of NetWare 5 to be utilized. IPX compatibility, when enabled, provides support for applications requiring IPX. This means the server will not broadcast services using RIP and SAP, but the server will process IPX requests that arrive at the server.

on the
Job

IPX compatibility mode is needed only if pure IP is being used and IPX is not the primary protocol stack on the network.

The Domain Name Service tab is a key component for IP if your network is connected to the Internet. As you recall, the Domain Name Service (DNS) is what translates novell.com to an IP address such as 111.111.110.23. The Domain Name Service tab allows you to enter the IP addresses of known DNS servers either on the internal network or provided by your Internet Service Provider. Multiple addresses can be listed, and NetWare 5 will start at the top of the list and work down until the name is either resolved or the list is exhausted.

The last tab on the Protocol Properties window is the SNMP (Simple Network Management Protocol) tab. This protocol is becoming more widely used. Products such as Novell's Managewise and Compaq's Insight Manager use SNMP to gather data. These utilities allow a network administrator to retrieve data about various hardware components or network traffic. Certain thresholds can be set to allow the administrator to set alarms so they can be notified if there is an abnormal number of errors on the network. These tools are especially important in larger network situations.

CERTIFICATION SUMMARY

In this chapter, we looked at some of the custom installation options for NetWare 5. To customize a NetWare installation use the Customize option on the Installation summary screen. From there you can select five options. We discussed two of these five options: File System and Protocols. The other three options are covered elsewhere in this book.

With the File System Properties you can customize your server by making changes to volume configuration. The options available with the File System Properties are the following:

- View free space
- Create, modify, or delete a partition
- Create, modify, or delete a volume
- Mount a volume

When creating volumes, remember that a Traditional NetWare volume must be created on a traditional NetWare partition, and an NSS volume can be created only on an NSS partition.

We also looked at integrating different protocols on a NetWare server. With NetWare 5 you now have the option for IP or IPX. With IP you need an IP address and a subnet mask to tell which part of the IP address is the network address and which is the host address. With IPX you must specify a frame type and an IPX network number, which should be the same for computers on the same cable segment.

 TWO-MINUTE DRILL

- ❑ Once all the basic information is entered in NetWare 5, you will be able to customize the following options: NetWare operating system, file system, protocols, NDS, NDPS, additional products and services.

- ❑ To customize your NetWare installation you simply select the Customize button on the summary screen during the installation.

There are other configuration tasks, such as selecting certain options or entering information.

❑ You may have one server that does not need block suballocation and another that requires block suballocation but not compression on the volume. The File System Properties give you the flexibility to make changes to your volumes and configure them the way you want them.

❑ The options available with the File System Properties are view free space; create, modify, or delete a partition; and mount a volume.

❑ A volume divides a partition. With the volume parameters you can work with two type of volumes: *Traditional volume* and *NSS volume*.

❑ If you have a partition that has free space available, you can select it and then click on the New Volume button to create a volume.

❑ It is important to remember that you must mount a volume in order to use it. You can mount volumes before or after the installation is complete, or when the server reboots.

❑ At least two of three components are required to use IP. The first is the IP address of the network card; the second component is the subnet mask; the last component of IP is the *gateway*, which is the IP address of a router that connects the network to another network such as the Internet.

❑ There are different frame types that can be used with IPX, with Ethernet_802.2 being the most common, since the introduction of NetWare 3.12.

❑ The last three tabs in the Protocol Properties screen are the IPX Compatibility tab, the Domain Name Service tab, and the SNMP tab. These tabs allow further configuration options.

❑ The Domain Name Service tab is a key component for IP if your network is connected to the Internet.

❑ The last tab on the Protocol Properties window is the SNMP (Simple Network Management Protocol) tab, which is becoming more widely used. Products such as Novell's Managewise and Compaq's Insight Manager use SNMP to gather data.

❑ When creating volumes, remember that a Traditional NetWare volume must be created on a traditional NetWare partition, and an NSS volume can be created only on an NSS partition.

❑ With NetWare 5 you now have the option for IP or IPX. With IP you need an IP address and a subnet mask to tell which part of the IP address is the network address and which is the host address.

❑ With IPX you must specify a frame type and an IPX network number, which should be the same for computers on the same cable segment.

❑ IPX compatibility mode is needed only if pure IP is being used and IPX is not the primary protocol stack on the network.

SELF TEST

The Self-Test questions will help you measure your understanding of the material presented in this chapter. Read all the choices carefully, as there may be more than one correct answer. Select all correct answers for each question.

1. Which of the following is not listed as an option when customizing your network installation?

   A. NetWare Operating System

   B. NDPS

   C. DNS

   D. NDS

2. At which customization component could you choose whether to load Console One after the installation is completed (or the server reboots)?

   A. NetWare Operating System

   B. NDPS

   C. Administration

   D. Protocols

3. On which of the following partition types can a traditional NetWare volume exist? (Choose all that apply.)

   A. Traditional NetWare partition

   B. Traditional NetWare volume

   C. NSS NetWare partition

   D. NSS NetWare volume

4. When creating a volume on a network server, which of the following options must be selected during creation or you will not be able to use the volume?

   A. Suballocation

   B. Migration

   C. Mount Volume on Creation

   D. Volume Name

5. Which options are available when mounting a volume with the Mount Volumes option in File Systems Properties of NetWare 5? (Choose all that apply.)

   A. Mount volumes immediately

   B. Mount volumes in 15 minutes

   C. DO NOT mount volumes at all

   D. Mount volumes upon server reboot

6. Which protocols does the Protocols tab in Protocols Properties show? (Choose all that apply.)

   A. RPC

   B. IPX

   C. SNMP

   D. IP

   E. DNS

   F. NDS

7. When configuring the IP information under protocols, which components are required? (Choose all that apply.)

   A. IP address

   B. Subnet mask

   C. Gateway

   D. Internal network number

8. When configuring IPX under protocols, which components are required? (Choose all that apply.)

A. Frame type

B. Network address (IPX Internal Network Number)

C. IPX address

D. Gateway

9. Which component under Protocol Properties resolves an address such as http://www.syngress.com to an IP address?

A. NDS

B. IP

C. Gateway

D. DNS

10. What does SNMP stand for?

A. Simple Novell Migration Process

B. Standard Network Management Protocol

C. Simple Network Management Protocol

D. Standard Novell Migration Protocol

11. When configuring the volumes on a NetWare server, which mounting option should you choose if the only components you are going to install are on the SYS: volume?

A. Reboot immediately

B. Mount volumes immediately

C. Mount volumes after server reboots

D. Do NOT mount volumes

12. On which of the following partition types can an NSS NetWare volume exist? (Choose all that apply.)

A. Traditional NetWare partition

B. Traditional NetWare volume

C. NSS NetWare partition

D. NSS NetWare volume

13. Which options are available when you customize you NetWare File System? (Choose all that apply.)

A. View free space available

B. Create or delete a partition

C. Mount a volume

D. Create or delete a volume

14. Which of the following is not a tab on the NetWare Operating System Properties window?

A. Language

B. Server Properties

C. License

D. Protocols

15. You are configuring your NetWare volumes. Upon customizing the File System you notice that you have only one partition showing: BIG DOS. In order to have a traditional NetWare volume on your server, what do you have to do?

A. Add an NSS partition

B. Add another BIG DOS partition

C. Add a traditional volume

D. Add a traditional partition

17

Setting Up the Network File System

CERTIFICATION OBJECTIVES

17.01	Introduction to Planning
17.02	System-Created Directories
17.03	Possible Directory Structures
17.04	Creating Additional Volumes
17.05	Designing Directory Structures

The network file system can store critical data and applications on a server so they can be shared by many users. The careful design of the network file system is one of your most important network administrator tasks. If the network file system is not designed with the needs of the organization in mind, it will cause problems in the future.

In the first section of this chapter, we discuss planning a file system. The second section examines the system-created directories, and the third section offers possible directory structures. Finally, in sections four and five, we discuss creating additional volumes and designing directory structure, respectively.

Introduction to Planning

Before you plan a network file system, you must understand how the NetWare file system is organized. A NetWare network file system is made up of volumes, folders (or directories), and files. NetWare uses a hierarchical tree structure, similar to MS-DOS and Windows 95, where a volume is the parent of a folder and a folder is the parent of files. Volumes are comprised of logical partitions of one or many disks. Each volume will have a top-level folder, the root folder, containing all other folders and files. Folders are created within volumes; and files, containing applications and data, are created within folders. Figure 17-1 shows the relationship between volumes, folders, and files. We use the terms *directories* and *folders* interchangeably throughout this chapter.

In Figure 17-1, the NetWare NWADMIN program is used to visually depict the relationship between a volume, folders, and files. In this example, the name of the volume is FIVE-NW5_SYS:. It contains several directories, Accounting and General Ledger. These directories contain other subdirectories and files. When viewed from NWADMIN, the volume has a file cabinet icon.

FIGURE 17-1

The NetWare network file system showing the relation among volumes, folders, and files

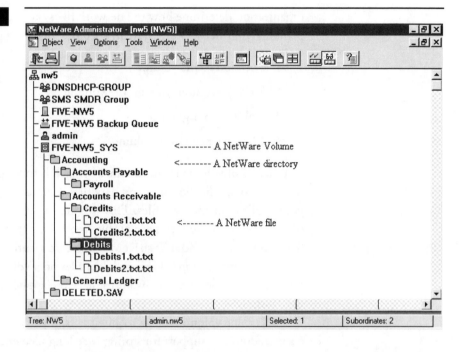

A volume exists on a NetWare server; it does *not* exist on a NetWare client. Actually, if you view a server volume from a Windows 95 client, it will have a folder icon. Think of a volume as one level higher than a normal folder in the Windows 95 tree structure.

exam
ⓦatch

Remember that a volume contains a directory, and the directory contains the application and data files.

During installation of a server, a default volume, called SYS:, is created. It contains NetWare system directories that hold NetWare Loadable Modules (files with an extension of *.NLM), Local Area Network (*.LAN) drivers, and other system files. Other volumes may be created at installation and also with the NWCONFIG.NLM once the server is installed.

Now that we have reviewed the background of a NetWare network file system, let's look at planning the network file system. The needs of the organization determine how the network file system is organized. In planning your network file system, keep the following points in mind:

- Location of the volume
- Storage requirements on the volume
- Volume configuration
- Maintenance of the volume

In terms of volume location, one approach is to keep the default volume, SYS:, free of application files and data files. Create a separate volume for your application and data files. This will prevent data files, which grow quite large, from causing space problems on the SYS: volume and vice versa. Separating system and user space will also ease security administration. So, locate your application folders and data files on a volume other than the SYS: volume. You may even want to place the application data on another disk entirely.

Concerning volume storage requirements, if you are using Macintosh clients, additional support for storing Mac long filenames will need to be added. Mac filename support (MAC.NAM) takes up additional storage on the volume. UNIX clients also require additional long filename space support. Thus, you will need to account for additional disk overhead when storing Macintosh or UNIX filenames on a given volume.

The configuration of your volume requires careful planning. When discussing volume configuration, we need to explore fault tolerance. Fault tolerance describes the safeguards a system has when it encounters a hardware failure or software problem that prevents proper data access. Many mission-critical applications cannot afford to be down and must be up 99.9 percent of the time. Their system needs to be highly fault tolerant. There are various ways to implement fault tolerance.

Another important aspect of volume configuration is *performance.* Volume placement may be determined by disk read and disk write access times. If you place your most important applications on a fast bus, such as a SCSI bus, then reads and writes will improve.

One of the methods NetWare provides for fault tolerance is disk mirroring. *Disk mirroring* is when two disks, located on the same disk controller and of equal partition sizes, are an exact copy of each other. For example, if you have two disk partitions of 500 megabytes each, they can be mirrored. Your total storage is not 1,000 megabytes (or 1 gigabyte) but merely 500 megabytes. The reason for this reduction is the duplicate copy. NetWare allows the volumes to be mirrored during install time or at a later time.

exam
ⓌatcH

When mirroring two disk partitions, they must be of equal size.

Another fault-tolerant technique NetWare provides is disk duplexing. This is a slight variation disk mirroring. *Disk duplexing* uses disk mirroring with two disk controller cards instead of one. Remember, disk mirroring uses one disk controller card and the disk controller card is connected to the bus in a server PC.

If fault tolerance is important to your organization, then place an additional drive in the server and mirror the two disks. Remember, with mirroring, you lose the capacity of one of the disks because it is an exact duplicate of the other. Mirroring also impacts performance with disk writing because the operating system must write twice. However, disk reads may be enhanced because data can be read from multiple disks. Mirroring is called for when your system must be up a high percentage of the time, say 95% or higher. If one of the disks goes bad, then you would break the mirror, install another disk, format it, and remirror it with the good disk. While this substitution is going on, your users will still be able to operate. If you had not implemented disk mirroring and your disk had become bad, then your users would be unable to use the server resources until the corrupted disk was replaced. This could take hours, even if a tape backup existed. Mirroring would have alleviated this problem.

If performance is importance to your organization, then you could spread a volume over many disks, thereby increasing the disk read time. Concurrent disk reads will occur, which speeds up access to your server. You will not incur the disk write performance impact that you would with disk mirroring; however, if your system went down, there would be no immediate online recovery. Your users would not be able to operate their applications. This approach—called *spanning*—is called for if speed is your goal at the risk of losing the redundancy provided by mirroring.

If fault tolerance and performance are equally important to your organization, mirroring is possible, but you should implement disk duplexing. By placing an additional disk controller in the server, your network file system will receive the benefit of faster disk accesses with the added benefit of duplicating your application and data. The disk writes would still take a performance hit but not as big a hit as disk mirroring, where a single disk controller card is used. Also, the disk reads would experience even better performance than under disk mirroring because there are the two disk controllers. Using the two disk controllers provides for concurrent disk reads.

Finally, with respect to configuration, review the needs of your organization up front. Then, choose your method to implement. Overall, disk duplexing offers the advantages of fault tolerance and performance, but the disadvantage is the cost of the additional hardware. Mirroring offers redundancy at a lower cost because there is a single disk controller.

The importance of volume maintenance is an often overlooked, but critical, task. Monitor the available space on your volumes periodically. Actually, if a volume gets low on disk space, the operating system will warn you; however, take a look at it routinely. This could cause critical applications and files not to be written to disk. You can review volume sizes from a client computer. If space becomes critically low on a given volume, the free space on a disk can be used to expand that volume. You can look at volumes with the NWADMIN software program. For a view of volume statistics, see Figure 17-2. Notice that the amount of disk space used for the volume, FIVE-NW5_SYS, is about 84%. You will also need to watch for the number of directory entries becoming too large. You may have space on the disk available, but if the number of your directory entries is too high, you cannot create any new directories. In this case, you will need to increase the SET parameter, Maximum Percent of Volume Used By Directory, at the file server console. You can type in the following command at the server prompt:

```
FIVE-NW5: SET MAXIMUM PERCENT OF VOLUME USED BY DIRECTORY = 85
```

This parameter can be set from a low value of 5 to a high value of 85.

FIGURE 17-2

Viewing a volume's
statistics with NWADMIN

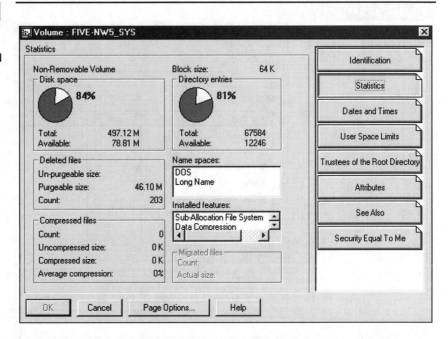

Another consideration is the *block suballocation* parameter. This allows greater use of disk space because files can be stored in smaller unused portions of the disk. Suballocation allocates smaller block sizes than under previous versions of NetWare, which in turn reduces overall fragmentation. There is some slight server memory overhead.

In terms of volume maintenance, the amount of space available to a user on a volume can be restricted with the NWADMIN utility. Figure 17-3 illustrates the restriction of user space on a volume. One reason to limit user space is to keep user files from growing so large that they cause critical application data to not be written to disk.

Keep an eye on the size of the error log files created by Transaction Tracking System (TTS) and the volume repair process (VREPAIR.NLM). These files are stored on the SYS: volume and grow over time. Compression is turned on for a volume by default. Compression will store the data more efficiently on disk, but your server will incur more processor overhead.

FIGURE 17-3

Restricting user space on a
volume with NWADMIN

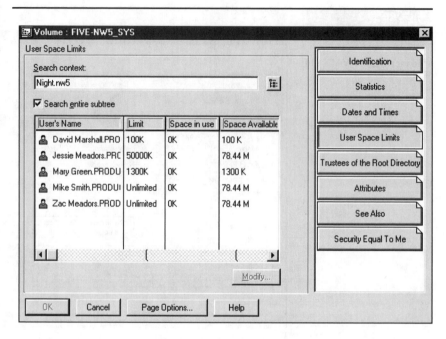

***The error log files created by TTS and VREPAIR are
SYS:\TTS$LOG.ERR and VOL$LOG.ERR.***

Another technique used for volume maintenance is the VREPAIR
program. This is analogous to SCANDISK for DOS and Windows
computers. VREPAIR will detect and repair volume problems such as File
Allocation Table (FAT) inconsistencies and mirror problems. In order to
run VREPAIR, the volume must be dismounted. In order to dismount a
volume, APPS, and then run VREPAIR on that volume, issue the following
commands at the server prompt:

```
FIVE-NW5_SYS: DISMOUNT VOLUME-NAME
FIVE-NW5_SYS: LOAD VREPAIR
```

When VREPAIR loads, it will prompt you to repair a volume.

***In order to repair a volume with VREPAIR, the volume must be
dismounted.***

System-Created Directories

Now, that we have investigated planning the network file system, let's take a look at the system-created directories. Remember, during a NetWare server installation, the SYS: volume is created. On that volume, NetWare will create several default system directories to store its necessary programs and files. The system-created directories of a NetWare 5.0 server are shown in Figure 17-4. In this example, the server, FIVE-NW5 contains the volume, SYS.

exam
Ⓦatch

*A volume name is typically represented as **servername_volumename:**.*
*For example, for a server named **FIVE-NW5** and a volume of **SYS:**, the*
*volume name is **FIVE-NW5_SYS:**.*

FIGURE 17-4

System-created directories
seen with a Windows 95
client

```
Exploring - SYS on Five-nw5                                          _ □ ×
File  Edit  View  Tools  Help
All Folders                      Contents of 'SYS on Five-nw5'
    Dekalbtech          ▲         Accounting        Vol$log.err
    dekalbtech                    docs
    Five-nw5                      etc
        SYS                       java
            Accounting            javasave
            docs                  Login
            etc                   Mail
            java                  ndps
            javasave              Netbasic
            Login                 ni
            Mail                  night
            ndps                  perl
            Netbasic              public
            ni                    Queues
            night                 Readme
            perl                  system
            public                _swap_.mem
            Queues                memuse
            Readme                shell.properties
            system                Tts$log.err
        Nw5
        nw5
◄                        ►    ◄                              ►
21 object(s) (plus 2 hidden)    2.03GB
```

Table 17-1 describes the more important system-created directories.

exam
ⓦatch

An easy way to remember the important system-created directories is with the acronym SiMPLE. This stands for SYSTEM, MAIL, PUBLIC, LOGIN, and ETC.

The SYS: directory contains NLMs used by the ADMIN user. Various LAN drivers and other NLMs are in this directory. Also, the NDS database is stored here. The MAIL directory holds users' mail if you are using NetWare MAIL software. The PUBLIC directory contains the NetWare

TABLE 17-1 System-Created Directories		
System-Created Directory	**Description**
SYSTEM	Holds administrator NLMs
MAIL	Exists for backwared compatibility with bindery-based services
PUBLIC	Holds user command and NWADMIN
LOGIN	Contains login commands
ETC	Holds TCP/IP programs and files
JAVA and JAVASAVE	Contains Java Console commands
QUEUES	Has subdirectories with a *.QDR extension; each representing a NetWare Print Queue object
CDROM$$.ROM	Indexes files for mounted CD-ROM volumes
DELETED.SAV	Has deleted files removed from directories
LICENSE	Contains license-related files
NDPS	Holds Novell Distributed Printing Service subdirectories and files
NETBASIC	Contains NetBASIC support files
NI	Has NetWare installation files
PERL	Holds PERL script files
README	Has Readme text files

Administrator program, NWADMIN, and other Windows-based administrator tools. Another important tool here is NDS Manager for managing the NDS partition and replicas and NAL (NetWare Application Launcher). NPTWIN95 is an executable program also located in the SYS: directory. NPTWIN95 allows a printer to be attached to a NetWare client. It must be run at the NetWare client that has a shared printer attached to it. The LOGIN directory holds a few commands, such as LOGIN, MAP, and CX, that give the user at a workstation access to basic network tools prior to actually logging in and being authenticated by a NetWare server. The ETC directory contains TCP/IP and DNS related files. For example, this is where the HOSTS file is located.

Now that we have reviewed the system-created directories, let's take a look at possible directory structures.

Possible Directory Structures

In considering possible directory structures, take a look at you users' needs.

I suggest that you consider the following types of directories when organizing a directory structure:

- User home directories
- Application and program directories including configuration files
- Shared data directories

Typically, users need to have home directories so they can store their data files. It is wise to create a home directory off either the SYS: volume or a separate volume. Each user should have a parent directory created under the home directory. This will ease administering network security, since you can isolate users to their own home directory.

Users need to have full access to their own home directories so they can add, delete, modify, file scan, and copy their own files. Users typically do not need access to other users' home directories. For a view of how users' data could be created, refer to Figure 17-5. In this example, the users have directories created in a home directory and are stored on the SYS: volume.

When the users log in, as long as a home directory is created, the files they create and edit for an application can be stored in their own home directory. You could implement a security scheme where one user could not even change directories to the parent directory, HOME, thus preventing them from even "seeing" another user's files. You would implement this with the MAP ROOT command. In Figure 17-5, if set up properly, user Jess could not see user Zac's files nor store data in Zac's home directory.

The following statement shows how a MAP ROOT would be set to create an artificial root ceiling (virtual root) for the user JOE. If the user named JOE logs in and attempts to change to the real root directory, the

FIGURE 17-5

Possible directory structures created on the SYS: volume

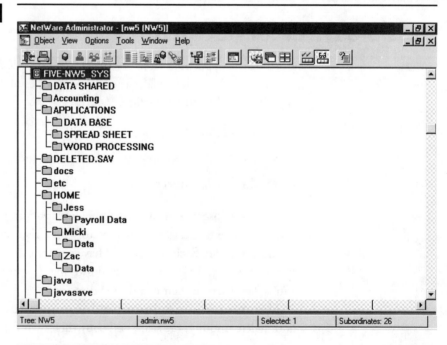

FROM THE CLASSROOM

Security Considerations for File System Design

When designing the file system structure for a NetWare server, don't forget to include file system security as one of your major considerations. Allowing users to store and access files at a volume's root directory can lead to exponentially compounding security problems and administrative headaches. A more prudent strategy is to leave the SYS: volume alone and to create another volume for placing additional directories for applications, user home directories, print queues, and other directories for data that quickly fill up the

unused disk space. Be careful not to put directories that users will access directly at the volume's root, but instead, create placeholder directories that will hold subdirectories. Later, when you grant file system trustee rights, you will have a file system structure that takes advantage of rights inheritance without excessive rights too high in the file system structure and will eliminate the need for most IRFs.

—Dan Cheung, CNI, MCNE, MCT

artificial ceiling will prevent him from doing so. His root directory i s \USERS\JOE on SERVER5 and volume SYS: instead of \.

```
MAP ROOT H:=SERVER5_SYS:\USERS\JOE
```

Also in this example, you can see how it is possible to separate the APPLICATIONS directory from the HOME directory. In the APPLICATIONS directory, you could place word processing, spreadsheet, and database programs and configuration files. The users could have read and file scan access to these directories. This would enable them to execute the appropriate application in one directory and store the necessary data in their own secured home directory. From a security standpoint, you would not want to give the users write, erase, or modify access to the APPLICATIONS directory. You don't want your users deleting the applications used by themselves and others; so, read and file scan should suffice.

Let's say that multiple users need to access a single data file. That data file can be put in a shared directory, and the users could be given access to that shared directory. This type of situation could happen, for example, in a payroll application where payroll clerks need to access the same file. Instead of placing this shared file in just one of the users' home directories, the file should be placed in the DATA SHARED directory, as seen in Figure 17-5. If a file that needs to be shared is placed in a single user's home directory, other users would need access to that directory. However, the disadvantage is that since other users can now see the shared file, they can also see files that may not relate to the application, which could cause a security breach. So, if a file needs to be shared, place it in a common directory. Assign appropriate rights to that directory and place the users in a group that has access to that directory.

Finally, if the workstations need a particular version of DOS, a directory for each version could be placed in the PUBLIC directory. Then, when the user logs in, a login script would map to this directory to get the correct version of DOS.

CERTIFICATION OBJECTIVE 17.04

Creating Additional Volumes

Volumes, including SYS:, may be created at server installation time, or they may be created later. In order to create additional volumes or add disk space to a current volume segment, you must use the LOAD NWCONFIG module at the file server console. For example at the console prompt for a server called FIVE-NW5:

```
FIVE-NW5: NWCONFIG
```

Next, select Standard Disk Options, NetWare Volume Options, and you will see the current volumes listed. Table 17-2 shows a list of options and keys used.

You can create a new volume or you can increase the size of a volume. For both processes, you must have free space available on the disk. In order

TABLE 17-2	Option	Button Name	Function
Commands to Modify Volumes	Save	ESC or F10	Save changes to a volume.
	Delete	DEL	Delete a volume.
	Mount/Dismount an existing volume	<ENTER>	Mount or dismount a volume.
	Modify Volume Parameters	<ENTER>	Change parameters.
	Help	<F1>	Get help on creating or changing a volume.
	Ins	<F3>	Add volume segments.

to add a volume, you must create a NetWare disk partition on it. In NWCONFIG, choose Standard Disk Options and then Modify disk partitions and Hot Fix. Next, choose the disk device where you want the NetWare partition to be placed. Then, choose Create NetWare disk partition and choose a size of the partition, from Free Space, that you want your partition to be. The default is the entire partition. You will also need to decide on a Hot Fix amount. The default Hot Fix size is probably best and is automatically determined by your NetWare partition size. Hot Fix is a fault tolerance technique where the data is written to a special reserved area of the disk, the Hot Fix, if other sectors go bad. Data will be written to the Hot Fix, or redirection, area only if an area of the disk is corrupt.

Once a NetWare partition has been created, you can get back to the main NWCONFIG menu and then select Standard Disk Options, and NetWare Volume Options. You will see listed the volumes that are currently available. To add a new volume segment, press INSERT or F3, and the Volume Disk Segment List will appear. This shows the NetWare partitions that were created earlier. You can add or modify a volume segment only from available free space.

Press ENTER on the volume disk segment to choose either to make the segment a new volume or make this segment part of another volume.

If you choose to make the segment a new volume, you must provide a new volume name. The following naming requirements apply to a new volume name:

■ The volume name must be unique.

■ The volume name cannot begin with an underscore (_) character.

■ It must be from 2 to 15 characters in length.

■ It can include these characters: a–z, A–Z, 0–9, ( )&%$#@!_.

Once the name has been entered, the volume size must be entered.

The range of valid sizes is from 1 to the partition size. If the partition size is 350MB, then valid numbers are from 1 to 350MB. If you don't choose all of the volume, then the difference is left as free space. You can then use this free space to place another volume. However, you can have up to 32 volume segments for each NetWare partition. After a volume has been created, there will be a column on the Volume Disk Segment List screen that shows a status of N indicating a new volume that is still in RAM. You must press F10 to save this to the disk. A summary of the status codes follows:

■ S indicates it is a System volume or SYS:.

■ M indicates the volume is part of a disk mirror.

■ E means an existing volume.

■ N means new volume.

After pressing F10 to save the volume, you must enter the administrator password to confirm. You must enter the distinguished NDS name for the Admin user. For example, if Admin is located in the NW5 organization unit, then for the Administrator Name prompt, you must enter **.ADMIN.NW5** followed by the correct password. A message will appear indicating that the volume was installed. Then you need to mount the volume.

A volume must be mounted before it can be used. The SYS: volume automatically gets mounted as the server boots up. Application volumes have to be mounted manually at the file server console in NWCONFIG or they can get mounted by placing an entry in the AUTOEXEC.NCF file for the server. To mount a volume named APPS, the entry would be the following:

```
FIVE-NW5_SYS: MOUNT APPS
```

You can modify or view volume information, as shown in Table 17-3.

Finally, you cannot dismount a volume while it is in use. File compression and block suballocation cannot be changed from here. Data migration is the process of moving data from the server hard disk to a secondary storage device such as tape or an optical disk. This optimizes hard disk utilization and is transparent to the users.

CERTIFICATION OBJECTIVE 17.05

Designing Directory Structures

Before designing directory structures, you will need to get an idea of your organization's needs and then do some careful planning.

Here are some things to consider when designing directory structures:

- Will applications need to reside on a single volume or multiple volumes?
- Do application and data files need to reside on the same volume or directory?

TABLE 17-3	Volume Information	Contents
Volume Information	Volume Name	Volume Name (Example: SYS:)
	Volume Block Size	Block Size (default of 64 KB Blocks)
	Status	Mounted or Dismounted
	File Compression	ON or OFF
	Block Suballocation	ON or OFF
	Data Migration	ON or OFF

■ Should shared data files and non-shared data files reside on the same volume or directory?

By placing multiple applications on multiple volumes, you are in fact spreading the application across multiple disks. This would enhance overall speed of the applications, since concurrent disk reads and writes could occur.

If you place your applications on one volume and your data files on another, you also enhance system performance. Because applications are typically read intensive and data is typically write intensive, you will split the reads and writes, which will in turn improve throughput. One volume is for reading only; the other is for writing only.

You also receive the same benefit by placing shared data files on volumes separate from non-shared volumes. You are splitting up the disk writes across multiple disks on multiple volumes. Refer to Figure 17-6 for a possible directory structure design.

FIGURE 17-6

Possible directory structure design

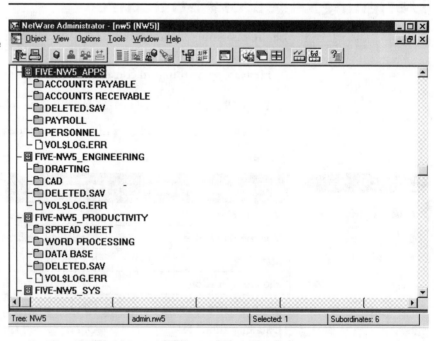

In Figure 17-6, you can see that the applications have been placed on different volumes. There is a volume for ENGINEERING, PRODUCTIVITY (which could contain generic office-related software), and APPS (which has organization-specific software).

CERTIFICATION SUMMARY

As we have mentioned several times in this chapter, it is best to plan your directory structure up front. This may entail performing user needs analysis to fully understand what is needed. Many organizations have problems down the road, when this initial analysis is not done.

Make sure you consider whether your organization has performance or fault tolerance as its objective. In NetWare, you have several fault-tolerant techniques: server mirroring, disk duplexing, disk mirroring, and the Hot Fix redirection process. If fault tolerance is your objective, then mirroring is adequate. However, if performance is your objective, then mirroring is not the best choice. If both are necessary, implement disk duplexing.

Be mindful of the system-created directories. They contain many programs that are used by NetWare. It is best not to place your critical applications on the SYS: volume.

In creating additional volumes, you can create a volume segment only on a NetWare partition. You can either create a new volume or extend a current volume. A partition can have up to 32 volume segments. A volume can be created only from available free space. Use the utility NWCONFIG at the file server console to create additional volume segments.

 # TWO-MINUTE DRILL

❑ The network file system can store critical data and applications on a server so they can be shared by many users. The careful design of the network file system is one of your most important network administrator tasks.

❑ A volume exists on a NetWare server; it does *not* exist on a NetWare client. Think of a volume as one level higher than a normal folder in the Windows 95 tree structure.

❑ During installation of a server, a default volume, called SYS:, is created. It contains NetWare system directories that hold NetWare Loadable Modules (files with an extension of *.NLM), Local Area Network (*.LAN) drivers, and other system files.

❑ *Fault tolerance* describes the safeguards a system has when it encounters a hardware failure or software problem that prevents proper data access.

❑ *Disk duplexing* uses disk mirroring with two disk controller cards instead of one, while disk mirroring uses one disk controller card.

❑ If fault tolerance and performance are equally important to your organization, mirroring is possible, but you should implement disk duplexing.

❑ Remember, with mirroring, you lose the capacity of one of the disks because it is an exact duplicate of the other.

❑ Overall, disk duplexing offers the advantages of fault tolerance and performance but the disadvantage is the cost of the additional hardware.

❑ *Block suballocation* parameter allows greater use of disk space because files can be stored in smaller unused portions of the disk.

❑ The error log files created by Transaction Tracking System (TTS) and the volume repair process (VREPAIR.NLM) are stored on the SYS: volume and grow over time.

❑ VREPAIR will detect and repair volume problems such as File Allocation Table (FAT) inconsistencies and mirror problems.

❑ The SYS: directory contains NLMs used by the ADMIN user. Various LAN drivers and other NLMs are in this directory. Also, the NDS database is stored here.

❑ Consider the following types of directories when organizing a directory structure: user home directories, application and program directories including configuration files, and shared data directories.

❑ When designing the file system structure for a NetWare server, don't forget to include file system security as one of your major considerations.

❑ In order to create additional volumes or add disk space to a current volume segment, you must use the LOAD NWCONFIG module at the file server console.

❑ The following naming requirements apply to a new volume name: the volume name must be unique; the volume name cannot begin with an underscore (_) character; it must be from 2 to 15 characters in length; it can include these characters: a–z, A–Z, 0–9, ( )&%$#@!_.

❑ If the partition size is 350MB, then valid numbers are from 1 to 350MB. If you don't choose all of the volume, then the difference is left as free space.

❑ Application volumes have to be mounted manually at the file server console in NWCONFIG or they can get mounted by placing an entry in the AUTOEXEC.NCF file for the server.

❑ When designing directory structures, consider the following: will applications need to reside on a single volume or multiple volumes? Do application and data files need to reside on the same volume or directory? Should shared data files and non-shared data files reside on the same volume or directory?

❑ In creating additional volumes, you can create a volume segment only on a NetWare partition. You can either create a new volume or extend a current volume. A partition can have up to 32 volume segments.

SELF TEST

The Self-Test questions will help you measure your understanding of the material presented in this chapter. Read all the choices carefully, as there may be more than one correct answer. Select all correct answers for each question.

1. What is the name of the software program used to create additional volumes?

   A. NWADMIN

   B. NWCONFIG

   C. VREPAIR

   D. MOUNT

2. What fault-tolerant technique redirects the data to a reserved area in case part of the disk becomes corrupt?

   A. Disk mirroring

   B. Disk duplexing

   C. Server mirroring

   D. Hot Fix

3. Which fault-tolerant technique uses two disk controllers?

   A. Disk mirroring

   B. Server mirroring

   C. Disk duplexing

   D. Hot Fix

4. Identify the system-created directories. (Choose all that apply).

   A. SYSTEM

   B. APPS

   C. PUBLIC

   D. SYS

5. Identify the default NetWare volume.

   A. SYS:

   B. APPS

   C. MAIL

   D. PUBLIC

6. What must be done to a volume prior to runningVREPAIR on it? (Choose all that apply.)

   A. It must be mounted.

   B. It must be dismounted.

   C. It must have been created on an NT server.

   D. You issue VREPAIR to run it.

7. How can you create a virtual root on a directory?

   A. MAP ROOT

   B. LOAD NWCONFIG

   C. VREPAIR

   D. MAP DEL

8. What must a disk have before a volume can be created?

   A. It must be deleted.

   B. It must have a NetWare partition.

   C. It must be dismounted.

   D. It should have an NT partition.

9. How many volume segments can a NetWare partition contain?

   A. 1

   B. 2

   C. 16

   D. 32

10. What is the best approach when performance and fault tolerance are important?

   A. Disk mirroring

   B. Hot Fix

   C. Server mirroring

   D. Disk duplexing

11. Which of the following are valid volume names? (Choose all that apply).

   A. APPS

   B. _PAYROLL

   C. ACCTS_REC

   D. ENG_2

12. What option button allows you to save changes in NWCONFIG? (Choose all that apply.)

   A. F10

   B. DELETE

   C. ENTER

   D. ESC

13. What system-created directory has TCP/IP related files?

   A. SYSTEM

   B. MAIL

   C. ETC

   D. PUBLIC

14. What are some things to watch for on a volume? (Choose all that apply.)

   A. Percentage of space available

   B. Size of log files

   C. File corruption

   D. Limiting user space

15. What is true about creating a volume? (Choose all that apply.)

   A. It must be done on a dismounted volume.

   B. It must be taken from free space.

   C. It must be done on a NetWare partition.

   D. It must be done on a mounted volume.

18

Using the Server Console

CERTIFICATION OBJECTIVES

18.01   NetWare Server Overview

18.02   Executing Console Commands

18.03   Loading and Unloading NLMs

18.04   Server Configuration Files

18.05   Customizing the Server
         Configuration Files

18.06   Creating Server Batch Files

18.07   Accessing the Server Console
         from a Workstation

18.08   Protecting Your Server

18.09   Loading Support for Java Applications
         on the NetWare 5 Server

18.10   Using the NetWare ServerTop

T he NetWare server console is where the administrator performs fundamental server management and configuration tasks. It is from the server console that NLMs are loaded so that network services are made available. From the console prompt NLM utilities can be accessed, server configurations performed, and server commands run.

In this chapter we will discuss some of the commands that can be executed at the console prompt. We will also explore server configuration files and how you can edit them.

You will find it efficient to remotely manage the NetWare server from a workstation, and Remote Console lets you do this. Security is also a constant issue with networks, and we will look into it briefly.

A new item introduced in NetWare is Console One, a Java-based application that gives NetWare its first marketed graphical user interface (GUI). We will see how Console One makes administration easier to manage.

Novell has tried server console GUI before, but it was received with hostility by the CNE community. It was compared to X-Window for UNIX and was considered slow and cumbersome to use. The Java GUI is required only during the install process. Once NW5 is installed, the command to load the GUI can be commented out of the NCF file. This feature was generally well received by CNIs during the 529 classes presented at Novell.

CERTIFICATION OBJECTIVE 18.01

NetWare Server Overview

When a NetWare server loads, a lot of rapidly scrolling text is displayed on the monitor's screen, as the configuration information processes and NLMs load, to bring the server up. The NetWare 5 server has many screen types, most of them associated with NLM utilities and enhancements. The basic server screen is the NetWare Console, which comes in two formats. The first is the standard text console, which looks like a DOS command prompt. The second is the graphical Java-based Console One.

The standard server console screen looks similar to a DOS prompt. Figure 18-1 shows what a basic server console screen looks like.

Different types of commands can be executed at the console prompt. For example, NLMs can be loaded or unloaded, and NetWare utilities, such as NWCONFIG and DHCPCFG, can be loaded to configure the server. The server can be brought down from the Server Console prompt, as well as restarted. The new Console One has some extended capabilities that the traditional console does not have. You can use Console One to browse and organize network resources, add accounts, and configure existing accounts. Figure 18-2 shows an example of what Console One looks like. From Console One, you can set access to network resources, as well as access remote server consoles on other servers. The first release of Console One has

---

FIGURE 18-1

Basic server console screen

```
            Hardware setting: Slot 1, I/O ports FF90h to FF9Fh, Interrupt Ah
            Node address: 00805F3198C1
            Frame type: ETHERNET_802.2
            Board name: CPQNF3_1_E82
            LAN protocol: IPX network 00000208

Compaq NetFlex-3 & Netelligent Ethernet HSM
            Version 2.41    April 9, 1998
            Hardware setting: Slot 1, I/O ports FF90h to FF9Fh, Interrupt Ah
            Node address: 00805F3198C1
            Frame type: ETHERNET_II
            Board name: CPQNF3_1_EII
            LAN protocol: ARP
            LAN protocol: IP Address 151.125.75.5 Mask FF.FF.0.0(255.255.0.0)
                        Interfaces 1

10-17-1998  10:41:22 am:    RSPX-4.12-28
            Remote console connection granted for 00010100:00805F6F248F


Tree Name: EMA_TREE
Bindery Context(s):
    .CORP.NYC.EMA

FS1:
```

FIGURE 18-2

Console One Java
application

FIGURE 18-2

Console One Java
application

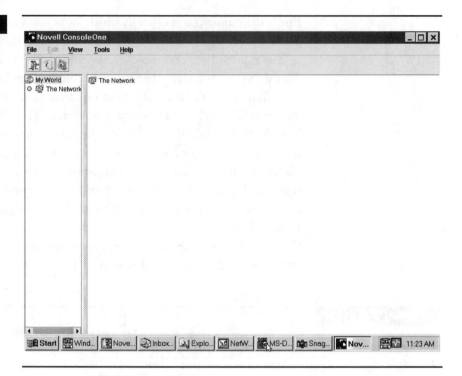

some capabilities of NetWare Administrator, but not all of them. Other
tasks that can be accomplished with Console One are managing local files
and folders, as well as hosting other Java applets.

CERTIFICATION OBJECTIVE 18.02

Executing Console Commands

There are many different commands that can be executed at the server
console screen, and this is something you need to know for the exam. Pay
particular attention to how certain things are loaded or unloaded at the
console prompt.

In addition to knowing how to load and unload items, you also should know some key combinations to help you navigate from one screen to the next.

Navigating the Server Console

To successfully manage a server from the console prompt, you should know how to navigate to other screens that are loaded when other NLMs running in the background. There are a couple of key sequences to become very familiar with as a NetWare engineer.

The first one is the ALT-ESC combination, which goes through the various screens loaded on a server. As you press ALT-ESC, you will move from screen to screen until you get to the one you want. A second way to navigate from one screen to another is to use the CTRL-ESC combination, which brings up a list of what is loaded on the server. This can serve two purposes—it summarizes what is running on the server and is a quick way to jump from screen 1 to screen 12.

Navigating Console One

With Console One you can browse a number of resources with the various menus available. The left window pane allows you to browse the different container objects, while the right window pane shows the actual contents of the resources.

With Console One running on the server, there are two key items in the left-hand window—the My Server and Shortcuts containers allow for management of local and remote server operations. Maneuvering around Console One is done with a mouse or other pointing device. To get to the properties on an object you can right-click and select Details. This is similar to the process in NetWare Administrator.

CERTIFICATION OBJECTIVE 18.03

Loading and Unloading NLMs

To add additional network services or to access a server utility, you will need to know the name of the NLM to load. Sometimes you may need to know the order of how a group of NLMs must be loaded. The two most basic commands are LOAD and UNLOAD. These are used in conjunction with the name of a particular NLM installed on the server. For example:

```
NWCONFIG
INETCFG
CDROM
```

These are just a few of the NLMs that can be loaded. When you want to unload an NLM, the most common way to do it is to type **UNLOAD** and the name of the NLM afterward. Some NLMs allow you to unload them from their menu. For example, if you type **MONITOR**, you can then exit the MONITOR utility by pressing the ESC key while on the monitor screen. You will be prompted if you want to exit MONITOR. Alternatively, you can type **UNLOAD MONITOR**, and monitor will be unloaded.

on the
Job

Unlike earlier versions of NetWare, you no longer need to use the LOAD command when loading NLMs. Just typing the NLM's filename will automatically load the module. Using LOAD is optional. For example, to load MONITOR.NLM, just type MONITOR at the server prompt.

CERTIFICATION OBJECTIVE 18.04

Server Configuration Files

To optimize and tune your server to make it run efficiently, you must learn how to edit server configuration files. There are also two ways to do this, but the easiest one that I recommend is using the NWCONFIG utility. The NWCONFIG utility gives an administrator quick and easy access to the two most important NetWare Configuration Files (NCF): STARTUP.NCF and AUTOEXEC.NCF.

exam
Watch

INSTALL.NLM has been replaced by NWCONFIG.NLM in NetWare 5.

FIGURE 18-3

NWCONFIG utility and
NCF file option

```
NetWare Configuration

┌──────────────────────────────────────────────────────────────┐
│                    Configuration Options                     │
├──────────────────────────────────────────────────────────────┤
│ Driver Options         (load/unload disk and network drivers)│
│ Standard Disk Options  (configure NetWare partitions/volumes)│
│ NSS Disk Options       (configure NSS storage and volumes)   │
│ License Options        (install or remove licenses)          │
│ Copy Files Options     (install NetWare system files)        │
│ Directory Options      (install NDS)                         │
│ NCF files Options      (create/edit server startup files)    │
│ Multi CPU Options      (install/uninstall SMP)               │
│ Product Options        (other optional installation items)   │
│ Exit                                                         │
└──────────────────────────────────────────────────────────────┘


Use the arrow keys to highlight an option, then press <Enter>.
```

To get to the NWCONFIG utility type **NWCONFIG** at the console prompt. This will allow you to look at and edit your main startup files, as shown in Figure 18-3. However, with NetWare there will be other NCF files that you may need to edit or at least look at.

CERTIFICATION OBJECTIVE 18.05

Customizing the Server Configuration Files

To edit the NCF files or other files that can be edited with a text editor, you can use EDIT.NLM to load the NetWare text Editor (see Figure 18-4). If you include a path and filename after the EDIT command, you can

FIGURE 18-4

EDIT utility in NetWare

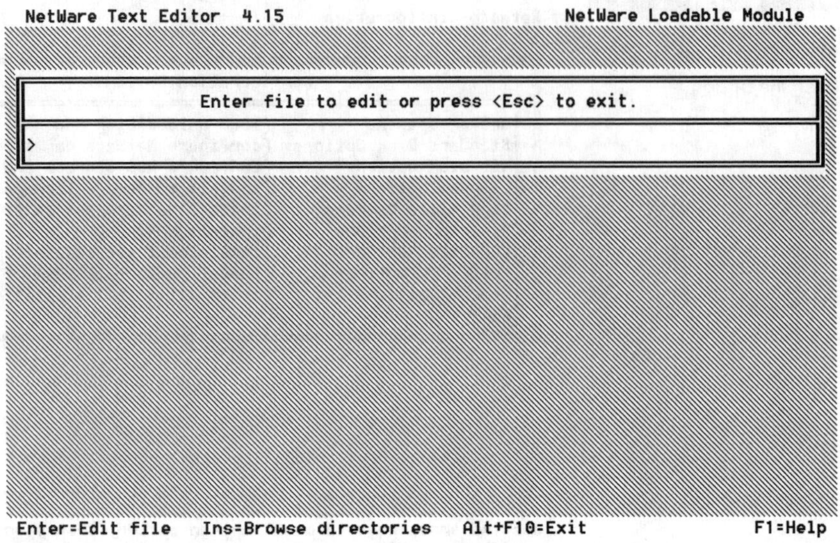

```
NetWare Text Editor  4.15                        NetWare Loadable Module

          ┌──────────────────────────────────────────────────────┐
          │        Enter file to edit or press <Esc> to exit.      │
          ├──────────────────────────────────────────────────────┤
          │ >                                                      │
          └──────────────────────────────────────────────────────┘




Enter=Edit file    Ins=Browse directories   Alt+F10=Exit          F1=Help
```

immediately open the file for editing. If you do not enter a path and filename after the EDIT command, you will be prompted for them.

NetWare NCF files, with the exception of STARTUP.NCF, can be edited with any text editor on a workstation. To edit NCF files from a workstation, though, you will have to know where the file exists on the server. Many times, NCF files are in either the SYSTEM directory on the SYS: volume, or, for example, stored with their other program files in the case of Computer Associates' ARCSERVE for NetWare product.

exam
Watch

STARTUP.NCF can only be edited using EDIT.NLM or NWCONFIG.NLM, since it resides on the DOS partition of the hard drive physically located on the server box.

Creating Server Batch Files

When it comes to simplifying commands and grouping configuration statements together, you will want to use server batch files. These batch files should reside on the SYS: volume in the SYSTEM directory.

To create the files, you can use any ASCII text editor. Just make sure that the file is saved in the appropriate location—the SYSTEM directory on the SYS: volume.

Accessing the Server Console from a Workstation

Many NetWare administrative tasks must be done at a workstation. NetWare has had a utility called RCONSOLE available for administrators to remotely access the server's console. As shown in Figure 18-5, RCONSOLE looks exactly like the server's console. The major difference is the keystroke sequence used to navigate from screen to screen.

Before RCONSOLE will work, two NLMs must be loaded: REMOTE.NLM and RSPX.NLM. To load the NLMs, type **REMOTE** (follow with the **RCONSOLE** password) and **RSPX** at the console prompt. You can then access the server with RCONSOLE.

Many times, REMOTE and RSPX will be loaded in one of the startup files so that, by default, the administrator will have remote access. When this is the case, the password for the remote console is entered immediately after the RSPX statement. Exercise 18-1 will show you how to do this.

EXERCISE 18-1:	**Editing a Server Configuration File**

1. At the server console, type **NWCONFIG**.
2. At the NWCONFIG menu, choose the option to edit NCF files.

FIGURE 18-5

RCONSOLE on a
Windows 95 workstation

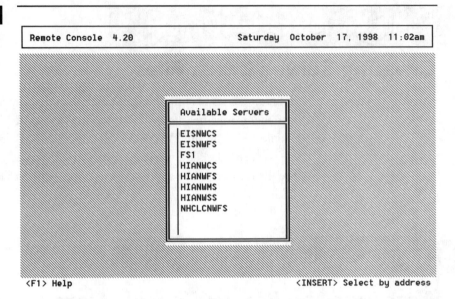

```
Remote Console  4.20                    Saturday  October  17, 1998  11:02am


                        ┌─────────────────────────┐
                        │    Available Servers    │
                        ├─────────────────────────┤
                        │ EISNWCS                 │
                        │ EISNWFS                 │
                        │ FS1                     │
                        │ HIANWCS                 │
                        │ HIANWFS                 │
                        │ HIANWMS                 │
                        │ HIANWSS                 │
                        │ NHCLCNWFS               │
                        │                         │
                        │                         │
                        │                         │
                        └─────────────────────────┘


<F1> Help                                        <INSERT> Select by address
```

3. Select the AUTOEXEC.NCF file and it will open on your screen.

4. Within the NCF file, add a line similar to the following:

   RSPX *password*

5. Press the ESC key and you will be prompted to save your AUTOEXEC.NCF file.

6. Unload any modules that are loaded and then type **DOWN** at the server console. This will bring the server down and allow you to reboot.

7. Once the server is back up and everything is loaded, go to a workstation and open a DOS window.

8. Type **MAP** to be sure you have a search drive mapped to the SYS:PUBLIC directory. If not, type **MAP ROOT INS S1:=*SERVERNAME*\SYS:PUBLIC**.

9. When you know you have a drive map searched to the PUBLIC directory, type **RCONSOLE**.

10. You may get a message that Windows 95 may interfere with the proper operation of RCONSOLE, press ENTER to continue.

11. The next prompt asks whether you want to use SPX or Asynchronous communications. Choose SPX.

12. You should now see your server's name listed. Select it by pressing ENTER.

13. You should be prompted for the password you entered in Step 4. Enter your password.

14. You should now see your server's console. Navigate around with the keystrokes shown in Table 18-1. When you have finished, press ALT-F2 to exit the remote console session.

Navigating the Console with RCONSOLE

In Windows 95, there are some keystrokes that cannot be used to navigate the console remotely because they already do something else. The ALT-ESC and CTRL-ESC combinations we looked at earlier will not work with RCONSOLE because they are compiled into RCONSOLE.EXE. There are four main keystrokes with RCONSOLE, as shown in Table 18-1.

Another NEW component of NetWare 5 is RCONSOLEJ. Along with the RCONSOLE.EXE in the public directory is RCONJ.EXE, which runs a Java-based remote console utility. The Java-based management on the server cannot be seen with RCONSOLE, so Novell included RCONSOLEJ to manage the Java-based management piece remotely. Figure 18-6 shows the RCONSOLEJ connection screen. For the exam, make sure you that you know this utility exists.

TABLE 18-1	Keystroke	What Happens
RCONSOLE Keystrokes	ALT-F1	Brings up the RCONSOLE menu, giving you a series of options
	ALT-F2	Prompts to see if you want to exit your RCONSOLE
	ALT-F3	Moves you ahead one screen on the server (similar to ALT-ESC directly on the server)
	ALT-F4	Moves you back one screen on the server

FIGURE 18-6

RCONSOLEJ on a
Windows 95 workstation

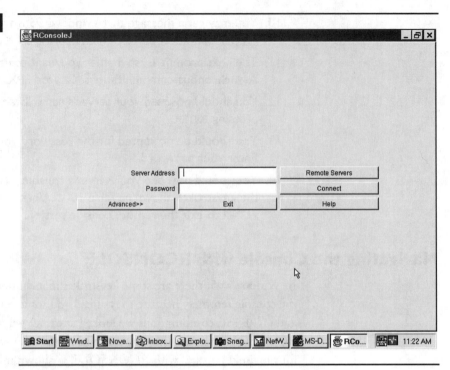

CERTIFICATION OBJECTIVE 18.08

Protecting Your Server

With any network, security is a primary concern. One of the first things to
do is make it physically inaccessible to unauthorized people by keeping it in
a locked room. Some administrators go further and actually remove the
keyboard from the server so that it can be monitored and managed only by
remote access. Another recommendation (from the Novell Web site) is to
use a power-on password, along with other passwords that can be put in
place at the server.

Using **SECURE CONSOLE**

One way to secure the server from tampering is to use the SECURE CONSOLE feature, which does the following:

- Prevents NLMs from being loaded
- Prevents keyboard entry into the operating system debugger
- Prevents anyone from changing the date and time on the server

The one thing to keep in mind about using this command is that it cannot be undone until the server is taken down and rebooted. Once this is done, the server is back to a state of being nonsecure. Also note that emote management has the same restrictions as being on the server directly.

Using **SCRSAVER** to Secure the Server

NetWare 5 has some new and different features, as you have discovered throughout this book. One of these is the new SCRSAVER utility that replaces the console-locking feature of MONITOR. There is no longer an option to lock the console in MONITOR with NetWare 5.

To load the SCRSAVER module you simply type:

```
SCRSAVER {options}
```

As with previous versions of NetWare, when the screensaver kicks in on a server, you see a snake for each processor in the server. With NetWare 5 you have the ability to lock the console with the SCRSAVER module. When the snake is crawling across the monitor, you simply press a key, and then you will be prompted for a username and password. When a key is pressed, you must do the following:

1. At the Login box, press ENTER to highlight the username field.

2. Enter the username. (The username must have write rights to the ACL for the Server object.)

3. Press ENTER again to highlight the password field.

4. Type the password for the user.

5. Press ENTER twice, and the console is now unlocked.

When SCRSAVER is loaded, the default is to have the server locked when the screensaver kicks in.

Loading Support for Java Applications on the NetWare 5 Server

Java has taken the computer world by storm, and Java-based applications are consequently proliferating. NetWare 5 comes with Java support, which makes NetWare 5 even more versatile as a Web server.

With the built-in Application Program Interfaces supporting Java, developers can write object-oriented, multithreaded, dynamically-linked applications using the Java language. This makes NetWare 5 one of the most powerful servers for Java applications.

Using the NetWare ServerTop

With NetWare 5 there is a new look and feel with the GUI interface of Console One. The GUI interface is actually known as the ServerTop. This is basically like the desktop in Windows 95.

The GUI interface makes NetWare come to life with a point-and-click style of Windows NT and Window 95/98. In the left-hand corner is the Novell menu, similar to the Start Menu in the various Windows products.

CERTIFICATION SUMMARY

Managing a server is the key component to successful network administration. With NetWare 5, an administrator has more tools available than ever before. In this chapter we looked at managing the server with the NetWare Console and the new Console One, GUI-based management tool.

Being able to navigate and know the appropriate commands makes you a successful server administrator. The other piece to Console Management is being able to do it remotely and configure the server to do so. We looked briefly at RCONSOLE and RCONSOLEJ, which I am sure you will see on the exam.

Along with the console comes the ability to view and edit the Server Configuration Files. The two most important of these are STARTUP.NCF and AUTOEXEC.NCF. Remember that NetWare has a built-in EDIT utility to edit text files and create batch files.

NetWare 5 comes with a couple of ways to secure the server. The first step is to physically secure the server by limiting access to it. Remember that SECURE CONSOLE can secure the server from attacks. The new SCRSAVER replaces the old console lock function of MONITOR. In order to begin the process of locking the console using SCRSCAVER, you press ENTER at the login box to highlight the Username field, and then enter the Username. The Username must have Write rights to the ACL for the Server object.

We briefly mentioned that NetWare 5 has support for Java applications. Along with Java support comes the new SERVER TOP that gives NetWare administrators a graphical user interface for managing their servers.

 # TWO-MINUTE DRILL

❑ The NetWare server console is where the administrator performs fundamental server management and configuration tasks. NLMs are loaded from the server console, to make network services available. From the console prompt, NLM utilities can be accessed, server configurations performed, and server commands run.

❏ A new item introduced in NetWare is Console One, a Java-based application that gives NetWare its first marketed graphical user interface.

❏ The NetWare 5 server has many screen types, most of them associated with NLM utilities and enhancements. The basic server screen is the NetWare Console, which comes in two formats. The standard text console, which looks like a DOS command prompt, and the Java-based graphical user interface of Console One

❏ To successfully manage a server from the console prompt, you should know how to navigate to other screens that are loaded when other NLMs running in the background. There are a two keystroke sequences to become very familiar with as a NetWare engineer: ALT-ESC and CTRL-ESC.

❏ To add additional network services or to access a server utility, you will need to know the name of the NLM to load. Sometimes you may also need to know the sequence in which a group of NLMs must be loaded. The two most basic commands are LOAD and UNLOAD. These are used in conjunction with the name of a particular NLM installed on the server.

❏ To optimize and tune your server, you must learn how to edit server configuration files. There are two ways to edit server configuration files. The easiest method is to use the NWCONFIG utility. The NWCONFIG utility gives an administrator quick and easy access to the two most important NetWare Configuration Files (NCF): STARTUP.NCF and AUTOEXEC.NCF.

❏ To edit the NCF files or other files that can be edited with a text editor, you can use EDIT.NLM to load the NetWare text Editor.

❏ To simplify commands and to group configuration statements together, you want to use server batch files. These batch files should reside on the SYS: volume in the SYSTEM directory. To create server batch files you can use any ASCII text editor.

❏ NetWare has had a utility called RCONSOLE available for administrators to remotely access the server's console. RCONSOLE looks exactly like the server's console. The major difference between the server's console and RCONSOLE is the sequence of keystrokes used to navigate from screen to screen.

❑ In Windows 95, there are some keystrokes that cannot be used to navigate the console remotely, for example ALT-ESC and CTRL-ESC. There are four main keystrokes with RCONSOLE: ALT-FI, ALT-F2, ALT-F3, and ALT-F4.

❑ Security is a primary concern with any network. Recommended methods for securing a network server include making it physically inaccessible by keeping it in a locked room, removing the keyboard so that it can be monitored and managed only by remote access, and (from the Novell Web site) use a power-on password along with other passwords.

❑ The SECURE CONSOLE command prevents NLMs from being loaded, prevents keyboard entry into the operating system debugger, and prevents anyone from changing the date and time on the server. The important thing to keep in mind about using the SECURE CONSOLE command is that it cannot be undone until the server is taken down and rebooted, which will return the server to a nonsecure state. The same restriction is valid for remote management as well.

❑ The new SCRSAVER utility in NetWare 5 replaces the console locking feature of MONITOR for previous versions of NetWare.

❑ NetWare 5 comes with Java support, which makes NetWare 5 even more versatile as a Web server.

❑ There is a new look and feel with the GUI interface of Console One in NetWare 5. The GUI interface is actually known as the ServerTop, which is similar to the desktop in Windows 95.

SELF TEST

The following Self-Test questions will help you measure your understanding of the material presented in this chapter. Read all the choices carefully, as there may be more than one correct answer. Choose all correct answers for each question.

1. To load NLMs and to get to the NWCONFIG utility, you would use the _____, which is the text version of this utility:

   A. Console One

   B. NetWare Console

   C. Console Monitor

   D. All of the above

2. To load NLMs and get to the NWCONFIG utility, you would use the _____, which is the graphical version of this utility:

   A. Console One

   B. NetWare Console

   C. Console Monitor

   D. All of the above

3. Which of the following can you use to remotely manage a server from a workstation as if you were in front of the server typing on the workstation? (Choose all that apply.)

   A. CONSOLER

   B. RCONSOLE

   C. REMCON

   D. RCONSOLEJ

4. What are the names of the two main NCF files that are used during server startup?

   A. AUTOEXEC.NCF

   B. STARTUP.NCF

   C. AUTOSTART.NCF

   D. START.NCF

5. Which of the following would you use to view and edit NCF files?

   A. INETCFG.BAT

   B. INSTALL.BAT

   C. NWCONFIG.NLM

   D. INETCFG.NLM

6. In order for RCONSOLE to work properly, you have to have which NLM loaded on the server with a password following the statement to load it?

   A. REMOTE.NLM

   B. RSPX.NLM

   C. REMOTESPX.NLM

   D. NWCONFIG.NLM

7. Which keystroke combination do you use to bring up a menu on RCONSOLE to select a server screen to view?

   A. ALT-ESC

   B. ALT-F4

   C. ALT-F2

   D. ALT-F1

8. Which command would you type at the server console to disable the ability to load any new NLMs?

A. LOCK CONSOLE

B. SECURE CONSOLE

C. SCRSAVER

D. LOCK SERVER

9. Which utility replaced the console lock feature of MONITOR?

A. RCONSOLE

B. MONITOR LOCK

C. SCRSAVER

D. SECURE CONSOLE

10. NetWare 5 supports _____, which is an application interface used by programmers to develop graphical intranet/Internet applications.

A. Java

B. GUI

C. IPL

D. RFT

11. The new graphical interface of the NetWare 5 Server is known as _____.

A. Server Desktop

B. Console Top

C. Server Top

D. Console Desktop

12. The RCONSOLE utility can be found in which directory and volume?

A. VOL1:PUBLIC

B. SYS:SYSTEM

C. SYS:PUBLIC

D. VOL1:SYSTEM

13. Which command do you type to remove an NLM loaded in memory?

A. LOAD UNINSTALL

B. UNLOAD

C. DISABLE

D. UNDO

14. Which key combination would you use to bring up a list of available screens on a NetWare server?

A. ALT-ESC

B. CTRL-L

C. ALT-L

D. CTRL-ESC

15. Which key combination would you use to change screens one by one at the server console?

A. ALT-ESC

B. CTRL-L

C. ALT-L

D. CTRL-ESC

16. Which utility can be used to edit the NCF files on a NetWare server? (Choose all that apply.)

A. EDIT.NLM

B. Any text editor

C. EDITOR.NLM

D. LOADER.NLM

CERTIFIED NOVELL ENGINEER

19

Optimizing the Network and Server

CERTIFICATION OBJECTIVES

19.01   Memory Overview

19.02   Memory Allocation and Deallocation

19.03   Virtual Memory

19.04   Monitor Statistics

19.05   Server Buffer and Packet Parameters

19.06   Block Suballocation

19.07   Enabling File Compression

19.08   Packet Burst

19.09   Large Internet Packets

A good network engineer must be able to make a server work as efficiently as possible. In this chapter we will look at how memory can affect a server's performance. Knowing some of the tricks of the trade will help you determine when you have to add memory or make the server use memory more efficiently.

We will look at optimizing the server with some common settings related to communication across the network. We will also discuss hard drive configuration and how it can affect server performance.

If there is one thing you will see on your exam for Advanced Administration, it will be troubleshooting and optimization wrapped up into one. Be sure to understand each of the items under the objectives here. This will also help build on some of the other CNE exams.

CERTIFICATION OBJECTIVE 19.01

Memory Overview

We have seen that NetWare requires a minimum of 64MB of RAM and can access up to 4GB of RAM. When a server is loaded, the SERVER.EXE file is executed, and all remaining memory is cache memory. Cache memory is available for NLM programs and other services and processes. Data stored in cache is stored in 4-kilobyte blocks, which are called *cache buffers*.

Two other items that NetWare uses are logical memory addressing and protected memory spaces. *Logical memory addressing* allows NetWare to use memory efficiently because fragmentation of memory is minimal, which results in faster memory response. The exam will not go into great detail here, but we wanted to mention it so that you would at least know what it is. *Protected memory space* is memory set aside for applications or NLMs that might not be stable. Protected memory space is separate from the server kernel, which means that if the application or NLM that is loaded in the protected memory space fails, it will not affect the server. This keeps the server from crashing due to unstable applications or NLMs.

More and More Memory

NetWare is considered a self-tuning operating system. One fact of computing today is that more and more memory is needed to support what is done within a network environment.

There are so many things we can do with today's Network Operating Systems that we need to keep a close eye on how memory is used. With e-mail, fax, web servers, Internet gateways, and the many other items, a lot of applications can be loaded on a Network Server.

Server Performance

If there is one thing that can hurt a server's performance, it is too little memory. We all know that physical memory is known as RAM (Random Access Memory). RAM is where programs and modules are loaded that are used on the server. The hard drive can be considered a place where programs and modules reside, but RAM is where they are loaded to be used on the server.

Types of Memory

There are different types of memory: permanent storage, RAM, and virtual memory. Examples of *permanent storage* are a floppy disk and hard drive. We have already discussed RAM.

The third form of memory is *virtual memory*, which is an extension of RAM. Figure 19-1 shows the different memory types. If a server needs, for example, 100MB (or 100 million bytes) of RAM and has only 96MB of RAM installed, then it has to find 4 additional MB of RAM. Computer operating systems do this by creating a swap file on the hard drive. A *swap file* is a temporary file that stores information from RAM that is not being used at this moment in time but will be needed in the future. This is quicker and more efficient than unloading and loading a file or module. If this seems confusing now, that is okay. You will understand it better when you read the section on virtual memory later in this chapter.

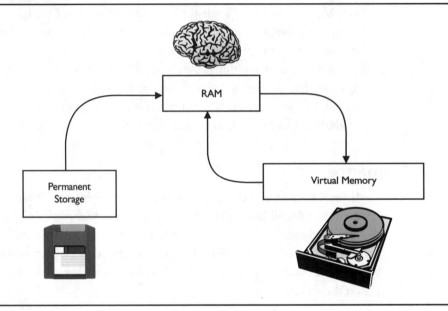

FIGURE 19-1 Different types of memory

CERTIFICATION OBJECTIVE 19.02

Memory Allocation and Deallocation

When you are troubleshooting and optimizing a server, you have to understand how memory is used within NetWare 5. One thing to know for the exam is how memory allocation and deallocation work.

When NLMs are loaded, a certain amount of memory is allocated to that specific NLM. The exam will not go into specific detail on how much memory NLM "A" uses or NLM "B" uses but there are two key points to remember. The first is that with NetWare 5, virtual memory is available. The second is that there is a routine, called *garbage collection* that is run when memory is deallocated. Figure 19-2 shows a graphical representation of garbage collection. Each section of the drawing is a block of memory. The free sections have been taken care of by the garbage collection routine.

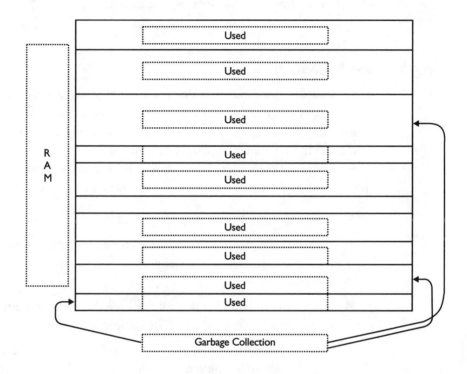

FIGURE 19-2   Garbage collection freeing up memory

Garbage collection is a memory recovery process that periodically collects allocated memory that is now free. The memory is returned to the cache for use by other NLMs or programs.

CERTIFICATION OBJECTIVE 19.03

Virtual Memory

As we discussed earlier, NetWare 5 has a new feature that allows items stored in RAM to be swapped to the hard drive. This frees up RAM for other purposes and can make the server more efficient. You can expect to see this on the exam, and as an administrator you will be customizing your servers with different virtual memory configurations.

Configuring Virtual Memory

There are a series of commands that you can use to manage the virtual memory configuration on your server console. These items can help you in establishing, deleting, and changing the swap file configuration on the server. Table 19-1 shows some of these commands.

Swap file configuration may not have to be dealt with in every case. For the exam, though, these are some things to know about virtual memory:

- There can be only one swap file per volume.

- The swap file on the SYS volume is created by default. Other swap files have to be created manually. Swap files can be stored on other volumes besides SYS.

- Swap files can be added to a volume even if it is not mounted. The swap file will be created when the volume is mounted.

- When a volume is unmounted, the swap file is deleted. To create a swap file when the volume is mounted again, you must go through the steps shown in Table 19-1. The exception to this is the SYS volume where the swap file is created by default.

- Swap files are not a set size. They change as the requirements of the swap file change.

Disk Thrashing

In some cases you may observe a server that is doing a lot of swapping. If RAM is running low, the swap file will be utilized more and more causing the hard drive(s) to *thrash*. This means that the hard drive is being accessed constantly to swap information in the swap file with RAM.

TABLE 19-1	Items	What To Do...
Configuration Items for Virtual Memory	Get HELP on the SWAP command	Type **HELP SWAP** at the console prompt
	Bring up a Virtual Memory Information screen	Type **SWAP** at the console prompt
	Create a swap file; parameters include MIN, MAX, and MIN FREE	Type **SWAP ADD** *volume_name [parameter=x]* at console prompt
	Delete swap file	Type **SWAP DEL** *volume_name* at console prompt
	Change parameters for a swap file	Type **SWAP PARAMETER** *volume_name parameter=x* at console prompt
	Set alert for excessive memory swapping	Type **SET AVERAGE PAGE IN ALERT THRESHOLD =** *x* at console prompt

Thrashing can cause extra wear and tear on the hard drives and may even can lead to premature hard drive failure. The reason it is called thrashing is due to the sound that is made by a hard drive constantly being accessed.

To curb disk thrashing add more RAM to the server. Even though virtual memory makes up for a shortage of RAM, it is not the recommended way to have your server operate. Virtual memory is meant to improve performance by taking idle tasks out of RAM to free it up for active processes. This makes the server more efficient. RAM should be used for the active processes, not for virtual memory. There are some things you can watch as other signs to tell you that more RAM is needed in the server. We will take a look at these in the next section.

CERTIFICATION OBJECTIVE 19.04

Monitor Statistics

If there is not enough memory in the server, you will see performance degradation. As a CNE you will spend a lot of time at the NetWare console monitor. To check whether the physical RAM is sufficient, go to the MONITOR. On the menu of AVAILABLE OPTIONS choose SYSTEM RESOURCES and then select SERVER MEMORY STATISTICS. Then choose Cache Buffer Memory (see Figure 19-3).

When determining what is using the memory you can use another option in MONITOR to see which NLMs are using large amounts of memory. Exercise 19-1 will take you through the process of checking the NLMs running on your server.

EXERCISE 19-1

Viewing Memory Information with MONITOR

1. If MONITOR is not loaded, type **MONITOR** at the console prompt.

2. From the Available Options menu choose Loaded Modules.

3. Highlight one of the loaded modules. This will display the information and statistics on that module in the upper part of the monitor screen.

4. Press TAB to expand the information window.

5. Check the module's Allocated Memory. The information includes such things as allocated memory in use and percent of memory in use. Press F1 on each of the information options. This will give you a description of each of the statistics.

6. Press TAB to return to the list of loaded modules.

7. Check the memory statistics for two other modules.

8. To free memory allocated for a highlighted module, press F4 when the module is highlighted.

These are just a few of the things that you can do to determine how much memory is available, as well as what is using the memory. Once these two items are determined, you can make a decision on upgrading RAM, changing some of the settings with cache, or leaving the server as is, if it is running at peak performance.

FIGURE 19-3

Cache buffer memory

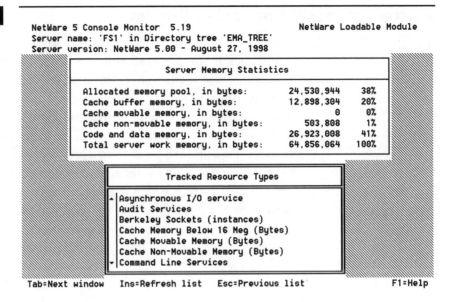

```
NetWare 5 Console Monitor  5.19                NetWare Loadable Module
Server name: 'FS1' in Directory tree 'EMA_TREE'
Server version: NetWare 5.00 - August 27, 1998

┌─────────────────────────────────────────────────────┐
│                Server Memory Statistics               │
├─────────────────────────────────────────────────────┤
│  Allocated memory pool, in bytes:     24,530,944  38% │
│  Cache buffer memory, in bytes:       12,898,304  20% │
│  Cache movable memory, in bytes:               0   0% │
│  Cache non-movable memory, in bytes:     503,808   1% │
│  Code and data memory, in bytes:      26,923,008  41% │
│  Total server work memory, in bytes:  64,856,064 100% │
└─────────────────────────────────────────────────────┘

      ┌───────────────────────────────────────┐
      │          Tracked Resource Types        │
      ├───────────────────────────────────────┤
      │ ▲ Asynchronous I/O service             │
      │   Audit Services                       │
      │   Berkeley Sockets (instances)         │
      │   Cache Memory Below 16 Meg (Bytes)    │
      │   Cache Movable Memory (Bytes)         │
      │   Cache Non-Movable Memory (Bytes)     │
      │ ▼ Command Line Services                │
      └───────────────────────────────────────┘

  Tab=Next window   Ins=Refresh list   Esc=Previous list        F1=Help
```

Server Buffer and Packet Parameters

When computers communicate on a network, they send packets of information across a medium. When a computer, in this case a server, receives these packets, something has to be done with them. NetWare uses what are known as *packet receive buffers* to store incoming data until the server can process it.

Increasing Maximum Packet Buffers

As an administrator you may notice that a server is dropping workstation connections, or slowing down in its communication across the network. This may be due to an incorrect setting of the packet receive buffers.

Again, using MONITOR you can view and change the maximum packet receive buffers setting. On the Available Options screen choose Server Parameters and then Communications. The upper window will display various communication parameters. This window doesn't list all the parameters and you can use the arrow keys to scroll through the list, where you will see maximum packet receive buffers. Figure 19-4 shows an example of what the MONITOR screen looks like. You can increase the value of the parameter and press ENTER. A good guideline is to set the value of the maximum packet receive buffers to twice the size of the minimum packet receive buffers.

FIGURE 19-4

Setting maximum packet receive buffers in MONITOR

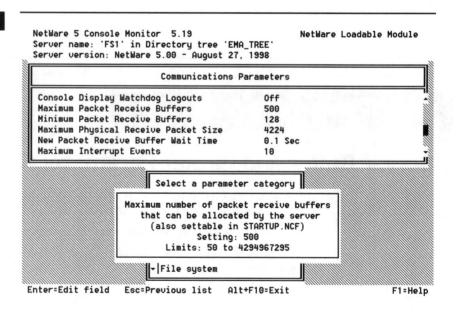

```
NetWare 5 Console Monitor  5.19                 NetWare Loadable Module
Server name: 'FS1' in Directory tree 'EMA_TREE'
Server version: NetWare 5.00 - August 27, 1998
┌──────────────────────────────────────────────────────────────────┐
│                      Communications Parameters                     │
├──────────────────────────────────────────────────────────────────┤
│ Console Display Watchdog Logouts          Off                   ▲  │
│ Maximum Packet Receive Buffers            500                      │
│ Minimum Packet Receive Buffers            128                      │
│ Maximum Physical Receive Packet Size      4224                  █  │
│ New Packet Receive Buffer Wait Time       0.1 Sec                  │
│ Maximum Interrupt Events                  10                    ▼  │
└──────────────────────────────────────────────────────────────────┘
                ┌─────────────────────────────────┐
                │    Select a parameter category  │
                ├─────────────────────────────────┤
                │ Maximum number of packet receive buffers │
                │   that can be allocated by the server    │
                │     (also settable in STARTUP.NCF)       │
                │            Setting: 500                  │
                │       Limits: 50 to 4294967295           │
                └──────────────────────────────────────────┘
                     ▼ File system

Enter=Edit field    Esc=Previous list    Alt+F10=Exit          F1=Help
```

Minimum Packet Receive Buffers

Along with maximum packet receive buffers, there are minimum packet receive buffers. If minimum packet receive is set to higher than 10 and the server doesn't respond to the network requests, you can increase this setting, similar to increasing the maximum packet receive buffer setting.

In MONITOR, select the Server Parameters and Communications from the Available Options screen. Scroll through the list with the arrow keys and select Minimum Packet Receive Buffers. You can increase or decrease this value the same as you did with the maximum packet receive buffers. The rule of thumb here is to allocate at least two packet buffers for each workstation connected to the server.

CERTIFICATION OBJECTIVE 19.06

Block Suballocation

To optimize the use of disk space NetWare uses what is known as *block suballocation*. Disk space is divided into blocks just as memory is divided into blocks. The default setting for some operating systems is 4- or 16-kilobyte blocks. This makes for inefficient use of disk space. Figure 19-5 illustrates how disk space is allocated.

As you see in Figure 19-5, a disk can be divided into 4K blocks. When this is done a block is a block, no matter what the file size is. For example, if a 2K file is written to disk, a whole 4K block is allocated to that 2K file, leaving 2K of unusable space. If you think about the number of files on a disk over time, this can add up to quite a bit of wasted space.

With block suballocation that same 2K file is written to disk, using 512-byte blocks, which means 4 blocks are used, and the remaining 4 blocks are left free and available for other files. One thing to remember is that block suballocation can be set only when a volume is created. If a volume exists without block suballocation and has existing data, you cannot simply set the volume for block suballocation.

FIGURE 19-5	Disk space with and without block suballocation

4K Blocks

Block suballocation
with
512-byte blocks

CERTIFICATION OBJECTIVE 19.07

Enabling File Compression

Another factor in disk space optimization is *file compression*. When a volume is created on a NetWare server, file compression is enabled by default. If file compression is not enabled on a volume, you can enable it at a later time with a SET statement. The nice thing about file compression on NetWare is that you can enable it and disable with NetWare Administrator or at the DOS command line with FLAG.EXE.

There are a series of parameters that can be used to determine how file compression works on a NetWare server. One of these is *Days Untouched Before Compression*. If files are used regularly, they will not be compressed. Files are compressed only if they haven't been used for the number days set in this parameter.

Another key SET parameter is *Minimum Percentage Compression Gain*. If compressing a file will not save any disk space, then the file will not be compressed. I've seen a lot of files that are compressed by other programs stored on a volume, but NetWare will not compress them again, because nothing is gained in doing so. One thing to remember is that there must be enough disk space available to uncompress a file in order to use it. If the volume cannot accommodate the file with the space needed, you may not be able to access the file.

Disabling File Compression

File compression is enabled or disabled at the volume level and if it was not enabled originally when the volume was created, it can be enabled later, even with data existing on the volume.

The opposite, however, is not true. Once file compression is enabled, you cannot disable it unless you re-create the volume. File compression can be temporarily suspended using the SET command. The parameter Enable File Compression can be used to suspend file compression.

Using NetWare Administrator to Configure File Compression

You can use NetWare Administrator to configure compression for a file or a directory. There are a couple of different settings you can configure. The attributes are either *Immediate Compress* or *Don't Compress*.

There are two things that are needed before you can configure these options with NetWare Administrator. The first is to make sure that file compression is enabled for the volume, and that you have the Modify right for the files and directories you want to configure. Using the ADMIN account or an equivalent will give these rights throughout the file system. In Exercise 19-2 you will make changes to some files on your NetWare Server.

Configuring Compression Attributes

1. Open NetWare Administrator by selecting it from the appropriate directory.

2. Find one of the Server Volumes in the Directory Tree.

3. Select a file that you want to change the compression configuration on.

4. From the Object Menu choose Details, or right-click the file and choose Details.

5. Choose the Attributes option on the right of the details window. The following illustration shows the result of selecting the Attributes option on the details window.

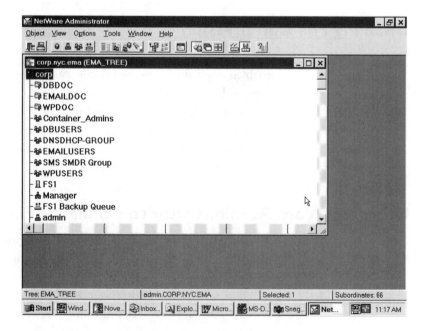

6. From the File Attributes you can choose either Immediate Compress or Don't Compress.

7. Choose OK and then select a Directory.

8. From the Object Menu choose Details, or right-click the Directory and choose Details.

9. Choose the Attributes on the right of the Details window.

10. From the File Attributes choose either Immediate Compress or Don't Compress.

11. Choose OK.

on the **Job**

When you choose a directory to change the attributes on, the attributes of all the files in that directory are changed.

CERTIFICATION OBJECTIVE 19.08

Packet Burst

When communicating across the network, data is sent in packets. NetWare can use the Packet Burst protocol to speed up communications (see Figure 19-6). Normal communications are sent packet by packet. In this scheme, one packet is sent and then an acknowledgment packet is sent back, creating an inefficient means of communicating.

With *packet burst* a whole group or "burst" of packets can be sent at once. An acknowledgment still has to be sent, but only one acknowledgment is needed for a group of packets. Without using packet burst, one acknowledgment would be needed for each packet. Packet burst creates more efficient communication for two reasons: data is transferred more quickly to and from a client or server, and less network traffic is generated.

One other side to this is that packet burst monitors packet communication and retransmits only missing packets. In normal communications if a packet is not received properly and other packets have been received, the communication has to back up to the error and retransmit from there.

FIGURE 19-6   Packet burst versus normal NCP communication

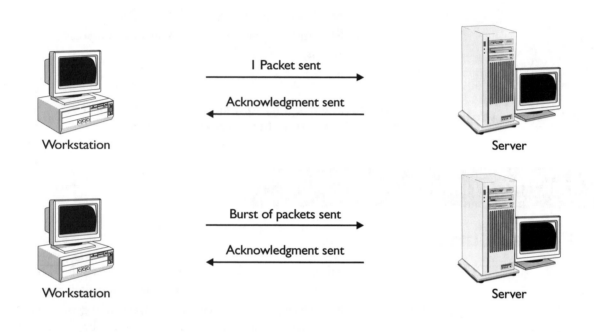

If a client is using packet burst and encounters a server that is not using packet burst, then the communication defaults down to normal NCP communication. So remember that both ends of the communication medium need to be using packet burst for the results to be worthy.

CERTIFICATION OBJECTIVE 19.09

Large Internet Packets

Large Internet Packets (LIP), allows the maximum size of internetwork packets to be larger than in previous versions of NetWare. The earlier maximum was 576 bytes. In versions earlier than NetWare 4.11, the client would have to negotiate with the server to agree on a packet size. Ethernet and Token Ring architectures can support packet sizes larger than 576 bytes. LIP allows the client to use a packet size based on the maximum size supported by the router.

To configure a Windows 95/98 workstation using the NetWare client to use LIP, you can do the following. On the workstation open up the Control Panel in Windows 95 and open the Network applet. Highlight the Novell NetWare Client and click the Properties button. In the Advanced Settings Tab, verify that Large Internet Packets support is enabled. LIP is automatically enabled at the workstation and server. Click Apply, Exit the applet, and close Control Panel.

CERTIFICATION SUMMARY

Ensuring that a network server is working as efficiently as possible is an important administrative task. In this chapter we discussed some of the basics and tried to focus on what you may see on your exam.

One big factor in server performance is the amount of RAM installed. Remember that a minimum of 64MB of RAM is needed for a NetWare 5 server. There are different types of memory. The first is RAM, which is used by the "live" active applications and NLMs. The second is virtual memory, which is an extension of RAM that is stored in a swap file on a volume. We also touched briefly on a couple of new items for NetWare: Logical Memory Addressing, which keeps memory fragmentation to a minimum, and Protected Memory, which allows for applications or NLMs that are not stable to be loaded and not crash the server. Also remember that a routine known as garbage collection frees up memory that has been released by NLMs that were unloaded.

The Console statements you can use to configure virtual memory are listed in Table 19-1.

NetWare MONITOR is a utility you can use to gauge and monitor memory and communication statistics, to determine how much memory is available, as well as what is using the memory.

Cache Buffer Memory will help you determine whether the amount of physical memory is adequate. You can also look at Loaded Modules to see which modules are taking up large amounts of memory.

In the area of network communication you can make sure your minimum and maximum packet receive buffers are set to appropriate standards. Two rules of thumb here are to set the value of the maximum packet receive buffers to twice the size of the minimum packet receive buffers, and to allocate at least two packet buffers for each workstation connected to the server.

Block suballocation controls how data is stored on the hard drive(s). Enabling block suballocation results in more efficient use of space on the hard drive(s). Block suballocation must be set when the volume is created. It cannot be set once the volume is in use and has data on it without recreating the volume.

File compression is another way to optimize space on the hard drive(s). File compression is turned on by default, and can be enabled later if it isn't on when the volume is created. The thing to remember here though is that file compression cannot be turned off on a volume without recreating the volume. However, it can be suspended.

Two other communication optimization settings are packet burst and Large Internet Packets. Packet burst allows a burst or group of packets to be sent versus one packet at a time. This helps speed up communications, as opposed to between clients and servers and cuts down on network traffic. Large Internet Packets allows the workstation to use a larger packet size when communicating across the network.

 TWO-MINUTE DRILL

❑ NetWare requires a minimum of 64MB of RAM and can access up to 4GB of RAM.

❑ When a server is loaded, the SERVER.EXE file is executed. Afterwards, all remaining memory is cache memory.

❑ Cache memory is available for NLM programs and other services and processes. Data stored in cache is stored in 4-kilobyte blocks, which are called cache buffers.

❑ NetWare is considered a self-tuning operating system.

❑ Physical memory is known as RAM (Random Access Memory). RAM is where programs and modules are loaded that are used on the server.

❑ There are different types of memory—permanent storage, RAM, and virtual memory.

❑ When NLMs are loaded, a certain amount of memory is allocated to each specific NLM.

❑ There are two key points to remember about memory in NetWare 5—first, that virtual memory is available, and second, that a routine called garbage collection is run when memory is deallocated.

❑ Garbage collection is a memory recovery process that periodically collects previously allocated memory that has been freed. The memory is returned to the cache for use by other NLMs or programs.

❑ NetWare 5 has a new virtual memory feature that allows items stored in RAM to be swapped to the hard drive. This frees up RAM for other purposes and can make the server more efficient.

❑ There are a series of commands that you use to manage the virtual memory configuration on your server console. They enable you to establish, delete, and change the swap file configuration on the server.

❑ If RAM is running low, the swap file is utilized more frequently, causing the hard drive(s) to thrash. To curb disk thrashing add more RAM to the server.

❑ Use MONITOR to check if physical RAM is sufficient, and to determine which NLMs are using large amounts of memory.

❑ NetWare uses packet receive buffers to store incoming data until the server can process it. NetWare has parameters that specify the maximum and minimum packet receive buffer amounts. Using MONITOR, you can view and change the maximum and minimum packet receive buffers settings.

❑ To optimize the use of disk space, NetWare uses what is known as block suballocation. Block suballocation can be set only when a volume is created.

❑ When a volume is created on a NetWare server, file compression is enabled by default. If file compression is not enabled when the volume is created, it can be enabled at a later time with a SET statement. You can enable and disable file compression with NetWare Administrator or at the DOS command line.

❑ Once file compression is enabled, you cannot disable it unless you re-create the volume. File compression can be temporarily suspended using the SET command. The parameter Enable File Compression can be used to suspend file compression.

❑ You can use NetWare Administrator to configure compression for a file or a directory. There are two different settings you can configure, including Immediate Compress or Don't Compress.

❑ NetWare can use the Packet Burst protocol to speed up communications. With packet burst, a whole group or "burst" of packets can be sent at once. One acknowledgment is sent for a group of packets versus one acknowledgment for each packet.

❑ Large Internet Packets (LIP) allows the maximum size of internetwork packets to be larger than the earlier maximum size of 576 bytes. LIP allows the client to use a packet size based on the maximum size supported by the router.

SELF TEST

The following Self-Test questions will help you measure your understanding of the material presented in this chapter. Read all the choices carefully, as there may be more than one correct answer. Choose all correct answers for each question.

1. What is the minimum amount of RAM needed for a NetWare 5 server?

   A. 48MB RAM

   B. 64MB RAM

   C. 96MB RAM

   D. 128MB RAM

2. If a server doesn't have enough physical memory installed, it will use _____ memory, which is an extension of RAM.

   A. Hard drive

   B. Read Only

   C. Virtual

   D. Logical

3. When an NLM releases the memory it was using when it is unloaded, which routine has to be run to recover the memory so the server can make it available for other NLMs or processes?

   A. Memory clean-up

   B. RAM Optimization

   C. Memory Reallocation Process 4

   D. Garbage collection

4. What do you type at the console prompt to create a swap file on a volume?

   A. SWAP ADD *volume_name [parameter=x]*

   B. ADD SWAP *volume_name [parameter=x]*

   C. SWAP *volume_name [parameter=x]*

   D. SWAP CREATE *volume_name [parameter=x]*

5. Where can a swap file be created? (Choose all that apply.)

   A. On a mounted volume

   B. On an unmounted volume

   C. On any NetWare Volume

   D. On the C: Drive

6. When your server is doing a lot of swapping of data between RAM and the hard drive, this is known as _____.

   A. Heavy swapping

   B. Disk thrashing

   C. Garbage collection

   D. Virtual memory overload

7. In NetWare, what happens when data is received by the network card, but cannot be processed by the server?

   A. The data is lost.

   B. The data is stored in a swap file.

   C. The data is stored in packet receive buffers.

   D. The server will crash if this happens.

8. What is the minimum recommended setting for packet receive buffers?

   A. Twice that of maximum packet receive buffers

   B. Half that of maximum packet receive buffers

   C. At least ten packets per workstation connected to the server

   D. At least two packets per workstation connected to the server

9. What do you call it when data is stored more efficiently in 512-byte blocks on a NetWare volume?

   A. Virtual memory

   B. Block suballocation

   C. Logical Memory Addressing

   D. File compression

10. To save disk space, NetWare 5 uses _____ to store data on a server. This can be enabled after the server has been in service for awhile, but cannot be disabled without re-creating a volume.

    A. File compression

    B. Block suballocation

    C. Packet burst

    D. Protected storage area

11. What is used to send more than one packet at a time to make server communication more efficient and reduce network traffic?

    A. Block suballocation

    B. Packet burst

    C. Virtual memory

    D. Multipacket compression

12. NetWare uses _____ to be able to transmit packets at more than 576 bytes each.

    A. Large Packet Burst Protocol

    B. Virtual IP Protocol

    C. Large Internet Packets

    D. Memory Burst Packets

13. What utility can you use to change the maximum packet receive buffers parameter? (Choose all that apply.)

    A. A SET statement at the console prompt

    B. NWADMIN

    C. MONITOR

    D. SYSCON

14. What is the maximum amount of memory a NetWare 5 server can access?

    A. 64MB RAM

    B. 256MB RAM

    C. 1GB RAM

    D. 4GB RAM

15. Which of the following do you type at the console prompt so that the server will display an alert on the console whenever excessive swapping occurs?

    A. SET AVERAGE PAGE IN ALERT THRESHOLD = x

    B. SET PAGE ALERT THRESHOLD AVERAGE = x

    C. SET AVERAGE ALERT IN PAGE THRESHOLD = x

    D. SET PAGE ALERT AVERAGE THRESHOLD = x

20

Backing Up Servers and Workstations

CERTIFICATION OBJECTIVES

20.01   Introduction to Storage Management
         Services

20.02   Choosing a Backup Strategy

20.03   Backing Up a NetWare Server

20.04   Restoring Data

Choosing a backup strategy is one of the most important decisions you will make as a network administrator. You can have the best hardware and software combination with the fastest configured server, but if it crashes and you do not have a backup, it is all over and your company can incur catastrophic costs.

In this chapter we will discuss the process of selecting a backup solution that fits your company's needs. We will also walk through the steps of backing up and restoring server and workstation data.

Introduction to Storage Management Services

Novell NetWare 5 has bundled a backup-and-restore product for simple to complex networks. This combination of services is called *Storage Management Services* (SMS).

The backup process involves three key components:

1. The *host server*   A NetWare server that is running the backup program

2. The *target*   A NetWare server or workstation that is to be backed up

3. The *console workstation*   The machine that is used to submit the backups and restoration jobs

The host uses an application of SMS to communicate with modules running on the targets. This application will read the information on the targets and send it to the storage device. Figure 20-1 illustrates this process.

A TSA (Target Service Agent) is a program that runs on the target. It allows the SMS application to back up the data on the target.

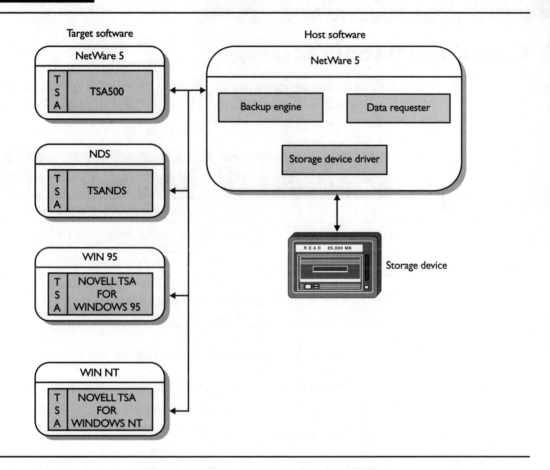

FIGURE 20-1   SMS backup modules

The SMS suite allows you to back up the following types of information and devices:

- NetWare DOS partition
- NDS
- NetWare file system
- GroupWise database
- Windows NT and Windows 95 workstations

CERTIFICATION OBJECTIVE 20.02

Choosing a Backup Strategy

We have three options when choosing our backup strategy: full backup, incremental backup, or differential backup. The following table describes each option.

Type of Backup	Data That Will Be Backed Up	State of Archive Bit
Full	Back up all data every time.	Cleared
Incremental	Back up any file that has been created or modified since last backup.	Cleared
Differential	Back up all files that have been modified or created since last full backup.	Not Cleared

You can use these options in one of three ways:

1. Full backup in combination with incremental backups
2. Full backup in combination with differential backups
3. Full backup every time

e x a m
Ⓦ a t c h

Never combine differential and incremental backups. The incremental backup will not contain all of the information that has been changed since the last full backup.

Time Requirements

When you choose your backup strategy, be sure to also consider the amount of time it takes to back up and restore your data. Figure 20-2 shows the amount of data backed up for each backup strategy.

FIGURE 20-2

Amount of data backed up
with the three backup
options

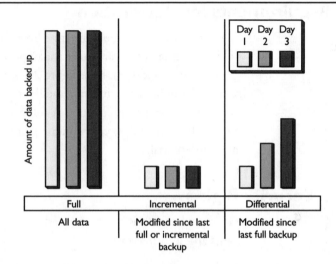

With this information in mind, let's look at the amount of time needed
to perform these backups. Figure 20-3 shows us the time needed to back up
data with each backup option.

Looking at the graph in Figure 20-3, you'll notice that a full backup
requires the most amount of time. A full backup with incremental backups
requires the least amount of time. And a full backup with differential
backups will take longer and longer to back up as the week goes by, until
the time required equals the full backup alone.

FIGURE 20-3

Backup time needed for
each backup option

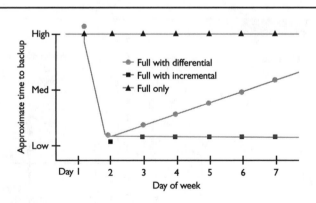

Time Requirements for Restoration

When restoring data, the same time lines for backing up your data do not hold true. In fact, they are quite the opposite, as illustrated in Figure 20-4.

According to the graph in Figure 20-4, a full backup is the fastest to restore. A full backup with incremental is the slowest; you would need to restore each tape in sequence. A full backup with differential is in the middle somewhere; you would restore the full backup and then the latest differential.

Backup Security Rights

The person you assign as backup administrator must be given the following rights and information:

■ To back up the file system, the administrator needs Read and File Scan rights to the file system.

■ To back up NDS, the administrator needs Browse object and Read property rights to the tree.

■ The administrator must also know the passwords of all hosts and target being backed up.

on the job

If the administrator needs to restore the file system or NDS, the administrator will need to have the Create right.

FIGURE 20-4

Time needed to restore data from each backup option

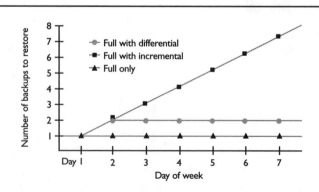

FROM THE CLASSROOM

Backing Up Wisely

Deciding whether to back up the file system is not hard. What is usually a less obvious, yet critical, decision is what to do with the NDS database. Don't forget to back it up. True, it is a distributed, replicated database; but waiting for the synchronization to happen between replicas can be time-consuming and can crowd the bandwidth while critical information is being updated, especially if done over WAN links. Including NDS as part of the backup is prudent and a time saver in the long run, particularly if you've ever experienced a catastrophic disk failure on a server containing several partitions' worth of Master Replicas and have to restore everything.

—By Dan Cheung, CNI, MCNE, MCT

CERTIFICATION OBJECTIVE 20.03

Backing Up a NetWare Server

In this section, we will discuss the steps for backing up servers and workstations. In the previous sections, we talked about time requirements, backup types, and the need to back up your data. Now let's put this knowledge to use.

Backing Up Your Servers and Workstations

SMS can be used to backup and restore data on your server and workstations, using two utilities:

- NWBACK32
- NetWare Backup/restore

There are a series of NLMs that comprise the NetWare backup/restore program that runs on a server. NWBACK32 is a program that runs on a workstation. Both of these programs are included in the NetWare 5 operating system.

The NWBACK32 program is used to configure and send jobs to the NetWare backup/restore program running on a host server. The NetWare backup/restore program processes the job; creates the session; and, once communication is established with the target, it conducts the backup or restoration. See the following illustration of the NWBACK32 interface.

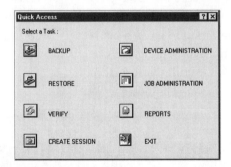

Backup Terminology

Before going further in our discussion, let's review some terms:

- A *target* is any NetWare server or workstation that has the appropriate TSA running. The TSA allows the target to be backed up.

- *TSA (Target Service Agent)* is a program the processes the data between a specific target and the backup host.

- A *host* is a NetWare server that is running the backup/restore program. The server must have a tape device attached to it.

- A *child* is a set of data that has no subordinates. An example of this is a file.

- A *parent* is a set of data that has other sets of data subordinates. An example of this is a directory.

NetWare Backup/Restore Program Guidelines

When using the backup/restore program, keep the following guidelines in mind:

- Load the Backup/Restore program on a server that has the backup device attached.

- Ensure the host server has enough disk space on the volume SYS: (1MB is sufficient).

- Make sure that your media device is large enough to accommodate the data.

- Limit access to the backup program to preserve data integrity.

- Ensure that the error log and backup logs are in the appropriate name space for your system.

- Monitor the size of the temporary files on the SYS: volume. It can get quite large.

- Do not allow any configuration of your server during a backup session.

Backing Up a Novell NetWare 5 Server

There are several pieces of software that must be loaded before you start a backup session. These files differ according to the type of information you are backing up (host or target). In Exercise 20-1, we will walk through the steps required to back up a NetWare 5 file system and NDS.

EXERCISE 20-1

Using the NetWare Backup/Restore Program to Back Up NDS and the File System

1. Make sure the backup device's interface is loaded.

2. If you are using a print queue for reports, make sure it is dedicated and configured.

3. Load the appropriate TSAs. The following table lists the TSAs required to back up NDS and the file system.

To Back Up	At This Console	Enter This Command
NetWare 5 Host server	NetWare 5 host	TSA500
NetWare 5 target	NetWare 5 target	TSA500
NDS	NetWare 5 server with a replica	TSANDS

4. On your NetWare server, load the NetWare backup/restore NLM.

5. At your console workstation, load the NWBACK32.EXE, which is located in the SYS: Public directory.

6. List the information you want to back up.

7. Select the location the information is going to be backed up to.

8. Choose your backup type.

9. Select a schedule for the backup.

10. Enter a description for the backup session.

11. Submit the backup job.

12. Make sure the tape is in the backup unit.

13. Start the backup.

14. Insert tapes as needed.

You can also use the NetWare backup/restore program to back up your Windows 95 and Windows NT workstations that are attached to your network. In Exercise 20-2 we will use SMS to back up a workstation. These steps are similar to the steps used to back up a server.

EXERCISE 20-2

Backing Up Workstations (Win95 and Win NT)

1. Load TSAPROXY at your server console.

2. Load your workstations' TSA (Windows 95 or Windows NT).

3. Load the NetWare backup/restore program at the server.

4. On your console workstation, load the NWBACK32.EXE program.

5. Identify the information you want to back up on the target.

6. Identify the location where the tape unit exists.

7. Specify your backup type.

8. Select a backup schedule.

9. Enter a description for the backup.

10. Submit your backup job.

11. Make sure that the tape is in the backup unit.

12. Start the backup.

13. Add tapes as needed.

CERTIFICATION OBJECTIVE 20.04

Restoring Data

What good are backups if you cannot restore them? In Exercise 20-3 we will go through the steps necessary to restore the data from a host server, target server, or target workstation.

The basic steps required to restore data are the same for a host, target, or workstation.

EXERCISE 20-3

Restoring Data

1. Make sure that your tape device driver is loaded.

2. Load any necessary TSAs.

3. Load the NetWare backup/restore NLM.

4. Load the NWBACK32.EXE program.

5. Select the target you want to restore data to.

6. Log in to the target if necessary.

7. Find the tape that has the data to be restored.

8. Select the tape device.

9. Select the session name to be restored.

10. Pick the data you want restored.

11. Select a schedule.

12. Submit your restore.

That is all there is to restoring data. One thing to keep in mind is to pick a backup method that fits your company's needs. If time is important during a backup session, pick a faster backup method (full with differential). But remember that this option requires a fair amount of time to restore. You must consider both ends of the cycle when choosing the backup/restore method for your company.

QUESTIONS AND ANSWERS

If I have Windows 3.x workstations, can I use SMS to back them up?	No. SMS currently backs up only Windows 95 and Windows NT.
I run a 24 × 7 server; which backup method is best for me?	Full with incremental; however, if you need to do a restore, it will take longer.
Can I back up my NDS and file system at the same time?	Yes. Load TSANDS and TSA500 on the server to be backed up.
I am the backup administrator and the server will not allow me to restore any data.	Make sure you have the required rights to restore data. They are different from the rights needed to back up data.
Can SMS be used in place of another nationally known backup program?	Yes. SMS is fully integrated into NetWare 5. It has a rerun scheduler to allow you to set a backup schedule.

CERTIFICATION SUMMARY

In this chapter, we discussed the importance of backing up your servers and workstations. We have described the different types of backups available and how you should go about selecting your method.

We walked through the entire SMS backup and restoration process. These exercises were designed to give you a feel of what it is like to use these tools. It is important to realize that SMS is a critical part of NetWare, while the backup programs are only a small component of SMS. There are many commercially available backup programs, so you need to understand the processes involved in deciding which methods to use.

 # TWO-MINUTE DRILL

- ❑ Novell NetWare 5 has bundled a backup-and-restore product for simple to complex networks. This combination of services is called Storage Management Services (SMS). The backup process involves three key components: the host server, the target, and the console workstation.

- ❑ We have three options when choosing our backup strategy: full backup, incremental backup, or differential backup. You can use these options in one of three ways: full backup in combination with incremental backups, full backup in combination with differential backups, and full backup every time.

- ❑ A full backup requires the most amount of time to complete. A full backup with incremental backups requires the least amount of time to complete. A full backup with differential backups will take longer and longer to complete, until the time required equals the full backup alone.

- ❑ A full backup is the fastest to restore. A full backup with incremental is the slowest; you would need to restore each tape in sequence. A full backup with differential is in the middle somewhere; you would restore the full backup and then the latest differential.

- ❑ A backup administrator must be given the following rights and information: Read and File Scan rights to back up the file system, and Browse object and Read property rights to the NDS tree to back up NDS. The administrator must also know the passwords of all hosts and target being backed up.

❑ SMS can be used to back up and restore data on your server and workstations using two utilities: NWBACK32 and NetWare Backup/restore.

❑ There are a series of NLMs that comprise the NetWare backup/restore program that runs on a server. NWBACK32 is a program that runs on a workstation. Both of these programs are included in the NetWare 5 operating system.

❑ The NWBACK32 program is used to configure and send jobs to the NetWare backup/restore program running on a host server. The NetWare backup/restore program processes the job; creates the session; and, once communication is established with the target, it conducts the backup or restoration

❑ Pick a backup method that fits your company's needs. If time is important during a backup session, pick a faster backup method (full with differential). But remember that this option requires a fair amount of time to restore. You must consider both ends of the cycle when choosing the backup/restore method for your company.

SELF TEST

The following Self-Test questions will help you measure your understanding of the material presented in this chapter. Read all the choices carefully, as there may be more than one correct answer. Choose all correct answers for each question.

1. What does SMS stand for?

   A. Storage Management Server

   B. Storage Management System

   C. Selective Management System

   D. Self Management System

2. What type of information will SMS back up?

   A. NetWare DOS partition

   B. NDS

   C. NetWare file system

   D. Windows NT and Windows 95 workstations

   E. All of the above

3. Can you mix differential and incremental backups?

   A. Yes

   B. No

4. Which backup strategy requires the most amount of time?

   A. Full

   B. Full with Differential

   C. Full with Incremental

5. What basic rights are needed on the file system to back it up?

   A. Read

   B. Read and File Scan

   C. Read and Compare

   D. Browse

6. What rights are needed for NDS to back it up?

   A. Browse

   B. Read

   C. Browse and Compare

   D. Browse and Read

7. What is the purpose of NWBACK32?

   A. To configure and load your backup device

   B. To view error logs

   C. To configure and send backup jobs to the host

   D. To modify name space for the backup

8. What is a target?

   A. A server that all data is backed up to

   B. A server that is backed up running a TSA

   C. A workstation that is backed up running a TSA

   D. Both A and B

9. What does TSA stand for?

   A. Target Service Agent

   B. Terminate and Stay Active

   C. Target Service Advisor

   D. Target System Advisor

10. What is a host?

    A. A server running the backup/restore program with a tape drive

    B. A server running a TSA with a tape drive

    C. A server running a TSA and the backup/restore program

    D. A server directing the backup process.

11. To run the backup/restore program, how much space is needed on the host's SYS: volume?

    A. 10MB

    B. 1MB

    C. 1GB

    D. 10GB

12. What is the console command to back up a NetWare 5 host server?

    A. NWBACK32

    B. TSAHOST

    C. TSANDS

    D. TSA500

13. What is the console command to back up NDS on a NetWare 5 server?

    A. NWBACK32

    B. TSAPROXY

    C. TSANDS

    D. TSA500

14. What is the console command to load the TSA to back up a workstation?

    A. TSAWKSTN

    B. TSANT

    C. TSAPROXY

    D. TSANDS

CERTIFIED NOVELL ENGINEER

21

Using DNS/DHCP Services

CERTIFICATION OBJECTIVES

21.01	DNS/DHCP Overview
21.02	Installing DNS/DHCP Services
21.03	Configuring and Starting DHCP Services
21.04	Exporting and Importing DHCP Databases
21.05	Configuring and Starting DNS Services
21.06	Exporting and Importing DNS Databases

N etWare 5 is geared toward the Internet. With NetWare 5, it is easier than ever to set up a Web server, configure a LAN to enable Web surfing, and set up your own intranet. First, of course, you need to configure some components in NetWare 5 that will make this process easier for end users. Remember that one of the goals of a good network administrator is to make network access easier for our users.

The first component to configure is DNS (Domain Name Service). We discussed this briefly in Chapter 16. Domain Name Service enables you to surf the Web or establish a server on the Internet. The second component to configure is DHCP (Dynamic Host Configuration Protocol). This component of NetWare also makes the administrator's job a little easier.

DNS/DHCP Overview

Before NetWare 5, the main (or core) protocol was IPX, which was Novell's mainstay for a long time. With the explosion of the Internet in the past 10 years, the need for IP support became more pressing. Previous versions of NetWare supported IP, but not natively. The NCP (NetWare Core Protocol) was supported only over IPX. With NetWare 5, it is now supported over IP.

What this means for NetWare is that administrators can make DNS and DHCP part of the NDS. With these services integrated into the NDS, we now have a central place from which to administer them. Having centralized administration of enterprise network components makes NetWare an easier network operating system to work with.

Domain Name Service

The Domain Name Service is a very important part of the Internet. It takes numeric IP addresses and ties them to a name that is easy for people to remember. We have all seen commercials that advertise www.something.com. These URLs are easy for us to remember. Novell's Web site, for example, is http:\\www.novell.com.

This sounds simplistic, but remember, computers use numbers. All Web sites have an IP address associated with them but we would prefer to use the common language names instead. This is where the Domain Name Service comes into play. It runs on a server and basically manages a database that matches Internet names to IP addresses. There are many different DNS servers on the Internet, and they learn from each other.

Dynamic Host Configuration Protocol

When you have a large network that uses TCP/IP as its main protocol, you don't want to have to go to each workstation to configure the IP portion. With IP, remember that you need at least an IP address and a subnet mask configured before the workstation will function properly.

Along with these two most basic components, you often have to configure a gateway IP address, as well as an IP configuration for your DNS servers. This all takes time and it would be nice if we could have a computer simply give us all this information each time we log in to the network, and DHCP (Dynamic Host Configuration Protocol) does exactly this. It dynamically configures the host (workstation) with its IP information.

Installing DNS/DHCP Services

When NetWare 5 is installed, the files to run DNS/DHCP services are automatically copied to the SYS: volume. To complete the installation and use DNS/DHCP services you have to do the following:

1. Extend the NDS schema and create the appropriate objects.

2. Install the Novell client on the machine that will run the management console for DNS/DHCP services.

3. Install the management console and NWADMIN32 snap-in files.

These three steps should be done in the order given. There are three ways to extend the NDS schema. The first is to install the DNS/DHCP services during the initial NetWare installation. The second way is to install the services later using the NetWare installation program from the GUI interface. The third is to use the DNIPINST.NLM. NWADMIN32 with the additional objects, as shown in Figure 21-1.

Exercise 21-1 will take you through extending the NDS schema and creating the needed objects for DNS/DHCP services.

FIGURE 21-1

NWADMIN32 with extended schema

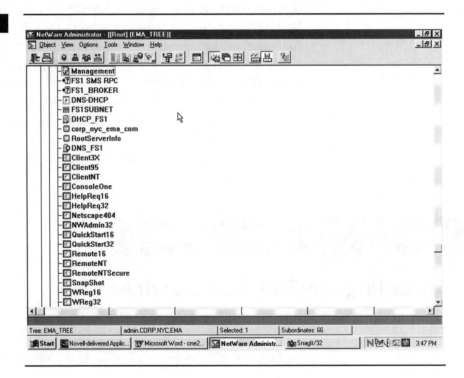

Using the NetWare Installation to Install DNS/DHCP Services

1. First, launch the NetWare Installation program by clicking the Novell menu button and then selecting Install.

2. In the Installed Products window, click the New Product button.

3. You must provide the path to the source files. You can use the Browse button to find the files needed.

4. One you provide the path, click OK.

5. In the Additional Products and Services window, select the Novell DNS/DHCP Services box and click Next.

6. Now you must authenticate yourself to NDS. Type the Full Distinguished Name of a user with Supervisor/Admin rights to the [Root], and then enter the password. Click OK.

7. You must now enter the context in which you want the object for DNS/DHCP services to reside.

8. Once you enter the context, click Next; in the Summary window, click the Finish button.

9. Once the installation is complete, you can click Yes to reboot your server.

Of course this is only the first step in the complete installation of DNS/DHCP services. Now we will look at the installation of the management console piece and the NetWare Administrator snap-in files.

In order to manage the objects in the NDS that were created when you first installed the services, you must install the DNS/DHCP Management Console. You must also install the snap-in files for NWADMIN32. Fortunately, this is all one process. To install the DNS/DHCP Management Console, complete Exercise 21-2. For this exercise make sure that you are logged in as your Admin user or the equivalent.

EXERCISE 21-2	**Installing the DNS/DHCP Management Console and NWADMIN32 Snap-In Files**

1. Choose Start, Run, and Browse.

2. Browse to the SYS:PUBLIC\DNSDHCP\SETUP.EXE and click OK.

3. Read the welcome screen and click Next.

4. Next you will see the path to install the files. For this exercise, keep the default and click Next.

5. The files will copy to their destinations and then you will see a screen that says Copy the Snap-in files. Click Next.

6. You will be prompted for a path to install the files.

7. Type **SYS:PUBLIC\WIN32** and click OK.

8. Click Next. You will be prompted to view the README file. Click Yes and read the file.

9. Close the file when you have finished and click OK.

Now that you have these items installed, you can administer the objects. In the next section we will look at configuring and starting the services.

CERTIFICATION OBJECTIVE 21.03

Configuring and Starting DHCP Services

Now that we know how to install the components necessary to have DHCP/DNS services on our servers, we must configure them. To do this, we need to complete a couple of items.

The first is to decide which server will be our DHCP server, if we have more than one server. Once we make this decision, we can configure the IP information that we want the DHCP server to assign to the workstations. The next thing we need to do is start the DHCP service once it is configured.

To configure and start the service we can use the snap-in to NWADMIN32. From the Tools menu, we can configure the service as shown in Figure 21-2.

There is another way to launch the Management Console in Windows 95 and Windows NT: a shortcut is created on your desktop during installation. The one difference between these two methods is that when you launch the console from NWADMIN32, the tree you are browsing is the target NDS tree. When you launch Management Console from the desktop, you will be prompted for the target NDS tree.

Within the DNS/DHCP Management Console there are two tabs that allow you to configure each service. The first tab is the DNS Service tab, as shown in Figure 21-3. The tab and window look similar to most of the configuration windows in NetWare: a list is on the left and information is

FIGURE 21-2

DNS/DHCP items in the Tools menu of NWADMIN32

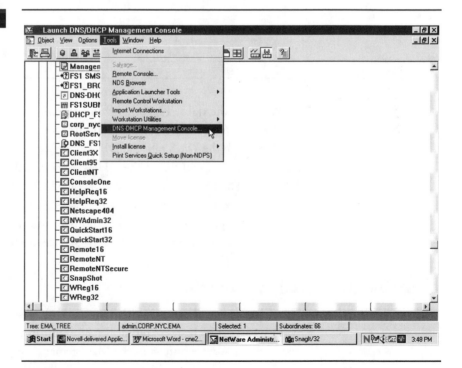

FIGURE 21-3

The DNS tab in the
Management Console

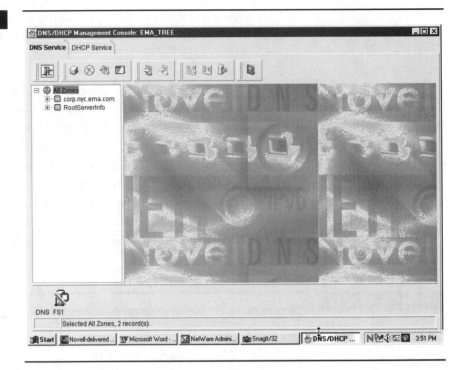

displayed on the right. The other thing you will notice is that there is a
third window with more configuration information.

Along with the DNS tab, the DHCP tab has configuration items for that
service. The look and feel of the DHCP tab is a little different than the
DNS tab. The DHCP tab has a couple of subtabs within the window that
show server configuration items, as well as an Options tab. There are still
three windowpanes with the DHCP information. Figure 21-4 shows the
Management Console with the DHCP Service tab in the foreground.

Creating the DHCP Server Object

Our focus here will be on configuring the DHCP service. The first thing
you have to do is create a DHCP Server object in the tree. To do this, you
can click the Create button in the Management Console DHCP Service
window; then click DHCP Server; and, finally, click OK. Now you have to

FIGURE 21-4

FIGURE 21-4

The DHCP tab in the
Management Console

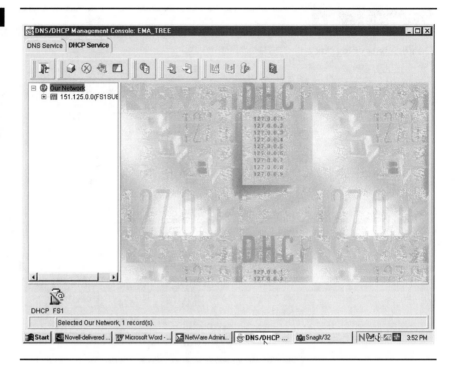

select which server in your tree you want to be the DHCP server. If you
have only one server, the decision is easy; if you have more than one server,
then your preplanning should tell you which one to use. Once you
determine which server will be the DHCP server, you can click the Create
button and you will see the DHCP server you created in the bottom
window. If you click the object in the bottom window, a details screen
will appear.

Creating the Subnet Object

A network can be subdivided into smaller networks called *subnets*. Now that
we have a DHCP server, we have to be able to set up a subnet. To set up
and configure the subnet information for your network, create another
object called the Subnet object. When you select Subnet, you will be
presented with a dialog box like the one in Figure 21-5.

FIGURE 21-5

Create Subnet dialog box

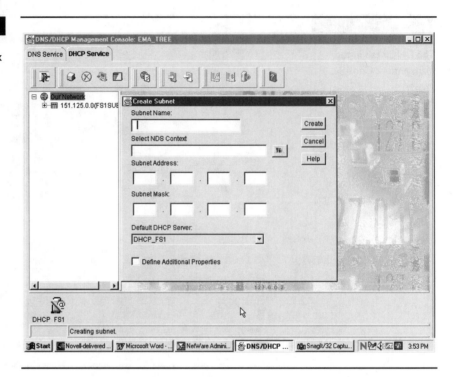

You must enter the information shown in Figure 21-5 to properly configure the Subnet object. The name can be anything you want. The Subnet address and Subnet mask are specific to your network. This information could be provided by your ISP, or by Internic if you have a set of IP addresses directly from them.

Creating the Subnet Address Range (SAR) Object

Once you have your Subnet object defined, you have to configure the Subnet Address Range object that tells the server what address it can give to workstations. To create this object, you must have the Subnet object highlighted and click the Create button on the toolbar. The Create DHCP objects dialog box then changes. You will see two additional objects since the Subnet object is now a container. Select Subnet Address Range and then you will be prompted to enter some information, as shown in Figure 21-6.

FIGURE 21-6

Create Subnet Address
Range window

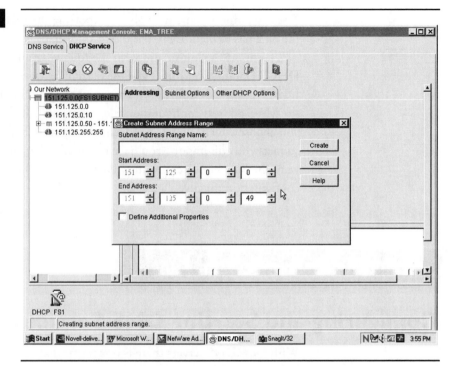

Name the object and then enter the starting and ending addresses of your subnet range. When you click Create, the object is added to the NDS.

In this particular section, we are simplifying a couple of the items because we want to focus on the test-specific items: installation and basic configuration. Other Novell courses and exams go into further detail on DNS and DHCP for the Master CNE course track.

CERTIFICATION OBJECTIVE 21.04

Exporting and Importing DHCP Databases

When upgrading a server, you may have previous DHCP information configured. When this is the case, you can use the DNS/DHCP Management Console to import this DHCP configuration information.

The key point to remember about importing the DHCP information is that the data has to be in DHCP 2.0 or 3.0 format.

To import the information, do the following: First, click the Import DHCP Database button. Type the path or browse to the path of the DHCP information file. If you are importing a DHCP 2.0 file, you can use the MAC address configuration file. Now you will see a window that will let you choose which subnets you want to import. After you select which subnets you will import, you have to specify where in the NDS tree you want the Subnet objects created. Next, select a DHCP server to manage the configuration; finally, click OK.

CERTIFICATION OBJECTIVE 21.05

Configuring and Starting DNS Services

With most DNS servers there is one server that keeps the DNS information. This server generally queries other DNS servers on the Internet for updates. This is true in a network configuration having replica name servers that allow for load balancing and prevents us from having a single point of failure on the network. The updates are made on one master server, and the replica servers get the updates from this master server. Configuration updates to replica servers are called *zone transfers*.

With DNS in NetWare 5, the information and configuration is stored in NDS objects. These objects are replicated throughout the network just like any other NDS objects, for fault tolerance. DNS information is stored in *zones*. A zone contains all the information about a certain part of the domain name space. An object in the NDS represents the zone. The DNS Zone object can represent three kinds of zones:

- A standard DNS zone
- An IN-ADDR.ARPA zone
- An IP6.INT zone

There are two types of zone objects within these three zone types: the primary DNS zone or a secondary DNS zone. When you create a DNS Server object in the NDS, you are creating a server that can respond to DNS queries. To create the object, click the Create object on the DNS Service tab and then click DNS Server. When you click OK you will then be prompted to select which Server object you want to designate as a DNS Server object. You must name the server and then enter a Domain that the DNS server will be in.

Along with the DNS Server object comes the DNS Zone object. The Zone object is a container object that contains all the information for a single DNS zone. If you need to have multiple domains, you must have multiple domain objects. To create a Zone object, click the All Zones object on the DNS Services tab and click the Create button on the toolbar. Choose Zone and click OK. You will see a screen similar to Figure 21-7.

FIGURE 21-7

Create Zone window

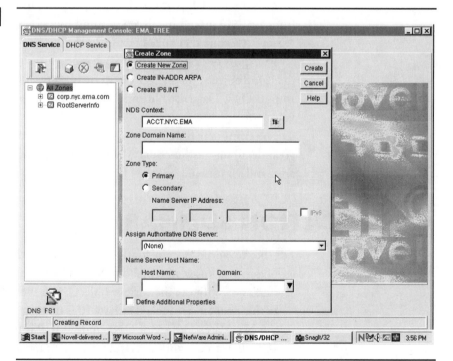

Once the Zone object is in the tree, we can create a Resource Record object that contains the details that actually perform the name resolution. The types of resource records include CNAME records, MX records, and PTR records. The key point for the exam is that once a resource record is created, it cannot be modified. To change a resource record you must delete it and then re-create it.

To learn more about DNS configuration, go to http://www.novell.com and check into the various AppsNotes and other documentation that is available on this subject.

CERTIFICATION OBJECTIVE 21.06

Exporting and Importing DNS Databases

As with the DHCP portion of NetWare, you can import DNS information from a BIND master file. Keep in mind that you will get an error if you try to import a zone that already exists in the tree.

To export or import DNS information, you simply have to expand all the Zone objects, then select the Zone objects, and click the Export or Import DNS Database button. Follow the prompts to move the data where you want it.

The exam may have you go through a basic export, but will not go into great detail on this function. Make sure you understand how to get to the area, and you should be ready for the questions.

CERTIFICATION SUMMARY

For the Advanced Administration exam, the key thing to remember is that as long as you know a little about NWADMIN, and know how to get around and configure the various objects, you should be okay.

In this chapter, we looked at how IP is playing an increasingly important role in NetWare. The use of DNS and DHCP is becoming more common. DHCP allows a network operating system to dynamically configure its clients with IP information, making network administration easier. Along with this you can also establish your NetWare server as a DNS server, and handle IP-to-Internet name resolution. DNS is the service that assigns easy-to-remember names to numeric IP addresses, which allows us to remember how to get to http:\\www.novell.com on the Web.

The primary tool for managing DNS and DHCP in NetWare 5 is the DNS/DHCP Management Console. Make sure you are familiar with DNS/DHCP Management Console. Be familiar with the basic buttons discussed in this chapter. You will use the Create button on the exam. Know what the different objects in the Management Console are. NDS drives NetWare, and knowing the basics of what these objects are will help you tremendously on the exam.

TWO-MINUTE DRILL

- ❑ The first component to configure is DNS (Domain Name Service).
- ❑ The second component to configure is DHCP (Dynamic Host Configuration Protocol).
- ❑ Before NetWare 5, the main (or core) protocol was IPX, which was Novell's mainstay for a long time.
- ❑ The Domain Name Service is a very important part of the Internet. It takes numeric IP addresses and ties them to a name that is easy for people to remember.
- ❑ With IP, remember that you need at least an IP address and a subnet mask configured before the workstation will function properly.
- ❑ To complete the installation and use DNS/DHCP services, you have to do the following: extend the NDS schema and create the appropriate objects; install the Novell client on the machine that will run the Management Console for DNS/DHCP services; install the Management Console and NWADMIN32 snap-in files.
- ❑ In order to manage the objects in the NDS that were created when you first installed the services, you must install the DNS/DHCP Management Console. You must also install the snap-in files for NWADMIN32.

❑ To configure and start the service we can use the snap-in to NWADMIN32.

❑ Within the DNS/DHCP Management Console there are two tabs that allow you to configure each service.

❑ To create a DHCP Server object in the tree, you can click the Create button in the Management Console DHCP Service window; then click DHCP Server; and, finally, click OK.

❑ A network can be subdivided into smaller networks called subnets. To set up and configure the subnet information for your network, create another object called the Subnet object.

❑ Once you have your Subnet object defined, you have to configure the Subnet Address Range object that tells the server what address it can give to workstations.

❑ To create this object, you must have the Subnet object highlighted and click the Create button on the toolbar.

❑ When upgrading a server, you may have previous DHCP information configured. When this is the case, you can use the DNS/DHCP Management Console to import this DHCP configuration information.

❑ DNS information is stored in *zones*. A zone contains all the information about a certain part of the domain name space. An object in the NDS represents the zone.

❑ The DNS Zone object can represent three kinds of zones: a standard DNS Zone, an IN-ADDR.ARPA zone, and an IP6.INT zone.

❑ Along with the DNS Server object comes the DNS Zone object. The Zone object is a container object that contains all the information for a single DNS zone.

❑ As with the DHCP portion of NetWare, you can import DNS information from a BIND master file. Keep in mind that you will get an error if you try to import a zone that already exists in the tree.

❑ For the Advanced Administration exam, the key thing to remember is that as long as you know a little about NWADMIN, and know how to get around and configure the various objects, you should be okay.

SELF TEST

The following Self-Test questions will help you measure your understanding of the material presented in this chapter. Read all the choices carefully, as there may be more than one correct answer. Choose all correct answers for each question.

1. What does DNS stand for?

    A. Domain Name Service

    B. Dynamic Name Service

    C. Dynamic Name System

    D. Domain Name Systems

2. What does DNS do for a network client?

    A. Resolves filenames to volumes

    B. Resolves Internet names to IP addresses

    C. Resolves Computer Names to Domains in Windows NT

    D. Dynamically Assigns IP addresses to workstations

3. What does DHCP do for a network client?

    A. Resolves filenames to volumes

    B. Resolves Internet names to IP addresses

    C. Resolves Computer Names to Domains in Windows NT

    D. Dynamically Assigns IP addresses to workstations

4. In order to integrate DNS/DHCP into the NDS tree, what steps have to be taken? (Choose all that apply.)

    A. The NDS schema has to be extended.

    B. The Management Console must be installed on the workstation.

    C. The snap-in files have to be installed for NWADMIN32.

    D. DNS has to be given rights to the [Root] of the tree.

5. What are three ways to install DNS/DHCP services on a NetWare server? (Select three.)

    A. Install the services during the original installation.

    B. Use RCONSOLE during the initial installation.

    C. Install from the Installation program GUI after the original installation.

    D. Use DPIPINST.NLM to install the services after the original installation.

6. What does DHCP stand for?

    A. Dynamic Host Connection Protocol

    B. Dynamic Host Configuration Process

    C. Dynamic Host Configuration Protocol

    D. Domain Host Configuration Protocol

7. Where is the SETUP located for the Management Console installation?

    A. SYS:PUBLIC\SETUPDHCP.EXE

    B. SYS:PUBLIC\DNSDHCP\SETUP.EXE

    C. SYS:PUBLIC\DHCPDNS\SETUP.EXE

    D. SYS:PUBLIC\DHCP\SETUP.EXE

8. What are the two ways to launch the Management Console? (Choose all that apply.)

   A. From NWADMIN95

   B. From NWADMIN32

   C. From the desktop shortcut created during installation

   D. From the Start menu in the Control Panel

9. Which object should be created first for proper configuration of the DHCP service?

   A. DHCP Server object

   B. Subnet object

   C. Subnet Address Range object

   D. Subnet Scope

10. What format do the DHCP files have to be in, in order to import them into the tree? (Choose all that apply.)

    A. DHCP 2.0 file

    B. DHCP 1.0 file

    C. DHCP 3.0 file

    D. DHCP 4.0 file

11. What are the three zone types with DNS? (Select three.)

    A. A standard DNS zone

    B. An IN-ADDR.ARPA zone

    C. An IP3.INT zone

    D. An IP6.INT zone

12. When installing DNS/DHCP services, what must you do after selecting the default location and product you want to add?

    A. Enter the location to install the product to.

    B. Authenticate yourself to the CD.

    C. Authenticate yourself to NDS.

    D. Authenticate yourself to DNS.

13. Before NetWare 5, what was the only protocol that supported NCP?

    A. TCP/IP

    B. IPX/SPX

    C. ARP

    D. NCP

14. A person is using his Web browser to go to Novell's Web site. He doesn't know the IP address of the Web site, but he knows that the URL is http:\\www.novell.com. What service allows a user to simply type the Web site name and have the server resolve that name to its IP address?

    A. DHCP

    B. IP Resolution

    C. NDS

    D. DNS

15. When you do not want to configure each workstation manually with its TCP/IP configuration, you can use which service?

    A. DNS

    B. NDS

    C. IP

    D. DHCP

22

Installing a
Web Server

CERTIFICATION OBJECTIVES

22.01   Introduction to the FastTrack Web
        Server

22.02   Installing the FastTrack Web Server

22.03   Configuring the FastTrack Web
        Server

22.04   Troubleshooting the Web Server

Many enterprises today rely increasingly on the Internet, particularly the World Wide Web. Others are extending Internet services internally in an intranet. The popularity of the Internet fueled the interest in a common data format that is both searchable and linkable in a nonstructured manner. The tools used to access this common data are available for all types of workstation operating systems.

CERTIFICATION OBJECTIVE 22.01

Introduction to the FastTrack Web Server

The FastTrack Web Server, which is included on the NetWare 5 CD-ROM, is also available from Netscape through Novonyx, a partnership formed between Novell and Netscape in 1997 for research and development and product management. Netscape's FastTrack Web Server enables a full-service intranet without replacing an existing NetWare network infrastructure. It allows an enterprise to meet their business requirements for:

- Integrated network security
- High performance
- Use of virtual private network (VPN) technology
- Publishing of Web documents
- Internet *or* intranet use

CERTIFICATION OBJECTIVE 22.02

Installing the FastTrack Web Server

The installation can be performed from any Windows 95, Windows 98, or Windows NT client workstation that is running Novell's NetWare Client 32. It can be installed to any NetWare 4.11 or later server in which the logged-in user has administrative rights. There are prerequisites to installing the FastTrack Web Server:

- There must be a NetWare server with sufficient space to unpack the Web server files and subsequently install them.

- There must be a NetWare client with at least 100MB of free space in the default TEMP directory.

- The installer must have administrative rights to the destination NetWare server.

exam
ⓦatch

The FastTrack Web Server installation must occur from a Windows 95, Windows 98, or Windows NT 4.0 workstation.

Minimum Requirements

The client used to install the FastTrack Web Server must run one of the following operating systems along with the Novell Client 32 for that operating system:

- Microsoft Windows 95
- Microsoft Windows 98
- Microsoft Windows NT Workstation 4.0

The client must also have a Web browser program installed, such as Netscape Communicator, which is included on the NetWare 5 CD-ROM in the Products\Netscape\Win32 directory. There must be a CD-ROM drive accessible from the client, and the client must have 100MB of free disk space to store temporary files.

The target NetWare 5 Server, which will run the FastTrack Web Server software, must

- Be configured for the IPX protocol and DNS (Domain Name Server), and support long filenames. Although NetWare 5 servers have LONG.NAM long filename support added to all volumes at installation, this may not be the case with a server that has been upgraded from a prior version of NetWare.

- Have a minimum of 64MB of RAM; more is recommended.

- Have a minimum of 100MB of free space in the SYS: volume.

The installing user must have administrative rights to the SYS: volume of the target NetWare 5 server. In addition, the installer must have the following information available during the FastTrack Web Server installation process:

- IP address of the target NetWare server, subnet mask of the network, and IP default gateway address

- DNS hostname of the target server

- Address of the DNS server used for IP address resolution

Installation

The installation file for FastTrack Web Server is on the NetWare 5 CD-ROM under the Products\Novonyx subdirectory. FastTrack Web Server uses a client/server installation method, which consists of the steps in Exercise 22-1.

EXERCISE 22-1

Installing FastTrack

1. Verify that all prerequisites are met.

2. Log in to the workstation and place the NetWare 5 CD-ROM in the drive.

3. Navigate to the Products\Novonyx subdirectory.

4. Double-click the file SETUP.EXE.

5. Click Finish to start the unpacking of the server files. After they have unpacked, a screen prompting for FastTrack Setup appears. Click Next.

6. Click Yes to accept the license agreement.

7. The next screen prompts for the destination of the FastTrack Server files. Click the Browse button to locate the appropriate destination server and SYS: volume. Note that the files can be installed only into the root of SYS:.

8. The next dialog box sets a host name and IP address, as illustrated in Figure 22-1. By default, the server's IP address is used for both. Verify the values and click Next.

9. The next dialog box requests the TCP port number for the Web services. The standard port number used on the World Wide Web is 80. Verify this value and click Next.

10. An administration TCP port number is used for accessing the administration components of the Web server over the TCP/IP protocol. The installation program automatically assigns a random port number to this value (see Figure 22-2). If the random value is acceptable, document it. If not, type the correct value and click Next; then click OK for the informational dialog box.

11. Type the name and password of the FastTrack Web Server administrator and click Next.

12. Click OK for the informational dialog box about utilizing Lightweight Directory Access Protocol (LDAP).

FIGURE 22-1

FastTrack Server host name configuration

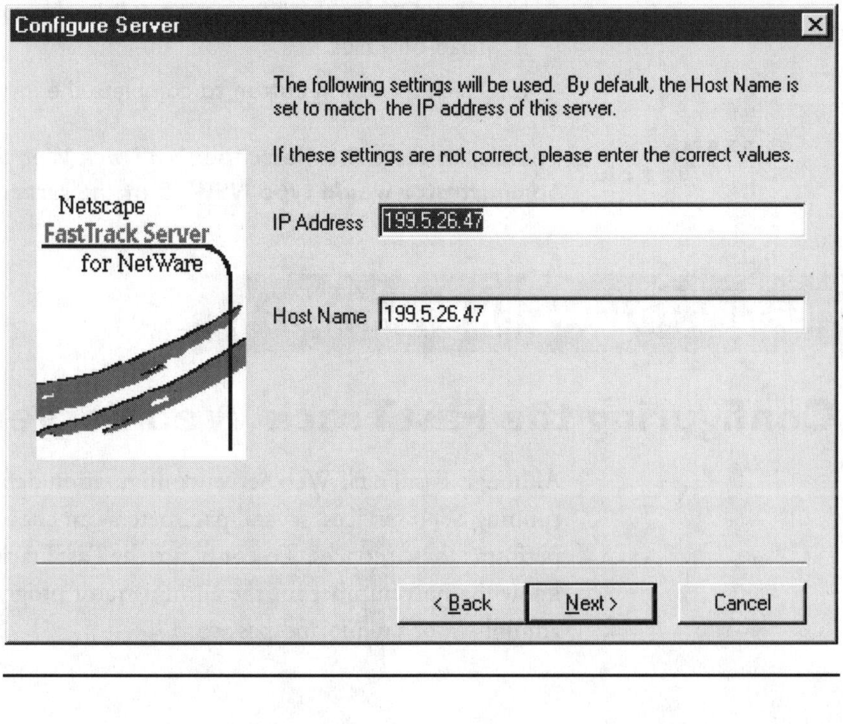

FIGURE 22-2

Administration port
number assignment

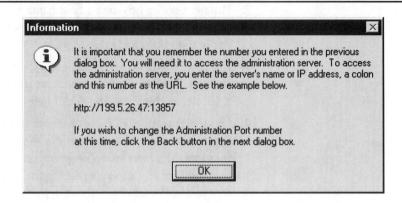

Information

It is important that you remember the number you entered in the previous dialog box. You will need it to access the administration server. To access the administration server, you enter the server's name or IP address, a colon and this number as the URL. See the example below.

http://199.5.26.47:13857

If you wish to change the Administration Port number at this time, click the Back button in the next dialog box.

OK

13. If desired, click Yes to make changes to the AUTOEXEC.NCF file to run the FastTrack Web Server upon server startup; then click Next to start copying files. This step adds the line NSWEB to the AUTOEXEC.NCF file.

14. Click OK for the informational dialog box about overwriting read-only files.

15. Click the Finish button to complete the installation.

exam
Watch

In order to start the Netscape FastTrack Web Server, the administrator would type NSWEB at the server's console prompt.

Configuring the FastTrack Web Server

Although FastTrack Web Server configuration defaults are sufficient for running Web services, several parameters can change how the Web server performs these services. To configure the FastTrack Web Server, you must know the port number for the administrator program, as well as the administrator's name and password.

Beginning Configuration

1. Log in at a client workstation.

2. Start the Web browser program.

3. In the address box, where you normally type the URL, type **http://*hostname:portnumber*** and press ENTER. If the host name of the Web server is set for the IP address of 111.22.33.4, and the port number is 10888, type **http://111.22.33.4:10888**.

4. The Web browser will access the administrative security page of the Web server, and a prompt will appear for the administrator's name and password. Type the administrator's name and password that was used during installation of the server and click OK.

5. The configuration page will appear, as shown in Figure 22-3.

FIGURE 22-3

FastTrack Server
Administration page

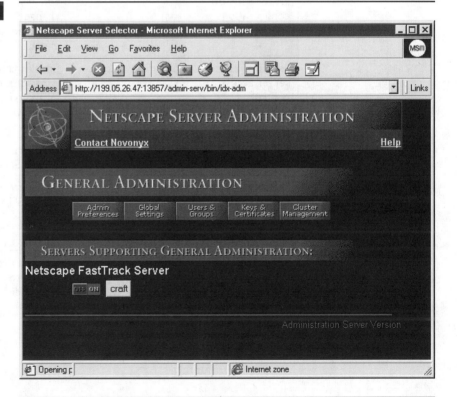

Admin Preferences

On the FastTrack Web Server Administration page, the Admin Preferences button leads to a page that enables shutting down the server. On the left pane of that page, there are sections with the different types of administration options. All administration preference options that are available for the FastTrack Web Server are listed in Table 22-1.

TABLE 22-1

Admin Preferences Options

Option	Section	Function
Shut down administration server	Shut Down	Shuts down the administration server. The administration server is the first Web server in a cluster.
Administration server daemon configuration	Network Settings	Allows the TCP port for the administration server to be changed. The server must be restarted for settings to take effect.
Administration server access control	SuperUser Access Control	Enables limiting the workstations that the admin user can log in from. Also, can change the admin user's name and password.
Encryption On/Off	Turn On/Off SSL	Enables encryption at the Secure Sockets Layer (SSL).
Security Preferences	Security Preferences	Configures the Secure Sockets Layer (SSL).
Administration server options	Logging Options	Sets the logging level.
View Access Log	View Access Log	Sets the number and types of entries to appear in the log, as well as displays the log.
View Error Log	View Error Log	Sets the number and types of entries to appear in the log, as well as displays the log.

Web services can be started and stopped from the Admin Preferences page.

Global Settings

The Global Settings page (see Figure 22-4) consists of a single option: Configure Directory Service. The directory service is the database of the users and groups that can access the FastTrack Web Server services. There are three options:

1. Local Database
2. LDAP Directory Server
3. Novell Directory Services

FIGURE 22-4

Global settings page

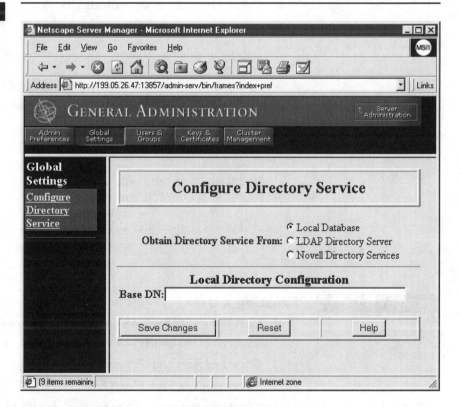

The default user database is a local database. If the enterprise has an Lightweight Directory Access Protocol (LDAP) service running, the users and groups configured in that database may be used. Novell Directory Services (NDS) can supply the user database, as well. Please note that, when selecting the database, the users and groups set must be created and maintained in that database.

Users and Groups

The Users and Groups page is used for creating and maintaining users in the local database. The administrator can

■ Create new and manage existing users

■ Create new and manage existing groups

■ Create and manage organizational units

■ Import an external database or export the local database

When importing a database, the data must be in *LDIF (LDAP Data Interchange Format)*. LDIF is a text format. The basic format of LDIF entries is

```
[<id>]
dn: <distinguished name>
objectClass: <object class>
objectClass: <object class>
...
<attribute type>:<attribute value>
<attribute type>:<attribute value>
...
```

EXERCISE 22-3

Creating a User

1. Launch the URL **http://hostname:portnumber**, which opens the Users and Groups page of the administration server.

2. Click the Users and Groups button.

3. In the left pane, click New User.

4. Specify the last name, full name, and user ID. Note that when a given name and last name (surname) are entered first, the full name and a

user ID (in the format of first initial of first name concatenated with the last name) are automatically completed. User IDs must be unique.

5. Place the user in an Organizational Unit using the Add New User To list.

6. Click Create User.

QUESTIONS AND ANSWERS

Laura has the FastTrack Web Server running on her NetWare 5 network. The CEO has mandated a new policy that only management users can have access to intranet content, which is currently being served by the FastTrack Web Server. Laura has all the management users created and grouped in NDS. What is the fastest way for Laura to implement the new policy?	Laura can go to the Global Settings page and change the user database to Novell Directory Services. Then she can apply the correct security to the users already set up in NDS.

Keys and Certificates

The Keys and Certificates page offers Secure Sockets Layer (SSL) configuration options. The FastTrack Web Server uses SSL to ensure privacy when communicating with other SSL-enabled applications. This is required for many enterprises because data can pass through many computers on its way from source to destination. SSL uses encryption to secure that data.

Keys refers to a public key encryption. In public key encryption, the user is granted two keys, one public and one private. The public key can be given to everyone, or every host on the network. The private key is kept private. When a file is sent to a server, the sender encrypts it with that server's public key. When the receiving server gets the file, it uses the private key to decode the file. Only that private key can decode the file, which means only that server can see it.

Certificates refers to a Certification Authority, or CA. The CA is a third party—either a department in the enterprise, or a public company—that issues certificates to verify the identity of the party.

Keys and certificates interact in the following manner:

1. For *server authentication,* a client tries to access a server using SSL.

2. The server signs a certificate with its public key and sends it to the client.

3. The client uses the public key and checks whether the CA accepts it.

4. If accepted, the client compares information in the certificate with the information received from the CA. A match will consider the site authenticated.

5. For *client authentication* the process continues: The client signs the certificate, including its public key, and sends it to the server.

6. The server uses the public key to verify that the owner of the certificate is the one who signed it.

7. If the CA is not a listed *trusted CA*, the server ends communication. If it is a trusted CA, the client has been authenticated.

The options for keys and certificates are summarized in Table 22-2.

TABLE 22-2

Options for Keys and Certificates

Option	Section	Function
Create Alias	Create Alias	Creates a name that will be associated to both a key and a certificate
Remove Alias	Remove Alias	Removes the alias, making the associated key pair and certificate unusable
List Aliases	List Aliases	Lists all aliases for server
Generate Key Pair	Generate Key	Displays a message for how to generate a public / private pair of keys
Change Key Pair File Password	Change Key Password	Can change the public / private key file password
Request a Server Certificate	Request Certificate	Assists in requesting a certificate from a CA through either electronic mail or a hypertext transfer protocol
Install a Server Certificate	Install Certificate	Installs a certificate that is received from a CA
Manage Server Certificates	Manage Certificates	Allows the administrator to manage the certificates that are installed to an alias

FIGURE 22-5

Adding servers to a cluster

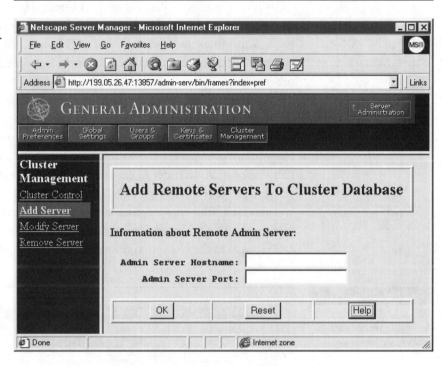

Cluster Management

Clusters are groups of Web servers that are associated with each other and share a common configuration. They all share a single administration server, and any configuration options changed on the administration server are automatically utilized by the other cluster servers. The Cluster Management option (see Figure 22-5) allows an administrator to add, remove, and modify servers in a cluster.

CERTIFICATION OBJECTIVE 22.04

Troubleshooting the Web Server

When connectivity to a Web server cannot be established, first verify that connectivity exists physically between the server and the workstation. The

TCP/IP-based PING (Packet InterNet Groper) utility at the workstation and the PING.NLM utility on the server can verify that connectivity exists both to and from the workstation. If PING does not return a response, then either TCP/IP is not set up correctly or the network connections are otherwise disabled.

For example, if 111.222.3.4 were the server's IP address, the user would type **PING 111.222.3.4** at the DOS prompt. At the server, the administrator would load PING and then type the IP address at the appropriate prompt. If PING works, there might be a problem with the name resolution. In order to check if the name is being resolved to the IP address, the user might type **PING** *hostname* at the DOS prompt.

FastTrack Web Server comes with a Web-enabled administration page (see Figure 22-6). The administration page can be accessed from the same central page as the configuration pages. On the initial page that is accessed

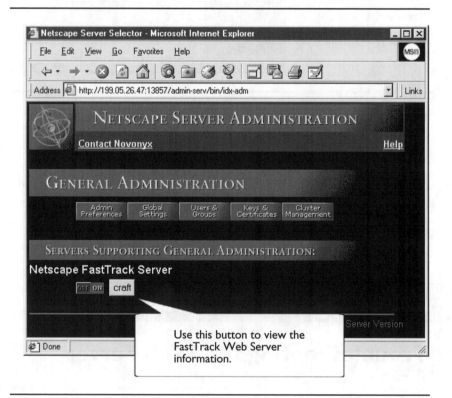

FIGURE 22-6

Accessing the server's administration pages

from a Web browser using the http://*Servername:portnumber* URL, there is a button listing the name of the server. That button initiates the administration page for that server.

Web services can be toggled on and off from the first page reached. If Web services have stopped, an administrator can turn the server off and then on again to restart them.

In order to view information about the server, the administrator can select the View Server Settings option in the left pane (see Figure 22-7). This page displays the IP address of the server, the host name, the directories for Web services, and other settings. In the case where a server's host name is not being resolved with its IP address, the administrator should check the DNS setting on this page. If the server is using a special port number, other than the standard 80, this page will reveal which port number that is.

QUESTIONS AND ANSWERS

Aaron is running the FastTrack Web Server on his NetWare 5 network. He has used the default settings during installation. Aaron has published the network standards on the server, and sent e-mail notification to all the network users that the server is available and giving its address. One user called and reported that the information was failing. Aaron discovered that the user had typed the address as http://*servername*:8080. What is the problem?

The user has tried to access the server content with a port number that is not being used by Web services. The default port number is 80.

If the configuration of the server has somehow changed, the Restore Configuration option is invaluable. It allows an administrator to select the date of the configuration to which to return the server. When some clients can authenticate to the server and others cannot, there may be a problem with encryption. To test for encryption as a root cause, select the Encryption On/Off page and turn encryption off. Then attempt connection again with the problem client workstations.

FIGURE 22-7

Server settings page for troubleshooting

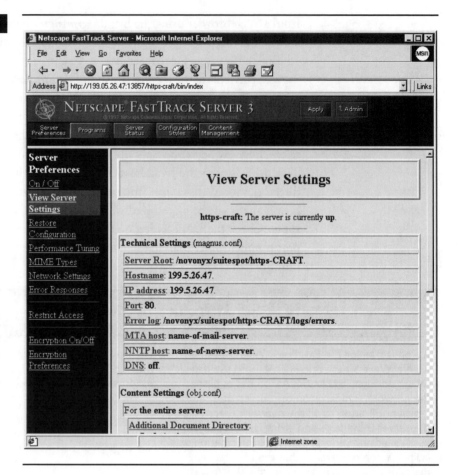

If the Web server is not performing correctly, also check the access and error logs. These can be viewed by selecting the Server Status button. Also available on this page is the ability to monitor the Web server's current activity: the administrator can monitor the server while the client attempts connection.

CERTIFICATION SUMMARY

FastTrack Web Server is available from Netscape as part of the Novell and Netscape partnership that created Novonyx. It enables a NetWare 5 server to perform Web services on the network.

The minimum requirements for installing FastTrack are

- A client workstation running Windows 95/8 or NT 4.0, NetWare Client 32, with 100MB of free space on the hard drive

- A server running NetWare 4.11 or later, 100MB of free space on SYS, with at least 64MB of RAM

- An installer with administrative rights to the server's SYS: volume

The server installation is run from the client workstation by accessing the NetWare 5 CD-ROM, navigating to Products\Novonyx, and running SETUP.EXE. During installation, the Web services port and administration port are established.

To configure the FastTrack Web server, the server must be started on the NetWare server. To start the server, the administrator can type **NSWEB** at the server console prompt. From a workstation, the administrator would type **http://***Servername:portnumber* to access the administration Web page.

Configuration of the server includes

- Determining which of three locations the user and group information is stored: local database, LDAP, or NDS

- Creating and managing a cluster of servers

- Managing the users and groups

- Establishing keys and certificates for the security of the server

When troubleshooting Web server problems, first establish that there is network connectivity between the client and server. The PING utility can verify connectivity. Second, name resolution should be verified.

The administration pages include a Server Status page where the Web server activity can be monitored. It also contains access and error logs that display access success and failures, as well as specific errors that occur.

TWO-MINUTE DRILL

❑ The FastTrack Web Server, which is included on the NetWare 5 CD-ROM, enables a full-service intranet without replacing an existing NetWare network infrastructure.

❑ FastTrack Web Server installation can be performed from any Windows 95, Windows 98, or Windows NT client workstation that is running Novell's NetWare Client 32. It can be installed to any NetWare 4.11 or later server in which the logged-in user has administrative rights.

❑ The client used to install the FastTrack Web Server must run Microsoft Windows 95, Microsoft Windows 98, or Microsoft Windows NT Workstation 4.0, along with the Novell Client 32 for that operating system. The client must also have a Web browser program installed. There must be a CD-ROM drive accessible from the client, and the client must have 100MB of free disk space to store temporary files.

❑ The target NetWare 5 server, which will run the FastTrack Web Server software, must be configured for the IPX protocol and DNS (Domain Name Server), support long filenames, have a minimum of 64MB, and have a minimum of 100MB of free space in the SYS: volume.

❑ The installing user must have administrative rights to the SYS: volume of the target NetWare 5 server, and must know the following information: the IP address of the target NetWare server, the subnet mask of the network, the IP default gateway address, the DNS host name of the target server, and the address of the DNS server used for IP address resolution

❑ The installation file for FastTrack Web Server is on the NetWare 5 CD-ROM under the Products\Novonyx subdirectory. FastTrack Web Server uses a client/server installation method.

❑ To configure the FastTrack Web Server, you must know the port number for the administrator program, as well as the administrator's name and password.

❑ On the FastTrack Web Server Administration page, the Admin Preferences button leads to a page that enables shutting down the server. On the left pane of that page, there are sections with the different types of administration options.

❑ The Global Settings page consists of a single option: Configure Directory Service. The directory service is the database of the users and groups that can access the FastTrack Web Server services. There are three options—Local Database, LDAP Directory Server, and Novell Directory Services.

❑ The Users and Groups page is used for creating and maintaining users in the local database. The administrator can create new and manage existing users, create new and manage existing groups, create and manage organizational units, and import an external database or export the local database.

❑ The Keys and Certificates page offers Secure Sockets Layer (SSL) configuration options. The FastTrack Web Server uses SSL to ensure privacy when communicating with other SSL-enabled applications.

❑ Clusters are groups of Web servers that are associated with each other and share a common configuration. They all share a single administration server, and any configuration options changed on the administration server are automatically utilized by the other cluster servers. The Cluster Management option allows an administrator to add, remove, and modify servers in a cluster.

❑ When connectivity to a Web server cannot be established, one of the first things to verify is that connectivity exists physically between the server and the workstation. The TCP/IP-based PING (Packet InterNet Groper) utility at the workstation and the PING.NLM utility on the server can verify that connectivity exists both to and from the workstation. If PING does not return a response, then either TCP/IP is not set up correctly, or the network connections are otherwise disabled.

SELF TEST

The following Self-Test questions will help you measure your understanding of the material presented in this chapter. Read all the choices carefully, as there may be more than one correct answer. Choose all correct answers for each question.

1. Jack has attempted to install the FastTrack Web Server, but cannot seem to find the option in the NWCONFIG.NLM Product Options screen. How can he install the server?

   A. He should load PINSTALL.NLM and look for the option there.

   B. He can Load NOVONYX.NLM to start the setup.

   C. He can access SETUP in the PRODUCTS\NOVONYX directory on the NetWare 5 CD-ROM.

   D. He can access SETUP from the SYS:NOVONYX directory.

2. Which of the following is a requirement for the client to run the FastTrack Web Server setup?

   A. The client must have 100MB of RAM.

   B. The client must have more than 32MB of RAM.

   C. The client must have Windows 3.1 installed.

   D. The client must be running the NetWare Client 32.

3. Which of the following is not a minimum requirement of the target server for FastTrack Web Server installation?

   A. Must have 32MB of free hard disk space.

   B. Must have long filenames enabled.

   C. Must have 100MB of free space on SYS:.

   D. Must have 32MB of RAM.

4. Which information is needed by the installer during FastTrack Server installation?

   A. IP address of the target server

   B. Volume name where the server files will be placed

   C. IPX address of the target server

   D. DHCP server name and address

5. Karen received an error when trying to install FastTrack to the SYS:WEB directory. Why?

   A. FastTrack can be installed only to non-SYS: volumes.

   B. The FastTrack files must be placed in the FastTrack directory.

   C. FastTrack cannot be installed to a WEB directory because it creates it later by default.

   D. FastTrack can be installed only into the root of the SYS: volume.

6. Which of the following will load the FastTrack Web Server at the server console?

   A. FSWEB

   B. NSWEB

   C. FASTRACK

   D. FTWEB

7. Barry set up his server WEBSTER, with address 10.1.21.98, to use port 8080 for Web services, and to use port 11188 for administration. Which of the following will start the administration page?

   A. WEBSTER\11188

   B. WEBSTER\SYS\11188

   C. http://10.1.21.98/8080

   D. http://Webster:11188

8. Which button will enable limiting which workstations can be used to access the administration server?

   A. Admin Preferences

   B. Users and Groups

   C. Keys and Certificates

   D. Global Settings

9. Which of the following is not an option for providing users and groups for the Web Server?

   A. LDAP

   B. NDS

   C. NT Domain

   D. Local database

10. Which of the following is the required file format for importing a file into the local database of the FastTrack Web Server?

    A. LDIF

    B. LDAP

    C. NDS

    D. ASCII

11. What name is used in association with a key pair and certificate?

    A. CA

    B. Alias

    C. Host name

    D. IP Address

12. If configuration changes are made on an administration server, which servers do they affect in the cluster?

    A. Only the administration server

    B. All servers, even those outside the cluster

    C. All cluster servers

    D. Any server in the cluster except the administration server

13. Which utility will help determine if connectivity exists between client and server?

    A. NSWEB

    B. FTCHECK

    C. NetWare Administrator

    D. PING

14. Gil has determined that all Web services are failing from the FastTrack Web Server. He has determined that connectivity exists and configuration is correct. What should Gil check next?

    A. The IP Address
    B. He should run PING.NLM
    C. Whether the FastTrack Web Server is "on"

15. If Gil further determines that the FastTrack Web Server is running, what else could he do?

    A. Check that DNS is configured correctly.
    B. Check that the Web services port number is correct.
    C. Read the error and access logs.
    D. Stop and restart the service for Web.

23

Securing the Directory Tree

CERTIFICATION OBJECTIVES

23.01   NDS Default Rights

23.02   Guidelines for Implementing
         NDS Security

23.03   Centralized Versus Distributed
         Administration

23.04   Suggested Administrative Roles and
         Rights Assignments

Netware administration requires a thorough knowledge of Novell Directory Services (NDS). NetWare 5's security consists of both file system security and NDS object security. Together, they provide a flexible security system for managing access to network resources, including files and directories.

NDS, or object, security uses the same terminology, and similar concepts, as file system security. These concepts govern the security access and how such access can be granted between objects:

- Trustee rights
- Inheritance of rights
- Inheritance rights filter
- Security equivalence
- Effective rights

NDS Default Rights

It benefits an administrator to understand the default rights granted to objects in the NDS tree. These rights generate the minimum security required to protect network resources and the flexibility to use the NetWare network as soon as it has been installed.

Object rights enable a trustee to perform tasks on an NDS object. The object rights are listed in Table 23-1.

Property rights are applicable to the values of an object's details. Table 23-2 lists the property rights. When a trustee is granted a property right, it can perform actions on that property of the object. In order to shorten the

TABLE 23-1

Overview of Object Rights

Right	Function
Supervisor	Supervisor is the combination of all other object rights.
Browse	Browse allows a trustee to view the object in the NDS tree. When the Browse right is removed or filtered, the objects cannot be seen in the NDS tree.
Create	Create lets a trustee add new objects to the NDS tree.
Delete	Delete lets a trustee delete objects from NDS as long as the trustee also has the Write right for All properties of the object in question.
Rename	Rename lets a trustee rename another NDS object.

TABLE 23-1

Overview of Object Rights

process of granting property rights, there is the option of granting the same right to All properties of the object in one step, as shown in Figure 23-1.

Right	Function
Supervisor	The Supervisor property right grants the total of the property rights to the property in question.
Compare	Compare allows a trustee to compare a property's value to a set value. It lets the trustee search for a match but not read the value itself.
Read	Read lets the trustee view the property value. When Read is granted, the Compare right is automatically granted.
Write	Write lets a trustee add a new value, and change or delete a value of the property.
Add Self	The Add Self right lets the trustee change a property's value to its own object for properties that include NDS objects as options.

TABLE 23-2

Property Rights Overview

FIGURE 23-1

Effective rights for All
properties

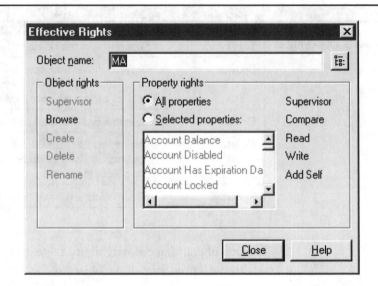

Trustee Assignments

Trustee assignments are the rights granted to an object for a file, directory,
object, or property. An administrator assigns trustee rights explicitly for
objects in order to grant rights beyond the default. Any NDS object can
receive a trustee assignment to any other object, including groups,
Organizational Units, and printers. The only time an NDS object right
affects file system rights is when an object has been granted, or has
inherited, the Supervisor or Write right to a Server object. When the
Supervisor or Write right is assigned to a Server object, the trustee receives
supervisor rights at the file system level.

NetWare administrators provide security by granting rights only to those
users who require them. The default trustee assignments for users are listed
in Table 23-3.

exam
Ⓦatch

*The Admin object can be disabled, renamed, moved, and deleted like
any NDS object. Its rights can be changed so that it no longer has
administrative access. This should be done only after another Admin
object has been created.*

TABLE 23-3   Default Trustee Assignments

Trustee	Object Right	Property Right	File Right	Object/Property/File System and Reason
Admin	[S]			[Root]—granted at installation so that Admin has access to entire NDS tree. This right flows down the entire tree, giving Admin Supervisor rights at the server level that in turn, give Supervisor rights to the server's file system.
[Public]	[B]			[Root]—granted at installation so that all users can browse tree and change contexts before logging into the tree.
Container object			[RF]	SYS:PUBLIC directory of all servers contained—Read and File Scan inherited by users in container so they can execute files stored in PUBLIC.
Container object			[C]	SYS:MAIL directory of servers contained—User objects can create their own MAIL directory upon user creation
User object		[RC]		All Properties of own User object—Read allows users to see their own object values. Compare allows users to compare value with another.
User object		[WR]		Login Script property of own User object—Read allows users to see and execute their own login scripts. Write allows users to change their own login scripts.
User object		[WR]		Print Job configuration of own User object—Read allows users to see and execute their own print jobs. Write allows users to change their own print job configuration.
User object		[R]		Network address property of the [Root] object—this flows down the tree and is applied to all servers, so that users can communicate with servers by reading the server's network address.
User object		[R]		Group Membership property of the [Root] object—this flows down the tree and is applied to all objects, so that User objects can determine the group membership.

Trustee assignments for objects and property rights flow down the tree. The only exception to this rule is when the right is blocked by the Inherited Rights Filter (IRF). Explicit trustee assignments at a lower level in the NDS tree will replace all the inherited trustee assignments. When an individual property right has been assigned to a trustee, it will override the All properties rights assignment.

So that you can view the rights assigned to an object, the Access Control List (ACL) property of the object contains the trustee assignments to that object.

Security Equivalence

Security equivalence is the state of one object gaining the same rights as another object without being explicitly granted those rights. It helps manage rights through the ability to place users in groups and grant the rights to the groups, and the user then becomes security equivalent to the group.

The following rules apply to rights gained through security equivalence:

- There is no way to filter out security equivalent rights with the IRF.
- Each object is security equivalent to each of the container objects that lead from the object to the [Root]. This means that user JOE.WEST.ACME is security equivalent to both the Organization Acme and the Organizational Unit West. Also, each object is security equivalent to [Root].
- Each object is security equivalent to the [Public] trustee.
- An object is security equivalent to each of the objects listed in its Security Equals property page.

Inherited Rights

Inherited rights are rights to objects or files and the All properties property rights that flow down to subordinate container units, and the leaf objects contained within them. Inherited rights begin as explicit trustee assignments at a container level. For example, the Admin object receives the Supervisor trustee assignment to objects at the [Root] level. For each container unit below the [Root], the Supervisor right is an inherited right and can be blocked.

Inherited Rights Filter

The *Inherited Rights Filter* (IRF) is used to block only inherited rights. This filter cannot block security equivalence or explicit trustee assignments. The IRF can be applied to inherited object rights, inherited All properties property rights, and inherited selected properties property rights. The IRF cannot grant any further rights. An IRF can be enabled for any object, property, file, or directory.

exam
ⓦatch

Although the Supervisor right for objects and properties can be revoked by the IRF, file system Supervisor rights cannot be revoked by an IRF.

Effective Rights

Effective rights are the collective actions that a trustee can take on an object after all the security factors are calculated. In taking two objects, Object A and Object B, and discussing Object A's access to Object B, the effective rights are the ones that finally govern what actions Object A can take on Object B. When discovering the effective rights, follow these steps:

1. All explicit trustee rights assigned to Object A would be calculated for Object B itself.

2. The sum of all rights assigned to Object A going back from Object B's container to the [Root] would be calculated, with only those rights not filtered by the IRF being added.

3. Add all rights gained through security equivalence, either explicit security equivalence or through group membership and the [Public] trustee.

Inheritable Rights

Under any container object in the NetWare Administrator in NetWare 5, there is a new object right: Inheritable (see Figure 23-2). The Inheritable

FIGURE 23-2

Inheritable selected
property for password
management

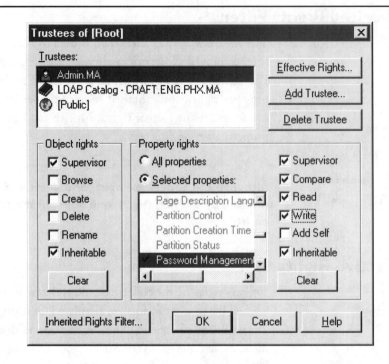

right will allow or disallow the inheritance of object or property rights to a
container object. This right specifically allows the creation of an
administrator over selected properties such as passwords.

When the Inheritable right is selected, objects and containers below
that container in the NDS tree inherit the trustee assignment. When the
Inheritable right is not selected, the trustee assignments are effective only for
that container object. The Inheritable option is selected by default for
object rights and all property rights. It is not selected by default for specific
property rights.

CERTIFICATION OBJECTIVE 23.02

Guidelines for Implementing NDS Security

Implementing NDS security involves defining the additional rights needed for users to access and manage what is required. Specifying additional rights when they are not needed can create security holes in an NDS design scheme. When an object has been granted *managed rights*—that is, the object has the Write object right to another object's Access Control List (ACL)— it can modify anything pertaining to that object. Managed rights should be granted only when absolutely necessary. Some administrative actions require this level of capability:

- Modifying the schema requires Write right to the [Root]'s ACL.

- Merging two trees requires the Write right to the [Root] ACLs of both NDS trees.

- Partitioning the NDS database requires the Write right to the Server object's ACL that contains the target partition.

- Changing the Profile, the Group, or the Security Equivalence of an object requires the Write right to the object's ACL.

When implementing NDS security, the use of auditing can ensure that NDS security is implemented correctly. *Auditing* is a feature that can assist in monitoring and recording how users access network resources. The audit system ensures that the network is secure, since it is capable of monitoring and recording relevant network transactions, the user who performed the transaction, and the timestamp of the transaction.

Auditing is configured at the container level in NDS and the volume level for the file system. Audit policies specify the items and/or users to monitor. Audit log files appear as NDS objects in the directory tree. Since the log files are objects within NDS, the access to audit information and configuration is controlled by NDS security.

QUESTIONS AND ANSWERS

Carla has just been hired as a NetWare network administrator. For her first assignment, she has been asked to make sure that no users have been granted access to the Human Resources servers, files, or NDS container. How can Carla perform this task?	Carla can implement NDS auditing and check to see if any users have accessed the objects in question.

CERTIFICATION OBJECTIVE 23.03

Centralized Versus Distributed Administration

Traditionally, network administration has rested on a single user or group of users who had access to an entire network (see Figure 23-3). In large enterprises, this structure did not mirror the actual distribution of responsibilities. An enterprise that is either logically or physically separated into large business units may wish to divide up the responsibilities of network management among multiple network administrators.

Due to its hierarchical structure, Novell Directory Services offers the ability to distribute administration responsibilities (see Figure 23-4). Each container can have separate administrators. Additionally, with the Inheritable right option, administrators with limits to their functions, such as password administrators, can be created.

FIGURE 23-3 Centralized administrative control

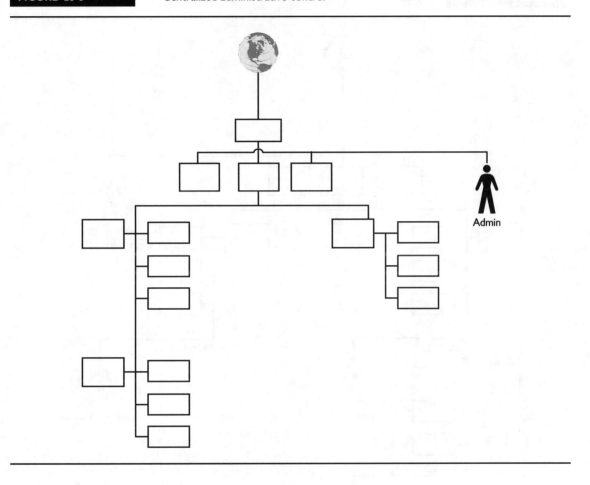

FIGURE 23-4   Distributed administrative control

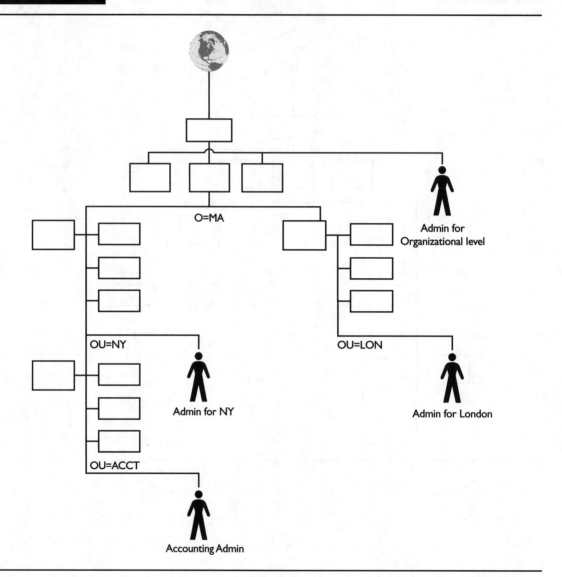

O=MA

Admin for
Organizational level

OU=NY

Admin for NY

OU=LON

Admin for London

OU=ACCT

Accounting Admin

Suggested Administrative Roles and Rights Assignments

There are several types of administrative roles applicable to network management:

- Distributed, container administrators
- File system, or server, administrators
- Installers
- Help Desk
- Password administrators
- NDS partition administrators

Container Administrators

Container administrators are User objects that have been given the capability of managing a container object and all the objects within it. Container administrators can administer over the objects within the container, and can administer the file system of servers in that container when having the Supervisor object right to the container. In order to block file system administrative rights, use an IRF to block the Supervisor right to the Server and Volume objects. The container administrators will be able to manage lower-level containers and their objects unless an IRF is placed on those containers after their own administrator organizational roles have been created.

Container administrators have the ability to create new objects within the container. They can manage existing objects within the container and delete them. With the Supervisor object right granted or inherited to Server and Volume objects, the container administrator has file system administrative rights. The container administrator can create new subcontainers and manage them as well through the inheritance of the Supervisor object rights.

EXERCISE 23-1

Creating a Container Administrator

1. Log in to NetWare with a user that has administrative capabilities, such as the original Admin object.

2. In the NetWare Administrator, navigate to the container over which the container administrator will preside. Select the container and press the INSERT key.

3. From the Object Creation dialog box, select Organizational Role. Click OK.

4. Type the name of the Organizational Role and click Create.

5. After the object is created, right-click the Organizational Role and select Rights to Other Objects.

6. Grant all object rights for the container object so that the Organizational Role has Supervisor rights to the container. Click OK to save the changes and close the dialog box.

7. Double-click the Organizational object to view its details. In the Occupant Role box, add the User object(s) who will manage that container.

8. Additionally, the Admin User object should be given explicit Supervisor rights to the Organizational Role.

9. An IRF of Browse and Read on the Organizational Role itself will prevent the occupants from changing its rights.

File System Administrator

File system administrators, or server administrators, are capable of managing the files and directories residing on NetWare servers. They do not have additional NDS object or property rights other than those required for file system administration.

The file system administrator does not have the ability to create, manage, or delete objects within the NDS tree. The file system administrator is able to create, manage, delete, and salvage any files on the NetWare server(s) to which the file system administrator is assigned.

EXERCISE 23-2

Creating a File System Administrator

1. Log in to NetWare with a user that has administrative capabilities, such as the original Admin object.

2. In the NetWare Administrator, navigate to the container over which the container administrator will preside. Select the container and press the INSERT key.

3. From the Object Creation dialog box, select Organizational Role. Click OK.

4. Type the name of the Organizational Role and click Create.

5. After the object is created, right-click the Organizational Role and select Rights to Other Objects.

6. Assign to the Organizational Role the Supervisor object right to the server(s) that will be managed. Click OK to save the changes.

7. In order to block other administrators from managing the server through inherited rights, place an IRF of Browse on the Server object(s).

Installers

One of the roles in an enterprise network is that of an installer. An installer can either install new servers into the Novell Directory Services tree or install applications onto a server. Many organizations do not retain Certified Novell Engineers (CNEs) on staff, but prefer that a CNE perform installations. In this case, the installer role is one that needs some special attention.

In order to install servers into NDS, the installer needs to have two types of rights:

1. The Create right for the container into which the server will be installed is required for the installation process to create Server and Volume objects in the tree.

2. The Supervisor right for the container is required to add a partition replica or partition root of the NDS database.

These rights are the same as those of the container administrator. However, the additional step that should be taken for installers is one of expiration (see Figure 23-5). When the installer is contracted from another company, the userID created for that installer should have an expiration date set that will disable the ID after a specified date. However, the User object itself can be added to the container administrator Organizational Role.

Application installers may require Write rights to the [Root] if the application being installed is NDS enabled and changes the schema.

FIGURE 23-5

Account expiration dates set on Login Restrictions page

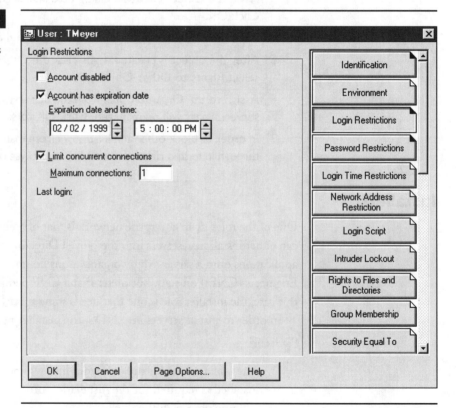

Otherwise, most applications require file system rights to the directory in which they are being installed. These rights do not necessarily have to include Supervisor rights to the Server or Volume objects, or even other directories and files on the server. Additionally, an application installer may require some extra NDS object rights.

In creating an application installer role, the installer must have the following rights and capabilities:

- The Create right to the target directory that will include the application after installation. This is often called APPS on the server.

- The Read and File Scan rights to the target directory, so the installer can verify that the files were installed to the server.

- Create object right to the container in which new group or directory map objects may be created for use with the application.

The Help Desk

There are several roles that a Help Desk can play for an enterprise network, as listed in Table 23-4. As a central call center, the Help Desk simply takes calls and transfers them to the correct support entity. As a service desk, the Help Desk can act as an application support center, a user administrator, a server administrator, or a tree administrator.

QUESTIONS AND ANSWERS

Acme has hired a vendor to provide Help Desk services. The vendor will connect to Acme's network with a WAN link. If Acme's security policy is such that only the Global Admin group will have Supervisor rights to any container objects or the [Root], what is the highest level of services that the Help Desk can provide remotely?

The Help Desk will be able to provide server administration and user administration, since neither of these options requires Supervisor rights at the container or [Root] level.

TABLE 23-4	Administrative Role	Function	Rights Required
Help Desk Administrative Roles and Rights	Call Center	Transfers calls to support entities	None
	Application Support	Triages problems with applications	None
	User Administration	Adds and manages users on the network	Create, Delete, and Rename object rights for applicable containers
	Server Administrator	Remotely supports server, backups, files, and directories. Manages volume capacity	Supervisor object rights for the applicable servers
	Tree Administrator	Manages all objects within the NDS tree, can partition the database, can remotely install applications, and manages workstations through Z.E.N.works	Supervisor object rights at the [Root]. Explicit Supervisor object rights for any objects that must be managed but have an IRF.

Password Administrators

Password administrators are User objects whose only administrative access is that which is required to change and manage passwords. This is one of the most common help requests for end users. In distributing administration responsibilities throughout a NetWare 5 network, the password administrator role can be granted to many users without concern over severe security violations, because the administrative capabilities are limited.

EXERCISE 23-3

Configure a Password Administrator

1. Log in to the NetWare network as a user with Supervisor object rights in the container in which the password administrator will reside and that it will manage.

2. In the NetWare Administrator, navigate to the container object over which the password administrator will preside and right-click it.

3. Select Trustees of this Object.

4. Select Add Trustee and choose the User object that will be the password administrator (this can be an Organizational Role or Group, too).

5. Click Selected Properties.

6. Scroll through the list and select Password Management so that it is checked.

7. Select the Compare, Read, Write, and Inheritable options.

Partition Administrators

Partitioning the NDS database in a poor design can greatly increase the network bandwidth or cause problems for users attempting to authenticate and log in, resulting in slow response time. For these reasons, enterprises should restrict partitioning operations from all but a few select users.

In order to restrict partition operations from container administrators, remove the container administrators' Supervisor rights to their respective containers and grant them all other rights to the container. Installers will require the Supervisor right, but that role should have an expiration date. The partition administrator should have the Supervisor right granted to it for each applicable container.

CERTIFICATION SUMMARY

Novell Directory Services (NDS) contains both object and property rights. These rights must be understood in order to implement NDS security. Object rights are Supervisor, Browse, Create, Delete, and Rename. Property rights are Supervisor, Compare, Read, Write, and Add Self.

Trustee assignments are the explicit rights granted to an object. Security equivalence is when Object A is granted the equivalent rights to Object B's explicit rights by its association to that object. Inherited rights are the rights that flow down the tree. The Inherited Rights Filter (IRF) is a block for rights that can flow down the tree. The IRF does not block any other rights. Effective rights are the sum total of the rights that are available to an object when accessing another object. A special right is the Inheritable right, which is new to NetWare 5. This right enables inheritance for selected property rights.

When implementing NDS security, managed rights that allow an object the Write right to an object's ACL should be restricted to only those users who require such access. Auditing can be utilized to ensure that NDS security is working as required.

Centralized administration is when a single administrator or administrator group has complete control of the entire NDS tree. Distributed administration is when the various administrative responsibilities have been granted to different groups across the enterprise network.

The different types of administrative roles are

- **Container administrators**   Management responsibilities over a particular container

- **File system administrators**   Management responsibilities over a particular server

- **Installers of servers**   Supervisor right over the container in which the server is installed, but should be an account with an expiration date

- **Installers of applications**   Responsible for installing applications onto server(s) and creating the groups and directory map objects associated with them

- **Help Desk User administrators**   Manage user accounts

- **Help Desk Server administrators**   Manage servers remotely

- **Help Desk Tree administrators**   Total control over entire tree

- **Password administrators**   Responsible for responding to password change requests

- **Partition administrators**   Manage the NDS database and the placement of replicas and partitions

Many of these roles are similar in capability, although they are used for different actions.

TWO-MINUTE DRILL

❑ NetWare 5's security consists of both file system security and NDS object security.

❑ *Trustee assignments* are the rights granted to an object for a file, directory, object, or property.

❑ An administrator assigns trustee rights explicitly for objects in order to grant rights beyond the default.

❑ *Security equivalence* is the state of one object gaining the same rights as another object without being explicitly granted those rights.

❑ *Inherited rights* are rights to objects or files and the All properties property rights that flow down to subordinate container units, and the leaf objects contained within them.

❑ *Auditing* is a feature that can assist in monitoring and recording how users access network resources.

❑ The *Inherited Rights Filter* (IRF) is used to block only inherited rights. This filter cannot block security equivalence or explicit trustee assignments.

❑ Container administrators are User objects that have been given the capability of managing a container object and all the objects within it.

❑ Password administrators are User objects whose only administrative access is that which is required to change and manage passwords.

SELF TEST

The Self-Test questions will help you measure your understanding of the material presented in this chapter. Read all the choices carefully, as there may be more than one correct answer. Select all correct answers for each question.

1. What type of rights make up NetWare 5's security system? (Choose all that apply.)

    A. Property rights

    B. Object rights

    C. Database rights

    D. File system rights

2. Which of the following represents the explicit rights granted to an object?

    A. Trustee assignments

    B. Security equivalence

    C. Inherited rights

    D. Effective rights

3. Which of the following rights cannot be blocked by an IRF? (Choose all that apply.)

    A. Trustee assuagements

    B. Security equivalence

    C. Inherited rights

    D. Effective rights

4. Which of the following object rights can be blocked by the IRF? (Choose all that apply.)

    A. Supervisor

    B. Create

    C. Browse

    D. Delete

5. Which of the following rights will allow a selected property to be inherited from a container?

    A. Supervisor

    B. Read

    C. Add Self

    D. Inheritable?

6. Which of the following is considered a hole in NDS security?

    A. Granting managed rights

    B. Granting unneeded rights

    C. Granting inherited rights

    D. Creating an IRF for Supervisor

7. Acme's standard Organizational Role for container administrators is to have the Supervisor right at the container level. The Human Resources group cannot allow access to the HR server by any but the HR administrator, who is not a container administrator. How can the server be managed separately?

    A. By granting managed rights to the container administrator

    B. By moving the server to another container

    C. By creating an IRF for Supervisor on the Server object

    D. By creating an IRF for Supervisor on the files and directories in the HR server

8. The .ORGROLE.WEST.ACME has the Supervisor right to the .WEST.ACME container. How can the occupant be prevented from changing the ORGROLE object properties itself?

   A. Create an IRF of Browse and Read on ORGROLE.WEST.ACME

   B. Create an IRF of Supervisor and Browse on ACME

   C. Create an IRF of Read and Compare on WEST.ACME

9. Which object rights does the file system administrator need in NDS?

   A. Supervisor object rights to the container

   B. Supervisor object rights to the Organizational Role

   C. Supervisor object rights to the Server object

   D. Supervisor object rights to the [Root]

10. How can administrators other than the file system administrator be prevented from managing a server and its files and directories through inherited rights?

    A. They cannot be prevented.

    B. Create an IRF of Supervisor on the container object.

    C. Create an IRF of Browse on the container object.

    D. Create an IRF of Browse on the Server object.

11. Even though a server installer requires the same rights as the container administrator, what additional step should be taken on this role?

    A. Additional rights should be granted to the APPS directory.

    B. Managed rights should be granted at the [Root].

    C. An expiration date should be set on the installer User object.

    D. The password should be changed on the installer User object

12. An application installer will require which of the following object rights in NDS?

    A. Supervisor rights at the [Root]

    B. Supervisor rights at the container object

    C. Supervisor rights at the Server object

    D. Create rights at the container object

13. Which of the following roles provided by a Help Desk do not require NDS rights?

    A. Call Center

    B. User Administrator

    C. Tree Administrator

    D. Server Administrator

14. Which rights are required for the Password Management property when creating a password administrator?

    A. Supervisor

    B. Read, Compare, and Inheritable

    C. Compare, Read, and Write

    D. Compare, Read, Write, and Inheritable

15. If the ACME Corporation places all of its servers in the SERVERS.WEST.ACME container, which rights are required by partition administrators?

    A. Supervisor rights to the [Root]

    B. Supervisor rights to all containers

    C. Supervisor rights to the SERVERS.WEST.ACME container

    D. Supervisor rights to the ACME organization

24

Maintaining NDS

CERTIFICATION OBJECTIVES

24.01   Understanding Replication
         and Synchronization

24.02   Preventative Maintenance

24.03   Troubleshooting NDS Inconsistencies

24.04   Repairing NDS

24.05   Recovering from a Crashed
         SYS: Volume

T

hink for a minute about what network engineers spend the most time doing, and you'll realize that most of our time is spent maintaining the network. For a NetWare network, that means that you must maintain *NDS*—the Novell Directory Services database of user, server, and other objects—that is the heart and soul of your network.

The first section of this chapter helps you to understand *replication* and *synchronization*; that is, how NDS *partitions* are created and copied to other servers, and how changes to NDS are spread throughout the network for the benefit of the users at all of your sites. In the next section, we learn preventative maintenance techniques for keeping NDS problems from happening in the first place. With NDS, as with most things in life, preventing a problem is much easier than fixing it. However, if your NDS management tools report inconsistencies in the database or you notice strange things happening on the network, the third section of this chapter shows you how to troubleshoot NDS problems by using the tools provided in NetWare, followed by a section on how to repair the damage once you find it. The final section of the chapter explains how to recover your server if the unthinkable happens and you lose the SYS: volume that houses your NDS database.

CERTIFICATION OBJECTIVE 24.01

Understanding Replication and Synchronization

Replication and synchronization might at first sound like something you'd hear the chief engineer on an interstellar starship discuss. However, the NDS concepts of replication and synchronization are just as critical to an earth-bound enterprise. This section explains what replication and synchronization are, and how to make sure that these essential processes are working properly and efficiently.

Replication

Replication is important to a network administrator whether you manage a large or small network. In small networks, replication backs up NDS and provides *fault tolerance*, that is, another place to access a copy of NDS if the master copy is not accessible. In large networks, replication also allows users quick access to the Directory from a local server. An understanding of replication begins with an understanding of NDS and why it needs to be backed up and distributed across large networks.

The NDS Database

As you've already learned, the Novell Directory Services (NDS) database, also called the Directory, is a database that contains the names, property values, and rights of the objects that make up the network. These objects include users, print queues, servers, and server volumes, among others. The Directory is used for *authentication* to make sure that a user has the right to log in to the network; it is also used for *access control* to make sure that users have the right to do specific things with other objects. For example, when a user logs in, the authentication process checks the NDS database to make sure that the user's password is correct and that the user is allowed to log in from that workstation and at that time of day. As soon as the user tries to access files, the access control process checks to make sure that the user has rights to the files.

As shown in Figure 24-1, within the Directory, objects are grouped into *containers,* either Organizations or Organizational Units. There is usually only one organization container in a tree, although some large trees have more than one. Typically, an Organization container will hold only the Admin object, along with smaller containers called Organizational Units. These Organizational Units are the preferred containers for holding groups of users, printers, and other objects that are physically close to each other or are grouped together because they are part of the same workgroup. When the structure of the Directory is drawn out, as in Figure 24-1, it resembles a cross between an organization chart and the view that Windows Explorer gives you of a hard drive's directories and files. This structural representation is called a directory *tree* because of the way the structure branches out.

FROM THE CLASSROOM

The NDS "Tree"

Students are sometimes confused by Novell's description of the structure of the Directory as being like a "tree." It might be more accurate to refer to the structural drawing as an upside-down tree because, as you can see in Figure 24-1, the [Root] is at the "top" of the tree. In fact, it might have made more sense had Novell referred to the structure as a pyramid rather than a tree, since most directories more closely resemble a pyramid. Novell even explicitly tells NDS designers to have their tree resemble a pyramid, with few

containers and objects at the top, and greater numbers toward the bottom. Perhaps the engineers at Novell decided to use "tree" rather than "pyramid" because the word "pyramid" can have negative associations in the world of business. In any case, just think of the drawn-out structure of an NDS database as an upside-down tree, or as the roots of a tree spreading out underground, and you'll have the picture that you need.

—*By Dan Cheung, CNI, MCNE, MCT*

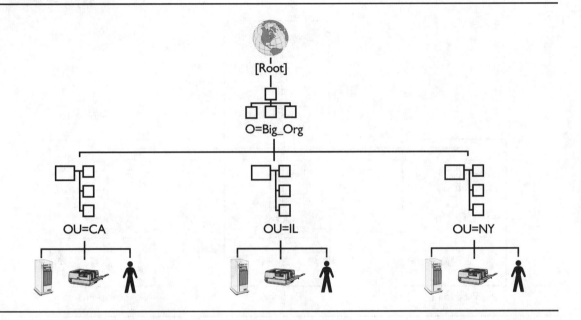

FIGURE 24-1   NDS database with three organizational units grouping objects by state

Partitions

Often the Directory will be split up into pieces. Each piece is called a *partition*. As shown in Figure 24-2, the rule is that you must separate partitions along the boundaries of containers. That is, you cannot put part of a container in one partition and another part of that same container in another partition, unless you are splitting off a subcontainer of the original container. It is possible, however, to have more than one container in a partition. In Figure 24-2, the Big_Org and IL containers are both part of the same partition.

As shown in Figure 24-3, NDS would not allow you to put the user and printer in the CA container into a separate partition, because they are not in

FIGURE 24-2   This Directory is split into three partitions along container boundaries

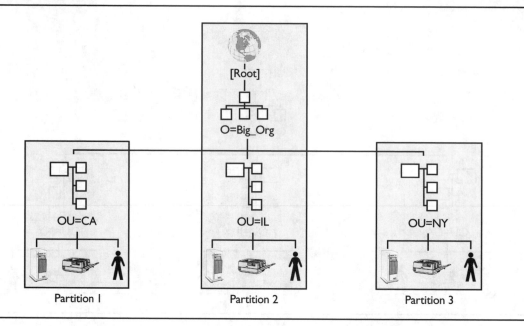

a subcontainer. The ALB subcontainer can be split from the NY container, because this split follows the rule that partitions must be done along container boundaries. If you really need to split the user and printer containers from the CA partition into their own partition, you could create a subcontainer to move them to, and then partition off the subcontainer.

Although partitions up to now have been called "Partition 1," "Partition 2," and so on, partitions actually have unique names that you will see in the NetWare administrative tools that help you manage partitions. As shown in Figure 24-4, the names of the partitions correspond to the names of the containers that they encompass, which are highest in the *tree*, closest to the [Root].

There is one more term regarding partitions that you need to know. A partition that is above another partition in the tree is called a *parent* of the partition that is below it. A partition that is below another partition in the tree is called—you guessed it—a *child* of the partition above it. In Figure 24-5, the NY and CA partitions are child partitions of the [Root] partition.

FIGURE 24-3   It is not possible to create a partition that splits a container unless you are splitting off a subcontainer

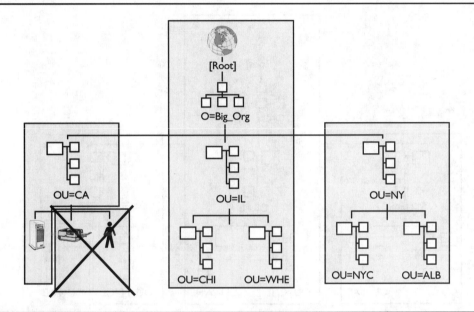

FIGURE 24-4   Names of partitions correspond to names of containers they encompass

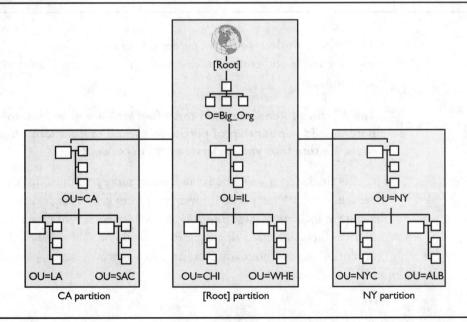

FIGURE 24-5   A child partition can also be the parent of a partition below it in the tree

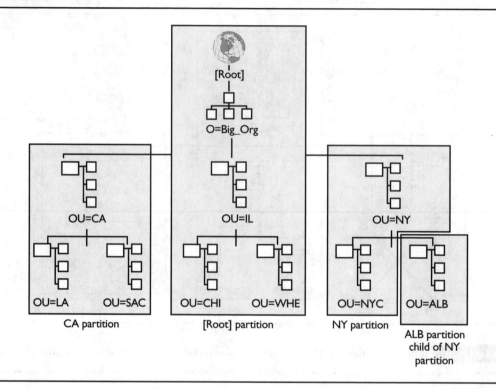

The [Root] partition is a parent partition because it encloses the Big_Org and [Root] containers that are higher in the tree than the NY and CA partitions.

The Advanced Administration test often includes questions on the parent/child relationship of partitions as well as questions on partition roots. Be sure that you understand these concepts.

Any single server *volume* can hold one or more partitions. In past versions of NetWare, partitions were created to keep a single server from having to maintain a large directory. Novell has improved newer versions of NDS to the point that a single partition should be able to handle 100,000 or more objects without any problems. As a general practice, partitions are created and placed on several servers so that no single server being down will make the NDS database inaccessible to users. In fact, to even further decrease the possibility of an individual server being a single point of failure, copies of partitions should be made and placed on several servers. These copies of partitions are called *replicas*.

The following Questions and Answers section offers a quick reference for exam situations that might come up regarding partitions.

QUESTIONS AND ANSWERS

You are asked to create a partition.	Use NDS Manager. Select a container (a container will sometimes be specified) and use the Create Partition command.
You are asked whether it is possible to put some of the users from one Organizational Unit into one partition, and some into another.	Following the rule that partitions must be done along container boundaries, you know that it is not possible to put some of the users into one partition and some into another partition unless you first create a new subcontainer to put the users into.
You are shown a picture of an NDS tree, similar to Figure 24-5, and are asked what the partition root of the CA partition is. (On an exam, the partition will probably be highlighted instead of named.)	Knowing that the partition root is the container closest to the [Root] directory, you answer that the CA container is the partition root of the CA partition.
You are shown a picture of an NDS tree, similar to Figure 24-5, and are asked what the partition root of the middle partition is.	Knowing that the partition root is the container closest to the [Root] directory, you answer that the Big_Org container is the partition root of the [Root] partition.
You are shown a picture of an NDS tree, similar to Figure 24-5, and are asked which partitions are parents.	Knowing that parents are partitions with subordinate partitions below them, you select the answer that lists the [Root] and NY partitions.
You are shown a picture of an NDS tree, similar to Figure 24-5, and are asked which partitions are children.	Knowing that child partitions have partitions above them in the tree, you select the answer that lists the CA, NY, and ALB partitions.

Replicas

You should have replicas, or copies of partitions of the NDS database, on more than one server for two important reasons.

First, users must be able to access the Directory to log in to the network and use network drives and printers. By having copies of each partition on more than one server, you protect users by allowing them to find a replica of the NDS partition that they need on another server if the server from which they usually access the Directory is not accessible.

Second, users can log in to the network and use network resources more quickly if they can access the NDS database on a server that is close to them or that they can connect to with a high-speed connection. Placing replicas on servers that users can access quickly will speed up everything they do. And believe me, if you've ever tried to do a job on a workstation that's separated from a necessary partition by a slow WAN link, then you know how important quick access to a replica can be.

on the
job

One of the most important rules to remember when you are managing replicas is this: "Don't Span the WAN." This means don't place a partition on one side of a slow WAN link and a replica of that partition on the other side of a WAN link, or else the link's bandwidth will be almost entirely used by NDS attempting to synchronize the replicas. Novell says that you can consider separating replicas across the WAN link if the link is a T1 or faster, but it really depends on how much traffic is going across the link. The best rule of thumb might be "Don't span the WAN unless absolutely necessary, and not unless you have a link with high bandwidth and low traffic and you can reasonably expect the link to stay that way." Not a concise rule, perhaps, but one that will serve you well.

TYPES OF REPLICAS   A *master replica* is created automatically when you create a partition. There can be only one master replica of any given partition. Master replicas are like the read/write replicas described next, with one important difference: If you want to change the boundaries of a partition in any way, you must be able to access the master replica of that partition. If the master replica becomes damaged, or the server that hosts it goes down, another replica can be promoted to master replica. Master replicas send out changes made to NDS objects that they contain, and can also be used to authenticate logins.

Read/write replicas are copies of the master replica that also send out the changes made to the NDS objects that they contain. Novell recommends creating at least two read/write replicas for each master replica. These read/write replicas should not be placed across a slow WAN link, however, as the slow transmission speed may make it impossible for the replicas to *synchronize* with each other when a change is made to an NDS object. Read/write replicas can also be used to authenticate logins.

Read-only replicas receive updates from master and read/write replicas, but do not allow their NDS objects to be modified. Since they do not allow changes to be made to their objects, it follows that they do not send out any updates to other replicas. Read-only replicas cannot be used to authenticate logins. They mainly exist because the original X.500 Proposal incorporated them when Novell was developing NDS. They allow placement of a replica for fault tolerance that does not generate outgoing synchronization traffic, although they do receive incoming synchronization updates from the master replica.

Subordinate references are created automatically by NDS when a server's hard drive holds a replica of a partition, but not a replica of its child partition. For example, let's say that a partition is created for the SoCal container in the CA container, and that a partition is created for the LA container in the SoCal container, as shown in Figure 24-6. If a server has a replica of the SoCal container, but does not have a replica of the LA partition, then NDS will create subordinate references that will point to the LA partition. Subordinate references cannot be created or accessed by users or administrators, only by NDS. You cannot modify objects in subordinate references (remember, there are no objects, only pointers), and you cannot use subordinate references to authenticate logins.

FIGURE 24-6	Subordinate references will be created for servers that hold a replica of the SoCal partition, but don't hold replicas of partitions further down the tree from the SoCal partition

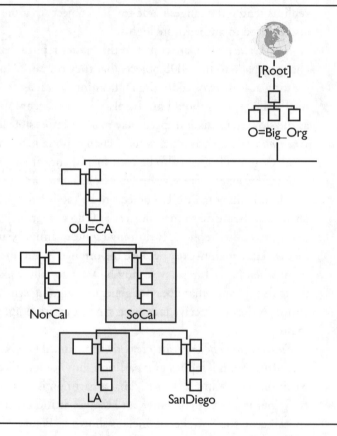

exam
ⓦatch

Novell loves to test on subordinate references. You are quite likely to get a question in which you have to figure out which servers in a tree hold subordinate references.

The following Question and Answer section contains some things to watch for in exams that relate to replicas and tells you how to respond to the clues.

QUESTIONS AND ANSWERS

You are asked if a master replica is most like a read/write, read-only, or subordinate reference replica.	Choose the answer that says that a master replica is most like a read/write replica.
You are asked which replica you must have access to when changing the boundaries of a partition.	Choose the master replica of a partition. Remember that the unique thing about a master replica is that you must be able to access it when changing partition boundaries.
You are asked which types of replicas allow you to make changes to the NDS objects that they contain.	Choose the answer that lists master and read/write replicas. Remember that read-only and subordinate reference replicas are modified only by NDS, not by administrators.
You are asked which servers in a list of servers hold subordinate references.	Choose servers that hold replicas of partitions, but not replicas of the children of those partitions.

Synchronization

When military special forces–type teams begin a critical mission, they always synchronize their watches to make sure that they can coordinate their actions, even though they're in different places looking at different watches. In much the same way, NDS must make sure that all copies of a section of the NDS tree contain the same information. To make things even more interesting, NDS must do two different types of synchronization to make sure that the database is updated properly: NDS synchronization and time synchronization.

NDS Synchronization

NDS is truly a marvel of modern programming. There are few database systems that can split off parts of the database and synchronize copies of the parts. The Directory is what is known as a *loosely consistent* database, which means the database maintains its integrity even if there are slight differences in replicas for a short period of time. NDS does continuously check all replicas, however, to see if objects in those replicas have been added, deleted, or modified. NDS then makes changes to the appropriate replicas to make sure that they all contain the most up-to-date information. This process is called *NDS synchronization.*

Time Synchronization

In order to keep track of which updates are the latest, NDS must also synchronize the time between all of the servers in the network. In fact, it would probably be impossible to keep a distributed database up-to-date if every server's clock was set to a different time. The process that NetWare servers use to coordinate and agree on a correct time is called *time synchronization.*

CERTIFICATION OBJECTIVE 24.02

Preventative Maintenance

It's normal to think of maintenance as something that you do on an ongoing basis. However, in "maintaining" NDS, there are things that you can do before NDS is installed, as well as after it's installed, to help prevent problems from happening in the first place.

Before NDS Is Installed

You should follow the procedures discussed in the next subsections to ensure that NDS can be maintained properly once installed.

Network Traffic

It is important when designing the NDS tree, before NDS is even installed on the servers, to plan the number and placement of replicas and partitions.

Although the network traffic generated by NDS synchronization is relatively minor in small networks, large networks with many replicas will generate a fair amount of traffic as updates travel between the replicas. Therefore, it is important not to have too many replicas and not to place replicas of a partition across slow or expensive network links. Otherwise, synchronization traffic will use up too much line capacity. Also, if updates are not received regularly, as can happen on very slow lines, the NDS database can literally get "out of sync."

Quality Equipment

The importance of quality equipment cannot be stressed enough. You should always try to get the best quality network hardware that your organization can reasonably afford. Stick with name brands that are known to have a record of quality and compatibility. Besides being reliable, getting name brand equipment affords you the luxury of being able to find replacement parts, drivers, and service more easily than with most cheaper, no-name equipment. Defective hardware can cause many problems that can affect NDS, and hardware problems are often very difficult to track down.

After NDS Is Installed

After NDS is installed, follow the suggestions given next, to provide ongoing maintenance for NDS and to prevent problems from occurring in the future.

Backing Up the NDS Database

Most current backup software is also capable of backing up the Directory. Take care to set the backup program to back up NDS as well as the files on the server if the program is capable of it. A daily copy of NDS may be even more important than a daily backup of files because NDS may change much more in the course of a day than most of the files on the server in some organizations. You particularly want to back up NDS if you do not have replicas of your Directory on other servers. If you don't have replicas on other servers and your SYS: volume crashes, you'll need to restore from tape, so be sure to have that tape ready!

Managing SYS: Volume Space

NDS is stored on the SYS: volume of the server. If SYS: gets full, NDS will lock the Directory and allow no further changes to the NDS database until space is freed up. For this reason, most organizations keep only what's absolutely necessary on the SYS: volume and put data, print queues, and applications on other server volumes. You can check how full the SYS: volume is in NetWare 5 by loading MONITOR.NLM at the server prompt, going to the Available Options window, and selecting Volumes. A list of volumes and their percentage of use is shown in Figure 24-7.

Updating NDS Network Servers with Patches

Novell never stops working on NetWare, and they release *patches* to the network operating system on a regular basis. DS.NLM is the file to look for and place on each server. If you do update the DS.NLM file, make sure that you update it on all of the servers on the network. Otherwise, the different versions of Directory Services might not communicate perfectly with each other.

FIGURE 24-7

The Monitor screen shows a great deal of valuable information, including how much of a volume is being used

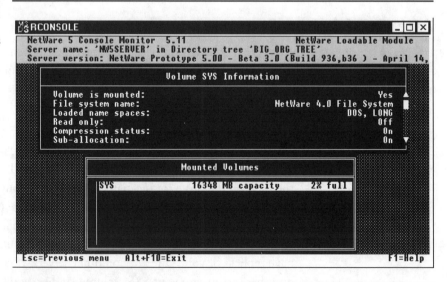

It is a good idea to wait two to four weeks before putting any patch on a production server —that is, a server used daily by the organization for ongoing business. Problems with patches are often not discovered right away. If you want to experiment with a brand-new patch, build a test network that does not connect to your production network and experiment in the test environment. The patch should be put into place only when you are fully convinced that it will not cause problems with existing software.

CERTIFICATION OBJECTIVE 24.03

Troubleshooting NDS Inconsistencies

Sometimes NDS problems are readily apparent and will make themselves known quickly and unmistakably. Other problems in the Directory may take a bit of detective work to find. This section discusses NetWare tools that help you troubleshoot NDS problems.

Readily Apparent Problems and Symptoms of Problems with NDS

NDS error messages are generated whenever replicas are unable to synchronize completely. These messages can be viewed in the file server error log, TTS$LOG.ERR, but the best way to keep track of NDS is to enter the following command at the server command prompt:

```
SET DSTRACE=ON
```

Then press ALT+ESC until you have toggled to the Directory Services screen. Any message similar to the following message means that synchronization is not going as it should and that the NDS database may need repair:

```
SYNC:  End sync of partition <name>. All processed=no
```

When users complain of problems similar to those listed here, NDS may need to be repaired:

- ■ User is prompted for a password, but does not have a password.

- ■ Workstations lose connection to network resources in ways that cannot be consistently or easily duplicated.

- ■ Logins are taking much longer than they should.

NDS Problems That Take Some Detective Work

By using NetWare utilities, you can look for inconsistencies in the NDS database before they manifest themselves in the form of a major problem. These utilities include NetWare Administrator, NDS Manager, and DSRepair.

exam
ⓦatch

Novell tests include simulations of NetWare Administrator and NDS Manager, in which you will have to perform simulated operations in each program. What's worse, you may have to take the test on a computer running Windows 3.1 in 640x480 mode. If possible, practice using both of these utilities on a computer similar to the one just described, so that you won't be thrown off by the different look of the screen at the exam.

In NetWare Administrator, look for objects in the tree with question-mark icons or unrecognizable, strange names. Some of these objects are temporary and normal; but, if any of these strange objects persist for more than a couple of days, it is likely that the Directory needs to be repaired.

In NDS Manager, select Check Synchronization from the Object menu to check the first server in a replica ring (see Figure 24-8). (A replica ring includes all servers with a replica of a particular partition.) Select Partition Continuity from the Object menu to check the replicas on all of the servers in the replica ring. NDS Manager will let you know if there are any problems with NDS synchronization.

Finally, DS Repair, which is loaded from the server prompt, can be used to check the synchronization status of all replicas on the server that DS Repair is run from. Figure 24-9 shows the Report Synchronization Status command in DS Repair.

FIGURE 24-8

Check Synchronization and
Partition Continuity
commands in NDS Manager

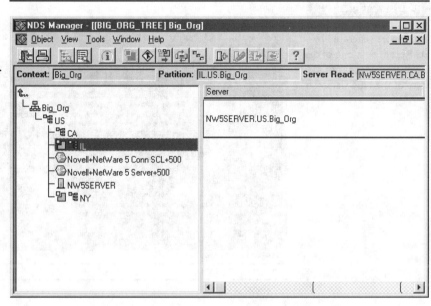

FIGURE 24-9

Report Synchronization
Status command
in DS Repair

Figure 24-10 shows the report generated by DS Repair. Review
the report for indications of synchronization problems with partitions
and replicas.

FIGURE 24-10

The report generated by
DS Repair gives one of the
most detailed looks at the
state of the NDS database

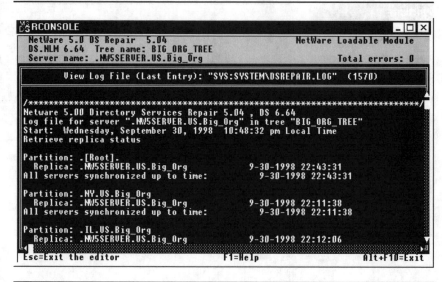

CERTIFICATION OBJECTIVE 24.04

Repairing NDS

NetWare also provides some very good tools for repairing problems with
NDS. This section will show you how to use DS Repair and NDS Manager
to fix inconsistencies in the NDS database.

A quick hint, though, before discussing the NetWare repair utilities.
Many problems in NDS that are related to synchronization will go away on
their own if the servers are left alone for a while and synchronization is

allowed to "catch up." For example, you might want to wait until the next Monday so that the servers can synchronize over the weekend when most organizations experience less network traffic. If the problem seems to be severe, however, don't wait—use one of the tools discussed in the following sections.

DS Repair

In the preceding section, you saw how DS Repair can be used to discover problems in the NDS database. Well, DS Repair also happens to be one of the easiest ways to repair a damaged database. Simply select Unattended Full Repair from the main menu and let DS Repair examine the database, find problems, and repair them (see Figure 24-11).

A few words of caution, however. The Directory will be locked part of the time that Unattended Full Repair is running, which means that users may not be able to use network resources during the time the NDS database is locked. Also, it is possible, though not likely, for DS Repair to delete or

---

FIGURE 24-11

The Unattended Full Repair command in DS Repair is often the quickest and easiest way to find and repair inconsistencies in the NDS database

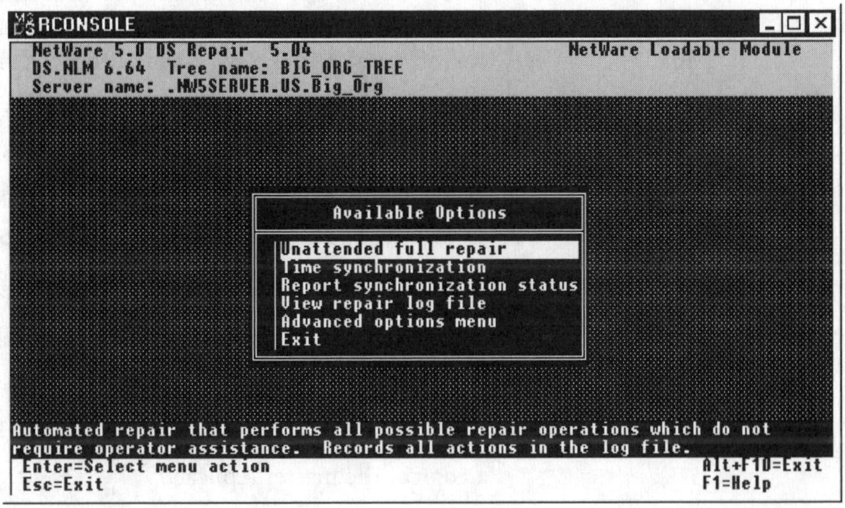

```
RCONSOLE                                                              _ □ ✕
NetWare 5.0 DS Repair  5.04                        NetWare Loadable Module
DS.NLM 6.64   Tree name: BIG_ORG_TREE
Server name: .NW5SERVER.US.Big_Org



                        ┌─────── Available Options ───────┐
                        │ Unattended full repair          │
                        │ Time synchronization            │
                        │ Report synchronization status   │
                        │ View repair log file            │
                        │ Advanced options menu           │
                        │ Exit                            │
                        └─────────────────────────────────┘


Automated repair that performs all possible repair operations which do not
require operator assistance.  Records all actions in the log file.
 Enter=Select menu action                                  Alt+F10=Exit
 Esc=Exit                                                   F1=Help
```

corrupt objects or portions of the Directory. Make sure that you back up the Directory before running any repair program on it.

NDS Manager

NDS Manager is used for repairing partitions and replicas, and also for creating them, deleting them, merging them, and working with them in other ways.

One of the most important repair functions of NDS Manager is its ability to promote a read/write replica to a master replica. If a master replica becomes damaged, a read/write replica can be promoted to a master replica, and the damaged master replica is automatically demoted to a read/write replica and then synchronized with the new, uncorrupted master replica.

To promote a read/write replica to a master replica, follow the steps outlined in Exercise 24-1.

EXERCISE 24-1

Promoting a Read/Write Replica to a Master Replica

1. Start NDS Manager.

2. Click once on the server that hosts the read/write replica that you want to promote to master. A list of the replicas hosted by the server appears in the right-hand pane of the NDS Manager window.

3. Right-click the partition that you want to promote.

4. Select Change Type from the pop-up menu.

5. Select Master from the types of replicas displayed.

6. Click OK. The read/write replica will now be promoted to master and the master demoted to read/write.

NDS Manager also can perform repair operations with some useful tools in the Object menu:

- **Replica...Receive Updates**   Deletes the replica and replaces it with a copy of the master replica.

- **Replica...Send Updates**   Forces immediate synchronization with all other servers in the replica ring.

CERTIFICATION OBJECTIVE 24.05

Recovering from a Crashed SYS: Volume

Did you ever think about what would constitute your worst possible day? It's pretty likely that a crashed SYS: volume would figure into it prominently. Exercise 24-2 tells you what to do when disaster strikes and you have to restore your server's SYS: volume.

EXERCISE 24-2

Restoring a Server's SYS: Volume

1. Take a deep breath. After all, you've been conscientious about backing everything up, right?

2. Make a list of the replicas that were on the downed server. Do this by running NDS Manager from another, working server and clicking the downed server's object. The list of replicas that were on the downed server will show up in the right-hand pane of the NDS Manager window. If there were any master replicas on the downed server, promote read/write replicas on other servers to master.

3. Click the downed server's object in NDS Manager and delete it. Yikes!

4. In NetWare Administrator, delete the downed server's volume objects from the tree.

5. Use NDS Manager's Object...Partition Continuity command to clean up any lingering NDS inconsistencies in the partition that the server resided in.

6. Set up the new hard disk and reload NetWare, making sure to put the server back into the same context in the tree that it was in before.

7. Use NDS Manager to restore all replicas that used to be on the server from other servers in the replica ring. Promote read/write replicas back to master replicas if necessary.

8. Restore any third-party system files and/or nonsystem files to the volume. (Your SYS: volume should have only system files and nonsystem files that are essential on it, right?)

9. Check to make sure that the bindery context is correct by going to the Monitor screen on the server and selecting Server Parameters from the Available Options menu as shown in Figure 24-12.

10. Next, select Directory Services as shown in Figure 24-13.

11. Finally, scroll down to the Bindery Context line in the Directory Services Parameters window, as shown in Figure 24-14.

12. If the context is correct, then your server should be fully recovered!

FIGURE 24-12

The Monitor screen now includes the information and settings that were in the SERVMAN utility in former versions of NetWare

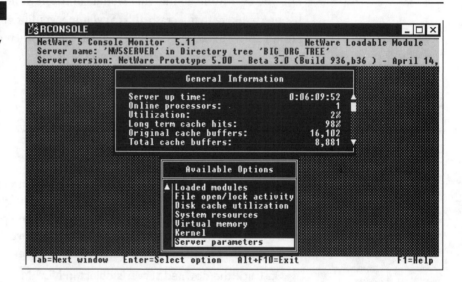

FIGURE 24-13

Many server settings can easily be changed from the Server Parameter menu

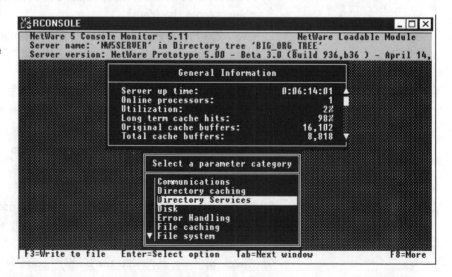

FIGURE 24-14

The context shows up in the Bindery Context line, and also in the pop-up help window

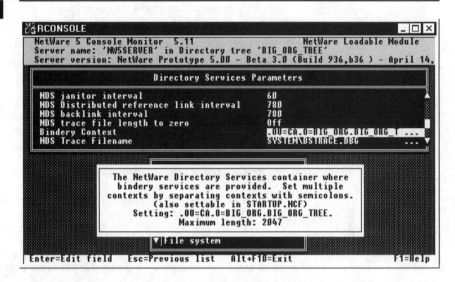

```
RCONSOLE                                                          _ □ ×
┌─────────────────────────────────────────────────────────────────────┐
│ NetWare 5 Console Monitor  5.11                  NetWare Loadable Module│
│ Server name: 'NW5SERVER' in Directory tree 'BIG_ORG_TREE'              │
│ Server version: NetWare Prototype 5.00 - Beta 3.0 (Build 936,b36 ) - April 14,│
│ ┌─────────────────── Directory Services Parameters ───────────────────┐│
│ │ NDS janitor interval                    60                          ▲││
│ │ NDS Distributed reference link interval 780                          ││
│ │ NDS backlink interval                   780                          ││
│ │ NDS trace file length to zero           Off                          ││
│ │ Bindery Context                         .OU=CA.O=BIG_ORG.BIG_ORG_T ...││
│ │ NDS Trace Filename                      SYSTEM\DSTRACE.DBG        ... ▼││
│ │    ┌───────────────────────────────────────────────────────┐        ││
│ │    │  The NetWare Directory Services container where        │        ││
│ │    │  bindery services are provided.  Set multiple          │        ││
│ │    │ contexts by separating contexts with semicolons.       │        ││
│ │    │      (also settable in STARTUP.NCF)                    │        ││
│ │    │  Setting: .OU=CA.O=BIG_ORG.BIG_ORG_TREE.               │        ││
│ │    │           Maximum length: 2047                         │        ││
│ │    └───────────────────────────────────────────────────────┘        ││
│ │                    ▼│File system                                     ││
│ └─────────────────────────────────────────────────────────────────────┘│
│ Enter=Edit field    Esc=Previous list    Alt+F10=Exit         F1=Help  │
└─────────────────────────────────────────────────────────────────────┘
```

CERTIFICATION SUMMARY

The NDS database, Directory, or tree, holds information about every object that makes up the network, including users, servers, printers, and other network resources. Objects are primarily grouped into containers called Organizational Units. Organizational Units and the Admin object are usually held in an Organization container just below the [Root] of the tree. The NDS database can be split up into partitions, along the boundaries of the partitions. Partitions are named for the container that they encompass that is closest to the [Root] of the tree, called the partition root. Partitions that are higher in the tree than other partitions are called parents of the lower partitions, which are called child partitions. Replicas are copies of partitions, placed on multiple servers for fault tolerance and to improve access to the Directory. The replicas use NDS synchronization and time synchronization to update information among them.

Preventative maintenance is done to minimize the possibility of corruption of the NDS database. Techniques include partition and replica placement, the use of quality equipment, backup of the Directory, monitoring of the free space on the SYS: drive, and applying patches and updates to the DS.NLM file.

Inconsistencies in the NDS database may be readily apparent or more difficult to discover. The command SET DSTRACE=ON can be used at the server prompt to monitor NDS synchronization. User complaints can also be a sign of NDS problems. NetWare Administrator, NDS Manager, and DS Repair are NetWare utilities to find and repair errors in the NDS database.

You can recover a server's SYS: volume by following these steps:

■ Remove it and its volume objects from NDS.

■ Reinstall the system software onto a new hard drive.

■ Restore its NDS database from replicas on other servers or from tape backup.

■ Restore user files.

■ Last, verify the context using the Monitor utility from the server prompt.

TWO-MINUTE DRILL

❑ Most of a network engineer's time is spent maintaining the network. For a NetWare network, that means maintaining the Novell Directory Services database of user, server, and other objects.

❑ Replication is important to a network administrator whether the network is large or small. In small networks, replication backs up NDS and provides fault tolerance or another place to access a copy of NDS if the master copy is not accessible. In large networks, replication also allows users quick access to the Directory from a local server.

❑ You should have replicas, or copies of partitions of the NDS database, on more than one server for two reasons: first, to enable users to access the Directory in order to log in to the network and use network drives and printers; second, to allow users to use network resources more quickly by enabling them to access the NDS database on a server that is close to them, or that they can connect to with a high-speed connection.

❑ A master replica is created automatically when you create a partition. There can be only one master replica of any given partition. If you want to change the boundaries of a partition in any way, you must be able to access the master replica of that partition.

❑ Read/write replicas are copies of the master replica that also send out the changes made to the NDS objects that they contain. Novell recommends creating at least two read/write replicas for each master replica.

❑ Read-only replicas receive updates from master and read/write replicas, but do not allow their NDS objects to be modified.

❑ Subordinate references are created automatically by NDS when a server's hard drive holds a replica of a partition, but not a replica of its child partition.

❑ NDS must make sure that all copies of a section of the NDS tree contain the same information. NDS must do two different types of synchronization to make sure that the database is updated properly: NDS synchronization and time synchronization.

❑ The NDS Directory is a loosely consistent database, or a database that maintains its integrity even if there are slight differences in replicas for a short period of time. However, NDS continuously checks all replicas to see if objects in those replicas have been added, deleted, or modified. NDS then makes changes to the appropriate replicas to make sure that all replicas contain the most up-to-date information. This process is called NDS synchronization.

❑ In order to keep track of which updates are the latest, NDS must also synchronize the time between all of the servers in the network.

❑ When designing the NDS tree, it is important to plan the number and placement of replicas and partitions.

❑ Most backup software is also capable of backing up the Directory. Take care to set the backup program to back up NDS, as well as the files on the server, if the program is capable of it.

❑ NDS is stored on the SYS: volume of the server. If SYS: gets full, NDS will lock the Directory and allow no further changes to the NDS database until space is freed up.

❑ Novell releases patches to the NetWare network operating system on a regular basis. DS.NLM is the file to look for and place on each server. If you update the DS.NLM file, make sure that you update it on all of the servers on the network.

❑ NDS error messages are generated whenever replicas are unable to synchronize completely. These messages can be viewed in the file server error log (TTS$LOG.ERR). The best way to keep track of NDS is to enter the following command at the server command prompt: SET DSTRACE=ON

❑ By using NetWare utilities, you can look for inconsistencies in the NDS database before they manifest themselves in the form of a major problem. These utilities include NetWare Administrator, NDS Manager, and DS Repair.

❑ DS Repair is one of the easiest ways to repair a damaged database. Simply select Unattended Full Repair from the main menu, and let DS Repair examine the database, find problems, and repair them.

❑ NDS Manager is used for repairing partitions and replicas, and also for creating, deleting, merging, and otherwise working with them. One of the most important repair functions of NDS Manager is its ability to promote a read/write replica to a master replica.

SELF TEST

The following Self-Test questions will help you measure your understanding of the material presented in this chapter. Read all the choices carefully, as there may be more than one correct answer. Choose all correct answers for each question.

1. Which statement about the Directory is not true?

   A. The Directory is used for authentication.

   B. The Directory contains program and data files.

   C. The Directory is used by the access control process.

   D. The Directory contains the names, property values, and rights of the objects that make up the network.

2. The Directory can be split into pieces called

   A. Containers

   B. Boundaries

   C. Organizational Units

   D. Partitions

3. It is possible to have more than one container in a partition.

   A. True

   B. False

4. Partitions are named

   A. For the biggest container in the partition

   B. Partition 1, Partition 2, and so on, in order of creation

   C. For the container in the partition that is highest in the tree, closest to the [Root]

   D. For the container that has the most User objects in it

5. A parent partition is a partition that

   A. Has a partition below it in the tree

   B. Is used to contain the most important Directory objects

   C. Contains more than one Organizational Unit

   D. Is used by educational organizations to group the User objects of the parents of their students

6. Copies of partitions are called

   A. Replicants

   B. Partition Mirrors

   C. Backup Partitions

   D. Replicas

7. Replicas are placed on more than one server for which of the following two reasons:

   A. Users run network applications from replicas.

   B. Users can access a replica of a partition if the server that they usually get it from goes down.

   C. A replica contains licensing information and must therefore be on each server.

   D. Users can access Directory information more efficiently if there is a replica containing the information that they need on a server that is close to them.

8. Which type of replica can be created only by NDS, not by an administrator?

   A. Read-only

   B. Subordinate References

   C. Master

   D. Read/Write

9. The Directory is a database that maintains its integrity even if there are slight differences in replicas for a short amount of time. This type of database is called

   A. Loosely consistent

   B. Fault tolerant

   C. Consistently integrated

   D. Loosely synchronized

10. Servers keep track of and agree on a common time through a process called

    A. NDS synchronization

    B. Time coordination

    C. Time synchronization

    D. Polling

11. To minimize network traffic, you should

    A. Make sure to put replicas on both sides of a WAN link.

    B. Do everything possible not to put replicas on both sides of a WAN link.

    C. Place all replicas of a partition on the same server.

    D. Not create replicas for any partition but the master partition.

12. When purchasing hardware for your network, you should

A. Buy the least expensive that you can find, since the only difference between brands is the price, and you need to save the company's money.

B. Buy whatever the salesperson recommends, because the salesperson will offer an unbiased, knowledgeable recommendation.

C. Buy the best quality, brand-name hardware that your organization can reasonably afford.

13. Backing up files is important, and it is at least as important to back up

    A. Programs

    B. Passwords

    C. The NDS database

    D. NLMs

14. To easily see how full the SYS: volume is, you can use

    A. INSTALL.NLM

    B. The DISKSIZE command

    C. NDS Manager

    D. MONITOR.NLM

15. When updating NDS with a new DS.NLM patch, you should

    A. Patch all servers on the network.

    B. Just patch the first server that was placed on the network, and it will automatically patch the rest.

    C. Just patch the first server that was placed on the network, since that is the only server that needs to be patched.

    D. Patch all servers on the network that host a master replica.

16. The status of NDS synchronization can best be monitored by

    A. Looking at the TTS$LOG.ERR error log file once every few weeks

    B. Using MONITOR.NLM

    C. Typing the **Set DSTRACE=ON** command at the server command prompt and toggling to the Directory Services screen by pressing ALT+ESC

    D. Typing **MONITOR DSTRACE** at the server command prompt and toggling to the Directory Services screen by pressing ALT+ESC

17. Which of the following is not a sign that NDS may need to be repaired?

    A. User is prompted for a password, but does not have a password.

    B. Workstations lose connection to network resources in ways that cannot be consistently or easily duplicated.

    C. Logins are taking much longer than they should.

    D. A user can log in on only one workstation at a time.

18. While in NetWare Administrator, you notice strange objects in the tree. You should

    A. Delete the objects immediately, since they will cause problems with NDS.

    B. Check the tree again in a couple of days. If the strange objects are still there, use one of the repair utilities provided with NetWare.

    C. Rename the objects to something recognizable.

    D. Do nothing. NDS sometimes gives strange names to permanent objects in the tree.

19. Besides looking for strange objects in NetWare Administrator, you can use the following utilities provided with NetWare to check the status of the NDS Database:

    A. Partition Manager and DSSTATUS

    B. NDS Manager and DSSTATUS

    C. NDS Manager and DSREPAIR

    D. Partition Manager and DSREPAIR

20. Which of the following are the two most common utilities for repairing problems in the Directory?

    A. NDS Manager

    B. NDS Repair

    C. DS Fix

    D. DS Repair

21. A DS Repair Unattended Full Repair should be run

    A. As soon as you suspect a problem with the Directory, even if users are logged in

    B. After backing up the Directory, at a time that not many users are logged in

    C. After backing up the Directory, even when users are logged in

    D. A maximum of once per month per number of replicas on the server

22. When a master replica becomes corrupted

    A. You should use NDS Manager to promote a read/write replica to master.

B. NDS will automatically promote a read/write replica to master.

C. You shouldn't worry, because a master replica is just the name given to the first read/write replica to be created.

D. Your only course of action is to restore an old copy of the replica from a tape or other backup device.

23. When a server goes down, you can find out which replicas and what types of replicas were on the server:

A. By using the REPLICAS <SERVERNAME> command from the command prompt of a working server.

B. By relying on the photographic memory that all CNE's are genetically blessed with.

C. By running NDS Manager from a working server and clicking the downed server's icon.

D. By restoring the Directory to a new hard drive and then running NDS Manager from that new hard drive.

25

Mobile Clients

CERTIFICATION OBJECTIVES

25.01   Introduction to Mobile Clients

25.02   Connecting Remotely

25.03   Using Remote Connections

25.04   Installing NetWare Connect on
         the Server

25.05   Configuring NetWare Connect

I n today's increasingly mobile workplace, enterprises find that it is a business requirement to offer remote networking capabilities to associates.

- In large cities, pollution control efforts have pushed businesses to present work-at-home alternatives to associates who travel by car.

- Travelling employees find that they need to "plug in and dial up" to the corporate network to update their associates on the business trip progress.

- Service organizations whose employees are off-site need to offer those employees access to the network from remote locations.

- Some organizations have found that offering a limited dial-up access to other organizations, or customers, is required for doing business.

CERTIFICATION OBJECTIVE 25.01

Introduction to Mobile Clients

A *mobile client* is a workstation or laptop used by a user that works from remote locations. Mobile clients are generally laptop or notebook computers with modems installed on them. They connect to the network via a dial-up telephone line. Another type of connection for mobile clients is through an ISDN (Integrated Services Digital Network) adapter and ISDN line that offer higher bandwidth compared to typical modems and telephone wires.

Remote Node versus Remote Control

There are two ways that mobile clients connect to the network: as a remote node client or as a workstation remotely controlling a local client.

When a client connects to the network via PPP (Point to Point Protocol), it can connect network drives and access network resources the same as though connected locally to the network. A remote connection protocol, PPP connects the workstation to the network at the physical and MAC layer of the applicable protocol stack (either IP or IPX). The network, transport, and upper-layer protocols transmit over that. The workstation uses the modem much the way it would a network interface card (NIC). This is called a *remote node*.

The benefit of a remote node is that end users need not change how they use their workstation from the way they use it on the network (aside from initializing the remote connection, of course). The drawback is that the bandwidth of the link is small compared to a network connection, making the transfer of data and execution of network applications extremely slow.

Remote nodes are suitable for applications that boot off the hard drive of the mobile client and need to have network connectivity only for small data transfers such as intranet access, electronic messaging, and word processing applications. Remote nodes are not suitable for applications that boot from the network or for database applications in which the database is located on the network. Figure 25-1 illustrates the remote node process.

When a client connects to the network and takes control of a workstation that exists on the network, that client is considered to be running by *remote control*.

A remotely controlled workstation is one attached to the network and has remote control software installed and running. It waits for a connection, which usually occurs through a direct modem connection or over the network. Once a connection is established, the remotely controlled workstation sends presentation data to the controlling workstation (display, keyboard, and mouse) so that the controlling workstation can manipulate applications and data on the workstation that is connected to the network.

The benefit of remote control is that it can take optimal advantage of low bandwidth since the data being exchanged is minimal. The drawbacks to remote control are these:

- It requires multiple workstations in order to be implemented. Each connection requires two workstations: one remote and the other connected to the network. For multiple workstations to be accessed simultaneously, there must be several workstations available on the network.

FIGURE 25-1	Remote node

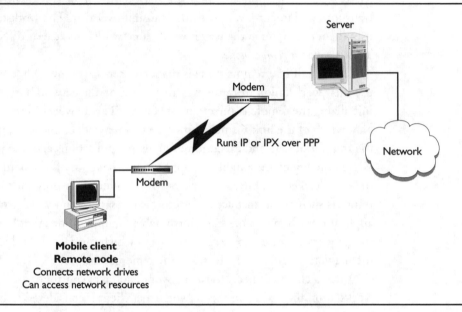

The network nodes lack security since they must always be up and running.

Special remote control software must be running on each of the workstations involved in a connection—both the network node and the mobile client.

A remote control workstation is suitable for access to databases and applications that are located on the network. A remote control workstation is not suitable for large numbers of mobile clients, or a secure environment. Figure 25-2 illustrates the remote control process.

exam
Watch

Remote nodes are mobile clients that access the network using the modem as if it were a network interface card. Remote control workstations wait for a connection from a mobile client and allow it to take over its functions by sending presentation data over the wire.

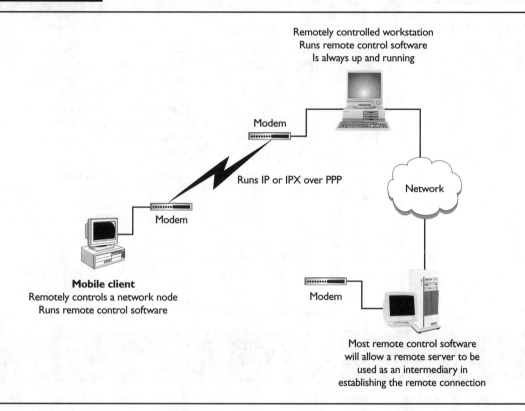

FIGURE 25-2

Remote control

Remotely controlled workstation
Runs remote control software
Is always up and running

Modem

Runs IP or IPX over PPP

Network

Modem

Mobile client
Remotely controls a network node
Runs remote control software

Modem

Most remote control software
will allow a remote server to be
used as an intermediary in
establishing the remote connection

CERTIFICATION OBJECTIVE 25.02

Connecting Remotely

NetWare 5 comes equipped with NetWare Connect, a remote dial-in connectivity software product from Novell that is now part of NetWare Internet Access Server (NIAS). NetWare Connect supports the services listed in Table 25-1 to the NetWare 5 network.

TABLE 25-1	Acronym	Service Name	Services Offered
Remote Access Services	ARAS	Appletalk Remote Access Services	Remote connection services for Macintosh computers.
	NCS	NASI Connection Services	Dial-out services for network-connected computers and remote control support for PCs and Macintoshes, if dedicated workstations for remote control and appropriate software are installed on the network.
	PPPRNS	PPP Remote Node Services	Remote connection services for DOS/UNIX/Windows computers to dial in and act as remote nodes over Point to Point Protocol over IP or IPX.
	RAMA	Remote Access Management Agent	Allows remote access to be controlled by any SNMP (Simple Network Management Protocol)–based console on the network.

QUESTIONS AND ANSWERS

Bruce has installed a NetWare 5 network and implemented the NetWare Connect PPPRNS service on a server with several attached modems. To test the service, Bruce used his home computer, which had Windows 95 and NetBEUI installed on it. Why would Bruce receive errors?	The PPPRNS service will allow network nodes to run over IP or IPX, but not over NetBEUI. Bruce should reconfigure the Windows 95 workstation to use IP or IPX and the NetWare client software.

CERTIFICATION OBJECTIVE 25.03

Using Remote Connections

Microsoft Windows 95, Windows 98, and Windows NT 4.0 are equipped with a native remote access software called Dial-Up Networking. Dial-Up

Networking can establish remote node connections to NetWare Connect servers, among other types of remote access servers.

EXERCISE 25-1

Configuring a Windows 95/8 Dial-Up Networking Connection

1. Double-click the My Computer icon on your desktop.

2. Double-click the Dial-Up Networking icon.

3. Double-click the Make New Connection wizard icon.

4. Type an appropriate name and verify or select the correct modem device; then click Next.

5. Type the correct area code and phone number; then click Next.

6. Click Finish.

7. The default settings will work for many networks, but some may require different settings. To edit the properties of the connection, right-click each of them and select Properties. You will get a dialog box, shown here.

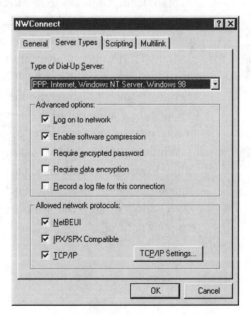

Remote Clients

There are several types of remote clients supported by NetWare Connect:

- **Macintosh Remote Nodes** Supported by Appletalk Remote Access Services (ARAS)

- **DOS Remote Nodes** Supported by PPPRNS (Point to Point Protocol Remote Node Service)

- **Windows 3.x Remote Nodes** Supported by PPPRNS

- **UNIX Remote Nodes** Supported by PPPRNS

- **Windows 95/98** Supported by PPPRNS

- **Windows NT Workstation 4.0** Supported by PPPRNS

- **Windows Remote Control** Supported by NCS (NASI Connection Service)

Macintosh clients can obtain the Appletalk Remote Access 1.0 or 2.0 program from Apple computer to access the ARAS service. To dial out of the network, a Macintosh workstation needs the Mac2NCS redirector software available from Novell on the MAC Client disk installed.

Many UNIX clients have native support for remote node connections over PPP. However, DOS and Windows 3.1x clients require PPPRNS client software for dialing into the network. Win2NCS software can be installed for dialing out of the network through the server's pool of modems or to wait for a remote control connection.

Windows 95/98 and NT 4.0 support remote node connections over PPP. However, you may need to install the Win2NCS software if dial-out capabilities are required from a network-connected workstation using the server's modems or if the workstation will be waiting for a connection to be remotely controlled.

Installing Win2NCS

1. On the NetWare 5 CD, access the PRODUCTS\WIN2NCS directory.

2. Double-click SETUP.EXE.

3. At the welcome screen, click Next.

4. Click the Custom button.

5. At the Installation Options dialog box, select the desired option for configuration files location. Then click Next. The Win2NCS Installation Options menu is shown here.

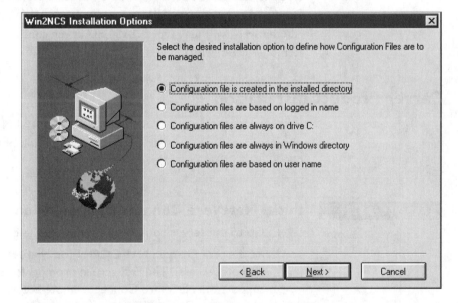

6. Either accept the default directory for the Win2NCS application or select a new one and click Next.

7. Select the COM port or ports that Win2NCS will be granted access to. Make sure to de-select any COM ports used by hardware other than a modem, such as a serial mouse. Click Next.

8. Win2NCS will copy files and locate the modems assigned to the COM ports selected. Then it will create a new Win2NCS program group. If desired, click Yes to view the README file. Click OK to finish.

CERTIFICATION OBJECTIVE 25.04

Installing NetWare Connect on the Server

NetWare 5 comes equipped with the NetWare Connect files as part of the system. There is no need to run an installation process to copy those files to the server. In order to begin the process of finalizing the installation, simply type the command **NWCCON** at the console prompt. NWCCON is the Remote Access Configuration program. It is a NetWare Loadable Module. Alternatively, you may type **NIASCFG** at the console prompt and select Remote Access, which will then prompt the NWCCON program to run.

Server Product Installation

Since NetWare Connect files are included as part of NetWare 5, server product installation consists of initial configuration of the NetWare Connect components.

EXERCISE 25-3

Initial NetWare Connect Configuration

1. Go to the server console and switch to the console prompt.

2. At the prompt, type **NWCCON** (or type **NIASCFG** and select Remote Access). The first screen prompts for schema extension to support the NetWare Connect remote access properties of NDS objects (see Figure 25-3).

3. When asked for instructions, select No.

4. Press ENTER to continue installation.

5. The next screen will prompt for synchronous adapters (see Figure 25-4). Select Yes if you have ISDN (not terminal adapters) or X.25 adapters. Otherwise, select No.

6. Next, there is a screen for asynchronous adapter boards. Press ENTER to configure AIO ports (asynchronous input/output).

7. Select the correct adapter from the list. If using a standard modem, select Serial Port (COMx) (see Figure 25-5)

FIGURE 25-3

Schema extension

8. Press ENTER to continue.

   The NWCCON program will search for modems attached to the ports on the adapter (see Figure 25-6).

9. After the modems have been discovered, press ENTER to continue.

FIGURE 25-4

Synchronous adapters

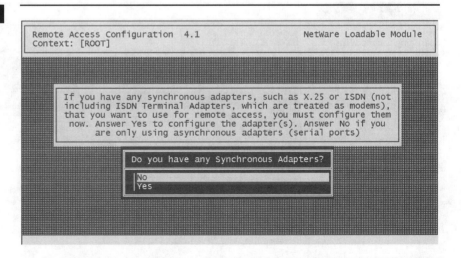

FIGURE 25-5

Serial adapter list

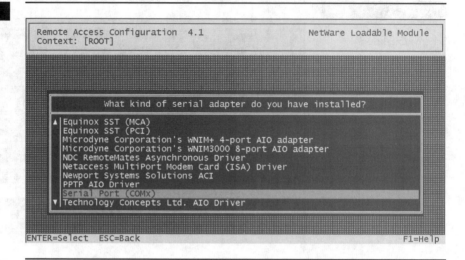

```
Remote Access Configuration  4.1                    NetWare Loadable Module
Context: [ROOT]



┌───────────────────────────────────────────────────────────────────────┐
│             What kind of serial adapter do you have installed?          │
├───────────────────────────────────────────────────────────────────────┤
│▲ Equinox SST (MCA)                                                      │
│  Equinox SST (PCI)                                                      │
│  Microdyne Corporation's WNIM+ 4-port AIO adapter                       │
│  Microdyne Corporation's WNIM3000 8-port AIO adapter                    │
│  NDC RemoteMates Asynchronous Driver                                    │
│  Netaccess MultiPort Modem Card (ISA) Driver                            │
│  Newport Systems Solutions ACI                                          │
│  PPTP AIO Driver                                                        │
│  Serial Port (COMX)                                                     │
│▼ Technology Concepts Ltd. AIO Driver                                    │
└───────────────────────────────────────────────────────────────────────┘

ENTER=Select   ESC=Back                                          F1=Help
```

10. Next, select the types of services that NetWare will offer: ARAS, NCS, PPPRNS, or RAMA. When selecting PPPRNS, you are prompted for the services to offer—either IP or IPX—then the addresses that are required for the service: an IP address and subnet mask, IP Header compression, and range of addresses for the IP

FIGURE 25-6

Searching for modems

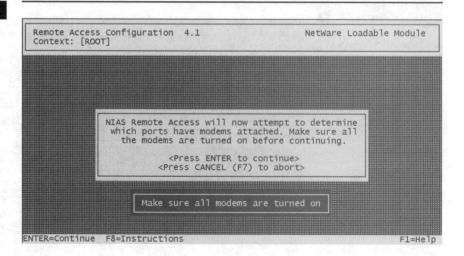

```
Remote Access Configuration  4.1                    NetWare Loadable Module
Context: [ROOT]




        ┌───────────────────────────────────────────────────┐
        │  NIAS Remote Access will now attempt to determine  │
        │  which ports have modems attached. Make sure all   │
        │    the modems are turned on before continuing.     │
        │                                                     │
        │            <Press ENTER to continue>               │
        │          <Press CANCEL (F7) to abort>              │
        └───────────────────────────────────────────────────┘

              ┌─────────────────────────────────────────┐
              │  Make sure all modems are turned on      │
              └─────────────────────────────────────────┘

ENTER=Continue   F8=Instructions                                 F1=Help
```

FIGURE 25-7

Basic configuration
complete

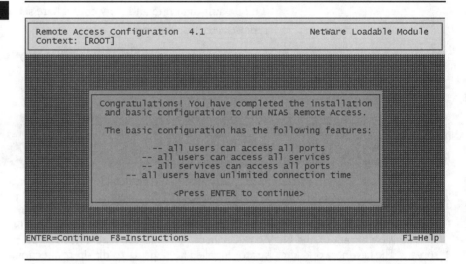

```
Remote Access Configuration  4.1                    NetWare Loadable Module
Context: [ROOT]




             Congratulations! You have completed the installation
             and basic configuration to run NIAS Remote Access.

             The basic configuration has the following features:

                        -- all users can access all ports
                        -- all users can access all services
                        -- all services can access all ports
                     -- all users have unlimited connection time

                            <Press ENTER to continue>




ENTER=Continue   F8=Instructions                                      F1=Help
```

service, and an IPX network address for the IPX service. Note that the addresses for IP and IPX should not already be in use on the network. You are then prompted to run INETCFG to bind the protocols to the adapter.

11. When you have finished selecting the services, press ESCAPE to return to the NWCCON program. The installation portion has completed and you will see the screen shown in Figure 25-7.

exam
ⓦatch

When a modem is connected directly to a serial port, the correct adapter to use is Serial Adapter (COMx). If another adapter is used, such as a Digiboard multiport adapter that extends the serial ports on a server, the Serial Adapter (COMx) is not used.

When the installation is complete, the default configuration is as follows:

- Bidirectional (both dial-in and dial-out) connections are enabled for all ports.

- Ports and services are enabled for all users.

- Established connections have no time limits.

■ The default data rate and flow control are set to match the modem type selected for that port.

■ For each modem, data bits are set at 8, parity to none, and stop bits are set at 1.

QUESTIONS AND ANSWERS

Acme Corporation has a strict corporate policy that no user can dial out of the network from a network-connected workstation. There are no modems installed on workstations and no modem lines available except on the NetWare Connect servers. The new network administrator installed a NetWare 5 server with NetWare Connect standard installation. Why does this violate Acme's policies?	The default configuration for a NetWare Connect server is that all ports allow dial-in and dial-out connections. In order to meet Acme's policy requirements, the NetWare Connect server would need to be configured to restrict ports to dial-in connections only.

CERTIFICATION OBJECTIVE 25.05

Configuring NetWare Connect

Once NetWare Connect has been installed on the server, it needs to be configured for the environment that it will service. Configuration occurs at either the server console or from within NDS. The items that can be configured are listed in Table 25-2.

Configuration at the Server Console

The NWCCON NetWare Loadable Module enables configuration of NetWare Connect at the server console after NetWare Connect has been installed. The administrator simply types the command **NWCCON** at the

TABLE 25-2	Configured Option	Application	Function
Configuration Options	Ports	NWCCON	Allows the modification of port names, data rates, and modem types. This is useful if the modem has difficulty in connecting or if the modems are changed.
	Port Groups	NWCCON	Enables the grouping of ports.
	Synchronous Interfaces	NWCCON	Allows the modification of synchronous adapter configuration parameters.
	Security	NWCCON	Enables restriction of ports or services so that only authorized users can access them or so that they are available only during specified time periods.
	Services	NWCCON	Allows modification of the parameters for the ARAS, PPPRNS, NCS, and RAMA services.
	Users	NetWare Administrator	Allows modification of the services and ports applicable to individual users.
	Container objects	NetWare Administrator	Allows modification of the services applicable to groups of users, but modified at the container object level.

server prompt and a Remote Access Options configuration screen opens (see Figure 25-8).

By selecting any option on the first NWCCON screen, the administrator can modify any parameter for the NetWare Connect server. Each NetWare Connect server on the network can have different services, port types, groups, and applicable security. The option to Generate Configuration Report creates a file displaying the configuration of the server's remote access parameters. An administrator can use the configuration report to verify specified settings, troubleshoot configuration problems, and document the server's configuration.

FIGURE 25-8

Remote access
configuration

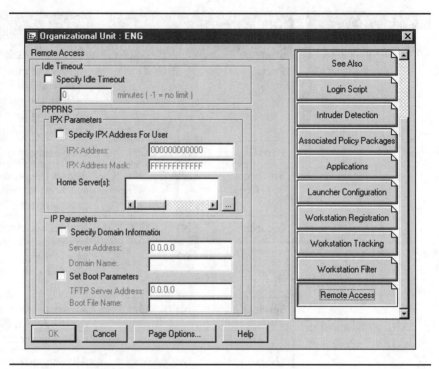

EXERCISE 25-4

Configuring Security for Ports and Services

1. From the server console, load NWCCON.

2. Select Configure Security; then select Restrict Ports by User.

3. Select a port, and then press the INSERT key. Select users and groups
   with the F5 key and press ENTER to add them to the list of
   authorized users for that port. Press ESCAPE twice.

4. Select Restrict Service by User, select a service. and press ENTER.

5. Press the INSERT key, select users and groups with the F5 key, and
   press ENTER to add them to the list of authorized users for that
   service. Press ESCAPE twice.

Global parameters are the key to server configuration and they affect all
users who dial in to that server. These parameters do not affect other servers.
The options available in the Global Parameters are listed in Table 25-3.

TABLE 25-3

Global Parameters for a
NetWare Connect Server

Parameter	Default	Function
Default Maximum Connect Time	−1	Defines the maximum amount of time that a client is allowed to be connected during a single session. −1 is equivalent to no limit.
Idle Time Before Disconnection	−1	Specifies the maximum amount of time during which a mobile client does not send data to NetWare Connect before it is disconnected. −1 equals no limit.
Dialback Wait Time	30 seconds	Specifies the number of seconds that the server waits before dialing back the client when configured for dial-back security.
Dialback Busy Retry Count	3	Specifies the number of times the server will attempt to connect to a client after being contacted when dial-back security is used.
Dialback busy retry interval	30 seconds	Specifies the number of seconds that the server will wait after receiving a busy signal during a dial-back when using dial-back security.
Dial-out restrictions	N/A	Defines the telephone numbers authorized to be used when dial-out is attempted through the NCS service.

Configuration Within NetWare Administrator

The NDS schema must be accessed with a snap-in DLL (data link library) file before remote access configuration options will appear in the NetWare Administrator program. To extend the schema for a Windows 95/98 workstation, copy the NWCADM95.DLL to the C:\WINDOWS directory of the workstation. Run the NWADMN95.EXE program once; then exit. Open the Registry Editor by choosing Start | Run; type **REGEDIT**, and press ENTER. Navigate to HKEY_CURRENT_USER | Software | NetWare | Parameters | NetWare Administrator | Snapin Object DLLs Win95. Click the Edit menu; select New | String Value. Type the name **NWCADM95.DLL**. When created, double-click the entry and type

C:\WINDOWS\NWCADM95.DLL. Then run NetWare Administrator again and the schema will include options for remote access in both container objects and User objects.

Container objects include remote access parameters for an idle timeout and protocol (IP and IPX) parameters for PPPRNS service, as shown in the following illustration. The users within the container will inherit these parameters.

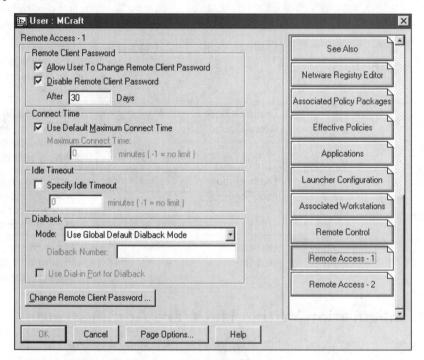

The Idle Timeout option sets how long the connection can remain open while there is no data being sent between the server and client. The PPPRNS options for IPX enable setting an IPX address for connected users and home servers. The IP parameters can specify a DNS (Domain Name Service) server and domain name. If required, the IP parameters include a TFTP (Tiny File Transfer Protocol) server and boot file for remote boot configuration, which is usually used for UNIX-based routers that use a common configuration.

Any changes made within the NetWare Administrator will apply to a user regardless of which NetWare Connect server the user is accessing. User objects have the same optional parameters as container objects, as well as others (see Figures 25-9 and 25-10). The additional parameters include the following:

- An option for the remote client password, which determines whether the user can change the password and can set an expiration date on the remote client password.

- Limitation for the connect time, so that each user can have a different maximum connect time.

- Dial-back options that can differ for each user.

- The ability to change the remote client password.

- Appletalk Remote Access Parameters (ARAS) to set the Appletalk zone.

FIGURE 25-9

User object remote access parameters

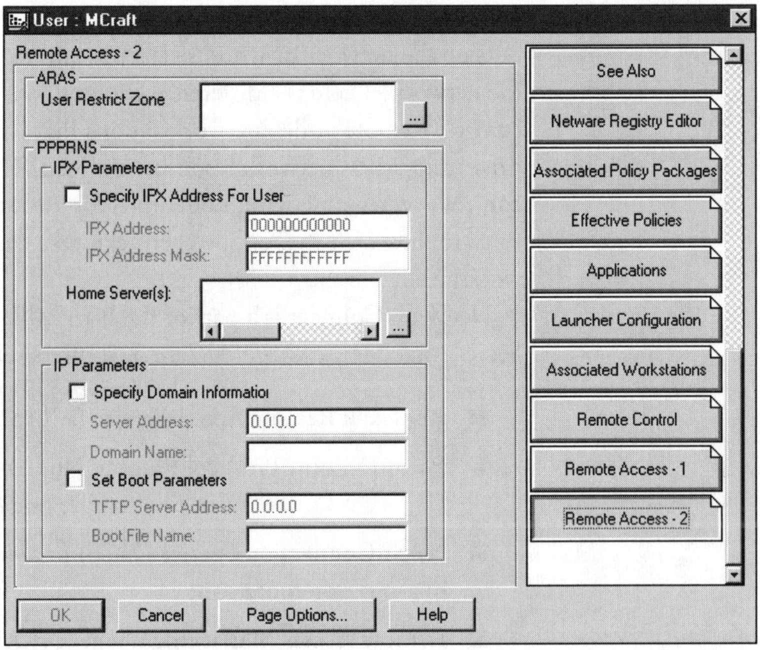

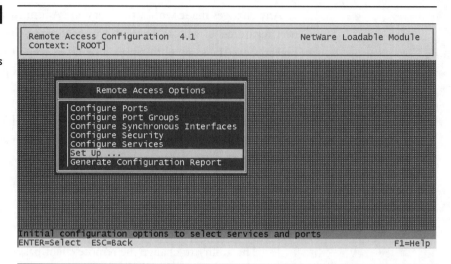

FIGURE 25-10

Additional User object
remote access parameters

CERTIFICATION SUMMARY

Mobile clients are essentially users who log in from multiple workstations outside the network or who use laptops and require dial-up connectivity to the network. There is a difference between a remote node and remote control. Remote nodes are workstations that connect and can map network drives and access network resources over a dial-up connection. Remote control is when a network node waits for a connection using special software in which the mobile client can take control of the network workstation.

NetWare Connect is a part of the NIAS (NetWare Internet Access Server) that comes with NetWare 5. It offers four remote service options:

- Appletalk Remote Access Service (ARAS) for Appletalk remote nodes
- Point to Point Protocol Remote Node Service (PPPRNS) for DOS/UNIX and Windows remote nodes
- NASI Connection Service (NCS) for Macintosh/DOS and Windows dial-out or remote control
- Remote Access Management Agent (RAMA) to assist in managing

NetWare Connect supports DOS, Windows 3.1*x*, Windows 95/98, Windows NT, Macintosh, and UNIX clients. The Windows 95/98, NT, and UNIX clients have remote node software native to the operating system. In Windows 95/98 and NT 4.0, this software is called Dial-Up Networking. In order to dial out of the network or to wait for a remote control connection, the Win2NCS or Mac2NCS software must be installed on the Windows or Macintosh workstation.

The NetWare Internet Access Server files are installed with NetWare 5. However, the initial installation on the server must be loaded through the NWCCON (or NIASCFG | Remote Access) NetWare Loadable Module. The installation process adds and configures dial-in/dial-out ports, remote services, and modems.

The NWCCON program also configures NetWare Connect after it has been installed on the server. At the server, the administrator can configure the ports, the modems, the services offered, and the applicable security.

Additionally, the NetWare Administrator has remote access parameters applicable to users. The parameters available within NetWare administrator are the idle timeout, remote client passwords, AppleTalk zones, and IP or IPX parameters.

 # TWO-MINUTE DRILL

❑ A *mobile client* is a user's workstation or laptop that works from remote locations.

❑ There are two ways that mobile clients connect to the network: as a remote node client or as a workstation remotely controlling a local client.

❑ NetWare 5 comes equipped with NetWare Connect, a remote dial-in connectivity software product from Novell that is now part of NetWare Internet Access Server (NIAS).

❑ Microsoft Windows 95, Windows 98, and Windows NT 4.0 are equipped with a native remote access software called Dial-Up Networking.

❑ Dial-Up Networking can establish remote node connections to NetWare Connect servers, among other types of remote access servers.

❑ When a client connects to the network and takes control of a workstation that exists on the network, that client is considered to be running *remote control.*

❑ The NWCCON NetWare Loadable Module enables configuration of NetWare Connect at the server console after NetWare Connect has been installed.

❑ Container objects include remote access parameters for an idle timeout and protocol (IP and IPX) parameters for PPPRNS service.

SELF TEST

The Self-Test questions will help you measure your understanding of the material presented in this chapter. Read all the choices carefully, as there may be more than one correct answer. Select all correct answers for each question.

1. What two ways can a mobile client connect to the network?

    A. Remote Node and NASI

    B. Remote Control and Remote Node

    C. Remote Control and NCS

    D. PPPRNS and AIO

2. What is the most suitable use for a remote control workstation?

    A. When there are multiple mobile clients needed

    B. When all applications boot from the mobile client hard drive

    C. For electronic messaging (e-mail)

    D. When applications or databases are located on the network

3. What options are available from NetWare Connect?

    A. ARAS, RNS, NIAS, NWCCON

    B. WIN2NCS, MAC2NCS, PPPRNS, NIASCFG

    C. ARAS, PPPRNS, NCS, RAMA

    D. ARAS, MAC2NCS, NWCCON, RAMA

4. Which of the following is used in managing the NetWare Connect Server?

    A. ARAS

    B. PPPRNS

    C. NCS

    D. RAMA

5. What type of connection does dial-up networking create?

    A. Remote node

    B. NCS

    C. RAMA

    D. Remote control

6. Which of the following software must be installed for a Windows PC to dial out of the network using a NetWare Connect server's modems?

    A. MAC2NCS

    B. WIN2NCS

    C. Dial-up networking

    D. PPPRNS

7. Which of the following is the server's Remote Access Configuration program?

    A. NetWare Administrator

    B. Win2NCS

    C. Mac2NCS

    D. NWCCON

8. Where do Macintosh clients get the ARAS client software?

    A. It is on the MAC Client Install disk.

    B. It can be obtained from Apple Computer Corporation.

C. It can be downloaded from Novell's Web site.

D. It is native to the client.

9. When NWCCON loads for the first time, what does it prompt for?

A. A user ID that has rights to extend the NDS schema

B. Selection of a synchronous adapter

C. Selection of an asynchronous adapter

D. Configuration of modems.

10. What is the default modem configuration for data bits, parity, and stop bits?

A. 7, none, 1

B. 8, none, 0

C. 7, none, 0

D. 8, none, 1

11. If a modem needs troubleshooting because it has difficulty in connecting, which of the following should be modified?

A. Security

B. Services

C. Ports

D. Users

12. Acme's dial-in hours are limited to after-hours only. No clients should connect during business hours. Which option can implement this policy?

A. Security

B. Services

C. Ports

D. Users

13. Which option in NWCCON will affect the configuration of multiple servers?

A. Services

B. Ports

C. Port Groups

D. None

14. What can an administrator do to verify settings for a server?

A. Search for remote access parameters in NetWare Administrator.

B. Run Win2NCS to verify settings.

C. Run a NetWare Connect Compare event against a standard file to see the deviations.

D. Generate a Configuration Report from NWCCON.

15. Where can an Idle timeout value affect users in only a particular container? Global parameters in NWCCON

A. Configure Services in NWCCON

B. NetWare Administrator Remote Access property page of the container

C. Configure Ports in NWCCON

CNE

CERTIFIED NOVELL ENGINEER

Part III

Networking Technologies

26

Network Services

CERTIFICATION OBJECTIVES

26.01   Networking Technologies

26.02   Network Services

26.03   Network Management

I n this chapter you will learn a great deal about networking as a whole, not only in logic, but in physical nature as well. The Networking Technologies exam is one of the most challenging because the topics covered don't lend themselves to a "hands-on" approach. For the Network Administration exam you can pull from field or lab experience, but the Networking Technologies questions challenge you to know what makes a network function, both at a software and hardware level. Furthermore, much of the material must be memorized, as anyone who has taken this exam will tell you.

CERTIFICATION OBJECTIVE 26.01

Networking Technologies

The basic task of networking is the sharing of information between two entities. When two people talk to each other and share information, they are networking. In the computer world the sharing of information and services is also known as networking. Services are included in this definition because, for example, printing and Internet access are services that can be provided by a computer to another computer on a network.

Before computer networks were available to share information and services, people had to use disks and switch boxes. The term "sneaker net" used to be a very popular one describing the sharing of files by copying to a floppy disk and "running" it to another computer. The thing to remember about networking in a computer environment is that you must have at least two things (usually computers) that want to share information. You then need a medium for them to communicate over. This medium can be a network cable, or possibly even a wireless connection. There are different types of networking that fall into different networking models, which we will look at now.

Computer Networking Models

The technologies of networking are broken down into three areas:

1. Centralized computing
2. Distributed computing
3. Collaborative computing

There are also two areas to look at with networking services: client/server and client/network. We will look at each of these briefly. The exam may not ask directly about these areas, but this knowledge will help you better understand exactly what makes a network tick.

A mainframe computer is the heart of *centralized computing*. In a centralized computing environment, you have a series of terminals attached to a mainframe computer that handles all the service and computing work. The terminals are nothing more than input/output devices. In a computer today, the CPU what handles all of the processing.

Distributed computing is what you see more today. The processing tasks are shared between the workstation and the server. The workstation has its own processing capabilities and the server also has processing capabilities. *Collaborative computing* is when two or more computers share in processing the same task, which can help in load balancing. This type of computing is more common when there are servers doing different parts of the same applications.

The services area has two categories. The first is the client/server approach, which is the most common network service platform in use today. The *client/server* network consists of workstations that are computers and servers that are computers. The distributed computing model conforms to this kind of network service environment. The way that applications are handled can be distinct in different environments. In some cases the application will run completely on the workstation, and the data is saved on the server. An example of this is a word processing program where the data is saved in the user's directory on the server. Another way applications can be handled is with a front end on the workstation and a back end on the server. An example of this is a database program that has a client piece that runs on the workstation. The back end on the server does much of the database processing.

In a *client/network* approach, the workstation logs into a set of services, not a particular server. This is what Novell Directory Services is and how NetWare can work for you.

Network Sizes

There are three different computer network sizes:

1. Local Area Network (LAN)

2. Metropolitan Area Network (MAN)

3. Wide Area Network (WAN)

Novell only hits on two of the three. The MAN is rarely used anymore. LAN and WAN are terms you have probably heard before. A *LAN* typically does not exceed 10 kilometers. A LAN is usually for a small company, building, or location. LAN speeds are measured in megabits per second.

A *WAN* is a group of LANs. WANs can span a city, country, or even the world. WAN speeds are measured in kilobits per second. WANs are broken down into enterprise and global. An *enterprise network* is what connects LANs of a single organization. A *global network* is similar to the Internet in that it connects various LANs of the same organization at different locations.

Network Components

Every network requires certain things to be considered a network:

1. Two or more entities with information to share

2. A common communications pathway

3. Rules for communicating

The way these things come together is in network services, transmission media, and protocols. When two or more individuals share something, they use *network services*. In order for communication to happen you need a *transmission medium* such as a cable, satellite, or infrared connection. Communicating across a medium is one step in communication. If the receiving party cannot understand you, then there is no communication. This is where protocols come into play. *Protocols* are the rules that enable communication to happen.

CERTIFICATION OBJECTIVE 26.02

Network Services

Network services are a combination of hardware and software that is shared by networked computers. Within the computer industry there are service requestors and service providers. S*ervice providers* are a combination of hardware and software that provide services or fulfill a particular role. For the CNE, remember that servers are service providers. They provide only services. The *service requestor* requests services from service providers. For the CNE, remember that workstations/clients are service requestors.

The other piece to network services is the peer relationship between computers. Sometimes you will see an environment where a computer fills both roles of service provider and service requestor. These enable *peer-to-peer networking*, the computers request services from peer servers and provide services to other peers requesting services Windows 95 is an example of an operating system that has built-in peer-to-peer networking capabilities.

Now that we know that there are service providers, service requestors, and peers we can break network services into two distinct categories:

1. Server centric

2. Peer-to-peer networking

Server-centric networks are more common, and NetWare is an example of the type of software that enables a computer to provide network services. There are strict guidelines as to what a computer does in a server centric environment. Each computer fills the role of either a service requestor or service provider. In a server-centric environment one computer cannot fill both roles. In a *peer-to-peer* environment a computer can be either a requestor, a provider, or both.

File Services

File services provide the ability to move, back up, synchronize, and handle general everyday file storage and management. One of the main functions of file services is file transfer. File transfer is any service that handles saving, retrieving, and moving of files for network clients. Another function of file services is file storage and data migration. There are different types of storage that you may see on the exam:

- **Online storage** Storage devices containing data that is immediately available to the computer, such as hard drives.

- **Nearline storage**   Can be a CD-ROM jukebox or a carousel, which isn't immediately available but does not require the user to do anything special to access it.

- **Offline storage**   Removable tape cartridges fall into this category. This requires a user to insert the tape to get to the data.

The main thing that you need to know for the exam regarding file services is when to implement them. You must decide when to use the various types of storage in your network. I cannot explain in detail here when to use them because of all of the different possibilities when it comes to network services. I will give you the basic information for you to make your own inferences.

There is also *file update synchronization,* which allows us to have multiple copies of a file, and the operating system will synchronize our files to the most current. There is one drawback here though. If both files change, we currently cannot merge the changes from both, only the newer of the two. The most basic feature in a network requires the use of file services. For the exam, know that these functions are needed in order to do most file management functions.

Print Services

Print services allow us to print, fax, and copy across the network. . These services provide an important function of networking. For example, sharing printers on a network helps reduce costs because not everyone needs their own printer.

The functions associated with print services revolve around allowing multiple users to access a printer, along with queuing those requests. With the distributed print services, management of printing and configuration is integrated into NDS. True communication between the workstation and the printer via the network allows distributed print services to work. Centralized administration and almost automatic setup and configuration of the printer drivers on the workstation are key benefits of distributed print services.

exam
ⓦatch

Make sure you understand when network print services should be implemented. There are so many different scenarios that it is hard to tell you exact ways to do things. From the information you'll be given in the questions, come up with your own inference as to when to implement print services. If you need to share a printer, fax capabilities, or copying functions, then print services will be used.

Message Services

Message services bring e-mail to mind, but it actually includes much more. Not only does messaging give you e-mail, but it also gives us the ability to transfer graphics, audio, video, and binary information. This allows for integrated voice and e-mail and workgroup applications. One thing to consider when choosing to implement messaging services is your LAN or WAN speed. Video and audio can consume a lot of bandwidth, while simple e-mail and voice mail usually do not consume a lot of bandwidth. If e-mail, audio, or video will be transmitted across the network, you need to have messaging services in place.

Application Services

Application services run applications for clients. Sounds simple, doesn't it? You may wonder why we don't see file services doing this piece. File services handle the transfer of data. Application services transfer the processing power from the client to a server to run the application. Processing power can also be shared, as it can in file services.

This service has a couple of functions. Server specialization is a big one. One server may handle your voice mail system or your telephone switch. This service also allows for scalability and growth because applications today may be on their own separate server. If this is the case and your application is suffering due to high demands, you could simply upgrade the server or get a new, higher performing server to give the application more processing power. This way, all servers do not need to be upgraded simultaneously, thus saving money and resources. If you find that you will need to run applications from your servers or do basic application execution across the network, then application services will be used.

Database Services

This is another area where specialization is important. *Database services* provide a server with the ability to process and handle the database back end for clients. Most databases are client/server, which means that the processing is divided up between the server and the client.

There are two aspects of database services to be concerned with for the exam: distributed data and replication. *Distributed data* is a way to break the database into smaller units while making it look like one large database. This makes for cooperative processing between various computers. *Replication* enables multiple copies of a database. This can be more efficient, since the database can be maintained and accessed locally. The challenge with using replication is synchronizing all the copies into one so that data is kept current. One other advantage to this is the fault tolerance provided by having multiple copies. In environments with large SQL database applications, for example, database services are used.

CERTIFICATION OBJECTIVE 26.03

Network Management

Being a good administrator includes managing the network. The network management scheme can be broken down into five areas, which were on the original 200 Series exam and may be on the new 565 exam. We will look at each briefly.

Configuration Management

Configuration management is the tracking and controlling of inventories, software distribution, service agreements, service requests, and procurement files. The main goal of network management is to track and keep records on past, current, and future network configurations. Good documentation is vital to servicing and maintaining your network.

Fault Management

Fault management involves everything an administrator does to prevent, diagnose, test, and repair network failures. The main goal is to isolate faults in the network quickly to keep it functioning. Good fault management will not guarantee a network without problems, but it will help identify problems before they become unmanageable or catastrophic.

Security Management

Every network needs *security management* to protect it from physical harm and unauthorized use of valuable data. This covers securing the operating system and the hardware as well. Locating your servers in an area that everyone has access to gives them a chance to get their hands on the server physically, potentially causing intentional or accidental harm. Securing the operating system and the file system prevents unauthorized people from accessing information.

Accounting Management

Accounting management is concerned with the tracking and evaluating of network costs and how they affect your current and future business. Knowing the trade-off between performance and cost for improved performance, are important to maintaining a successful and up-to-date network.

Performance Management

As an administrator keeping an eye on how the network performs is vital to success. *Performance management* and fault management go hand-in-hand. Identifying bottlenecks, performing trend analysis, and making future performance predictions are the major components to performance management.

CERTIFICATION SUMMARY

As stated in the beginning of this chapter, this exam is not a given easy pass, even though you might think it would be straightforward. Preparing for this exam is nothing more than pure memorization.

In this chapter we looked briefly at the basic axiom of networking: sharing information. To have a network with computers you need three things: two or more computers who want to share something, a medium to transmit the communication, and rules to govern the communication. These boil down to network services, transmission medium, and protocols.

We also looked at the different networking models: centralized computing, distributed computing, and collaborative computing.

There are different network sizes: LAN and WAN. A LAN is local to a building or campus, while a WAN can span a country or the world. We also looked at server-centric versus peer-to-peer networking. In a server-centric environment a computer is either a service requestor or service provider. In a peer-to-peer environment computers can fill both roles simultaneously.

One other area that you may see on the exam is the different types of services in networking. File services manage files: moving, backing up, and synchronizing them. Print services allow network users to print, fax, and copy across the network. Messaging services give us not only e-mail, but voice mail and the ability to transfer graphics, audio, and video. Application services allow users to run the applications from the network. Database services manage the front-end and back-end processing of database applications. We looked briefly at distributed data and replication.

Network Management was on the original 200 exam, and we briefly looked at the different areas: configuration management, fault management, security management, account management, and security management.

TWO-MINUTE DRILL

❑ The basic task of networking is the sharing of information between two entities.

❑ The technologies of networking are broken down into three areas: centralized computing, distributed computing, and collaborative computing.

❑ A mainframe computer is the heart of *centralized computing*. In a centralized computing environment, you have a series of terminals attached to a mainframe computer that handles all the service and computing work.

❑ In *distributed computing*, the processing tasks are shared between the workstation and the server. The workstation has its own processing capabilities, and the server also has processing capabilities.

❑ *Collaborative computing* is when two or more computers share in processing the same task, which can help in load balancing. This type of computing is more common when there are servers doing different parts of the same applications.

❑ There are three different computer network sizes: Local Area Network (LAN), Metropolitan Area Network (MAN), and Wide Area Network (WAN).

❑ Every network requires certain things to be considered a network: two or more entities with information to share; a common communications pathway; and rules for communicating.

❑ There are three types of storage: online storage, nearline storage, and offline storage.

❑ *Distributed data* is a way to break the database into smaller units while making it look like one large database. This makes for cooperative processing between various computers.

❑ *Replication* enables multiple copies of a database. This can be more efficient, since the database can be maintained and accessed locally.

❑ *Configuration management* is the tracking and controlling of inventories, software distribution, service agreements, service requests, and procurement files.

❑ *Fault management* involves everything an administrator does to prevent, diagnose, test, and repair network failures.

SELF TEST

The Self-Test questions will help you measure your understanding of the material presented in this chapter. Read all the choices carefully, as there may be more than one correct answer. Select all correct answers for each question.

1. What three things are needed for a network? (Choose all that apply.)

    A. Two more computers that need to share something

    B. A communication medium

    C. Rules for communication

    D. A rules medium

2. Which of the following is not a computer networking model?

    A. Collaborative

    B. Synchronized

    C. Centralized

    D. Distributed

3. Which type of computer networking model has a mainframe computer at the heart of the network?

    A. Collaborative

    B. Centralized

    C. Synchronized

    D. Distributed

4. Which network does not usually exceed 10 kilometers in size?

    A. LAN

    B. WAN

    C. MAN

    D. PAN

5. What gives us the rules needed to communicate successfully on a network?

    A. Two or more computers that need to share something

    B. The transmission medium

    C. The protocols

    D. The network packets

6. What are the two distinct categories of network services? (Choose all that apply.)

    A. Server mainframe

    B. Server centric

    C. Peer-to-peer

    D. Client/server

7. What are the three types of storage in file services? (Choose all that apply.)

    A. Online storage

    B. Offline storage

    C. Internal storage

    D. Nearline storage

8. Which type of storage with file services would include a CD-ROM jukebox?

A. Online storage

B. Offline storage

C. Internal storage

D. Nearline storage

9. Which service gives us the ability to fax or copy documents across the network?

A. File services

B. Print services

C. Message services

D. Backup services

10. Which service enables video and audio to be transferred across the network?

A. File services

B. Print services

C. Message services

D. Backup services

27

Transmission Media and Connections

CERTIFICATION OBJECTIVES

27.01   Media Types

27.02   Cable Media

27.03   Wireless Media

27.04   Public and Private Network Services

27.05   Transmission Media Connections

I n the previous chapter we looked at the three things necessary to make a network. One of these was a transmission medium for the clients to communicate across. No communication will happen across a network unless a communications medium carries the signals.

If there is one thing that you will troubleshoot a lot, it is your transmission media. There are different types of transmission media and this is what we will look at here. We will discuss cost factors as well as cable media types and types of wireless media. We will describe the different types of hardware that may be involved in how your network is connected to itself and possibly to the outside world.

CERTIFICATION OBJECTIVE 27.01

Media Types

When selecting media for a computer network there are a few factors to keep in mind:

- Cost
- Ease of installation
- Capacity
- Attenuation
- Immunity from interference

Cost

The cost of the media is an important consideration when confronted with other possible choices. When comparing different transmission media, it is useful to make a chart listing each of the choices, side by side. Certain implementations may cost more, or less, depending on the layout of the facility, the number of workstations, and other factors. You can make some assumptions regarding the cost per foot, for example, of the medium itself.

This will give you an estimated cost and help you decide which medium you will use.

Installation

Ease of installing the cable is another important factor to consider. Often a third-party company will do the installation for you, but you still have to consider the difficulty in installing particular media types. The more difficult something is to install, the more likely the cable provider is to charge you more.

Capacity

The *capacity* refers to what a transmission medium can support for data transfer. Referred to frequently as *throughput*, the capacity varies from cable type to cable type or wireless type to wireless type. Bandwidth is measured in hertz or cycles per second that a medium can physically accommodate. This is one area that can be a bottleneck in your network if you're not careful in choosing the transmission medium.

Attenuation

Different types of transmission media can transport information for only a certain distance before they start encountering problems, such as signals becoming weak, a distortion in the information the farther it travels, and generally losing their clarity. This is known as *attenuation*. When a signal attenuates, it loses strength or becomes unreadable by the receiver.

Electromagnetic Interference

With any electrical equipment there is a chance for interference from other electrical items, including the atmosphere and the weather. *Electromagnetic interference* occurs when the signal in the transmission media is interfered with by other electronic signals, which ends up distorting the signal to the point that the receiver cannot successfully interpret the information.

Cable Media

Now that we've looked at the considerations that must be made when selecting a transmission medium, we will look at the different types of cable media. Cable media use electronic signals or light conducted across copper or glass to communicate from one end to the other. There are three main types. The first is called *twisted-pair cable*, which is a series of individual copper cables encased in plastic. There is also *coaxial cable*, which is similar to what we use today for television and VCR connections. The last and the most expensive is *fiber-optic cable*, which is made up of glass or plastic fibers.

Twisted-Pair Cable

Twisted-pair is the most common type of cable used today in computer networking. Used heavily in LAN systems, twisted-pair cable uses a series of individually wrapped copper wires encased in a plastic sheathing. Each cable is individually encased in plastic and then the overall outer shell is plastic as well. Each cable inside is twisted together with another. Most cable today comes with eight cables or wires, making four pairs. The cable is twisted to cut down on crosstalk. *Crosstalk* is when two wires in close proximity inadvertently share information due to interfering with each other. Figure 27-1 shows a simple example of twisted-pair cable.

Twisted-pair cabling is made up of 22- or 26-gauge copper wire. There are two types of twisted-pair cable:

- Shielded twisted-pair (STP)
- Unshielded twisted-pair (UTP)

FIGURE 27-1

Twisted-pair cabling

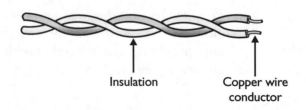

Insulation   Copper wire
                  conductor

Unshielded is the more common of the two types of twisted-pair. Unshielded twisted-pair is a series of pairs of wires twisted together with their own distinct plastic insulation, and then the group of wires are encased in a plastic sheathing that holds all the other wires together as shown in Figure 27-2.

There are five types of twisted-pair cabling as ranked by the Electrical Industries Association:

- *Category 1 (CAT 1)*   Low speed data and voice; less than 4 Mbps
- *Category 2 (CAT 2)*   Low speed data and voice; less then 4 Mbps
- *Category 3 (CAT 3)*   Data; 10–16 Mbps (100 possible)
- *Category 4 (CAT 4)*   Data; less than or equal to 20 Mbps
- *Category 5 (CAT 5)*   Data; High speed 100 Mbps

Typically, twisted-pair cable consists of RJ-45 or RJ-11 ends. RJ-11 ends are what you see for most telephones. RJ-45 is similar but wider than the RJ-11 connector. RJ-45 has an 8-pin connection and RJ-11 has a 4-pin connection.

When considering the factors we described earlier in this chapter, we see the following:

- **Cost**   Less expensive than other forms of transmission media.
- **Installation**   Installation is easy and necessary equipment is relatively inexpensive.

FIGURE 27-2

Unshielded twisted-pair cable

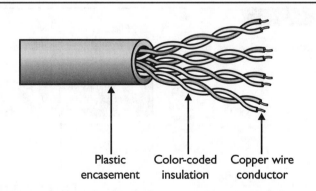

Plastic encasement   Color-coded insulation   Copper wire conductor

- **Capacity**   UTP can support from 1 Megabit per second to 1 Gigabit per second at distances of 100 meters. Most common are 10 Mbps and 100 Mbps.

- **Attenuation**   UTP attenuates more quickly than other types due to the copper conductor. For this reason, distance is limited.

- **Interference**   The copper conductor is very susceptible to interference from outside signals.

Shielded twisted-pair cable is similar in features to UTP. The main difference is the extra shielding that STP has. Figure 27-3 illustrates this difference.

Shielded twisted-pair cable has enhanced protection with a foil wrap and extra shielding outside the individual twists inside the cable. The considerations for STP are as follows:

- **Cost**   More expensive than UTP but less expensive than other forms of transmission media like coax and fiber.

- **Installation**   Similar to UTP but there are a few other considerations. Certain STP implementations will use special connectors. STP also requires an electrical ground like that of coax.

- **Capacity**   STP can support from 500 Megabits per second at distances of 100 meters. The most common is 16 Mbps. This is not widely implemented at over 155 Mbps.

FIGURE 27-3

Shielded twisted-pair cable

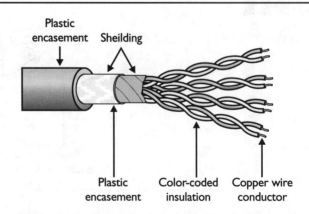

- **Attenuation**   STP attenuates more quickly than other types due to the copper conductor. For this reason, distance is limited.

- **Interference**   The copper conductor is very susceptible to interference from outside signals. STP is better than UTP due to the protection given by the extra shielding.

Coaxial Cable

Coaxial cable is made up of two conductors that share a common axis. This is where the name comes from. Figure 27-4 shows an example of a coaxial cable.

The inside of the cable is made up of a solid or stranded copper wire typically surrounded by foam. Next is an outer wire mesh tube that further protects the signal travelling along the inner wire. The outside is a tougher plastic encasement that protects all the inner components.

There are different types of coax that are used in computer networking. The main difference is the ohm ratings and size standard:

- 50 OHM RG-8/RG-11 (Thick Ethernet)

- 50 OHM RG-58 (Thin Ethernet)

- 75 OHM RG-59 (Cable Television)

- 93 OHM RG-62 (ARCNet)

When connecting coaxial cables the most common type of connection is a T-connector. Another type of connection that is used is the "vampire" tap.

FIGURE 27-4

Coaxial cable

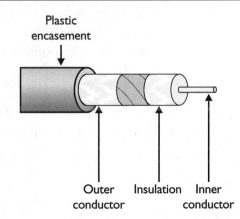

Plastic
encasement

Outer
conductor   Insulation   Inner
conductor

T-connectors are more generally used, since thick coax is no longer common. Remember in either case, the cable has to be grounded on one end only and terminated on both ends. If the cable isn't grounded and terminated, you will not be able to successfully communicate across the medium. Coax has the following considerations:

- **Cost** Increases as the cables get bigger in diameter and depends on the construction of the internal conductor. Thin coax is relatively inexpensive (less than STP and CAT 5 UTP). Thick coax can be more expensive than STP or UTP.

- **Installation** The initial installation of coax is easy. Most of the coax cabling situations use one long cable (referred to as a drop) that connects each computer to the network.

- **Capacity** Current limitations allow for transmission speeds somewhere between twisted-pair and fiber-optic cables. The most common speed is 10 Mbps.

- **Attenuation** The attenuation of coax is less than either form of twisted-pair. Nowadays distance in the thousands of meters is possible.

- **Interference** The inner copper is limited in resistance but the shielding makes the resistance better or equal to STP.

Fiber-Optic Cable

Distinctly different than both twisted-pair and coax, fiber-optic cable is made up of a light conducting glass or plastic core. More reflective material, called cladding, surrounds the core, and then the outer plastic sheath protects the inside. Figure 27-5 shows different configurations of fiber-optic cable.

Common types of fiber-optic cable include the following:

- 8.3 micron core/125 micron cladding single-mode

- 62.5 micron core/125 micron cladding multimode

- 50 micron core/125 micron cladding multimode

- 100 micron core/140 micron cladding multimode

FIGURE 27-5

Fiber-optic cable

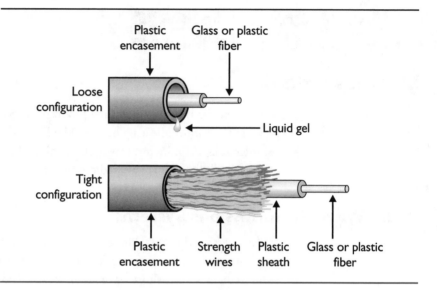

When deciding on a transmission medium consider the following:

- **Cost**   Fiber cable used to be much more expensive than coax or twisted-pair but the costs are coming down. The major cost is doing the installation.

- **Installation**   Installation is much more challenging than with coax or twisted-pair.

- **Capacity**   The optical nature of fiber allows for high bandwidth over great distances. The current capacity is 100 Mbps to 2 Gbps at distances of 2 to 25 kilometers.

- **Attenuation**   Attenuation is much less in fiber-optic cables versus any copper conductor cables. Attenuation for fiber-optic cable is measured in kilometers.

- **Interference**   Due to the fact that the signal is a light transmission, there is no chance for interference as along as the surrounding covering and cladding are not harmed in any way.

CERTIFICATION OBJECTIVE 27.03

Wireless Media

Wireless media transmit without a physical connection, like a cable, between the communicating bodies. The Earth's atmosphere could be considered as a conductor, if we get technical about it. The three common types we will discuss here are radio wave, microwave, and infrared light.

Radio Wave Transmissions Systems

Radio waves are those transmissions that fall into the 10 KHz and 1 Ghz range in the electromagnetic spectrum. The following are included in the radio frequency area: short wave radio, VHF television and FM radio, and UHF television and radio.

Attenuation can be the result of atmospheric conditions with radio wave transmission. Foggy, rainy, or cloudy weather can greatly affect how well the information can be transmitted. There are three classes of radio wave transmissions:

1. Low-power single frequency
2. High-power single frequency
3. Spread spectrum

The *low-power* radio wave is a single frequency that is used in a short distance over an open area. The *high-power* radio is also a single frequency transmission that can cover greater distances and even go through dense materials. *Spread spectrum* uses multiple frequencies simultaneously.

Microwave Transmission Systems

Microwave transmission systems exist in the form of terrestrial and satellite. *Terrestrial systems* are earth-based and use directional parabolic antennas. The terrestrial-based transmission is direct or line of sight, which means it requires an unobstructed path. *Satellite microwave systems* communicate from a directional parabolic antenna to a geosynchronous satellite in Earth's orbit.

Infrared Transmission Systems

Another type of wireless media is *infrared*, which uses light emitting diodes or injection laser diodes to transmit signals. The receiving piece is a photodiode. The signal can be line of sight or it can be received after being bounced off walls. This type of medium is most useful in small, open environments. The signal cannot penetrate walls or other opaque surfaces.

CERTIFICATION OBJECTIVE 27.04

Public and Private Network Services

One other common area that is often overlooked is the public or private networks available for connecting people all over the world. You may not see this on the exam, but it is worth mentioning. The reason I say that is the Internet is a combination of public and private networks. The most commonly known network is the *public switched telephone network* (PSTN). A dial-up account uses the PSTN to communicate with various routers and service providers all over the country. T1 and T3 lines and other forms of connectivity with telephone companies make up the backbone of what we call the Internet.

CERTIFICATION OBJECTIVE 27.05

Transmission Media Connections

In order to use the mediums available, whether it is cable or wireless, we need a way to connect the computer to the medium. This is where the transmission media connection comes into play.

Network Connectivity Devices

There are various types of network connectivity devices. From the ends that go on a cable to the network interface board that is installed in your computer you have a series of different types of network connectivity devices that you use every day. The ones we will look at here are transmission media connectors, network interface boards, modems, repeaters, hubs, bridges, and multiplexers. The first three are what we use to connect a computer to a media segment. The other four are for connecting various media segments to form a larger network.

Transmission Media Connectors

There are different kinds of transmission media connectors that we can use to connect to a cable segment on the network. Figure 27-6 shows some common media connectors.

The transmission media connector is what plugs into the connection on the back of the computer. The RJ-45 connector is commonly used with twisted-pair. The BNC connector is commonly used with coaxial cable. The DB-25 and DB-15 connectors are commonly used for printers and serial connections, respectively.

FIGURE 27-6

Transmission media connectors

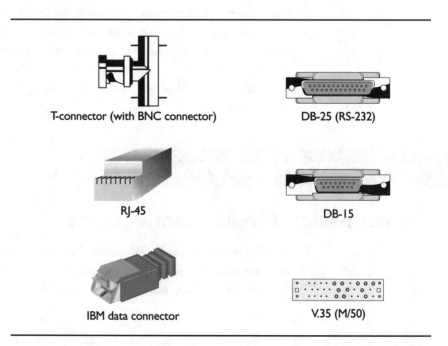

T-connector (with BNC connector)

DB-25 (RS-232)

RJ-45

DB-15

IBM data connector

V.35 (M/50)

Network Interface Boards

Network Interface Boards are the logic boards that allow us to connect the transmission media connector to our computer and form the physical path in order to communicate. The *Network Interface Board*, more commonly known as a Network Interface Card (NIC), has an internal transceiver that converts the information from the computer into a form that can travel across the medium.

Modems

A *modem* stands for modulator/demodulator. The modem converts the digital signals from a computer into an analog signal that can transfer across a phone line or microwave transmission.

Repeaters

Earlier we looked at the limitations of some media used in today's networks. When attenuation occurs we need a way to increase the signal in order to reach the distance we need. A *repeater* boosts the signal in order to expand the total distance for what we need. Many hubs are repeaters.

Hubs

In order to connect various cable segments we need a central point to plug everything together. A *hub* brings all the cable segments together. A hub can be a multiport repeater. There are different types of hubs: active, passive, multiport repeaters, and switches. Active hubs are repeaters because the regenerate or boost the signal. A passive hub is just a connectivity point and is not a repeater. A multiport repeater is a hub that regenerates the signal to all ports. A switch is smarter in that it repeats to only the port that is connected to the receiving host.

Bridges

Bridges connect various segments of a network and allow for filtering of transmissions to certain segments. Bridges are similar to switches in that they send information only on to segments that the information is destined for.

Multiplexing

Sometimes the entire bandwidth is not used efficiently and we need something to allow us to use the entire medium by transmitting multiple signals. A *multiplexer* (MUX) combines two or more separate signals onto one transmission medium.

Internetwork Connectivity Devices

With today's variety of networks, we need a way to connect them together. This is where internetwork connectivity devices come into the spectrum of network hardware. Here we will take a brief look at routers, brouters, and CSU/DSUs.

Routers and Brouters

Routers and brouters connect to logically different networks. A good example of this is a company's network that is connected to the Internet. Perhaps they receive stock market information from another company. In this scenario they would probably have two routers connected to their network. The separate networks are referred to as subnetworks or subnets. The collection of subnetworks makes up the internetwork. Figure 27-7 shows an example of what a network would look like with routers in place. Brouters are the same as routers except that they can also do bridging.

CSUs/DSUs

Similar to a modem, a *CSU/DSU* is used to transfer data to a special format. The difference, however, is that a CSU/DSU is a digital-to-digital converter. The modem is a digital-to-analog conversion device. CSU/DSU stands for Channel Service Unit/Digital Service Unit. The CSU/DSU prepares the information from a LAN to be transmitted across the WAN. They work in conjunction with routers in some cases.

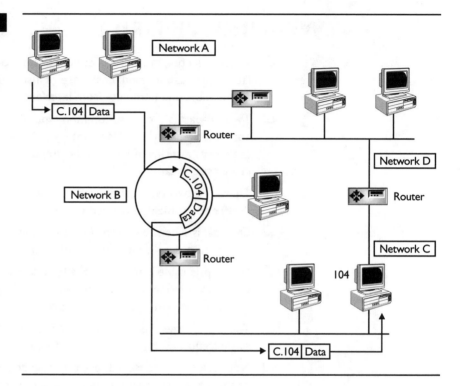

FIGURE 27-7

An internetwork with routers

CERTIFICATION SUMMARY

In this chapter we looked at the different considerations we need to make when deciding on how to connect the network. For the exam you will see a few questions out of this chapter. The five big factors for network connectivity are cost, installation, capacity, attenuation, and interference.

We also looked at cable media. The different types include unshielded twisted-pair, shielded twisted-pair, coaxial cable, and fiber-optic cable. Wireless media includes the radio waves, microwave transmission systems, and infrared transmission systems.

We also took a brief look at the different network connectivity types from network cards to routers.

TWO-MINUTE DRILL

❑ When selecting media for a computer network, there are a few factors to keep in mind: cost, ease of installation, capacity, attenuation, and immunity from interference.

❑ Twisted-pair is the most common type of cable used today in computer networking. Used heavily in LAN systems, twisted-pair cable uses a series of individually wrapped copper wires encased in a plastic sheathing.

❑ There are two types of twisted-pair cable: shielded twisted-pair (STP) and unshielded twisted-pair (UTP).

❑ *Crosstalk* is when two wires in close proximity inadvertently share information due to interfering with each other.

❑ Fiber-optic cable is made up of a light conducting glass or plastic core. More reflective material, called cladding, surrounds the core, and then the outer plastic sheath protects the inside.

❑ There are three classes of radio wave transmissions: low-power single frequency, high-power single frequency, and spread spectrum.

❑ Network Interface Boards are the logic boards that allow us to connect the transmission media connector to our computer and form the physical path in order to communicate.

❑ The *Network Interface Board*, more commonly known as a Network Interface Card (NIC), has an internal transceiver that converts the information from the computer into a form that can travel across the medium.

SELF TEST

The following Self-Test questions will help you measure your understanding of the material presented in this chapter. Read all the choices carefully, as there may be more than one correct answer. Choose all correct answers for each question.

1. Which of the following is not one of the five factors to consider when choosing a transmission media type?

   A. Ease of installation

   B. Capacity

   C. Insinuation

   D. Immunity from interference

2. What do you call the condition when a signal becomes weak as it travels along the medium?

   A. Distance Limitation Factor (DLF)

   B. Attenuation

   C. Attentuation

   D. Electromagnetic Interference (EMI)

3. What is the distance limitation of unshielded twisted-pair?

   A. 100 meters

   B. 500 meters

   C. 300 meters

   D. Unlimited

4. Which category of unshielded twisted-pair allows for data transmission speeds up to 20 Mbps? (Choose all that apply.)

   A. CAT 1

   B. CAT 3

   C. CAT 5

   D. CAT 2

   E. CAT 4

5. What is the inner conductor in coaxial cable made of?

   A. Aluminum

   B. Glass

   C. Plastic

   D. Copper

6. What is the rating and size standard for Thin Ethernet?

   A. 50 OHM RG-8/RG-11

   B. 50 OHM RG-58

   C. 50 OHM RG-59

   D. 93 OHM RG-62

7. Which type of transmission media is made up of an inner core of glass or plastic?

   A. UTP

   B. STP

   C. Coax

   D. Fiber

8. Which form of wireless media falls into the 10 KHz to 1 Ghz range in the electromagnetic spectrum?

   A. Radio wave transmission

   B. Microwave transmission

C. Infrared transmission

D. Terrestrial transmission

9. What type of transmission media connector is commonly used with twisted-pair cabling?

A. T-connector

B. RJ-45

C. DB-15

D. V. 35

10. What type of network connectivity device is used to change a digital signal to analog?

A. Router

B. Bridge

C. Network card

D. Modem

CNE
CERTIFIED NOVELL ENGINEER

28

The OSI Model's Lower Layers

CERTIFICATION OBJECTIVES

28.01   The OSI Model

28.02   The Physical Layer

28.03   The Data Link Layer

Ham information travels from one network node to another is the basis of network communication. For any type of communication to take place in an environment comprised of diverse network devices, the syntax or *protocol* of the communication must be standard. When the protocol is different between two machines, it is similar to a person speaking French to someone who understands only Japanese—virtually no communication takes place even though both are trying.

One of the most widely accepted models for understanding networking protocols is the OSI (Open Systems Interconnection) reference model, which was created by the ISO (International Organization for Standards) in 1977.

CERTIFICATION OBJECTIVE 28.01

The OSI Model

The *OSI model* defines the rules for network communications. When one network device contacts another network device, the communication must meet several criteria in order to be intelligible:

- Network access must be managed so that devices do not constantly interrupt each other's communication.

- The electronic or optical bits must use the same representation on the media. For example, if a positive three (+3) volts is equal to a one (1) bit on the sending device, but equal to a zero (0) bit on the receiving device, then the data cannot be understood.

- The devices must be able to communicate on the physical media, and if there are changes between a sending device's physical media and a receiving device's physical media, then a translating device must be able to move the data appropriately. (A device on a fiber optic ring cannot send data to a device on an Ethernet segment unless there is a connecting device present that can translate the data.)

- Guarantees of data delivery must be available to ensure network reliability.

The OSI model provides the following framework on which developers may base future network communication protocols. The model consists of seven layers: Application, Presentation, Session, Transport, Network, Data Link, and Physical. A simple mnemonic device is the sentence *All People Seem To Need Data Processing*. (That is, the first letter of each word corresponds to the first letter of an OSI reference model layer.)

Protocol Stacks

The layers of the OSI model divide the requirements for network communications into subtasks. Each layer handles its own designated tasks, and then passes the information on to the next layer. In real implementations, the separate protocols are analyzed and categorized by the OSI layer function(s) that they contain. The subtasks, or protocols, are grouped together to complete a full task. This creates a *protocol stack* (see the diagram in Figure 28-1).

FIGURE 28-1

Protocol stack

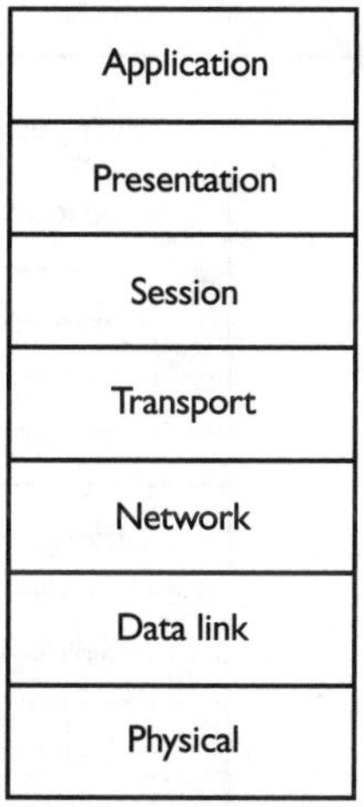

| Application |
| Presentation |
| Session |
| Transport |
| Network |
| Data link |
| Physical |

Peer Layer Communication Between Stacks

When two devices communicate over a network, they must be running the same protocol stack. As data travels through each layer of the stack on the sending device, it gets formatted for that protocol layer (see Figures 28-2 and 28-3):

1. A protocol header including the protocol subtasks (control information) is added to the data packet.

2. The data is forwarded to the next lower layer.

When the receiving device accepts the data, it follows a corresponding action at the peer protocol layer:

1. Data is assembled into small packets.

2. The protocol header is reviewed for the control information (or subtasks) and stripped off the data packet.

3. The data is forwarded to the next higher layer.

FIGURE 28-2

Peer layer communication

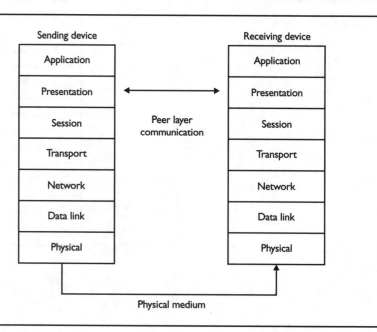

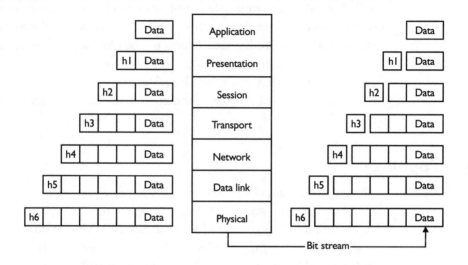

FIGURE 28-3   OSI Model and protocol layer headers data is broken down into small packets.

The two lowest layers of the OSI model are the Physical and the Data Link layers, also called Layer 1 and Layer 2, respectively. The Physical Layer specifies the physical media, electrical signaling, and bitstream. The Data Link Layer is the first layer of logic above the Physical Layer. It adds structure to the Physical Layer bitstream by grouping those bits into small groups of data called *frames*.

CERTIFICATE OBJECTIVE 28.02

The Physical Layer

The subtasks of the Physical Layer are to transmit bits over the physical media, or network cabling. The Physical Layer defines the physical structure (topology) of the network cabling, the signaling format, and synchronization of the electronic pulses that the network devices interpret as *bits*, and the transmission methods in order to utilize bandwidth.

Connection Types

The Physical Layer can specify one of two types of connections: multipoint or point-to-point (see Figures 28-4 and 28-5). A *multipoint connection* allows multiple network devices to exist on the physical media simultaneously. Network connections are typically multipoint connections. A *point-to-point connection* allows only two network devices to exist on the physical media simultaneously. A remote access connection is an example of a point-to-point connection. Another example is a printer connected to a PC.

Physical Topology

The physical layout of the network is the *physical topology*. Network devices can be connected together in various configurations.

The *star* topology consists of a central hub or MSAU (multistation access unit, a Token Ring hub) to which each device is connected by a single dedicated cable (see Figure 28-6). Both Ethernet 10BaseT and Token Ring

| FIGURE 28-4 | Multipoint connection examples |

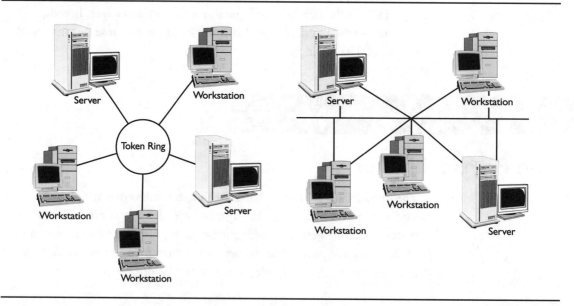

FIGURE 28-5

Point-to-point connection examples

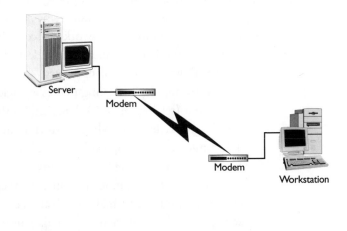

FIGURE 28-6

Physical star topology

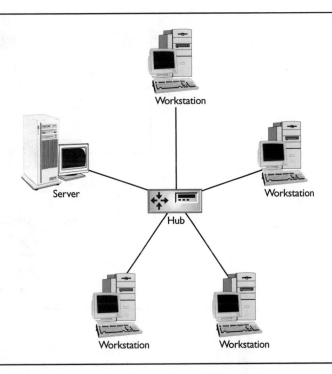

are cabled in a physical star topology. The star topology has the benefit of being fairly easy to troubleshoot, since a media failure for a single network device is limited to that network device's cable. Furthermore, media failure is generally limited to a single network device, keeping an entire segment from failing when a problem occurs.

The *bus* topology is configured as a single cable with each network device tied into it (see Figure 28-7). Each end of the bus must be terminated to avoid signal reflections. Most network nodes attach to the single cable with a T-connector and drop cable. The most common type of physical bus topology is an Ethernet Thicknet coaxial cable or Thinnet coaxial cable network. The bus topology has the advantage of using less cable and being easy to configure. The main disadvantage to a bus topology is that the entire segment is affected if there is a media failure. Thus, it is difficult to troubleshoot the source of the problem.

FIGURE 28-7

Bus topology

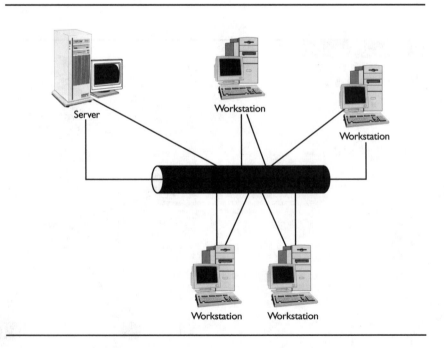

The *ring* topology is circular (see Figure 28-8). Each device has a cable connected to the next device. There are typically ring-in and ring-out ports in order to connect the network devices. Data travels from the ring-out port of one device to the ring-in port of the next and travels around the ring. The signal is normally kept strong (avoiding attenuation) through the incorporation of a receiver (ring-in port) and transmitter (ring-out port) on each network device. The main advantage to a ring topology is that it is fairly easy to troubleshoot. A disadvantage is that in a single ring configuration, a media failure will cause the entire ring to malfunction.

The *mesh* topology is most prevalent in Wide Area Networks, since its redundancy provides a high level of reliability. In a full mesh topology, each network device is connected to each of the other network devices

FIGURE 28-8

Ring topology

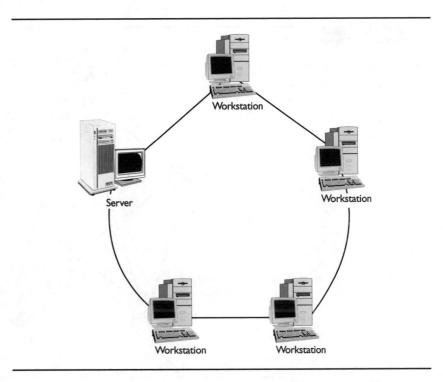

(see Figure 28-9). More common is a hybrid mesh network, where several (not all) network devices are configured with multiple network links. The biggest advantage to a mesh topology is its fault tolerance. If a link becomes unavailable, the network remains functional.

The *cellular* topology is wireless. The network is comprised of multiple areas, called cells, that are serviced by a wireless hub. Wireless communication takes place between the network devices and the hubs. The central hub then forwards any signals that are destined outside the network to another hub; otherwise, signals remain within the cell. The advantage to a cellular topology is that it is simple to install. A disadvantage is that the hub is a single point of failure for any particular cell. More importantly, the wireless communications are easier to capture, so communications should be encrypted to protect secure data.

FIGURE 28-9

Full mesh topology

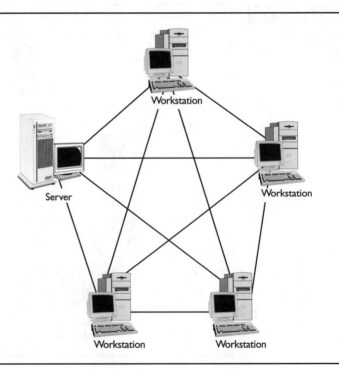

Signaling

Signaling is the way that data is transmitted across the network. Each signal is formatted in such a way that it is understood as data. This format is known as encoding or modulation. The difference between encoding data and modulating data is that *encoding* creates a digital signal and *modulation* creates an analog signal.

Digital Signaling

Most networks use digital signals, which are transmitted as discrete voltage levels. Digital signals can have more than one signal level and represent more than one binary bit. The encoding schemes follow and are shown in Figure 28-10:

- *Unipolar encoding* uses either a negative or a positive voltage plus a zero voltage to represent data. Unipolar does not use both positive and negative voltage. For example: Negative three volts might be a 1 bit and zero volts might be a 0 bit. Teletype (TTY) interfaces use unipolar encoding. It requires a separate clocking system to synchronize the signals between sender and receiver.

- *Polar encoding* uses both negative and positive voltage, but no zero voltage. For example, negative three volts might be a 1 bit and positive three volts might be a 0 bit. This scheme is less susceptible to noise, since the difference between the 1 and 0 voltage levels is twice as large as the unipolar scheme. This scheme requires a separate clocking signal to synchronize the sender and receiver.

- *Return to zero (RZ) encoding* determines the one 1 or 0 bit from the transition between the positive or negative voltage to zero. This scheme eludes much noise interference because noise will interfere with a voltage, not with the transition.

- *Non-return to zero (NRZ) encoding* specifies that a 1 bit is equal to a transition, and a 0 bit is equal to no transitions. This means that for 0 bits the signal remains at the same voltage, whether it is positive or negative. This scheme requires a separate clocking mechanism.

■ *Biphase encoding* requires a transition for each bit, which makes it self-clocking. An absence of a transition shows that there is an error. There are two types of biphase coding schemes: Manchester and Differential Manchester. *Manchester encoding* represents a 1 bit as a low-to-high mid-bit transition, and a 0 bit as a high-to-low mid-bit transition. Manchester encoding is used for Ethernet. *Differential Manchester encoding* uses a mid-bit transition only for clocking. If there is the presence of a transition at the beginning of the bit cell, it is a 0 bit of data; otherwise an absence is a 1 bit. Differential Manchester is used for Token Ring.

FIGURE 28-10

Data encoding schemes

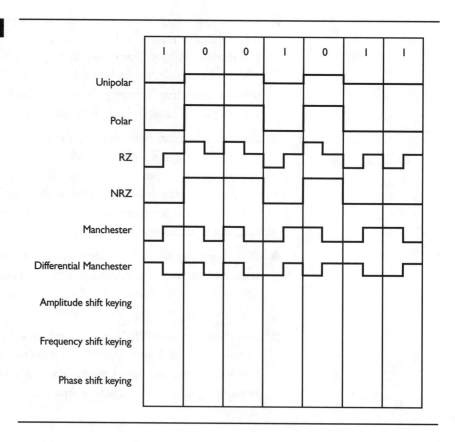

Analog Signaling

Modulation translates digital data into an analog carrier signal using the analog characteristics. Most analog signals use the telephone system for transmission.

Amplitude is one of the characteristics of an analog signal. *ASK,* or *amplitude shift keying* modulates the carrier's amplitude between two or more levels. The highest voltage reached for a "1" bit might be twice as high as that reached for a 0 bit. (If the signal were an ocean wave, this change in amplitude is the difference between three-foot waves and ten-foot waves—the height of the wave is affected.) ASK is susceptible to interference, attenuation, and amplification.

Frequency shift keying (FSK) modulates data by assigning two different frequencies, or number of analog signal waves per time period, to the 1 and 0 bit. For example, when the signals are transmitted at the faster frequency rate, they are interpreted as a 1, and at the slower frequency, they are interpreted as a 0 bit for each bit-time period.

Phase shift keying (PSK) shifts the phase of the analog signal to indicate a value. A lack of phase shift over a bit-time period indicates a different value. It is not unusual to combine the various methods.

Bit Synchronization

When data is encoded in digital transmissions or modulated into analog signals, it needs to synchronize the bits between the sending network device and the receiving network device. This clocking or timing system is called *bit synchronization.*

Asynchronous communications normally begin with a start bit and end with a stop bit. During idle times, the network devices are not synchronized.

Synchronous communications require a clocking mechanism to maintain synchronization during the transmission. When an encoding scheme has a guaranteed state change during the transmission, it is considered self-clocking. Other bit synchronization options are to have a separate clock signal, or use oversampling. *Oversampling* is where the receiver samples the data faster than the sender sends it and uses the nondata samples as a clocking method.

Baseband and Broadband Transmissions

There are two ways of managing bandwidth, or the allocated capacity, within bounded media: *baseband* or *broadband.* Baseband transmissions use the entire bandwidth of the media, and are typically used for digital data across LANs. Broadband transmissions have the option of dividing up the bandwidth into channels, which can carry a different signal. Broadband networks can carry multiple conversations simultaneously on the same media.

Multiplexing Methods

Multiplexing provides a way of enabling both broadband and baseband to support multiple data channels. Frequency Division Multiplexing (FDM) utilizes different frequencies for each data conversation. Time-Division Multiplexing (TDM) divides the bandwidth into timeslots. Each timeslot represents a different conversation and is cycled in a round-robin fashion. TDM can be used with baseband, but if a timeslot is unused, it continues to be unused and bandwidth is wasted. Statistical Time-Division Multiplexing (StatTDM) can dynamically allocate timeslots to multiple machines and identifies the owner of the data conversation with a control field in each timeslot so that the data can be allocated correctly.

CERTIFICATION OBJECTIVE 28.03

The Data Link Layer

The Data Link Layer, or Layer 2, is the first layer to begin managing the data transmission. It organizes the bits into small groups called *frames*, identifies errors, introduces data flow control, and addresses devices on the network. There are two sublayers within the Data Link Layer: Media Access Control and Logical Link Control.

The two sublayers of the Data Link Layer are the Media Access Control, which controls how multiple network devices share the same media channel, and Logical Link Control, which controls the establishment and maintenance of links between communicating devices.

Logical Topology

The logical topology of the network represents the path that data transmission will take around the network. The logical topology is different from the physical topology, or layout, since data flows from device to device requiring both an inflow and outflow on the same wire. There are two main logical topologies: ring and bus. The ring topology sends data from device to device. Token Ring, which uses a physical star topology, has a logical ring topology. The bus topology sends signals the entire length of the network segment such that all devices receive the signal. The devices read the address of the signal to determine whether it was a signal meant for them. Ethernet uses a logical bus topology, and can be wired into either physical bus or physical star topologies.

Media Access Control

The way that network devices determine which are allowed to transmit data and when is called *media access control.* Types of media access control comprise of contention, token passing, and polling.

FROM THE CLASSROOM

Using the OSI Reference Model for Troubleshooting

The OSI Reference Model has practical applications on production networks. If you use a protocol analyzer to capture data packets on a network, you will notice that it can reveal information that can save you a lot of time in troubleshooting network communications problems. However, you must understand what happens to data at each of the seven layers. The packet data capture trace will break down the information according to the seven layers. Some commonly used protocol analyzers are LANalyzer, which comes with Novell's ManageWise product and Network Monitor, which is packaged with NT Server in a cut-down version. Both of these products will help tremendously in analyzing your network's data traffic, but an in-depth knowledge of the OSI layers, and how they work, is essential.

—*By Dan Cheung, CNI, MCNE, MCT*

Contention enables all network devices to access the network whenever there is data to transmit. Multiple simultaneous data transmissions cause collisions. In order to avoid collisions, the network device uses *carrier sensing* to determine whether there is data currently being transmitted. If there is no data currently being transmitted, the network device sends its own data. *Collision detection* is used when the network device transmit its data at the same time as another transmission takes place. The device determines that a collision has occurred, and sends out a jamming pattern to make all network devices aware of the collision. Then the device stops transmission, waits a random amount of time, and resumes transmission. The combination of these two methods is called CSMA/CD (Carrier Sense Multiple Access with Collision Detection). Ethernet uses CSMA/CD. Appletalk uses a variation of this called CSMA/CA (Carrier Sense Multiple Access with Collision Avoidance), which attempts to avoid collisions rather than detect them.

Token-passing enables a network device to access the network only when it has received the token, or small, specially-formatted frame. The token is passed around the ring until it reaches a network device that needs to transmit data. That network device transmits its data and then passes the token to the next. Token Ring and FDDI both use a method of token passing. Because of the methods that token passing employs, it has better performance on a network with a heavy load, since there are no collisions, and there are no retransmissions due to collisions.

Polling has a central device to regulate the network traffic and device access. The central device polls each network device to determine whether there is data to be sent. When a device needs to send data, it is enabled to do so at the point that it is polled.

Data Link Layer Addressing

The MAC address, also called the physical address or hardware address, is assigned in the Data Link Layer. A unique number on the network segment identifies each network device. When data is transmitted, the data includes the MAC address to identify which network device to send the data to. As data is received, a network device can read the MAC address in the data frame header to determine whether the data is intended for itself.

Some MAC addresses can be assigned manually, but most are assigned by the network interface card (NIC) manufacturer. Ethernet manufacturers assign a six-byte address to the NIC. The first three bytes of that address are assigned to the manufacturer by the IEEE (Institute of Electrical and Electronics Engineers). The remaining three bytes are assigned serially by the manufacturer. This results in a unique MAC address for every device on a network. Note that MAC addresses are typically written in a 12-character hexadecimal notation. Each of the characters represents 4 bits.

exam

ⓦatch

Ethernet MAC addresses are six bytes in length. The first three bytes are the manufacturer's assigned number, and the remaining three bytes are allocated serially to ensure that there are no duplicate Ethernet MAC addresses.

Transmission Synchronization

At the Physical Layer, there is a method of synchronizing bits. At the Data Link Layer, there is a method of synchronizing the transmission of frames between sender and receiver. In an asynchronous transmission, the start and stop bits establish the transmission of each frame. *Parity* is used to check for errors, where an extra bit is added to the frame to guarantee an even or odd sum of all the 1 bits in a frame. This means that the parity bit can be either a 0 or a 1, depending on the sum of the bits before parity is added. If there is an inconsistent sum, the frame is considered invalid.

Synchronous transmission requires a clocking mechanism, whether that is a string of control characters, or a separate channel dedicated to synchronization. The error control used is typically a cyclic redundancy check (CRC). The CRC uses a computed number based on the bits being transmitted and an algorithm. When the data is received, the same calculation is made and compared to the CRC number stored in the header to determine whether an error has occurred.

Isochronous transmission uses a separate common timing device to provide clocking. This is seldom used, since that separate device becomes a single point of failure for the entire network.

Connection Services

In order to control the logical connection, there are two services offered: flow control and error control. *Flow control* manages the amount of data transmitted. When the sending device and the receiving device negotiate a rate that is mutually acceptable and retain that rate during the entire data transmission, it is guaranteed rate flow control. When the sending and receiving devices negotiate a rate during the data transmission, depending on the bandwidth availability, it is window flow control. A static window flow control uses set sizes of windows. A sliding window flow control will use a dynamically sized window that can maximize the available bandwidth.

Error control consists of cyclic-redundancy check (CRC), or the lack of receipt of expected acknowledgments. The CRC will indicate corrupt data. The receiver may send a negative acknowledgment (NAK), which will prompt the sender to resend the transmission. When a sender does not receive an expected acknowledgment, it indicates data loss. The sender waits a predetermined time period for an acknowledgment, and if the acknowledgment is not received, the sender retransmits the data.

CERTIFICATION SUMMARY

The OSI (Open Systems Interconnection) reference model was created by the ISO (International Organization for Standards). The model defines the modular approach to networking, in which seven layers take on the task of networking and divide it into subtasks. The layers are Application, Presentation, Session, Transport, Network, Data Link, and Physical. Each layer at the sending device will communicate with its peer layer on the receiving device.

The lower layers of the protocol stack are the Physical (Layer 1) and Data Link (Layer 2) Layers. The Physical Layer defines the physical topology and the signaling of the bitstream. Physical connections can be either multipoint (with multiple devices sharing the media) or point-to-point (with only two devices sharing direct communication).

The physical topology, or layout, of the network can be in a star, bus, ring, mesh, or cellular configuration. Signaling can be either digital or analog. Digital encoding schemes format the data at discrete voltage levels. Various schemes are Unipolar, Polar, Return-to-Zero (RZ), Non-Return to Zero (NRZ),

Manchester, and Differential Manchester. Analog signals are in a wave format, and can use amplitude, frequency, or phase shifts to format the data.

Bit synchronization is required to synchronize the sending and receiving devices. The clocking mechanism can be in the coding scheme itself, a separate signal, or a method of oversampling data.

The two types of bandwidth used are baseband and broadband. Baseband utilizes the entire media bandwidth capacity for the transmission. Broadband uses a channelized bandwidth, in which multiple conversations can take place simultaneously.

In order to utilize bandwidth for multiple data conversations, the media can use a form of multiplexing. Even baseband media can use some form of multiplexing to send multiple data transmissions simultaneously. Frequency division multiplexing uses different frequencies for different data conversations. Time Division Multiplexing and Statistical Time Division Multiplexing use timeslots for different data conversations.

The Data Link layer consists of two sublayers: Logical Link Control (LLC) and Media Access Control (MAC). The Data Link layer defines the logical topology, or the path that the data travels around the network. This path can be either a ring or bus topology.

The Media Access Control is the way that the devices access the media in order to send data. This can be either a contention, token passing, or polling method. The contention method used for Ethernet is Carrier Sense Multiple Access with Collision Detection (CSMA/CD). The token-passing method is used for Token Ring and FDDI. Polling is rarely used, since it requires a central device to poll the network for data and this is a single point of failure.

MAC addresses, also known as physical or hardware addresses, are used to identify devices on the network segment. Most MAC addresses are specified by the NIC manufacturer, although some may be manually specified. Ethernet NICs are assigned a six-byte address: three bytes for the manufacturer identification and three bytes assigned to identify the NIC within that manufacturer.

Transmission synchronization is managed by a clocking mechanism that can either be a start and stop bit (asynchronous), separate signal (synchronous), or a separate device (isochronous). Connection services include flow control and error control. Flow control can be a guaranteed rate, or a windowed flow control. When windows are defined as set sizes, they are considered a static window flow control. When the windows are dynamically agreed upon at any size, they are considered a sliding window flow control.

TWO-MINUTE DRILL

❑ For any type of communication to take place in an environment comprised of diverse network devices, the syntax or *protocol* of the communication must be standard.

❑ The *OSI model* defines the rules for network communications. When one network device contacts another network device, the communication must meet several criteria in order to be intelligible.

❑ In real implementations, the separate protocols are analyzed and categorized by the OSI layer function(s) that they contain. The subtasks, or protocols, are grouped together to complete a full task. This creates a *protocol stack*.

❑ The OSI model consists of seven layers: Application, Presentation, Session, Transport, Network, Data Link, and Physical. A simple mnemonic device is the sentence *All People Seem To Need Data Processing*.

❑ When two devices communicate over a network, they must be running the same protocol stack.

❑ The Physical Layer defines the physical structure (topology) of the network cabling, the signaling format, and synchronization of the electronic pulses that the network devices interpret as *bits*, and the transmission methods in order to utilize bandwidth.

❑ A *multipoint connection* allows multiple network devices to exist on the physical media simultaneously. Network connections are typically multipoint connections.

❑ A *point-to-point connection* allows only two network devices to exist on the physical media simultaneously.

❑ The *star* topology consists of a central hub or MSAU (multistation access unit, a Token Ring hub) to which each device is connected by a single dedicated cable.

❑ The *bus* topology is configured as a single cable with each network device tied into it. Each end of the bus must be terminated to avoid signal reflections.

❑ The *mesh* topology is most prevalent in Wide Area Networks, since its redundancy provides a high level of reliability. In a full mesh topology, each network device is connected to each of the other network devices. More common is a hybrid mesh network.

❑ The *cellular* topology is wireless. The network is comprised of multiple areas, called cells, that are serviced by a wireless hub. Wireless communication takes place between the network devices and the hubs.

❑ The difference between encoding data and modulating data is that *encoding* creates a digital signal and *modulation* creates an analog signal.

❑ *Unipolar encoding* uses either a negative or a positive voltage plus a zero voltage to represent data.

❑ *Polar encoding* uses both negative and positive voltage, but no zero voltage.

❑ *Return to zero (RZ) encoding* determines the one 1 or 0 bit from the transition between the positive or negative voltage to zero.

❑ *Non-return to zero (NRZ) encoding* specifies that a 1 bit is equal to a transition, and a 0 bit is equal to no transitions.

❑ *Biphase encoding* requires a transition for each bit, which makes it self-clocking.

❑ Modulation translates digital data into an analog carrier signal using the analog characteristics. Most analog signals use the telephone system for transmission.

❑ *Frequency shift keying (FSK)* modulates data by assigning two different frequencies, or number of analog signal waves per time period, to the 1 and 0 bit.

❑ *Contention* enables all network devices to access the network whenever there is data to transmit. Multiple simultaneous data transmissions cause collisions. In order to avoid collisions, the network device uses *carrier sensing* to determine whether there is data currently being transmitted.

❑ *Token passing* enables a network device to access the network only when it has received the token, or small, specially formatted frame. The token is passed around the ring until it reaches a network device that needs to transmit data.

❑ *Polling* has a central device to regulate the network traffic and device access. The central device polls each network device to determine if there is data to be sent.

❑ Transmission synchronization is managed by a clocking mechanism that can either be a start and stop bit (asynchronous), separate signal (synchronous), or a separate device (isochronous).

SELF TEST

The Self-Test questions will help you measure your understanding of the material presented in this chapter. Read all the choices carefully, as there may be more than one correct answer. Select all correct answers for each question.

1. Which organization created a reference protocol stack model for networking?

   A. ISO

   B. OSI

   C. IEEE

   D. CCITT

2. When multiple layers create a single network communication, what is that called?

   A. sublayer

   B. protocol stack

   C. time division

   D. frequency division

3. Which of the following is the correct order of the OSI protocol model layers from top to bottom?

   A. Physical, Data Link, Session, Network, Application, Presentation, Transport

   B. Application, Data Link, Session, Presentation, Network, Transport

   C. Session, Network, Transport, Data Link, Application, Physical, Presentation

   D. Application, Presentation, Session, Transport, Network, Data Link, Physical

4. What type of connection enables multiple devices to be on the same media simultaneously?

   A. Transport

   B. Point-to-point

   C. Frequency division

   D. Multipoint

5. Which of the following can be the physical topology of a network?

   A. multipoint or point-to-point

   B. ring or bus

   C. star, ring, bus, mesh, or cellular

   D. baseband or broadband

6. When data is encoded, what form is it sent in?

   A. digital

   B. ASK

   C. analog

   D. broadband

7. Which of the following is a form of biphase encoding?

   A. Unipolar

   B. Non-return to zero

   C. Manchester

   D. RZ

8. When data is transmitted at a faster rate for a 1 bit and slower for a 0 bit, which of the following formats is it being sent in?

   A. Phase shift keying

   B. Amplitude shift keying

   C. Frequency shift keying

   D. Frequency time division

9. When an encoding scheme includes a guaranteed state change per bit time, which of the following clocking schemes will it use?

   A. oversampling

   B. separate device

   C. self-clocking

   D. separate signal

10. Which of the following transmission types will allow multiple data conversations on the same media?

    A. Broadband

    B. Data Link

    C. Baseband

    D. MAC

11. Which method will dynamically allocate timeslots to conversations, and use a control field to identify the owner of the conversation?

    A. FSK

    B. FDM

    C. TDM

    D. StatTDM

12. Which of the following are logical topologies?

    A. multipoint or point-to-point

    B. ring or bus

    C. star, ring, bus, mesh, or cellular

    D. baseband or broadband

13. Which of the following will Ethernet use to access the media?

    A. CSMA/CD

    B. CSMA/CA

    C. token passing

    D. polling

14. How long is an Ethernet MAC address?

    A. 4 bytes

    B. 3 bytes

    C. 6 bytes

    D. 12 bytes

15. Which of the following transmission synchronization methods is seldom used because it has a single point of failure?

    A. Isochronous transmissions using separate device

    B. Asynchronous transmissions using start and stop bits

    C. Synchronous transmissions using separate signals

    D. Synchronous transmissions using oversampling

MICROSOFT CERTIFIED SYSTEMS ENGINEER

29

The OSI Model's Middle Layers

CERTIFICATION OBJECTIVES

29.01   The Middle Layers of the OSI Model

29.02   The Network Layer

29.03   The Transport Layer

The OSI reference model provides seven subtasks that create a total network communication. Usually the first two layers are coupled into an actual specification, such as Ethernet. This modular approach to networking allows a Network and Transport Layer specification to be united with various Physical and Data Link specifications. For example, TCP/IP (a Transport/Network Layer protocol) can run over either Token Ring or Ethernet, among other physical/data link specifications. For that matter, so can IPX/SPX. So, while the lower two layers of the OSI model tend to be tightly coupled, the middle layers are similarly implemented.

CERTIFICATION OBJECTIVE 29.01

The Middle Layers of the OSI Model

The middle layers of the OSI reference model are the Network Layer (Layer 3) and the Transport Layer (Layer 4). These two layers provide routing through an internetwork, and reliability in the form of end-to-end flow control.

CERTIFICATION OBJECTIVE 29.02

The Network Layer

The Network Layer (Layer 3) is responsible for moving data to its destination across an internetwork. This may involve moving the data across multiple networks. The task of moving data involves several functions:

- Addressing of the network and node
- Knowledge of the routes to the various networks
- Switching the data when multiple redundant paths exist
- Managing the efficiency of the data delivery
- Utilizing a gateway when required

Network Layer Addressing

The Network Layer provides for a logical address of the network node. This is in addition to the MAC address, or physical address, provided at the Data Link Layer. The logical network address uniquely identifies each network that takes part in the internetwork (see Figure 29-1). An administrator normally assigns network addresses, and each workstation on the same network shares the same network address. Some implementations, such as IP, will also assign a logical node address at the Network Layer. Other implementations, such as IPX, will use the MAC address as the logical node address.

The network address is important to the routing function. Routers will maintain a routing table that lists the available network addresses and the path to take to reach them. The routing table can be either statically maintained by an administrator or dynamically created through the implementation of a routing protocol.

FIGURE 29-1

Network addresses assigned to each network, even if it has no workstations

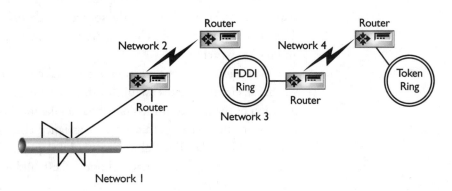

Service Addressing

The Network Layer offers services to the other protocol layers. Since there are multiple services available, there must be some way to distinguish them from each other. In order to specify a source or destination service, these services have an address that can be identified in the header of the packet.

The addresses at the Network Layer include the following:

- Logical network address representing the network that is shared by multiple devices.

- Logical node address representing the device, which can sometimes also be the MAC address.

- Service address representing the process running on the node.

exam
ⓦatch

It is sometimes useful to think of Network Layer addresses in the way a letter is addressed through the U.S. Post Office. The network address is like a street, since many nodes (like houses) can exist on it. The node address is the house number and the service address is the person in the house who can receive the letter.

Switching

Switching is the method of moving data through a network where multiple redundant paths exist between the source and destination (see Figure 29-2). The three major types of switching are circuit switching, message switching, and packet switching.

Circuit switching is the creation of a virtual circuit through a network, where the circuit remains established for switching and this is the minimum duration of the data transmission. It has a guaranteed data rate, but can be inefficient, since bandwidth cannot be assigned elsewhere if a circuit is established but idle. The Public Switched Telephone Network (PSTN) uses a circuit switching system. Each phone call establishes a dedicated link for the duration of the call.

Message switching does not establish a circuit. Instead, each message is considered independent of all other messages. The message contains the

FIGURE 29-2

Switching establishes a
single path as needed when
multiple paths exist

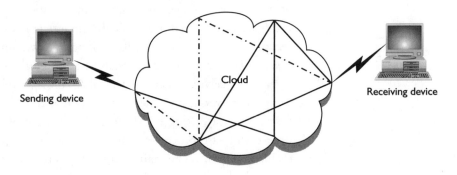

Sending device

Cloud

Receiving device

source and destination node addresses, and is forwarded through the
internetwork from device to device on a *store-and-forward* basis. This is
where the routing device selects the next best hop to send the message from
the options available to it. Each message could conceivably take a different
route through the internetwork. Message switching is more efficient than
circuit switching and avoids network congestion, since the messages are sent
on the best available routes at the time that they are forwarded. The
disadvantage to message switching is the delay introduced by the storing of
messages before they are forwarded from device to device.

Packet switching provides the best of both circuit switching and message
switching, while avoiding their disadvantages. Packet switching breaks
messages down into packets that follow their own route through the
internetwork. Since independent packets do not always follow the same

route, this is called *independent routing*. One form of packet switching is *datagram packet switching*, which treats each packet as though it were complete, rather than part of a larger message. In order to manage datagrams that arrive out of sequence at the receiving device, the packet header includes a sequence number that the receiving device uses to reassemble the message. Since datagrams are smaller than messages, the packets are transmitted both quickly and efficiently in comparison to message switching. The other form of packet switching is called *virtual-circuit packet switching,* which establishes a logical circuit between the sender and receiver. When the virtual circuit is established, the devices use it for data conversation. The main advantage to packet switching is that it has a lower delay, using RAM more often instead of disk storage for store-and-forward processes if the packets are small (packets can be variable in length). The main disadvantages to packet switching are that there is a higher incidence of lost packets because there is a greater number of them to lose, and a requirement for more processing power to handle the packets on each switching device.

Cell switching is a form of packet switching that is used by ATM (Asynchronous Transfer Mode) networks. The main difference between cell switching and packet switching is that, instead of breaking messages down into variable length packets, the message is broken down into small, fixed-length cells. For example, an ATM cell is 53 bytes long. The fixed length of the cell creates a much faster and efficient network, which is always utilizing RAM for store-and-forward processes. This is due to absence of a header containing packet length information.

Routing

When data is moved between two different networks, the two networks become an internetwork. The process of moving the data across an internetwork is called *routing*. Routers use a routing table to refer to the available paths to various networks. An administrator can create the table, in the form of *static routes*, or a routing protocol can be used to dynamically create and maintain the routing table.

Route selection is the ability to determine which route will be the most efficient to use to forward data to its final destination. *Cost* is the number assigned to a link, or route, to give it a relative priority. In the area of cost, the link with the least assigned cost is the first to be selected. One way of determining cost is the number of *hops*, which is the number of routers that have to be hopped over before the destination is reached. A factor in cost can also be time, sometimes calculated in the form of *ticks*, which are a time period of 1/18 of a second.

Route Discovery

Route discovery is performed by a routing protocol, of which there are two types: *distance vector* and *link state*. Each type of routing protocol handles route discovery in a different way.

Distance vector routers periodically (every 60 seconds for IPX RIP) broadcast their entire routing table to their neighbors, and depend on secondhand information for updates to their tables. The larger the internetwork, the longer it takes for the network routers to synchronize their routing tables, known as *convergence*, and the more inefficient this method becomes. Distance vector protocols depend on hops for the cost metric. This route selection criteria can be cumbersome when a slow link has fewer hops than a faster link.

Link state routers broadcast only their immediately known routes to the network, and rebroadcast this information only when a new router is added, or in infrequent periods. This results in only firsthand information being broadcast, and a small amount of information per broadcast. Link-state routing protocols are both efficient and converge quickly. They depend on an assigned or calculated cost metric that incorporates the speed of the link. These route selection criteria will result in a fairly optimal use of the network links.

exam
ⓦatch

RIP (Routing Information Protocol) is a distance vector protocol. There is a RIP version for IPX/SPX and two RIP versions (RIP I and RIP II) for TCP/IP. The link state protocol for IPX/SPX is NLSP (Network Link State Protocol) and OSPF (Open Shortest Path First) is a link state protocol for TCP/IP.

Connection Services

The connection services for the Network Layer include both flow control and error control. Network layer flow control is based on the capability of the internetwork infrastructure. This is also a form of *congestion control,* since the primary goal of this flow control is to manage the amount of data transmitted over any given route to a network. Network flow control uses the following methods:

- Guaranteed transmission rates negotiated by the sending and receiving devices
- Static-sized window flow control
- Dynamic window, or sliding window, flow control

These methods are the same methods implemented at the Data Link Layer, although they are applied to the Network Layer, and thus are represented in the header of the Network Layer datagram.

Error control at the Network Layer attempts to mitigate data loss through the identification of faulty data. Although the Network Layer can detect lost, duplicate packets, or even out-of-sequence packets, these services are usually handled at the Transport Layer. The Network Layer does implement the cyclic-redundancy check (CRC) to control errors. Each time a packet passes through a router, the packet header information changes to correct the next hop address. At this time, and for each hop, the CRC is recalculated.

Gateway Services

At the Physical Layer, the connectivity is at the shared media. At the Data Link Layer, the connectivity is at the shared media and over bridges. At the Network Layer, connectivity can be routed, where routers and devices are using the same Network Layer protocol. Gateways are used for protocol translation at any layer, but typically are implemented at the Network Layer and above to translate between two different protocol stacks. The most common gateway service is between an IBM mainframe environment running SNA traffic and a client-server environment running either IPX/SPX or TCP/IP. Although a gateway can use a single network interface card and the same shared media for both the input and the output traffic, the traffic flows between two logically separate networks.

FROM THE CLASSROOM

Commonly Used Protocol Suites at the Middle Layers

Protocol suites are combinations of individual protocols that work closely together, so they are often treated as a single protocol. The two best-known protocol suites on NetWare networks are the IPX/SPX and the TCP/IP protocol suites. They also happen to be implementations at the Network Layer (Layer 3) and Transport Layer (Layer 4) of the OSI Reference Model. They are, respectively, components of the IPX protocol stack (also called the NetWare protocol stack) and the TCP/IP protocol stack (also called the Internet protocol stack), which encompass implementations at other layers of the OSI Model.

Internetwork Packet Exchange (IPX) provides the Network and Transport Layer implementation for the IPX/SPX protocol stack. Sequenced Packet Exchange (SPX) is a Transport Layer implementation and must rely on IPX to provide routing information. Likewise, Internet Protocol (IP) is the Network Layer implementation for the TCP/IP protocol stack. However, IP protocol, unlike IPX, does not implement any Transport Layer functions. The Transmission Control Protocol (TCP) and the User Datagram Protocol (UDP) provide Transport Layer functions.

In both the IPX protocol stack and the TCP/IP protocol stack, there is a single Network Layer protocol that enables multiple Transport Layer implementations.

—By Dan Cheung, CNI, MCNE, MCT

CERTIFICATION OBJECTIVE 29.03

The Transport Layer

The Transport Layer (Layer 4) is the interface to processes and upper-layer protocols running on a network device. At the sending device, the Transport Layer receives the data from the process. It allows the lower protocols to handle the moving of data to the device and then takes the data and delivers it to the receiving process, which is identified by a port or a socket. The main concern for the process is that the data will be received *reliably*. Reliability does not guarantee data delivery, but it does identify whether it was received correctly and whether retransmission is required.

Transport Layer Addressing

Service addresses at the Network Layer are the access point to the Transport Layer processes. Since a service can receive data from multiple network devices, or have multiple data conversations, a *connection identifier* (sometimes known as the *socket* or *port*) is used to specify the data conversation.

A transaction identifier is used to specify the request/response exchange between a sender and receiver. This type of exchange is known as a *transaction*.

Address/Name Resolution

In order to access another network device, end users find that it easier to use an alphanumeric name (for example, SERVER-FS1) rather than a numeric address (230.44.63.101). However, since all addressing is based on the network address, and not on the alphanumeric name, the address and the name must somehow be mapped to each other so that workstations can resolve which name is associated with which address. This process is known as *address/name resolution*.

Requesting workstations may initiate address/name resolution because they have a name for the device, but no address, or sometimes vice versa (an IP address but not the name). When this happens, the requester broadcasts a special packet that is sent to either the name or the address of the destination machine. The packet asks the destination machine to respond with its address or name.

Service providers may broadcast address/name resolution information on a periodic basis. An example of this is SAP (Service Advertising Protocol) in the IPX/SPX protocol stack. It broadcasts the service provider's name, address, and available services to the network.

Directory services can maintain the name and address mapping of network devices. In this scenario, a requesting device accesses the directory, such as NDS, and acquires the name or address of an applicable device.

Message Segment Development

The Transport Layer takes messages from upper-layer protocols and divides them into segments or packets, which results in segments that are suitably sized for lower-layer protocols. Each segment is identified with a unique sequence number so that the data can be reassembled correctly.

When small messages from multiple services or upper layers are sent to the same destination, the Transport Layer can combine them into a single message. This *aggregation* of messages is performed to enhance network efficiency. The connection identifier of the packet is placed in the header of the packet so that the correct destination services receive their relevant data transmissions.

Connection Services

The Transport Layer implements several connection services in order to perform reliable data transmissions. These connection services include segment sequencing, end-to-end flow control, and error control.

Reordering the segments after they have arrived at the destination is called *segment sequencing*. Since the Transport Layer creates the segments at the sending device, when the segments arrive at the destination device, the destination Transport Layer must reconstruct them into the message that is ready for the upper-layer protocols.

Transport Layer flow control is considered end-to-end because the only devices involved are the sending and receiving devices, or each end. Acknowledgments (ACK) and negative acknowledgments (NAK) from the receiving device let the sender know whether the data was received correctly. There are two special types of ACK packets: *go back n* ACKs request retransmission of the last *n* number of packets and *selective repeat* ACKs request retransmission of specific packets that were not received, or were in error.

Error control detects corrupted, delayed, duplicate, or lost packets. The use of unique segment sequence numbers enables detection of duplicate packets. The use of a timeout value detects packets that have outlived their expected delivery time, and allows them to be discarded. Cyclic Redundancy Check (CRC) is a checksum value algorithm applied to the header and data of a packet, appended to the segment at the sending device. CRC is performed only at the sending and receiving devices, not during the data transmission for the Transport Layer. When the packet is received at the Transport Layer of the receiving device, it performs the same calculation and compares it to the value sent with the packet to verify its validity.

CERTIFICATION SUMMARY

The middle layers of the OSI protocol reference model are the Network Layer (Layer 3) and the Transport Layer (Layer 4). These two layers are responsible for moving data to its destination on an internetwork, and for enabling its reliable transmission.

The Network Layer is responsible for the routing of data across routers and networks. The Network Layer is responsible for routing data across an internetwork, including the knowledge and maintenance of routes and the network addressing.

The address provided at the Network Layer is applied to each separate network on the internetwork. Some Network Layer protocols provide for a node address; others utilize the Data Link Layer MAC address or physical address as the node address. The other address used is the service address to specify which process the data is being sent from or sent to on the nodes.

Switching is the transmission of data through an internetwork that has multiple redundant paths. There are several types of switching. *Circuit switching* is the method of creating a virtual circuit, or path, through the network from the sender to the destination, which remains open for the duration of the data transmission. *Message switching* sends each message over the network on whichever path is currently most efficient. Messages can be sent over different paths. This is also known as *store-and-forward,* since the messages are stored on each switching node and then forwarded to the next node. *Packet switching* is similar to message switching, except that the message is broken down into small, variable-length packets before being sent across the network on the most efficient path. The small size allows most packets to be handled in RAM. The packets are each identified with sequence numbers so that they can be reassembled at the receiving node. *Cell switching,* which is used in ATM (Asynchronous Transfer Mode), is a variation of packet switching in which the packets are small and fixed in length.

Routing is the moving of data across an internetwork. The administrator may create a static route table to identify the available routes, or a dynamic routing protocol can be used to identify updates to the network. Distance vector routing protocols use a hop count to identify the distance to the next route for route selection, and the address of the route for the direction or vector that the data should be moved in. Distance vector protocol routers periodically broadcast their entire routing table to neighboring routers. This means that they depend on secondhand information. Link state routing protocols use a cost metric to identify the priority of the routes for route selection. Each link state router broadcasts updates of only directly connected routes to the rest of the network, meaning that routers get firsthand information.

The Network Layer offers both flow control and error control. The Network Layer also offers gateway services that can translate between two different protocol stacks on the same media, or same type of media. This is typically implemented for mainframe access on a LAN.

The Transport Layer is responsible for the reliable data transmission between the sender and receiver. This layer is concerned with the service addresses, ensuring that data is sent from the correct service and received by the correct service for that particular data conversation, which is identified with a connection identifier.

Name and address resolution occur where the sending node may know the name of a network device, but not the address or vice versa. In these cases, the sending node sends a broadcast with the name or address of the destination, requesting the missing information to be provided. The broadcast packet is received by all nodes and when the destination node reads it, it responds with its information. Name and address resolution data can be sent out in a broadcast format to be able to advertise available network services. This information can be kept within a name server, or it can be kept within directory services.

Message sizes from the upper layers may be too large for lower layers to understand, so the Transport Layer can break the message into packets or segments. Each segment is identified with a sequence number so that it can be reconstructed at the receiving device. In some cases, messages can be concatenated into packets in order to take advantage of network bandwidth. Each different message that is aggregated is given an identifier for its particular conversation.

The connection services at the Transport Layer are geared towards reliable transmission of data. There is an end-to-end flow control that uses ACK and NAK (acknowledgments and negative acknowledgments) packets to verify transmission or request retransmission of data. Error control uses a checksum, or CRC, to verify that data is not corrupted. The ACKs and NAKs handle lost or delayed packets. Sequencing is used to ensure that each packet is assembled correctly, and using a unique sequence number guarantees that duplicate packets can be detected and discarded.

✓ TWO-MINUTE DRILL

❑ The middle layers of the OSI reference model are the Network Layer (Layer 3) and the Transport Layer (Layer 4). These two layers provide routing through an internetwork, and reliability in the form of end-to-end flow control.

❑ The Network Layer (Layer 3) is responsible for moving data to its destination across an internetwork. This may involve moving the data across multiple networks.

❑ The network address is important to the routing function. Routers will maintain a routing table that lists the available network addresses and the path to take to reach them.

❑ *Message switching* does not establish a circuit. Instead, each message is considered independent of all other messages. The message contains the source and destination node addresses, and is forwarded through the internetwork from device to device on a *store-and-forward* basis.

❑ Since independent packets do not always follow the same route, this is called *independent routing*. One form of packet switching is *datagram packet switching*, which treats each packet as though it were complete, rather than part of a larger message.

❑ An administrator can create the table, in the form of *static routes,* or a routing protocol can be used to dynamically create and maintain the routing table.

❑ The addresses at the Network Layer include the following: logical network address representing the network that is shared by multiple devices, and logical node address representing the device, which can sometimes also be the MAC address.

❑ At the Physical Layer, the connectivity is at the shared media. At the Data Link Layer, the connectivity is at the shared media and over bridges. At the Network Layer, connectivity can be routed, where routers and devices are using the same Network Layer protocol.

❑ *Route discovery* is performed by a routing protocol, of which there are two types: *distance vector* and *link state*.

❑ Since a service can receive data from multiple network devices, or have multiple data conversations, a *connection identifier* (sometimes known as the *socket* or *port*) is used to specify the data conversation.

❑ When small messages from multiple services or upper layers are sent to the same destination, the Transport Layer can combine them into a single message. This *aggregation* of messages is performed to enhance network efficiency.

❑ Reordering the segments after they have arrived at the destination is called *segment sequencing*.

❑ Cyclic Redundancy Check (CRC) is a checksum value algorithm applied to the header and data of a packet, appended to the segment at the sending device.

❑ Switching is the transmission of data through an internetwork that has multiple redundant paths. There are several types of switching. *Circuit switching*, *Message switching*, also known as *store-and-forward* and *Packet switching*.

❑ The connection services at the Transport Layer are geared towards reliable transmission of data. There is an end-to-end flow control that uses ACK and NAK (acknowledgments and negative acknowledgments) packets to verify transmission or request retransmission of data..

❑ The Network Layer offers both flow control and error control. The Network Layer also offers gateway services that can translate between two different protocol stacks on the same media, or same type of media.

❑ Sequencing is used to ensure that each packet is assembled correctly, and using a unique sequence number guarantees that duplicate packets can be detected and discarded.

❑ The Transport Layer is responsible for the reliable data transmission between the sender and receiver. This layer is concerned with the service addresses, ensuring that data is sent from the correct service and received by the correct service for that particular data conversation, which is identified with a connection identifier.

SELF TEST

The Self-Test questions will help you measure your understanding of the material presented in this chapter. Read all the choices carefully, as there may be more than one correct answer. Select all correct answers for each question.

1. Which of the following are the middle layers of the OSI reference model?

   A. Application and Presentation

   B. Session and Data Link

   C. Network and Transport

   D. Transport and Physical

2. True or False: The Network Layer will move data across only a single network; the Transport Layer must be involved to go between two networks on an internetwork.

   A. True

   B. False

3. Which of the following layers is responsible for routing and network addresses?

   A. Transport

   B. Session

   C. Physical

   D. Network

4. What method is used to get data to the correct process on a node, such as to the printing process on a print server?

   A. Use of service address, or port

   B. Implementation of distance vector

   C. Implementation of link state protocols

   D. Use of cell switching

5. Which of the following is the creation of a virtual path on a network that is maintained as open for the duration of the data conversation?

   A. Message switching

   B. Packet switching

   C. Cell switching

   D. Circuit switching

6. Which of the following uses small variable length segments of data that are typically sent from switch to switch in RAM?

   A. Message switching

   B. Packet switching

   C. Cell switching

   D. Circuit switching

7. How long is a tick?

   A. 1/8 of a second

   B. 1/18 of a minute

   C. 1/16 of a second

   D. 1/32 of a second

8. Which of the following are types of routing protocols?

   A. Distance vector and cell switching

   B. Distance vector and packet switching

   C. Route selection and link state

   D. Distance vector and link state

9. Which layer performs another CRC each time the data crosses a router?

    A. Session
    B. Network
    C. Transport
    D. Application

10. What process does a gateway perform?

    A. Routing
    B. Switching
    C. Protocol translation
    D. Vectoring

11. What does the term *reliability* mean at the Transport Layer?

    A. Data transmission is guaranteed.
    B. Data retransmissions do not need to be performed.
    C. Errors do not occur.
    D. Transmissions are acknowledged and retransmissions requested.

12. What does a connection identifier do?

    A. Identifies a data conversation
    B. Identifies a transaction
    C. Identifies a session
    D. Identifies the vector travelled

13. If all a workstation knows is the name for a network device, what process does it use to determine the address to send it to?

    A. Connection identifier
    B. Transaction identifier
    C. Address/name resolution
    D. Service advertising

14. What is used to reassemble segments into messages?

    A. Connection identifier
    B. Sequence number
    C. Transaction identifier
    D. Service advertising

15. At the Transport Layer, when is a CRC performed?

    A. At each router that is crossed
    B. At each node that receives a broadcast
    C. At the sending and receiving devices
    D. At the server

CERTIFIED NOVELL ENGINEER

30

The OSI Model's Upper Layers

CERTIFICATION OBJECTIVES

30.01   Upper Layers of the OSI Model

30.02   The Session Layer

30.03   The Presentation Layer

30.04   The Application Layer

The lower layers of the OSI reference model include all the specifications needed for the structure and data flow of an internetwork. The upper layers, Session, Presentation, and Application, are responsible for the network services. End users perceive the network from using these services, and the lower layer protocols are transparent to them.

CERTIFICATION OBJECTIVE 30.01

Upper Layers of the OSI Model

The three upper layers of the OSI reference model are the Session layer (Layer 5), the Presentation layer (Layer 6), and the Application layer (Layer 7). The Session layer establishes connections and their releases. The Presentation layer handles translation, which is the process allowing different types of computers to communicate. The Application layer owns the services used by end users to access the network.

CERTIFICATION OBJECTIVE 30.02

The Session Layer

The Session layer (Layer 5) creates and destroys *sessions* or dialogs between applications running on the sender and receiver. Session layer connections are an established data conversation between the sender and receiver devices. The connection is established regardless of the path that any data travels over the internetwork.

exam Watch

The Session layer is usually considered to be the source location of remote procedure calls (RPCs). RPCs transmit data over the internetwork in a manner that is transparent to the end user.

Some sessions in NetWare are established between the client and the server. One way to view sessions in NetWare is to view the connected stations in the MONITOR.NLM. The session is established before a login can occur.

Dialog Control

When two network nodes communicate, the data conversation is called a *dialog*. The ways that a dialog can be established between the two network nodes are described in Table 30-1.

Session Administration

Session administration provides a method of identifying the participants of a dialog. Managing dialogs at the Session layer involves three basic tasks:

1. Establishing the connection
2. Transmitting the data
3. Releasing the connection

Secure Session layer dialog connections can be initiated with a valid name and password. The Session layer will also assign a Connection ID to the dialog. Also, the Session layer will specify the services that are requested.

The Session layer dialog will continue with a data transfer. During the transmission, the lower-layer protocols will be exchanging acknowledgments (ACKs) and negative acknowledgments (NACKs) to manage the flow of data. A Session layer dialog may be interrupted due to a network condition. However, the Session layer will not know of the interruption until notified by a lower-layer protocol, when it does not receive an expected acknowledgment. The Session layer then informs upper layers of the interruption in service.

The procedures that release the dialog at the Session layer are in place so that there is an orderly end to the session. This means that any resources used by the dialog will be released for others to use. If there is an abrupt

Dialog Type	Direction	Description
TABLE 30-1 Dialog Types Simplex	One-way communication	In simplex transmissions, data travels in only one direction. There is one device that is a transmitter and one that is a receiver. An example is a radio transmission. The advantages of simplex are that it is fairly inexpensive and easy to implement. The disadvantages include the lack of reliability and the inability to respond directly.
Half-duplex	Alternating two-way communication	Each device at the two ends of a half-duplex acts as both a transmitter and receiver. However, the data can travel in only one direction at a time, so the devices take turns. The advantage is that there is bidirectional communication, and the equipment is not as expensive as full-duplex. The disadvantages are that only one device can transmit at a time and there is some turnaround overhead.
Full-duplex	Simultaneous two-way communication	Each device at the two ends of a full-duplex acts as both a transmitter and receiver at all times. Data transmits in both directions simultaneously. The advantage is the simultaneous bidirectional data transmission. The disadvantage is that the equipment is more expensive and complex than the simplex and half-duplex equipment.

termination release of the dialog, such as from a network error condition, some implementations of the Session layer enable communication to resume where it left off.

The Presentation Layer

The Presentation layer (Layer 6) handles data formatting. It will translate data into a mutually agreed upon format or *transfer syntax*. This enables an application to send data from one type of workstation (such as a Windows 95 PC) to a different type of workstation (such as a Macintosh), and have that data be in a readable format. The Presentation layer is also responsible for

- Data translation, inclusive of compression and expansion
- Encryption and decryption

Data Translation

Data translation is simply the transfer from one syntax to another. There are various approaches to data translation. At the bit level, the *bit order translation* is the agreement between the sender and receiver of whether to read each byte from the first bit received or the last bit received. At the byte level, *byte order translation* is the agreement between the sender and receiver of whether to read from the first byte or last byte. The first byte method (used by Motorola processors) is called *big endian.* The last byte method (used by Intel processors) is called *little endian.*

The method of file compression and expansion is dependent on the types of characters and file syntax that are understood by the operating system being used. File compression is typically implemented in a replacement of typical bit or byte sequences by a smaller set of bits or bytes. Before compression can take place, the file headers specific to the operating system may be stripped off. Then, at the receiving station, the appropriate file headers may be added after the reverse expansion replacement of bits/bytes is made.

In some cases, the characters may need to be translated. An example of this is when data is being transferred between an IBM mainframe and an

Intel workstation. IBM mainframes use EBCDIC (Extended Binary Coded Decimal Interchange Code, also referred to as Extended ASCII) and Intel workstations use ASCII (American Standard Code for Information Interchange).

Encryption

Encryption is the ability to secure a data transmission through a secret code so that it can traverse the internetwork without fear of being read by someone other than the intended recipient. Not only does encryption secure the data from a user at the receiving network node, but it also protects the data from being read even if it was copied from the network, or *sniffed*, onto a different network node.

exam
ⓦatch

Decryption is the process of deciphering the code in an encrypted file.

There are many types of encryption available. One popular method is *public key encryption*. Public key encryption uses two keys: a public key and a private key. A user who signs up for public key encryption is given the public key to hand out to others. Some public keys are managed by directory services, such that accessing the directory service will allow all users to use the public key. The private key is given to the user, or managed in a directory service under the user's ID, and is never handed out. The public and private keys are mutually encrypting/decrypting algorithms.

For example, when a user wants to send an encrypted file to another user, the user will encrypt the file with the public key. The public key will perform an encrypting algorithm on the file at the Presentation layer. The message will then travel through the protocol stack, across the network to the receiving node, up the protocol stack to the receiving Presentation layer. There may be some notification about the encrypted file. The user would then use the private key (in whatever method that the encryption program requires) to decrypt the file.

Some networks require a high level of security, and they may implement automatic encryption at the Presentation layer. This method is more likely to be managed by a network directory service or other network-wide security service so that the encryption is transparent to the end user.

The Application Layer

The Application layer (Layer 7) is responsible for the user interface. It specifies the interface and manages communication between network services. Such network services include but are not limited to

- Virtual terminal programs such as RCONSOLE (NetWare's remote console application)

- File transfer such as NCOPY (NetWare's file copying program)

- Directory services such as Novell Directory Services through NetWare Administrator

- Network management such as SNMP (Simple Network Management Protocol)

- Electronic messaging such as GroupWise (an e-mail and groupware product from Novell)

Service Advertising

Although many services share a common advertising method, each network service may use a different type of service advertising, or none at all.

There is a method of actively advertising services. This is usually in the form of a broadcast message that is sent on a periodic basis, like SAP (Service Advertising Protocol). Some advertising protocols are implemented at lower layers of the protocol stack. The Application layer is responsible for ensuring that the lower-layer protocol is notified that the service is available. The network clients will then know what services are available when they receive the advertisement.

Directory services is a form of passive service advertisement implemented at the Application layer. Novell Directory Services, or NDS, provide a global hierarchical listing of all network resources. Those resources and their applicable services are available to the network by viewing the directory. At the base level, the directory is available to users so that they may search for services. NDS-aware applications can access the directory and find the services so that this process is transparent to the end user.

Service Use Methods

In order to utilize services, there must be an access method. The Application layer will communicate with lower-layer protocols to ensure that the service can be used. This involves some cooperation between the sending and receiving devices.

Some applications are not network aware, but they must have some access to the network. In these applications, the Application layer protocol interfaces with the operating system in a form of *OS call interception.* For example, NCP (NetWare Core Protocol) responds to the shell in the NetWare 32-bit client. In turn, the NetWare 32-bit client shell intercepts the application calls and determines whether the application needs to be accessing the network or the operating system. The NetWare client then redirects the application to the network if that is the destination. This type of interaction is depicted by an application that is saving a file to a network file server, rather than the local drive. When the user types the file location and name, such as F:\PUBLIC\FILE.TXT, the application sends a call to the operating system (OS) to access the F: drive. The NetWare client intercepts this call and, knowing that F: is a mapped drive, redirects the save action to the network file server.

Some applications are created with networking features incorporated into the application. These can be RPC (remote procedure call) applications. They incorporate the Session layer protocol implementation of RPCs. Typical applications that use RPCs are electronic messaging or network-aware databases.

Some applications use *agents* on the client. This is typical of a remote backup system, or of SNMP. In both of these systems, the agent sits on the client and serves as an interface between the operating system and the network application. In the case of remote backups, the agent advertises the workstation's files for backup and restore purposes. This does not make those files available for network access by any other application or network device. In the case of SNMP, the agent is given instructions as to which events to notify the SNMP server with, either programmed within the agent itself, or available to the network application to adjust. When an event occurs, the SNMP agent notifies the SNMP server.

CERTIFICATION SUMMARY

The three upper layers of the OSI protocol reference model are Session, Presentation, and Application. These are also known as Layer 5 (Session), Layer 6 (Presentation), and Layer 7 (Application).

The Session layer is responsible for the establishment, maintenance, and release of dialogs between two network devices.

The Session layer dialog control can be one of three types. Simplex is a one-way communication in which there is one transmitting device and one receiving device. Half-duplex is a two-way communication in which both devices can transmit and receive, but must take turns doing so. Full-duplex is a two-way communication in which both devices transmit and receive simultaneously.

The Session layer manages the establishment of connections, the transfer of data during the connection, and the close of the connection to release resources. The Session layer is the base of remote procedure calls (RPCs).

The Presentation layer is responsible for the syntax transfer of data. It has several ways of managing this. The methods of data translation that the Presentation layer may employ include bit order translation, byte order translation, and compression/expansion. The Presentation layer is also responsible for the data format as it relates to encryption.

The Application layer is responsible for network services. It provides access to advertising protocols at lower layers. The Application layer will use OS call interception to redirect non-network-aware applications to the network when necessary. The Application layer services may incorporate

RPCs within the application for transparent network access. Other methods of service access and use include using an agent on the workstation that interacts with a centralized network application.

✓ TWO-MINUTE DRILL

❑ The lower layers of the OSI reference model include all the specifications needed for the structure and data flow of an internetwork.

❑ The upper layers—Session, Presentation, and Application—are responsible for the network services.

❑ The Session layer (Layer 5) creates and destroys *sessions*, or dialogs, between applications running on the sender and receiver.

❑ The Session layer is usually considered to be the source location of remote procedure calls (RPCs).

❑ RPCs transmit data over the internetwork in a manner that is transparent to the end user.

❑ When two network nodes communicate, the data conversation is called a *dialog*.

❑ The Presentation layer (Layer 6) handles data formatting. It will translate data into a mutually agreed upon format or *transfer syntax*.

❑ *Encryption* is the ability to secure a data transmission through a secret code so that it can transverse the internetwork without fear of being read by someone other than the intended recipient.

❑ The Application layer (Layer 7) is responsible for the user interface. It specifies the interface and manages communication between network services.

SELF TEST

The Self-Test questions will help you measure your understanding of the material presented in this chapter. Read all the choices carefully, as there may be more than one correct answer. Select all correct answers for each question.

1. Which layers of the OSI protocol model are perceived by the end user?

   A. Lower layers: Physical and Data Link

   B. Middle layers: Network and Transport

   C. Upper layers: Session, Presentation, and Application

2. True or False: When the Session layer establishes a connection between a sender and receiver, it creates a specific path through the network.

   A. True

   B. False

3. The type of dialog communication that requires only one receiver and one transmitter is

   A. Simplex

   B. Half-duplex

   C. Full-duplex

4. The type of dialog that provides for simultaneous bidirectional data transmission is

   A. Simplex

   B. Half-duplex

   C. Full-duplex

5. Session layer dialog data transfer depends on what for dialog interruptions?

   A. Nonreceipt of acknowledgments at lower layers

   B. Nonreceipt of ACKs at the Session layer

   C. End-to-end flow control

   D. Application layer notification messages

6. What is another term for formatting data?

   A. ACK

   B. Transfer syntax

   C. Bit order

   D. RPC

7. What type of data translation is the agreement of the sender and receiver to read data from the first or last bit of each received byte?

   A. Byte order

   B. Character code

   C. Compression

   D. Bit order

8. Which of the following methods is used to secure data at the Presentation layer?

   A. Compression

   B. Bit order translation

   C. Encryption

   D. ASCII

9. Which of the following are services offered at the Application layer? (Choose all that apply.)

   A. Electronic messaging

   B. Network management

   C. Virtual terminal

   D. File transfer

10. What service at the Application layer will enable non-network-aware applications to access the network?

    A. Agents

    B. Remote procedure calls

    C. Service advertising

    D. OS call interception

Part IV

Networking Directory Services Design and Implementation

CNE
CERTIFIED NOVELL ENGINEER

31

Assessing the Network

CERTIFICATION OBJECTIVES

31.01   Defining the NetWare Design and Implementation Process

31.02   Identifying the Design and Implementation Team

31.03   Assessing Business Needs

31.04   Previewing Case Company Information

The NetWare Design and Implementation process is a methodical, well laid-out plan to building a successful network. This plan, as developed by Novell, has proven itself time and time again in networks of all sizes and is the same one that Novell's own consulting group uses when they are called in to design networks. This process is based on a variant or subset of the linear SDLC (System Design Life Cycle Model), which we will cover in the first section of this chapter. Following the Novell Design and Implementation model will help ensure a network that is easy to use, manage, and build upon in the future.

CERTIFICATION OBJECTIVE 31.01

Defining the NetWare Design and Implementation Process

When a company makes a decision to invest in a network, someone has to make the decisions concerning network planning.

As a network consultant, you will be dealing with an information services (IS) manager or another person in the corporate structure that has decided upon a NetWare network. Your first concern will be to answer some very basic questions concerning the implementation of the network presented to you by the IS manager:

- What is the process for installing the NetWare operating system on the network?

- What are the resource needs and demands in terms of people and hardware?

- How long will the planning and implementation take?

However, before you can answer these questions, you must find out the goals and priorities of the IS manager, including such things as performance, fault tolerance, and accessibility. Once you know the goals of the IS manager, the NetWare Design and Implementation process can begin and the questions of the IS manager can be answered.

System Design Life Cycles

To gain the most insight into designing, implementing, maintaining, and revising an information system, we are going to look at a tool that is used by programmers and system designers: the System Design Life Cycle (SDLC). This tool is a consistent and methodical approach to designing and is used throughout the information processing industry. Figures 31-1 and 31-2 illustrate a linear SDLC and an incremental SDLC, respectively.

There are different styles of an SDLC, such as linear, structured, incremental, and modified spiral. The difference between the various SDLC models is the extent to which the different phases occur linearly or concurrently. For example, in a linear model, each phase is completed before moving on to the next phase. On the other hand, in an incremental model, each phase is overlapped with the previous phase.

FIGURE 31-1

Linear SDLC

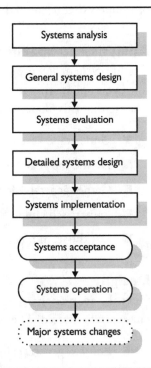

FIGURE 31-2 Incremental SDLC

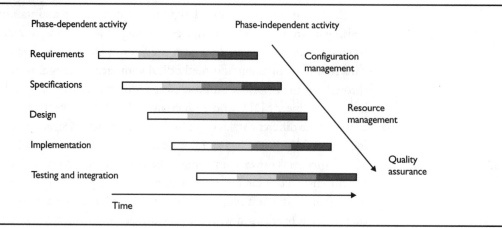

All of these styles have several steps in common and each variation has procedures that relate to the following phases.

Analysis and Specification

The life cycle of any project begins with the analysis and specification phase. It is in this phase that the project scope and requirements are identified. The steps in this phase should include the following as a minimum:

- Understand and state the business need of the system.
- Define the goals, constraints, and resources needed.
- Gather general information on the project.
- Prepare schedules.
- List the team members' responsibilities and assignments.

Design

Once the analysis and specifications phase has been defined, the design phase can be started. The design phase will include the following:

- Propose generic solutions.

■ Propose alternative solutions.

■ Design a specific solution.

Implementation

After a specific solution has been chosen, or at least a partial solution has been designed, the implementation phase can begin. Whether the solution involves new hardware, software, or just configuration of existing systems, try to complete the following:

■ Define implementation-specific milestones.

■ Develop and test a working solution.

■ Implement a pilot solution.

■ Test the pilot solution.

■ Gain customer acceptance.

■ Implement the final solution.

■ Document the solution and train users.

■ Test the final solution.

■ Gain customer acceptance.

Maintenance

Once the system has been implemented, maintenance begins. During the other phases, decisions were made concerning the design of the system. The maintenance phase includes tasks to help you evaluate the validity of your decisions. It is also in this phase that the decision to start the SDLC process again is made.

■ Perform on-going system checks and performance reports.

■ Perform maintenance until maintenance costs exceed the cost of a new system.

■ Retire the solution; at this point you should have already prepared by starting the SDLC process again.

The NetWare Design and Implementation Process

The NetWare Design and Implementation process is a subset of a standard SDLC and uses a linear approach. However in actual use, the process is very iterative and nonlinear. This will become evident as you progress through this chapter and the subsequent chapters covering the design and implementation process. The NetWare Design and Implementation process is shown in Figure 31-3. Only the first six steps are covered in the Design and Implementation test; the remaining steps are covered in other NetWare tests. In this section we will define the phases in the NetWare NDS Design Cycle model and what procedures are performed in each phase.

Project Approach Phase

The first phase in the NetWare NDS Design Cycle process contains only one process, preparing for NDS design, as shown in the following illustration of Phase 1.

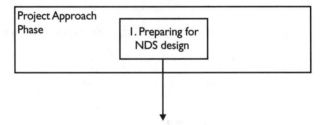

The following tasks make up this process:

- Assemble the project team.
- Gather the business information related to the network design.
- Train the project team.
- Determine the scope of the design process.
- Schedule preliminary project design.

These steps help establish realistic expectations to ensure that the design and implementation process proceeds on course without too many surprises

FIGURE 31-3

Novell SDLC

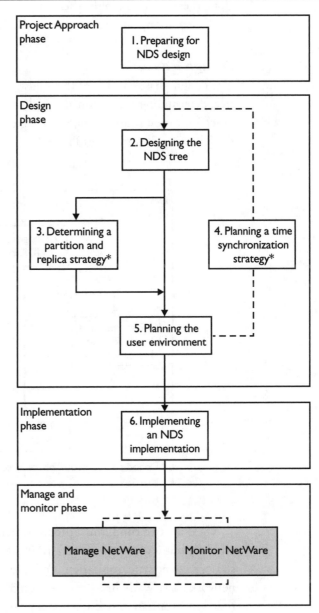

* Denotes a conditional procedure

along the way. This is also where members of the design and implementation team will be given an idea of their roles in the project.

Design Phase

The design phase consists of the following processes: designing the NDS tree, determining a partition and replication strategy, planning a time synchronization strategy, and planning the user environment, as shown in the following illustration of Phase 2.

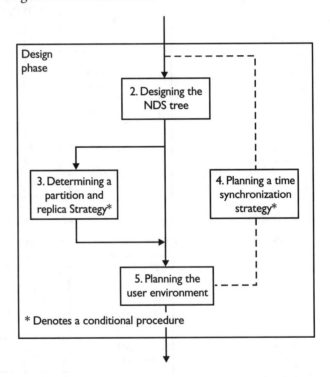

There are two conditional procedures in this phase: the time synchronization strategy and determining a partition and replication strategy. Time synchronization is conditional because it is used only if your network has a WAN link or more then 30 servers. In addition, designing time synchronization is also a nonsequential process that can be performed independent of other procedures within the design phase. As for the partition and replication strategy, this process can be employed only if you have more than one server.

- **Designing the NDS tree**   This procedure includes an NDS objects-naming standards document and the design of the upper and lower layers of the NDS directory tree. This process will ensure an efficient, well-designed tree that is easy to use for network users and easy to manage for network administrators. It is also a critical step for the next procedure—designing the partition and replication strategy that will be used.

- **Determining a partition and replica strategy**   This procedure includes designing how the tree will be partitioned, placement of the partitions, and where the replicas of the partitions will be stored. Careful planning will help provide scalability for the directory tree, fault tolerance, and accessibility of the directory tree across the network.

- **Planning a time synchronization strategy**   Within this procedure, it will be decided whether or not time synchronization should be designed for the network or if the default time synchronization will be used. Time synchronization is used to provide timestamps to NDS events and other applications such as file systems and messaging applications. This procedure will be necessary for networks containing WAN links and/or more than 30 servers, to ensure fault tolerance of time synchronization without creating undue traffic on the network.

- **Planning the user environment**   In this procedure, login scripts will be defined. NDS security and the use of aliases, directory maps, and Profile objects also will be designed. This procedure will make network services more intuitive to administer and easier for the user. Some of the tasks include standardizing NDS object use, standardizing the file system directory structures, and developing strategies for mobile users.

Implementation Phase

The third and last phase in the design and implementation objectives is the procedure for implementing an NDS implementation, as shown in the following illustration of Phase 3.

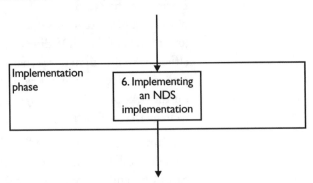

Implementing an NDS implementation: This procedure develops the strategies for setting up servers, workstations, and other network components. A network lab is also set up in this procedure to help work out the problems and glitches that will be encountered when setting up the subsequent pilot program. Other procedures covered in this process are defining the various tasks involved, drafting time-line documents, assigning tasks to team members, and the coordination of the implementation with other groups within the company. The first actual implementation is the pilot program. The IS department is usually the best group to use for the pilot program because of their computer literacy skills and expectations. The time-line documents are used to plot the proper sequence of steps for the tasks involved. The implementation schedule is the single most visible procedure to the company and, should it disrupt or impact the company's operation, it will become a direct reflection on you, the network consultant.

Manage and Monitor Phase

The manage and monitor phase contains the two procedures that take up most of the system administrator's time: the management and monitoring of a NetWare network, as shown in the following illustration of Phase 4.

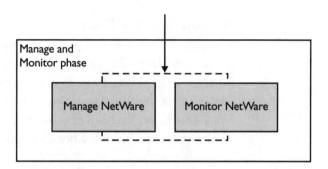

- **Manage NetWare** This procedure includes creating users and other objects, configuring printing, setting security, and maximizing performance. These topics are covered in the NetWare 5 Administration and NetWare 5 Advanced Administration chapters of this book.

- **Monitor NetWare** Monitoring NetWare includes understanding the server memory, troubleshooting performance, and troubleshooting NDS. This procedure is covered in the NetWare 5 Advanced Administration and the NetWare 5 Service and Support chapters of this book.

CERTIFICATION OBJECTIVE 31.02

Identifying the Design and Implementation Team

The design and implementation team will be composed of employees from the IS department or an outside consulting firm, or a combination of both. No matter where the team members come from, it is critical to the success of the project that all team members work well together, are able to express their concerns, and provide feedback and suggestions during the project. It is best to compose the team of individuals with various job responsibilities so that concerns and expectations from different areas of the company can be addressed. Each team member should have his or her role in the project clearly defined regarding responsibilities, priorities, and expectations of how team members should interact with each other.

Assembling the Team

Assigning team members depends on what resources are available to you. If you have a large IS department, you most likely will assemble your team from within its ranks. If you do not have such a luxury, hiring an outside consultant or consulting group could be an option. If you're really in a pinch, sometimes the team may be just one or two people such as a network administrator and his or her boss. The following questions will help you find team members:

- How is your IS department organized?
- Who administers the workstations?
- Who administers the servers?
- Who manages software updates on the workstations and servers?
- Who administers the printers?
- Who tests new software on the workstations and servers?
- Who knows the network layout and protocols used?
- Who trains the support staff and users?

The answers to these questions will help you determine who should be part of the team. Keep in mind that the more diversity you have on the team, the better design you will develop.

Team Roles

While a lot of companies simply do not have the resources for a separate team member for each and every role, many teams have members that serve multiple roles in the team. Even though it would be nice to have a different person in each role, this is seldom the case due to limited resources. While the number of members is not important, the main concern is that the task of each role is addressed. The following roles have been proven to be effective in the NetWare Design and Implementation process:

- **IS manager**   Someone, no matter the size of the company, must make decisions and take responsibility for the design and implementation of the network. This is the role of the IS manager. The IS manager is responsible for overseeing the entire process and serves as the motivational force of the project. The IS manager's responsibilities include the following:

■ Choose the team members.

■ Coordinate all procedures with the team members.

■ Act as a liaison to upper management.

■ Secure necessary resources for the project.

■ Manage cost and scheduling of the project.

■ Assume overall responsibility for the project.

■ **NDS expert**   The NDS expert is responsible for the overall design of the directory tree and security thereof. This includes partitioning the tree, replication, and time synchronization. It is the goal of the NDS expert to design the tree so that it is easy for users to use, administration is simple, and maintenance of tree is made as easy as possible. Since it is assumed that the NDS expert has a thorough knowledge of NetWare, this position also serves as a team leader. The NDS expert's responsibilities include the following:

■ Help choose team members.

■ Act as a liaison to other departments within the company and the team.

■ Guide the overall network design to match the company organization and fulfill the company's needs, keeping in mind the need for network security.

■ Be responsible for the design of the directory tree.

■ **Server specialist**   The server specialist is responsible for the performance and stability of the NetWare network during the project. The server specialist's responsibilities include the following:

■ Ensure the success of the pilot program.

■ Provide server-related information to other team members.

- Check disk space requirements and monitor space on the servers.

- Back up servers and verify the backups.

- Record all IPX and IP addresses used and following the standards set by the project team concerning frame types and protocols used on the network.

- **Workstation specialist** The workstation specialist is responsible for ensuring that the workstations have access to all the resources on the network needed by the user. The workstation specialist's responsibilities include the following:

  - Make sure the NetWare client files are up-to-date.

  - Automate workstation software updates as much as possible.

  - Maintain consistent client configuration files.

  - Make sure a consistent naming convention is used within client configuration files.

  - Verify that the application software is compatible with the NetWare client software.

  - Check the function of the login scripts and bindery services if used.

  - Make network accessible for traveling users.

- **Application specialist** The application specialist is responsible for testing and ensuring that the current applications used on the network are compatible with the new NetWare server software. The application specialist's responsibilities include the following:

  - Create current login scripts to access applications.

  - Create current menu programs to access applications.

  - Make sure that any applications planned for the future are compatible.

- **Printing specialist** The printing specialist handles the printing needs of the users. The printing specialist's responsibilities include the following:

- See that all printers are set up and accessible to users.

- Verify that printer drivers are installed and configured correctly.

- Make sure that any printer requiring bindery services is configured correctly.

- Set up Point and Print correctly for Win 95 / Win 98 clients.

- **Connectivity specialist**   The connectivity specialist is responsible for the routing, protocols, telecommunications, and any other connectivity issues in the design and implementation process. The connectivity specialist's responsibilities include the following:

  - Monitor network packet traffic load.

  - Check network bandwidth utilization.

  - Know the correct use of bridges, routers, and switches.

  - Maintain WAN links.

  - Make sure that remote access solutions are adequate.

- **Testing lab coordinator**   The testing lab coordinator performs the network setup and runs tests on the networking software with the current applications. The testing lab coordinator will also run diagnostics, compile statistics on performance, and ensure software stability. The testing lab coordinator's responsibilities include the following:

  - Set up the lab environment.

  - Gather all network information to simulate in the lab.

  - Verify that all application software is up-to-date.

  - Obtain resources for the lab via the IS manager.

  - Provide test results to the other members of the team.

- **Education and training coordinator**   The education and training coordinator is responsible for assessing the skills of the team members and then providing for any necessary training that may be required. The coordinator also sees that network users receive necessary training. The education and training coordinator's responsibilities include the following:

- Identify and provide implementation and administration guidelines.
- Train members of the project team.
- Train the network administrators.
- Train users.
- Secure budget for training via the IS manager.
- Define the scope of the training.

Assessing Business Needs

Networks in business are a relatively new concept. Not long ago in the corporate environment, mainframe and minicomputers were used for mission-critical and line-of-business applications. These systems used centralized processing methods and were able to support hundreds of people on a single host. Since all of the processing was performed on the host computer, the clients were merely dumb terminals on the user's desktop. The applications used were limited to accounting, sales orders, and distribution, with a few systems offering primitive e-mail and word processing capabilities. There was no concept of PCs using GUI front ends to perform many diverse tasks such as groupware workflow solutions, desktop database management, word processing, Internet e-mail, and file transfer. When PC-based LANs were first introduced to the corporate world, they were employed in a limited fashion, usually to upper management to share spreadsheet, database data, and printers. The LANs were installed with no foresight into future expansion hampering smooth transitions into new resources and services that could be delivered with newer technologies, as they became available.

The network consultant assessing the needs of a business today, must keep in mind the mistakes made in the past and plan for the future in the designs provided for a client.

CERTIFICATION OBJECTIVE 31.04

Previewing Case Company Information

In order to create a successful NetWare 5 network, you must first have the appropriate company information assembled. This information is obtained by the various team members and compiled to form the documents to design and implement the NetWare network. The following is a list of the documents that will have to be obtained in order to perform the design process:

- Project team role checklists
- Company background information
- Organization charts
- LAN topology
- WAN topology
- Location maps
- Resource lists
- Workflow information

Each team member will need different documents to carry out his or her responsibilities in the design phase. Some of these documents will be needed by more than one team member and will be used to derive different types of information. The following are guidelines as to what documents are needed and how they relate to each team role:

- **IS manager**

Organization charts	Structure of the company
Resource lists	People, hardware, and software
Workflow information	How information flows in the company

- **NDS expert**

Organization charts	Divisions and workgroups within the company
LAN topology	Resources and how they are grouped
WAN topology	Number of remote sites, WAN link speeds, and time synchronization
Location maps	Partition, replication, and time synchronization
Workflow	Tree(s) and container design

- **Server specialist**

LAN topology	Number of servers, the version of NetWare they are running, and how they are used in the network
WAN topology	Number of remote servers, the version of NetWare they are running, and how they are used in the network
Location maps	The location of the servers
Resource lists	The number of servers in each location and type of clients

- **Workstation specialist**

Resource lists	Number and types of clients

■ Application specialist

LAN topology	Servers storing applications and access methods
Resource lists	License counts and versions of applications
Workflow information	Location needs for applications

■ Printing specialist

Resource lists	Number of printers, location, print driver versions, and user access

CERTIFICATION SUMMARY

The Novell NDS Design Cycle process is based upon a subset of the linear SDLC model and is composed of four phases. The Novell Design and Implementation process involves a total of nine processes, six of which are covered on the test.

The six processes are as follows:

1. Preparing for NDS design

2. Designing an NDS tree

3. Determining a partition and replica strategy

4. Planning a time synchronization strategy

5. Planning the user environment

6. Implementing an NDS implementation.

Of the six processes, two are conditional: determining a partition and replication strategy, and planning a time synchronization strategy.

The partition and replication strategy is not used on networks with only one server and the time synchronization strategy is used only when there are more than 30 servers or a WAN environment exists.

The design and implementation team is comprised of an IS manager, NDS expert, server specialist, workstation specialist, connectivity specialist, application specialist, printing specialist, testing lab coordinator, and the education and training coordinator.

TWO-MINUTE DRILL

❑ The System Design Life Cycle (SDLC) is a consistent and methodical approach to designing and is used throughout the information processing industry.

❑ There are different styles of an SDLC, such as a linear, structured, incremental, and modified spiral. The difference between the various SDLC models is the extent to which the different phases occur linearly or concurrently.

❑ The life cycle of any project begins with the analysis and specification phase.

❑ The design phase will include the following: propose generic solutions, propose alternative solutions, and design a specific solution.

❑ After a specific solution has been chosen, or at least a partial solution has been designed, the implementation phase can begin.

❑ Once the system has been implemented, maintenance begins. During the other phases, decisions were made concerning the design of the system and the maintenance phase includes tasks to help you evaluate the validity of your decisions.

❑ The NetWare Design and Implementation process is a subset of a standard SDLC and uses a linear approach.

❑ While a lot of companies simply do not have the resources for a separate team member for each and every role, many teams have members that serve multiple roles in the team.

❑ The Novell Design and Implementation process involves a total of nine processes, six of which are covered on the test:

  ❑ Preparing for NDS design

  ❑ Designing an NDS tree

  ❑ Determining a partition and replica strategy

  ❑ Planning a time synchronization strategy

  ❑ Planning the user environment

  ❑ Implementing an NDS implementation.

❑ The design and implementation team is comprised of an IS manager, NDS expert, server specialist, workstation specialist, connectivity specialist, application specialist, printing specialist, testing lab coordinator, and the education and training coordinator.

SELF TEST

The Self-Test questions will help you measure your understanding of the material presented in this chapter. Read all the choices carefully, as there may be more than one correct answer. Select all correct answers for each question.

1. Who should arrange a visit to a site where the company recently went through a NetWare Design and Implementation project?

    A. IS manager

    B. NDS expert

    C. Server specialist

    D. Printing specialist

2. Which of the following best describes the resource list?

    A. It is a list of the budgets allocated to each phase of the project.

    B. It is a list of the servers in the current network.

    C. It is a list comprised of only the new servers to be implemented.

    D. It is a list containing only the printers planned for the network.

3. It is the responsibility of the _____ to assign team members to roles based on their skill sets?

    A. NDS expert

    B. Integration expert

    C. Team leader

    D. IS manager

4. The implementation team starts to install the file servers and discovers there is not enough room for all of the applications that have to be loaded. Which team member didn't meet the expectations of his or her assigned role?

    A. Server specialist

    B. Resource specialist

    C. NDS expert

    D. Testing Lab coordinator

5. Which of the following documents would be used to determine the number of file servers that needed to be upgraded?

    A. Server list

    B. LAN topology

    C. Resource list

    D. WAN topology

6. What document defines the layout of the existing network?

    A. Organization chart

    B. LAN topology

    C. Company background

    D. Resource list

7. Which document would be used to determine how many workstations are on the network?

    A. Organization chart

    B. LAN topology

    C. Company background

D. Resource list

8. Assembling the team and training the team members is included in the _____ phase of the project.

A. Project approach

B. Design

C. Implementation

D. Manage and monitor

9. During the _____ phase, the project team can make a realistic determination of what can be expected from the project.

A. Project approach

B. Design

C. Implementation

D. Manage and monitor

10. In which procedure do you establish what client requester software is currently in use and plan upgrades to the newest version?

A. Planning a time synchronization strategy

B. Implementing an NDS implementation.

C. Developing a migration strategy

D. Managing and monitoring the network

11. Which of the following statements are true? (Choose all that apply.)

A. Small networks are easier to design and implement than larger ones.

B. There is no need to design a time synchronization strategy in a WAN environment.

C. The team must have at least seven members, one for each role.

D. You must design a time synchronization strategy for networks that contain more than 30 servers.

12. The Naming Standards document is created during which procedure?

A. Designing an NDS tree

B. Determining a partition and replication strategy

C. Planning the user environment

D. Preparing for NDS design

13. You have just completed determining a partition and replica strategy and planning a time synchronization strategy. What step should come next?

A. Implementing an NDS implementation.

B. Designing an NDS tree

C. Planning the user environment

D. Preparing for NDS design

14. What is the single most important procedure in the design and implementation of a NetWare network?

A. Planning a time synchronization strategy

B. Planning the user environment

C. Determining a partition and replica strategy

D. Designing an NDS tree

32

Defining and Justifying the Network Solution

CERTIFICATION OBJECTIVES

32.01   Defining a Network Solution

32.02   Creating a Design and
        Implementation Schedule

32.03   Calculating the Costs, Benefits, and
        Risks

32.04   Selling the Solution

32.05   Launching the Design and
        Implementation Process

N etWare-certified engineers are frequently requested to review network systems in order to troubleshoot them, add network components to them, or redesign them. Many engineers know, simply from their certification studies and experience, that there are other problems within a network system when they are working on one aspect of it. In any case, an engineer may know of a solution that will

- Satisfy a business requirement
- Enhance business productivity
- Resolve a persistent or anomalous problem
- Resolve the original problem

Many network solutions come with an associated cost for hardware, software, downtime costs, and charges for engineering time spent in development and implementation. When costs are involved, businesses accept solutions that are presented with the problems they resolve, the costs, the scope of the work to be performed, and the time it would take to implement. This requires a bit of salesmanship on the part of the engineer. This process is shown in Figure 32-1.

CERTIFICATION OBJECTIVE 32.01

Defining a Network Solution

Before a network solution can be defined, there must be a phase of exploration or discovery. This phase involves gathering data about the network to ensure that the correct network solution is put into place. For example, if there is a router on the network that will run solely on TCP/IP, but a solution is built on IPX/SPX, there can only be two consequences:

1. The solution will be rejected
2. The solution will be implemented and will fail.

FIGURE 32-1

Solution process

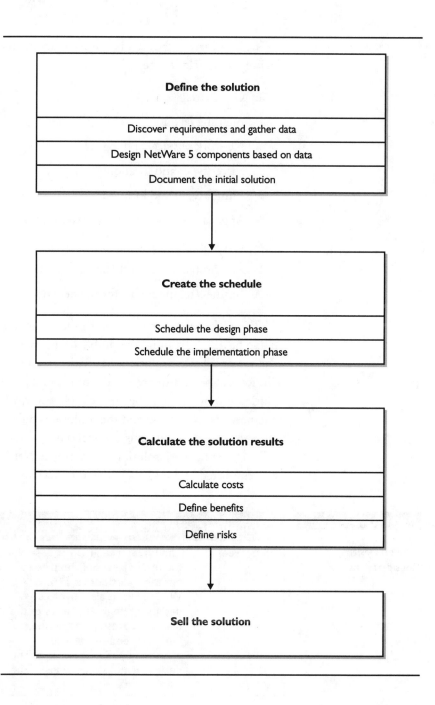

The information that can be gathered about an enterprise network environment includes the following:

- Org charts
- Building layouts
- Network physical and logical layout
- Server types and locations
- Printer types and locations
- Applications and operating systems in use
- Network protocols
- Any problems currently being experienced by the business
- Business requirements for the network

The two last requirements are the most important. The network solution should be defined around the problems it solves, as well as the business requirements for the solution. Many times, an engineer will present a solution but neglect to present the problem it solves. The result is that the solution is more likely to be rejected. However, when the business requirements are defined and the solution is built to fulfill those requirements, the solution is better received.

When the network solution is a complete NetWare 5 implementation, the items listed in Table 32-1 should be reviewed.

TABLE 32-1	Component	Implications	Design Decisions
Solution Design Considerations	NDS Tree	The NDS Tree involves designing the upper layers of the tree to optimize partitioning across WAN links. It also involves designing the lower layers of the tree to represent the business function needs—these are reflected by the Org charts. The design includes the names of the tree objects.	Decide the NDS tree design and naming convention.

	Component	Implications	Design Decisions
TABLE 32-1 Solution design considerations *(continued)*	Servers	Server design involves how time synchronizes across WAN links. It places the servers physically on the network and logically in the NDS tree. It sets standards for the server data store and hardware requirements. The type of protocols used on the network are specified for servers depending on the way the servers are used—for example, an Intranet server would typically require TCP/IP.	Decide the time synchronization scheme, the server placement, NDS object placement, and server hardware and configuration standards.
	Workstations	Workstations can be managed in NetWare 5 to a certain extent, and more so with extensions of Z.E.N.works or ManageWise. The workstation type may force protocols selected for the server. For example, Apple workstations may require AppleTalk.	Decide whether and how workstations are managed and which protocols are required.
	Printers	Printers are managed by a print server or NDPS Manager. In either case, at least one server on the network is affected. Some printers require TCP/IP or use DLC, and may affect what protocols and what configuration the printers will require.	Decide whether to use Print servers or NDPS Managers on the network, and any required protocols.
	Applications	Applications for a NetWare 5 can be installed on servers or on workstations. Server-installed applications that run on workstations will affect the network performance, and their placement should be considered carefully.	Decide which applications should be installed on the network.

The initial network solution is what could be called "hand-grenade close." That is, it will satisfy the business requirements, but may not have taken all design implications into consideration. The naming convention, the time synchronization scheme, the protocols, and so on, may all be changed in some small ways to fit the actual business requirements better. This will require a true "design and development" phase for the final network solution.

The solution should be documented. Documentation of the network solution can be presented to decision-makers later on if they are not the people that the engineer first submits the solution to. Additionally, the documentation provides a foundation for the schedule.

CERTIFICATION OBJECTIVE 32.02

Creating a Design and Implementation Schedule

In order to provide an idea of the scope of work to be done, a schedule of the design work and implementation work must be created. A schedule will need the task description, start and target end dates, assigned person, and percentage of completion. The schedule is basically a project plan, much like a Gantt chart shown in Figure 32-2. Note that the chart has been truncated for display, and misses some critical schedule items.

Design Phase

For a full NetWare 5 implementation, the design phase schedule will consist of the following major steps. Each of these steps will have several subtasks associated with it that may be different, depending on the environment. For example, when implementing NetWare 5 in an existing network there would be a Design subtask to "Select the installation method" (which would be migration, in-place-upgrade, and so on). But that task would not be in a schedule for a network that was completely new, since there could only be one choice—new installation.

FIGURE 32-2

Sample schedule Gantt chart

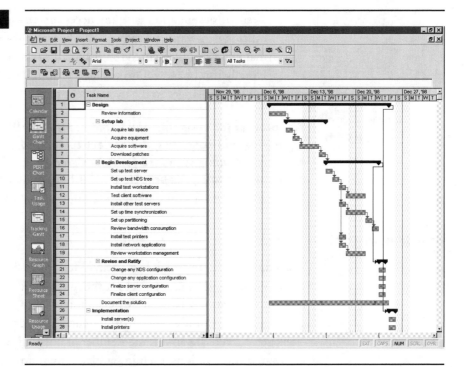

1. **Organize and educate the team** In a small network, this may be one person. She may not need any NetWare or environment education. In a large network, the work should be divided, since there is so much to consider and do (such as install multiple servers rather than one). Some people will need education on either or both.

2. **Create a naming standard** This will maintain consistency throughout the implementation if done first.

3. **Design the NDS tree, servers, and workstations** Even when an NDS tree already exists, it should be reviewed, and redesigned if it needs optimization. This design will be more detailed than the initial network solution.

4. **Create a lab** This phase involves specifying a space, gathering software and acquiring hardware. When possible, in order to prevent errors and downtime, it should not be part of the production network.

5. **Test the design and make any necessary changes**   Always use existing hardware and software configurations for testing the changes that will be implemented to verify that the method is correct. Usually this phase will make many technical changes to the process, but fewer changes to the overall design.

exam
ⓦatch

The process for designing and implementing NetWare 5 includes organizing and educating the project team, understanding NDS and creating a naming standard for it, designing the NDS tree, creating the implementation approach, establishing a lab and pilot, migrating clients and servers, and maintaining daily operations.

Implementation Phase

The implementation schedule is tricky. Most engineers, after having spent months in a lab, are eager to just get the implementation over with. They may believe that they have already encountered any possible situation that could exist in the production environment, so there is no need for an initial "look-see." There are an infinite number of possibilities for software and hardware configurations, even in standard environments. The only way to mitigate errors is to start with a test group, or pilot.

The pilot is a miniature implementation of the final rollout. It may go smoothly, it may not. Usually it does not, even for the best thought-out deployments. The pilot phase should be followed by a return to the lab. A backout, or contingency plan should accompany the pilot. Once the first or subsequent pilots has reached the acceptance criteria, and mitigated unforeseen problems, the final implementation should be completed. Make sure to include the following major steps in the implementation schedule:

■ **Notification**   No matter how well the technical execution of the project goes, the lack of notification will cause it to be perceived as a failure. There are two levels of notification: management and end user. Management should be notified first, with a memo and short meeting. Management may provide additional acceptance criteria for their group. After they agree to the rollout, the end-users can be notified with a memo or e-mail, and with flyers posted near the involved group.

■ **Install the infrastructure components**   This consists of setting up the back-end components that can be installed without disturbing the existing environment. This usually is the installation and configuration of new server hardware and software.

■ **Roll out the pilot group**   The technical rollout will probably bring about a review of the process. There may be an easier, better, or faster way to implement the project that could not be tested in the lab. Existing server data will need to be migrated, printers set up, and workstations updated with the new client access software. The rollout should meet the acceptance criteria.

■ **If there is a failure, perform the backout plan**   The contingency plan should be able to uninstall anything that was installed, and return configuration to its prior state.

■ **Educate the pilot group**   The end users will need some training or documentation about how the new system works in general, as well as how it will work in their environment.

■ **Review and support the pilot group**   The end users will require technical assistance for performing their jobs in the new environment. This phase may also highlight some problems that need to be reviewed in the lab.

■ **Return to the lab**   Any problems that were encountered during the implementation or support period should be reviewed and either fixed or explained.

■ **Roll out the remaining groups**   The remaining rollouts should include the exact same steps that the pilot rollout includes—from notification to support. There can be more than one phase of rollout, especially in large environments.

■ **Maintain operations**   In a small environment, the same team that performs the project will probably also maintain the network. In a large environment, these are more likely to be separate groups. This will require that the daily operations support team is educated and able to support the new technology.

CERTIFICATION OBJECTIVE 32.03

Calculating the Costs, Benefits, and Risks

A cost-benefit analysis and risk assessment should be completed as part of any network solution. These two views of the solution will impact its acceptance by upper management.

The cost-benefit analysis will state the actual and expected costs. These costs will include

- New hardware and hardware upgrade costs
- New software and licensing costs
- Hourly or set costs for hired engineering assistance
- Travel or other expenses
- Training costs

The hardware and software costs will be estimated based on the initial network solution design. Note that the design phase may add to these costs, through an identified need for an additional server or discovery of additional end users, etc. The estimated costs should include a "cushion" or variance of a percentage of the total cost, so that additions or changes do not impact the final implementation of the project. A typical variance is a 10 to 20 percent of the total cost of the project (inclusive of the time and expense costs).

The schedule of the work will primarily impact the cost of engineering assistance. When an engineer is contracted for work of this sort, he will know what costs to include in the cost-benefit analysis. When a network administrator is creating the cost-benefit analysis, the need for engineering assistance should be included, whether or not the administrator plans to implement the project with help. Many administrators require assistance for daily support when they implement projects themselves. These costs can be obtained from value-added resellers or network integrators.

Travel expenses and other expenses will need to be included, but can only be estimated. Travel may be required between sites. Other expenses can include training materials, and minor equipment such as extra printer cables. Training costs are an expense, but they are also calculated in the productivity lost due to people being trained during work hours.

The benefits portion of the cost-benefit analysis should estimate the decrease in daily or maintenance costs on an ongoing basis. It should also answer each of the business requirements that the network solution provides. There are numerous examples of the benefits and their associated reduction in costs for most network software and hardware solutions. The solution's vendor will typically post a benefits review on their website and/or distribute it in paper form upon request. Novell has a link to their benefits analysis for NetWare 5 at **http://www.novell.com/netware5**. The specific page is **http://www.novell.com/netware5/fab.html**.

Risk assessments will discuss the risk of not implementing the solution, and any risks associated with implementing the solution. As an example of the "not" side, one of the major concerns in the industry currently is the Year 2000 crisis. If a solution is put in place to answer the need for Year 2000 compliance, the risk of not implementing that solution is that both network malfunctions and miscalculations within applications may occur. Other risks will include the loss of being able to provide the business requirements, continued degradation in network performance, and associated productivity degradation.

On the other hand, there are always risks to implementing a solution. These risks will include the downtime associated to changing network infrastructure components and the possibility that the solution will not work as presented by a vendor. Such risks should be mitigated by the inclusion of a contingency plan.

I have run into many customers who have lost money through not implementing a solution. One customer told me his worst experience and it has always stuck with me. This customer did not install a RAID array because at the time the cost was well over $10,000. The unthinkable happened—the server's single drive failed—and it was 16 hours before the new drive was installed and the last backup's data was restored. That particular piece of equipment logged time assessments and associated charges. The final result was that for every hour lost from the time of the last backup until the server was running again, the customer lost an approximate $30,000, which totaled about $1,000,000. Needless to say, the RAID array was installed on a pair of servers, one which was a hot-spare to the other. And the same configuration was required for all servers then on, to prevent this from happening again. A cost-benefit analysis and risk assessment would have prevented the problem in the first place.

CERTIFICATION OBJECTIVE 32.04

Selling the Solution

Many NetWare-certified engineers work for value-added resellers and network integrators. They are typically in a position to sell a solution to customers. Even when network administrators want to install NetWare 5 into "their" networks, there is a stage of selling the solution to management.

The documented solution, scheduled scope of work, cost benefit analysis and risk assessment are all sales tools. The approach to management in order to sell the solution should be made after these items are created. The documents are "take-aways" for management. Sometimes, a network administrator will request a solution for a problem and review it with the vendor. However, that network administrator must still present the solution to the individuals who can approve these costs, and so, the information must be in a format that can be passed along.

Launching the Design and Implementation Process

It is a big day when management has finally approved the implementation of a major undertaking like installing NetWare 5. The basis for the launch of the design and implementation process has already been created in the form of the defined solution, schedule, and analyses. Also, any information gathered for the initial solution will be needed for further analysis.

The first thing to do is review the schedule and start with the steps involved. There may be the need to assign a project manager to ensure that the schedule is met. The team must be organized and assigned to the project. This will start with an initial team meeting. At this point, the project begins according to schedule with the design phase.

CERTIFICATION SUMMARY

The overall process for getting from a problem to a solution starts with the Definition of the Solution. This step has several subtasks. There is the discovery of the requirements and data gathering, the initial solution design and the documentation of the solution.

The second part of the process is to create a design and implementation schedule. This schedule has two phases. The Design phase includes the following steps:

- Organize and educate the team
- Create a naming standard
- Design the NDS tree, servers, and workstations
- Create a lab
- Test the design and make any necessary changes

The Implementation phase includes these following steps:

- Notification
- Install the infrastructure components
- Roll out the pilot group
- If there is a failure, perform the backout plan
- Educate the pilot group
- Review and support the pilot group
- Return to the lab
- Roll out the remaining groups
- Maintain operations

Each of these steps for both design and implementation will consist of several subtasks that are dependent on the environment and project goals.

The next step is to create a cost-benefit analysis and risk assessment. The cost-benefit analysis should define the estimated costs of software, hardware, implementation and expenses. Plus it should include a percentage for variance. The benefits should review the monetary and the intrinsic benefits of the solution. The risk assessment should define the risks of not implementing the solution as well as the risks of implementing the solution.

The final step is to present the solution, its schedule and analyses to management in order to gain acceptance, or "sell" the solution.

Once the solution is accepted, it can begin by assigning the project team members and leader. Then it will start implementing according to the schedule created.

 TWO-MINUTE DRILL

❑ Before a network solution can be defined, there must be a phase of exploration or discovery. This phase involves gathering data about the network to ensure that the correct network solution is put into place.

❑ In order to provide an idea of the scope of work to be done, a schedule of the design work and implementation work must be created.

❑ The process for designing and implementing NetWare 5 includes organizing and educating the project team, understanding NDS and creating a naming standard for it, designing the NDS tree, creating the implementation approach, establishing a lab and pilot, migrating clients and servers, and maintaining daily operations.

❑ A cost-benefit analysis and risk assessment should be completed as part of any network solution.

❑ A typical variance is a 10 to 20 percent of the total cost of the project (inclusive of the time and expense costs).

❑ The benefits portion of the Cost Benefit Analysis should estimate the decrease in daily or maintenance costs on an ongoing basis.

❑ There are an infinite number of possibilities for software and hardware configurations, even in standard environments. The only way to mitigate errors is to start with a test group, or *pilot.*

❑ The pilot phase should be followed by a return to the lab.

❑ A backout, or contingency plan, should accompany the pilot.

SELF TEST

The following Self-Test questions will help you measure your understanding of the material presented in this chapter. Read all the choices carefully, as there may be more than one correct answer. Choose all correct answers for each question.

1. When should an engineer define a network solution?

   A. When asked to resolve a network problem

   B. When noticing the need for it while resolving a different problem or working on the network

   C. When asked to define the solution

   D. All of the above

2. What two results will happen if an incorrect solution is presented? (Select two.)

   A. The solution will be rejected.

   B. If accepted, there will be no impact on the network.

   C. If accepted, the solution will succeed after implementation.

   D. If accepted, the solution will fail after implementation.

3. Which of the following represent documents that would not be useful for a solution definition? (Choose all that apply.)

   A. Org charts

   B. Building layouts

   C. List of names of every employee

   D. Server types

4. Which of the following are the five design decisions that should always be included in a NetWare 5 initial solution definition?

   A. NDS tree, servers, users, physical security, redundancy

   B. NDS tree, servers, workstations, applications, printers

   C. Servers, workstations, users, NDS security, redundancy

   D. Applications, Internet printers, workstations, redundancy, server location

5. Aside from the task description and start date, what else should be included in a schedule? (Choose all that apply.)

   A. Target end date

   B. Person assigned to the task

   C. Person managing the task

   D. Cost of implementation

6. After the team has been organized, the naming standard has been created and the tree designed, what is the next step?

   A. Notification

   B. Implementation of the Pilot

   C. Execute the backout plan

   D. Create the lab

7. What additional step should take place if there is a separate group maintaining daily operations in a network environment for Maintaining Operations step?

    A. There is no additional step.

    B. The end users will require extra support from the project team.

    C. The operations team should be trained/educated to take over the new support.

8. What two documents should be created after the solution and schedule are completed?

    A. Scope of work

    B. Final design solution

    C. Cost-benefit analysis

    D. Risk assessment

9. Which of the following positions will require an engineer to sell a network solution?

    A. Network administrator

    B. Contractor

    C. Consultant

    D. Any engineer or administrator

10. What is the first step for launching the design and implementation?

    A. Gathering data

    B. Organizing the team and educating them

    C. Designing the NDS Tree

    D. Establishing a lab

33

Designing the Directory Tree

CERTIFICATION OBJECTIVES

33.01   Creating a Naming Standards Document

33.02   NDS Naming Standard

33.03   Guidelines for the Upper Layers

33.04   Assessing Other Design Considerations

Designing a technical solution is a form of preventative maintenance. A network designed to operate with the existing infrastructure will perform better than one that ignores the current environment. But design work does not stop there. Whenever a portion of the network infrastructure is upgraded, added, or retired, the network design should be reviewed for the impact that the change will have on the organization's information technology needs.

Such changes can affect even the most detailed items. For example, if a business acquires and merges with another business and then integrates an existing Novell Directory Services Tree into its own, there will be two sets of naming standards, and probably two different NDS designs. These two standards and designs will need to be integrated into a single naming standard and a single design that is optimized to work on the newly combined network.

Design work and setting standards may seem like a static decision process, but they simply have a longer-lasting impact than most other decisions. These items should be revisited on a periodic basis—more often when the enterprise experiences a great deal of change or growth, and less often if the enterprise is fairly static. For every enterprise, these items should be reviewed any time a major change is made.

CERTIFICATION OBJECTIVE 33.01

Creating a Naming Standards Document

When planning the Novell Directory Services environment, the first task to complete is to decide the naming standards. *Naming standards* are the details of how to assign names to container objects, servers, end users, printers, and other network resources. A naming standards document includes the written instructions for naming network resources and gives examples of names for each type of network resource.

There are many reasons to define naming standards:

- A standard naming convention can assist users in locating resources by including location information.

- It can ensure that duplicate names will not exist.

- It can facilitate network management by making it easier for administrators to recognize which resources are being accessed by which users.

QUESTIONS AND ANSWERS

Jolene is a new network administrator given the task of redesigning the NDS Tree in preparation for upgrading to NetWare 5. In reviewing the network, Jolene finds that the servers have names of cartoon characters. Is this a standard that Jolene should maintain after the upgrade?

Unless the network is for a cartoon creator and each server holds the work done for that character, this naming standard is not easy for new users to understand. Jolene should probably evaluate a naming standard that will better describe the server's function and/or location within the enterprise, and then implement that naming standard during the migration to NetWare 5.

A naming standards document should include the following information:

- **The naming standard for each network resource or service** This would include printers, volume names, and directory services organizational information such as NDS trees and containers.

- **The naming standards for servers, hosts, and other service providers**   Many network operating systems have the requirement that server names be unique on the network. The same is true for NDS, regardless of which Tree or context the servers are located in.

- **The naming standards for end users' login IDs**

- **A list of the information required about each network resource**   For example, a requirement to have the building and floor number entered into each Location property for a network resource, service, or user.

- ■ **An example of the naming standard format**
- ■ **A reference list to assist in name creation**   For example, if using the IATA airport codes for each major city represented by an Organizational Unit, a reference list of the IATA codes would be required.

For all network names, consistency throughout the network will make it easy for end users and administrators to decipher and use the names.

CERTIFICATION OBJECTIVE 33.02

NDS Naming Standard

NDS has several different types of objects within it. The Tree name describes the NDS database available for access. There can be multiple Trees on a single network. There are three types of objects within the Tree:

- ■ [Root], which cannot be given a different name
- ■ Container objects, which organize the NDS tree into a hierarchical structure
- ■ Leaf objects, which represent the resources that are available within the tree

Each object's Distinguished Name must be unique within NDS. The Distinguished Name of an object is the concatenation of the object's Common Name and the context of that object within the tree. The context is the location of the object within the NDS tree. With the exception of servers, multiple objects can have the same Common Name, but not the same Distinguished Name.

For example, a User object named DMEYER is located in the Organizational Unit PHX, which is located in the organization MA. The Common Name is DMEYER. The Distinguished Name is .DMEYER.PHX.MA. If another user's Common Name is DMEYER but it is located in the LON

Organizational Unit under the MA organization, the Distinguished Name .DMEYER.LON.MA is unique, even though the Common Name DMEYER is not.

exam
ⓦatch

The uniqueness of object Distinguished Names is not limited to the type of object. If a printer is named DELT and a server is also named DELT, they cannot exist in the same context.

Keep in mind that, for all NDS objects (not including the name of the NDS Tree itself), an underscore or a space can be used as part of a name. However, they are interpreted as the same. That means that the name PTR WEST and PTR_WEST would be the same name in NDS. The use of spaces in a Distinguished Name requires quotation marks placed around the name. NDS is case insensitive. The name Jcraft is interpreted the same as JCRAFT.

NDS reserves some characters that cannot be used in object names:

- The period (.) is used to separate name segments in Distinguished Names.

- The plus (+) sign is used to tie names with multiple name attributes and is typically seen for Bindery objects.

- The equal sign (=) is used in typeful names, such as .CN=ADMIN.O=MA.

- The slash (/) is not allowed with Microsoft Windows naming rules inherent in the operating system.

Tree and Container Units

When there are multiple trees in an enterprise network, their names should be different from each other to avoid confusion for end users. Many enterprise networks implement at least two trees: one for testing and the other for production use. The tree, therefore, should be clearly named according to its purpose. This prevents users from attempting to access the wrong tree. Many trees include the name of the corporation as part of, or the entire, Tree name. Sometimes an underscore character is used to concatenate the corporation name with a descriptor. The use of spaces is not allowed for tree names.

The following are some examples of tree names for the ACME Corporation:

- **NDSTEST**   The tree used for testing in NDS
- **ACME**   The corporate tree
- **ACME_PHX**   The Phoenix branch's tree, kept separate because of a different network administrative group
- **ACME_RESEARCH**   The Research division's tree, kept separate for security purposes

Container object names will affect each user that is contained within that container. Container units, such as the Organization name and the Organizational Units are used during an end user's login, and when locating other network resources. Many times, the user will need to type in a full context to log in or when accessing a printer. The more letters used in a container object, the more cumbersome the Distinguished Name. It is a good rule of thumb to limit container unit names to four or fewer letters (see Figure 33-1).

For enterprise networks that span multiple cities around the world, the design of the NDS tree hierarchy will typically include location information, such as cities, states or provinces, and buildings. This division is normally held at upper layers of the tree in order to make partitioning at that level mirror the WAN links. At the lower layers of the tree, the design tree will likely be logically divided to mirror the corporate structure. A small network might be based completely on the logical divisions, or may simply contain all objects in the Organization container. When devising a naming standard for container objects, take into account the need to limit the number of characters in the name, as well as the meaning that might be attached to the object.

Examples of container object names include the following:

- **PHX**   Represents a city (Phoenix)—location oriented.
- **MI**   Represents a state (Michigan)—location oriented.

FIGURE 33-1

Login requires knowledge of OU names

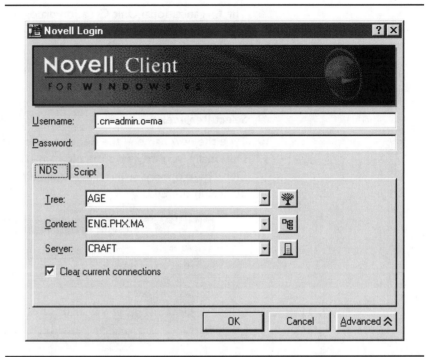

- **OPS** Represents a company division (Operations)— organization oriented.

- **ENG** Represents a business unit (Engineering)— organization oriented.

Naming and Renaming Container Objects

1. Log in to the NDS tree with a user account that has administrator access to the tree.

2. In the NetWare Administrator, navigate to the Organization and highlight it.

3. Press the INSERT key.

4. From the Object Creation dialog box, select Organizational Unit and click OK.

5. The Organizational Unit Creation dialog box will appear. Give the OU an appropriate name.

6. Click Create.

7. To Rename an OU, highlight the OU.

8. Click the Object menu.

9. Select Rename.

10. Type the new name in the Rename dialog box (as shown below). Optionally, you may save the old name or create an alias for the OU. These options will facilitate the name change for existing objects in the OU.

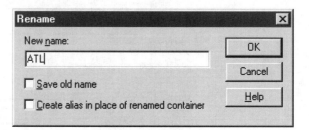

Server and Volume Names

Server names have a requirement of being unique on a network. If two servers exist in separate contexts, across WAN links, or even if they exist in separate NDS trees, they cannot have the same name. The reason for this unique name requirement is due to the way that NetWare servers send out advertisements. When servers advertise their services, they use their Common Name, rather than their Distinguished Name, and the advertisement is exclusive of the tree, so any client will see it in order to log in to it. If an administrator changes the name of the tree, or merges two trees, the users will still be able to locate the servers they used before. Note that the unique server name applies to any version of a NetWare server.

Servers can be named according to location or function, or a concatenation of both. In large enterprise networks, the final option is typically exercised. In many cases, the need for a serial number at the end of a name is required because multiple servers exist in the same location and perform the same function. Examples of server names include the following:

- **BLDG1EAST**   A location-oriented server (server is located in the East portion of Building 1)

- **FS**   A function-oriented server (FS stands for File Server)

- **PHXFS01**   A serially numbered, location- and function-oriented server (server is located in Phoenix, provides file services, and is the first in a series)

Volume names do not need to be unique on a server. In fact, each server in the same context can have identical volume names without fear of conflict within NDS. The reason for this is that within NDS, the volume name is concatenated with the server name. Since all NetWare servers have a SYS: volume, this rule must be performed automatically when the server is installed in the NDS tree. Therefore, the SYS: volume on server PHXFS01 is named PHXFS01_SYS. The remaining volumes on a server can be named according to the data that they store. Examples of volume names are the following:

- APPS (for a volume containing applications)

- DATA (for a volume containing information)

- HOME (for a volume containing only user home directories)

Leaf Object Names

Leaf objects represent the resources of the network itself. They include users, groups, printers, workstations, and many other types of objects. These four types usually constitute the majority of objects within an NDS tree, and their names should be defined so that an administrator can manage the objects without trying to determine which object refers to which user, group, printer, workstation, or other resource.

Naming User objects is a critical area for defining standards. It is difficult, once an ID has been defined for a user, to change that ID. So user IDs should be considered static. Several items should be considered when creating a user ID. The first is the interaction with other programs. For example, many messaging systems integrate with the network operating system and use the same login ID as a mailbox name. This is true for Novell's GroupWise messaging product. Those messaging systems must interact with other, possibly older, messaging systems. Several older messaging systems will not work with a mailbox (the ID) that has more than eight characters. If the ID is truncated down to eight characters, there can be multiple names that are the same and misrouted mail or other mail problems may result.

As a security measure, some networks implement a user-naming scheme that is difficult to discern even if you know the user's name. For example, the user's employee number may be used as the User object name.

Limiting user IDs to eight characters can apply to home directories. If the home directory is on a volume of a server that does not support long names, then the directory would be restricted to eight characters. If the workstation operating system, such as DOS, does not support long names, then the workstation will not display the correct directory name for that home directory.

Because user IDs apply to individual users, they should utilize some form of the user's name. If an administrator wants to create a user ID for a function—such as *contractor*, *receptionist*, or *student*—it is more appropriate to use an Organizational Role object. The user ID should be able to provide for unique common names. As organizations grow, the likelihood that two users will have the same name increases. Using a concatenation of first and last names, in some form, helps. So does the use of middle initials. But even then, there is the possibility that two people will have the same name. This means that there should be some ability to serialize the names. An example of user IDs includes the following, using Thomas Robert Smithson as the example name:

- **TRSMITH1** This is an eight-character name format, requiring the first initial, the middle initial, five characters of the last name, and a digit to serialize it up to nine persons.

- **TSMITHSO** This is an eight-character name format, requiring the first initial, and the first seven characters of the last name.

■ **TOMS**   This is a format using the person's nickname or first name, and first initial of the last name.

■ **TSMITH01**   This is an eight-character name format that uses the first initial, the first five characters of the last name, and two digits to serialize the IDs up to 99 persons.

The information that an enterprise requires to be entered for each User object should be defined. Templates can be created to ensure that the information is included at the object's creation (see Figure 33-2). For example, if the department's and user's locations are required for all users in each department, the administrator can create templates for each department that detail that information. The administrator can also use the template for other purposes, such as predefining the file system rights that those department users should automatically be granted.

FIGURE 33-2

A template object can assist in implementing naming standards

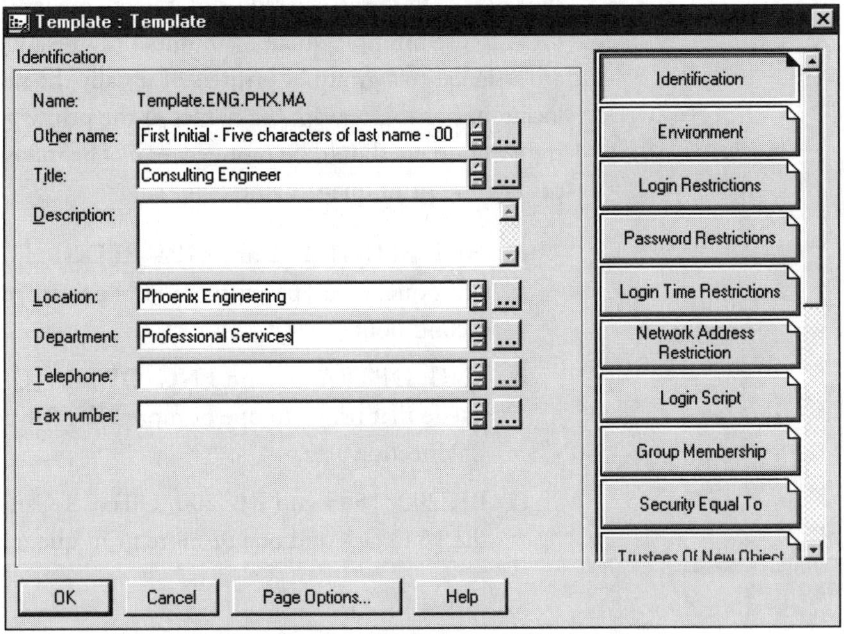

Template : Template

Identification

Name:	Template.ENG.PHX.MA
Other name:	First Initial - Five characters of last name - 00
Title:	Consulting Engineer
Description:	
Location:	Phoenix Engineering
Department:	Professional Services
Telephone:	
Fax number:	

Identification
Environment
Login Restrictions
Password Restrictions
Login Time Restrictions
Network Address Restriction
Login Script
Group Membership
Security Equal To
Trustees Of New Object

OK   Cancel   Page Options...   Help

Groups are objects that can group users logically. Groups are typically used to grant special rights to objects or files to a group of users. They should then be given a name to demonstrate the purpose of the group. For example, if a group is created to provide access to a particular printer, the group's name might be PTRX_GRP.

Printers and Printing objects have an added dimension in NetWare 5 due to the inclusion of Novell Distributed Printing Services (NDPS). Traditionally, there were Print Queues, Print Servers, and Printer objects. NetWare 5's NDPS added Brokers, NDPS Managers, and NDPS Printers. A naming standard might do well to include all of these types of objects. Since the majority of the objects will be NDPS Printers, Printer Servers, and Print Queues, and since they represent the resources needed by the users, they should be named carefully. When a user prints to a printer, they need to know what type of printer it is and where it is located. A naming standard that mirrors this usage is usually successful. Print queues are usually associated with a particular printer. For that reason, the addition of the letter Q to the associated printer name makes it easily identifiable. In order to use multiple queues, a number can be added. Sometimes, queues are assigned to a group of printers of usually the same type and in the same location. For this reason, the names of the printers should be serialized and the print queue should be more general. The following are examples of printer and print queue names:

- **HP4_BLDG1_FL2 and HP4_BLDG1_FL2_Q** A printer and print queue that prints to an HP4 printer in building 1 on the second floor.

- **ENG_OPTRA_01 and ENG_OPTRA_Q** A printer and print queue that prints to one or more OPTRA printers in the Engineering area.

- **BJC200_1543 and BJC200_Q01** A Canon BubbleJet printer at the 1543 jack and one or more print queues.

Workstations are objects used by the Workstation Manager component of Z.E.N.works. When Z.E.N.works imports workstations into NDS, it automatically assigns a standard name to the PC. The administrator can customize the naming standard for workstations. Since these objects represent only Windows PCs, the workstations already have an assigned NetBIOS name. This may or may not be in use as a unique name on the network. That depends on whether the workstation utilizes peer-to-peer networking or participates in Windows NT Domains, which force a unique name. The default-naming standard in Z.E.N.works is to concatenate that NetBIOS computer name with the node address, which is always unique on a network. The options for names are shown in Table 33-1.

TABLE 33-1

Workstation Naming Options

Option	Function
Computer	Represents the NetBIOS name assigned to a Windows PC.
Network Address	Represents the node address assigned to the network interface card in the PC. This can be either the IPX address or the IP address. If using DHCP, using the IP address is not recommended since it may change.
OS	Is a short name of the operating system running on the workstation? For example, Windows 98 is WIN98.
Container	Represents the container that the workstation exists in.
CPU	Represents the type of processor installed in the PC, such as 80486 or Pentium.
DNS	Represents the IP Domain name assigned to the workstation.
Server	Represents the home server for the user of the workstation.
User	Represents the user ID of the user that is assigned to the workstation.

EXERCISE 33-2	**Using the Workstation Policy to Standardize Workstation Names**

1. Log in to the NDS tree with administrative access to the NDS tree.

2. Navigate to the container in which the Workstation Policy will be created.

3. Press the INSERT key.

4. Select Policy Package and click OK.

5. From the first dialog drop-down box, click the down arrow and select Win95 User Package. Type an appropriate name. Check the box to Define Additional Properties and click Create.

6. The properties for the User Policy Package will appear. Check the Workstation Import Policy option at the bottom of the first dialog box. Then click Details.

7. The Workstation Import Policy will appear as shown in the following illustration of the Workstation Naming page.

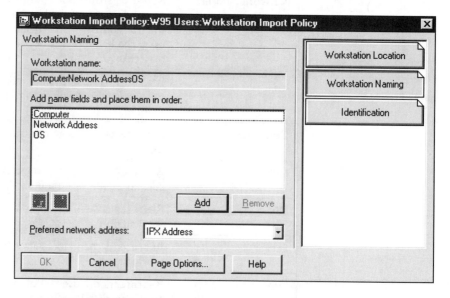

8. Select the Workstation Naming property page button. Note that Computer and Network Address are selected.

9. Click Add.

10. Select CPU and click OK.

11. Highlight CPU and move it to the top of the list using the up-arrow button.

12. Look at the Workstation Name box; note that it states the name will be CPUComputerNetworkAddress. Click OK to save the changes and close the dialog box. Click OK on the Policy Package to save the policy.

on the
Job

Although Exercise 33-2 creates a naming convention for workstations, further steps must be taken to import workstations that use this convention.

CERTIFICATION OBJECTIVE 33.03

Guidelines for the Upper Layers

When creating an NDS design, keep in mind not only today's needs, but also the future needs of the enterprise. This is not an exact science. Future mergers, mass building moves, and corporate restructuring are rarely known far in advance of their actual implementation. If any are known at the time the tree is being designed, their needs should be incorporated into the design. For example, if two business units currently share a building, but one will split off and move into a separate building at some point in the future, then the use of two location-oriented Organizational Units for the two business units will facilitate the move of the servers and appropriate partitioning of NDS after the move has been completed.

NDS is so flexible that nearly any type of configuration can be used. However, the optimal designs are those that take advantage of the infrastructure in place. The top section of an NDS tree includes the [Root], the Organization, and the first level of Organizational Units. This part of the tree serves as a foundation for the rest of the tree.

The first step is to name the tree. The tree represents the largest organization of the business. NDS can handle global conglomerates that have multiple business lines and subsidiaries. Administration can be distributed accordingly.

Optionally, the tree can use the Country object. This is created directly below the [Root] object. It is rarely implemented, because its use forces multiple Organization objects for the same organization.

The next step is to name the Organization object. There is at least one Organization object in each tree, although multiple Organization objects may exist. It is recommended that the number of Organization objects be limited. The Organization objects could represent the separate businesses running within a conglomerate. Figure 33-3 displays a tree with two separate Organization objects.

The last step of the NDS upper-layer specification is to design the first layer of Organizational Units (see Figure 33-4). There are two approaches to this layer. One is to use a regional-, or location-oriented design. The other is to use a departmental-, or organization-oriented design. When the company is organized into various regions that include multiple cities, the use of regional OUs mirrors both the organization and the location. At this level of the tree, you want to avoid a location OU at the building or floor level of detail. Using a regional approach will facilitate partitioning of the NDS database because it may mirror some of the company's WAN links.

| FIGURE 33-3 | NDS tree with two Organizational objects |

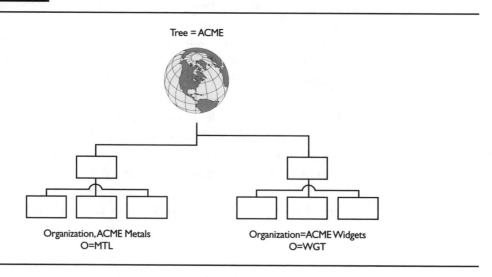

Tree = ACME

Organization, ACME Metals
O=MTL

Organization=ACME Widgets
O=WGT

FIGURE 33-4   Designing first layer of Organizational Units

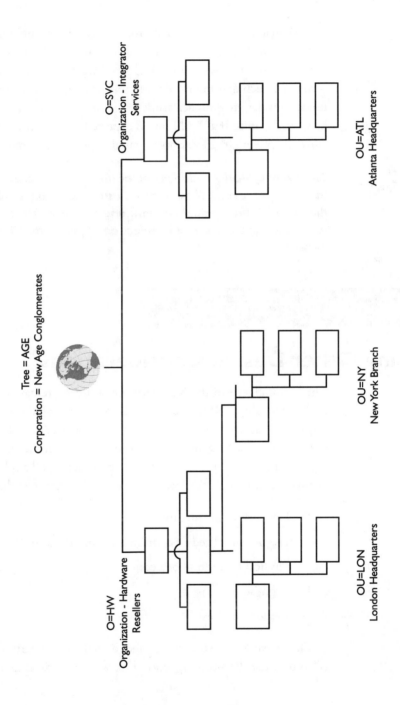

The organization-oriented approach at this level would mirror the organization chart at its first layer. Again, this may be a regional organization. Otherwise, it is a high-level view of the divisions of the company. Each division may have subdivisions and, below that, business units. This design approach works only for those companies that do not have WAN links. If a WAN link is expected in the future, even if it is not currently present, the location-oriented approach is recommended.

The exam typically includes one or more questions about NDS design at the upper layers. The questions usually contain exhibits or diagrams of the physical network and corporate structure at a high level. Then you are asked to select an appropriate NDS design for this network.

CERTIFICATION OBJECTIVE 33.04

Assessing Other Design Considerations

The bottom layers of the NDS tree constitute the remaining OUs in the hierarchical NDS structure. The lower containers will mirror the organizational structure, representing the divisions, departments, and workgroups. The Organizational Units will contain the leaf objects representing users, groups, printers, workstations, and applications. Other factors that will affect the lower layer of the tree are the following:

- Network infrastructure
- Use of centralized or distributed administration
- Physical location of devices
- Login scripts
- Bindery services

The network infrastructure applies directly to the partitioning of the NDS database. Partitioning works best when partitions do not span WAN links. There is a certain amount of network traffic that takes place within a partition, and less traffic between partitions. So, when spanning a WAN link, more network traffic is created across it. Since WAN links tend to be slower and retain a higher cost for the network traffic sent across them, any chance to reduce or prevent unnecessary WAN traffic should be exercised. This, in effect, requires that container objects do not span WAN links.

Centralized distribution is the use of a single administrator or administrative group that has total control over the entire network. Distributed administration is the use of multiple administrative groups that reside at various locations within the enterprise. When using central administration, a shallow design, one with few nested Organizational Units, assists in that management since it is easier to search and find resources.

Distributed administration lends itself to a deeper NDS tree design. The administrative groups can be hierarchical. If so, the lower layers of the tree can mirror this administrative design.

The location of resource leaf objects should be close to the users that access those resources. For example, if a lower-layer OU represents a specific workgroup, the server and the printer that the workgroup utilizes should be placed within the same OU or in an OU nearby in the tree. This will aid users in locating their resources and ensure that the resources are kept within the same NDS partition.

The use of login scripts should be considered when designing the NDS tree. Users execute the script for the container in which their User object is located. In order to prevent the need to maintain multiple identical login scripts for users who are in the same physical building, those users are best kept within the same OU.

Bindery services can be enabled on a server, and the server can point to up to 16 containers within the NDS tree. If there are more than 16 containers that need access to the bindery service on a server, those containers may be combined until there are 16 or fewer contexts required for bindery services.

exam
ⓌatcH

Partitions should not span WAN links. The design of the NDS tree will affect the partitioning scheme. An OU must be completely contained within a partition.

CERTIFICATION SUMMARY

When implementing a new or upgraded NetWare network, design of the NDS tree is one of the first exercises to complete. Design work does not remain static for the life of a network. When changes are made to the network infrastructure, the impact to the NDS tree should be managed and may require some redesign of the tree.

Naming standards are part of design work. The name standards should be documented for reference. The naming standard document provides a means for deciphering names and it should contain the instructions for the name, examples of the name, any additional required information that each NDS object of that type should contain, and reference material for consistent names.

The NDS naming standard should define the tree name, the organization name(s), and the name(s) for Organizational Units. The use of short container unit names is recommended.

Servers must have unique names on the entire internetwork. This applies to servers that reside in different trees, different containers, and on different local networks. The server name should refer to the server's function and location. If multiple servers exist in the same location and perform the same function, the server name can be serialized. Volume names are unique, because they concatenate the name of the server with an underscore and the name of the volume.

Leaf object names should be defined for the objects in the tree. User objects generally refer to the user they are assigned to. Since multiple users may have the same name, the name can be serialized. Printer objects should refer to the printer type and its location. Group names should refer to the purpose of the logical grouping of those users. Workstation names can be automated through the use of a Workstation Import Policy.

The upper layers of the NDS tree include the [Root], the Organization object(s), and the first level of Organizational Units. There should be one Organization object for each major subsidiary of a conglomerate, or only one Organization object for a single-purpose business. The first level of Organizational Units should reflect the major locations of the internetwork. This method assists partitioning.

Other things to keep in mind when designing the tree are the impact of network infrastructure on the NDS tree as it applies to partitioning, centralized versus distributed administration, the location of devices and their associated users, how login scripts will be used, and the use of bindery services on servers.

✓ TWO-MINUTE DRILL

- ❏ *Naming standards* are the details of how to assign names to container objects, servers, end users, printers, and other network resources.

- ❏ NDS has several different types of objects within it. The tree name describes the NDS database available for access. There can be multiple trees on a single network.

- ❏ There are three types of objects within the tree: [Root], which cannot be given a different name; Container objects, which organize the NDS tree into a hierarchical structure; and leaf objects, which represent the resources that are available within the tree.

- ❏ The uniqueness of object Distinguished Names is not limited to the type of object. If a printer is named DELT and a server is also named DELT, they cannot exist in the same context.

- ❏ NDS reserves some characters that cannot be used in object names: period (.), plus (+) sign, and equal sign (=).

- ❏ The slash (/) is not allowed with Microsoft Windows naming rules inherent in the operating system.

- ❏ If two servers exist in separate contexts, across WAN links, or even if they exist in separate NDS trees, they cannot have the same name.

- ❏ Leaf objects represent the resources of the network itself. They include users, groups, printers, workstations, and many other types of objects.

- ❏ Centralized distribution is the use of a single administrator or administrative group that has total control over the entire network.

- ❏ Distributed administration is the use of multiple administrative groups that reside at various locations within the enterprise.

SELF TEST

The Self-Test questions will help you measure your understanding of the material presented in this chapter. Read all the choices carefully, as there may be more than one correct answer. Select all correct answers for each question.

1. What are naming standards?

   A. Setting IP addresses for Domain Name Service.

   B. Specifying the names of the administrators of the network.

   C. Definitions of the names used for network resources.

   D. Setting the language for the network.

2. With the exception of _____, multiple objects can have the same _____ name, but not the same _____ name.

   A. Printers, Typeful, Typeless

   B. Servers, Common, Distinguished

   C. Tree, Typeless, Typeful

   D. Servers, Distinguished, Common

3. Which of the following is not an acceptable NDS tree name?

   A. Ema

   B. MA_TREE

   C. My_Own_Nds_Tree

   D. NDS TREE

4. ACME bought the WIDGET Corporation and subsequently merged NDS trees. Now, the tree is being redesigned. In order to use a different container object name, which option should the administrator take?

   A. Create a new container object and move all objects to the new container.

   B. Create a new tree with a few servers, and then gradually migrate users into the brand new design.

   C. Rename the OU and select Create Alias in place of renamed container.

   D. Create a new container object and copy all objects to the new container.

5. Which of the following can have the same name as a NetWare 5 server participating in the GRAY_NDSTREE tree if they are on the same internetwork?

   A. A NetWare 5 server participating in the BLUE_NDSTREE

   B. A NetWare 4.11 server located in the GRAY_NDSTREE but in a different OU

   C. A NetWare 3.11 server running only bindery

   D. None of the above

6. What is the default naming standard for Workstation Import Policies?

   A. Computer NetworkAddress

   B. OS NetworkAddress CPU

   C. NetworkAddress Computer

   D. User Computer OS

7. True or False: When designing the upper layers of the NDS tree, if any future additions or moves of the enterprise are known they should be incorporated into the design.

   A. True

   B. False

8. Where are Country objects located in the NDS tree?

   A. Below the Organization object

   B. Below the first level of Organizational Units

   C. Above the Organization object

   D. Anywhere except below the [Root] object

9. ACME is adding a NetWare 5 network to their network that uses mainframes. The network has three locations: Phoenix, Detroit, and Boston. The ACME organization contains three major divisions: Sales, Manufacturing, and Headquarters. HQ exists in Detroit. Sales and Manufacturing have departments in all three cities. Which of the following would be optimal for the first layer of OUs?

   A. SALES, MFG, HQ

   B. ACME

   C. PHX, DET, HQ

   D. PHX, DET, BOS

10. GENTEX has created a new design for resources that mirrors the administration in the network, which is central. All resources, including printers and servers, are located in .OU=RES.OU=LAX.O=GTX. Users are located in .OU=USERS.OU=CITY.O=GTX, where CITY can be one of 16 different cities in the United States or Canada. Will this be an optimal design?

    A. Yes.

    B. No.

CERTIFIED NOVELL ENGINEER

34

Implementing Time Synchronization Strategies

CERTIFICATION OBJECTIVES

34.01   Determining a Partition Boundary Strategy

34.02   Reviewing Time Synchronization Issues

34.03   Planning a Time Synchronization Strategy

W hether you work for an organization with a small one-site network or an organization with a large multisite network, it's important that you understand how to determine the best placement of Directory *partitions,* as well as how to keep time *synchronized* among the servers on your network. The first section of this chapter will show you how to partition your Directory, also called the NDS database. The second section will review time synchronization concepts, and the last section will show you how to correctly set up time synchronization on your servers.

CERTIFICATION OBJECTIVE 34.01

Determining a Partition Boundary Strategy

Determining a partition boundary strategy usually begins with a look at the Directory, since the design of the Directory tree will determine where it is possible to create partitions and place *replicas.* After a quick review of what a Directory looks like, we'll move on to partitioning and placement of partitions.

A Brief Review of the NDS Database

As you recall from previous chapters, the NDS database, or Directory, is a database that organizes all of the objects that make up the network. Network administrators create objects that represent users, servers, printers, and other network resources, and create container objects to help organize them. The NetWare Administrator program is the easiest way to look at and work with the Directory. As seen in Figure 34-1, NetWare Administrator shows the Directory in what might be described as a cross between an organization chart and the Windows Explorer view of your hard drive. Because of the way the Directory branches out, it is commonly referred to as the NDS tree, or simply, the tree.

The view of Big Org's tree in Figure 34-1 is like an organization chart in that it branches out and divides the tree by geographic region. It is also like the Windows Explorer view of a hard drive with the smaller NDS containers shown below and to the right of bigger NDS containers, the way that smaller hard drive directories are shown below and to the right of bigger hard drive directories. Figure 34-2 shows that when you double-click

FIGURE 34-1

NetWare Administrator shows a visual representation of Big Org's NDS tree

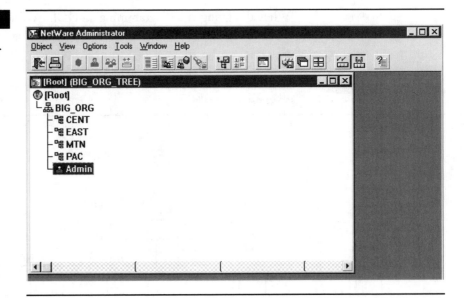

on a container, it opens to show you its contents, just like a directory does in Windows Explorer.

FIGURE 34-2

Double-clicking on NDS containers will show you the contents—also called leaf objects—of that container

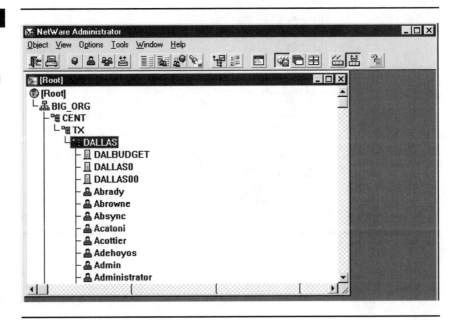

When designing and diagramming an NDS tree, however, it would be more common to show Big Org's tree horizontally, as in Figure 34-3.

FIGURE 34-3 NDS designs usually show trees horizontally, even though NetWare Administrator shows them vertically

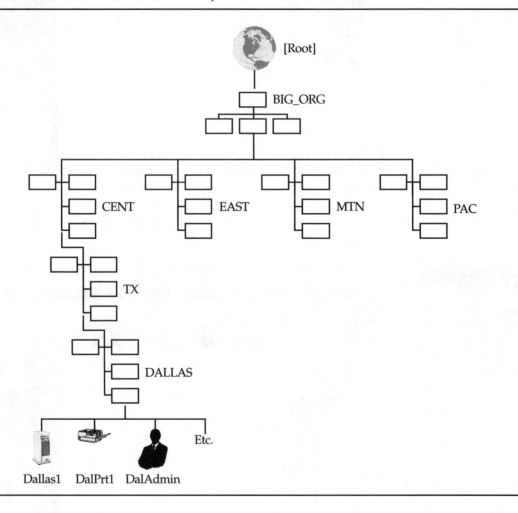

exam
Watch

It might be a good idea to get a piece of paper and practice turning a vertical NetWare Administrator view of an NDS tree into a horizontal design view, and vice versa. Novell's exams may have you create objects in NetWare Administrator based on a design, or may have you select a design based on a NetWare Administrator view.

As Figure 34-3 suggests, a Directory may include information for objects that are separated by great distances. Also, as more and more users, printers, workgroups, and other objects are added to the tree, the NDS database can get very large and complex. Creating partitions by splitting the Directory into smaller pieces helps to prevent the problems that can occur when the NDS database is too large, or is too spread out. Partitioning does the following:

- Helps the network load balance—or share the responsibility of maintaining the database among the servers on the network— instead of relying on one server to do all of the work.

- Also helps prevent synchronization problems by keeping the different portions of the tree physically close to the administrators that make changes to those portions of the tree.

- Allows you to place copies of the partitions, called replicas, on more than one server, ensuring that a copy of every partition will always be available to the users of the network.

Replicas, as you may remember, are copies of partitions. Three replicas of each partition are automatically created by NetWare on nearby servers, assuming that there are enough servers to host that many replicas. Network administrators can create additional replicas if they want an extra measure of protection, or if they want to place a replica close to the users that will be using that partition of the Directory for login authentication or other purposes.

Partitioning Issues

When designing a network and planning for partitions, two main factors will determine how you organize the Directory tree. The first factor is the geographic placement of the servers on the network. Will all servers be in one building or will they be spread out across a campus, city, state, country, or even the entire planet? The second factor is the way that your organization is divided into workgroups, and the printers and other resources that support those workgroups.

Geographic Placement of Servers

Your first consideration in partitioning will always be the physical location of the servers that make up the network. Since you never want to have NDS synchronization creating network traffic across slow WAN links, it only makes sense to plan to create a container for each major geographic location and create your first partitions along the boundaries of those containers. In Figure 34-4, we see that the network administrator for a nation-wide company has created four upper-level containers for each of the time zones in which the organization does business.

FIGURE 34-4

Create upper-level containers by building, city, time zone, or country, depending on the size of your network

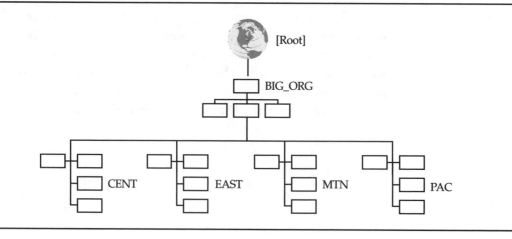

Since each time zone roughly corresponds to a geographic section of the United States, this is a good strategy. The administrator will now be able to partition the upper levels of the NDS tree along the boundaries of each container. The result would look like Figure 34-5.

The administrator is still not done, however, unless there is only one office in each of the four time zones. Remember the oft-repeated rule from earlier chapters: "Don't span the WAN," meaning that you will want to further partition the tree until you have made a container (and partition) for each office that is separated from another office by a WAN link. Otherwise, in order for the partition to stay synchronized, a great deal of network traffic will have to flow across the WAN line. For example, say that the company has offices in Kansas City, KS and in Dallas, TX. Both cities are in the same time zone, but are separated by a WAN link. You would therefore want to create separate partitions under the CENT partition for both locations, as shown in Figure 34-6.

FIGURE 34-5   Partitions of the upper levels of the tree are shown in gray

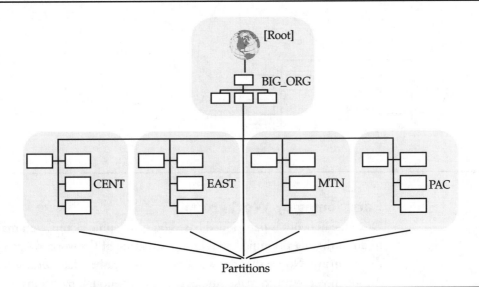

Partitions

FIGURE 34-6   Each part of the organization that is separated by a WAN link should be in its own partition

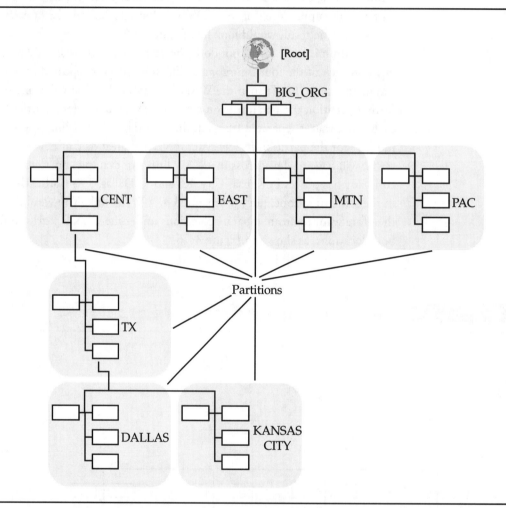

Partitioning by Workgroup

Once the network is partitioned based on geographic factors, you may want to do further partitioning based on the structure of the workgroups within the company. Notice that the word *may* is used rather than *should*. Although you want to make sure that you have enough partitions to efficiently divide and load balance your network, you do not want to create unnecessary partitions that generate extra traffic on the network.

Novell recommends that you partition your tree based on geographic factors, and partition further only under three special circumstances:

- If the total number of objects (users, printers, servers, and others) grows to more than 3,500, consider further partitioning.

- If you need a partition to be managed by a specific administrator or group of administrators close to the users and other resources in that part of the tree, consider further partitioning.

- If a single partition has more than 10 to 15 replicas, consider splitting that partition, because synchronizing more than 10 replicas of a single partition can stretch the already amazing capabilities of NetWare.

exam
ⓌatcH

Be sure to memorize the preceding three rules. Novell tends to regard its guidelines as set in stone, especially for exam questions.

Transitive Synchronization

All versions of NetWare prior to NetWare 5 required that you set up servers to communicate using a protocol called *IPX*. However, NetWare 5 was designed so that you now have the option to set up servers to exclusively use a protocol called *IP* (*Internet Protocol*). Novell did this for several reasons:

- Since the Internet uses IP, it is now easier for NetWare servers to connect to the Internet and to act as Web servers.

- IP, unlike IPX, is an easily routable protocol; that is, it can communicate between networks over routers.

- Many programs and network utilities are designed to work over IP, but not IPX.

A potential problem arises, though, when you set up a new NetWare 5 server that uses only IP into an existing IPX network. Servers that use only IP cannot synchronize replicas with servers that use only IPX.

Novell's solution to this problem is called *transitive synchronization.* With transitive synchronization, at least one server must be set up to use both IP and IPX. This server is called a *source server.* Each source server manages synchronization among *target servers,* or servers that use only one of the two protocols. As Figure 34-7 shows, the source server acts as a go-between, allowing IP-only servers to send and receive updates from IPX-only servers. Transitive synchronization is enabled automatically as soon as a server is set up to use multiple protocols.

Transitive synchronization is also used to reduce WAN traffic. Unlike earlier versions of NetWare, NetWare 5 does not require every server to synchronize continuously with its *replica ring*—that is, every other server that holds a replica of the same partition. Instead, the source server checks a target server to see if it has received an update from the other servers in the replica ring. If so, the source server synchronizes with the target, but not with every other server in the ring. This effectively means that the source server communicates with only one server and reduces network traffic by not having to synchronize with multiple servers.

FIGURE 34-7

A source server that uses both IP and IPX updates target servers that use only one of the two protocols

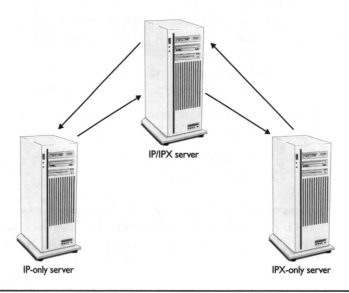

IP/IPX server

IP-only server

IPX-only server

on the **Job**

Although the terms replica ring *and* replica list *are interchangeable, Novell documentation favors* **replica list.**

The source server checks with the target server if it has not received an NDS update within a specified period of time. This period of time is called the *NDS inactivity synchronization interval.* The default is 60 minutes, but you can set the inactivity synchronization interval to any amount of time between 2 and 1,440 minutes by typing the following command at the server prompt:

```
SET NDS INACTIVITY SYNCHRONIZATIONAL INTERVAL=x (minutes)
```

WAN Traffic Manager

Another tool new to NetWare 5 is the *WAN Traffic Manager (WTM).* Previous versions of NetWare communicated all NDS updates immediately, without regard to the time of day, or the amount of traffic on the WAN. The WAN Traffic Manager allows you to control when NDS synchronization traffic will be allowed across WAN links.

You enable WTM by loading WTM.NLM at the server console. Once you load the *NLM,* the NDS *schema* is updated with a new object called a *LAN Area object* (see Figure 34-8).

FIGURE 34-8

The LAN Area object is new to NetWare 5

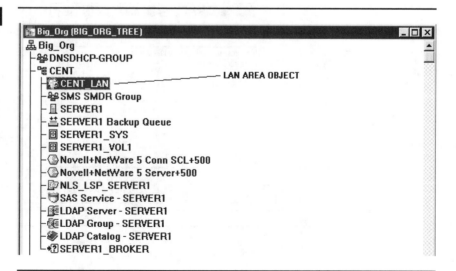

After creating a LAN Area object, you can add servers to it in much the same way that you can add users to a group. Within the LAN Area object, you can create WAN traffic policies that control when NDS synchronization traffic is allowed to flow across specified WAN links. The traffic policies are then applied to every server in the LAN Area object. NetWare 5 comes with predefined policies to make things easier for the administrator, and you will usually be able to find a predefined policy that meets your needs with little or no modification (see Figure 34-9).

Note that these policies affect only NDS synchronization traffic, not time synchronization traffic, or traffic generated by users or administrators.

exam
ⓦatch

Be sure to spend some time looking at the objects in a working NDS tree and become familiar with the location of the settings in each object. In an exam situation, you'll want to be able to go immediately to the setting that you're being asked to modify—remember, Novell exams are timed.

FIGURE 34-9

This predefined policy limits NDS synchronization traffic to 1:00 A.M. – 3:00 A.M.

LAN Area:CENT_LAN

WAN Policies

Predefined Policy Groups:
[1-3am ▼]

Policy Load Results:
No errors found in policy (1 - 3 am).
No errors found in policy (1 - 3 am, NA).

[Continue] [Load Group] [Advanced]

[OK] [Cancel] [Page Options...] [Help]

Identification
See Also
Servers belonging to LAN Area
Cost
WAN Policies

Now that you've read about partitions and replicas, here is a quick reference with things to look for on the exam, and an appropriate response.

QUESTIONS AND ANSWERS

An exam question shows you a diagram of an NDS tree and asks you where partitioning is appropriate.	Look for containers separated by WAN links, containers with over 3,500 objects, a container that must be locally administered, or a partition with more than 10 to 15 replicas.
The question asks for ways that WAN traffic can be minimized.	Look for answers that mention partitioning along container boundaries and/or WAN traffic manager.
The question shows you an NDS tree and asks you to point out an object that could be used to manage WAN traffic between servers.	Select the LAN Area object.
The question shows several servers and the protocols they communicate with, and asks which server is a source.	Select the server that uses both IP and IPX protocols.

CERTIFICATION OBJECTIVE 34.02

Reviewing Time Synchronization Issues

As you may recall from earlier chapters, a NetWare server must coordinate time with the other servers in the network in order to ensure that file and NDS updates are synchronized properly. In other words, the server needs to know if its NDS database and files are the most current version or if they have been updated elsewhere by a user or administrator. The server relies on *timestamps* to determine which version of a file or NDS database change is the latest version.

The time setup depends on whether your NetWare 5 network is using only the IPX protocol, IP protocol, or is using mixed IP/IPX protocols.

Time Setup in an IPX Environment

In an IPX environment, a NetWare server can be either a *time provider*, which gives time to other servers, or a *time consumer*, which receives the time from another server. A *secondary time server* is referred to as a time consumer. It will adjust its internal clock until that internal clock is synchronized with the time provider. Just to make things interesting, though, there are three types of time providers:

■ **Single-reference time server**   Provides the time to the other servers, all of which are secondary time servers if a single reference time server exists. Single reference time servers will not check the time with other NetWare servers, but can be connected to an external time source.

■ **Primary time server**   Provides the time to secondary servers, but checks with other primary time servers and "votes" on the correct time. Each primary time server gets one vote as to what the correct time is, and adjusts its clock until synchronized with the other servers on the network.

■ **Reference time server**   Participates in the polling process with primary time servers, but gets 16 "votes" and does not adjust its clock. All primary time servers therefore end up synchronized to the reference time server.

Students often find the section on time servers to be challenging, particularly because the terms for each type of server are very similar to each other. It's often difficult to keep them straight when trying to memorize the relationships between them.

Some simple charts make the relationships between the types of time servers easier to remember. It may be even more beneficial to draw the charts once or twice; then try to draw them again from memory. Once you can draw the charts from memory, you can always draw them quickly at the beginning of your Novell exam on the scratch paper provided, and then refer to them if you come across any questions about time servers.

S's go together:
Single reference servers provide only *to*
Secondary servers

And, for the other types, remember RPS = Really Pretty Simple:

Reference servers provide to	**Really**
Primary servers, which provide to	**Pretty**
Secondary servers	**Simple**

Time Setup in an IP or Mixed IP/IPX Environment

In an IP or mixed IP/IPX environment, you can set up time servers in the same way that you would set up a pure IPX network, with primary, secondary, reference, and single reference time servers. You also have the option of running a module that is new to NetWare 5 called NTP.NLM. *NTP* (*Network Time Protocol*) is an open standard that allows a server using the IP protocol to receive the time from a trusted time source such as the U.S. Naval Observatory. Using NTP gives your time setup an extra measure of fault tolerance, since the time servers that provide time to NTP use accurate atomic clocks and are unlikely to go down. The server receiving the time from an NTP source then provides time to the secondary time servers on the rest of the network.

Under the NTP terminology, a server using NTP is either a *server* or a *peer*. A server provides time and does not synchronize its clock with other sources. The Naval Observatory would be an example of an NTP server because it provides time, but never looks to other sources for the correct time.

A peer, on the other hand, can synchronize its clock with other peers. For example, you might set one NetWare 5 server to get the time from the Naval Observatory and another NetWare 5 server to get the time from the Lawrence Livermore Lab. The two NetWare 5 servers might then synchronize the time between them. In this instance, the two NetWare 5 servers would be peers, because they are synchronizing the time with each other. The Naval Observatory and Lawrence Livermore Labs would not be peers, because they are providing the time without synchronizing their time to other sources.

Planning a Time Synchronization Strategy

By default, NetWare sets up the first server in the network as a single reference time server and all subsequent servers as secondary time servers. This setup works just fine if your network is in only one location with no WAN links and if you have less than 30 servers. If your network does cross WAN links, or grows beyond 30 servers, then you will have to plan a time synchronization strategy to make sure that all of the servers on your network are keeping accurate time.

Novell refers to anything other than a default setup as a time provider group. A time provider group must have the following:

- In an IPX-only network, at least one reference time server and two primary time servers

- In a mixed IP/IPX network using NTP, a NetWare 5 server using the IP protocol set up as an NTP server or peer to provide the time to secondary servers

The reference time server or main NTP time source should be the server that is the closest to the "center" of the network. For example, in an organization with branches across the United States, a server in a city somewhere in the middle of the country would be a good choice for a reference or NTP server.

After deciding which location will host the reference or NTP server, you should plan for one server at each location that is separated from other locations by a WAN link to act as a primary or peer time server. Every other server should be set up as a secondary time server.

Figure 34-10 shows a sample time synchronization plan for a company with branches in Dallas, Chicago, and Sacramento.

Finally, you need to decide how your servers will communicate with each other. By default, NetWare servers communicate time synchronization

FIGURE 34-10 The geographical location of the branches of your organization help determine
which type of time server to place at each location

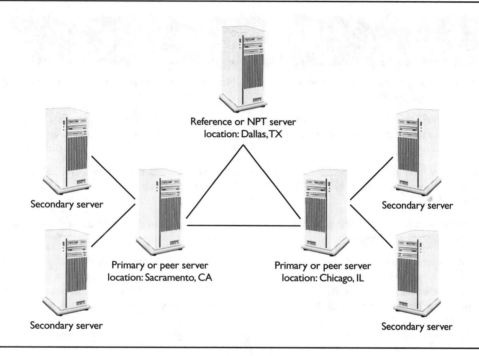

Reference or NPT server
location: Dallas, TX

Secondary server

Secondary server

Primary or peer server
location: Sacramento, CA

Secondary server

Secondary server

Primary or peer server
location: Chicago, IL

information through the *Service Advertising Protocol (SAP)*. SAP is a
broadcast protocol, which means that it sends messages to no particular
address—everyone on the network gets the message. This method is useful
because everything attached to the network gets time updates from the
server; but it is not efficient because SAP generates a lot of traffic.

The alternative is to manually set how a server will communicate with
other time sources. By setting up a custom configuration, your servers will
communicate time information directly to only the servers that you specify,
and will not generate excess network traffic by sending out SAP broadcasts
to everything on the network. You create and save these settings in a file
called TIMESYNC.CFG by using the Monitor NLM utility.

Look for the following situations on exam questions relating to time synchronization strategies.

QUESTIONS AND ANSWERS

You are asked if you should use NTP in a network that uses only IPX.	No, NTP requires at least one server to use the IP protocol.
You are asked whether a custom setup is needed for a network in a single location with 31 servers.	Yes, because Novell recommends a custom setup whenever the number of servers exceeds 30, even if all of the servers are at a single location.
You are asked which utility should be used to customize time settings: TIMESYNC, SERVMAN, or MONITOR.	NetWare 5 uses the MONITOR utility to configure time settings.
You are asked which type of NTP server can synchronize with other servers.	Peer servers can synchronize with other peer servers.
You are asked which time source would be better overall: a reference server set maintained by the network administrator or an external trusted time source such as the U.S. Naval Observatory.	As reliable as network administrators may be, they can't match the accuracy of a trusted time source with an atomic clock. Choose the external trusted time source.

EXERCISE 34-1

Customizing Time Synchronization Settings

Complete the following steps to set up a server with customized time synchronization settings:

1. Go to the server or use Rconsole from a workstation to access the server's console prompt.

2. At the console prompt, type **MONITOR**; then press ENTER. You should see a screen similar to Figure 34-11. Scroll down to the Time parameter. NetWare 5 configures time settings through the Monitor screen. Previous versions of NetWare used the Servman NLM to configure time settings.

3. Once in the Time section of the MONITOR utility, begin by setting TIMESYNC Configured Sources to ON (see Figure 34-12). After setting TIMESYNC Configured Sources to ON, be sure to tell the server which sources to synchronize with.

FIGURE 34-11

Configuring time settings
through the Monitor
screen

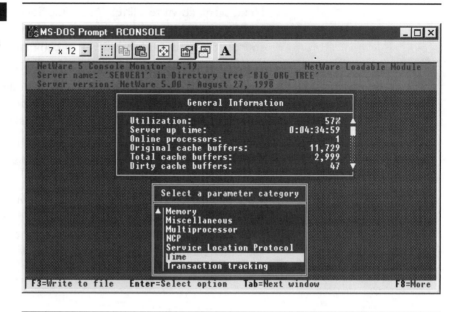

FIGURE 34-12

Setting TIMESYNC
Configured Sources
to ON

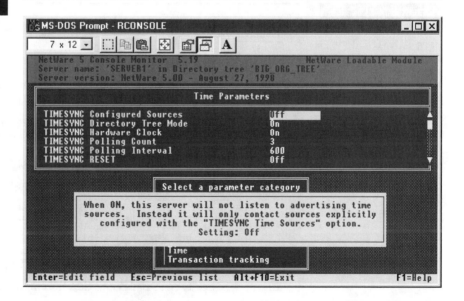

4. Next, scroll down to TIMESYNC Time Sources and press ENTER. Now, type in the server name or IP address, if using IP, of the time sources that you want the server to communicate with (see Figure 34-13). Separate the names of the time sources with semicolons.

5. Finally, you can tell the server which type of time server it should act as, by scrolling down to TIMESYNC Type, pressing ENTER, and entering the name of the time server type (see Figure 34-14).

6. Scroll through the other Time options and read the pop-up windows that explain the other parameters that can be modified to further customize the TIMESYNC.CFG settings.

7. Keep in mind that if a server cannot communicate with any of the time sources specified in TIMESYNC.CFG, it will automatically fall back to SAP as a method of communicating time information with the other servers on the network.

FIGURE 34-13

Using TIMESYNC Time Sources

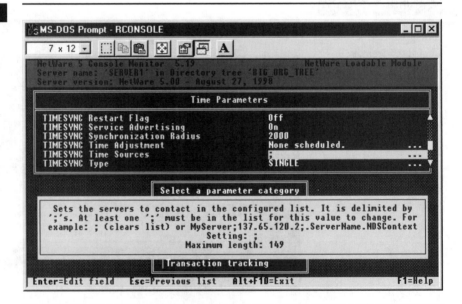

FIGURE 34-14

Configuring time servers
for efficiency and fault
tolerance

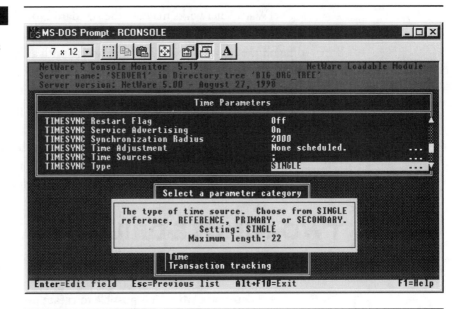

CERTIFICATION SUMMARY

Understanding the structure of the NDS database will help you plan the
partitioning and replication of portions of the database. Partitioning and
replication should be done to minimize WAN traffic and provide users with
quick access to the portions of the tree that they need. Partitioning may also
be appropriate when the number of objects in a container grows above
3,500 objects, when there are more than 10 to 15 replicas of a partition,
when a container needs to be locally administered, or when it seems
appropriate for members of a workgroup to have a container to themselves.

Transitive synchronization is a method by which servers that use only
either the IP or IPX protocol can synchronize through a server that uses
both protocols. This method of synchronization does not require a server
to contact every other member of the replica ring.

The WAN traffic manager (WTM) is configured via the LAN Area
object in NetWare Administrator and is used to set policies regarding the
time and method of NDS synchronization.

NetWare 5 networks may use the standard Novell scheme of single-reference, reference, primary, and secondary time servers to synchronize time on the network. NetWare 5 networks with at least one server running the IP protocol may use NTP (Network Time Protocol) to obtain the time from a trusted time provider. NTP servers provide time but do not synchronize with other time providers, while NTP peers can synchronize the time with other NTP peers.

NetWare time servers can synchronize the time either through SAP (Service Advertising Protocol), or they can be configured to communicate directly with specified servers. Custom setups are done using the Monitor utility.

TWO-MINUTE DRILL

- ❑ Determining a partition boundary strategy usually begins with a look at the Directory, since the design of the Directory tree will determine where it is possible to create partitions and place *replicas*.

- ❑ Partitioning does the following: helps the network load balance; helps prevent synchronization problems; allows you to place copies of the partitions, called replicas, on more than one server.

- ❑ When designing a network and planning for partitions, two main factors will determine how you organize the Directory tree: the geographic placement of the servers on the network; and the way your organization is divided into workgroups, plus the printers and other resources that support those workgroups.

- ❑ Since you never want to have NDS synchronization creating network traffic across slow WAN links, it only makes sense to plan to create a container for each major geographic location and create your first partitions along the boundaries of those containers.

- ❑ "Don't span the WAN" means that you will want to further partition the tree until you have made a container (and partition) for each office that is separated from another office by a WAN link.

- ❑ Novell recommends that you partition your tree based on geographic factors, and partition further only under three special circumstances: if the total number of objects (users, printers, servers, and others) grows to more than 3,500; if you need a partition to be managed by a specific administrator or group of administrators close to the users and other resources in that part of the tree; or if a single partition has more than 10 to 15 replicas.

❏ With transitive synchronization, at least one server must be set up to use both IP and IPX. This server is called a *source server.*

❏ Unlike earlier versions of NetWare, NetWare 5 does not require every server to synchronize continuously with its *replica ring*—that is, every other server that holds a replica of the same partition.

❏ Although the terms *replica ring* and *replica list* are interchangeable, Novell documentation favors *replica list.*

❏ The source server checks with the target server if it has not received an NDS update within a specified period of time. This period of time is called the *NDS inactivity synchronization interval.*

❏ The WAN Traffic Manager allows you to control when NDS synchronization traffic will be allowed across WAN links.

❏ In an IPX environment, a NetWare server can be either a *time provider,* which gives time to other servers, or a *time consumer,* which receives the time from another server. A *secondary time server* is referred to as a time consumer.

❏ Remember: *RPS = **R**eally **P**retty **S**imple: **R**eference servers=**R**eally; **P**rimary servers=**P**retty; and **S**econdary servers=**S**imple.*

❏ In an IP or mixed IP/IPX environment, you can set up time servers in the same way that you would set up a pure IPX network, with primary, secondary, reference, and single reference time servers.

❏ In NTP terminology, a server using NTP is either a *server* or a *peer.* A server provides time and does not synchronize its clock with other sources. A peer, on the other hand, can synchronize its clock with other peers.

❏ NetWare servers communicate time synchronization information through the *Service Advertising Protocol (SAP).* SAP is a *broadcast protocol,* which means that it sends messages to no particular address—everyone on the network gets the message.

❏ By setting up a custom configuration, your servers will communicate time information directly to only the servers that you specify, and they will not generate excess network traffic by sending out SAP broadcasts to everything on the network.

❏ By setting up a custom configuration, your servers will communicate time information directly to only the servers that you specify, and they will not generate excess network traffic by sending out SAP broadcasts to everything on the network.

❏ NetWare 5 uses the MONITOR utility to customize time settings: TIMESYNC, SERVMAN, or MONITOR.

❏ If a server cannot communicate with any of the time sources specified in TIMESYNC.CFG, it will automatically fall back to SAP as a method of communicating time information with the other servers on the network.

SELF TEST

The Self-Test questions will help you measure your understanding of the material presented in this chapter. Read all the choices carefully, as there may be more than one correct answer. Select all correct answers for each question.

1. Which of the following terms is not commonly used when referring to the database that holds information about the objects that comprise the network?

    A. The Directory

    B. The tree

    C. The NDS database

    D. The Container

2. A diagram of an NDS tree, often drawn when planning the structure of the tree, shows the tree branching out:

    A. Upward

    B. Vertically

    C. Horizontally

    D. From the first server

3. NetWare will automatically create _____ replica(s) of each partition, if there are enough servers to hold the replicas.

    A. 4

    B. 3

    C. 2

    D. 1

4. Which of the following are the two main factors in determining the boundaries of partitions?

    A. The way in which users and resources are organized into workgroups.

    B. Partitions should be placed wherever upper management thinks is best.

    C. Each type of object, such as Printer, User, and Server, should be in a separate partition.

    D. The geographic placement of servers on the network.

5. Which of the following would not be a reason to create a partition that is not required by the "Don't span the WAN" rule?

    A. The number of objects in a partition exceeds 3,500.

    B. You want part of the tree to be managed by a specific administrator.

    C. A partition has more than 10 to 15 replicas.

    D. You want to reduce network traffic.

6. Transitive synchronization accomplishes which of the following two functions? (Choose all that apply.)

    A. Synchronizes replicas from one language to replicas from another language, for example, from English to Spanish.

B. Synchronizes replicas on IP-only servers with replicas on IPX-only servers.

C. Synchronizes NetWare 4 replicas with NetWare 5 replicas.

D. Reduces WAN traffic by not requiring every server holding a replica of the same partition to communicate with every other server in the replica ring.

7. After _____ (this period of time) elapses in a transitive synchronization setup, the source server will check with the target server to see if an update is necessary:

A. The inactive NDS interval

B. The synchronization interval set time

C. The NDS inactivity synchronization interval

D. The WTM inactivity synchronization interval

8. Which of the following is not a step in enabling the WAN Traffic Manager?

A. Enter the **SET WAN TRAFFIC MANAGER=ON** command at the console prompt.

B. Load WTM.NLM at the console prompt.

C. Create a LAN Area object.

D. Set the traffic policy by modifying the LAN Area object.

9. Which of the following is not a time provider?

A. Reference time server

B. Single-reference time server

C. Primary time server

D. Secondary time server

10. If at least one server on the network is running IP, it can be configured to receive time from a trusted source such as the U.S. Naval Observatory, using

A. NetWare Time Protocol

B. Network Time Protocol

C. Naval Time Protocol

D. NetWare Trusted Protocol

11. Under the NTP method of time synchronization, what is the name for a time source that can adjust its clock after checking with other time sources?

A. Server

B. Primary

C. Peer

D. Transceiver

12. You will need to set up a custom time synchronization scheme if which of the two circumstances occur? (Choose all that apply.)

A. Your network grows beyond 30 servers.

B. There are WAN links in your network.

C. The server keeps telling you that "It's Hammer Time!"

D. Your network grows beyond 20 servers.

13. Your network's reference time server or main NTP time source should be located

A. On the first server to be installed on the network

B. On a server residing in the [Root] partition of the NDS tree

C. On a server that is in the geographical center of the network

D. On a server dedicated solely to time synchronization.

14. By default, NetWare networks communicate time information through a broadcast protocol called

A. SPAM

B. SAP

C. NAP

D. PAS

15. On a NetWare 5 server, you set up custom time synchronization by modifying the TIMESYNC.CFG file:

A. By using the SERVMAN utility

B. By using the EDIT utility

C. By issuing SET commands from the console prompt

D. By using the MONITOR utility

35

Creating an Accessibility Plan

CERTIFICATION OBJECTIVES

35.01   Creating a User Accessibility Needs
        Analysis Document

35.02   Creating an Accessibility Guideline
        Document

35.03   Creating an Administrative Strategies
        Document

The core function of NDS is to simplify your access to network resources. It accomplishes this by giving you a logical view of your network resources with a single tool for administration with NetWare Administrator and one login. Your access to the network resources is dependent on several components, your client software, login scripts, and NDS objects. While your client software will allow you initial access to the network, your NDS objects and login scripts create your individual environment.

In this chapter, we will learn how to plan our users' environment and allow them access to the resources they need.

Creating a User Accessibility Needs Analysis Document

When developing a user-environment plan, the first step is to create an accessibility needs analysis document. You create this document by gathering usability information from the users.

You should keep the following in mind when determining your users' needs:

- Application needs
- Physical network needs
- Need to access legacy network services

Application Needs

You need to gather as much information you can about the applications and data files your users need, and then ask yourself the following questions:

- Are there applications and data that everyone needs access to?
- Are there groups of users in a container that need access to specific applications?

- Do your DOS and Windows users have any shared needs?

- Do your shared applications have any hardware or operating system requirements?

- Which shared applications need to be launched manually by your users?

- Which shared applications need to be launched automatically by your users?

- Are there groups in multiple containers that need access to applications and data?

- Are any applications used across your WAN?

- Are any users dependent on applications running at specific times?

Physical Network Needs

You should also gather information about your users' needs regarding physical network resources. A physical network resource can be defined as one of the following:

- *Networked:* for example, printers, plotters, and scanners

- *Network storage devices:* for example, CD-ROM towers, jukeboxes, and disk arrays

When considering physical network needs, ask the following questions:

- Do all the your users in the same container have the same access needs?

- Are there any resources that everyone will need access to?

- Do you have any resources that are shared across a WAN?

- How are you planning on modifying users' access to resources?

- What network OS and workstation OS are you using?

Needs to Access Legacy Network Services

If you have any NetWare 3 resources on your network, you will need to consider a guideline for creating bindery context.

Your NetWare server can support 16 containers with bindery context, which allows you the flexibility to place the NetWare 3 resources where they are needed in the NDS tree. Ask the following questions when considering the use of legacy network services:

■ Do I have any bindery-based physical network resources?

■ Do I have any bindery-based applications and who uses them?

You should figure out how many users need accesses to the bindery-based resources and provide them access to the specific containers that have the resource.

CERTIFICATION OBJECTIVE 35.02

Creating an Accessibility Guideline Document

Now that we have gathered the information, we need to create our accessibility guideline. This guideline will address how our NDS objects are utilized to create our users' environment.

There are two points to keep in mind when you are creating your accessibility guideline:

■ You want to create a centrally managed user environment.

■ You want to keep the management of NDS resources as simple as possible.

When you create an accessibility guideline document, consider which NDS objects you will use to create your users' environment, and how you will design your security plan to restrict access to network resources. You need to keep the following scenarios in mind when designing your security plan:

■ You want to restrict access to network resources by the placement of User NDS objects in the NDS yree.

■ Restrict access by granting specific object rights to a particular NDS object.

Table 35-1 is Novell's Suggested NDS Accessibility Guidelines. You will want to use this table as a guide and implement the suggestions when they are appropriate.

TABLE 35-1

Novell's Suggested
Accessibility Guidelines

Topic	Suggestions for Accessibility Guidelines
Container policy package objects	Specify where container policy package object should be used. Place container policy package at the highest possible level of the tree without spanning the WAN. Rule of thumb: have one container policy package for each geographic.
User policy package object	Specify where user policy package objects should be used. Place user policy packages in the same container as the users who will access them.
Application object	Specify where application objects should be used. Place application objects close to users who access them. If your network has multiple geographic locations connected by a WAN, create application objects in the containers that represent the physical locations. If you have multiple application servers at one location, create application objects for each application on each server.
Group objects	Specify where group objects can be used. Use group objects only when all group members are in the same physical location. The number of group members should not exceed 1500 in most situations. If possible, keep users assigned to the group within the same partition.
Profile objects	Specify where and how profile objects can be used. Create profile login scripts when user objects needing the same access exist in more than one container. If you allow multiple profile login scripts in a container, identify how they should be used. Profile login scripts require more maintenance than container login scripts, but they are still easier to manage than user login scripts.

TABLE 35-1	Topic	Suggestions for Accessibility Guidelines
Novell's Suggested Accessibility Guidelines *(continued)*	Organizational role objects for network administrators	Specify a level at which organizational role objects should be created. Create organizational role objects with two members: the network administrator and the backup administrator.
	Directory map object	Because directory map objects ease administration, identify the names of directory map objects to be used throughout the organization and the data they represent.
	Alias objects	Alias objects have many uses. To limit their use, specify their limitations. For example, identify which objects can or cannot use an alias.
	User login scripts	Specify when to implement a user login script so that the user can access applications and data files.
	IRFs for containers	Specify how NDS inherited right filters are used and which rights can be blocked.
	Data directories and drive mappings	If you have applications, such as e-mail and word processing, that are company wide, create a standard for the directory structure and drive mapping. For example, the standard could always map drive M to the user object's personal mailbox, with a search drive X always mapped to the e-mail application directory. Each server's directory structure would be the same for these applications. This eases administration and helps mobile users access resources.
	Security precautions	Identify precautions related to specific security practices. For example, you could warn network administrators to avoid granting the Supervisor NDS right to the server objects, because this right is inherited by the file system.
	(Source: Novell's Study Guide for Course 575)	

Creating an Administrative Strategies Document

In this section, we will use the information we have gathered to design a strategy that will address the following concerns:

- Common login scripts
- Creation of security guidelines
- Design strategy for legacy services
- Structure of a standard file system
- Client configuration
- Mobile user design

We will discuss each point in further detail. We need to keep two principles in mind as we explore this section:

1. We need to manage our users centrally.
2. We need to simplify our management of the network resources.

Common Login Scripts

Login scripts are used to provide users additional access to network services. Login scripts can be associated to several NDS object types:

- User NDS object
- Profile NDS object
- Organization NDS object
- Organizational Unit NDS object

Login scripts are used with the four NDS object types to provide access to network services. Using the needs analysis and accessibility documents we have created, we need to address the following questions:

■ Does everyone in a container need a common environment? Do they have similar needs? If the answer is yes, we should create a container login script. This will create a common environment for all users in that container.

■ Now that we have created a common environment for access to common resources (such as printers and scanners), is there a special user that has needs that are not shared by anyone else in the container? If the answer is yes, you should consider creating a user login script. This will allow you to further customize the environment for that user without affecting anyone else in the container.

■ Now that we have identified common use of needs within the same container and the individual use of needs for login scripts, we need to consider the use of login scripts for users with common needs but that are in different containers. Do you have users in different containers that need access to the same network resources? If the answer is yes, you should create a Profile object and give the object a login script. Once you have created the NDS object and script, you need to associate users to this NDS object. This will allow users from different containers to access their common network resources.

If you follow these simple guidelines, your administration of network resources and users will be greatly reduced.

 on the **job**

You should avoid using personal login scripts. This will add greatly to your administrative duties if you have to manage all of your user login scripts.

Security Guidelines

In this section we will discuss the different levels of network administrator security and the default user security system.

There are several levels of network administrators: enterprise administrators, container administrators, backup administrators, password administrators, and server administrators. All of these administrators have NDS security rights that allow them to perform only the security functions that the job requires. We will cover these in more detail.

Enterprise Administrator

The *enterprise administrator* has the highest level of security. The rights for this administrator start at the [Root] of the NDS tree and flow through all objects and the file system. This administrator is usually the person that sets up the specialized administrators. This object is controlled by an Organizational Role object and is usually placed in a hidden container in the NDS tree.

Container Administrator

In a large LAN or a WAN environment, you may want to divide the management of administration among several *container administrators*. These administrators have full control over their containers but not outside their container. To create container administrators, create an Organizational Role object, grant the necessary rights, and then associate the users that will be the container administrator.

Backup Administrator

A backup administrator is usually used in large LAN and or WAN environments. This position is used for backing up and restoring the network data. The backup administrator has no object rights in the container. They cannot create or modify users in this role. They do have full file system rights and the ability to install servers. They do not have the partition capability. To create a backup administrator, create an Organizational Role object, give the role the necessary rights, and then associate the appropriate users with the object.

Password Administrators

The *password administrator* is perfect for organizations that utilize a help desk. This administrator has limited rights for User objects, groups, login scripts, and passwords. The administrator cannot create or modify objects, install or partition servers, and has no file system rights. Use the Organizational Role object to create this object. You give the necessary rights and associate any necessary User objects.

Server Administrator

The *server administrator* is your do-it-all administrator. This administrator type is used to manage the server's health and fitness. This administrator can change passwords, group memberships, and login scripts. They cannot install servers or manage the partitions of your tree. This administrator has full file system right to the following volumes and directories: Public, Apps, and Users. To create a server administrator, create an Organizational Role object and assign the appropriate NDS rights, then assign the appropriate user associations.

Default User Security

Table 35-2 lists the default security account settings used by NetWare when you create a user.

Design Strategy for Legacy Services

Any NetWare 4.*x* server through NetWare 5 can support services for bindery-based network resources through the use of the SET BINDERY CONTEXT command. This will allow up to 16 containers to act as hosts for bindery-based services.

When a client or application requests access for Bindery objects, it will search the containers that have bindery services enabled. When you are designing services for your legacy services, consider the following questions:

■ Where in the network are the bindery-based resources located?

■ What objects in my NDS tree need access to the bindery resources?

TABLE 35-2		
User Account Security Defaults	**Parameter**	**Default Value**
	Account Has Expiration Date	NO
	Limit Current Connections	YES
	Maximum Connections	2
	Require Password	YES
	Minimum Password Length	6
	Force Periodic Password Changes	YES
	Days Between Change	Less than or Equal to 45
	Require Unique Passwords	YES
	Limit Grace Logins	YES
	Grace logins Allowed	3
	Intruder Detection/Lockout	
	Detect Intruder	YES
	Intruder Detection Threshold	
	Incorrect Login Attempts	3
	Bad Login Count Retention Time	0 Days 0 Hours 15 Minutes
	Lock Account after Detection	YES
	Length of Lockout	0 Days 0 Hours 30 Minutes
	(Source: Novell's Study Guide for Course 575)	

Standard File System

To reduce the time spent on file system administration, you need to consider the following questions when designing your file structure:

- How many volumes am I going to have on each server?
- Are my volumes going to have specific functions, such as USERS, DATA, and APPS?

- Do I have storage considerations for my users?
- What drive-letter mapping rules have I created?
- Have I considered the accessibility of my file system throughout the system and implemented necessary aliases?

Client Configuration

To reduce administrative overhead, you need to develop a standard Client32 configuration. This configuration will be the same if you are working with Windows 95 or Windows 3.11. To develop this configuration, consider the following questions:

- What is the name context?
- Do you have a preferred server; if so, what is the name?
- What is the preferred tree?
- What is the first network drive letter?

Mobile User Design

NetWare allows your users access to the network from any location within the tree. This places different demands on network resources, and with this in mind, we must design an accessibility plan that accommodates mobile users. Mobile users and remote users different types of users and, we must understand the distinction between the two.

Remote User

A *remote user* is a user that connects to your LAN, authenticates, and then logs in to their home context. All access and activity resides in their home container with their remote User NDS object. A remote user requires very little planning or specialized configuration on your part. Some examples of remote users are listed below:

- A user who uses their notebook computer to dial in to the LAN to send and receive e-mail and accesses their files and data.
- A user who uses their notebook to dial in to the LAN to access printers.

These people have very little impact on the NDS tree design. They are considered local access users in the design of the tree.

Mobile User

A *mobile user* needs access to information in the container they are currently in, as well as their home container.

Mobile users have a large impact on the NDS tree design. They require additional NDS objects to support their mobility. Here's an example of a mobile user:

> A desktop support engineer who supports several hundred users in a multicontext environment needs access to the local applications, as well as to the IS staff container for their applications.

There are several types of mobile users. You have mobile users that use a notebook to travel around the LAN/WAN, and you have users that use a workstation in each location they travel to.

Access Needs of Mobile Users

To create an effective mobile user accessibility plan, you need to consider the following questions:

- Where is the mobile user gaining access to the network?
- Does the mobile user need access to information at each location or is all of their information local to their home container?
- Does the mobile user carry a notebook or use a local workstation?
- How often and how long are they at this particular location?

Administration of Mobile Users

You can administer your mobile users by leveraging the following options:

- **Typeful Relative Distinguished Name** User knows the Full Distinguished Name when logging in to the network from a remote location.

- **Login scripts** You can create elaborate login scripts that will automate and customize the mobile user environment when the user logs in.

- **Alias object** You can create alias objects for mobile users and place them in the required areas to make it easier for the users to access the network.

- **Contextless login** If you are running NetWare 5 and NDS Catalog Services, you can configure your Novell client software to use the contextless login services. This will eliminate the need to provide your NDS context when logging in. If more than one user exists with the same user name, a list of options will appear for your user to select their ID.

- **Client configuration** You can configure your users' Novell client workstation to log in to a preferred server or tree.

CERTIFICATION SUMMARY

In the previous sections you were presented with questions you need to ask yourself in order to create an effective user environment. There were two main topics you should have kept in mind as we went through the chapter:

- We need to manage our users centrally.

- We need to simplify our management of the network resources.

This chapter was broken down into three main topics: Accessibility Needs, Accessibility Guidelines, and Administrative Strategies. We walked through the methodologies and strategies to gather the necessary information so we can make the right decisions.

 ## TWO-MINUTE DRILL

❑ When developing a user-environment plan, the first step is to create an accessibility needs analysis document. You create this document by gathering usability information from the users.

❑ Your NetWare server can support 16 containers with bindery context, which allows you the flexibility to place the NetWare 3 resources where they is needed in the NDS tree.

❑ There are two points to keep in mind when you are creating your accessibility guideline: you want to create a centrally managed user environment and you want to keep the management of NDS resources as simple as possible.

❑ Login scripts are used to provide users additional access to network services, and login scripts can be associated to several NDS object types.

❑ Login scripts are used with the four NDS object types to provide access to network services.

❑ There are several levels of network administrators: enterprise administrators, container administrators, backup administrators, password administrators, and server administrators.

❑ The *enterprise administrator* has the highest level of security. The rights for this administrator start at the [Root] of the NDS tree and flow through all objects and the file system.

❑ In a large LAN or a WAN environment, you may want to divide the management of administration among several *container administrators*.

❑ A *backup administrator* is usually used in large LAN and or WAN environments. This position is used for backing up and restoring the network data.

❑ The *password administrator* is perfect for organizations that utilize a help desk. This administrator has limited rights for User objects, groups, login scripts, and passwords.

❑ The *server administrator* is your do-it-all administrator. This administrator type is used to manage the server's health and fitness.

❑ Any NetWare 4.*x* server through NetWare 5 can support services for bindery-based network resources through the use of the SET BINDERY CONTEXT command.

❑ To reduce administrative overhead, you need to develop a standard Client32 configuration. This configuration will be the same if you are working with Windows 95 or Windows 3.11.

❑ NetWare allows your users access to the network from any location within the tree. This places different demands on network resources, and with this in mind, we must design an accessibility plan that accommodates mobile users.

❑ A *remote user* is a user that connects to your LAN, authenticates, and then logs in to their home context.

❑ Mobile users have a large impact on the NDS tree design. They require additional NDS objects to support their mobility.

❑ *Typeful Relative Distinguished Name* is when the user knows the Full Distinguished Name when logging in to the network from a remote location.

❑ You can create alias objects for mobile users and place them in the required areas to make it easier for the users to access the network.

❑ If you are running NetWare 5 and NDS Catalog Services, you can configure your Novell client software to use the contextless login services.

❑ You can configure your users' Novell client workstation to log in to a preferred server or tree.

SELF TEST

The Self-Test questions will help you measure your understanding of the material presented in this chapter. Read all the choices carefully, as there may be more than one correct answer. Select all correct answers for each question.

1. When creating an accessibility plan what is your first step?

    A. Create an accessibility guideline document.

    B. Create an administrative strategies document.

    C. Create an accessibility needs analysis document.

2. When determining your Physical Network Needs, which would not be included in the list?

    A. Jukebox

    B. Disk arrays

    C. CD-ROM towers

    D. Local printer

3. On your NetWare server, how many containers can support Bindery context?

    A. 6

    B. 16

    C. 32

    D. unlimited

4. You want to create a centrally managed user environment, True or False?

    A. True

    B. False

5. Where does an Enterprise Administrator receive their security rights?

    A. From their user objects home container

    B. From their current container

    C. From the [Root] of the NDS tree

    D. From the Organization object.

6. What File system rights does the password administrator have?

    A. Read and Write

    B. Read, Write, and Create

    C. Read and File Scan

    D. None

7. Place an "M" in the far right box for Mobile User or an "R" in the far right box for a Remote User.

A.) Someone who dials into the LAN and uses resources in their home container	
B.) Someone who dials into the LAN for e-mail	
C.) Someone who travels to multiple sites and uses a local computer to access local information	
D.) An IS staff engineer that supports several hundred users in a multicontext environment	

36

Conducting a NetWare Implementation

CERTIFICATION OBJECTIVES

36.01   Creating the Directory Tree

36.02   Managing Partitions and Replicas

36.03   Implementing and Managing Time
         Synchronization

36.04   Merging NDS Trees

36.05   Providing Network Access

Novell Directory Services (NDS) was introduced with NetWare 4 and replaces the NetWare 3.x bindery that was used to store user and object information. The NDS database is hierarchical and is compliant with the X.500 standard for directory services. NDS offers much more functionality and is more robust than the bindery, but it is also more complicated to manage. Transitioning a company to NetWare requires an in-depth understanding of NDS concepts, which we will cover in detail in this chapter. Upon completion of this chapter, you should be able to identify the NDS model to use for an organization, the implementation scheme to use, and many of the details required for designing and implementing a Novell network.

CERTIFICATION OBJECTIVE 36.01

Creating the Directory Tree

The first step in implementing NetWare is to design and create the NDS tree. There are several approaches to designing NDS trees, and tree design is an important issue in NetWare implementation projects. A lack of planning can cause major problems when an organization grows, because the NDS tree may have to be completely restructured. Network administrators must take care to model the NDS tree after an organization and anticipate its growth; otherwise, the administrator may have to recreate the tree from scratch.

There are several factors that must be considered when designing an NDS tree, including the model tree to use, the naming standard, the implementation model, and the detailed design tree. A properly designed NDS tree will make resources easy to find and use, provide redundancy, minimize network traffic, and minimize administrative costs. NDS design should be performed with a top-down approach. Begin at the high level and move down to detailed design issues.

Assessing the Situation

The first step in beginning a project is to establish what the organization has and what it needs. This information will be used to make basic decisions on which approach to take, what the timeline is for the implementation, and what the costs and benefits are. The following are some of the resources that must be identified:

- Company structure
- Information processing requirements
- Available resources
- Existing infrastructure

Each of these items plays an important role in the decision making and planning processes. Let's discuss each of these and how they apply to the NDS design and implementation.

Company Structure

Company structure includes several factors. The single most important factor to assess is how the company assesses its workgroups, because this will be used to decide the structural model to use. A workgroup is the unit a company uses to group its employees; perhaps an organization breaks its workgroups down by location or by administrative departments. Whatever the method, there is a corresponding structural design model. We will cover structural design models in more detail.

Information Processing Requirements

Information processing requirements are the cornerstone of any implementation plan. Requirements drive decisions such as the types of services that will be implemented, how administration is delegated, the plan's timeframe, and acceptable costs.

Available Resources

Available resources include several types, but in the Novell context it primarily refers to manpower. Manpower is probably the single most important resource to identify in the planning stages of an implementation, because this will drive the implementation model you choose. If all manpower is centralized and adequate to roll out NetWare to an entire organization at once, you will use one implementation approach. If each division has its own administration and will have to implement on its own time schedule, you will use a different implementation approach.

Existing Infrastructure

Existing infrastructure is very important to identify. If all locations of an organization are connected over WAN links, it will affect the implementation approach you use. If no locations have WAN connections, you cannot install a centralized directory structure; it will have to be developed at each location and merged later.

These factors establish a basic approach; once you assess these items, you can begin the next step of creating a design and an implementation approach.

Defining the Network Solution

As with any project, a major stepping stone is planning and approval for the project. Several factors to use in a Novell implementation are as follows:

- *Define the solution.* Identify all the components of the solution, including software, WAN links, hardware, and technical personnel.

- *Create an implementation schedule.* Create a timeline for the project. Is the timeline you generated feasible? Do you have the resources to meet it?

- *Calculate the costs.* What are the costs of the project? Make sure you calculate the costs and the benefits, as well as any risks involved.

Launching the Design and Implementation Process

An NDS tree should be designed to model the company's structure. The first step is to identify which structural model to use for the organization. The method an organization uses to establish its workgroups is the method you should use when deciding what type of model to use for the NDS tree. We will discuss the four models most commonly used to design a ree:

- **Administrative model**   This model is ideal for companies with clearly established administrative workgroups. For this model, start by identifying workgroups that will be used as organizational units for the company. We will take an example of the CORP organization that is made up of three distinct administrative workgroups: Sales, Marketing, and Accounting. The tree structure for CORP will resemble the one shown here:

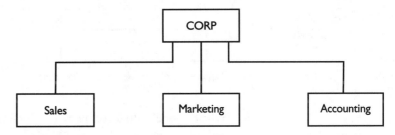

- **Geographical model**   This model is ideal for companies with multiple locations, in which the geographical location is used to establish the workgroups of the company. For this model, establish the geographical locations that define the workgroups, and use them as organizational units. If CORP consists of three main offices in San Diego, Chicago, and Atlanta, the tree structure will resemble the one shown here:

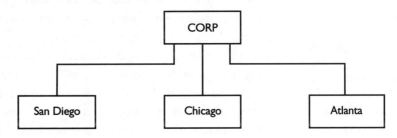

■ **Divisions model**   If a company organizes its workgroups by the type of project they are working on, the Divisions model is probably the one to use. For example, CORP makes computer equipment and has three major workgroup divisions: the Desktop division, the Laptop division, and the Peripherals division. Each division has its own set of departments as separate entities. The Divisions model would be ideal for this type of company, and would resemble the model shown here:

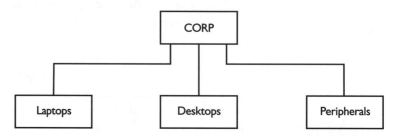

■ **Hybrid model**   In a company in which the boundaries separating workgroups are mixed, a combination of any of the other three models can be used to make up a Hybrid model. For example, CORP is made up of a central office that is divided into three administrative workgroups, and two field offices that are organized by divisional workgroups. The model might look like the one shown in Figure 36-1.

Choosing an Implementation Approach

Once you assess the tree model, you should then choose an implementation approach. The implementation approach refers to the granularity with which an organization will deploy NetWare. In other words, will it deploy NetWare from an organizational level to all divisions at once, or will start at the department level and later merge everyone into a single tree? Implementation approaches fall into three main categories: Departmental, Divisional, and Organizational. The method to use depends on the structure of the company,

FIGURE 36-1   The Hybrid Model NDS tree

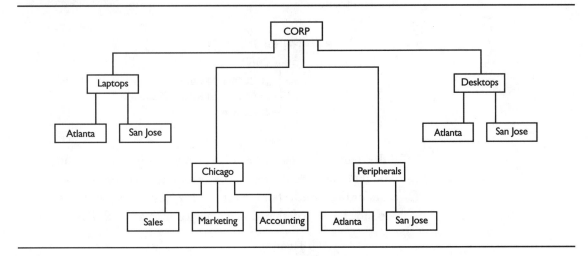

the type of LAN or WAN connections between departments and divisions, and the structure of an organization's network administration staff.

■ **Departmental implementation**   The Departmental implementation is designed to allow multiple trees that will be merged at a later date. The idea behind this approach is that departments will install their own trees at their own pace, without requiring a coordinated effort by entire divisions of the organization. Each department should design their tree with the understanding that it will be merged with other trees in their divisions at a later date.

The guidelines for a Departmental implementation are that the company has multiple locations that make coordination difficult, and that there are no WAN links to connect the remote trees. If the company as a whole is moving to NetWare, each administrator should design their own tree with a unique organization name and a unique tree name. Shown here is a simple tree using this implementation:

If the trees will be merged at a later date, an additional container should be added to the top of the Tree. The Tree shown next contains the same leaf objects as the Tree just shown, but this one shows a Tree designed to be merged with another Tree:

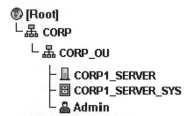

■ **Divisional implementation**   The Divisional implementation takes the Departmental method a step further. In this type of implementation, there is still no unified organizational conversion to NDS, but different divisions as a whole move to NetWare at the same time. This type of implementation still involves the development of several NDS trees, but takes place on a larger scale. This implementation may be based upon the Workgroup, Geographical, or Administrative models, depending on which one matches the company structure. This implementation requires that each division understand the role of its own departments in developing their own tree.

■ **Organizational implementation**   From a planning standpoint, the
Organizational implementation approach is larger in scale than
Departmental and Divisional implementations. It assumes the tree
will be designed and installed for the entire organization at the same
time, and will require much more up-front planning than the other
two methods. This implementation will require a solid understanding
of the organization as a whole. This method is recommended when
all locations have WAN links connecting them and the organization
is simple enough that the entire company can move to a Novell
NDS-based network without impacting operations

Designing the Directory Tree

The second step in designing an NDS tree is to establish naming standards.
This includes naming standards for such things as user accounts, Printer
objects, and Server objects. Naming standards assist in making the NDS
tree easy to use and easy to administer. For example, if you standardize user
names as first initial followed by last name, every user will know their login
name. If you don't set these standards, it can be confusing for new users
who are unable to contact an administrator.

Resource names are especially important. If you establish that Printer
objects will begin with PTR_, it will be easy for users to identify that object.
If you further establish that all accounting department printers will begin
with PTR_ACCT_, it becomes even easier for users to locate the resources.
Failure to establish a naming standard can result in numerous problems,
such as users contacting an administrator every time they need access to a
different printer. If users cannot locate resources or understand the naming
scheme, administrative costs go up.

Once you establish the naming standards, you should generate a naming
standards document. This document includes all schema objects you intend

to use and the naming convention to use for those objects. This document will ensure that naming is consistent across multiple Trees in the event that the organization deploys NetWare at a divisional or departmental level.

Naming standards become extremely important when bindery emulation is used. Bindery emulation can cause problems if you have two user accounts or two printers with the same name in different containers. If the bindery context is set to include both containers, you will have two objects in the "virtual" bindery with the same name. Since the bindery context can contain up to 16 containers, an administrator should take care not to have duplicate names in any of the containers used in the bindery context.

To set the bindery context, type the following at the server prompt:

```
set bindery context =  <context1>;<context2>;…
```

where context is a container to include in the bindery services. Separate multiple context entries with semicolons.

EXERCISE 36-1

Installing Directory Services

Once the NDS tree model is developed, the naming scheme chosen, and the implementation type selected, you can go about installing NDS on your servers. We will go through installing NDS on a single server, but the basic process will apply on additional servers in a tree. These steps assume you have an NDS-capable server and that you did not install NDS as part of the server installation.

1. At the server console prompt, load the installation module. On NetWare 4.11 servers, the syntax is as follows:

```
load install
```

On NetWare 5 servers, the syntax is either:

```
load nwconfig
```

or:

```
nwconfig (the LOAD command is optional with Netware 5)
```

2. At the installation module screen, select Directory Options from the main menu. This screen is shown here:

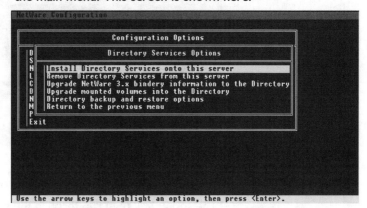

3. Select Install Directory Services onto this server; then select Create a New DS Tree. If you had already completed this operation on a server and created the tree, you could choose the option to Install into Existing Tree.

4. Press ENTER to go past the warning screen. Select Yes when asked to create the Tree, and press ENTER again.

5. Enter a name for the tree. We will call our tree CORPTREE. Press ENTER.

6. Select your time zone from the list.

7. We will leave the settings for time server type at the default of Single Reference at the next screen. If this were the second or third server in this tree you would choose Secondary (see the section on time server types). Press F10 to continue.

8. At the next screen, enter the top-level organization and initial organizational units. For this example we will use the information shown next. Enter the administrator's name, enter a password for the administrator, press ENTER, retype the password to verify it, then press ENTER again. Press F10 to continue.

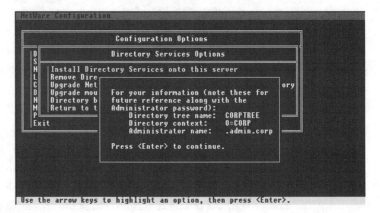

9. Select Yes when asked to Save Directory Information and Continue.

10. The server will then run through the process of creating the NDS database and adding NDS security information to the volumes. The volumes will be dismounted and then mounted again; then a screen giving the results will appear, as shown here:

NDS is now installed on the server, and you can begin adding containers and objects to your tree.

Managing Partitions and Replicas

The NDS database can get very large when thousands of objects and containers are added, and having the entire database reside on one server would be a problem. Imagine a network that had ten thousand users all being authenticated on one server. To begin with, the server would be very heavily utilized performing authentication. The network containing that server would experience high utilization because all activity that required NDS access would have to access the central server. Also, what would happen if the server went down? All users on the network would be locked out of the network until access was restored. To prevent these types of problems, Novell offers partitioning and replicas of the NDS database.

Partitions

Partitioning is the process of dividing the NDS database into smaller pieces; partitions are distinct units of NDS data. Partitioning allows the directory database to be divided up into manageable pieces, rather than having to remain a large single database. Partitions and replicas (discussed in a moment) allow an NDS database to be spread over several servers instead of the entire structure residing on a single server. Take an example of the hybrid tree we looked at in Figure 36-1. If we partition that NDS Tree, we could end up with a set of partitions that look like the ones in Figure 36-2.

Each of the partitions just shown is a piece of the NDS database. The naming convention for partitions is the name of the highest level container in the partition. In our example, Partition 1 is LAPTOP, Partition 2 is CHICAGO, Partition 3 is the Root Partition, and Partition 4 is DESKTOPS.

FIGURE 36-2   Dividing the NDS database into partitions

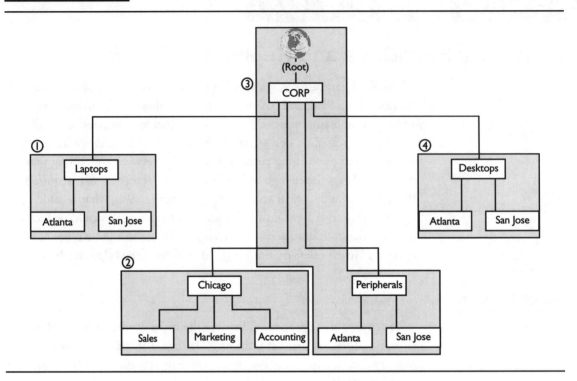

Creating Partitions

In early versions of NetWare 4, partition operations were handled through the NetWare Administrator application, but that has changed with recent releases. Partitions are now managed using NDS Manager (NDSMGR32.EXE for Win 95), the Novell application for creating, deleting, and managing partitions, replicas, and schemas. This application is in SYS:PUBLIC\WIN95 for IntranetWare and SYS:PUBLIC\WIN32 for NetWare 5.

Partitions are created for several reasons. First, if you wanted to move the Sales container to a different location in your tree, you would first have to make it a partition. Second, if there are two servers that all the sales staff use, you would want to create a Sales partition and put replicas of that partition on the two servers.

Replicas

Replicas contain the NDS data for objects in a partition; think of replicas as the boundaries of partitions. All the replicas together collectively form the directory. NDS uses four types of replicas:

- **Master replica**   When a partition is defined, the original replica is called the master replica. There is only one master replica for each partition, and these can be used for authentication (such as user authentication).

- **Read/Write replica**   A read/write replica is a copy of the master that replicates changes back and forth with the master. If the master is lost, a R/W can be promoted to the master. Read/write replicas can also be used for authentication.

- **Read-Only replica**   A read-only replica is designed to increase NDS browsing by providing a replica that cannot be modified, but can be used for searching and viewing objects (cannot be used for user authentication).

- **Subordinate reference**   A subordinate reference is a pointer to a child replica, and is created when a server has a copy of the parent but not the child. If a replica of the child is later added to a server that has a subordinate reference, the subordinate reference is automatically deleted.

All the replicas for a partition make up the *replica list* for the partition. NetWare servers synchronize all replicas in a replica list as long as there are no problems with the Tree or communications between the servers. The default method in which Novell servers create replicas of partitions is that the first server in the tree gets a master copy of the [Root], the second and third servers get a read/write replica, and the fourth and above servers get no replicas. An administrator must manually create replicas on those servers.

Partitioning Strategy and Issues

When working with partitions and replicas, there are some design strategies and issues involved. A few of the general guidelines are as follows:

- **Bindery services** If bindery services will be enabled, make sure every server in the tree contains either a master or read/write copy of all replicas containing partitions used in the bindery context.

- **Maximize bandwidth** If a group of users have to authenticate or access resources over a WAN link, you are wasting bandwidth. You should keep replicas local to the users that access them, which accomplishes two goals. First, there is no need to access the information in a partition over the WAN link, and replica synchronization traffic is kept off the WAN link. Also, Novell recommends limiting NDS partitions to 1000 objects to maximize performance.

- **Provide fault tolerance** Novell recommends at least three copies of a replica to provide fault tolerance. There must be a master replica for any replica list, and a read/write replica can be promoted to a master in the event the master is lost. If you have no read/write replicas and the master is lost or corrupted, you will have to restore the information either from backup or manually create the objects.

CERTIFICATION OBJECTIVE 36.03

Implementing and Managing Time Synchronization

Time synchronization is important in Novell networks because of the importance of timestamps on events that occur. In any network environment, communications that are transmitted by multiple hosts may not arrive in the same order they were sent. When this happens, the receiving host must have a way of sorting the received information, and timestamps on the packet are often the method servers use. If the sending hosts have clocks that are not synchronized, information may be sorted incorrectly. Time synchronization is a key component of Novell networking.

The Novell Time Synchronization Model

Novell servers use time synchronization for timestamps on several NetWare services, including file systems, NDS, various network applications, and various messaging systems. All of these systems require timestamps on communications, and incorrectly set clocks can cause loss of synchronization and data corruption.

Novell servers use TIMESYNC (A NetWare Loadable Module) to coordinate time on the network. Before we discuss how NetWare 5 handles time, let's look at an example of Novell time synchronization on a small network. This model is shown here:

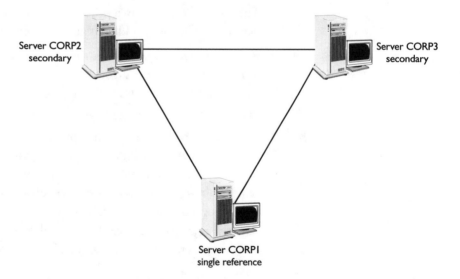

Server CORP2
secondary

Server CORP3
secondary

Server CORP1
single reference

In this illustration, each of the Novell servers load TIMESYNC.NLM, and this module synchronizes time over the network using NetWare Core

Protocol (NCP) over IPX. One of the servers (in this case CORP1) is configured as a single reference, which means all other servers on the network look to it for a time source. The other two servers are configured as secondary time servers and take their time from CORP1 (or one another in some instances). This model is well suited to small networks with no external time sources.

There are four types of time servers in a Novell environment:

- **Single Reference Server**   This server provides time to secondary time servers. This type of server is usually used for small networks with few secondary time servers. When this type of server is used, it is assumed it will be the only server providing time on the network (that is, it does no synchronization with other servers).

- **Primary Time Server**   This server provides time to secondary time servers. This type of server is used in larger networks because there can be multiple primary time servers on a network. Primary time servers vote among themselves to synchronize the network time. There must be at least two primary time servers on a network (if you have only one, you would configure a single reference).

- **Reference Time Server**   This time server uses an external time source to synchronize its clock, and provides that time to primary and secondary time servers. This type of server is used to ensure that network time is not only synchronized, but also accurate.

- **Secondary Time Server**   This time server receives its time from a time server and provides time synchronization to network client workstations. This server does no voting on network time synchronization (most servers on the network will be secondary time servers). A secondary time server can take its time from any type of time server (single reference, primary, reference, or another secondary), but they generally take it from one of three time provider types.

An example of time synchronization in a more complex network is shown in Figure 36-3.

In this illustration, only three servers participate in time voting: CORP1, CORP6, and CORP8. Secondary servers do not vote; they only receive

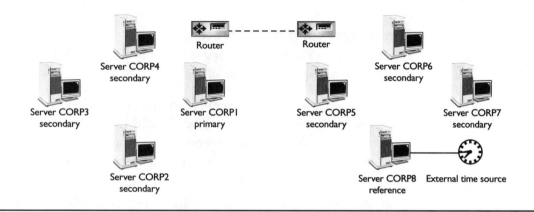

FIGURE 36-3 Time synchronization in a complex network

their time from a time source. Single reference servers assume there are no other servers and do not vote; the only two server types that participate in time voting are primary and reference time servers. Also, once secondary time servers find a time source, they will attempt to stay synchronized with that time source. If that time source becomes unavailable, they will look for another. Time sources advertise themselves on the network using Novell's Service Advertisement Protocol (SAP).

NetWare 5 Time Synchronization

With NetWare 5, traditional IPX-based TIMESYNC communications have been replaced/combined with *Network Time Protocol (NTP)*. NTP is a standards-based (RFC 1305), TCP/IP-based time synchronization protocol, and any servers that use NTP must have the IP stack loaded. The NTP.NLM provides NTP services on NetWare 5 servers. By default, NetWare 5 servers will automatically use TIMESYNC for network time synchronization whether the servers are using IPX or IP as their transport protocol. When NTP is loaded, NTP takes over as the time source on the network, and will then manage and set the clocks. When NTP is used, TIMESYNC's role in network time synchronization is then reduced to responding to NCP time requests, and any servers on the network running IPX and TIMESYNC must become secondary time servers.

Time Synchronization Strategy

When implementing time synchronization in a NetWare environment, there are a few basic guidelines to follow:

- *Scale your strategy.* Plan your network synchronization based upon the size of the network. Using the Novell default of one single reference is fine for small networks, but will not work for larger networks. Be familiar with each of the time server types and implement them to fit your network.

- *Maximize bandwidth.* Plan your time servers to minimize WAN traffic. If you have multiple WAN links, try to have a time source local to each LAN. This prevents secondary servers from synchronization across the links.

- *Plan time synchronization strategy.* If you plan to merge Trees in the future, all servers must be coordinated. Plan your strategy to accurately keep time throughout the entire network.

CERTIFICATION OBJECTIVE 36.04

Merging NDS Trees

If you have two separate network trees developed by two separate organizations, and the organizations merge, what happens to the trees? Will you have to scrap one of them and add the servers of that tree into the NDS tree of the original? The answer is no. Novell provides, through the use of the server-based DSMERGE utility, the ability to merge two separate trees.

When you merge two trees, one is specified as the source and the other is the target. The servers and objects in the source tree become resources in the target tree, and the top-level object, [Root], disappears from the source. This illustration shows two trees before being merged:

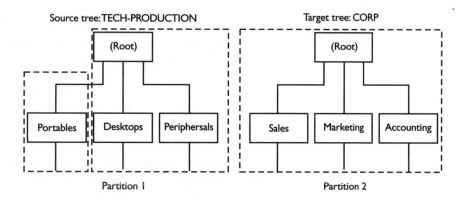

When DSMERGE is run on the two trees, the [Root] disappears from the source Tree but remains for the target tree. All partitions under the source become partitions under [Root] of the target. In the illustration just shown, the tree will look like the one shown here:

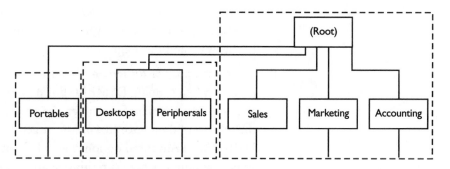

Notice that the partitions of the source tree are now partitions under CORP's [Root]. CORP's original partition structure did not change; the new partitions were simply added under it.

Running **DSMERGE**

Before you run the DSMERGE utility, there are several prerequisites that must be met, and several steps that must be followed in order to ensure a successful merge. We will start with the prerequisites.

■ *No alias or leaf objects can exist at the [Root] level of the source tree.* Using NWAdmin, check the [Root] level of the source tree, and either move these objects to a container below [Root] or delete them.

■ *There can be no duplicate container names at the [Root] level of the source and target trees.* The O=(*organization*) must be unique on each tree, and since the two trees will be merged at the [Root] level, all container names at that level must be unique. If duplicate names exist, either rename the containers with duplicate names or move the containers' objects to a different container and delete the containers.

■ *There can be no active connections on either tree.* You should check the MONITOR screen on all servers and ensure there are no active connections.

■ *Both trees must be running the same version of NDS.* If they are not, upgrade NDS on all servers running the lower version that have replicas of [Root] (ideally you should upgrade NDS on all servers in the tree).

■ *All servers with a replica of [Root] must be available during the merge operation.* Check to ensure every server in the Tree with a replica of [Root] is up and running.

■ *The schema must be the same on both trees.* You will get an error message when running DSMERGE if they are not. Use DSREPAIR to import the schema of the target tree on the source, then import the schema of the source tree on the target tree. Do this by using DSREPAIR | Advanced options menu | Global schema options | Import remote schema. Run this operation from the servers that have the master replica of [Root] on both trees.

These are prerequisites steps for running DSMERGE. Some additional steps that are strongly recommended by Novell are as follows:

1. *Run DSREPAIR | Report synchronization status and ensure there are no errors.* Resolve any errors that you find.

2. *Run DSREPAIR | Time Synchronization and ensure time is in sync for both trees.* Novell recommends making the servers in the source tree reference the servers in the target tree for time.

3. *Rebuild the operational schema on the master replica on both trees.* Run DSREPAIR | Advanced options menu | Repair local DS database | and set the Rebuild Operational Schema to Yes.

Once the prerequisites are met, you can begin the merge process.

1. *Load DSMERGE.* The DSMERGE utility runs from a NetWare server and is loaded from the NetWare console prompt by typing **load dsmerge**. The DSMERGE screen is shown here:

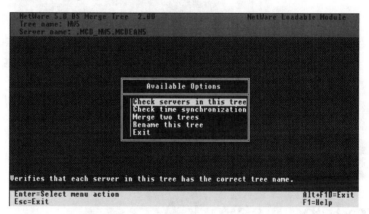

2. *Ensure that all servers are up.* Use the Check Servers in This Tree option from the main DSMERGE screen. This will return the status of all the servers, and they should all be UP. Possible values include UP, Error *<code>*, Unknown, and Wrong Tree.

3. *Check time synchronization to ensure that all servers in the Tree are synchronized.* Choose the Check Time Synchronization option from the main DSMERGE screen. The In Sync value for all servers should be Yes.

4. *Run the DSMERGE Operation.* From the server that contains the master replica of the source tree, choose the Merge Two Trees option. This screen is shown here:

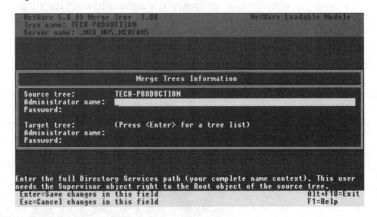

Enter the Administrator's name (including context), and the password; then choose the target tree, and enter the information for the administrator. Once this is done, press F10 to perform the operation.

CERTIFICATION OBJECTIVE 36.05

Providing Network Access

There are several tasks an administrator must complete in order to finalize an NDS Tree project and provide network access. These tasks include items such as security, creating miscellaneous objects required for ease of use, enabling travelling user access, and many more. There are two basic types of access to address when setting up a NetWare environment: file system access and NDS access. *File system access* is the rights that users have to the files that physically reside on the volumes of the servers. *NDS access rights* are the rights that objects (such as user accounts) have to other objects (such as printers, and login script profiles). Let's start with file system rights.

File System Rights

File system concepts have not changed considerably since NetWare 3.*x*, though there have been some attributes added, and the NetWare Administrator utility can now be used to administer file system rights. Rights still flow down from directories to subdirectories based upon inheritance filters; rights assigned to a directory will flow down to any subdirectories under that directory unless the inheritance filter is modified.

File system rights differ from NDS rights. Although there are similarities, such as the inheritance of rights, NDS rights do not translate to file system rights. The exception to this rule is the NDS Supervisor object right to a file server; if you assign a user Supervisor rights to a server, they will automatically get Supervisor access to all volumes on the server.

NDS Rights

Security is a key concern when designing trees. There are several steps involved in securing an NDS tree, and they range from basic setup to advanced inheritance of rights. Let's take a look at the procedures for establishing basic security on an NDS tree.

Inheritance

Much like file systems, rights assigned to a top-level container will flow down to children of that container unless the inheritance filter is modified. An administrator should be extremely careful not to assign rights any higher on the tree than is required.

Groups Versus Containers

There are two basic methods for assigning object rights to multiple users. The first method is to assign these rights by container. Assigning access rights for an NDS object to a container will give those rights to any users in that container. This scenario works well for small workgroups or situations in which users from a single container will be the only ones accessing a particular resource. The second method is to use groups, which works well with larger workgroups and scenarios in which users from multiple containers need access to a single resource.

Establishing an Administration Strategy

There are two basic methods for assigning administrative privileges. The first is to use to the NetWare defaults of the Admin account. This method will suffice for small networks that have centralized administration, but is not very secure for environments that have distributed administration. For these environments, you should use container administrators, which involves creating an account that has Supervisor object rights to a single container. This allows workgroup administrators to handle their own administration without compromising security on the other containers.

The first major step in completing the tree is to add the lower levels of the NDS tree. When an administrator starts building out the tree, the planning stages such as naming standards come into play. An administrator must create any required objects such as user accounts, print queues, printers, and print servers.

CERTIFICATION SUMMARY

In this section, we have covered the basic concepts behind installing and administering NDS in a NetWare environment. Before an administrator begins any NDS implementations, they must carefully plan and design the NDS tree from the top down, then address issues such as partition and replica management, as well as time synchronization. The administrator must choose an implementation plan, and plan for future growth and merging of the NDS trees, and plan for client access to the file servers in the tree. Rolling out NDS to a large corporation is a big task, but careful planning can keep the contingencies to a minimum.

✓ TWO-MINUTE DRILL

- ❑ The first step in implementing NetWare is to design and create the NDS Tree.

- ❑ Existing infrastructure is very important to identify. If all locations of an organization are connected over WAN links, it will affect the implementation approach you use.

- ❑ Several factors to use in a Novell implementation are as follows: define the solution, create an implementation schedule, and calculate the costs.

- ❑ There are four models most commonly used to design a tree: the Administrative model, the Geographical model, the Divisions model, and the Hybrid model.

- ❑ The Administrative model is ideal for companies with clearly established administrative workgroups. For this model, start by identifying workgroups that will be used as organizational units for the company.

- ❑ The Geographical model is ideal for companies with multiple locations where the geographical location is used to establish the workgroups of the company.

- ❑ If a company organizes its workgroups by the type of project they are working on, the divisions model is probably the one to use.

- ❑ In a company where the boundaries separating workgroups are mixed, a combination of any of the other three models can be used to make up a hybrid model.

- ❑ *Partitioning* is the process of dividing the NDS database into smaller pieces; partitions are distinct units of NDS data.

- ❑ The Departmental implementation is designed to allow multiple Trees that will be merged at a later date.

- ❑ The Divisional implementation takes the Departmental method a step further. In this type of implementation, there is still no unified organizational conversion to NDS, but different divisions as a whole move to NetWare at the same time.

❑ From a planning standpoint, the Organizational implementation approach is larger in scale than Departmental and Divisional implementations. It assumes the tree will be designed and installed for the entire organization at the same time, and will require much more up-front planning than the other two methods.

❑ Bindery emulation can cause problems if you have two user accounts or two printers with the same name in different containers.

SELF TEST

The Self-Test questions will help you measure your understanding of the material presented in this chapter. Read all the choices carefully, as there may be more than one correct answer. Select all correct answers for each question.

1. In a company that has three regional offices, and each office is a separate entity, which model would be suited for the design of the NDS Tree?

   A. Administrative model

   B. Geographical model

   C. Divisions model

   D. Hybrid model

2. How many containers can be set for a bindery context?

   A. 5

   B. 15

   C. 16

   D. 25

3. If you assign Supervisor rights to a Server object in a tree for a user account, what rights will the user account have to the file system?

   A. None

   B. Supervisor

   C. It will be dependent upon what rights the user account has been explicitly assigned.

4. What application is used in NetWare to manage partitions?

   A. Netware Administrator

   B. NDS Manager

   C. INSTALL.NLM

   D. DSREPAIR.NLM

5. What is the prerequisite to move a container of an NDS tree?

   A. There are no requirements; using Netware Administrator you can simply move the container.

   B. The container must be the top level of a partition.

   C. A container cannot be moved.

   D. The container must be exported then imported to move it.

6. By default, what types of [Root] replicas of the NDS tree will the third and fourth servers installed into the tree get?

   A. They will both get read/write.

   B. They will both get read-only.

   C. The third server will get a read/write; the fourth server will get none.

   D. The third server will get a read-only; the fourth server will get none.

7. What time synchronization model would be suited to a small network with two servers and no external time sources?

A. Single reference

B. Multiple primary

C. External reference

D. All secondary

8. What is the minimum number of primary servers needed to configure your network with primary and secondary servers?

A. One

B. Two

C. Three

D. Five

9. What types of servers participate in voting on the network?

A. Single reference

B. Primary

C. Reference

D. Secondary

10. By default, what file is used to configure TIMESYNC settings on a Novell server?

A. SYS:ETC\TIMESYNC.CFG

B. SYS:SYSTEM\TIMESYNC.CFG

C. SYS:SYSTEM\TIME.CFG

D. SYS:ETC\TIME.CFG

11. What file is used to configure NTP settings on a Novell server?

A. SYS:ETC\NTP.CFG

B. SYS:SYSTEM\NTP.CFG

C. SYS:SYSTEM\TIMESYNC.CFG

D. SYS:ETC\TIMESYNC.CFG

12. What happens to the partitions of the source tree when two trees are merged?

A. The partitions become a single partition under [Root] of the target.

B. The partitions become a single partition under a specified parent partition.

C. The partitions keep their structure and become partitions under [Root] of the target.

D. The partitions cannot be attached to the target. They must be merged into [Root] on the source tree before the tree is merged with the target.

13. Leaf objects at the [Root] of the source tree will be added to the [Root] of the target tree when the trees are merged.

A. True

B. False

14. How are Netware Services for Macintosh installed?

A. From a PC client workstation

B. From the server console using INSTALL

C. From a Mac client workstation

D. From the server console using MONITOR

15. What line below does not belong in the NET.CFG file, under the NetWare DOS Requester section?

A. Preferred Tree = CORP

B. Name Context = "ou=users.ou=corp"

C. Bind ipx to NE2000

D. First Network Drive = F

Part V

NetWare Service and Support

37

Network
Troubleshooting

CERTIFICATION OBJECTIVES

37.01   Preventing Problems

37.02   Troubleshooting the Network

37.03   Reference Sources

I n this chapter, we will explore the steps you can take to prevent problems from occurring on your network. We'll discuss what steps to take when problems do occur and how to use research tools to quickly resolve problems and get your network up and running again as quickly as possible.

CERTIFICATION OBJECTIVE 37.01

Preventing Problems

Preventing problems is crucial to a successful, stable network environment for your customers, and should be your number one goal as a NetWare administrator. Although there are many different types of problems, and you cannot anticipate each one, most of the problems you will encounter on a network fall into one of four basic categories:

1. Problems in the physical environment

2. Electrical problems

3. Viruses

4. Security problems

We will cover these in the next four sections.

Problems in the Physical Environment

The computer's physical environment will either help to ensure its long life or its slow demise. Temperature, humidity, and air quality all play an important part in the equation, and any one of them can make or break a system. Temperature is the single most important consideration. The difference between the ambient temperature (the temperature of the room the computer is sitting in) and the temperature inside the computer can be as much as 40 degrees or more. All electrical devices generate heat while under power, and computers and their components are no exception. Today's Pentium II processors with the huge built-in heat sink must be kept cool.

One of the symptoms of a computer not having adequate ventilation is *chip creep*, wherein chips in the computer will creep up out of their socket and lose contact. This can show up as any number of problems, such as the system hanging for no apparent reason after running for a while. Check the CPU and power supply fans on a regular basis for correct operation and clogged ventilation slots. Make sure the holes in the case are cleaned out and the room temperature is kept consistent.

on the **Job**

One reason for keeping computers on all the time is to maintain a consistent temperature inside the computer. This will reduce thermal stress on the components.

Air quality and humidity also play a role in ensuring a healthy computer environment. Dust and dirt in the air will collect over time on all of the components inside the computer. The fan blades inside the computer and power supply will collect dust and dirt, thus reducing the volume of airflow. The ventilation slots in the computer case will clog with dust, further reducing air flow, and dirt will collect on the surface of the electrical components, reducing heat transfer from the component surface to the air surrounding the component. Humidity should be kept at a comfortable level: if it's too dry, the likelihood of static electricity increases; if it's too moist, the chance for condensation occurring inside the computer increases. Static electricity can invisibly destroy an IC chip, and condensation will promote corrosion on electrical contacts inside the computer.

on the **Job**

After receiving new equipment, allow the equipment to sit a few hours to adjust to room temperature before turning it on. This will reduce the thermal stress on the equipment and the chance of condensation building up inside the equipment.

Electrical Problems

Environmental problems can slowly destroy a computer; electrical problems can destroy a $50,000 dollar server in less then a second. Maintaining a safe electrical environment is mandatory.

Electrical problems fall into four basic categories: static electricity, crosstalk, line noise, and transients.

Static Electricity

Static electricity is an invisible, sometimes silent computer killer. It flourishes in a low humidity environment, and its effects can be devastating to computer equipment. It is not the actual static electricity that destroys components, but the discharge of the static charge to a component. It is also known as *Electro-Static Discharge (ESD)* and can be felt only above 3,000 volts, although it only takes about 20 volts to destroy the component. I imagine you have, at some time in your life, rubbed your shoes against a carpeted floor and "shocked" someone when you touched them afterwards. When you did this, you were merely discharging the 3,000 + volts of static electricity that had built up in your body. Keeping this in mind, can you imagine what that shock could do to an IC chip? I don't have to tell you that it will pretty much blow its internals into the next century. To prevent this from happening, always ground yourself by using an ESD wrist strap while working on equipment (except for monitors!) and ensure that all of your equipment is grounded properly. Always keep spare components in the antistatic packaging they come in, and handle components without touching the metal parts. Try to avoid placing equipment on or around carpeted floors. However, if the carpet cannot be avoided, use antistatic mats or antistatic spray on the carpet. Keeping the room's humidity in check will also cut down on the chance of ESD striking your equipment.

Crosstalk

Crosstalk is when two separate wires (such as LAN cables, serial cables, or power cords) interfere with each other's magnetic fields. This can surface, for example, as garbled data over a serial printer or excessive errors on a LAN segment. The best defense against crosstalk is to ensure that proper grade cable and cords are used and that the cables and cords are not piled on top of each other. Keeping the cabling neat and orderly not only prevents crosstalk, it also makes it easier to find and service cables.

Line Noise

Line noise is low in both voltage and current. Its cause can be traced to another device such as a microwave oven, fluorescent light ballast, or an electric motor used by an elevator. Line noise may surface as a pattern of disturbance on the network that occurs only during certain times of the day. For example, Mary is complaining that often when she attempts to log in after her lunch break, it takes a long time and sometimes she has to keep retrying until the server accepts her log in info. It turns out that her network drop runs right behind the microwave on the other side of the wall and just when Mary logs in after lunch, somebody is using the microwave to heat up their lunch. The best solution to eliminate line noise is to route LAN cables away from all other electrical devices including motors, fluorescent lights, and microwave ovens, and to make sure all electrical equipment is grounded properly.

on the
Ü o b

Line noise can be described as being either RFI (Radio Frequency Interference), which is caused by devices that transmit RF, such as radio transmitters and microwave ovens, or EMI (Electromagnetic Interference), which can be caused by lights and motors.

Transients

Transients are momentary power line disturbances. The most common types are spikes and brownouts. A spike is a sudden increase in the voltage that may last only a few milliseconds or a second or two. Lightning strikes or blackouts occurring down the power line from your receptacle may cause spikes. A brownout is when the line voltage drops below the normal 115-120 volts. Brownouts may be caused by overloaded circuits or when demand on the power company is too high. Brownouts can last much longer than a few seconds and steps should be taken to protect your computers from them. A surge suppressor, which uses suppressor diodes, will protect your equipment from spikes. However, the best prevention for both spikes and brownouts is to install a UPS (Interruptible Power Supply) rated to support your power requirements for at least 15 minutes. The longer the UPS can supply the power, the better.

Surge suppresser devices are also available for modem phone lines, LAN cables, and serial lines. All of these products can help prevent power problems.

Viruses

Viruses have been around causing havoc on LANs since the beginning. What better way to transmit a virus to a bunch of PCs than on a network? There are two types of viruses: those that do nothing but aggravate a user or administrator with stupid messages or the like, and data-destroying viruses. Both types of viruses disrupt the normal flow of data processing and should be eradicated and prevented from attacking your system. Viruses usually attach themselves to executable code such as .EXE, .COM, .NLM, .DLL, and .OVL files. These files can enter your system by users downloading the infected file from a Web site or bulletin board, or users bringing in disks given to them by friends. The virus is activated when the infected program is loaded into memory and executed. Some of the newer viruses out there are Word macro viruses. Word macro files are really just VBA (Visual Basic for Applications) script files and, hence, provide easy transport into a workstation. They are simple to write and deploy. On the other hand, .NLM and the Java .class type viruses are much harder to program and deploy. Nevertheless, .NLM and .class viruses do exist and need to be prevented. The following is a list of some actions you, as administrator, can take to reduce the likelihood of having your server or workstations infected:

- Back up your server(s) on a regular basis.

- Routinely scan your server(s) and workstations for viruses using a third-party product.

- Flag all executable files in the PUBLIC and LOGIN directories as READ and FILE SCAN only.

- Scan all software for viruses before installing. This should include commercial software, even though infection from commercial software is extremely rare.

- Discourage or prohibit users from downloading software from the Internet and/or bulletin board systems, or install special virus scanning software on your communication points of entry (that is, your firewall and e-mail gateway).

Security

There are four types of threats to security on a network:

- **Interruption**   The network becomes inaccessible to the users because an employee trips over a poorly placed network cable, which is ripped out of a server or hub.

- **Destruction**   Destruction of data or hardware can be caused by a disgruntled employee or by a virus that has found its way into your system.

- **Corruption**   Data stored on the server becomes corrupted and unusable because of a hard disk crash.

- **Disclosure**   Data that should be inaccessible (such as payroll data) is downloaded from the server and posted in a public access area.

Some of these security threats are easier to manage than others. However, if the proper steps are taken, the risks can be minimized as follows:

- Limit log ins to one session.

- Enforce periodic password changes.

- Force unique passwords.

- Limit log ins for users so that users can log in only from one or a group of workstation addresses or a LAN segment.

- Assign file and directory access rights.

- Limit log in times to business hours.

- Turn off modems and Internet access after business hours.

- Employ servers with redundant power supplies.

- Use either disk mirroring or RAID disk systems.

- Keep the servers and cable plant equipment behind locked doors with controlled access.

CERTIFICATION OBJECTIVE 37.02

Troubleshooting the Network

Even when all possible steps have been taken to prevent problems from occurring on the network, problems can and will occur. Knowing how to tackle these problems with a sound troubleshooting model will not only save valuable time in fixing the problem, but will also aid in achieving your goals of minimal down time.

The Novell Troubleshooting Model

Novell has defined a five-step troubleshooting model that will aid in resolving problems and restoring your network to service in a timely matter:

1. **Try a quick fix/gather basic information.** Check the obvious first. Has the client's network cable come out of the NIC? Is the printer online? Did the user check the toner cartridge? Does the problem appear only on one workstation, a few, or all of them? What is it the user is doing when the problem occurs? These are the first steps in the troubleshooting model. It may seem obvious, but I cannot count the number of times a printer or network cable has worked loose somehow and was the problem. If it turns out not to be so obvious, ask questions. Users and customers can provide good clues as to what the problem may or may not be. Ask the user to duplicate the problem, if possible. Sometimes it can just be a case of the user not knowing how the particular application or resource on the network works. Build a good rapport with your users; they can make your troubleshooting life easier.

2. **Develop a plan to isolate the problem.** If your quick fix attempts, such as unloading and reloading PSERVER.NLM in an effort to "unfreeze" a stuck print server, fail to fix the problem, you will need to develop hypotheses about the problem and prioritize them. You will have to weigh the probability of the solution working and the

time it will take to try it. If a possible solution has only a 10 percent chance of working, but will take only five minutes to try, you may want to try that first rather than a solution that has a 70 percent chance of correcting the problem but will take two hours to try. The amount of time the network is down is inversely proportional to the job life of an administrator.

3. **Execute the plan**.   Once you have developed hypotheses concerning the problem, start applying the solutions one at a time until the problem is resolved. Often, inexperienced administrators will take the shotgun approach—instead of taking a logical, step-by-step approach, they fire both barrels at the problem, hoping that changing everything at once will correct the problem. This approach has a very serious flaw in it. While it may fix the problem, it in no way helps to prevent the problem from recurring, and the solution remains undocumented.

4. **Ensure user satisfaction.**   Once the problem has been solved, have the user or your customer try it out. Ask the user if the problem is solved and, if so, explain what you found and what you did to correct the problem. If not, return to Step 1. Start at the beginning and give it another try. Was something overlooked the first time? Have the symptoms changed? Having your customer or boss satisfied is your number one goal, and letting them in on what went wrong, and what was done to correct it, makes for good customer relationships.

5. **Document the solution and take steps to avoid or prepare for recurrence.**   The last, and one of the most important steps, is documenting what was done to solve the problem. In your system logbook, write a good clear description of the problem and the exact sequence of steps taken to resolve it. Include the date, time of day, the equipment involved, and, of course, what it was that fixed the problem. One of the biggest mistakes made by administrators of all skill levels is to neglect the logbook. How many times have you thought to yourself, "I'll write it down when I get a chance." For many administrators, they never get that chance until whatever it was they were going to write down, is forgotten. Rest assured, if you don't document the problem, it will come back and haunt you.

Diagnostic Tools

The trick to becoming a master troubleshooter is to know how to use tools to quickly isolate the problem to as few components as possible. For example, when working with client workstation or server connection problems, the diagnostic program PING.EXE, which is used on clients, and PING.NLM, which is used on servers, can be used to see if TCP/IP is functioning correctly. Both versions of PING work by sending a UDP packet to another host, which in turn returns a response to the sending host. If a ping to another node is successful, you can assume TCP/IP is configured correctly.

There is an equivalent tool for IPX called IPXPING.NLM. This tool works just like PING.NLM, except it uses an IPX packet. Another useful tool is COMCHECK.EXE, which can be used on both client workstations and servers, and will show what stations are communicating. In order to run COMCHECK.EXE on a server, the server must be brought down, and then COMCHECK.EXE is run from DOS with either the VLM or NETX drivers loaded.

Another useful tool for communication problems is LANalyzer by Novell. LANalyzer is a software-based protocol analyzer that requires nothing but an ordinary PC and a supported NIC card. LANalyzer works by putting the NIC card into promiscuous mode that allows the NIC card to receive all packets, not just the packets directly addressed to it. You can configure LANalyzer to filter out packets by station, type, and a host of others, which will allow you to see exactly what is occurring on the cable. There are also other tools on the market, some free and some very expensive, that can help pinpoint problems on your network. Spend time learning the various tools at your disposal; it will be time well spent.

CERTIFICATION OBJECTIVE 37.03

Reference Sources

As any administrator can attest to, as the number of devices on the network increases, the problems increase logarithmically. It is impossible to know everything about every piece of equipment or software in a typical network today. Realizing this, Novell stresses three troubleshooting resources, which we will discuss next.

The Support Connection CD

Novell publishes the *Support Connection CD*, which contains all of the Technical Information Documents (TIDs) Novell has published and made available over the years, in the form of files, patches, and product documentation. The Support Connection CD uses a browser-type interface as a front end to the wealth of information found inside (see Figure 37-1).

The home page of the Support Connection CD organizes the contents into four main categories: What's New, Product Documentation, Product Support, and Program Information. Table 37-1 lists the contents under each section.

You will become a faster troubleshooter if you familiarize yourself with the contents under each heading. Also, the service and support test contains questions about finding certain types of information on the Support Connection CD. The most useful areas on the CD for you, as an administrator, are the Files (patches), TIDs, and Hot Issues. Learn and know these locations because the exam will contain a question or two about them.

FIGURE 37-1

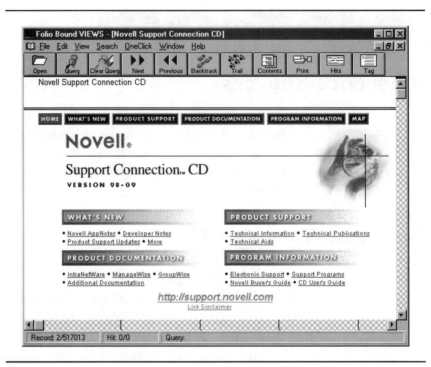

FIGURE 37-1

Novell's Support
Connection CD

NetWire on CompuServe

In the early days of NetWare, the World Wide Web did not exist. Novell
was faced with a dilemma concerning the delivery of patches and technical
information to its customer base. Knowing that maintaining a BBS
(Bulletin Board System) would be adequate in the beginning, Novell
quickly learned that a key to success with customer support, hence success
in sales, was to make their technical support information and files globally
available. Novell turned to CompuServe to provide a *Forum* where
customers could locate information, files, patches, and share questions and
answers with other NetWare users. CompuServe was by far the largest
business/consumer, computer-accessed information service with over seven
IBM 370 mainframe computers and POP (point of presence) connections
worldwide. Even if CompuServe did not provide a POP within a local

TABLE 37-1	What's New	Product Support	Product Documentation	Program Information
	Novell AppNotes	Tech Info	intraNetWare	Electronic Support
Contents of Novell's Support Connection CD	DeveloperNotes	TIDs	ManageWise	Electronic Incident
	Product Support Updates	Top 100 TIDs	GroupWise	NSC CD
	Binders and Sleeves	Hot Issues	Additional Documentation	Support Forums
	Files			Fax Response
	Novell Labs			Support Programs
	Technical Publications			Premium Service
	Novell AppNote			Preferred Service
	Novell DevNotes			Advanced Technical Training
	NPD Bullets			Novell Telephone Support
	GroupWare Professional Guide			Novell Buyer's Guide
	Tech Aids			CD User's Guide

calling area, it could and still can be accessed from Tymnet, Sprint Net, and other third-party networks, and now, of course, via the Internet as well.

While Novell still maintains a Forum on CompuServe, most of the content, except for the message boards, has been moved to Novell's Web site.

on the
job

In order to access the Novell forum on CompuServe, you must first set up a CompuServe account. For information on setting up an account, point your browser to http://www.compuserve.com.

Once you have established a CompuServe account and have the CompuServe client software installed, you will be able to access the Novell Forum on CompuServe. After logging in to CompuServe type **NetWire** in the Page scroll-down list box and click the *Go* button. From the Novell Forum Table of Contents page (see Figure 37-2) you can navigate to the different available sections.

Click the Support Forums button on the right-hand side of the screen to bring up the Forum menu. Select Message Boards by clicking on the Message Board button to display the message categories available for

FIGURE 37-2

Novell CompuServe Forum

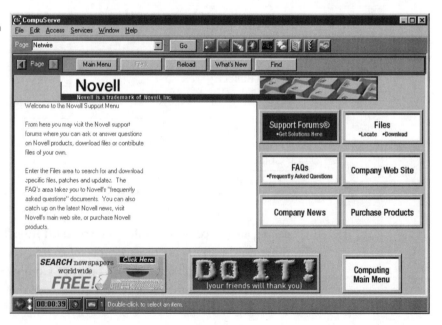

reading and posting (see Figure 37-3). From here, you can post questions to the NetWire sysops, and read other users questions and answers. This is an excellent medium for exchanging ideas and experiences with other NetWare users.

Novell's Web Site

Novell's Web site is also an excellent source of information for troubleshooting. This is the next best thing to sliced bread for a NetWare administrator. Here you access all of the latest TIDs, Hot Issues, and Files (patches) that Novell has made available for their product line. While the Support Connection CD is current when it is issued each month, some new patch or TID might get posted the day after the CD is stamped. Another

---

FIGURE 37-3

Message categories available on Novell CompuServe Forum

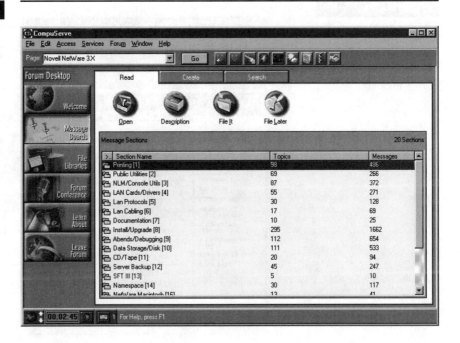

---

benefit of Novell's Web site is that access to it is free! The screenshot in Figure 37-4 is the home page of **http://www.novell.com**.

However, as an administrator troubleshooting a problem, **http://support.novell.com** (shown in Figure 37-5) is where you want to start your search for a solution.

Novell also maintains an ftp site at **ftp.novell.com**, but it appears that Novell is moving the content from the ftp site over to the Web site at this time.

exam
ⓌⒶⓉⒸⒽ

Remember these two Web sites. The exam will most likely have a question or two concerning which Web site you should visit to retrieve a patch or get product information.

FIGURE 37-4

www.novell.com
home page

FIGURE 37-5

support.novell.com home page

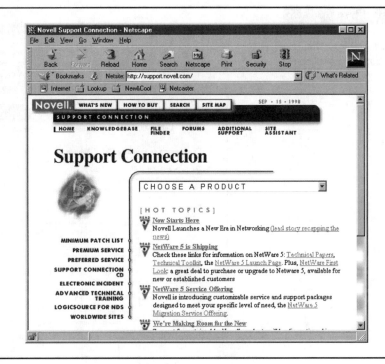

From the **http://support.novell.com** page, you can access the Minimum Patch List, Premium Service, Preferred Service, Support Connection CD, Electronic Incident, Advanced Technical Trainning, Logicsource for NDS, and the Worldwide Sites. In about the middle of the page, you will see a drop-down list box. Using this list box, you can go directly to a particular product Knowledgebase search page. From here you can search on key words for TIDs pertainning to the product category. Figure 37-6 shows a sample TID.

You will need to know this Web site like the back of your hand. Just about anything concerning troubleshooting Novell's products can be found here, and you will be spending most of your troubleshooting time here.

FIGURE 37-6

Sample TID from the
http//support.novell.com
page

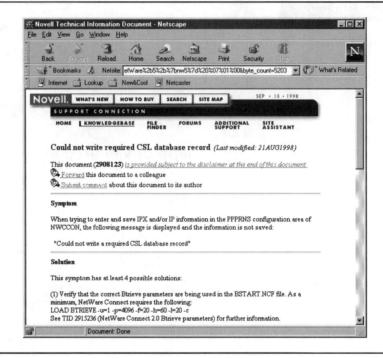

The Support Source

What was once the Microhouse Technical Library is now part of the
Support Source product from Microhouse International. The *Support
Source* is a combination CD-ROM/Web-based product that not only serves
as the front end to the Microhouse Technical Library, but also allows
additional modules to be purchased and integrated into the search engine.

The Support Source indexes thousands of technical documents, spec
sheets, white papers, product reviews, and other troubleshooting and service
information on virtually all PC products. Figure 37-7 is a screenshot of the
main page of Support Source with all of the available modules installed.

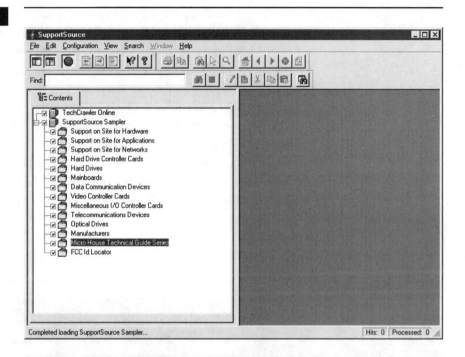

FIGURE 37-7

Main page of
Support Source

FROM THE CLASSROOM

The Value of Using Online Support Resources

Getting to know what is on the Support Connection CD, Support Source CD, and Online Documentation (formerly DynaText) will save you a lot of time and money. Knowing how to navigate these resources efficiently will get you answers quickly. Although the information on a CD will not be as current as what's on a Web site or as immediate as calling a vendor help desk, it will give you a starting point. An additional advantage of using the CD-based resources, is that you do not need to rely on a network or an Internet connection, which is very handy when troubleshooting a network or internetworking connectivity problem! Finally, most of the questions handled by Novell's Help Desk can be answered directly from Online Documentation and the Support Connection CD. Imagine the money you can save if you can narrow questions down after first utilizing CD-based resources.

—By Dan Cheung, CNI, MCNE, MCT

There are two basic ways a search or query can be formed. The first method is to use the *Query Assistant*. This is the same interface as used in the old Microhouse Technical Library. First, select the information category you want to search. In Figure 37-7, all content is selected. To deselect a particular category, simply click the check box to the left of the category. Next, start the Query Assistant by clicking on the binoculars icon in the toolbar located on the bottom row, furthest right. The Query Assistant screen will appear as shown in Figure 37-8.

From the tabs located on the top of the dialog box, choose the type of item you wish to search for. In Figure 37-8, I have chosen Data Communication Devices. From here, you can further narrow the query.

FIGURE 37-8

Support Source Query
Assistant

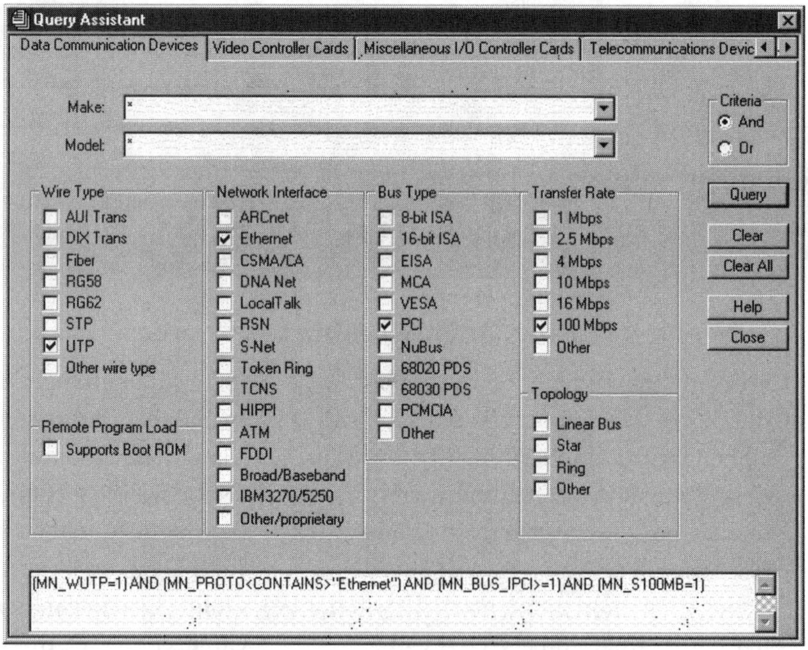

I have decided to search for information on an Ethernet adapter that uses UTP wiring, that is a PCI bus type, and that is 100Mbps in speed. Next, I click the Query button that starts the search engine. The search engine will then contact the Support Source Web site to perform the search for the information requested, and my results are returned, in order of relevance, in the left-hand pane as shown in Figure 37-9.

From the results returned in the left-hand pane, I double-click the FAST ETHERLINK XL. The search engine will then go out to the Support Source Web site and retrieve the information that is subsequently displayed on the right-hand pane.

FIGURE 37-9

Query results in Support
Source Query Assistant

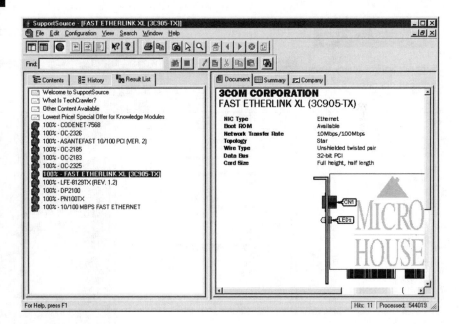

The other way to construct a query is by hand. To do this, you simply select the category(s) and/or module(s) you would like to search from in the contents pane on the left and type your query into the Find list box located below the toolbar on the top left of the screen. You can construct your query using Boolean operators, such as AND and OR. In Figure 37-10, I have set up a query to search the category of motherboards that contain ASUS and Pentium in the description.

To execute this query, I would click the binocular with the lighting bolt through it located to the immediate left of the Find list box. The results are returned just as in the first method; matches are placed in the left pane by order of relevance. Then, to retrieve information, I simply double-click the item.

on the **job**

A demo version of Support Source can be downloaded from Microhouse's Web site at http://www.Microhouse.com.

FIGURE 37-10

Support Source query using
Boolean operators

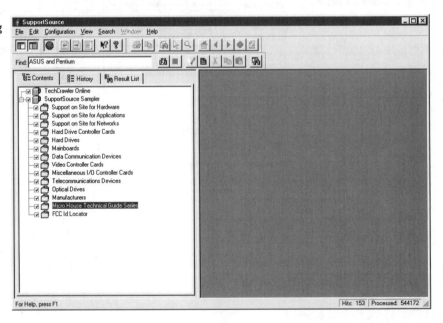

CERTIFICATION SUMMARY

In this chapter, we have covered the fundamental troubleshooting methods, including Novell's five-step troubleshooting model and static protection measures. We discussed the importance of documenting problems and resolutions, and explored how to use research tools to aid in troubleshooting.

Some things to look out for on the test include knowing which research tool to use to identify an unknown NIC card, motherboard, or cable type, and which tool(s) can be used to locate files and patches. The performance portions of the Service & Support test involve using the Support Connection CD from Novell and the Support Source product from Microhouse. You will be presented with questions such as "What is the TID number for using SBACKUP with a HP5000 tape drive?" You will have to decide which tool to use and then actually use the product during the test.

TWO-MINUTE DRILL

- ❑ Most network problems fall into one of four basic categories: problems in the physical environment, electrical problems, viruses, and security problems

- ❑ The computer's physical environment will either help to ensure its long life or its slow demise. Temperature is the single most important consideration in a computer's physical environment. Air quality and humidity also play a role in ensuring a healthy computer environment.

- ❑ Electrical problems fall into four basic categories: static electricity, crosstalk, line noise, and transients.

- ❑ The Administrator can take the following actions to prevent virus infection: Back up server(s) on a regular basis; routinely scan server(s) and workstations for viruses; flag all executable files in the PUBLIC and LOGIN directories as READ and FILE SCAN only; scan all software for viruses before installing; and discourage users from downloading software from the Internet; or install special virus scanning software on communication points of entry.

- ❑ There are four types of threats to security on a network: Interruption, Destruction, Corruption, and Disclosure.

- ❑ The Administrator can minimize security risks by taking the following steps: Limit logins to one session; enforce periodic

❑   password changes; force unique passwords; limit log ins for users; assign file and directory access rights; limit login times to business hours; turn off modems and Internet access after business hours; employ servers with redundant power supplies; use either disk mirroring or RAID disk systems; maintain controlled access to servers and cable plant equipment.

❑   The steps in Novell's five-step troubleshooting model include (in order): Try a quick fix/gather basic information; develop a plan to isolate the problem, execute the plan; ensure user satisfaction; and document the solution, taking steps to avoid or prepare for recurrence.

❑   The trick to becoming a master troubleshooter is to know how to use tools to quickly isolate the problem to as few components as possible.

❑   Novell publishes the *Support Connection CD*, which contains all of the Technical Information Documents (TIDs) Novell has published and made available over the years in the form of files, patches, and product documentation.

❑   Novell turned to CompuServe to provide the NetWire *Forum* where customers could locate information, files, patches, and share questions and answers with other NetWare users. Most of the content, except for the message boards, has been moved from the CompuServe forum to Novell's Web site.

❑   Novell's Web site is also an excellent source of information for troubleshooting. Here you access all of the latest TIDs, hot issues, and files (patches) that Novell has made available for their product line. Another benefit of Novell's Web site is that access to it is free! Novell also maintains an ftp site at **ftp.novell.com**, but it appears that Novell is moving the content from the ftp site over to the Web site at this time.

❑   The Support Source product from Microhouse International was once the Microhouse Technical Library. The Support Source is a combination CD-ROM / Web-based product that not only serves as the front end to the Microhouse Technical Library, but also allows additional modules to be purchased and integrated into the search engine. The Support Source indexes thousands of technical documents, spec sheets, white papers, product reviews, and other troubleshooting and service information on virtually all PC products.

SELF TEST

The following Self-Test questions will help you measure your understanding of the material presented in this chapter. Read all the choices carefully, as there may be more than one correct answer. Choose all correct answers for each question.

1. Which of the following resources could you use to locate patches for NetWare 4.11? (Select two.)

    A. Novell's Web site

    B. The Norton Utilities

    C. Novell's Support Connection CD

    D. Ontrack Data Recovery for NetWare

2. For what types of problems would you use the Novell Support Connection CD? (Select two.)

    A. You need an old software patch that was written months ago.

    B. You want to see the physical layout of a popular network board.

    C. You need to find the jumper settings on a specific ASUS system board.

    D. You need to access an application note about a NetWare 3.12 printing problem.

    E. You need the latest version of CLIB.NLM.

3. You want to ask a Novell sysop a question concerning print queues in NetWare. Which tool will allow you to do this?

    A. Novell's Support Connection CD

    B. Novell's Web page

    C. NetWire on CompuServe

    D. Support Source

4. Why would you find IBM mentioned in the Novell Support Connection CD?

    A. Its internal network uses NetWare 4.11.

    B. It manufactures servers.

    C. IBM had a problem with an Intel NIC board running in a PS/2 486.

    D. It writes special interface code for Novell.

5. You are working on a user's computer that hangs intermittently. You take the following steps to troubleshoot the problem:

    > You check around to see if others on the network are having similar problems.
    > You prioritize your hypotheses about the problem.
    > You eliminate one possibility at a time until you find the answer.
    > You record the problem and your solution in the system logbook.
    > You explain the problem and its solution to the user.

    How many of these steps fall into Novell's troubleshooting model?

    A. Three of the steps

    B. Five of the steps

    C. Two of the steps

    D. Four of the steps

6. How should you always store and transport network components?

   A. In Styrofoam to eliminate static build-up

   B. In bubble wrap to cushion the components

   C. In the packaging they came in

   D. In anti-static bags

   E. None of the above

7. Which command would you use to access the Novell technical information on CompuServe?

   A. Go BigRed

   B. Go SupportCD

   C. Go NovellHelp

   D. Go Netwire

8. Which of the steps outlined below would be part of simplifying a network so that you can isolate a problem? (Select two.)

   A. Comment out the AUTOEXEC.BAT and CONFIG.SYS files.

   B. Remove cards one at a time to expose conflicts.

   C. Disconnect the cable running from the NIC to the data jack.

   D. Power off and on the server and workstations to see if they start correctly.

9. Name two services that NetWire provides:

   A. Exchanging information with other NetWare users and administrators

   B. The steps to becoming a CNE

   C. All of Novell's product manuals

   D. Technical support for various networking problems

10. Novell offers online support via which of the following two methods?

    A. FTP

    B. Telnet

    C. WWW

    D. SMTP

11. How can you find information on Novell's World Wide Web server?

    A. Click the bookshelf button

    B. Use the GO command

    C. Use the Folio Bound Views query tool

    D. Click hyperlinked text or graphics

12. From which support resource would you find the most current patch kit for NDS?

    A. NDS for NT

    B. Novell's Support Connection CD

    C. Support Source

    D. Novell's Web page

13. Which types of problems would you use Support Source for? (Select two.)

    A. Locating an AppNote about the SBACKUP program.

    B. The most current HAM driver for a hard disk. It must be the latest version.

C. You need to find a Novell document that includes the words "ODI", "NIC", and "INTERRUPT".

D. You need to identify an unknown I/O adapter card.

E. You need to know the MASTER/SLAVE settings for a hard drive.

14. Which path is the correct URL for Novell's www server?

A. http://www.netwire.com

B. http://www.netware.com

C. http://www.novellinc.com

D. http://www.novell.com

15. What is the purpose of the GO button in CompuServe?

A. To GO to a forum

B. To log in to CompuServe

C. To post a message on a forum

D. To GO to http://www.novell.com

16. How many volts of ESD energy does it take to destroy a computer component?

A. 2000

B. 20

C. 1

D. 200

17. What are some of the benefits of implementing an ESD control program? (Select three.)

A. Fewer mysterious intermittent problems

B. Less need for spare parts inventory on hand

C. Less network down time

D. Possibility of obtaining refunds for damaged merchandise

38

Installing and Troubleshooting Network Interface Cards and Cables

CERTIFICATION OBJECTIVES

38.01   Ethernet Networks

38.02   Token Ring Networks

38.03   FDDI Networks

38.04   ATM Networks

I n this chapter, we will start with a discussion of the basics of Ethernet and Token Ring networks, cabling types, bus types of adapter cards for both Ethernet and Token Ring, configuring adapter cards and troubleshooting the same. We will end the chapter with a brief discussion of the highlights of FDDI and ATM networks.

Ethernet Networks

Ethernet-based networks are by far the most popular networks in use today. What is an Ethernet network? *Ethernet* is a type of network cabling and signaling specification (OSI Model layers 1 [Physical] and 2 [Data Link]) originally developed by Bob Metcalfe while working for Xerox in the late 1970s. In 1980, Digital Equipment Corp. (DEC), Intel, and Xerox (the origin of the term *DIX*, as in DEC/Intel/Xerox) began joint promotion of this baseband, CSMA/CD computer communications network over coaxial cabling, and published the "Blue Book Standard" for Ethernet version 1. This standard was later enhanced and, in 1985, Ethernet II was released.

How Ethernet Works

Ethernet is a baseband, CSMA/CD (Carrier Sense, Multiple Access / Collision Detection) transmission protocol. *Baseband* is a type of signal transmission that allows only one frequency to carry information on the cable. On the other hand, *broadband* can support more than one signal on the cable by using frequency division techniques.

Information is transmitted in *bits* on an Ethernet network. A bit is the smallest amount of information that can be represented. A bit is represented as a single binary digit that can be either a 1 or a 0. A sequence of bits is called a *frame*. An Ethernet frame is comprised of bits and defines what each bit represents. Speeds in Ethernet networks range from 10MBps to 1 gigabits per second, and possibly faster in the future.

The sequence of events, which occur when a NIC (Network Interface Card) sends data out on the cable, is as follows. First, the NIC "listens" to the cable to see if there is another frame being transmitted by another station. If there is traffic present on the cable, the NIC listens until the cable is "clear." Once the NIC "senses" that the cable is clear to use, it transmits its frame onto the cable. This is the *Carrier Sense Multiple Access* part of the CSMA/CD protocol. Should everything go okay, the sequence starts over: first listen, and then send.

Now, if two NICs should start to transmit at the same time, a collision occurs. The two different signals from the NICs actually run into each other on the cable and corrupt both of the frames. The two NICs that transmitted the frames will detect the collision and then wait a random amount of time to attempt a re-send of their respective frames. This is the *Collision Detection* part of the CSMA/CD protocol.

FROM THE CLASSROOM

How CSMA/CD Devices "Listen" for Collisions

Network boards, currently manufactured for use in computers with Intel-based CPUs, use carrier sensing to "listen" for collisions after they have transmitted the bits making up data packets. The "sensing" is actually the NIC detecting an increase in voltage on the medium. This also triggers the collision light, found on some NICs and hubs, to flash. When the NIC detects the change in voltage, it knows to retransmit the bits using a countdown delay algorithm, which calculates a random delay before retransmitting. The physical characteristics of electrical impulses are much like the action of water ripples encountering each other. The height of the ripple when they collide is the combined height of both. In the case of electrical impulses colliding, the voltage of the collision is the combined voltages of the separate signals.

—By Dan Cheung, CNI, MCNE, MCT

Ethernet Cabling Types

The Ethernet protocol originally specified coaxial type cabling. However, as with most standards in this industry, the protocol has been expanded to include different cable types such as unshielded twisted pair (UTP) and fiber optic.

Coaxial cable is a single piece of cable comprised of "jackets" of material. The innermost material is a copper core that carries the signal. An insulator, usually made of plastic, covers this inner core. Over the insulator is a jacket made of shielding wire, and the outer case is made of an abrasion resistant material. If you were to look at a cross-section of coaxial cable, it would look like the rings of a tree.

10Base5 (Thicknet) Ethernet

The 10Base5 (Thicknet) topology uses an external transceiver to attach a device to the network (see Figure 38-1). The transceiver is attached to the (DEC/Intel/Xerox) DIX connector on the NIC via an (Attachment Universal Interface) AUI cable. The transceiver attaches to the Thicknet cable by means of a clamping device that uses "fangs" to pierce the cable to make the connection. This type of connection is referred to as a *vampire tap*. Both ends of the Thicknet cable must be terminated with a 50ohm terminator to prevent signal "bounce back," with only one end using a grounded terminator. This provides electrical safety.

Here are some guidelines to follow when implementing Thicknet in your network:

- The 5-4-3 rule must be followed.
- Segments can be no longer than 500 meters or 1,640 feet.
- The entire network cannot exceed 2,500 meters or 8,200 feet.
- Transceivers can be placed no closer than 2.5 meters or 8 feet on the Thicknet.
- AUI cables can be as short as necessary; however, they can be no longer than 50 meters from the transceiver to the NIC.

FIGURE 38-1   Ethernet 10Base5 and 10Base2 physical topology

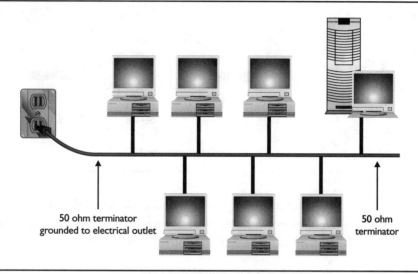

50 ohm terminator
grounded to electrical outlet

50 ohm
terminator

- The maximum number of nodes per network segment is 100. This includes all repeaters.

- One, and only one, of the ends of the cable segment must be grounded.

10Base2 (Thinnet) Ethernet

The 10Base2 (Thinnet, also cheaper net) topology is a coax cable type that uses the transceiver built into the NIC to translate the signals from the NIC to the network. 10Base2 uses either RG-58A/U or RG-58C/U coax cable, which has an impedance of 50 ohms and is terminated on both ends with a 50-ohm terminator, one of which must be grounded. The cable uses a British Naval Connector (BNC) on each end to connect to a "T" connector, which in turn is connected to the NIC or network device (see Figure 38-2).

One of the main advantages of using 10Base2 cabling in your network is the cost. RG-58 cable is cheap, plentiful, and easy to install. However, there are two severe drawbacks to using 10Base2. First, it is limited to 10MBps in

FIGURE 38-2

T connector with cables
attached

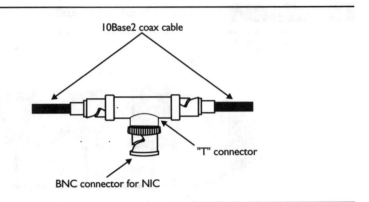

speed; secondly, when you experience a break in the cable, it takes the rest of the devices on the segment down with it. Here are some guidelines to keep in mind while working with 10Base2 cabling:

- The 5-4-3 rule must be followed.

- The minimum cable distance between clients is .5 meters or 1.5 feet.

- AUI or drop cables are not used; the network cable is connected directly to the NIC via a "T" connector.

- The maximum number of nodes per segment is 30. This includes clients and repeaters.

- The maximum length of the network cabling cannot exceed 925 meters or 3,035 feet.

- The cable segments must be terminated at each end with a 50-ohm terminator. One of these terminators must be grounded.

10BaseT / 100BaseTX (Twisted-Pair) Ethernet

Most of today's networks are wired with the 10BaseT cabling specification because of its cheaper cost, higher data rates, and greater support in the marketplace. Unlike the physical and logical linear bus topology used in 10Base2 and 10Base5 networks, 10BaseT uses a physical star, logical linear bus topology. Figure 38-3 shows the physical star topology of 10BaseT.

10BaseT uses a *UTP (unshielded twisted pair)* cable to connect devices. UTP cabling is classified into categories, the two most popular being

FIGURE 38-3   10BaseT physical star topology

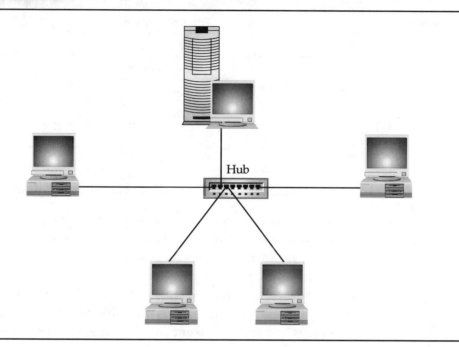

Category 3 and Category 5. Category 3 cabling is a voice/data–grade type of cable, which can be used for data communications; however, it can handle transmission speeds of only up to 10MBps. Category 5 cable, on the other hand, is a higher-grade cabling system capable of handling transmission speeds of up to 100MBps. It is used with 100BaseTX, also known as *Fast Ethernet.*

While both Category 3 and Category 5 cables contain four pairs of wire, only two of the pairs are used to carry the electrical signals. One pair is used for transmitting and the other for receiving. Both categories use a RJ45-type connector at each end of the cable to attach to the NICs, HUBs, and other devices on the network. The RJ45 connector resembles an oversized RJ11 telephone-type connector, except the RJ45 has eight separate connector "fingers," and the RJ11 has only four. Both ends of the cable are wired into the connector the same way. This is referred to as *being wired straight through.* Table 38-1 lists the pin assignments for the RJ45 connector.

Pin Number	Signal
1	Transmit Data +
2	Transmit Data −
3	Receive Data +
4	Not Used
5	Not Used
6	Receive Data −
7	Not Used
8	Not Used

TABLE 38-1

RJ45 Pin Assignments

Sometimes you may need to connect just two NICs together; like when you have one server and one client to connect together to perform some form of off-network work. Another situation may be the need to chain two hubs together and the hub does not have an "uplink" or cross-over switch on one of the ports. A cross-over cable can be used in these situations to connect the devices together. A cross-over cable simply has the transmit and receive pairs "crossed over" to one another. Table 38-2 shows the pin assignments for 10BaseT cross-over cable.

Categories 3 and 5 cable are very similar to telephone wiring and companies have been known to use existing telephone wiring to wire their network; however, this practice is discouraged. The 802.3 standard that

First RJ45 Pins	Signal	Second RJ45 Pins
1	Transmit Data +	3
2	Transmit Data −	6
3	Receive Data +	1
4	Not Used	4
5	Not Used	5
6	Receive Data −	2
7	Not Used	7
8	Not Used	8

TABLE 38-2

10BaseT Cross-Over Cable Pin Assignments

defines the type of UTP cable that can be used with 10BaseT networks calls for exactly two or more twists per inch for Category 5 cable, and three to four twists per foot for Category 3 cable. This reduces the cross-talk between the pairs of wires. Most, if not all, of the old telephone wiring found in buildings does not meet this requirement and, therefore, should not be used for data.

Some of the advantages of using 10BaseT / 100Base TX topology are

- 10BaseT is a star-based topology. This means that instead of a linear bus design, as used in 10Base2 where a single cable runs to each device, each device in a 10BaseT network is connected to a central hub with its own cable. Should a single cable fail, it is easier to pinpoint the problem and the rest of the network is not affected.

- 10BaseT allows you to set up your network one segment at a time, adding segments as your network grows. This makes 10BaseT more flexible in network design than other topologies.

- 10BaseT is one of the cheapest media types that can be used. While a little more expensive than 10Base2, the other benefits greatly outweigh the cost.

The following are some guidelines that should be followed when using the 10BaseT topology:

- The maximum length for a UTP cable segment is 100 meters or 328 feet.

- The maximum number of workstations is 1,024.

- The maximum number of nodes on a segment is 512.

- The wire used should be 22, 24, 26 American Wire Gauge (AWG) and be rated for impedance of 85 to 115 ohms at 10MHz.

100Base-T4 (Twisted-Pair) Ethernet

100Base-T4 supports an operating rate of 100MBps over Category 3, 4, or 5 UTP wiring. Unlike 10Base-T wiring, all four pairs of wires are used in the 100Base-T4. The four pairs are labeled D1 through D4; pairs D1 and D2 are unidirectional and D3 and D4 are bidirectional. Table 38-3 lists the RJ45 pin assignments for 100Base-T4.

TABLE 38-3

RJ45 Pin Assignments for
100Base-T4

Node (NIC)	Function	Hub
1	Transmit D1	1
2	Transmit D1	2
3	Receive D2	3
4	Bidirectional D3	4
5	Bidirectional D3	5
6	Receive D2	6
7	Bidirectional D4	7
8	Bidirectional D4	8

While not as common as 100Base-TX, 100Base-T4 allows the use of Category 3 cable, which may enable companies that are wired with Category 3 cable a migration path to 100MBps without having to completely reconstruct their wiring infrastructure.

CERTIFICATION OBJECTIVE 38.02

Token Ring Networks

The *Token Ring* network architecture was developed by IBM to provide a method to integrate their mainframe and minicomputers into PC-based networks. Originally designed to operate at 4MBps, it was quickly upgraded to provide a transmission speed of 16MBps to compete with the 10MBps Ethernet standard. Token Ring networks do not use a shared-access architecture. Instead, they use a token-passing media access method that is defined by the IEEE 802.5 standard. Unlike Ethernet networks, Token Ring networks pass a token from station to station. Instead of having the nodes listen to the network as to when it is safe to transmit, the node must first be in possession of the token to transmit. Token Ring networks use a physical star topology; however, they operate as a logical ring topology.

How Token Ring Works

As mentioned earlier, Token Ring networks use a token-passing media access method to transmit data across the network. Each node acts as a repeater that receives token and data frames from its *nearest active upstream neighbor (NAUN)*. After the node has processed the frame, the frame is passed downstream to the next attached node. Each token makes at least one trip around the entire ring, and then returns to the originating node. Stations that indicate problems send a "beacon" to identify an address of the potential failure.

A Token Ring network is physically wired as a star (see Figure 38-4); each node is connected to a *Multiple Station Access Unit (MSAU)*, as in a 10BaseT network, in which each node is connected to a hub. Over the years, the term *MSAU* has been dropped and is now referred to as a *hub* in the industry.

FIGURE 38-4

Logical view of the Token Ring topology

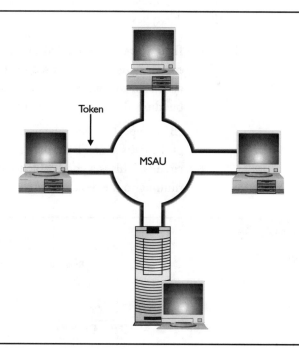

Token Ring MSAUs or hubs have an *RO (Ring Out)* and an *RI (Ring In)* port that are used to add additional MSAUs or hubs to the network in order to increase the number of nodes that can be attached to the network segment. The RI and RO ports allow you to extend the ring by simply connecting a patch cable from the RO port on one MSAU to the RI port on the other MSAU, and then connecting the first MSAU's RI port to the second MSAU's RO port. Figure 38-5 shows two IBM 8228 MSAUs connected together using the RI and RO ports.

Token Ring Cabling Types

As designed by IBM, Token Ring originally used *STP (Shielded Twisted Pair)* cable. However, like everything else in the computer industry, IBM has expanded the standard to include over ten different cable standards, including STP, UTP, and fiber-optic cable. We will briefly go over some of the more popular IBM cable standards and then the connectors used with these cable types:

- **IBM Type 1** A braided shield surrounds two twisted pairs of solid copper wire. Type 1 is used to connect terminals and distribution panels, or to connect between wiring closets located within the same building. Type 1 uses 22 AWG wire with a solid core.

- **IBM Type 2** This type uses a total of six twisted pairs of wire. Two of the pairs are STP for data and four are UTP used for telephone circuits. This is a good cable to use to reduce the number of cables running to the desk.

FIGURE 38-5

Two 8228 MSAUs connected

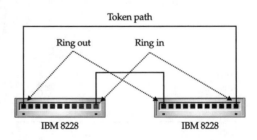

- **IBM Type 3**   Type 3 cable is very similar to Ethernet Category 5 cable. The cable uses four twisted pairs of 24 AWG solid-core wire with two twists per inch. Type 3 cable cannot be used for 16MBps data because it lacks the shielding found in Type 1 and Type 2 cable.

- **IBM Type 5**   Type 5 cable is a fiber-optic cable type that is primarily used on the main ring (or backbone ring). Type 5 can use either 100-um or 140-um optical fibers in one fiber jacket.

- **IBM Type 6**   This cable is composed of a braided shield surrounding two twisted pairs of 26 AWG stranded copper wire. This cable supports shorter cable runs than Type 1; however, because it is made of stranded copper wire, it is more flexible. Type 6 cable is IBM's standard for patch cables.

- **IBM Type 8**   This is the type of cable well suited for use under carpet. It is made of 26 AWG stranded-core STP.

- **IBM Type 9**   Type 9 cable is the same as Type 6, except its outer casing is made to be fire resistant and is used in plenums (air ventilation ducts).

- **Categories 3, 4, and 5**   This is the same type of cable used in Ethernet 10/100 BaseTx networks. Categories 3 and 4 cable can be used with 4MBps Token Ring, and Category 5 is well suited for use with 16MBps Token Ring.

Token Ring cables use one of three different types of connectors: the IBM data connector, 9 pin D connector, and the RJ45 connector. The IBM data connector is referred to as being a unisex connector because the "plug" and "socket" are physically the same; that is, any two connectors can connect together. The IBM data connector can be found on both ends of the patch cables used to connect IBM 8228 MSAUs together or on the end of a client drop cable that connects to the MSAU.

The 9 pin D connector is the same shape and size as the 9 pin serial port connector used on most PCs today. This connector is used to connect to older Token Ring NIC cards.

The third, and now most popular, is the RJ45 connector. The RJ45 connector and Category 5 cable are fast becoming the combination of choice for Token Ring installations. Most all of the Token Ring equipment sold today, NICs and MSAUs, have abandoned the IBM data connector and the 9-pin connectors and now use of RJ45 (sockets and plugs) and Category 5 cable.

Network Card Types

Network cards (NICs) come in an array of bus types, speeds, and features. We will first explore the different cable topologies supported by NICs, the bus types available, and then we will discuss how to configure Ethernet and Token Ring cards.

Network Adapter Connectors

When choosing a NIC, the first concern is the topology. For example, not much sense in buying a Token Ring card to use in your Ethernet network, is there? The vast majority of Ethernet cards are offered with three different types of connectors and combinations of these: BNC, AUI or DIX, and the RJ45 socket. The BNC style is used for 10Base2 networks; the AUI or DIX is used for 10Base5; and the RJ45 is used with 10/100BaseTx type networks. As mentioned earlier, Ethernet cards may have one, two, or all three of these connectors to enable them to be used with most network cable topologies, and only one connector can be used at a time. Keep in mind that while a 10/100BaseTx card may have all three connectors on board, the only connector that can be used for 100MBps operation is the RJ45. Neither 10Base2 nor 10Base5 topologies can support 100MBps operation. Token Ring NICs are available with either or both a 9-pin connector and RJ45 socket. Both types of connectors used on Token Ring cards can support either 4MBps or 16MBps transmission speeds.

Network Adapter Bus Types

Since the PC was introduced back in 1981, various system board bus architectures have been used. The following is a list of the bus architectures used and their features.

- **ISA (8 bit)**   Industry Standard Architecture. This was the original bus design used in the first PCs. It uses an 8-bit data path and supports only eight hardware interrupts of which only 2, 3, 4, 5, and 7 are available for use; the others were reserved for system use. This bus, running at only 4.77MHz, by today's standards is extremely slow. The ISA 8-bit slot will accept only ISA 8-bit cards.

- **ISA (16 bit)**   Industry Standard Architecture. Here the original bus was expanded by increasing the bus width to 16 bits and the bus speed to 8MHz. The interrupts also increased to 16 with 2, 3, 4, 5, 7, 9, 10, 11, 12, and 15 available for use. This bus slot will accept ISA (16 bit) and ISA (8 bit) cards.

- **MC (32)**   Micro Channel. This was IBM's new high-performance architecture for their PS/2 line of computers and servers. This bus uses a 32-bit data path and 10MHz speed. The interrupt settings along with I/O ports, address ranges, and DMA channels for cards in these slots are performed with a setup program supplied by IBM. IBM kept the Micro Channel design proprietary and licensed its use. Needless to say, very few manufacturers licensed the technology and it was a failure in the marketplace. You can use only MC cards in MC slots.

- **EISA (32 bit)**   Extended Industry Standard Architecture. EISA was the industry's answer to IBM's MC technology. It was designed by the "Gang of Nine": AST, Compaq, Epson, Hewlett-Packard, NEC, Olivetti, Tandy, Wyse, and Zenith. This standard also employed a 32-bit data path with a speed of 8MHz, and, like MC, the EISA cards used in these slots are configured with software. However, unlike MC, EISA slots can accept both ISA 8-bit and ISA 16-bit cards. This feature, along with the non-proprietary design of EISA, made it a success in the server marketplace.

- **VLB VESA (Video Electronics Standards Association) Local Bus**   VESA Local Bus was a short-lived bus extension to the ISA 16-bit. It used an extended ISA 16-bit slot with a speed of up to 40MHz based on the CPU and was configured with jumpers on the card. It was used primary in workstations for video cards and hard disk controllers. The VLB slot would also accept ISA 8-bit and 16-bit cards; however, it quickly disappeared from the marketplace due to the PCI bus.

■ **PCI** Peripheral Component Interface. The PCI bus is now the industry de facto standard bus. It sports a 32-bit data path and a 33MHz asynchronous speed with a theoretical throughput of 132MBps. In addition, the PCI bus controller on the system main board will automatically assign an interrupt to the adapter. The PCI slot accepts only PCI cards. However, since most adapter cards are now available in the PCI architecture, this should not present a problem.

■ **PCMCIA** Personal Computer Memory Card International Association. This interface was first developed for use in portable laptop or notebook computers to serve as an expansion slot that most small portable computers lacked. The card is approximately the size of a credit card and is inserted into a slot located on the computer. Various peripherals have been designed for PCMCIA, such as modems, NICs, and hard drives. Most people in the industry now refer to it as PC card.

exam
ⓦatch

PCMCIA (Personal Memory Card International Association) standard is also covered in the course, although mentioned only briefly, and Novell omits the fact that everyone else now calls it PC card, because people can't memorize computer industry acronyms.

Network Adapter Configuration

All network adapters must be configured before using them. The card must have the interrupt, I/O port address, and memory address set. A fourth parameter, the DMA channel, is used on higher-performance cards. All of these parameters are set by various methods depending on the type of card. On older cards, most of the settings are done with jumpers. Figure 38-6 shows an Ethernet card with all of the jumpers labeled.

Jumper-type cards are configured by either "shorting" or "closing" two pins with a jumper or leaving the pins open. The documentation for the

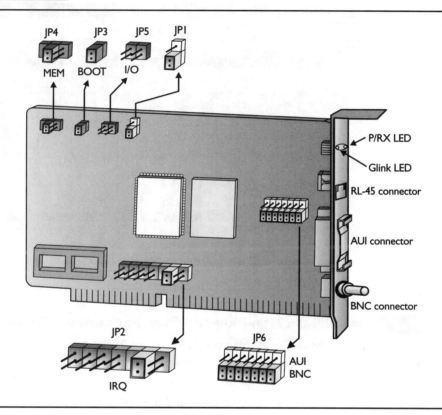

FIGURE 38-6   Network adapter card jumper locations

adapter will have the correct jumper settings listed. Newer cards use a "jumperless" design. These cards are configured via software provided by the manufacturer or by Windows 95/98 Plug-and-Play. Figure 38-7 is a screenshot of a utility to configure a "jumperless" card.

Figure 38-7 shows the settings that apply to a particular card. Also note that some cards can have their Ethernet or Token Ring address overridden via the software configuration. Normally, the Ethernet and Token Ring addresses are "burned" into the card at the factory; however, to allow more flexibility in network designs, manufacturers have started to include this feature in their cards.

FIGURE 38-7

Screenshot of a "jumperless" NIC configuration utility

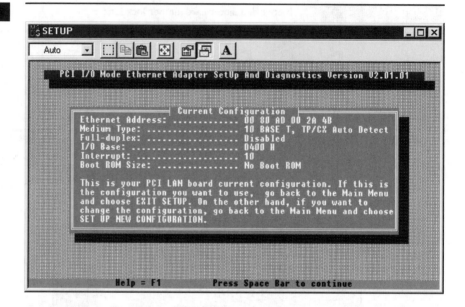

EXERCISE 38-1

Installing a Non-Plug-and-Play, jumperless, ISA 16-bit NIC

1. From Device Manager in Windows 95/98, determine which interrupts, I/O address ranges, and memory addresses are free for use and make a note of them.

2. Shut down the computer and then remove the power cord and cover.

3. Insert the NIC into an available 16-bit ISA slot. Be sure to screw the card into place, making sure the card is inserted fully and securely into the slot.

4. Replace the cover and power cord and power on the computer.

5. After the first POST beep sounds, press F8. This will bring up the Microsoft Windows 95/98 Startup Menu. If the choice of Previous version of DOS is present, select it. If not, select Safe Mode.

6. From the DOS command line or from a DOS window in safe mode, run the NIC card configuration utility that came with the card.

7. Set the card to use one of the free interrupts, I/O address range, and memory addresses, as noted in Step 1.

8. Save the configuration to the card and exit the utility. Reboot the computer and allow it to start up normally.

9. Windows 95/98 may or may not recognize the new NIC. If Windows does not recognize the NIC, use the Add Hardware Wizard to add the NIC.

10. From the Start Menu, choose Control Panel | System | Device Manager | Expand Network Adapters to check and/or change the resource settings to match the configuration of the card.

Troubleshooting Ethernet

Unfortunately, even in a perfect network design, problems do crop up and have to be resolved. The following are some guidelines to use while troubleshooting Ethernet. In the next section, we will cover Token Ring troubleshooting.

When troubleshooting any type of network, check the obvious physical problems first. For example, make sure all connections and connectors are tight and secure in their sockets or couplers. Check that cable lengths are within the Ethernet specifications and that the cable used is the correct type. Always follow the 5-4-3 rule when working with coax Ethernet networks, and don't exceed the specified number of nodes on a segment. The following are some other steps to take in troubleshooting Ethernet:

■ If you are using 10/100BaseTx, make sure the correct number of twists are used in the cable to meet the specification.

■ Check for electrical interference from other equipment. Keep the network cables separated from the power and monitor cords on the computer.

■ Check for excessive shielding on coax cable connectors and make sure it is not grounding out or coming in contact with the center pin.

■ If you are using coax, make sure that the coax cables are not coiled together tightly.

■ Check for invalid frame types, if you have "Server not found" error messages.

- Check for network adapter card settings to make sure they are not conflicting with other adapter cards.

Troubleshooting Token Ring

As with Ethernet troubleshooting, in Token Ring troubleshooting, check the obvious physical problems first. Make sure all cable connections are tight and secure, check cable lengths to make sure they are within specifications, and that the number of nodes does not exceed the limit. Other things to check include the following:

- Check that any base I/O, DMA shared memory, or interrupt settings do not conflict with other adapters.

- Make sure the version of the server driver or client driver software is compatible with the network adapter you are using. Sometimes drivers will load without error but will not work with the model of board you are using.

- Check the wiring between MSAUs for proper RO and RI connections. If you suspect a bad MSAU, wire the ring around it and see if that solves the problem. If the problem disappears, then you know you have a bad MSAU. Be careful when mixing MSAUs from different manufacturers in your network. Electrical characteristics between manufacturers may show slight differences that can show up as intermittent problems.

CERTIFICATION OBJECTIVE 38.03

FDDI Networks

FDDI (Fiber Distributed Data Interface) follows the IEEE 802.5 standard for accessing the network just like Token Ring. However, unlike the Token Ring topology, FDDI uses two fiber-optic cables in a dual counter rotating ring configuration and operates at 100MBps instead of the 4MBps or

16MBps as used in Token Ring. FDDI uses LEDs or lasers to generate the light that is used d to carry the information through the fiber-optic cable, and travels in only one direction on each cable. On one cable, data flows in one direction and, on the other cable, data flows in the opposite direction, as shown in Figure 38-8.

The dual counter rotating rings serve two purposes. First, while one ring is being used for normal data traffic, the second ring can be used for backups and other services. This can be a big consideration in a 24-hour production environment. Second, should you lose a ring, such as a fault at one of the stations, those stations located on either side of the break can isolate the break in the fiber by forming a single ring (wrapping) from their own ports. This provides for fault tolerance.

There are two different station types on an FDDI network—a Class A and a Class B station. A *Class A station* is called a Dual Attached Station (DAS) and is connected to both rings. A *Class B station* has a connection to only one ring, and is called a Single Attached Station (SAS). This type of station would be a good choice for unstable network devices. Since the

FIGURE 38-8

Logical diagram of the FDDI topology

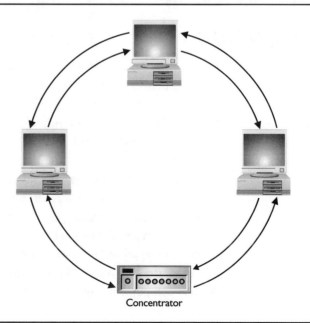

Concentrator

station is attached to only one ring, should the station fail, data will continue unhindered on the second ring.

The ability to isolate a break in a cable makes FDDI an extremely reliable network cabling topology. FDDI also overcomes some of the performance problems of Token Ring by using a higher bandwidth. Other advantages of FDDI include the following:

■ Much greater distances can be achieved with FDDI because it uses fiber-optic cable. Fiber-optic cable can theoretically span hundreds of miles, whereas the Token Ring network diameter is measured in feet.

■ Fiber-optic cable is very difficult to tap into, thus increasing network security.

■ Fiber-optic cable is not susceptible to electrical interference and does not conduct electricity.

CERTIFICATION OBJECTIVE 38.04

ATM Networks

Asynchronous Transfer Mode (ATM) is by far the hottest technology in today's networks. ATM works on a wide array of mediums and speeds from copper wire to fiber-optic cable, from 155MBps to over 2.448GBps (OC48). The most common in use in LANs is on fiber-optic cable running at a speed of 155MBps. While ATM is currently being used mostly for backbones in LANs and the Internet, ATM is becoming a general-purpose transport protocol to deliver voice, data, video, and sound to the desktop. ATM uses cells in a switched environment, transmitting information very much like a packet-switching service, such as frame relay. The cells are 53 bytes in length and the protocol allows for stringent service qualities that can differ by application. For example, different Qualities of Service (QOS) can be delivered by ATM, like assigning a lower priority to data cells of a file copy compared to higher priority video cells. Since video transmission requires a higher sustained rate of transfer to reproduce the picture correctly, the video cells will be sent before the data cells that do not depend on speed to copy correctly.

QUESTIONS AND ANSWERS

My customer wants to upgrade his Arcnet network to Ethernet 10Base2. Can I just change the cards in the clients and reuse the old coax cable?	No, Arcnet used a RG-62/U cable and 93-ohm terminators. 10Base2 uses RG-58A/U or RG-58C/U coax cable with 50-ohm terminators.
I need to run Ethernet 802.2, Ethernet 802.3, and Ethernet II on my network. Do I have to have three NICs in my server to support these different frame types?	No, you can bind up to four protocols or frame types to one NIC.
Can I connect my company's art department, which uses Apple computers on a Token Ring network, to the rest of my company's Ethernet network?	Yes. The cheapest way to accomplish this is to add a Token Ring card to a server that already has an Ethernet card installed, and configure it to act as a router. There are also more expensive solutions out in the market that can provide higher throughput.
Our company just bought 100 10MBps NICs that support Full Duplex. However, when I configure the NICs for Full Duplex, the network does not seem any faster. Why is that?	You are most likely still using shared media hubs and concentrators and your NICs have switched themselves back to Half Duplex operation. To take advantage of Full Duplex operation on your network, you have to use switches instead of hubs.
My EISA NIC in my server just stopped working. The only spare NIC I have is a 16-bit ISA NIC card. Will this NIC work in place of my EISA NIC?	Yes, 8- and 16-bit ISA cards will work in EISA slots. This is one of the advantages of the EISA slot design.
My NetWare console screen keeps displaying messages about a "router configuration error." What does this mean?	You most likely have a second server on the same network segment that has a different network address bound to the frame type used by the first server. All servers on the same segment must have the same network address.
I just set up a new server on my network, and whenever I use the Display Servers command from this server, no other servers are found. Why is this?	The most likely cause is that the wrong frame type is being used on this server. Make sure that the correct frame type is being used and that the correct protocols are bound to the NIC.

CERTIFICATION SUMMARY

In this chapter, we have covered four of the most common topologies used in modern networks, discussed the basics in setting up the related cards, and suggested troubleshooting steps that apply to them. Things to prepare for on the Service and Support section of the exam are network segment lengths, termination of segments, the basic operation of the different topologies, and the 5-4-3 rule. You should also be familiar with the different bus types used and what types of network cards are supported in each of the bus types.

TWO-MINUTE DRILL

❑ Ethernet is a type of network cabling and signaling specification (OSI Model layers 1 [Physical] and 2 [Data Link]) originally developed by Bob Metcalfe while working for Xerox in the late 1970s.

❑ Ethernet is a baseband, CSMA/CD (Carrier Sense, Multiple Access / Collision Detection) transmission protocol. *Baseband* is a type of signal transmission that allows only one frequency to carry information on the cable.

❑ The Ethernet protocol originally specified coaxial type cabling. However, as with most standards in this industry, the protocol has been expanded to include different cable types, such as unshielded twisted pair (UTP) and fiber optic.

❑ The Token Ring network architecture was developed by IBM to provide a method to integrate their mainframe and minicomputers into PC-based networks. Originally designed to operate at 4MBps, it was quickly upgraded to provide a transmission speed of 16MBps to compete with the 10MBps Ethernet standard.

❑ Token Ring networks use a token passing media access method to transmit data across the network. Each node acts as a repeater that receives token and data frames from its nearest active upstream neighbor (NAUN). After the node has processed the frame, the frame is passed downstream to the next attached node.

Each token makes at least one trip around the entire ring, and then returns to the originating node.

❏ Token Ring originally used STP (Shielded Twisted Pair) cable. However, IBM has expanded the standard to include over ten different cable standards, including STP, UTP, and fiber-optic cable.

❏ Topology is the first concern when choosing a NIC. The vast majority of Ethernet cards are offered with three different types of connectors and combinations of connectors—BNC, AUI or DIX, and the RJ45 socket.

❏ The bus designs commonly in use include ISA (8 bit), ISA (16 bit), MC (32), EISA (32 bit), VLB VESA (Video Electronics Standards Association) Local Bus, PCI, and PCMCIA.

❏ All network adapters must be configured before they can be used. The card must have the interrupt, I/O port address, and memory address set. A fourth parameter, the DMA channel, is used on higher-performance cards. All of these parameters are set by various methods depending on the type of card.

❏ When troubleshooting any type of network, check the obvious physical problems first.

❏ To troubleshoot an Ethernet network, follow these steps:

1. If using 10/100BaseTX, make sure the correct number of twists are used in the cable to meet the specification.

2. Check for electrical interference from other equipment. Keep the network cables separated from the power and monitor cords on the computer.

3. Check for excessive shielding on coax cable connectors and make sure it is not grounding out or coming in contact with the center pin.

4. If using coax, make sure that the coax cables are not coiled together tightly.

5. Check for invalid frame types, if you have "Server not found" error messages.

6. Check for network adapter card settings to make sure they are not conflicting with other adapter cards.

❑ To troubleshoot a Token Ring network, use the following steps:

1. Check that any base I/O, DMA shared memory, or interrupt settings do not conflict with other adapters.

2. Make sure the version of the server driver or client driver software is compatible with the network adapter you are using.

3. Check the wiring between MSAUs for proper RO and RI connections.

❑ FDDI (Fiber Distributed Data Interface) follows the IEEE 802.5 standard for accessing the network. FDDI uses two fiber-optic cables in a dual counter rotating ring configuration and operates at 100MBps.

❑ Asynchronous Transfer Mode (ATM) is the hottest technology in today's networks. ATM works on a wide array of mediums and speeds from copper wire to fiber-optic cable, from 155MBps to over 2.448GBps (OC48). The most common in use in LANs is on fiber-optic cable running at a speed of 155MBps.

SELF TEST

The following Self-Test questions will help you measure your understanding of the material presented in this chapter. Read all the choices carefully, as there may be more than one correct answer. Choose all correct answers for each question.

1. You have been asked to help troubleshoot a Token Ring network. Which of the following suggestions may help? (Select three.)

   A. The custom statistics of a Token Ring board are useful in finding internal errors.

   B. Make sure all of the network adapter cards are using the same data rate.

   C. Since Token Ring node addresses are set manually, check for duplicates with other network resources.

   D. A useful solution in working with MSAUs is to remove all of the patch cables from the MSAU, reset all of the ports with initialization or setup tools, and then reconnect the patch cables back to the MSAU.

2. What is the purpose of the COMCHECK utility?

   A. It is used to isolate physical communication problems between computers.

   B. It can be used to reconfigure network board address.

   C. It is the only tool used to configure addresses of nodes manually.

   D. It works like Check-It Pro to discover any type of IRQ or address conflict.

3. Which of the following cable lengths are correct for 10BaseT?

   A. 75 meters and 0.4 meters

   B. 10 meters, 75 meters and 175 meters

   C. 10 meters

   D. 0.4 meters, 10 meters, 75 meters, and 175 meters

4. Which of the following statements best describes the function of an I/O address?

   A. It causes the CPU to service a device.

   B. It serves as a mail address for the CPU to communicate with a device.

   C. It allows devices to directly access memory without the CPU.

5. What is a DMA Channel?

   A. Digital Multi Access service is a new telephone service similar to ISDN.

   B. It is used by a device to pass information directly to the CPU, bypassing memory.

   C. It allows devices to write directly to memory without intervention by the CPU.

   D. It is a baseband subchannel used with ATM.

6. What are two advantages of PCI?

A. It is 32 bits wide with a maximum of 133MBps at 33MHz.

B. Like DMA, it requires no processor to work.

C. It is scalable to 64-bit processing.

D. It uses quad-sized words for increased data transfer rates.

7. Which of the following statements are true about ATM?

A. It is a fiber-optic bus-wired network that controls media access with token-passing technology.

B. It is a LAN specification using dual counter-rotating rings.

C. It is any network that uses fiber optics.

D. It uses packet-switching technology.

8. For a station to transmit data on a Token Ring network, it must grab a token as the token passes by, and add data to the token frame. What happens when the destination station receives that token?

A. The destination station alters the direction of the sending token so the token does not have to travel all the way around the ring.

B. The destination station copies the data from the frame, reverses two bits of the frame, and sends the token back into the ring.

C. The destination station takes the data from the frame and sends the token back to the sending station.

D. The destination station sends a token, indicating that it received the frame.

9. What do the RI and RO ports on a MSAU do?

A. They generate beacons for COMCHECK to use.

B. They reverse the bits in the token pattern on the token's return trip.

C. They are used to connect one MSAU to another.

D. They send out RI and RO signals to the network when the token is lost.

10. You work at an electrical plant that connects many of its departmental offices and process control networks together within a campus environment. The company wants you to rebuild the network to avoid the substantial problems with electrical interference. Which technology would you use?

A. ARCNET

B. FDDI

C. PCNET-2

D. 10BaseT

11. When the workstation boots up, the NIC's driver fails to load. Which of the following is the most likely reason?

A. The workstation is out of environment space.

B. The network is down.

C. The address for the board has not been configured.

D. The memory manager has not excluded the correct address range.

12. Of the following cable types, which one should be used for 10Base2?

   A. RG-62A/U

   B. RG-58U

   C. RG-58A/U

   D. UTP/TR

13. You are planning the installation of a new network. You want to present to your manager the advantages of FDDI over other types of cable. Which of the following is not an advantage of FDDI?

   A. Network boards are relatively cheap and easy to maintain because of advances in technology.

   B. FDDI can be run at extremely long distances, much farther than 10BaseT.

   C. Ground isolation is possible because FDDI does not conduct electricity.

   D. Reliability is increased because there is no susceptibility to EMI.

14. You are installing a "jumperless" Ethernet network board. From the following, select some or all of these steps in the correct order:

   1. Set termination.

   2. Boot the computer.

   3. Physically install the network board in an expansion slot.

   4. Configure the network board for IRQ, DMA, Port Address, and/or I/O Address.

   5. Configure node address.

      A. 3, 2, 4

      B. 1, 5, 3, 4, 2

      C. 1, 3, 2

      D. 3, 2, 5

      E. 4, 1, 3, 2

15. Why should you not use RG-58U coaxial cable for an Ethernet network?

   A. You can use RG-58U for 10Base2.

   B. It does not meet the IEEE specification.

   C. Cable impedance is too low and signals will "bounce" back.

   D. It has only a single shield and Ethernet requires two shields.

39

Installing and Troubleshooting Network Storage Devices

CERTIFICATION OBJECTIVES

39.01   Hard Drives

39.02   Using RAID Devices

39.03   CD-ROM Drives on NetWare

39.04   Magneto-Optical Drives

In this chapter, we discuss the various mass storage devices NetWare supports and the interface types used with these devices. NetWare supports a large array of IDE, ATA, ATAPI, and SCSI devices right out of the box without the need for any special software drivers. Devices such as hard drives, tape drives, CD-ROM, and removable media can all be installed into a NetWare server with no more trouble than physically installing the device and loading a driver for it. NetWare provides more flexibility and functionality in storage device support than any other networking product. As part of NetWare Peripheral Architecture (NWPA), a host adapter module (HAM) and a custom device module (CDM) now replace the traditional storage device driver (DSK). However, there are some important guidelines that should be followed to ensure a successful implementation of the storage device.

CERTIFICATION OBJECTIVE 39.01

Hard Drives

Hard drives are one of the most critical components of a server and the reason servers and LANs came into existence. In the early 1980s, hard disk drives were very expensive, and businesses could not afford to equip every PC with one. What was needed was a way to share the expensive hard disk between users. Hence, NetWare was born to satisfy this need.

The hard drive itself has not changed much in basic design over the last 20 years; all hard drives store information on platters that are coated with a metallic compound that can hold a magnetic "charge." This platter is spun at a high rate of speed and a mechanical arm, with a read/write head attached to the end of it, is moved over the platter's surface and reads or writes changes in the magnetic flux on the platter. These changes in flux represent the bits that make up the bytes of information stored on the disk. Figure 39-1 represents a typical hard disk with the major components labeled.

While Figure 39-1 shows a hard disk drive with a stepper motor, a "voice coil" in modern hard disk drives has replaced the stepper motor. The stepper motor design used a rack and pinion method to move the head assembly across the platter. The stepper motor shaft acted as the pinion and the head assembly acted as the rack. The stepper motor would receive pulses of electricity to rotate the shaft in small fractional turns that in turn would move

FIGURE 39-1

A typical hard disk and its components

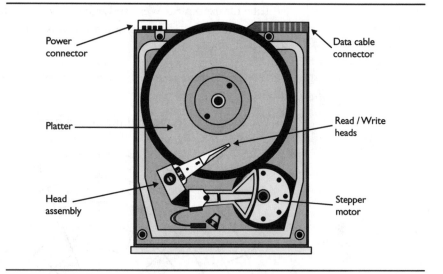

Power connector

Data cable connector

Platter

Read / Write heads

Head assembly

Stepper motor

the head assembly across the platter(s). In modern hard disks, a mechanism called a *voice coil* is used to position the read /write heads. There is no mechanical connection between the voice coil and the head assembly. The head assembly is moved into position by a servomechanism that uses a magnetic field. This method provides for much faster seek times than the stepper motor design.

A hard disk may have as few as one platter or as many as six or more. For each side of a platter, there is a corresponding read/write head. Some drive designs may not use both sides of a particular platter; thus, you may have a drive with 6 platters but only 11 sets of heads. This is done because the internal case design of the hard disk does not have room for a read/write head on the bottom platter. The platters are broken up into concentric rings that grow in diameter from the inside of the platter to the outside. These rings are called *tracks*. A *cylinder* is comprised of the same track on all of the platters. The tracks are further broken down into sectors. The *sector* is the smallest storage unit on the disk. A typical sector holds 512 bytes of data and there are anywhere from 17 to over 50 sectors per track. The capacity of a hard disk can be determined by the following formula:

```
Cylinders * Heads * Sectors * 512 = Bytes
```

Take for example a Western Digital Caviar Model 2420 drive. It has 989 cylinders or tracks, 15 heads, and 56 sectors per track. Plugging in the numbers we get:

```
989 (cylinders) * 15 (heads) * 56 (Sectors) * 512 (bytes
per sector) = 425.3MB
```

The concept of sectors and tracks on a hard disk platter is illustration here:

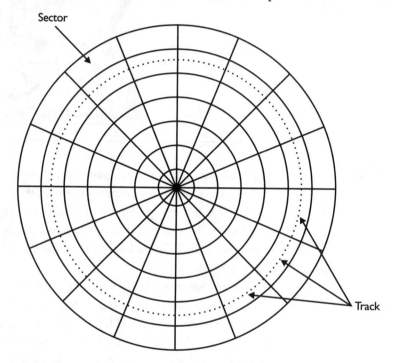

Hard Drive Interface Types

Hard drives come in a variety of interface types from the original ST412/ST506 to the SCSI-Ultra Wide. The interface type determines the transfer speed of data from the hard drive to the system bus, and whether the drive controller is built into the drive or requires an external controller card. The following are some types of hard drives:

- **ST412/ST506** IBM selected a Xebec controller for its PC-XT hard disk adapter that combined features from two existing Seagate

Technology Company interfaces referred to as the ST412 and ST506 interfaces; hence the interface name ST412/ST506. This interface supported one channel, which in turn supported two drives. Because the IBM XT had an 8-bit bus and a 4.77Mhz clock speed, the controller had a maximum transfer rate of 2MB per second to and from the motherboard using the motherboard's DMA controller. When the IBM AT was introduced with its 16-bit bus and a faster clock rate, the WD1003 disk controller was used. The AT used the PIO (Programmed Input/Output) method, which supported transfer rates of 3.3MBps instead of the DMA method, which was still limited to 2MBps. The AT was designed with two separate hardware I/O address and interrupt levels to support two hard disk controllers. However, the AT BIOS would support only the first controller or channel, which limited the computer to only two disk drives. The interface required an external controller card and used two cables to transfer information from the controller to the hard disk. The first cable was a control cable with a 34-pin connector. This cable carried the signals to the hard disk, such as what track or sector to move to and read. One control cable could support up to two drives. The second cable was the data cable that carried the actual data to and from the drive. This cable had 20 pins, and each drive required its own cable. The ST412/ST506 interface design was capable of a transfer rate of 5MBps, however, because of the controller transfer-to-motherboard limitations, 5MBps could not be achieved.

■ **ESDI** Enhanced Small Device Interface was an IBM design intended to be used in higher performance workstations and servers. It offered a higher density of sectors to a track and came with either a single 40-pin connector or, like the ST-506, two connectors. Even though the ESDI drive may have come with the same type of connectors as the ST-506, they were logically incompatible. A ST-506 controller would not work with an ESDI drive. ESDI could support data transfer rates as high as 15MBps and used the MFM encoding technology. Another feature introduced with the ESDI was the ability to store drive parameters on the disk itself, which eliminated the need to configure the drive in the computer's BIOS ROM.

- **IDE** Integrated Drive Electronics incorporates the controller electronics into the drive. It was found that shortening the length of the data cable increased the transfer rates from the drive to the controller. IDE/ATA/ATAPI types are shown in the following illustration. Since each drive has its own controller built in, and you can have two drives on one cable, a method had to be devised to differentiate between the two drives. This lead to the development of the *Master/Slave system* where each IDE drive can act as either a master or slave. If two drives are used on the channel, one of the drives must be configured as the master and the other drive must be configured as the slave so that only one controller is seen by the system. The IDE specification also allows for an additional channel that allows up to four IDE hard disks in the computer, of which the second pair of drives must also be configured as Master/Slave.

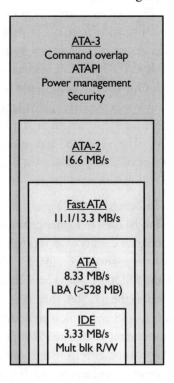

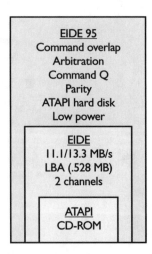

- **SCSI** Small Computer System Interface was around before the IBM PC and was used mainly with UNIX and Apple systems in the early 1980s. SCSI is well suited for multitasking systems such as

NetWare because it allows for processing simultaneous requests. The following is a list of SCSI Advantages:

- **Reduced CPU demand for increased system performance**   SCSI is capable of independently processing I/O requests, freeing up the system CPU for other tasks.

- **Multiple device support**   SCSI can support up to seven devices (15 for wide SCSI) from one bus slot. Each adapter can have up to eight peripheral LUNs (16 for wide SCSI), so increasing disk storage simply requires adding adapters and drives.

- **External device support**   Whereas IDE/EIDE support only up to four internal devices, SCSI allows for external devices to be added. These devices can be tape drives, CD-ROMs, and other SCSI devices.

- **Expanded peripheral support**   Many devices come with a SCSI interface, such as disks, CD-ROM drives, tape drives, scanners, and removable media like Zip drives.

- **Hardware and software compatibility**   SCSI is an established international standard supported by virtually every OS and hardware platform via software drivers.

- **Multitasking capability**   SCSI is capable of performing multiple I/O tasks, which increase overall system performance.

- **SCSI supports RAIDS**   CSI is the only technology that supports RAID levels other than Level 1 on NetWare. To use disk striping or disk striping with parity, you must use SCSI devices.

Other the years, SCSI is continuously evolving and now offers a wide array of speeds and features. The following is a list of the types of SCSI in use today:

- **Single-ended SCSI**   Single-ended SCSI is a term applied to standard SCSI devices that are fully compliant with standard SCSI specifications. This includes SCSI, SCSI-2, Ultra SCSI, Fast Wide SCSI-2, and Ultra Wide SCSI.

- **SCSI**   First type of SCSI, uses an 8-bit bus, is capable of supporting seven devices, and has a transfer rate of 5MBps.

■ **Narrow SCSI 2**   This version of SCSI passes data through the SCSI bus along an 8-bit data path and provides support for up to seven devices. This device uses a 50-pin SCSI connector that connects via cable to the host adapter. Data transfer rates of up to 10MBps can be achieved with cable lengths of 3m or less.

■ **Ultra SCSI 2**   Ultra SCSI 2 is an enhancement of the SCSI 2 specification that allows for up to 20MBps transfer rates. Cable length requirements are very important or slower transfer rates will result; with four or fewer devices installed, maximum cable length is 3 meters or less; with more than four devices installed, cable length is 1.5 meters or less.

■ **Fast Wide SCSI 2**   This version of SCSI passes data through the SCSI bus along a 16-bit data path and provides support for up to 15 devices. It uses a 68-pin SCSI connector that connects via cable to the host adapter. Data transfer rates of up to 20MBps can be achieved with cable lengths of 3 meters or less.

■ **Ultra Wide SCSI 2**   Ultra Wide SCSI 2 is an enhancement to the Fast Wide SCSI 2 specification that allows for up to 40MBps burst data transfer rates. Cable length requirements are very important or slower transfer rates will result; with four or fewer devices installed, maximum cable length is 3m or less; with more than four devices installed, maximum cable length is 1.5 meters or less.

■ **Ultra2 SCSI**   Ultra2 SCSI uses a new technology called Low Voltage Differential, which allows for longer cable lengths (12 meters) with up to 80MBps burst data transfer rate. Drives and adapters utilizing this technology are backward compatible with older SCSI technology. Most of the devices that utilize this interface will support the 16-bit wide SCSI format and will incorporate a high-density 68-pin interface.

■ **Differential SCSI**   Differential SCSI is a special version of SCSI that allows for cable lengths of up to 25 meters. To utilize this technology, a special differential host adapter is required and is not compatible with standard SCSI devices. Differential SCSI technology has a dual data path built in and compares one line to its counterpart to interpret the data being read or written. All differential devices require external line termination because Differential SCSI specifications do not call for on-board termination.

Setting Jumpers on the Hard Drive and Controller Card

Most hard disk drives and controller cards use jumpers to configure the different parameters of the drive or controller. In this section, we will first describe the jumpers that are required for IDE type drives; then we will discuss the SCSI jumpers. Finally, we will discuss the jumpers typically found on controllers and describe their configuration.

IDE Drive Configuration

IDE drives have only one configuration setting you need to be concerned about. This setting is the Master/Slave/Single Drive jumper, or the CS jumper if the system uses the Cable Select method instead of the Master/Slave method. Most systems use the Master/Slave/Single Drive setting jumpers. If the drive is the only drive in the system, then the Single setting is used. If the drive is to be the first drive of two on the channel, then the Master setting is used; and if the drive is to be the second drive on the channel, then the Slave setting is used. Setting the drive type is done by "shunting" pins together with a jumper shunt. This jumper shunt electrically connects the two pins together. Figure 39-2 shows how a jumper shunt is placed over the pins, and Figure 39-3 shows the different pin configurations possible.

FIGURE 39-2

The jumper settings for a Western Digital Caviar drive

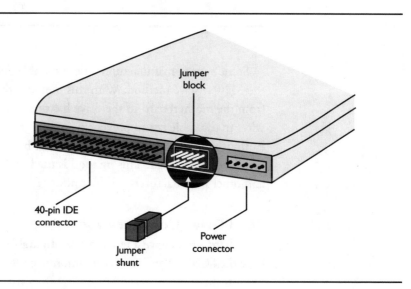

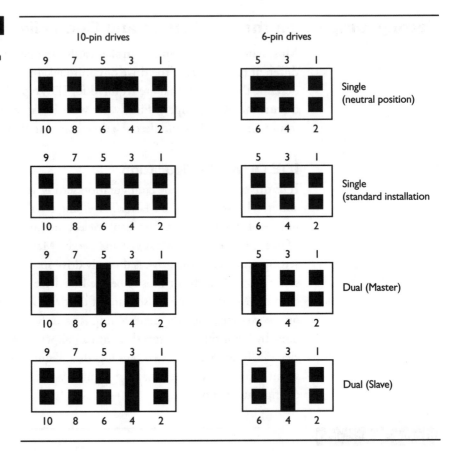

FIGURE 39-3

Jumper block showing pin positions

Some system manufacturers use the Cable Select mechanism instead of the Master/Slave method. With this method, the 40-pin cable that connects from the motherboard to the drive has one of these mechanisms on the wires in the cable cut to prevent the signal from reaching the second drive. Both drives in a Cable Select system must have the jumper labeled C/S or Cable Select shunted. This method is used by Compaq, Hewlett Packard, and other manufacturers on their newer PCs.

SCSI Drive Configuration

SCSI hard drives have a few more configurable settings, but in most cases, only the SCSI ID and the termination need to be set. Like the IDE drives discussed earlier, SCSI drives are configured with jumpers that shunt pins together. On a SCSI disk, it is the ID of the drive that distinguishes it from any other devices that may also be on the bus. On an 8-bit SCSI controller, there are eight IDs available, but only seven can be used for devices. One address, typically ID 7, is used for the controller card itself. On a 16-bit SCSI controller, up to 15 devices can be connected to the bus. The 16-bit SCSI controller also requires an address for itself. Figure 39-4 shows the jumper location and a chart showing the various settings for the SCSI ID.

Unlike the IDE drive, the SCSI drive must be terminated, if it is the last device on the bus. Over the years, manufacturers have devised a few ways to terminate the SCSI bus. One of the more modern ways is to include a built-in terminating resistor in the hard drive, which can be turned on or off with a jumper. Figure 39-5 shows a drive with a built-in terminating resister. If this were the last physical device on the bus, you would place a jumper on Pins 15 and 16 (farthest left pair on the jumper block) to enable the terminator.

While built-in termination facilities are convenient, older SCSI drives required a separate resistor(s) in a socket on the PCB board of the drive or plugged into the last connector on the SCSI cable. These older-style SCSI drives requiring a physically separate termination resistor are slowly being replaced by the drives with built-in termination.

Another often overlooked feature of the SCSI bus is that the devices are assigned priority based on their SCSI ID number. For example, if you had a tape drive and a hard drive on the SCSI bus, you could place the hard drive at SCSI ID 0 and the tape device at ID 6. This would help prevent tape drive requests from slowing down requests to the hard drive. This will not speed up the tape drive, or for that matter, the hard drive, but will give priority to requests for the hard drive over the tape drive when they arrive in the SCSI controller command queue at the same time.

IDE Controller Configuration

IDE controllers come in two flavors—either they are built into the motherboard, or they are separate cards inserted into the bus slots in the computer. In either case, the controllers have to have the same parameters configured. Most motherboards used today support two IDE channels that

FIGURE 39-4 Wide SCSI jumper block

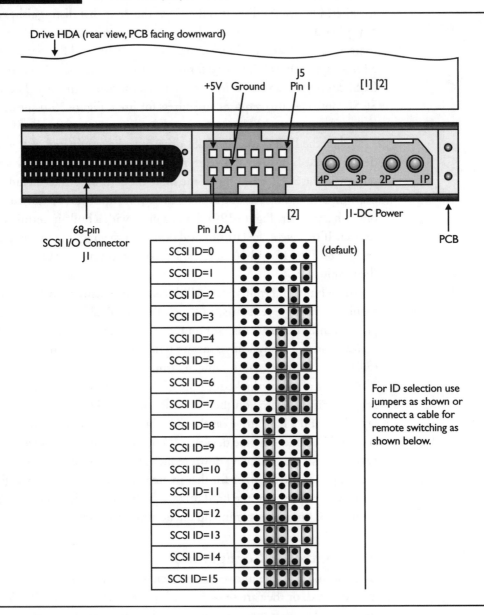

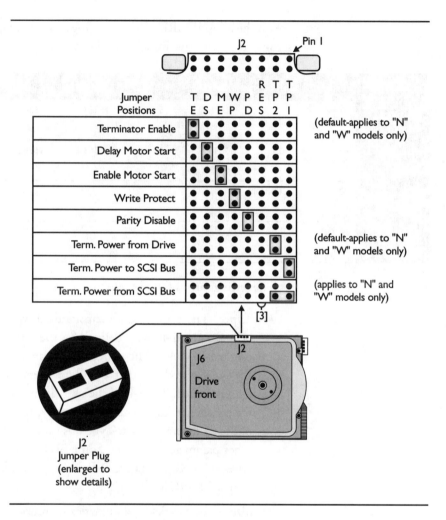

FIGURE 39-5

SCSI terminator jumper positions

can support up to a total of four drives. The controller on these motherboards is configured from the BIOS setup screen. In order to access this screen, the computer is powered off and then on. Once the computer powers up, a memory check runs, and it is during this memory check that a message should appear instructing which key sequences to press to enter the BIOS setup menu. On most BIOS setup screens, the hard disk parameters are on the STANDARD CMOS settings screen. There are eight different settings for each drive installed in the system:

Hard Disk	Type	Size	Cyls	Heads	Precomp	Landing	Sector	Mode
Primary Master	47 (User)	10.1	16383	16	16383	16383	63	LBA
Primary Slave	47 (User)	10.1	16383	16	16383	16383	63	LBA
Secondary Master	47 (User)	CD-ROM						AUTO
Secondary Slave	NONE							

The settings are as follows:

- **Type**   There are 47 different standard type values. Type numbers between 1 and 46 were defined for the earlier hard drives used in the original IBM AT. These predefined parameter sets are a holdover in the BIOS and drives that would use them are no longer manufactured. Type 47 is the user-definable type and allows all of the parameters to be entered manually. If this type is chosen, the rest of the fields must be set. Type 0 is for a SCSI drive and requires no other parameters to be set. Some BIOS may even have another type—CD-ROM. The CD-ROM type would be used if the device were a CD-ROM drive.

- **Size**   The size field is automatically computed once the other parameters are entered. This field will display the capacity of the drive.

- **Cyls**   This field holds the number of cylinders or tracks on the disk.

- **Heads**   This field holds the number of heads the drive has.

- **Precomp**   This field holds the cylinder that precompensation starts. This is yet another holdover from the earlier AT disks. This value is typically set to the number of cylinders in the newer drives.

- **Landing Zone**   This field is another holdover from the earlier AT disks. This parameter specified which track the heads were to be returned to or "parked" during drive shutdown. The drives of today automatically park themselves when they are shut down.

- **Sector** This field holds the number of sectors to a track. This is the smallest addressable space on a hard disk drive.

- **Mode** The mode field specifies the addressing method used to map the drive. The different modes are Normal, LBA, Large, and Auto. The Auto value, if offered, is the best to use because the controller will determine which modes the drive supports and will choose the best one.

If the computer uses a built-in controller on the motherboard, the interrupt, I/O port, and DMA channels (if used) are typically configured from another screen in the BIOS setup program. This screen is usually found under a peripheral setup screen. Some BIOSs do not allow the primary or secondary channel configurations to be changed and are hard-coded into the BIOS. Of the BIOSs that do allow the parameters to be changed, most will allow the assignment of the interrupt, I/O port, and DMA channel to be used for each channel. On systems that have a separate controller card in one of the bus slots, the interrupt, I/O port, and DMA channel (if used) are configured with jumpers or dip switches. The standard configuration for IDE controllers is interrupt 14, I/O port 0x01F0 for the primary channel and interrupt 15, and I/O port 0x0170 for the secondary channel.

SCSI Controller Configuration

Since SCSI controllers can either be integrated into the motherboard or inserted as an adapter card in an open bus slot in the computer, they follow the same basic configuration steps. If the controller is integrated in the motherboard, the BIOS setup program is used to configure the different parameters for the controller. The model of the SCSI controller used on the motherboard determines the parameters that can be configured. However, most, if not all, allow the selection of interrupt, I/O port, and DMA channels used. If the controller is a separate card, the parameters are set via jumpers, switches, or through a software configuration program.

If the computer is equipped with only a SCSI drive, the SCSI controller must have a BIOS to enable the SCSI drive to act as a boot device. This BIOS can be enabled or disabled, if needed. Most high-performance SCSI controllers are configured with software that is supplied by the vendor or by the BIOS located on the controller. The SCSI controller BIOS setup program can be accessed from the boot screen when the SCSI controller runs its self-check program.

Hard Drive Cabling

Both IDE and SCSI devices must be connected with a cable that meets the manufacturer's specifications for length and impedance. Both IDE and SCSI internal devices use a ribbon cable to connect the drive to the controller. On the ribbon cable, one of the edges of the cable has red markings, which means this is the Pin1 side of the cable/connector, which in turn connects to Pin 1 on the drive and on the controller. When installing a drive and cable, be certain that the side of the cable with the red marking is in fact connected to the correct pin, or damage to the drive and/or controller may result.

IDE drives use a ribbon cable that has a 40-pin connector on either end that, in turn, is connected to the hard drive on one end and the controller on the other. A third 40-pin connector may be present on the cable to allow connection to a second IDE drive. This cable cannot exceed 18 inches in length. The electrical signals used on the cable are time-sensitive and, if the cable is too long, the signals will not reach the destination before the next signal is placed on the cable, and this can result in data corruption or "Drive not found" messages. Also, when installing an IDE cable, do not use tight rubber bands to bunch the cable together. Let the cable lie loose and as far away as possible from other components in the computer. For an IDE drive, only use 40-pin ribbon cables that are 18 inches or less in length.

SCSI devices come in a wide variety and each specification has its own cable requirements. Most internal SCSI drives use ribbon cable with either a 50-pin connector or a 68-pin connector. SCSI note: devices should be spaced evenly on the cable, but no closer than .3 meters apart to prevent impedance mismatching.

Do not confuse the different types of ribbon cable. A floppy drive cable has 34 wires, an IDE type ribbon cable has 40 wires, and a SCSI cable has 50 or 68 wires.

Formatting the Hard Drive

Hard drives, whether IDE or SCSI, require two levels of formatting. The first level is referred to as the low-level format. This low-level format actually lays out the physical sectors on the platters. In the original XT and AT drives, you had to perform a low-level format before the disk could be high-level formatted. This low-level format process involved loading the DOS DEBUG.COM and issuing a GO command to a certain address. This started a program in the controller's ROM to low-level format the drive. Today, hard drives are shipped low-level formatted and require a special program from the manufacturer to low-level format the drive again. In most cases, this will never be needed.

After the low-level format is done, or should the disk already have been low-level formatted at the factory, you need to run FDISK.COM to partition the disk. FDISK is used to break the disk up into separate sections for placing different operating systems on the disk, such as DOS and NetWare, or to break a large disk up into smaller partitions that can be used later for additional drives or extended partitions. FDISK.COM is a DOS program that is executed from a DOS prompt. With FDISK, partitions can be created, deleted, assigned drive letters, and can be set active. A partition that is to serve as the BOOT partition must be set as the active partition in FDISK. There can be only one active partition per disk. When installing NetWare 5, you will be using FDISK to create a DOS boot partition of at least 50MB and setting this partition active; the remaining space on the drive will be used for a NetWare volume.

The second level format (high-level) lays out the FAT (File Allocation Tables) and the file structure for storing information on the drive. Under DOS, the program used is simply called FORMAT.COM and is executed from the DOS prompt. When you format a disk with DOS for use in a NetWare file server, you will want to make the DOS partition bootable by placing the DOS system files on the disk. The command to do this is **FORMAT C: /S**. The /S is a switch that instructs the format command to place the DOS systems files on the drive that makes the disk bootable. You will have to use only the DOS format command on the DOS boot partition; NetWare formats its own volumes automatically as you create or extend them.

CERTIFICATION OBJECTIVE 39.02

Using RAID Devices

Networks have become much more than just simple file and print servers; they can now hold critical business information and are expected to be available 24 hours a day, 365 days a year, to provide mission-critical data processing tasks. These demands on the network are being met by disk systems using RAID (redundant array of independent disks). RAID comes in different types, but all of them offer varying levels of data protection. In this section, we will take a look at the most popular RAID levels used with NetWare.

- **RAID Level 1** This is the same as disk mirroring, which is covered in the next section.

- **RAID Level 3** This level uses a parity disk to store redundant information on several disks. The algorithm used distributes the data from each virtual disk block evenly across corresponding blocks of all array members but one, the parity disk, and writes the parity of the distributed data in the corresponding block of the parity disk. RAID Level 3 provides excellent I/O performance for large blocks of sequentially located data such as image processing.

- **RAID Level 5** This level uses storage capacity equal to one of the disks in the array to store the parity computed from the data stored on the other disks in the array. In this respect, it is similar to RAID Level 3. It differs, however, in that the array's disks operate independently of each other, and the redundant data is distributed across all disks in the array. RAID Level 5 can also have a "hot spare" drive in the array. Should a drive fail in the array, the hot spare is automatically brought online, and the data from the failed drive can be rebuilt on the fly on the hot spare.

Since RAID Levels 3 and 5 are highly disk-operation intensive, they are implemented in NetWare only via hardware. The vendor of the RAID disk system provides special disk drivers for NetWare to use with the array. NetWare sees the RAID array as a single, logical partition that can be divided into one or many volumes like a single disk. There are some operating systems that can emulate RAID Levels 3 and 5 through software; however, these implementations are simply too slow to be considered viable solutions. NetWare provides no built-in support for RAID except for RAID Level 0 and RAID Level 1, which will be discussed in the next section.

Disk Mirroring and Disk Duplexing

Disk mirroring and disk duplexing are two data protection methods that NetWare can provide out of the box and without any special hardware or software. *Disk mirroring* is implemented with one controller and two hard drives. *Disk duplexing* is implemented with two disk drives and two controllers.

Disk Mirroring

Disk mirroring (RAID Level 1) uses two disk drives attached to one controller. When disk mirroring is used, NetWare issues two write instructions, one to each disk when a write request is made. This means that instead of one disk of data, you have two disks with identical information on both. One of the drawbacks to mirrored drives is that write requests are slower than on a nonmirrored drive because two write requests must be made, one to the mirrored (original) drive and one to the mirror drive. However, when reading data from a mirrored pair, the reads can be faster because the data may be read from either of the disks. One of the disks will inevitably have its heads closer to the requested data and return quicker from the request. This fact holds true only for SCSI disks.

While it is a common practice to use two identical drives for mirroring, the two hard drives can be of different sizes, but if they are, the mirrored drive (the one holding the original data) has to have the smaller capacity. If the mirrored drive is the one with larger capacity, the system will not be able to create a mirror of the first on the smaller second drive.

Under NetWare, should one of the two drives fail, a message will be sent to the console screen, and the system will continue with no interruption to service. Unless the server supports hot-swap drives, the server will have to be brought down and the defective drive replaced. Once the server is rebooted, NWCONFIG will have to be loaded on the server and the mirrored pair reestablished with the new drive. NetWare will then start the mirroring process to synchronize the mirrored pair.

If you are mirroring IDE disks, you should duplex them by mirroring them on separate adapters or on different channels of IDE/ATA adapter, with each channel or adapter configured to support one drive. This is necessary because IDE drives have a design limitation that prevents them from continuing normally after one of the drives fails.

EXERCISE 39-1

Mirroring Partitions

You must have two disks, either IDE or SCSI, NetWare partitions of equal size on both drives, and Hot Fix enabled on all partitions.

1. Make sure all partitions are deleted from the disk that will be mirrored to an existing disk.

Make sure you do not delete the partitions from the disk containing data you want to mirror.

2. On the disk that the partition will be mirrored to, create one or more new partitions to match those on the disk containing the data. Do not create any volumes. Be sure to enable Hot Fix on the new partitions.

3. Type **NWCONFIG** at the server console and select Standard Disk Options.

4. From the Available Disk Options menu, select Mirror/Unmirror Disk Partitions. A Disk Partition Mirroring Status window appears. This window lists each device and its mirrored status. For example:

```
Mirrored: Logical Partition 3
Not Mirrored: Logical Partition 4
Out of Sync: Logical Partition 5
```

The meaning of each status is as follows:

- **Mirrored** The partition is mirrored to another partition.

- **Not Mirrored** The partition is not mirrored to another partition.

- **Out of Sync** The partition is mirrored to another partition, but is currently out of sync.

5. From the Disk Partition Mirroring Status window, select the disk partition containing the data you want to mirror to another partition. A Mirrored Disk Partitions list appears. This window displays any hard disks that are currently mirrored to the partition you selected. You now specify the empty partition to be mirrored to the selected partition.

6. Click Insert. The system displays the Available Disk Partitions list, a list of all partitions that can be mirrored to the first partition.

on the
● o b

Do not mirror one partition to another partition on the same disk. Doing this eliminates fault tolerance.

7. Select the empty partition from the Available Disk Partitions list. The system mirrors the two partitions to each other so that one partition becomes synchronized with the data from the other partition.

Mirroring can take a long time, depending on the size of the partitions, the amount of data to be mirrored, and the speed of the drive(s)/controller(s) combination. You can view the status of mirroring, abort the mirroring, and start the mirroring again by entering the following commands at the server console:

- **MIRROR STATUS**   Displays a list of logical partitions and their mirroring status, such as Being Remirrored. If a partition is being mirrored, the percent complete is also displayed.

- **ABORT REMIRROR** *logical_partition_number*   Stops the mirroring process on a designated partition. While NetWare is remirroring a pair of drives, server performance can drop. You can use the command ABORT REMIRROR to increase server performance during production hours.

- **REMIRROR PARTITION** *logical_partition_number*   Remirrors a designated partition to a previously mirrored set. NetWare automatically remirrors partitions when they become unsynchronized. This command could be used if you had to stop the remirroring process during production hours and wanted to resume remirroring after hours.

Disk Duplexing

Disk duplexing uses two disk drives just like disk mirroring does; however, instead of using one controller for both disks, disk duplexing uses two controllers, one for each disk. Using a second controller offers a higher degree of fault tolerance over disk mirroring because, if one controller should fail, the system continues on with the other controller and hard disk. For maximum performance, the same type of controllers and disk drives should be used. Implementing disk duplexing is identical to the procedure for disk mirroring.

CERTIFICATION OBJECTIVE 39.03

CD-ROM Drives on NetWare

CD-ROM drives can enhance your network environment by adding flexibility to your resources for a multitude of information. NetWare 5 supports both E/IDE or SCSI CD-ROM drives both for installation purposes and use as a volume. CD-ROMs under NetWare also use the NWPA; that is, IDEATAPI.HAM and IDECD.CDM for IDE CD-ROMs. However, CD-ROMs require one additional piece of software, either CD9660.NSS for CDs adhering to the ISO9660 format or CDHFS.NSS for CDs adhering to the Apple HFS format. To mount a CD-ROM volume, simply type **CD9660.NSS** for ISO9660 CDs or **CDHFS.NSS** at the system console prompt. You can still mount CD-ROMs using the old **CDROM.NLM**; however, using this command loads both CD9660.NSS and CDHFS.NSS modules. CDROM.NLM no longer has any other commands associated with it. NetWare 5's new NWPA eliminates the need for any of the old CDROM commands such as CD DEVICE LIST and CD VOLUME LIST.

on the !ob

In NetWare 5, it is no longer necessary to use the LOAD command when loading or executing command files at the server console. NLMs and NCF files and drivers can all be loaded now by simply typing the name of the module to load at the command prompt.

QUESTIONS AND ANSWERS

I have a tall computer case and I need an IDE cable that is 26 inches in length to reach from the controller to the disks. Can't I just buy a length of cable and snap the ends on it and use it?	No, IDE cables cannot be longer than 18 inches.
I just replaced my SCSI controller in my server. Now when I boot the server, the following message appears: "No SCSI Boot Device Found" and the server just hangs there. What's wrong?	The SCSI controller's BIOS needs to be enabled to allow it to boot from the SCSI drive.
I just replaced my IDE drive in my server and now when I boot it, I get a "Controller Failure" message. Is my disk too large for my controller?	Most likely not. You probably forgot to jumper the drive as a Master or Single Drive in a one-drive system.
After installing a new RAID subsystem, NetWare does not see it in NWCONFIG. What is going on here?	The RAID system you installed most likely requires special HAM and CDM drivers. Check with the vendor for the correct drivers to use with the RAID system.
Whenever I use the command **CDROM** to mount my CD, NetWare loads the CDHFS.NSS module. The CD is in ISO9660 format. Why does NetWare load the Apple support module?	In NetWare 5, the command to mount a CD-ROM volume is **CD9660.NSS**. To mount an Apple format CD-ROM, use **CDHFS.NSS**. The command **CDROM** will load both modules by default.
Can I use my old SCSI I drives on my Fast Wide SCSI controller?	Yes, you can with the proper SCSI cable adapter(s). However, your controller will use the slower transfer speed for all devices on the cable.
Someone told me that you can use a floppy drive cable for an IDE hard drive in an emergency. Is this true?	Absolutely not. While the 34-pin floppy cable will plug into an IDE drive and controller, you will be short 6 wires and the drive will not work.

Magneto-Optical Drives

Magneto-optical drives (*M-O*) are used mainly for archiving and for data-intensive applications, such as CAD and CAM. M-O drives should not be confused with *Write Once Read Many* (*WORM*) drives that can be written to only once. M-O drives use laser beams and magnetism to record the information on the disk. These drives are slower than a hard drive, yet faster than most tape drives, which makes them ideal for archival and backup purposes. M-O drives come in many configurations and can be internal, external, single drive, and jukebox types.

CERTIFICATION SUMMARY

In this chapter, we have discussed the most common types of storage devices used on NetWare and how they are configured and implemented. On the Service and Support certification test, watch out for cable lengths, the way drives are addressed, CMOS and SCSI Ids, and the speed of read/write operations on single disks versus RAID devices. Other concepts to remember are cable types and the difference between IDE and SCSI cables, what the basic disk-related error messages mean, how CD-ROMs are handled by NetWare, and the difference between mirroring and duplexing drives.

 # TWO-MINUTE DRILL

❑ NetWare supports a large array of IDE, ATA, ATAPI, and SCSI devices right out of the box without the need for any special software drivers.

❑ Most hard disk drives and controller cards use jumpers to configure the different parameters of the drive or controller.

❑ IDE controllers come in two flavors—built into the motherboard or separate cards inserted into the bus slots in the computer.

❏ SCSI devices come in a wide variety, and each specification has its own cable requirements. Most internal SCSI drives use ribbon cable with either a 50-pin connector or a 68-pin connector.

❏ If the computer uses a built-in controller on the motherboard, the interrupt, I/O port, and DMA channels (if used) are typically configured from another screen in the BIOS setup program.

❏ Since RAID Levels 3 and 5 are highly disk-operation intensive, they are implemented in NetWare only via hardware.

❏ *Disk mirroring* is implemented with one controller and two hard drives. *Disk duplexing* is implemented with two disk drives and two controllers.

❏ *Magneto-optical drives (M-O)* are used mainly for archiving and for data-intensive applications such as CAD and CAM. M-O drives should not be confused *with Write Once Read Many (WORM)* drives that can be written to only once.

SELF TEST

The Self-Test questions will help you measure your understanding of the material presented in this chapter. Read all the choices carefully, as there may be more than one correct answer. Select all correct answers for each question.

1. What is the single biggest cause of SCSI problems?

   A. Memory addressing problems

   B. Slow data transfer rates

   C. Plug-and-Play incompatibilities

   D. ID settings or termination

2. When you boot your server with a SCSI disk, you receive the message WARNING: POSSIBLE BUS CONTENTION. What do you do?

   A. Check that the adapter has been jumpered to enable the BIOS.

   B. Make sure Pin 1 of the SCSI cable is properly attached to drive.

   C. Check whether the SCSI adapter and the hard disk have different SCSI ID numbers.

   D. Make sure the SCSI bus has been terminated.

3. What does spanning mean?

   A. Distributing a volume in segments over multiple drives

   B. The storage distribution of a data file

   C. Using disk mirroring in a server

   D. Creating more than one NetWare volume per partition

4. What procedure differs between installing an IDE disk and installing a SCSI disk?

   A. Deciding device position on the bus

   B. Attaching cables to the devices

   C. Setting the CMOS disk type in the setup program

   D. Configuring the controller adapter

5. How many devices can a wide SCSI controller support?

   A. 7

   B. 8

   C. 16

   D. 15

6. If you wanted to automatically mount a CD-ROM drive as a NetWare volume when the server boots, what line would you add to AUTOEXEC.NCF file?

   A. LOAD "CDROM"

   B. LOAD ISOCDROM

   C. ISO9660.NSS

   D. CD9660.NSS

7. Your server has an IDE hard disk that has stopped working. When you try to boot the server, you get this error message: Disk Controller Failure. What could be wrong?

   A. Make sure the disk is jumpered as Master.

   B. Check to make sure NetWare is configured for an IDE drive.

C. Make sure the drive or the cable is terminated.

D. Change the I/O port address in CONFIG.SYS.

8. You are working on a server that has two IDE hard drives installed in it. You check the drive cable and find it faulty. You check your parts supply but the only replacement cable you have is cable on a floppy drive. Will this cable work?

A. Yes, it is the same.

B. Yes, just flip the connector over.

C. No, it will not work.

D. Yes, just twist the wire for pin 34 & 33.

9. You are installing a SCSI hard disk. What do you set the CMOS disk type setting to?

A. 0

B. 1

C. 46

D. 47

10. Which CMOS type number would you enter for a User Definable Type for an IDE drive?

A. 44

B. 47

C. 49

D. 45

11. When booting a server with a SCSI disk, you receive the message: No Bootable SCSI Device Found. What do you do?

A. Make sure the SCSI ID of the hard drive is 0.

B. Set the jumper on the controller to BIOS/Enabled.

C. Run FDISK.COM on the drive.

D. Use The Norton Utilities to check the drive.

12. You are unable to boot a server from the IDE hard drive. You can boot the server successfully from a floppy and access the CMOS. No drive type settings are cleared. Which hardware component has failed?

A. BIOS

B. CMOS battery

C. IDE drive

D. CPU

13. How is Pin 1 marked on a hard disk ribbon cable?

A. The pin is opposite the color of Stripe1.

B. There is no way to tell.

C. Pin 1 is square; all of the other pins are round.

D. Pin 1 has a color stripe.

14. Which of the following are issues when planning the SCSI Bus layout? (Choose three.)

A. Cabling

B. SCSI addresses

C. Termination

D. Disk configuration

15. What is the priority of the SCSI Adapter?

    A. 7

    B. 0

    C. 1

    D. 6

16. Which of the following are important considerations when working with CD-ROM drives in a NetWare 5 server? (Choose two.)

    A. NetWare 5 does not support IDE CD-ROM drives.

    B. Performance degradation can occur when a CD-ROM drive is placed on the same SCSI bus as a hard disk.

    C. A CD-ROM is much slower than a hard disk.

    D. CD-ROM drives should not be placed above hard disks in a multiple bay because the strong magnetic field generated by the CD-ROM may damage data on the hard disk.

17. Which tasks might you perform when installing an IDE CD-ROM drive and mounting a CD as a NetWare 5 volume? (Choose two.)

    A. Set the drive's master/slave parameters.

    B. Set the drive's ID number.

    C. Use the CD DEVICE LIST command.

    D. Load CD9660.NSS.

18. An IDE drive uses what size connector?

    A. 50-pin

    B. 40-pin

    C. 35-pin

    D. 25-pin

19. Where is the Hot-Fix Redirection Area located?

    A. In a special area of high memory

    B. In a NetWare logical partition

    C. In a NetWare physical partition

20. You have been asked to load and enable the CDROM.NLM on NetWare 5. Choose three things that loading the CDROM.NLM will allow you to do.

    A. List a volume

    B. Mount a volume

    C. Write to a CD

    D. None of the above

CERTIFIED NOVELL ENGINEER

40

Troubleshooting the DOS Workstation

CERTIFICATION OBJECTIVES

40.01 The Workstation's Communication with the Server

40.02 Troubleshooting Hardware Conflicts

40.03 DOS Versions

U nderstanding the elements that comprise a DOS client/workstation will benefit the Network Administrator in troubleshooting the network. There are primarily two areas where problems could occur, namely software and hardware.

In the first section we will discuss the workstation's communications with a NetWare server. We will look at the software components necessary for a workstation to connect to a server. Next, we will discuss the problems with hardware conflicts, and finally, we will discuss DOS versions.

CERTIFICATION OBJECTIVE 40.01

The Workstation's Communication with the Server

In this section, we will explore the client INSTALL process, the programs and files used on a client and setting up the client NIC (Network Interface Card). We will also investigate the NetWare Watchdog, the Remote Boot features, and troubleshooting with TRACK.

What Occurs During the INSTALL Process?

Let's take a look at the installation process. First, you need to load the install CD, either in a server or local CD-ROM drive. If you do an install from the server, you will need to mount the CD volume on the server and then map a drive to that volume from the workstation. Of course, you would have already had a client installed in the first place in order to connect to a NetWare server, but, you could have booted from a client floppy and then installed the local hard drive from the NetWare server.

Assuming you are installing for the first time, place the install CD in the local CD-ROM drive. Change your directory location to the CD and type the command **INSTALL**. Refer to the example below for executing INSTALL from the CD-ROM, which happens to be D: drive:

```
D:\> INSTALL
```

The initial INSTALL screen will prompt you to select the language, such as English, that INSTALL will display to you on the screen. Next, you'll see copyright information, which you will read and then press any key to continue with the install process. Next, you will see the screen similar to the following:

```
Select the type of Installation desired
    NetWare Server Installation
    Client Installation
```

Once you get the INSTALL screen, you will select the option to perform a client install. After selecting a client install, another install screen will appear. It will ask you to decide which type of client to install. In the case of installing a DOS workstation, you'll need to choose the option ANetWare DOS/WINDOWS Client (VLM)@. The final INSTALL screen for a client appears below:

```
1.  Enter the destination directory:
    C:\NWCLIENT
2.  Install will modify your AUTOEXEC.BAT and CONFIG.SYS files and
    make backups.  Allow changes ? (Y/N): Yes
3.  Install support for MS Windows ? (Y/N): No
4.  Configure your workstation for backup by a NetWare server running
        software such as SBACKUP ? (Y/N) No
5.  Select the driver for your network board.
     Highlight here and press <Enter> to see the list.
6.  Highlight here and press <Enter> to install.
```

The Network Administrator must answer several installation questions. (I've shown sample responses to the questions—these appear in bold.) The following is a list of questions that require answers as part of the install process:

- Where will the installation files be stored?

- Should the installation process modify AUTOEXEC.BAT and CONFIG.SYS?

- Do you want MS-Windows support?

- Should a NetWare server back up the client?

- What type of driver is to be used on the client?

The default destination directory for the installation process to place the client files is C:\NWCLIENT. If you want to create a client floppy, then you'll need to change the default drive location to A:. Unless you have a reason to change the location, it is best to use the standard NWCLIENT directory.

An important decision to make is whether INSTALL will update your AUTOEXEC.BAT and CONFIG.SYS files. If it does modify them, then your PC will be set to automatically boot as a client when powered on. You will need to remember to place the required DOS boot files on the disk or the PC won't boot in the first place. You can use SYS A: to place boot files on the floppy. You can also create a bootable floppy by issuing FORMAT A: /S; however, if you do this after you install the client files, then you will need to install the client again

If you do choose to modify these files, INSTALL creates backups of the older versions. These are called AUTOEXEC.BNW and CONFIG.BNW and can be copied to the original files if necessary.

exam
ⓦatch

The NetWare Workstation INSTALL process will prompt you to update AUTOEXEC.BAT and CONFIG.SYS. It will then back up the old files and generate a *.BNW extension of each.

Load Windows support only if you are running MS-Windows. The installation will modify various sections of the Windows installation files: SYSTEM.INI, PROGRAM.INI, and WIN.INI.

If the client will be backed up by a NetWare server running Novell's SBACKUP, then choose support for that option. If you do choose this option, then another installation screen will appear. This screen will prompt you for additional information such as the SMS (Storage Management Services) Server name doing the backup, the workstation name being backed up, the DOS hard drive(s) holding the data to be backed up, and the hard drive location where you want data restored.

The final decision is which type of driver will be installed. This is one of the most important decisions you will make during the workstation install. The question here is what type of Network Interface Card are you using? You will need to choose the driver (i.e., NIC device driver) for the NIC physically installed on your client. There are about 50 to 60 drivers that come on the install CD; however, if your driver is not listed, you will need to insert the disk that came with the NIC. Some newer drivers may not be on the INSTALL CD.

exam
Watch

The NIC software device driver must match the type of NIC installed on the client PC.

Once you have made install decisions, go to Part 6 and press ENTER to actually install the client files. We will now take a look at the stand-alone and network files necessary for a client PC to connect to a NetWare server.

Files and Programs Used on DOS Workstations

In order for a DOS workstation to communicate with a NetWare server in a network environment it must use stand-alone boot files and network boot files. The standalone files are necessary for a PC to boot but this does not necessarily mean the PC has network connectivity. That is where the network files come in. Network files will be loaded after the stand-alone (nonnetwork) files are loaded. They will reside on the PC in RAM and stay there as TSR (Terminate and Stay Resident) programs. On NetWare, these are called the *requester*, or redirector, files.

In a nutshell, these determine whether a request is local or coming over the network. If local, they pass the request to DOS and the DOS files handle the request. If there is a network request, the network TSRs pass the request through the NIC, down the cable, and to a NetWare server for processing. For example, when you take a directory listing of drive A:, the DIR request is passed to DOS for processing. However, when you perform a DIR listing on a network drive that has been mapped to G:, for example, then the network TSRs intercept the request and pass it to a NetWare server. They do this because DOS has no idea what a server and volume mean, and a mapped drive points to a server and volume.

The standalone and network files needed for a PC to boot up and have network connectivity are as follows:

- **IO.SYS**   Required hidden file providing basic I/O handling
- **MSDOS.SYS**   Required hidden file that deals with file management

- **COMMAND.COM**   Required non-hidden file that is the command interpreter

- **CONFIG.SYS**   Optional DOS boot file needed for some workstation settings

- **AUTOEXEC.BAT**   Optional DOS boot file needed to run STARTNET.BAT

- **STARTNET.BAT**   NetWare workstation batch file that is used to load the programs to allow the workstation to connect to a server

- **NET.CFG**   A configuration file used by the programs loaded in STARTNET.BAT

When the DOS workstation boots, IO.SYS, MSDOS.SYS, and COMMAND.COM are executed. Next, if CONFIG.SYS and AUTOEXEC.BAT are on the root directory of the boot drive, they are executed, in order. Let's look at some of the commands that would be placed in the CONFIG.SYS and AUTOEXEC.BAT files that relate to a workstation's connectivity to the network. Incidentally, these are samples that INSTALL would create if you selected the option to modify AUTOEXEC.BAT and CONFIG.SYS during the installation process. The contents of a sample CONFIG.SYS file looks like this:

```
FILES=40
DEVICE=C:\WINDOWS\COMMAND\HIMEM.SYS
LASTDRIVE=Z
```

In this file, the setting FILES = 40, indicates that DOS can open 40 files concurrently. The DEVICE statement tells DOS to use Extended Memory (XMS); otherwise, DOS cannot access RAM above 1 MB.

LASTDRIVE=Z tells DOS that the last drive on this workstation will be Z:. A setting equal to Z: allows DOS to take advantage of 26 drive letters, from A: to Z:. This is particularly important when the DOS workstation needs to access a server's network drive. To set a network drive, a logical drive letter must be mapped using the NetWare MAP command. Some of the drive letters, such as A: or C:, will be physical; other drive letters will be logical drives pointing to a server's physical drive. In order to map a logical drive letter to a server's physical disk, use the following command:

```
C:\>MAP H:=ONE_SYS:\PAYROLL
```

Note that the server is named ONE, the server has a volume named SYS:, and the directory being mapped is \PAYROLL.

e x a m
ⓦatch

A workstation can access at most 26 drive letters from A: to Z: by setting LASTDRIVE=Z in CONFIG.SYS.

An equally important file is the AUTOEXEC.BAT file. This file will be automatically executed once the PC boots. When a DOS workstation (or client) is installed, the install process stores some files in a specific directory, usually \NWCLIENT. One of the files it creates is the batch file STARTNET.BAT. INSTALL will also modify AUTOEXEC.BAT by inserting the @CALL statement in it. In the following example, the @CALL statement in the AUTOEXEC.BAT file is calling STARTNET.BAT which will, in turn, execute and then return control back to AUTOEXEC.BAT. Once STARTNET.BAT starts to run, it will execute several other programs. These will be explored later.

```
PATH=C:\DOS
PATH=%PATH%;C:\NWCLIENT
@CALL C:\NWCLIENT\STARTNET.BA
```

In this example, the DOS PATH is set in order for DOS programs to execute. In the second PATH statement, the install process has appended C:\NWCLIENT to the current PATH. Finally, the @CALL statement executes, which tells DOS to execute STARTNET.BAT. STARTNET.BAT is a batch file that executes NetWare-specific programs.

Now, let's explore the NetWare-specific files created during the installation process. INSTALL creates STARTNET.BAT and several other executable files, which are loaded in the drive and directory location specified in the first question you answered.

The follow list outlines the major files created by the INSTALL program.

- **LSL.COM (Link Support Layer)** Provides the dialog between the client's NIC and the protocol used.

- **NIC driver** Also known as the ODI (Open Data-Link Interface) MLID (Multiple Link Interface Driver), the NIC driver sends and receives messages to and from the LSL. ODI allows multiple NIC drivers and protocols to reside on the same PC.

- **IPXODI.COM** This loads the IPX/SPX (Internetwork Packet eXchange/Sequenced Packet eXchange) protocol. IPX/SPX is NetWare's native protocol. TCP/IP could be loaded here, which would provide Internet connectivity.

- **VLM.EXE (Virtual Loadable Module)** This program, also known as the NetWare DOS Requestor, acts as the "traffic cop" between DOS and the network. This program is actually a suite of other programs listed in Table 40-1.

The following is an example of a STARTNET.BAT file that will execute NetWare programs:

```
SET NWLANGUAGE=ENGLISH
C:\NWCLIENT\LSL.COM
C:\NWCLIENT\SMC9432.COM
C:\NWCLIENT\IPXODI.COM
C:\NWCLIENT\VLM.EXE
```

The first statement sets the NetWare language to English. Then, LSL is loaded. This is followed by the NIC driver, which happens to be an SMC9432 100 MBps card, the IPXODI module, and then the NetWare DOS Requester - VLM.

exam
ⓦatch

The NetWare network connection files must be executed in this order: LSL, NIC driver, IPXODI, and VLM.

The last file we need to discuss is a configuration file that is read by the network programs. This file is called NET.CFG. As the client PC boots, STARTNET.BAT is called to execute LSL, the NIC driver, IPXODI, and the VLM suite of programs. These four major programs read different

TABLE 40-1

The VLM Suite
of Programs

VLM module	Description
CONN.VLM	The connection table manager tracks network connections between a server and a workstation.
TRAN.VLM	The transport protocol supports other transport modules such as IPXNCP.VLM.
IPXNCP.VLM	This module creates IPX packets for use with servers that use NCP (NetWare Core Protocol).
SECURITY.VLM	Provides packet signature security.
NDS.VLM	Allows support for NetWare 4.1x and 5.0 servers.
BIND.VLM	Provides NetWare 3.1x bindery emulation.
NWP.VLM	Parent VLM protocol giving support for NDS, BIND, and FIO.
FIO.VLM	This module manages file input and output.
GENERAL.VLM	This provides functions for other VLMs.
REDIR.VLM	The module that handles DOS and NetWare redirection.
PRINT.VLM	This VLM works with DOS to handle printer redirection.
NETX.VLM	Provides compatibility for NetWare shell.
AUTO.VLM	The VLM that handles automatic workstation reconnection to a server.

sections of NET.CFG to initialize certain variables. A sample NET.CFG appears as follows:

```
Link Driver SMC943
     INT 10
     PORT 300
     MEM D0000
     FRAME Ethernet_802.2

NetWare DOS Requester
     FIRST NETWORK DRIVE = F
     PREFERRED SERVER = TMFIRM
     NAME CONTEXT = "OU=PAYROLL.O=HQ"
```

The first section sets the port, interrupt, base memory address, and frame type for the NIC. NetWare networks using the IPX/SPX protocol must specify a frame type. The NetWare DOS Requester section sets the first network drive for this client to F:. The preferred server will be TMFIRM, and the NDS context location is set to the Organization Unit PAYROLL and the Organization HQ. Now that we've discussed the software aspects of the workstation, let's look at the hardware setup, namely the NIC.

Setting Up a Workstation's NIC

In order to get the NIC to communicate correctly with the network software and the other hardware components in the PC, such as the CPU and RAM, you will need to configure it correctly. The following are some typical settings:

- Hardware interrupt (INT in NET.CFG)
- Base I/O port (PORT in NET.CFG)
- Base RAM address (MEM in NET.CFG)
- Frame type

Notice that these correspond to the variables in the NET.CFG file. Some NICs require you to configure settings manually; others will automatically configure the settings in software that comes with the NIC. Each manufacturer's NIC is different, so you'll have to look at the individual NIC and any documentation that comes with it to accurately configure your NIC. Refer to Table 40-2 as a guideline for determining whether you should manually set the NIC's settings or whether software will allow you to list and change the values.

The main thing to keep in mind is that the settings on your NIC cannot conflict with settings on other devices. You could use the DOS MSD diagnostic utility to determine hardware values currently used.

An *interrupt* is a signal that tells the CPU that a device needs some type of attention. Each hardware component will need a unique interrupt. Table 40-3 lists the most commonly used interrupts.

TABLE 40-2	NIC bus type	Description
Determining the Method of Hardware Configuration	ISA	Check the NIC for settings. There will either be jumpers or a series of on/off switches to configure your hardware settings.
	EISA, MCA, or PCI Local Bus	Execute the NIC's setup program to list and change hardware settings.

There are a number of interrupts available for use by a NIC. In our sample NET.CFG file shown earlier, an entry of INT 10 indicates INTerrupt 10, which was available, and is now used for our SMC9432 NIC.

The base I/O port is the communication channel used by a hardware device to send data to the CPU. Each I/O port uses an I/O address and each hardware device must have a unique I/O port address. Table 40-4 outlines some of the common ports used.

TABLE 40-3	Interrupt	Device
Commonly Available Hardware Interrupts	0	System timer
	1	Keyboard
	2	VGA/EGA controller
	3	Serial Port 2 (COM2:)
	4	Serial Port 1 (COM1:)
	5	Parallel Port 2 (LPT2:)
	6	Floppy disk controller
	7	Parallel Port 1 (LPT1:)
	8	Real-time clock
	9 – 12	Available
	13	Mathematical coprocessor
	14	IDE hard disk controller
	15	Available

TABLE 40-4	Device	Base I/O port address in hexadecimal
Commonly Used I/O Port Addresses	COM1	3F8
	COM2	2F8
	COM3	3E8
	COM4	2E8
	LPT1	378
	LPT2	278

If the I/O port address is not listed, then it is most likely available for use by new hardware such as an NIC. In our NET.CFG file shown earlier, we are using PORT 300 for the SMC9432 NIC.

The base memory address identifies the initial location in RAM that a hardware device will use to exchange data across the network. Some NICs don't require a setting because they don't use RAM. In that case, you don't need to specify one. Common locations used are D0000 and CC000. Looking back at our NET.CFG file, the SMC9432 card uses a MEM setting of D0000 as its RAM location.

Choosing the frame type is required for the IPX/SPX protocol; it is not required for TCP/IP. In earlier versions of NetWare, versions 2.x and 3.x, the NIC drivers used Ethernet 802.3 frame type packets. Starting in NetWare 4.x, the NIC drivers use Ethernet 802.2 frame type packets. If your network is using a mix of versions, then place both frame types in the NET.CFG for your NIC.

Once you have configured the hardware settings for your NIC, you can use it on the network. Remember, hardware settings cannot conflict with other devices in the PC.

NetWare's Watchdog Feature for Workstations

The watchdog feature is a technique, in which a NetWare server will send a packet, called the *watchdog packet*, to a workstation to ensure that the workstation is active. If the workstation does not respond to the server's request within a given amount of time, then the server will send another watchdog packet. If the workstation still does not respond to the server, the workstation is assumed to be inactive, and the server disconnects the workstations's connection. The server also notifies the Network Administrator by sending an alert to the server console screen.

Watchdog settings are made with the SET command at the NetWare server. Table 40-5 summarizes the watchdog parameters SET at the server console.

e x a m
ⓦa t c h

Watchdog parameters are set at the NetWare server console.

The following examples demonstrate how to use watchdog SET parameters at the server console for a server named SERVER-A:

```
SERVER-A: SET CONSOLE DISPLAY WATCHDOG LOGOUTS=ON
SERVER-A: DELAY BEFORE FIRST WATCHDOG PACKET=5
SERVER-A: SET NUMBER OF WATCHDOG PACKETS=35
SERVER-A: SET DELAY BETWEEN WATCHDOG PACKETS=25
```

TABLE 40-5   Summary of the Watchdog Parameters Using the Console SET Command

Parameter	Default Value	Range	Description
NUMBER OF WATCHDOG PACKETS	10	5 to 100	The quantity of packets the server sends before disconnecting a workstation connection.
DELAY BETWEEN WATCHDOG PACKETS	59.3 secs	9.9 secs to 10 mins 26.2 secs.	The interval of time between packets.
DELAY BEFORE FIRST WATCHDOG PACKET	4 mins 56.6 secs	15.7 secs to 14 days	The amount of time the server will wait before sending the initial watchdog packet.
CONSOLE DISPLAY WATCHDOG LOGOUTS	OFF	ON or OFF	Determines whether a server console message appears when a workstation is disconnected.

If these are set only at the server, then they will be lost the next time the server is booted. Place the SET parameters in AUTOEXEC.NCF to maintain the values the next time the server boots.

If your workstations are having connection problems, then you could display them to the server and see which workstations are not responding.

Using the Remote Boot Feature

You can remotely boot a diskless client PC as long as you have a boot PROM inserted into the PROM socket on the NIC. When the PC is booted, it uses boot images stored on the server to load files across the network. In order to use this feature, you will need to do the following:

1. Install a Remote Boot PROM (Programmable Read-Only Memory) chip.

2. Load RPL.NLM (Remote Program Load) on the server.

3. Load RPL.COM on the workstation if it is going across a source routing bridge.

4. Turn on the diskless workstation.

5. Log in to the server.

Using TRACK for Troubleshooting

If you don't have a device called a *sniffer* to display packets sent over a network, you can use NetWare's TRACK program. TRACK will display all server and RIP (Routing Internet Protocol) packets sent on the server. It can also be used to display workstation connection requests. TRACK is turned OFF by default. It must be turned on at the server console as shown in the following example:

```
SERVER-A: TRACK ON
```

To turn tracking off, simply type **TRACK OFF** as shown here:

```
SERVER-A:  TRACK OFF
```

There are two main types of requests that are TRACKed. When a server is receiving inbound information, an IN packet is sent. When the server broadcasts outbound information, an OUT record is sent. An example of a server's IN packet is the following:

```
IN [00001234:000034BCF12F] 6:11:05pm Get Nearest Server
```

exam
Ⓦatch *Get Nearest Server is requested by a workstation when the workstation needs to attach to a NetWare server.*

The first number after IN is the network address such as 00001234, while the second number, following the colon, is the workstation node, such as 000034BCF12F, that is requesting the nearest server. In this case, a workstation is sending a packet to the server so it is the server's IN packet. An example of a server's OUT packet is shown next:

```
OUT [00001234:000034BCF12F] 6:11:06pm Give Nearest Server
```

exam
Ⓦatch *Give Nearest Server is sent by the closest NetWare server. The server is then saying it will be used to authenticate the workstation.*

In this case, the server is responding to the workstation's initial attachment request and satisfies it. When a workstation initially boots and network connection software loads, the workstation sends out a Get Nearest Server command as a broadcast over the cable. A server can then respond with a Give Nearest Server command, and the workstation will initially attach to that server.

If you see an OUT packet's node address consisting of all F's, then this is a broadcast packet. A broadcast is sent to all nodes on the network. See the following example for a partial OUT packet with a broadcast:

```
OUT [00001234:FFFFFFFFFFFF]
```

exam
Ⓦatch *A packet of all F's is a broadcast packet sent to all workstations on the network.*

Another useful tool is the DISPLAY console command to determine whether a server or network is available. If, for some reason, a workstation is not able to connect to a server, then the DISPLAY SERVERS command can be executed as follows:

```
SERVER-A: DISPLAY SERVERS
```

This will generate a list of servers that have broadcast their server names on the network. If the server is not in the list, then the server is the problem. If the server is in the list, then the workstation may be the problem. To make sure the workstation is at fault, try connecting to the server from another workstation. If you are still unable to connect, then the workstation is most likely the culprit. However, you might also try connecting to another server from the workstation that is having the problem.

The DISPLAY command can also be used to determine why a workstation cannot connect to a given network. It is issued at the console as follows:

```
SERVER-A: DISPLAY NETWORKS
```

Note that TRACK and DISPLAY will show only IPX numbers, so if you are using TCP/IP, they will not be displayed.

CERTIFICATION OBJECTIVE 40.02

Troubleshooting Hardware Conflicts

In terms of troubleshooting hardware conflicts, make sure that no two devices share the same interrupt, base I/O port address, or base memory address. Refer to the commonly used settings of each of these given earlier in the chapter. If your NIC has a conflict with another device, then you will not be able to connect to the network, even if your PC boots.

If you do experience a hardware conflict, you can change it either with a hardware setting or by using the setup disk that comes with the NIC. Refer to Table 40-4 to help you determine which method to use. You can always change settings in the Link Driver section of the NET.CFG to test your settings. For example, an SMC8000 NIC has one of two possible settings listed on the card itself. If one does not work, then you can change the settings in NET.CFG for the other settings.

Types of PC Memory

There are various types of PC memory. The first kind ranges from address location 0 to 640K. This is called *conventional memory* and is used by applications and some DOS programs. From 640K to 1,024K (or 1MB) the memory is called *Upper Memory Blocks (UMB)* and is reserved for shadow ROM. From 1MB to the total amount of RAM on the PC is called *extended memory* (also known as XMS). On 386 PCs and higher, the total amount of RAM cannot exceed 4GB. The first 64K of XMS is called the High Memory Area (HMA). It is used to load device drivers and TSRs to free conventional memory. Only one program at a time can occupy HMA. To use HMA and XMS, you will need a device driver called HIMEM.SYS. Expanded Memory (known as EMS) uses 16K pages in a 64K-page UMB window. Some older programs use EMS; this type of memory is not directly addressable by the CPU.

In terms of optimizing PC memory, you could run the DOS MEMMAKER program, which will alter AUTOEXEC.BAT and CONFIG.SYS in an attempt to load various programs into higher memory. This will free up conventional memory for applications that require it. Also, the network boot files, LSL, the NIC driver, IPXODI, and VLM, automatically load in extended memory if it is available.

CERTIFICATION OBJECTIVE 40.03

DOS Versions

Just a brief word on DOS versions. DOS has gone through various revisions from version 1.0 to version 6.22 and now version 7 is built into Windows 95. Most likely your clients will be running DOS 5 and higher. The

NetWare license disk is bootable and has a copy of Digital Research DOS v. 7.0 (DRDOS 7), which includes all of the utilities necessary for creating a DOS partition on the server hard drive.

CERTIFICATION SUMMARY

In summary, a PC needs both hardware and software in order to connect to a network server. After resolving hardware conflicts with regard to interrupt, base I/O port address, and base memory address, you will need to install the client software. If you have conflicts, the PC will not be able to connect to the network.

Client software is installed from the NetWare CD by typing **INSTALL**. This procedure will copy over network files to the destination directory you give it. The files are LSL, the NIC driver, IPXODI, and VLM. You must choose the correct NIC driver that goes along with the NIC. If you do not pick the correct one, you will not get access to the network.

INSTALL will create a STARTNET.BAT that will execute the network files. If any of the network files do not get loaded, then the PC will not gain network access.

You will also need to choose the appropriate frame type on your network. Ethernet 802.3 is the default for versions 2.x and 3.x, while Ethernet 802.2 is the default for 4.x and higher. If you get the wrong frame type, the workstation will not be able to communicate.

However, if all of the above work successfully, then you should be able to gain network access. You can then log in and use mapped network directories and captured network printers.

TWO-MINUTE DRILL

- ❏ The default destination directory for the installation process to place the client files is C:\NWCLIENT.
- ❏ The NetWare Workstation INSTALL process will prompt you to update AUTOEXEC.BAT and CONFIG.SYS. It will then back up the old files and generate a *.BNW extension of each.

❑ In order for a DOS workstation to communicate with a NetWare server in a network environment, it must use stand-alone boot files and network boot files.

❑ The NetWare network connection files must be executed in this order: LSL, NIC driver, IPXODI, and VLM.

❑ The watchdog feature is a technique where a NetWare server will send a packet, called the *watchdog packet*, to a workstation to ensure the workstation is active.

❑ You can remotely boot a diskless client PC, as long as you have a boot PROM inserted into the PROM socket on the NIC.

❑ If you don't have a device called a *sniffer* to display packets sent over a network, you can use NetWare's TRACK program.

❑ A packet of all Fs is a broadcast packet sent to all workstations on the network.

SELF TEST

The Self-Test questions will help you measure your understanding of the material presented in this chapter. Read all the choices carefully, as there may be more than one correct answer. Select all correct answers for each question.

1. By setting _____, in the _____ file, we allow a client to take advantage of the full range of drive letters.

    A. LSL and AUTOEXEC.BAT

    B. Watchdog and TRACK

    C. LASTDRIVE=Z and CONFIG.SYS

    D. LASTDRIVE=A and AUTOEXEC.NCF

2. What is the name of the technique whereby a server determines whether a workstation is active?

    A. VLM

    B. Extended memory

    C. TRACK

    D. Watchdog

3. What is the name of the program that is used to display network connection traffic on the server?

    A. DISPLAY SERVERS

    B. DISPLAY NETWORKS

    C. TRACK ON

    D. TRACK OFF

4. What server file must contain watchdog parameters if they are to become permanent?

    A. AUTOEXEC.BAT

    B. CONFIG.SYS

    C. AUTOEXEC.NCF

    D. DOS Requestor

5. What do all Fs represent in a packet's node address?

    A. It is a broadcast.

    B. It is used to represent a watchdog packet being removed from the network.

    C. It indicates failure of a packet to be acknowledged by a server.

    D. It indicates failure of a packet to be acknowledged by a workstation.

6. What is the name given the NetWare DOS Requester program?

    A. The NIC driver you loaded for your NIC

    B. IPXODI.COM

    C. VLM.EXE

    D. NET.CFG

7. What is the load order of the DOS client boot files?

    A. NIC driver, VLM.EXE, IPXODI.COM, LSL.COM

    B. LSL.COM, VLM.EXE, IPXODI.COM, NIC driver

C. LSL.COM, NIC driver,
   IPXODI.COM, NET.CFG,
   STARTNET.BAT

D. LSL.COM, NIC driver,
   IPXODI.COM, VLM.EXE

8. What is the name of the NetWare
   configuration read by the network
   programs?

   A. VLM.EXE

   B. AUTOEXEC.BAT

   C. CONN.VLM

   D. NET.CFG

9. What is the default directory where client
   files are installed?

   A. \NWCLIENT

   B. /NWCLIENT

   C. \STARTNET.BAT

10. What is the name of the process to get a
    diskless workstation network connectivity?

    A. Watchdog

    B. Remote Boot

    C. TRACK

    D. NetWare DOS Requester

11. What type of memory ranges from 0 to
    640K?

    A. XMS

    B. EMS

    C. Conventional

D. HMA

12. If STARTNET.BAT fails to load
    automatically, what file should you
    investigate first?

    A. NET.CFG

    B. VLM.EXE

    C. AUTOEXEC.NCF

    D. AUTOEXEC.BAT

13. What is the default frame type for
    NetWare 4.x servers?

    A. Ethernet 802.2

    B. Ethernet 802.3

    C. Ethernet_II

    D. Ethernet 802.5

14. What device driver is needed for HMA
    and XMS?

    A. LOMEM.SYS

    B. NET.CFG

    C. VLM.SYS

    D. HIMEM.SYS

15. What memory ranges from 1MB to a
    maximum of 4GB?

    A. XMS

    B. EMM

    C. HMA

    D. UMB

41

Troubleshooting Network Printing

CERTIFICATION OBJECTIVES

41.01   An Overview of Network Printing

41.02   General Printer Troubleshooting

41.03   Troubleshooting Print Queues

41.04   Troubleshooting Print Server and Printer Objects

Printing plays one of the most important roles in a computer environment. At some time or another, everyone in an organization will need to print. Troubleshooting printer problems is an important part of the network administrator job.

The first section of this chapter gives an overview of network printing. Next, we examine general printer troubleshooting and explore the topic of print queue troubleshooting. Finally, we discuss troubleshooting Print Server and Printer objects.

CERTIFICATION OBJECTIVE 41.01

An Overview of Network Printing

Before you begin troubleshooting printers, you need to understand some general printing concepts. We know that in a stand-alone environment a PC can print to a local printer port, such as LPT1. In this case, the printer is physically attached to the PC. The user issues the print request, and the print job is sent to a local print queue. A print queue is a directory that holds print jobs until they are printed. Once printed, the print job is deleted from the print queue. If the printer is online, the print job will be printed from the print queue and then removed. If the printer is offline, the print job will be held in the print queue and printed at a later time. A printer physically attached to a workstation PC is known as a local printer. The term *local printer* indicates that the printer is on a workstation PC, is not shared, and no users can access this printer through the network.

exam
ⓌatcH

A local printer is attached to a stand-alone PC or workstation and cannot be accessed through the network.

Now, if we were in a networked environment, we could print to a network printer. The overall process of the print job being sent to the print queue would be similar to the stand-alone situation, but the location of the print queue and actual printer would be somewhere else in the network. That is the key difference.

In a network, if the printer is not physically attached to the local printer port, for example, LPT1, we can still print to it, but we must "trick" the local printer port. We do this by a process known as *capture*. The local printer port is captured, and the print job is redirected to a print queue located on a NetWare server. A NetWare server that manages the printing process is called a *print server*. On a NetWare workstation the physical printer port then becomes a logical printer port. The user issues the print request, and the print job will be sent to LPT1.

Assume a workstation with no local printer attached to LPT1. When the print request is initiated, instead of the print job really being sent to a local printer, it will be sent to a print queue on a NetWare server. Then the print server that manages that particular print queue will send the print job to the correct LPT port that has the attached printer. In a NetWare network, a physical printer can be attached to a server or workstation. A printer can also be attached directly to the network and this is known as a *network printer*. In a 10/100 BASE T network, for example, the network printer would attach directly to a network hub.

exam
Ⓦatch

A networked printer can be attached to either a server, a workstation, or directly to the network.

Figure 41-1 shows the required printing objects you need to create in order to set up network printing. In order to implement network printing, the Network Administrator must create a Print Queue object. This object will reference a volume on a NetWare server. Required properties for this object are as follows:

- Print Queue object name
- NetWare Volume name where the [*VolumeName*]:\QUEUES directory will be created.

The Print Queue object name will be used to link the print queue to the logical printer. A Printer object must also be created. This is not an actual printer but represents a logical printer somewhere in the network. Here are a few of the important properties:

- Printer port: LPT*n* or COM*n* where *n* is the port number
- Location: Manual load or Auto load

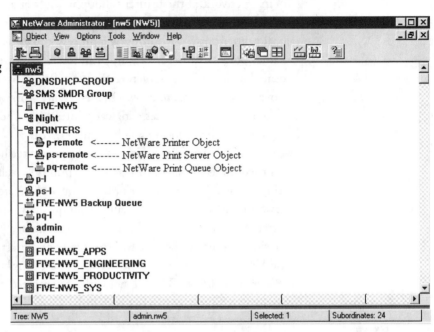

The Manual load location is used for a printer attached directly to a workstation. The Auto load location indicates a printer attached directly to a server. Manual load implies that you, as the Network Administrator, must run NPRINTER.EXE, or the Windows-based utility, NPTWIN95.EXE, on the client. This must remain there in order for any print jobs to be sent to that printer. Once loaded, just minimize it; then the user who uses the PC can run other applications. The printer port is the LPT or COM number that has the actual physical printer connected to it.

exam
ⓦatch

Manual load is used when the printer is physically attached to a workstation. That workstation must be running NPRINTER.EXE or NPTWIN95.EXE. Auto load is used when the printer is physically attached to a server. That server must be running PSERVER.NLM and PSERVER.NLM will automatically load NPRINTER.EXE. In either case, NPRINTER.EXE must be loaded.

You will also need to assign a Printer object name. Next, you will need to assign the print queue name to the Printer object name using NWADMIN.

This step links the two together. See Figure 41-2, which shows the NWADMIN screens for creating the three necessary printing objects.

The Print Server object requires a name and the name of the printer that it manages. It must be loaded on the NetWare server you designate as a print server. To make a print server, just execute PSERVER on the file server console as follows:

```
FIVE-NW5: PSERVER
```

A print server is a NetWare server with PSERVER.NLM loaded.

So, the print queue is assigned to a printer and a printer is assigned to a print server. Now, all the components are linked together.

Assign print queues to printers and assign printers to print servers.

FIGURE 41-2

Creating the necessary printing objects: a Printer, a Print Server, and Print Queue

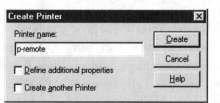

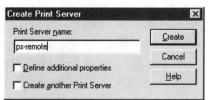

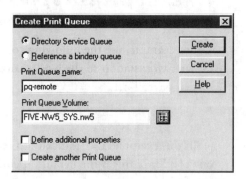

Once these are created, your workstations must then redirect their local printer port to the print queue you created. Once the user issues a print request, the print job will be sent to the print queue that the LPT[*number*] has been redirected to. That means it will be stored on a NetWare volume. Next, the print server will see that there is a print job in the print queue. It will then send the print job to the designated printer. Remember, in order to use a printer attached to a workstation, a PC must CAPTURE its local printer port, which will be redirected to a print queue. The following command will redirect a print job in DOS-mode to a network queue, named pq-remote in the printers organization unit:

```
D:\SYSTEM> capture q=.pq-remote.printers.nw5
```

Then, a CAPTURE SHOW command can be issued to verify which port is CAPTUREd or redirected to which print queue. LPT1 is the default CAPTUREd port.

CAPTURE can redirect other LPT ports as well. To CAPTURE the LPT2 port to a particular printer, use the following command:

```
D:\SYSTEM> capture L=2p=.p-remote.printers.nw5
```

Using CAPTURE SHOW is a good troubleshooting tool to make sure the print job goes to the right printer. If the correct LPT port is not CAPTUREd to the correct print queue, then the print job might go to the wrong printer. You could also create a CAPTURE in Windows 95 by choosing Control Panel | Printers.

exam
ⓦatch

To redirect a print job to a printer attached to a workstation or print server, the workstation's local printer port must be CAPTUREd.

For example, use the following command to CAPTURE the LPT1 port on your workstation so the workstation can print to a network printer named payroll-prt:

```
D:\PUBLIC> capture L=1 P=payroll-prt
```

In this example, L=1 indicates to redirect or capture LPT, port number one (1). Since this is the default, it could be left off the command; it is there just for clarity.

CERTIFICATION OBJECTIVE 41.02

General Printer Troubleshooting

The troubleshooting process is an important aspect of network printing. The two major areas for general printer troubleshooting are the following:

1. Software

   - Print Queue object
   - Print Server object
   - Printer object

2. Hardware

In terms of troubleshooting from a software viewpoint, first check your printer definitions and assignments using NWADMIN. You may want to document these configurations. It is important to know which Print Queue object is assigned to which printer and then which printer is assigned to which print server. If the print job does not print, you could look at your configurations and determine why. We will explore these in detail in a later section.

Regarding hardware problems, check the printer first. Make sure it is on and the cable is plugged in. Also, make sure the correct printer is checked as the default printer. Another problem could be the printer is not using the correct print device driver. Perform a test page print. These basic tips require minimal effort. Next, check for possible hardware interrupts. If the printer has a conflicting interrupt with another device, that could be your problem. You can use Device Manager in Windows 95 to discover hardware interrupts conflicts.

One good troubleshooting technique is to print to the printer as a local printer if you cannot print to it through the network. In other words, if you cannot print to the printer through the network, reconnect the printer cable directly into a PC and attempt to a print request. If it does not print, you know you have a problem with the printer, cable, or printer port on the PC. If the printer still does not print, then change the cable. If it does not print after changing the cable, then it is a possible printer problem. If it prints when you change the cable, then the cable may well be the problem. If you finally get the printer to print locally but not through the network, then you can assume it is a software-related problem. One of the printing objects, Print Queue, Printer, or Print Server, is configured incorrectly. In DOS mode, you could issue the following command to print directly to the LPT port and test your local print connection—if it prints, your printer and cable are good:

```
C:\> DIR > LPT1
```

Now, let's look at a few issues with different categories of printers. Typically, you will use a dot matrix, ink jet, or laser printer in your network. In terms of dot matrix printers, make sure you use quality ribbons. Low-quality ribbons will yield poor quality output. Also, dot matrix ribbons dry out over time if not used. Check the printing head for dust and dirt particles and make sure there is enough free air around it in order to distribute heat. Don't turn the knob while the printer is on. This could damage the internal motor. As a final check, make sure self-test is working. This is a good troubleshooting technique since it ensures the printer is working at all.

Concerning ink jet printers, make sure the correct paper is used. If the supply of ink is low, replace the cartridge. Also, clean the nozzles but make sure you follow the instructions of the manufacturer carefully. Also, try printing a test page.

Everyone wants to print to laser printers. Their quality is very good and they make less noise. Check the paper supply, toner level, and look for paper jam error messages. Keep the manufacturer's guide close by. If you get errors unfamiliar to you, you can check the guide for possible problems.

Start out with the basics when troubleshooting printers. Once you check for these problems, move on to the more advanced tools outlined for the different categories of printers.

CERTIFICATION OBJECTIVE 41.03

Troubleshooting Print Queues

If your print job never reached the print queue, then you have a few possible items to check. First look at the Print Queue object Job List screen. See Figure 41-3 for the Print Queue Job List for a Print Queue object named pq-remote. If the job is not in the print queue, then maybe the Printer, Print Server, and Print Queue object configurations are incorrect. This can be verified with the Assignments screen for a Print Queue object. Figure 41-4 shows the Assignments screen for a Print Queue object. It could be your print queue is assigned to an unlisted printer. Then, your print job would not print to the printer you thought you were printing to.

FIGURE 41-3

Viewing the Print Queue Job list

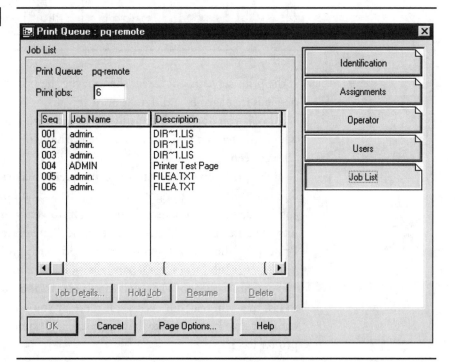

FIGURE 41-4

Verifying print server and
printer assignments for a
print queue

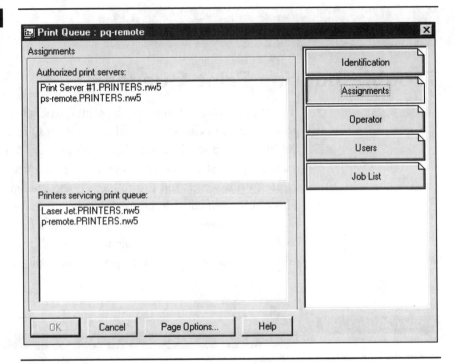

If the print server is not listed, then maybe the printer servicing your print queue is managed by a different print server.

Also, if you don't see the print job in the print queue, maybe the user who requested the job, cannot use the print queue, so check this on the Users screen.

If the print job makes it to the print queue, make sure it is not on hold. Someone with enough rights could put the job on hold. You can use the Job List screen and then scroll to the right to verify the status of your print jobs. The status codes are as follows: Held, Active, Ready, Paused, and Printing. If the status shows Active, the printer is probably off or stopped. You can get Job Details for a particular job and check the job's status.

Sometimes the job is so small that it gets in and out of the print queue so fast that you may not even see it there. If you know the jobs are small, consider that it may already have printed, and someone closer to the printer has it.

FROM THE CLASSROOM

Troubleshooting Printing from User Applications

If a user has trouble printing from an application, check the obvious things first. This may seem trite, but it's often overlooked. Check to see that the printer is on and all connections are properly seated. Don't forget to check if the printer is on line. If the user can print from another application, check to see if the proper port is specified. This should not be a problem with Windows 95 or NT workstation if you have a default printer selected. If this is the case, make sure that the default printer is online and that pause print is not checked. NetWare-aware applications, such as versions of WordPerfect that were marketed when Novell used to own it, printed to selected NetWare print queues if it detected a network connection to a NetWare server with Print Queue objects on it. Non-NetWare-aware applications need to have a valid LPT port redirected to a Print Queue object (NetWare 3.*x* and later) or a Printer object (if NetWare 4.*x* or 5).

—By Dan Cheung, CNI, MCNE, MCT

To determine where your job was sent, you could issue the CAPTURE SHOW, or just CAPTURE SH. This will tell you the print queue where the job is being sent. The following example shows where CAPTURE SHOW is executed at the DOS command line; following the command, is a partial sample of the output:

```
F:\SYSTEM> CAPTURE SHOW
LPT1  Capturing data to print queue
pq-remote.printers.nw5
LPT2  Capturing data to print queue payroll.printers.nw5
```

Another method to determine which Print Queue you are using is to issue NPRINT with the /D option:

```
F:\PUBLIC> NPRINT filea.txt q=.pq-remote.printers.nw5 /D
```

In Windows 95, you can verify the correct print queue by choosing Control Panel | Printers; selecting the printer; and right-clicking on

Properties | Details. A button called Capture Printer Port... will allow you to set and verify printer captures.

Sometimes jobs in the print queue have a status of Ready but do not print. Here are some items to check:

- Other jobs may be ahead of the current print job.
- The print server could be down.
- The print queue is not assigned to a printer.
- The print server is not configured to manage the printer.
- The print job could be waiting on a different form to be mounted on the printer.
- The printer may be offline.

Occasionally, print jobs are held in Adding status. This might happen when the application is generating graphics, particularly in engineering organizations where CAD/CAM is used. Another reason is that CAPTURE includes No Autoendcap (the NA option) and the TI=0 (No Timeout). This will cause jobs to be stuck with the Adding status.

Another factor to investigate is the amount of disk space on the server volume where the Print Queue object is assigned. You could use NWADMIN to view the volume statistics of a volume to ensure you do not run out of disk space. This will cause the job not to be printed because it cannot be placed in the print queue.

exam
ⓦatch

A print queue is required to have a server volume assignment.

The Print Queue object is one of the most complicated to troubleshoot. This is where the Print Server and Printer objects come together and where all print jobs end up.

Troubleshooting Print Server and Printer Objects

Now let's take a look at troubleshooting Print Server objects. the following are some reasons your print job might not be printed:

- PSERVER.NLM is not loaded on a NetWare Server.
- The printer is not assigned to the print server.
- PSERVER.NLM is loaded, but a print server has not been selected.

The PSERVER.NLM utility must be loaded on a print server to enable network printing. To execute PSERVER.NLM, enter the following on a NetWare Server:

```
FIVE-NW5: PSERVER
```

Then, you must select the print server name you want to load. Once this is done, then the NetWare becomes a print server. After pressing ENTER on the correct NDS context, you will see a screen similar to the following:

Current Context
PRINTERS.NW5
Contents of current context
Engineering-Print-Server PS-REMOTE

You are then required to enter the correct print server name. You will need to choose the one that manages the print queue and printer you need; otherwise, your print job won't print. If you created the print server with a password, then you'll need to enter the print server password. Otherwise, your print server will not load, and you won't be able to print.

The next screen will be the Printer List screen. It will list the printers managed by this print server:

```
┌──────────────────────────────────────────────────────────┐
│  ┌────────────────────────────────────────────────────┐  │
│  │                   Printer List                     │  │
│  └────────────────────────────────────────────────────┘  │
│                                                          │
│  ┌────────────────────────────────────────────────────┐  │
│  │  P-REMOTE.PRINTERS.NW5                      0       │  │
│  │                                                    │  │
│  │  ENG-PRT.PRINTERS.NW5                       I       │  │
│  └────────────────────────────────────────────────────┘  │
│                                                          │
└──────────────────────────────────────────────────────────┘
```

You must then select the printer assigned to your print queue. Since a print server can manage multiple printers, be sure you choose the correct printer number.

After this is completed, you will get a screen with detailed information about the printer's properties on it. This screen includes the status of the printer and as well as some other information:

- Printer name.
- Type: Manual load or Auto load.
- Address: Hardware address of the NIC for the print server.
- Current Status: Printing or waiting.
- Queues serviced: A list will appear showing all queues serviced.
- NetWare server: The name of the server that is the print server.
- Print queue: Current print queue defined.
- Print job ID and description: This is the same as the Job list for the print queue.

You can also get print server information while in PSERVER. This screen will give you information such as NetWare version, print server's advertising name, the number of printers serviced by this print server, the number of print queues serviced, and most importantly, the current status. You want to see Running as the status. However, you could Unload the PSERVER or even Unload after printing current job. Troubleshooting a print server is the same whether the printer is attached to print server or a workstation.

Now, let's take a look at troubleshooting a printer. If the printer is attached to the print server, then make sure PSERVER is running with the correct print server and printer. Again, make sure your print queue is assigned to the printer loaded. You don't need to worry about loading NPRINTER for a printer attached to a print server because PSERVER does it for you. That is what is meant by Auto load: it automatically loads the NPRINTER utility. Beware that your printer will not print if you have Auto load selected on the printer configuration and the printer is really attached to a workstation. By the same token, if you have Manual Load selected on the printer configuration and the printer is physically attached to the print server, the printer will not print.

If the printer is attached to a workstation, troubleshooting is a bit more complex. Remember, for another PC to use a printer that is attached to a workstation, the workstation must have NPRINTER.EXE, or the Windows-based NPTWIN95.EXE, running. These should be running in the background on the workstation. If NPRINTER is not running, then the print job will not print. If the user at the workstation unloads NPRINTER, then the print requests will be held in the print queue but will print only after NPRINTER is brought back up. Figure 41-5 shows a screen view of NPTWIN95.EXE. This displays the printer named LaserJet, which is serviced by the print server named PRINT_SERVER_#1. You can also see it's assigned to LPT1.

exam
ⓦatch

A printer attached to a workstation is called a remote printer or network printer.

FIGURE 41-5

The NPTWIN95.EXE
(NPRINTER) utility loaded
on a workstation with a
printer attached

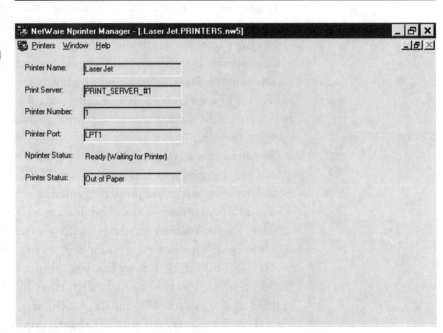

CERTIFICATION SUMMARY

We discussed the overall printing process in a NetWare 5.0 network.
Workstations can access printers that are attached to either a print server, a
workstation, or directly to the network. The necessary NDS objects are a
Print Server, a Print Queue, and a Printer. The Print Server object manages
the printing process and requires PSERVER to be loaded at the NetWare
server console. The Print Queue object is a directory on a volume that holds
the print jobs temporarily. Once printed, the print jobs are deleted from the
queue. The Printer object, in NetWare, is not the physical printer, but a
logical representation of the physical printer. First, create all the objects,
then assign the print queue to the printer. Next, assign the printer to the
print server. Be sure to select whether NPRINTER (or NPTWIN95) needs
to be loaded manually or automatically. If the printer is physically attached
to a print server, Auto Load must be selected. PSERVER will then

automatically load NPRINTER. If the printer is physically attached to a workstation, Manual Load must be selected. Then, you will need to run NPRINTER on the workstation in the background.

Troubleshooting hardware entails basics such as making sure the power on the printer is on, checking cables, and changing toner cartridges and ribbons. If your remote network printer does not print at all, try printing a test page locally to the printer. If that works, then you have a software problem and it is most likely a configuration issue.

Concerning software troubleshooting, make sure you assign your print queue to the correct printer and the correct printer to the correct print server. A printer can service multiple print queues, and a print server can mange multiple printers. Document your configuration so it will be easier to troubleshoot when the time comes.

 # TWO-MINUTE DRILL

- ❏ A local printer is attached to a stand-alone PC or workstation and cannot be accessed through the network.

- ❏ A NetWare server that manages the printing process is called a *print server.*

- ❏ A networked printer can be attached to either a server, a workstation, or directly to the network.

- ❏ Manual load is used when the printer is physically attached to a workstation. That workstation must be running NPRINTER.EXE or NPTWIN95.exe.

- ❏ Auto load is used when the printer is physically attached to a server. That server must be running PSERVER.NLM, and PSERVER.NLM will automatically load NPRINTER.EXE.

- ❏ To redirect a print job to a printer attached to a workstation or print server, the workstation's local printer port must be CAPTUREd.

- ❏ Occasionally, print jobs are held in Adding status. This might happen when the application is generating graphics, particularly in engineering organizations where CAD/CAM is used.

- ❏ A print queue is required to have a server volume assignment.

SELF TEST

The Self-Test questions will help you measure your understanding of the material presented in this chapter. Read all the choices carefully, as there may be more than one correct answer. Select all correct answers for each question.

1. Which of the following objects are required when setting up network printing? (Choose all that apply.)

    A. Print Server

    B. Print Queue

    C. Printer

    D. NT Server

2. If your network printer does not print, what should you do?

    A. Delete all the objects and recreate them.

    B. Attempt to print to the printer locally by connecting it to a local printer port.

    C. Attach the printer to a 10 BASE T port.

    D. Empty the print queue.

3. What is required when creating a print queue? (Choose all that apply.)

    A. A server volume assignment

    B. A Print Queue name

    C. A Printer name

    D. NPRINTER must be loaded.

4. What configuration setting is required on the Printer object if the physical printer is attached to a print server?

    A. Manual Load

    B. Auto Load

    C. A volume assignment

    D. You must assign it to LPT1.

5. What is the name of the utility that must be loaded on a PC workstation, that has a printer attached to it, if it is to be a network printer? (Choose all that apply.)

    A. Manual Load

    B. NPRINTER

    C. NPTWIN95

    D. Print Server

6. What is the name of the utility that will redirect a workstation's LPT port to a network printer?

    A. NPRINT

    B. CAPTURE

    C. NPRINTER

    D. PSERVER

7. What must be loaded on a NetWare server to make it a print server?

    A. NPRINTER

    B. CAPTURE

    C. NPRINT

    D. PSERVER

8. If a print job stays in the queue but never actually prints, what could be the problem?

    A. The job could be on hold.

    B. PSERVER was not be loaded on the workstation.

    C. The CAPTURE command was not run at the server.

    D. NPRINTER is not running on the server.

9. What commands will show where a print job has been sent? (Choose all that apply.)

    A. NPRINT /D

    B. CAPTURE SH

    C. CAPTURE SHOW

    D. NPRINTER

10. How must the printer be configured in order to print to a printer attached to a workstation?

    A. Set it as Manual Load.

    B. Run CAPTURE /D.

    C. Set it as Auto Load.

    D. Run NPRINTER on the server.

11. Where do print jobs go prior to actually being printed?

    A. Print Queue

    B. Printer

    C. Physical printer

    D. To a workstation with NPRINTER running

12. Which default port is CAPTURE designed to use?

    A. LPT1

    B. COM1

    C. LPT2

    D. COM2

13. What should you look for when maintaining the physical printers? (Choose all that apply.)

    A. Use good quality ribbons.

    B. Watch for messages on the printer.

    C. Run NPRINTER on the workstation.

    D. Delete all the NDS objects.

14. If your printer constantly has the Adding status, what could be the problem?

    A. Your workstation could be generating graphics.

    B. NPRINT is not running on the server.

    C. PSERVER is not running on the workstation.

    D. Your ribbon is low quality.

15. What is the utility to actually print a DOS text document?

    A. NPRINTER

    B. NPRINT

    C. PSERVER

    D. NPTWIN95

42

Troubleshooting the Server and the Network

CERTIFICATION OBJECTIVES

42.01   Installing Server Software Updates

42.02   Understanding Server Abends and Lockups

42.03   Troubleshooting Performance Bottlenecks

42.04   Using LANalyzer to Diagnose Performance Problems

42.05   Developing Disaster Recovery Options

CERTIFICATION OBJECTIVE 42.01

Installing Server Software Updates

If software development companies released new versions of their product every time they discovered a problem, we'd be deluged with program versions. On the other hand, the complexity of today's software requires timely updates to resolve product incompatibilities and bugs. Novell, like most software companies, addresses this update issue through the release of *patch kits* or *service packs*.

Well over half of the Novell Support Center calls are resolved by installing these updates, individual NLM (NetWare Loadable module) updates, or device driver updates. As a proactive approach to managing the network, you

FROM THE CLASSROOM

Patch Kit Documentation

Patches, updates, and service packs can be found on the CD-ROM or downloaded from http://support.novel.com. However, trying to find the directions on how to install the patch could be somewhat maddening. Most patches come as self-extracting executables and, unfortunately, the installation instructions could be accessed only after uncompressing all the directories and files. If you encounter this situation, run the executable on a workstation in a directory you've created to access the documentation text files and don't forget to

examine the directory structure that it creates. Most, if not all, server patches must be installed on the server hard drive's DOS partition and enabled through INSTALL.NLM (NetWare 3.*x* and 4.*x*) or NWCONFIG.NLM (NetWare 5). Fortunately, the newest patch kits and service packs from Novell's support Web site have installation instructions available as a separate downloadable file, but the individual updates and NLMs may not have these instructions available separately.

—*Dan Cheung, CNI, MCNE, MCT*

need to periodically check for product updates and apply the appropriate updates to the network. We'll discuss the various operating system updates for NetWare 3.12, NetWare 4.11, and NetWare 5.0; how to locate them; and the steps involved in installing patches for these server versions.

Operating System Updates

NetWare OS service patches can be obtained from the Novell Support Connection CD, from any authorized Novell support provider, or from the Novell Support Web site (http://support.novell.com). Although the Web site offers the most current patch kits, some of the updates can be rather large. If you have a low-speed Internet connection, you may want to use the Web to determine what patches are available, and then obtain them elsewhere.

Novell names server patch kits with the OS version number or name, PT (Passed Testing) or SP (Support Pack), and a revision number or letter. A PT indicates that a patch has been tested against a specific known problem. The SP designation means the update addresses all products included within a NetWare version. Since SP updates are tested as a complete suite, they should not be installed piecemeal.

NetWare 3.12 doesn't use the Support Pack format, in which all (or at least most) of the operating system updates are applied from a single update. The 3.12 PT kit does apply all the current OS patches, but it doesn't update the client-side software. Support Packs for NetWare 4.11 and NetWare 5.0 apply both the server and the client applications software updates (with the exception of the NetWare workstation client itself).

Other updates, such as Directory Service or TCP/IP communications updates, use the product identification and a revision number or letter.

The following are some examples of patch kit names:

IWSP5B.EXE	IntraNetWare service pack 5, rev B
312PTD.EXE	NetWare 3.12 patch kit D
DS411H.EXE	Directory Services update rev H for NetWare 4.11
VRPNNW5A.EXE	Vrepair Update Rev A for NetWare 5.0

Patches that install as an NLM or through the Novell PATCHMAN manager can be either dynamic or semistatic. *Dynamic* patches can be loaded or unloaded while the server is running. *Semistatic* patches can be loaded after the server becomes operational, but can't be removed from memory without downing the server. *Static* patches are applied directly to the SERVER.EXE file and permanently modify the server executable. Novell's utilities for applying static patches will always create a backup of the SERVER.EXE if there is sufficient space on the server DOS partition. Don't install static patches without a backup or the original copy of your server CD or disks available.

Installing Service Packs on NetWare 4.11 or 5.0

Before installing updates to a production server, be sure you have a current backup. From a workstation, copy the latest service pack to a directory on the server and run the executable file. This will extract the entire service pack to the same directory as the executable, and you can then delete the source file.

At the server console (or via RCONSOLE), enter the following:

```
LOAD INSTALL (for NetWare 4.11)
```

or

```
NWCONFIG (for NetWare 5.0)
```

Choose the Product Options menu, and choose Install a Product Not Listed. Press the F3 key to insert a path to the directory in which the service pack is located. Be sure to prefix the path with the volume name (for example, SYS:\SYSTEM\PATCHES\IWSP5). Follow the prompts to complete the service pack installation, and reboot the server.

It's also possible to installation patches to one server from a directory on another server by using the server name, volume, and path when specifying the location of the service pack. INSTALL or NWCONFIG will prompt for a valid login account and password on the source server or tree. This account must have rights to the service pack directory.

Installing Patches on a NetWare 3.12 Server

Before installing updates to a production server, be sure you have a current backup. From a workstation, copy the latest PT to a directory on the server and run the executable file. At the server console (or via RCONSOLE), enter the following:

```
LOAD PATCH312
```

At the prompt, select Copy OS Patches to the Server, and enter the source path to the patch kit (i.e., SYS: SYSTEM\PATCHES\312PTC). Exit the Patch Manager upon completion and restart the server.

If this is the first time you have installed patches on a NetWare 3.12 server, the PATCH312.NLM may not be in the SYS: SYSTEM directory. If necessary, copy the PATCH312.NLM file from the patch kit directory to SYS: SYSTEM, or load it using the full path to the PATCH directory.

Device Driver Updates

Device drivers interface between the network operating system and hardware devices such as hard drives and network interface boards. Although NetWare ships with support for numerous device drivers, updates to these drivers are available only directly from the third-party vendor.

All NetWare device drivers are loaded as NLMs, but are usually identified by the extension *.DSK* (for disk drivers) or *.LAN* (for network adapters). Newer drivers, called *NWPA* (NetWare Peripheral Architecture) drivers, also function as disk drivers, but consist of a *HAM* (host adapter module) and a *CDM* (custom device module). NWPA drivers require both of these files to function, but they provide support for a wider range of hardware devices, such as CD-ROM drives, tape devices, and RAID controllers. NWPA drivers provide better performance than DSK drivers. NetWare 5 requires NWPA compliant drivers and will not load the older DSK drivers.

Device driver updates are generally downloaded directly from the vendor and then copied to either the SYS: SYSTEM directory on the server or the local DOS partition of the server, or both. Since disk drivers have to load before NetWare volumes are mounted, they will always need to be copied to the local DOS partition. After copying, shut down the server and restart it to load the new version.

Understanding Server Abends and Lockups

Unexpected server failures appear as either system abends or lockups. The term *abend* is an acronym for ABnormal END of program. Upon detecting an invalid condition, for whatever reason, NetWare will terminate the active process and display an abend message on the screen. Dreaded as they are, the alternative would be to continue the process and risk significant data corruption.

Server lockups, unlike abends, usually offer no clues to the problem. Typically, the server keyboard and the console screen become unresponsive. Server utilization may be 100 percent and it may be impossible to perform a normal shutdown of the system.

We'll discuss both of these types of server failures and some methods for resolving them.

CPU-Detected Errors

Most NetWare abends are CPU-detected errors. When the CPU detects the error, either an interrupt or an exception will be generated. The failure of an external device will generate an *interrupt*. The processor itself generates *exceptions* when an invalid instruction is detected.

Exceptions can be further classified as faults, traps, or aborts, based on how they are reported and whether the failed instruction can be reinitiated.

Abend-related exceptions can be either processor detected or *NMI* (nonmaskable interrupt). NMI errors are hardware-generated errors and are almost never related to the operating system itself.

Starting with NetWare 4, NetWare takes advantage of the paging architecture of the Intel processor. The architecture allows individual pages of memory to be flagged as present, not present, readable, writable, read protected, or write protected. Exceptions resulting from paging or segmentation can allow the operating system to fix the page fault by restoring processor registers to their state before processing began. Novell SET parameters can enable or disable page fault emulation, giving you the choice between continuing program execution or generating an abend.

Consistency Check Errors

A less common abend is a *consistency check failure*. Consistency checks are constantly being performed by the operating system at virtually every corner, testing such things as communication processes, memory access, and disk I/O. An abend generated by a failed consistency check is a code-detected error, not a CPU-detected error. Failed consistency checks always indicate some degree of memory corruption and, consequently, some degree of data corruption is also likely.

Consistency check failures can be generated by corrupt program files, outdated LAN or workstation drivers, bad network packets, or a variety of hardware failures.

How Netware 4.11 and Netware 5 Handle Abends

Prior to NetWare 4.11, the only options for handling a server abend was to shut down and restart the server or attempt to terminate the process using NetWare's internal debugger. Since processes themselves are often interdependent, terminating a process from the debugger could lead to further problems.

NetWare 4.11 and NetWare 5 provide limited recovery options for server abends. These options can allow the server to continue operations, while suspending the offending process. Improvements to the abend process include the following:

- Updated abend messages that provide additional error information.
- An ABEND.LOG file that includes the abend message as well as a list of processes running at the time.

■ The SECURE CONSOLE command no longer disables DOS. This allows abend logging and automatic server restarts to occur when the console is secured.

■ New SET parameters to allow the server to recover from abends:

■ Auto restart after abend

■ Auto restart after abend delay time

■ CPU hog timeout amount

■ Hung unload wait delay

Table 42-1 lists the values for each of these parameters and their effects on the operating system.

TABLE 42-1		NetWare 4.11 and NetWare 5 Abend Recovery Options
Set Parameter	**Default**	**Possible Values**
Auto Restart after Abend	1	**0** Do not try to recover from the abend. **1** For page faults, suspend the offending process and leave the server running. For NMI or software exceptions, force a delayed restart (based on the Auto Restart after Abend Delay value). **2** Force a delayed restart of the server for all software and hardware abends. **3** Force an immediate restart of the server for all software and hardware abends.
Auto Restart after Abend Delay Time	2	Indicates the number of minutes the server will wait after an abend before automatically restarting itself. Supported values are 2 to 60 minutes.
CPU Hog Timeout Amount	60	Indicates the number of seconds the server will wait before terminating a process that has not relinquished control to the CPU. Supported values are 0 (disabled) to 3,600 seconds.
Hung Unload Wait Time (NetWare 5 only)	30	Number of seconds to wait for an NLM to unload before prompting the user to shut down the address space in use by the application.

Analyzing Abend Messages

Let's look at a sample abend message screen:

```
(1) System halted Sunday, October 24, 1998 10:26:10 pm CDT
(2) Abend on P00: General Protection Processor Exception (Error code 00000002)
(3) OS version: Novell NetWare 5.00 August 27, 1998
(4) Running Process: Server 04 Process
(5) Stack: 80 AA 73 D0 07 10 72 D0 00 00 00 00 97 42 00 00
           46 40 00 00 FF FF FF FF 00 00 00 00 00 00 00 00
           01 00 00 00 D6 97 00 FC 00 00 00 00 00 00 00 A9
(6) Additional Information:
The CPU encountered a problem executing code in LOADER.EXE. The problem may be
in that module or in data passed to that module by a process owned by
SERVER.NLM.
(7) Press:
  "Y" to copy diagnostic image to disk (COREDUMP).
  "X" to update ABEND.LOG and then exit.
```

The numbers in parentheses in the preceding listing are for instructional purposes, and are not part of an abend message. The following is a line-by-line explanation of the sample abend output shown above:

Line 1   Date and time the abend occurred.

Line 2   Text of the abend message. This may allow you to determine if the abend was generated by the CPU or the operating system.

Line 3   Operating system version.

Line 4   The name of the process thread executing at the time of the abend. Although this process was active at the time of the abend, it may not be the cause of the abend.

Line 5   This is a partial stack dump for the current running process. Novell Technical Support may request this when diagnosing an abend.

Line 6   This line provides additional information about the NLM that was running at the time the abend occurred.

Line 7   This line indicates that the AUTO RESTART AFTER ABEND was set to manually restart the server. When you're troubleshooting a recurring abend, you'll probably want to set this parameter to manual restart.

The default setting in NetWare 4.11 and 5.0 servers (see Table 42-1) will instruct the server to suspend the offending process and continue to operate. With this setting, line 7 will display the server name and a number in brackets, i.e., DALLAS_FS<1>:

The number in brackets indicates the number of threads that have been stopped since the server was started. Subsequent abends will increment this number.

Server Lockups

Server lockups can be either full or partial. A *full lockup* suspends all processes, and no one can log in to the server. The server keyboard cannot control the system, and server screens appear frozen. *Partial lockups* will often allow users to continue to work, but you may not be able to load or unload modules. In some cases, new users are unable to log in, but existing connections continue to function.

Server lockups are typically the result of a process thread that is caught in a loop, waiting for some other process. They can also be caused by processes that lock access to a resource. Other threads that require access to the resource cannot run until the resource is released.

In the case of a process loop, the CPU Hog Timeout and Hung Unload Wait time parameters in Table 42-1 will force the process to relinquish control to the operating system. Server lockups can also be caused by the same things that cause server abends: for example, hardware failures, corrupted application files, and outdated drivers or NLMS.

NetWare 5, unlike earlier versions, is *preemptive*, which means it allows the OS to take control of the processor at any time, regardless of the state of programs currently running.

Troubleshooting Server Abends and Lockups

There are six basic steps to troubleshooting and eliminating server abends and lockups:

1. Gather information about the problem.
2. Evaluate the available data and identify likely causes for the failure.
3. Identify and test solutions.
4. Use debugging tools, as necessary.
5. Resolve the problem.
6. Document the problem and the resolution.

Step 1: Gather Information About the Problem

Get the facts, just the facts. Find out what changes were most recently made to the system. Determine what processes were running on the affected server and whether any other processes were recently terminated. Examine the abend log and server operating system error logs. Generate a complete hardware configuration for the server and a list of the associated drivers that were loaded. Check the Novell Web site for known issues and current patch revisions.

Download and get familiar with Novell's CONFIG.NLM and its companion Windows-based Config Reader. This NLM will automate the process of documenting the loaded disk and network drivers, as well as all the other NLMS running on your server. The Config reader can periodically download the current NetWare patch list and compare it against the configuration report generated by CONFIG.NLM. It will identify any Novell modules that are outdated. You can also add third-party modules and versions to the list and develop a baseline list of NLM versions.

Step 2: Evaluate the Available Data and Identify Likely Causes for the Failure

Often, the process of collecting the data in Step 1 will result in an obvious fix.

In particular, look at the most recent changes to the system. Was a new application installed that downgraded an NLM, such as NetWare's CLIB? Was the hardware (and subsequent software drivers) changed? Does the Novell Support Connection address the specific problem you've encountered and list a solution?

Is the server OS up-to-date and have all the appropriate patches (both Novell and third-party) been applied? Can the offending process be identified by commenting out specific applications in the server startup process?

Once you have reviewed all the facts, develop a list of options for resolving the problem, in order of probability.

Step 3: Identify and Test Solutions

Novell always recommends applying known patches to the server prior to performing any other troubleshooting. If you ever have to escalate a problem to Novell Support, they will usually attempt to duplicate the problem in-house, and they will always use a fully patched system. The patch kits were developed to resolve specific issues, including server abends, and it can save you considerable time by applying these before attempting to resolve the problem yourself.

In the case of a suspected hardware component failure, try swapping it with a known good component. Don't use the shotgun approach if you can avoid it, since the object is to identify and document the specific system failure.

If the problem appears to be software related, try unloading specific components or start with a bare system and begin adding components until you can identify the offending process.

Don't be afraid to ask for help. Talk to other engineers in your company or contact Novell for support. Time permitting, you can also use the Novell

Web site forums to discuss the problem with Novell volunteer sysops and your peers in the industry. The forums are at http://support.novel.com/forums/scfindex.htm.

Step 4: Use Debugging Tools, as Necessary

If you haven't been able to resolve the problem using the previous steps, you'll have to locate and use additional tools to research the problem. This might involve the use of a protocol analyzer to gather information about the network conversations occurring at the time of the abend, or a wire tester to determine if the physical cable plant is defective. Some third-party utilities can isolate processes in server memory and notify you if they exceed their memory boundaries.

As a last (and extreme) step, you'll need to take a core dump and send it to Novell Technical Services for analysis. This core dump takes a snapshot of the server memory at the time of the abend and writes it to disk. A server with 128 megabytes of RAM will generate a 128-megabyte core dump file, and you'll have to find some acceptable media for transferring it to Novell. If Novell determines that the problem is a result of a software bug in the OS, they will provide you with a patch for the problem. Obviously, this is not a quick process.

Step 5: Resolve the Problem

Having isolated the problem and determined a solution, you are ready to apply the fix. In a multiserver environment, look at the other servers and determine if the solution should be applied to all of them. For example, if the problem is a result of an out-of-date version of Directory Services, are all of your NetWare 4.x and NetWare 5.0 servers running up-to-date DS versions?

Step 6: Document the Problem and the Resolution

Keep a log of all significant outages and the steps taken to resolve the problem. This will greatly reduce the amount of time required to resolve similar issues in the future.

Troubleshooting Performance Bottlenecks

Network bottlenecks will manifest themselves in poor network performance, end-user dissatisfaction, and lost productivity. Since the primary role of the network is to move data between the server and user computers, it's easy to identify critical components that can choke the network. They fall into four general categories:

- Disk I/O
- Network I/O
- Server CPU
- Server bus I/O

Overall network throughput is limited by the performance of each of these components and, in many cases, resolving a single network performance problem or upgrading one network component may not provide an overall performance gain. Instead, we have to look at the network as a whole and identify the areas most likely to be slowing the system, using both built-in server monitoring tools and third-party utilities.

An important part of monitoring and troubleshooting network performance is the development of baseline performance statistics, using tools such as Novell's LANalyzer. Novell ManageWise also provides excellent long-term trend performance data. As the network grows, resource contention can become a problem. Without knowing the baseline performance of the server and the network, it becomes difficult to identify degraded performance.

Having decided that there is a problem with network performance, we'll address each of the four component categories until we've isolated and resolved the issue.

Disk I/O Problems

A network server with a single hard disk drive is a very likely candidate for this type of network bottleneck. A single drive has only one set of read/write heads available for all users on the system. A fast server with a large amount of cache memory can help, but a better solution is to implement some level of *RAID* (redundant array of independent disks). RAID allows us to add read/write heads, each operating independently and thereby servicing significantly more simultaneous requests. In addition, most RAID controllers provide their own processor and cache memory, freeing up the CPU and the operating system for other tasks.

In a heavily loaded environment, particularly one with high bandwidth into the server (such as FDDI, ATM, or Fast Ethernet), the disk subsystem will significantly impact overall network performance. Under light loads, however, disk requests are much more likely to be serviced directly from server cache, reducing the requirements for higher performance disk components.

Network I/O Problems

Network I/O problems can be relatively easy to diagnose. Relatively low-cost software solutions, such as Novell's LANalyzer, can be used to detect bandwidth problems. Even without a traffic analyzer, you can detect network I/O problems simply by using the built-in statistics available on the LAN information screens on a NetWare 4.*x* or 5.*x* server.

These statistics are available in the Monitor utility and will vary depending on the network topology and the number of custom statistics the vendor includes in their network driver. Typically, network I/O problems will result in transmit or receive failure messages, and problems are manifested by consistently high or rapidly increasing error counts.

It's important to remember that cable faults can also be responsible for these errors, so don't overlook the physical network when troubleshooting these errors. Assuming the cable plant is not at fault, resolving network I/O problems usually requires adding hardware. In smaller environments, you can simply add network adapters in the server and reduce the number of users on each segment. In larger environments, you may need to increase the bandwidth of the network router or switch, or upgrade the network to a faster media.

CPU Problems

Assuming your network server is of fairly recent vintage, it's unlikely you'll experience CPU performance problems in a NetWare environment. NetWare servers running on an Intel 80486 processor have been known to handle hundreds of user connections. Still, newer technologies, such as streaming video and database engines, continue to place greater burdens on the server CPU. NetWare's Monitor utility has a CPU utilization counter that can help you determine when to push for a server CPU upgrade. However, don't rule out the possibility that third-party software is improperly configured for your network. If you suspect this, work with the software vendor to determine if the application is properly tuned for your environment.

Another alternative to upgrading the server CPU is to move some server processes, like mail handling or tape backup, to another system. You may also be able to upgrade network or disk controllers to bus-mastering devices, thereby reducing the server CPU task requirements.

Bus I/O Problems

The *bus* refers to the system bus on the network server. It's the backbone of the server and allows all system peripherals—including network adapters, disk controllers, and memory—to communicate with the CPU. This close relationship between the CPU and the bus makes it difficult to determine when performance problems are bus related.

High-performance servers are designed specifically to overcome bus performance problems. If your server doesn't use current technology to provide high-performance bus throughput, then you should consider upgrading. Again, the use of bus-mastering interface adapters can significantly improve overall bus performance.

CERTIFICATION OBJECTIVE 42.04

Using LANalyzer to Diagnose Performance Problems

Earlier, I mentioned that Novell's LANalyzer could be used to monitor network performance. LANalyzer is a relatively low-cost software-based network monitor that uses off-the-shelf hardware. For best results, I'd recommend a low-end Pentium system, with Windows 95 and 16–32 MB of RAM. The network adapter and its associated driver must support *promiscuous mode.* This mode allows the adapter to listen to all packets on the wire, not simply those addressed to it. Most adapters support this, but check with the manufacturer if you are not sure. An ideal LANalyzer PC would be a laptop system with a PC-Card network adapter—this portability comes in handy when testing multiple network segments.

An important component of the LANalyzer is the NetWare Expert. Whenever the NETWORK, SERVER, or ROUTER thresholds are exceeded, an error is generated and the appropriate box turns red. Clicking on the box brings up the error log and NetWare Expert Help screen. On my test network, I set the alarm levels very low to generate these messages. New alarms appear in red. The NetWare Expert provides an explanation of the alarm and suggests ways to fix it. The NetWare Expert provides an online explanation of network error messages and offers suggestions for resolving the error.

Network Errors

The most common network errors reported by LANalyzer include CRC/alignment errors and fragments. CRC/alignment errors are damaged packets, in which the Frame Check Sequence of the packet is invalid or does not divide evenly by eight (the number of bits in a byte). These errors are often associated with physical cable problems. Fragment errors are also packets with an invalid FCS, but the packet size is less than 64 bytes. In an Ethernet network, normal network packet collisions will generate fragment errors. A high number of fragment errors usually indicates that the network is overloaded. Under low utilization, a large number of fragment errors indicates a faulty network adapter somewhere on the segment.

Less common errors, including oversize packets, undersize packets, and jabber errors are typically generated by software driver bugs. Contact the network vendor for support on these errors.

Determining Baseline Network Performance

One of the most useful features of the LANalyzer is its ability to capture trend data. Up to six months of network performance can be tracked to develop a performance baseline by which to compare future network throughput. Since LANalyzer can monitor only a single network segment, you'll need to run it against each LAN segment you wish to track.

Novell recommends using at least one month's trend information when establishing a baseline to monitor the following:

- Utilization (in percentage)
- Errors/second
- Kilobytes/second
- Packets/second

In addition, LANalyzer will identify the most active servers, routers, and users on the network.

Once you have established baseline performance, you can set the alarm thresholds in LANalyzer to alert you when network activity or error rates increase significantly. I normally set my threshold values at 30 to 50 percent above the peak baseline, to avoid false alarms by short-term utilization spikes.

Diagnosing Overloaded Servers and Networks

Overloaded networks are a result of a network design that cannot handle the amount of traffic being transmitted by the attached devices. Overloads are manifested by significant delays in launching applications or by disconnected sessions (NetWare clients will usually report an error sending/receiving from the network when a session is disconnected).

Network overload can be caused by increased numbers of workstations on the LAN, an increase in the number or size of applications loaded from the network, increased Internet traffic, or the movement of large files (such as video) across the network.

Network overload can be easily detected by monitoring the network utilization and error rates as reported by LANalyzer and comparing the results to your benchmark statistics.

CERTIFICATION OBJECTIVE 42.05

Developing Disaster Recovery Options

This section deals with restoring data and network operations in the event of a disaster. Data loss can occur as a result of hardware failure, intentional or accidental user intervention, or from external sources, such as software virus attacks.

Planning for a Disaster

Recovering from a disaster can be significantly easier if you plan ahead. You should develop a written plan that outlines the steps required to prevent data loss following a disaster. This plan should take into consideration the amount of time required to restore the data, the number of users who require immediate access, and the cost of continued network downtime. These requirements will determine the level of redundancy required by the network. Your plan should also consider methods of maintaining off-site backups.

Recovering from a Disaster

Regardless of the level of fault tolerance built into the network, the disaster recovery plan should assume that the server, some number of user workstations, and a minimum cable plant would need to be completely rebuilt. In the event of a major disaster, such as a fire or flood, this is the typical initial requirement. Other aspects of the plan should include the following:

- Running VREPAIR to repair damaged network volumes
- Using DS Repair or NDS Manager to restore NDS information
- Operating system and backup software reinstallation steps
- Restoring user data and trustee rights from backups
- Use of third-party software to recover data
- Using professional data recovery services

Your network maintenance procedures may preclude the necessity of using the final two options, but you should be aware (at least for the purposes of Novell's testing) of their existence.

Using VREPAIR to Repair Damaged Volumes

The VREPAIR.NLM is used to correct minor volume errors that can prevent a network volume from mounting. It can also be used to remove name space entries from a volume directory table. VREPAIR is most often run after a NetWare server abend—volumes that are not closed properly will often have mismatched data on the primary and backup copies of their file allocation tables.

The default setting for VREPAIR allows it to load and attempt to repair a damaged volume automatically whenever a volume mount fails. You can manually invoke VREPAIR with the LOAD command. After loading VREPAIR, use the ALT+ESC key combination to switch to the console prompt and dismount the volume to be repaired (this will allow you to load VREPAIR from the SYS: volume before dismounting it).

Do not attempt to use VREPAIR on volumes that have suffered a serious hardware failure—VREPAIR permanently deletes damaged files and directory table entries. If no other copy of the data exists, then third-party tools or consulting services should be used to attempt to restore the data.

After loading VREPAIR, you may need to load name space modules for VREPAIR support. Determine the name spaces loaded on a volume and load the name space support modules required. The most common name spaces are V_MAC for Macintosh name space, V_OS2 for OS/2, and V_LONG for long name space support. NetWare 4 and 5 both use V_LONG for OS/2 and Windows long name support, while NetWare 3.12 and earlier versions use OS2.NAM for long name support.

On a volume with a large number of reported errors, run VREPAIR repeatedly until no errors are reported.

Using DS Repair to Repair NDS Damage

While the use of DS Repair is covered elsewhere, it should be included in the disaster recovery plan and the procedures for repairing individual directory service partitions and replicas should be documented. As a network administrator, you should be familiar with the DS Repair interface and how to perform DS Repair operations.

Restoring Data and Trustee Assignments from Backups

The most common method of restoring network operations after a disaster consists of reinstalling the network operating system and restoring the user data from backups. Your disaster recovery plan should cover this aspect in detail and should also discuss methods for storing and retrieving tapes in a timely manner, particularly when the current backups are stored off-site.

An important part of your backup procedures should include periodic testing of the restore process. Backup tapes have a finite shelf and usage life, and tape drives should be periodically cleaned and serviced.

Backups must be kept current. While incremental or differential backups may significantly reduce the amount of time required to perform the backup, you'll need to look at the amount of time required to restore from a full backup and subsequent incremental backups when you develop your restoration procedures.

Using Third-Party Software to Recover Data

In the event of a hardware failure, you may want to attempt to recover data using a third-party utility designed specifically for rebuilding NetWare volumes. The Novell course discusses the use of Ontrack Data Recovery for NetWare (ODR for NetWare). ODR allows you to recover files from a downed server, rebuild the file table on a volume, examine or change data on any server disk sector, and perform a media analysis on a server disk. ODR for NetWare consists of three utilities:

- *NetFile 4* is the file recovery tool and file editor.
- *NetDisk 4* allows you to examine and modify the data on any server disk sector.
- *NetScan 4* is used to repair damaged NetWare volumes and perform media testing.

ODR for NetWare will create emergency boot disks with the minimum files necessary to boot the network (the server O/S files, CLIB, STREAMS, and disk controller drivers).

Using Professional Data Recovery Services

In the event that your backups fail and the data cannot be recovered by any other means, you may elect to hire a professional data recovery service.

Companies such as Ontrack will physically dismantle a failed hard drive and perform a sector-by-sector recovery of as much data as possible. These services are typically very expensive and can take days or even weeks to complete. However, in many cases, there may be no alternative.

The key to successful data recovery is providing the recovery service with a disk that has not been significantly altered since the disk failure. Attempting to repair a damaged disk using software utilities or reinstalling the operating system will usually destroy data that might otherwise have been recovered.

CERTIFICATION SUMMARY

This chapter deals with the procedures for troubleshooting the server and the network. As we've seen, both hardware and software issues have to be addressed when maintaining the server and the network.

NetWare is an extremely complex product, and a regular part of keeping your server healthy includes tracking and installing product updates.

We reviewed the underlying causes of server abends and how to resolve them.

We looked at the four hardware bottlenecks in a server and how to detect and overcome them. We saw a sample network analyzer and learned how it can help diagnose network problems.

We discussed the importance of a disaster recovery plan and what steps are involved in developing and documenting a basic plan. Finally, we described Novell and third-party utilities for use in disaster recovery.

 # TWO-MINUTE DRILL

❑ As a proactive approach to managing the network, you need to periodically check for product updates and apply the appropriate updates to the network.

❑ Most, if not all, server patches must be installed on the server hard drive's DOS partition and enabled through INSTALL.NLM (NetWare 3.x and 4.x) or NWCONFIG.NLM (NetWare 5).

❏ The SP designation means the update addresses all products included within a NetWare version. Since SP updates are tested as a complete suite, they should not be installed piecemeal.

❏ Patches that install as an NLM or through the Novell PATCHMAN manager can be either dynamic or semistatic. *Dynamic* patches can be loaded or unloaded while the server is running. *Semistatic* patches can be loaded after the server becomes operational, but they can't be removed from memory without downing the server.

❏ *Static* patches are applied directly to the SERVER.EXE file and permanently modify the server executable.

❏ Before installing updates to a production server, be sure you have a current backup. From a workstation, copy the latest PT to a directory on the server and run the executable file.

❏ Unexpected server failures appear as either system abends or lockups. The term *abend* is an acronym for ABnormal END of program.

❏ A less common abend is a *consistency check failure*. Consistency checks are constantly being performed by the operating system at virtually every corner, testing such things as communication processes, memory access, and disk I/O.

❏ *Partial lockups* will often allow users to continue to work, but you may not be able to load or unload modules.

❏ NetWare 5, unlike earlier versions, is *preemptive*, which means it allows the OS to take control of the processor at any time, regardless of the state of programs currently running.

❏ Additional tools to research the problem. Might involve the use of a protocol analyzer to gather information about the network conversations occurring at the time of the abend or a wire tester to determine if the physical cable plant is defective.

❏ *RAID* (redundant array of independent disks) allows us to add additional read/write heads, each operating independently and thereby servicing significantly more simultaneous requests.

❑ Even without a traffic analyzer, you can detect network I/O problems simply by using the built-in statistics available on the LAN information screens on a NetWare 4.*x* or 5.*x* server.

❑ The *bus* refers to the system bus on the network server. It's the backbone of the server and allows all system peripherals, including network adapters, disk controllers, and memory, to communicate with the CPU.

❑ The network adapter and its associated driver must support *promiscuous mode*. This mode allows the adapter to listen to all packets on the wire, not simply those addressed to it .

❑ An important component of the LANalyzer is the NetWare Expert. Whenever the NETWORK, SERVER, or ROUTER thresholds are exceeded, an error is generated and the appropriate box turns red.

❑ The VREPAIR.NLM is used to correct minor volume errors that can prevent a network volume from mounting. It can also be used to remove name space entries from a volume directory table.

❑ ODR for NetWare consists of three utilities: *NetFile 4,* which is the file recovery tool and file editor; *NetDisk 4,* which allows you to examine and modify the data on any server disk sector; and *NetScan 4,* which is used to repair damaged NetWare volumes and perform media testing.

❑ NetWare 5, unlike earlier versions, is *preemptive*, which means it allows the OS to take control of the processor at any time, regardless of the state of programs currently running.

❑ The key to successful data recovery is providing the recovery service with a disk that has not been significantly altered since the disk failure. Attempting to repair a damaged disk using software utilities or reinstalling the operating system will usually destroy data that might otherwise have been recovered.

SELF TEST

The Self-Test questions will help you measure your understanding of the material presented in this chapter. Read all the choices carefully, as there may be more than one correct answer. Select all correct answers for each question.

1. Prior to placing a call to the Novell Support Center, you should

   A. Remove all patch files to determine if a patch is the cause of the problem.

   B. Obtain the latest NetWare 3.12 Support Pack (SP).

   C. Obtain, test, and apply all applicable product and driver updates.

   D. Obtain LANalyzer traces of suspect network activity.

2. The three types of server NLM patches are the following:

   A. Static, semistatic, and dynamic

   B. Core, peripheral, and client

   C. Static, semidynamic and dynamic

   D. Internal, external, and transparent

3. NetWare 5 discontinues support for which of the following?

   A. Support Pack (SP) updates

   B. DSK and LAN drivers

   C. DSK drivers

   D. Symmetric multiprocessing

4. Which of the following faults cannot be corrected by the NetWare 5 operating system?

   A. Page faults

   B. Segmentation errors

   C. NMI errors

   D. None of the above

5. In the event of a server abend, the server name will be appended by a number in brackets. This number indicates

   A. The number of threads executing at the time of the abend

   B. The number of threads that have been stopped since the server was started

   C. The number of the thread that generated the abend

   D. Nothing in particular, other than that the server has abended at some time

6. NetWare 5, unlike earlier versions of NetWare, offers

   A. Preemptive multitasking

   B. Multithreaded operations

   C. Nonpreemptive multitasking

   D. Page fault processing

7. XYZ Corporation has a single NetWare 4.11 server running on a 200 MHz Pentium with 64MB of RAM and an 8GB Enhanced IDE drive. The server's Fast Ethernet interface adapter is connected to an Ethernet switch. The

server supports 200 users. Which component in this network is most likely the cause of network bottlenecks?

A. Disk I/O

B. Network I/O

C. Server CPU

D. Server bus I/O

8. The use of bus-mastering interface cards and disk controllers can

A. Reduce the amount of traffic on the network

B. Improve overall network performance, at the cost of increased server CPU overhead

C. Improve overall network performance, by reducing the server CPU overhead

D. Allow you to specify the frequency of adapter interrupts

9. Promiscuous mode drivers allow an interface adapter to

A. Broadcast to all other stations on the wire

B. Receive and retransmit all packets on the wire

C. Receive all packets on the wire

D. All of the above

10. A sudden increase in network traffic could be a result of

A. Excessive network collisions

B. Cable faults

C. The new Internet connection

D. An overloaded server

11. The correct way to remove a name space entry from a NetWare volume is to

A. Use VREPAIR and invoke the Remove Name Space option.

B. Use the command line Remove Name Space (name) from Volume (volume name).

C. Use the INSTALL (NetWare 4.12) or NWCONFIG (NetWare 5) utility.

D. Dismount the volume, unload the name space NLM, and remount the volume.

12. The primary function of DS Repair is to

A. Remove unwanted servers and volumes from directory services

B. Repair a volume after a directory services abend

C. Perform repairs on directory service partitions and replicas

D. Repair the file allocation table on a damaged server volume

13. Every disaster recovery plan should provide

A. Step-by-step procedures for restoring data from backups

B. Installation procedures for loading the network operating system

C. Procedures for running VREPAIR

D. All of the above

14. Of the following SET parameters, which is supported only by NetWare 5?

    A. Auto Restart after Abend

    B. Hung Unload Wait Time

    C. Auto Restart after Abend Delay Time

    D. CPU Hog Timeout Amount

15. The most common cause of fragment errors on an Ethernet network is

    A. LAN driver bugs

    B. Improperly configured routers

    C. Physical cable problems

    D. High network traffic

Part VI

intranetWare: Integrating Windows NT

CERTIFIED NOVELL ENGINEER

43

Introduction to Windows NT

CERTIFICATION OBJECTIVES

43.01   Windows Product Overview

43.02   Logging In to Windows NT

43.03   Windows NT Default Accounts

43.04   The Windows Registry

43.05   Windows NT Utilities and Programs

43.06   Adding Users to the
Local Workstation

Although Microsoft is a relative newcomer to the networking market, it has been an industry leader in client operating systems (OS) since the first IBM personal computer rolled off the assembly line. Microsoft's first OS, MS-DOS, was command-line based and proved challenging for most end users to work with. After several revisions, Microsoft introduced the first version of its Windows product line, which replaced the command-line interface with a graphical user interface (GUI, pronounced *gooey*), that was much more intuitive to use. As Windows gained in popularity, it evolved to include several different versions.

Because of its popularity, you will probably find at least one member of the Windows family product line already integrated with almost every Novell network you encounter. While there are several versions of Windows products in use today, the Novell certification exam covers only the three main products: Windows 95 (basics), Windows NT Workstation 4.0, and Windows NT Server 4.0, which are also the most commonly deployed. You need to understand the different features and capabilities of Windows before you can learn how to integrate it into your Novell network.

CERTIFICATION OBJECTIVE 43.01

Windows Product Overview

Before you can master the Windows family product line, you need to understand what each product was designed for and how each one functions. While each Windows product was developed for a distinct purpose, you will notice that they possess several common traits. The most noticeable similarity is the common user interface and desktop features, which give a consistent environment across the product line. For example, if you needed to modify network settings on any of these three operating systems, you would go to the Network icon in the Control Panel. Another commonality is their ability to run 32-bit (Win32) applications and maintain backward compatibility with 16-bit (Win16) applications, although you cannot always run software designed for Windows 95 on a Windows NT machine.

Windows 95

When Windows 95 was released, it was the first desktop operating system able to utilize the capabilities of the new 32-bit processors. However, because the computer industry had already invested heavily in 16-bit hardware and software, it had to maintain compatibility with existing computer components in order to remain competitive. As a result, Microsoft was challenged to provide a flexible operating system that could handle new components as they were released, yet maintain compatibility with existing systems. The first step in achieving this goal was to ensure that most of the computer systems already in use could run the new operating system without a costly upgrade. Therefore, the minimum requirements were set as follows:

- 386SX or better
- 4MB RAM 40MB hard disk space available

As we mentioned previously, most hardware had been developed using 16-bit technology. Windows 95 retained compatibility with most of the existing hardware devices, or *legacy* devices, and provided support for the emerging plug-and-play technology. Using plug-and-play, the operating system can automatically detect when a new device is attached to the computer, even if the computer is currently running, and complete the hardware installation. This took much of the configuration burden away from the end user.

Software was almost as expensive as the hardware components, and the industry could not afford to upgrade the operating system and all the applications at one time. Therefore, Windows 95 had to be able to run the older Windows 3.1 and MS-DOS applications, yet also allow for development of newer Win32 applications. Older Windows applications used the method of *cooperative multitasking* to simulate a multitasking system. Although you could have more than one application open at a time, the operating system would only process information from one window at a time. In order for an application to get processor time, the currently active process would have to voluntarily, or *cooperatively*, relinquish control. This caused problems with applications that had a tendency to hog system resources. In addition, all applications shared the same memory area. If one of the processes terminated abnormally or wrote into another application's memory space, the entire system suffered the consequences.

Windows 95 introduced the concept of *preemptive multitasking,* which lets the operating system judge when an application has to relinquish system time to another process. This prevents applications from hogging the processor's time by having the operating system police time allotments. Also, each application is given its own memory address space to prevent processes from bumping into each other, resulting in a much more stable operating system. Preemptive multitasking is provided for Win32 applications and some MS-DOS applications. However, to provide backward compatibility with Win16 processes, Windows 95 created a *virtual machine (VM).* The virtual machine encloses all non-Win32 applications—16-bit, 32-bit, and some MS-DOS applications—in a special memory address block and provides a single queue to the processor. To the applications, it looks as if it is really running on a Windows 3.1 machine.

While Windows 95 can act as a stand-alone desktop operating system, it can also function as a client in a Novell NetWare network or a Windows NT domain. Windows 95 also comes with basic peer-to-peer networking support that allows the computer to participate in a workgroup, which is discussed in Chapter 44. This flexibility gives Windows 95 an edge in the client operating system market, but falls short as a true network server. Other than the capability of controlling remote access to a computer's resources through shares and permissions, topics that will be discussed later in the chapter, there is no mechanism to prevent unauthorized local access.

Windows NT Workstation 4.0

When you compare Windows NT Workstation with Windows 95, you might come to the conclusion that Windows NT is an upgraded version of Windows 95. However, there are as many differences as there are similarities. In the area of hardware support, Windows 95 provides support for MS-DOS device drivers and plug-and-play technology, whereas Windows NT does not. However, Windows NT does include support for multiple processors—two in an out-of-box installation—while Windows 95 can handle only one. In addition, Windows NT has higher minimum hardware requirements than Windows 95:

- 486DX 33MHz or better processor
- 16MB or more RAM
- 120MB hard disk space available

Windows NT also has different capabilities from Windows 95 in software support. Windows NT also supports preemptive multitasking, but unlike Windows 95, it does not discriminate between16-bit and 32-bit applications. Therefore, each application is supported in its own memory address space, whether it is a 16-bit or 32-bit process. With Windows 95, processor-intensive applications have a tendency to slow down the system, but Windows NT Workstation has been optimized for these types of applications. Windows NT also provides support for Microsoft's popular BackOffice product family—Microsoft SQL Server for client/server databases, Exchange for e-mail services, and SNA for connectivity to IBM systems.

Security has become a major concern in information technology, and Windows 95 falls short where local security is concerned. Windows NT Workstation rectifies this by providing a mandatory log in, or *WinLogon* (discussed in a later section) and the NTFS file system. By requiring users to log in, only authorized users can access the resources on the local machine. When you add the NTFS file system, which allows permissions and rights to be assigned at the local level, only validated users can access resources to which they have been granted access. This enhances the security of the operating system on the local level.

As with Windows 95, Windows NT Workstation can act as a stand-alone desktop operating system, as a member of a workgroup, and as a network client on a Novell NetWare network or a Windows NT domain. However, Windows NT is not necessarily the best choice for the home or small office user. When you need to make a decision between deploying Windows 95 or installing Windows NT Workstation, you need to consider several important issues.

QUESTIONS AND ANSWERS

Is local file system security an issue?	If it is, then you will need to look at Windows NT Workstation.
Which platform best matches the existing hardware and software?	Unless your company has a big upgrade project, because of legacy MS-DOS applications or devices that utilize only MS-DOS drivers, you may want to deploy Windows 95.
Do you need to run processor-intensive applications?	Windows 95 loses some of its performance with mathematically-intensive applications, such as certain graphics and drawing packages, whereas Windows NT was optimized for processor-intensive applications.
Does your environment use plug-and-play hardware that does not require legacy device drivers?	Plug-and-play is not available in Windows NT, making Windows 95 the choice in this scenario.

While the certification exam focuses on Windows NT, you are required to know the basics of Windows 95. Know when Windows 95 is appropriate and when Windows NT Workstation is required.

Windows NT Server 4.0

Windows NT Server has all the features of Windows NT Workstation, yet it brings the operating system up to the server level. Windows NT Server was designed as the operating system for Microsoft's BackOffice Server and components—Microsoft SQL Server, Microsoft Exchange Server, Microsoft SNA Server, and Microsoft Systems Management Server (SMS)—and provides Internet server capabilities by bundling the *Microsoft Internet Information Server (MIIS)*. In addition, it can function as a file, print, or application server in a Novell NetWare network or a Windows NT domain.

Microsoft has given Windows NT Server some additional functionality in the hardware area. First, it has the capability to run up to four processors—instead of two—in an out-of-the-box installation for improved performance. Second, Windows NT Server has fault tolerance built in through software-based *Redundant Array of Inexpensive Disks (RAID)*. However, these additional features and functionality, surprisingly, raise Windows NT Server's minimum hardware requirements only slightly:

- 486DX 33MHz
- 16MB of RAM
- 130MB hard disk space available

Windows NT Server uses the Windows NT Directory Services (NTDS), formerly known as Microsoft Domain Services, as its counterpart to Novell's NetWare Directory Services and can authenticate user domain log in requests. Unlike Windows NT Workstation, which only supports ten inbound concurrent client connections, Windows NT Server can handle an unlimited number of inbound and outbound connections. Windows NT Server also provides import and export directory replication, while Windows NT Workstation can only import.

However, directory replication in Microsoft terminology is a bit different than Novell's directory replication. With Novell, the phrase refers to placing copies of a Master Replica of an NDS partition, which contains the NDS information, on servers across the network, while Microsoft means the copying of files from a source (export) computer to a destination (import) machine.

CERTIFICATION OBJECTIVE 43.02

Logging In to Windows NT

Before you can access any of the resources on a Windows NT machine, you must first go through the mandatory login process, known as the *WinLogon* process, in which you must provide a valid user name and password. This feature of Windows NT provides several advantages, particularly when you have multiple users accessing the same computer.

- **Consistency**   Individual configurations, such as network connections or desktop settings, can be retained for each local user of the computer.

- **Flexibility**   Users can have more than one account, with each account having different rights and permissions.

- **Security**   When used in conjunction with the NT File System (NTFS), users can allow or deny other users access to their local files.

The WinLogon process is initiated each time the machine is powered on or restarted, and after a local user logs off. At this step in the process, the computer disallows any keystroke sequence other than CTL-ALT-DEL, and will display a dialog box, such as that shown in Figure 43-1. This provides you with two layers of security on your Windows NT machine. First, it prevents access to the computer's resources from anyone without a valid username and password combination. Second, it defeats password capture programs by halting all user-mode programs.

Once you press the CTL-ALT-DEL keystroke sequence, you are presented with a login dialog box that allows you to either enter your username and password or shut down the computer. When you supply your credentials to the operating system, the WinLogon process will pass that information to the *Local Security Authority (LSA)* process, which then queries the *Security Accounts Manager (SAM)* for verification. If your username and password are invalid, you are denied access to the machine. However, if the SAM validates your credentials, the LSA will generate an

---

FIGURE 43-1

Initial logon screen

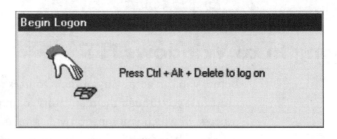

access token with your rights and pass it back to the WinLogon process. At this point, you will be allowed to access any of the computer's resources that your login ID grants you.

Do not get confused by the terminology. Novell uses the term log in when you authenticate to the network, while Microsoft uses the term log on. If you get a question on the certification exam regarding this process, read through it very carefully.

CERTIFICATION OBJECTIVE 43.03

Windows NT Default Accounts

As we mentioned in the previous section, you will need to have a valid username and password in order to successfully log in to a Windows NT computer. Windows NT comes with several default accounts that allow for different levels of access through rights and permissions. A *right* allows the user to perform some form of activity on the machine, such as log on locally, shut down the server, or back up files and directories. A *permission* authorizes a user to access and use an object, such as a file, an application, or a printer. (Rights and permissions are discussed in more detail in Chapters 44 and 46.) The default accounts, Administrator, Guest, and Initial User (Workstation only), are discussed in the following subsections.

Administrator Account

The Administrator account is similar to Novell's Admin account, and gives the user complete control over a Windows NT machine's configuration and user settings. Examples of the tasks that you can perform with the Administrator account are

■ **Disk Management**   The Administrator account permits you to partition, format, and restructure disks resident on a Windows NT computer.

■ **Printer Management** You have the rights and permissions to install, remove, and connect to printers, as well as to modify printer settings.

■ **Shared Directory Management** You are able to create, delete, rename, and connect to shared directories. In addition, you can allow or disallow access to these directories.

■ **Security Policy Management** Security policies are the set of security settings that control a user's access to the network and to network resources. Each user is given their own security policy in which these values are stored. Under the Administrator account, you can create or modify a user's access rights through their security policy.

■ **Operating System Management** The Administrator is given total control over all of the components that make up the operating system. Examples of changes that can be made include the installation or removal of hardware, the modification of device driver settings, the addition or deletion of applications, and the creation or deletion of users.

Because the Administrator account has such broad powers, it is highly recommended that you rename it to prevent hackers from using a known account. If you are planning on using Novell's integration tools, you should rename this account to match the Novell Admin account. While you can rename or disable this account, you cannot delete it.

Guest User Account

The Guest account is used to provide limited access to the resources on a Windows NT computer. This allows the occasional user, such as a company employee visiting from another location, to access network resources without a permanent account. Because of the restrictions placed on this account, any changes to desktop settings or additional network connections are discarded once the user logs off. This provides a consistent environment for traveling users.

When you install Windows NT, the Guest account is created with a blank password. On Windows NT Workstation, this poses a security threat by allowing anyone on the network access to the machine. To remedy this problem, it is recommended that you either put a strong password on the account or you disable it. With Windows NT Server, the Guest account is disabled by default. While you may disable this account, you may not delete or rename it.

Initial User Account (NT Workstation)

The Initial User Account is present only if you installed Windows NT Workstation without networking capabilities. It is given a name during the installation process, and has the same rights and permissions as the Administrator account. While this account can be renamed or deleted, it cannot be disabled.

CERTIFICATION OBJECTIVE 43.04

The Windows Registry

Earlier versions of Windows stored operating system information in text files that were given special extensions based on the type of file, such as configuration (CFG), initialization (INI), or system (SYS). These files were stored in a variety of locations, and, if you needed to make a change, you would have to locate the appropriate file. The current version of Windows changed the way that Windows stores system information by consolidating the numerous configuration files into a single database called the *Registry*. By doing so, Windows centralizes the location of operating system settings and user information.

The Registry itself is organized into a hierarchical structure that is similar to the file system structure. Having a database rather than a myriad of files scattered about the hard drive is an obvious advantage over the old version of Windows. However, Windows also uses the Registry to maintain multiple user configurations on the same machine. This is done through the manner in which the Registry is organized, as shown in Figure 43-2. In

FIGURE 43-2

Registry Editor and the
various Registry
components

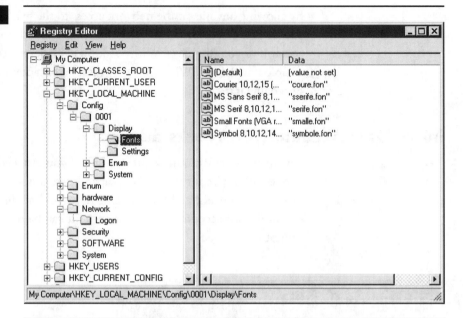

order to make it efficient, the Registry is broken down into two parts: the
Subtree and the Hive.

Subtree

As we stated previously, the Registry is a hierarchically structured
database that is organized in a manner similar to the file system. With
the file system, you have root folders that logically group files and other
folders. The Registry applies this concept to its database structure and
uses a *subtree* to logically group operating system information. There are a
total of five subtrees, each holding a specific type of information, that makes
up the Registry.

The first subtree, HKEY_LOCAL_MACHINE, contains all of the
computer's hardware information. Applications, device drivers, and the
operating system use this information when they need to access data on a
particular device. When a Windows NT machine boots, the boot process
determines which device drivers to load by referencing this subtree.

The HKEY_USERS subtree contains the system default settings and the security settings for each user. This information is used by the operating system to determine what each user is allowed to view and access on the computer. Examples of the data stored in this subtree are default user settings, network settings, and control panel settings. When a user logs into a Windows NT machine, this data is copied into the subtree called HKEY_CURRENT_USER.

As we have mentioned, the HKEY_CURRENT_USER subtree obtains its information from the HKEY_USERS subtree. This data is kept for each user that has logged in to the machine, and includes such items as keyboard layout, software used, desktop settings, and remote access definitions.

The HKEY_CLASSES_ROOT subtree stores all software configuration information for the computer. This includes such items as screen location and colors, recently accessed files, executable location and name, and any other information the vendor has defined.

The HKEY_CURRENT_CONFIG subtree stores the active hardware profile. This subtree obtains its initial data from the subtree called HKEY_LOCAL_MACHINE subtree when the user logs in and maintains it for the active hardware profile.

exam

ⓦatch

You need to remember the purpose of each Registry key in order to pass the Novell certification exam.

Hive

A hive is made up of three components: keys, subkeys, and values. A hive also has two files associated with it: a data file and a log file. A *key* is similar to a folder in the file system, but instead of holding subdirectories and files, it holds subkeys and values. *Subkeys* are analogous to subdirectories, and aid in breaking down the Registry into a more organized structure. *Values* are comparable to files, and just as files have attributes associated with them, so do values. These attributes are composed of a name, a data type, and a configuration parameter. The name is used as a label, or variable, just as you would name a file. The data type can be compared to an extension on a file, and is used to associate a specific data type with the value. The configuration parameter is the actual data, or value, that is used.

Editing the Registry

There are several methods used to modify Registry settings:

- Control Panel
- Novell's integration tools
- REGEDT32.EXE
- Software install and uninstall programs
- System Policy Editor
- Windows NT Setup program
- Various other third-party utilities, such as Norton's WinDoctor or Quarterdeck's CleanSweep

One thing to be aware of is that Microsoft's Registry Editor program, REGEDT32.EXE, is the last method you should use to modify Registry settings. Since the Registry is the most critical component in the Windows operating system, be very careful whenever you make changes to it. It is important to maintain current backups of the Registry, especially when you need to make a change to the system, such as installing or removing system components.

CERTIFICATION OBJECTIVE 43.05

Windows NT Utilities and Programs

When working with Windows NT, it helps to remember that everything is considered an *object*. Each object has various properties associated with it that define the object to the operating system. By modifying an object's properties, you are able to alter its appearance and its behavior within the system. Windows NT comes with a variety of programs and utilities to aid you in configuring and maintaining the different objects residing within the operating system. You will need to familiarize yourself with these utilities and programs in order to function effectively in Windows NT. The most commonly used programs are discussed in the following subsections.

My Computer

The My Computer utility, shown in Figure 43-3, allows you to manage and maintain your file system. As we mentioned in the preceding paragraph, everything in Windows NT is an object. With the Windows NT file system, there are three objects that are used—folders, files, and shortcuts. *Folders* are used to hold directory information, other folders (subdirectories), and files. When you use My Computer to look at a folder's or file's properties, you will notice that you have a General tab and a Sharing tab. The General tab contains information about that object, such as name, location, creation date, and local security attributes. The Sharing t ab allows you to remove access from or grant access to an object by users on the network. With the My Computer utility, you can delete, rename, or modify security attributes to both files and folders. However, while you can create folders, you must create files using other applications.

FIGURE 43-3

The My Computer utility

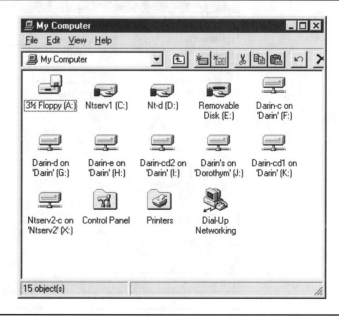

Shortcuts can be thought of as pointers to another object. For example, if you wanted to create an icon on the desktop that will start a particular application, you would create a shortcut. When you examine a shortcut's properties through the My Computer utility, you will notice that there is a General tab and a Shortcut tab. The General tab contains the same type of information that a file or folder would have. The Shortcut tab contains the exact name and location of another object, such as an executable program or a batch file. Some shortcuts have other tabs that allow you to modify the appearance and memory usage of the target when it runs. With the My Computer utility, you can create, delete, rename, or modify shortcuts.

Windows NT Explorer

Windows NT Explorer, shown in Figure 43-4, offers some of the same functionality as the My Computer utility, but it expands on it. When you first launch Windows NT Explorer, you are presented with a window that is

FIGURE 43-4

The Windows NT
Explorer window

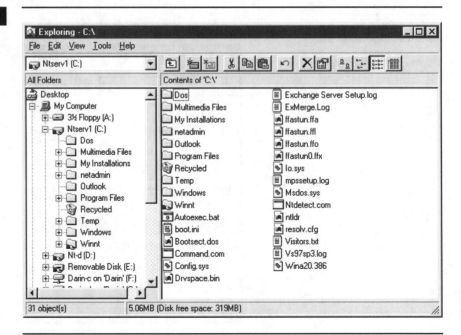

divided into two panes. The left pane displays your folders in a tree-type design, and the right pane shows the files and shortcuts in the highlighted folder. In addition, you are provided with a search routine to assist in locating a particular file or folder, and you are able to create drive mappings.

Network Neighborhood

The Network Neighborhood utility, which allows you to access network resources, is present only if you have installed the networking components. It is a graphical utility that uses intuitive icons to display what type of resource is being viewed. For example, Figure 43-5 shows two workstations depicted by a computer icon next to their names. When you activate Network Neighborhood, it displays several types of resources: the Entire Network icon, workstations, and servers in your workgroup, and any resources that you are already accessing. Through this utility, you can connect to printers, create drive mappings, and explore available resources.

Control Panel

The Control Panel, displayed in Figure 43-6, allows you to modify the Windows Registry settings. These settings contain information about the

---

FIGURE 43-5

Network Neighborhood

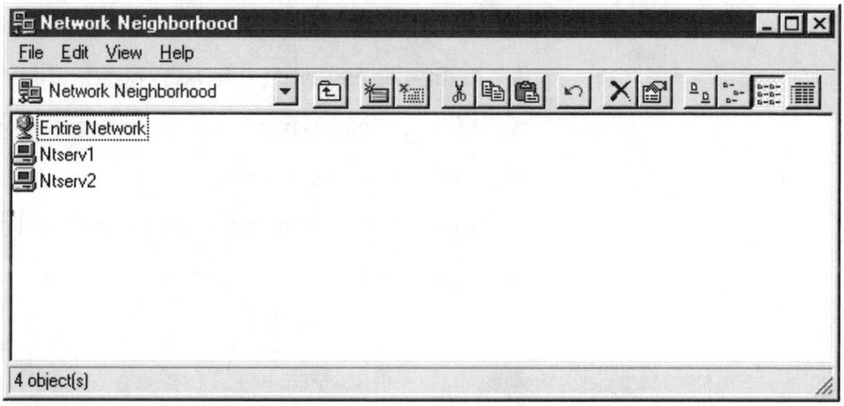

FIGURE 43-6

The Control Panel

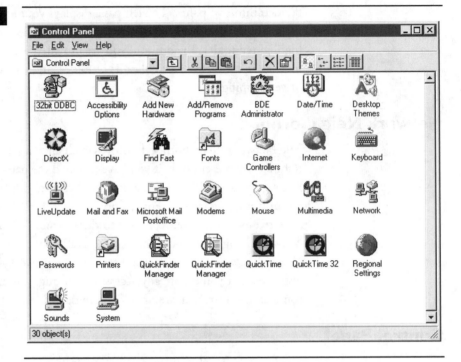

hardware, software, and user configuration. Some examples of the types of actions you can perform include

- Adding, configuring, and removing hardware devices
- Adding or removing software applications
- Adding a screensaver (with or without a password)
- Modifing network settings
- Accessing the Printers folder to install or delete printers

Disk Administrator

Disk Administrator, shown in Figure 43-7, is used to manage and maintain the hard drives on a Windows NT computer. Some of the functions of Disk Administrator include

- Creating and deleting partitions
- Creating and deleting logical drives
- Creating, deleting, formatting, and labeling volumes
- Changing drive letter assignments
- Creating and deleting stripe sets (fault tolerance)
- Viewing drive information

Disk Administrator is covered more thoroughly in Chapter 44.

FIGURE 43-7

The Disk Administrator utility

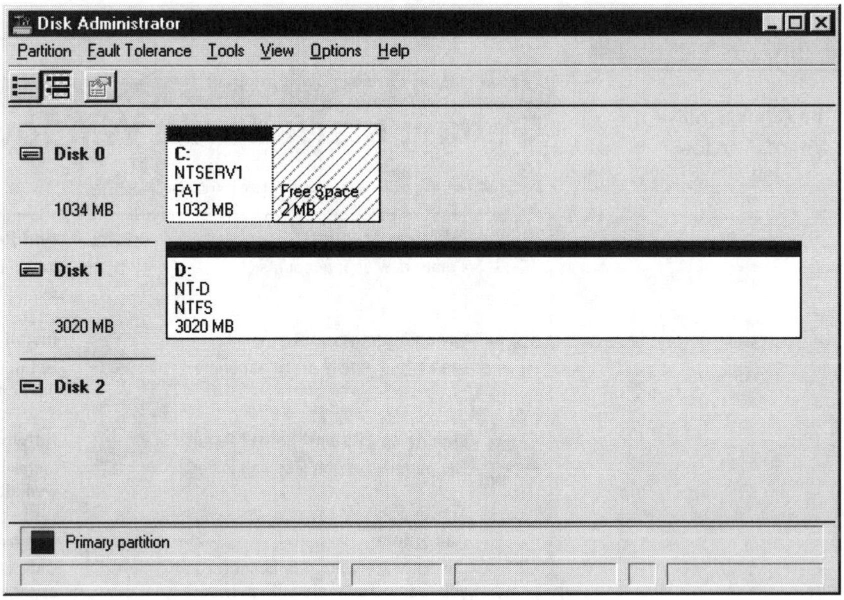

Adminstrative Wizards

Administrative Wizards is more of a user interface that provides quick access to the various Microsoft Windows configuration tools. As Figure 43-8 shows, you can create new user accounts, manage group accounts, set permissions on files and folders, install printers, add and remove programs, install modems, install or update network client workstation, and check for license compliance.

Server Manager

Server Manager, shown in Figure 43-9, is available only on Windows NT Server, but it allows you to configure domains and manager computers connected to the Server. Some of the functions of Server Manager include

- Adding and removing computers from a domain
- Displaying users connected to a particular computer on the domain

FIGURE 43-8

The Administrative Wizards window

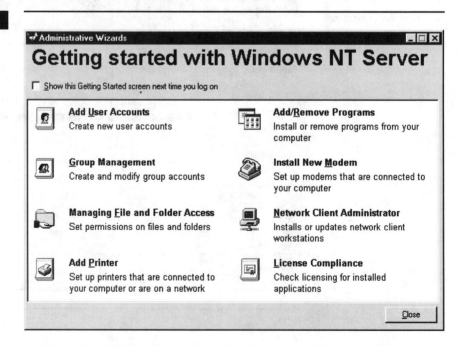

FIGURE 43-9

Server Manager utility

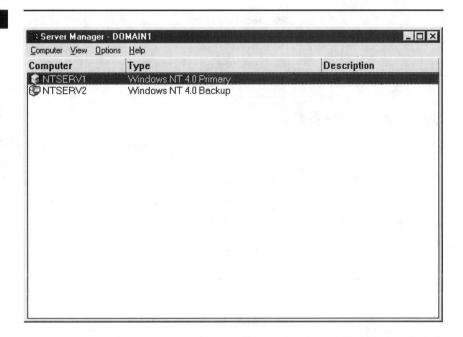

- Sending messages to users connected to the domain
- Displaying open and shared resources, such as files or printers
- Promoting a backup domain controller to a primary domain controller
- Manually synchronizing servers with the primary domain controller
- Managing and maintaining directory replication

Event Viewer

The Event Viewer, displayed in Figure 43-10, is used to view Windows NT system logs. These logs contain useful information about system events. There are three types of logs used by Windows NT:

- Application Log   Contains information on application-related events, such as application failures

- **Security Log**   Contains security-related events, such as login failures or file access events
- **System Log**   Contains information on hardware events, such as component failures

System Policy Editor

The System Policy Editor, shown in Figure 43-11, is used to directly edit the Registry settings that affect the users' working environment, or *policies*. These policies can be set up by the Administrator account, or an account with equivalent privileges, to control settings like the following:

- Desktop settings
- Access to various settings, such as the Run command from the Start menu
- Access to various resources

FIGURE 43-10

Event Viewer utility

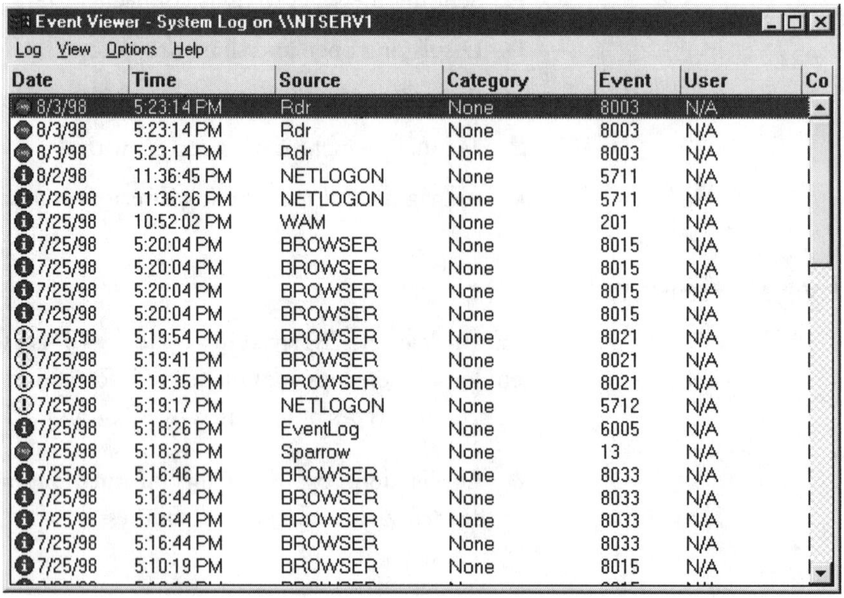

Date	Time	Source	Category	Event	User	Co
8/3/98	5:23:14 PM	Rdr	None	8003	N/A	I
8/3/98	5:23:14 PM	Rdr	None	8003	N/A	I
8/3/98	5:23:14 PM	Rdr	None	8003	N/A	I
8/2/98	11:36:45 PM	NETLOGON	None	5711	N/A	I
7/26/98	11:36:26 PM	NETLOGON	None	5711	N/A	I
7/25/98	10:52:02 PM	WAM	None	201	N/A	I
7/25/98	5:20:04 PM	BROWSER	None	8015	N/A	I
7/25/98	5:20:04 PM	BROWSER	None	8015	N/A	I
7/25/98	5:20:04 PM	BROWSER	None	8015	N/A	I
7/25/98	5:20:04 PM	BROWSER	None	8015	N/A	I
7/25/98	5:19:54 PM	BROWSER	None	8021	N/A	I
7/25/98	5:19:41 PM	BROWSER	None	8021	N/A	I
7/25/98	5:19:35 PM	BROWSER	None	8021	N/A	I
7/25/98	5:19:17 PM	NETLOGON	None	5712	N/A	I
7/25/98	5:18:26 PM	EventLog	None	6005	N/A	I
7/25/98	5:18:29 PM	Sparrow	None	13	N/A	I
7/25/98	5:16:46 PM	BROWSER	None	8033	N/A	I
7/25/98	5:16:44 PM	BROWSER	None	8033	N/A	I
7/25/98	5:16:44 PM	BROWSER	None	8033	N/A	I
7/25/98	5:16:44 PM	BROWSER	None	8033	N/A	I
7/25/98	5:10:19 PM	BROWSER	None	8015	N/A	I

FIGURE 43-11

System Policy Editor

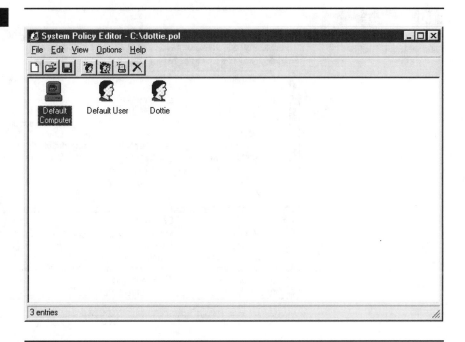

CERTIFICATION OBJECTIVE 43.06

Adding Users to the Local Workstation

As we mentioned earlier in the chapter, the WinLogon process requires a valid username and password in order to grant a user access to the Windows NT machine's resources. Microsoft has provided the User Manager utility to manage and maintain user accounts. There are actually two versions of the User Manager utility, one for Windows NT Workstation and Windows NT Servers that are installed as stand-alone servers (User Manager), and another one for Windows NT Servers that are installed as Domain Controllers (User Manager for Domains). The only difference between the two versions is that the User Manager for Domains utility also administers user accounts on the network.

User Manager is accessed under the Administrative Tools folder from Start | Programs. When you start the User Manager utility, you are presented with a window similar to the one shown in Figure 43-12.

FIGURE 43-12

User Manager utility

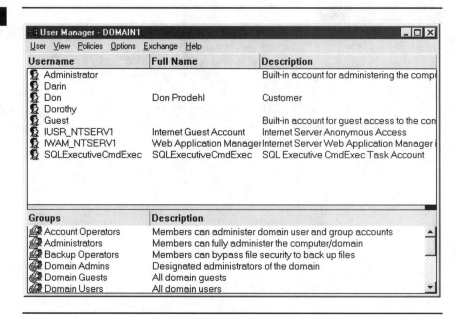

As you can see, the window is organized into two sections—a user account section, which we will discuss next, and a group section, which we will discuss in a later chapter. To modify an existing user, you can highlight the name of the account and select one of the options from the User menu, or you can simply double-click the name of the account. When you do so, you are presented with the same dialog box, shown in Figure 43-13, that is displayed when you add a new account.

There are five fields to complete for each account:

- **Username**　Required. A unique name used to log in to a Windows NT computer.

- **Full Name**　The user's full name. This option is highly useful for large companies that may have more than one individual with the same first and last name, or when there are several individuals who have the same initials.

- **Description**　Any type of descriptive information about the user, such as the user's location or their phone number.

FIGURE 43-13

User Properties Dialog
Box from the User
Manager Utility

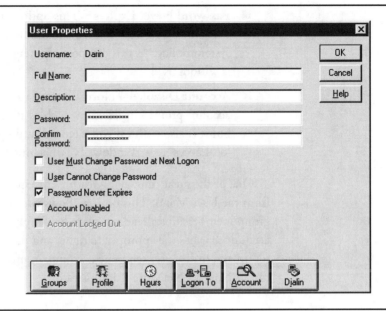

■ **Password** Required, although a blank password is considered a valid entry. This field is limited to a maximum of 14 characters, and displays asterisks (*) instead of the characters you type.

■ **Confirm Password** Required, although a blank password is considered a valid entry. This field must exactly match the Password field, and is used to ensure that what you thought you typed is what you really typed.

Along with these five fields, User Manager also permits you to select one of several options on the user account:

■ **User Must Change Password at Next Log In** This option is set by default, and requires the user to change their password the next time they log in.

■ **User Cannot Change Password** Normally used when you have several users who utilize the same user account, such as the Guest account. This option ensures that the password will remain unchanged unless modified by an account with Administrator privileges.

- **Password Never Expires**   This option allows an account to retain the same password, even if a Maximum Password age is set in the system policy. As this can pose a potential security threat, this option is seldom used.

- **Account Disabled**   Normally used to temporarily disable an account prior to its deletion, such as after an employee is terminated, but it is also useful if you have a travelling user who will not need local access to a Windows NT machine for a long period of time.

One of the great timesaving features in User Manager is the Copy option from the User Menu. This option allows you to create a new account with group memberships already in place by simply copying an existing user account that has the appropriate rights and permissions. Therefore, you can set up and utilize user template accounts in much the same way that you can in Novell's NetWare Administrator.

CERTIFICATION SUMMARY

In this chapter, we laid the foundation for your journey through the Windows family product line, and have examined the characteristics of the main products that you will be tested on. The utilities and tools that are used with Windows are similar amongst the three products, and are accessed via graphical interfaces that are designed to perform a specific task. As you must have a local account on a Windows NT Server, or Windows NT Workstation, we have gone over the method used to create accounts.

TWO-MINUTE DRILL

- ❑ The minimum requirements for Windows 95 are 386SX or better processor, 4MB RAM, and 40MB available hard disk space.
- ❑ Windows 95 introduced the concept of preemptive multitasking, which lets the operating system judge when an application has to relinquish system time to another process.

❑ Windows 95 created a virtual machine (VM) to provide backward compatibility with Win16 processes. The virtual machine encloses all non-Win32 applications—16-bit, 32-bit, and some MS-DOS applications—in a special memory address block and provides a single queue to the processor.

❑ Windows 95 can function as a client in a Novell NetWare network or a Windows NT domain. Windows 95 also comes with basic peer-to-peer networking support that allows the computer to participate in a workgroup. Other than the capability of controlling remote access to a computer's resources through shares and permissions, there is no mechanism to prevent unauthorized local access.

❑ The minimum hardware requirements for Windows NT are 486DX 33 MHz or better processor, 16MB or more RAM, and 120MB available hard disk space.

❑ Windows NT supports preemptive multitasking, but it does not discriminate between16-bit and 32-bit applications. In Windows NT each application is supported in its own memory address space, whether it is a 16-bit or 32-bit process. Windows NT also provides support for Microsoft's popular BackOffice product family—Microsoft SQL Server for client/server databases, Exchange for e-mail services, and SNA for connectivity to IBM systems.

❑ Windows NT Workstation provides a mandatory login, or WinLogon, and the NTFS file system. Only authorized users can access the resources on the local machine. The NTFS file system allows permissions and rights to be assigned at the local level, insuring that only validated users can access resources to which they have been granted access.

❑ Windows NT Workstation can act as a stand-alone desktop operating system, as a member of a workgroup, and as a network client on a Novell NetWare network or a Windows NT domain.

❑ Windows NT Server was designed as the operating system for Microsoft's BackOffice Server and components. It can function as a file, print, or application server in a Novell NetWare network or a Windows NT domain. Windows NT Server has the capability to run up to four processors in an out-of-the-box installation for improved performance. Windows NT Server has fault tolerance built in through software-based Redundant Array of Inexpensive Disks (RAID). Windows NT Server's minimum hardware requirements are 486DX 33MHz, 16MB of RAM, and 130MB available hard disk space.

❑ Windows NT Server uses the Windows NT Directory Services (NTDS) as its counterpart to Novell's NetWare Directory Services and can authenticate user domain login requests. Windows NT Server can handle an unlimited number of inbound and outbound connections. Windows NT Server also provides import and export directory replication

❑ The WinLogon process is initiated each time the machine is powered on or restarted, and after a local user logs off. This provides you with two layers of security on your Windows NT machine. First, it prevents access to the computer's resources from anyone without a valid username and password combination. Second, it defeats password capture programs by halting all user-mode programs.

❑ Windows NT comes with several default accounts that allow for different levels of access through rights and permissions— Administrator, Guest, and Initial User (Workstation only).

❑ Windows consolidates the numerous configuration files into a single database called the Registry. The Registry itself is organized into a hierarchical structure that is similar to the file system structure. Windows also uses the Registry to maintain multiple user configurations on the same machine.

❑ The Registry uses a subtree to logically group operating system information. There are a total of five subtrees, each holding a specific type of information, that make up the Registry.

❑ A hive is made up of three components—keys, subkeys, and values. A hive also has two files associated with it—a data file and a log file.

❑ There are several methods used to modify Registry settings, includingControl Panel, Novell's integration tools, REGEDT32.EXE, software install and uninstall programs, System Policy Editor, Windows NT Setup Program, or other third-party utilities. Microsoft's Registry Editor program, REGEDT32.EXE, is the last method you should use to modify Registry settings. Since the Registry is the most critical component in the Windows operating system, be very careful whenever you make changes to it. It is important to maintain current backups of the Registry, especially when you need to make a change to the system.

❑ Windows NT comes with a variety of programs and utilities to aid you in configuring and maintaining the different objects residing within the operating system, including: The My Computer utility, Windows NT Explorer, the Network Neighborhood utility, the Control Panel, and the Disk Administrator.

❑ Administrative Wizards is a user interface that provides quick access to the various Microsoft Windows configuration tools.

❑ Server Manager is available only on Windows NT Server, and allows you to configure domains and manager computers connected to the Server.

❑ The Event Viewer is used to view Windows NT system logs. These logs contain useful information about system events. There are three types of logs used by Windows NT—Application Log, Security Log, and System Log.

❑ The System Policy Editor is used to directly edit the Registry settings that affect the users' working environment or policies. These policies can be set up by the Administrator account, or an account with equivalent privileges, to control settings.

❑ The User Manager utility is used to manage and maintain user accounts. There are two versions of the User Manager utility—User Manager, for Windows NT Workstation and Windows NT Servers that are installed as stand-alone servers, and User Manager for Domains for Windows NT Servers, which are installed as Domain Controllers. One of the great timesaving features in User Manager is the Copy option from the User Menu. This option allows you to create a new account with group memberships already in place by simply copying an existing user account that has the appropriate rights and permissions. Therefore, you can set up and utilize user template accounts in much the same way that you can in Novell's NetWare Administrator.

SELF TEST

The following Self-Test questions will help you measure your understanding of the material presented in this chapter. Read all the choices carefully, as there may be more than one correct answer. Choose all correct answers for each question.

1. Which of the following utilities would you use to create a new user account?

   A. Server Manager

   B. Control Panel

   C. Network Neighborhood

   D. User Manager

2. The Registry is

   A. Composed of various INI and CFG files

   B. A hierarchically structured database

   C. Found in the C:\WINNT\REGISTRY directory

   D. Seldom accessed

3. Windows 95 requires _____ MB of RAM.

   A. 4

   B. 8

   C. 16

   D. 32

4. You would use the _____ utility to monitor Windows NT system events.

   A. My Computer

   B. Windows NT Explorer

   C. Event Viewer

   D. User Manager

5. Your supervisor has decided to catch up with current technology and wants to replace the current client operating system, but since he knows nothing about computers he has turned to you for advice. You know that you have some MS-DOS applications that are critical to the business, but are unable to replace them at this time. You would recommend which of the following products:

   A. Windows for Workgroups 3.11

   B. Windows 95

   C. Windows NT Workstation

   D. Windows NT Server

6. The process used to log on to a Windows NT machine is called the

   A. WinLogin

   B. Windows Login

   C. WinLogon

   D. Windows Logon

7. The _____ utility is used to configure domains and computers connected to the domain.

   A. Control Panel

   B. My Computer

   C. Server Manager

   D. User Manager for Domains

8. Which of the following are default accounts set up by Windows NT during installation?

   A. Administrator

   B. Admin

   C. Initial User

   D. Guests

9. Windows NT Server can handle up to _____ inbound concurrent users.

   A. 5

   B. 10

   C. 20

   D. Unlimited

10. The order that the WinLogon authenticates a user is:

   A. WinLogon -> Local Security Authority (LSA) -> Security Accounts Manager (SAM) -> LSA -> WinLogon

   B. WinLogon -> SAM -> LSA -> SAM -> WinLogon

   C. WinLogon -> LSA -> SAM -> WinLogon

   D. WinLogon -> SAM -> LSA -> WinLogon

11. The Initial User account is present only when:

   A. You install Windows NT Workstation with networking capabilities.

   B. You install Windows NT Server with networking capabilities.

   C. You install Windows NT Workstation without networking capabilities.

   D. You install Windows NT Server without networking capabilities.

12. All of a Windows NT computer's hardware configuration settings are stored in the _____ Registry key.

   A. HKEY_USER

   B. HKEY_LOCAL_MACHINE

   C. HKEY_HARDWARE

   D. HKEY_CLASSES_ROOT

13. You need to create a new partition on your Windows NT server and format it with NTFS. To do so, you would use

   A. Disk Administrator

   B. My Computer

   C. Server Manager

   D. User Manager

14. You are asked to choose the office's new desktop operating system. Since security has become quite a concern, the new client operating system must allow for file-level security. You respond with:

   A. Windows 95

   B. Windows NT Workstation

   C. Windows NT Server

   D. Apple

15. What do you call it when the operating system decides when an application has used up its processing time?

   A. Preemptive multitasking

   B. Cooperative multitasking

   C. Judgmental multitasking

   D. Decision multitasking

44

Introduction to Windows NT Networking

CERTIFICATION OBJECTIVES

44.01   Windows NT Networking Models

44.02   Supported Protocols in Windows NT

44.03   Supported File Systems in Windows NT

44.04   Using Disk Administrator to Manage the File System

44.05   Creating Shares and Granting Permissions

Now that you have mastered the basics of Windows NT on the client level, it is time to explore how Windows NT performs on the network level. First, we will gain an understanding of how Windows NT can function in a network environment by exploring the different networking models used in a Windows NT network. Next, we will study how Windows NT communicates between Windows NT and other operating systems through the protocols that it supports. We will then move on to examine the underlying file system structures available on the Windows NT platform and how they are managed through the Disk Administrator utility. Finally, we will learn how to set up file and directory shares.

CERTIFICATION OBJECTIVE 44.01

Windows NT Networking Models

In order to understand how Windows NT operates in a networking environment, you will need to learn the basic types of networking models used in a Windows NT network. A network model can be thought of as a blueprint that defines the characteristics and functionality of a network. By understanding the various networking models, you will be better equipped to assign a role to a Windows NT machine in your network. This section will discuss the fundamental models used in the Windows NT networking environment—the workgroup model and the domain model.

The Workgroup Model

A *workgroup* is a collection of computers that have been logically grouped together for the purpose of sharing resources. However, a workgroup is a peer-to-peer arrangement that does not require a central server to provide access to network resources. Instead, the individual workstations bear the responsibilities of account administration, resource management, and security policies by maintaining their own security database locally, also known as the *Security Accounts Manager (SAM)*.

For example, if Mary needed to access files that are on Tom's computer, as shown in Figure 44-1, she would need an account on his workstation that contains the appropriate privileges to access the files. If Andy required access to Connie's printer, he would need an account on Connie's computer that grants him access to the printer. In each case, a copy of the SAM is resident on the workstation, making individual workstation account management a requirement. Unless you have a small network, this forced *decentralization* of resources can prove cumbersome to administer since you must rely on each individual to administrate user accounts on the local machine.

Another problem with using the workgroup model occurs when you have a network that spans a WAN link. Accessing resources over a WAN link could prove to be too slow for practical use, especially for applications that are time dependent. One problem that I have seen with application access over a slow WAN link is that applications will time-out if they do not receive a confirmation within a prescribed time limit. Backup applications can also cause problems, including obtaining a reliable backup, when they span a WAN link since they utilize a large amount of bandwidth.

| FIGURE 44-1 | The workgroup model |

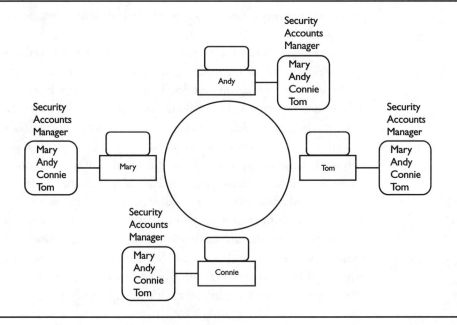

There are situations in which you may want to pursue the workgroup model for your network. Because it is simple to design and implement, it is a good model for a network that consists of a few workstations that are located in close proximity to each other. However, keep in mind that Windows NT workstations are restricted to a maximum of ten concurrent inbound connections. If a member of the workgroup maintains files or databases that everyone else needs access to, you should consider the domain model.

The Domain Model

The *domain model* takes the workgroup model and upgrades it for the enterprise. A Windows NT domain is comprised of network servers and computers that have been logically grouped together for the purpose of sharing resources. Unlike the workgroup model, a Windows NT domain requires a Windows NT server to provide access to network resources. The server, known as a *primary domain controller (PDC)*, is responsible for maintaining the master database, or directory, that contains user and resource accounts for all workstations in the domain. This provides centralized administration of user accounts and security settings, as shown in Figure 44-2.

One of the advantages to a centralized directory database is that it eliminates the need for maintaining separate accounts on each workstation, as is required by the workgroup model. This drastically cuts down on the time and coordination required to maintain multiple databases on a network, which can be cumbersome on a large network. A second benefit is that users are required to log in only once to access any of the resources on the network. This single-point log in cuts down on the number of accounts and passwords that users need to remember, again unlike the workgroup model.

Centralized administration has other benefits for the network administrator. Instead of having to manage and maintain the accounts on every workstation, the administrator can log in from any workstation in the domain and create a single account. Network security settings can also be customized for the entire network from one central location, providing for more efficient use of the administrator's time. In addition, the administrator

FIGURE 44-2

The domain model

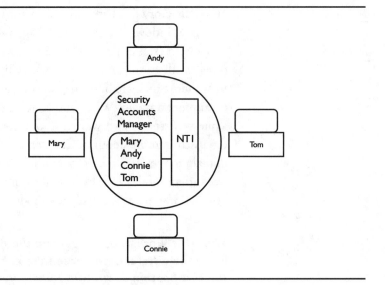

can manage and maintain resources from his or her workstation, allowing for ease of sharing important resources.

When dealing with domains, it helps to understand the terminology that is used. For instance, any workstation running a version of Windows that has networking capability—Windows for Workgroups, Windows 95, Windows 98, Windows NT Workstation—is capable of joining a domain. These computers are then called *member computers*. Also, any computer running Windows NT as its operating system (except those configured as domain controllers) must also have a computer account in the domain in order for a user to log in to that computer. A Windows NT server is slightly different from the desktop operating systems because it can play multiple roles in a domain—*primary domain controller (PDC), backup domain controller (BDC), and member server*. When a Windows NT server stores the original, or copies, of the directory database, it is a *domain controller*. If it contains the master copy of the directory database, it is a *primary domain controller*. With domains, there can be only one primary domain controller at any given time on the network. Hence, all other controllers are *backup domain controllers*. If a Windows NT server machine does not store a copy of the directory database, it is called a *member server.* We will explore the roles of Windows NT server in Chapter 45.

You can establish multiple domains in a Windows NT network, but in order for them to communicate you will need to implement a *trust.* Trusts in Windows NT are built to allow one domain access to resources located on another domain. When you establish a trust relationship, you can set up a one-way trust, a two-way trust, or a complete trust. (Trusts will be discussed in more depth in Chapter 45.) Because of the complexity of the domain model, it is much more difficult to plan and implement than the workgroup model; but, because the domain model can support a larger number of users, it is usually the model of choice.

While the workgroup model and the domain model are very similar, know the differences between them. You may be asked questions on the certification exam that require you to know when you would prefer one model over the other.

Supported Protocols in Windows NT

Just as human beings must have a common language in order to successfully communicate with each other, machines must use a common *protocol* to exchange information. When data is passed between computers, it is packaged in a specific manner that is dependent upon the protocol used for the transmission. Unless the sender and the receiver are using the same protocol, the receiver will be unable to interpret the information.

Windows NT has the ability to deploy multiple protocols at the same time. However, protocols do utilize processor time and take up memory space, which can slow down the computer, or even the entire network if you use too many or the wrong kinds of protocols for your network environment. When you plan your protocol scheme, you will need to consider the following:

- What types of file-sharing services will be needed?
- What types of printing services will be required?
- What applications will be used?

To ensure compatibility with most operating systems, Windows NT comes with several protocols—TCP/IP, NetBEUI, NWLink IPX/SPX Compatible, DataLink Control (DLC), and AppleTalk. You can either deploy a protocol during the installation process or you can use the Networking icon in the Control Panel to install one later, as shown in Figure 44-3. In the next sections, we will discuss the protocols that you will most likely use.

FIGURE 44-3

The Networking icon allows you to modify protocol settings

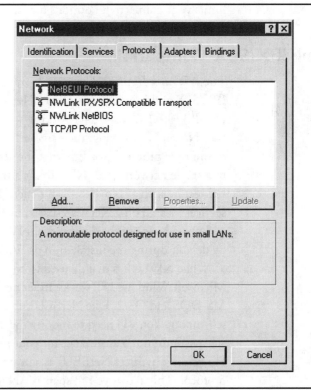

NetBEUI

Of all the protocols used in Windows NT, Microsoft's *NetBIOS Extended User Interface (NetBEUI)* is the easiest one to implement because it is not only self-configuring, but self-tuning as well. In Windows 95 and NT Workstation, it is one of the protocols selected by default. For smaller networks, such as workgroups or networks that do not use WAN links, it is a fast protocol that has very low memory requirements. However, there are several major disadvantages to using NetBEUI that have led Microsoft to recommend its use only on small to medium-sized networks.

The main shortcoming with NetBEUI is that it is not a *routable* protocol. This means that a second protocol that is routable (such as IPX or IP) will become necessary to encapsulate NetBEUI packets, if your network traffic has to cross a router. Another problem with NetBEUI is that there are few platforms, primarily Windows and OS/2, that support it. This limits your connectivity options for current and future network growth.

NWLink IPX/SPX Compatible

The *NWLink IPX/SPX Compatible protocol* is Microsoft's version of IPX/SPX and is NDIS-compliant. Network Device Interface Specification (NDIS) is to Microsoft Networking what Open Data-Link Interface (ODI) is to Novell Networking; they are both specifications that allow the binding of multiple protocols (or Ethernet frametypes, in the case of NetWare) to a single network card. NWLink is a transport protocol that relies on a redirector, such as Novell's 32-bit client for Windows, to access file or print services located on a NetWare-based network. However, because of the widespread use of mixed networks, NWLink is one of the protocols selected by default during the installation of Windows NT.

While NWLink is mainly used to connect Novell NetWare networks with Microsoft Windows NT workstations and domains, it is also supported by MS-DOS and OS/2. Like NetBEUI, it is also self-configuring but not self-tuning. You will need to modify the default configurations in order to achieve optimum performance for your particular network environment. However, it bypasses NetBEUI as a protocol of choice because it is a routable protocol. This allows you to span WAN links and provide network services to remote sites. NWLink also has some major limitations, like that only one Ethernet frametype is supported at a time on Ethernet networks. If the frametype is set to "Auto" in the Properties Page for NWLink, and both Ethernet_802.2 and Ethernet_802.3 frametypes are detected, Ethernet_802.2 will become the default frametype and all Ethernet_802.3 traffic will not be detected. If NetWare Client for NT is installed, it is capable of reading all IPX Ethernet frametypes.

TCP/IP

The most popular protocol used in today's network environment is the *Transmission Control Protocol / Internet Protocol (TCP/IP) protocol.* Originally designed to connect wide area networks together, TCP/IP is a routable protocol that makes connecting any two networks together that support TCP/IP relatively easy. TCP/IP is a published industry standard that is maintained by the Institute of Electrical and Electronics Engineers (IEEE), and is therefore a nonproprietary protocol that any vendor is free to use in their hardware or software products. Since TCP/IP is one of the oldest protocols, it has proven itself to be reliable and vendors have responded by using it in their products. One good example that you are most likely to run into is printers that run off TCP/IP.

The Internet has had an enormous influence on the popularity of TCP/IP. With the rapid growth of the Internet, more products are being developed to be Internet-aware. As TCP/IP is the protocol used to connect to the Internet, these new products are being designed around TCP/IP. Some examples of Internet-aware products are various games that allow you to play against another individual on the Internet and fax modems that will allow you to send a fax over the Internet rather than a phone line.

TCP/IP also comes with support for Simple Network Management Protocol (SNMP), Dynamic Host Configuration Protocol (DHCP), and Windows Internet Name Service (WINS). *SNMP* is used to monitor and manage network resources, such as downed printers, and there are several network management tools that rely on this protocol. *DHCP* functions as an IP address distributor, in that it assigns the computers on a network an IP address, and then reclaims it once a computer leaves the network. In offices that have many computers but relatively few IP addresses, this is an address-preserving mechanism that relieves the administrator of the burden of manually tracking and maintaining every IP address. *WINS* is the method used in a Windows NT network to dynamically manage and maintain NetBIOS names and their associated IP addresses.

Other Protocols Used on a Windows NT Network

The *DataLink Control (DLC)* protocol is used primarily to connect to IBM mainframes and AS/400 systems. While the main reason this protocol is supported is because of the number of IBM and AS/400 systems currently in use today, HP JetDirect printers also use this protocol to enable network printing capability. *Appletalk* is the protocol used to connect to Apple computers. Although there is very little that you need to study about these two protocols, it is important to at least remember what each acronym stands for and what platform they connect to.

exam
Watch

Know what each protocol's acronym is and what each protocol is used for.

CERTIFICATION OBJECTIVE 44.03

Supported File Systems in Windows NT

Just as a protocol is necessary for communication to take place, the operating system must have a method to manage and store data on the hard disk. A *file system* provides the file structure and defines the attributes that can be assigned to individual files and directories. Windows NT includes three files systems—CDFS, FAT, and NTFS—that you can deploy based upon your file storage needs. When you install Windows NT, you are required to choose the file system, or systems, that you wish to deploy. However, Windows NT not only includes the capability to install multiple file systems, but also provides the Disk Administrator utility to manage and maintain your file system. Since *CDFS* is the CD-ROM file system, which permits read-only access, it will not be discussed further.

FAT

Making its debut with MS-DOS, the *File Allocation Table (FAT)* is still one of the oldest file systems in use today and is supported by MS-DOS, Windows, and OS/2. This support is primarily provided for backward compatibility with older software applications that have been written around the FAT file system. Although it has been revised several times to upgrade its capabilities, all versions of FAT utilize the same basic underlying methods to store and manage data.

The FAT file system uses the file allocation table as an index to translate a file or directory name into its physical location on the disk. However, the index is maintained in a first-come, first-served manner in which each new entry is placed in the next available spot. There is no sorting mechanism available for FAT, resulting in longer disk access times as the number of files increases. If a volume on a Windows NT computer exceeds 400MB, you might consider using *NTFS* for that volume's format.

Files are stored on the disk in the same manner as the file allocation table. When you add a file to the disk, the file system places that file on the first available area on the hard disk. If the file is larger than the space available in that spot, a file pointer is added to the end of the file. The pointer contains the address location of the next chunk of that file. This routine continues until the entire file has been saved to the disk. As files are added and deleted from the disk, files are spaced farther away from each other and are segmented down into many more pieces. The result is slower disk access time and, possibly, lost data over a period of time. Many field technicians are now recommending that a disk defragmenting utility, such as Microsoft's Disk Defragmenter, become part of the normal maintenance routine on computers that support NTFS.

When you utilize the FAT file system on a computer, you must be sure that file system security is not an issue. This is due to the fact that FAT supports only read-only (RO), system (S), hidden (H), and archive (A) attributes. Even if you set a file as read-only, it is still possible to modify the file by turning off the read-only attribute. This poses a problem in environments that require a medium to high level of security, yet at the same time provides for low overhead, as there are fewer security settings that need to be stored.

NTFS Overview

The *Windows NT File System (NTFS)* makes up for the restrictions imposed by the FAT file system. First, the size restriction of 400MB is increased to 16 *exabytes* (EB). To put this into its proper context, an exabyte is equal to 1,024 terabytes (TB), which is in turn equal to about 1,024 gigabytes (GB). Since it is rare to find an exabyte hard disk, this gives you a virtually unlimited amount of disk storage capacity. However, this does come with a price in that NTFS does not work well with volumes smaller than 400MB, and cannot be used to format floppy disks.

NTFS has file compression built into the file system structure, whereas you must use a third-party utility with FAT. However, this compression is on an individual file basis rather than on a volume basis. This makes up in part for the overhead associated with NTFS, as you are given the capability to set file-level security. Since NTFS allows for a range of permissions associated with files and directories, which will be discussed in the next section, there is more storage used per file. There is also the capability of tracking access events and file modifications through NTFS, and there is no equivalent when using FAT.

Windows NT comes with a utility to convert FAT partitions into NTFS partitions; but, unless you are absolutely certain that you wish to perform this operation, it is to be avoided. This is due to the fact that there is no utility to convert NTFS back into FAT. This can become a problem if you need to boot back into MS-DOS to make a repair on the system, as MS-DOS does not understand the NTFS file system. For this reason, many Windows NT servers have a small FAT partition to store the operating system files and then use NTFS for the rest of the hard disk.

FAT Versus NTFS

When deciding whether to use FAT or NTFS, consider the following questions:

QUESTIONS AND ANSWERS	
What size is the volume?	If it is over 400MB, you should consider using NTFS.
Will you need to access the volume from MS-DOS or OS/2?	If so, you should consider using FAT.
Will you require file-level security?	Since FAT has no file-level security, you will need to use NTFS.
Is file compression required?	If so, you will need to use NTFS unless you have a third-party utility that can handle compression.

Keep in mind that MS-DOS is unable to recognize NTFS volumes. You may wish to utilize both file systems in case you ever need to boot into MS-DOS to make a system repair.

Know when you need to use the FAT file system versus the NTFS file system. The above list of questions should help you make the determination, but exam questions have been known to throw in more than one of these elements.

Using Disk Administrator to Manage the File System

As we learned in Chapter 43, the Disk Administrator utility is used to manage and maintain the hard disk. To run the utility, you would select the following: Start | Programs | Administrative Tools (Common) | Disk Administrator, which

FIGURE 44-4

The Disk Administrator
utility

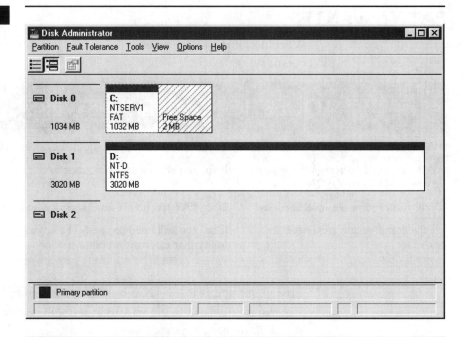

brings up the window shown in Figure 44-4. However, in order to use
Disk Administrator, you must be logged in with an administrator account
because it gives you complete control over the hard disks associated with the
Windows NT machine. These tasks will be discussed in the following sections.

Partitioning the Hard Disk

When you partition a disk, you are selecting an area of free space that will
be formatted with a particular file system. You have two basic types of
partitions: primary partitions and extended partitions. The *primary partition*
is the partition you would normally boot with. In order to create a primary
partition, you would perform the steps outlined in Exercise 44-1:

EXERCISE 44-1

Partitioning the Hard Disk

1. Highlight an area of free space on one of the disk rows.

2. Select Partition | Create. You will receive a dialog box indicating the minimum and maximum sizes permitted for the new primary partition.

3. Enter the size of the new partition and click OK.

If you wish to create an *extended partition*, you would follow the same steps, except you would select Partition | Create Extended.

Volume Sets

A *volume set* is made up of areas of free space resident in a partition. When you gather up the free space, you assign a drive letter to it so that the operating system can reference it. However, before you can actually use the new volume set, you must first format it with a file system, such as FAT or NTFS. The following steps are used to create a volume set:

EXERCISE 44-2

Creating a Volume Set

1. Highlight the areas of free space that you will include in the volume set.

2. Select Partition | Create Volume Set. This will bring up the Create Volume Set dialog box that lists the maximum and minimum sizes for the new volume set.

3. In the dialog box, enter the size of the volume and then click OK.

CERTIFICATION OBJECTIVE 44.05

Creating Shares and Granting Permissions

As we mentioned earlier in the chapter, Windows NT allows you to share resources through shares and permissions. A *share* makes the resource available to other users located on the local machine or over the network. However, shares alone do not allow access to files or printers. Instead, shares are combined with *permissions*, which define what type of access each user or group of users is permitted to the resources. In this section, we will explore how you set up shares and set the appropriate permissions.

Creating Shares for Resource Access

When you share a directory, you are permitting network users access to your resources. For this reason, care must be taken in assigning the appropriate permissions to a shared directory to avoid unauthorized access to the directory's contents. There are several ways to create a share on a directory, and each method is dependent upon how you are logged in to the network and how your network is configured. The first type of directory share that we will look at is the *local computer share*. In order to share a directory on a Windows NT workstation or Windows NT server, you must be logged in as a member of the Administrators group or Power Users group. However, in this scenario, the Windows NT server cannot be a domain controller but must be a member server.

Whether you can share directories on the network depends on how you are logged in. If you wish to share a directory on a Windows NT server that is acting as a domain controller, you must be logged in to that server with an account that is a member of the Administrators group or the Server Operators group. However, to share a directory that is located on a remote computer, you must be logged in with a domain account that is a member of the Administrators or Server Operators local group. In addition, you must use the Server Manager utility if you wish to share a directory remotely, which will be discussed in a later chapter.

When sharing a directory on the local computer, whether you are just sharing a directory on the local machine or on the domain, you will use the procedure outlined in Exercise 44-3:

EXERCISE 44-3

Sharing a Directory

1. Log in to the computer with the appropriate rights. If you are just sharing the directory on a member computer or server, you need to log in with an account that is a member of the Administrators group or the Power Users group. However, you must be logged in with an

account that is a member of the Administrators or Server Operators group in order to share a directory on the domain.

2. Run Windows Explorer.

3. Bring up the options menu on the directory that you wish to share by right-clicking it.

4. Select the Sharing option to bring up the Properties dialog box with the Sharing tab already selected, as shown in the following illustration. You can also get to this point by selecting the Properties option and then selecting the Sharing tab.

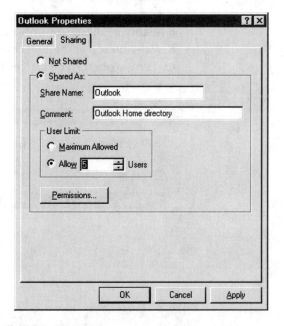

5. Click Shared As. You will note that the other options, such as Share Name and User Limit, will become active and allow you to make changes. The default Share Name is the name of the directory, but you can change this by typing in anything that you wish.

6. You can enter an optional description of the directory in the Comment box. This helps users locate the correct directory, if you use good descriptions.

7. The User Limit box has two choices—Maximum Allowed and Allow x Users. These options allow you to set a limit to the number of connections that can be established with the directory at any given time. If you select Maximum Allowed and the directory resides on a Windows NT workstation, you are limited to ten concurrent connections. However, a Windows NT server allows an unlimited number of connections.

8. Click the Permissions button to bring up the Access Through Share Permissions dialog box, as shown in the following illustration. The first thing you will notice is that the group Everyone, meaning everyone on the network, is given Full Control permissions to the directory by default. In order to change this, you can either use the Remove button at the bottom of the dialog box, then begin to add users manually, or you can modify the permissions to the group Everyone.

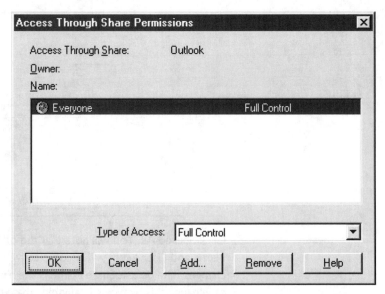

9. Exit the Access Through Share Permissions dialog box by clicking OK.

10. Begin sharing the directory and close the Properties dialog box by clicking OK.

As you can see from step 8, the group Everyone is given Full Control to a directory share by default. Also, Everyone in Microsoft Networking is not the same as the NetWare Bindery Services–based (NetWare 3.12 and earlier) default group Everyone. The Microsoft Everyone is analogous to the [Public] trustee in NDS—that is, *any* client with a connection to the network can access the shared resource, without having to authenticate. Since it is a rare occurrence that you will want to give anyone connected to the network full rights to a file, without first authenticating, you will want to modify the permissions associated with the directory. In order to do so, you will need to use the Add and Remove 2buttons to include or exclude users from having access. To assign rights other than Full Control, you can highlight the user with a single left-click and select the appropriate right from the drop-down list under Type of Access.

Windows NT allows four types of share permissions:

- **No Access**   While remote users are permitted to establish a connection, they are unable to access or view the contents of a directory.

- **Read**   Similar to the standard Read property rights, remote users are permitted to view the directory's contents, display files located in the directory and display their properties, execute programs resident in the directory, and view any subdirectories and their associated contents.

- **Change**   Grants the same access permissions as Read, and allows a remote user to add files to the directory, create subdirectories, modify data in the files, change file attributes, and delete files and subdirectories.

- **Full Control**   Grants the same access permissions as Read and Change, and allows remote users to modify file permissions and take ownership of files.

exam
ⓦatch

You need a thorough understanding of share permissions in order to pass the Novell examination because of the security implications of file shares. We will review this material again in Chapter 46.

Granting Permissions

You can also share resources by setting file and directory permissions, which not only apply to local users, but also to users who log in remotely. However, this is true only if the volume that contains the files or directories resides on an NTFS volume. If the volume type is FAT, anyone on the local machine can gain access to the data and could even delete data. However, you can protect data on a FAT volume from remote access by using shares or permissions.

The Windows NT permissions are similar to file system rights in NetWare, and the concepts are the same. If you grant permissions to a directory, those permissions flow down to the files and subdirectories that reside in that folder. The only exception to this rule is when you set permissions on an individual file basis. In this case, the file-level permissions will override the directory permissions that have been set. Because of the administrative nightmare that can occur by setting permissions on a file-level basis, this type of access is rarely used. However, keep this in mind, as there are instances when you will want to utilize this type of access.

When you grant permissions, you should always grant access rights to groups rather than to individual users. This makes it easier to manage the large file systems that are part of every network, especially if you need to make an access change to multiple users. However, in order to grant permissions to files or directories, you must meet one of the following criteria:

- **You must be the owner/creator of the file or directory**   When you create a file, you are by default the owner. However, Windows NT does allow for users with administrative accounts, such as members of the Administrators group, to take ownership of files or directories. The key point to remember is the owner.

- **Possess the Change Permissions permission to the file or directory**   The Change Permissions permission will be discussed shortly.

- **Possess Full Control access to the file or directory**   As we will see later in this section, Full Control gives a user all rights to a file or directory.

When you set permissions on a file or directory, you use either the Windows NT Explorer or the My Computer utility. Windows NT does discriminate between the permissions that you can assign at the directory and file levels. For each type, there is a set of standard permissions that you can assign. *Standard permissions* are composed of different types of access rights, known as *individual permissions*, and should look quite familiar:

- Change Permissions (P)
- Delete (D)
- Execute (X)
- Read (R)
- Take Ownership (O)
- Write (W)

Now that you have seen the individual permissions, we will put them together with the standard permissions assigned to files. Table 44-1 lists the standard permissions with their associated individual permissions.

Directory level permissions are similar; but, instead of four types of standard permissions, there are a total of seven standard permissions. Another difference is that the permissions assigned to new files within a folder are slightly different than the permissions assigned to the folder itself.

	File Permission	Individual Permissions	Description
TABLE 44-1 Standard File Permissions and How They Relate to Individual Permissions	No Access	None	No access is permitted to the file, even if they have been given other access rights through use of a group or explicitly set permissions.
	Read	RX	Users are allowed to view, and execute, if appropriate, the contents of the file.
	Change	RWXD	Gives the user the same access rights as Read, but adds the right to modify or delete the file.
	Full Control	RWXDPO	Gives the user the same access rights as Change, but adds the Change Permissions and Take Ownership permissions.

Table 44-2 sums up the directory permissions, new file permissions, and how they are associated with individual permissions.

Permission	Individual Permissions		Description
	Assigned to the Folder	Assigned to New Files	
No Access	None	None	No Access always means no access, even when given access through other group membership.
List	RX	None	Users can list the files that reside in the directory, or files located in a subdirectory.
Read	RX	RX	Users can read the contents of files and execute files in the directory.
Add	WX	None	Users can add files to the directory. However, users do not have privileges to view the directory contents.
Add and Read	RWX	RX	Combines the privileges of Read and Add.
Change	RWXD	RWXD	Gives the same access rights as Add and Read, but adds the ability to modify the contents of the directory and delete files.
Full Control	All	All	Gives the same permissions as Change, but adds the capability to change the permissions to, or take ownership of, the directory and its files.

When you set permissions on a file or directory, you will need to perform the steps outlined in the following exercise:

Setting Up Permissions

1. Start either the Windows NT Explorer utility or the My Computer utility.
2. Right-click the directory or file for which you wish to set permissions. On the pop-up menu, select the Properties option.
3. Select the Security tab.
4. Click the Permissions button to bring up the Permissions dialog box, shown in the following illustration.

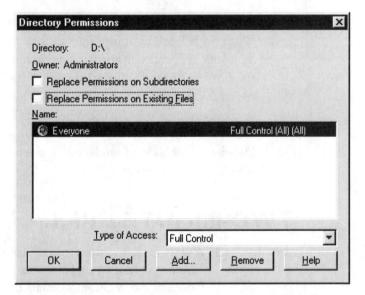

5. Add or remove groups using the Add and Remove buttons located on the bottom of the dialog box.
6. Highlight each group, or groups, that you wish to assign certain permissions. To change permissions, use the Type of Access list box.
7. When you have finished, click OK to close the dialog box.

Two other items that need to be discussed in more detail are Replace Permissions on Subdirectories and Replace Permissions on Existing Files.

If you are modifying current access rights, you can also replace permissions that are set on the associated subdirectories by checking the Replace Permissions on Subdirectories check box. By the same token, you can replace permissions on existing files by selecting the Replace Permissions on Existing Files check box.

Remember the different file and directory permissions, and their associated individual permissions. Also keep in mind that you cannot secure local files that reside on a FAT volume. These issues come up rather frequently in the Novell certification exam.

CERTIFICATION SUMMARY

In this chapter, we have explored the basic networking models used by Windows NT and examined their differences. From understanding how Windows NT works in a network environment, we went on to discover the different protocols that are supported by Windows NT to establish communications with other operating systems. From there, we progressed to the file systems used by the Windows NT operating system, and how to share the files and directories that reside on the different volumes. This knowledge will lay the foundation for the next step in the learning process, Windows NT server networking.

✓ TWO-MINUTE DRILL

❑ A workgroup is a peer-to-peer arrangement of computers that have been grouped together in order to share resources, in which individual workstations maintain their own security databases (the Security Accounts Manager) and do not require a central server to provide access to network resources.

❑ A Windows NT domain is comprised of network servers and computers, logically grouped together for the purpose of sharing resources, in which a Windows NT server is a primary domain controller (PDC) to provide access to network resources. The

PDC is responsible for maintaining the master database (directory) containing user and resource accounts for all workstations in the domain.

❑ Windows NT has the ability to deploy multiple protocols at the same time. When planning a protocol scheme, you will need to consider the types of file-sharing and printing services needed, and the types of applications to be used. Windows NT comes with several protocols—TCP/IP, NetBEUI, NWLink IPX/SPX Compatible, DataLink Control (DLC), and AppleTalk.

❑ Of all the protocols used in Windows NT, Microsoft's *NetBIOS Extended User Interface (NetBEUI)* is the easiest one to implement because it is not only self-configuring, but self-tuning as well. It is one of the protocols selected by default in Windows 95 and NT Workstation

❑ The NWLink IPX/SPX Compatible protocol is Microsoft's version of IPX/SPX and is NDIS-compliant. NDIS, Network Device Interface Specification, allows the binding of multiple protocols to a single network card.

❑ Transmission Control Protocol/Internet Protocol (TCP/IP) is the most popular protocol used in today's network environment. Designed to connect wide area networks together, TCP/IP is a routable protocol that makes connecting any two networks together that support TCP/IP relatively easy.

❑ The DataLink Control (DLC) protocol is used primarily to connect to IBM mainframes and AS/400 systems. This protocol is supported because of the number of IBM and AS/400 systems currently in use, and because HP JetDirect printers use this protocol to enable network printing capability.

❑ Appletalk is the protocol used to connect to Apple computers.

❑ File Allocation Table (FAT) is one of the oldest file systems in use today and is supported by MS-DOS, Windows, and OS/2. This support is primarily provided for backward compatibility with older software applications written around the FAT file system.

❑ The *Windows NT File System (NTFS)* makes up for the restrictions imposed by the FAT file system. NTFS gives a virtually unlimited amount of disk storage capacity, but it does not work well with volumes smaller than 400MB, and cannot be used to format floppy disks.

❑ Partitioning a hard disk involves selecting an area of free space on the disk that will be formatted with a particular file system.

❑ There are two basic types of partitions—primary partitions and extended partitions. The primary partition is the partition the computer normally boots with.

❑ A volume set is made up of areas of free space resident in a partition. When you gather up the free space, you assign a drive letter to it so that the operating system can reference it. Before you can actually use a new volume set, you must format it with a file system.

❑ When you share a directory, you are permitting network users access to your resources. Care must be taken in assigning the appropriate permissions to a shared directory to avoid unauthorized access to the directory's contents.

❑ You can also share resources by setting file and directory permissions, which apply to local users and users who log in remotely. This is true only if the volume that contains the files or directories resides on an NTFS volume.

❑ If the volume type is FAT, anyone on the local machine can gain access to the data and could even delete data. You can protect data on a FAT volume from remote access by using shares or permissions.

SELF TEST

The following Self-Test questions will help you measure your understanding of the material presented in this chapter. Read all the choices carefully, as there may be more than one correct answer. Choose all correct answers for each question.

1. The maximum size that a FAT partition can handle is

    A. 100MB

    B. 200MB

    C. 300MB

    D. 400MB

2. The networking model that requires the individual workstations to maintain their own accounts is the

    A. Domain model

    B. Workgroup model

    C. Peer-to-Peer model

    D. NDS model

3. If you want to connect a Windows NT network to a Novell NetWare network, you would use which of the following protocols?

    A. IPX / SPX

    B. NetBEUI

    C. NWLink IPX / SPX Compatible

    D. TCP/IP

4. The _____ contains the master directory database for the domain.

    A. Windows NT workstation

    B. Primary domain controller

    C. Member server

    D. Backup domain controller

5. The _____ utility is used to manage and maintain the hard disk.

    A. Disk Administrator

    B. My Computer

    C. User Manager

    D. Windows NT Explorer

6. When you create a share, the Everyone group is given which type of access by default?

    A. Add

    B. Add and Read

    C. Change

    D. Full Control

7. You need to give Connie access to the MYDATABASE directory located on your Windows NT workstation. The MYDATABASE directory is stored on a FAT volume and is maintained by the workstation administrator. Also, since your company hasn't received a workstation for Connie, she has been using your computer to access the network. In order to give Connie access rights to the directory, you would need to

    A. Create a share.

B. Set up the appropriate permissions.

C. Tell Connie the name of the directory.

D. Nothing. You can't give her rights to the directory because you are not the owner of the MYDATABASE directory.

8. An NTFS volume can store a maximum of

A. 16EB

B. 16GB

C. 16TB

D. 16MB

9. The Windows NT Domain Model provides which of the following advantages over the workgroup model? (Choose all that apply.)

A. Centralized Administration

B. Decentralized Administration

C. Multiple Logins

D. Single Login

10. You are creating a special directory called PRODUCT_SPECS on the NTSERV1 server for users of the Engineering Department to deposit product specification files. These files will need to be viewed by the Marketing Department in order to create a marketing strategy. The NTSERV1 server uses only NTFS for its file system. Based on the above information, you would need to give the Marketing Department _____ permissions to the PRODUCT_SPECS directory.

A. Add

B. Change

C. Read

D. Write

11. Which of the following describes the workgroup model? (Choose all that apply.)

A. Centralized Administration

B. Decentralized Administration

C. Used for large groups of users

D. Used for small groups of users

12. Johnny is given membership to the Engineering, Marketing, and Sales groups. He needs to access the MYDATABASE directory located on the NTSERV1 server. Engineering is given Read, Add, and Change permissions to the directory; Marketing has Read permissions; and Sales is given No Access. Which of the following rights does Johnny have to the MYDATABASE directory?

A. Add

B. Change

C. No Access

D. Read

13. Which of the following statement(s) describes the domain model? (Choose all that apply.)

A. Centralized Administration

B. Decentralized Administration

C. Used for small groups of users

D. Used for large groups of users.

14. When you grant access rights, you should always

    A. Assign rights to groups and assign users to groups.

    B. Assign rights to users and assign groups to users.

    C. Assign rights to groups and assign groups to users.

    D. Assign rights to groups and assign users to groups.

15. In order to share a directory locally on a Windows NT workstation or a Windows NT server, you must be logged in as a member of which group(s)?

    A. Administrators group

    B. Backup Operators group

    C. Power Users group

    D. Server Operators group

CERTIFIED NOVELL ENGINEER

45

Windows NT Domain Networking

CERTIFICATION OBJECTIVES

45.01   NT Directory Services (NTDS)

45.02   Domain Server Roles

45.03   Setting Up Domain Controllers

45.04   Adding a Workstation or Server to a Domain

I n the previous chapter, we explored the different components necessary in a Windows NT network. As you learned, Windows NT has two basic networking models, the workgroup model and the domain model. This chapter will delve deeper into Windows NT server–based networking by examining Microsoft's NT Directory Services and the different roles played by a Windows NT server. Understanding these topics is critical to passing the Novell certification exam.

CERTIFICATION OBJECTIVE 45.01

NT Directory Services (NTDS)

As you recall from the previous chapter, the workgroup model is a peer-to-peer networking environment that requires each workstation to manage and maintain its own user accounts database and security settings. With this type of network environment, administration of user accounts and access rights is decentralized and requires cooperation and coordination among the members of the workgroup. For all but the smallest of businesses, this type of administration is undesirable due to the amount of work involved in maintaining the network.

In the domain model, as shown in Figure 45-1, the user account database and security settings are maintained on a central server, called the *primary domain controller*. Since the user account database and security settings reside in a single location rather than being spread throughout the network, administration is centralized. This form of network administration is more desirable to companies since it takes fewer individuals to maintain the network.

Formerly known as Microsoft Domain Service, NT Directory Services (NTDS) is based on the concept of domains and is a replicated database system. The master Directory database resides on the primary domain controller (PDC) and is replicated to the backup domain controllers (BDC), a process we will discuss more thoroughly later. While it is a replicated database system, it is not a distributed database system as is

FIGURE 45-1   The domain model

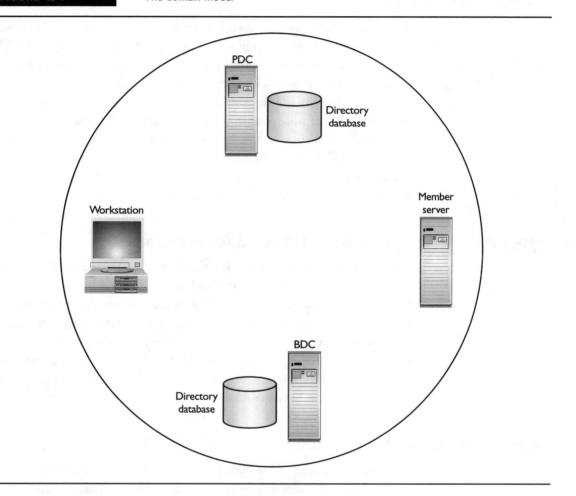

Novell Directory Services (NDS). In a distributed database system, the database is *partitioned* and stored in parts. In contrast, a replicated database system copies and stores the *entire* database.

There are several key features to NTDS that you will need to comprehend in order to pass the exam. These features, discussed in the following paragraphs, can be compared to Novell's NDS.

Single Network Logins

Since user account administration is centralized in a Windows NT domain environment, only one account and password combination is required in order for a user to access network resources. This is accomplished by having the user log into the network rather than into individual servers, much as with NDS. The database keeps track of what resources the user is permitted to access, as well as what permissions are granted to any single resource. Because of this, the user can log in to the domain from any workstation on the network. This feature relieves users of having to remember multiple account names and passwords, and it gives them the ability to access any resources they need without having to log out and log back in.

Integration with Windows NT–Based Applications

The basic feature of every network is the ability to share resources, whether the resource is a file, printer, or application. Originally, networks were designed around file and printer sharing; but, more recently, application servers have become more popular. Application servers provide a network with the ability to process and distribute data much the way that mainframes are used, but at a lower cost. There are several applications that work with NTDS, such as the Windows BackOffice product line, to provide application services to users on the network.

Single Point of Administration

Since the master copy of the Directory database resides on the primary domain controller, administrators are given the ability to manage and maintain the network from a single location. This allows the administrator to make one change on the network rather than at several different points on the network. Changes are then propagated throughout the network by directory replication.

Directory Replication

As we mentioned earlier in this section, NTDS is a replicated database system. The primary domain controller *replicates*, or copies, the master Directory database to the backup domain controllers. However, this also represents a single point of failure in the network with regard to administrative activities. Should the PDC fail, all administration activities are halted until it is reinstated to the network, or the administrator manually promotes a BDC to a PDC.

CERTIFICATION OBJECTIVE 45.02

Domain Server Roles

As we saw in Figure 45-1, a Windows NT server can perform one of several roles in a Windows NT domain environment—primary domain controller (PDC), backup domain controller (BDC), and member server. The role given to a Windows NT server is assigned during installation, and care must be taken due to the limitations of role assignment. The next subsections will describe the characteristics of each type of server role.

Primary Domain Controller (PDC)

The most important server in a domain environment is the primary domain controller, or PDC. The PDC is responsible for storing the master copy of the Directory database, which contains all user account information for the entire domain. When a modification to the Directory database is required, such as adding a workstation to the domain, the PDC must be online and accessible from the network in order to complete any administrative changes. This is because you can have only one PDC operating in the domain at any given time.

Since the PDC contains the master copy of the Directory database, it can also provide authentication services to the domain. When a user attempts to log into the network, the PDC will verify the login credentials provided by the user against the Directory database. By doing so, the PDC becomes the central security point in the domain. However, should a PDC fail, a backup domain controller can provide authentication services to the domain. This is made possible through Directory replication, which is controlled by the PDC. Periodically, the PDC will copy the master Directory database to all backup domain controllers in the domain, which provides for fault tolerance.

One of the problems associated with PDCs is server failure. When a PDC fails, or communication to the PDC is lost, no administrative changes can be made. To rectify this potential problem, a BDC can be promoted to a PDC (at which time the PDC is automatically demoted to a BDC). The process of promoting a BDC to a PDC is not automatic; it must be manually performed by an administrator. If you have advance notice that a PDC must be taken offline, such as for preventive maintenance, you can demote a PDC to a BDC and then promote a BDC to a PDC. However, you cannot demote a PDC to a member server without reinstalling the Windows NT server software. This is primarily because the structure of the Registry is slightly different between a domain controller and a member server. Even though you cannot demote a PDC to a member server, a PDC can still function as a file, print, or application server. While there are minor differences in the Registry structure, those areas that are affected do not interfere with the functionality of these types of services.

Backup Domain Controllers (BDC)

Backup domain controllers (BDCs) are used for two primary reasons: login authentication and fault tolerance. Periodically, the PDC will replicate copies of the master Directory database to BDCs to ensure that the BDCs have an updated copy. The BDC uses its copy of the Directory database to unload some of the login authentication responsibilities from the PDC. Imagine if you worked on a medium-to-large network, and everyone attempted to log in at the same time in the morning. If everyone tried to authenticate to the same domain controller, there would be a severe drain on system resources that would result in a bottleneck and some very upset users. However, since BDCs have a copy of the Directory database, they can take some of the burden off the PDC and allow for faster login times.

Another reason to have at least one backup domain controller is for fault tolerance. If you manage to lose the primary domain controller, such as with a hard disk failure or a corrupted Directory database, you can recover through the BDC. In this case, you would promote a BDC to a PDC and allow it to remain the PDC until you could get the original PDC back online. By performing this step you are allowing administrative changes to the network, since only a PDC can perform those types of modifications. However, the BDCs can continue to perform login authentication services to the network, even though a PDC is not available.

You are permitted to have as many BDCs on the network as you wish, but Microsoft recommends that you have at least one for fault tolerance. However, when you choose to install a server as either a backup domain controller or a member server, care must be taken to choose wisely. If you install a Windows NT server as a BDC, you will be unable to revert it back to a member server without a full reinstall, and vice versa. However, if you install a Windows NT server as a BDC, you still retain the functionality of a file, print, or application server just as you would with a PDC.

Member Servers

A member server is used primarily to provide application, file, or printer services to the network. The most common use of a member server is to support applications services, such as the Microsoft BackOffice product family. In this regard, a member server is similar to a domain controller. However, member servers do not store copies of the Directory database and, therefore, cannot provide logon authentication services for the domain. While at first glance this may seem to be a disadvantage, it is actually a benefit if you plan to utilize application services that require a lot of processing power or will be heavily accessed. Without the extra overhead of providing logon authentication, a member server can utilize the additional resources for other services.

Before you plan your network layout, remember that domain controllers cannot be demoted to a member server without a complete reinstall. This rule also holds true for a member server: a member server cannot be promoted to a domain controller without a complete reinstall. Again, the reason lies in the structure of the Registry, which differs enough between a domain controller and a member server to cause problems without a full reinstall.

Remember that you cannot switch a Windows NT server between a domain controller and a member server without a full reinstallation of the Windows NT server operating system.

CERTIFICATION OBJECTIVE 45.03

Setting Up Domain Controllers

Before you begin the installation process on a new Windows NT server, you must determine what role the server will play on your network. Planning the server role is a critical step during the installation process since you cannot convert a domain controller to a member server, or vice versa, without reinstalling the Windows NT server operating system. As we discussed in the preceding section, this is due to the differences in the Registry structure between a domain controller and a member server. Therefore, you will need to take a look not only at your current network structure, but you should also take into account any future network expansion plans. By identifying your network needs in advance, you will save some time and grief in the long run.

There are several key questions that you should answer to help determine a Windows NT server's role in a domain:

- *Is this the first server installed on the network?* If so, it will be the primary domain controller since a PDC is required to provide permission to join the network. However, if it is not the first server installed on the network, it will have to be a backup domain controller or a member server as you can have only one primary domain controller on the network at any given time.

■ *Do you have any backup domain controllers on the network?*
If you do not, you should consider installing the server as a BDC. It is highly recommended that you have at least one BDC for fault tolerance purposes. Remember that if your primary domain controller crashes, you will be unable to perform any administrative modifications on the network until it is brought back online or a BDC has been manually promoted to a PDC.

■ *Are you installing at a remote site (or a site that spans a WAN link)?*
If you are planning to provide network servers to a remote location, you may want to see if a BDC is already at that location. If not, it is highly recommended that you install a BDC at a remote location to cut down on the traffic generated by logon authentications.

■ *Does the network severely slow down in the morning hours or right after lunch?* Generally, this is the time that most users log in to your network. Consequently, this is the time that network traffic is at a peak and you may need another BDC to help facilitate authentication.

■ *Will the server provide application services that will be heavily accessed?*
If so, you will want to install the server as a member server to avoid the additional overhead of logon authentication.

Keeping these items in mind will help determine what role your server should play in a Windows NT domain.

The Domain Logon Process

If you recall from Chapter 43, before a user can access any local resources, he must log in to a Windows NT machine. This process, known as the *WinLogon process*, is initiated every time the computer is restarted and displays a login dialog box that requires a CTRL-ALT-DEL keystroke sequence. This keystroke sequence brings up the Logon Information dialog box that allows you to supply your access credentials in the form of a user name and password. From there, your access credentials are passed to the

Local Security Authority (LSA) for routing to the Security Accounts Manager (SAM) for verification. The results are then passed back to the LSA for routing to the WinLogon process. If you have been validated, you are then allowed access to local resources. However, if you are not validated, the WinLogon process will deny access until valid credentials are presented.

The WinLogon process is used whenever you attempt to gain entry to a Windows NT workstation that is not a member of a domain, whether the workstation is a stand-alone machine or a member of a workgroup. In a domain environment, the login process has to be modified because authentication occurs through a domain controller rather than the local machine. To log in to a domain, you must go through a mandatory *NetLogon* process as shown in Figure 45-2.

As you can see in Figure 45-2, there are several more steps that must be completed in order to successfully log in to a domain:

1. You are first presented with a login dialog box, which requests a user name and password, from the WinLogon process. These credentials are passed to the LSA.

2. The LSA routes the login request and information to the local, or client, NetLogon process. This process is part of the workstation's network client.

FIGURE 45-2   The NetLogon process authenticates a user to the domain

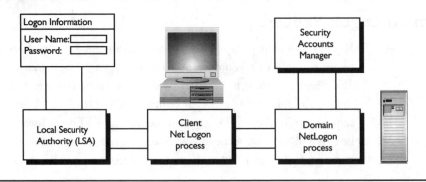

3. The client NetLogon process takes the request from the LSA and routes it to the NetLogon process that runs on a domain controller, which can be either a primary domain controller or a backup domain controller.

4. The domain controller's NetLogon process takes the login request and passes it to the Security Accounts Manager (SAM), which also resides on the domain controller, for validation.

5. The SAM checks the login credentials against the Directory database. The results, whether a denial or an *access token* that contains the user's security access information, are then passed back down to the domain's NetLogon process.

6. The domain's NetLogon process routes the results back to the client NetLogon process at the workstation.

7. The client NetLogon process forwards the information back to the LSA.

8. The LSA returns the login results to the WinLogon process.

9. If the credentials were not validated, the WinLogon process denies the login attempt. However, if the user name and password were authenticated, a new session is initiated for the user at the workstation.

exam
☜atch
Do not get confused between the client NetLogon process and the domain controller NetLogon process. The way to differentiate between the two is that one is at the client, or workstation, level (client NetLogon process) and the other is at the domain, or network, level (domain controller NetLogon process).

Creating and Administering Domain User Accounts

When you create a new user account on the *local machine*, you use the User Manager utility. However, in order to create a new user account on a *domain*, you must use the User Manager for Domains utility. While the look and feel of both applications is very similar, the location of their respective databases is different. As you recall from Chapter 44, the User Manager utility maintains all accounts in a database that resides on the workstation. With the User Manager for Domains utility, the Directory database resides on a domain controller. However, you can modify the Directory database only on the primary domain controller because it contains the master copy. The master database is then replicated, or copied, to the backup domain controllers.

Each time you create a user or group account in a Windows NT domain, the account is assigned a *security identifier*, also known as a SID. The SID is a unique number that is assigned once and is never reused. This means that if you accidentally delete an account, you will not be able to reassign the SID even if you re-create the account with the same exact settings. If the account was assigned ownership of any shared resources, an account deletion would remove access to those resources. SID assignment is an automatic process that is completed by the Windows NT operating system, and is not used by the system administrator.

The SID is also used to assign security access rights to resources. Each resource has an *Access Control List (ACL)* that contains a list of SIDs that are permitted to access the resource. When a user successfully logs on to a domain, an access token is generated and attached to the user's workstation. The access token contains the account's SID, and every activity performed by the user is associated with the SID. When a user attempts to access a resource, the user's account SID is compared against the resource's ACL. If a match is found, the user can then access the resource. For example, Figure 45-3 shows Tom's attempt to access a network printer. Tom's SID, 023453, is compared against the printer's ACL. Since a match is found, Tom is permitted to access the network printer.

To create and administer domain user accounts, you must understand the method of assigning user rights. In Windows NT, as with Novell's NetWare, permissions and rights are assigned at the group level rather than at the user level. Users are then assigned membership to the appropriate groups that give them access rights to network resources. Using this philosophy, administration of user accounts is simplified because you are managing groups of users, as opposed to individual accounts. For example, if you have 50 people who access the same database, you can assign the necessary rights to a database group and then grant the individual users membership in the group. If you need to modify the access rights at a later time, you have to make the change to only the one group. However, user accounts have no permissions granted to them by default.

FIGURE 45-3

The ACL is compared to a process SID

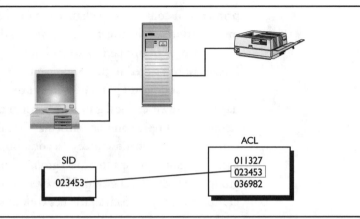

Windows NT applies the group concept to grant user rights for performing system administration tasks. For example, Windows NT comes with a Server Operator group that grants the appropriate permissions for backing up and restoring files. By using this group, you can grant multiple individuals, such as members of your Information System Division, the right to back up and restore files. If you need to revoke these privileges later, all you need to do is remove them from the group.

There are two types of groups that are used in the Windows NT network environment: global groups and local groups. These groups will be discussed in the following sections.

exam
ⓦatch

Study local and global groups and understand them thoroughly. You must be able to differentiate between the two and know the default groups in order to pass the certification exam.

Local Groups

Local groups are used to assign access rights to resources located on the local Windows NT machine. For example, if you installed a new printer on the Engineering Department's server, you could create a local group and assign permissions to access the printer to that group. At this point, recalling our permissions assignment rule of assigning permissions to groups and placing users in groups, you would grant membership to the local group for each user. If at some point you needed to modify permissions to access the printer, you could merely change the local group's permissions and the modification would affect all members in the group.

Since local groups permit access only to local resources, the group's information is stored in the local machine's account database. This has the advantage of offloading some of the burden from the domain's Directory database. However, local groups can assign rights and permissions only to resources that reside on that particular machine. It cannot grant rights or permissions to global resources. In addition, you are limited to assigning only users and global groups to a local group—that is, you cannot assign a local group to another local group. However, you can include users and global groups from any domain in the network in which a trust relationship has been established (trust relationships are covered in detail in Chapter 47).

Windows NT comes with several default groups that can aid the network administrator in assigning rights and permissions. These groups, which cannot be deleted or renamed, are listed in Table 45-1.

To create a local group, use the User Manager for Domains utility. Once you have User Manager for Domains running, perform the following steps.

1. Select (highlight) any users you would like to include in the new local group and select the User option from the menu bar.

2. Select the New Local Group option. This will bring up the New Local Group dialog box with a list of the user accounts that you had selected, as shown in the following illustration.

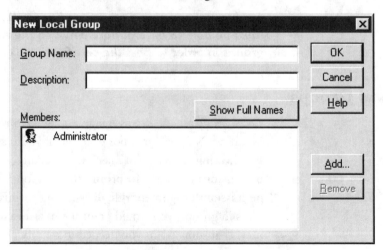

	Group Name	NT Workstation	NT Server	Description
TABLE 45-1 Default Local Groups for Windows NT Workstation and NT Server	Administrators	X	X	Full access to the local computer.
	Account Operators		X	Used to manage and maintain user and group accounts.
	Backup Operators	X	X	Allows back up and restore operations to files regardless of the user's permissions.
	Guests	X	X	Allows access permissions for users who do not use the system often, such as traveling users.
	Power Users	X		Permits members to set networking options and share files.
	Print Operators		X	Grants create, delete, install, share, and modification access rights to printers on the server.
	Replicator	X	X	Used by the replicator server to manage and maintain security during the file replication process.
	Server Operators		X	Grants the appropriate rights and permissions to perform administrative duties on the server such as backup and restore operations, server shut down, change the server time, lock the server, and share resources.
	Users	X	X	Allows members to perform normal, day-to-day operations such as managing files and running applications.

3. Enter a name in the Group Name text box.

4. Enter an optional description in the Description text box. Even though this field is optional, you will find network administration much easier if you include a brief description.

5. If you need to add or remove additional users, or if you simply forgot to select user accounts prior to opening the New Local Group dialog box, you can use the Add and Remove buttons in the Members section to add and remove accounts.

The Show Full Names button allows you to view the information stored in the Full Name field of the account. This feature can be useful, for example, if you have two users with the same first and last names, and have included middle names in the Full Name field. While most people believe that the odds are against this type of situation arising, it will occur on the larger networks at some point in time with some of the more common last names, such as Smith or Thomas. I have actually seen a network in which there were three users with the same first and last name, and two of them had the same middle initial.

Global Groups

Global groups are very similar to local groups, except they gather user accounts from the entire domain. The information pertaining to a global group is stored in the Directory database on the domain controllers. Because of this, only user accounts from the domain can be stored in a global group. This also means that global groups cannot contain local groups or other global groups. However, a trusted domain can use global groups, making it easy to allow administrators from one domain to assign access rights to users in your domain. This is performed by adding global groups to local groups, allowing the global group to inherit rights from the local group.

Windows NT provides for three built-in, or default, global groups: Domain Administrators, Domain Guests, and Domain Users. Since these are global groups, they are used to grant access rights across the domain. Each global group is utilized for a different purpose:

■ *Domain Administrators*   The Domain Administrators group, known as Domain Admins, is used to perform administrative functions, such as adding new workstations and granting/revoking access rights on domain accounts. When the Domain Admins global group is created, it is automatically added to the local Administrators group on every Windows NT machine in the domain. By doing so, it allows the domain administrator to remotely manage workstations and servers in the domain.

exam
ⓦatch

Note that Novell documentation incorrectly lists the Domain Admins group as Domain Administrators. While this may seem a minor point, you will see several questions regarding global groups on the certification exam.

■ *Domain Guests*   The Domain Guests global group is used to provideguest-level accounts across the domain, just as the local group Guests is used to provide guest-level access on the local machine. When the Domain Guests group is created, it is automatically added to each Windows NT machine's local Guests group. You would use this group if you wished to provide limited network access to roaming users.

■ *Domain Users*   The Domain Users group encompasses all user accounts on the domain. When a new domain account is added to the network, it is automatically added to this group. This allows users to log in from different workstations on the domain. However, since this global group contains all users on the network, including the Administrator account, care must be taken to which privileges are granted or denied to this group. For example, if you give the Domain Users group No Access rights to log on locally to the domain controller, you have effectively blocked out everyone from managing that domain controller.

When you are presented with questions on the Novell certification exam that list both local and global groups, remember that global groups are always prefixed by the word Domain. When you create a global group, you are creating a group that is to be used on the domain level, rather than the client level. The Domain Users group encompasses all user accounts on the domain level. Therefore, you must use the User Manager for Domains utility to create, delete, or modify global groups. When you create a global group, you will perform the following steps:

1. Start the User Manager for Domains utility by selecting Start|Programs|Administrative Tools (Common)|User Manager for Domains. You must be already logged in with administrative privileges.

2. Highlight all users that you wish to include in the global group. Alternatively, you can ensure that no users are highlighted if you wish to make assignments later.

3. Select the New Global Group option from the User menu. A dialog box will appear, similar to this one.

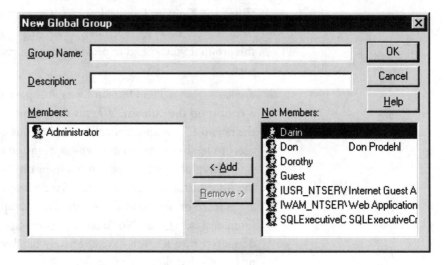

4. Give your new group a name in the Group Name text box.

5. You can give an optional description of the Global group in the Description text box.

6. From the Not Members area of the dialog box, select one or more user accounts and click the Add button. This will add the user account(s) to the global group.

7. Choose the OK button when you have finished.

Alternatively, you could have also removed users by selecting accounts from the Member portion of the dialog box and selecting the Remove button.

FROM THE CLASSROOM

Granting Permissions to Users for Domain Resources

Just as with NetWare network resources, Microsoft Windows NT domain resources should have groups assigned permissions to use them, rather than individual user accounts. However, don't forget that NT domains have two main types of groups: local and global. Additionally, don't confuse an NT global group with an NDS global group, which is nothing more than a group composed of users from multiple NDS contexts. With NT domains, the recommended method of assigning permissions to domain resources can be remembered with the acronym AGLP: (1) add user *A*ccount to a (2) *G*lobal group, which is added to a (3) *L*ocal group (4) to which you assign *P*ermissions.

—*By Dan Cheung, CNI, MCNE, MCT*

CERTIFICATION OBJECTIVE 45.04

Adding a Workstation or Server to a Domain

This is part of the Windows NT security system that stops unknown workstations from accessing any part of the domain. There are actually two methods that are used to allow a workstation to join the domain. The first method does not require the administrator to go to the workstation to add it to the domain as long as you provide the user with the appropriate steps to complete the process.

1. Log into the domain as Administrator and start the Server Manager utility. This is performed by choosing Start|Administrative Tools (Common)|Server Manager.

2. Select Add to Domain from the Computer menu item. The Add Computer to Domain dialog box, shown below, will appear.

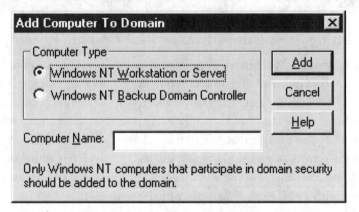

3. The Computer Type field allows you to choose either the Windows NT Workstation or Server, or the Windows NT Backup Domain Controller. Normally, you would select the default of the workstation/server combination.

4. Enter the computer name in the Computer Name text box and click the Add button.

5. Select Close.

At this point, the user can perform the next steps, or the administrator can go to the Windows NT machine and complete the rest of the process. However, if you have a large number of users, such as after a building move or installing a new network, you will probably want to have a set of instructions already prepared and distributed for the next steps.

6. At the Windows NT machine, start the Control Panel by choosing Start|Settings|Control Panel.

7. Select the Network icon.

8. Select Change.

9. Click Member of Domain. Type the name of the domain that you wish to join.

10. Select the OK button. This brings up the Welcome to Domain dialog box.

11. Select Close. When the Restart Machine dialog box appears, select Yes.

This method does not require the administrator to visit the Windows NT machine that will be added to the network. However, the next method of adding a workstation to the domain *requires* the administrator to go to the workstation, and may not be the best choice for larger networks.

1. At the Windows NT workstation, select the My Computer icon.

2. Bring up the Control Panel and choose the Network option.

3. Select Change.

4. Click the Domain option. In the text box, enter the name of the domain the workstation is being added to.

5. Enable the Create a Computer Account in the Domain option by clicking the check box. This will prompt you for a user name and password. You must use an account that has domain administrative rights or you cannot complete the process.

6. Select the OK button. This will bring up the Welcome to Domain dialog box, which you close by selecting the OK button.

7. Select Close to close the Network dialog box. At this point, you will be prompted to restart the workstation.

Regardless of which method you use to add a workstation to the domain, it is imperative that the primary domain controller for the domain is running and accessible to the machine. Recall from earlier in the chapter that no administrative changes, including adding a workstation to the domain, can be performed if the PDC is offline.

exam
ⓦatch
You will need to know both procedures for adding a workstation to the domain for the exam. One particular item to watch out for is which method would require the administrator to physically go to the workstation.

CERTIFICATION SUMMARY

In this chapter, we discussed how NTDS works to provide a Windows NT domain with network services. We have also seen how a Windows NT server can function in that network, whether as a domain controller or as a member server. By bringing these concepts together, you can better understand a Windows NT network and the underlying characteristics of each part of the network on a basic level.

Because one common administrative task is to grant permissions to users to access network resources, we discussed the concepts of local and global groups. Finally, we described the steps involved in adding a workstation to the domain. By understanding these concepts, you are now ready to delve into the realm of Windows NT security, which will further add to your understanding of how permissions and rights are assigned to users and how Windows NT provides security to its users.

TWO-MINUTE DRILL

❑ In the domain model the user account database and security settings are maintained on a central server, called the *primary domain controller*.

❑ Formerly known as Microsoft Domain Service, NT Directory Services (NTDS) is based on the concept of domains and is a replicated database system.

❑ NTDS is a replicated database system. The primary domain controller *replicates*, or copies, the master Directory database to the backup domain controllers.

❑ The most important server in a domain environment is the primary domain controller, or PDC.

❑ Since the PDC contains the master copy of the Directory database, it can also provide authentication services to the domain.

❑ Backup domain controllers (BDCs) are used for two primary reasons: login authentication and fault tolerance.

❑ A member server is used primarily to provide application, file, or printer services to the network.

❑ Before you begin the installation process on a new Windows NT server, you must determine what role the server will play on your network.

❑ Before a user can access any local resources, he must log in to a Windows NT machine. This process, known as the *WinLogon process*, is initiated every time the computer is restarted and displays a login dialog box that requires a CTRL-ALT-DEL keystroke sequence.

❑ When you create a new user account on the *local machine*, you use the User Manager utility. However, in order to create a new user account on a *domain*, you must use the User Manager for Domains utility.

❑ Each time you create a user or group account in a Windows NT domain, the account is assigned a *security identifier*, also known as a SID.

❑ The SID is also used to assign security access rights to resources. Each resource has an *Access Control List* (ACL) that contains a list of SIDs that are permitted to access the resource.

❑ *Local groups* are used to assign access rights to resources located on the local Windows NT machine.

❑ *Global groups* are very similar to local groups, except they gather user accounts from the entire domain. The information pertaining to a global group is stored in the Directory database on the domain controllers.

❑ Windows NT provides for three built-in, or default, global groups: Domain Administrators, Domain Guests, and Domain Users.

❑ The Domain Administrators group, known as Domain Admins, is used to perform administrative functions, such as adding new workstations and granting / revoking access rights on domain accounts.

❑ The Domain Guests global group is used to provide guest-level accounts across the domain, just as the local group Guests is used to provide guest-level access on the local machine.

❑ The Domain Users group encompasses all user accounts on the domain. However, since this global group contains *all* users on the network, including the Administrator account, care must be taken about which privileges are granted or denied to this group.

❑ Even if you have a valid user account and password, you will be unable to access resources on a domain from a Windows NT machine unless the computer has been added to the domain.

❑ When adding a workstation to the domain, it is imperative that the primary domain controller for the domain is running and accessible to the machine.

SELF TEST

The Self-Test questions will help you measure your understanding of the material presented in this chapter. Read all the choices carefully, as there may be more than one correct answer. Select all correct answers for each question.

1. Microsoft's NTDS is a _____ database system.

    A. Distributed

    B. Partitioned

    C. Replicated

    D. Stored in parts

2. The _____ stores the master copy of a domain's Directory database.

    A. Backup Domain Controller

    B. Member Server

    C. Primary Domain Controller

    D. Windows NT Workstation

3. The primary reason(s) that BDCs are used include these. (Choose all that apply.)

    A. Administrative modifications

    B. Directory replication

    C. Fault tolerance

    D. Login authentication

4. Your boss is complaining that login times are at an unacceptable level during the morning and after lunch hours. After checking the network, you determine that you need an additional server to provide login services. Since a member server on your network is scheduled to be taken permanently offline soon, you decide you will use it to help the situation. To prepare the member server to provide login authentication services, you will need to perform which of the following?

    A. Reinstall Windows NT Server as a Backup Domain Controller.

    B. Reinstall Windows NT Server as a Primary Domain Controller.

    C. Install Service Pack 3 with logon authentication services enabled.

    D. Nothing. It will already handle login authentication.

5. ACME has just established a remote site in Hong Kong, and you will need to install a server at their site. The new site will connect to the company domain using a dedicated T1 link. You should install their server as a

    A. Backup Domain Controller

    B. Member Server

    C. Primary Domain Controller

    D. Member Server with networking options

6. To log in to a domain, you must go through a mandatory _____ process.

    A. CTRL-ALT-DEL

    B. Domain Logon

    C. WinLogon

    D. NetLogon

7. In order to create or manage user accounts on a domain, you would use the _____ utility.

A. Windows NT Explorer

B. User Manager

C. Server Manager

D. User Manager for Domains

8. A _____ is used to assign access rights to resources located on the local Windows NT Machine.

A. Global Group

B. Local Group

C. Permissions Group

D. Rights Group

9. You have a new employee who will need to back up and restore files, shut down the server, and share server resources. Which of the following local group(s) would assign the employee all of the necessary rights?

A. Administrators

B. Backup Operators

C. Domain Admin

D. Server Operators

10. A global group can contain which of the following?

A. Other Global Groups

B. Local Groups

C. User Accounts

D. Domain Groups

11. Which of the following are default Global Groups? (Choose all that apply.)

A. Admin

B. Domain Admin

C. Guests

D. Domain Guests

12. In order for a workstation to log in to a domain, it must first be _____.

A. Authenticated

B. Added to the domain

C. Added to a workgroup

D. Have a valid user name and password

13. What must be done before an administrator can add a workstation to the domain without visiting the workstation?

A. Add the computer account in Server Manager.

B. Add the computer account in User Manager.

C. Add the computer account in User Manager for Domains.

D. Nothing. There is no need to visit the workstation.

14. The domain's NetLogon process has just received an access token from the SAM to permit a user to log in to the network. The domain NetLogon process passes the access token to

A. Local Security Access (LSA)

B. Client NetLogon

C. WinLogon

D. Client SAM

15. Local groups can contain which of the following? (Choose all that apply.)

A. Local Groups

B. Global Groups

C. User Accounts

D. Computer Accounts

CERTIFIED NOVELL ENGINEER

46

Managing Windows NT Security

CERTIFICATION OBJECTIVES

46.01   Windows NT Security

46.02   Policies

46.03   User Profiles

46.04   System Policies

W hen you stop to think about computer security, you will find that the term *computer security*, or just *security*, covers quite a bit of ground. First, you have physical security, in which you must ensure that your users' workstations are not logged into the network while they are away.

Next, you have Internet security, which relies on things such as *firewalls*. A firewall is a control device that prevents certain communications both from coming into the network via the Internet, and from going out to the Internet from the network. These communications can take the form of specific protocols or IP addresses, and the control device usually involves both hardware and software.

The third security consideration is *network security*. Network security, for the purposes of this chapter, includes activities such as controlling and monitoring user activities on the network. There are other aspects to network security, such as virus protection, but all forms of security overlap at some point. However, since these forms of security are not covered on the Novell certification exam, they will not be covered in this book.

CERTIFICATION OBJECTIVE 46.01

Windows NT Security

When a user logs in to Windows NT, a security access token is generated by the Windows NT security system and attached to the user's process. This access token contains the following information:

- User SID, which is the *security identifier* for that user account
- Group SIDs, one SID for each group that the user belongs to
- Other information, such as user name and group name(s) the user has been assigned

As we mentioned in Chapter 45, an SID is a unique number that is automatically assigned by Windows NT when you create a user or group account. If the account were accidentally deleted, you would be unable to reuse the SID even if you re-created the account with all of the original properties. This ensures that each SID is completely unique to the network. The SIDs associated with the user account are used to grant or deny access to objects every time the user initiates a process, as shown in Figure 46-1.

If the user were to start a process, such as accessing a printer, the user's security access token would be attached to the new process. Since the file is a resource, it is an *object* that has an *access control list (ACL)* associated with it. The ACL contains the SIDs of user and group accounts that have permission to access the resource, and their respective permissions to the object. The Windows NT security system will compare the user's access token against the ACL associated with that object. If the Windows NT security system cannot find a match, the process is denied access to the object. A match, on the other hand, will allow the process to access the object with the permissions listed in the ACL.

FIGURE 46-1

A user's desktop icons for printing

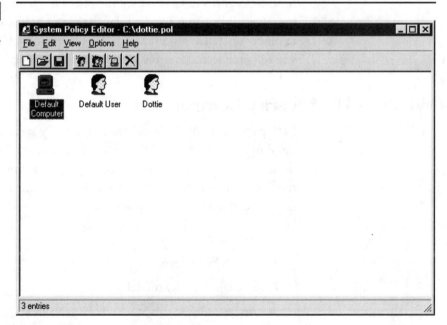

Besides granting or denying access to system resources, the Windows NT security system is responsible for monitoring user activities on the network. Every time a user accesses a file or makes an operating system change, the user is initiating a *process* that has his or her security access token attached to it. Contained in the access token are the user's SID and a list of group SIDs. The Windows NT security system uses the SIDs contained in the access token to log user activity, a process known as *auditing*.

exam
Ⓦatch

Unless you have worked with the concept of objects and processes before, this section can get a little confusing. Remember that an object is associated with a resource, and that a process is associated with an activity. These terms will be used again in this chapter, as well as on the Novell certification exam.

While ACLs and SIDs are used by the Windows NT security system to grant or deny access to resources, there is much more to the security system. When discussing the Windows NT security system, it helps to break down the system into two categories: security components and resource access controls. *Security components* are the actual implementations of the security system, while *resource access controls* are methods of controlling access to resources or system modification. We will examine security components and resource access controls in the next subsections.

Windows NT Security Components

Each component of the Windows NT security system is used to either monitor or regulate user activities on the network. These activities range from logging into Windows NT through performing a desktop modification. Windows NT implements several methods to assist with desktop and network security needs:

- Mandatory logon
- NTFS file system
- Domain security model
- Audit trails

The mandatory logon process requires a user to press the CTRL-ALT-DEL keystroke sequence prior to logging into a Windows NT machine. Until this keystroke sequence has been completed, all other processes are suspended. This ensures that password-capture programs cannot steal your access credentials as you log in. By requiring a username and password to access a Windows NT machine's resources, you are also ensuring that the security system can successfully track the user's activities through auditing policies.

While the mandatory logon process is one of the security implementations used in Windows NT, it cannot prevent access to files on the local computer by itself. This is especially true when the FAT file system is in use on the computer. As we discussed in Chapter 44, there is no provision for file-level access controls with the FAT file system. While you can secure FAT directories over the network using shares, you cannot secure FAT files and directories from local access. Even if there were a method to prevent unauthorized access to these files, the user could simply reboot the machine with an MS-DOS bootable disk and bypass the mandatory logon process. However, by using another implementation of the Windows NT security system, the NTFS file system, you are able to initiate file-level access. NTFS not only allows you to set permissions on a file-level basis, it also prevents access using the MS-DOS bootable disk trick. Since MS-DOS uses the FAT file system, it cannot read data on an NTFS partition. Windows NT does not allow for the creation of an NTFS bootable disk, which further prevents access to files stored by NTFS.

The domain security model is yet another implementation of the Windows NT security system. Just as you must initiate the WinLogon process to gain access to a Windows NT machine's resources, you must first initiate the NetLogon process to gain access to network resources. Authentication procedures in a domain are regulated by the primary and backup domain controllers because they contain a copy of the Directory database. However, only the primary domain controller can make administrative modifications to the network. This is because the master copy of the Directory database resides only on the primary domain controller. The Directory database also contains security information, such as rights and permissions, which grant or deny access to network resources.

Audit trails are used to monitor a user's activities on the network. As we mentioned earlier, when the mandatory login process authenticates a user's credentials, an access token is attached to the user's process. The access token contains the user's SID and each group SID that the user belongs to. Through these SIDs, the Windows NT security system can log information on the user's activities while they are logged into a Windows NT network. Audit trails cover all security-related activities, including other system events, which are then placed into logs that are viewable by the administrator. Audits are covered more thoroughly later in this chapter.

Resource Access Controls

Resource access controls cover more than just file and printer access. They also include user environmental controls such as access to desktop features or installing new applications to a Windows NT machine. The Windows NT security system uses several methods to enable the administrator to control a user's activities on the network:

- User accounts
- User rights
- User profiles
- System policies

Since Windows NT requires the user to log in to the domain in order to access network resources, each user must have a valid user account. When the administrator creates a user account, all of the rights and permissions that will be required by the user to access system resources must be assigned. Normally, user rights are assigned to groups rather than to individual user accounts, and users are assigned to groups. However, you can assign access rights directly to the user account, even though this form of account management is much more difficult to maintain whenever there are administrative changes.

User profiles also allow you to control resource access, but in this case the resources are the users' working environments. When you are dealing with many users on the network, it is not always wise to allow them to make changes to the system configuration. This is because most users are unfamiliar with the operating system and the types of problems that can arise from a misconfigured environment. (User profiles will be discussed in more depth later in this chapter.) Most often, user profiles are used in conjunction with system policies. System policies allow the administrator to control user access to certain features in Windows NT.

CERTIFICATION OBJECTIVE 46.02

Policies

Now that you have been exposed to the various security mechanisms used by the Windows NT security system, it is time to take a closer look at policies. As we mentioned in the previous section, policies are used to control what a user can do on the network. There are four types of policies that are used by Windows NT:

- Account policies
- User rights policies
- Auditing policies
- System policies

With the exception of system policies, policies are configured with the User Manager for Domains utility and can be configured only if you are logged in with an administrative account. However, system policies must be managed using the System Policy Editor, which also requires you to log in with an account that has administrative privileges. System policies will be discussed later in the chapter since they are typically used with profiles to control user activity.

Account Policies

Account policies are used to set domain-level user account security options. This means that one account policy is used throughout the domain, rather than configured for each account. To access the Account Policy dialog box, you would select the Account option from the Policies menu in User Manager for Domains. When you select this option, you will see a dialog box similar to this one:

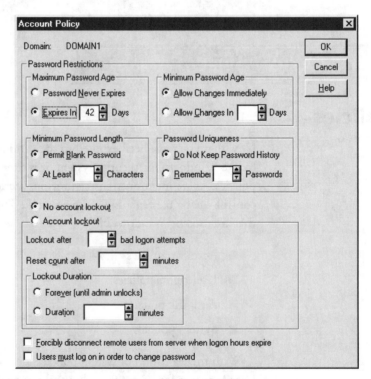

There are several options that you can set to control user account parameters. The dialog box is broken down into two major sections: Password Restrictions and Account Lockout. Each of the options should be familiar to you from working with Novell NetWare systems, but we will take a look at the options in Table 46-1.

TABLE 46-1	Option	Description
Account Policy Options	Maximum Password Age	You can choose a maximum password age, measured in days, to expire passwords automatically; or you can choose to never expire passwords.
	Minimum Password Age	You can set how long a user must wait before modifing an account password, or you can allow the user to change a password as often as desired. Again, a specific interval is measured in days.
	Minimum Password Length	You can set the minimum character size for a user account password, or you can permit a blank password. For security purposes, it is never advisable to allow blank passwords.
	Password Uniqueness	You can either allow users to recycle their passwords without any restrictions, or you can set a limit on how many passwords it will take to reuse one. For security reasons, most system administrators will set this property to 5.
	No Account Lockout	By selecting this option, the network will not lock out an account if an invalid password is entered.
	Account Lockout	This option will allow you to configure account lockout options, and it is recommended by most system administrators for security purposes.
	Lockout After	Sets the number of attempts the user is permitted before the account is locked out. Normally set to 3 attempts.
	Reset Count After	Sets the time interval before resetting the lockout account.
	Lockout Duration	The time period that the account is locked out before permitting more attempts.
	Forcibly Disconnect Remote Users	This option is used to close a user's open files and then disconnect them from the network. Normally used to ensure that there are no open files when system backups begin.
	Users Must Log on in Order to Change Password	Forces a user to log on to the network before changing the password.

User Rights Policies

User rights policies are used to control various activities a user account can perform on a computer. These types of activities range from accessing the computer from the network to loading/unloading device drivers, and are normally associated with an administrative account. In order to access the User Rights Policy dialog box, such as the one shown in Figure 46-2, you must select the User Rights option from the Policies pull-down menu in User Manager for Domains.

Some of the options that the administrator can perform are listed below:

- Access this computer from the network
- Add workstation to domain
- Back up files and directories
- Change system time
- Force shutdown from a remote system
- Load and unload device drivers
- Log on locally
- Manage auditing and security logs
- Restore files and directories
- Shut down the system
- Take ownership of files or other objects

While there are other user rights that you can assign, you would need to select the Show Advanced User Rights check box, as shown in Figure 46-2. In order to assign or revoke a user right, you would need to perform the following steps in the User Rights Policy dialog box:

1. Select the right to be assigned from the Right drop-down list.

2. Under Grant To, select the Add button if you wish to assign a user right.

3. Under Grant To, select the user or group account from whcih you wish to revoke rights, and select the Remove button.

FIGURE 46-2

FIGURE 46-2

The User Rights dialog box

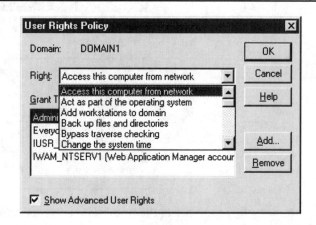

While most of the user rights are intuitive, be sure you understand what each right allows a user to perform.

Audit Policies

Audit policies are used in conjunction with user accounts to monitor user activities on the network, such as file access or account modifications. However, since Windows NT defaults to no auditing, audit policies cannot be used unless you have enabled the auditing feature. This is due to the additional amount of overhead in processor time and disk space that the auditing feature uses, and you must use caution when selecting which events to audit. To enable auditing, you would complete the following steps in the User Manager for Domains utility:

1. Select the Audit option from the Policies menu, which brings up the Audit Policy dialog box, as shown here:

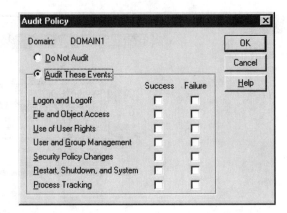

2. Select the Audit These Events radio button to enable auditing.

3. You can monitor the success or failure of any of the events shown by clicking on its respective Success or Failure check box.

Once an event is selected for auditing, an entry is placed into the security log and can be viewed with the Event Viewer utility. Table 46-2 describes the events that you can monitor with an Auditing Policy. You can audit specific objects by using either the My Computer or Windows NT Explorer utilities and right-clicking on the object to be audited. This will allow you to select the object's Properties menu and access the Auditing tab. However, remember that whenever you enable auditing, you will use system resources to monitor the events you choose. Because of the processor and hard disk overhead, you will want to be very selective about which events you wish to monitor.

When you wish to view the events for objects that you are auditing, you need to go into the Event Viewer utility and select the log that you wish to view. As we mentioned in Chapter 43, the Event Viewer has three different types of logs that you can view: application log, security log, or system log. Once you have chosen a log to view, you must double-click a specific event to view detailed information about the event.

	Event	Description
TABLE 46-2 The Events That You Can Monitor with an Auditing Policy	Logon and Logoff	Useful for tracking user time usage, or to monitor attempts to break into the network.
	File and Object Access	Enables tracking of file, directory, and printer access.
	Use of User Rights	Tracks the user's use of User Rights.
	User and Group Management	Enables auditing of user and group management changes. Useful if you have some portion of the network being remotely managed.
	Security Policy Changes	Used in secure environments to track the individuals who made changes to the network security policies.
	Restart, Shutdown, and System	Monitors system restart, shutdown, and system events.
	Process Tracking	Tracks process events. A process is any activity started on the network.

CERTIFICATION OBJECTIVE 46.03

User Profiles

User profiles allow the administrator to control a user's environmental settings from the network. Environmental settings include items such as the user's desktop configuration, startup applications, and automatic network connections. These types of configuration settings are typically set by the user according to personal preferences, and are retained in configuration files known as *user profiles*. By storing the environmental settings in user profiles, the operating system can automatically load the user's configuration from the previous logon session. This is obviously a benefit to the user, who does not have to take the time to reconfigure the workstation.

By retaining a user's environment in configuration files, the operating system can store multiple profiles on the same workstation. Since Windows NT requires a user to log on with a valid username and password, the configuration file for each user can be stored separately based on the user name. This works extremely well if you have an office where multiple users must share the same workstation. Let's say, for example, that Mary and Jeff share the same workstation. If the operating system stored only one user profile, this would prove an annoyance to Mary and Jeff unless they agree on exactly the same environmental settings. However, since Windows NT bases user information on the username, Mary and Jeff will each have their own environment restored without conflicting with each other.

Another benefit to utilizing user profiles is when you have a user who logs into the network from different workstations. The first time a user logs into the workstation, the operating system bases the user's profile on a default profile. As modifications are made, the new settings are stored for the user on that workstation. Since the profile is typically stored on the workstation, the user would have to update each workstation they log into each time they wished to make any changes in order to retain consistency. However, you can store these settings on the network, in a file known as a *roaming profile*, and have the user access them from any workstation they log in to. This allows the user to modify environmental settings from any workstation and retain those settings regardless of which workstation he or she is using.

As we mentioned, the individual user profiles are originally loaded from the default user profile. This file is located in the profiles directory of the system root directory, typically C:\WINNT\PROFILES. When the user logs into a workstation for the first time, the system creates a subdirectory in the profiles directory that has the same name as the user's username. Several other subdirectories are created that contain specific desktop settings. The default user profile is then copied to this directory and used for the remainder of the user's session. When the user logs back into the workstation—or the network, as in the case of a roaming profile—the settings are restored.

There are three types of user profiles that can be used by the administrator to control a user's environmental settings: local user profile, roaming user profile, and mandatory user profile.

Local User Profile

The *local user profile* is initially created the first time the user logs into the workstation and is based on the default user profile. As modifications are made, the system stores this information in a file, called NTUSER.DAT, located in the user's profile directory. The next time the user logs into the workstation, the NTUSER.DAT file is merged with the Registry information to recreate the same environment the user had when they logged off the workstation.

If you wish to use only local user profiles, you would not enter the path to the profile directory under the user account properties as shown in below. When you do this, Windows NT will automatically default to the profile stored in the C:*systemroot*\\PROFILES*username* folder that is located on the workstation. (Remember that the *systemroot* directory is by default called WINNT but may have been changed during installation.) The obvious disadvantage to using only local user profiles is that the user will be unable to utilize roaming profiles.

Roaming User Profile

A roaming user profile is used to allow the user's environment to follow him or her across the network. In order to perform this function, the profile must be stored on the network in a location in which the user account expects to find it. You do this by accessing the user account properties from User Manager for Domains, and then setting the profile path to the location of the user profile. Once the profile path is set, you need to ensure that the profile directory has been shared and that the user account has read, write, and modify permissions to the profile directory itself. Without these settings, the user account cannot load or modify the profile information from the network.

When the user logs into the network for the first time, the default roaming profile is copied to the user's roaming profile and to the local profile. As the user makes changes to the workstation's configuration, these modifications are made to both the local and roaming profiles. The next time the user logs into the network, the network compares the timestamps between the user's roaming profile and the user's local profile. If the roaming profile has the later time stamp, it is copied to the local workstation and overwrites the local profile. However, if the local profile has the later timestamp, the user is given the option to retain the local profile settings or to download the roaming profile to the local machine. Once the user logs off the network, all modifications that were made to the profile are made to the local and the roaming profiles. In this manner, the roaming profiles are kept current and synchronized with the workstation.

Mandatory User Profile

When the administrator needs to ensure that the user obtains the same workstation configuration every time he logs into the network, he would use mandatory profiles. The mandatory profile is similar to the roaming profile in that it is stored on the network and that it is copied from the network to the local user profile. However, there are several differences between the two types of user profiles. First, the mandatory profile is stored in a file called NTUSER.MAN rather than the usual NTUSER.DAT file used for roaming and local user profiles. Second, each time the user logs into the network the mandatory profile is copied over the user's local profile without comparing timestamps or allowing the user to specify which profile to use. Third, if the user should make any changes to the workstation's configuration, the modifications are discarded at the time the user logs off.

CERTIFICATION OBJECTIVE 46.04

System Policies

As we saw in the previous section, user profiles not only establish default settings for new user accounts, they also control environmental settings. In contrast, system policies are used to control *specific* user activities in Windows NT and can be used in conjunction with user profiles to control most facets of the user's interaction with Windows NT. Some of the more commonly used features of system policies are listed below:

- Permit users to connect and/or remove printer connections through Print Manager
- Disable the Run command on the Start menu
- Require users to process the login script before initiating any other processes
- Control automatic program execution through the Startup folder
- Lock and unlock specific program groups
- Specify what types of changes a user can make to an unlocked program group
- Disable the Save Settings menu option in Program Manager, File Manager, and the Print Manager

As you can see, system policies enable the administrator to control user activities on the workstation at various levels. In order to create or modify a system policy, you will need to use the System Policy Editor (shown earlier in Figure 46-1) rather than the User Manager for Domains application that you use to manage and maintain other types of policies. With the other policies—account, audit, and user rights policies—the network operating system is responsible for ensuring their enforcement. However, system policies are utilized and enforced on the workstation level through the Registry.

Recalling our discussion of the Registry from Chapter 42, remember that the Registry stores information for each user's hardware and software configuration settings. When you create a system policy, the configuration settings are stored in a file called NTCONFIG.POL. This file must be stored in the NETLOGON share, which is a shared directory, located in the *<winnt_root>*\SYSTEM32\REPL\IMPORT\SCRIPTS directory. By placing NTCONFIG.POL in the NETLOGON share, you are enabling a standard policy for every Windows NT computer in the domain. However, the system policy used by a workstation is based on the user's login domain and not the computer's domain. This has been known to cause confusion, as most people forget that the computer can be set up as part of one domain while the user can log on to a different domain.

Since system policies directly affect the Registry, you need to understand how the Registry is modified before attempting to establish one. System policies are broken down into two categories: system policies for users and system policies for computers. System policies for users will allow you to manage user desktop settings, such as disabling the Run command from the Start menu or locking down program groups. This type of policy modifies the HKEY_CURRENT_USER section of the Registry. System policies for computers will allow you to manage login and network settings, such as forcing a user to wait for the login script to process or set up which applications process during startup, and modifies the HKEY_LOCAL_MACHINE portion of the Registry.

As we stated earlier, NTCONFIG.POL contains policy information. When a user logs into a domain, the system checks to see if this file exists. If it does, the system copies the information into the local computer's Registry in the areas discussed previously—that is, user policy information is copied into HKEY_CURRENT_USER and computer policy information is copied into HKEY_LOCAL_MACHINE. The system also compares the settings in NTCONFIG.POL against the settings in the user's profile (NTUSER.DAT) file. If the settings are different, the system will always use the settings from the system policy.

CERTIFICATION SUMMARY

The purpose of this chapter is to introduce you to the features of Windows NT security, which is one of the most important features of any network. There are several aspects of Windows NT security, ranging from the mandatory login process to setting up mandatory environmental configurations. Each component is dependent on every other component in some way, no matter how minor it may seem, and a thorough understanding will enable you to protect your network and its resources and pass this portion of the Novell certification exam.

 TWO-MINUTE DRILL

❑ A *firewall* is a control device that prevents certain communications both from coming into the network via the Internet and from going out to the Internet from the network. These communications can take the form of specific protocols or IP addresses, and the control device usually involves both hardware and software.

❑ Network security, for the purpose of this chapter, includes activities such as controlling and monitoring user activities on the network.

❑ When a user logs in to Windows NT, a security access token is generated by the Windows NT security system and attached to the user's process.

❑ An SID is a unique number that is automatically assigned by Windows NT when you create a user or group account.

❑ Since the file is a resource, it is an *object* that has an *access control list (ACL)* associated with it. The ACL contains the SIDs of user and group accounts that have permission to access the resource, and their respective permissions to the object.

❑ *Security components* are the actual implementations of the security system, while *resource access controls* are methods of controlling access to resources or system modification.

❑ Each component of the Windows NT security system is used to either monitor or regulate user activities on the network. These activities range from logging into Windows NT through performing a desktop modification.

❑ While the mandatory logon process is one of the security implementations used in Windows NT, it cannot prevent access to files on the local computer by itself.

❑ Just as you must initiate the WinLogon process to gain access to a Windows NT machine's resources, you must first initiate the NetLogon process to gain access to network resources.

❑ When the mandatory login process authenticates a user's credentials, an access token is attached to the user's process.

❑ Resource access controls cover more than just file and printer access. They also include user environmental controls such as access to desktop features or installing new applications to a Windows NT machine.

❑ When you are dealing with many users on the network, it is not always wise to allow them to make changes to the system configuration.

❑ There are four types of policies that are used by Windows NT: account policies, user rights policies, auditing policies, and system policies.

❑ User rights policies are used to control various activities a user account can perform on a computer. These types of activities range from accessing the computer from the network to loading/unloading device drivers.

❑ User profiles allow the administrator to control a user's environmental settings from the network. Environmental settings include items such as the user's desktop configuration, startup applications, and automatic network connections.

❑ A roaming user profile is used to allow the user's environment to follow him across the network.

❑ When the administrator needs to ensure that the user obtains the same workstation configuration every time he logs into the network, he would use mandatory profiles.

❑ User profiles not only establish default settings for new user accounts, they also control environmental settings. In contrast, system policies are used to control *specific* user activities in Windows NT and can be used in conjunction with user profiles to control most facets of the user's interaction with Windows NT.

❑ When you create a system policy, the configuration settings are stored in a file called NTCONFIG.POL. This file must be stored in the NETLOGON share, which is a shared directory located in the *<winnt_root>*\SYSTEM32\REPL\IMPORT\SCRIPTS directory.

❑ NTCONFIG.POL contains policy information. When a user logs into a domain, the system checks to see if this file exists. If it does, the system copies the information into the local computer's Registry in the areas previously discussed.

SELF TEST

The Self-Test questions will help you measure your understanding of the material presented in this chapter. Read all the choices carefully, as there may be more than one correct answer. Select all correct answers for each question.

1. In general, a firewall is
   A. A hardware device that prevents certain communications from coming into the network from the Internet
   B. Software device that prevents certain communications from coming into the network from the Internet
   C. Hardware device that prevents certain communications from going out of the network to the Internet
   D. All of the above

2. You would use a(n) _____ policy to set domain-level user account security options:
   A. Account
   B. Auditing
   C. User Rights
   D. System

3. A user's environmental settings are controlled using:
   A. Account Policies
   B. User Profiles
   C. User Rights Policies
   D. System Policies

4. System policies are created and maintained through which of the following utilities?
   A. System Policy Editor
   B. System Profile Editor
   C. User Manager
   D. User Manager for Domains

5. A security access token includes (Choose all that apply.)
   A. User's security identifier
   B. All group SIDs the user has been assigned membership
   C. A list of all objects to which the user has been granted access
   D. Permissions to objects to which the user has been granted access

6. The Manage Auditing and Security Logs right is assigned using which of the following policies:
   A. Account
   B. Auditing
   C. User Rights
   D. System

7. SIDs associated with the user account are used to
   A. Grant or deny access to applications
   B. Grant or deny access to files
   C. Grant or deny access to objects
   D. Grant or deny access to printer

8. To allow the user to log into any workstation and obtain the same environmental settings, you would enable a

   A. Local User Profile

   B. Mandatory User Profile

   C. Roaming User Profile

   D. System Policy

9. In order to disable the Run command from the Start menu, you would modify which of the following policies?

   A. Account

   B. Audit

   C. User Rights

   D. System

10. Windows NT security components include which of the following?

    A. User Accounts

    B. User Rights

    C. Mandatory Logon

    D. System Policies

11. You are the network administrator for a small law firm that works on high-profile cases. In the past, users were on the honor system to use unique passwords when they expired, but you have noticed that most users just reset the old password. To increase security, you decide to implement a new account policy to force users to use unique passwords for every 5 cycles. To accomplish this task, you would set which option under the account policy dialog box?

    A. Maximum Password Age

    B. Maximum Password Length

    C. Password Uniqueness

    D. Users Must Log on in Order to Change Password

12. The mandatory logon process is used in conjunction with _____ to control access to files on the local machine.

    A. Audit Trails

    B. FAT File System

    C. Domain Security Model

    D. NTFS File System

13. A local user profile is stored in which of the following files?

    A. C:\WINNT\PROFILES\ NTUSER.DAT

    B. C:\WINNT\PROFILES\ *username*\NTUSER.DAT

    C. C:\WINNT\PROFILES\ NTUSER.MAN

    D. C:\WINNT\PROFILES\ *username*\NTUSER.MAN

14. The file that holds system policy information is located in which of the following directories?

    A. C:\WINNT\SYSTEM\REPL\ EXPORTS\SCRIPTS

    B. C:\WINNT\SYSTEM\REPL\ IMPORTS\SCRIPTS

    C. C:\WINNT\SYSTEM32\REPL\ EXPORTS\SCRIPTS

    D. C:\WINNT\SYSTEM32\REPL\ IMPORTS\SCRIPTS

15. The Windows NT security system controls user activity on the network through which of the following? (Choose all that apply.)

    A. User accounts

    B. Audit trails

    C. User profiles

    D. Mandatory logon

16. You have enabled auditing on your Windows NT network and need to monitor any changes in user and group accounts. To complete this task, you would audit which of the following events?

    A. File and Object Access

    B. Process Tracking

    C. Security Policy Changes

    D. User and Group Management

17. Mandatory user profiles are stored in which file?

    A. NTUSER.DAT

    B. NTUSER.MAN

    C. NTUSER.POL

    D. NTUSER.SYS

CNE
CERTIFIED NOVELL ENGINEER

47

Multiple Domain Windows NT Networking

CERTIFICATION OBJECTIVES

47.01   Trusts

47.02   Domain Models

W henever you deal with a Microsoft Windows NT network, you are almost certain to be working in a domain environment. For the Advanced Administration exam, the key thing to remember is that as long as you know a little about NWADMIN and know how to get around and configure the various objects, you should be okay. As we mentioned in Chapter 44, domains are networking schema used in a Windows NT network. There are four domain models—the single domain, single master domain, multiple master domain, and complete trust—that can be implemented in a Windows NT network. However, domains rely heavily upon trust relationships in order to communicate among/between themselves. In this chapter, we will explore the different domain models and how trust relationships allow a Windows NT network to function as a single administrative unit.

CERTIFICATION OBJECTIVE 47.01

Trusts

Since trust relationships are an integral part of most Windows NT networks, you need a thorough understanding of how they work with the different domain models. Recall from Chapter 44 that a domain is comprised of network servers and computers that have been logically grouped together for the purpose of sharing resources. A *trust relationship*, or simply *trust*, is a communications and administrative link between two domains that permits the sharing of resources and account information. Without the implementation of trust relationships, individual domains have no method of communicating with each other and, therefore, no method of sharing resources.

Trusted Versus Trusting

When implementing a trust relationship, one domain contains user accounts that require access to resources located in the second domain. As shown in Figure 47-1, the domain containing the user accounts is called the *account domain*, and the domain containing the resources is called the *resource domain*. In order for the account domain to access resources in the resource domain, the resource domain must trust the accounts domain. Since the resource domain trusts the account domain, the resource domain is said to be the *trusting domain*. The account domain then becomes the *trusted domain*. This point can cause some confusion, and it helps to have a mnemonic to remember it by. The easiest method to remember which is the trusting domain and which is the trusted domain is to remember that the account domain contains user accounts, such as Ed. The resource domain must *Trust-Ed*.

With Figure 47-1 in mind, another source of confusion is the manner in which the arrow is drawn. This is because you would normally picture the arrow to start from the trusted domain and point to the trusting domain. However, while the resource domain uses the accounts from the trusted

FIGURE 47-1   The accounts domain is the trusted domain and the resource domain is the trusting domain

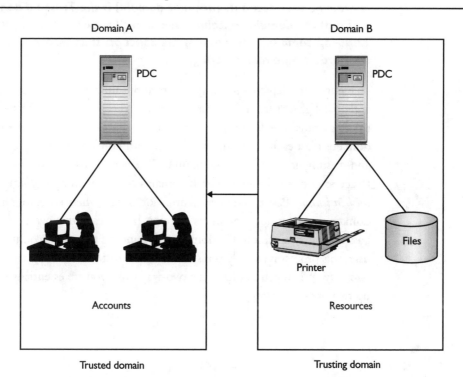

Domain A

PDC

Accounts

Trusted domain

Domain B

PDC

Files

Printer

Resources

Trusting domain

domain, security permissions are assigned by the resource domain. This permits the resource domain to control access to the resources in their domain. For example, let's say that John is in Domain A and needs to access a file located in Domain B. Since Domain B is the resource domain, a trust relationship is implemented so that Domain B is the trusting domain and Domain A is the trusted domain. The network administrator in Domain B would grant John the necessary permissions to access the file, rather than the administrator from Domain A. As you can see, this permits Domain B to control who has access to the file, or the resources in their domain. Microsoft permits up to 128 incoming, or trusted, trust relationships and an unlimited number of outgoing, or trusting, trust relationships in a Windows NT network.

exam
ⓦatch

Do not confuse the trusted domain with the trusting domain. The Novell certification exam will require you to know that the domain containing user accounts (account domain) is the Trust-Ed domain and that the domain containing resources (resource domain) is the Trust-ing domain. This is one of the concepts that most people have the hardest time remembering.

Figure 47-1 depicts a *one-way trust* relationship, which allows remote users and global groups from the trusted domain to access resources located in the trusting domain. A *two-way trust*, shown in Figure 47-2, occurs when both domains trust each other equally; that is, both domains become the trusted and trusting domains at the same time. This permits users in both domains to access resources located in both domains and allows for *pass-through authentication*. Pass-through authentication occurs when a user logs in to a domain that does not contain his account. In this case, the logon domain will pass the logon request to the domain that contains the user account. To the user, this process is entirely transparent when trust relationships are set up correctly. When you implement a two-way trust, you are essentially setting up two one-way trusts.

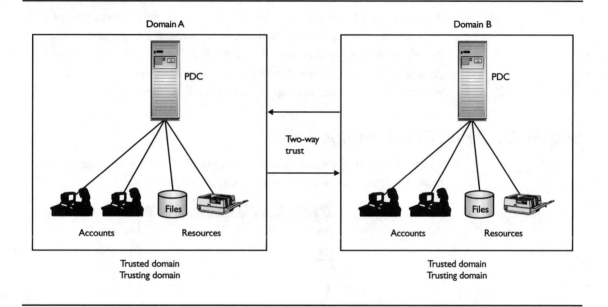

FIGURE 47-2 An example of a two-way trust relationship

Using Groups with Trust Relationships

As we learned in Chapter 46, Windows NT uses local groups to assign permissions to local resources, and global groups to assign permissions across the domain. When you are dealing with groups across domain boundaries, you place global groups from the trusted (account) domain into local groups in the trusting (resource) domain, just as you would in a single domain situation. The trusting domain would then assign the necessary permissions to access its resources in the local group.

In order to maintain a semblance of order, always use the built-in (default) global and local groups whenever the situation permits. One of the problems with network administration is keeping track of all the different groups and what permissions are assigned to them. Whether your are working with a Novell network or a Windows NT network, by keeping the number of groups as small as possible, it will be easier to ensure that you do not accidentally give a user permissions that they should not have.

Setting Up Trust Relationships

Trust relationships are set up using the User Manager for Domains utility from the Trust Relationships dialog box, as depicted here:

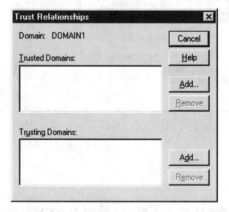

Implementing a trust relationship is performed in two steps:

1. The trusted domain completes the trusting section of the Trust Relationships dialog box.

2. The trusting domain completes the trusted section of the Trust Relationships dialog box.

Trust relationships cannot be implemented until you log in to the primary domain controller with administrative rights, such as using the Administrator account. If you are initiating a trust relationship with a domain in which you do not have administrative rights, you must coordinate with that domain's administrator. The procedure for completing a one-way trust relationship is shown in Exercise 47-1.

EXERCISE 47-1

Complete a One-Way Trust Relationship

On the *trusted* domain's PDC, perform the following steps:

1. Open the User Manager for Domains utility.

2. Under the Policies menu, select Trust Relationships. This will bring up the Trust Relationships dialog box.

3. Next to the Trusting Domains list box, click the Add button.

4. Enter the trusting domain's name in the text box. When completed, you will be asked for a password.

5. Enter and confirm a password to be used in establishing the trust. This password is used only during the establishment of the trust relationship. After the trust has been implemented, the primary domain controller will change this password to an unknown password that cannot be retrieved and is part of the Windows NT security system. However, if the trusting domain has a separate administrator, you will need to supply them with the password you have entered to ensure that they can complete their part in the process.

From the *trusting* domain, complete the following steps:

1. Open the User Manager for Domains utility.

2. From the Policies menu, select Trust Relationships.

3. Next to the Trusted Domain, click the Add button.

4. Enter the trusted domain's name in the text box that appears. You will be prompted for a password.

5. Enter the same password that was used by the trusted domain. This step is imperative, as the trust cannot be established unless the correct password is supplied.

6. A dialog box will appear asking if you wish to establish the trust relationship. Click OK.

7. Click OK on the confirming message that appears.

8. Select Close.

While the steps in Exercise 47-1 can be completed in either order, Microsoft states in its documentation that this is the preferred method of implementation. If you need to set up a two-way trust, you would again perform the above procedure. The difference here is that the trusted domain becomes the trusting domain, and the trusting domain becomes the trusted domain. In a two-way trust scenario, you will notice that the same domain names appear in both the Trusted Domains and Trusting Domains sections of the Trust Relationships dialog box.

Remember that when you set up a trust relationship, you are setting up a trust between two specific domains. This trust is not transferable to another domain. As an example, take a look at Figure 47-3. In this figure, you have three domains: Marketing, Sales, and Engineering. In this scenario, Marketing uses the resources in both the Sales and Engineering domains and is therefore the trusted domain. Sales and Engineering become the trusting domains. There are two one-way trusts established: one between the Marketing domain and the Sales domain, and one between the Marketing domain and the Engineering domain. Even though the Marketing domain is the trusted domain to both Sales and Engineering, this does not grant access to resources between the Sales and Engineering domains.

You may be required to demonstrate knowledge that trust relationships are not transferable. Be careful when analyzing trust relationship questions.

CERTIFICATION OBJECTIVE 47.02

Domain Models

As we saw in Chapter 44, a Windows NT network will utilize either the workgroup model or the domain model as its networking schema. In a *workgroup model,* resources and user account administration are decentralized because each workstation must store and use its own security accounts database. Since the SAM database is restricted to 40 MB, you are limited in the number of user, group, and computer accounts that a workstation can maintain. In addition, any administrative changes will have to be performed on each workstation that contains the account to be modified.

FIGURE 47-3

Trust relationships are not transferable

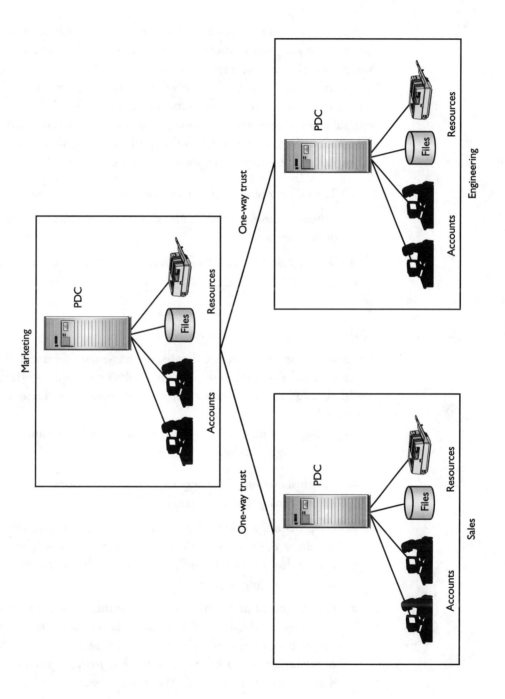

A better solution for most networks is to utilize the *domain model* for its networking needs. Microsoft has defined four different domain models—single domain, single master domain, multiple master domain, and complete trust—that will allow you to customize your network according to your particular requirements. Each model will provide you with different features and functionality, but be careful when selecting the most appropriate model for your network as reconfiguration is a hassle. As you design your network's layout, bear in mind:

- The number of user, group, and computer accounts required

- Whether administration of user and group accounts is centralized or decentralized

- Whether administration of resources is centralized or decentralized

- Future network growth

Single Domain Model

The first domain model we will discuss, the single domain model, is actually the easiest one to design and implement. As shown in Figure 47-4, this model places all accounts—user, group, and computer—and resources into one domain.

By placing everything on your network into a single domain, you will gain the following advantages:

- **Easy installation**   The only requirement is to install the first server as the primary domain controller.

- **Simple configuration**   Since all resources and accounts reside in one domain, there are no trust relationships (which will be discussed later in this chapter) to configure. All of your network's servers and workstations join the same domain.

- **Centralized administration of user accounts**   Since there is only one Directory database, all accounts reside on one PDC. Local and global groups need to be defined only once, whereas in a multidomain network, you need to define multiple groups, depending on which domain the resources were located.

FIGURE 47-4   The single domain model contains all accounts and resources

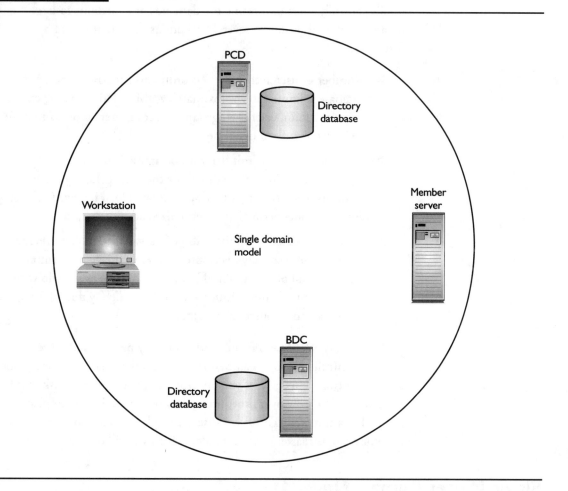

- **Centralized administration of network resources**   All of the network's resources reside in the same domain, so resource administration is centralized.

- **Ideal for small organizations**   Organizations that are relatively small will not require the additional servers that would be required by a multidomain network (PCDs and additional BDCs).

Even with all of the advantages that a single domain brings a network, it falls painfully short of meeting the demands of a medium-to-large organization. This is due to several limitations that are imposed by this model:

- **Number of user accounts**   According to Microsoft, the SAM database is limited to approximately 40MB. This size restriction limits the number of user, group, and computer accounts that the SAM can handle at one time.

- **No decentralized administration of user accounts**   Larger organizations will want to distribute the management of user accounts to assist in cutting down the workload involved. The single domain model permits only centralized administration.

- **No decentralized administration of network resources**   Larger organizations typically distribute resource management among departmental or geographical boundaries, much as they do with user accounts. Political issues within the company may also require decentralized resource management.

As with any Windows NT network, you may need to add more backup domain controllers if logon authentication begins to take an unacceptable amount of time. However, if you are working on a small network that has the potential to grow over time, it may still be a good idea to implement the single domain model. This is because the single domain model can easily become a single master domain model, which we will discuss next.

Single Master Domain Model

In a single master domain model, you have two or more domains. As depicted in Figure 47-5, one domain functions as the master domain and contains the user accounts for the domain. Since user and computer accounts reside in the master domain, it is also called the account domain. All other domains, which contain resources such as files and printers, are resource domains in this model. Each resource domain communicates with the master domain through the use of one-way trust relationships. Referring back to our discussion of trust relationships earlier in this chapter, the account domain is considered the trusted domain and all resource domains are considered the trusting domains.

With this model, you retain the centralized administration that is inherent in a single domain model, and users benefit by having a single account and password because all users must log into the domain through the master domain. However, because you are working with a single SAM database, the maximum number of accounts that a single master domain model can handle is still limited by the 40 MB restriction placed on the SAM database. In addition, local groups must be defined in both the master domain and the resource domain(s).

FIGURE 47-5

The single master domain consists of an accounts domain and one or more resource domains

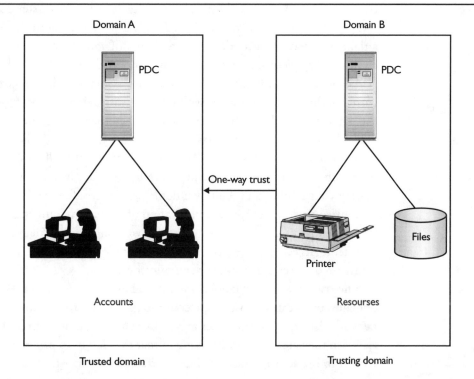

Resource administration in the single master domain model can be either centralized or decentralized administration, giving you added flexibility in tailoring your network. However, if you choose to decentralize your resource administration, you must keep in mind that resource administrators have no control over global group membership. Therefore, it is important that there is some coordination and trust between account administrators and resource administrators in order to keep a secure network.

Multiple Master Domain Model

The multiple master domain model is much more complicated than the single master domain model. In this domain, user accounts still reside in the account domain and network resources in the resource domains. However, you are essentially taking the single master domain and multiplying it. In order to communicate among the individual single master domains, a two-way trust must be established between each and every master domain to each and every other master domain. This is depicted in Figure 47-6, although only two master domains are shown (if you think that this looks confusing, try picturing three or four master domains).

As you can see in Figure 47-6, each resource domain still trusts their corresponding master domains with one-way trust relationships. However, the slight twist to this is that they also trust the other master domain(s). While Novell documentation states that this is not required, it is recommended on a Windows NT network to ensure that all trust relationships are implemented and that resource access is not denied. By placing your resources in their own domains, you are allowing for centralized or decentralized administration of network resources. As with the single master domain, users will still have to log into the master domain in order to access resources, but by using multiple master domains you can centralize or decentralize network administration.

Since two-way trust relationships are established between all master domains, users can still use one account to gain access to all authorized network resources. When a user logs in from a domain other than the one to which they are assigned, the domain that they log in to passes the login request to the appropriate domain. For example, say that John is a salesman

FIGURE 47-6 Trust relationships are more complicated in the multiple master domain model

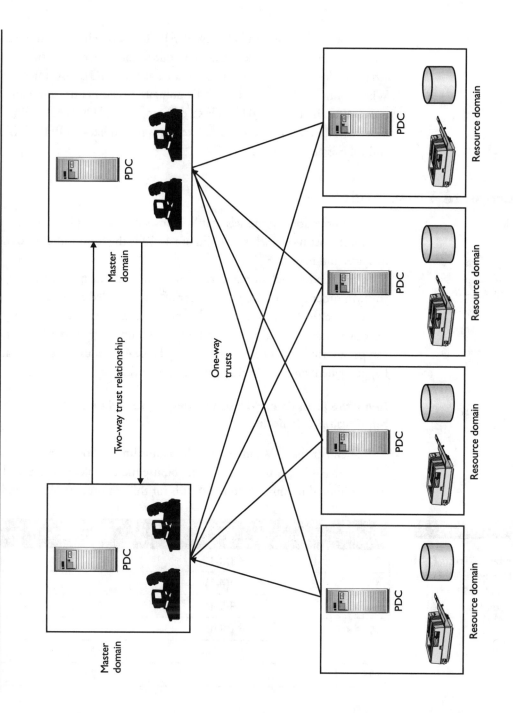

who normally logs into the HEADQUARTERS domain in Baltimore. John finds that he needs to make a trip out to the Phoenix location to attend a sales meeting, which is designated as the PHOENIX domain. When John logs into the PHOENIX domain, his authentication request is passed to the HEADQUARTERS domain. If HEADQUARTERS authenticates the request, the access token is passed back to PHOENIX, and John is able to log in.

Complete Trust Model

Out of all the domain models that Windows NT can implement, the complete trust model (shown in Figure 47-7) is the most difficult to install, manage, and maintain.

In this model, each domain trusts every other domain with a two-way trust. In order to calculate the number of trusts needed for each domain, you can use the formula $n(n-1)$, where n is the number of domains. By looking at the formula, you can tell that the number of trust relationships can get enormous after a period of time. Table 47-1 illustrates what can happen when you start building a large network.

Know the formula n(n-1), as you may be tested on trust relationship calculations.

Remember that a Windows NT domain is limited to 128 inbound trusts. From Table 47-1, you can see that if you use the complete trust model you will be limited to only 11 domains. It is for this reason that Novell and

TABLE 47-1	Number of Domains	n(n-1)	Number of Trusts
Number of Trusts Related to Number of Domains in a Complete Trust Relationship	3	3(3-1)	6
	4	4(4-1)	12
	5	5(5-1)	20
	10	10(10-1)	90
	11	11(11-1)	110
	12	12(12-1)	132

FIGURE 47-7

Trust relationships in a complete trust

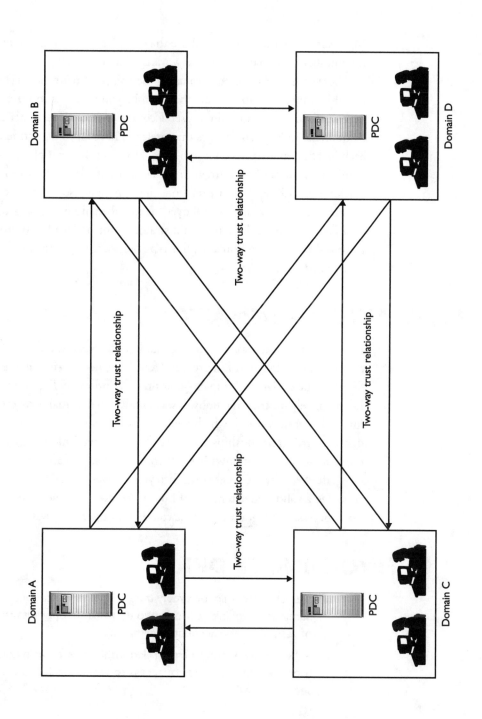

Microsoft agree that you should use the complete trust model only when the number of domains in the network is relatively small.

There are some advantages to using the complete trust model. For one thing, it is a scalable model that permits you to use centralized or decentralized administration of user accounts and resources. This can be desirable in large companies that prefer to have an IS department at each location manage its own resources. However, the complex trust administration can be a burden to manage, and if a trust is broken you are stuck reestablishing the trust relationships. There is also a network security issue, since you have no control over the membership of global groups that are outside the local domain administrator's control. In addition to the trust relationships between domains, this type of model requires complete trust between administrators.

CERTIFICATION SUMMARY

Domains are the central networking modules to every Windows NT network, and Microsoft has provided four basic networking models to facilitate the design and implementation of Windows NT networks. Domains rely on trust relationships to join isolated domains together to form a larger network in which you can share resources. This chapter has discussed trust relationships and the different domain models that are implemented in a Windows NT network. Because you are learning how to integrate Windows NT networks into your Novell IntranetWare networks, you need a solid understanding of how a Windows NT network is essential for a successful integration of the two different operating systems.

 # TWO-MINUTE DRILL

- ❏ A *trust relationship*, or simply *trust*, is a communications and administrative link between two domains that permits the sharing of resources and account information.

- ❏ When implementing a trust relationship, one domain contains user accounts that require access to resources located in the second domain.

❑ The domain containing the user accounts is called the *account domain*, and the domain containing the resources is called the *resource domain*.

❑ Since the resource domain trusts the account domain, the resource domain is said to be the *trusting domain*. The account domain then becomes the *trusted domain*.

❑ A *two-way trust* occurs when both domains trust each other equally; that is, both domains become the trusted and trusting domains at the same time. This permits users in both domains to access resources located in both domains and allows for *pass-through authentication*.

❑ Windows NT uses local groups to assign permissions to local resources, and global groups to assign permissions across the domain.

❑ In order to maintain a semblance of order, always use the built-in (default) global and local groups whenever the situation permits.

❑ Trust relationships are set up using the User Manager for Domains utility from the Trust Relationships dialog box.

❑ In a two-way trust scenario, the same domain names appear in both the Trusted Domains and Trusting Domains sections of the Trust Relationships dialog box.

❑ Remember that when you set up a trust relationship, you are setting up a trust between two specific domains. This trust is not transferable to another domain.

❑ In a *workgroup model*, resources and user account administration are decentralized because each workstation must store and use its own security accounts database.

❑ A better solution for most networks is to utilize the *domain model* for its networking needs.

❑ Microsoft has defined four different domain models—single domain, single master domain, multiple master domain, and complete trust—that will allow you to customize your network according to your particular requirements.

❑ Even with all of the advantages that a single domain brings a network, it falls painfully short of meeting the demands of a medium-to-large organization

❑ In a single master domain model, you have two or more domains. One domain functions as the master domain and contains the user accounts for the domain. Since user and computer accounts reside in the master domain, it is also called the account domain.

❑ The account domain is considered the trusted domain, and all resource domains are considered the trusting domains.

❑ Resource administration in the single master domain model can be either centralized or decentralized administration, giving you added flexibility in tailoring your network.

❑ The multiple master domain model is much more complicated than the single master domain model. In this domain, user accounts still reside in the account domain and network resources in the resource domains.

❑ Each resource domain still trusts their corresponding master domains with one-way trust relationships. However, the slight twist to this is that they also trust the other master domain(s).

❑ By placing your resources in their own domains, you are allowing for centralized or decentralized administration of network resources.

❑ Since two-way trust relationships are established between all master domains, users can still use one account to gain access to all authorized network resources.

❑ Out of all the domain models that Windows NT can implement, the complete trust model (shown in Figure 47-7) is the most difficult to install, manage, and maintain.

❑ There are some advantages to using the complete trust model. For one thing, it is a scalable model that permits you to use centralized or decentralized administration of user accounts and resources.

❑ The complex trust administration can be a burden to manage, and if a trust is broken you are stuck reestablishing the trust relationships. There is also a network security issue.

❑ Domains rely on trust relationships to join isolated domains together to form a larger network in which you can share resources

SELF TEST

The Self-Test questions will help you measure your understanding of the material presented in this chapter. Read all the choices carefully, as there may be more than one correct answer. Select all correct answers for each question.

1. In a trust relationship, the domain containing user accounts is called the _____ domain. (Choose all that apply.)

   A. Account
   B. Resource
   C. Trusted
   D. Trusting

2. The _____ domain model places all user accounts and resources in one domain.

   A. Complete trust
   B. Single
   C. Single master
   D. Multiple master

3. You are designing a network that follows the complete trust domain model. Your network will be composed of seven domains. How many trust relationships will you have to establish?

   A. 35
   B. 42
   C. 49
   D. 56

4. John needs to log in to the Windows NT network. His home account resides in the HEADQUARTERS domain, but he is currently at a site that is designated as the PHOENIX domain. Which domain will John be authenticated from?

   A. HEADQUARTERS
   B. PHOENIX
   C. Neither
   D. Both

5. Which of the following are attributes of the single master domain model? (Choose all that apply.)

   A. Centralized Account Administration
   B. Decentralized Account Administration
   C. Centralized Resource Administration
   D. Decentralized Account Administration

6. You establish a trust relationship with which of the following utilities?

   A. Server Manager
   B. User Manager
   C. User Manager for Domains
   D. Windows NT Explorer

7. You are about to establish a two-way trust relationship between the Headquarters domain and the Sales domain. Since Sales contains the resources, it will be the

trusting domain and Headquarters will be the trusted domain. In the Trust Relationships dialog box, which step must be performed first to establish the two-way trust if a one-way trust already exists?

A. Headquarters will add the Sales domain to the Trusted portion of the dialog.

B. Sales will add the Headquarters domain to the Trusted portion of the dialog.

C. Headquarters will add the Sales domain to the Trusting portion of the dialog.

D. Sales will add the Headquarters domain to the Trusting portion of the dialog.

8. In the multiple master domain model, which trust relationships must be established? (Choose all that apply.)

A. The resource domains must trust their corresponding master domains with one-way trusts.

B. The master domains must trust every other master domain with a one-way trust.

C. The resource domains must trust their corresponding master domains with two-way trusts.

D. The master domains must trust every other master domain with a two-way trust.

9. In the single master domain model, which trust relationship must be established?

A. The master domain must trust the resource domains with a one-way trust.

B. The resource domains must trust the master domain with a one-way trust.

C. The master domain must trust the resource domains with a two-way trust.

D. The resource domains must trust the master domain with a two-way trust.

10. After a trust relationship has been established, how can you obtain the new password in case something happens to the trust?

A. By using the Trust Relationships menu in User Manager for Domains

B. By using the Trust Relationships menu in Server Manager

C. By using the Trust Relationships menu in Windows NT Explorer

D. You can't.

11. A Windows NT network can handle _____ inbound trust relationships and _____ outbound trust relationships.

A. 64, 128

B. 128, 64

C. 128, unlimited

D. unlimited, 128

12. In a complete trust model, you are limited to how many domains on the network?

A. 5

B. 7

C. 9

D. 11

13. You are about to establish a trust relationship between the Headquarters domain and the Sales domain. Since Sales contains the resources, it will be the trusting domain and Headquarters will be the trusted domain. In the Trust Relationships dialog box, which step must be performed first to begin the trust?

   A. Headquarters will add the Sales domain to the Trusted portion of the dialog.

   B. Sales will add the Headquarters domain to the Trusted portion of the dialog.

   C. Headquarters will add the Sales domain to the Trusting portion of the dialog.

   D. Sales will add the Headquarters domain to the Trusting portion of the dialog.

14. Which of the following are attributes of the single domain model?

   A. Centralized Account Administration

   B. Decentralized Account Administration

   C. Centralized Resource Administration

   D. Decentralized Resource Administration

15. The _____ domain model requires that all domains trust each other with two-way trusts.

   A. Complete trust

   B. Single

   C. Single master

   D. Multiple master

48

Integrating Windows NT Workstations

CERTIFICATION OBJECTIVES

48.01   Benefits of Integrating Windows NT Workstations with NDS

48.02   NDS Integrated Messaging Multiprotocol Support Management

48.03   32-Bit NetWare Administrator on an NT Workstation

48.04   Windows NT Workstation Benefits

48.05   Introduction to the NetWare Client for Windows NT

48.06   Managing Windows NT Workstation Users and Desktops

48.07   Introduction to the Novell Workstation Manager

48.08   Creating and Configuring the NT Client Configuration Object

48.09   Introduction to the Novell Application Launcher (NAL)

M ost networks today are going to be a mixture of various client operating systems. For the most part you will see Windows 95 or Windows 98. You are also going to run into Windows NT Workstation, which can be a little challenging. The exam is going to focus more on the client than you might expect. NetWare and Z.E.N.works are an integral part of proper administration.

The focus of this chapter is workstation and application administration. We will look at details such as using NetWare Administrator to administer a workstation. There are a lot of things you can do with an NT workstation as a client on a NetWare network. We will also discuss using the NAL and implementing it with Windows NT.

Benefits of Integrating Windows NT Workstations with NDS

With NetWare you've probably realized that the more that can be integrated into NDS, the easier it is to administer. The reason for this is that 40 percent of a network administrator's time is spent going to the workstation to configure something. With NetWare5 and Z.E.N.works, remote administration of the workstation can be done from a single point of administration. Centralized management via NDS is a big plus for NetWare. Now with support for Windows NT workstation management, not only can policies be managed from NDS, but so can application distribution.

The nice part about integrating the workstation into NDS is that you don't have to worry about two passwords, one for the NT workstation and another for logon to the NetWare network. With NDS integration it is easy to keep these two components synchronized.

With the two-account situations existing with an NT workstation on a NetWare network, you can use NetWare's Workstation Manager to automatically generate accounts on the workstation when the user logs in to the network. Without this feature you would have to create two accounts: one on the workstation and one in NDS. The centralized administration of policies, profiles, and workstation components makes it easy to handle a diverse network environment.

NDS Integrated Messaging Multiprotocol Support Management

The Windows NT client lets you take advantage of multiple protocols. Both IPX and IP are supported. The NT client actually uses what Microsoft calls NWLINK, which is their IPX compatible protocol. This means that a Windows NT workstation can function easily in a diverse environment that may have Windows NT servers as well as NetWare servers.

The NetWare client for Windows NT supports both ODI and NDIS standards. ODI and NDIS standards allow a network adapter to have multiple protocols bound to network board drivers. Thus, both IPX and IP can be bound to the same network adapter.

32-Bit NetWare Administrator on an NT Workstation

The 32-bit NetWare Administrator runs on an NT workstation. The same file can be used by both Windows 95 and 98 as well as Windows NT. The filename is NWADMN32.EXE and it is located in the SYS:PUBLIC/WIN32 directory. NWADMIN32 allows administration of the User objects in the directory tree. Figure 48-1 shows NWADMN32.EXE.

FIGURE 48-1

32-bit NetWare
Administrator for
Windows NT

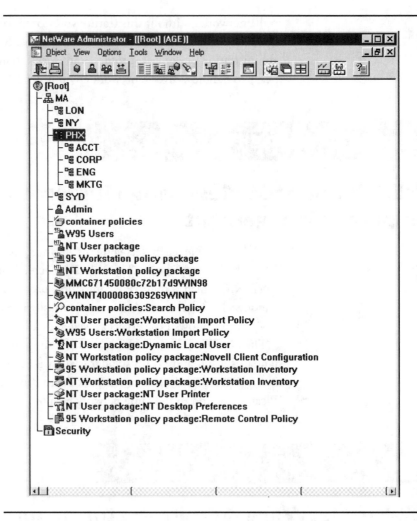

Management of Local NT Workstation User Accounts in NDS

As mentioned previously, user accounts can be administered from NDS. This also handles the accounts on the workstation. Because NT has workstation accounts stored locally on the workstation, the proper configuration must be in place for NT Workstation to have its accounts managed from NDS. Figure 48-2 shows the options available with NT Workstation objects.

FIGURE 48-2

NWADMN32 and NT
Workstation objects

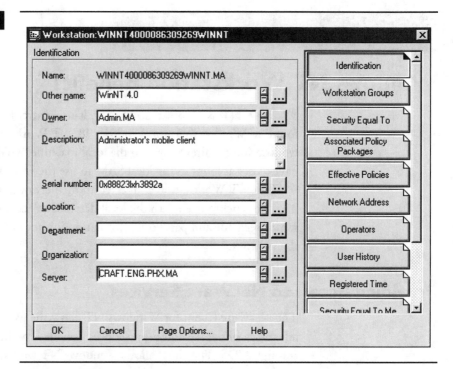

Distribution and Management of Network Applications

When you set up and configure users' workstations, make sure the applications are readily available to the user. As an administrator you can either install the application to each workstation or install the application as a shared application on the network.

With this in mind, you have to remember that the user must still have an icon to click on in order to use the application. This is where the NetWare Application Launcher (NAL) comes in. With NAL you can manage and distribute applications and updates from NDS using NWADMIN32. This keeps the administration centralized and simpler.

Windows NT Workstation Benefits

Windows NT as a workstation has built-in security features that are not found in Windows 95 and Windows 98. NT Workstation as a stand-alone workstation requires a login to the local machine, which means you have to have a user account in the local SAM to use the workstation.

With NT Workstation connected to the network, the NetWare account must be synchronized with the local database of accounts so it will keep the same username and password information for both the workstation and the network.

Providing Access to NetWare Services

The NetWare Client for Windows NT allow the workstation to take full advantage of the file and print services provided by the NetWare server through NDS. The client allows Windows NT workstations to access bindery print services and bindery file services on previous versions of NetWare. W e will look more at the NetWare Client for Windows NT in the next section.

Introduction to the NetWare Client for Windows NT

The NetWare Client for Windows NT was designed for the workstation to take full advantage of services offered by NetWare and NDS that are not offered in Windows NT.

There are several advantages to using this client, and you may see this on the exam:

- Full NDS support
- Full access to services
- Network security
- Automatic reconnection
- Automatic client updates
- Multiprotocol support

Installing the NetWare Client for Windows NT

The NetWare Client is pretty straightforward to install. There are some requirements though in terms of hardware. First, you have to be running Windows NT 3.51 or 4.0 Workstation. To install the basic client pieces you will need 10MB of disk space. To install the Administrator utilities you will need 16MB of additional disk space.

Along with the requirements comes the method of installation. There are three ways to install the client software. The first is the basic local install at the workstation. The second is a network install from a shared directory on the network. With this method you must have some client on the system to access the information. This is usually the method chosen for an upgrade. The third method is the unattended installation. There are two ways to do an unattended installation. The unattended installation uses a basic configuration file, UNATTEND.TXT, to answer most of the questions answered during the installation. The other method that is also unattended but more of an upgrade, is the Automatic Client Update. We will look at this more later in the chapter.

To install the NetWare client for Windows NT you use the SETUPNW.EXE from the PRODUCTS/WINNT/I386 directory on the CD. The CD is an autorun and will come up with the WINSETUP.EXE, which then allows you to select what you want to install. When the Windows

NT selection is chosen, the SETUPNW.EXE is executed. You will follow various prompts and then have to REBOOT when the client is installed. With the unattended installation there are some switches that you can use to accomplish the type of install you want. The /U switch is for the unattended install. Along with this switch is the /ACU switch for automatic client upgrades.

Updating the Client with Automatic Client Update (ACU)

If there are users with different versions of the client software, you can update everyone to the same basic network installation. First, you must enable the ACU component. To do this you have to copy the NetWare client I386 directory to the server so workstations can get to the object. Next, you must grant users Read and File Scan rights to the directory. Once you have these two steps completed, add a line to the login script to run the update component.

Managing Windows NT Workstation Users and Desktops

The key to successful management of workstations with Z.E.N.works and NetWare Administrator is association with the appropriate objects. NetWare5 enables you to have NT policies and profiles integrated into the NDS. Figure 48-3 shows some of the things you can do with an NT policy package in NetWare Administrator.

This again means centralized management and control of not only the workstation but also the users, since policies can now be managed within NetWare Administrator without having to use a separate policy editor.

FIGURE 48-3

NT policy package in
NetWare Administrator

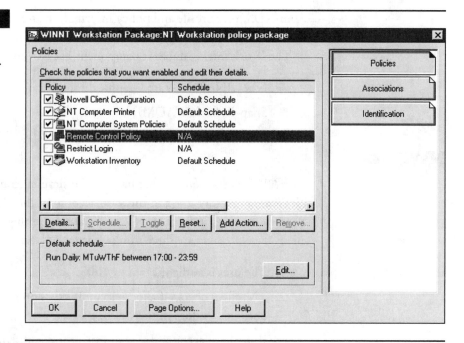

CERTIFICATION OBJECTIVE 48.07

Introduction to the Novell Workstation Manager

In order for all this to come together, there is a piece to the puzzle that we
have not yet discussed. This piece is the Workstation Manager, which is a
component of the Client that runs and interacts with the NDS Workstation
and Policy packages.

Workstation Manager makes it possible to administer both the local
Windows NT user accounts and the NetWare objects in NDS. Tying
these two items together makes for simpler and more efficient administration.
The Workstation Manager also gives us the ability to centrally administer

from NDS, user profile and policy information and computer/workstation profile and policy information.

The Workstation Manager component has two components:

■ NWGINA (NetWare Graphical Identification and Authentication)

■ Snap-In for NWADMIN for NT

NWGINA

The *NWGINA module* is what handles the simultaneous login to the NetWare Directory tree and the local account at the NT workstation. When a user logs in from an NT workstation running the NetWare client for NT, there are three things that take place:

1. The user is authenticated to NDS.

2. The client checks if a local account exists on the workstation; if it does exist, it logs in there also.

3. If the local account does not exist, the client dynamically creates a user and then logs the user in.

exam
Watch

You will probably see this mentioned on the exam so be sure to know that the NWGINA component handles the synchronization and management of local NT Workstation accounts and the User account/object in NDS.

Snap-In for the NT Client Configuration Object

The snap-in component is important to the centralized administration of NT configurations. The snap-in is configured using the ADMSETUP utility. The one thing to remember here is that the snap-in can be used only by the user who installed it.

Creating and Configuring the NT Client Configuration Object

Create the NT Configuration object just like any other NDS object. Select the container you want the object to be in and press the INSERT key or choose the Create button on the Toolbar. Scroll down through the list of available objects and then choose NT Configuration.

Once the object is imported, you can manage the following items:

■ Administer NT Workstation user accounts.

■ Configure components of the workstation configuration from NDS.

■ Works with the client piece to create local NT workstation accounts when the user logs in.

■ Manage items such as policies, profile information, and login screen banner.

These are the main items to remember for the exam. Now we will look at a couple of items that are important when it comes to administering the workstation from NDS.

Associating Users with the NT Client Configuration Object

Once you have the NT Configuration object configured the way you want it, you have to associate with your user, group, or container. To do this you use the Associations tab in the Details window for the NT Configuration object.

exam
Watch

The NT Configuration object can be created and then associated with a user, group, or container.

Managing User Profiles and System Policies

Along with the association is the basic configuration of the object. The main thing that is configured is the policy information and profile. The policy information replaces the old NTCONFIG.POL that would be used in previous versions of NetWare before Z.E.N. Works came about.

With Windows NT there is also profiles information. The profile information makes up the user portion of the policy configuration as well as desktop and start menu icons and layout. This can be centrally managed within NDS making an administrator's job much easier.

CERTIFICATION OBJECTIVE 48.09

Introduction to the Novell Application Launcher (NAL)

The Novell Application Launcher gives the network administrator a powerful tool for application management, which includes managing the desktop icons.

There are two ways to use NAL. There is the standard NAL, which incorporates a window of its own on the desktop with the applications for the user, and there is the NAL Explorer, which allows you to incorporate icons on the Start Menu and the desktop.

Installing and Configuring NAL

The application launcher is a default piece of NetWare. I highly recommended using the Z.E.N.works start pack update and use that version because there is more flexibility with that update. Applications are better managed with Z.E.N.works being part of your NDS.

NAL configuration has a couple of pieces to it. First, there are Application objects that have the information about where the application exists and how it executes and runs. This is shown in Figure 48-4. Second, you must associate the Application object with a container, user, or group.

Novell recommends having an application container that holds the Application objects and then you can create application groups that are associated with the application. The group can be assigned rights and the users you want to use the application will be members of the group.

FIGURE 48-4

Application object creation

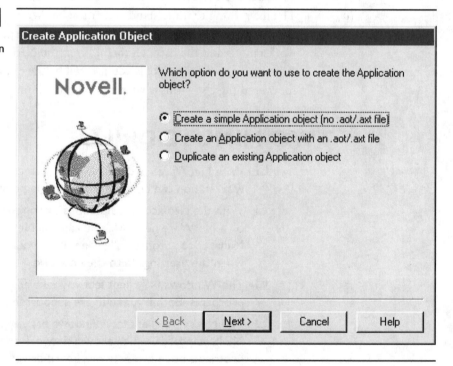

CERTIFICATION SUMMARY

When managing Windows NT and integrating Windows NT into a NetWare environment, take advantage of using NDS to manage your NT workstations. The first thing we discussed is that the integration will prevent administrators from having to manage two passwords. Windows NT workstations have their own local password and user account to log in to the operating system. When the workstation is integrated with the NetWare NDS, the Workstation Manager portion of the client will take advantage of Windows NT Configuration objects.

We looked briefly at what the NetWare Client for NT gives you as advantages to the normal NetWare Client that comes with NT Workstation. The main thing to understand is that the NetWare Client for NT and Workstation Manager will help you centrally manage and administer your workstations and the users on them. From the NAL to the NetWare Administrator the main tools you use will be the ones you use everyday for everything else—this is what centralized administration is all about.

TWO-MINUTE DRILL

❑ With NetWare5 and Z.E.N.works, remote administration of the workstation can be done from a single point of administration.

❑ With the two-account situations existing with an NT workstation on a NetWare network, you can use NetWare's Workstation Manager to automatically generate accounts on the workstation when the user logs in to the network.

❑ The Windows NT client lets you take advantage of multiple protocols. Both IPX and IP are supported.

❑ The NetWare client for Windows NT supports both ODI and NDIS standards, which allow a network adapter to have multiple protocols bound to network board drivers.

❑ Because NT has workstation accounts stored locally on the workstation, the proper configuration must be in place for NT.

❑ There are three ways to install the client software. The first is the basic local install at the workstation. The second is a network install from a shared directory on the network. The third method is the unattended installation.

❑ To install the NetWare client for Windows NT you use the SETUPNW.EXE from the PRODUCTS/WINNT/I386 directory on the CD. The CD is an autorun and will come up with the WINSETUP.EXE, which then allows you to select what you want to install.

❑ The Workstation Manager component has two components: NWGINA (NetWare Graphical Identification and Authentication); and Snap-In for NWADMIN for NT.

❑ When the workstation is integrated with the NetWare NDS, the Workstation Manager portion of the client will take advantage of Windows NT Configuration objects.

❑ The *NWGINA module* is what handles the simultaneous login to the NetWare Directory tree and the local account at the NT workstation.

❑ The snap-in is configured using the ADMSETUP utility. The one thing to remember here is that the snap-in can be used only by the user who installed it.

❑ Once you have the NT Configuration object configured the way you want it, you have to associate with your user, group, or container. To do this, you use the Associations tab in the Details window for the NT Configuration object.

❑ There are two ways to use NAL. There is the standard NAL, which incorporates a window of its own on the desktop with the applications for the user, and there is the NAL Explorer, which allows you to incorporate icons on the Start Menu and the desktop.

❑ In NAL configuration, there are Application objects that have the information about where the application exists, and how it executes and runs, and you must associate the Application object with a container, user, or group.

SELF TEST

The Self-Test questions will help you measure your understanding of the material presented in this chapter. Read all the choices carefully, as there may be more than one correct answer. Select all correct answers for each question.

1. What utility will automatically generate a user account on the local Windows NT workstation if one does not exist?

   A. NetWare Client for NT

   B. NetWare Administrator

   C. Workstation Manager

   D. Workstation Administrator

2. What two standards does the NetWare Client for NT support that allow for multiple protocols to be bound to the network card? (Choose all that apply).

   A. ODI

   B. NDS

   C. DOI

   D. NDIS

3. Where is the 32-bit NetWare Administrator utility found?

   A. On the root of the SYS: volume

   B. Under VOL1:SYSTEM

   C. Under SYS:PUBLIC

   D. Under SYS:PUBLIC\WIN32

4. Which of the following is not an advantage of using the NetWare Client for NT as mentioned in this chapter?

   A. Full access to all volumes

   B. Full NDS support

   C. Full access to services

   D. Automatic reconnect feature

5. What EXE do you use to install the NetWare Client for NT?

   A. INSTALL.EXE

   B. SETUPNW.EXE

   C. SETUP.EXE

   D. NWSETUP.EX

6. What switch will take advantage of the Automatic Client Update configuration?

   A. /U

   B. /ACU

   C. /CU

   D. /AU

7. What are the two components that make up the Workstation Manager component? (Choose all that apply.)

   A. GINA

   B. NWGINA

   C. Snap-ins for NWADMIN32

   D. Snap-ins for NWADMN32

8. What utility do you use to configure the snap-in for NetWare Administrator for Workstation Manager?

   A. SETUP

   B. ADMCONFIG

   C. ADMSETUP

   D. CONFIG

9. What type of object do we need to properly administer NT workstations?

   A. NDS NT object

   B. NT object file

   C. NWADMN32

   D. NT Configuration object

10. What is the name of the tab that assigns an Application object to a user?

    A. Assignment

    B. Association

    C. Application

    D. Group

11. What types of objects can be associated with an Application or client Configuration object? (Choose all that apply.)

    A. Organization

    B. Organizational Unit

    C. User

    D. Group

12. Which tab in NetWare Administrator enables profile configuration?

    A. Profile

    B. Policy

    C. Profile/Policy

    D. Policy/Profile

13. What happens when a user logs in to an NT workstation that has no user account locally in its user database?

    A. The user cannot log in until both accounts are created.

    B. As long as Workstation Manager is in place, then the local account will be created automatically.

    C. The user is deleted from the Tree and then cannot log on the network.

    D. The account will be created even if Workstation Manager is not.

14 Where is the SETUPNW.EXE located if I want to install the NetWare Client for Windows NT? (Choose all that apply.)

    A. SYS:PUBLIC

    B. PRODUCTS\WINNT\I386.

    C. SYS:PUBLIC\WIN32

    D. PROCUTS\WINNT\I386\NAL

    E. On the installation CD

15. What are the three types of installations that can be done with the NetWare Client for Windows NT Workstation? (Choose all that apply.)

    A. Basic local install

    B. Unattended install

    C. Network install from shared directory

    D. NetWare Administrator 32-bit

MICROSOFT CERTIFIED SYSTEMS ENGINEER

49

Integrating NetWare and Windows NT Domains

CERTIFICATION OBJECTIVES

49.01   Benefits of Integrating Windows NT Domains with NDS

49.02   Introduction to the Novell Administrator for Windows NT

49.03   Installing and Configuring Novell Administrator for Windows NT

49.04   Synchronizing NetWare and Windows NT Users and Groups

N ow that you have learned how to integrate Windows NT Workstation with NDS, it is time to learn how to integrate your Windows NT domains with NDS. Managing Windows NT domains with NDS simplifies administration because you can use one application to manage the whole network.

CERTIFICATION OBJECTIVE 49.01

Benefits of Integrating Windows NT Domains with NDS

Administering Windows NT domains and NDS without integrating the two would result in the following problems:

- You would have to use two different account managers: the User Manager for domains application for Windows NT and the NetWare Administrator for NDS accounts.

- You would double your workload by maintaining two separate directory databases.

- You would have to manually migrate users from Windows NT to the NDS database.

Trying to maintain a Windows NT network and NDS without integrating the two also provides a larger margin for error, which can take an enormous amount of time to track down. Instead, you can easily access NDS and Windows NT resources and centrally manage both environments by integrating the two networks into a single, coherent unit. In this section, we will explore these benefits in more detail.

Reducing Redundant Administration by Managing Windows NT Domains from NetWare Administrator

NetWare 5 allows you to centrally administer the two systems from NDS using the NetWare Administrator application. This not only reduces the workload on the administrator, but decreases the potential for errors. If you make a mistake using NetWare Administrator, you know the mistake was replicated to the Windows NT domain. However, rectifying the mistake is easy because once you correct the error using NetWare Administrator, it is automatically corrected on the Windows NT domain. In this case, you are spared having to look at both systems to determine which one contained the error in the first place.

Allowing Access to Both Windows NT and NetWare Resources and Services

If you don't synchronize the two networks, users will have to remember two different accounts in order to access both NetWare and Windows NT network resources. If, on the other hand, you synchronize the two platforms, you can maintain the goal of one user, one account. While both systems will still have separate accounts, the account information can be standardized between the two systems and logins can be accomplished simultaneously without the user being aware of it.

CERTIFICATION OBJECTIVE 49.02

Introduction to the Novell Administrator for Windows NT

In order to integrate Windows NT domains into NetWare networks, you use the Novell Administrator for Windows NT. This will allow you to administer all users in NDS with NetWare Administrator from a central location. In addition, the need for trust relationships between domains is eliminated, since network resources are now handled by NDS.

There are several components to the Novell Administrator:

■ NDS Schema Extensions
■ NetWare Administrator Snap-In Service

- NDS Event Monitor
- NDS Object Replication Service
- Integration Utility

This section will introduce you to each component and its function.

You will need to know these Novell Administrator components for the exam.

NDS Schema Extensions

As we mentioned in the previous chapter, NDS is an extensible database that allows you to add additional schema extensions. A *schema* defines the NDS object and the various properties that are associated with that object. NDS is an object-oriented database that allows you to include objects that are not even developed yet. In order for NetWare to manage Windows NT objects, you must provide it with a blueprint of the objects, or extend its awareness to include them. This is performed through the installation of Novell Administrator for Windows NT by administrators with the Supervisor right to the [Root] object.

Extending NDS to store Windows NT objects is the first step. Next, you must extend the NetWare Administrator in order to manage those objects. The Novell Administrator for Windows NT snap-in service modules provide this functionality to NetWare Administrator, as we'll see in the next section.

NetWare Administrator Snap-In Service

The Novell Administrator snap-in service allows the network administrator to centrally manage Windows NT domains through the NetWare Administrator as Windows NT Server objects. Synchronization between NDS and Windows NT is transparent to the administrator and makes the routine administration tasks easier, since you will not have to migrate users from Windows NT to NDS manually. Through the snap-in service, Windows NT users and groups are stored in NDS as native NDS objects and are referenced to the Windows NT Server object that stores the Windows NT domain account.

NDS Event Monitor

The NDS Event Monitor is an NLM (NDSDM.NLM) that is implemented on a NetWare server. Its job is to scan the NDS database for object modifications such as creation or deletion of objects and attribute value changes. When it detects that an object has changed, it then transfers the changes to the NDS Object Replication Service, which we discuss in the next section. The NDS Event Monitor can also ensure that synchronization with a Windows NT system is completed, even if the Windows NT system or its connection fails. When a failed Windows NT system comes back online, the NDS Event Monitor will submit the appropriate changes to the Windows NT system. This ensures that the NetWare network and the Windows NT network are synchronized with each other while also providing fault tolerance. The administrator can configure how often NDS events are synchronized with a Windows NT system through the Novell Administrator. This feature is important, as it can significantly cut down on network traffic between the two systems.

The main requirement of the NDS Event Monitor is that it must be present on each server in the Directory tree that contains a master or read/write replica. Since a subordinate reference and a read-only copy will not allow for NDS changes, NDS Event Monitor should not run on servers that contain these replicas.

NDS Object Replication Service

The NDS Object Replication Service resides on the Windows NT primary domain controller (PDC) and any backup domain controllers (BDCs) that are administered using NDS. When a change occurs to certain objects in NDS, the NDS Event Monitor passes those changes to the NDS Object Replication Service. When the NDS Object Replication Service receives the changes, it first formats the modifications to fit the Windows NT SAM database. Once reformatting is complete, it makes the changes in the SAM database. Since the PDC contains the master copy of the domain's SAM database, changes are not made on the BDCs. Should the PDC fail, NDS information is synchronized with a BDC only if it has been promoted to a PDC. If there is no PDC online during a synchronization, NDS will hold onto (queue) the appropriate modifications until a PDC is available.

Integration Utility

When you first begin the process of integrating a Windows NT network into a NetWare network, you must synchronize the existing users between both networks. In order to accomplish this task, the Novell Administrator includes an integration utility, IGRATE.EXE, that takes the existing user and group information from the Windows NT SAM database and imports them into NDS. Subsequently, it then takes existing user and group information from NDS and synchronizes it with the Windows NT system. After a successful integration, any modifications are handled by the NDS Event Monitor and the NDS Object Replication Service components of the Novell Administrator.

exam
ⓦatch

Remember that the IGRATE.EXE application is used during the initial integration process.

Integration Security

Network security is important to every administrator, and hackers use any method they can to gain entry to your network. The Novell Administrator for Windows NT provides for a secure communications channel between a Windows NT network and a NetWare network by establishing a private, authenticated NDS connection. The connection is not shared by any other process nor is it viewable when browsing the network. If a hostile entity attempts to locate your secure connection, it is much more difficult for them to find you if that connection is not advertised over the network.

Installing and Configuring Novell Administrator for Windows NT

Before you install the Novell Administrator for Windows NT, you must meet some system requirements.

For the Windows NT network, you will need the following:

■ Windows NT Server functioning as a PDC. The NetWare Client for Windows NT must be installed on the PDC.

■ IPX Protocol installed on the PDC. IPX is the native protocol of NetWare. (This step is necessary only if the NetWare 5 server is not using pure IP.)

■ Access to a user account with administrative privileges to the domain.

For the NetWare network, you will need the following:

■ NetWare Server, 4.1 or higher. The NetWare Administrator must be installed.

■ Access to a user account with administrative privileges to the NDS Directory tree that you will extend the schema. The Windows NT domain object will be placed in this tree.

Installing the Novell Administrator for Windows NT is accomplished through the SETUP.EXE executable, and uses a graphical user interface that is similar to Microsoft's Installation Wizard process. The following steps guide you through the installation process.

1. Log in to the NetWare server with an account that has administrative rights.

2. Go to the Novell Administrator for Windows NT folder and run SETUP.EXE. You will be presented with three pages: product

overview, installation overview, and license agreement. Note that if you decline the license agreement the installation process will terminate.

3. On the Select Components dialog box, select each component that should be installed. On the initial installation, you should mark all components and then select the Next button.

4. The Select Novell Directory Services Tree dialog box is used to select which Directory tree's schema will be extended. You must have administrative privileges on the tree whose schema will be extended or the installation will fail. Once you have completed your select, click the Next button to continue.

5. The Select NDS Context for NetWare Server dialog box contains two components: the NDS Tree that you have selected to extend the schema (from the previous dialog box), and the Select Context textbox. If you have selected the wrong NDS tree, you can use the Back button to return to the Select Novell Directory Services Tree dialog box. However, if you are ready to proceed, select the context that contains the NetWare server on which you will install the Novell Administrator for Windows NT components. When you have completed your selection, click on the Next button.

6. The Select Novell NetWare Servers dialog box will allow you to select on which NetWare servers you will install the Novell Administrator for Windows NT components, which includes the NDS Event Monitor. As stated earlier in this section, the NDS Event Monitor must be placed on each NetWare server that contains a master or read/write replica. Note that only NetWare servers that exist in the context you chose in the Select NDS Context for NetWare Server dialog will appear. If you need to install the Novell Administrator for Windows NT components on an additional server that exists in another context, you will have to perform the installation process a second time.

7. Next, you will see the Select NT Domains and Workgroups dialog box, where you are specify where to install the NDS Object

Replication Service (ORS). This phase may take a few minutes, depending on the size of your network, because the setup program must scan the network for all Windows NT domains and workgroups on the network. In order to successfully complete this phase, ensure that you select only those domains and/or workgroups to which you have administrative privileges.

8. In the Select NDS Context for Domain or Workgroup System Object dialog box, you will need to specify the context for the Windows NT Server object that will be created at the end of the installation. Valid NDS objects that can store the Windows NT Server object are (O) Organization or OU (Organizational Unit).

9. The Review Installation Choices dialog box lets you verify your selections. At this stage, it is a good idea to double-check that you have not made an incorrect selection. If you do find an error, use the Back button to return to the page that contains the incorrect selection and modify it. The settings on any pages that follow the error will still retain their settings. Once you select the Next button, you will be prompted to log in to the Windows NT domain that you selected from the Select Windows NT Domains and Workgroups page.

10. Log in to the Windows NT domain with an account that contains administrative privileges.

The installation program will now extend the tree's schema and copy the files listed in Table 49-1.

The last step is to review the Setup Complete dialog box displaying the results of the installation process. If you select the Launch the Integration Utility Now, IGRATE.EXE will begin, and you can synchronize the user and group accounts between Windows NT and NetWare . However, if you choose to run this process at a later date, you can launch the integration utility from the NetWare Administrator.

exam
ⓦatch

Become familiar with the dialog boxes presented during the installation of Novell Administrator for Windows NT.

TABLE 49-1	Files Copied to Netware Server	Files Copied to Windows NT PDC (C:\WINNT\SYSTEM32 Directory)
Files Copied During the Installation of Novell Administrator for Windows NT	SYS:SYSTEM\NDSDM.NLM	MWAAGENT.EXE
	SYS:PUBLIC\WINNT\ASMCLNT.DLL	MWA.CFG
	SYS:PUBLIC\WINNT\ASMNTWNT.DLL	MWABE.CFG
	SYS:PUBLIC\WINNT\ASMORS.DLL	ASMORS.DLL
	SYS:PUBLIC\WINNT\ASMWIRE.DLL	ASMWIRE.DLL
	SYS:PUBLIC\WINNT\IGRATE.EXE	LIBAUTH.DLL
	SYS:PUBLIC\WINNT\LIBAUTH.DLL	LISTEN.DLL
		NTSAM.DLL
		NWINTER.DLL
		ASMCLNT.DLL
		HA3300W32.DLL

CERTIFICATION OBJECTIVE 49.04

Synchronizing NetWare and Windows NT Users and Groups

As we mentioned earlier in the chapter, the IGRATE.EXE integration utility is a component of the Novell Administrator for Windows NT. Its function is to synchronize existing Windows NT users and groups with NDS during the initial integration process. Since the NDS Event Monitor and NDS Object Replication Service maintains Directory database synchronization once the two platforms have been integrated, you will not need to run IGRATE.EXE more than once.

You can launch the integration utility either from the NetWare Administrator or from the command line as a stand-alone utility. When you start the utility, you are presented with a dialog box. From this utility, you can perform the following integration tasks:

- Integrate NDS User to Windows NT.
- Integrate Windows NT Users to NDS.
- Synchronize existing Windows NT users with existing NDS users.

Each of these tasks will be explained in the following subsections.

Integrating NDS Users to Windows NT

Since Windows NT cannot store all of the information that is present in an NDS User object, the integration utility can replicate only the information that Windows NT can store. Unfortunately, Windows NT does not offer extensibility to include NDS objects. Since you will be managing the network from NDS, this is not necessarily a bad thing. However, if you add new information to the User object in NDS, that new information cannot be synchronized with the Windows NT User object unless the Windows NT User object contains that field.

To replicate an NDS User object to Windows NT, perform the following steps in the integration utility:

1. Select the NDS User object that is not present in Windows NT.
2. Select the domain where the Windows NT user resides.
3. Click the Integrate to NT button.
4. Confirm that you wish to integrate this user.
5. Select the Continue button.

Integrating Windows NT Users to NDS

Since NDS can store more information than Windows NT, you will not lose any information during the integration, or any subsequent synchronization, process. As long as you manage your Windows NT User objects from NDS, you will not need to replicate Windows NT User objects to NDS after the initial synchronization has been completed. However, if User Manager for Domains is used to perform user management, you will need to synchronize the User objects again manually.

To replicate a Windows NT User object to NDS, perform the following steps from the integration utility:

1. In the NDS Context and Users portion of the dialog box, select the context where the Windows NT users will be replicated to.

2. Select the Windows NT user that does not have an NDS user account.

3. Click the Integrate to NDS button. At this point, a User object will appear on the NDS tree, and the Windows NT User object will change to the standard NDS user icon.

4. Select Continue.

Synchronizing Existing NDS Users with Existing Windows NT Users

During the synchronization process, you will encounter situations in which there is a Windows NT User object and an NDS User object for the same individual. When you encounter this type of situation, you can merge the attributes of both User objects by designating the Windows NT User object as a Common User object. However, when duplicate information exists between these two objects, the NetWare attributes will be retained, and the Windows NT attributes will be overwritten.

To synchronize Windows NT and NDS User objects, perform the following steps from the integration utility:

1. In the NDS Context and Users portion of the dialog box, select the NDS User.

2. In the Available NT User and Groups portion of the dialog box, select the Windows NT User object.

3. Click on the Synchronize button.

e x a m
Ⓦ a t c h

Become familiar with the IGRATE.EXE integration utility and know how to perform the three integration tasks.

Configuring User Properties

The User Properties button on the integration utility's main page allows you to change the user properties of the User object when synchronizing or replicating that object. The User Property Options dialog box that appears contains two tabs—Passwords and Other Properties with the Passwords tab displayed when you bring up the dialog. Recall that one of the goals of a well designed network is "one account, one password." In order to accomplish this goal, you will need to ensure that the password is synchronized between NDS and Windows NT. The Passwords tab allows you to specify how the password synchronization phase is completed. The options are as follows:

- *No password required.* This option will remove the password from both accounts, and may jeopardize network security.

- *Generate a random password.*

- *Use new password.* If enabled, you will need to enter and confirm the new password.

- *Require password change at next login.*

- *Don't allow user to change password.* This option is generally used for a Guest account.

The Other Properties tab controls the method of merging Windows NT User account properties into NDS. If you leave the default of Use NDS Default option, NDS User account properties will be retained when there is a conflict between existing accounts. The other option, Use NDS Template, will allow you to integrate multiple Windows NT user accounts without having to enter the information that is not migrated from the Windows NT User object because there was no field present under Windows NT for the information.

exam
ⓦatch
Know the different options available under the Passwords and Other Properties tabs, as the exam will most likely have a question or two on them.

Replicating New NDS Users to Windows NT

Once you have integrated your Windows NT users into NDS, you should not use User Manager for Domains to manage Windows NT users. If you do, any changes that you make will not be replicated to NDS and will be overwritten by NDS parameters during the next synchronization. Instead, you would use the NetWare Administrator to manage and maintain both Windows NT and NetWare accounts through NDS. When you receive a new user who requires access to the Windows NT network, you will need to replicate their NDS User object to Windows NT. While you can perform the replication process from the integration utility, it is highly recommended (and assumed on the Novell examination) that you will use the NetWare Administrator. The procedure to replicate an NDS User object from the NetWare Administrator is as follows:

1. Right-click the User object to be replicated.

2. Click the Details item from the pop-up menu.

3. Click on the Application Servers button.

4. Use the Add button to select the domain that the user is to be replicated to.

Using NetWare Administrator

One interesting note about the NetWare Administrator is that you can manage Windows NT objects whether they are integrated into NDS or not. Since the NetWare Administrator's schema must be extended to store and manage Windows NT objects, it already has all the information necessary to manage those objects. If you work in a security-conscious network environment, you may not want to integrate some Windows NT User objects with NDS. This is especially true if the individual works solely in the Windows NT environment and does not require the services provided by NDS. However, when taking the Novell certification exam, assume that all Windows NT users will want to use the services provided by NDS.

In addition to Windows NT User objects, NetWare Administrator can also handle Windows NT Group assignments. In order to make a Windows NT Group assignment to a Windows NT User object, regardless of whether they are integrated into NDS, you simply pull up the Details of the Windows NT Group object and make your assignments through the Members page. Here, you simply click the Add button to add Windows NT User objects to the Windows NT Group object.

Since everything is an object to NDS, you can manage Application Server objects as easily as you can manage other objects. The purpose of the Application Server object is to manage communications between the Event Monitor that resides on the NetWare server and the ORS that resides on the Windows NT Server. As you recall from an earlier section, the NDS Event Monitor tracks modifications made to objects that will require synchronization with a Windows NT network. When it finds that a change has been made, it alerts its counterpart on the Windows NT Server, the NDS Object Replication Service (ORS), and passes those changes to it. The ORS then validates the data it has received by formatting it for the SAM database and makes the modifications required. Through the Network Settings page of the Application Server object, you can configure the protocol settings and the synchronization interval to Windows NT.

The Application Server object also allows you to configure password and login restrictions for users that are associated with the Application Server through the System Modals page of the Application Server object. The options on this page are relatively intuitive.

exam
ⓦatch

Become familiar with the Network Settings page for the Novell Certification exam, as the NDS Event Monitor and ORS are important features of Directory database synchronization.

CERTIFICATION SUMMARY

In this chapter, we have discovered that managing an NetWare network and a Windows NT network can be a burden unless you have integrated the two.

Without integration, you are stuck managing two different networks from two separate management utilities. However, Novell has provided you with several integration tools that allow you to extend the schema of NetWare to become Windows NT aware, and to integrate and manage your Windows NT objects with NDS. Through the components of Novell Administrator, and the snap-in modules available to the NetWare Administrator, your routine administrative activities will be easier to manage.

TWO-MINUTE DRILL

❑ If you make a mistake using NetWare Administrator, you know the mistake was replicated to the Windows NT domain.

❑ A *schema* defines the NDS object and the various properties that are associated with that object.

❑ The NDS Event Monitor is an NLM (NDSDM.NLM) that is implemented on a NetWare server.

❑ The NDS Object Replication Service resides on the Windows NT primary domain controller (PDC) and any backup domain controllers (BDCs) that are administered using NDS.

❑ You can launch the integration utility either from the NetWare Administrator or from the command line as a stand-alone utility.

❑ The Other Properties tab controls the method of merging Windows NT User account properties into NDS.

❑ If you select the Launch the Integration Utility Now, IGRATE.EXE will begin, and you can synchronize the user and group accounts between Windows NT and NetWare.

❑ Synchronization between NDS and Windows NT is transparent to the administrator and makes the routine administration tasks easier, since you will not have to manually migrate users from Windows NT to NDS.

❑ The User Properties button on the integration utility's main page allows you to change the user properties of the User object when synchronizing or replicating that object.

❑ When you receive a new user who requires access to the Windows NT network, you will need to replicate their NDS User object to Windows NT.

❑ In order to make a Windows NT Group assignment to a Windows NT User object, whether or not they are integrated into NDS, you simply pull up the Details of the Windows NT Group object and make your assignments through the Members page.

❑ When you first begin the process of integrating a Windows NT network into an NetWare network, you must synchronize the existing users between both networks

❑ The purpose of the Application Server object is to manage communications between the Event Monitor that resides on the NetWare server and the ORS that resides on the Windows NT Server.

❑ The main requirement of the NDS Event Monitor is that it must be present on each server in the Directory tree that contains a master or read/write replica.

❑ Installing the Novell Administrator for Windows NT is accomplished through the SETUP.EXE executable, and uses a graphical user interface that is similar to Microsoft's Installation Wizard process.

❑ During the synchronization process, you will encounter situations in which there is a Windows NT User object and an NDS User object for the same individual. In that case, you can merge the attributes of both User objects by designating the Windows NT User object as a Common User object.

❑ Once you have integrated your Windows NT users into NDS, you should not use User Manager for Domains to manage Windows NT users. If you do, any changes that you make will not be replicated to NDS and will be overwritten by NDS parameters during the next synchronization.

❑ The purpose of the Application Server object is to manage communications between the Event Monitor that resides on the NetWare server and the ORS that resides on the Windows NT Server.

❑ The NDS Event Monitor tracks modifications made to objects that will require synchronization with a Windows NT network. When it finds that a change has been made, it alerts its counterpart on the Windows NT Server, the NDS Object Replication Service (ORS), and passes those changes to it.

Self Test

The Self-Test questions will help you measure your understanding of the material presented in this chapter. Read all the choices carefully, as there may be more than one correct answer. Select all correct answers for each question.

1. Components of the Novell Administrator include which of the following? (Choose all that apply.)

    A. NetWare Administrator Snap-In Service

    B. NDS Event Monitor

    C. NetWare Client for Windows NT

    D. Auto-reconnect service

2. The NetWare Administrator Snap-In Service allows the administrator to

    A. Manage and maintain NDS accounts from a central location

    B. Manage and maintain Windows NT Workstation accounts from a central location

    C. Manage and maintain Windows NT domain accounts from a central location

    D. Extend NDS's knowledge of Windows NT Workstation.

3. Which of the following is the Novell Administrator component used to initially synchronize a Windows NT system's SAM database with the NetWare NDS database?

    A. NDS Schema Extensions

    B. IGRATE.EXE

    C. NetWare Administrator

    D. NDS Event Monitor

4. During the installation of Novell Administrator for Windows NT, which of the following dialog boxes lets you choose the servers through which the NDS Event Monitor is installed?

    A. Select Components

    B. Select Novell Directory Services Tree

    C. Select NDS Context for NetWare Server Search

    D. Select Novell NetWare Servers

5. Which of the following occurs when you synchronize an existing Windows NT User object with an existing NDS User object for the same person?

    A. Duplicate information is discarded.

    B. Duplicate information is overwritten by the NDS attributes.

    C. Duplicate information is overwritten by the Windows NT attributes.

    D. You cannot synchronize existing Windows NT User objects with an existing NDS User object for the same person.

6. The integration utility, IGRATE.EXE, provided with the Novell Administrator for Windows NT allows you to perform which of the following integration tasks? (Choose all that apply.)

A. Replace Windows NT objects with NDS objects.

B. Synchronize Windows NT objects with NDS objects.

C. Replace NDS objects with Windows NT objects.

D. Synchronize NDS objects with Windows NT objects.

7. You need to configure the synchronization interval between your Windows NT network and NetWare. When you pull up the Details page of the Application Server object, you would make changes to the synchronization interval using which of the following pages?

A. Identification

B. System Modals

C. Network Settings

D. NDS Event Monitor

8. The NDS Object Replication Service:

A. Runs on a NetWare server and monitors object modifications.

B. Runs on a Windows NT PDC and monitors object modifications.

C. Runs on a NetWare server and synchronizes changes between NDS and Windows NT.

D. Runs on a Windows NT PDC and synchronizes changes between NDS and Windows NT.

9. The NDS Event Monitor NLM is

A. NDSDM.NLM

B. NDSEVENT.NLM

C. NDSEVMON.NLM

D. MONITOR.NLM

10. You have just received a request for a new user who will require access to the NetWare and Windows NT networks. After you complete their NDS account, you would use which of the following pages in NetWare Administrator to replicate their NDS User object to Windows NT?

A. Application Server

B. Windows NT Properties

C. Files and Directories

D. Group Memberships

11. You need to modify the manner in which the integration between NDS and Windows NT handles User object properties when there is a duplication of data. You would use the _____ tab located in User Properties of the User object.

A. Integration Options

B. Other Properties

C. Passwords

D. Windows NT User Object Properties

12. The NDS Event Monitor:

A. Runs on a NetWare server and monitors object modifications.

B. Runs on a Windows NT PDC and monitors object modifications.

C. Runs on a NetWare server and synchronizes changes between NDS and Windows NT.

D. Runs on a Windows NT PDC and synchronizes changes between NDS and Windows NT.

13. You are installing the Novell Administrator and have reached the Select NDS Context for Domain or Workgroup System Object dialog box. Which of the following container objects can store the Windows NT Server object? (Choose all that apply.)

A. [Root]

B. O

C. OU

D. CN

14. To integrate an NDS User object into Windows NT, you would use which of the following buttons in IGRATE.EXE?

A. Integrate to NDS

B. Integrate to NT

C. Synchronize

D. User Properties

15. During the installation of Novell Administrator for Windows NT, which of the following dialog boxes lets you choose where the NDS Object Replication Service, ORS, is installed?

A. Select Novell Directory Services Tree

B. Select NT Domains and Workgroups

C. Select NDS Context for NetWare Server Search

D. Select NDS Context for Domain or Workgroup System Object

A

Self-Test
Answers

Answers to Chapter 1 Self Test

1. **B.** Resetting a user's forgotten password is a reactive administrative responsibility. The other examples are also administrative responsibilities, but they are considered proactive, since they are not in reaction to a problem.

2. **D.** A change for users at the Organizational Unit level, especially when that change spans a WAN link between two distant cities, can make problems for a network. The Network Planning group should be able to review the need and respond to Mary's request.

3. **B.** A printer on a network server is a resource on the network.

4. **C.** Both the resource, in this case the CD-ROM hardware, and the service, in this case the CD-ROM sharing program, must be available to access the CD-ROM drive from a network station.

5. **C.** NDS stands for Novell Directory Services, a database of network resources and organizational objects used for secured network access.

6. **E.** A through D can all be organized in NDS. Files and directories appear in the Volume object, as well as Directory Map. Printers have an associated object in the tree. Applications are available as an object when using the NetWare Application Launcher, and a Computer object exists that can be used to organize workstations.

7. **D.** There are many different configurations that might force Gene to require four different login IDs for the four separate servers. However, if the NetWare servers were all in the same NDS tree, there would be only one login ID required to gain access via NDS.

8. **A.** The root object is the base of the tree and is a special container-like object that cannot contain any Leaf objects other than Aliases. Only Country and Organization objects can be placed in the root of the NDS tree.

9. **B.** The organizational role was created to handle those positions requiring different security levels that are rotated frequently among users.

10. **C.** The most efficient way to grant Ed's request is to create a Profile object and copy Patti's script into the Profile object.

11. **D.** The schema is the structure designating which NDS objects can be placed in NDS.

12. **A.** An object signifies a network resource, and has properties, which are fields used to store information known as values.

13. **B.** Rights are the security access that can be granted to objects.

14. **D.** File system rights, directory rights, NDS object rights, and NDS property rights can all be granted in NDS.

15. **C.** Jack can enable the security by changing the property rights for the Telephone property so that only HR and network administrators have Read rights. This will effectively hide the telephone number from unauthorized users and other administrators.

Answers to Chapter 2 Self Test

1. **D.** NLMs are NetWare Loadable Modules.

2. **A.** The ODI specification is the Open Data-link Interchange, a modular approach to network client software.

3. **C.** Only one NIC is needed to run multiple protocols under ODI.

4. **D.** An MLID has a .LAN extension. TOKEN.LAN is the Multiple Link Interface Driver for a Token-Ring NIC.

5. **C.** The CLIENT32.NLM handles all the layers above the Network layer.

6. **A.** The order for loading the ODI components is MLID, LSL, IPX or IP, CLIENT32.

7. **B.** FALSE. NDPS is an optional component that can be added if selected.

8. **B.** The Account Disabled feature of the Login Restrictions properties will maintain the HR policy and make the on-leave process more efficient.

9. **C.** Dan can edit the login time restrictions. This will manage the backup and allow maximum remote access time for the users.

10. **A.** Gordon can edit the Network Address restrictions and restrict each user to the network address of their associated workstation.

11. **D.** Intruder Detection policies are established in the Intruder Detection property of the container object. This allows each container to use different policies for Intruder Detection.

12. **B.** After Joe left for the meeting, the intruder attempt reset interval changed to 0 from 2 because it had been more than 20 minutes since the last incorrect login attempt.

13. **A.** NetWare 5's authentication process does not send passwords across the wire, but uses an encrypted user code.

14. **C.** Order of execution for login scripts is Container, Profile, User, or if no User login script, Default.

Answers to Chapter 3 Self Test

1. **C.** The login name is the User object name. In this case, the naming convention makes it JustHerf.

2. **A.** A context is a location in the NDS tree.

3. **D.** The context of the user ID is required for the NDS tree to find the User object and allow it to log on.

4. **C.** The Distinguished Name does not depend on abbreviations, but on the User object's context in the NDS tree. It begins with a leading period and ends with the last container until the [Root] of the tree is reached.

5. **D.** A Relative Distinguished Name is the user's name and context location relative to the current context

6. **A.** A Typeful Name includes the abbreviation for the type of object in the name, such as CN for Common Name or OU for Organizational Unit, and an equal sign (=) before the name of that object.

7. **B.** A Typeless Name does not include the abbreviations or equal sign in it.

8. **A.** User objects can be created and managed in Console One, a new utility that runs as a graphical Java application on the NetWare server console.

9. **D.** The NetWare Client 32-compatible executable for NetWare Administrator is located in SYS:PUBLIC\WIN32. It is NWADMN32.EXE.

10. **C.** To start user creation, the Manage Objects option is selected first from NETADMIN's main window.

11. **B.** Console One can view the NDS tree of the server it is running on or any other NDS tree on the network.

12. **A.** UIMPORT is used to create a large number of NDS users by importing information from another database.

13. **A, C, D.** The steps for running UIMPORT are (1) extract the data, (2) generate a control file, and (3) run UIMPORT against the data and control files.

14. **B.** NLS (NetWare License Services) provides a single administration point for NetWare and NetWare product licenses.

15. **C.** Users automatically inherit the rights that a container has.

Answers to Chapter 4 Self Test

1. **C.** The ability to share printers reduces costs, since multiple users can share a single resource.

2. **B.** A print server is a service that manages the print action.

3. **D.** The Print Queue Volume is the NetWare volume in which print jobs are stored before they are serviced.

4. **A.** The printer type should be Other/Unknown for printers connected to workstations, or for printers connected to network print devices.

5. **D.** The user installs the NetWare Client 32 that comes with NetWare 5, since it incorporates the NDPS client.

6. **A.** The Printer Agent acts like a legacy NetWare Print Queue, Print Server, and Printer all in one.

7. **B.** The Printer Gateway enables communication from the client to the non-NDPS printer.

8. **B, C, D.** RMS (Resource Management Service), ENS (Event Notification Service), and SRS (Service Registry Service) are all offered by the NDPS Broker.

9. **A.** RMS manages resources, including printer drivers, so that they can be downloaded and installed from a central location.

10. **D.** Typing **LOAD NWCONFIG** will start the NLM that can prompt for product installation, including that of NDPS.

11. **A, B, C.** The gateways included in the Printer Agent installation dialog reflect the corporations that collaborated on the NDPS creation: Hewlett-Packard, Novell, and Xerox.

12. **D.** Selecting the Resynchronize Database Files option will create a new index file from the database file when the option is executed.

13. **B.** Since the NDPS Broker is shared by the servers of both offices, if it went down, then no one could print in either office. The NDPS

Manager is separate on each server, so it could go down and affect a single office, leaving the other running fine.

14. **C.** The Spooling location property is the Printer object's storage area.

15. **C.** The Set Defaults button on the Printer Control Page of the NDPS Printer object properties in the NetWare Administrator will manage the default configuration that users will receive when connecting to that printer.

Answers to Chapter 5 Self Test

1. **B.** The volume is the largest storage unit, since it can span disks (which includes the NetWare partitions).

2. **C.** SYS: is the first volume created on each NetWare 5 server. It can be the only volume, or there can be multiple volumes.

3. **A, B, C, D.** All of these utilities can be used to manage the NetWare file system.

4. **A.** To display volume object information, the NLIST command is used with the VOLUME object type specified.

5. **A.** The NDIR command with the last accessed option /AC and the logical operator EQ for *equal to* and the value of the last accessed date will display all files accessed on that date.

6. **B.** The NDIR command can display directory space information when used with the /SPA switch.

7. **D.** NetWare's FILER utility can be used to undelete files by selecting the Salvage Deleted Files option.

8. **F.** The NetWare Administrator program has full file management features and can move, copy, rename, delete, and salvage files and directories.

9. **C.** Chris can use the NetWare Administrator to view the directory's properties and see if Restrict Size has been checked.

10. **D.** George can look at the Modifier and Modified Date Information, which are properties of the file in NetWare Administrator.

11. **D.** Joe can use the root feature of the MAP command with MAP R H:=THE_X/FILES:HOME*username.*

12. **D.** The MAP C option will change a regular drive to a search drive.

13. **B.** George should edit the home directory property in the User object so that it points at the new home directory name. He should also review the login script to verify that it is not using the old name, but is actually using the home directory property of the user.

14. **A.** Jan can select the Move radio button and dynamically change a copy command to a move command if it is executed in NetWare Administrator.

15. **C.** David can use the NetWare Administrator and restrict user space limits on the volume object for each user in the HQ container.

Answers to Chapter 6 Self Test

1. **E.** Any NDS object can be a trustee of a file or directory when granted access rights to it.

2. **C.** Rights granted to the [Public] trustee are available to any user, whether logged in or not.

3. **A.** Read Only is a file system attribute, not a trustee right. Read is a trustee right.

4. **D.** Inheritance is when a right flows down the directory structure.

5. **B.** The IRF (Inherited Rights Filter) controls inheritance.

6. **C.** Organizational Units that are parents of a User object offer an implied security equivalence, such that the rights granted the Organizational Unit are automatically granted to the child User object, but it does not show up in the Security Equal To property page.

7. **D.** Effective rights are those that are in effect for a given directory or file, and are calculated from rights inherited, filtered, granted explicitly, or through equivalence.

8. **D.** Aconat's effective rights are [RFECW] to the VOL1:DATA\DB directory.

9. **C.** Through inheritance, George has effectively granted any user access to the files that the business units have requested remain secure.

10. **D.** The Delete Inhibit attribute overrides the Erase trustee right.

11. **B.** The A (Archive Needed) flag is set automatically by NetWare to indicate that the file has changed since the last backup. This enables incremental and differential backups to select the files that have changed and then back them up.

12. **C.** When the Read Only attribute is set on a file, it automatically sets Delete Inhibit and Rename Inhibit.

13. **D.** The X attribute cannot be removed once it is set for a file.

14. **A.** The RIGHTS command can make a user a trustee of a file.

15. **C.** The N flag is used to flag files as "normal," which means that they have the read/write and shareable attributes.

Answers to Chapter 7 Self Test

1. **C.** The Container script executes first, then the Profile script, then the User script or the Default script if there is no user script.

2. **B.** The script will not execute because the User object is not in the correct container. Container scripts execute for users who are Child objects of the container.

3. **B.** Profile scripts are used for special purposes, such as location-specific or global scripts.

4. **D.** Gordon can assign the profile to each user's Login Script property page in the Profile script property.

5. **A.** User login scripts are difficult to maintain because there can be multiple scripts requiring changes whenever network resources change.

6. **D.** Jack cannot change the default script because it is compiled as part of the LOGIN executable.

7. **A.** The %LOGIN_CONTEXT variable represents the context that the User object belongs to.

8. **B.** Linda can use the variable called %HOME_DIRECTORY in a MAP command statement in the container login script and remove all the user scripts.

9. **C.** The MAP DISPLAY OFF command will hide the drive mappings as they execute in a login script. It does not work on the command line.

10. **C.** The pound sign, #, must be used to execute an external DOS command from a login script.

11. **C.** The DISPLAY command displays a text file in raw format.

12. **A.** The INCLUDE command with the context of the container will execute that container's script.

13. **B.** Using a profile script for testing prevents users from accidentally running an unproven script.

14. **C.** He can teach users to change the variables from the Variables button on the Script tab.

15. **B.** If using a different PHASERS.WAV file on the client workstation, the login script will execute that sound file, rather than the one that is issued with Client 32.

Answers to Chapter 8 Self Test

1. **C.** Z.E.N.works integrates with NDS to deliver desktop management.

2. **D.** Z.E.N.works does not provide teleconferencing.

3. **A.** Schema extensions can be cleared from a check box during Z.E.N.works installation.

4. **C.** Z.E.N.works can be installed to more than one tree simultaneously during installation, depending on the options selected by the installer.

5. **A, B, D.** Enterprises consider security, ease of use, and bandwidth when selecting a remote control solution.

6. **B.** Since Z.E.N.works uses workstation address information in NDS, the Remote Control Agent does not need to advertise.

7. **C.** WSRIGHTS grants users the correct rights to be able to register workstations into a container unit.

8. **B.** The WSREG32 executable is used to register NT workstations.

9. **C.** The workstation import policy must be created in a user policy package before the workstation can be imported.

10. **D.** Veronica can verify the success of a registration by viewing the C:\WSREG32.LOG file.

11. **A.** The NT Workstation's Remote Control Agent installation program is NTASCFG.EXE.

12. **B, C.** There is a remote control policy associated with user policy packages and another remote control policy associated with workstation policy packages.

13. **D.** The workstation and user policies for remote control may be different from each other. In this case, the more restrictive policy is used for the remote control security.

14. **A.** The Windows 3.1 Help Requester executable is SYS:PUBLIC\HLPREQ16.EXE.

15. **A.** The workstation logs into the network and launches the workstation registration application (WSREG16.EXE or WSREG32.EXE) to synchronize with NDS.

Answers to Chapter 9 Self Test

1. **D.** Application icons appear in a user's NAL window when they have been associated to a User object, a Group object for which that user is a member, or a parent container unit of the User object.

2. **B, C.** The application object must have the Windows 3.1 and Windows 4.0 options selected in its properties for it to appear in both. Those that are configured for Windows 3.1, but not Windows NT 4.0 will not appear. So Jay will only see the exact same applications if they have been configured for both operating systems.

3. **C.** The NetWare Administrator is used to configure applications for NAL. Under Windows NT, it is NWADMNNT.EXE.

4. **A.** NAL uses a wrapper technology that launches the OS-specific NAL executable after detecting which OS is running.

5. **D.** SNAPPSHOT is used to detect configuration changes after an application installs and then write them to a file.

6. **B.** The .AOT file is used to store configuration information that changes during application installation.

7. **B.** There are two discovery processes run for each application. One is run prior to

installation to establish a baseline; the second is run to determine what configuration changes have been made by the setup process.

8. **B.** FALSE. Simple applications do not require snAppShot to create an application object.

9. **D.** In an enterprise network where inheritance travels up the tree to the [Root], adding an application to the Applications property page of the Organization will enable it for lower level container objects.

10. **C.** The administrator can create an Application Folder object, then create folders in it and organize the Application objects within them.

11. **D.** The Application icon is controlled in the application object through the Application Icon button on the Identification property page.

12. **C.** George can show his client the Command Line Parameters property on the Environment page of the application object and then create Application objects for each custom switch required by the client.

13. **B.** The Show Distribution Progress property will display a progress bar during application execution. It is used to display the progress during an application distribution.

14. **A.** The execution command is @\\SERVER\SYS\PUBLIC\NAL /A=.APP.OU.O

15. **C.** The NAL /U! command executed on the command line will unload NAL but leave NAL-launched applications open.

Answers to Chapter 10 Self Test

1. **C.** The NetWare Administrator is used to manage the Workstation Manager NDS objects.

2. **A.** The NT desktop preferences policy exists within an NT User Package.

3. **B.** The default-polling schedule for the Workstation Manager client component is ten minutes.

4. **D.** The Novell client configuration policy can configure NetWare/IP.

5. **C.** The inventory of each workstation will appear in the Workstation Inventory property page of that object's details.

6. **C.** The NetWare client configuration information is not maintained in the workstation inventory.

7. **A.** The NT Desktop Preferences policy manages roaming profiles.

8. **C.** To use the TOM.POL file, Tom must create a 95-computer system policies policy with the remote update option pointing to TOM.POL.

9. **A.** The NT Actions policy had already executed the run-once option for the user, so it did not need to execute again. Taylor could have used the Workstation Package to ensure that the actions affected each workstation, not each user, a single time.

10. **C.** The difference in the number of workstation policy checkboxes is directly related to the numbers of actions added to the Workstation Policy Package. Each time a new action is added, another checkbox is added.

11. **C.** The difference in the number of workstation policy check boxes is directly related to the number of actions added to the Workstation Policy Package. Each time a new action is added, another check box is added.

12. **B.** Penny can put the switches into the Command Parameters box.

13. **C.** The 95 computer printer policy will configure a printer and print queue on Windows 95 workstations. There is not a 95-user printer policy currently.

14. **D.** The NetWare Settings button has an option within it to enable a banner page for a print queue.

15. **A.** The dynamic local user policy manags NT user accounts.

16. **C.** The Volatile User is removed from the local workstation accounts after the user logs out of the workstation.

Answers to Chapter 11 Self Test

1. **C.** NDS establishes security through the rights granted for each NDS object.

2. **B.** A trustee is an object that was granted rights to another object.

3. **A.** The Organizational Role object can contain multiple or rotating occupant objects, thereby facilitating applying the same rights to multiple users. A Group object can also be used this way.

4. **D.** The Read [R] right is not an object right. It is a property right.

5. **A.** The Create [C] right is not a property right. It is an object right.

6. **C.** George can grant the [B] object right of the Printer object to [Public].

7. **B.** The Browse right is granted to [Public] for the tree [Root].

8. **D.** The default property rights that a User object is granted to its own Login Script property are [RW]. These enable the user to read, modify, and execute the user login script.

9. **B.** Inheritance is the method through which rights flow down the NDS tree.

10. **A.** Security equivalence is the method through which an object is granted the same rights as another object's explicit trustee assignments.

11. **D.** The Inherited Rights Filter, or IRF, is used to block inherited rights from flowing down the tree.

12. **C.** The effective rights are the actual rights that an NDS object has when it is accessing another object.

13. **D.** The IRF is subtracted from the inherited rights when adding up all the rights that create the effective rights.

14. **C.** Although each of these options is a possibility, the most likely cause is that the users having problems had depended on their Security Equivalence to the user object that was changed for network access.

15. **A.** The four-step troubleshooting method does not include "Create a test security scenario."

Answers to Chapter 12 Self Test

1. **C.** FINANCE.SMITHNSON The full name includes the complete path from object back to the [Root] of the directory tree.

2. **D.** The Common Name is simply the object name.

3. **A, C.** Since the name has the complete path from the object back to the [ROOT] and it uses the attribute abbreviations, it is a Typeful Distinguished Name.

4. **A.** Notice first that the name has to start with a dot because it is a Distinguished Name. Second, because it is Typeless, you don't use the attribute abbreviations.

5. **B.** Use the .LXM_1024.EFGH.1234 name to access the resource. Using the complete name allows JFREDER to use the resource without changing her current context.

6. **B.** Move him to the HDQTRS container because he accesses resources primarily in that

container and this will place the user near the resources. Since the user is physically located in the Headquarters location and using resources primarily at that location, it makes the most sense to move him to the HDQTRS container.

7. **D.** There is no root login script.

8. **B.** **JDOE.MKTNG** is the correct answer since it leads up to the current context.

9. **B.** NetWare 5 introduces Contextless Login, which allows a user to log in regardless of their location in the directory tree.

10. **C.** Object context identifies the location of the object in the directory tree.

11. **A.** Organization can be directly under the [Root] object.

12. **A.** Since Bsmith shares the same current context at the HP_LJ_4, he is in the CLOTHING container.

13. **D.** Remember: Relative Distinguished Name + Current Context = Distinguished Name

14. **B.** The [Root] object is the entry point, or highest point in the directory tree.

15. **B.** A Country object is sometimes used directly below the [Root] to signify a location.

Answers to Chapter 13 Self Test

1. **B.** NetWare 5 has two installation interfaces: GUI and text-based.

2. **B, C, D.** By default the server installation program assigns a random Server ID Number per server; however, you can customize this number to fit your filter needs or registered numbers. This address is unique among all servers.

3. **D.** The default volume in NetWare is SYS:

4. **A.** By default NetWare creates only one partition.

5. **B.** The default block size for a hard disk of this size is 16K.

6. **C.** NetWare suballocation breaks blocks into 512-byte sections.

7. **A.** The default for file compression is enabled.

8. **A, B, C.** Data migration works with all three of these devices.

9. **A.** NetWare 5 uses Ethernet_II as its default frame type for TCP/IP.

10. **D.** NetWare 5 uses Ethernet 802.2 as its default frame type for IPX.

11. **B.** CDM stands for Custom Device Module.

12. **A.** HAM stands for Host Adapter Module.

13. **A, B, C, D, E.** As well as English.

14. **A.** The minimum processor for NetWare 5 is a 486/66.

15. **D.** A port value is a memory location associated with a hardware port.

16. **D.** A slot number identifies each piece of hardware.

17. **A, B, C, D.** A server name can be between 2 and 47 characters with dashes and underscores.

Answers to Chapter 14 Self Test

1. **B.** The in-place upgrade involves the installation of NetWare 5 on an existing server. The old system files are overwritten, and the bindery and file system are then upgraded into the NDS structure.

2. **B, C, D, E.** NetWare 2.*x* must be upgraded to NetWare 3.1*x* or NetWare 4.*x* before moving to NetWare 5.

3. **B, C.** Answers A and D are advantages of an across-the-wire migration.

4. **C.** If your existing server meets minimum requirements, this would be considered an advantage. Both A and B are disadvantages of an in-place upgrade.

5. **C.** The across-the-wire migration can take the bindery and file information from multiple servers and migrate them to another more powerful server that has had NetWare 5 already installed on it.

6. **D.** The Novell Upgrade Wizard is the graphical modeling and upgrade utility used to simplify the process of migrating a NetWare 3.1*x* server across the wire to a NetWare 5 server.

7. **A, C, D, E.** Answer B is incorrect. You do not have to migrate all the existing volumes at once. The Novell Upgrade Wizard gives you the opportunity to select individual volumes to migrate.

8. **A.** Extra hardware will be required. Since the across-the-wire method upgrades bindery and volume information to another server, new hardware is necessary.

9. **C.** A PS/2 or serial mouse is recommended but not required.

10. **E.** All of the items listed are software requirements before the upgrade process can begin. You will also need the Novell Client for DOS and Windows 3.1*x* if you will be accessing the installation files from the network.

11. **D.** UPGRDWZD.EXE is a self-extracting file that can be found in the directory \PRODUCTS\UPGRDWZD on the NetWare 5 Operating System CD-ROM.

12. **C.** All of the steps are for the in-place upgrade. However, you must first take down the server and exit to DOS.

13. **B.** The Novell Upgrade Wizard can be run from either a Windows 95 or Windows NT workstation.

14. **A.** You must run the verification process from the Project window to make sure that there will be no conflicts or errors during the migration. You will also have options available to you to correct any conflicts.

15. **D.** With the in-place upgrade, you reboot the server. But this occurs as the last step in the upgrade process, not as a post-upgrade task.

Answers to Chapter 15 Self Test

1. **C.** NetWare Administrator is used to manage and secure NDPS printing components.

2. **B.** The operator role has administrative control over the NDPS printer.

3. **A.** ENS (Event Notification Service), RMS (Resource Management Service), and SRS (Service Registry Service) are the services made available by the NDPS broker.

4. **D.** The NDPS Broker object stores its databases in the SYS:NDPS\RESDIR directory.

5. **B.** The NDPS manager must be created before an NDPS printer agent can be made available from a NetWare 5 server.

6. **B.** The Client for NetWare that comes with NetWare 5 is NDPS enabled.

7. **C.** A list of the printers and how they are used by end users will help determine which printers can be migrated to NDPS.

8. **D.** NDPS printers offer security through the use of NDS, automatic download of printer drivers, and management capabilities.

9. **B.** The schema does not need to be extended to include NDPS objects on a NetWare 5 network.

10. **C.** NDPS components and legacy print queue components can coexist on the same NetWare server.

11. **C.** The Novell Upgrade Wizard can be used to migrate existing legacy printing components to NDPS components on NetWare 5.

12. **B.** The Novell gateway can be used with any printer, especially if there is no third-party or applicable gateway available.

13. **D.** The NPRINTER.NLM program must be loaded on a server that is sharing its own printer on the network in the legacy network.

14. **C.** The NDPS Manager must be loaded on any server that is sharing out its own attached printer to the network through NDPS.

15. **A.** The best method of removing a print queue from a network is to disable the queue first; then later remove it from NDS, which automatically removes the queue directory.

Answers to Chapter 16 Self Test

1. **C.** DNS is not an option while customizing the server. It is, however, a tab in the Protocols section.

2. **A.** NetWare Operating System is where you can decide whether to load Console One.

3. **A.** Traditional NetWare volumes can exist only on traditional NetWare partitions.

4. **C.** The volume has to be mounted in order to be used.

5. **A, D.** When mounting volumes the two options available are mount immediately or mount when server reboots.

6. **B, D.** IPX and IP are the protocols that can be configured from the Protocols tab.

7. **A, B.** The IP address and subnet mask are required.

8. **A, B.** The frame type and network address are required. The network address may be detected automatically if there are other servers on the network.

9. **D.** DNS (Domain Name Service) resolves Internet names to IP addresses.

10. **C.** SNMP stands for Simple Network Management Protocol.

11. **C.** Since the volumes are not needed, you can mount the volumes after the server reboots.

12. **C.** NSS NetWare volumes can exist only on NSS NetWare partitions.

13. **A, B, C, D.** All of the above options are available.

14. **D.** Protocols is an option only on the main Customization window.

15. **D.** In order for a traditional volume to exist, a traditional partition must exist first.

Answers to Chapter 17 Self Test

1. **B.** NWCONFIG. This is the NetWare 5 software tool that allows you to add volumes.

2. **D.** Hot Fix. This technique redirects data to a reserved disk area, the Hot Fix.

3. **D.** Disk duplexing. This uses two disk controller cards.

4. **A, C.** The system-created directories are SYSTEM and PUBLIC.

5. **A.** SYS. SYS is the default volume created at install time.

6. **B, D.** The volume must be dismounted prior to running VREPAIR.

7. **A.** MAP ROOT. This can be used to create a virtual root.

8. **B.** It must have a NetWare partition.

9. **D.** 32. A partition can contain 32 volume segments.

10. **D.** Disk duplexing. This provides fault tolerance and best performance.

11. **A, C, D.** A volume cannot have an initial underscore character.

12. **A, D.** Both F10 and ESC allow you to save.

13. **C.** The ETC directory contains TCP/IP related files.

14. **A, B, C, D.** All of these are important to watch.

15. **B, C.** To create a volume, you must take space from the free space available and it must be on a NetWare partition.

Answers to Chapter 18 Self Test

1. **B.** The NetWare Console is the text equivalent to Console One.

2. **A.** The Console One utility is the graphic equivalent to NetWare Console.

3. **B, D.** RCONSOLE and RCONSOLEJ both allow for remote management of the server.

4. **A, B.** AUTOEXEC.NCF and STARTUP.NCF are the two main startup NCF files on a NetWare server.

5. **C.** The NWCONFIG.NLM file makes it easy to view and edit the NCF files.

6. **B.** RSPX has to be loaded at the server in order for RCONSOLE to function properly.

7. **D.** ALT-F1 will bring up the menu allowing you to choose which screen to view.

8. **B.** SECURE CONSOLE allows an administrator to disable the ability to load NLMs.

9. **C.** SCRSAVER locks the console when the screensaver kicks in.

10. **A.** Java is a new language supported by NetWare for Internet and intranet application development.

11. **C.** Server Top is the graphical interface that administrators can use to manage a server.

12. **C.** The PUBLIC directory on the SYS: volume contains RCONSOLE.

13. **B.** UNLOAD is the command you type to unload an NLM from memory.

14. **D.** CTRL-ESC give you a list of available screens on a NetWare server.

15. **A.** ALT-ESC navigates through the screens on a NetWare server one at a time.

16. **A, B.** The NetWare EDITOR or any other text editor can be used to edit NCF files.

Answers to Chapter 19 Self Test

1. **B.** The minimum amount of RAM that a NetWare 5 server requires is 64MB.

2. **C.** Virtual memory is an extension of physical memory or RAM.

3. **D.** Garbage collection recovers memory for other processes to use on a NetWare 5 server.

4. **A.** SWAP ADD is the command used to create a swap file on a volume.

5. **A, B, C.** Swap files can be created on mounted or unmounted volumes, and can be

created on any volume on a NetWare 5 server, but only one per volume.

6. **B.** Disk thrashing occurs when there is a lot of swapping of data on a computer.

7. **C.** Packet receive buffers store data that has been received by the network card as packets but cannot be processed by the server.

8. **D.** The rule of thumb is to allocate at least two packet buffers for each workstation connected to the server.

9. **B.** Block suballocation uses 512-byte blocks to use hard drive space on a NetWare 5 server better.

10. **A.** File compression can be enabled after a server has been in use for a while and saves space by compressing files on the volume.

11. **B.** Packet burst allows a NetWare 5 server to send multiple packets at once as long as the server or client on the other end is also using packet burst.

12. **C.** Large Internet Packets allows a NetWare Server to communicate using packets larger than 576 bytes.

13. **A, C.** MONITOR and a SET statement will change this parameter.

14. **D.** NetWare 5 can access up to 4GB of RAM.

15. **A.** SET AVERAGE PAGE IN ALERT THRESHOLD = x is the correct SET statement to configure the server to display an alert if excessive swapping is occurring.

Answers to Chapter 20 Self Test

1. **B.** SMS is a suite of applications that includes the backup/restore program.

2. **E.** SMS will also back up your GroupWise Database.

3. **B.** No, this will cause data loss.

4. **A.** Full, all data is backed up during this session.

5. **B.** Read and File Scan are required; you must be able to scan the directory for the file and then read it.

6. **D.** Browse and Read rights are required; to back up NDS you must be able to browse and read the NDS information.

7. **C.** The purpose of NWBACK32 is to configure and send backup jobs to the host; this is your management interface for SMS.

8. **A, B, C.** A target is a workstation or server that is running the appropriate TSA that allows them to be backed up.

9. **A.** TSA stands for Target Service Agent. A TSA is loaded for each type of backup you want to do; for example, TSANDS for the NDS and TSA500 for the file system.

10. **A.** A host is a server running the backup/restore program with a tape drive. This is the server that all other data is backed up to.

11. **B.** You will need at least 1MB of space for error logs.

12. **D.** TSA500 will back up the file system.

13. **C.** TSANDS is the TSA for the NDS directory.

14. **C.** TSAPROXY will allow you to back up a Windows 95 or Windows NT workstation.

Answers to Chapter 21 Self Test

1. **A.** DNS stands for Domain Name Service.

2. **B.** DNS resolves Internet names to IP addresses.

3. **D.** DHCP assigns an IP and IP configuration to the client.

4. **A, B, D.** The first three must be done to complete the installation of DNS/DHCP services.

5. **A, C, D.** These options are the ones you can use to install these services.

6. **C.** DHCP stands for Dynamic Host Configuration Protocol.

7. **B.** The location is on the SYS: volume under PUBLIC, DNSDHCP.

8. **B, C.** The two options are from NWADMIN32 and the desktop.

9. **A.** The DHCP Server object should be created first to tie the other objects together in the tree properly.

10. **A, B.** The files have to be in DHCP 2.0 or 3.0 format.

11. **A, B, C.** IP3.INT is not a zone.

12. **C.** You must authenticate yourself in order to create the objects in NDS.

13. **B.** IPX/SPX was the only protocol that supported NCP until NetWare 5, which supports IP natively.

14. **D.** The Domain Name Service resolves URLs to their IP addresses.

15. **D.** DHCP (Dynamic Host Configuration Protocol) allows for automatic IP configuration of a client workstation by the server.

Answers to Chapter 22 Self Test

1. **C.** Jack can run SETUP from the PRODUCTS\NOVONYX directory on the NetWare 5 CD-ROM.

2. **D.** The client must be Windows 95/8 or NT 4 running the NetWare Client 32 and have at least 100MB of free space on the hard drive.

3. **A.** 32MB of free hard disk space is not a minimum requirement of the target server for FastTrack Web Server installation.

4. **A.** The IP address of the server is required during installation.

5. **D.** FastTrack can be installed only into the root of the SYS: volume.

6. **B.** NSWEB typed at the server console will load the FastTrack Web Server.

7. **D.** **http://webster:11188** will start the administration page from a Web browser.

8. **A.** The Admin Preferences button contains an option to limit the workstations that may access the administration server.

9. **C.** NT Domain is not an option for providing users and groups for the FastTrack Web Server.

10. **A.** LDIF, or LDAP Data Interchange Format, is the required file format for importing into the FastTrack Web Server database.

11. **B.** The alias is created to be used in association with a key pair and certificate.

12. **C.** When configuration changes on the administration server, all servers within the cluster are affected.

13. **D.** PING will help determine whether connectivity exists between client and server.

14. **C.** Gil should check to see whether the FastTrack Web Server is running.

15. **A, B, C, D.** All of these.

Answers to Chapter 23 Self Test

1. **A, B, D.** Object, property, and file system rights all make up the NetWare 5 security system.

2. **A.** Trustee assignments are the explicit rights granted to an object.

3. **A, B, D.** The only rights that can be blocked by the IRF are inherited rights.

4. **A, B, C, D.** All object rights can be blocked by the IRF.

5. **D.** The Inheritable right will allow a selected property to be inherited from a container.

6. **B.** Granting unneeded rights is considered a hole in NDS security.

7. **C.** The server can be managed separately for HR if there is an IRF for the Supervisor right on it.

8. **A.** An IRF of Browse and Read on the Organizational Role itself will prevent the occupants from changing its rights.

9. **C.** The file system administrator requires the Supervisor right to the server(s) being administered.

10. **D.** Placing an IRF of Browse on the Server object(s) will prevent other administrators from seeing the object in the NDS tree and being able to manage it.

11. **C.** Because the installer role is often provided by contracted, short-term CNEs, the installer User object should be given an expiration date.

12. **D.** The application installer will require the Create right in the container so that the installer may create Groups and Directory Map objects that will work in conjunction with the newly installed applications.

13. **A.** A Call Center does not require any NDS rights.

14. **D.** The rights required for a password administrator to the Password Management property are Compare, Read, Write, and Inheritable.

15. **C.** In this configuration, the partition administrators would require the Supervisor right to the SERVERS.WEST.ACME container.

Answers to Chapter 24 Self Test

1. **B.** The Directory contains program and data files. Files are not stored in the directory, although objects are created for files in NDS so that you can assign access rights to the files.

2. **D.** Partitions. In fact, NDS manager, the utility used to create and manage partitions, used to be called Partition Manager.

3. **A.** TRUE. In fact, it would be somewhat unusual to see a tree in which every container was in a separate partition.

4. **C.** For the container in the partition that is highest in the tree, closest to the [Root]. If partitions were named according to the other listed options, partition names would be even harder to associate with their partition.

5. **A.** Has a partition below it in the tree. As you probably remember, a partition that has a partition above it in the tree is called a child.

6. **D.** Replicas. There's no logical reason why copies of partitions are called replicas instead of one of the other options, but *replica* is a short word that serves the purpose.

7. **B, D.** Users can access a replica of a partition if the server that they usually get it from goes down. Users can access Directory information more efficiently if there is a replica containing the information that they need on a server that is close to them.

8. **B** Subordinate References. Objects in read-only replicas can be modified only by NDS once they are created, but an administrator still creates read-only replicas.

9. **A.** Loosely Consistent. Again, a seemingly arbitrary term, but an important one to learn.

10. **C.** Time Synchronization. Polling, as you've learned in other chapters, is part of the time synchronization process, but not the name of the process itself.

11. **B.** Do everything possible not to put replicas on both sides of a WAN link. Otherwise, the replicas will generate network traffic as they try to synchronize with each other.

12. **C.** Buy the best quality, brand-name hardware that your organization can reasonably afford. Not only will such hardware be more reliable, but it will be easier to find drivers for it.

13. **C.** The NDS database. After all, the NDS database may change more in a day than any of the other options listed.

14. **D.** MONITOR.NLM. The new version of MONITOR.NLM shows a lot of useful information.

15. **A.** Patch all servers on the network. All servers must be patched in order for Directory Services to be able to communicate properly, and the process of patching all servers does not happen automatically.

16. **C.** Typing the **Set DSTrace=On** command at the server command prompt, and toggling to the Directory Services screen using ALT-ESC. Once activated, the Directory Services screen will show you the NDS synchronization process as it is happening. Review the TTS$LOG.ERR file if you need to look at how synchronization was going hours or days ago.

17. **D.** A User can log in on only one workstation at a time. The number of workstations that a user can log in to at one time is set by the network administrator, and is not a sign of a problem with NDS.

18. **B.** Check the tree again in a couple of days. If the strange objects are still there, use one of the

repair utilities provided with NetWare. Objects with strange names will sometimes show up temporarily in the tree, but if they persist beyond a couple of days, they likely represent a problem with the NDS database that should be repaired.

19. **C.** NDS Manager and DSREPAIR. Partition Manager is an old name for what is now called NDS Manager. DSSTATUS does not exist, as far as I know.

20. **A, D.** NDS Manager and DSREPAIR are the most commonly used NDS repair utilities. Oddly, not many third parties have shown an interest in developing NDS repair utilities.

21. **B.** After backing up the Directory, at a time that not many users are logged in. Since an Unattended Full Repair has a remote possibility of corrupting objects, it should be run only after backing up the Directory. Also, since the Directory will be locked and inaccessible during part of the process, you should run the Unattended Full Repair only when there are as few users logged in as possible.

22. **A.** You should use NDS Manager to promote a read/write replica to master. An uncorrupted master replica is necessary for changing partition boundaries, and NDS will not promote an uncorrupted replica to master automatically.

23. **C.** By running NDS Manager from a working server, and clicking on the downed server's icon. This is the easiest choice unless you truly have a photographic memory.

Answers to Chapter 25 Self Test

1. **B.** The two ways in which a mobile client connects to a network are as a remote node or remote control.

2. **D.** The most suitable use for a remote control workstation is when applications or databases are located on the network.

3. **C.** The four options available from NetWare Connect are ARAS, PPPRNS, NCS, and RAMA.

4. **D.** RAMA is used for managing the NetWare Connect Server over SNMP.

5. **A.** Dial-Up Networking creates a remote node connection over PPP.

6. **B.** The Win2NCS software is used by Windows network workstations to dial out of the network using a NetWare Connect server's pool of modems.

7. **D.** NWCCON.NLM is the server's Remote Access Configuration program.

8. **B.** The ARAS client software can be obtained from Apple.

9. **A.** When NWCCON loads for the first time, it prompts for a user ID that has sufficient rights to extend the NDS schema.

10. **D.** The default modem configuration is 8 data bits, no parity, and 1 stop bit.

11. **C.** Ports should be modified when modems require troubleshooting.

12. **A.** Security can limit the times that mobile clients are allowed to connect.

13. **D.** No option in NWCCON will affect the configuration of multiple servers.

14. **D.** In order to verify server settings, an administrator can generate a configuration report from NWCCON.

15. **C.** The Idle timeout value of the Remote Access property page for a container object will be inherited by all users in that container.

Answers to Chapter 26 Self Test

1. **A, B, C.** The three items that are needed are two or more clients, a transmission medium, and rules.

2. **B.** Synchronized is not a computer networking model.

3. **B.** Centralized computing uses mainframes.

4. **A.** A LAN is usually for a small company and does not exceed 10 kilometers.

5. **C.** The protocols set the rules for successful communication.

6. **B, C.** Server centric and peer-to-peer are the two distinct network services categories.

7. **A, B, D.** The three types of storage in file services are online, offline, and nearline.

8. **D.** Nearline storage includes CD-ROM carousels.

9. **B.** Print services give us the ability to fax and copy.

10. **C.** Message services allow for video and audio to be transferred across the network.

Answers to Chapter 27 Self Test

1. **C.** Insinuation is not one of the factors; attenuation is.

2. **B.** Attenuation is what happens when the signal gets weaker as it travels along the media.

3. **A.** UTP has a distance limit of 100 meters.

4. **C, E.** CAT4 and CAT5 both support data transmission at 20MBps.

5. **D.** Copper makes up the conductor in coaxial cable.

6. **B.** 50 ohm RG-58 is used for Thin Ethernet.

7. **D.** Fiber has an inner core of plastic or glass.

8. **A.** Radio wave transmission falls into the 10 KHz to 1 Ghz range.

9. **B.** RJ-45 is used with twisted-pair cabling.

10. **D.** A modem is used to change a digital signal to analog.

Answers to Chapter 28 Self Test

1. **A.** The ISO, or International Organization for Standards created the OSI (Open Systems Interconnection) reference model.

2. **B.** Multiple protocol layers stack upon each other to create a single network communication. This is called a protocol stack.

3. **D.** The correct order of the OSI protocol reference model is Application, Presentation, Session, Transport, Network, Data Link, and Physical.

4. **D.** A multipoint connection enables multiple devices to share the same media.

5. **C.** The physical topology of a network can be a star, ring, bus, mesh, or cellular.

6. **A.** Encoding data results in it being sent in a digital format.

7. **C.** Manchester, as well as Differential Manchester, is a form of biphase encoding.

8. **C.** FSK, or frequency shift keying, will shift the frequency from a faster rate to a slower rate in order to specify a 1 bit or 0 bit.

9. **C.** Any encoding scheme that includes a guaranteed state change per bit time is self-clocking.

10. **A.** Broadband transmissions allow multiple data conversations on the same media.

11. **D.** StatTDM, or Statistical Time Division Multiplexing, will dynamically allocate time slots to conversation, using a control field to identify the owner of the data.

12. **B.** The two logical topologies are ring or bus.

13. **A.** Ethernet uses CSMA/CD, or carrier sense multiple access with collision detection to access the media.

14. **C.** An Ethernet MAC address is 6 bytes in length.

15. **A.** The separate device used for clocking in isochronous transmissions is the single point of failure for the network.

Answers to Chapter 29 Self Test

1. **C.** The Network and Transport protocol layers are the middle layers of the OSI reference model.

2. **B.** FALSE. The Network layer is responsible for moving data across an entire internetwork.

3. **D.** The Network layer is responsible for routing, and uses a unique network address to identify the different networks on an internetwork.

4. **A.** The service address, or port, is used to identify the destination process on the destination node.

5. **D.** Circuit switching uses a virtual circuit on the network and keeps it open for the duration of a data conversation.

6. **B.** Packet switching uses small, variable-length segments or packets of data that are sent from switch to switch in RAM.

7. **B.** A tick lasts 1/18 of a second and is a measurement of time for routing.

8. **D.** Both distance vector and link state are types of routing protocols.

9. **B.** The Network layer will perform the CRC each time the data crosses a router, since the header information changes with the new addressing information for the next hop.

10. **C.** A gateway performs protocol translation between two disparate protocol stacks at the Network layer or above.

11. **D.** Reliability at the Transport layer means that data transmissions are acknowledged by the receiver and retransmissions are requested if errors occur.

12. **A.** A connection identifier, or port, identifies the data conversation.

13. **C.** A workstation uses address/name resolution to determine the address for a network device when it knows only the device's name.

14. **B.** A sequence number is used to reassemble segments into messages in the correct order.

15. **C.** At the Transport layer, the CRC is performed only at the sending and receiving devices.

Answers to Chapter 30 Self Test

1. **C.** The end user perceives the network through the upper layers.

2. **B.** FALSE. When the Session layer establishes a connection, it is transparent to the path that the data travels over the network.

3. **A.** Simplex communication requires only one receiver and one transmitter device.

4. **C.** Full-duplex communication provides for simultaneous bidirectional data transmission.

5. **A.** Session layer dialog data transfer depends on the nonreceipt of acknowledgments at lower layers for dialog interruptions in order to notify upper layers.

6. **B.** Transfer syntax is another term for data formatting at the Presentation layer.

7. **B.** Bit-order translation is the agreement of the sender and receiver to read data from either the first or last bit of each received byte.

8. **C.** Encryption is used to secure data at the Presentation layer.

9. **A, B, C, D.** Electronic messaging, network management, virtual terminal, and file transfer are all examples of services offered at the Application layer.

10. **D.** OS Call Interception enables non-network-aware applications to access network services.

Answers to Chapter 31 Self Test

1. **A.** It is the responsibility of the IS manager to act as a representative of the company when dealing with other companies in this fashion.

2. **B.** The Resource List contains all of the resources that are part of the network. This includes old and new servers, printers, and other devices that provide services to the users of the network.

3. **D.** This is the responsibility of the IS manager. Sometimes the IS manager will ask for input from other members of the team such as the NDS Expert, who typically serves as the Team Leader. There is no such thing as the Integration Expert in the NetWare Design and Implementation model.

4. **A.** It is the responsibility of the Server Specialist to ensure that there is enough storage space for the applications. The Server Specialist could have avoided this by following the specifications set forth by the Testing Lab Coordinator. There is no such thing as a Resource Specialist in the NetWare Design and Implementation model.

5. **C.** The Resource List would have the necessary server information recorded to determine which file servers needed to be upgraded. There is no such thing as a Server List in this model.

6. **B.** The LAN Topology is a diagram of the existing network.

7. **D.** The Resource List contains the number and types of workstations on the network.

8. **A.** These steps are performed in the Project Approach phase.

9. **A.** The Project Approach phase determines what the resulting network will consist of and the services it will provide.

10. **A.** This would be an issue that would be covered in the Implementing an NDS Implementation.

11. **A, D.** Only A and D are correct answers. You must design a time synchronization strategy for any type of WAN, and a team can have as few as one member taking on all of the roles.

12. **A.** One of the steps during the designing of the NDS tree is to draft a Naming Standards document.

13. **A.** The next step is Planning the User Environment. For the exam, it is very important to know the phases and procedures of the NetWare NDS Design Cycle process.

14. **D.** Designing the NDS tree properly helps you set up NDS so that it works efficiently, is easy for network users to use, is easy for administrators to manage, and can be merged if needed. It also lays a foundation for successful completion of determining a Partition and Replica Strategy.

Answers to Chapter 32 Self Test

1. **D.** An engineer can define network solutions whenever a need for the solution is apparent.

2. **A, D.** The two possibilities that can result when an incorrect solution is presented is that it is rejected, or if accepted it will fail at implementation.

3. **C.** The only information that will not affect a network solution would be the names of every employee.

4. **B.** The five areas that should be identified in a NetWare 5 solution include NDS tree, servers, workstations, applications, and printers. This does not prevent the inclusion of other factors

such as redundancy, although they would appear as a component of an area, such as servers.

5. **A, B.** The target end date and person assigned to the task, as well as the percentage of completion should be added to the task description and start date for each task in the schedule.

6. **D.** The next step is to create the lab.

7. **D.** When there are two separate groups—one project, the other operations—the operations team will need to be educated on the new support requirements in order to maintain operations.

8. **C, D.** The Cost Benefit Analysis and Risk Assessment should be created after the solution is defined and schedule created.

9. **D.** Any engineer or administrator will need to sell a network solution to management and decision makers, regardless of their position in or outside the enterprise.

10. **B.** The first step to launch the design and implementation is to organize the team and educate them.

Answers to Chapter 33 Self Test

1. **C.** Naming standards are the definitions of the names used for network resources.

2. **B.** With the exception of servers, multiple objects can have the same common name, but not the same Distinguished name.

3. **D.** NDS TREE is not an acceptable tree name because tree names cannot include spaces.

4. **C.** The administrator can rename the OU and select Create Alias in Place of Renamed Container to facilitate the change for users.

5. **D.** All NetWare servers must have unique names.

6. **A.** The default naming standard for Workstation Import Policies is the concatenation of Computer with Network Address.

7. **A.** TRUE. When designing the upper layers of the NDS tree, if any future additions or moves of the enterprise are known, they should be incorporated into the design.

8. **C.** Country objects are placed above the Organization object, directly beneath the [Root].

9. **D.** The optimal design for the first layer of OIs is PHX, DET, and BOS.

10. **B.** No, this is not an optimal design because the users are not located in the tree next to the resources that they use.

Answers to Chapter 34 Self Test

1. **D.** The Container. A container is an object representing an organization, organizational unit, or group in the NDS database that is used to group and organize User, Printer, and other objects.

2. **C.** Horizontally. The vertical arrangement that NetWare Administrator uses works well for showing long lists of objects below the containers, while the horizontal arrangement on a planning diagram makes it easy to see the logical places to partition the tree.

3. **B.** NetWare creates the first three replicas, but you can use NDS Manager to create more than three, if appropriate.

4. **D.** Geographic placement and workgroup organization. These are always the starting points, because they logically divide the company by WAN link and function. Resources common to locations and workgroups can then be grouped in the same partition for efficient access and management.

5. **D.** Partitioning actually creates more network traffic, because replicas will be created for each new partition. As the replicas communicate with each other to synchronize, more network traffic will be generated.

6. **B, D.** Transitive synchronization uses an IP/IPX server as a translator for IP-only and IPX-only servers as they synchronize, and allows servers to "check in" for updates from a specified server instead of contacting every other server holding a replica of that partition.

7. **C.** The NDS inactivity synchronization interval. Yep, you have to memorize it. It might show up on the exam. In fact, you might even have to type it out.

8. **A.** SET WAN TRAFFIC NANAGER=ON might sound like it would work, but is not an actual step in enabling the WAN Traffic Manager. SET commands generally enable something that is already loaded with the main parts of NetWare. Since WTM is not something that everyone will use, its functionality was put into an NLM so as not to use memory unless really needed by that particular server.

9. **D.** Secondary time server. A secondary time server is still a time server, in that it provides time to the workstations on the LAN, but relative to the other types of NetWare time servers, it is considered a time consumer, because it never provides time information to another NetWare server.

10. **A.** Network Time Protocol. This is an open standard that can be used by any network operating system that uses the IP protocol.

11. **C.** Peer. A peer is somewhat akin to a primary time server under the standard NetWare time synchronization setup, since its main role is to provide time to other servers while still being able to adjust its clock after consulting with other time sources.

12. **A, B.** Novell's recommendation is that you set up a custom time scheme if the network has any

WAN links or grows beyond 30 servers. With the advances in WAN-link technologies, and the greater speeds of modern WAN links, this recommendation may be amended in the near future.

13. **A.** On a server that is in the geographical center of the network. What you're really shooting for is a position that is central to the other servers in terms of the time that it takes for a signal to go from the central point outwards to the remote servers. If your network is made up of similar hardware in every part of the network, then the geographical center of your network is usually also the temporal center of your network.

14. **A.** SAP (Service Advertising Protocol). The alternative is to set up a custom configuration in the MONITOR utility, where servers will communicate time information directly to specified servers.

15. **D.** By using the MONITOR utility. In NetWare 5, most of the parameters that used to be set in the SERVMANutility are now set in the MONITOR utility.

Answers to Chapter 35 Self Test

1. **C.** Create an accessibility needs analysis document

2. **D.** Local printer. A local printer does not need to be considered when planning access to networked devices.

3. **B.** 16. a NetWare 5 server can support up to 16 containers with Bindery context.

4. **A.** TRUE. This will allow for easier administration of users and resources.

5. **C.** The [Root]. Rights received from the [Root] object flow through the entire tree.

6. **D.** None. A password administrator does not have any file system rights.

7.

A.) Someone who dials into the LAN and uses resources in their home container?	**R,** A person who dials into and accesses only information in his/her local container is considered a local user and has little impact on the NDS design.
B.) Someone who dials into the LAN for e-mail?	**R,** Someone who only dials in to check e-mail is a remote user, they have no special impact on the NDS design past the initial remote user NDS object creation.
C.) Someone who travels to multiple sites and uses a local computer to access local information?	**M,** If you have users that travel to different locations or need access to information in different containers, this person is considered a Mobile user.
D.) In IS staff engineer that supports several hundred users in a multicontext environment?	**M,** If you have users that travel to different locations or need access to information in different containers, this person is considered a Mobile user.

Answers to Chapter 36 Self Test

1. **B.**   The Geographical model is suited to companies that use locations as the separation for their workgroups.

2. **C.**   A bindery context can be set for up to 16 containers.

3. **B.**   Assigning an individual, group, or container Supervisor rights to a Server object

will give them Supervisor rights to the server's file system.

4. **B.**   In NetWare, the NDS Manager is used to manage partitions. Early versions of Netware 4 had this functionality implemented into the Netware Administrator, but it was split off to a separate application later.

5. **B.**   To move a container, you must make it the top level of a partition using NDS Manager and you can then move it, also using NDS Manager.

6. **C.**   By default, the first server gets the master partition of [Root], the second and third servers get read/write partitions, and every server after that gets none.

7. **A.**   For small networks with no external time source, install one server as a single reference and the rest as secondary.

8. **A.**   If you want to install a network with primary servers, it is recommended that you use at least two primary servers. If you do not have enough servers to warrant multiple primaries, you should use the single reference model.

9. **B, C.**   Only primary and reference servers participate in voting. A single reference server assumes there are no other servers, and secondary servers do not vote.

10. **B.**   By default, Novell servers use SYS:SYSTEM\TIMESYNC.CFG for settings for time synchronization

11. **A.**   NetWare uses the SYS:ETC\NTP.CFG to configure NTP.

12. **A.**   Partitions of the source tree maintain their structure and are joined to the target under [Root]. The [Root] on the source tree is deleted.

13. **B.**   FALSE. There can be no Leaf objects at the [Root] of the source tree when two trees are merged. They must either be deleted or moved into containers.

14. **B.** Use the INSTALL NLM (NWCONFIG for NetWare 5) to install NetWare services for Macintosh, under product options.

15. **B.** All lines above except C are used by the DOS Requester.

Answers to Chapter 37 Self Test

1. **A, C.** Novell's Web site and Support Connection CD contain patches for NetWare. The Norton Utilities and Ontrack Data Recovery for NetWare are simply utilities and do not contain patches for NetWare.

2. **A, D.** You will find patches and AppNotes on the Support Connection CD. For the latest patches, always check the Novell Web site first and for hardware information, turn to the Support Source.

3. **C.** Novell NetWire on CompuServe is where you can ask questions that are answered by a group of veteran sysops and other knowledgeable CompuServe enthusiasts in the Novell Forums.

4. **B.** IBM manufactures servers that can run NetWare. The names of customers who had specific problems are not given in the TIDs. The Novell Labs Bulletin reports on tests performed on third-party products by Novell engineers, and you will see the names of many different manufacturers here.

5. **B.** This is the entire five-step troubleshooting model.

6. **E.** This is a bit of a trick question. Novell recommends static-shielding bags, not antistatic bags. Static-shielding bags have a metallic grey-silver look to them. Your best bet here is the packaging they came in. The manual emphasizes that antistatic bags and static-shielding bags are not the same. Static-shielding bags are the proper bags for

transporting and storing components, and are usually tinted gray-silver.

7. **D.** Go Netwire.

8. **A, B.** IRQ and memory problems are the two most common problems with network clients.

9. **A, D.** Only A and D are directly available on NetWire. The steps to becoming a CNE (CNE progress charts) are available on the Novell Web site and most, not all, of the Novell product manuals are found on the Novell Web site.

10. **A, C.** FTP: (ftp.novell.com) and WWW: (http://support.novell.com).

11. **D.** You navigate the Novell Web site like any other Web site by clicking on hyperlinks.

12. **D.** Remember, Novell's Web page has the most up-to-date patches. Support Source does not have the patches; NDS for NT is simply a Novell product; and Novell's Support Connection CD may not have the latest.

13. **D, E.** Support Source is your number-one tool for hardware problems and issues.

14. **D.** This is one URL you should never forget.

15. **A.** The GO button is used to navigate to CompuServe forums and services.

16. **B.** Computer components can be destroyed with as little as 20 volts of electricity.

17. **A, B, C.** All of these items are benefits of an ESD program.

Answers to Chapter 38 Self Test

1. **A, B, D.** Answer C is the only one here that would be incorrect. By default, Token Ring addresses are burned in at the factory and are unique. Even though some cards allow the node address to be set by software, this is not an option as far as the test is concerned.

2. **A.** COMCHECK tests only for physical communications between nodes; it has no other functions.

3. **C.** 10 meters is the only correct answer here. 10BaseT cable must be between 0.6 meters (2 feet) and 100 meters (328 feet).

4. **B.** An I/O port is an address the CPU uses to send and receive data from.

5. **C.** DMA channels are used for direct access to system RAM. This allows for greater speeds in memory transfers between devices such as NICs and system memory.

6. **A, C.** PCI is today's standard for bus designs in PCs.

7. **D.** While ATM can be run on fiber-optic cable, it can also be used over copper. Answer B describes FDDI and many different protocols that can run over fiber-optics, which discounts Answer C.

8. **B.** Don't forget this important fact: once the station has received the token, the two bits are flipped and returned to the sending station.

9. **C.** The only purpose of the RI and RO ports is to connect two MSAUs together. The other answers are simply meaningless.

10. **B.** Of the technologies listed, FDDI is the only one not susceptible to electrical interference.

11. **D.** This is one of the most common problems with drivers not loading correctly.

12. **C.** Of the cable types listed, only RG-58A/U meets the IEEE specification for 10Base2.

13. **A.** A is the only incorrect answer here. FDDI boards are still expensive compared to other types.

14. **A.** For a "jumperless" network card, you must first install the card into the computer, boot the computer, and then run the software to configure the card. There is no such thing as a terminator on a network card and the node address is "burned in" at the factory.

15. **B.** Memorize the types of coax cable specified for 10Base2 and 10Base5.

Answers to Chapter 39 Self Test

1. **D.** Most SCSI problems are due to devices not having their address set correctly or terminated correctly.

2. **C.** This error message could indicate that the drive and SCSI adapter are set to the same device number. The adapter is typically set to 7. The first SCSI device is set to 0.

3. **A.** A NetWare volume can have up to 32 segments over multiple drives.

4. **A.** Deciding device position on the bus.

5. **D.** A wide SCSI bus can handle up to 15 devices, 16 including the controller. Remember, the controller requires an ID, too.

6. **D.** CD9660.NSS would be the only one that would work. Answer A is close; however, quotation marks are not used in this command.

7. **A.** This error message is a dead giveaway that the hard drive is jumpered incorrectly.

8. **C.** Remember, you cannot use anything but a 40 pin, 18-inch or shorter cable on a IDE drive.

9. **A.** 0 is used for no device or a SCSI drive.

10. **B.** Type 47 is reserved for user-defined types.

11. **B.** If your boot device is a SCSI drive, you must have a controller with a BIOS that can support boot devices.

12. **B.** The CMOS battery is dead and all of the CMOS settings have been lost. Replace the battery and reconfigure the CMOS.

13. **D.** All ribbon cables that are used on hard drives use a red or similar marker to denote Pin 1.

14. **A, B, C.** Cabling such as length, SCSI addressing, and the termination placement and/or type all play a role in the design of the SCSI bus.

15. **A.** Most SCSI controllers default to a SCSI ID of 7. You can change this value on most adapters but it is not recommended.

16. **B, C.** CDROM drives are much slower than a hard drive and hence can slow down access to the other devices located on the SCSI bus.

17. **A, D.** Like hard drives, IDE CDROMs require their master/slave parameters to be set, and LOAD CD9660.NSS is used to mount the volume.

18. **B.** 40 pin connectors are used with IDE type drives. Remember this!

19. **C.** The Hot Fix area is an area set aside on the NetWare partition for dynamically moving information from bad sectors on the disk to known good areas on the disk.

20. **D.** CDROM under NetWare 5 loads only CD9660.NSS and CDHFS.NSS; it provides no other functionality.

Answers to Chapter 40 Self Test

1. **C.** Setting LASTDRIVE=Z in the CONFIG.SYS file will allow the client PC to use all 26 drive letters from A: to Z:.

2. **D.** The Watchdog feature is a technique whereby the server will send packets to the workstation. After several unsuccessful attempts, the server will determine that the workstation is inactive and disconnect it from the network.

3. **C.** TRACK ON is used to display network connection information. It can be used as a substitute for a sniffer.

4. **C.** The AUTOEXEC.NCF is one of the server console's boot files. It contains the SET parameters.

5. **A.** A broadcast packet will have all Fs in the node address field.

6. **C.** VLM, or Virtual Loadable Module, is the NetWare DOS Requester program that sits in RAM as a TSR on the client PC. It manages traffic and redirects local versus network requests.

7. **D.** The correct load order is LSL.COM, NIC driver, IPXODI.COM, and VLM.EXE.

8. **D.** NET.CFG is the configuration file read by the executable network programs LSL.COM, the NIC driver, IPXODI.COM, and VLM.EXE.

9. **A.** The default location is \NWCLIENT on C: drive.

10. **B.** The Remote Boot feature allows a diskless workstation to connect to the network.

11. **C.** Conventional memory ranges from 0 to 640K.

12. **D.** AUTOEXEC.BAT. Look here first because STARTNET.BAT is called from AUTOEXEC.BAT. It may be REMarked out.

13. **A.** Ethernet 802.2 is the default frame type for NetWare 4.*x*.

14. **D.** HIMEM.SYS is the device driver needed for HMA and XMS.

15. **A.** XMS or Extended Memory ranges from 1MB to 4GB.

Answers to Chapter 41 Self Test

1. **A, B, C.** All three of these objects are required to initiate network printing.

2. **B.** If you cannot printer through the network, attach the printer to a local printer port and print locally.

3. **A, B.** Both are required. A volume contains the directory in which the print jobs will reside until printed.

4. **B.** Auto Load. This must be set if the printer is attached to the print server. Otherwise, if set to Manual Load, the printer will not print.

5. **B, C.** NPTWIN95 is the Window-based version of NPRINTER. NPRINTER must be loaded on the workstation.

6. **B.** CAPTURE will redirect the LPT port.

7. **D.** PSERVER must be loaded.

8. **A.** The job could be on hold. PSERVER runs on a server. CAPTURE and NPRINTER run on a workstation.

9. **A, B, C.** These will all show the print queue where a job has been sent.

10. **A.** Manual Load must be set and then NPRINTER needs to be loaded on the workstation that has the printer attached to it.

11. **A.** They go to a print queue, which is a directory used to temporarily store the print requests.

12. **A.** CAPTURE 's default port is the parallel port named LPT1.

13. **A, B.** Use good quality ribbons and check printer messages.

14. **A.** Your workstation could be generating graphics that could slow the printing process. Add more RAM either at the workstation or the printer.

15. **B.** NPRINT prints documents.

Answers to Chapter 42 Self Test

1. **C.** Obtain, test, and apply all applicable product and driver updates. Novell Support requires that product testing and debugging be performed on a fully patched version of the system.

2. **D.** Static, semi-static, and dynamic. Static patches are permanently applied to the server

executable, while semi-static and dynamic patches are loaded after the server is started.

3. **C.** DSK drivers. NetWare 5 requires all disk drivers to use the NWPA specification.

4. **C.** NMI errors. NMI errors are hardware related and will always result in a complete server shutdown. The paging architecture of the Intel processor allows NetWare 4.11 and 5 to fix either page faults or exception errors.

5. **B.** The number of threads that have been stopped since the server was started. If additional abends occur, this number will increment for each thread that is terminated.

6. **A.** Preemptive multitasking. NetWare 5 can take control of the processor, regardless of the state of any processes running in the system.

7. **A.** Disk I/O. In this environment, the single IDE drive is attempting to service all read/write requests. Implementing RAID on a bus-mastering controller would undoubtedly improve overall network performance.

8. **C.** Improve overall network performance, by reducing CPU overhead. Bus-mastering devices can free up the system processor from managing bus operations.

9. **C.** Receive all packets on the wire. Novell's LANalyzer requires a network card and driver that support promiscuous mode to allow the analyzer to capture and review all network traffic.

10. **C.** The new Internet connection. A sudden increase in traffic after the addition of a new service or application is probably not coincidental.

11. **A.** Use VREPAIR and invoke the Remove Name Space option. This is the only method to safely remove name space from a volume.

12. **C.** Perform repairs on directory service partitions and replicas. DSREPAIR allows us to fix and resynchronize the directory service

database, its partitions, and the replicas of each partition.

13. **D.** All of the above. A comprehensive disaster recovery plan should provide step-by-step procedures to follow for all of these tasks.

14. **B.** Hung Unload Wait Time. When an NLM is unloaded, the NetWare 5 operating system will wait the specified amount of time and then prompt the administrator to shut down the address space in use by the application.

15. **D.** High network traffic. Fragment errors are most commonly caused by Ethernet collisions, as a result of high network utilization.

Answers to Chapter 43 Self Test

1. **D.** User Manager. Remember that User Manager is the Windows NT Workstation and Server (nondomain controllers) version, and that User Manager for Domains is the Windows NT Server version for domain controllers.

2. **B.** A hierarchically structured database. It replaced the myriad of INI and CFG files used in Windows 3.1 and Windows for Workgroups 3.11.

3. **A.** 4MB of RAM. Even though most documentation states that 16MB is a recommended minimum, remember that the Microsoft / Novell stated minimum hardware requirements is 4MB.

4. **C.** Event Viewer. Remember the keyword is *event*, which includes application events, system events, and security events.

5. **B.** Windows 95. DOS applications are legacy applications. DOS aplications will run under Windows NT as long as they don't make any direct hardware calls. While Windows for

Workgroups 3.11 could work in this scenario, the question asks about current technology.

6. **C.** WinLogon. You must be able to differentiate between Novell terminology and Microsoft terminology. Novell uses *log in*, whereas Microsoft calls it *log on*.

7. **C.** Server Manager. While the Control Panel is used to configure a computer, it is not used to configure a computer connected to the domain. The My Computer icon is used to locate file resources on the local computer. User Manager for Domains may sound right, but it is used to administer accounts rather than configure computers.

8. **A, C.** Admin is a Novell administration account. While Guests may seem correct, the Guest account is not plural. You will need to look carefully at questions on the exam to avoid falling into this type of trick question.

9. **D.** Unlimited. Windows NT Workstation can handle only 10 inbound concurrent connections, but since Windows NT Server *is* a server operating system, it is built to handle as many connections to it as you can make.

10. **A.** WinLogon -> LSA -> SAM -> LSA -> WinLogon. You will need to remember the correct order for the examination.

11. **C.** You install Windows NT Workstation without networking capabilities. This account is not present with Windows NT Server.

12. **B.** HKEY_LOCAL_MACHINE. You must remember what each Registry key is used for.

13. **A.** Disk Administrator. Server Manager may seem like the correct choice, but it is not used to modify the hard disk format.

14. **B.** Windows NT Workstation. While Windows NT Server can be used as a client operating system, this is not desirable due to the cost involved. Windows 95 does not allow for file-level security.

15. **A.** Preemptive multitasking. Remember that cooperative multitasking leaves the decision to give up processor time to the application.

Answers to Chapter 44 Self Test

1. **D.** 400MB. Even though newer versions of FAT, such as FAT32, can handle up to 4GB of storage on a partition, the Novell examination tests you on the original FAT.

2. **B.** Workgroup model. While the workgroup model is based on the peer-to-peer networking model, the correct answer is workgroup.

3. **C.** NWLink IPX / SPX Compatible. While IPX / SPX is Novell's standard protocol in earlier versions of NetWare, Microsoft uses its own version of IPX / SPX.

4. **B.** Primary Domain Controller. Remember that the Directory database for the domain must reside on a domain controller. In addition, the master copy can be contained only on the primary domain controller.

5. **A.** Disk Administrator. You would use the My Computer or Windows NT Explorer to create and manage shares or permissions to files and directories. The User Manager utility is used to create and manage user and group accounts.

6. **D.** Full Control. The other permissions are contained within the Full Control access right. Because of this, care must be taken to assign the appropriate access rights after you create the share.

7. **A.** Tell Connie the name of the directory. This is really a trick question, as the keywords are *FAT volume*. You can secure only directories that reside on an NTFS volume from remote access. Local access is not restricted when you use FAT.

8. **A.** 16EB. An NTFS partition can handle up to 16 *exabytes*, which is equivalent to 1,024 *terabytes*.

9. **A, D.** Centralized Administration and Single Login. With the workgroup model, administration is decentralized because the accounts database is stored on the local machine, as opposed to a central location. Because of the decentralized nature of the workgroup model, multiple login accounts are required.

10. **C.** Read. The keyword is *viewed*. While you could assign any of the other permissions, you assign only those rights that are absolutely necessary to the task at hand.

11. **B, D.** Decentralized Administration and Used for small groups of users. Remember that in a workgroup, users must manage and maintain accounts at the workstation. Also, because of limitations on inbound concurrent connections on Windows NT workstation and on the accounts database, the workgroup model doesn't work very well with large groups of users.

12. **C.** No Access. Whenever you have No Access permissions, it supercedes all other permissions.

13. **A, D.** Centralized Administration and Used for small groups of users. Since the Directory database resides on a primary domain controller, administration of user accounts is centralized. Also, the domain model can scale to handle large groups of users.

14. **A.** Assign rights to groups and Assign users to groups. It's always easier to manage groups than to manage users.

15. **A, C.** Administrators group or Server Operators group. You will need to differentiate between sharing a directory locally and sharing it over the domain.

Answers to Chapter 45 Self Test

1. **C.** Replicated. The other choices describe Novell's NDS database system.

2. **C.** Primary Domain Controller. The master copy of the domain's Directory database resides on the PDC because the PDC is responsible for administrative changes and directory replication.

3. **C, D.** Fault tolerance and Login authentication. BDCs do not perform administrative modifications or directory replication. These are functions of the primary domain controller.

4. **B.** Reinstall Windows NT Server as a Backup Domain Controller. Only a domain controller can provide login authentication services, and the only way to convert a member server to a domain controller, or vice versa, is reinstalling the Windows NT server operating system.

5. **A.** Backup Domain Controller. This scenario would necessitate local logon authentication services in case of a loss of link.

6. **D.** NetLogon. While CTL-ALT-DEL will initiate the logon process, it is only one part of the whole process. The WinLogon process is used only for local workstation or workgroup access, and there is no such process as the Domain Logon process.

7. **D.** User Manager for Domains. Whenever you need to work with user or group accounts, you would use the User Manager for *Domains* utility.

8. **A.** Global Group. Global groups assign resources across the domain.

9. **D.** Server Operators. You would not want to give him complete control over the server with Admin, nor complete control over the network as a Domain Admin (plus it's a global group). While Backup Operators would assign the necessary rights to backup and restore files, it would not allow the employee to shut down the server or share server resources. Only Server Operators will assign all of the correct rights.

10. **C.** User Accounts. Global groups can contain only user accounts.

11. **B, D.** Domain Admin and Domain Guests. When trying to remember the default global groups, remember that all three start with the word *Domain*.

12. **B.** Added to the domain. This is a little bit of a trick question, which you will need to watch out for on the Novell exam. While it is true that you must be authenticated to log in to the domain, the question specifically targeted a workstation as opposed to a user. A valid username and password is required only during authentication or when the administrator is attempting to add the workstation to the domain. However, the administrator must use a username and password combination that has administrative privileges, which that answer did not specify.

13. **A.** Add the computer account in Server Manager. The User Manager and User Manager for Domains utilities are for user and group accounts. Workstation accounts are handled by Server Manager.

14. **A.** Domain NetLogon goes to the Client NetLogon. You must know the proper sequence of events during the NetLogon process in order to pass the Novell certification exam.

15. **B, C.** Local groups can contain only global groups or user accounts.

Answers to Chapter 46 Self Test

1. **D.** All of the Above. Remember that a firewall controls communications between your network and the Internet, and that there are both hardware and software firewalls available in the marketplace.

2. **A.** Account. You must ensure that you know the various types of policies available under Windows NT and what each type of policy is used for.

3. **B.** User Profiles. The easiest way to differentiate between policies and profiles is to remember that a policy, much like at the workplace, is used to control user activity. A profile describes the user environment.

4. **A.** System Policy Editor. All other profiles are created and maintained by the User Manager or User Manager for Domains utilities.

5. **A, B.** User's Security Identifier and All Group SIDs the User Has Been Assigned Membership. Each object has an access control list (ACL) that contains the permissions, not the security access token.

6. **C.** User Rights. Actually, this was a trick question because you would normally associate an auditing policy with the Manage Auditing and Security Logs right. However, you must be prepared for these types of trick questions on the exam.

7. **C.** Grant or Deny Access to Objects. Remember that applications, files, and printers are considered objects under Windows NT.

8. **C.** Roaming User Profile. The easiest way to remember the file extension is that the profile *roams* with the user.

9. **D.** System Policy. Remember that system policies control *specific* user activities.

10. **C.** Mandatory Logon. The other choices are resource access controls.

11. **C.** Password Uniqueness. You can specify how many passwords the system will remember under Password Uniqueness.

12. **D.** NTFS File System. NTFS controls file level security and is used in conjunction with the mandatory logon process to control access to files on the local machine. Note that the FAT

file system has no file-level security controls, and is therefore an incorrect answer.

13. **B.** C:\WINNT\PROFILES*username*\ NTUSER.DAT. Local user profiles are stored in a subdirectory of the Profiles directory in a file called NTUSER.DAT. Do not confuse local user profiles with mandatory user profiles, which have the MAN extension.

14. **D.** C:\WINNT\SYSTEM32\REPL\IMPORT S\SCRIPTS. System policies on the domain are located in this directory on the primary domain controller and are exported to the backup domain controllers.

15. **A, C.** User Accounts and User Profiles. The mandatory logon process controls only the initial logon process and does not control user activities on the network. Audit trails are used to monitor, rather than control, user activities.

16. **D.** User and Group Management. Security Policy Changes would monitor policies, rather than account information.

17. **B.** NTUSER.MAN. Remember that the mandatory user profile uses the MAN extension.

Answers to Chapter 47 Self Test

1. **A, C.** The Novell examination will mix the Account and Trusted terms.

2. **B.** Single. The Single Master Domain Model actually has two domains, one for accounts and one for resources.

3. **B.** 42. The formula for calculating trust relationships in a complete trust model is $n(n-1)$.

4. **A.** HEADQUARTERS. The domain that contains the user account performs the authentication even when the user logs in from another domain.

5. **A, C, D.** Centralized Account Administration, Centralized Resource Administration, and Decentralized Account Administration. Since resources are placed in separate domains, you can centralize or decentralize resource administration. However, since all user accounts reside in one domain, you are stuck with centralized account administration.

6. **B.** User Manager for Domains. The trick to remembering which utility establishes trust relationships is the word *Domains.*

7. **D.** Sales will add the Headquarters domain to the Trusting portion of the dialog. This question establishes the fact that a one-way trust already exists. Therefore, in completing the two-way trust, you must reverse the roles of the two domains.

8. **A, D.** The resource domains must trust their corresponding master domains with one-way trusts, *and* the master domains must trust every other master domain with a two-way trust. This ensures that users can access their accounts from any domain in the network.

9. **D.** The resource domains must trust the master domain with a one-way trust. A two-way trust is used only in the multiple master domain and complete trust domain models.

10. **D.** You can't. The password is not obtainable through any application or utility. If a trust relationship is broken, you will have to reestablish the trust.

11. **C.** Unlimited, 128. Inbound trust relationships are limited to 128 and unlimited outbound trust relationships.

12. **D.** 11. Twelve domains will go beyond the 128 inbound connection limit. If you forget, use the formula $n(n-1)$ to calculate the possible number of trust relationships until you pass 128.

13. **C.** Headquarters will add the Sales domain to the Trusting portion of the dialog. Remember that the trusted domain adds the trusting domain first.

14. **A, C.** Centralized Account Administration and Centralized Resource Administration. Since all user accounts and resources reside in one domain, decentralized administration is not possible.

15. **A.** Complete Trust. The complete trust model uses two-way trusts between every domain, and is the most complex to manage and maintain.

Answers to Chapter 48 Self Test

1. **C.** The Workstation Manager allows the user account to be created.

2. **A, D.** NDIS and ODI are the standards that allow for multiple protocols to be supported on one network card.

3. **D.** The application exists at the WIN32 directory under PUBLIC.

4. **A.** Full access to volumes is not an advantage, and in fact would be inadvisable.

5. **B.** The SETUPNW.EXE is what needs to be executed to install the NetWare Client for NT.

6. **B.** The /ACU will take advantage of the Automatic Client Upgrade.

7. **B, D.** NWGINA and NWADMN32 are the two components that make up the Workstation Manager.

8. **C.** The ADMNSETUP utility configures NDS to work correctly.

9. **D.** The NT Configuration object allows for proper administration.

10. **B.** The Association tab allows you to associate the Application object to a user.

11. **B, C, D.** Organizational Unit, User, and Group objects can be associated with an Application or client Configuration object.

12. **C.** The Profile/Policy tab is where configuration takes place.

13. **B.** A could be true, but for this scenario it is not.

14. **B, E.** The files are in PRODUCTS\WINNT\I386 and on the CD.

15. **A, B, C.** These are the main types of installations available.

Answers to Chapter 49 Self Test

1. **A, B.** NetWare Administrator Snap-In Service and NDS Event Monitor. Know which components are part of the Novell Administrator for the certification exam.

2. **C.** Manage and Maintain Windows NT domain accounts from a central location. Domain accounts are different than workstation accounts.

3. **B.** IGRATE.EXE. The IGRATE.EXE application is used only during the initial synchronization.

4. **D.** Select Novell NetWare Servers. This page determines which servers the NDS Event Monitor will be installed on. Remember that the NDS Event Monitor must be installed on a server containing a master or read-write replica.

5. **B.** Duplicate information is overwritten by the NDS attributes. Whenever there is a conflict between Windows NT and NDS, remember that NDS always prevails.

6. **B, D.** Synchronize Windows NT Objects with NDS Objects and Synchronize NDS objects with Windows NT Objects. There is no actual replacement performed, as Windows NT

requires a user account to be stored in its SAM database. The integration process just makes this fact transparent to the user and the administrator.

7. **C.** Network Settings. Do not confuse the System Modals page with synchronization.

8. **D.** Runs on a Windows NT PDC and synchronizes changes between NDS and Windows NT. The NDS Event Monitor tracks object modifications.

9. **A.** NDSDM.NLM. You will need to remember the NLM for the certification exam.

10. **A.** Application Server. When you use the Application Server page, you are specifying which domain the new user will belong to.

11. **A.** Other Properties. The Other Properties tab allows you to specify to retain NDS settings or to use a template object to handle duplicate data.

12. **A.** Runs on a NetWare server and monitors object modifications. The NDS Event Monitor works in conjunction with the NDS Object Replication Service module to perform Directory database synchronization. Changes are tracked by the NDS Event Monitor, and modifications to the SAM database are made by ORS.

13. **B, C.** O and OU. The [Root] object cannot store the Windows NT Server object.

14. **B.** Integrate to NT. Know which buttons in IGRATE.EXE perform which integration / synchronization procedures.

15. **B.** Select NT Domains and Workgroups. The Select NDS Context for Domain or Workgroup System Object dialog is used to set the NDS context in which the Windows NT Server object will be stored.

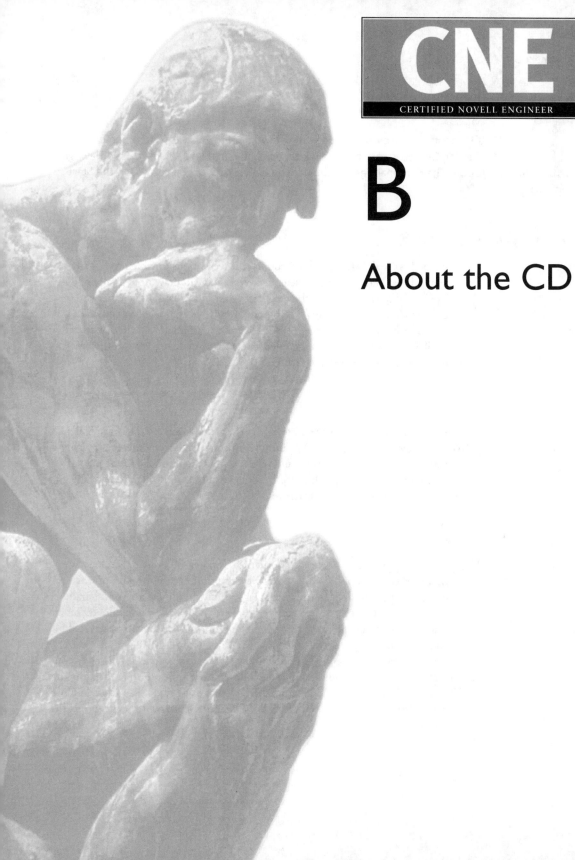

B

About the CD

T his CD-ROM contains a browser-based testing product, the *Personal Testing Center*. The Personal Testing Center is easy to install. Just click Setup and you will be walked through the installation. The Personal Testing Center program group will be created in the Start Programs folder.

Test Type Choices

With the Personal Testing Center, you have three options in which to run the program: Live, Practice, and Review. Each test type will draw from a pool of over 400 potential questions. Your choice of test type will depend on whether you would like to simulate an actual CNE exam, receive instant feedback on your answer choices, or review concepts using the testing simulator. Note that selecting the Full Screen icon on Internet Explorer's standard toolbar gives you the best display of the Personal Testing Center.

Live

The Live timed test type is meant to reflect the actual exam as closely as possible. You will have between 90 and 120 minutes to complete the various exams. You will have the option to skip questions and return to them later, move to the previous question, or end the exam. Once the timer has expired, you will automatically go to the scoring page to review your test results.

Managing Windows

The testing application runs inside an Internet Explorer 4.0 browser window. We recommend that you use the full-screen view to minimize the amount of text scrolling you need to do. However, the application will initiate a second iteration of the browser when you link to an Answer in Depth or a Review Graphic. If you are running in full-screen view, the second iteration of the browser will be covered by the first. You can toggle between the two windows with ALT-TAB, you can click your taskbar to maximize the second window, or you can get out of full-screen mode and arrange the two windows so they are both visible on the screen at the same time. The application will not initiate more than two browser windows, so you aren't left with hundreds of open windows for each Answer in Depth or Review Graphic that you view.

Saving Scores as Cookies

Your exam score is stored as a browser cookie. If you've configured your browser to accept cookies, your score will be stored in a cookie named History. If you don't accept cookies, you cannot permanently save your scores. If you delete the History cookie, the scores will bedeleted permanently.

Using the Browser Buttons

The test application runs inside the Internet Explorer 4.0 browser. You should navigate from screen to screen by using the application's buttons, not the browser's buttons.

JavaScript Errors

If you encounter a JavaScript error, you should be able to proceed within the application. If you cannot, shut down your Internet Explorer 4.0 browser session and relaunch the testing application.

Practice

When choosing the Practice exam type, you have the option of receiving instant feedback as to whether your selected answer is correct. The questions will be presented to you in numerical order, and you will see every question in the available question pool for each section you chose to be tested on.

As with the Live exam type, you have the option of continuing through the entire exam without seeing the correct answer for each question. The number of questions you answered correctly, along with the percentage of correct answers, will be displayed during the post-exam summary report. Once you have answered a question, click the Answer icon to display the correct answer.

You have the option of ending the Practice exam at any time, but your post-exam summary screen may reflect an incorrect percentage based onthe number of questions you failed to answer. Questions that are skipped are counted as incorrect answers on the post-exam summary screen.

Review

During the Review exam type, you will be presented with questions similar to both the Live and Practice exam types. However, the Answer icon is not present, as every question will have the correct answer posted near the bottom of the screen. You have the option of answering the question without looking at the correct answer. In the Review exam type, you can also return to previous questions and skip to the next question, as well as end the examby clicking the Stop icon.

The Review exam type is recommended when you have already completed the Live exam type once or twice, and would now like to determine which questions you answered correctly.

Questions with Answers

For the Practice and Review exam types, you will have the option of clicking a hyperlink titled Answers in Depth, which will present relevant study material aimed at exposing the logic behind the answer in a separate browser window. By having two browsers open (one for the test engine and one for the review information), you can quickly alternate between the two windows while keeping your place in the exam. You will find that additional windows are not generated as you follow hyperlinks throughout the test engine.

Scoring

The Personal Testing Center post-exam summary screen, called Benchmark Yourself, displays the results for each section you chose to be tested on, including a bar graph similar to the real exam, which displays the percentage of correct answers. You can compare your percentage to the actual passing percentage for each section. The percentage displayed on the post-exam summary screen is not the actual percentage required to pass the exam. You'll see the number of questions you answered correctly compared tothe total number of questions you were tested on. If you choose to skip a question, it will be marked as incorrect. Ending the exam by clicking the END button with questions still unanswered lowers your percentage, as these questions will be marked as incorrect.

Clicking the END button and then the HOME button allows you to choose another exam type or test yourself on another section.

C

About the
Web Site

Access Global Knowledge Network

As you know by now, Global Knowledge Network is the largest independent IT training company in the world. Just by purchasing this book, you have also secured a free subscription to the Global Knowledge Network Web site and its many resources. You can find it at

http://access.globalknowledge.com

You can log on directly at the Global Knowledge site, and you will be e-mailed a new, secure password immediately upon registering.

What You'll Find There. . .

The wealth of useful information at the Global Knowledge site falls into three categories:

Skills Gap Analysis   Global Knowledge offers several ways for you to analyze your networking skills and discover where they may be lacking. Using Global Knowledge Network's trademarked Competence Key Tool, you can do a skills gap analysis and get recommendations for where you may need to do some more studying. (Sorry, it just might not end with this book!)

Networking   You'll also gain valuable access to another asset: people. At the Access Global site, you'll find threaded discussions, as well as live discussions. Talk to other CNE candidates, get advice from folks who have already taken the exams, and get access to instructors.

Product Offerings   Of course, Global Knowledge also offers its products here, and you may find some valuable items for purchase—CBTs, books, or courses. Browse freely and see if there's something that could help you take that next step in career enhancement.

CNE
CERTIFIED NOVELL ENGINEER

D

The Career Center

You might be tempted to think that your work is finished once you have achieved your CNE certification. Nothing could be further from the truth. Now that you have the certification, you need a job that is going to provide opportunities to use your certification. You might also look for a job that will allow you to obtain additional certifications. Finding that job can be difficult if you don't know where to look or what to look for.

The "Help Wanteds": Planning Your Attack

Looking at the title of this section, you might think you were going to war. Well, it's not quite as bad as that, but a job-hunting campaign, like a military campaign, should have a strategy. Many people start with the attitude that if you have no idea what you're looking for, then you won't be disappointed with what you find. There's probably some truth in that, but I would add that you probably won't find the job that's right for you, either.

I also like to use the analogy of courtship when explaining the importance of having a strategy for your search. If you've never stopped to think about your perfect mate, then chances are you don't really know what you're looking for. If you go ahead and get married anyway, you could find yourself in a marriage that is going to lead to a messy divorce or many years of unhappiness.

Getting fired or quitting a job isn't as bad as getting a divorce, but it's not much fun. In my career I've had good and bad jobs, jobs that have gone from good to bad, and jobs that have gone from bad to good. I've been hired, fired, and I've "moved on to other opportunities" (I quit). All of these changes required decisions from me, and a lot of thought had to go into those decisions.

In the next few pages I'm going to try to help you develop a job search strategy. Since I am both a certified professional and a technical recruiter, I'll try to give you a little insight from both sides of the table.

**recruiter
@dvice**

Before talking to a headhunter or recruiter, put together an information packet that includes a résumé, a cover letter, a skills list, a project list, and maybe even references. The more information you provide, the easier it will be for a headhunter or recruiter to place you.

The Job Search

We begin with the job search. Time seems to be the biggest factor for most folks when it comes to looking for a new job. How long is this going to take? That's a tough question. The answer depends on the market, on the type of job you are looking for, and your personal situation.

The ideal situation to be in when searching for new job is to have a job you already like. That might not make sense at first, but think about it for a minute. If you don't feel like you have to leave your current job, you aren't going to feel as much pressure to take a less than optimal new job. You will spend more time learning about new opportunities and educating yourself about what you're getting into.

With more time, you may broaden your search and consider areas or industries that you might not have considered under a time crunch. You'll feel better about holding out for a higher salary or a better signing bonus. Most importantly, you will not be rushed into a decision that is going to shape the rest of your life. You will have time to decide what you want, and then to develop a strategy for how you are going to get it.

Incidentally, recruiters love to find people who are under the gun, because recruiters know that they can get these people on board faster and at a lower cost. However, a manager will recognize that this type of person may not be around for long, because the person may be getting into a job he isn't suited for. Remember that recruiters make recommendations, but it's managers who make decisions.

If you happen to find yourself "between jobs" at the moment, don't sweat it. If you are certified, or are getting certified, the jobs are out there. Just relax and take some time to focus on your strategy. Then implement that strategy.

If you aren't currently in a job, you may actually have an advantage over someone who does have a job. You have an abundance of one of the world's most limited resources: spare time!

Networking 101

You have heard someone say, "It's not what you know, but whom you know." There is some truth in that. Networking has two big benefits for you if it's done right. The first benefit is contacts. The second benefit is association.

The contacts benefit is fairly straightforward, so we'll talk about that one in a second. Let's talk about associations first, since that's the one that might not be so obvious. One very common method of networking is to join professional groups like software user groups. Even if you don't attend the meetings, you can tell people that you're a card-carrying member of the XYZ group.

If the XYZ group has a reputation for being a very technical and prestigious group, chances are your value just went up in the mind of the recruiter. By the way, you are also demonstrating the capacity to be social. Most recruiters aren't interested in even the most technically proficient people, if they can't relate to other people.

Let's say for a moment that you did join a users group or any type of social organization, and you actually attended the meetings. Whom might you meet there? Well, you might meet me or one of my fellow recruiters. That could prove helpful.

You might also meet directors, project managers, senior technical leads, or entrepreneurs. All of these people are always on the lookout for talent—it's ingrained in them. Every time they meet someone new, the question they ask themselves is, "Could I use this person?"

If you can prompt someone to ask that question about you, and answer "yes", then you have probably just found yourself a job. At a minimum, you have gained recognition from an influential person inside the organization. That puts you about a light-year ahead of your competitors who are answering ads from the Sunday paper.

recruiter
@dvice

Make yourself a list of questions before going into an interview. You don't even have to memorize them. Take notes, and press for information if you aren't satisfied with the answers. Remember that you are interviewing the company just as much as they are interviewing you.

Using Placement Services

I have mixed feelings about placement services. I think placement services are excellent vehicles for finding entry-level positions. If you have just finished your CNE, then a placement service might be a good choice for you.

However, if you've had your CNE for a while, or if you already have a lot of industry experience, then be careful of placement services. Most services make their money by doing a volume business. You register with the service, and the service attempts to place you in the first job request they receive for which you are qualified.

Placement services rarely take the time to investigate the jobs into which they are placing people. Many times the placement services get their list of job positions right out of the newspaper. Many of the opportunities that you will find through placement services are temporary staffing positions.

This might be just what you need to build a résumé. However, for an experienced individual looking for a full-time position as a senior technical lead, listing a number of temporary staffing positions on your résumé may do you more harm than good.

If you choose to use a placement service, consider using one of the nationwide services like Kelly Technical Services or AeroTek. I have been impressed in the past with the speed at which these services have filled positions, and with the quality of applicants that these services attract. Also, if you are willing to travel, the nationwide services may be able to find you a specific type of job.

To sum it up, my advice on placement services is not to discount them. Just make sure that the type of job you are looking for is the type of job that the service fills on a regular basis.

Going Online

By now, I hope I don't need to tell you that you can find a wealth of information on the Internet. This includes company marketing information, securities exchange information, and recruiting information. Almost all of the Fortune 500 companies, and many of the smaller ones, provide a way to submit résumés either through an e-mail address or through a Web form.

If you submit your résumé through e-mail, be sure that you clearly indicate what file format it's in. Pick something common like RTF format or Microsoft Word 6.0/95 format. When you submit your résumé via e-mail, you can be reasonably sure that someone is going to print it out and read it.

Here's a situation where you need to plan for the least common denominator. All your high resolution color graphics, watermarks, and textures may look great at home, but when printed on the high-volume laser printer at the recruiter's office, they become distracting. Guess what happens to résumés that are distracting and hard to read. That's right—straight in to the trash. I've thrown away dozens of résumés because they were just too much work to read.

When submitting your résumé via an online form, you need a slightly different strategy. Think keywords. There's a good chance that all of that information you are entering is being stored in a database. At some point, someone is going to run a query against that database that goes something like this, "Show me all of the CNEs with at least TWO YEARS' WORK EXPERIENCE."

You've got to get as many keywords as you can into the information you are entering in the database. That way, your name will come up more often. As you can imagine, trying to maximize keywords can lead to some pretty hilarious text, but it works. It also demonstrates that you understand how computer systems work. That isn't lost on recruiters.

If you happen to be just what a company is looking for, then submitting your résumé online might be a good idea. However, it's been my experience that submitting a résumé online isn't much better than mailing in a resume to the attention of the personnel director.

I'm not fond of this method, because it lacks a certain personal touch. Also, you really have no idea who is receiving your résumé. It might be someone in the personnel department at a company, or it might be someone at a placement office that has the contract for the company you are interested in.

Whenever I submit my résumé, I always identify the job I'm looking for, then I find out who is responsible for filling that position. This often requires a little inside knowledge. Try to find someone in the organization who will give you an exact job title and the name of a manager responsible for filling that position.

An excellent source for this type of information is ex-employees. Most will be more than happy to give you the inside scoop. They will probably also be willing to tell you what to look out for. Finding an ex-employee and taking him or her out to lunch may be one of the best investments you ever make.

After a personal contact, such as a phone call or a lunch appointment, I then submit my résumé to that person. That person then becomes my sponsor. He or she passes my résumé on to whoever needs to see it, hopefully with some positive remarks. That is a level of personal contact that just can't be achieved through an online submittal process.

Getting the Advice of Peers

Once you have identified a company that you want to work for, you need to get the lay of the land. You need to gather intelligence. Try to make some contacts within the company, and try to meet some people who have interviewed with the company before. This is usually easier said than done, but you can get some really valuable information.

Ask around. You might just get lucky and find someone who has successfully, or unsuccessfully, done what you are trying to do. Try to figure out what works and what doesn't. Be careful, though. If you start asking too many questions, you might tip your hand to either a vindictive supervisor or a coworker planning on interviewing for the same position you are. Know who your friends are.

Now is the right time for you to make a friend at the company you are interested in. There is nothing better than inside information. Find someone who is willing to check the internal postings a couple of times a week, or someone who knows someone.

This might be easier than you think. Many companies are now offering finders fees for technical talent. If an employee submits someone's résumé, and the candidate is eventually hired, that employee may have earned a bonus of a few thousand dollars. You would be amazed how many "friends" you'll have if you have the potential of putting a few thousand dollars in their pocket.

The Interview

So far, so good. You've been granted an interview. This is no time to forget about your strategy! On the contrary, now is the time to redouble your efforts. This may be your only face-to-face interaction with the company of your dreams. You've got to make a good impression, and you are going to be limited in the amount of time you have to do that.

Try to ask pointed questions that demonstrate that you know programming. For example, you might ask a technical interviewer about their applications and languages being used. Find out whether the company has a 100 percent 32-bit desktop, and whether the Y2K issue is presenting any problems.

All of these are great questions if you are talking to a technical interviewer. These are not appropriate questions if you are talking to someone from the human resources department, or a senior nontechnical manager. If you're talking to a vice president or a senior manager, don't talk technical, talk business. Ask whether the company has done a Total Cost of Ownership (TCO) analysis, and if so, what were the results. Ask what the acceptable Return on Investment (ROI) is for a capital project.

If you aren't comfortable with these questions, stick to something simpler like asking what projects are in the works for improving productivity, improving reliability, or reducing support costs. These are the issues that business people wrestle with every day. If you want to relate to these folks, you've got to speak their language, and you've got to talk about things that they care about.

When answering questions, give direct, concise answers. If you don't know the answer, admit it, then offer your best guess. Guessing is acceptable, as long as you identify your answer as a guess. Don't ever try to pass yourself off as something you are not. A technical interviewer will smell a phony as soon as the answers start to stink.

Working with a Headhunter

As someone looking for a job, I loved working with headhunters. As a recruiter, I hate competing with them. So for the purpose of this discussion, I'm going to try to think like someone looking for a job.

The really nice thing about headhunters is that most of them are paid a finder's fee that is a percentage of the salary of the person hired. Consequently, the more money you make, the more money your headhunter makes. This is one of the few situations in life where your agent's best interests are truly your best interests. Also, most headhunters don't get paid at all unless they fill a position. They work fast, and usually with remarkable results.

There are some things to watch out for, though. There are people out there calling themselves career consultants, or even headhunters. They want you to pay them a few hundred dollars to build a résumé and to tell you what your ideal job is.

First, you don't need someone to tell you what your ideal job is. You should be able to figure that out on your own. Second, if these people even have a placement service, you would be amazed how many times your ideal job just happens to be the position they are trying to fill. Third, there are too many good recruiters and headhunters out there who don't charge you a dime. You should never, ever pay someone to find you a job! Now give me a second to get off my soapbox…

I guess I get so excited about this topic because I know some really good headhunters who do excellent work. When they make a placement, the company is happy, the employee is happy, and the headhunter makes a little money. But there are always a few who give the rest of the recruiting industry a bad name, because they've taken clients' money and left them in the same job, or a worse job.

Headhunters often specialize in a particular type of job, location, or industry. If you are looking for something specific, ask around and find a headhunter who has concentrated on that area. Not only will this person know what is going on in her specialty, she can help tailor your presentation to that area. That's the real benefit. Think of these specialists as insiders for hire—only you're not paying the bill!

Even if you don't need a specialist, before you contact a headhunter, try to narrow down your goals. Headhunters aren't in the business of being career counselors. They are in the business of finding you the job you're looking for. That's not to say that they won't help you. On the contrary, they will probably give you a great deal of attention. But only you know what you want.

Put together a professional-looking résumé listing every skill you have. Also put together a cover letter that details what type of job you are looking for, what kind of salary and benefits package you need, and any other interesting bits of information about yourself. This is the documentation that is going to catch the eye of a headhunter.

Your headhunter will then probably take you out to lunch, and you two will have a chat. By the time you're ordering dessert, you will probably have defined your job requirements even more precisely. You may also leave with a list of things to do. The list might include making enhancements to your résumé, researching companies, and maybe even scheduling an interview.

On the other hand, the headhunter may tell you point blank that you just aren't qualified for what you want to do, and that there is no way he or she could place you in the job you're looking for. That's hard to hear, but it's probably an honest assessment.

Remember that headhunters only make money if you make money. If a headhunter tells you that you're not qualified, you need to decide whether to continue pursuing this job with another headhunter, or look for another job for which you are better suited.

My advice is to swallow your pride, open your mind, and see what the headhunter has to say. Chances are, he's going to have some ideas that you might not have considered. At a minimum, you should be able to find out why you aren't qualified and what you need to do to get qualified for the job of your dreams.

One final thought on this topic. A lot of people worry that a headhunter is going to rush them into a job that they won't enjoy, just so the headhunter can get paid. Well, in the first place, you're the decision-maker. Only you can decide whether or not to take a job.

Second, a growing trend in the industry is that headhunters don't get paid their full commission until the client has held the job for more than six months. I like this trend because once again, your best interests dovetail with the headhunter's. There's little incentive for a headhunter to put you in a job you're not going to enjoy.

Working with headhunters has been a very positive experience for me. Some of the best jobs I've ever had have come through headhunters. If you find one you like, they are an excellent resource for taking your career where you want it to go.

Preparing for the Interview

Start with a little research. You need to be able to talk intelligently about the company you are interviewing with, the industry that company is in, and how you can help this company achieve its goals. At a minimum, you should check out the company's Web site and learn its mission statement, objectives, and goals. You need to demonstrate that you know where this company wants to go and how they are planning to get there.

You can also check out one of the online investment firms to gather information, if the company you're researching is publicly traded. Know what the financial status of the company is. Know whether there are any planned mergers or acquisitions.

You should also try to get a feel for the technology being used in the company. This information could be a little more difficult to obtain than financial information; you may need to find an insider. Be careful of making any recommendations about technology during an interview. After all, you don't want to tell someone how to do his job or step on someone's toes. You might, however, be able to identify some troublesome areas that your skills could ease.

Acing the Interview

I wish I could give you a nice, simple formula for ensuring success in an interview. If one exists, I haven't found it, and I don't know anyone who has.

By definition, an interview occurs when two or more people get together for the purpose of filling a job. When you get two people together, there exists the possibility for conflict. Unfortunately, you can do everything right and still have a lousy interview simply because your personality clashed with the personality of the person doing the interviewing.

One of the things that you might consider doing is buying a couple of books, audio tapes, or videos about interviewing or personal selling. There are lots of tapes on how to sell, and quite a few about interviewing. All of them will give you some ideas for building a personal relationship with someone in a very short amount of time.

Try to avoid obvious gimmick techniques like commenting on something you see in the person's office. I was on a sales call one time with a junior sales representative who made the mistake of complementing a manager about the large fish he had mounted on the wall. The manager looked right at the rep and said, "I hate that damn fish. My boss goes on all of these company-sponsored fishing trips, spends a fortune, and then decorates our offices with his stupid fish." The sales call was over before it even began.

This may sound like a cliché, but be yourself. Don't put on airs; don't try to be something you aren't. Most people are not good actors, and most recruiters can spot a performance very quickly. When a recruiter interviews you, he or she wants to get a sense of who you are—not just what you know. Don't make it hard on the recruiters by putting on a show.

When being interviewed, you should appear confident about yourself and your abilities. Practice showing confidence by standing in front of a mirror and "introducing yourself" a few times. Tell your mirror image how happy you are to have an opportunity to interview for the position. Then briefly explain to yourself what your qualifications are and why you would be a good fit for the position. (But avoid telling yourself that you are the *best* candidate for the position. You never know that, and you might be setting yourself up for feeling "robbed" if you're not eventually hired.) Finally, ask yourself a few questions about the job and your own plans, and then answer them. Try this technique. I guarantee it will be the toughest interview you ever have.

Now let's talk for a moment about interview etiquette. I've never seen a formal guide to interview etiquette, but there is certainly an informal set of expectations.

For example, most recruiters are tolerant of a candidate being ten minutes late. Five minutes early is preferable, but ten minutes late is acceptable. Beyond ten minutes, your chances for a successful interview begin to drop precipitously. If you are going to be more than ten minutes late, you definitely need to call, and you can probably expect to reschedule your interview.

Another piece of etiquette involves who speaks first in the interview. Once introductions are made, and everyone is comfortable, the interviewer will ask the first question. That question may be followed by another series of short-answer "warm-up" questions, or the interviewer may ask a more open-ended question.

Open-ended questions are designed to give the person being interviewed an opportunity to talk openly or to bend the conversation towards a topic he or she wants to discuss. Recognize the different types of questions and respond appropriately. If you speak out of turn or fail to answer appropriately, you are running the risk of annoying the interviewer and having your interview cut short.

Incidentally, if the interviewer asks you a trick question, and it's obvious that it is a trick question, call him on it. Let him know that you're not afraid to call a donkey a donkey. Most interviewers will appreciate this and probably accord you a little more respect as a result.

Following Up on the Interview

Always follow up on an interview. This can be done with a simple thank-you card, or phone call.

You're trying to accomplish several things with the follow-up: refreshing the memories of the decision makers (who may have interviewed numerous candidates), projecting a positive impression, and demonstrating interest and eagerness to work for this company.

Don't worry about looking desperate; you are more likely to come off as confident and professional. Never worry about following up an interview with a phone call to check the status of your application. In many companies, the people doing the interviewing are also the people doing real work. Interviewing is not their primary responsibility. Consequently, applications sometimes slip through the cracks. It may be up to you to keep the ball rolling by continuing to call and ask questions. You might get hired through persistence alone.

( )
recruiter
advice

Never stop looking for your perfect job. You should test the waters and go out on an interview or talk to a headhunter once every six months. High-tech industries change rapidly, and with that change comes a myriad of new opportunities.

Glossary

Access Control Entries (ACE) Specifies auditing and access permissions for a given object for a specific user or group of users.

Access Control List (ACL) File and print servers also check the access control list (ACL) of each resource before allowing a user to access a file or use a printer. If the user, or a group to which the user belongs, is not listed in the ACL, the user is not allowed to use the resource.

access mask Every ACE must have an access mask. An access mask tells the ACE which attributes are available for a particular object type. The ACE can then grant permissions based on that mask. For example, a file can set Read, Write, Execute, Delete, Take ownership, and Change permissions because an access mask defines these attributes. (See also **Access Control Entries**.)

access methods The rules governing the use of the physical network by various devices.

account lockout Can be set to lock out an account after a certain number of unsuccessful logon attempts. (Three bad attempts is a common choice.) This prevents hackers from breaking into your account.

account policies Set from the User Manager to change how passwords are used. This is where you can set the account lockout policy to help prevent your system from being hacked into.

across-the-wire migration This upgrade method can take the bindery and volume information from multiple NetWare 3.1x servers and upgrade them to another, more powerful, server that has had NetWare 5 already installed.

Administrator account One of the two built-in NT user accounts. The Administrator account manages the workstation's user accounts, policies, and resources. This account cannot be locked out or disabled. The Administrator account even has control over the files owned by other users. (See also **guest account**.)

Alerter Service used by the Server and other services. This service broadcasts the logged on user name in the NetBIOS name table, which can be considered a security breach.

alerts Critical security controls that help perform real-time monitoring. Enabled by configuring the Performance Monitor.

Application layer OSI layer that provides a consistent way for an application to save files to the network file server or print to a network printer. (2) TCP/IP layer that is the highest layer in the TCP/IP model. It is used by applications to access services across a TCP/IP network. Examples of applications that operate at this layer are a Web browser, file transfer program (FTP), and a remote login program.

applications There are two types of applications: simple and complex. A simple application is one that does not require any configuration on the workstation in order to run. A complex application may require registry entries, INI file changes, text file changes, and multiple files to be copied.

asset Anything that is of value and needed for the operation of the corporation.

ATM (Asynchronous Transfer Mode) A cell-switching protocol. ATM uses cell switching which is marked by its small, fixed length cells. (See also **Ethernet**, **Token Ring**, and **FDDI**.)

auditing policies An important component of the Monitoring Security Effectively controls. Auditing measures the system against a predefined system setting to ensure that no changes have occurred. The Windows NT security system uses the SIDs contained in the access token to log user activity, a process known as auditing. (See also **security identifier (SID)**).

availability Ensuring that information and vital services are accessible when required.

backup administrator Usually used in large LAN and or WAN environments. This position is used for backing up and restoring the network data.

Backup Domain Controllers (BDC) After a domain has been created, the entire account database is basically mirrored on each BDC, and the PDC keeps the information updated within five minutes by default. (See also **PDC**.)

baseband A type of signal transmission that allows only one frequency to carry information on the cable. (See also **broadband**.)

bindery-style logon Require a user to attach or log on to a server before gaining access to services on the server.

binding The linking of network components on different levels to enable communication between those components.

bits Information is transmitted in bits on an Ethernet network. A bit is the smallest amount of information that can be represented. A bit is represented as a single binary digit that can be either a 1 or a 0. A sequence of bits is called a frame.

block suballocation Disk space is divided into blocks just as memory is divided into blocks.

bridges Used to connect similar LAN segments. Bridges look at the destination and source address of a network packet and decide whether to pass that packet on to the LAN segment. A bridge can be used to filter out traffic for a local subnet and prevent it from passing onto an unnecessary LAN segment.

broadband Signal transmission that can support more than one signal on the cable by using frequency division techniques. (See also **baseband**.)

bus topology When the computers in your network are all connected in a row along a single cable or segment. (See also **star topology** and **ring topology**.)

C2 A security evaluation level assigned to a specific product, by the National Computer Security Center (NCSC), a division of the National Security Association (NSA), after a period of detailed product review and attestation. The C2 level of "trust" is one level that can be granted to an evaluated product. The defined levels of trust, in increasing levels of trust (or security), are D, C1, C2, B1, B2, B3, and A1. NT 3.5 with the Service Pack 3.0 has the C2 level of trust.

callback security Security feature implemented within RAS. When a user is configured to use callback and dials in to a RAS server, the server disconnects the session and then calls the client back at a preset telephone number or at a number provided during the initial call.

cellular topology Wireless topology in which the network is comprised of multiple areas, called cells, that are serviced by a wireless hub. Wireless communication takes place between the network devices and the hubs.

change control Manages any negative affects that changes can have on the network so that they are minimized.

child partition A partition that is below another partition in the tree is called a child of the partition above it, which is the parent partition. (See also **parent partition**.)

CIFS (Common Internet File Sharing) An enhanced version of SMB services that is available for use over the Internet. (See also **SMB**.)

Client 32 A 32-bit software application that is available for DOS, Windows 3.1*x*, Windows 95/98, and Windows NT 4.0 workstations.

client/server messaging One program on one computer talking to another program (usually on another computer).

client/server model Model in which data is requested by the client from the server. The server fulfills this request and sends the data to the client. The client does any processing that it wishes on the data and sends the modified data back to the server.

coaxial (or coax) cable One of the three types of physical media that can be used at the OSI Physical Layer. A coaxial has one strand (a solid-core wire) that runs down the middle of the cable. Around that strand is insulation. There are two different types of commonly used Ethernet coaxial cables: thickwire and thinwire. (See also **twisted-pair cable** and **fiber-optic cable**.)

Computer Browser Default service that maintains an up-to-date list of computers and provides the list to applications when requested. Provides the computer list displayed in the Select Computer and Select Domain dialog boxes; and in the main Server Manager window.

confidentiality The protection of information in the system so that unauthorized persons cannot access it.

console workstation The machine that is used to submit the backups and restoration jobs. (See also **host server** and **target**.)

container administrator In a large LAN or a WAN environment, you may want to divide the management of administration among several container administrators. These administrators have full control over their containers but not outside their container.

Container object A container object in NDS is like a directory (or folder) in a directory tree. It can contain Leaf objects or other Container objects. Container objects are used to organize the tree structure. (See also **Leaf object**.)

contextless login With contextless login you can authenticate from any point on the network simply by typing your login name and password, without knowing the location of your User object in the NDS tree.

corrective security controls Used to correct security holes that have been exploited.

Country object   Special container object for country locations. Country objects can be placed only in the root. (See also [**Root**].)

CSNW   One of the two installable network components, CSNW is the client redirector and NWLink is the IPX/SPX-compatible network transport protocol. (See also **NWLink**.)

cryptography   See **public key cryptography**, **secret key cryptography**, and **symmetric cryptography**.

Data Link layer   OSI layer that handles many issues for communicating on a simple network.

data striping   Process that allocates data evenly among the drives, improving reliability and access times. (See also **RAID**.)

decision tree   A query-like structure that graphically represents the filter expression. In a decision tree, statements are linked together by colored AND, OR, and NOT tabs. Combined, these statements specify the kinds of data you want to capture or display. (See also **filtering**.)

detective security controls   Ascertain when security holes are in the process of being exploited.

Dial-Up Networking (DUN)   Dialing-out service that is set up when RAS is installed as a service. DUN allows you to connect to any dial-up server using the Point-to-Point protocol (PPP) as a transport mechanism allowing for TCP/IP, NetBEUI or IPX/SPX network access over your analog modem, ISDN, or X.25 Pad devices.

Dial-Up Networking server   Allows Windows 98 to host a single dial-up network connection. Any client with support for PPP can dial-in using either IP, IPX, or NetBEUI as their connection protocol. Windows 98 can then act as a server sharing its files and printers just as it does on a LAN, or it can act as a gateway for an IPX or NetBEUI network.

directories   Organizational units for file storage. (See also **files**.)

directory replication   An NT default service that makes an exact copy of a folder and places it on another server.

directory replicator   Default service that replicates directories and the files in the directories between computers.

directory synchronization   The NT process of synchronizing the Backup Domain Controllers with the Primary Domain Controller on a periodic basis. (See also **Backup Domain Controller** and **Primary Domain Controller**.)

directory tree   An NDS directory tree is a database of objects. Every object in a directory has a relationship to every other object in the directory.

Disaster Recovery Plan (DRP)   Plan for recovery of necessary systems and data to support the core processes necessary to run the business. (See also **Business Recovery Plan**.)

discretionary access Access control when the person who created the file or folder is the owner and is responsible for securing those files and folders.

Disk Administrator A program that creates and manages partitions.

Disk Cache Manager Manages disk caching by reducing the amount of I/O traffic to your hard drive. It does this by storing frequently used data in physical memory rather than having to read it each time from your hard drive.

disk caching Storing frequently used data in electronic memory rather than having to read it each time from your hard drive.

disk duplexing Disk duplexing uses two disk drives just like disk mirroring does; however, instead of using one controller for both disks, disk duplexing uses two controllers, one for each disk. Using a second controller offers a higher degree of fault tolerance over disk mirroring because if one controller should fail, the system continues on with the other controller and hard disk. (See also **RAID** and **disk mirroring**.)

disk mirroring Disk mirroring (RAID Level 1) uses two disk drives attached to one controller. When disk mirroring is used, NetWare issues two write instructions, one to each disk when a write request is made. (See also **RAID** and **disk duplexing**.)

disk thrashing (See **thrashing**.)

distinguished name A distinguished name begins with a leading period, starts with the common name of the resource, and then lists each container unit up the tree to the [Root]. Each object has a unique distinguished name in the tree. A distinguished name can locate an object no matter what the current context is set at. (See also **relative distinguished name**.)

DMA (Direct Memory Access) A process whereby some devices can directly access memory on the system without the intervention of the CPU.

DNS zone file Contains one host name, one IP address, and a record type.

domain A group of computers containing domain controllers that share account information and have one centralized accounts database. The four domain models—single domain, complete trust, master domain, and multiple-master domain—represent various stages of growth and decentralization. The multiple master domain is actually two or more master domain models joined by a two-way trust. (See also **domain model**.)

domain mode Under the domain model, a Windows NT Server acts as a domain controller. The domain controller authenticates users into the domain before they can access resources that are a part of the domain. (See also **domain controller**.)

domain controller Serve two purposes in the NT environment: to authenticate users and grant them access to other resources within the network. (See also **Primary Domain Controller** and **Backup Domain Controllers**.)

Domain Name Service (DNS)   Performs name resolution of host names to IP addresses. DNS was created because numerical IP addresses are too difficult for humans to remember.

Dynamic Host Configuration Protocol (DHCP)   Assigns TCP/IP configuration parameters on networked clients.

dynamic routing   Protocols that advertise the routes they are familiar with and pass on the metrics, number of other routers, or hops, required to get from their host to another network, either directly or indirectly through another router.

effective rights   The actual rights that an object has, by determining which rights have been inherited, which have been filtered, and which have been directly granted to the object or granted through Security Equivalence.

Electronics Communications Privacy Act (ECPA)   Prevents you from eavesdropping on the activities of an intruder, even if you own the system, unless you post a message to indicate that all activities are subject to being monitored.

Emergency Repair Disk (ERD)   Can be used to restore a Windows NT system back to the configuration it had the last time you updated your Emergency Repair Disk. This disk can repair missing Windows NT files and restore the registry to include disk configuration and security information.

encapsulation   The process of encoding data for transmitting it across the network.

encrypted authentication   Methods for secure network transmission that include the simple Password Authentication Protocol (PAP), which permits clear-text passwords and the Shiva Password Authentication Protocol (SPAP) used by Windows NT workstations when connecting to a Shiva LAN Rover.

enterprise administrator   Has the highest level of security. The rights for this administrator start at the [Root] of the NDS tree and flow through all objects and the file system.

Ethernet   A baseband, CSMA/CD (Carrier Sense, Multiple Access / Collision Detection) transmission protocol. A type of network cabling and signaling specification originally developed by Bob Metcalfe while working for Xerox in the early 1970s. (See also **baseband** and **broadband**.)

Event Log   Default service that records system, security, and application events in the Event Log.

Event Notification Service (ENS)   Provides event notification for print jobs and status.

Event Viewer   The tool within Windows NT used to review audited events. Event Viewer has three logs that record system, security, and application related events, known as the System log, the Security log, and the Applications log, respectively.

FastTrack Web Server   Available from NetScape as part of the Novell and NetScape partnership that created Novonyx. It enables a NetWare 5 server to perform Web services on the network.

FAT (File Allocation Table) file system
The FAT file system is predominantly used for other operating systems such as Windows 3.x and Windows 95. To support backward compatibility, Windows NT fully supports the FAT file system. This is also because of FAT's universal acceptance and accessibility through other operating systems. Does not support Windows NT security features and does not offer any of the robust NTFS features. (See also **NTFS**.)

FAT32   The Windows 98 32-bit upgrade to the FAT file system that originally came from DOS. The benefits of FAT32 include optimal use of disk space and larger partition sizes than the maximum 2 GB (gigabyte) size allowed by FAT. *Note: Windows 98 supports only FAT and FAT32 files systems, and Windows NT does not support FAT32.*

fault tolerance   Recovery from operational failure control due to the system's ability to withstand hardware failures and software errors. Windows NT provides fault tolerance by allowing the redundancy of data by simultaneously writing files to multiple disks, and by replicating the contents of file directories to other servers on the network.

FDDI (Fiber Distributed Data Interface)
Follows the IEEE 802.5 standard for accessing the network just like Token Ring. However, unlike the Token Ring topology, FDDI uses two fiber-optic cables in a dual counterrotating ring configuration and operates at 100MBps instead of the 4MBps or 16MBps as used in Token Ring. (See also **Ethernet**, **Token Ring**, and **ATM**.)

fiber-optic cables   One of three types of physical media that can be used at the Physical layer to carry digital data signals in the form of modulated pulses of light. An optical fiber consists of an extremely thin cylinder of glass, called the core, surrounded by a concentric layer of glass, known as the cladding. There are two fibers per cable—one to transmit and one to receive. (See also **coaxial cable** and **twisted-pair cable**.)

file compression   Factor in disk space optimization that makes the most efficient use of hard disk space.

files   Files are data units such as graphics, documents, executable applications, and text files.

filtering   An effective security monitoring control that allows the system administrator to specify expressions to capture data either by protocol or network address. The filter expressions are represented by a decision tree. (See also **decision tree**.)

finger   Tool used to gather information about users on any machine running a finger server.

firewall   Software that prevents unauthorized traffic between two networks by examining the IP packets that travel on both networks. Firewalls look at the IP address and type of access the packet requires (such as FTP or HTTP) and then determine if that type of traffic is allowed.

FTP Publishing Service   Default service that, in Windows NT 4.0, FTP is part of Internet Information Server (IIS).

full-duplex dialogs   Used by OSI Session layer to let data flow in both directions simultaneously.

full synchronization   In a full synchronization, the PDC sends a copy of the entire user accounts database to a BDC.

fully qualified domain name (FQDN) Identifies the type of service by preceding the domain name with a service name.

garbage collection   A routine that is run when memory is deallocated.

gateway   A device that enables two dissimilar systems that have similar functions to communicate with each other.

global groups   Created on domain controllers and used to assign local permissions to domain users. The sole purpose of a global group is to gather users together at the domain level so that they can be placed in the appropriate local groups. (See also **local groups.**)

group accounts   Accounts used for grouping together users who perform the same function or require access to the same resources. If it were not for group accounts, you would have to grant access to resources on a per-user basis.

guest account   One of the two built-in NT user accounts. The guest account is for the one-time or occasional user. (See also **Administrator account.**)

half-duplex dialogs   Used by OSI Session layer to allow data to flow in two directions, but only one direction at a time. With half-duplex dialogs, replies and acknowledgements are possible.

HARDWARE   Registry subtree that contains information about the hardware that is detected upon system startup. Such information might include device settings, interrupts, and information about hardware components.

Hardware Abstraction Layer (HAL)   The layer between the operating system and the hardware located in the computer. Separates the kernel from the hardware to provide an intermediary layer, so that the Windows NT kernel does not have to perform communication with the hardware. HAL is what makes NT portable to other architectures.

Hardware Compatibility List (HCL)   A compilation of computer systems and hardware that have been tested for compatibility with Windows NT.

host server   A NetWare server that is running the backup program. (See also **target** and **console workstation.**)

Hot Fix   Method whereby, transparent to the user, when an error occurs because of a bad sector, the file system moves the data that was located in this sector (if possible) to another sector, and labels the original sector as bad. A feature of NTFS and SCSI hardware, but not the FAT file system.

HTTP (Hypertext Transfer Protocol)   The protocol that you use to connect to the Internet to view Web pages.

impersonation Technique for a server process to access objects that it doesn't have permissions to. If the client process has proper access permissions, the server process impersonates the client process in order to access the object.

Inherited Rights Filter (IRF) The system used to prevent rights from flowing down the tree from a parent container object. The IRF lists those rights that should not be inherited.

in-place upgrade Method of upgrading to NetWare 5.0 that will overwrite the system files on an existing server and upgrade the bindery and file system to an NDS structure.

Integrated Services Digital Network (ISDN) Connections that take place over digital lines and provide faster and more reliable connectivity. The primary benefit of ISDN is its speed and reliability. ISDN is commonly found in two speeds: 64kbps and 128kbps.

integrity The protection of information in the system from unauthorized, unanticipated, and unintentional modification, ensuring that data is accurate and complete.

Internet layer TCP/IP layer that is responsible for handling the communication from one computer to another computer. It accepts a request to send data from the Transport layer. The Internet layer consists of two protocols, the Internet Protocol (IP) and the Internet Control Message Protocol (ICMP Internet Mail Service (IMS). The Internet Mail Service enables users on Microsoft Exchange Server to send messages to, and receive messages from, users on the Internet.

internetworks Repeaters, bridges, and routers are devices used to link individual LANs together to form larger internetworks. (See also **repeaters**, **bridges**, and **routers**.)

Internet Protocol (IP) Provides packet delivery for all other protocols within the TCP/IP suite.

IP address Uniquely identifies a computer on the network. It is 32 bits long, with four octets separated by dots (.). This number is then converted to binary and used as a unique identifier.

IPX/SPX Protocol used to connect Novell Networks.

IT Security Control Model The relationship between corporate business objectives and IT Security controls or Windows NT Security features. An effective security model has three objectives: confidentiality, integrity, and availability.

Large Internet Packets (LIP) New feature in NetWare 5.0 that allows the maximum size of internetwork packets to be larger than in previous versions of NetWare.

Last Known Good Configuration Allows the user to restore the system to the last working system configuration. When used, it discards any changes to the configuration since the last working system configuration.

Leaf object Represents resources in the NDS tree. A Leaf object does not contain any other objects.

Legal Notice Corporation-specific message that appears whenever a user logs on the system warning them that only authorized users may access the system and that they are being monitored. Set through the Registry Editor or System Policy Editor. (See also **Registry Editor** and **System Policy Editor**.)

Local Area Network (LAN) A collection of computers connected in a geographically close network.

local groups Defined on each machine and may have both user accounts and global groups as members but cannot contain other local groups. (See also **global groups**.)

Local Security Authority The heart of the NT security subsystem. It creates security access tokens, authenticates users, and manages the local security policy.

Logical Link Control layer One of the sublayers of the Data Link layer. It controls the establishment and maintenance of links between communicating devices. (See also **Media Access Control layer** and **Data Link layer**.)

logical memory addressing Logical memory addressing allows NetWare to use memory efficiently because fragmentation of memory is minimal, which results in faster memory response.

login script Enables authentication for access to any NetWare 5 server, printers, and other network resources.

logon scripts Used to start applications or set environment variables for a computer upon startup.

loosely consistent The NDS Directory is what is known as a *loosely consistent* database, which means the database maintains its integrity, even if there are slight differences in replicas for a short period of time. NDS does continuously check all replicas, however, to see if objects in those replicas have been added, deleted, or modified. NDS then makes changes to the appropriate replicas to make sure that they all contain the most up-to-date information. This process is called *NDS* synchronization.

MAC (Media Access Control) A networked computer's unique address of its network interface card (NIC). Data is transported over networks in packets that always contain the source and destination MAC addresses. A bridge reads this information off the packets it receives to fill its routing table.

mandatory logon NT uses mandatory logon to force everyone to logon before it grants access to the system.

mandatory profile Used when the administrator needs to ensure that the user obtains the same workstation configuration every time they log into the network.

master replica Created automatically when you create a partition. There can be only one master replica of any given partition.

Media Access Control layer   One of the sublayers of the Data Link layer. It controls how multiple network devices share the same media channel. (See also **Logical Link Control layer** and **Data Link layer**.)

mesh topology   Network topology most prevalent in Wide Area Networks, since its redundancy provides a high level of reliability. In a full mesh topology, each network device is connected to each of the other network device.

Messenger   Default service that sends and receives messages sent by administrators or by the Alerter service. This service is stopped when the Workstation service is stopped.

Microsoft Challenge Handshake Authentication Protocol (MS-CHAP)   An encrypted login protocol used by remote users.

mirroring   Enables Windows NT to read files from, and write files to, two disks simultaneously. Entire disks (or sets of disks) can be mirrored or just partitions on each disk. If one drive fails, the second continues to function as normal.

mobile client   A workstation or laptop used by a user that works from remote locations. Mobile clients are generally laptop or notebook computers with modems installed on them.

monitoring controls   Include violation and exception reporting which help management determine whether their systems are being compromised.

multipoint connection   A connection that allows multiple network devices to exist on the physical media simultaneously. Network connections are typically multipoint connections.

nbstat   Tool used to display the contents of the remote computer's NetBIOS name table. The information listed in the NetBIOS name table can be used to determine the Domain name or workgroup the machine is in and the currently connected users. The information may also be used to uncover the Administrator's account, due to the fact that account SIDs are displayed in the name cache.

NDPS (Novell Distributed Print Services)   Printing service created by Novell in partnership with Hewlett-Packard and Xerox, NDPS incorporates new technology functions.

NDS security   Implemented by assigning trustee rights to the NDS objects, or the properties of those objects.

NDS synchronization   Process in which NDS continuously checks all replicas to see if objects in those replicas have been added, deleted, or modified. NDS then makes changes to the appropriate replicas to make sure that they all contain the most up-to-date information.

NetBEUI (NetBIOS Extended User Interface)   NetBEUI, the built-in protocol of Microsoft networking, supports communication in a Microsoft-only environment when the network is small and composed of a single network segment. NetBEUI is a nonroutable protocol, meaning that its packets contain no routing information and cannot pass through routers into other network segments. NetBEUI protocol is best suited for Local Area Networks that do not connect to the Internet. (See also **NetBIOS**.)

NetBIOS   Protocol used when Microsoft networking is required in a large multisegment network. NetBIOS has many similarities to NetBEUI except for the fact that it can be routed into other network segments when combined with either the TCP/IP or NWLink protocols in a form known as an encapsulated protocol. (See also **NetBEUI** and **NWLink**.)

Net Logon   Default service that performs authentication of account for primary domain and backup domain controllers, and also keeps the domain directory database synchronized between the primary domain controller and the backup domain controllers of he domain. For other computers running Windows NT, supports pass-through authentication of account logons. Used when the workstation participates in a domain.

netstat   Tool used to display the status of the TCP/IP stack including what ports are open and what connections are active.

NetWare Application Launcher (NAL)   The component of Z.E.N.works that handles application management and software distribution. NAL centralizes application administration by creating application objects in Novell Directory Services (NDS). The application objects can then be secured using NDS security. (See also **Z.E.N.works**.)

NetWare Connect   A remote dial-in connectivity software product from Novell that is now part of NetWare Internet Access Server (NIAS).

Network DDE   Default service that provides a network transport as well as security for DDE (Dynamic Data Exchange) conversations.

Network DDEDSDM   Dynamic Data Exchange Share Database Manager manages the shared DDE conversations. It is used by the Network DDE service.

Network Interface Card (NIC)   Also called an adapter card or interface card, it is installed in a computer to allow it to communicate with other computers over a network. A NIC changes the parallel signals inside the computer into serial signals that go over the network cable.

Network layer   OSI layer that manages addressing and delivering packets on a complex internetwork such as the Internet. Internetworks are joined by devices known as routers, which utilize routing tables and routing algorithms to determine how to send data from one network to another.

Network Monitor   Tool used to monitor packets of information that are sent from or received by the computer where you are running the program, including broadcast and multicast frames. The Microsoft System Management Server includes an advanced Network Monitor tool, which allows you to capture frames sent to and from any computer on the network, edit and transmit frames on the network, and capture frames from remote computers running Network Monitor Agent on the network.

NLMs (NetWare Loadable Modules)
Applications that run on a NetWare server.

Novell Directory Services (NDS)   The service used by NetWare to organize resources throughout an entire network. It is a database of user IDs and resources. NDS stores network resources in a tree structure that is similar to a directory tree.

NTFS (New Technology File System) The file system exclusive to Windows NT 4.0. Utilizes Windows NT file and directory security features so it is more secure than FAT.

NT LM Security Support Provider Default service that provides Windows NT security to RPC (Remote Procedure Call) applications that use transports other than named pipes.

NWAdmin The single point of administration for User objects is the NetWare Administrator program, also referred to as NWAdmin.

NWLink Microsoft's implementation of the IPX protocol that allows connectivity between the Windows NT and the Novell NetWare environments. (See also **CSNW**.)

object rights Object rights enable a trustee to perform actions on an NDS object. The object rights are Browse, Create, Delete, Rename, and Supervisor.

Organization object A high-level container object placed directly in the root or under country units. This object usually represents the company. (See also [**Root**] and **Container object**.)

Organization Unit object Container objects placed below the Organization level unit. This creates a subgroup within the tree in order to organize the network resources.

OSI (Open Systems Interconnection) Defines the rules for communication between network devices.

packet Small, manageable pieces of data that are transmitted over the network.

packet burst Data transmission in which a whole group or "burst" of packets can be sent at once. An acknowledgement still has to be sent, but only one acknowledgement for a group of packets versus one acknowledgement for each packet.

packet receive buffers Store incoming data until the server can process it. Two parameters that can be set in the packet receive buffer are the maximum and minimum packet receive buffer, referring to how much space is allocated to store data.

parent partition A partition that is above another partition in the NDS directory tree is called a parent of the partition that is below it. (See also **child partition**.)

partitioning The process of dividing the database into multiple parts. This is beneficial because when one server with a part of the NDS database (called a *replica*) on it goes down, the resources in that replica can still be accessed.

pass-through authentication Occurs when you choose a domain to log on to from your NT computer, but your computer doesn't have an account in that domain.

password administrator Used in organizations that utilize a help desk. This administrator has limited rights for User objects, groups, login scripts, and passwords.

Performance Monitor   Configured to monitor system performance, to gather vital information on system statistics, and to analyze and graphically display information. Can also be configured to send alerts when a hacker may be attempting to compromise security. There are four ways to view the information gathered by the Performance monitor: chart, alert, log, and report.

Physical Layer   Bottom OSI layer that is only concerned with moving bits of data on and off the network medium. The Physical Layer does not define what that medium is, but it must define how to access it.

PING (Packet InterNet Groper)   A standard TCP/IP network utility that sends packets from one machine to another in order to determine whether there is a valid network route between them.

plug-and-play   The operating system can automatically detect when a new device is attached to the computer, even if the computer is currently running, and complete the hardware installation.

point-to-point connection   A connection that allows only two network devices to exist on the physical media simultaneously. A remote access connection is an example of a point-to-point connection.

Point-to-Point Protocol (PPP)   Enables links between two points with no devices in between.

Point-To-Point Protocol Multilink Protocol (PPP-MP)   An Internet standard allowing multiple protocols, such as NetBEUI and IPX, to be encapsulated within IP datagrams and transmitted over public backbones such as the Internet.

Point-to-Point Transmission (PPT)   Many computer networks use point-to-point transmission methods, where there may be one to dozens of points between the two ends (email is a good example of this). Each point is only concerned with transferring data from itself to the next point downstream.

Point-to-Point Tunneling Protocol (PPTP)   Microsoft PPTP is a transport mechanism under which remote users can connect to corporate networks through secure channels creating connections commonly referred to as Virtual Private Networks (VPNs). There are two implementations of PPTP today, one is a North American version featuring 128-bit encryption and the other is an exportable version with 40-bit encryption. (See also **Virtual Private Networks.**)

preemptive multitasking   Process that lets the operating system judge when an application has to relinquish system time to another process.

Presentation layer   OSI layer that ensures that data sent by the Application layer and received by the Session layer is in a standard format and if not, it converts the data.

Primary Domain Controller (PDC)   The central server in the network that maintains the security database for that domain.

print device   The actual hardware that prints the document. The three basic types of print devices are raster, PostScript, and plotter.

print driver   The software that allows an application to communicate with printing devices. Print drivers are composed of three files, which act together as a printing unit: printer graphics driver, printer interface driver, and characterization data file.

print job   Source code consisting of both data and commands for print processing. All print jobs are classified into data types. The data type tells the spooler what modifications need to be made to the print job so it can print correctly on the printing device.

print monitor   Controls access to the printing device, monitors the status of the device, and communicates with the spooler, which relays this information via the user interface. Controls the data going to a printer port by opening, closing, configuring, writing, reading, and releasing the port.

printer pooling   An efficient way to streamline the printing process. It sends print jobs to a pool of printing devices, in which only one printing device actually prints the document.

print processor   Completes the rendering process. (See also **rendering**.)

print router   Routes the print job from the spooler to the appropriate print processor.

print spooler   A service that actually manages the print process.

printing software   Considered the printer. A printer is software that manages a specific printing device (or devices, in case of printer pooling). The printer determines how the print job gets to the printing device, via parallel port, serial port, or via the network.

printer   See printing software.

Privacy Act   See Electronics Communications Privacy Act (ECPA).

proactive administration   The collection of tasks that attempts to prevent errors and avoid problems on the network. Proactive administration results in less reactive administration. (See also **reactive administration**.)

property rights   Property rights allow a trustee to access the values of the properties information stored within NDS. The property rights are Compare, Read, Write, and Add or Delete Self, and Supervisor.

protected memory space   Memory set aside for applications or NLMs that might not be stable. Protected memory space is separate from the server kernel, which means that if the application or NLM that is loaded in the protected memory space fails, it will not affect the server. This keeps the server from crashing or abending due to unstable applications or NLMs.

protocols   Languages used by computers. In order for two computers to talk to each other they must speak the same language (use the same protocol).

proxy server   A local server between the client workstation and the Internet itself.

public key cryptography   Consists of a public key and a private key. The public key is given freely to anyone that needs it, and the private key is kept secret by the keys' owner and is stored in the user's security file.

RAID (Redundant Array of Inexpensive Disks)   Enables a system to segment data and store pieces of it on several different drives, using a process known as data striping. (See also **data striping**.)

RAM (Random Access Memory)   Physical memory where programs and modules are loaded that are used on the server.

reactive administration   The collection of tasks that fix problems as they arise. It is "reactive" to the situation at hand. (See also **proactive administration**.)

read-only replica   Receives updates from master and read/write replicas, but does not allow their NDS objects to be modified. (See also **master replica** and **read/write replica**.)

read/write replica   Copies of the master replica that also send out the changes made to the NDS objects that they contain. (See also **master replica**.)

REGEDT32.EXE   Executable that launches the Registry Editor. (See also **Registry** and **Registry Editor**.)

Registry   A powerful database that controls your computer by containing all your system and program configuration parameters. Contains the SAM and configuration data for applications, hardware, and device drivers. The Registry also contains data on user-specific information including settings from user-profiles, desktop settings, software configurations, and network settings.

Registry Editor   A Microsoft tool for searching the Registry. Both the new tool, REGEDIT.EXE, and the traditional registry editor, REGEDT32.EXE, are included. Some of the new features of REGEDIT.EXE include improved search capabilities and a Windows Explorer interface. (See also **Registry**.)

relative distinguished name   A relative distinguished name lists the path from the current context to the object, does not contain a leading period, and can have an ending period. The relative distinguished name can be confusing because it starts with the object that it is trying to reach, although it is intended to lead to that object from the current context. Remember that this type of name is locating a resource in a context relative to the current context. (See also **distinguished name**.)

Remote Access Service (RAS)   Enables users to connect over a phone line to your network and access resources as if they were at a computer connected directly to the network.

remote control   A program that grants a user remote control so they can administer a server. This variation of external networking allows the client to take full control of the machine; all input devices, like the keyboard and mouse, are routed to the remote client.

remote node   The external networking method employed by Windows NT Remote Access Services (RAS). The remote node method allows a remote client machine to dial into a server and attach itself to the network using various protocols. (See also **Remote Access Service**.)

Remote Procedure Call (RPC) Used by programmers to create an application consisting of multiple procedures; some run on the local computer, and others run on remote computers over a network. RPCs allow commands to be sent from one system to execute programs on another system.

Remote Procedure Call (RPC) Locator Default service that allows distributed applications to use the Microsoft RPC service and manages the RPC Name Service database. The server side of distributed applications registers its availability with this service. The client side of distributed applications queries this service to find available server applications.

Remote Procedure Call (RPC) Service Default service that is the RPC subsystem for Windows NT. It includes the endpoint mapper and other related services.

rendering The process of translating print data into a form that a printing device can read.

repeater Connects network cables by regenerating signals so they can travel on additional cable lengths.

replicas Copies of partitions. (See also **partitioning**.)

resource An entity that exists on the network. A service provides access to the resource.

resource domains Process of sharing resources, like printers and files, within a domain. Administered by the Resource Domain Controller.

Resource Management Service (RMS) Allows centralized printing resources such as print drivers, PDF (printer definition) files, and banners, to be downloaded to clients or printers.

rights The term used for security access to various network resources.

ring topology When the computers in a network form an electrical loop with their connecting cable. (See also **bus topology** and **star topology**.)

risk The measurement of exposure to possible harm or loss. The threat could be from a variety of sources, including market forces, disgruntled employees, competitors, or one's own inefficient/outdated processes.

roaming profile Workstation settings stored on the network to give a user the same environment, no matter which workstation they're logged into.

roaming user A user who logs on to the network at different times from different computers.

[Root] The top of the NDS tree. There is only one root object. It is created during the first server installation into the NDS tree. The [Root] can contain only Country objects or the Organization object. It does not contain any Leaf objects other than Alias objects, if the Alias represents a Country or an Organization.

routers Use the destination network address to see where a packet should go. (See also **routing**.)

routing   Process of forwarding a packet from one segment to another segment until it arrives at its final destination. A router makes decisions as to where to send network packets by looking at the network addresses of the packets it receives before passing them on.

routing table   Used by bridges to determine whether data is destined for the local network.

SAM (Security Access Manager)   A database that maintains all user, group, and workstation accounts in a secure database. (2) Registry subtree that contains all account and security information for local users on a nondomain controller and for all users in the current domain on a domain controller.

schema   NDS schema is the structure of objects that can be stored within the directory tree.

secret key cryptography   Secret key encrypts and decrypts messages using a single secret key called a bulk encryption key in the Key Management Server. Two examples of secret key cryptography are DES and CAST. The Key Management Server supports CAST 40 and CAST 64. DES and CAST 64 are available only in North America.

sector   The smallest storage unit on a hard disk. A typical sector holds 512 bytes of data.

Secure Attention Sequence   Invoked at logon by pressing CTRL-ALT-DELETE, this feature requires the user to acknowledge the notice by clicking the OK button in the message box before continuing.

SECURITY   Registry subtree that contains security information for the local machine on nondomain controllers and for the entire domain on domain controllers.

security descriptors   Describes the security attributes for an object, and has the following parts: Owner security ID, which identifies the owner of the object; Group security ID, which is only used by the POSIX subsystem; and Discretionary access control list (ACL), which identifies the groups and users who are allowed and denied access.

Security Equivalence   The ability to grant an object all the rights that another object has, simply by making them equivalent.

Security ID (SID)   Used to uniquely identify each user, NT Workstation, and Server on the network.

Security Log   A report where suspicious information can be filtered and tracked.

Security Reference Monitor   Verifies that the user has permissions to access the requested object, and then performs that action.

Server   Default service that provides remote procedure call RPC support, and file, print and named piping sharing using SMB services.

server administrator   This administrator can change passwords, group memberships, and login scripts.

server alerts   Used to send notification messages to users or computers. Server alerts are generated by the system, and relate to server and resource use. They warn about security and access problems, user session problems, printer problems, and server shutdown because of power loss when the UPS service is available.

Server Manager   A utility not only for managing servers, but for managing workstations and the domain. Allows the administrator to control most domain activity, including domain administration, setting up shares, configuring replication settings, modifying services, and monitoring user connections.

Service Registry Service (SRS)   Holds and advertises printer registration information (device type, address, and device-specific information) for public access servers so that users and administrators can find them.

services   Processes that run in the background of a Windows NT environment and may be started automatically at boot time or manually started and stopped by the Administrator or Server Operators. Services provide access to resources on the network. (See also **resource**.)

Session layer   OSI layer that manages dialogs between computers. It does this by establishing, managing, and terminating communications between the two computers. (See the three types of dialogs that the Session layer uses: **simplex dialogs**, **half-duplex dialogs**, and **full-duplex dialogs**.)

share   Created by granting a particular resource a share name. This name is what other users or devices recognize as the entity with which they have permission to access. (See also **share-level security**.)

share-level security   Used to give other users access to your hard drive via the network. The four types of share permissions are No Access, Read, Change, and Full Control.

Simple Network Management Protocol (SNMP)   An Internet standard for monitoring and configuring network devices. An SNMP network is composed of management systems and agents.

simplex dialogs   Used by the OSI Session layer to allow data to flow in only one direction. Since the dialog is one way, information can be sent, but not responded to, or even acknowledged.

SLIP (Serial Line Internet Protocol)   An older protocol used to carry TCP/IP over low-speed serial lines.

SMB (Server Message Block)   Services that form the backbone of Microsoft networking in the Windows NT environment. All file and printer sharing in Windows NT operate using the SMB services.

SOFTWARE   Registry subtree that contains software configuration information pertaining to the local computer.

Spooler   Provides print spooler services.

star topology   In a star topology, all computers are directly cabled to a hub. (See also **bus topology** and **ring topology**.)

star bus topology   If you replace the computers in a bus topology with the hubs from star topology networks, you get a star bus topology.

star ring topology   Also called star-wired ring. The smaller hubs are internally wired like a ring and connected to the main hub in a star topology.

Storage Management Services (SMS)   The combination of services that Novell NetWare 5 has bundled as a backup-and-restore product for simple to complex networks.

subnet mask   Used to hide part of the IP address in order to distinguish the network from the host on the network.

subordinate references   Created automatically by NDS when a server's hard drive holds a replica of a partition, but not a replica of its child partition.

swap file   A temporary file that stores information from RAM that is not being used at this moment in time but will be needed in the future. This is quicker and more efficient than unloading and loading a file or module. (See also **virtual memory**.)

switch   A common solution to traffic problems, a switch calculates which devices are connected to each port.

symmetric cryptography   So named because both the sender and receiver use a single key.

SYN Flood Attack   A flood of TCP connection requests (SYN) that can be sent to a server, effectively tying it up and causing the server to respond with a reset to all further connection requests.

SYSTEM   Registry subtree that contains all data that is essential for starting the system.

System Policy Editor   Tool that provides the ability to configure and maintain the environment and actions of users, groups and computers. Controls the same configurations as the Registry Editor. (See also **Registry Editor**.)

System User Access Form   Defines the appropriate level of access depending on the user's job responsibilities.

Systems Security Audit   An independent examination designed to determine whether adequate controls exist to ensure the following corporate IT objectives: effectiveness, efficiency, compliance, reliability of information, confidentiality, integrity, and availability.

target   The NetWare server or workstation that is to be backed up. (See also **host server** and **console workstation**.)

TCP/IP (Transmission Control Protocol/Internet Protocol)   An industry-standard suite of protocols designed for local and wide-area networking. Widely used for Internet communication.

Teardrop and Teardrop 2 Attacks   Attacks that can cause a system to halt by using up all available memory in the kernel.

Telnet   Terminal emulation for character-based communicating.

thrashing   Refers to the noise made when you have exceeded the amount of physical RAM in the system, your paging file is becoming full, and the system is looking for more available memory.

time synchronization   Process that NetWare servers use to coordinate and agree on a correct time.

Token Ring   Token Ring networks do not use a shared-access architecture. Instead, they use a token-passing media access method that is defined by the IEEE 802.5 standard. Unlike Ethernet networks, Token Ring networks pass a token from station to station. Instead of having the nodes listen to the network as to when it is safe to transmit, the node must first be in possession of the token to transmit. (See also **Ethernet**, **ATM**, and **FDDI**.)

tracert   Traces the path that a packet follows to its destination server.

Transport layer   OSI layer that ensures reliable delivery of data to its destinations. The Transport layer consists of two protocols, the Transmission Control Protocol (TCP) and the User Datagram Protocol (UDP).

trigger   Conditions that must be met before an action occurs.

Trivial File Transfer Protocol (TFTP)
Similar to the file transfer protocol, but does not require user authentication.

trust   A communications and administrative link between two domains that permits the sharing of resources and account information. There are two possible trust configurations, the one-way trust and the two-way trust. In a one-way trust, one domain trusts the users in the other domain to use its resources. A two-way trust is actually comprised of two one-way trusts. Each domain trusts the user accounts in the other domain.

trusted domain   Domain in which your workstation doesn't have an account. A user in one domain also can be authenticated to another domain by establishing trust relationships. (See also **trust**.)

trustee   Any object within NDS that is granted rights to another object. (See also **rights**.)

trust relationship   A one-way administrative and communicative link between two domains allowing one domain (the trusting domain) to honor authentication requests from users of another domain (the trusted domain). (See also **trust** and **trusted domain**.)

twisted pair   The most common Ethernet implementation used today. (See also **coaxial cable** and **fiber-optic cable**.)

typeful name   A distinguished name that includes the attribute abbreviation along with the name of the object. (See also **distinguished name** and **typeless name**.)

typeless name   A distinguished name without the attribute abbreviations. (See also **distinguished name** and **typeless name**.)

UNC (Universal Naming Convention)   Each computer in the domain or workgroup is given a "friendly name," which Windows NT converts into the TCP/IP address, MAC address, or other identifiable means of routing the information. The syntax for the UNC name is *copmutername\sharename*. A full UNC consists of the server's name and the name of the share on the server that you wish to use. The names are then put together in the format of \\<*Server Name*>\<*Share Name*>\ to form a UNC.

UPS (Uninterruptable Power Supply)   A device consisting of a stand-alone power source (a battery or a generator) and circuitry which will automatically and instantaneously switch from building power to backup power in the case of an outage.

user account   Represent users who access the resources on the domain. User accounts do not have to represent individuals; they can also be accounts for services, such as a SQL Server account.

User Manager for Domains   The administrative tool used to manage user accounts, groups, and policies. You can copy, rename, or delete user accounts with User Manager. The User Manager for Domains contains three policies that can be customized for different security needs, Account Policies, User Rights, and Auditing Policies. (See also **account policies, user rights**, and **auditing policies**.)

User Mode   Often referred to as nonprivileged processor mode, this is where most of Windows NT code is located. This is also where applications and the various subsystems are run. User Mode is designed to prevent applications from bringing down the operating system.

User object   Represents a person who accesses the network.

user profile   User profiles allow the administrator to control a user's environmental settings from the network. Environmental settings include items such as the user's desktop configuration, startup applications, and automatic network connections. These types of configuration settings are typically set by the user according to personal preferences, and are retained in configuration files known as user profiles.

user rights   Allow you to control which operations a user or group performs. Each right enables the user to perform specific operations on the computer.

Virtual File Allocation Table (VFAT)   With the Windows 95 operating system, enhancements were made to FAT, and the new version was called Virtual File Allocation Table (VFAT). VFAT enables the use of long filenames, while maintaining the 8.3 naming convention for older applications viewing the same file.

Virtual LANs (VLANs)   Restrict where the data can travel by configuring communications equipment to route data across specific paths.

virtual memory   An extension of RAM that allows items stored in RAM to be swapped to the hard drive. This frees up RAM for other purposes and can make the server more efficient. (See also **swap file**.)

Virtual Memory Manager (VMM) Responsible for the use of virtual memory and the paging file in the system.

Virtual Private Networks (VPNs)   Networks that use the connections already established by the protocols as its medium for transmission.

volatile user   The volatile user is removed from the workstation after logging out of the network.

Windows NT Diagnostics   Utility to view various system, resource, and environment information. Also used to monitor possible breaches of security.

wireless bridge   Provides wireless connectivity of remote Ethernet networks and is fully transparent to network protocol and applications.

wireless connectivity   Can be achieved through the use of existing cellular telephone links.

workgroup   A collection of computers that have been logically grouped together for the purpose of sharing resources.

Z.E.N.works (Zero Effort Networks) Novell's network management utility.

zone transfers   Configuration updates to replica servers are called zone transfers.

INDEX

10Base2 (Thinnet), 935-936
10Base5 (Thicknet), 934-935
10BaseT/100BaseTX (Twisted-Pair), 936-939
100Base-T4 (Twisted-Pair), 939-940

A

Abends. *see* Server abends and lockups
Access control
    Access Control List (ACL), 21-22, 596
    NDS database and, 617
Accessibility guideline document, 856-858
    accessing NDS objects and, 856
    centralized user environment and, 856
    Novell's suggested guidelines for, 857-858
Accessibility Options, 302
Accessibility plan, 853-869
    accessibility guideline document. *see*
        Accessibility guideline document
    administrative strategies document. *see*
        Administrative strategies document
    user needs document. *see* User needs
        document
Account expiration and lockout, 80
Account policies, 1156-1157
Across-the-wire migration, 404-405
    advantages/disadvantages of, 405
    Novell Upgrade Wizard and, 404, 411-414
    prerequisites for, 411-414

procedures for, 404-405
    steps in process, 418-421
Addressing
    host address, 460-461
    IP address, 460-461
    MAC address, 720-721
    Network Layer addressing, 731
    Transport Layer addressing, 738
Admin preferences, FastTrack Web Server,
    576-577
Administration
    proactive type, 6
    reactive type, 5
    security and
        centralized administration, 600-602
        distributed administration, 600-602
    server maintenance, 4
    workstation maintenance, 4
Administrative strategies document, 859-866
    common login scripts, 859-860
    legacy services, 862-866
    security guidelines, 860-862
Administrative Wizards, Windows NT, 1080
Administrators
    backup, 861
    container, 861
    enterprise, 861
    file system, 604-605
    password, 861-862
    server, 862

Analog signaling, 717
Appletalk, 1102
Application Layer (Layer 7), OSI, 753-755
  service advertising, 753-754
  service use methods, 754-755
Application Object Template (.AOT) files,
  256-257
Application services, 679-680
Applications, managing
  application design specialist, 774
  application directories and, 481
  application objects, 269-275
  complex applications, 263
  location and, 486
  NAL and, 251
  objects and property rights, 264-265
  scheduling application upgrades, 307-308
  simple applications, 263
  user needs document and, 854-855
  viewing inherited applications, 267-268
  see also NetWare Application Launcher
Asynchronous Transfer Mode (ATM) networks,
  952-953
Attributes. *see* File system attributes
Audit policies, 1159-1161
Authentication
  client, 580
  NDS database and, 617
  server, 579
  single login and, 9, 47
Automatic Client Update (ACU), 35, 1204

B

Backup, 535-550
  child and, 542
  as disaster recovery option, 1051-1052

  guidelines for, 543
  host and, 542
  for NDS and file system, 543
  for NetWare 5 Server, 543-544
  parent and, 542
  restoring data and, 545-546
  security rights and, 540-541
  Storage Management Services and,
    536-537
  target and, 542
  time requirements and, 538-540
  TSA and, 542
  types of
    differential, 538-541
    full, 538-541
    incremental, 538-541
  for workstations, 544
Backup administrator, 861
Backup domain controllers (BDC),
  1128-1129
Bandwidth
  baseband transmission, 718
  broadband transmission, 718
  partitioning strategies and, 886
  Remote Control Access (NEBO) and, 221
Baseband transmission
  bandwidth and, 718
  Ethernet and, 932
Bindery services, 886
Bit synchronization, 717
Bits, 932
Block size
  customizing, 381
  for simple installations, 376
Block suballocation
  disabling, 381
  optimizing disk space, 523-524

performance and, 475
    for simple installations, 377
Bridges, 699
Broadband transmission
    bandwidth and, 718
    Ethernet and, 932
Brouters, 700
Browser client, 49-50
Bus I/O problems, 1046-1047
Bus topology, 712
Bus types, network adapters, 944-946
    EISA (32-bit), 945
    ISA (8-bit), 945
    ISA (16-bit), 945
    MC (32), 945
    NICs and, 944-946
    PCI, 945-946
    PCMCIA, 945-946
    VESA Local Bus, 945-946

C

Cable media
    coaxial, 693-694, 934
    Ethernet networks and, 934
    fiber-optic, 694-695
    hard drives and, 976
    Token Ring networks and, 942-944
    twisted-pair
        shielded twisted-pair (STP), 690-693
        unshielded twisted-pair (UTP), 690-693
Cache Buffer Memory, 520-521
Cache buffers, 514
Call for Help dialog, 235
Capture
    CAPTURE command, 102
    capture process, 1013

capture switches
    capturing a printer port in Windows
        95, 103-104
    compared with CAPTURE
        command, 99-102
Career Center, 1277-1287
    interviewing, 1282-1287
        acing the interview, 1285-1287
        follow up, 1287
        preparation for, 1285
        working with a headhunter,
            1283-1285
    job search, 1278-1282
        networking and, 1279-1280
        online, 1281-1282
        placement services for, 1280-1281
Carrier Sense Multiple Access/Collision
    Detection (CSMA/CD), 932-933
CD-ROMs, 982-983
Cell switching, 734
Cellular topology, 713-714
Centralized administration
    domain networks and, 1096
    security and, 600-602
Certificates, 581
Change control, 446
Channel Service Unit/Digital Service Unit
    (CSU/DSU), 700
Child, backup, 542
Circuit switching, 732
Class A station, 951
Class B station, 951
Classes, 14
Client 32
    Advanced Settings page for, 103
    components required for connectivity,
        34-36

installation for Windows 95, 37-40
exercise for, 38-40
optional components, 37-38
types of installations, 37
installation for Windows NT, 41-42
integration with NDPS, 106
ODI specifications supported by, 33-36
printing management and, 103
software components (NLMs) included with, 33
workstation requirements for, 33
Clients
authentication and, 580
browser client, 49-50
installing and configuring multiple clients, 291-299
legacy services and client configuration, 864
minimum software version requirements for, 408-409
Cluster management, 581
Coaxial cable, 693-694, 934
Collision Detection, 932-933
COMCHECK, 912
Common Name, 352-354
Compatibility mode, 430
Complete trust, 1188-1190
Complex applications, 263
Computer System Policy, 306
CONFIG.NLM, 410
Configuration
CONFIG.NLM and, 410
DHCP, 556-561
DNS, 562-564
FastTrack Web Server, 574-581
file compression, 525
file system rights in NAL, 275-276

IDE controller, 971-975
IDE drives, 969-970
IP, 460-461
IPX, 461-462
Launcher, 254-255, 265-267
legacy services and client configuration, 864
multiple clients, 291-299
NDS for login, 361
NDS for resource access, 361-362
NetWare Connect, 660-666
NICs and, 946-948
Novell Administrator for Windows NT, 1221-1224
printers and print queues, 308-309
SCSI controller, 975
SCSI drives, 970-971
snAPPShot and, 258-263
virtual memory, 518-519
Workstation Manager, 296-298
Configuration management, networks, 680-681
Connectivity
design specialist for, 775
devices for. see Internetwork connectivity devices; Network connectivity devices
error control services, 722
flow control services, 722
multipoint type, 710
point-to-point type, 710
Connectors, NICs, 944
Consistency check errors, 1037
Console One
creating a user in, 72
navigation of, 497
overview of, 495-496

ServerTop and, 506
Console workstations, 536-537
Container administrators
    administrative strategies document and, 861
    creation of, 321-323
    definition of, 603-604
    security function of, 320-321
Container login script, 47
Container objects
    Country, 349-350, 352
    definition of, 10-11
    naming and, 806-808
    NDS database and, 319, 617
    Organization, 349-350, 352
    Organizational Units, 349-350, 352
Container script
    cascading, 200-201
    execution of, 187
    pitfalls to avoid, 202
    as property of container object, 187-188
Contention, 720
CONTEXT, 198
Context
    contextless login and, 356-357
    current context, 356
    naming and, 352-354
    object context, 356
    overview, 58-62
    resource access and, 354-357
Contextless login, 356-357
Control Panel, Windows NT, 1077-1078
Conventional memory, 1005
Country, as container object, 349-350, 352
CPU-detected errors, 1036-1037
CPU problems, 1046
Crosstalk, 906

CSMA/CD, 932-933
CSU/DSU, 700
Current context, 356
Custom Device Module (CDM), 416

D

Data
    distributed data, 680
    encoding, 715
    recovery, 1052-1053
    restoring, 545-546
Data Link Layer (Layer 2)
    addressing, 720-721
    connection services of, 722
    function of, 718
    logical topology of, 719
    media access control, 719-720
    modulation, 715
    transmission synchronization, 721
Data migration
    enabling, 381-382
    for simple installations, 377-378
Data translation
    bit order translation, 751
    byte order translation, 751
Database services
    distributed data and, 680
    network services, 680
    replication and, 680
Databases
    importing and exporting DHCP
        databases, 561-562
    importing and exporting DNS databases,
        563-564
Datagram packet switching, 734

DataLink Control (DLC), 1102
Default login script, 48
Default rights. *see* Novell Directory Services, rights in
Default script, 192-193
    commands in, 192
    using NO_DEFAULT statement with, 193
Default user security, 862, 863
Designing the network, assessment phase, 759-782
    design team for, 771-776
        application specialist, 774
        assembling the team, 772
        connectivity specialist, 775
        education and training coordinator, 775-776
        IS manager, 772-773
        NDS expert, 773
        printing specialist, 774-775
        server specialist, 773-774
        testing lab coordinator, 775
        workstation specialist, 774
    gathering information for, 759-779
    processes for, 759-782
        NetWare Design and Implementation, 766-771
        System Design Life Cycles, 763-765
    see also Network solutions
Desktop management
    Accessibility Options, 302
    Desktop Preferences policy and, 302
    Roaming Profiles options, 302-303
    Windows NT and Windows 95 options, 305-306

Device drivers, updates, 1035-1036
DHCP. *see* Dynamic Host Configuration Protocol
Diagnostic tools
    COMCHECK, 912
    IPXPING, 912
    LANalyzer, 912
    PING, 912
Dial-Up Networking, 652-653
Dialog control, 749
Differential backup, 538-541
Digital signaling, 715-716
Directories
    applications directories, 481
    creating, 144
    defined, 131
    deleting, 144
    designing directory structures, 485-487
        application location and, 486
        system performance and, 486
        volume information and, 485-486
    displaying directory information, 139
    file system structure and, 470-471
    moving, 144
    object properties and, 140
    renaming, 144
    shared directories, 482
    system created directories, 477-479
    user home directories, 479-481
Directory attributes, 168-171
Directory services
    modifying, 382
    simple installation and, 378

Directory tree
    assessing needs, 872-874
        available resources and, 873-874
        company structure and, 873
        existing infrastructure and, 874
        information processing requirements
            and, 873
    creation of, 872-882
        implementation, departmental, 877-878
        implementation, divisional, 878
        implementation, organizational, 878
        models, administrative, 875
        models, divisional, 876
        models, geographic, 875
        models, hybrid, 876
    design of. *see* Directory tree, designing
    importance of location in, 351
    introduction to, 18-20
    location or context and, 352-354
    NDS database component, 17
    NDS design and, 354
    object interaction in, 352-354
    resources access and, 20-22
    structure of, 318-319, 348-352, 617-623
        [Root] object, 346, 349-351
        container objects, 349-350, 617
        Country object, 349-350
        leaf objects, 346, 349-352
        Organization object, 346, 349-351, 617
        Organizational Unit, 346, 349-351, 617
        partitions, 619-623
Directory tree, designing, 801-823
    creating a naming standards document,
        802-804
        function and need for, 802-804
        information included in, 803-804

design fundamentals for, 348
guidelines for bottom layers, 818-819
guidelines for the upper layers, 815-818
installing NDS, 880-882
naming standards and, 879
naming standards document, 802-804,
    879-880
NDS naming standard, 804-815
    leaf object names, 809-815
    server and volume names, 808-809
    tree and container units, 805-808
    workstation naming options, 813-815
Disaster recovery options, 1049-1053
    data recovery services, 1052-1053
    DS Repair, 1051
    Ontrack Data Recovery, 1052
    planning for, 1049-1050
    restoring from backups, 1051-1052
    VREPAIR, 1050-1051
Disk Administrator, Windows NT, 1079,
    1105-1107
    creating a volume set with, 1107
    partitioning hard disk with, 1106-1107
Disk duplexing, 473, 979, 982
Disk I/O problems, 1045
Disk mirroring, 472-473, 979-981
Disk space, 523-524
Disk thrashing, 518-519
DISPLAY, 199
Distinguished Name, 59-60, 357-359
    dots and, 360
    leaf objects and, 352
    naming standards and, 805
Distributed administration, security, 600-602
Distributed data, 680

DNS. *see* Domain Name Service
DNS/DHCP services
    DNS/DHCP Management Console, 556
    installing, 553-556
    NWADMIN32 snap-in files for, 556
Documentation
    accessibility guideline document. *see*
      Accessibility guideline document
    administrative strategies document. *see*
      Administrative strategies document
    naming standards document, 802-804,
      879-880
    user needs document. *see* User needs
      document
Domain controllers, 1130-1141
    domain logon process, 1131-1133
    domain user accounts, 1133-1135
    global groups, 1138-1141
    local groups, 1135-1138
Domain logon process, 1131-1133
Domain models
    complete trust, 1188-1190
    multiple master domain,
      1186-1188
    single domain, 1182-1184
    single master domain, 1184-1186
Domain Name Service (DNS)
    configuring and running, 562-564
    customizing, 462
    exporting and importing DNS databases,
      564
    installing, 553-556
    overview, 552-553
    zone objects, 563-564
    zones types, 562

Domain networks, 1096-1098
    adding workstations or servers to,
      1142-1144
    centralized administration and, 1096
    domain components of, 1097
    trusts and, 1098
Domain server roles, 1127-1130
    backup domain controllers (BDC),
      1128-1129
    member servers, 1129-1130
    primary domain controller (PDC),
      1127-1128
Domain user accounts, 1133-1135
DOS. *see* Troubleshooting, DOS workstations
DOS boot partition, 383, 407
DOS version, NetWare Administrator, 71
Dot matrix printers, 1018
Drive mapping, 142-143, 249
Drivers. *see* Device drivers, updates
DS Repair
    as disaster recovery option, 1051
    repairing NDS, 635-636
    troubleshooting with, 632-634
DSMERGE, 892-894
Dynamic Host Configuration Protocol (DHCP)
    configuring and running, 556-561
    creating DHCP server object, 558-559
    creating Subnet Address Range object,
      560-561
    creating subnet object, 559-560
    exporting and importing DHCP
      databases, 561-562
    installing, 552-553
    overview, 552-553
Dynamic Local User policy, 309-310

E

EDIT, 499-500

Effective rights
definition of, 21, 334
determining, 334-336
IRF and, 335
NDS default rights, 597
planning File system rights and, 165-167

EISA. *see* Extended Industry Standard
Architecture

Electro-Static Discharge (ESD), 906

Electromagnetic interference (EMI), 907

Encoding, 715-716

Encryption, 579, 752

Enterprise administrator, 861

Error control, 722

Errors
Consistency check errors, 1037
CPU-detected errors, 1036-1037
network errors, 1047

Ethernet networks, 932-940
10Base2 (Thinnet), 935-936
10Base5 (Thicknet), 934-935
10BaseT/100BaseTX (Twisted-Pair),
936-939
100Base-T4 (Twisted-Pair), 939-940
cabling types for, 934
how it works, 932-933
troubleshooting, 949-950

Event Notification Service (ENS), 431

Event Viewer, Windows NT, 1081-1082

Explicit rights, 329

Extended Industry Standard Architecture (EISA),
945

Extended memory, 1005

F

Fast Ethernet, 937

FastTrack Web Server, 569-590
configuration of, 574-581
Admin preferences for, 576-577
Cluster management option, 581
Global settings for, 577-578
Keys and Certificates settings,
579-581
Users and Groups settings for,
578-579
installation of, 570-574
minimum requirement for, 571-572
prerequisites for, 570-571
overview of, 570
troubleshooting, 581-584

Fault tolerance, 472-475
disk duplexing and, 473
disk mirroring and, 472-473
partitioning strategies and, 886

FDDI. *see* Fiber Distributed Data Interface

FDISPLAY, 199

Fiber Distributed Data Interface (FDDI)
networks, 950-952

Fiber-optic cable, 694-695

File Allocation Table (FAT), 1103-1104

File attributes. *see* File system attributes

File compression, 524-525
configuring, 525
Days Untouched Before Compression, 525
disabling, 381, 525
enabling, 524-525
Minimum Percentage Compression Gain,
525
for simple installations, 377

File services, networks, 677-678
File system
    accessing system, 141-143
        drive mapping and, 142-143
        Network Neighborhood and, 141-142
    components of
        files, 131
        partitioned hard drive, 130
        volume directories, 131
        volume naming, 131
        volumes, 130-131
    customizing, 381
    directory structure and, 144
    displaying system information, 138-141
        directory information, 139
        directory object properties, 140
        file information, 140
        file object properties, 140
        NetWare Administrator and, 138-139
    file management, 144-146
    legacy services and, 863-864
    utilities for, 132, 145
    volume space usage and, 146-150
File system administrator, 604-605
File system attributes, 168-174
    file and directory attributes, 168-171
    implementing, 175-176
    planning attributes, 172-174
    setting attributes, 171-172
File system information, 138-141
File system rights, 158-168, 895
    Access Control List (ACL) and, 21-22
    assigning in multicontext environment, 363
    configuring in NAL, 275-276
    controlling directory access with, 320
    effective rights

        definition of, 21, 334
        determining, 334-336
        inheritance and, 335
        NDS security and, 597
        planning file system rights and,
          165-167
    granting rights from user object, 161-162
    granting rights to a group, 160-161
    Inherited Rights Filter (IRF) and, 21, 163
    list of rights for files and directories, 160
    managed rights and, 599
    NDS default rights and, 325-328
        [Public] trustee, 326
        object rights, 326-327
        property rights, 327
    NDS rights and, 895-896
    object rights, 20, 320, 323-324
    planning, 158-160, 167-168
    property rights, 21, 324-325
    security and, 158-168
    security equivalence, 21, 163-165
    trustees and, 20, 159-160, 320
    types available, 20
    see also Novell Directory Services, rights in
File system security, 157-183
    compared with NDS object security, 592
    definition of, 77
    file system attributes and, 168-174,
        175-176
    file system rights and, 158-168
    implementing, 174-176
    login concepts for, 42
    overview, 158
    trustee rights and, 175
File system, set up, 469-491
    directories

applications directories, 481
designing directory structures, 485-487
shared directories, 482
system created directories, 477-479
user home directories, 479-481
fault tolerance, 472-475
disk duplexing and, 473
disk mirroring and, 472-473
performance and, 472-474
overview, 470-471
performance, 472-475
block suballocation and, 475
directories design and, 485-487
fault tolerance and, 472-474
spanning and, 473
Transaction Tracking System (TTS) and, 475
planning, 471-476
volumes
configuration of, 472-474
creating or modifying, 482-485
location of, 472
maintenance of, 474-476
storage requirements for, 472
File systems, Windows NT
FAT, 1103-1104, 1105
NTFS, 1104, 1105
FILER, 135-137
Files
Application Object Template (.AOT) files, 256-257
copying, 145-146
defined, 131
displaying file information, 136, 140
for DOS workstations, 993-998

file system structure and, 470-471
.INI files, 256
managing with NetWare Administrator, 144-146
object properties and, 140
salvaging with FILER, 137
swap files and, 515
FIRE PHASERS, 198
Flow control, 722
Folders, 470-471
Frames, 932
Full backup, 538-541

G

Garbage collection. *see* Memory, allocation and deallocation
Gateway, IP, 461
Global groups, 1138-1141
Global Knowledge Network, 1276
Global settings, FastTrack Web Server, 577-578
Graphical User Interface (GUI)
Console One and, 506
installation, NetWare 5 and, 382
login utility, 207-208
Group objects, 352
GUI interface. *see* Graphical User Interface

H

Hard drives, 962-977
cabling for, 976
formatting, 976-977
IDE controller configuration, 971-975

IDE drive configuration, 969-970
interface types for, 964-968
overview, 962-964
partitioning, 130
SCSI controller configuration, 975
SCSI drive configuration, 970-971
Hardware
inventory management, 299-301
requirements for upgrade to NetWare 5, 406
Help Desk, 607-608
Help Desk Policy, 234
Help Request, 229-232
Call for Help dialog, 235
Help Desk Policy and, 234
launching from NetWare Application
Launcher (NAL), 232-234
Mail for Help dialog, 236
Host
address, 460-461
backup, 542
Host Adapter Module (HAM), 416
server, 536-537
Hubs, 699, 941-942

I

I/O problems
bus, 1046-1047
disk, 1045
network, 1045-1046
IDE. *see* Integrated Drive Electronics
IETF, 106
IF, THEN, ELSE, 199

Implementation
NetWare implementation. *see* NetWare
Implementation
network solutions. *see* Network solutions,
implementation phase
Implied security equivalence, 78
In-place upgrade method, 403-404
advantages/disadvantages of, 404
prerequisites for, 409-410
procedures for, 403
server preparation for, 410
steps in process, 415-418
upgrading into existing NDS structure,
409-410
INCLUDE, 200
Incremental backup, 538-541
Industry Standard Architecture (ISA), 945
Infrared transmission, 697
Inheritable rights, 597-598
Inheritance
explicit rights and, 329
file system rights and, 163
inheritable rights and, 597-598
inherited rights and, 596
object information and, 14
property rights and, 329
security equivalence and, 330
viewing inherited applications, 267-268
Inherited rights, 596
Inherited Rights Filter (IRF)
blocking inherited rights with,
332-333
definition of, 21
effective rights and, 335
file system rights and, 163

NDS default rights and, 597
security equivalence and, 596
.INI files, 256
Ink jet printers, 1018
INSTALL, 403, 990-993
Installation
    browser client, 49-50
    Client 32 for Windows 95, 37-40
    Client 32 for Windows NT, 41-42
    DHCP, 552-553
    DNS/DHCP services, 553-556
    Domain Name Server (DNS), 553-556
    FastTrack Web Server, 570-574
    ISA 16-bit NIC, 948-949
    licenses
        NetWare Administrator, 77
        NLS Manager, 75-76
    NDPS, 109-110
    NDS, 880-882
    NetWare 5, custom, 16-13
        integrating multiple protocols, 460-462
        modifying volume parameters, 457-459
        options, 456-457
        steps in process, 457
    NetWare Client for Windows NT,
        1203-1204
    NetWare Connect, 656-660
    Novell Administrator for Windows NT,
        1221-1224
    role of installer, 605-606
    Web browser, 49-50
    Workstation Manager, 296-298
    Z.E.N.works, 217-220
Installation, NetWare 5, 373-398
    adding products and services, 391

custom installations, options
    block size, 381
    data migration enabled, 381-382
    directory services, 382
    file compression disabled, 381
    file system, 381
    language, 380
    protocols and, 382
    Server ID Number, 379-380
    suballocation disabled, 381
file system set up, 385-393
    installing and configuring protocols,
        385-388
    installing NDS, 388-392
    time zone selection, 388
hardware set up, 383-384
    autodetecting storage devices, 384
    choosing regional settings, 384
    creating DOS partition, 383
    minimum hardware requirements
        and, 382-383
NetWare partition, creating, 385
overview of, 374
server
    finalizing installation of, 390
    licensing, 391
    naming, 385
simple installations, defaults
    block size, 376
    data migration disabled, 377-378
    directory services, 378
    file compression enabled, 377
    network boards, 379
    platform support modules, 379
    protocols and, 378

Server ID Number, 375
single partition, 375
storage devices, 378-379
suballocation enabled, 377
volume (SYS), 375
using GUI utility and, 382
volume SYS:, creating, 385
Integrated Drive Electronics (IDE)
controller configuration, 971-975
drive configuration, 969-970
drives, 966
Interface types, hard drives, 964-968
Internet Engineering Task Force (IETF), 106
Internet Packet Exchange/Sequenced Packet
Exchange (IPX/SPX), 32
Internet Printing Protocol (IPP), 106
Internet Protocol (IP)
customizing, 460-461
DHCP and, 553
DNS and, 552-553
gateway, 461
host address, 460-461
IP address, 460-461
NDPS and, 430
ODI and, 35
subnet mask, 460-461
support for, 552
Internetwork connectivity devices, 700-701
CSUs/DSUs, 700
routers and brouters, 700
Internetwork Packet eXchange (IPX)
compared with IP, 552
compatibility, 462
configuring, 461-462
ODI and, 35

Intruder detection and lockout, 45-46
intruder attempt reset interval, 46
intruder lockout reset interval, 46
login security and, 80
IP. *see* Internet Protocol
IPX. *see* Internetwork Packet eXchange
IPXPING, 912
IS (information services) manager, 772-773
ISA. *see* Industry Standard Architecture

J

Java APIs, 506

K

Keys, 579-581

L

LANalyzer, 1047-1049
diagnostics and, 912
monitoring network performance,
1048-1049
network errors, 1047
server and network overloads, 1048-1049
Language, custom options for, 380
LANs, 346, 675
Large Internet packets (LIP), 528-529
Laser printers, 1018
Launcher Configuration, 254-255, 265-267
Leaf objects, 10-13
defined, 11
directory tree structure and, 346
Directory tree structure and, 349-352

Distinguished Name and, 352
naming and, 809-815
NDS database and, 319
table and definitions of, 11-13
Legacy access, 855-856
Legacy services
administrative strategies document for, 862-866
client configuration, 864
mobile user, 864, 865-866
remote user, 864-865
standard file system, 863-864
Licensing
with NetWare Administrator, 77
with NLS Manager, 75-76
server installation and, 391
Line noise, 907
Link Support Layer (LSL), 35
Local area networks (LANs), 346, 675
Local groups, 1135-1138
Local printer, 1012-1013
Local Security Authority (LSA), 1068
Local user profile, 1163
Lockups. *see* Server abends and lockups
Logical memory addressing, 514
Logical topology, 719
Login, 42-49
authentication
login process and, 47
NDS and, 9
Z.E.N.works and, 221
contextless login, 356-357
intruder detection and lockout, 45-46
NTDS and, 1126
passwords, 80

process for, 47-49
restrictions, 43-45
Login Time Restrictions, 44
network address restrictions, 44
Password Restrictions, 44
security, 43, 79-80
Login identifier variables, 194-197
Login script commands, 197-200
CONTEXT, 198
DISPLAY, 199
external or DOS commands, 198
FDISPLAY, 199
FIRE PHASERS, 198
IF, THEN, ELSE, 199
INCLUDE, 200
MAP, 197-198
A REM, REMARK, 199
WRITE, 198-199
Login scripts, 47-48, 185-214
administrative strategies document for, 859-860
container scripts, 47, 187-188
creating, executing, debugging, 202-207
default scripts, 48, 192-193
designing systems, 193-202
cascading container scripts, 200-201
container script pitfalls, 202
login identifier variables and, 194-197
login script commands and, 197-200
executing NAL with, 277
GUI login utility and, 207-208
location of, 186
naming and, 363-364
order of execution, 186
overview, 186-193

PAUSE, 209
profile scripts, 47, 188-190
registering workstations and, 226-227
testing, 203
user scripts, 48, 190-192
uses of, 186
for Workstation Manager, 291-292
Login time restrictions, 44, 80
LoginID, 58

M

MAC address, 720-721
Magneto-optical drives, 984
Mail for Help dialog, 236
Maintenance
server, 4
workstation, 4
Maintenance, NDS, 615-646
crashed SYS volume and, 637-639
preventative, 628-631
backups and, 629
managing SYS: volume, 630
network traffic and, 628-629
quality equipment and, 629
updating servers, 630
repairing, 634-636
DS Repair, 635-636
NDS Manager, 636
replication and, 617-627
synchronization and, 627-628
NDS synchronization, 627-628
time synchronization, 628
troubleshooting, 631-634
DS Repair and, 632-634

error messages, 631-632
NDS Manager and, 632-633
NWADMIN and, 632
Managed rights, 599
Mandatory user profile, 1164-1165
MAP, 197-198
Map command options, 143
Master replica, 624-625
MC. *see* Micro Channel
Media. *see* Transmission media
Media access control (MAC), 719-720
contention, 720
MAC address and, 720-721
polling, 720
token-passing, 720
Member servers, 1129-1130
Memory
allocation and deallocation, 516-517
cache buffers and, 514, 520-521
conventional, 1005
extended, 1005
garbage collection and, 516
logical memory addressing, 514
overview, 514-516
permanent storage, 515
protected memory space, 514
RAM required, 514
swap files and, 515
upper memory blocks, 1005
viewing information with MONITOR,
520
virtual memory, 515, 517-519
configuring, 518-519
disk thrashing and, 518-519
Mesh topology, 713-714

Message services, network, 679

Message switching, 732

Metropolitan area network, 676

Micro Channel (MC), 945

Microwave transmission
  satellite systems, 697
  terrestrial systems, 696-697

Migration across-the-wire, 404-405
  advantages/disadvantages of, 405
  Novell Upgrade Wizard and, 404
  procedures for, 404-405

Migration from queue-based printing, 443-445

Mobile clients, 647-670
  NetWare Connect, 651-652
    configuration of, 660-666
    connecting to Dial-Up Networking
      with, 652
    installation of, 656-660
    remote access services of, 652
    remote clients supported by, 654
  remote control connection, 648-651
  remote node connection, 648-650

Mobile user
  access needs of, 865
  administration for, 865-866
  design for, 864
  legacy services and, 864, 865-866

Modems, 699

Modulation, 715

MONITOR, 519-520
  Cache Buffer Memory and, 520-521,
    520-521
  increasing maximum packet buffers, 522
  viewing memory information with, 520

Multiple Link Interface Driver (MLID), 34

Multiple master domain, 1186-1188

Multiple Station Access Unit (MSAU),
  941-942

Multiplexing, 700, 718

Multipoint connection, 710

Multitasking
  cooperative, 1063
  preemptive, 1064

My Computer, Windows NT, 1075-1076

N

Naming
  Common Name, 352-354
  Distinguished Name, 357-359, 360
  dots and, 360
  login scripts and, 363-364
  object information and, 14
  object location and, 352-354
  Relative Distinguished Name, 359, 360
  Typeful Names, 359
  Typeless Names, 359
  volumes and, 131, 474

Naming standards, 804-815, 879
  leaf object names, 809-815
  server and volume names, 808-809
  templates for, 811
  tree and container units, 805-808
  workstation naming options, 813-815

Naming standards document, 879-880
  function and need for, 802-804
  information included in, 803-804

NCOPY, 145

NDIR, 134-135

NDPS. *see* Novell Distributed Printing Services

NDS. *see* Novell Directory Services

Nearest active upstream neighbor (NAUN), 941

NETADMIN, 71

NetAdmin. *see* NetWare Administrator

NetBIOS Extended User Interface (NetBEUI), 1100

NetWare 3
legacy access needs and, 855
upgrading, 400-428

NetWare 5 Server
backup for, 543-544
installing NDPS on, 109-110
upgrading to, 400-428

NetWare Administrator (NWADMIN), 62
configuring NetWare Connect with, 663-666
displaying system information, 138-139
DOS version of, 71
file compression and, 525
file management with, 144-146
file system management and, 137-138
licensing with, 77
NWADMIN32 and
creating a user in, 69-71
snap-in files, 556-557
troubleshooting with, 632
volume maintenance with, 475
Windows NT workstations and, 1199-1200
managing network applications, 1201
managing user accounts, 1200

NetWare Application Launcher (NAL), 247-285, 896
Applications property page of, 255
configuring NDS and file system for, 256-276

enabling, 254-255
execution using login scripts, 277
features of, 250-253
application management, 251
OS and executables for, 253
security in, 251
single seat administration in, 251
software distribution and, 251
use of wrapper technology, 252
file system rights and, 275-276
Help Request and, 232-234
introduction to, 248-250
Launcher Configuration and, 254-255, 265-267
launching applications with, 277
objects and property rights and, 264-268
search drive mappings with, 249
snAPPShot and, 256-263
switches for, 278

NetWare Client, using with Windows NT, 1202-1204
Automatic Client Update (ACU) and, 1204
installation of, 1203-1204

NetWare Configuration Files (NCF), 498-500

NetWare Connect (NWCCON), 651-652
configuration
with NetWare Administrator, 663-666
options, 661
remote access configuration, 662
security for ports and services, 662-663
at server console, 660-663
connecting to Dial-Up Networking with, 652-653

installation, 656-660

remote access services of, 652

remote clients supported by, 654

NetWare Core Protocol (NCP), 430

NetWare design and implementation phases

design phase, 769

implementation phase, 770

manage and monitor phase, 770-771

project approach phase, 766-768

NetWare Graphical Identification and
Authentication (NWGINA), 1206

NetWare implementation, 871-900

directory tree, assessing needs, 872-874

available resources and, 873-874

company structure and, 873

existing infrastructure and, 874

information processing requirements
and, 873

directory tree, creating, 872-882

directory tree, defining network solution

implementation types, 877-878

organizational models, 875

directory tree, designing

installing NDS, 880-882

naming standards and, 879

naming standards document and,
879-880

merging NDS trees, DSMERGE, 890-894

network access, 894-896

administrative strategies for, 896

file system rights and, 895

NDS rights and, 895-896

partitions and replicas

partitions, 883-885

replicas, 885

time synchronization, 886-890

NetWare 5 Time Synchronization,
889-890

Novell Time Synchronization model,
887-889

strategies for, 890

NetWare Internet Access Server (NIAS), 651

NetWare Licensing Services (NLS), 74-76

NetWare Licensing Services (NLS) Manager,
74-76

NetWare Loadable Modules (NLMs)

Client 32 and, 33

loading/unloading, 497-498

managing NDPS with, 114

providing services via, 8

SYS default volume and, 471

NetWare Operating System, 457

NetWare Peripheral Architecture (NWPA),
416

NetWire on CompuServe, 914-917

Network access, 31-56

administrative strategies for, 896

browser client installation for, 49-50

Client 32 and, 32-42

installation for Windows 95, 37-40

installation for Windows NT, 41-42

overview, 33-36

enabling communication protocol for,
32-33

file system rights, 895

login

concepts of, 42-46

process for, 47-49

NDS rights, 895-896

Network address restrictions, 44, 80

Network boards, 378-379

Network communication, IPX/IP protocol
for, 32

Network connectivity devices, 698-700
  bridges, 699
  hubs, 699
  modems, 699
  multiplexer, 700
  Network Interface Card (NIC), 699
  repeaters, 699
  transmission media connectors, 698

Network design and implementation
  accessibility plan. *see* Accessibility plan
  assessment phase. *see* Designing the network,
    assessment phase
  directory tree. *see* Directory tree, designing
  NetWare implementation. *see* NetWare
    Implementation
  network solutions. *see* Network solutions
  partition boundaries. *see* Partitioning,
    stategies for
  time synchronization. *see* Time
    synchronization strategies

Network I/O problems, 1045-1046

Network Interface Board. *see* Network Interface
  Card

Network Interface Card (NIC), 33-34, 699,
  998-1000
  adapter bus types, 944-946
    EISA (32-bit), 945
    ISA (8-bit), 945
    ISA (16-bit), 945
    MC (32), 945
    PCI, 945-946
    PCMCIA, 945-946

    VESA Local Bus, 945-946
  installation of ISA NIC, 948-949
  network adapter configuration, 946-948
  network adapter connectors for, 944

Network Layer (Layer 3)
  addressing, 731, 732
  common protocols suites for, 737
  connection services of, 736
  gateway services of, 736-737
  overview, 730
  routing, 734-735
    route discovery, 735
    route selection, 734-735
    static routes, 734-735
  switching, 732-734
    cell switching, 734
    circuit switching, 732
    message switching, 732
    packet switching, 733-734

Network management, 680-681
  accounting management, 681
  configuration management, 680-681
  fault management, 681
  performance management, 681
  security management, 681

Network Neighborhood
  accessing file system with, 141-142
  Windows NT and, 1077

Network printer, 1013

Network services, 676-680
  application services, 679-680
  database services
    distributed data and, 680
    replication and, 680
  file services, 677-678

message services, 679
overview
    peer-to-peer networks, 677
    server-centric networks, 677
    service providers, 677
    service requestors, 677
print services, 678-679
Network solutions. *see also* Designing the
  network, assessment phase
calculate results
    benefits, 785, 792-794
    costs, 785, 792-794
    risks, 785, 792-794
create schedule for, 785
define the solution, 786
design phase, 788-790
gather information for, 786
implementation phase, 790-792, 795
sell the solution, 785, 794
solution design considerations, 786-788
see also Directory tree, designing
Network Time Protocol (NTP), 838
Networking, 671-685
components of
    network services, 676
    protocols, 676
    transmission media, 676
models for
    centralized computing, 674-675
    collaborative computing, 674-675
    distributed computing, 674-675
network management. *see* Network
  management
network services. *see* Network services
network size, 675-676

    LAN, 675
    MAN, 676
    WAN, 676
service platforms
    client/network, 675
    client/server, 675
NLIST, 132-133
NLM. *see* NetWare Loadable Modules
NLS. *see* NetWare Licensing Services
NLSMAN. *see* NetWare Licensing Services
  Manager
Novel Client Configuration policy, 296-298
Novell Administrator for Windows NT,
  1217-1224
installing and configuring, 1221-1224
integration security, 1220
integration utility, 1220
NDS event monitor, 1219
NDS object replication, 1219-1220
NDS schema extensions, 1218
snap-in service for, 1218-1219
Novell Application Launcher (NAL),
  1208-1209
Novell Directory Services (NDS), 617-624
access control and, 617
application management. *see* NetWare
  Application Launcher
authentication and, 617
backup, 543
container objects and, 10-11, 319, 617
defined, 17-18
design team and, 773
DS Repair and, 635-636
event monitor, 1219
file format and file location in, 17

hierarchical nature of, 9
installation of, 388-392, 880-882
    containers and, 390
    creating NDS tree, 389
    naming NDS tree, 390
    options for, 389
    passwords and, 390
introduction to, 9-18
leaf objects and, 10-13, 319
maintenance. *see* Maintenance, NDS
naming standard for. *see* Naming standards;
  Naming standards document
NDPS. *see* Novell Distributed Printing
  Services
NDS Manager
    repairing NDS with, 636
    troubleshooting with, 632-633
objects and, 17
    properties and values, 15-17
    replication and, 1219-1220
    schema of, 14-15
partitioning of, 18, 619-623, 826-836
printing and, 90-105 *see also* Novell
  Distributed Printing Services
profile and policy management in, 302-306
replication and, 624-627
resources access and, 20-22
rights in, 325-328, 592-598, 895-896
    effective rights, 594, 597
    explicit rights and, 329
    groups vs. containers, 895-896
    Inheritable rights, 597-598
    inherited rights, 328-331, 596, 895
    Inherited Rights Filter (IRF), 597
    object rights, 593

property rights, 329, 593
security equivalence, 330-331, 596
strategy for, 896
trustee assignments, 594-596
see also File system rights
security in
    login concepts for, 42
    management of, 9, 317-345
synchronization and, 627-628, 837-845
tree design and, 354, 360-362
    configuring NDS for login, 361
    configuring NDS for resource access,
      361-362
tree structure of
    introduction to, 18-19
    objects and, 10-11
    security and, 318-319
    see also Directory tree, structure of
values and, 17
Windows NT integration with,
  1198-1199
workstation management. *see* Workstation
  Manager
workstations, registering, 226-227
Z.E.N.works and, 216-221
see also Directory tree, designing
Novell Distributed Printing Services (NDPS)
    automatic driver downloads for, 430
    benefits of, 105-107
    bi-directional printing and, 430
    broker distribution in, 431
    creating NDPS Manager Object, 432-434
    creating NDPS Printer, 441
    creating objects for, 111-113
    gateways for, 108, 442

IETF support in, 106
installing on NetWare 5 Server, 109-110
integrated with Client 32 software, 106
IP environment and, 430
legacy components and, 441-442
managing, 114-120
NDPS Broker and, 108, 117
NDPS Client and, 108
NDPS Manager and, 108, 114-117, 118,
    432-434
NDPS Printer and, 118-120, 441
new features of, 430
overview of, 8
print server for, 431
Printer Agent and, 107, 431
Public Access Printer and, 92
queue-based printers and, 431
security roles for, 431
set up of, 109-114
structure of, 107-109
see also Upgrading to NDPS
Novell Time Synchronization model, 887-889
Novell Upgrade Wizard, 411-414
Novell Workstation Manager, 1205-1206
    NWGINA, 1206
    snap-in for NT Client configuration object,
        1206
Novell's Web sites, 917-920
NSS volume, 458
NTDS. *see* Windows NT Directory Services
NTFS. *see* Windows NT File System
NWADMIN. *see* NetWare Administrator
NWCCON. *see* NetWare Connect

NWCONFIG
    creating volumes with, 482-485
    editing configuration files with, 498-499
NWGINA, 1206
NWLink IPX/SPX Compatible protocol,
    1100-1101

Object context. *see* Context
Object properties
    directories, 140
    files, 140
    volumes, 147
Object rights, 320, 323-324, 593
    filtering, 333
    NDS default rights and, 326-327
Objects
    [Root] objects, 346, 349-351
    application management and, 264-265,
        269-275
    classes and, 14
    container objects, 10-11, 349-350, 352
    context and, 352-354
    Country objects, 349-350, 352
    DHCP Server objects, 558-559
    directory tree integration of, 352-354
    Group objects, 352
    leaf objects, 10-13, 346, 349-352
    naming, 352-354
    NDPS manager objects, 432-434
    as NDS database component, 17
    NDS schema and, 14-15
    Organization objects, 346, 349-350,
        349-351, 352

Organizational Unit objects, 346, 349-350, 349-351, 352
    properties and values of, 15-17
    rights for, 20
    Subnet objects, 559
    Volume objects, 352
    workstations and, 295-296
    zone objects, 563-564
Ontrack Data Recovery, 1052
Open Data-link Interface (ODI)
    client software for, 35-36
    IPX or IP compatibility drivers for, 35
    Link Support Layer driver for, 35
    Network Interface Card driver for, 33-34
Open Systems Interconnection (OSI) model
    lower layers, 705-727
        Data Link Layer. *see* Data Link Layer
        Physical Layer. *see* Physical Layer
    middle layers, 729-746
        Network Layer. *see* Network Layer
        Transport Layer. *see* Network Layer
    overview
        peer layer communication in, 708
        protocol stacks of, 707
    upper layers, 747-758
        Application Layer. *see* Application Layer
        Presentation Layer. *see* Presentation Layer
        Session Layer. *see* Session Layer
Operating system updates, 1033-1035
Optimization, 513-528
    allocation and deallocation of memory, 516-517
    block suballocation, 523-524
    file compression
        configuring, 525

        disabling, 525
        enabling, 524-525
    Large Internet packets (LIP) and, 528-529
    memory, overview
        growing demands for, 514-515
        server performance and, 514-515
        types of, 514-515
    MONITOR, 519-520
        Cache Buffer Memory and, 520-521
        increasing maximum packet buffers, 522
        viewing memory information with, 520
    packet burst and, 527-528
    server buffer and packet parameters, 521-524
    virtual memory, 517-519
        configuring, 517-518
        disk thrashing and, 518-519
Organization object
    as container object, 349-350, 352, 617
    directory tree structure and, 346, 349-351
Organizational Unit object
    as container object, 349-350, 352, 617
    directory tree structure and, 346, 349-351
OSI model. *see* Open Systems Interconnection

P

Packet buffers
    increasing maximum packet buffers, 522
    minimum packet receive buffers, 523
    packet receive buffers, 521
    see also Server buffer and packet parameters
Packet burst, 527-528

Packet switching, 733-734
   cell switching, 734
   datagram packet switching, 734
   independent routing in, 734
   virtual circuit packet switching, 734
Parent, back up, 542
Partitioning
   creating DOS partition, 383
   geographic placement of servers, 830-832
   hard disk and, 130
      extended partition, 1107
      primary partition, 1106-1107
   implementation of, 883-885
   NDS database and, 18, 619-623, 826-836
   partition administrators, 609
   partitioning by workgroup, 832-833
   for simple installations, 375
   strategies for
      bandwidth, 886
      bindery service, 886
      fault tolerance, 886
   transitive synchronization and, 833-835
   WAN traffic management and, 819, 835
Password
   administrators, 608-609, 861-862
   NDS installation and, 390
   restrictions, 44, 80
PAUSE, 209
PCI. *see* Peripheral Component Interface
PCMCIA. *see* Personal Computer Memory Card
  International Association
Performance, 472-475
   analyzing with LANalyzer, 1048-1049
   block suballocation and, 475
   directories design and, 485-487

fault tolerance and, 472-474
   spanning and, 473
   Transaction Tracking System (TTS) and,
      475
Peripheral Component Interface (PCI),
  945-946
Permanent storage, 515
Permissions, Windows NT, 1112-1116
Personal Computer Memory Card
  International Association (PCMCIA),
  945-946
Personal Testing Center, 1272-1274
   JavaScript errors and, 1273
   managing Windows for, 1272
   navigating with browser buttons on, 1273
   scoring, 1273, 1274
   testing options on, 1272-1274
      Live option, 1272
      Practice option, 1273
      Review option, 1274
Physical Layer (Layer 1)
   baseband and broadband transmissions of,
     718
   bit synchronization on, 717
   function of, 709
   multiplexing and, 718
   multipoint connection and, 710
   physical topologies of
      bus, 712
      cellular, 713-714
      mesh, 713-714
      ring, 713
      star, 710-711
   point-to-point connection on, 710

signaling
  analog signaling, 717
  digital signaling, 715-716
Physical topologies
  bus, 712
  cellular, 713-714
  mesh, 713-714
  ring, 713
  star, 710-711
PING, diagnostic tools, 912
Platform Support Modules (PSM), 379
Point-to-point connection, 710
Policies
  Computer System Policy, 306
  definition of, 238
  Desktop Preferences policy, 302
  Dynamic Local User policy, 309-310
  Novel Client Configuration policy, 296-298
  user, 289-290
  Windows NT, 1155-1166
    account policies, 1156-1157
    audit policies, 1159-1161
    system policies, 1165-1166
    user rights policies, 1158-1159
  Workstation Manager and
    user policy package, 289-290, 293, 294
    Workstation Import Policy, 293
    Workstation Inventory Policy and, 299
    workstation policy package, 289, 293
Polling, 720
Port Handler, 108
Presentation Layer (Layer 6), 751-753
  data translation, 751-752
    bit order translation, 751
    byte order translation, 751

encryption, 752
Primary domain controller (PDC), 1096,
  1127-1128
Print Device Subsystem (PDS), 108
Print queue, 90-92
  object for, 1014
  properties table of, 97
  troubleshooting, 1019-1022
Print server
  printing management and, 1013
  printing overview and, 91-92
  properties table of, 96
  troubleshooting and, 1023-1025
Print services, networks, 678-679
Printer Agent, 107
Printer gateways, 108
  Port Handler, 108
  Print Device Subsystem (PDS) for, 108
Printer object, 92, 1026
Printer properties, 98-99
Printers
  Dot matrix printers, 1018
  Ink jet printers, 1018
  Laser printers, 1018
Printing, 89-127
  Advanced Settings page, 103
  bi-directional, 105, 430
  capture process and, 1013
  capture switches and, 100-101
  configuring printers and print queues,
    308-309
  local printer and, 1012-1013
  NDS and, 90-92
  network printer, 443, 1013
  print queue, 97

print queue and, 90-92, 1014
print server and, 91-92, 96, 441, 1013
printer agent and, 441
printer object and, 92
printer properties for, 98-99
queue-based printers and, 437, 441
remote workstation printing
    set up at workstation, 95-103
    set up on server, 93-94
server-attached printers and, 443
troubleshooting. *see* Troubleshooting,
  network printing
Windows 95, capturing printer port in,
  103-104
workstation-attached printers, 443
see also Novell Distributed Printing Services
  (NDPS); Upgrading to NDPS
Proactive administration, 6
Problems. *see* Help Request
Profiles
defined, 238
profile script, 188-190
    assigning, 189-190
    definition of, 47
    uses of, 188
Roaming Profiles options, 302-303
user. *see* Desktop management, Desktop
  Preferences policy
Properties
application management and, 264-265
NDS database component, 17
objects for, 15-17
Property rights
filtering and, 333
inheritance and, 329

NDS default rights and, 327, 593
NDS objects and, 324-325
trustees and, 21
Protocols
compatibility mode (CMD) and, 386
CSMA/CD, 932-933
customizing, 382, 460-462
    configuring IP, 460-461
    configuring IPX, 461-462
    DNS, 462
    IPX Compatibility, 462
    SNMP, 462
IP, 386
IPX, 387
IPX/SPX, 32
NCP, 430
networking and, 676
SAP, 841
simple installations and, 378
SNMP, 106
TCP/IP, 32, 1101-1102
Windows NT supported, 1098-1102
    Appletalk, 1102
    DataLink Control (DLC), 1102
    NetBEUI, 1100
    NWLink IPX/SPX Compatible,
      1100-1101
    TCP/IP, 1101-1102
Public Access Printer, 92
Public switched telephone network (PSTN),
  697
[Public] trustee
definition of, 326
security equivalence and, 596

R

Radio Frequency Interference (RFI), 907

Radio wave transmission
  high-power frequency and, 696
  low-power frequency and, 696
  spread spectrum and, 696

RAID devices, 978-982
  disk duplexing, 979, 982
  disk mirroring, 979-981

RAM, 514

RCONSOLE, 501-504

Redundant array of independent disks (RAID).
  see RAID devices

Regional settings, 383

Registry, managing with snAPPShot, 256

Registry, Windows NT, 1071-1074
  editing methods for, 1074
  hive components of, 1073
  subtrees of, 1072-1073

Relative Distinguished Name
  context and, 59-61
  dots and, 360
  formula for, 359

REM, REMARK, 199

Remote boot, 1002

Remote clients. see Mobile clients

Remote control, 648-651

Remote Control Access (NEBO), 221
  configuring workstations for, 227-232
  Remote Control Agent and, 228-229
  Remote Control Policy and, 229-232

Remote node, 648-650

Remote procedure calls (RPCs), 748

Remote user, legacy services and, 864-865

Repeaters, 699

Replicas
  definition of, 18
  master replica, 624-625, 885
  read-only replicas, 625, 885
  read/write replicas, 625, 885
  replica list and, 885
  replica ring and, 834
  subordinate references and, 625, 885

Replication, 617-627
  database services and, 680
  implementation of, 885
  NDS database and, 617-619
  network traffic and, 629
  NTDS and, 1127
  partitions and, 619-623
  types of replicas, 624-627, 885

Resource Management Service (RMS), 432

Resources
  accessing
    directory tree and, 20-22
    setting context for, 354-357
    shortcuts for, 357-360
  definition of, 8
  list of, 8
  login scripts and, 363-364
  managing in multicontext environment,
    345-371
  NDS tree design and, 360-362
    configuring NDS for login, 361
    configuring NDS for resource access,
      361-362
  services associated with, 8
  sharing, 8

user rights and, 20-22, 363
Windows NT, access controls in, 1154-1155
Restrictions
  Login Restrictions, 43
  Login Time Restrictions, 44
  network address restrictions, 44
  Password Restrictions, 44
Rights. *see* File system rights
Rights inheritance. *see* Inheritance
Ring topology, 713
Roaming profiles options, 302-303
Roaming user profile, 1164
[Root]
  directory tree structure and, 346, 349-351
  NDS tree structure and, 318
  security equivalence and, 596
Route discovery, 735
Routers, 700
Routing, 734-735
  route selection, 734-735
  static routes, 734-735

S

Schema, NDS, 14-15
  object information and
    attribute information, 14
    inheritance, 14
    naming, 14
    subordination, 14
  objects classes and, 14
SCRSAVER, 505-506
SCSI. *see* Small Computer System Interface
SDLC. *see* System Design Life Cycles
Secondary Time Server, 378, 838

SECURE CONSOLE, 505
Security
  account expiration and lockout, 80
  certificates and, 581
  file system rights and. *see* File system rights
  file system security and. *see* File system security
  intruder detection and lockout, 45-46, 80
  keys and, 579-581
  login security
    concepts of, 42-46
    network security type, 77, 79-80
  login time restrictions, 80
  managing in NDS, 9
  NDPS roles and, 431
  NDS. *see* Security, NDS
  NetWare Connect and, 662-663
  Remote Control Access (NEBO) and, 221
  restrictions and
    network address restriction, 80
    passwords, 80
    restrictions in NDS, 43-45
  security equivalence
    definition of, 21
    file system rights and, 163-165
    implied, 78
    inheritance and, 330
    NDS default rights and, 596
  server security
    definition of, 77
    login and, 43
    SCRSAVER and, 505-506
    SECURE CONSOLE and, 505
  user objects and, 78-79

Windows NT. *see* Windows NT, security
Security Accounts Manager (SAM), 1068, 1094
Security equivalence
    definition of, 21
    file system rights and, 163-165
    implied, 78
    inheritance and, 330
    NDS default rights and, 596
Security guidelines, 860-862
    backup administrator, 861
    container administrator, 861
    default user security, 862
    enterprise administrator, 861
    password administrator, 861-862
    server administrator, 862
Security, NDS, 317-345, 591-614
    auditing, 599-600
    blocking inherited rights, 332-333
    centralized vs. distributed administration,
        600-602
    definition of, 42, 77
    directory access and, 320-325
        container administrators and, 320-321
        object rights and, 320, 323-324
        property rights and, 324-325
        trustees and, 320
    guidelines for implementing NDS security,
        336-337, 599-600
    NDS default rights and, 325-327, 592-598
        [Public] trustee, 325-327
        effective rights, 334-336, 594, 597
        inheritable rights, 597-598
        inherited rights, 596
        Inherited Rights Filter (IRF), 597
        object rights, 326-327, 593

property rights, 327, 593
        security equivalence, 596
        trustee assignments, 594-596
    NDS rights inheritance and, 328-331
    suggested administrative roles for
        container administrators, 603-604
        file system administrator, 604-605
        Help Desk, 607-608
        installers, 605-606
        partition administrators, 609
        password administrators, 608-609
    troubleshooting, 337-338
Security rights, backup, 540-541
Self tests
    accessibility plan, 869
    accessibility plan, answers, 1258-1259
    assessing the network, 780-782
    assessing the network, answers, 1256
    back up, 549-550
    back up, answers, 1249-1250
    designing the directory tree, 822-823
    designing the directory tree, answers,
        1257
    DNS/DHCP services, 567-568
    DNS/DHCP services, answers, 1250
    FastTrack Web Server, 588-590
    FastTrack Web Server, answers,
        1250-1251
    file system, managing, 154-156
    file system, managing, answers,
        1240-1241
    file system security, 181-183
    file system security, answers, 1241
    file system, set up, 490-491
    file system, set up, answers, 1248

implementing time synchronization strategies, 846-848

implementing time synchronization strategies, answers, 1257-1258

installation, NetWare 5, 396-397

installation, NetWare 5, answers, 1245-1246

integrating NetWAre and Windows NT Domains, 1233-1235

integrating NetWAre and Windows NT Domains, answers, 1269

introduction to intraNetWare, 27-29

introduction to intraNetWare, answers, 1238

login scripts, 212-214

login scripts, answers, 1241-1242

maintenance, NDS, 643-646

maintenance, NDS, answers, 1252-1253

managing resources in multicontext environment, 367-371

managing resources in multicontext environment, answers, 1245

mobile clients, 669-670

mobile clients, answers, 1253

multiple domain Windows NT networking, 1193-1195

multiple domain Windows NT networking, answers, 1267-1268

NDS security, 343-344

NDS security, answers, 1244-1245

NetWare Application Launcher (NAL), 283-285

NetWare Application Launcher (NAL), answers, 1243

NetWare implementation, 899-900

NetWare implementation, answers, 1259-1260

network access, 52-53

network access, answers, 1238-1239

network interface cards and cables, 957-959

network interface cards and cables, answers, 1260-1261

network solutions, 798-799

network solutions, answers, 1256-1257

network troubleshooting, 925-926

network troubleshooting, answers, 1260

networking technologies, 684-685

networking technologies, answers, 1253-1254

optimizing network and server, 532-534

optimizing network and server, answers, 1249

OSI, middle layers, 743-745

OSI, middle layers, answers, 1255

OSI, upper layers, 757-758

OSI, upper layers, answers, 1255-1256

performing a custom installation, 466-467

performing a custom installation, answers, 1247-1248

printing, 125-127

printing, answers, 1239-1240

security, NDS, 612-614

security, NDS, answers, 1251-1252

server console, 510-511

server console, answers, 1248-1249

storage devices, 986-988

storage devices, answers, 1261-1262

transmission media and connections, 703-704

transmission media and connections, answers, 1254

troubleshooting, DOS workstations, 1008-1009

troubleshooting, DOS workstations, answers, 1262

troubleshooting, server and network, 1056-1058

troubleshooting, server and network, answers, 1263-1264

upgrading NetWare 3.1 to Netware 5, 422

upgrading NetWare 3.1 to Netware 5, answers, 1246-1247

upgrading to NDPS, 452-454

upgrading to NDPS, answers, 1247

user objects, 85-87

user objects, answers, 1239

Windows NT, 1090-1091

Windows NT, answers, 1264-1265

Windows NT Domain networking, 1147-1148

Windows NT Domain networking, answers, 1266

Windows NT, networking, 1119-1121

Windows NT, networking, answers, 1265

Windows NT, security, 1170-1172

Windows NT, security, answers, 1266-1267

Windows NT, workstations, 1212-1213

Windows NT, workstations, answers, 1268-1269

Workstation Manager, 314-316

Workstation Manager, answer, 1243-1244

Z.E.N.works, 243-245

Z.E.N.works, answers, 1242-1243

Server

    abends. *see* Server abends and lockups

    administrator for, 862

    authentication and, 579

    host, 536-537

    lockups. *see* Server abends and lockups

    maintenance of

        administrator responsibilities and, 4

        updating servers, 630

    names and, 808-809

    optimizing performance on, 514-515

    security and, 43

        SCRSAVER, 505-506

        SECURE CONSOLE, 505

    Server Manager, Windows NT, 1080-1081

    updates for, 1032-1036

        device driver updates, 1035-1036

        operating system updates, 1033-1035

Server abends and lockups, 1036-1043

    abend recovery options, 1037-1038

    analyzing abend messages, 1039-1040

    consistency check errors, 1037

    CPU-detected errors, 1036-1037

    server lockups, 1040

    six step process for, 1041-1043

Server buffer and packet parameters, 521-524

    increasing maximum packet buffers, 522-524

    packet receive buffers, 521

Server console, 493-509

    accessing from workstation, 501-504

    configuration files for

EDIT and, 499-500
        NWCONFIG and, 498-499
    creating server batch files with, 501
    executing commands with, 496
    loading/unloading NLMs with, 497-498
    navigating, 497
    overview of, 494-496
    RCONSOLE and, 501-504
    security for, 504-506
        SCRSAVER, 505-506
        SECURE CONSOLE, 505
    support for Java applications on, 506
    using ServerTop on, 506
Server ID Number
    customizing, 379-380
    simple installations and, 375
Server Manager, Windows NT, 1080-1081
ServerTop, GUI interface, 506
Service Advertising Protocol (SAP), 841
Service Registry Service (SRS), 431
Services
    list of, 8
    resources associated with, 8
Session Layer (Layer 5), 748-750
    dialog control, 750
    dialog control and, 749
    session administration and, 749
Shares, Windows NT, 1108-1111
Shielded twisted-pair (STP) cables, 690-693, 942
Signaling
    analog, 717
    digital, 715-716
Simple applications, 263
Simple Network Management Protocol (SNMP),
    106

customizing, 462
    printer management and, 106
Single domain, 1182-1184
Single login authentication, 9, 47
Single master domain, 1184-1186
Single Reference Time Server, 378
Small Computer System Interface (SCSI)
    controller configuration, 975
    drive configuration, 970-971
    drives, 966-968
snAPPShot
    Application Object Template (.AOT) files
        and, 256-257
    creating applications with, 258
    managing registry and .INI files with, 256
    set up and configuration of, 258-263
Software
    distribution, 251. see also NetWare
        Application Launcher; snAPPShot
    inventory management and, 299-301
    requirements for upgrade to NetWare 5,
        408
Solutions. see Network solutions
Spanning, 473
Star topology, 710-711
Storage devices, 961-988
    autodetection of, 384
    CD-ROMs, 982-983
    hard drives, 962-977
        cabling for, 976
        formatting, 976-977
        IDE controller configuration,
            971-975
        IDE drive configuration, 969-970
        interface types for, 964-968

overview, 962-964
SCSI controller configuration, 975
SCSI drive configuration, 970-971
RAID devices, 978-982
disk duplexing, 979, 982
disk mirroring, 979-981
simple installations and, 378-379
Windows NT and, 984
Storage Management Services (SMS)
console workstations and, 536-537
host server and, 536-537
target and, 536-537
Subdirectories, 132
Subnet Address Range (SAR), 560
Subnet mask, 460-461
Subnets, 559-560
Subnet Address Range (SAR), 560
Subnet object, 559
Subordination, object information, 14
Support Connection CD, 913, 915
Support Source, 920-924
Swap files, 515
Switching, 732-734
cell switching, 734
circuit switching, 732
message switching, 732
packet switching, 733-734
Synchronization
NDS inactivity synchronization interval, 835
NDS synchronization, 627-628
NetWare 5 Time Synchronization, 889-890
network traffic and, 629
Novell Time Synchronization model,
887-889

strategies for. *see* Time synchronization
strategies
time servers for, 888
transitive, 834-835
transmission synchronization, 721
SYS
default volume and, 471-472
installation, NetWare 5 and, 375
managing volume space on, 630
NetWare Loadable Modules (NLMs) and,
471
repairing crashed SYS volume, 637-639
as system created directory, 478
SYSCON, 62
System Design Life Cycles (SDLC)
analysis and specification phase, 764
design phase, 764-765
implementation phase, 765
incremental SDLC, 764
linear SDLC, 763
maintenance phase, 765
System performance. *see* Performance
System policies
remote update of, 305-306
Windows NT, 1165-1166
Workstation Manager and, 304-306
System Policy Editor, 1082-1083

T

Target, 536-537, 542
Target Service Agent (TSA), 536
Time consumer, 838
Time synchronization, 886-890

NDS inactivity synchronization interval, 835

NDS synchronization, 627-628

NetWare 5 Time Synchronization, 889-890

network traffic and, 629

Novell Time Synchronization model, 887-889

time servers for, 888

transitive, 834-835

transmission synchronization, 721

Time synchronization strategies

customizing time synchronization settings, 842

guidelines for, 890

planning, 840

time setup in IP or mixed IP/IPX environment, 839

time setup in IPX environment, 838-839

timestamps and, 837

Time zone, 388

Timestamps, 837

Token-passing, 720

Token Ring networks, 940-944

cabling for, 942-944

how it works, 941-942

troubleshooting, 950

Topologies, logical, 719

Topologies, physical

bus topology, 712

cellular topology, 713-714

mesh topology, 713-714

ring topology, 713

star topology, 710-711

TRACK, DOS workstations, 1002-1004

Traditional volume, 458-459

Transaction Tracking System (TTS) and, 475

Transients, 907

Transitive synchronization, 834-835

Transmission Control Protocol/Internet Protocol (TCP/IP), 32, 1101-1102

Transmission media, 687-704

cable media

coaxial, 693-694

fiber-optic, 694-695

twisted-pair, 690-693

connections, 697-701

internetwork connectivity devices, 700-701

network connectivity devices, 698-700

networking and, 676

overview of

attenuation, 689

capacity, 689

ease of installation, 689

electromagnetic interference, 689

media cost and, 688-689

public and private services and, 697

wireless media

infrared, 697

microwave, 696-697

radio waves, 696

Transmission synchronization, 721

Transport Layer (Layer 4), 738-740

acknowledgements, 740

address/name resolution, 738-739

connection services of, 739

Cyclic Redundancy Check (CRC) and, 740

message segment development of, 739

segment sequencing in, 739
Transport Layer addressing, 738
Tree names, 805-806
Tree structure. *see* Directory tree, structure of
Troubleshooting, DOS workstations
    DOS versions and, 1005-1006
    files and programs and, 993-998
    INSTALL process and, 990-993
    remote boot feature of, 1002
    setting up NIC, 998-1000
    TRACK and, 1002-1004
    troubleshooting hardware conflicts,
      1004-1005
    watchdog feature of, 1000-1002
Troubleshooting, NDS, 631-634
    DS Repair and, 632-634
    error messages and, 631-632
    NDS Manager and, 632-633
    NWADMIN and, 632
Troubleshooting, network, 901-929
    diagnostic tools
      COMCHECK, 912
      IPXPING, 912
      LANalyzer, 912
      PING, 912
    electrical problems, 905-907
      crosstalk, 906
      line noise, 906-907
      static, 906
      transients, 907
    environmental problems, 902-903
      air quality, 905
      humidity, 905
      temperature, 904-905
    five-step model for, 910-911

references for
    NetWire on CompuServe, 914-917
    Novell's Web sites, 917-920
    Support Connection CD, 913, 915
    Support Source, 920-924
security and
    risk minimization, 909
    types of threats, 909
viruses, 908
    preventative measures, 908
    types of viruses, 908
Troubleshooting, network printing,
    1011-1029
    dot matrix printers, 1018
    hardware problems and, 1017
    ink jet printers, 1018
    laser printers, 1018
    overview of, 1012-1017
    Print Object problems, 1025
    Print Queue problems, 1019-1022
    Print Server problems, 1023-1025
    problems printing from user applications,
      1021
    software problems, 1017
Troubleshooting, NICs
    Ethernet, 949-950
    Token Ring, 950
Troubleshooting, server and network,
    1031-1058
    disaster recovery options, 1049-1053
      data recovery services, 1052-1053
      disaster planning and, 1049-1050
      DS Repair, 1051
      Ontrack Data Recovery, 1052
      restoring from backups, 1051-1052

VREPAIR, 1050-1051
FastTrack Web Server and, 581-584
LANalyzer and, 1047-1049
  monitoring network performance with,
    1048-1049
  network errors and, 1047
  server and network overloads and,
    1048-1049
performance bottlenecks, 1044-1047
  bus I/O problems, 1046-1047
  CPU problems, 1046
  disk I/O problems, 1045
  network I/O problems, 1045-1046
server abends and lockups, 1036-1043
  abend recovery options, 1037-1038
  analyzing abend messages, 1039-1040
  consistency check errors, 1037
  CPU-detected errors, 1036-1037
  server lockups, 1040
  six step process for, 1041-1043
server updates, 1032-1036
  device driver updates, 1035-1036
  operating system updates, 1033-1035
Trustee
  [Public], 326
  assignments, 594-596
  definition of, 20, 320
  file system rights and, 159-160
  implementing rights for, 175
  role in controlling directory access, 320
Trusts
  domain networks and, 1098
  one-way trust relationship, 1176
  setting up trust relationships, 1178-1180
  trusted vs. trusting, 1174-1177
  two-way trust relationship, 1176

using groups with trust relationships,
    1177-1178
Twisted-pair cables
  shielded twisted-pair (STP), 690-693
  unshielded twisted-pair (UTP), 690-693
Two-minute drill
  accessibility plan, 866-868
  assessing the network, 780
  back up, 547-548
  designing the directory tree, 821-822
  DNS/DHCP services, 565-566
  FastTrack Web Server, 586-587
  file system, managing, 151-154
  file system security, 178-180
  file system, set up, 487-489
  implementing time synchronization
    strategies, 846-848
  installation, NetWare 5, 393-395
  integrating NetWAre and Windows NT
    Domains, 1230-1232
  introduction to intraNetWare, 24-26
  login scripts, 209-211
  maintenance, NDS, 640-642
  managing resources in multicontext
    environment, 364-366
  mobile clients, 667-668
  multiple domain Windows NT
    networking, 1190-1192
  NDS security, 340-342
  NetWare Application Launcher (NAL),
    280-282
  NetWare implementation, 897-898
  network access and, 52-53
  network interface cards and cables,
    954-956
  network solutions, 796-797

network troubleshooting, 925-926

networking technologies, 683

optimizing network and server, 530-532

OSI, middle layers, 743-745

OSI, upper layers, 756

performing a custom installation, 463-465

printing, 122-124

security, NDS, 611

server console, 507-509

storage devices, 984-985

transmission media and connections, 702

troubleshooting, DOS workstations, 1006-1007

troubleshooting, server and network, 1053-1055

upgrading NetWare 3.1 to Netware 5, 422

Upgrading to NDPS, 450-451

user objects, 82-84

Windows NT, 1086-1089

Windows NT Domain networking, 1145-1146

Windows NT, networking, 1116-1118

Windows NT, security, 1167-1169

Windows NT, workstations, 1210-1211

Workstation Manager and, 312-313

Z.E.N.works, 241-242

Typeful Names

definition of, 61-62

Distinguished Name and, 59-61

naming concepts and, 359

Relative Distinguished Name and, 59-61

Typeless Names

definition of, 61

naming concepts and, 359

U

UIMPORT, 73-74

Unshielded twisted-pair (UTP) cables, 690-693, 936

Updates. *see* Server, updates for

Upgrades, scheduling, 307-308

Upgrading NetWare 3.1 to Netware 5, 400-428

across-the-wire migration method, 404-405

advantages/disadvantages of, 405

prerequisites for, 411-414

procedures for, 404-405

steps in process, 418-421

confirming the upgrade, 422

DOS boot partition and, 407

hardware requirements for, 406

in-place upgrade method, 403-404

advantages/disadvantages of, 404

prerequisites for, 409-410

procedures for, 403

server preparation for, 410

steps in process, 415-418

upgrading into existing NDS structure, 409-410

installation of files, 415

minimum client versions for, 408-409

software requirements for, 408

Upgrading to NDPS, 429-454

broker distribution and

Event Notification Service (ENS), 431

Resource Management Service (RMS), 432

Service Registry Service (SRS), 431

configuring current printing information and, 437-438

creating NDPS Manager Object, 432-434

designing the NDPS system, 431-432

gathering current printing information, 435-436

migrating printing components, 439-446

    creating NDPS Printer, 441

    interoperability with legacy components, 441-442

    process for, 443-445

    scenarios for, 442-443

protocol choice and, 430

removing old printing components, 447

security roles and

    manager, 431

    operator, 431

    user objects, 431

testing migrated components, 446-447

upgrading software to NetWare 5 client, 434-435

Upper memory blocks (UMB), 1005

User access. *see* Accessibility plan

User accounts. *see* User objects

User needs document

    application needs, 854-855

    legacy access needs, 855-856

    physical network needs, 855

User object context. *see* Context

User objects, 57-87

    adding licenses and, 74-77

        NetWare Administrator, 76-77

        NLS Manager, 74-76

    administration utilities for, 62-63

    Console One and, 72

creation of, 63-74

loginID and, 58

management of, 57-87

NDS and, 58

NetWare Administrator (NWADMIN) and, 69-71

network security and, 77-80

    login security, 79-80

    types of, 77-78

properties of, 58, 64-68

[Root] object and, 63

UIMPORT and, 73-74

user object context and, 58, 59-62

User Package, Windows NT, 309-310

User policies, 289-290. *see also* Workstations, policies

User policy package, 293, 294

User profiles. *see* Desktop management, Desktop Preferences policy

User profiles, Windows NT, 1161-1165

    local user profile, 1163

    mandatory user profile, 1164-1165

    roaming user profile, 1164

User rights policies, 1158-1159

User script, 190-192

    definition of, 48

    execution of, 190

    maintenance difficulties with, 191

Users and Groups settings, FastTrack Web Server, 578-579

Utilities, file system management

    DOS XCOPY, 145

    FILER, 135-137

    NDIR, 134-135

    NetWare Administrator, 137-138

NetWare NCOPY, 145
NLIST, 132-133
Utilities, Windows NT, 1074-1083
Administrative Wizards, 1080
Control Panel, 1077-1078
Disk Administrator, 1079
Event Viewer, 1081-1082
My Computer, 1075-1076
Network Neighborhood, 1077
Server Manager, 1080-1081
System Policy Editor, 1082-1083
Windows NT Explorer, 1076-1077

Values, 15-17
VESA Local Bus. *see* Video Electronics Standards
Association
Video Electronics Standards Association (VESA),
945-946
Virtual circuit packet switching, 734
Virtual memory, 515
configuring, 518-519
disk thrashing and, 518-519
optimization, 517-519
Volume names, 808-809
Volume objects, 352
Volume space usage
restricting, 148
volume object properties and, 147
volume statistics and, 148
Volume (SYS:)
default volume and, 471-472
installation, NetWare 5 and, 375
managing volume space on, 630

NetWare Loadable Modules (NLMs) and,
471
repairing crashed SYS volume, 637-639
as system created directory, 478
Volumes
configuration of, 472-475
fault tolerance and, 472-475
performance and, 472-475
creating or modifying, 458-459, 482-485
customizing, 457-459
directory design and, 485-486
file system structure and, 131, 470-471
hard disk partition and, 130-131
location of, 472
maintenance of, 474-476
NWADMIN and, 475
VREPAIR and, 476
mounting, 459
naming, 131, 474
NSS volume type and, 458
NWCONFIG and, 482-485
object properties and, 147
storage requirements and, 472
traditional volume and, 458
volume statistics and, 147
VREPAIR, 476, 1050-1051

WAN traffic manager (WTM), 835
Watchdog, 1000-1002
Web browser, installation, 49-50
Web server. *see* FastTrack Web Server
Web sites
Global Knowledge Network, 1276

Novell Web site, 917-920
Wide area networks (WANs), 346, 676
Windows 95
    desktop options for, 305-306
    overview of, 1063-1064
    weakness as network server, 1064
Windows NT, 1059-1091
    adding users to local workstation with,
        1083-1086
    default accounts of, 1069-1071
        Administrator account, 1069-1070
        Guest account, 1070-1071
        Initial User Account, 1070-1071
    desktop options for, 305-306
    login in process for, 1067-1069
    Registry of, 1071-1074
        editing methods for, 1074
        hive components of, 1073
        subtrees of, 1072-1073
    Server 4.0 and, 1064-1066
    user management on, 309-310
        Dynamic Local User policy, 309-310
        User Manager, 1083-1084
    utilities for, 1074-1083
        Administrative Wizards, 1080
        Control Panel, 1077-1078
        Disk Administrator, 1079
        Event Viewer, 1081-1082
        My Computer, 1075-1076
        Network Neighborhood, 1077
        Server Manager, 1080-1081
        System Policy Editor, 1082-1083
        Windows NT Explorer, 1076-1077
    Workstation 4.0 and, 1064-1066
Windows NT Directory Services (NTDS)

directory replication of, 1127
integration with Windows NT
    applications, 1126
single network logins of, 1126
single point of administration on, 1126
Windows NT Explorer, 1076-1077
Windows NT File System (NTFS), 1104,
    1105
Windows NT, integrating with NetWare
    benefits of integrating with NDS,
        1216-1217
        accessing Windows NT and NetWare
            resources, 1217
        reducing redundant administration,
            1216-1217
    Novell Administrator for Windows NT,
        1217-1224
        installing and configuring,
            1221-1224
        integration security on, 1220
        integration utility of, 1220
        NDS event monitor, 1219
        NDS object replication, 1219-1220
        NDS schema extensions, 1218
        NetWare Administrator snap-in
            service, 1218-1219
    synchronizing NetWare and Windows
        NT users and groups, 1224-1229
        configuring user properties, 1227
        integrating NDS users to Windows
            NT, 1225
        integrating Windows NT users to
            NDS, 1225
        replicating new NDS users to
            Windows NT, 1224-1229

synchronizing existing NDS users with
Windows NT users, 1226
using NetWare Administrator with,
1228-1229
Windows NT, networking, 1093-1121,
1123-1148
adding workstation or server to a domain,
1142-1144
creating shares and, 1108-1111
Disk Administrator and, 1105-1107
creating a volume set with, 1107
partitioning hard disk with, 1106-1107
domain controllers, 1130-1141
domain logon process, 1131-1133
domain user accounts, 1133-1135
global groups, 1138-1141
local groups, 1135-1138
domain models, 1096-1098, 1180-1190
complete trust, 1188-1190
multiple master domain, 1186-1188
single domain, 1182-1184
single master domain, 1184-1186
domain server roles, 1127-1130
backup domain controllers (BDC),
1128-1129
member servers, 1129-1130
primary domain controller (PDC),
1127-1128
file systems supported by, 1102-1105
FAT, 1103-1104, 1105
NTFS, 1104, 1105
granting permissions on, 1112-1116
NTDS. *see* Windows NT Directory Services
protocols supported by, 1098-1102
Appletalk, 1102

DataLink Control (DLC), 1102
NetBEUI, 1100
NWLink IPX/SPX Compatible,
1100-1101
TCP/IP, 1101-1102
resource access and, 1108-1111
security on. *see* Windows NT, security
trusts and, 1174-1180
setting up trust relationships,
1178-1180
trusted vs. trusting, 1174-1177
using groups with trust relationships,
1177-1178
workgroup model of, 1094-1096
workstations. *see* Windows NT,
workstations
Windows NT, security, 1149-1172
components of, 1152-1154
Novell Administrator and, 1220
overview of, 1150-1152
policies of, 1155-1166
account policies, 1156-1157
audit policies, 1159-1161
system policies, 1165-1166
user rights policies, 1158-1159
resources access controls on, 1154-1155
user profiles of, 1161-1165
local user profile, 1163
mandatory user profile, 1164-1165
roaming user profile, 1164
WinLogon and, 1065, 1067-1069
Local Security Authority (LSA),
1068
Security Accounts Manager (SAM),
1068

Windows NT, workstations, 1197-1213
    Automatic Client Update (ACU) and,
        1202-1204
    benefits of, 1202
    integrating with NDS, 1198-1199
    managing users and desktops, 1204-1205
    multiple protocol support for, 1199
    NetWare Administrator and, 1199-1200
        managing network applications, 1201
        managing user accounts, 1200
    NetWare Client and, 1202-1204
    Novell Application Launcher (NAL),
        1208-1209
    Novell Workstation Manager, 1205-1206
        NWGINA, 1206
        snap-in for NT Client configuration
          object, 1206
    NT client configuration object
        associating users with, 1207
        managing user profiles and system
          policies with, 1208
WinLogon, 1067-1069
    Local Security Authority (LSA), 1068
    Security Accounts Manager (SAM),
        1068
    Windows NT security, 1065
Workgroup networks, 1094-1096
    decentralized nature of, 1095
    limitations of, 1096
Workstation Import Policy, 293
Workstation Inventory
    managing, 299-301
    property page for, 300
    Workstation Inventory Policy and, 237-238,
        299-301

Workstation Manager, 287-316
    configuring printers and print queues,
        308-309
    installation and configuration
        configuring for Novell Client,
          296-298
        login script for, 291-292
        policy packages for, 293-296
        switches and functions for, 291
    installing and configuring multiple clients
        with, 291-298
    introduction to, 288-290
    managing profiles and policies with
        desktop setting, 302-303
        system policies, 304-306
    managing workstation inventory with,
        299-301
    policies list for, 289-290
    printing and, 308-309
    scheduling application upgrades for,
        307-308
    services of, 289
    Windows NT user management and,
        309-310
    see also Novell Directory Services, profile
        and policy management
Workstations
    back up, 544
    configuring for Remote Control Access,
        227-232
    creating objects for Z.E.N.works,
        221-225
    Help Request application and, 229-232
    import policy for, 222
    maintenance of, 4

managing hardware and software inventory
on, 299-301
naming and, 813-815
objects, associating to workstation policies,
295-296
policies and, 289-290, 293
registration with NDS and, 222, 226-227
see also Workstation Manager
WRITE, 198-199

XCOPY, 145

Z.E.N.works. *see* Zero Effort Networks
Zero Effort Networks (Z.E.N.works), 216-245
configuring workstations for Remote Access
Control, 227-232

creating workstation objects for, 221-225
features of, 216-217
Help Request application and, 232-237
installing, 217-220
component options, 219
operating system options, 219
set up options, 218
print management in. *see* Workstation
Manager, printing
Remote Control Access (NEBO) and, 221
Workstation Inventory Policy and,
237-238
workstation management in. *see*
Workstation Manager
workstation registration program for,
226-227
see also NetWare Application Launcher
Zone objects, 563-564
Zone transfers, 562
Zones, 562

Custom Corporate Network Training

Train on Cutting Edge Technology   We can bring the best in skill-based training to your facility to create a real-world hands-on training experience. Global Knowledge has invested millions of dollars in network hardware and software to train our students on the same equipment they will work with on the job. Our relationships with vendors allow us to incorporate the latest equipment and platforms into your on-site labs.

Maximize Your Training Budget   Global Knowledge provides experienced instructors, comprehensive course materials, and all the networking equipment needed to deliver high quality training. You provide the students; we provide the knowledge.

Avoid Travel Expenses   On-site courses allow you to schedule technical training at your convenience, saving time, expense, and the opportunity cost of travel away from the workplace.

Discuss Confidential Topics   Private on-site training permits the open discussion of sensitive issues such as security, access, and network design. We can work with your existing network's proprietary files while demonstrating the latest technologies.

Customize Course Content   Global Knowledge can tailor your courses to include the technologies and the topics which have the greatest impact on your business. We can complement your internal training efforts or provide a total solution to your training needs.

Corporate Pass   The Corporate Pass Discount Program rewards our best network training customers with preferred pricing on public courses, discounts on multimedia training packages, and an array of career planning services.

Global Knowledge Training Lifecycle   Supporting the Dynamic and Specialized Training Requirements of Information Technology Professionals

- Define Profile
- Assess Skills
- Design Training
- Deliver Training
- Test Knowledge
- Update Profile
- Use New Skills

College Credit Recommendation Program   The American Council on Education's CREDIT program recommends 53 Global Knowledge courses for college credit. Now our network training can help you earn your college degree while you learn the technical skills needed for your job. When you attend an ACE-certified Global Knowledge course and pass the associated exam, you earn college credit recommendations for that course. Global Knowledge can establish a transcript record for you with ACE, which you can use to gain credit at a college or as a written record of your professional training that you can attach to your resume.

Registration Information

COURSE FEE: The fee covers course tuition, refreshments, and all course materials. Any parking expenses that may be incurred are not included. Payment or government training form must be received six business days prior to the course date. We will also accept Visa/MasterCard and American Express. For non-U.S. credit card users, charges will be in U.S. funds and will be converted by your credit card company. Checks drawn on Canadian banks in Canadian funds are acceptable.

COURSE SCHEDULE: Registration is at 8:00 a.m. on the first day. The program begins at 8:30 a.m. and concludes at 4:30 p.m. each day.

CANCELLATION POLICY: Cancellation and full refund will be allowed if written cancellation is received in our office at least six business days prior to the course start date. Registrants who do not attend the course or do not cancel more than six business days in advance are responsible for the full registration fee; you may transfer to a later date provided the course fee has been paid in full. Substitutions may be made at any time. If Global Knowledge must cancel a course for any reason, liability is limited to the registration fee only.

GLOBAL KNOWLEDGE: Global Knowledge programs are developed and presented by industry professionals with "real-world" experience. Designed to help professionals meet today's interconnectivity and interoperability challenges, most of our programs feature hands-on labs that incorporate state-of-the-art communication components and equipment.

ON-SITE TEAM TRAINING: Bring Global Knowledge's powerful training programs to your company. At Global Knowledge, we will custom design courses to meet your specific network requirements. Call 1 (919) 461-8686 for more information.

YOUR GUARANTEE: Global Knowledge believes its courses offer the best possible training in this field. If during the first day you are not satisfied and wish to withdraw from the course, simply notify the instructor, return all course materials, and receive a 100% refund.

In the US:

CALL: 1 (888) 762-4442

FAX: 1 (919) 469-7070

VISIT OUR WEBSITE:

www.globalknowledge.com

MAIL CHECK AND THIS FORM TO:

Global Knowledge

Suite 200

114 Edinburgh South

P.O. Box 1187

Cary, NC 27512

In Canada:

CALL: 1 (800) 465-2226

FAX: 1 (613) 567-3899

VISIT OUR WEBSITE:

www.globalknowledge.com.ca

MAIL CHECK AND THIS FORM TO:

Global Knowledge

Suite 1601

393 University Ave.

Toronto, ON M5G 1E6

REGISTRATION INFORMATION:

Course title _____

Course location _____ Course date _____

Name/title _____ Company _____

Name/title _____ Company _____

Name/title _____ Company _____

Address _____ Telephone _____ Fax _____

City _____ State/Province _____ Zip/Postal Code _____

Credit card _____ Card # _____ Expiration date _____

Signature _____

LICENSE AGREEMENT

THIS PRODUCT (THE "PRODUCT") CONTAINS PROPRIETARY SOFTWARE, DATA AND INFORMATION (INCLUDING DOCUMENTATION) OWNED BY THE McGRAW-HILL COMPANIES, INC. ("McGRAW-HILL") AND ITS LICENSORS. YOUR RIGHT TO USE THE PRODUCT IS GOVERNED BY THE TERMS AND CONDITIONS OF THIS AGREEMENT.

LICENSE: Throughout this License Agreement, "you" shall mean either the individual or the entity whose agent opens this package. You are granted a non-exclusive and non-transferable license to use the Product subject to the following terms:

(i) If you have licensed a single user version of the Product, the Product may only be used on a single computer (i.e., a single CPU). If you licensed and paid the fee applicable to a local area network or wide area network version of the Product, you are subject to the terms of the following subparagraph (ii).

(ii) If you have licensed a local area network version, you may use the Product on unlimited workstations located in one single building selected by you that is served by such local area network. If you have licensed a wide area network version, you may use the Product on unlimited workstations located in multiple buildings on the same site selected by you that is served by such wide area network; provided, however, that any building will not be considered located in the same site if it is more than five (5) miles away from any building included in such site. In addition, you may only use a local area or wide area network version of the Product on one single server. If you wish to use the Product on more than one server, you must obtain written authorization from McGraw-Hill and pay additional fees.

(iii) You may make one copy of the Product for back-up purposes only and you must maintain an accurate record as to the location of the back-up at all times.

COPYRIGHT; RESTRICTIONS ON USE AND TRANSFER: All rights (including copyright) in and to the Product are owned by McGraw-Hill and its licensors. You are the owner of the enclosed disc on which the Product is recorded. You may not use, copy, decompile, disassemble, reverse engineer, modify, reproduce, create derivative works, transmit, distribute, sublicense, store in a database or retrieval system of any kind, rent or transfer the Product, or any portion thereof, in any form or by any means (including electronically or otherwise) except as expressly provided for in this License Agreement. You must reproduce the copyright notices, trademark notices, legends and logos of McGraw-Hill and its licensors that appear on the Product on the back-up copy of the Product which you are permitted to make hereunder. All rights in the Product not expressly granted herein are reserved by McGraw-Hill and its licensors.

TERM: This License Agreement is effective until terminated. It will terminate if you fail to comply with any term or condition of this License Agreement. Upon termination, you are obligated to return to McGraw-Hill the Product together with all copies thereof and to purge all copies of the Product included in any and all servers and computer facilities.

DISCLAIMER OF WARRANTY: THE PRODUCT AND THE BACK-UP COPY OF THE PRODUCT ARE LICENSED "AS IS." McGRAW-HILL, ITS LICENSORS AND THE AUTHORS MAKE NO WARRANTIES, EXPRESS OR IMPLIED, AS TO RESULTS TO BE OBTAINED BY ANY PERSON OR ENTITY FROM USE OF THE PRODUCT AND/OR ANY INFORMATION OR DATA INCLUDED THEREIN. McGRAW-HILL, ITS LICENSORS, AND THE AUTHORS MAKE NO GUARANTEE THAT YOU WILL PASS ANY CERTIFICATION EXAM BY USING THIS PRODUCT. McGRAW-HILL, ITS LICENSORS AND THE AUTHORS MAKE NO EXPRESS OR IMPLIED WARRANTIES OF MERCHANTABILITY OR FITNESS FOR A PARTICULAR PURPOSE OR USE WITH RESPECT TO THE PRODUCT. NEITHER McGRAW-HILL, ANY OF ITS LICENSORS, NOR THE AUTHORS WARRANT THAT THE FUNCTIONS CONTAINED IN THE PRODUCT WILL MEET YOUR REQUIREMENTS OR THAT THE OPERATION OF THE PRODUCT WILL BE UNINTERRUPTED OR ERROR FREE. YOU ASSUME THE ENTIRE RISK WITH RESPECT TO THE QUALITY AND PERFORMANCE OF THE PRODUCT.

LIMITED WARRANTY FOR DISC: To the original licensee only, McGraw-Hill warrants that the enclosed disc on which the Product is recorded is free from defects in materials and workmanship under normal use and service for a period of ninety (90) days from the date of purchase. In the event of a defect in the disc covered by the foregoing warranty, McGraw-Hill will replace the disc.

LIMITATION OF LIABILITY: NEITHER McGRAW-HILL, ITS LICENSORS NOR THE AUTHORS SHALL BE LIABLE FOR ANY INDIRECT, SPECIAL OR CONSEQUENTIAL DAMAGES, SUCH AS BUT NOT LIMITED TO, LOSS OF ANTICIPATED PROFITS OR BENEFITS, RESULTING FROM THE USE OR INABILITY TO USE THE PRODUCT EVEN IF ANY OF THEM HAS BEEN ADVISED OF THE POSSIBILITY OF SUCH DAMAGES. THIS LIMITATION OF LIABILITY SHALL APPLY TO ANY CLAIM OR CAUSE WHATSOEVER WHETHER SUCH CLAIM OR CAUSE ARISES IN CONTRACT, TORT, OR OTHERWISE. Some states do not allow the exclusion or limitation of indirect, special or consequential damages, so the above limitation may not apply to you.

U.S. GOVERNMENT RESTRICTED RIGHTS: Any software included in the Product is provided with restricted rights subject to subparagraphs (c), (1) and (2) of the Commercial Computer Software-Restricted Rights clause at 48 C.F.R. 52.227-19. The terms of this Agreement applicable to the use of the data in the Product are those under which the data are generally made available to the general public by McGraw-Hill. Except as provided herein, no reproduction, use, or disclosure rights are granted with respect to the data included in the Product and no right to modify or create derivative works from any such data is hereby granted.

GENERAL: This License Agreement constitutes the entire agreement between the parties relating to the Product. The terms of any Purchase Order shall have no effect on the terms of this License Agreement. Failure of McGraw-Hill to insist at any time on strict compliance with this License Agreement shall not constitute a waiver of any rights under this License Agreement. This License Agreement shall be construed and governed in accordance with the laws of the State of New York. If any provision of this License Agreement is held to be contrary to law, that provision will be enforced to the maximum extent permissible and the remaining provisions will remain in full force and effect.

MCSE
MICROSOFT CERTIFIED SYSTEMS ENGINEER

Don't let the real test be your first test!

Microsoft Certified
Professional
Approved Study Guide

GET CERTIFIED WITH PROVEN CURRICULUM-BASED LEARNING METHODOLOGY FROM GLOBAL KNOWLEDGE™, THE WORLD'S LARGEST INDEPENDENT IT TRAINING COMPANY

MCSE Windows NT Workstation 4.0 Study Guide
(Exam 70-73)
Syngress Media, Inc.
ISBN: 0-07-882492-3
$49.99 USA
$71.95 CANADA
CD-ROM Included

MCSE Windows NT Server 4.0 Study Guide
(Exam 70-67)
Syngress Media, Inc.
ISBN: 0-07-882491-5
$49.99 USA
$71.95 CANADA
CD-ROM Included

MCSE Windows NT Server 4.0 in the Enterprise Study Guide
(Exam 70-68)
Syngress Media, Inc.
ISBN: 0-07-882490-7
$49.99 USA
$71.95 CANADA
CD-ROM Included

MCSE Networking Essentials Study Guide
(Exam 70-58)
Syngress Media, Inc.
ISBN: 0-07-882493-1
$49.99 USA
$71.95 CANADA
CD-ROM Included

MCSE TCP/IP on Windows NT 4 Study Guide
(Exam 70-59)
Syngress Media, Inc.
ISBN: 0-07-882489-3
$49.99 USA
$71.95 CANADA
CD-ROM Included

MCSE Exchange Server 5.5 Study Guide
(Exam 70-81)
Syngress Media, Inc.
ISBN: 0-07-882488-5
$49.99 USA
$71.95 CANADA
CD-ROM Included

MCSE Internet Information Server 4.0 Study Guide
(Exam 70-87)
Syngress Media, Inc.
ISBN: 0-07-882560-1
$49.99 USA
$71.95 CANADA
CD-ROM Included

MCSE Windows 98 Study Guide
(Exam 70-98)
Syngress Media, Inc.
ISBN: 0-07-882532-6
$49.99 USA
$71.95 CANADA
CD-ROM Included

MCSE Certification Press Core Four Boxed Set
Syngress Media, Inc.
ISBN: 0-07-882568-7
$159.99 USA
$233.99 CANADA
4 CD-ROMs Included

MCSE Certification Test Yourself Practice Exams by Syngress Media, Inc. • ISBN: 0-07-211854-7 • $39.99 USA/$57.95 CANADA
A+ Certification Test Yourself Practice Exams by Syngress Media, Inc. • ISBN: 0-07-211877-6 • $39.99 USA/$57.95 CANADA
A+ Certification Study Guide by Syngress Media, Inc. • ISBN: 0-07-882538-5 • $49.99 USA/$71.95 CANADA

AVAILABLE AT YOUR LOCAL BOOK OR COMPUTER STORES

OR CALL OSBORNE/MCGRAW-HILL: 1-800-262-4729

www.osborne.com

OSBORNE
***REQUIRED READING** for the Information Age*

Prepare for the CNE NetWare 5 exams using the most effective Test-Prep CD-ROM available!

COVERS ALL THE REQUIRED CORE EXAMS PLUS ONE ELECTIVE:

- Networking Technologies (Exam 50-632)
- NDS Design and Implementation (Exam 50-634)
- Service and Support (Exam 50-635)
- NetWare 5 Administration (Exam 50-639)
- NetWare Advanced Administration (Exam 50-640)
- intraNetWare: Integrating Windows NT elective (Exam 50-636)

Includes full version of CNE NetWare 5 TEST YOURSELF Personal Testing Center, covering six exams.

Reinforces your knowledge and improves your test-taking skills with challenging practice exams.

Packed with powerful exam preparation tools, this CD-ROM will increase your chances of passing the exams.

ON THE CD YOU'LL FIND:

- Extensive, full-featured Web site: full Web site links all CD-ROM components together for fast access through your Web browser.

- Complete electronic version of the study guide with fully hyperlinked table of contents.

- CNE NetWare 5 TEST YOURSELF Personal Testing Center with more than 450 questions, offering a realistic exam experience.

- TEST YOURSELF Personal Testing Center software, featuring:

Practice Mode—Pause the exam and link back to the text for in-depth answers to questions.

Live Exam Mode—Take realistic, timed exams that simulate the Test Center environment.

Assess Yourself tool—Use it to pinpoint your weak knowledge areas that require further study.

Benchmark Yourself tool—Chart your improvement from exam to exam with the personalized scoring feature so that you know when you're ready for the real exam.